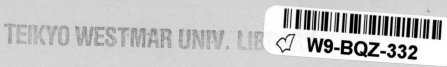

HISTORIC
DOCUMENTS
OF
1988

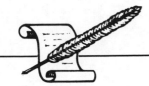

HISTORIC
DOCUMENTS
OF
1988

Cumulative Index, 1984-1988

Congressional Quarterly Inc.

Congressional Quarterly Inc.
1414 22nd St. N.W., Washington, D.C. 20037

The following have granted permission to reprint copyrighted material: from the Introduction to the *Amnesty International Report 1988*, © Amnesty International; from John L. Palmer, Timothy Smeeding, and Barbara Boyle Torrey, eds., *The Vulnerable* (Washington, D.C.: The Urban Institute Press, 1988), 115-117, reproduced by permission; from *Health Risks of Radon and Other Internally Deposited Alpha-Emitters: BEIR IV*, © 1988 by the National Academy of Sciences.

The Library of Congress cataloged the first issue of this title as follows:

Historic documents.   1972—
    Washington. Congressional Quarterly Inc.

    1. United States — Politics and government — 1945— — Yearbooks.
2. World politics — 1945— —Yearbooks. I. Congressional Quarterly Inc.

E839.5H57   917.3'03'9205   72-97888

ISBN 0-87187-493-8

ISSN 0892-080X

Historic Documents of 1988

Editor: Hoyt Gimlin
Production Editor: Kerry V. Kern
Editorial Assistant: Jamie Holland
Contributors: Bryan de Boinville, Juliet Bruce, Daniel C. Diller, James R. Ingram, Mary McNeil, Charles J. Moseley, Patricia Pine, Susanna Spencer, Stephen F. Stine, D. Park Teter, Margaret C. Thompson
Indexer: Victoria Agee

PREFACE

Historic Documents of 1988 carries through a seventeenth year the project Congressional Quarterly began with *Historic Documents of 1972*. The purpose of this series is to give students, scholars, librarians, journalists, and citizens convenient access to documents of basic importance in the broad range of public affairs.

To place the documents in perspective, each entry is preceded by a brief introduction explaining the historical background, the main points, reactions to the document, and in some cases subsequent developments. We believe these introductions will become increasingly useful as the issues recede from public view.

Historic Documents of 1988 contains official statements, Supreme Court decisions, reports, special studies, speeches, presidential debates, international agreements, papal pronouncements, impeachment charges, and an arctic explorer's field notes. These are documents related to events that we judged to be of lasting significance or interest. Where space limitations prevented the publication of a full text, we chose excerpts that convey the document's essential thoughts.

Documents published in this volume reflect the big events of 1988. Election-year politics held the national spotlight, while numerous peace initiatives and goodwill gestures marked the international scene.

George Bush became the first vice president in this century to be elected directly to the American presidency. As the successor to Ronald Reagan, Bush extended Republican control of the White House for at least four more years. But his victory was not accompanied by a Republican majority in the House or Senate. Democrats continued their hold on Congress, and enlarged it slightly in the November 1988 election. This volume records highlights of the election campaign and its outcome.

The nation's political concerns, aside from the election, focused on federal budget deficits and the growing national debt. Many of the nation's lending institutions remained insolvent but not officially bankrupt, as the government searched for ways to replenish depleted deposit-insurance funds. Also in 1988, federal authorities received but took little action on several studies into the causes of the October 1987 stock market crash.

After years of discussion and debate, Congress extensively revised the nation's welfare system to add work incentives. The year opened with the United States and Canada signing a trade treaty to make the two countries virtually one market. Canadians debated the question most of the year and gave their assent in a national election that amounted to a referendum.

For much of the world, 1988 was peaceful. The level of hostility and distrust declined in many regions, perhaps most of all between the United States and Soviet Union. Two meetings between President Reagan and Soviet leader Mikhail S. Gorbachev were marked by a newfound and sometimes exuberant harmony. They signed a missile-reduction treaty in Moscow in May, and Gorbachev announced further unilateral reductions when he addressed the United Nations in December. He spoke to the General Assembly of a new era of Soviet cooperation with the West.

Gorbachev had set out on an even bolder program in his homeland. In 1988 he went further than before in challenging old ideology and loosening the government's rein on Soviet society in the hope of reinvigorating a stagnant economy. He signed an international pact for the withdrawal of Soviet troops from Afghanistan.

Cease-fire agreements stopped the seven-year war between Iran and Iraq, and at least temporarily ended the fighting between the Nicaraguan government and U.S.-aided "contras." In southern Africa, the principals in the related areas of strife signed a peace pact that was years in the making. It called for an end to a civil war in Angola and for the formation of an independent Namibia, free from South Africa's control. In the Middle East, the Palestinians' uprising in Israeli-occupied territories drew support from Arab capitals for the Palestine movement's assertion of "statehood."

As major new developments in such issues unfold, *Historic Documents* will chronicle them, along with new matters of great public interest.

Hoyt Gimlin, Editor

How to Use This Book

The documents are arranged in chronological order. If you know the approximate date of the report, speech, statement, court decision, or other documents you are looking for, glance through the titles for that month in the table of contents.

If the table of contents does not lead you directly to the document you want, turn to the index at the end of the book. There you may find references not only to the particular document you seek but also to other entries on the same or a related subject. The index in this volume is a five-year cumulative index of *Historic Documents* covering the years 1984-1988.

The introduction to each document is printed in italic type. The document itself, printed in roman type, follows the spelling, capitalization, and punctuation of the original or official copy. Where the full text is not given, omissions of material are indicated by the customary ellipsis points.

CONTENTS

January

Report on Radon
Excerpts from *Health Risks of Radon and Other Internally Deposited Alpha-Emitters,* issued January 5 by the Committee on Biological Effects of Ionizing Radiations 3

Reports on the Stock Market Crash
Excerpts from the January 18 report of the Presidential Task Force on Market Mechanisms (the Brady Commission) and from the May 16 report of the Working Group on Financial Markets 9

Court on Student Newspaper Censorship
Excerpts from the majority opinion in the Supreme Court's 5-3 ruling January 13 in *Hazelwood School District v. Kuhlmeier,* ruling that public school officials have broad power to censor school newspapers, plays, and other "school-sponsored activities," and from the dissent of Justice William J. Brennan, Jr. 37

Court on Disruptive Handicapped Students
Excerpts from the Supreme Court's 6-2 ruling January 20 in *Honig v. Doe,* barring the unilateral expulsion of disruptive handicapped students, and from the dissent of Justice Antonin Scalia 47

State of the Union Address
Text of President Ronald Reagan's seventh State of the Union address, delivered January 25 to a joint session of Congress ... 57

February

New Jersey Supreme Court on Surrogate Mothers
Excerpts from the unanimous decision of the New Jersey
Supreme Court, "In the Matter of Baby M," issued
February 3   71

Grand Jury Indictments of General Noriega
Excerpts from the federal grand jury indictments, announced
February 5, bringing criminal charges against Panamanian
military leader Gen. Manuel Antonio Noriega and sixteen
associates   81

State Department Report on Human Rights Practices
Excerpts from the State Department's *Country Reports on
Human Rights Practices for 1987*, released February 10   93

President's Economic Report, Economic Advisers' Report
Text of the Economic Report of the President and excerpts from
the Annual Report of the Council of Economic Advisers, issued
February 16   117

President Reagan's Budget Message
Text of President Ronald Reagan's annual budget message to
Congress, released February 18 with the 1989 budget   149

Papal Encyclical on Social Concerns
Excerpts from the papal encyclical, "Social Concerns of the
Church," issued February 19 by Pope John Paul II   165

Court on Press Freedom
Excerpts from the Supreme Court's 8-0 decision February 24 in
Hustler Magazine, Inc., et al. v. Falwell, ruling that satire—
even if "outrageous"—enjoys First Amendment protection, and
from the concurrence of Justice Byron R. White   175

March

Kerner Report Update
Text, except for the summary, of "The Kerner Report Updated:
Race and Poverty in the United States Today," issued March 1
by the 1988 Commission on the Cities   185

Carnegie Report on Urban Schools
Excerpts from *An Imperiled Generation: Saving Urban Schools*,

a study released March 15 by the Carnegie Foundation for the
Advancement of Teaching 195

Scientists' Report on Ozone Depletion
Excerpts from the Executive Summary of the Ozone Trends
Panel report, issued March 15, substantiating depletion of the
earth's protective ozone layer 221

Report on Privatization
Excerpts from *Privatization: Toward More Effective
Government,* issued March 18 by the President's Commission
on Privatization 229

Central American Cease-Fire
Text of the agreement signed March 23 in Sapoá, Nicaragua,
calling for a cease-fire and other measures to end the civil war in
Nicaragua 241

April

**Impeachment and Conviction of Arizona Governor
Mecham**
Text of three articles of impeachment against Arizona governor
Evan Mecham, filed February 8 by the state House and voted on
April 4 by the state Senate 249

Agreements on Afghanistan
Main portions of the documents signed April 14 comprising the
negotiated settlement regarding Afghanistan 257

Report on Aviation Safety
Excerpts from the final report and recommendations of the
Aviation Safety Commission, issued April 18 267

Court on Alcoholism and Veterans' Benefits
Excerpts from the Supreme Court's 4-3 ruling April 20 in
Traynor v. Turnage and *McKelvey v. Turnage,* upholding the
Veterans Administration's authority to characterize any
alcoholism not connected with psychiatric illness as a problem
that was essentially the veteran's own fault, and from the
dissent of Justice Harry A. Blackmun 277

Reparations for Japanese-American Internees
Excerpts from the *Congressional Record* of Senate debate April
20 on reparations for interned Japanese-Americans 287

Assessing American Education
Excerpts from *American Education: Making It Work*, by
Secretary of Education William J. Bennett, issued April 26 ...   297

May

Report on Nicotine Addiction
Excerpts from "The Health Consequences of Smoking: Nicotine
Addiction," issued May 16 by the surgeon general   309

Science Board Panel on Strategic Missile Defense
Excerpts from the "Report of the Defense Board Task Force
Subgroup on Strategic Air Defense" (SDI Milestone Panel),
released May 20   323

**Public Health Service Report on Length of
Hospitalization**
Excerpts from the National Center for Health Services Research
and Health Care Technology Assessment report, "Trends in
Hospital Average Lengths of Stay, Casemix, and Discharge
Rates, 1980-85," issued May 24   333

Trade Bill Vetoes
Texts of President Reagan's messages informing the House of
Representatives on May 24 of his veto of the Omnibus Trade
and Competitiveness Act of 1988 and on September 28 of his
veto of the Textile Apparel and Footwear Trade Act of 1988 ..   339

Sweden's Pioneer Law on Farm-Animal Rights
Excerpts from a press release by the Swedish Ministry of
Agriculture explaining the Animal Protection Act passed by
Sweden's Parliament on May 27   347

Reagan-Gorbachev Summit
Excerpts from remarks by President Ronald Reagan and Soviet
leader Mikhail Gorbachev at the opening ceremony of the U.S.-
Soviet summit in Moscow May 29, from Reagan's remarks at the
Danilov Monastery May 30, from Reagan's remarks at Spaso
House May 30, from Reagan's and Gorbachev's toasts at the
state dinner May 30, from Reagan's remarks at Moscow State
University May 31, from toasts by the two leaders at a dinner
hosted by Reagan May 31, from remarks by Reagan and
Gorbachev at the exchange of ratification instruments for the
INF Treaty June 1, from the joint U.S.-Soviet communiqué
June 1, and from the president's news conference June 1   353

June

Reports on Math and Science Education
Excerpts from "The Mathematics Report Card: Are We
Measuring Up?" and "The Science Report Card: Elements of
Risk and Recovery," issued June 7 and September 22 by the
National Assessment of Educational Progress 377

Toronto Economic Summit
Excerpts from the Political Declaration, issued June 20, and the
Economic Declaration, issued June 21, at the Toronto Economic
Summit 391

Court on Private Clubs
Excerpts from the majority opinion of Justice Byron R. White in
the Supreme Court decision June 20 in *New York State Club
Association, Inc. v. City of New York et al.,* unanimously
upholding the constitutionality of a New York City ordinance
outlawing discrimination against women by private clubs, and
from the concurring opinions of Justice Sandra Day O'Connor
and Justice Antonin Scalia 399

Pope John Paul's Visit to Austria
Excerpts from the remarks of Pope John Paul II at the former
Mauthausen concentration camp and to the leaders of the
Austrian Jewish Community in Vienna, and from the welcoming
remarks of Paul Grosz on the Jewish Community's behalf, all
made on June 24 405

Presidential Commission Report on AIDS
Excerpts from the "Report of the Presidential Commission on
Human Immunodeficiency Virus Epidemic," issued June 24 .. 415

Soviet Party Conference
Excerpts from the report June 28 by Mikhail Gorbachev, as
general secretary of the Central Committee, to the nineteenth
All-Union Party Conference at the Kremlin Palace of
Congresses in Moscow 447

Court on Independent Counsel
Excerpts from the Supreme Court's 7-1 ruling June 29 in
Morrison v. Olson, upholding the constitutionality of the law
providing for the appointment of a special prosecutor, or
independent counsel, to investigate alleged wrongdoing by high
executive officials, and from the dissent of Justice Antonin
Scalia 465

U.S. District Court Order to Bar Closing of PLO Office
Excerpts of the order and opinion issued June 29 by Judge
Edmund L. Palmieri in U.S. District Court, Southern District of
New York, allowing the PLO mission to the United Nations to
remain open 479

July

Excommunication of Archbishop Lefebvre
Texts of the Vatican document announcing Archbishop
Lefebvre's excommunication, dated July 1, and of a papal letter
to the archbishop's followers, dated July 2, as released to the
public July 11 489

Ethics Investigation of Edwin Meese III
Excerpts from the "Report of Independent Counsel: In Re Edwin
Meese III," filed July 5 by James C. McKay and others with a
three-judge panel of the United States Court of Appeals for the
District of Columbia 495

Endowment Report on the State of the Humanities
Excerpts from the text of "Humanities in America: A Report to
the President, the Congress, and the American People," issued
July 8 by the National Endowment for the Humanities 517

Iran-Iraq Truce
Text of President Ali Khamenei's letter of July 18 to UN
Secretary General Javier Pérez de Cuéllar accepting UN
Resolution 598 on behalf of Iran 529

Democratic National Convention
Speeches at the Democratic national convention in Atlanta as
delivered by Michael S. Dukakis and Lloyd Bentsen accepting
the Democratic party's nominations for president and vice
president, respectively, July 21, and by former presidential
candidate Jesse L. Jackson, July 19 533

Democratic Party Platform
Text of the 1988 Democratic party platform, "The Restoration of
Competence and the Revival of Hope," adopted July 19 by
delegates to the Democratic party convention in Atlanta 557

Trade Pact with Canada
Texts of a letter from President Ronald Reagan to the Speaker of
the House and president of the Senate transmitting the Canada-

United States Free Trade Agreement to Congress, July 25, and
of the president's remarks at White House ceremonies,
September 28, at which he signed legislation implementing the
agreement 571

King Hussein's Speech Severing West Bank Ties
Excerpts from the text of King Hussein's speech July 31
renouncing his government's claims to the West Bank 579

August

Republican National Convention
Speeches at the Republican national convention in New Orleans
as delivered by President Ronald Reagan August 15, by Sen.
Dan Quayle accepting the vice presidential nomination August
18, and by Vice President George Bush accepting the
presidential nomination August 18 589

Republican Party Platform
Text of the Republican party platform, "An American Vision:
For Our Children and Our Future," adopted August 16 by
delegates to the Republican party convention in New
Orleans 615

Report on the Downing of an Iranian Airliner
Excerpts from the news briefing at the Pentagon August 19 at
which Secretary of Defense Frank C. Carlucci and Adm. William
J. Crowe, Jr., chairman of the Joint Chiefs of Staff, presented
the results of an investigation into the circumstances of the
missile firing July 3 from the U.S. Navy frigate *Vincennes* that
shot down an Iranian commercial airliner over the Persian
Gulf 703

September

Presidential Debates
Texts of the presidential debates between George Bush and
Michael S. Dukakis, held September 25 and October 13 721

Apostolic Letter on Women
Excerpts from the apostolic letter, "On the Dignity and Vocation
of Women," issued August 15 in Rome by Pope John Paul II .. 785

October

Space Shuttle *Discovery*'s Tribute to *Challenger* Victims
Texts of tributes delivered in orbit October 2 by the five
astronauts of the space shuttle *Discovery* to the seven persons
who died in the *Challenger* disaster January 28, 1986   795

Vice Presidential Debate
Text of the 1988 vice presidential debate held October 5 between
Sen. Dan Quayle of Indiana, the Republican nominee, and Sen.
Lloyd Bentsen of Texas, the Democratic nominee   799

Peary's Polar Notes
Photographic reproduction of the page from Robert E. Peary's
notes containing his sextant readings that were thought to have
been written at the nothernmost point of his 1909 expedition to
the North Pole, as discovered at the National Archives by
Dennis Rawlins and disclosed October 12 by the *Washington
Post*   831

Harvard Report on the Presidential Press Conference
Excerpts from "Reviving the Presidential News Conference,"
issued October 12 by the Harvard Commission on the
Presidential Press Conference   835

Revision of the U.S. Welfare System
Excerpts from President Ronald Reagan's remarks October 13 on
signing the Family Support Act of 1988, revising the welfare
system   847

South Korean President's United Nations Address
Excerpts from an address by President Roh Tae Woo delivered
October 18 before the United Nations General Assembly   853

EPA Report of "Greenhouse Effect" on America's Climate
Excerpts from the draft report, "The Potential Effects of Global
Climate Change on the United States," issued October 20 by the
Environmental Protection Agency   861

Indictment of Ferdinand and Imelda Marcos
Excerpts from the "Outline of Superseding Indictment" issued
October 21 by the U.S. attorney's office in Manhattan
summarizing the indictments against former Philippine
president Ferdinand Marcos, his wife Imelda, and eight
associates, as handed down by the U.S. District Court, Southern
District of New York   867

Creation of Department of Veterans Affairs
Excerpts from President Ronald Reagan's speech October 25 at a
ceremony at Fort McNair, Washington, D.C., at which he signed
into law the bill establishing a cabinet-level Department of
Veterans Affairs 873

Study of Child Poverty in America and Abroad
Excerpts from the conclusions of the chapter, "Patterns of
Income and Poverty: The Economic Status of Children and the
Elderly in Eight Countries," from *The Vulnerable,* a
compilation of studies on children and the elderly, released
October 26 by the Urban Institute 877

November

Amnesty International's Report on Human Rights
The Introduction to *Amnesty International Report 1988,* issued
November 2 by Amnesty International Publications 883

Postelection Statements by Bush and Dukakis
Vice President George Bush's victory statement November 8 and
excerpts from postelection press conferences held November 9
by Bush in Houston, Texas, and Michael S. Dukakis in
Boston, Massachusetts 891

Palestinian Declaration of Independence
Excerpts from the Palestinian National Council's "Declaration of
Independence," asserting statehood for the Palestinian people,
adopted at the council's November 15 conference in Algiers ... 905

Proposals to Overcome Savings and Loan Crisis
Excerpts from the speech, "Deposit Insurance for the Nineties,"
delivered November 30 by FDIC chairman L. William Seidman
before the National Press Club in Washington, D.C. 913

December

SEC Report on Corporate Takeovers
Excerpts from the report, "Do Bad Bidders Become Good
Targets?" by Mark L. Mitchess and Kenneth Lehn, issued
December 4 by the Securities and Exchange Commission 921

CONTENTS

Gorbachev's Speech to the United Nations
Excerpts from the address delivered December 7 by Soviet leader
Mikhail Gorbachev to the United Nations General Assembly ..   927

Interagency Report on Forest-Fire Policy
Excerpts from the Fire Management Policy Review Team's
"Report on Fire Management Policy," issued December 14 ...   941

Angola-Namibia Peace Accord
Excerpts from the "Agreement Among the People's Republic of
Angola, the Republic of Cuba, and the Republic of South
Africa," signed December 22 at the United Nations   947

Defense Panel's Proposals to Close Military Bases
The Executive Summary from the commission report, "Base
Realignments and Closures," presented December 29 to
Secretary of Defense Frank C. Carlucci   951

Cumulative Index, 1984-1988   955

January

Report on Radon 3

Reports on the Stock Market Crash 9

Court on Student Newspaper Censorship 37

Court on Disruptive Handicapped Students ... 47

State of the Union Address 57

REPORT ON RADON
January 5, 1988

A National Research Council (NRC) committee on January 5 reported its findings from a three-year study into the health risks of exposure to radon, an odorless and colorless radioactive gas produced by the decay of uranium in the soil and rocks. Minute and apparently harmless amounts of radon are almost everywhere in the environment. But the gas can build up to dangerous levels in underground mines and buildings, which it enters through drainage pipes, cracks in the foundation, and other openings. Radioactive particles emitted from the gas can lodge in the small passages of the lungs and cause cancer, especially among cigarette smokers. A key finding was that the risk to smokers was "10 or more times greater than in non-smokers."

The Environmental Protection Agency (EPA), which together with the Nuclear Regulatory Commission requested the study in 1984, had estimated that 8 to 12 percent of the 75 million American homes might have elevated radon levels. The results of a ten-state survey it conducted in August 1987 indicated that the number of affected homes might be even higher. Above-normal radon levels—a measurement expressed in technical terms as above four picocuries of radiation per liter of air—were detected in 21 percent of the 11,600 homes that the agency surveyed.

Just how extensive the problem might be still remained unclear. All authorities have had difficulty in trying to determine the precise national dimensions of radon's contribution to indoor air pollution. The EPA had previously estimated that radon was the cause of 5,000 to 20,000 deaths from lung cancer annually. The committee's study said the number was

3

probably in the middle range between the two figures. Jacob I. Fabrikant, the committee chairman, said in a newspaper interview that 13,000 deaths might "reasonably" be attributed to radon each year. The National Cancer Institute estimated that all causes of lung cancer claimed the lives of 136,000 Americans in 1987, and that 85 percent of the 150,000 new cases resulted from smoking.

Fabrikant, a professor of radiology and biophysics at the University of California at Berkeley, and eleven other scientists comprised the committee, formally known as the Committee on the Biological Effects of Ionizing Radiations. The report on their study, titled Health Risks of Radon and Other Internally Deposited Alpha-Emitters, *was the fourth that this standing committee of the NRC had issued on radiation exposure.*

The committee developed its risk estimates by analyzing extensive data from four epidemiological studies of 22,000 uranium miners in the United States, Canada, and Sweden. Fabrikant said that advanced statistical techniques were used to determine the extent to which the information could be applied to a more general population. Not surprisingly, the committee found that health risks increased with increases in the amount and length of exposure to radon. The risks continue long after exposure has ceased, it added.

Anthony V. Nero, Jr., an expert in indoor air pollution but not a member of the committee, wrote in Scientific American *magazine's May issue, "The average indoor level [of radon] represents a radiation dose about three times larger than the dose most people get from X-rays and other medical procedures in the course of their lifetime." He added that "hundreds of thousands of Americans living in houses that have high radon levels receive as large an exposure of radiation yearly as those people living in the vicinity of the Chernobyl nuclear power plant did in 1986...." An accident in April 1986 at the Chernobyl nuclear power plant near Kiev in the Soviet Union released massive amounts of radiation into the environment. (Chernobyl Nuclear Accident, Historic Documents of 1986, p. 383)*

The NRC committee did not address the matter of how to keep buildings free of radon. However, the National Research Center of the National Association of Home Builders has been doing research in New Jersey on the most cost-effective way of radon-proofing new homes. The research project is sponsored by the EPA, the New Jersey Builders Association, and the New Jersey Department of Community Affairs.

On September 12, the EPA and surgeon general's office issued a public advisory, recommending that every house in the United States be tested for radon. The following month, Congress passed legislation to provide the states $30 million over three years to help them develop radon testing and abatement programs.

Following are excerpts from Health Risks of Radon and Other Internally Deposited Alpha-Emitters, *issued by the Committee on Biological Effects of Ionizing Radiations, January 5, 1988:*

Overview [Chapter 1]

Introduction

This report addresses demonstrated and potential health effects of exposure of human populations to internally deposited alpha-emitting radionuclides and their decay products. It emphasizes carcinogenic effects and, where possible, presents quantitative risk estimates for cancer induction. The largest part of the report deals with health effects of exposure to radon and its progeny, primarily because of a need to characterize the lung-cancer risk associated with exposure to radon and its short-lived daughters in indoor domestic environments. The report also addresses health effects of exposure to other groups of radionuclides and their progeny that emit alpha particles—the isotopes of polonium, radium, thorium, uranium, and the transuranic elements.

Several alpha-emitting radionuclides occur naturally in our environment; others are produced for industrial, military, and medical applications. Recent attention has focused on the alpha-emitting radioisotopes because of their presence in drinking water, in indoor air in buildings, and in mines and because of their potential release into the environment from the nuclear fuel cycle (including radioactive waste disposal) and from accidents during space exploration. The radionuclides of concern are mainly radon-222 and radium-226 and their alpha-emitting daughter products and the transuranic elements plutonium-238 and -239.

Alpha-emitting radionuclides can be absorbed into the tissues of the body and irradiate adjacent cells after inhalation or ingestion, after entry through a wound in the skin, or after injection for diagnostic or therapeutic purposes. Radiation effects depend not only on the physical properties of emitted radiation, but also on the physiology and biochemistry of the exposed person and the physical and chemical characteristics of the radionuclides, which control their deposition, transport, metabolism, excretion, and reuse in the body. The health effects of radiation in humans include cancer induction, genetic disease, teratogenesis (induction of developmental abnormalities), and degenerative changes. The most important target tissues for cancer induction and degenerative changes are the respiratory tract, bone, liver, and the reticuloendothelium system.

Both natural and man-made alpha-emitting radionuclides in our environment can pose a risk to human health, but the natural sources currently make the largest contribution to human exposure. Among the natural sources, inhaled radon and radon decay products indoors are the largest contributors to population exposure and might be responsible for a large number of lung-cancer deaths each year. That has led to recommendations, now being implemented, for national studies to assess the magnitude of the problem, for adopting remedial action levels of radon progeny in the indoor environment, and for introducing mitigation procedures to take effect at or below such levels to reduce population exposures from this source. . . .

This report attempts to respond to a broad range of scientific questions related to current public health issues. Not all the questions can be addressed directly. There is considerable variation in the amount of data on each radionuclide from epidemiological studies and animal investigations. Epidemiological data are available on some alpha-emitting radionuclides, such as radon and its daughters, radium, and thorium. Little human information is available, however, on the transuranic elements, so dependence must be placed on animal experiments. As in all experimental animal studies, the extent to which the results can be extrapolated to humans and the confidence that can be placed on such extrapolation are uncertain. Even when human data were available, the committee has tried to rely on its own studies using newly developed methods for the analysis of occupational cohort data rather than relying solely on published information. The committee has also used novel statistical methods to analyze interspecies comparisons of the risks associated with different radionuclides when human data were insufficient. The committee recognizes that these analyses are preliminary and that large uncertainties are inherent in such extrapolations. Nevertheless, the committee believes that the methods introduced here will help to point the way to more detailed comparisons as additional data from epidemiological and animal studies become available. . . .

Summary of Findings

Most primordial radionuclides are isotopes of heavy elements and belong to the three radioactive series headed by uranium-238, thorium-232, and uranium-235. These contribute significantly to the general population collective dose equivalent. The relevant radionuclides in the body include the isotopes of uranium, radium, radon, polonium, bismuth, and lead; these enter the body by inhalation or by ingestion of food and water and only rarely through wounds in the skin. They follow normal chemical metabolism, and the concentrations of the long-lived radionuclides are usually maintained at equilibrium or increase slowly with age. The shorter-lived radionuclides disappear by decay, but might be continually replenished by renewed intake.

Radon

The evaluation of the lung-cancer risk associated with radon and its progeny has been the most challenging task of the committee. Numerous studies of underground miners exposed to radon daughters in the air of mines have shown an increased risk of lung cancer in comparison with nonexposed populations. Laboratory animals exposed to radon daughters also develop lung cancer. The abundant epidemiological and experimental data have established the carcinogenicity of radon progeny. Those observations are of considerable importance, because uranium, from which radon and its progeny arise, is ubiquitous in the earth's crust, and radon in indoor environments can reach relatively high concentrations. Although the carcinogenicity of radon daughters is established and the hazards of exposure during mining are well recognized, the hazards of exposure in other environments have not yet been adequately quantified. . . .

Research in the United States and other countries has provided data on concentrations of radon and radon progeny in homes. The studies have also described the sources of radon and determinants of its concentration. A few exploratory epidemiological investigations of the lung-cancer risk associated with radon-daughter exposure in homes have been carried out, but the study populations have been small and the results inconclusive. The committee judged these exploratory studies to be inadequate for the purposes of risk estimation. . . .

Radium

The main sources of information on the health effects of radium deposited in human tissues are the U.S. cases of occupational exposure (mostly in dial painters and radium chemists) and medical exposure to radium-226 and radium-228 and the German cases of repeated injection of radium-224 into patients for treatment of ankylosing spondylitis in adult life or tuberculosis in childhood. Malignant effects are almost exclusively the induction of skeletal tumors and of carcinomas in the paranasal sinuses and mastoid air cells. The evidence of induction of leukemia is weak, except at doses far greater than those in occupational, environmental, or therapeutic exposures currently encountered. . . .

Uranium

. . . Uranium is ubiquitous in rocks and soil and is a trace element in foods, particularly crops or cereals, and in drinking water. Wide geographical differences have been noted. . . .

Uranium compounds may induce detrimental health effects due to both chemical toxicity and alpha-radiation damage. Animal experiments have demonstrated a specific toxic effect of uranium on the kidney, but with little evidence of toxic effects on other organs.

Radon [Chapter 2]

Underground mining was the first occupation associated with an increased risk of lung cancer. Uranium ores contain particularly high concentrations of radium, and radon-daughter exposure has been associated with lung cancer in uranium miners. Miners of other types of ore can also be placed at risk by the combination of a sufficiently strong source of radon and inadequate ventilation.

Radon progeny are also present in the air of dwellings. Their source is the underlying soil, but building materials, water used routinely in the building, and utility natural gas also contribute. The concentration of radon progeny in dwellings is highly variable and depends mainly on the pressure in the house and on the ventilation.

Because of their wide distribution, radon daughters are a major source of exposure to radioactivity for the general public, as well as for special occupational groups. The estimated dose to the bronchial epithelium from radon daughters far exceeds that to any other organ from natural background radiation. The recent recognition that some homes have high concentrations of radon has focused concern on the potential lung-cancer risk associated with environmental radon. . . .

Most lung cancers are caused by cigarette smoking; only 5-10% of the total cases occur in lifelong nonsmokers. . . . The risk of lung cancer for a smoker is some 10 times higher than that for a nonsmoker, and up to 20 times higher for heavy smokers. Because cigarette smoking predominates as the cause of lung cancer, the committee needed to address separately the risks of radon-daughter exposure for smokers and for nonsmokers. . . .

The committee recognizes that smoking is the most important risk factor for lung cancer and . . . has evaluated the interaction between smoking and radon-daughter exposure as comprehensively as possible. The committee has accepted that smoking and radon exposure combine in a fashion that is multiplicative (or nearly so) on the relative-risk scale. . . .

REPORTS ON THE
STOCK MARKET CRASH
January 8 and May 16, 1988

The stock market crash of October 1987 spawned official reports from the regulatory agencies looking into the cause of the crash. The first inquiry to be reported in 1988, however, came not from a federal agency but from a presidentially appointed group of five businessmen prominent in the nation's financial markets. They constituted the Presidential Task Force on Market Mechanisms, popularly known as the Brady Commission. The commission's report, submitted to President Ronald Reagan on January 8, received wide publicity and drew close attention in Congress, which since the market plunge had been pondering whether new regulatory mechanisms should be required to prevent another crash.

Nicholas F. Brady, the commisssion's chairman, was a Wall Street financier who had served as a Republican senator from New Jersey in 1982, filling out an unexpired term. In August 1988, Reagan named him secretary of the Treasury, replacing James A. Baker III, who had resigned to run George Bush's presidential campaign. A victorious Bush said Brady would remain in the post.

The Brady report was followed on January 26 by a preliminary study of financial markets prepared for Congress by the U.S. General Accounting Office. On January 29 came a staff report to the Commodity Futures Trade Commission (CFTC), and on February 2 a staff report to the Securities and Exchange Commission (SEC), which regulates the stock markets.

President Reagan on March 18 named a high-level, interagency com-

mittee, the Working Group on Financial Markets, to examine the various proposals for market reform and report back to him within sixty days on what should be done to "enhance investor confidence" in the markets. The Working Group, headed by Treasury undersecretary George D. Gould, made its interim report on May 16. Other members were the chairmen of the Federal Reserve System (Alan Greenspan), CFTC (Wendy Gramm), and SEC (David S. Ruder).

Brady Report Findings

The key conclusion of the Brady Commission was that the stock market and the marketplaces where stock index futures and other derivative instruments were traded had become essentially one market. An initial surge of selling in mid-October 1987 became a rout when control mechanisms failed and the "market segments" became disconnected, the report said. In the resulting turmoil, it added, the nation's financial system "approached breakdown."

The market's volatility culminated in the most precipitous decline in stock market history, eclipsing even the famous 1929 stock market crash. The report's account of what happened was characterized by blunt language and a wealth of detail. The first day of the crisis was summed up this way: "All told, Monday, October 19 was perhaps the worst day in the history of U.S. equity markets." But it was the next day that intermarket links became "completely disconnected," leading to a "free fall in both [stock and futures] markets." The task force credited the Federal Reserve Board (the "Fed") and a number of major corporations with stopping the slide. The "timely intervention" of the Fed, the report said, restored "liquidity and confidence," and "buyback" announcements by the corporations "turned the market around." (Stock Market Crash, Historic Documents of 1987, p. 833)

A five-year bull market—the Wall Street term for a long period of rising stock prices—preceded the crash. The Dow Jones Industrial Average, a widely observed index of New York Stock Exchange trading, plunged 508 points on October 19. The index fell that day from 2246.73 to 1738.74, reflecting an unprecedented 22.6 percent decline in value of the stocks it recorded.

During the years of the bull market, a huge increase in trading took place in stock futures, including both stock options and the broader stock-index futures. Futures trading, centered in Chicago, permitted investors to bet on the direction of stock-price movements or to protect themselves against unexpected price changes. The stock markets and futures markets were linked, the Brady task force determined, by "financial instruments, trading strategies, market participants and clearing and credit mechanisms." Movements in the stock markets were transmitted to the stock market through sophisticated computer-based strategies.

The task force said that a relative handful of "institutions" such as pension and endowment funds, money management funds, and investment banking houses had been the major participants in the market's plunge. In an interview with the editors and reporters of the New York Times on January 12, Brady said he found the role of the institutions on October 19 to be "mind boggling."

In its main conclusion the task force said, "Stocks, stock index futures and options constitute one market." It went on to assert that the market collapse could be "traced to the failure of these market segments to act as one. Institutional and regulating structures designed for separate marketplaces were incapable of responding to intermarket pressures."

Brady Report Recommendations

Based on its "one-market" conclusion, the task force recommended that margins (down payments required for the purchase of stocks or futures) be "consistent" from market to market "to control speculation and financial leverages." The report also called for "circuit-breakers"— price limits in the futures market and trading halts in the stock market. It recommended a single agency to coordinate all intermarket activities and suggested the Federal Reserve Board as the agency to carry out that job. Certain current duties of the SEC in supervising the stock market and the CFTC in supervising the futures market could remain with those two regulatory bodies under the new arrangement that it envisioned.

In the New York Times interview, Brady said he was "convinced" that if the changes the task force recommended had been in place "you would not have had that fall we had in October." Brady's task force was created by President Reagan on October 21, 1987. The four other members were John R. Opel, Robert G. Kirby, Howard M. Stein, and James C. Cotting.

Reaction, Other Reports

While much of the reaction to the Brady report was favorable, the response on Wall Street was largely critical. Securities industry executives were particularly dissatisfied with the report's proposal for circuit-breakers. The Washington Post called the report "excellent," and Rep. John Dingell, D-Mich., chairman of the House Energy and Commerce Committee, termed its recommendations "not only acceptable but good." The Wall Street Journal quoted a leader of the futures industry as saying that the report had become "the bible in Washington."

The SEC report generally concurred with the Brady report, endorsing the proposal that a single agency regulate the markets. However, where the Brady report suggested the Federal Reserve Board as the single regulator, the SEC looked upon itself as the logical choice. The SEC, in legislative proposals it approved May 26, asked that it be given authority to regulate stock futures and to close down the nation's stock exchanges in the event of another market crisis. SEC Chairman Ruder argued that *his agency, because of its existing regulatory authority, had the highest claim on the overall job. John J. Phelan, Jr., chairman of the New York Stock Exchange, testifying February 5 before the Senate Banking Committee, agreed that a single federal agency should regulate financial markets, but he carefully avoided saying which agency it should be.*

Alan Greenspan of the Federal Reserve Board rejected suggestions that the Fed become the super-regulator. His view was reflected in the May 16 report of the Working Group on Financial Markets, on which he served. Of the four members of that interagency review group, only Ruder pushed for regulatory consolidation. He differed from the general view of the other three—Gould, Greenspan, and Gramm—that government regulation of financial markets was already sufficient. The three-member majority recommended only one major new restriction, that trading be halted in the New York and Chicago markets for one hour whenever the Dow Jones Industrial Average dropped as much as 250 points. The New York Stock Exchange and the Chicago Mercantile Exchange, which trades in both commodity and stock-market futures, announced July 7 that they would adopt the recommendation if the SEC approved their plan. A market shutdown was envisioned in several of the reports as a "circuit-breaker," a way to keep the failure of one market from connecting with and causing failure in another.

Responses to the Working Group

"The report by the inter-agency group represented an almost total victory for the futures industry," commented the New York Times, *"since it hews closely to nearly all of the industry's basic viewpoints." The futures industry opposed proposals to increase regulation in the purchase of futures, as well as those suggesting a single-agency "super-regulator."*

In Congress, the Working Group's handiwork drew the scorn of some senior Democrats. The interagency report was a "do-nothing" solution, said Sen. William Proxmire, D-Wis., chairman of the Senate Banking Committee, at a hearing before his committee on May 24. Rep. Edward J. Markey, D-Mass., chairman of the House Subcommittee on Telecommunications and Finance, used a football metaphor to express his criticism: "After being handed a game plan for market reform by the Brady Commission, the Working Group went into a two-month huddle, came out and punted." There was general agreement that because of the differing views represented in the various reports, no remedial legislation was likely to be enacted by Congress until 1989 or beyond.

Following are excerpts from the January 18, 1988, report of the Presidential Task Force on Market Mechanisms (the Brady Commission) and from the May 16, 1988, report of the Working Group on Financial Markets:

PRESIDENTIAL TASK FORCE ON MARKET MECHANISMS

Executive Summary

Introduction

From the close of trading Tuesday, October 13, 1987, to the close of trading Monday, October 19, the Dow Jones Industrial Average declined by almost one third, representing a loss in the value of all outstanding United States stocks of approximately $1.0 trillion.

What made this market break extraordinary was the speed with which prices fell, the unprecedented volume of trading and the consequent threat to the financial system.

In response to these events, the President created the Task Force on Market Mechanisms. Its mandate was, in 60 days, to determine what happened and why, and to provide guidance in helping to prevent such a break from happening again.

The Market Break

The precipitous market decline of mid-October was "triggered" by specific events: an unexpectedly high merchandise trade deficit which pushed interest rates to new high levels, and proposed tax legislation which led to the collapse of the stocks of a number of takeover candidates. This initial decline ignited mechanical, price-insensitive selling by a number of institutions employing portfolio insurance strategies and a small number of mutual fund groups reacting to redemptions. The selling by these investors, and the prospect of further selling by them, encouraged a number of aggressive trading-oriented institutions to sell in anticipation of further market declines. These institutions included, in addition to hedge funds, a small number of pension and endowment funds, money management firms and investment banking houses. This selling, in turn, stimulated further reactive selling by portfolio insurers and mutual funds.

Portfolio insurers and other institutions sold in both the stock market and the stock index futures market. Selling pressure in the futures market was transmitted to the stock market by the mechanism of index arbitrage. Through the period of the decline, trading volume and price volatility increased dramatically. This trading activity was concentrated in the hands of a surprisingly few institutions. On October 19, sell programs by three portfolio insurers accounted for just under $2 billion in the stock market; in the futures market three portfolio insurers accounted for the equivalent in value of $2.8 billion of stock. Block sales by a few mutual funds accounted for about $900 million of stock sales.

The stock and futures market handled record volume of transactions and had a generally good record of remaining available for trading on October 19 and 20. However, market makers were unable to manage smooth price transitions in the face of overwhelming selling pressure.

13

Clearing and credit system problems further exacerbated the difficulties of market participants. While no default occurred, the possibility that a clearinghouse or a major investment banking firm might default, or that the banking system would deny required liquidity to the market participants, resulted in certain market makers curtailing their activities and increased investor uncertainty. Timely intervention by the Federal Reserve System provided confidence and liquidity to the markets and financial system.

One Market

Analysis of market behavior during the mid-October break makes clear an important conclusion. From an economic viewpoint, what have been traditionally seen as separate markets—the markets for stocks, stock index futures, and stock options—are in fact one market. Under ordinary circumstances, these marketplaces move sympathetically, linked by financial instruments, trading strategies, market participants and clearing and credit mechanisms.

To a large extent, the problems of mid-October can be traced to the failure of these market segments to act as one. Confronted with the massive selling demands of a limited number of institutions, regulatory and institutional structures designed for separate marketplaces were incapable of effectively responding to "intermarket" pressures. The New York Stock Exchange's ("NYSE") automated transaction system ("DOT"), used by index arbitrageurs to link the two marketplaces, ceased to be useful for arbitrage after midday on October 19. The concern that some clearinghouses and major market participants might fail inhibited intermarket activities of other investors. The futures and stock markets became disengaged, both nearly going into freefall.

The ability of the equity market to absorb the huge selling pressure to which it was subjected in mid-October depended on its liquidity. But liquidity sufficient to absorb the limited selling demands of investors became an illusion of liquidity when confronted by massive selling, as everyone showed up on the same side of the market at once. Ironically, it was this illusion of liquidity which led certain similarly motivated investors, such as portfolio insurers, to adopt strategies which call for liquidity far in excess of what the market could supply.

Regulatory Implications

Because stocks, futures and options constitute one market, there must be in place a regulatory structure designed to be consistent with this economic reality. The October market break illustrates that regulatory changes, derived from the one-market concept, are necessary both to reduce the possibility of destructive market breaks and to deal effectively with such episodes should they occur. The guiding objective should be to enhance the integrity and competitiveness of U.S. financial markets.

Analysis of the October market break demonstrates that one agency must have the authority to coordinate a few critical intermarket issues cutting across market segments and affecting the entire financial system; to monitor activities of all market segments; and to mediate concerns across marketplaces. The specific issues which have an impact across marketplaces and throughout the financial systems include: clearing and credit mechanisms; margin requirements; circuit breaker mechanisms, such as price limits and trading halts; and information systems for monitoring activities across marketplaces.

The single agency required to coordinate cross-marketplace issues must have broad and deep expertise in the interaction of the stock, stock option and stock index futures marketplaces, as well as in all financial markets, domestic and global. It must have broad expertise in the financial system as a whole.

The Task Force compared these requirements with possible alternative regulatory structures, including: existing self-regulatory organizations, such as the exchanges; existing government regulatory agencies; namely the Securities and Exchange Commission and the Commodity Futures Trading Commission; the Department of the Treasury; the Federal Reserve Board; a combination of two or more of these; and a new regulatory body.

Conclusion

Our understanding of these events leads directly to our recommendations. To help prevent a repetition of the events of mid-October and to provide an effective and coordinated response in the face of market disorder, we recommend:

- One agency should coordinate the few, but critical, regulatory issues which have an impact across the related market segments and throughout the financial system.
- Clearing systems should be unified across marketplaces to reduce financial risk.
- Margins should be made consistent across marketplaces to control speculation and financial leverage.
- Circuit breaker mechanisms (such as price limits and coordinated trading halts) should be formulated and implemented to protect the market system.
- Information systems should be established to monitor transactions and conditions in related markets.

The single agency must have expertise in the interaction of markets— not simply experience in regulating distinct market segments. It must have a broad perspective on the financial system as a whole, both domestic and foreign, as well as independence and responsiveness.

The Task Force had neither the time nor the mandate to consider the full range of issues necessary to support a definitive recommendation on the choice of agency to assume the required role. However, the weight of the evidence suggests that the Federal Reserve is well qualified to fill that role. . . .

Introduction

From the close of trading on Tuesday, October 13, 1987, to the close of trading on October 19, 1987, the Dow Jones Industrial Average ("Dow") fell 769 points or 31 percent. In those four days of trading, the value of all outstanding U.S. stocks decreased by almost $1.0 trillion. On October 19, 1987, alone, the Dow fell by 508 points or 22.6 percent. Since the early 1920's, only the drop of 12.8 percent in the Dow on October 28, 1929, and the fall of 11.7 percent the following day, which together constituted the Crash of 1929, have approached the October 19 decline in magnitude.

The significance of this decline lies in the role that the stock market plays in a modern industrial economy, both as a harbinger and a facilitator of economic activity. Stock price levels can have an important effect on the confidence and, hence, the behavior of both businesses and households. Further, equity markets are a primary means by which businesses and industries raise capital to finance growth and provide jobs. Gross sales of newly issued common stock increased substantially over the course of the 1982 to 1987 bull market, reaching $56.3 billion in 1986 and $27 billion in the first six months of 1987. However, the importance of stock sales is greater than simply the amount of funds raised. New equity capital and public equity markets are essential to financing innovative business ventures which are a primary engine of the nation's economic growth.

Moreover, publicly traded equities are a repository of a significant fraction of U.S. household wealth. Households directly own about 60 percent of all U.S. publicly owned common stock, which was worth approximately $2.25 trillion before the October market decline. Households hold another $210 billion of common stock through mutual funds and $740 billion through pension funds. Thus, in the early fall of 1987, the stock market accounted for approximately $3.2 trillion of household wealth.

Equity markets are also inextricably tied to the wider financial system through the structure of banks and other financial institutions. Given the importance of equity markets to the economy and to the public, effectively structured and functioning equity markets are critical. . . .

What made the October market break extraordinary was the speed with which prices fell, the unprecedented volume of trading and the consequent dislocations of the financial markets. Thus, whatever the causes of the original downward pressure on the equity market, the mandate of the Task Force was to focus on those factors which transformed this downward pressure into the alarming events of the stock market decline and to recommend measures to ensure, as far as possible, that future market fluctuations are not of the extreme and potentially destructive nature witnessed in October 1987.

Fundamental causes of the recent market decline should not, of course, be ignored. To the extent that existing imbalances in the budget, foreign transactions, savings, corporate asset positions and other fundamental factors are perceived to be problems, they merit attention.

The events of October demonstrated an unusual frailty in the markets. Only 3 percent of the total shares of publicly traded stock in the U.S. changed hands during this period, but it resulted in the loss in stock value of $1 trillion. That such a relatively small transaction volume can produce such a large loss in value over such a short time span suggests the importance of determining the extent to which market mechanisms themselves were an important factor in the October market break. The work of the Task Force, therefore, focused on the individual marketplaces and the interrelationship of existing market mechanisms, including the instruments traded, the strategies employed and the regulatory structures.

The Task Force's findings and conclusions are based significantly on the primary transaction data and information that we accumulated. Recognizing the importance of determining as much as possible about each transaction, the Task Force spent much of its time gathering and then analyzing transactions on the New York Stock Exchange ("NYSE"), Chicago Mercantile Exchange ("CME"), Chicago Board of Trade ("CBOT"), American Stock Exchange ("Amex") and the Chicago Board Options Exchange ("CBOE")....

The Bull Market

All major stock markets began an impressive period of growth in 1982. Spurred by the economic turnaround, the growth in corporate earnings, the reduction in inflation and the associated fall in interest rates, the Dow rose from 777 to 1,896 between August 1982 and December 1986. Other factors contributing to this dramatic bull market included: continuing deregulation of the financial markets; tax incentives for equity investing; stock retirements arising from mergers, leveraged buyouts and share repurchase programs; and an increasing tendency to include "takeover premiums" in the valuation of a large number of stocks....

The Market Break

Introduction

On Wednesday morning, October 14, 1987, the U.S. equity market began the most severe one-week decline in its history. The Dow stood at over 2,500 on Wednesday morning. By noon on Tuesday of the next week, it was just above 1,700, a decline of almost one third. Worse still ... the S&P 500 futures contract would imply a Dow level near 1,400.

This precipitous decline began with several "triggers," which ignited mechanical, price-insensitive selling by a number of institutions following portfolio insurance strategies and a small number of mutual fund groups. The selling by these investors, and the prospect of further selling by them, encouraged a number of aggressive trading-oriented institutions to sell in anticipation of further declines. These aggressive trading-oriented institutions included, in addition to hedge funds, a small number of pension and endowment funds, money management firms and investment banking houses. This selling in turn stimulated further reactive selling by portfolio insurers and mutual funds. Selling pressure in the futures market was transmitted to the stock market by the mechanism of index arbitrage. Throughout the period, trading volume and price volatility increased dramatically. This may suggest that a broad range of investors all decided to reduce their positions in equities. In reality, a limited number of investors played the dominant role during this tumultuous period.

The Days Before the Break
(October 14 to 16)

Wednesday, October 14. The stock market's break began with two events which contributed to a revaluation of stock prices and triggered the reactive selling which would exacerbate the decline the following week. At 8:30 a.m., Eastern Time, the government announced that the merchandise trade deficit for August was $15.7 billion, approximately $1.5 billion above the figure expected by the financial markets. Within seconds, traders in the foreign exchange markets sold dollars in the belief that the value of the dollar would have to fall further before the deficit could narrow. . . .

The second event was the announcement early Wednesday that members of the House Ways and Means Committee were filing legislation to eliminate tax benefits associated with the financing of corporate takeovers. While rumors of the legislation had been circulating on Wall Street for several weeks, its actual announcement had a galvanizing effect on investors, particularly risk arbitrageurs, who specialize in buying shares of takeover candidates. . . . As risk arbitrageurs came to appreciate the seriousness of the legislative initiative, they began to liquidate their positions, collapsing the prices of takeover shares. These stocks had led the bull market up and now, during the week of October 14 to October 20, they would begin to lead it back down again.

In response to these events, the equity market declined immediately on Wednesday's opening. The S&P 500 futures contract fell sharply as trading-oriented investors sold. . . .

The morning decline was followed by another 45 point decline between 12:15 p.m. and 1:15 p.m. This midday decline was the result mainly of selling in the futures market by portfolio insurers and, then, the transmission of this selling activity back into the stock market by the actions of index arbitrageurs who bought futures and sold stocks. . . .

At the end of Wednesday there was a sell-off by trading-oriented institutions. Institutional sellers moved large blocks in the stock market and sold futures as well. In the last half hour, the Dow fell 17 points. Index arbitrage sales were $140 million, 15 percent of volume.

For the day, the Dow was down an historic 95 points on volume of 207 million shares. . . .

Thursday, October 15. Selling in Tokyo and London overnight continued the pattern seen in New York and Chicago on Wednesday. When the U.S. markets opened, they were greeted by heavy selling from portfolio insurers. . . .

Despite the opening, the Dow recovered during the day and was down only four points at 3:30 p.m. In the last 30 minutes of trading, however, it fell another 53 points to close down 57 points for the day. This sharp decline on heavy volume so late in the day bewildered investors. . . .

Friday, October 16. Despite the sell-off at the close on Thursday in the U.S., trading in Tokyo on Friday was quiet. London was closed because of a freak hurricane. . . .

The stock market was relatively quiet until 11:00 a.m., with the Dow down only seven points, when futures selling by portfolio insurers picked up significantly, running over 2,000 contracts, or $300 million of stock, an hour. . . .

The stock market rallied briefly but then plummeted 70 points between noon and 2:00 p.m. Index arbitrage selling was active, accounting for about 16 percent of NYSE volume between 1:00 p.m. and 2:00 p.m. Large block transactions accounted for about half the volume in the 30 stocks making up the Dow. After a technical trading rally fizzled at about 2:30 p.m., the decline quickened in the last half hour of trading. Between 3:30 p.m. and 3:50 p.m., the Dow fell 50 points, then recovered 22 points in the last 10 minutes of trading. . . .

The Dow was off 108 points, the largest one day drop ever, on volume of 338 million shares. . . .

The Three Days in Perspective. During October 14 to 16, the Dow fell by over 250 points. The selling was triggered primarily by two proximate causes: disappointingly poor merchandise trade figures, which put downward pressure on the dollar in currency markets and upward pressure on long term interest rates; and the filing of anti-takeover tax legislation, which caused risk arbitrageurs to sell stocks of takeover candidates resulting in their precipitate decline and a general ripple effect throughout the market. The market's decline created a huge overhang of selling pressure—enough to crush the equity markets in the following week. . . .

Monday, October 19

In Tokyo, the Nikkei Index, Japan's equivalent of the Dow, fell 2.5 percent. Investors in London sold shares heavily, and by midday the market index there was down 10 percent. Selling of U.S. stocks on the London market was stoked by some U.S. mutual fund managers who tried to beat the expected selling on the NYSE by lightening up in London. One mutual fund group sold just under $90 million of stocks in London.

Selling activity shifted to the U.S. when the equity markets opened. At

9:15 a.m., the MMI futures opened down 2.5 percent from an already weak close on Friday. Fifteen minutes later the S&P 500 futures also opened down under heavy selling pressure by portfolio insurers. During the first half hour of trading, a few portfolio insurers sold futures equivalent to just under $400 million of stocks, 28 percent of the public volume.

By the scheduled 9:30 a.m. opening on the NYSE, specialists faced large order imbalances. In the DOT system alone, almost $500 million of market sell orders were loaded before the market opened. Of this total, $250 million were sales by index arbitrageurs responding to an apparent record futures discount. The remaining $250 million included straight sell programs by a few portfolio insurers permitted by their clients to sell stocks as well as futures; this group would sell more or less consistently from the opening to the closing bell. There were also large sell orders on the floor for blocks of individual stocks by a small number of mutual funds.

Faced with this massive order imbalance, many specialists did not open trading in their stocks during the first hour. Nevertheless, volume was impressive; in the first half hour alone, about $2 billion crossed the tape. Of this total, about $500 million, roughly 25 percent of volume in this period, came from one mutual fund group. Slightly less came from the execution of orders in the DOT system for index arbitrageurs and portfolio insurers. In addition, even as these trades were being executed through DOT, another $500 million of sell orders were being loaded into the system backlog. Thus, sell orders from a few institutional traders overwhelmed the stock market at the opening.

During the first hour, the reported levels of the S&P and Dow indices reflected out-of-date Friday closing prices for the large number of stocks which had not yet been opened for trading. The result was an apparent record discount for the futures relative to stocks. Based on this apparent discount, index arbitrageurs entered sell-at-market orders through DOT, planning to cover by later purchases of futures at lower prices. However, specialists ultimately opened their stocks at sharply lower levels, in line with the prices at which futures had opened earlier. As this fact became evident, index arbitrageurs realized they had sold stock at prices lower than expected. By 10:30 a.m., when most stocks had opened, the Dow was around 2,150 compared with the Friday close of near 2,250.

Starting around 10:50 a.m., these arbitrageurs rushed to cover their positions through purchases of futures. The result was an immediate rise in the futures market. By 11:00 a.m., futures were at a premium, and the stock market in turn began an hour-long rally....

Even as the futures and then the stock markets rallied, one portfolio insurance client began to modify its selling strategy in response to the anticipated volume of sales....

Thus, one hour into the trading day, two mechanisms were operating at high volume through DOT to transmit futures selling pressure to the stock market: index arbitrage and the diversion of portfolio insurance sales from the futures market into straight stock sell programs....

The selling pressure in futures led to discounts of historic size. In response to these huge discounts, three mechanisms came into play to transmit selling pressure from futures to stocks. First, index arbitrage executed $1.7 billion of program sales through DOT, matched by equivalent futures purchases. Second, there were additional straight program sales of stock equal to $2.3 billion. More of this was portfolio insurance selling diverted from the futures market to the stock market by the large discount. Taken together, arbitrage programs and straight sell programs totaled $4 billion, almost 20 percent of the sales on the first 600 million share day in the NYSE's history. These program sales would no doubt have been even higher if the DOT system had functioned more effectively after 2:00 p.m. Third, some indeterminant portion of the $41 billion of purchases was diverted from more expensive stocks to cheaper futures.

Starting around 11:40 a.m., portfolio insurance sales overwhelmed the rally. Between then and 2:00 p.m., the Dow fell from 2, 140 to 1,950, a decline of just under 9 percent. The last 100 points of this decline occurred after reports began circulating that the NYSE might close. The break below 2,000 was the first time this level had been penetrated since January 7, 1987. Over these two hours, the futures index fell 14.5 percent. Portfolio insurance activity intensified. Between 11:40 a.m. and 2:00 p.m., in the futures market portfolio insurers sold approximately 10,000 contracts, equivalent to about $1.3 billion and representing about 41 percent of futures volume exclusive of market makers (i.e. locals). In addition, portfolio insurers authorized to sell stock directly sold approximately $900 million in stocks on the NYSE during this period. In the stock and futures markets combined, portfolio insurers contributed over $3.7 billion in selling pressure by early afternoon.

Throughout most of this period, index arbitrage had succeeded in transmitting futures selling pressure back to the stock market. After about 2:00 p.m., index arbitrage slowed because of concerns about delays in DOT and the consequent ineffective execution of basket sales. . . .

The result of the withdrawal of some index arbitrage and diverted portfolio insurer sales from the DOT system was that neither mechanism was sufficient to keep the stock and futures markets from disconnecting. Enormous discounts of futures relative to stocks were free to develop as the futures market plummeted, disconnected from the stock market.

The rest of Monday afternoon was disastrous. Heavy futures selling continued by a few portfolio insurers. In the last hour and one half of futures trading, these institutions sold 6,000 contracts, the equivalent of $660 million of stock. With some index arbitrageurs unwilling to sell stock through DOT, they also withdrew from the futures side of their trading, denying buying support to the futures market, allowing it to fall to a discount of 20 index points. In addition, the appearance of this dysfunctionally large discount inhibited buyers in the stock market. With these stock buyers gone, the Dow sank almost 300 points in the last hour and one quarter of stock trading, to close at 1,738. Portfolio insurance futures selling continued even after stocks closed.

All told, Monday, October 19 was perhaps the worst day in the history of U.S. equity markets. By the close of trading, the Dow index had fallen 508 points, almost 23 percent, on volume of 604 million shares worth just under $21 billion. Even worse, the S&P 500 futures had fallen 29 percent on total volume of 162,000 contracts, valued at almost $20 billion.

This record volume was concentrated among relatively few institutions. In the stock market, the top four sellers alone accounted for $2.85 billion, or 14 percent of total sales. The top 15 sellers as a group accounted for $4.1 billion, or about 20 percent to total sales. The top 15 buyers purchased $2.2 billion, almost 11 percent of total volume. In the futures market the top 10 sellers accounted for sales equivalent to $5 billion, roughly 50 percent of the non-market maker total volume.

The contribution of a small number of portfolio insurers and mutual funds to the Monday selling pressure is even more striking. Out of total NYSE sales of just under $21 billion, sell programs by three portfolio insurers made up just under $2 billion. Block sales of individual stocks by a few mutual funds accounted for another $900 million. About 90 percent of these sales were executed by one mutual fund group. In the futures market, portfolio insurer sales amounted to the equivalent of $4 billion of stocks, or 34,500 contracts, equal to over 40 percent of futures volume, exclusive of locals' transactions; $2.8 billion was done by only three insurers. In the stock and futures markets together, one portfolio insurer sold stock and futures with underlying values totaling $1.7 billion. Huge as this selling pressure from portfolio insurers was, it was a small fraction of the sales dictated by the formulas of their models.

Tuesday, October 20

Overnight the Tokyo and London stock markets declined dramatically, falling just under 15 percent. In the U.S., the Federal Reserve issued a statement just before the equity market's opening that it would provide needed liquidity to the financial system. On U.S. equity markets, the start of trading Tuesday stood in marked contrast to Monday. Both stock and futures markets opened with dramatic rises. On the NYSE, many stocks could not open due to "buy-side" order imbalances. The majority of these imbalances were made up of "market orders," primarily from value-oriented investors and traders with short stock or futures positions. The NYSE specialists, burdened with more than $1 billion in stock inventories at Monday's close, opened stocks at higher levels and reduced their inventories. In the first hour, the Dow index rose just under 200 points. . . . In the futures market, the S&P 500 contract opened up 10 percent at 223. Buying pressure came from aggressive trading-oriented institutions who wanted to buy the market but were unsure how quickly they could get execution on the NYSE. Buying pressure also came from traders wanting to close out short positions after hearing rumors about the financial viability of the CME's clearinghouse. These rumors were unfounded, although two New York investment banks had to wait until late in the afternoon before receiving variation margin payments totaling about $1.5 billion from the CME clearinghouse. The rumors did affect Tuesday's trading, with futures volume dropping 22 percent below Monday's level.

The morning rally in the futures market ended abruptly at 10:00 a.m., as heavy selling by portfolio insurers and traders overwhelmed buying. Portfolio insurance selling in the first hour totaled the equivalent of almost $900 million of stock. The futures contract quickly moved to an enormous discount (as large as 40 index points) as the market went into freefall, plummeting 27 percent between 10:00 a.m. and 12:15 p.m. By the end of this period, portfolio insurance sales for the day totaled the equivalent of $1.75 billion of stock; by the end of the day it added up to 40 percent of futures activity of public sellers. At its low, the S&P 500 futures contract price implied a Dow level of about 1,400. Contributing greatly to this freefall was the lack of index arbitrage buying which would normally have been stimulated by the huge discount of futures to stock.... As on Monday afternoon, the primary linkage between the two markets had been disconnected.

The stock market also ran out of buying support by midmorning and began to follow the futures market down. Although individual stocks were opening and closing again at various times all morning and early afternoon, record or near-record volume was executed in every half hour period. During the first two hours, 259 million shares were traded. Selling pressure was widespread, much of it from mutual funds who were dealing with expected redemptions, portfolio insurers who were switching from selling futures to selling stocks, and some index arbitrageurs. In addition, the large discount between futures and stocks acted as a "billboard," worrying many investors that further declines were imminent. By 12:30 p.m., the Dow had fallen to just above 1,700.

At this point a number of exchanges closed trading temporarily. The CBOE suspended trading at 11:45 a.m., based on its rule that trading on the NYSE must be open in at least 80 percent of the stocks which constitute the options index it trades. At 12:15 p.m., the CME announced a trading suspension in reaction to individual stock closings on the NYSE and the rumor of the imminent closing of the NYSE itself.

During Tuesday morning, the dynamics of trading in stocks and futures had become dysfunctional. The futures market was falling under selling pressure from portfolio insurers. Normally, the large discount would have attracted buyers; under the current circumstances, however, some potential buyers were afraid of the credit risk perceived to exist in futures and many stock investors were simply not authorized to buy futures. In addition, index arbitrage activity was limited because DOT was no longer available to some market participants. Because of the futures discount, those market professionals who could sell stocks did so. At the same time, the huge discount at which futures were selling made stocks look "expensive" and stifled buying demand in the stock market. The stock market "drafted" down in the wake of the futures market. The result was sell-side order imbalances in both markets, leading to the near disintegration of market pricing.

Closing the futures market had a number of marked effects on the equity market. On the sell side, it disconnected most of the portfolio insurers from the market. On the buy side, there was no longer a "cheap" futures alternative to buying stocks. Finally, the negative psychology of the "billboard" effect was eliminated. The reaction time of the stock market was dramatic: the Dow rallied 125 points in the next 45 minutes.

When the futures market reopened just after 1:00 p.m., it was still at a substantial 17 point discount to stocks. Many of the effects which had rallied the stock market were reversed. Portfolio insurers resumed selling futures and the stock market began drafting down again. The Dow lost almost 100 points in the next half hour.

By early Tuesday afternoon, the equity market was again in freefall and needed reassurance. This came from a series of announced stock buyback programs by major corporations. By committing to these programs, the corporations provided needed support for the future level of their stocks. The buying power represented by these announced programs would ultimately total over $6 billion by Tuesday evening. Around 2:00 p.m., the combined effect of buybacks already announced and those expected turned the equity market around. The Dow rallied 170 points between 2:00 p.m. and 3:30 p.m. After a decline in the last 30 minutes induced by program sales, the Dow closed with a new gain for the day of over 100 points, the largest gain on record.

Although Monday was the day of the dramatic stock market decline, it was midday Tuesday that the securities markets and the financial system approached breakdown. First, the ability of securities markets to price equities was in question. The futures and stock markets were disconnected. There were few buyers in either market and individual stocks ceased to trade. Investors began to question the value of equity assets.

Second, and more serious, a widespread credit breakdown seemed for a period of time quite possible. Amid rumors, subsequently revealed to be unfounded, of financial failures by some clearinghouses and several major market participants, and exacerbated by the fragmentation and complexity of the clearing process, the financial system came close to gridlock. Intermarket transactions required funds transfers and made demands for bank credit almost beyond the capacity of the system to provide.

Summary

Although the equity market's behavior during this week was complex and rich in detail, several important themes emerge. First, reactive selling by institutions, which followed portfolio insurance strategies and sought to liquidate large fractions of their stock holdings regardless of price, played a prominent role in the market break. By reasonable estimates, the formulas used by portfolio insurers dictated the sale of $20 to $30 billion of equities over this short time span. Under such pressure, prices must fall dramatically. Transaction systems, such as DOT, or market stabilizing mechanisms, such as the NYSE specialists, are bound to be crushed by such selling pressure, however they are designed or capitalized.

Second, a few mutual funds sold stock in reaction to redemptions. To the market their behavior looked much like that of the portfolio insurers, that is, selling without primary regard to price. Third, some aggressive trading-oriented investors, seizing the profit opportunity presented by the predictable forced selling by other institutions, contributed to the market break. Fourth, much of the selling pressure was concentrated in the hands of surprisingly few institutions. A handful of large investors provided the impetus for the sharpness of the decline.

Fifth, ... futures and stock market movements were inextricably related. Portfolio insurers sold in the futures market, forcing prices down. The downward price pressure in the futures market was then transmitted to the stock market by index arbitrage and diverted portfolio insurance sales. . . .

Finally, there were periods when the linkage between stock and futures markets became completely disconnected, leading to a freefall in both markets.

The juxtaposition of a record 508 point decline on Monday and a record 102 point bounceback on Tuesday suggests that these trading forces outstripped the capacity of market infrastructures. . . .

Market Performance

. . . The most immediately striking fact about the performance of the equity market during the market break is that, in the face of selling pressure of unprecedented severity, it handled a record volume of transactions. . . .

The extent to which trading in listed stocks and the S&P 500 futures contract was suspended during the critical days of October 19 and 20 was, in light of the pressures brought to bear, surprisingly limited. . . .

However, the performance of financial markets cannot be judged solely in terms of volumes traded. The terms on which trades were executed are equally important. Effective market making mechanisms should sustain fair and orderly trading in several critical respects. At best, market mechanisms should smooth out temporary fluctuations in market prices. At a minimum, they should not exacerbate price fluctuations. Also, trading should be conducted on an equitable basis. Similar orders entered under equal conditions should not be executed on widely different terms. In neither of these respects did market mechanisms perform effectively during the critical days of the October market break. . . .

Equal Access to Trading Opportunities

The extreme volatility of market prices on October 19 and 20 subjected all market participants, and particularly small investors, to capriciously different treatment.

Price variations as large and erratic as those that occurred on October 19 and 20 can be inherently discriminatory. An investor selling stock, or futures contracts, near the close on Monday suffered a loss of 10 to 12 percent compared to investors who sold either an hour earlier or the next morning. In contrast, an investor who bought at or near the open on Tuesday morning paid from 10 to 20 percent more than one who bought either at the previous afternoon's close or two hours later.

In addition to these discrepancies, small investors were at an apparent disadvantage in speed of order execution. Part of the disadvantage stemmed from an understandable difficulty experienced by small investors in reaching retail brokers, which was widely reported but impossible to quantify after the fact. Another part of the problem was, however, attributable to delays and failures of the automated, small-order-oriented processing systems of both the NYSE and the OTC market. . . .

These system failures, coupled with natural delays in processing orders at the retail level, meant that small investor orders were executed at random times and, therefore, at prices that varied widely from those in existence when purchase or sale decisions were made. The unequal speed at which trades were executed did not necessarily disadvantage small investors. In some cases, delays in execution—for example, of buy orders entered prior to the opening on Monday—might have been substantially beneficial to some small investors. However, the existence of unequal access would almost necessarily have created at least an appearance of unfairness. . . .

New York Stock Exchange Specialists

The performance of NYSE specialists during the October market break period varied over time and from specialist to specialist. . . . At this critical time, specialists were willing to lean against the dominant downward trend in the market at a significant cost to themselves.

The limited nature of some specialists' contributions to price stability may have been due to the exhaustion of their purchasing power following attempts to stabilize markets at the open on October 19.

However, for other specialists, lack of purchasing power appears not to have been the determining factor in their behavior. It is understandable that specialists would not sacrifice large amounts of capital in what must have seemed a hopeless attempt to stem overwhelming waves of selling pressure. Nevertheless, from the final hours of trading on October 19 through October 20, a substantial number of NYSE specialists appear not to have been a significant force in counterbalancing market trends. . . .

Clearing and Credit

Difficulties with the clearing and credit systems further exacerbated the difficulties of market makers and other market participants during the market break. Because of the five day settlement rule for stocks, these concerns were less immediate in the stock markets than in the futures and options markets, where settlement is made the next day. However, in the stock market, the unprecedented volume led to an unusually large number of questioned trades. . . . Uncertainties concerning the ultimate disposition of questioned trades added to other uncertainties regarding the financial condition of specialists and other broker-dealers on October 19 and 20.

Settlement problems in the futures and options markets also contributed to these uncertainties. . . .

In this atmosphere of uncertainty, the mere possibility that commercial banks might curtail lending to clearinghouse members was enough to raise questions and feed rumors about the viability of those firms and clearinghouses. However, timely intervention by the Federal Reserve helped assure a continuing supply of credit to the clearinghouse members. At 8:15 a.m. on Tuesday morning, it was announced that:

> The Federal Reserve Bank affirms its readiness to serve as a source of liquidity to support the economic and financial system.

Notwithstanding these assurances, there were continued difficulties on Tuesday. For example, because of delays in the CME clearing process, two major clearinghouse members with margin collections of $1.5 billion due them on Tuesday did not receive their funds until after 3:00 p.m., many hours later than normal. . . .

Although the cash, credit and the timing demands of the current clearinghouse system raised the possibility of a default, none occurred. On the other hand, the mere possibility that a clearinghouse might default, or that liquidity would disappear, contributed to volatility on Tuesday in two important ways.

First, some market makers did curtail their market making activities, especially in the case of block trading where temporary commitments of capital were required, because they feared that loans or credit lines from their commercial bankers might be exhausted or withdrawn. Second, uncertainties about the activities and viability of the clearinghouses, as well as major broker-dealers, appear to have increased investor uncertainty in the already turbulent atmosphere of October 20.

These uncertainties intensified market fluctuations and the sense of panic evident that day. Had decisive action not been taken by the Federal Reserve, it appears that far worse consequences would have been a very real possibility. . . .

One Market: Stocks, Stock Index Futures, and Stock Options

Analysis of market behavior during the crucial days in mid-October makes clear an important conclusion. From an economic viewpoint, what have been traditionally seen as separate markets—the markets for stocks, stock index futures, and stock options—are in fact one market. Under ordinary circumstances these marketplaces move sympathetically, linked by a number of forces. The pathology which resulted when the linkages among these market segments failed underlay the market break of October.

Many mechanisms link these marketplaces. The instruments—stocks, stock index futures and stock options—are fundamentally driven by the same economic forces. The same major investment banks dominate the trading among all three segments, both in executing orders for others and for their own accounts. In addition, many of the same institutions are responsible for a large amount of the trading in all three instruments, and particularly in stocks and index futures.

Many of the trading strategies discussed in this Report also serve to link these marketplaces. Index arbitrage provides a direct linkage between the stock and index futures markets. Faced with increasingly chaotic markets in October, portfolio insurers, to the extent possible, abandoned their reliance on the futures markets to execute their strategies and switched to selling stocks directly, underlining the commonality among market function. Another link is the routine use of the futures markets by institutions investing in index funds as a fast and low-cost entry and exit vehicle to the stock market. And, of course, a host of hedging strategies for individual stock positions employ counterbalancing purchases and sales by market makers in these marketplaces.

Market makers in these markets routinely hedge their positions by trading in two markets. For example, market makers in the S&P 100 option hedge by using the S&P 500 futures contract, and some NYSE specialists and market makers in futures and options constantly monitor up-to-the-minute prices in other markets on electronic screens. Market makers tend to carry minimal positions from day-to-day, providing liquidity for normal market moves but not for the kind of abnormally large swings experienced in October 1987.

Clearing procedures in the several market segments produce further intertwining. While it is not yet possible to cross-margin positions, proceeds from sales in one market segment may provide funds needed to pay for purchases in another. Fears that a clearinghouse in one market segment might be unable to deliver funds owed to investors can ignite concern throughout the system, as it did in October.

In sum, what may appear superficially to be three separate markets—for stocks, stock options, and stock index futures—in fact behaves as one market. . . .

Just as the failure of sellers to understand that they were trading in a single equity market exacerbated the market break, so, too, did the breakdown of certain structural mechanisms linking these separate market segments. Unopened stocks inhibited trading in the derivative instruments. . . .

Under normal circumstances, index arbitrage acts as one of the primary bridges between stock and futures markets. By midday October 19, this arbitrage became difficult. First, transactions backed up in the DOT system, and then, on subsequent days, access to the system was denied to these traders. However, had the system functioned more effectively, this linkage would have been incapable of transmitting the full weight of the estimated $25 billion of selling dictated by portfolio insurance strategies.

Even as direct arbitrage between stocks and futures failed, portfolio insurers provided some indirect arbitrage when they switched from selling futures to selling stocks. The amount of such indirect arbitrage was limited by, among other things, structural and regulatory rigidities. . . .

Differences in margin and clearinghouse mechanisms contributed further to the failure of linkages within the single equity market. Many investors, not fully understanding margin and clearing mechanisms in futures, responded to rumors of payment failures, and the reality of late payments, by the CME clearinghouse, by refusing to buy in the futures market.

The decisions of lenders were also influenced by concerns over inconsistencies among the several markets. The complexity of clearing massive volumes of stocks, options, and futures through separate clearinghouses caused some lenders to hesitate in extending credit. The consequent threat of financial gridlock posed the prospect of major financial system breakdown on October 20, prompting the Federal Reserve to boost investor confidence by promising to inject liquidity into the market.

A number of factors ultimately contributed to the failure of the stock and futures markets to function as one market. As the markets became disengaged, a near freefall developed in both markets. Sellers put direct downward pressure on both markets. As large discounts developed between futures and stocks, those investors who could, switched from selling futures to selling stocks. Those unable to switch continued to sell futures, driving these prices down further. . . .

The pathology of disconnected markets fed on itself. Faced with a surfeit of sellers and a scarcity of buyers, both markets—futures and stock—were at times on October 19 and 20 nearly in freefall.

The ability of the equity market to absorb the huge selling pressure to which it was subjected in mid-October depended on its liquidity. . . .

The liquidity apparent during periods of normal volume provided by the activities of market makers and active traders on both sides of the market is something of an illusion. Liquidity sufficient to absorb the selling demands of a limited number of investors becomes an illusion of liquidity when confronted by massive selling, as everyone shows up on the same side of the market at once. As with people in a theatre when someone yells "Fire!", these sellers all ran for the exit in October, but it was large enough to accommodate only a few. . . .

Regulatory Implications

. . . The analysis of the October market break demonstrates that one agency must have the authority to coordinate a few but critical intermarket regulatory issues, monitor intermarket activities and mediate intermarket concerns.

This "intermarket"—across markets—agency need not take responsibility for all "intramarket"—within one market—regulatory issues. Such matters as securities registration, tender offer rules, and regulation of stock and option trading practices should be left to the SEC, which has the required expertise in these areas. Intramarket issues in futures markets should remain within the purview of the CFTC, which has expertise in the design and regulations of futures contracts and markets.

However, there are a few important intermarket regulatory issues which must be considered jointly and simultaneously across market segments to ensure that the intermarket systems operate harmoniously. These are issues which cannot be decided from the perspective of a single marketplace. Doing so imposes pervasive, unavoidable and possibly destabilizing influences on other related marketplaces and on the interrelated market system as a whole. . . .

The October experience demonstrates that the issues which have an impact across related markets, and throughout the financial system, include clearing and credit mechanisms, margin requirements, circuit breaker mechanisms, such as price limits and trading halts, and information systems for monitoring intermarket activities. . . .

The critical requirement for the intermarket agency is broad expertise in the financial system as a whole because the greatest potential risk of intermarket failure is to the financial system as a whole, rather than to individual market segments. . . .

In addition, this intermarket agency needs to serve a broad constituency. Since intermarket activities affect the health of the financial system, this constituency is not dominated by the active market participants so prominent in the October episode. Nor is this constituency limited to individual investors, the majority owners of U.S. equities. The intermarket agency serves the broader constituency of all those who have a stake in the financial system.

Because of its broad constituency, this agency needs the independence to resist demands of partisan political and economic interests, particularly those of active market participants. The stakes are simply too high, the potential adverse consequences of market failure too pervasive. . . .

Joint SEC-CFTC Responsibility. A single regulator, created through joint SEC-CFTC responsibility, could be achieved through a merger of the two agencies, a formal joint committee arrangement, or strict requirements for coordination of intermarket regulatory issues. This alternative would bring together the expertise of the SEC and CFTC with respect to specific types of instruments and intramarket regulatory issues. Nonetheless, combining two agencies with intramarket expertise . . . would not necessarily produce effective intermarket regulation. . . .

Joint Federal Reserve-SEC-CFTC Committee. The addition of the Federal Reserve would supplement the intramarket expertise of the SEC and CFTC with the broad financial system expertise of the Federal Reserve.

Although this alternative has attractive aspects, there are drawbacks. . . .

. . . [T]he health of the financial system depends upon effective intermarket regulation. This argues for investing the responsibility in a single responsive agency with the authority to act promptly, rather than assembling a committee representing several agencies.

The Federal Reserve. In most countries, the central bank, as part of its broader responsibility for the health of a nation's financial system, is the intermarket regulator. The Federal Reserve has a primary responsibility for the health of the U.S. financial system. The Federal Reserve works closely with the Department of the Treasury to achieve this goal. This responsibility, and the Federal Reserve's accumulated expertise in discharging this responsibility, are arguments in its favor as the appropriate intermarket agency. . . .

Finally, there are precedents for the Federal Reserve as an intermarket agency. The Federal Reserve already has formal responsibility for margin requirements on stocks and stock options. Adding futures margins to the Federal Reserve's purview would be a logical extension of its current responsibilities and is not a major change. Also, the Federal Reserve regulates bank lending to securities market participants.

Despite these advantages, there are drawbacks to the Federal Reserve as the intermarket agency. Intermarket coordination would be a new responsibility, involving the burden of additional tasks. . . . Another problem with the Federal Reserve as the intermarket agency is the danger that market participants may take on more risk in the expectation that the Federal Reserve will bail them out in a crisis. . . .

The Department of the Treasury. The Treasury Department possesses most of the advantages of the Federal Reserve. It has broad financial system perspective and expertise, international standing in a variety of markets, financial strength, prestige and influence.

However, unlike the Federal Reserve, the SEC, and the CFTC, which are structured as independent agencies, the Treasury is part of the executive branch. Because the Secretary of the Treasury and the Treasury staff serve at the pleasure of the President, it has less independence as a regulatory agency.

A New Regulatory Body. It would be possible to establish a new regulatory body designed to coordinate intermarket issues. This alternative appears to be more expensive than, and inferior to, harnessing the accumulated expertise and standing of an existing agency. . . .

Intermarket Issues

Intermarket issues are those which systematically and unavoidably impose influences on all markets. The few important intermarket issues which need to be harmonized by a single body include clearing and credit mechanisms, margin requirements, circuit breaker mechanisms such as price limits and trading halts, and information systems for monitoring intermarket activities. . . .

Clearing and credit mechanisms need to be unified. With separate clearing houses for each market segment, no single clearing corporation has an overview of the intermarket positions of market participants. . . .

The complexity and fragmentation of the separate clearing mechanisms in stocks, futures and options—in conjunction with massive volume, violent price volatility, and staggering demands on bank credit—brought the financial system to the brink on Tuesday, October 20. Some clearing-houses were late in making payments. There were rumors concerning the viability of clearinghouses and market participants. This in turn affected the willingness of lenders to finance market participants under the uncommitted lending arrangements common in the industry. This crisis of confidence raised the spectre of a full-scale financial system breakdown and required the Federal Reserve to provide liquidity and confidence. The complexity of the clearing and credit mechanisms, rather than a substantive problem of solvency, was at fault. . . .

. . . While margins on stocks and options are already within the Federal Reserve's regulatory purview, futures margins are currently determined by futures exchanges, and thus are not subject to intermarket oversight. Futures margins should be consistent with effective stock margins for professional market participants such as broker-dealers, and cross-margining should be implemented.

Margins have two fundamental characteristics. First, margin requirements affect intramarket performance risk. Margins serve as a performance bond to secure the ability of market participants to meet their obligations. Second, margins represent collateral; thus, margin requirements control the leverage possible in the investment in any financial instrument. . . .

However, margins are more than a financial performance control mechanism. All margin requirements have one aspect in common; margins are collateral and control the effective economic leverage achievable in any financial instrument. . . .

It has been long recognized that margin requirements, through leverage, affect the volume of speculative activity. Controlling speculative behavior is one approach to inhibiting overvaluation in stocks and reducing the potential for a precipitate price decline fueled by the involuntary selling that stems, for example, from margin calls. . . .

The October experience illustrates how a relatively few, aggressive, professional market participants can produce dramatic swings in market prices. Moreover, the mid-October episode demonstrates that such pressures are transmitted from marketplace to marketplace and, at times, pressures concentrated in one market segment can have traumatic effects on the whole system. Low futures margins allow investors to control large positions with low initial investments. The clear implication is that margin requirements affect intermarket risk and are not the private concern of a single marketplace. . . .

Speculation by professional market participants is, however, a realistic concern. In the stock market, professionals are not subject to the 50 percent margin requirement applicable to individuals. Professionals, such as broker-dealers, can invest in stocks on 20 percent to 25 percent margin. The same professionals can take equivalent positions in stock through the futures market on much lower margin.

To protect the intermarket system, margins on stock index futures need to be consistent with margins for professional market participants in the stock market. Such requirements need not produce equal margins in futures and stocks but should reflect the different structure of the two related market segments. . . .

Circuit breaker mechanisms involve trading halts in the various market segments. . . . To be effective, such mechanisms need to be coordinated across the markets for stocks, stock index, futures and options. Circuit breakers need to be in place prior to a market crisis. . . .

Circuit breakers have three benefits. First, they limit credit risks and loss of financial confidence by providing a "time-out" amid frenetic trading to settle up and ensure that everyone is solvent. Second, they facilitate price discovery by providing a "time-out" to pause, evaluate, inhibit panic, and publicize order imbalances to attract value traders to cushion violent movements in the market.

Finally, circuit breaker mechanisms counter the illusion of liquidity by formalizing the economic fact of life, so apparent in October, that markets have a limited capacity to absorb massive one-sided volume. Making circuit breakers part of the contractual landscape makes it far more difficult for some market participants—pension portfolio insurers, aggressive mutual funds—to mislead themselves into believing that it is possible to sell huge amounts in short time periods. . . .

There are perceived disadvantages to circuit breaker mechanisms. They may hinder trading and hedging strategies. Trading halts may lock investors in, preventing them from exiting the market. However, circuit breakers in a violent market are inevitable. . . .

The October experience illustrates the need for a trading information system incorporating the trade, time of the trade and the name of the ultimate customer in every major market segment. This is critical to assess the nature and cause of a market crisis to determine who bought and who sold. This information can be used to diagnose developing problems as well as to uncover potentially damaging abuses. . . .

Conclusion

One intermarket system mandates one agency to coordinate the few critical intermarket regulatory issues—clearing and credit arrangements, margins, circuit breakers and information systems. This intermarket agency need not be involved in detailed intramarket regulatory issues in which the SEC, the CFTC and the self regulatory organizations have expertise. The expertise required of the intermarket agency is evident from the nature of the task. . . .

Although exchanges may not be pleased with the prospect of intermarket regulations, the Task Force has concluded it is essential to ensure the integrity of financial markets. . . .

INTERIM REPORT OF THE WORKING GROUP ON FINANCIAL MARKETS

Introduction and Summary

On March 18, 1988, the Working Group on Financial Markets was established by Executive Order to provide a coordinating framework for consideration, resolution, recommendation, and action on the complex issues raised by the market break in October of 1987. The Working Group was charged with developing effective mechanisms to enhance investor confidence, to protect the quality and fairness of markets for all participants, and to preserve the continued orderliness, integrity, competitiveness, and efficiency of our nation's financial markets. This is an interim report on our progress, actions, and recommendations. . . .

The Working Group reached early agreement on a number of important premises for our deliberations:

- The existence of large debt and equity portfolios held by institutions and the increased level of principal activities by investment firms have led to increased demand for portfolio hedging strategies and market liquidity.
- It is unrealistic (and perhaps counterproductive) to try to undo the changes in financial markets or market strategies brought about by improvements in telecommunications and computer technology.
- The role of fundamental economic forces should be emphasized when evaluating the October decline. Stock prices prior to the collapse had reached levels that seemed to be in excess of those justified by real earnings potential and reasonable discount factors. The inevitable reassessment of economic fundamentals by market investors was an important part of the selling pressure and price decline in October.
- The size and speed of the decline initiated by fundamental reevaluation of equity values was exacerbated on October 19 by a number of factors:
  —volume overwhelmed trade processing capacity;
  —many participants pulled back from the markets because of fear and shock—and because of uncertainties and concerns over (i) the accuracy and timeliness of information, (ii) counter-party solvency,

(iii) credit availability, and (iv) *de facto, ad hoc* market closures or other market disruptions.

—the financial system came under great stress in the credit, clearing, and settlement area.

- The Working Group agrees with the Brady Report conclusion that the stock, options, and futures markets are closely linked.
- The priority goals of the Working Group, therefore, have been to address the major uncertainties and to focus on reductions in possible systematic risk. In this respect, the Working Group followed the agenda established by the Brady Report, which also assigned first priority to the systemic risks identified during the market break.

As a result, the Working Group was able to concentrate its initial efforts on developing the most important system protections, in close consultation with self-regulatory organizations and market participants. The Working Group's conclusions and recommendations, more fully described in the body of the Report and its appendices, are as follows:

1. A "circuit-breaker" mechanism should be put in place that operates in a coordinated fashion across all markets, using pre-established limits broad enough to be tripped only on rare occasions, but which are sufficient to support the ability of payment and credit systems to keep pace with extraordinarily large market declines.
2. A significant number of important initiatives should be implemented in a timely fashion to improve further the operation of the credit, clearing, and settlement system—beyond the notable and valuable changes the markets have made already. Although these initiatives are complex and technical, they would result in highly significant improvements in the vital linkages within the credit markets.
3. Current minimum margins for stocks, stock index futures, and options provide an adequate level of protection to the financial system. Prudential maintenance margin percentages required for carrying an individual stock should be significantly higher than the percentage margin required for a futures contract on a stock index.
4. Contingency planning, including the continuation of the Working Group, is an important, ongoing responsibility that the Working Group members are implementing.
5. Capital adequacy is being addressed in material ways by the markets and should continue to be reviewed and improved whenever necessary.
6. Markets already are making—and should continue to make—significant efforts to enhance the operational capacity of trade-processing systems and to improve the fairness and quality of order executions for all investors, large or small.
7. The Working Group should continue to function as a coordinating and consulting mechanism for intermarket issues.

The Working Group can continue to be effective by monitoring the progress of its recommendations, by serving as a consultative and coordinating forum, and by expediting resolution of the remaining issues. The Working Group also believes that the structural weaknesses exposed by the October break can be overcome through cooperative efforts of the relevant government agencies, self-regulatory bodies, market participants, and the Congress.

Continuing Coordination

The Working Group believes that its continuation, in its existing configuration, is an excellent way to continue the process of addressing intermarket issues. Much as been accomplished in a short time frame, but work on a number of issues has not been completed. The Brady Task Force and others have recommended that some additional regulatory mechanism be established to resolve these continuing issues. Recognizing this concern for coordination, the Working Group believes that cooperative efforts under the existing regulatory structure will be more effective and less disruptive than more formal, additional legislated structure. . . .

COURT ON STUDENT NEWSPAPER CENSORSHIP

January 13, 1988

In a 5-3 ruling handed down January 13, the Supreme Court upheld the broad powers of public school authorities to control the content of student publications. In so doing, it continued a recent trend toward curtailing students' rights. In 1985 the Court had ruled that school officials did not need a warrant or probable cause to search students (Court on Student Searches, Historic Documents of 1985, p. 13); *and in 1986, it held that officials could discipline a student for using vulgar language.* (Court on Students' Free Speech, Historic Documents of 1986, p. 731)

Writing for the majority in the case of Hazelwood School District v. Kuhlmeier, *Justice Byron R. White said a school "need not tolerate student speech that is inconsistent with its basic educational mission, even though the government could not censor similar speech outside the school." The First Amendment was not violated, White added, when school officials exercised "editorial control over the style and content of student speech in school-sponsored expressive articles," so long as the officials' actions were "reasonably related to legitimate pedagogical concerns."*

The case arose when the principal of Hazelwood East High School in Hazelwood, Missouri, deleted two pages from the May 13, 1983, issue of the Spectrum, *the school newspaper produced by a journalism class. The pages contained an article on the problems faced by pregnant teenagers and one on the effects of parents' divorce on their children. The first article mentioned three pregnant students, but not by name; nevertheless the school's principal, Robert E. Reynolds, thought they could be identified. He also considered the article inappropriate for younger students. The article on divorce, he said, should have included responses from the parents who were discussed in the piece, and their comments for publication should have been obtained.*

After the pages were deleted, three student editors took Reynolds and the Board of Education to court. They based their case on a 1969 landmark Supreme Court case, Tinker v. Des Moines Independent Community School District, *which upheld the rights of high school students to wear black armbands to protest the Vietnam War. Students did not "shed their constitutional rights at the schoolhouse gate," the Court then held.*

The Hazelwood students lost in district court, but the U.S. Court of Appeals for the Eighth Circuit reversed that ruling, holding that the First Amendment rights of the journalism students had been violated.

Limits on Free Speech?

In overturning the appellate court's ruling, Justice White rejected its view that a school paper constituted a "public forum" for the expression of students' viewpoints and was thus protected from editorial intrusion. White cited the Tinker *case in his opinion, agreeing that rights did not stop at the school gate. But, he continued, protected free-speech rights did not extend to expression that carries "the imprimatur of the school." A public school, White wrote, must be able "to set high standards for student speech that is disseminated under its auspices—standards that may be higher than those demanded by some newspaper publishers or theatrical producers in the 'real' world—and ... refuse to disseminate student speech that does not meet those standards."*

Justices William J. Brennan, Jr., Thurgood Marshall, and Harry A. Blackmun dissented, saying the decision would give free reign to Orwellian "thought police" exercising "mind control" over a captive student audience. The Court's majority, Brennan wrote, "teaches youth to discount important principles of government as mere platitudes. The young men and women of Hazelwood East expected a civics lesson but not the one the court teaches them today."

Mixed Reaction, Uncertain Impact

The decision was immediately hailed by school administrators who said it would put to rest concerns about their right to exert control over student publications. Jonathan Howe, president of the National School Boards Association, said school officials now might be less reluctant for student newspapers to be established.

Janet Benshoof, a staff attorney for the American Civil Liberties Union, which assisted the students in their suit, called the decision "a serious undermining of press rights." "The 5-to-3 majority is basically correct in upholding the authority of educators over students of this age," said a New York Times *editorial on January 15. "But the Court's affirmation puts heavy responsibility on how educators will use that authority. . . . The student journalists made mistakes but deserved commendation as well as correction. They tackled tough subjects, where many school newspapers content themselves with publishing community billboards. They did so in a serious way."*

The impact of the decision on colleges and universities was uncertain; previous decisions held college students to be adults, subject to prevailing legal standards. In a footnote, White noted that the Hazelwood *ruling did not address whether college officials had the same authority as high school officials to censor student material. "Ultimately, I think that the Court won't apply this decision to the college press," said Mark Goodman, director of the Student Press Law Center, a national advocacy group for high school and college newspapers.*

> *Following are excerpts from the majority opinion in the Supreme Court's 5-3 ruling January 13, 1988, in* Hazelwood School District v. Kuhlmeier, *ruling that public school officials have broad power to censor school newspapers, plays, and other "school-sponsored activities," and from the dissent of Justice William J. Brennan, Jr.:*

<u>No. 86-836</u>

Hazelwood School District et al., Petitioners *v.* Cathy Kuhlmeier et al.	On writ of certiorari to the United States Court of Appeals for the Eighth Circuit

[January 13, 1988]

JUSTICE WHITE delivered the opinion of the Court.

This case concerns the extent to which educators may exercise editorial control over the contents of a high school newspaper produced as part of the school's journalism curriculum.

I

Petitioners are the Hazelwood School District in St. Louis County, Missouri; various school officials; Robert Eugene Reynolds, the principal of Hazelwood East High School, and Howard Emerson, a teacher in the school district. Respondents are three former Hazelwood East students who were staff members of Spectrum, the school newspaper. They contend that school officials violated their First Amendment rights by deleting two pages of articles from the May 13, 1983, issue of Spectrum.

Spectrum was written and edited by the Journalism II class at Hazelwood East. The newspaper was published every three weeks or so during the 1982-1983 school year. More than 4,500 copies of the newspaper were distributed during that year to students, school personnel, and members of the community.

The Board of Education allocated funds from its annual budget for the printing of Spectrum. These funds were supplemented by proceeds from sales of the newspaper. . . .

The practice at Hazelwood East during the spring 1983 semester was for the journalism teacher to submit page proofs of each Spectrum issue to Principal Reynolds for his review prior to publication. On May 10, Emerson delivered the proofs of the May 13 edition to Reynolds, who objected to two of the articles scheduled to appear in that edition. One of the stories described three Hazelwood East students' experiences with pregnancy; the other discussed the impact of divorce on students at the school.

Reynolds was concerned that, although the pregnancy story used false names "to keep the identity of these girls a secret," the pregnant students still might be identifiable from the text. He also believed that the article's references to sexual activity and birth control were inappropriate for some of the younger students at the school. In addition, Reynolds was concerned that a student identified by name in the divorce story had complained that her father "wasn't spending enough time with my mom, my sister and I" prior to the divorce, "was always out of town on business or out late playing cards with the guys," and "always argued about everything" with her mother. Reynolds believed that the student's parents should have been given an opportunity to respond to these remarks or to consent to their publication. He was unaware that Emerson had deleted the student's name from the final version of the article.

Reynolds believed that there was no time to make the necessary changes in the stories before the scheduled press run and that the newspaper would not appear before the end of the school year if printing were delayed to any significant extent. He concluded that his only options under the circumstances were to publish a four-page newspaper instead of the planned six-page newspaper, eliminating the two pages on which the offending stories appeared, or to publish no newspaper at all. Accordingly, he directed Emerson to withhold from publication the two pages containing the stories on pregnancy and divorce. He informed his superiors of the decision, and they concurred.

Respondents subsequently commenced this action in the United States District Court for the Eastern District of Missouri seeking a declaration that their First Amendment rights had been violated, injunctive relief, and monetary damages. After a bench trial, the District Court denied an injunction, holding that no First Amendment violation had occurred.

The District Court concluded that school officials may impose restraints on students' speech in activities that are " 'an integral part of the school's educational function' "—including the publication of a school-sponsored newspaper by a journalism class—so long as their decision has " 'a substantial and reasonable basis.' " The court found that Principal Reynolds' concern that the pregnant students' anonymity would be lost and their privacy invaded was "legitimate and reasonable," given "the small number of pregnant students at Hazelwood East and several identifying characteristics that were disclosed in the article." The court held that Reynolds' action was also justified "to avoid the impression that [the school] endorses the sexual norms of the subjects" and to shield younger students from exposure to unsuitable material. The deletion of the article on divorce was seen by the court as a reasonable response to the invasion of privacy concerns raised by the named student's remarks. Because the article did not indicate that the student's parents had been offered an opportunity to respond to her allegations, said the court, there was cause for "serious doubt that the article complied with the rules of fairness which are standard in the field of journalism and which were covered in the textbook used in the Journalism II class." Furthermore, the court concluded that Reynolds was justified in deleting two full pages of the newspaper, instead of deleting only the pregnancy and divorce stories or requiring that those stories be modified to address his concerns, based on his "reasonable belief that he had to make an immediate decision and that there was no time to make modifications to the articles in question."

The Court of Appeals for the Eighth Circuit reversed [the ruling]. The court held at outset that Spectrum was not only "a part of the school adopted curriculum" but also a public forum, because the newspaper was "intended to be and operated as a conduit for student viewpoint." The court then concluded that Spectrum's status as a public forum precluded school officials from censoring its contents except when " 'necessary to avoid material and substantial interference with school work or discipline ... or the rights of others.' " (quoting *Tinker* v. *Des Moines Independent Community School Dist.* (1969)).

The Court of Appeals found "no evidence in the record that the principal could have reasonably forecast that the censored articles or any materials in the censored articles would have materially disrupted classwork or given rise to substantial disorder in the school." School officials were entitled to censor the articles on the ground that they invaded the rights of others ... only if publication of the articles could have resulted in tort liability to the school. The court concluded that no tort action for libel or invasion of privacy could have been maintained against the school by the subjects of the two articles or by their families. Accordingly, the court held that school officials had violated respondents' First Amendment rights by deleting the two pages of the newspaper.

We granted certiorari [calling up the case for review], and we now reverse.

II

Students in the public schools do not "shed their constitutional rights to freedom of speech or expression at the schoolhouse gate." They cannot be punished merely for expressing their personal views on the school premises—whether "in the cafeteria, or on the playing field, or on the campus during the authorized hours"—unless school authorities have reason to believe that such expression will "substantially interfere with the work of the school or impinge upon the rights of other students."

We have nonetheless recognized that the First Amendment rights of students in the public schools "are not automatically coextensive with the rights of adults in other settings," *Bethel School District No. 403* v. *Fraser* (1986), and must be "applied in light of the special characteristics of the school environment." A school need not tolerate student speech that is inconsistent with its "basic educational mission," even though the government could not censor similar speech outside the school. Accordingly, we held in *Fraser* that a student could be disciplined for having delivered a speech that was "sexually explicit" but not legally obscene at an official school assembly, because the school was entitled to "disassociate itself" from the speech in a manner that would demonstrate to others that such vulgarity is "wholly inconsistent with the 'fundamental values' of public school education." We thus recognized that "[t]he determination of what manner of speech in the classroom or in school assembly is inappropriate properly rests with the school board" rather than with the federal courts. It is in this context that respondents' First Amendment claims must be considered. . . .

A

We deal first with the question whether Spectrum may appropriately be characterized as a forum for public expression. The public schools do not possess all of the attributes of streets, parks, and other traditional public forums that "time out of mind, have been used for purposes of assembly, communicating thoughts between citizens, and discussing public questions." *Hague* v. *CIO* (1939). . . .

The policy of school officials toward Spectrum was reflected in Hazelwood School Board Policy 348.51 and the Hazelwood East Curriculum Guide. Board Policy 348.51 provided that "[s]chool sponsored publications are developed within the adopted curriculum and its educational implications in regular classroom activities." The Hazelwood East Curriculum Guide described the Journalism II course as a "laboratory situation in which the students publish the school newspaper applying skills they have learned in Journalism I." . . . Journalism II was taught by a faculty member during regular class hours. Students received grades and academic credit for their performance in the course.

School officials did not deviate in practice from their policy that production of Spectrum was to be part of the educational curriculum and a "regular classroom activit[y]." The District Court found that Robert Stergos, the journalism teacher during most of the 1982-1983 school year, "both had the authority to exercise and in fact exercised a great deal of control over *Spectrum*."...

... In sum, the evidence relied upon by the Court of Appeals fails to demonstrate the "clear intent to create a public forum." ... Accordingly, school officials were entitled to regulate the contents of Spectrum in any reasonable manner. It is this standard, rather than our decision in *Tinker*, that governs this case.

B

The question whether the First Amendment requires a school to tolerate particular student speech—the question that we addressed in *Tinker*—is different from the question whether the First Amendment requires a school affirmatively to promote particular student speech. The former question addresses educators' ability to silence a student's personal expression that happens to occur on the school premises. The latter question concerns educators' authority over school-sponsored publications, theatrical productions, and other expressive activities that students, parents, and members of the public might reasonably perceive to bear the imprimatur of the school. These activities may fairly be characterized as part of the school curriculum, whether or not they occur in a traditional classroom setting, so long as they are supervised by faculty members and designed to impart particular knowledge or skills to student participants and audiences....

... A school must be able to set high standards for the student speech that is disseminated under its auspices—standards that may be higher than those demanded by some newspaper publishers or theatrical producers in the "real" world—and may refuse to disseminate student speech that does not meet those standards. In addition, a school must be able to take into account the emotional maturity of the intended audience in determining whether to disseminate student speech on potentially sensitive topics, which might range from the existence of Santa Claus in an elementary school setting to the particulars of teenage sexual activity in a high school setting. A school must also retain the authority to refuse to sponsor student speech that might reasonably be perceived to advocate drug or alcohol use, irresponsible sex, or conduct otherwise inconsistent with "the shared values of a civilized social order," or to associate the school with any position other than neutrality on matters of political controversy. Otherwise, the schools would be unduly constrained from fulfilling their role as "a principal instrument in awakening the child to cultural values, in preparing him for later professional training, and in helping him to adjust normally to his environment." *Brown. v. Board of Education* (1954).

Accordingly, we conclude that the standard articulated in *Tinker* for determining when a school may punish student expression need not also be the standard for determining when a school may refuse to lend its name and resources to the dissemination of student expression. Instead, we hold that educators do not offend the First Amendment by exercising editorial control over the style and content of student speech in school-sponsored expressive activities so long as their actions are reasonably related to legitimate pedagogical concerns. . . .

III

We also conclude that Principal Reynolds acted reasonably in requiring the deletion from the May 13 issue of Spectrum of the pregnancy article, the divorce article, and the remaining articles that were to appear on the same pages of the newspaper.

The initial paragraph of the pregnancy article declared that "[a]ll names have been changed to keep the identity of these girls a secret." The principal concluded that the students' anonymity was not adequately protected, however, given the other identifying information in the article and the small number of pregnant students at the school. . . . Reynolds therefore could reasonably have feared that the article violated whatever pledge of anonymity had been given to the pregnant students. In addition, he could reasonably have been concerned that the article was not sufficiently sensitive to the privacy interests of the students' boyfriends and parents, who were discussed in the article but who were given no opportunity to consent to its publication or to offer a response. The article did not contain graphic accounts of sexual activity. The girls did comment in the article, however, concerning their sexual histories and their use or nonuse of birth control. It was not unreasonable for the principal to have concluded that such frank talk was inappropriate in a school-sponsored publication distributed to 14-year-old freshmen and presumably taken home to be read by students' even younger brothers and sisters.

The student who was quoted by name in the version of the divorce article seen by Principal Reynolds made comments sharply critical of her father. The principal could reasonably have concluded that an individual publicly identified as an inattentive parent—indeed, as one who chose "playing cards with the guys" over home and family—was entitled to an opportunity to defend himself as a matter of journalistic fairness. . . .

Principal Reynolds testified credibly at trial that, at the time that he reviewed the proofs of the May 13 issue during an extended telephone conversation with Emerson, he believed that there was no time to make any changes in the articles, and that the newspaper had to be printed immediately or not at all. . . . We . . . agree with the District Court that the decision to excise the two pages containing the problematic articles was reasonable given the particular circumstances of this case. . . .

The judgment of the Court of Appeals for the Eighth Circuit is therefore *Reversed.*

JUSTICE BRENNAN, with whom JUSTICE MARSHALL and JUSTICE BLACKMUN join, dissenting.

When the young men and women of Hazelwood East High School registered for Journalism II, they expected a civics lesson. Spectrum, the newspaper they were to publish, "was not just a class exercise in which students learned to prepare papers and hone writing skills, it was a ... forum established to give students an opportunity to express their views while gaining an appreciation of their rights and responsibilities under the First Amendment to the United States Constitution. ..."

In my view the principal ... violated the First Amendment's prohibitions against censorship of any student expression that neither disrupts classwork nor invades the rights of others, and against any censorship that is not narrowly tailored to serve its purpose.

... The Court offers no more than an obscure tangle of three excuses to afford educators "greater control" over school-sponsored speech than the *Tinker* test would permit: the public educator's prerogative to control curriculum, the pedagogical interest in shielding the high school audience from objectionable viewpoints and sensitive topics; and the school's need to dissociate itself from student expression. ... None of the excuses, once disentangled, supports the distinction that the Court draws. *Tinker* fully addresses the first concern; the second is illegitimate; and the third is readily achievable through less oppressive means.

The Court is certainly correct that the First Amendment permits educators "to assure that participants learn whatever lessons the activity is designed to teach. ..." That is, however, the essence of the *Tinker* test, not an excuse to abandon it. Under *Tinker*, school officials may censor only such student speech as would "materially disrup[t]" a legitimate curricular function. Manifestly, student speech is more likely to disrupt a curricular function when it arises in the context of a curricular activity—one that "is designed to teach" something—than when it arises in the context of a noncurricular activity. ...

I fully agree with the Court that the First Amendment should afford an educator the prerogative not to sponsor the publication of a newspaper article that is "ungrammatical, poorly written, inadequately researched, biased or prejudiced," or that falls short of the "high standards for ... student speech that is disseminated under [the school's] auspices. ..." But we need not abandon *Tinker* to reach that conclusion; we need only apply it. The enumerated criteria reflect the skills that the curricular newspaper "is designed to teach." The educator may, under *Tinker*, constitutionally "censor" poor grammar, writing, or research because to reward such expression would "materially disrup[t]" the newspaper's curricular purpose.

The same cannot be said of official censorship designed to shield the *audience* or dissociate the *sponsor* from the expression. ...

... [T]he Court attempts to justify censorship of the article on teenage pregnancy on the basis of the principal's judgment that (1) "the students' anonymity was not adequately protected," despite the article's use of aliases; and (2) the judgment "that the article was not sufficiently sensitive to the privacy interests of the students' boyfriends and parents...."

But the principal never consulted the students before censoring their work. "[T]hey learned of the deletions when the paper was released...." Further, he explained the deletions only in the broadest of generalities.... The Court's second excuse for deviating from precedent is the school's interest in shielding an impressionable high school audience from material whose substance is "unsuitable for immature audiences."...

Tinker teaches us that the state educator's undeniable, and undeniably vital, mandate to inculcate moral and political values is not a general warrant to act as "thought police" stifling discussion of all but state-approved topics and advocacy of all but the official position.... Even in its capacity as educator the State may not assume an Orwellian "guardianship of the public mind," *Thomas* v. *Collins* (1945).

The mere fact of school sponsorship does not, as the court suggests, license such thought control in the high school, whether through school suppression of disfavored viewpoints or through official assessment of topic sensitivity. The former would constitute unabashed and unconstitutional viewpoint discrimination....

Since the censorship served no legitimate pedagogical purpose, it cannot by any stretch of the imagination have been designed to prevent "materia[l] disrup[tion of] classwork." Nor did the censorship fall within the category that *Tinker* described as necessary to prevent student expression from "inva[ding] the rights of others."...

Finally, even if the majority were correct that the principal could constitutionally have censored the objectionable material, I would emphatically object to the brutal manner in which he did so.... He objected to some material in two articles, but excised six entire articles. He did not so much as inquire into obvious alternatives, such as precise deletions or additions (one of which had already been made), rearranging the layout, or delaying publication. Such unthinking contempt for individual rights is intolerable from any state official. It is particularly insidious from one to whom the public entrusts the task of inculcating in its youth an appreciation for the cherished democratic liberties that our constitution guarantees.

The Court opens its analysis in this case by purporting to reaffirm *Tinker*'s time-tested proposition that public school students " 'do not shed their constitutional rights to freedom of speech or expression at the schoolhouse gate.' " That is an ironic introduction to an opinion that denudes high school students of much of the First Amendment protection that *Tinker* itself prescribed.... [T]he Court today "teach[es] youth to discount important principles of our government as mere platitudes." The young men and women of Hazelwood East expected a civics lesson, but not the one the Court teaches them today.

I dissent.

COURT ON DISRUPTIVE HANDICAPPED STUDENTS

January 20, 1988

School officials acting on their own cannot expel disruptive handicapped students from classrooms for more than ten days, the Supreme
Court ruled January 20, in a 6-2 decision. The case, Honig v. Doe, was
hailed as a victory by handicapped-rights advocates. It essentially
confirmed an interpretation of the 1975 Education for All Handicapped
Children Act (PL 94-142) that would require school officials to consult
with the families of handicapped children and follow specific procedures
before removing disruptive children. At the same time, school officials
were given an avenue of appeal in extremely difficult cases.

The decision, written by Justice William J. Brennan, Jr., applied to a
San Francisco case in which two school officials indefinitely suspended
two emotionally disturbed students because of their alleged disruptive
and violent behavior. The students' families filed the suit, claiming that
the 1975 act had been violated and that there were no exceptions to the
law's requirement that a handicapped student must remain in the
educational program designed by the school personnel unless a change
was mutually agreed on by the family and school officials. A district court
and the U.S. Circuit Court of Appeals for the Ninth Circuit upheld the
so-called "stay put" ruling.

Bill Honig, the California superintendent of public instruction, argued
that Congress did not intend the stay-put provision to be literally
enforced because that would mean dangerous or disruptive students
could remain in school during possibly lengthy review proceedings.
According to the U.S. Department of Education, 4.4 million children were

enrolled in special education programs in 1986-1987; 8.7 percent of them were described as "emotionally disturbed." An Education Department spokesman said the number that might be disruptive or dangerous probably was very small.

Majority, Dissenting Opinions

In upholding the lower court verdicts, Justice Brennan said on behalf of the Supreme Court's majority that to read a "dangerousness" exception into the statute would mean revising it. "We decline [Honig's] invitation to rewrite the statute," he said. "We think it clear ... that Congress very much meant to strip schools of the unilateral *[Brennan's emphasis] authority they had traditionally employed to exclude disabled students, particularly emotionally disturbed students, from school."*

He added that the law allowed school officials to seek prompt federal court intervention to remove a student if expulsion was necessary. Moreover, the 1975 act permitted school officials to suspend a highly disruptive student for up to ten school days while alternatives were sought. However, Brennan pointed out that the burden of proving that a child was dangerous rested with school officials.

Justices Antonin Scalia and Sandra Day O'Connor declined to join in the majority opinion because they said the issue was moot—that the students in question were no longer covered by the act.

Reaction

Attorneys in the case generally found the decision acceptable. It was "not so bad at all," said San Francisco attorney Asher Rubin, who represented Honig. The attorney for the students, Toby Rubin, said the Court "is telling school officials that the Education for All Handicapped Children [Act] means exactly what it says—you need to involve the parents and students when appropriate" before changing a student's placement.

The decision gave school officials "at least one outlet" when they were in disagreement with the disabled student's family, said Gwendolyn Gregory, deputy general counsel of the National School Boards Association. However, she predicted that the officials would perceive court intervention as cumbersome, and might become "more rigid" in making educational plans for handicapped children.

Sen. Tom Harkin, D-Iowa, said the 1975 law set forward a right of education for handicapped children but also recognized that the students' rights must be "properly balanced against the interests of state and local school officials to ensure a safe school environment." He added that "because the court correctly construed congressional intent, I see no need" for Congress to revise the law.

Following are excerpts from the Supreme Court's 6-2 ruling, delivered January 20, 1988, in Honig v. Doe, *barring the unilateral expulsion of disruptive handicapped students, and from the dissenting opinion by Justice Antonin Scalia:*

No. 86-728

Bill Honig, California Superintendent of Public Instruction, Petitioner	On writ of certiorari to the United States Court of Appeals for the Ninth Circuit
v.	
John Doe and Jack Smith	

[January 20, 1988]

JUSTICE BRENNAN delivered the opinion of the Court.

As a condition of federal financial assistance, the Education of the Handicapped Act requires States to ensure a "free appropriate public education" for all disabled children within their jurisdictions. In aid of this goal, the Act establishes a comprehensive system of procedural safeguards designed to ensure parental participation in decisions concerning the education of their disabled children and to provide administrative and judicial review of any decisions with which those parents disagree. Among these safeguards is the so-called "stay-put" provision, which directs that a disabled child "shall remain in [his or her] then current educational placement" pending completion of any review proceedings, unless the parents and state or local educational agencies otherwise agree. 20 U.S.C. §1415(e)(3). Today we must decide whether, in the face of this statutory proscription, state or local school authorities may nevertheless unilaterally exclude disabled children from the classroom for dangerous or disruptive conduct growing out of their disabilities. In addition, we are called upon to decide whether a district court may, in the exercise of its equitable powers, order a State to provide educational services directly to a disabled child when the local agency fails to do so.

I

In the Education of the Handicapped Act (EHA or the Act), Congress sought "to assure that all handicapped children have available to them . . . a free appropriate public education which emphasizes special education and related services designed to meet their unique needs, [and] to assure that the rights of handicapped children and their parents or guardians are protected." When the law was passed in 1975, Congress had before it ample evidence that such legislative assurances were sorely needed: 21

years after this Court declared education to be "perhaps the most important function of state and local governments," *Brown* v. *Board of Education* (1954), Congressional studies revealed that better than half of the Nation's eight million disabled children were not receiving appropriate educational services. Indeed, one out of every eight of these children was excluded from the public school system altogether; many others were simply "warehoused" in special classes or were neglectfully shepherded through the system until they were old enough to drop out. Among the most poorly served of disabled students were emotionally disturbed children: Congressional statistics revealed that for the school year immediately preceding passage of the Act, the educational needs of 82 percent of all children with emotional disabilities went unmet. See S. Rep. No. 94-168, p.8 (1975)(hereinafter S. Rep.).

Although these educational failings resulted in part from funding constraints, Congress recognized that the problem reflected more than a lack of financial resources at the state and local levels. Two federal-court decisions, which the Senate Report characterized as "landmark," demonstrated that many disabled children were excluded pursuant to state statutes or local rules and policies, typically without any consultation with, or even notice to, their parents. . . . Indeed, by the time of the EHA's enactment, parents had brought legal challenges to similar exclusionary practices in 27 other states.

In responding to these problems, Congress did not content itself with passage of a simple funding statute. Rather, the EHA confers upon disabled students an enforceable substantive right to public education in participating States, see *Board of Education of Hendrick Hudson Central School Dist.* v. *Rowley* (1982), and conditions federal financial assistance upon a State's compliance with the substantive and procedural goals of the Act. Accordingly, States seeking to qualify for federal funds must develop policies assuring all disabled children the "right to a free appropriate public education," and must file with the Secretary of Education formal plans mapping out in detail the programs, procedures and timetables under which they will effectuate these policies. Such plans must assure that, "to the maximum extent appropriate," States will "mainstream" disabled children, *i.e.*, that they will educate them with children who are not disabled, and that they will segregate or otherwise remove such children from the regular classroom setting "only when the nature or severity of the handicap is such that education in regular classes . . . cannot be achieved satisfactorily."

The primary vehicle for implementing these congressional goals is the "individualized educational program" (IEP), which the EHA mandates for each disabled child. Prepared at meetings between a representative of the local school district, the child's teacher, the parents or guardians, and, whenever appropriate, the disabled child, the IEP sets out the child's present educational performance, establishes annual and short-term objectives for improvements in that performance, and describes the specially designed instruction and services that will enable the child to meet those objectives. The IEP must be reviewed and, where necessary, revised at least once a year in order to ensure that local agencies tailor the statutorily required "free appropriate public education" to each child's unique needs.

Envisioning the IEP as the centerpiece of the statute's education delivery system for disabled children, and aware that schools had all too often denied such children appropriate educations without in any way consulting their parents, Congress repeatedly emphasized throughout the Act the importance and indeed the necessity of parental participation in both the development of the IEP and any subsequent assessments of its effectiveness. Accordingly, the Act establishes various procedural safeguards that guarantee parents both an opportunity for meaningful input into all decisions affecting their child's education and the right to seek review of any decisions they think inappropriate. These safeguards include the right to examine all relevant records pertaining to the identification, evaluation and educational placement of their child; prior written notice whenever the responsible educational agency proposes (or refuses) to change the child's placement or program; an opportunity to present complaints concerning any aspect of the local agency's provision of a free appropriate public education; and an opportunity for "an impartial due process hearing" with respect to any such complaints.

At the conclusion of any such hearing, both the parents and the local educational agency may seek further administrative review and, where that proves unsatisfactory, may file a civil action in any state or federal court. In addition to reviewing the administrative record, courts are empowered to take additional evidence at the request of either party and to "grant such relief as [they] determine[] is appropriate." The "stay-put" provision at issue in this case governs the placement of a child while these often lengthy review procedures run their course. It directs that:

> "During the pendency of any proceedings conducted pursuant to [§1415], unless the State or local educational agency and the parents or guardian otherwise agree, the child shall remain in the then current educational placement of such child. . . ."

The present dispute grows out of the efforts of certain officials of the San Francisco Unified School District (SFUSD) to expel two emotionally disturbed children from school indefinitely for violent and disruptive conduct related to their disabilities. In November 1980, respondent John Doe assaulted another student at the Louise Lombard School, a developmental center for disabled children. Doe's April 1980 IEP identified him as a socially and physically awkward 17 year old who experienced considerable difficulty controlling his impulses and anger. Among the goals set out in his IEP was "[i]mprovement in [his] ability to relate to [his] peers [and to] cope with frustrating situations without resorting to aggressive acts." Frustrating situations, however, were an unfortunately prominent feature of Doe's school career: physical abnormalities, speech difficulties and poor grooming habits had made him the target of teasing and ridicule as early as the first grade; his 1980 IEP reflected his continuing difficulties with peers, noting that his social skills had deteriorated and that he could tolerate only minor frustration before exploding.

On November 6, 1980, Doe responded to the taunts of a fellow student in precisely the explosive manner anticipated by his IEP: he choked the student with sufficient force to leave abrasions on the child's neck, and kicked out a school window while being escorted to the principal's office afterwards. Doe admitted his misconduct and the school subsequently suspended him for five days. Thereafter, his principal referred the matter to the SFUSD Student Placement Committee (SPC or Committee) with the recommendation that Doe be expelled. On the day the suspension was to end, the SPC notified Doe's mother that it was proposing to exclude her child permanently from SFUSD and was therefore extending his suspension until . . . the expulsion proceedings were completed. The Committee further advised her that she was entitled to attend the November 25 hearing at which it planned to discuss the proposed expulsion.

After unsuccessfully protesting these actions by letter, Doe brought this suit against a host of local school officials and the state superintendent of public education. Alleging that the suspension and proposed expulsion violated the EHA, he sought a temporary restraining order cancelling the SPC hearing and requiring school officials to convene an IEP meeting. The District Judge granted the requested injunctive relief and further ordered defendants to provide home tutoring for Doe on an interim basis; shortly thereafter, she issued a preliminary injunction directing defendants to return Doe to his then current educational placement at Louise Lombard School pending completion of the IEP review process. Doe re-entered school on December 15, 5½ weeks . . . after his initial suspension.

Respondent Jack Smith was identified as an emotionally disturbed child by the time he entered the second grade in 1976. School records prepared that year indicated that he was unable "to control verbal or physical outburst[s]" and exhibited a "[s]evere disturbance in relationships with peers and adults." Further evaluations subsequently revealed that he had been physically and emotionally abused as an infant and young child and that, despite above average intelligence, he experienced academic and social difficulties as a result of extreme hyperactivity and low self-esteem. Of particular concern was Smith's propensity for verbal hostility. . . .

Based on these evaluations, SFUSD placed Smith in a learning center for emotionally disturbed children. His grandparents, however, believed that his needs would be better served in the public school setting and, in September 1979, the school district acceded to their requests and enrolled him at A. P. Giannini Middle School. His February 1980 IEP recommended placement in a Learning Disability Group. . . . Like earlier evaluations, the February 1980 IEP noted that Smith was easily distracted, impulsive, and anxious; it therefore proposed a half-day schedule and suggested that the placement be undertaken on a trial basis.

At the beginning of the next school year, Smith was assigned to a full-day program; almost immediately thereafter he began misbehaving. School officials met twice with his grandparents in October 1980 to discuss returning him to a half-day program; although the grandparents agreed to the reduction, they apparently were never apprised of their right to challenge the decision through EHA procedures. The school officials also warned then that if the child continued his disruptive behavior—which included stealing, extorting money from fellow students, and making sexual comments to female classmates—they would seek to expel him. On November 14, they made good on this threat, suspending Smith for five days after he made further lewd comments. His principal referred the matter to the SPC, which recommended exclusion from SFUSD. As it did in John Doe's case, the Committee scheduled a hearing and extended the suspension indefinitely pending a final disposition in the matter. On November 28, Smith's counsel protested these actions on grounds essentially identical to those raised by Doe, and the SPC agreed to cancel the hearing and to return Smith to a half-day program at A. P. Giannini or to provide home tutoring. Smith's grandparents chose the latter option and the school began home instruction on December 10; on January 6, 1981 an IEP team convened to discuss alternative placements.

After learning of Doe's action, Smith sought and obtained leave to intervene in the suit. The District Court subsequently entered summary judgment in favor of respondents on their EHA claims and issued a permanent injunction. In a series of decisions, the District Judge found that the proposed expulsions and indefinite suspensions of respondents for conduct attributable to their disabilities deprived them of their congressionally mandated right to a free appropriate public education, as well as their right to have that education provided in accordance with the procedures set out in the EHA. The District Judge therefore permanently enjoined the school district from taking any disciplinary action other than a two- or five-day suspension against any disabled child for disability-related misconduct, or from effecting any other change in the educational placement of any such child without parental consent pending completion of any EHA proceedings. In addition, the judge barred the State from authorizing unilateral placement changes and directed it to establish an EHA compliance-monitoring system or, alternatively, to enact guidelines governing local school responses to disability-related misconduct. Finally, the judge ordered the State to provide services directly to disabled children when, in any individual case, the State determined that the local educational agency was unable or unwilling to do so.

On appeal, the Court of Appeals for the Ninth Circuit affirmed the orders with slight modifications. Agreeing with the District Court that an indefinite suspension in aid of expulsion constitutes a prohibited "change in placement" under §1415(e) (3), the Court of Appeals held that the stay-put provision admitted of no "dangerousness" exception and that the statute therefore rendered invalid those provisions of the California Education Code permitting the indefinite suspension or expulsion of disabled children for misconduct arising out of their disabilities. The court concluded, however, that fixed suspensions of up to 30 school days did not fall within the reach of §1415(e)(3), and therefore upheld recent amendments to the state education code authorizing such suspensions. Lastly, the court affirmed that portion of the injunction requiring the State to provide services directly to a disabled child when the local educational agency fails to do so.

Petitioner Bill Honig, California Superintendent of Public Instruction, sought review in this Court, claiming that the Court of Appeals' construction of the stay-put provision conflicted with that of several other courts of appeals which had recognized a dangerousness exception. . . . We granted certiorari to resolve these questions, and now affirm.

II

At the outset, we address the suggestion, raised for the first time during oral argument, that this case is moot. Under Article III of the Constitution this Court may only adjudicate actual, ongoing controversies. . . . That the dispute between the parties was very much alive when suit was filed, or at the time the Court of Appeals rendered its judgment, cannot substitute for the actual case or controversy that an exercise of this Court's jurisdiction requires. . . . In the present case, we have jurisdiction if there is a reasonable likelihood that respondents will again suffer the deprivation of EHA-mandated rights that gave rise to this suit. We believe that, at least with respect to respondent Smith, such a possibility does in fact exist. . . .

Respondent John Doe is now 24 years old and, accordingly, is no longer entitled to the protections and benefits of the EHA, which limits eligibility to disabled children between the ages of three and 21. . . . [T]hus the case is moot as to him. Respondent Jack Smith, however, is currently 20 and has not yet completed high school. Although at present he is not faced with any proposed expulsion or suspension proceedings, and indeed no longer even resides within the SFUSD, he remains a resident of California and is entitled to a "free appropriate public education" within that State. His claims under the EHA, therefore, are not moot if the conduct he originally complained of is " 'capable of repetition, yet evading review.' " *Murphy* v. *Hunt* (1982). Given Smith's continued eligibility for educational services under the EHA, the nature of his disability, and petitioner's insistence that all local school districts retain residual authority to exclude disabled children for dangerous conduct, we have little difficulty concluding that there is a "reasonable expectation" that Smith would once again be subjected to a unilateral "change in placement" for conduct growing out of his disabilities were it not for the state-wide injunctive relief issued below.

Our cases reveal that . . . we generally have been unwilling to assume that the party seeking relief will repeat the type of misconduct that would once again place him or her at risk of that injury. . . . No such reluctance, however, is warranted here. It is respondent Smith's very inability to conform his conduct to socially acceptable norms that renders him "handicapped" within the meaning of the EHA. . . . In the absence of any suggestion that respondent has overcome his earlier difficulties, it is certainly reasonable to expect . . . that he will again engage in classroom misconduct. Nor is it reasonable to suppose that Smith's future educational placement will so perfectly suit his emotional and academic needs that further disruptions on his part are improbable. Although JUSTICE SCALIA suggests in his dissent that school officials are unlikely to place Smith in a setting where they cannot control his misbehavior, any efforts to ensure such total control must be tempered by the school system's statutory obligations to provide respondent with a free appropriate public education in "the least restrictive environment"; to educate him, "to the maximum extent appropriate," with children who are not disabled; and to consult with his parents or guardians, and presumably with respondent himself, before choosing a placement. Indeed, it is only by ignoring these mandates, as well as Congress' unquestioned desire to wrest from school officials their former unilateral authority to determine the placement of emotionally disturbed children that the dissent can so readily assume that respondent's future placement will satisfactorily prevent any further dangerous conduct on his part. . . . Given the unique circumstances and context of this case, therefore, we think it reasonable to expect that respondent will again engage in the type of misconduct that precipitated this suit.

We think it equally probable that, should he do so, respondent will again be subjected to the same unilateral school action for which he initially sought relief. . . .

III

The language of §1415(e)(3) is unequivocal. It states plainly that during the pendency of any proceedings initiated under the Act, unless the state or local education agency and the parents or guardian of a disabled child otherwise agree, "the child *shall* remain in the then current educational placement." §1415(e)(3) (emphasis added). Faced with this clear directive, petitioner asks us to read a "dangerousness" exception into the stay-put provision on the basis of either of two essentially inconsistent assumptions: first, that Congress thought the residual authority of school officials to exclude dangerous students from the classroom too obvious for comment; or second, that Congress inadvertently failed to provide such authority and this Court must therefore remedy the oversight. Because we cannot accept either premise, we decline petitioner's invitation to re-write the statute. . . .

We think it clear . . . that Congress very much meant to strip schools of the *unilateral* authority they had traditionally employed to exclude disabled students, particularly emotionally disturbed students, from school. In so doing, Congress did not leave school administrators powerless to deal with dangerous students; it did, however, deny school officials their former right to "self-help," and directed that in the future the removal of disabled students could be accomplished only with the permission of the parents or, as a last resort, the courts. . . .

Our conclusion that §1415(e)(3) means what it says does not leave educators hamstrung. The Department of Education has observed that, "[w]hile the [child's] placement may not be changed [during any complaint proceeding], this does not preclude the agency from using its normal procedures for dealing with children who are endangering themselves or others." Such procedures may include the use of study carrels, time-outs, detention, or the restriction of privileges. More drastically, where a student poses an immediate threat to the safety of others, officials may temporarily suspend him or her for up to 10 school days. This authority . . . not only ensures that school administrators can protect the safety of others by promptly removing the most dangerous of students, it also provides a "cooling down" period during which officials can initiate IEP review and seek to persuade the child's parents to agree to an interim placement. And in those cases in which the parents of a truly dangerous child adamantly refuse to permit any change in placement, the 10-day respite gives school officials an opportunity to invoke the aid of the courts under §1415(e)(2). . . .

IV

We believe the courts below properly construed and applied §1415(e)(3), except insofar as the Court of Appeals held that a suspension in excess of 10 school days does not constitute a "change in placement." We therefore affirm the Court of Appeals judgment on this issue as modified herein. Because we are equally divided on the question whether a court may order a State to provide services directly to a disabled child where the local agency has failed to do so, we affirm the Court of Appeals' judgment on this issue as well.

Affirmed.

JUSTICE SCALIA, with whom JUSTICE O'CONNOR joins, dissenting.

Without expressing any views on the merits of this case, I respectfully dissent because in my opinion we have no authority to decide it. I think the controversy is moot. . . .

If our established mode of analysis were followed, the conclusion that a live controversy exists in the present case would require a demonstrated probability that *all* of the following events will occur: (1) Smith will return to public school; (2) he will be placed in an educational setting that is unable to tolerate his dangerous behavior; (3) he will again engage in dangerous behavior; and (4) local school officials will again attempt unilaterally to change his placement and the state defendants will fail to prevent such action. The Court spends considerable time establishing that the last two of these events are likely to recur, but relegates to a footnote its discussion of the first event, upon which all others depend, and only briefly alludes to the second. Neither the facts in the record, nor even the extra-record assurances of counsel, establish a demonstrated probability of either of them. . . .

STATE OF THE
UNION ADDRESS
January 25, 1988

President Ronald Reagan's seventh State of the Union address to a joint session of Congress—probably his last one to be delivered in person—portrayed a decidedly optimistic picture of his administration's accomplishments and the nation's future. Declaring that he wanted his last year in office to be "the best in eight," the president said, "We're not finished yet." He insisted that the administration still had a full agenda, including holdover legislation that Congress had not enacted.

The January 25 speech, and an accompanying thirty-nine-page legislative message, contained no surprising new promises or bold initiatives. Reagan repeatedly returned to the major themes of his presidency. "Our record," he said, is an "economic and social revolution of hope, based on work, incentives, growth, and opportunity." On the international scene, he added, "We've replaced 'Blame America' with 'Look up to America.'"

The upbeat assessment of the Reagan era carefully skirted developments that had badly eroded his political power. They included the Iran-contra scandal, failure to win approval of two Supreme Court nominees, and a string of legislative losses.

The president said surprisingly little about his chief 1987 accomplishment: the signing of a treaty with Soviet leader Mikhail S. Gorbachev to ban intermediate-range nuclear force (INF) missiles. The pact was discussed in only one paragraph of Reagan's eight-page speech. However, the president's brief call for the treaty's ratification did draw one of the most enthusiastic responses of his speech, which was interrupted thirty-

eight times by applause (INF Treaty, Historic Documents of 1987, p. 945). *"In addition to the INF treaty, we're within reach of an even more significant START [strategic arms reduction talks] agreement that will reduce U.S. and Soviet long-range missile, or strategic, arsenals by half,"* he said. *At the same time, the president renewed his appeal for his missile defense plan in space, known as the Strategic Defense Initiative (SDI), which faced funding cuts in Congress.*

On the highly controversial issue of U.S. military aid to the contras fighting the leftist Sandinista government in Nicaragua, the speech treated the subject in a relatively restrained manner, acknowledging that the Sandinistas had taken some steps toward democratic reform. A week later, the president went on national television to lobby more vigorously for contra aid. But the next day, February 3, the House of Representatives defeated his request. Congress subsequently did approve about $50 million in humanitarian aid for the contras.

Budget, Domestic Proposals

Turning to the budget, Reagan won a standing ovation—with the help of eye-catching props. Calling for an overhaul of the budget process, Reagan hoisted unwieldy stacks of paper weighing forty-three pounds and totaling 3,300 pages. They were the texts of budget bills that Congress passed in the waning hours of the 1987 session. Dropping the stack with a thud for effect, the president said, "Congress shouldn't send another one of these. No. And if you do, I will not sign it."

In his legislative message, Reagan proposed new budget procedures, among them a requirement that tax increases be approved by more than a simple majority. He again called for approval of untouched pieces of the Reagan agenda such as a constitutional amendment to require a balanced budget and a proposal to give the president a line-item veto enabling him to excise individual items from appropriations bills.

Other domestic policy issues spotlighted by the president's address and his relatively detailed legislative message read more like an inventory of lost causes than a pragmatic plan for legislative action. He revived proposals to allow prayer in schools, to create low-tax "enterprise zones" in low-income areas, and to ban abortions.

Free Trade, Antidrug Efforts

Some new items did surface in the speech, such as Reagan's call for congressional approval of the U.S.-Canadian Free Trade Agreement that he and Prime Minister Brian Mulroney signed January 2. Reagan said he was "determined to expand the concept, south as well as north." He added that trade would be his "foremost concern" when he met in February with President Miguel de la Madrid of Mexico (Trade Pact with Canada, p. 571). *Reagan also said he would unveil a policy to increase commercial enterprises in space, and he called for continued support for a manned space station.*

Reagan peppered his comments on domestic policy with references to strengthening the family. His previous State of the Union addresses included the introduction of civilian and military "heroes." The 1988 heroine was First Lady Nancy Reagan, whom he credited with leading the battle for a "drug-free America." After Mrs. Reagan acknowledged a standing ovation, her husband said, "Surprised you, didn't I?"

Democratic Response

"We've come to the end of an era," said Senate Majority Leader Robert C. Byrd, D-W.Va., in a televised response to the address. The Democratic response was a sharper and a more direct attack on Reagan than it had been the previous year. "The 'feel-good' slogans have gone flat with time," Byrd said. Byrd and House Speaker Jim Wright, D-Texas, contended that the legislative initiative had passed from the White House to the Democratic-controlled Congress. In reviewing the accomplishments of the 1987 congressional session, Wright noted that bills affecting highway, clean-water, and housing programs were passed in spite of Reagan's objections.

Following is the text of President Ronald Reagan's seventh State of the Union address, delivered to a joint session of Congress and nationally televised on January 25, 1988:

Mr. Speaker, Mr. President, and distinguished Members of the House and Senate: When we first met here 7 years ago—many of us for the first time—it was with the hope of beginning something new for America. We meet here tonight in this historic Chamber to continue that work. If anyone expects just a proud recitation of the accomplishments of my administration, I say let's leave that to history; we're not finished yet. So my message to you tonight is, put on your work shoes; we're still on the job.

History records the power of the ideas that brought us here those 7 years ago—ideas like the individual's right to reach as far and as high as his or her talents will permit; the free market as an engine of economic progress. And as an ancient Chinese philosopher, Lao-tzu, said: "Govern a great nation as you would cook a small fish; do not overdo it."

Well, these ideas were part of a larger notion, a vision, if you will, of America herself—an America not only rich in opportunity for the individual but an America, too, of strong families and vibrant neighborhoods; an America whose divergent but harmonizing communities were a reflection of a deeper community of values: the value of work, of family, of religion, and of the love of freedom that God places in each of us and whose defense He has entrusted in a special way to this nation.

All of this was made possible by an idea I spoke of when Mr. [Soviet leader Mikhail S.] Gorbachev was here—the belief that the most exciting revolution ever known to humankind began with three simple words: "We the People," the revolutionary notion that the people grant government its rights, and not the other way around.

And there's one lesson that has come home powerfully to me, which I would offer to you now. Just as those who created this Republic pledged to each other their lives, their fortunes, and their sacred honor, so, too, America's leaders today must pledge to each other that we will keep foremost in our hearts and minds not what is best for ourselves or for our party, but what is best for America.

In the spirit of Jefferson, let us affirm that, in this Chamber tonight there are no Republicans, no Democrats, just Americans. Yes, we will have our differences. But let us always remember what unites us far outweighs whatever divides us. Those who sent us here to serve them—the millions of Americans watching and listening tonight—expect this of us. Let's prove to them and to ourselves that democracy works even in an election year.

We've done this before. And as we have worked together to bring down spending, tax rates, and inflation, employment has climbed to record heights; America has created more jobs and better, higher-paying jobs; family income has risen for 4 straight years, and America's poor climbed out of poverty at the fastest rate in more than 10 years.

Our record is not just the longest peacetime expansion in history but an economic and social revolution of hope, based on work, incentives, growth, and opportunity; a revolution of compassion that led to private sector initiatives and a 77-percent increase in charitable giving; a revolution that at a critical moment in world history reclaimed and restored the American dream.

In international relations, too, there's only one description for what, together, we have achieved: a complete turnabout, a revolution. Seven years ago, America was weak and freedom everywhere was under siege. Today America is strong, and democracy is everywhere on the move. From Central America to East Asia, ideas like free markets and democratic reforms and human rights are taking hold. We've replaced "Blame America" with "Look up to America." We've rebuilt our defenses. And, of all our accomplishments, none can give us more satisfaction than knowing that our young people are again proud to wear our country's uniform.

And in a few moments, I'm going to talk about three developments— arms reduction, the Strategic Defense Initiative and the global democratic revolution—that, when taken together, offer a chance none of us would have dared imagine 7 years ago, a chance to rid the world of the two great nightmares of the postwar era. I speak of the startling hope of giving our children a future free of both totalitarianism and nuclear terror.

Tonight, then, we're strong, prosperous, at peace, and we are free. This is the state of our Union. And if we will work together this year, I believe we can give a future President and a future Congress the chance to make that prosperity, that peace, that freedom, not just the state of our Union, but the state of our world.

Toward this end, we have four basic objectives tonight. First, steps we can take this year to keep our economy strong and growing, to give our children a future of low inflation and full employment. Second, let's check our progress in attacking social problems, where important gains have been made but which still need critical attention. I mean schools that work, economic independence for the poor, restoring respect for family life and family values. Our third objective tonight is global: continuing the exciting economic and democratic revolutions we've seen around the world. Fourth and finally, our nation has remained at peace for nearly a decade and a half, as we move toward our goals of world prosperity and world freedom. We must protect that peace and deter war by making sure the next President inherits what you and I have a moral obligation to give that President: a national security that is unassailable and a national defense that takes full advantage of new technology and is fully funded.

This is a full agenda. It's meant to be. You see, my thinking on the next year is quite simple: Let's make this the best of 8. And that means it's all out—right to the finish line. I don't buy the idea that this is the last year of anything, because we're not talking here tonight about registering temporary gains, but ways of making permanent our successes.

And that's why our focus is the values, the principles, and ideas that made America great. Let's be clear on this point. We're for limited government because we understand, as the Founding Fathers did, that it is the best way of ensuring personal liberty and empowering the individual so that every American of every race and region shares fully in the flowering of American prosperity and freedom.

One other thing we Americans like—the future—like the sound of it, the idea of it, the hope of it. Where others fear trade and economic growth, we see opportunities for creating new wealth and undreamed-of opportunities for millions in our own land and beyond. Where others seek to throw up barriers, we seek to bring them down. Where others take counsel of their fears, we follow our hopes. Yes, we Americans like the future and like making the most of it. Let's do that now.

And let's begin by discussing how to maintain economic growth by controlling and eventually eliminating the problem of Federal deficits. We have had a balanced budget only eight times in the last 57 years. For the first time in 14 years, the Federal Government spent less in real terms last year than the year before. We took $73 billion off last year's deficit compared to the year before. The deficit itself has moved from 6.3 percent of the Gross National Product to only 3.4 percent. And perhaps the most important sign of progress has been the change in our view of deficits. You know, a few of us can remember when, not too many years ago, those who created the deficits said they would make us prosperous and not to worry about the debt, because we owe it to ourselves. Well, at last there is agreement that we can't spend ourselves rich.

Our recent budget agreement, designed to reduce Federal deficits by $76 billion over the next 2 years, builds on this consensus. But this agreement must be adhered to without slipping into the errors of the past: more broken promises and more unchecked spending. As I indicated in my first State of the Union, what ails us can be simply put: The Federal Government is too big and it spends too much money. I can assure you, the bipartisan leadership of Congress, of my help in fighting off any attempt to bust our budget agreement. And this includes the swift and certain use of veto power.

Now, it is also time for some plain talk about the most immediate obstacle to controlling Federal deficits. The simple but frustrating problem of making expenses match revenues—something American families do and the Federal Government can't—has caused crisis after crisis in this city. Mr. Speaker, Mr. President, I will say to you tonight what I have said before and will continue to say: The budget process has broken down; it needs a drastic overhaul. With each ensuing year, the spectacle before the American people is the same as it was this Christmas: budget deadlines delayed or missed completely, monstrous continuing resolutions that pack hundreds of billions of dollars' worth of spending into one bill—and a Federal Government on the brink of default.

I know I'm echoing what you here in the Congress have said, because you suffered so directly. But let's recall that in 7 years, of 91 appropriations bills scheduled to arrive on my desk by a certain date, only 10 made it on time. Last year, of the 13 appropriations bills due by October 1st, none of them made it. Instead, we had four continuing resolutions lasting 41 days, then 36 days, and 2 days, and 3 days, respectively. And then, along came these behemoths. This is the conference report—1,053 pages weighing 14 pounds. Then this—a reconciliation bill 6 months late, that was 1,186 pages long, weighing 15 pounds. And the long-term continuing resolution—this one was 2 months late and it's 1,057 pages long, weighing 14 pounds. That was a total of 43 pounds of paper and ink. You had 3 hours—yes, 3 hours—to consider each, and it took 300 people at my Office of Management and Budget just to read the bill so the Government wouldn't shut down. Congress shouldn't send another one of these. No. And if you do, I will not sign it.

Let's change all this. Instead of a presidential budget that gets discarded and a congressional budget resolution that is not enforced, why not a simple partnership, a joint agreement that sets out the spending priorities within the available revenues? And let's remember our deadline is October 1st, not Christmas. Let's get the people's work done in time to avoid a footrace with Santa Claus. And yes, this year—to coin a phrase—a new beginning: 13 individual bills, on time and fully reviewed by Congress.

I'm also certain you join me in saying: Let's help ensure our future of prosperity by giving the President a tool that, though I will not get to use it, is one I know future Presidents of either party must have. Give the President the same authority that 43 Governors use in their States: the right to reach into massive appropriation bills, pare away the waste, and enforce budget discipline. Let's approve the line-item veto.

And let's take a partial step in this direction. Most of you in this Chamber didn't know what was in this catchall bill and report. Over the past few weeks, we've all learned what was tucked away behind a little comma here and there. For example, there's millions for items such as cranberry research, blueberry research, the study of crawfish, and the commercialization of wildflowers. And that's not to mention the $.5 million or so—that—so that people from developing nations could come here to watch Congress at work. I won't even touch that. So, tonight I offer you this challenge. In 30 days I will send back to you those items as rescissions, which if I had the authority to line them out, I would do so.

Now, review this multibillion-dollar package that will not undercut our bipartisan budget agreement. As a matter of fact, if adopted, it will improve our deficit reduction goals. And what an example we can set: that we're serious about getting our financial accounts in order. By acting and approving this plan, you have the opportunity to override a congressional process that is out of control.

There is another vital reform. Yes, Gramm-Rudman-Hollings has been profoundly helpful, but let us take its goal of a balanced budget and make it permanent. Let us do now what so many States do to hold down spending and what 32 State legislatures have asked us to do. Let us heed the wishes of an overwhelming plurality of Americans and pass a constitutional amendment that mandates a balanced budget and forces the Federal Government to live within its means.

Reform of the budget process—including the line-item veto and balanced budget amendment—will, together with real restraint on government spending, prevent the Federal budget from ever again ravaging the family budget.

Let's ensure that the Federal Government never again legislates against the family and the home. Last September I signed an Executive order on the family requiring that every department and agency review its activities in light of seven standards designed to promote and not harm the family. But let us make certain that the family is always at the center of the public policy process, not just in this administration but in all future administrations. It's time for Congress to consider, at the beginning, a statement of the impact that legislation will have on the basic unit of American society, the family.

And speaking of the family, let's turn to a matter on the mind of every American parent tonight: education. We all know the sorry story of the sixties and seventies—soaring spending, plummeting test scores—and that hopeful trend of the eighties, when we replaced an obsession with dollars with a commitment to quality, and test scores started back up. There's a lesson here that we all should write on the blackboard a hundred times: In a child's education, money can never take the place of basics like discipline, hard work, and, yes, homework.

As a nation we do, of course, spend heavily on education—more than we spend on defense. Yet across our country, Governors like New Jersey's

Tom Kean are giving classroom demonstrations that how we spend is as important as how much we spend. Opening up the teaching profession to all qualified candidates, merit pay—so that good teachers get A's as well as apples—and stronger curriculum, as Secretary [of Education William J.] Bennett has proposed for high schools—these imaginative reforms are making common sense the most popular new kid in America's schools.

How can we help? Well, we can talk about and push for these reforms. But the most important thing we can do is to reaffirm that control of our schools belongs to the states, local communities and, most of all, to the parents and teachers.

My friends, some years ago, the Federal Government declared war on poverty, and poverty won. Today, the Federal Government has 59 major welfare programs and spends more than $100 billion a year on them. What has all this money done?

Well, too often it has only made poverty harder to escape. Federal welfare programs have created a massive social problem. With the best of intentions, government created a poverty trap that wreaks havoc on the very support system the poor need most to lift themselves out of poverty: the family. Dependency has become the one enduring heirloom, passed from one generation to the next, of too many fragmented families.

It is time—this may be the most radical thing I've said in 7 years in this office—it's time for Washington to show a little humility. There are a thousand sparks of genius in 50 States and a thousand communities around the Nation. It is time to nurture them and see which ones can catch fire and become guiding lights.

States have begun to show us the way. They have demonstrated that successful welfare programs can be built around more effective child support enforcement practices and innovative programs requiring welfare recipients to work or prepare for work. Let us give the States even more flexibility and encourage more reforms. Let's start making our welfare system the first rung on America's ladder of opportunity, a boost up from dependency, not a graveyard, but a birthplace of hope.

And now let me turn to three other matters vital to family values and the quality of family life. The first is an untold American success story. Recently, we released our annual survey of what graduating high school seniors have to say about drugs. Cocaine use is declining, and marijuana use was lowest since surveying began. We can be proud that our students are just saying no to drugs. But let us remember what this menace requires: commitment from every part of America and every single American, a commitment to a drug-free America. The war against drugs is a war of individual battles, a crusade with many heroes, including America's young people and also someone very special to me. She has helped so many of our young people to say no to drugs. Nancy, much credit belongs to you, and I want to express to you your husband's pride and your country's thanks. Surprised you, didn't I?

Well, now we come to a family issue that we must have the courage to confront. Tonight, I call America—a good nation, a moral people—to charitable but realistic consideration of the terrible cost of abortion on demand. To those who say this violates a woman's right to control of her own body: Can they deny that now medical evidence confirms the unborn child is a living human being entitled to life, liberty, and the pursuit of happiness? Let us unite as a nation and protect the unborn with legislation that would stop all Federal funding for abortion and with a human life amendment making, of course, an exception where the unborn child threatens the life of the mother. Our Judeo-Christian tradition recognizes the right of taking a life in self-defense.

But with that one exception, let us look to those others in our land who cry out for children to adopt. I pledge to you tonight I will work to remove the barriers to adoption and extend full sharing in family life to millions of Americans, so that children who need homes can be welcomed into families who want them and love them.

And let me add here: So many of our greatest statesmen have reminded us that spiritual values alone are essential to our nation's health and vigor. The Congress opens its proceedings each day, as does the Supreme Court, with an acknowledgment of the Supreme Being: Yet we are denied the right to set aside in our schools a moment each day for those who wish to pray. I believe Congress should pass our school prayer amendment.

Now, to make sure there is a full nine-member Supreme Court to interpret the law, to protect the rights of all Americans, I urge the Senate to move quickly and decisively in confirming Judge Anthony Kennedy to the highest Court in the land and to also confirm 27 nominees now waiting to fill vacancies in the Federal judiciary.

Here then are our domestic priorities. Yet if the Congress and the administration work together, even greater opportunities lie ahead to expand a growing world economy, to continue to reduce the threat of nuclear arms, and to extend the frontiers of freedom and the growth of democratic institutions.

Our policies consistently received the strongest support of the late Congressman Dan Daniel of Virginia. I'm sure all of you join me in expressing heartfelt condolences on his passing.

One of the greatest contributions the United States can make to the world is to promote freedom as the key to economic growth. A creative, competitive America is the answer to a changing world, not trade wars that would close doors, create greater barriers, and destroy millions of jobs. We should always remember: Protectionism is destructionism. America's jobs, America's growth, America's future depend on trade—trade that is free, open, and fair.

This year, we have it within our power to take a major step toward a growing global economy and an expanding cycle of prosperity that reaches to all the free nations of this Earth. I'm speaking of the historic free trade agreement negotiated between our country and Canada. And I can also tell you that we're determined to expand this concept, south as well as north.

Next month I will be traveling to Mexico, where trade matters will be of foremost concern. And, over the next several months, our Congress and the Canadian Parliament can make the start of such a North American accord a reality. Our goal must be a day when the free flow of trade, from the tip of Tierra del Fuego to the Arctic Circle, unites the people of the Western Hemisphere in a bond of mutually beneficial exchange, when all borders become what the U.S.-Canadian border so long has been: a meeting place, rather than a dividing line.

This movement we see in so many places toward economic freedom is indivisible from the worldwide movement toward political freedom and against totalitarian rule. This global democratic revolution has removed the specter, so frightening a decade ago, of democracy doomed to permanent minority status in the world. In South and Central America, only a third of the people enjoyed democratic rule in 1976. Today, over 90 percent of Latin Americans live in nations committed to democratic principles.

And the resurgence of democracy is owed to these courageous people on almost every continent who have struggled to take control of their own destiny. In Nicaragua the struggle has extra meaning, because that nation is so near our own borders.

The recent revelations of a former high-level Sandinista major, Roger Miranda, show us that, even as they talk peace, the Communist Sandinista government of Nicaragua has established plans for a large 600,000-man army. Yet even as these plans are made, the Sandinista regime knows the tide is turning, and the cause of Nicaraguan freedom is riding at its crest. Because of the freedom fighters, who are resisting Communist rule, the Sandinistas have been forced to extend some democratic rights, negotiate with church authorities, and release a few political prisoners.

The focus is on the Sandinistas, their promises and their actions. There is a consensus among the four Central American democratic Presidents that the Sandinistas have not complied with the plan to bring peace and democracy to all of Central America. The Sandinistas again have promised reforms. Their challenge is to take irreversible steps toward democracy.

On Wednesday my request to sustain the freedom fighters will be submitted, which reflects our mutual desire for peace, freedom, and democracy in Nicaragua. I ask Congress to pass this request. Let us be for the people of Nicaragua what Lafayette, Pulaski, and von Steuben were for our forefathers and the cause of American independence.

So, too, in Afghanistan, the freedom fighters are the key to peace. We support the Mujahidin. There can be no settlement unless all Soviet troops are removed and the Afghan people are allowed genuine self-determination. I have made my views on this matter known to Mr. Gorbachev. But not just Nicaragua or Afghanistan—yes, everywhere we see a swelling freedom tide across the world: freedom fighters rising up in Cambodia and Angola, fighting and dying for the same democratic liberties we hold sacred. Their cause is our cause: freedom.

Yet, even as we work to expand world freedom, we must build a safer peace and reduce the danger of nuclear war. But let's have no illusions. Three years of steady decline in the value of our annual defense investment have increased the risk of our most basic security interests, jeopardizing earlier hard-won goals. We must face squarely the implications of this negative trend and make adequate, stable defense spending a top goal both this year and in the future.

This same concern applies to economic and security assistance programs as well. But the resolve of America and its NATO allies has opened the way for unprecedented achievement in arms reduction. Our recently signed INF [intermediate-range nuclear-force missiles] treaty is historic, because it reduces nuclear arms and establishes the most stringent verification regime in arms control history, including several forms of short-notice, on-site inspection. I submitted the treaty today, and I urge the Senate to give its advice and consent to ratification of this landmark agreement. Thank you very much.

In addition to the INF treaty, we're within reach of an even more significant START [strategic arms reduction talks] agreement that will reduce U.S. and Soviet long-range missile, or strategic, arsenals by half. But let me be clear. Our approach is not to seek agreement for agreement's sake but to settle only for agreements that truly enhance our national security and that of our allies. We will never put our security at risk—or that of our allies—just to reach an agreement with the Soviets. No agreement is better than a bad agreement.

As I mentioned earlier, our efforts are to give future generations what we never had: a future free of nuclear terror. Reduction of strategic offensive arms is one step; SDI another. Our funding request for our Strategic Defense Initiative is less than 2 percent of the total defense budget. SDI funding is money wisely appropriated and money well spent. SDI has the same purpose and supports the same goals of arms reduction. It reduces the risk of war and the threat of nuclear weapons to all mankind. Strategic defenses that threaten no one could offer the world a safer, more stable basis for deterrence. We must also remember that SDI is our insurance policy against a nuclear accident, a Chernobyl of the sky, or an accidental launch, or some madman who might come along.

We've seen such changes in the world in 7 years. As totalitarianism struggles to avoid being overwhelmed by the forces of economic advance and the aspiration for human freedom, it is the free nations that are resilient and resurgent. As the global democratic revolution has put totalitarianism on the defensive, we have left behind the days of retreat. America is again a vigorous leader of the free world, a nation that acts decisively and firmly in the furtherance of her principles and vital interests. No legacy would make me more proud than leaving in place a bipartisan consensus for the cause of world freedom, a consensus that prevents a paralysis of American power from ever occurring again.

But my thoughts tonight go beyond this and I hope you'll let me end this evening with a personal reflection. You know, the world could never be quite the same again after Jacob Shallus, a trustworthy and dependable clerk of the Pennsylvania General Assembly, took his pen and engrossed those words about representative government in the preamble of our Constitution. And in a quiet but final way, the course of human events was forever altered when, on a ridge overlooking the Emmitsburg Pike in an obscure Pennsylvania town called Gettysburg, Lincoln spoke of our duty to government of and by the people and never letting it perish from the Earth.

At the start of this decade, I suggested that we lived in equally momentous times, that it is up to us now to decide whether our form of government would endure and whether history still had a place of greatness for a quiet, pleasant, greening land called America. Not everything has been made perfect in 7 years, nor will it be made perfect in 7 times 70 years, but before us, this year and beyond, are great prospects for the cause of peace and world freedom.

It means, too, that the young Americans I spoke of 7 years ago, as well as those who might be coming along the Virginia or Maryland shores this night and seeing for the first time the lights of this Capital City, the lights that cast their glow on our great halls of government and the monuments to the memory of our great men—it means those young Americans will find a city of hope in a land that is free.

We can be proud that for them and for us as those lights along the Potomac are still seen this night signaling, as they have for nearly two centuries and as we pray God they always will, that another generation of Americans has protected and passed on lovingly this place called America, this shining city on a hill, this government of, by, and for the people.

Thank you, and God bless you.

February

New Jersey Supreme Court
  on Surrogate Mothers 71

Grand Jury Indictments of
  General Noriega 81

State Department Report
  on Human Rights Practices 93

President's Economic Report,
  Economic Advisers' Report 117

President Reagan's Budget Message 149

Papal Encyclical on Social Concerns 165

Court on Press Freedom 175

NEW JERSEY SUPREME COURT ON SURROGATE MOTHERS

February 3, 1988

The surrogate motherhood contract in the highly publicized "Baby M" case was held illegal in a unanimous decision by the New Jersey Supreme Court on February 3. In overturning the ruling that a lower court judge made March 31, 1987, the state's Supreme Court said that paying money to a surrogate mother not only was illegal but was "perhaps criminal, and potentially degrading to women."

This case was the first court test of a surrogate motherhood contract. Under its terms Mary Beth Whitehead, a married mother of two children, agreed to become pregnant by artificial insemination with the sperm of William Stern, who was not her husband, and bear a child. Whitehead further agreed to give the infant to Stern and terminate her rights as the biological mother so that his wife, Elizabeth, could adopt the baby. In return, Stern agreed to pay Whitehead $10,000 and all medical expenses.

Although the court declared invalid any contract that provides money for a surrogate mother or includes her agreement to surrender the child at birth, the court found no legal objections to agreements in which a woman becomes a surrogate mother voluntarily and without pay, provided that she is not subject to a binding agreement to give up the baby. The question of giving up the baby is what brought this case to court.

Baby M—called Melissa Elizabeth by the Sterns and Sara by the Whiteheads—was born March 27, 1986. Whitehead gave the infant to the Sterns, but a few days later asked to take the baby back for a week and then refused to relinquish her.

To evade a court order awarding temporary custody to the Sterns, the Whiteheads fled to Florida. In tape-recorded telephone conversations with William Stern that were later presented as evidence, Mary Beth Whitehead threatened to kill the baby and herself if he tried to recover the infant, and she accused him of sexually molesting her nine-year-old daughter. The baby was recovered July 31 by private detectives hired by the Sterns, who were awarded temporary custody pending a final court ruling.

Lower Court Ruling

After seven weeks of hearings, Judge Harvey R. Sorkow of Bergen County Superior Court awarded custody to the Sterns and terminated Whitehead's parental rights. Noting the absence of previous New Jersey court tests of surrogacy, Sorkow held that the only applicable legal concepts were contract law principles and the parens patriae *principle, which gives courts broad authority to protect the interests of children and others unable to protect themselves. Sorkow found "clear and convincing evidence" that the baby's best interests would be served by placement in the father's sole custody.* (New Jersey Court on Rights of Surrogates, Historic Documents of 1987, p. 373)

While agreeing that the child's interests would be best served by granting custody to William Stern, the Supreme Court observed that "the mere fact that a child would be better off with one set of parents than with another is an insufficient basis for terminating the natural mother's rights." Nor can such termination be based on contract, according to the opinion written by Chief Justice C. J. Wilentz.

Wilentz rejected Sorkow's opinion that New Jersey adoption statutes do not apply in surrogacy cases. Wilentz cited these statutes, as well as New Jersey public policy, in holding the surrogacy contract invalid.

In its order that followed on April 6, spelling out the natural mother's visitation rights, the lower court noted that since the original trial Whitehead's marital problems had been resolved through divorce, that she had attained family stability with her new husband, and that she had "come to the realization that she will never have custody of Melissa, who will be raised by her father and stepmother."

Court Briefs, Pro and Con

Numerous friend-of-the-court briefs were filed with the Supreme Court, as they had been with the trial court. Those opposed to surrogacy included the Catholic Church, profamily organizations, and feminist spokespersons.

In the wake of the Baby M controversy, several states enacted laws prohibiting paid surrogacy. A New York task force organized by Gov. Mario Cuomo on May 28 recommended criminal penalties to halt *"making money from birth and human reproduction." In Michigan, a new law making it a felony to arrange a paid surrogacy contract carries penalties of up to five years in prison and $50,000 in fines.*

Supporters of surrogacy argued that opposition to the practice arose because of a few bad cases, and that these might have been avoided if higher standards had been imposed on those surrogacy contracts. Dr. Betsy Aigen, director of the Surrogate Mother Program in New York City and a founder of the American Organization of Surrogate Parenting Practitioners, estimated that there had been about 1,000 surrogate births in the previous twelve years. Only six of those surrogate mothers decided to keep their babies, a rate far lower, Aigen said, than among women who change their minds on adoptions.

Following are excerpts from the unanimous decision of the New Jersey Supreme Court, "In the Matter of Baby M," issued February 3, 1988:

The opinion of the Court was delivered by WILENTZ, C. J.

In this matter the Court is asked to determine the validity of a contract that purports to provide a new way of bringing children into a family. For a fee of $10,000, a woman agrees to be artificially inseminated with the semen of another woman's husband; she is to conceive a child, carry it to term, and after its birth surrender it to the natural father and his wife. The intent of the contract is that the child's natural mother will thereafter be forever separated from her child. The wife is to adopt the child, and she and the natural father are to be regarded as its parents for all purposes. The contract providing for this is called a "surrogacy contract," the natural mother inappropriately called the "surrogate mother."

We invalidate the surrogacy contract because it conflicts with the law and public policy of this State. While we recognize the depth of the yearning of infertile couples to have their own children, we find the payment of money to a "surrogate" mother illegal, perhaps criminal, and potentially degrading to women. Although in this case we grant custody to the natural father, the evidence having clearly proved such custody to be in the best interests of the infant, we void both the termination of the surrogate mother's parental rights and the adoption of the child by the wife/stepparent. We thus restore the "surrogate" as the mother of the child. We remand the issue of the natural mother's visitation rights to the trial court. . . .

We find no offense to our present laws where a woman voluntarily and without payment agrees to act as a "surrogate" mother, provided that she is not subject to a binding agreement to surrender her child. Moreover, our holding today does not preclude the Legislature from altering the current statutory scheme, within constitutional limits, so as to permit surrogacy contracts. Under current law, however, the surrogacy agreement before us is illegal and invalid.

I

Facts

In February 1985, William Stern and Mary Beth Whitehead entered into a surrogacy contract. It recited that Stern's wife, Elizabeth, was infertile, that they wanted a child, and that Mrs. Whitehead was willing to provide that child as the mother with Mr. Stern as the father.

The contract provided that through artificial insemination using Mr. Stern's sperm, Mrs. Whitehead would become pregnant, carry the child to term, bear it, deliver it to the Sterns, and thereafter do whatever was necessary to terminate her maternal rights so that Mrs. Stern could thereafter adopt the child. Mrs. Whitehead's husband, Richard, was also a party to the contract; Mrs. Stern was not. Mr. Whitehead promised to do all acts necessary to rebut the presumption of paternity under the Parentage Act. Although Mrs. Stern was not a party to the surrogacy agreement, the contract gave her sole custody of the child in the event of Mr. Stern's death. Mrs. Stern's status as a nonparty to the surrogate parenting agreement presumably was to avoid the application of the baby-selling statute to this arrangement.

Mr. Stern, on his part, agreed to attempt the artificial insemination and to pay Mrs. Whitehead $10,000 after the child's birth, on its delivery to him. In a separate contract, Mr. Stern agreed to pay $7,500 to the Infertility Center of New York ("ICNY"). The Center's advertising campaigns solicit surrogate mothers and encourage infertile couples to consider surrogacy. ICNY arranged for the surrogacy contract by bringing the parties together, explaining the process to them, furnishing the contractual form, and providing legal counsel.

The history of the parties' involvement in this arrangement suggests their good faith. William and Elizabeth Stern were married in July 1974, having met at the University of Michigan, where both were Ph.D. candidates. Due to financial considerations and Mrs. Stern's pursuit of a medical degree and residency, they decided to defer starting a family until 1981. Before then, however, Mrs. Stern learned that she might have multiple sclerosis and that the disease in some cases renders pregnancy a serious health risk. Her anxiety appears to have exceeded the actual risk, which current medical authorities assess as minimal. Nonetheless that anxiety was evidently quite real, Mrs. Stern fearing that pregnancy might precipitate blindness, paraplegia, or other forms of debilitation. Based on the perceived risk, the Sterns decided to forego having their own children. The decision had a special significance for Mr. Stern. Most of his family had been destroyed in the Holocaust. As the family's only survivor, he very much wanted to continue his bloodline.

Initially the Sterns considered adoption, but were discouraged by the substantial delay apparently involved and by the potential problem they saw arising from their age and their differing religious backgrounds. They were most eager for some other means to start a family.

The paths of Mrs. Whitehead and the Sterns to surrogacy were similar. Both responded to advertising by ICNY. The Sterns' response, following their inquiries into adoption, was the result of their long-standing decision to have a child. Mrs. Whitehead's response apparently resulted from her sympathy with family members and others who could have no children (she stated that she wanted to give another couple the "gift of life"); she also wanted the $10,000 to help her family.

Both parties, undoubtedly because of their own self-interest, were less sensitive to the implications of the transaction than they might otherwise have been. Mrs. Whitehead, for instance, appears not to have been concerned about whether the Sterns would make good parents for her child; the Sterns, on their part, while conscious of the obvious possibility that surrendering the child might cause grief to Mrs. Whitehead, overcame their qualms because of their desire for a child. At any rate, both the Sterns and Mrs. Whitehead were committed to the arrangement; both thought it right and constructive.

Mrs. Whitehead had reached her decision concerning surrogacy before the Sterns, and had actually been involved as a potential surrogate mother with another couple. After numerous unsuccessful artificial inseminations, that effort was abandoned. Thereafter, the Sterns learned of the Infertility Center, the possibilities of surrogacy, and of Mary Beth Whitehead. The two couples met to discuss the surrogacy arrangement and decided to go forward. On February 6, 1985, Mr. Stern and Mr. and Mrs. Whitehead executed the surrogate parenting agreement. After several artificial inseminations over a period of months, Mrs. Whitehead became pregnant. The pregnancy was uneventful and on March 27, 1986, Baby M was born.

Not wishing anyone at the hospital to be aware of the surrogacy arrangement, Mr. and Mrs. Whitehead appeared to all as the proud parents of a healthy female child. Her birth certificate indicated her name to be Sara Elizabeth Whitehead and her father to be Richard Whitehead. In accordance with Mrs. Whitehead's request, the Sterns visited the hospital unobtrusively to see the newborn child.

Mrs. Whitehead realized, almost from the moment of birth, that she could not part with this child. She had felt a bond with it even during pregnancy....

Nonetheless, Mrs. Whitehead was, for the moment, true to her word. Despite powerful inclinations to the contrary, she turned her child over to the Sterns on March 30 at the Whiteheads' home.

The Sterns were thrilled with their new child. They had planned extensively for its arrival, far beyond the practical furnishing of a room for her. It was a time of joyful celebration—not just for them but for their friends as well. The Sterns looked forward to raising their daughter, whom they named Melissa. While aware by then that Mrs. Whitehead was undergoing an emotional crisis, they were as yet not cognizant of the depth of that crisis and its implications for their newly-enlarged family.

Later in the evening of March 30, Mrs. Whitehead became deeply disturbed, disconsolate, stricken with unbearable sadness. She had to have her child. She could not eat, sleep, or concentrate on anything other than her need for her baby. The next day she went to the Sterns' home and told them how much she was suffering.

The depth of Mrs. Whitehead's despair surprised and frightened the Sterns. She told them that she could not live without her baby, that she must have her, even if only for one week, that thereafter she would surrender the child. The Sterns, concerned that Mrs. Whitehead might indeed commit suicide, not wanting under any circumstances to risk that, and in any event believing that Mrs. Whitehead would keep her word, turned the child over to her. It was not until four months later, after a series of attempts to regain possession of the child, that Melissa was returned to the Sterns, having been forcibly removed from the home where she was then living with Mr. and Mrs. Whitehead, the home in Florida owned by Mary Beth Whitehead's parents.

The struggle over Baby M began when it became apparent that Mrs. Whitehead could not return the child to Mr. Stern. Due to Mrs. Whitehead's refusal to relinquish the baby, Mr. Stern filed a complaint seeking enforcement of the surrogacy contract. He alleged, accurately, that Mrs. Whitehead had not only refused to comply with the surrogacy contract but had threatened to flee from New Jersey with the child in order to avoid even the possibility of his obtaining custody. . . . And that is precisely what she did. . . .

The Whiteheads immediately fled to Florida with Baby M. They stayed initially with Mrs. Whitehead's parents, where one of Mrs. Whitehead's children had been living. For the next three months, the Whiteheads and Melissa lived at roughly twenty different hotels, motels, and homes in order to avoid apprehension. From time to time Mrs. Whitehead would call Mr. Stern to discuss the matter; the conversations, recorded by Mr. Stern on advice of counsel, show an escalating dispute about rights, morality, and power, accompanied by threats of Mrs. Whitehead to kill herself, to kill the child, and falsely to accuse Mr. Stern of sexually molesting Mrs. Whitehead's other daughter.

Eventually the Sterns discovered where the Whiteheads were staying, commenced supplementary proceedings in Florida, and obtained an order requiring the Whiteheads to turn over the child. Police in Florida enforced the order, forcibly removing the child from her grandparents' home. She was soon thereafter brought to New Jersey and turned over to the Sterns. . . . Pending final judgment, Mrs. Whitehead was awarded limited visitation with Baby M.

The Sterns' complaint, in addition to seeking possession and ultimately custody of the child, sought enforcement of the surrogacy contract. Pursuant to the contract, it asked that the child be permanently placed in their custody, that Mrs. Whitehead's parental rights be terminated, and that Mrs. Stern be allowed to adopt the child, *i.e.,* that, for all purposes, Melissa become the Sterns' child.

The trial took thirty-two days over a period of more than two months. It included numerous interlocutory appeals and attempted interlocutory appeals. There were twenty-three witnesses to the facts recited above and fifteen expert witnesses.... The bulk of the testimony was devoted to determining the parenting arrangement most compatible with the child's best interests. Soon after the conclusion of the trial, the trial court announced its opinion from the bench. It held that the surrogate contract was valid; ordered that Mrs. Whitehead's parental rights be terminated and that sole custody of the child be granted to Mr. Stern; and after hearing brief testimony from Mrs. Stern, immediately entered an order allowing the adoption of Melissa by Mrs. Stern, all in accordance with the surrogacy contract. Pending the outcome of the appeal, we granted a continuation of visitation to Mrs. Whitehead, although slightly more limited than the visitation allowed during the trial.

Although clearly expressing its view that the surrogacy contract was valid, the trial court devoted the major portion of its opinion to the question of the baby's best interests. The inconsistency is apparent. The surrogacy contract calls for the surrender of the child to the Sterns, permanent and sole custody in the Sterns, and termination of Mrs. Whitehead's parental rights, all without qualification, all regardless of any evaluation of the best interests of the child. As a matter of fact the contract recites (even before the child was conceived) that it is in the best interests of the child to be placed with Mr. Stern. In effect, the trial court awarded custody to Mr. Stern, the natural father, based on the same kind of evidence and analysis as might be expected had no surrogacy contract existed.... The factual issues confronted and decided by the trial court were the same as if Mr. Stern and Mrs. Whitehead had had the child out of wedlock, intended or unintended, and then disagreed about custody....

On the question of best interests—and we agree, but for different reasons, that custody was the critical issue—the court's analysis of the testimony was perceptive, demonstrating both its understanding of the case and its considerable experience in these matters. We agree substantially with both its analysis and conclusions on the matter of custody.

The [trial] court's review and analysis of the surrogacy contract, however, is not at all in accord with ours. The trial court concluded that the various statutes governing this matter, including those concerning adoption, termination of parental rights, and payment of money in connection with adoptions, do not apply to surrogacy contracts. It reasoned that because the Legislature did not have surrogacy contracts in mind when it passed those laws, those laws were therefore irrelevant. Thus, assuming it was writing on a clean slate, the trial court analyzed the interests involved and the power of the court to accommodate them. It then held that surrogacy contracts are valid and should be enforced, and furthermore that Mr. Stern's rights under the surrogacy contract were constitutionally protected.

Mrs. Whitehead appealed.... [She] contends that the surrogacy contract, for a variety of reasons, is invalid. She contends that it conflicts with public policy since it guarantees that the child will not have the nurturing of both natural parents—presumably New Jersey's goal for families. She further argues that it deprives the mother of her constitutional right to the companionship of her child, and that it conflicts with statutes concerning termination of parental rights and adoption. With the contract thus void, Mrs. Whitehead claims primary custody (with visitation rights in [sic] Mr. Stern) both on a best interests basis . . . as well as on the policy basis of discouraging surrogacy contracts. . . .

The Sterns claim that the surrogacy contract is valid and should be enforced, largely for the reasons given by the trial court. They claim a constitutional right of privacy, which includes the right of procreation, and the right of consenting adults to deal with matters of reproduction as they see fit. As for the child's best interests, their position is factual: given all of the circumstances, the child is better off in their custody with no residual parental rights reserved for Mrs. Whitehead. . . .

II

Invalidity and Unenforceability
of Surrogacy Contract

We have concluded that this surrogacy contract is invalid. Our conclusion has two bases: direct conflict with existing statutes and conflict with the public policies of this State, as expressed in its statutory and decisional law. . . .

The surrogacy contract conflicts with: (1) laws prohibiting the use of money in connection with adoptions; (2) laws requiring proof of parental unfitness or abandonment before termination of parental rights is ordered or an adoption is granted; and (3) laws that make surrender of custody and consent to adoption revocable in private placement adoptions. . . .

Mr. Stern knew he was paying for the adoption of a child; Mrs. Whitehead knew she was accepting money so that a child might be adopted; the Infertility Center knew that it was being paid for assisting in the adoption of a child. The actions of all three worked to frustrate the goals of the statute. It strains credulity to claim that these arrangements, touted by those in the surrogacy business as an attractive alternative to the usual route leading to an adoption, really amount to something other than a private placement adoption for money.

The prohibition of our statute is strong. Violation constitutes a high misdemeanor, a third-degree crime carrying a penalty of three to five years imprisonment. The evils inherent in baby bartering are loathsome for a myriad of reasons. . . .

Under the contract, the natural mother is irrevocably committed before she knows the strength of her bond with her child. She never makes a totally voluntary, informed decision, for quite clearly any decision prior to the baby's birth is, in the most important sense, uninformed, and any decision after that, compelled by a pre-existing contractual commitment, the threat of a lawsuit, and the inducement of a $10,000 payment, is less than totally voluntary. Her interests are of little concern to those who controlled this transaction.

Although the interest of the natural father and adoptive mother is certainly the predominant interest, realistically the *only* interest served, even they are left with less than what public policy requires. They know little about the natural mother, her genetic makeup, and her psychological and medical history. Moreover, not even a superficial attempt is made to determine their awareness of their responsibilities as parents.

Worst of all, however, is the contract's total disregard of the best interests of the child. There is not the slightest suggestion that any inquiry will be made at any time to determine the fitness of the Sterns as custodial parents, of Mrs. Stern as an adoptive parent, their superiority to Mrs. Whitehead, or the effect on the child of not living with her natural mother.

This is the sale of a child, or, at the very least, the sale of a mother's right to her child, the only mitigating factor being that one of the purchasers is the father. Almost every evil that prompted the prohibition of the payment of money in connection with adoptions exists here. . . .

GRAND JURY INDICTMENTS
OF GENERAL NORIEGA
February 5, 1988

The U.S. Department of Justice announced February 5 that federal grand juries in Miami and Tampa, Florida, had indicted the military leader of Panama's government, Gen. Manuel Antonio Noriega, and sixteen associates and charged them with extensive federal narcotics violations, including drug smuggling and racketeering. Under terms of Panama's constitution, Noriega could not be extradited to the United States to stand trial as long as he remained in Panama. The indictments promptly became a factor in State Department negotiations with Noriega over conditions under which he would agree to resign as commander of Panama's Defense Forces—and hence as the country's strongman.

As he had done for the previous year, Noriega frustrated overt efforts by the Reagan administration to push him out of power. Noriega held fast during a wave of unrest in Panama during February and March, withstanding U.S. economic sanctions aimed at undermining his authority. During the political unrest, often punctuated by anti-Noriega street demonstrations in Panamanian cities, the country's figurehead president, Eric Arturo Delvalle, attempted to dismiss him as military commander. Noriega retaliated by having the National Legislature replace Delvalle with a new president of Noriega's choosing. A coup attempt by some senior military officers failed, and the participants ended up in jail. The economic sanctions had to be eased to reduce the misery they created among the Panamanian people.

On May 25, U.S. Secretary of State George P. Shultz announced that the negotiations with Noriega had ended in failure. The general refused

*to accept a deal, as described by Under Secretary of State Michael H.
Armacost, that would have required him to resign his military post and
leave the country at least until national elections could be held in May
1989. After that time, a new government would decide if he could return
to Panama. The U.S. government, in turn, would drop the economic
sanctions and the grand jury charges. Spain offered Noriega political
asylum, it was reported, on the condition that the United States not try
to extradite him for trial.*

Second Foreign Official Indicted

*Noriega was only the second senior official of a foreign government ever
indicted in the United States on drug-smuggling charges. The first was
Norman Saunder, chief minister of the Truks and Caicos Islands in the
Caribbean, who was convicted of similar charges in 1985.*

*The indictment of Noriega—in essence the U.S. government's acknowl-
edgment of his involvement in drug trafficking—was an embarrassment
to some American officials who as recently as mid-1987 praised him as an
ally in the Reagan administration's "war on drugs." The general first
came under substantial fire from U.S. leaders on June 26, 1987, when the
Senate passed a resolution, 84-2, accusing him of drug trafficking,
political corruption, election fraud, and the murder of an opposition
leader.*

*Noriega's drug-smuggling activities had been rumored for years, but he
previously had not fallen into Washington's disfavor—according to
numerous press accounts—because he gave the United States valuable
information. Rising to the head of Panama's military intelligence section
in 1970, Noriega was in a position to assist the United States in its quest
for security information about Cuba and, later, Nicaragua.*

*Noriega was an issue in the September 25 presidential campaign debate
between Vice President George Bush and Massachusetts Governor Michael
Dukakis. Dukakis, the Democratic nominee, said that Bush's long experience in government had not prevented him from "being involved in the
relationship between this [U.S.] government and Mr. Noriega and drug
trafficking in Panama." Bush contended that seven administrations had
dealt with Noriega, and the Reagan administration moved against Noriega
as soon as it had "hard evidence" of drug trafficking.*

Soon after the debate, the New York Times *quoted unidentified U.S.
officials as saying that as head of the Central Intelligence Agency in
1976, Bush learned that Noriega had bribed American soldiers to give him
information the United States obtained from an electronic eavesdropping
operation in Panama. But, according to the same account, his value to the
United States was then perceived to be greater than the damage he was
doing. Bush was among various U.S. officials over the years who were said
to have had access to intelligence reports about Noriega's activities,
included suspected drug trafficking.*

Noriega's Alleged Drug Role

In his intelligence post, and subsequently as commander of Panama's Defense Forces, Noriega assisted Colombian drug smugglers, according to U.S. Attorney Leon B. Kellner of Miami. Kellner said the twelve-count Miami indictment detailed the central role Noriega had played in the international narcotics trade and how he had misused his official positions to facilitate narcotics shipments through Panama to the United States.

Noriega was accused of receiving more than $4.6 million to arrange the safe movement of U.S.-bound cocaine from Medellin, Colombia. The indictment depicted an intimate business relationship between Noriega and the notorious Medellin drug cartel. Several of its leaders were named in the indictment.

While the Miami indictment dealt with the production and shipment of cocaine, the three-count Tampa indictment recounted the laundering of millions of dollars in U.S. currency through Panamanian banks and businesses, with Noriega's connivance, so that law-enforcement authorities could not trace the money to drug trafficking. According to the indictment, one of the principals in these operations, Steven Kalish, purchased a Boeing 727 aircraft for the Panamanian Defense Forces to fly the drug-sale money from the United States to Panama for laundering.

Agents of the Federal Bureau of Investigation, Drug Enforcement Administration, and the U.S. Customs Service jointly conducted the investigation leading to the Tampa indictment.

Following are excerpts from the federal grand jury indictments, announced February 5, 1988, bringing criminal charges against Panamanian military leader Gen. Manuel Antonio Noriega and sixteen associates:

MIAMI INDICTMENT

United States District Court
Southern District of Florida

United States of America
v.

Manuel Antonio Noriega	Ricardo Bilonick
Gustavo Dejesus Gaviria-Rivero	Luis Fernando Escobar-Ochoa
Pablo Escobar-Gaviria	Brian Alden Davidow
Luis Del Cid	Herman Velez
Roberto Steiner	William Saldarriaga
Francisco Chavez-Gil	Eduardo Pardo

David Rodrigo Ortiz-Hermida   Daniel Miranda
Amet Paredes   Jaime Gomez

Indictment

The Grand Jury charges that:

Count One

The Enterprise

1. At all times relevant to this Indictment, there existed an Enterprise, within the meaning of Title 18, United States Code, Section 1961 (4), that is, a group of individuals associated in fact which utilized the official positions of the defendant Manuel Antonio Noriega in the Republic of Panama to facilitate the manufacture and transportation of large quantities of cocaine destined for the United States and to launder narcotics proceeds.

2. The members of the Enterprise consisted of the defendants herein and others, including Panamanian military and civilian associates of Manuel Antonio Noriega and international drug traffickers who purchased from Manuel Antonio Noriega the use of his official positions and influence to assist and protect their narcotics and money laundering operations.

Roles in the Enterprise

3. Manuel Antonio Noriega was and is a high ranking officer in the military forces of the Republic of Panama. Manuel Antonio Noriega exploited his positions to obtain substantial personal profit by offering narcotics traffickers the safe use of the Republic of Panama as a location for transshipment of multi-hundred kilogram loads of cocaine destined for the United States; by permitting the shipment of ether and acetone in and through Panama; by allowing and protecting laboratory facilities for the manufacture of cocaine; by providing a safe haven for international narcotics traffickers; and by allowing the deposit of millions of dollars of narcotics proceeds in Panamanian banks.

a. Noriega's Official Positions: Through the use of his military positions, as set forth below, Manuel Antonio Noriega was able to expand and formalize his control over military, intelligence, law enforcement operations and other essential government functions in Panama....

b. Noriega's Association With The Medellin Cartel and Other Narcotics Traffickers: Manuel Antonio Noriega utilized his official positions to provide protection for international criminal narcotics traffickers, including an organization based in Medellin, Colombia, South America known by various names, including "The Medellin Cartel" (hereinafter "Cartel"), which consisted of controlling members of major Colombian cocaine manufacturing and distribution organizations. The Cartel operated to coordinate and consolidate the production, distribution, and importation of cocaine into the United States. Through the Cartel, major Colombian cocaine traffickers were able to pool resources, including raw materials, cocaine conversion laboratories, aircraft, vessels, transportation facilities, distribution networks, and cocaine to facilitate international narcotics trafficking. Cartel representatives sold cocaine and collected proceeds from illegal narcotics sales in a clandestine international market, which included the United States and Panama. In furtherance of its international drug trafficking business, the Cartel sought to obtain secure locations in Panama to conduct its operations and store its illegal proceeds.

4. Pablo Escobar-Gaviria and Gustavo Dejesus Gaviria-Rivero, among others, were leaders of the Cartel. Floyd Carlton-Cacerez flew drugs from Colombia to Panama and money from the United States to Panama for the Cartel under the protection of Manuel Antonio Noriega. After the murder in 1984 of Rodrigo Lara-Bonilla, the Minister of Justice of Colombia, Cartel leaders, including Pablo Escobar-Gaviria, Gustavo Dejesus Gaviria-Rivero, Jorge Ochoa-Vasquez, and Fabio Ochoa-Vasquez utilized Panama for the conduct of Cartel operations and as refuge from increased law enforcement activity in the Republic of Colombia.

5. Luis Del Cid was a member of the National Guard and the Defense Forces of the Republic of Panama. He acted as liaison, courier, and emissary for Manuel Antonio Noriega in his transactions with drug traffickers. At various times, he arranged for the transportation of payments to Noriega from the traffickers, including the Cartel.

6. Amet Paredes is the son of General Ruben Dario Paredes, former military commander of the National Guard of Panama. Amet Paredes, along with his now deceased brother, Ruben Dario Paredes-Jimenez, smuggled cocaine from Panama to the United States utilizing their connections with Manuel Antonio Noriega and Noriega's now deceased partner, Cesar Rodriguez, to obtain protection for their activities. In March 1986, co-conspirators Ruben Dario Paredes-Jimenez and Cesar Rodriguez travelled from Panama to Medellin, Colombia to make arrangements with the Cartel to acquire a load of cocaine. On or before March 19, 1986, they were murdered in Medellin, Colombia.

7. Ricardo Bilonick is a Panamanian civilian who was a part-owner of Inair Airlines, a Panamanian cargo airline used to ship cocaine for the Cartel from Panama to the United States. Bilonick maintained a close personal relationship with Noriega. Bilonick acted as Noriega's representative in several meetings with narcotics traffickers.

8. Brian Alden Davidow was a cocaine distributor based in Miami, Florida, who worked with Cesar Rodriguez, Ruben Dario Paredes-Jimenez and others. Brian Alden Davidow met with Manuel Antonio Noriega and others in Panama to arrange for secure transportation of cocaine destined for the Southern District of Florida.

9. Francisco Chavez-Gil made the initial arrangements for Floyd Carlton-Cacerez to meet with Cartel members Pablo Escobar-Gaviria and Gustavo Dejesus Gaviria-Rivero to arrange for protection by Manuel Antonio Noriega of cocaine shipments from Colombia to Panama.

10. David Rodrigo Ortiz-Hermida and Roberto Steiner were pilots who transported cocaine for the Cartel.

11. Eduardo Pardo and Daniel Miranda were pilots who worked for Cesar Rodriguez and Floyd Carlton-Cacerez and transported money from the United States to Panama.

12. Herman Velez, William Saldarriaga, Jaime Gomez and Luis Fernando Escobar-Ochoa were Colombian cocaine traffickers.

Purposes and Objects of the Enterprise

13. By utilizing his official positions, Manuel Antonio Noriega and trusted associates were able to assure drug traffickers that Panamanian military, customs, and law enforcement personnel would not interfere with their operations in Panama as long as substantial fees were paid to Manuel Antonio Noriega.

a. *Protection of Cocaine Shipments.* Members of the Cartel and other independent narcotics traffickers, with the assistance of Floyd Carlton-Cacerez, Ricardo Bilonick, Boris Olarte-Morales, Cesar Rodriguez and others, paid substantial fees to Manuel Antonio Noriega to protect cocaine shipments transported from Colombia through Panama to the United States. The cocaine was delivered to secure airstrips in Panama for transshipment.

b. *Protection and Assistance in Manufacturing Cocaine.* Manuel Antonio Noriega arranged for the transshipment and sale of ether and acetone, precursor chemicals used in the manufacture of cocaine hydrochloride, a Schedule II narcotic controlled substance, to members of the Cartel, including such chemicals previously seized by Panamanian authorities. Further, Manuel Antonio Noriega agreed to permit the Cartel to establish and supply a cocaine laboratory in Darien Province, Panama and to allow shipments of ether and acetone to enter Panama from the United States and Europe.

c. *Protection of Narcotics Traffickers.* In the spring of 1984, members of the Cartel and other cocaine traffickers fled Colombia as a result of increased law enforcement activities in that country. Manuel Antonio Noriega agreed to permit members of the Cartel and others to continue their narcotics business within the borders of Panama and to notify them if and when any law enforcement action was to be taken against them.

d. *Negotiations and Dispute Settlement.* Manuel Antonio Noriega, directly and through intermediaries, negotiated with narcotics traffickers. Failure to make adequate payment to, or the failure to obtain the prior approval of, Manuel Antonio Noriega for narcotics operations resulted in the seizure of drugs or other retaliatory measures by Manuel Antonio Noriega. In 1984, a dispute developed between the members of the Medellin Cartel and Manuel Antonio Noriega over the seizure of a cocaine laboratory in Darien Province, Panama despite payment by members of the Cartel to Manuel Antonio Noriega for protection of the laboratory. This dispute was mediated by Fidel Castro, Cuban head of State, in meetings with Manuel Antonio Noriega and others in Havana, Cuba.

e. *Protection of Shipments of Narcotics Proceeds From the Southern District of Florida to Panama.* Cesar Rodriguez, Floyd Carlton-Cacerez, and others transported large shipments of United States currency from the Southern District of Florida to Panama. Manuel Antonio Noriega assured the safe passage of hundreds of thousands of dollars of narcotics proceeds into Panamanian banks and arranged for the drug proceeds to be flown into Panama without interference by Panamanian customs or law enforcement authorities at civilian and military airfields.

The Racketeering Conspiracy

14. From in or about the Fall of 1981 to on or about March 21, 1986, in the Southern District of Florida, and elsewhere, the defendants:

Manuel Antonio Noriega
Gustavo Dejesus Gaviria-Rivero
Luis Del Cid
Francisco Chavez-Gil
David Rodrigo Ortiz-Hermida
Amet Paredes
Ricardo Bilonick
Brian Alden Davidow

and others known and unknown to the Grand Jury, including Pablo Escobar-Gaviria and Jorge Ochoa-Vasquez, named as co-conspirators but not co-defendants in this count, ... engaged in ... activities which affected interstate and foreign commerce in the United States, did unlawfully, willfully, and knowingly combine, conspire, confederate and agree with each other to conduct and participate, directly and indirectly, in the conduct of the affairs of the Enterprise through a pattern of racketeering activity as defined in [U.S. laws]. . . .

[Remaining counts, setting forth specific charges, are omitted]

TAMPA INDICTMENT

United States District Court
Middle District of Florida
Tampa Division

United States of America
v.
Manuel Antonio Noriega,
a/k/a "The General," "Tony,"
and
Enrique A. Pretelt,
a/k/a "Kiki"

Indictment

The Grand Jury charges that:

Count One

[Section 1 omitted]

II. The Agreement

From in or about November, 1982, through and including in or about December, 1984, in the Middle District of Florida, and elsewhere,

Manuel Antonio Noriega,

a/k/a "The General," "Tony,"

and

Enrique A. Pretelt,

a/k/a "Kiki,"

defendants herein, did knowingly, intentionally and unlawfully combine, conspire, confederate and agree together with each other and with various other persons whose names are both known and unknown to the Grand Jury, to commit offenses against the United States, that is, to import into the United States from places outside thereof in excess of 1,000 pounds of marihuana. . . .

III. Manner and Means

1. It was part of said unlawful conspiracy that Manuel Antonio Noriega and Enrique Pretelt, defendants herein, would and did arrange and plan with [Steven] Kalish, [Cesar] Rodriguez and other co-conspirators to transport large amounts of United States currency to the Republic of Panama, said money constituting the proceeds of marihuana importations and distributions into and within the United States.

2. It was further a part of said unlawful conspiracy that once the United States currency arrived in Panama, Manuel Antonio Noriega, Enrique Pretelt, Rodriguez, Kalish and other co-conspirators would and did deposit and cause to be deposited said United States currency into various financial institutions within the Republic of Panama.

3. It was further a part of said unlawful conspiracy that Manuel Antonio Noriega, Enrique Pretelt, Kalish, Rodriguez and other co-conspirators would and did then invest said proceeds in, *inter alia,* various businesses owned by Servicios Turisticos, S.A., a Panamanian corporation in which Noriega, Pretelt, Kalish and Rodriguez had an interest.

4. It was further a part of said unlawful conspiracy that Noriega, Pretelt, Kalish, Rodriguez and other co-conspirators would and did make arrangements to import approximately 1,400,000 pounds of marihuana into the United States.

5. It was further a part of said unlawful conspiracy that Noriega, Pretelt, Kalish, Rodriguez and other co-conspirators planned to continue laundering large sums of United States currency. . . . Said currency would be the proceeds of subsequent importations and distributions of mari-

huana and cocaine, some of which were to be accomplished by Kalish and his associates as well as other drug trafficking organizations.

6. It was further a part of said unlawful conspiracy that Noriega, Pretelt, Rodriguez, and other co-conspirators would and did misrepresent, conceal and hide, and cause to be misrepresented, concealed and hidden, the purposes of the acts done in furtherance of the conspiracy.

IV. Overt Acts

In furtherance of the aforesaid conspiracy and to effect the objects thereof, in the Middle District of Florida and elsewhere, one or more of the defendants committed and caused to be committed one or more of the following overt acts, among others:

1. In or about June, 1983, Kalish, Leigh Bruce Ritch ("Ritch") and others imported approximately 280,000 pounds of marihuana into the United States on board a barge brought into the coastal area of Louisiana.

2. During June, July and August, 1983, Kalish, Ritch and others distributed approximately 240,000 pounds of said marihuana in various locations within the United States including Tampa, Florida.

3. During June, July and August 1983, Kalish, Ritch and others collected approximately 60 million dollars in proceeds in the form of United States currency from the distribution of said marihuana in various locations within the United States including Tampa, Florida.

4. On or about September 22, 1983, Kalish transported approximately 2.5 million dollars of said proceeds in United States currency from Tampa, Florida, to Panama City, Panama.

5. On or about September 23, 1983, Kalish and Rodriguez deposited and caused to be deposited approximately two million dollars of said proceeds in United States currency into a Panamanian bank.

6. On or about September 23, 1983, Kalish gave $300,000 of said proceeds in U.S. currency to Noriega.

7. On or about October 11, 1983, Kalish transported approximately 2.5 million dollars of said proceeds in U.S. currency from Tampa, Florida, to Panama City, Panama.

8. On or about October 12, 1983, Pretelt, Rodriguez and Kalish deposited and caused to be deposited approximately two million dollars of said proceeds in United States currency into a Panamanian bank.

9. In or about October, 1983, Kalish purchased with $400,000 of said proceeds in United States currency a 25 percent interest in Servicios Turisticos, S.A., a Panamanian corporation, in which Noriega, Pretelt and Rodriguez had an interest.

10. In or about October, 1983, Kalish paid Rodriguez approximately $30,000 for a Panamanian passport in the name of Frank Brown.

11. On or about November 15, 1983, Ritch traveled to Panama from Tampa, Florida, and was introduced to Pretelt and Rodriguez by Kalish.

12. In or about November, 1983, at Noriega's request, Kalish purchased and caused to be purchased a Boeing 727 aircraft for the Panamanian

Force of Defense to be used, among other things, for the transportation from the United States to Panama of United States currency derived from illegal drug trafficking activities.

13. In or about December, 1983, Kalish and Noriega discussed the laundering through Panama of in excess of 100 million dollars in United States currency to be derived from the planned importations [of] in excess of 1,000,000 pounds of marihuana into the United States and the distribution thereof.

14. In or about December, 1983, Kalish, at Noriega's request, purchased a Bell 212 helicopter for the Panamanian Force of Defense and in exchange thereof received an irrevocable letter of credit issued by a Panamanian bank for the account of the Panamanian Force of Defense.

15. On or about December 23, 1983, Kalish gave Noriega in excess of $100,000 in cash and jewelry.

16. In or about January, 1984, Kalish met with Noriega and discussed the transshipment through Panama to the United States of a large quantity of marihuana.

17. On or about January 26, 1984, Kalish traveled from Tampa, Florida, to Medellin, Colombia, to arrange for the purchase of approximately 400,000 pounds of marihuana to be transhipped through Panama to the United States in containers as a legitimate cargo of plantains.

18. In or about January, 1984, Kalish made a down payment of approximately $250,000 in United States currency on four million dollars to be paid to Noriega, Pretelt and Rodriguez for Noriega's approval and authorization and their assistance concerning the importation described in Overt Act 17, above.

19. In or about January, 1984, Kalish traveled to Barranquilla, Colombia, to arrange for the purchase of approximately 1,000,000 pounds of marihuana to be imported into the United States on board a barge that was to be towed by a tugboat.

20. In or about January, 1984, at Tampa, Florida, Kalish paid $250,000 to Eugene Davis as partial payment for the use of a New York City, New York pier where the containerized shipment of marihuana would be offloaded.

21. In or about February, 1984, Kalish and Ritch made arrangements in Tampa, Florida, to purchase the Cari Cargo I, the vessel to be used in transporting the containerized shipment of marihuana.

22. In early February, 1984, Kalish gave an additional $250,000 in United States currency to Noriega, Pretelt and Rodriguez as a partial payment for Noriega's approval and authorization and their assistance concerning the containerized shipment of marihuana.

23. On or about February 17, 1984, Kalish, Noriega and Rodriguez met at Noriega's ranch in Panama where they discussed the progress of the containerized shipment of marihuana.

24. On or about February 20, 1984, Kalish paid Pretelt an additional $250,000 for the containerized shipment importation.

25. During March, 1984, Kalish, Noriega, Pretelt and Rodriguez met at Noriega's beach house in Panama to discuss the progress of the containerized shipment of marihuana importation.

26. During March, 1984, Noriega approved the issuance of a Panamanian diplomatic passport to Kalish.

27. On or about March 30, 1984, the Cari Cargo I arrived in Port Everglades, Florida, to be outfitted for the transportation of the containerized shipment of marihuana.

28. In or about April, 1984, Kalish paid $50,000 to a Panamanian shipping agent for the facilitation of the transportation of the containerized shipment of marihuana.

29. On or about April 13, 1984, Kalish traveled from Tampa, Florida, to Michigan where Kalish paid $250,000 to Eugene Davis as partial payment for the use of a New York City, New York, pier where the containerized shipment of marihuana was to be off-loaded.

30. During May, 1984, upon Noriega's authorization, Kalish paid $185,000 to an official of Panamanian Customs to obtain official Panamanian Customs seals indicating that the country of origin of the contents of the containerized shipment of marihuana was Panama.

31. On or about June 6, 1984, Kalish paid $300,000 as an additional payment to Eugene Davis for the use of the New York City, New York, pier where the containerized shipment of marihuana was to be off-loaded.

32. In or about June, 1984, the Cari Cargo I traveled from Port Everglades, Florida, to Colon, Panama.

33. In or about April, 1984, a barge to be used for the importation of approximately 1,000,000 pounds of marihuana traveled from Louisiana to Colon, Panama.

34. In or about June, 1984, said barge was towed by a tugboat traveled from Colon, Panama, to Barranquilla, Colombia, in order to be loaded with approximately 1,000,000 pounds of marihuana.

35. During the spring of 1984, the 400,000 pounds of marihuana to be shipped on board the Cari Cargo I was collected and packaged in Colombia for shipment to the United States.

36. During May, June and July, 1984, the 1,000,000 pounds of marihuana to be shipped to the United States via a tug and barge was readied for shipment in Barranquilla, Colombia.

All in violation of Title 21, United States Code, Sections 963 and 846.

Count Two

Between on or about December 1, 1983, and on or about October 31, 1984, in the Middle District of Florida and elsewhere, the defendants . . . did knowingly and intentionally attempt to import into the United States from a place outside thereof . . . a quantity in excess of fifty (50) kilograms of marihuana, to wit, approximately one million . . . pounds . . . that was to be on board a barge to be towed by a tugboat from Colombia to the United States. . . .

Count Three

Between on or about December 1, 1983, and on or about August 31, 1984, in the Middle District of Florida and elsewhere, the defendants ... did knowingly and intentionally attempt to import into the United States from a place outside thereof, and did aid, abet, counsel, command, procure and cause the attempted importation into the United States from a place outside thereof, approximately four hundred thousand (400,000) pounds of marihuana ... through Panama to the United States from Colombia via a containerized shipment disguised as a cargo of plantains.

STATE DEPARTMENT REPORT
ON HUMAN RIGHTS PRACTICES
February 10, 1988

"As we look back on human rights developments worldwide during the year 1987, there is no doubt that the attention of a great many observers focused on ... the Soviet Union." This statement is from the introduction of Country Reports on Human Rights Practices for 1987, *released by the State Department on February 17. The department has been required by law since 1961 to report to Congress annually on human rights developments abroad. Since 1979 these reports have applied to all member-countries of the United Nations, and before that only to countries that received U.S. aid. The 1,358-page document for 1987 reported on human rights activities in 169 countries.*

The focus on the Soviet Union resulted from changes being brought about in the third year of Mikhail S. Gorbachev's rule. The authors of the 1987 reports saw the changes as "more than cosmetic and less than fundamental." They explained: "The Soviet dictatorship ... remained in place. The secret police and its comprehensive network of informants remained the principal pillar on which the state edifice rests. A majority of political prisoners remained in jail. But ... there was some relaxation of totalitarian controls. Some political prisoners were released. The Soviets announced moves to end the truly barbarous practice of abuse of psychiatry. Emigration levels of ethnic Germans, Armenians, and Jews were higher than those of recent years. ... Plays and films could be seen that dealt with the realities of Soviet life more honestly than had been allowed in a long time. ..."

"On the other hand, we regret to say, the hopes and expectations voiced

in the spring of 1987 were not fulfilled by the end of the year," the authors of the report added. "We need to see what 1988 will bring." In Poland and Hungary, countries in the Soviet bloc, some progress could be detected. "Poland completed a full calendar year, for the first time in a long time, without a single person convicted and incarcerated for the mere expression of a dissenting political view," the document stated, adding: "It surely does not mean that political freedom has come to Poland, but it is progress of a sort."

Elsewhere in the world, the State Department noted "with satisfaction" that free elections had been held in South Korea and government controls had been relaxed in Taiwan. On the other hand, democracy suffered a setback in Haiti, where a futile attempt was made to hold the first presidential election in thirty years. On election day, November 29, squads of armed men—many of them believed to be followers of the ousted dictator, Jean-Claude Duvalier—attacked polling places throughout Haiti, killing at least thirty-four persons. The independently appointed Provisional Electoral Council, charged under the new constitution with overseeing the election process, cancelled the election to prevent further carnage.

The State Department noted "no progress toward respect for human rights in South Africa," and its reports from dozens of countries— especially in Africa, the Middle East, and Central America—continued to portray deplorable conditions. As the year drew to a close, Palestinians in the Israeli-occupied territories launched a wave of often-violent protests. Israeli forces responded with gunfire and beatings, creating new outcries of human rights violations.

Following are excerpts from the State Department's Country Reports on Human Rights Practices for 1987, released February 10, 1988:

South Africa

... The human rights situation in South Africa continued to deteriorate in 1987. A state of emergency, imposed in 1986 and giving police and military extraordinary arrest and detention powers, was renewed in June 1987. The Government also rewrote many of the emergency regulations in 1987 to "close the loopholes" and make it more difficult for the judiciary to intervene in questions relating to the state of emergency. The Government has used these powers to arrest an estimated 30,000 people since June 1986. The United Democratic Front (UDF), a loosely organized national movement of more than 600 antiapartheid groups, and various black trade unions have been special targets for detention. The government imposed harsher curbs on the media and brought its program of limited reforms to a virtual halt.

The level of political violence apparently declined in 1987 from previous years, although at least 500 people died as the result of such violence during the year. The shadowy war between South African security forces and the African National Congress (ANC) escalated. The banned ANC is headquartered in exile in Lusaka, Zambia, while many of its leaders, including Nelson Mandela, remain in long-term imprisonment in South Africa. . . .

Most of the deaths in 1987 resulted from violence within the black townships, and the vast majority of victims were blacks. Much of this violence resulted from fighting between political factions. Overall, however, violence resulting from political strife within the black community was less prevalent than in 1986, and so-called "necklace" killings, in which the victim is executed by a burning tire placed around his neck, declined dramatically in 1987. This was mainly due to the state of emergency but also to strong discouragement of such acts by internal and external black political groups, including the ANC. Fragmentary statistics indicated deaths resulting from necklacing declined from the hundreds in 1986 to perhaps no more than a dozen in 1987.

Many other deaths were the result of excessive use of force by police, who sometimes quelled demonstrations with live ammunition, tear gas, birdshot, hard rubber clubs, or rubber bullets. In April six people were killed when police fired on a demonstration of striking railroad workers. During 1987 the Government augmented security forces by accelerating the recruitment of "Kitsconstabels" ("instant police"—called that because their training periods were short); these special police constables were first introduced in the black townships in 1986. Government critics charge that they have been responsible for numerous abuses. In February four people were shot and killed by Kitsconstabels in Grahamstown.

Several deaths of persons in police custody occurred during the year, at least two of which appeared to be execution-style killings. In July ANC member Ashley Kriel was killed by police in a Cape Town home. An autopsy revealed that he had been shot in the back at point-blank range. In August Caiphus Nyoka, a high school student leader, was killed by police during a nighttime raid on his home in Daveyton, even though he had apparently offered no resistance. He had been shot in the forehead at close range. At the end of 1987, the Government had failed to provide any explanation or order any investigation in regard to Nyoka's death. . . .

The most serious violence resulting from political factional fighting in 1987 took place in Natal. In particular, clashes between UDF supporters and Inkatha members, who support KwaZulu Chief Mangosuthu Buthelezi, resulted in at least 268 deaths during the year in the Pietermaritzburg area. The violence around Pietermaritzburg accelerated beginning in September, and efforts by several groups to mediate an end to the violence were unsuccessful as of the end of 1987.

In addition, as a significant minority of blacks in South Africa espouse or condone violent opposition to apartheid, there were instances of violence and intimidation against blacks who were not complying with such protest activities as school or rent boycotts and strikes. Attacks by radical blacks on township government officials, black policemen, and other suspected "collaborators" continued, though at a lower rate than in 1986. The ANC helped fuel this violence since it continued to call on blacks to attack these so-called collaborators. The Government emphasized such intimidation as a justification for repressive actions against members of trade unions and community organizations. . . .

Disappearance [and Torture]

In recent years many people have disappeared, reportedly into police custody, for long periods. Some, missing for very long periods of time, are suspected by friends and associates to have been killed by security forces. South African law does not require notification of a person's family, lawyer, or any other person in the event of his detention or arrest, and prohibits the unauthorized publication of the name of any detainee if "the prevention of or combating of terroristic activities" is the reason for the detention.

Since August 1986, the Minister of Law and Order periodically has tabled lists of state of emergency detainees in Parliament. These lists, which appeared to be incomplete, only included detainees held for at least 30 days. As of the end of 1987, this constituted the Government's only official public accounting of emergency detainees. Human rights monitoring groups estimated that substantial numbers of detainees have not been named in the Government's lists and maintained that in most cases family members were not informed of emergency detentions. . . .

Many persons reported that they had been held in solitary confinement during their detention. Others gave accounts of torture by police, including applications of electric shocks to hands, feet, and genitals. Many former detainees in the Port Elizabeth area reported that police had supplemented routine beatings and electric shocks with repeated suffocation as a means of extracting information. According to their affidavits, police tied wet plastic or canvas bags around the heads of prisoners and repeatedly applied rubber innertubes over their noses and mouths to suffocate them, often to unconsciousness. Journalists and others detained in KwaNdebele during the year produced a number of eyewitness accounts detailing the apparently routine beatings suffered by detainees in that homeland.

Most torture occurred during and immediately following arrest. The chances of physical abuse taking place apparently diminish once a detainee is processed and made part of the general inmate population. Instances of abuse in prisons, while not unheard of, appear to be less frequent than at police stations. . . .

Police and other security force members were seldom held accountable in 1987 for abuse of detainees. While the Government conceded in some cases that such abuses occurred, the courts often imposed only token punishments on those found guilty. In 1987 the Government completed an investigation of credible allegations by Father Smangaliso Mkhatshwa,

Secretary General of the Southern African Catholic Bishops Conference, that he had been tortured while in detention. A court permitted one of the six accused SADF personnel to pay a small "admission of guilt" fine and absolved the other five soldiers. In October the Law and Order Minister, responding to the protests of Eastern Cape human rights activists, pledged to investigate charges of police torture of detainees....

On June 11, 1987, the Government renewed the June 1986 state of emergency and issued new regulations which tightened and extended those originally promulgated in June 1986. Under the revised 1987 rules, the period for which SADF members and police officers down to the rank of constable are empowered to detain persons was extended from 14 days to 30 days.... After 30 days the Minister of Law and Order may extend the detention for an indefinite period of time, limited only by the duration of the state of emergency. In June the Government issued new rules concerning the treatment of state of emergency detainees, giving them many of the rights granted to ordinary prisoners awaiting trial. However, in July an appeals court reaffirmed that emergency detainees may be denied access to lawyers and have no right to a hearing before the Minister extends the detention....

Uganda

In the period since it assumed control in January 1986, the National Resistance Movement (NRM) Government headed by Yoweri Museveni has established authority in the areas firmly under its control, primarily in the southern and western parts of Uganda. Remnants of previous regimes continue guerrilla activity in the north, as do political and criminal elements in the east. The NRM has promised that a new constitution will be drafted and presented to Ugandans for approval. Progress has been slow, and due to continued fighting in the north and east, the NRM may find it difficult to keep its pledge of a 4-year transitional period. In the interim, the 1980 Constitution is suspended and political activity not allowed, although parties exist nominally. The President exercises executive authority with the assistance of a Cabinet of his choosing. The National Resistance Council, while intended to serve in a legislative capacity, has in fact had little active responsibility.

The security structure of the Government is composed of the National Resistance Army (NRA) and the police. The NRA, a disciplined organization during its bush days, has absorbed soldiers from previous regimes and recruited those who did not fight for the NRA's goals before its assumption of power. Thus, discipline and morale have dropped, most notably in the contested areas, where fighting is keeping up to 50,000 troops in the field. NRA soldiers have committed burglaries and automobile hijackings at gunpoint, even in the uncontested areas of Kampala and West Nile....

The NRM has given a high public profile to its concerns about human rights abuses in Uganda and Africa, most recently in an October address by President Museveni at the U.N. General Assembly. Human rights and other organizations, including the international press, have noted favorably the contrasting approaches between the NRM and previous regimes. Nevertheless, in 1987 the goal of national reconciliation was undercut as continuing unrest in the northern and eastern regions of Uganda contributed to a deterioration of human rights, especially in the areas of military operations. There were frequent reports of execution of adversaries wounded in battle, of homes and fields burned, of occasional torture of prisoners in NRA custody, and of continued detention of those thought to be unsympathetic to the NRA. As a result of the fighting, thousands of persons—some reports indicate as many as 100,000 in 1987—have been displaced, including 2,000 to Kenya. The Commission of Inquiry into past human rights abuses, which Museveni established in 1986, continued to hear testimony in 1987 but did not issue any reports. The Commission plans to spend 2 years collecting evidence for the Attorney General, who will decide which cases should be prosecuted....

Amnesty International issued a special report in July 1987 in which it noted the positive steps the Government had taken to end human rights abuses in Uganda. It added, however, that it had a number of new concerns, based on many reports, including reports of extrajudicial killings by government troops in combat areas. Former Minister of Energy Andrew Kayiira was murdered on March 6, 2 weeks after his release from prison where he had been held on suspicion of preparing a coup. Five suspects have been charged with the murder. At the end of 1987, no trial date had been set, and the motivation for the killing remained unclear....

Reports of disappearance, common under previous regimes, markedly declined under the NRM Government. However, there were allegations, especially by church authorities, of disappearances in the north and east.

Torture and inhuman treatment are not sanctioned by Ugandan law, but for many years extreme forms of torture have taken place at detention centers, particularly military barracks, where political prisoners are often held illegally. The NRM Government has allowed the International Committee of the Red Cross (ICRC) to visit prisons in uncontested areas of the country and has cooperated in improving conditions in response to ICRC suggestions. However, the Government did not allow the ICRC access to military prisons throughout the year, although at year's end an agreement was reached between the Government and the ICRC to allow such visits. Human rights organizations such as Amnesty International have alleged inhuman treatment and torture by the NRA, which has its own detention centers outside the jurisdiction of Ugandan law....

Argentina

In the fourth year since its return to constitutional government, the Argentine people and their elected leaders continued to demonstrate in 1987 a strong commitment to democracy and the rule of law. Argentina is governed by a constitution with an elected president, bicameral legislature, and autonomous judiciary. In 1987 Argentina held its third successful national election in 4 years, following an extended campaign, free and open debate, dozens of rallies, and full press coverage. . . .

A political crisis occurred in 1987 concerning prosecution of military personnel for alleged abuses committed during the 1976 to 1983 period of military rule. The Government's attempt to bring a definitive end to the prosecutions through the so-called "punto final" law of December 1986 brought hundreds of cases to the federal courts early in the year. Following an April uprising by a group of military officers, Congress passed a "due obedience" law, the practical effect of which was to protect from prosecution all but an estimated 50 retired, and perhaps one or two active duty, officers. Some human rights activists and opposition leaders criticized the law, but all agree that it was adopted in full accord with constitutional requirements. Tensions over human rights trials lessened considerably in the latter half of the year.

The inefficiency of the judicial system and conditions in Argentine prisons provoked some protests in 1987, but reforms currently before Congress and new construction are expected to ameliorate the problems. . . .

Apparent politically motivated bombings rose substantially in 1987. Most were small explosions late at night, causing little damage or injuries. Targets covered the political spectrum, including the right, left, national parties, military, church, human rights groups, press, and judicial officials. The incidents clustered around high profile events, such as the Pope's visit in early April, the Easter week military crisis and military trials debate, and the September 6 national elections. The perpetrators never claimed formal responsibility for the bombings, and there is no consensus on the possible identity of the persons or groups responsible. There have been few arrests.

There were no known abductions, secret arrests, or disappearances linked to or condoned by the Government during 1987. . . .

In August President Alfonsin signed a decree providing pensions to spouses and minor children of victims who disappeared between 1976 and 1983. . . .

Amnesty International, the International Committee of the Red Cross, and a host of international human rights organizations enjoyed free access throughout Argentina. Eleven domestic human rights organizations operated openly in 1987, despite occasional bombings, death threats, and harassment from unidentified sources. During January and February, the organizations brought hundreds of charges to the federal courts related to disappearances during the years of military rule. . . .

Suspected Nazi war criminal Josef Franz Leo Schwamberger was arrested in November and is being held for possible extradition to the Federal Republic of Germany. Jewish organizations expressed satisfaction with the arrest and extradition but concern at the lengthy delay in locating and arresting the suspect. . . .

There is a current of anti-Semitism in Argentine society and occasional anti-Semitic incidents occur. In the final months of 1987, Argentina's Jewish community expressed concern at signs of increasing anti-Semitism. They specifically cited anti-Semitic remarks during a public Mass in September, anonymous threats following the Schwamberger arrest in November, and a November synagogue bombing. A draft bill providing criminal penalties for racial, religious, and other forms of discrimination is pending in Congress. . . .

Chile

Many fundamental political freedoms in Chile remained restricted during 1987. The implementation of laws which allowed for the legalization of political parties and the registration of voters provided somewhat greater freedom of association and assembly. Rights of private property, freedom of religion, and minority rights are respected, but freedom from arbitrary arrest and exile is limited. Freedoms of speech and of the press were expanded when the Government gave permission for the publication of two daily opposition newspapers. However, access to television by opposition groups remained virtually nonexistent. . . .

In 1987, as in the past, there were reliable and documented reports of torture and mistreatment of those detained by Chilean security forces. Some government ministries have tried to stop or at least control such abuses. . . .

. . . According to the Vicariate of Solidarity, the human rights organization of the Catholic Church, 51 persons died in acts of political violence during the year. Government officials state that terrorist groups in 1987 caused 42 deaths and 404 personal injuries in attacks which included 368 bombings. Chilean Human Rights Commission (CHRC) figures indicate that 43 deaths occurred due to political violence. The deaths and injuries resulted from both deliberate and random actions by leftwing and rightwing terrorists and by security and military forces.

Over half of the dead were leftist terrorists, with seven deaths attributed to the premature explosion of bombs reportedly being placed by these persons. Two deaths were attributed to rightwing extremists when shots were fired from vehicles at antigovernment demonstrators. In June 12 people, whom government reports tied to the FPMR [Manuel Rodriguez Patriotic Front], were shot by CNI officials in 5 separate incidents. In all five cases authorities maintained the victims were killed resisting arrest. Human rights organizations questioned these claims and sought a special judicial investigation of the incidents. A civilian court began investigating the deaths of 7 of these 12 people, but before it could establish if they had been summarily executed or not, the investigation was taken over by a military court. Since then this case has disappeared from the press, and human rights groups have no further information on it. . . .

Human rights organizations report that politically motivated kidnappings, unauthorized searches, and threats increased from 668 in 1986 to 792 in 1987. There were 85 individuals kidnaped in 1987. Although numerous complaints have been made to the courts, there have been no known arrests or prosecutions in any of these kidnaping cases. . . .

Torture continues to occur despite these efforts to stop it. The Vicariate reported 102 cases of torture in 1987, as compared to 130 cases in 1986, and 81 in 1985. The Vicariate has compared the statistics on torture with the number of people detained on charges of violating various state security laws. In 1987 there were 461 people detained, and 102 of them were subjected to torture, or 22.1 percent. In 1986 there were 773 people detained, and 130 tortured, or 16.8 percent. In 1985 the figures were 549 people detained and 81 tortured, or 14.7 percent. CHRC statistics indicate 118 cases of torture occurred in 1987, compared to 291 cases in 1986 and 166 cases in 1985. . . .

In late November, the legislative Junta approved a law which permits military unit commanders to refuse to comply with court orders seeking information on the activities of military units which may be involved in actions that infringe on human rights. Under this law military commanders may classify information relating to military patrols, involving the members of these patrols, as vital to national security. While the investigating courts may appeal to the Supreme Court, the information may still be denied to them. . . .

The Catholic Church continues to take the lead in defending human rights. It supplies legal counsel to those accused of politically related crimes and to victims of human rights abuses. Its Vicariate of Solidarity monitors the human rights situation throughout Chile, issues factual monthly reports on human rights violations, and protects and defends significant numbers of people. . . . The Vicariate remains a target of investigation by the military prosecutor who is looking into several terrorist-related incidents. Several lawyers for the Vicariate were subjected to court summonses, generally from military courts, on a variety of charges related to their legal work. The prosecutor, so far unsuccessfully, has sought access to the Vicariate's case files and bank records. . . .

Haiti

The attempt to establish democracy in Haiti after 30 years of dictatorship was thwarted by violence and murder on election day, November 29, 1987. The November elections had been designed to provide a peaceful and orderly transition of power from the current caretaker military-dominated National Governing Council (CNG) to a freely elected constitutional civilian government. However, on election day, squads of armed men, many of them believed to be followers of the ousted dictator, Jean-Claude Duvalier, attacked polling places throughout Haiti, killing at least 34 people. There is evidence that some Haitian military personnel participated in the carnage on election day. The independently appointed Provisional Electoral Council (CEP), charged under the Constitution with overseeing the electoral process, cancelled elections to avoid further bloodshed. . . .

The Haitian Armed Forces (Forces Armées D'Haiti—FAD'H) perform both defense and police functions, as an integrated organization of navy, army, air force, and police elements. The military came under criticism due to involvement of security force elements in human rights abuses and the Government's failure to investigate or prosecute these cases.

Haiti's most pressing problem remains its systemic economic distress. The poorest and most densely populated country in the Western Hemisphere, Haiti is plagued by malnutrition, infectious disease, and illiteracy. Soil erosion, deforestation, and periods of drought afflict the agricultural sector. The dire poverty of the majority of the population affects all aspects of Haitian life. Although expectations were raised and hopes were high following the fall of the Duvalier dictatorship, most Haitians still live in conditions of abject economic misery.

The human rights record of the CNG, even prior to the November elections, was mixed. The major accomplishment of 1987 was a referendum in which 42 percent of the population overwhelmingly approved a new Constitution establishing the legal basis for democratic institutions in Haiti. The Constitution provides for legislative, judicial, and executive branches of government headed by an elected President who appoints a Prime Minister; a bicameral legislature representing the nine regions of the country; and fundamental rights and freedoms for all Haitians.

Violence erupted in June and July as many Haitians perceived the CNG's promulgation of an election law restricting the powers of the constitutionally mandated independent electoral council as an attempt to subvert or circumvent the new Constitution. Weeks of violent antigovernment street demonstrations resulted in numerous deaths and injuries, some the result of inappropriate crowd control actions by Haitian security forces. Violence again rose steadily several weeks prior to the November elections, and the CNG failed to stop the violence or to provide the necessary security for a fair and orderly election....

... [U]nexplained killings have been attributed to hit squads or to men in green uniforms, who are accused of causing a "reign of terror" throughout the country. The arrests in February and September of two gangs revealed that, although gang members wore uniforms, none were members of the military. They and others perpetrating these murders and many lesser crimes appear to be common criminals, ex-Tonton Macoutes (members of the outlawed volunteers for National Security, the Duvalier family's brutal militia) and military personnel acting independently to take advantage of the chaotic situation, particularly in rural areas.

There have also been incidents of violence against soldiers. In July, a soldier was killed by persons who fired on him from a private vehicle. During the summer's unrest, homes of soldiers and police were frequent targets of mob violence.

The Constitution stipulates that all arrests occur openly, with warrants, and that all arrestees be brought before a judge. In the days preceding and immediately following the November 29 elections, approximately 50 young people who had organized "vigilante brigades" to protect their Port-au-Prince neighborhoods from preelection violence in the absence of police protection were reportedly rounded up by army units. Conclusive information regarding their whereabouts is unavailable. There are some claims that they are still being held, and other allegations that they were executed. Government officials state that they have no information concerning these alleged disappearances. . . .

Cambodia

The human rights situation in Cambodia is profoundly affected by the ongoing struggle for political control, which began in December 1978 when the Vietnamese army drove the Khmer Rouge Communist regime of Democratic Kampuchea out of Phnom Penh. Vietnam subsequently installed a puppet regime, the so-called People's Republic of Kampuchea (PRK), under former Khmer Rouge division commander Heng Samrin. Vietnam, through the Heng Samrin regime and its own occupation forces, controls most of Cambodia by force of arms. Widespread abuses of human rights in Cambodia stem largely from the occupation by at least 10 Vietnamese army divisions and an indigenous Communist countrywide, civil-military control apparatus which together maintain the Heng Samrin regime in power. This control is challenged by a three-part Khmer resistance movement, the Coalition Government of Democratic Kampuchea (CGDK), which holds Cambodia's seat at the United Nations. The resistance has implemented a guerrilla strategy and conducts operations throughout much of Cambodia from areas along the Thai-Cambodian border. . . .

According to Amnesty International, a variety of tortures is inflicted on political suspects detained for interrogation. The most commonly cited are lengthy and repeated beatings and whippings. Detainees are said to have been punched and kicked on the body, head, and extremities; struck with pistol and rifle butts, truncheons, wooden staves with sharpened edges, and bamboo or iron bars; and whipped with electrical or steel cables, chains, rubber hoses, or wet gunny sacks. The victim may be tied up during these assaults or blindfolded and hung upside down from the ceiling with ropes. There are credible reports that many other forms of torture are also used, including being buried alive, burning with powdered limestone or heated instruments, and the insertion of nails through the thigh muscles to the bone.

Both Amnesty International and the Lawyers Committee note that detainees undergoing interrogation in centers higher than the district level are generally held incommunicado in small and completely dark solitary confinement cells that are poorly ventilated and unsanitary. They are immobilized by shackles on both legs. Sometimes they are also handcuffed. The detainees are allowed no bedding or mosquito netting. Detainees whose ill-treatment during interrogation is being intensified are also deprived of food and water progressively to undermine their physical strength and resistance to illness. They may not bathe or go outside their cells to relieve themselves and are reportedly permitted no medication or medical attention.

The aim of this cruel treatment is apparently to compel detainees to confess to crimes and to inform on other suspects or persons considered opponents by the authorities. Although it is rarely reported that a suspect has been killed during the actual interrogation, there are frequent reports of detainees dying following interrogation, during the indefinite period of detention without charge or trial. Such deaths reportedly occur even though the torture is over and conditions have improved. The causes appear to be a combination of internal injuries sustained during torture, unattended diseases contracted during or after torture, and inadequate diet. Suicides also have been reported, as well as cases of detainees becoming insane after torture and ill-treatment. . . .

Forced labor by the PRK regime and directly by the Vietnamese military is common, although it is not primarily used as a sanction or means of racial, social, or other discrimination. The authorities have systematically conscripted Khmer civilians from throughout Cambodia for work on military-related projects in or near combat areas along the Thai-Cambodian border. The number of these forced laborers remained in the tens of thousands during 1987. . . .

Since 1981 the ICRC has sought permission from the Phnom Penh authorities without success to visit prisoners captured in combat. It has also been unsuccessful in persuading the resistance factions to allow them access to prisoners held at their military camps. The ICRC has also had no success in persuading Thai authorities to allow it access to Vietnamese prisoners held in Thai prisons, nor in persuading the PRK authorities to allow it access to a small number of Thai prisoners reportedly held in Cambodian prisons. Nevertheless, the ICRC has pursued a program to disseminate information about the proper treatment of prisoners of war and the role the ICRC traditionally plays during conflicts. . . .

Human rights violations in Cambodia have been the subject of intense international attention since 1978, when the United Nations Human Rights Commission and its subcommission on the Prevention of Discrimination and Protection of Minorities began investigating the problem. In February 1987, the Commission adopted the latest in a series of resolutions on Cambodia, reiterating its condemnation of persistent violations of human rights in Cambodia and reaffirming that the continuing occupation of Cambodia by foreign forces deprives the people of Cambodia of their right to self-determination. . . .

Republic of Korea

The year 1987 saw dramatic political change in the Republic of Korea (ROK), resulting in significant developments in the human rights situation there. Large street demonstrations broke out in June, partly the result of widespread disenchantment with the Government over the death of a student by torture at police hands in January and the highly unpopular decision by President Chun Doo Hwan on April 13 to end debate over constitutional revision.

Faced with continuing protests, on June 29 ruling Democratic Justice Party [DJP] Chairman Roh Tae Woo, President Chun's choice as his successor, announced far-reaching democratic reforms. In addition to acceptance of the opposition's demands for direct presidential elections, these proposals included the release of political prisoners, a sweeping amnesty, and restoration of civil rights, including those of opposition leader Kim Dae Jung. On July 1 President Chun accepted Roh's proposal.

In October ruling and opposition parties in the National Assembly passed a bipartisan constitutional revision bill, thus paving the way for Korea's first direct presidential election since 1971. The election took place on December 16. Four major candidates conducted a fiercely contested campaign, occasionally marred by violence. Nearly 90 percent of the electorate participated in the election, in which Roh Tae Woo emerged as the victor with a plurality of around 36 percent. These developments basically changed the political environment in Korea and provide the possibility for further improvement in the human rights environment.

The Korean Government describes itself as a liberal democracy, but power under the Constitution of the Fifth Republic was indisputably centered around President Chun. The Constitution creating the Fifth Republic in October 1980 was written under strict martial law conditions. The 1987 bipartisan revision—to take full effect on the inauguration of the new President February 25, 1988—is widely regarded as a key step in Korea's democratization. . . .

Korea is one of the world's most homogeneous societies. Its sociopolitical tradition emphasizes order, conformity, and a subordinate role for women. These attitudes, while changing somewhat, nevertheless retain great strength, coexisting uneasily at times with Western democratic ideals. This tradition and a heavily armed and unpredictable Communist North Korea, which invaded the South in 1950 and remains committed to reunifying the entire peninsula under its control, have caused successive South Korean governments to give top priority to maintaining external and internal security. . . .

Many Koreans have complained that the security threat from the North, which is genuine, has been used as a pretext by the Government to suppress legitimate internal dissent. Although the law enforcement agencies are well trained and generally well disciplined, excessive use of force has been a continuing problem, especially prior to June 29. Torture has also occurred. Although the Constitution provides for freedom of speech and press, in practice both have been abridged. The new Constitution promises to make these freedoms a reality. . . .

A major component of the democratization reforms announced June 29 by the ruling Democratic Justice Party Chairman Roh Tae Woo was the release of political prisoners. Consequently, in July and August, the Government released a large number of political prisoners in a series of special clemencies. During this time, the Government also granted amnesty and restored civil rights to more than 2,300 individuals, including prominent opposition politician Kim Dae Jung. In August the Government claimed that it was holding no more than about 100 political prisoners, all of whom it contended had been convicted by the courts of being ideological "leftists" and revolutionaries who sought to subvert society through violence and other means. Human rights groups acknowledged that large numbers of prisoners, mainly students, had been released, but claimed that the number of real political prisoners still being held was closer to 400.

During the summer numbers of people were arrested in connection with growing labor strife. Beginning in September, authorities began to apprehend significant numbers of suspected student activists, including key leaders of the National University Student Council Alliance ("Chondaehyop"). Many of these students were accused of violating the National Security Law by allegedly forming subversive organizations, plotting to undermine the presidential election, and fomenting social unrest....

During the latter half of 1987, the media was more open in its coverage of events. Although freedom of speech and press is provided for in the Constitution, in practice the expression of opposition viewpoints has often been restricted, sometimes severely.

Although National Assemblymen enjoy immunity from prosecution for remarks made within the Assembly, they are not immune from prosecution for what they write or say outside the chamber. Opposition parliamentarian Yoo Sung-Hwan was arrested in October 1986 for prior dissemination of an Assembly speech in which he suggested that the first priority of the Government's "national ideology" should be unification of the peninsula and not anticommunism. He was convicted in April 1987 of violating the national security law and sentenced to 1 year in prison. Yoo was released from custody in July 1987, however, and returned to active politics....

The Philippines

The Government of the Philippines oversaw the adoption of a new Constitution and the establishment of national democratic institutions during 1987. Despite continued evidence of overwhelming popular support for President Aquino and her reform agenda, political forces on both left and right sought to destabilize or overthrow her Government by force....

A stubborn Communist insurgency active in most of the country's 73 provinces continues to pose the major long-term challenge to democratic practices and the restoration of respect for human rights in the Philippines. A 60-day cease-fire negotiated late in 1986 between the Government and the Communist New People's Army (NPA) ended in February after political talks were terminated by representatives of the leftist National Democratic Front (NDF). During 1987 the NPA increasingly targeted for assassination government officials, private citizens, and labor leaders who resisted its influence. NDF spokesmen claimed responsibility for the October 28 murder of three American citizens, including two uniformed servicemen, near Clark Air Base. Communist rebels stepped up their killing of soldiers and police in Manila and other urban centers while launching offensives aimed at destroying bridges, power facilities, and other economic infrastructure in rural areas. . . .

Political killings are frequent in the Philippines and take place throughout the country. Because successful prosecution of political assassins is extremely rare, private vendettas are often pursued. Over 100 persons are believed to have died during the campaign culminating in nationwide congressional elections on May 11. At year's end, nearly 30 persons had been killed in violence related to nationwide local elections scheduled for January 18, 1988. Prominent figures are not immune from violence. During 1987 a cabinet member and the secretary general of a leading leftist political organization were among those murdered.

The official fact-gathering human rights institution in the Philippines is the constitutionally mandated CHR. In contrast to the CHR, which investigates all alleged violations of human rights, several private groups focus almost exclusively on allegations against government forces. The best known of these organizations is Task Force Detainees (TFD), whose broad definitions of human rights violations have the effect of increasing the number of reported incidents. TFD has been accused of using its statistics to support a politically motivated finding that the human rights situation in the Philippines is deteriorating.

The CHR and its predecessor, the Presidential Commission on Human Rights (PCHR), have received 123 reports of political killings since the February 1986 change of government. TFD reports 208 summary executions by government forces during the first 11 months of 1987 alone. This figure compares to 197 reported by the organization in all of 1986 and 517 in 1985. TFD also reports that 123 persons were killed during the first 11 months of 1987 in massacres—defined as politically motivated killings of groups of individuals. This figure is up, according to TFD, from 101 such victims in 1986, but less than the 276 claimed in 1985. TFD includes in its figures the deaths of 13 people during a protest march in January at Mendiola Bridge near the presidential palace in Manila and the February shooting of 17 unarmed villagers in Nueva Ecija province. Twenty-three soldiers charged with murder in the latter incident are about to go on trial. . . .

Political killings go largely unpunished in the Philippines. Several major cases involving the murder of a prominent political figure are presently being heard. During 1987 the only conviction in such a case was entered against eight defendants who were found guilty and sentenced to life in prison for the 1985 killing of Italian priest Tullio Favali. Most cases are never solved or prosecuted.

During 1987 human rights groups focused on proliferating anti-Communist citizens' self-defense groups as frequent perpetrators of political killings. A locally organized counterinsurgency measure, these groups vary considerably in character, ranging from unarmed neighborhood watch organizations which supplement police intelligence to quasi-legal paramilitary patrols. There are also illegal private armies and fanatical cults such as the Tadtad which kill Communist sympathizers along with other political opponents....

There is no convincing evidence that government officials are involved regularly in politically motivated disappearances. In some cases, however, citizens have been taken into custody by government authorities and held incommunicado for several days before being released or charged....

Trials in the Philippines are public. The Constitution guarantees that those accused of crimes shall be informed of charges against them and have the right to counsel. Defendants enjoy the presumption of innocence and the right to confront witnesses against them, to present evidence, and to appeal their convictions.

The right of defendants to a lawyer is well recognized in law and is generally carried out in practice in metropolitan Manila. It is much less frequently accorded in the provinces, however, where in many cases there are simply no lawyers available. Many defendants are released because of this, especially those charged with minor crimes. Those charged with a capital offense are usually held until a lawyer becomes available.

Judicial proceedings often continue for years. Many criminals, especially those who have expert legal representation, escape conviction and punishment. Efforts by the Aquino Government to reform the Philippine judiciary and to remove judges believed to be incompetent or corrupt have aggravated chronic docketing delays. Since the judicial appointments commission required by the new Constitution has not been implemented, no new judges have been appointed since February. The shortage of judges continues to be particularly severe outside the Manila area....

Human rights groups allege that military dissatisfaction with the amnesty program encourages some soldiers to kill their adversaries rather than take them prisoner. While isolated incidents of this nature may occur in remote areas where observers are few, there is no direct evidence to support charges that such conduct is common. The large number of Communist rebels regularly reported as having been taken captive by the AFP, more than 344 as of late 1987, contradict assertions that summary executions of prisoners are widespread....

Turkey

Turkey is a republic with a multiparty parliamentary system and a strong presidency. In 1987 Turkey completed a return to a full functioning democracy. A referendum, passed on September 6, restored all political rights to those former politicians who had been banned from politics by a provisional article of the 1982 Constitution. All charges against the formerly banned politicians for activities prior to the referendum were dropped. Prime Minister Turgut Ozal called for early national elections which took place on November 29. These were the first national elections since 1980 to include all prominent political leaders. Prime Minister Ozal's Motherland Party won the elections from a field of seven legal political parties....

Progress in the observance of human rights continued in 1987. The end of martial law in July 1987, the lifting of political bans in the September referendum, and recent court rulings removed many restraints on freedom of the press. In January the Government recognized, in principle, the right of Turkish citizens to appeal to the European Human Rights Commission, although it has yet to approve appeals to the European Human Rights Court, whose decisions are binding. In January 1988, Turkey signed the Council of Europe (COE) Convention for the Prevention of Torture and Inhuman or Degrading Treatment and announced its intention to sign a similar U.N. agreement. By signing, the Government of Turkey, for the first time, accepted official outside monitoring of places of detention, a step human rights organizations had long been advocating. Application for membership in the European Community has provided an additional impetus for bringing human rights practices into conformity with general Western European norms.

The Government prosecuted many persons accused of torturing detainees. Increased penalties for torture have been incorporated into the proposed revision of the penal code. The Government is also improving prison conditions by building new facilities and responding to prisoner demands. However, despite the Government's efforts to date, serious and repeated incidences of torture continue to be reported. . . .

. . . In its September 1987 File on Torture, Amnesty International charged that torture was "widespread" and "systematic," claiming that "almost 4 years after a civilian government came to power in November 1983, no effective measures have been taken to prevent torture." The Amnesty file included accounts of torture methods, centers of torture, sexual abuse, and death in custody. Helsinki Watch in its latest report concluded that "torture is still practiced in Turkey on a large scale." It also stated, however, that abuse or torture in prisons, apart from the initial detention period, has substantially decreased. . . .

Human rights advocates both in and outside of Turkey, including the Turkish Bar Association, have suggested that the most effective way to prevent torture or assertions of torture is to allow lawyers access to prisoners during the initial period of detention. Such access is being considered among proposed revisions to the criminal code. . . .

In August, following widespread hunger strikes by prisoners and parallel demonstrations by their friends and relatives outside the prisons, Turkish reporters were permitted for the first time to visit prisons and to report extensively on prison conditions. As a result of this press attention, conditions in many prisons appear to have improved. . . .

Estimates of the number of political prisoners held in Turkish jails vary greatly, depending on the source and the source's definition of political prisoner. The Government denies that it holds any political prisoners but points out that many persons have been imprisoned for terrorist acts or for other crimes committed in the course of pursuing ostensibly political goals during the 1970's. Human rights organizations believe that many people have been imprisoned under statutes proscribing "membership in illegal organizations," prohibiting propaganda aimed at promoting the hegemony of one class or ethnic group, and advocating the establishment of an Islamic state. They estimate that persons currently imprisoned for nonviolent activity under these statutes number several hundred.

Soviet Union

... This year saw some change in the Soviet handling of dissent. The limits of permissible dissent were expanded, and those who exceeded them usually were not subjected to imprisonment or exile. Instead, authorities used other means of intimidation short of court trial. These changes, although evident in Moscow and Leningrad, were barely felt elsewhere. Official attitudes toward dissent also seemed to harden as the year progressed. Unlike other government agencies, the KGB [Committee for State Security] has largely been exempted from the policy of "glasnost" (openness), and there is no indication of movement toward reform of that agency. Even in Moscow, the city where the most notable changes occurred, most dissident sources described the changes as primarily in the sphere of what it was possible to say and much less in what it was possible to do.

Reforms are taking place at the direction of the party and are primarily the product of political decisions, not the result of legal reform. The improvements in Soviet human rights performance which took place in 1987 have yet to be reinforced by reform laws, administrative regulations, and bureaucratic procedures which would help ensure that the rights of individuals are respected. Soviet authorities currently are reviewing their entire set of interlocking criminal codes, and Soviet officials have said repeatedly that significant reforms are expected. Their effect on the human rights of Soviet citizens will not be clear until the revised criminal code appears and is implemented.

Under current laws, those who exercise their rights continue to face the possibility of arrest, trial, and imprisonment; internment in a psychiatric hospital; or, more commonly, the loss of their jobs and opportunities for education, housing, and even medical treatment. Fear of these possibilities restrains the vast majority of the people in the Soviet Union from attempting to exercise the basic rights of freedom of speech, assembly, or religion.

Nevertheless, a small but apparently growing number of Soviet citizens have begun to organize unofficial groups and issue unofficial publications that provide a forum for public discussion of political, social, ecological, religious, and other current issues. At the same time, the official press has provided more open discussion of some historical, economic, social, and—to a lesser extent—political issues. While freedom of expression has been expanded and censorship relaxed, controls remained in place, and the current trends are neither stable nor legally defined....

Jewish, ethnic German, and Armenian emigration increased markedly, in contrast to the last several years. By the end of 1987, monthly average departures for ethnic Germans and Armenians compared favorably with those of the late 1970's; however, Jewish monthly average departures in 1987 were less than half those of the 1970's and far below the peak of 1979. Emigration of members of other ethnic groups remained negligible.

In January new Soviet regulations for travel abroad went into effect. In making family reunification the only legal basis for emigration, the regulations codified Moscow's longstanding refusal to recognize the "right to leave," a right included in the Universal Declaration of Human Rights. . . .

Prison and camp conditions have not improved this year; they may have grown worse, owing to more consistent implementation of regulations, which are harsh. Life in prison continues to be marked by isolation, poor diet and malnutrition, compulsory hard labor, beatings, frequent illness, and inadequate medical care. . . .

The Government continued to place selected political and religious activists in psychiatric hospitals, some of which fell under the jurisdiction of the Ministry of the Interior and not of the Ministry of Health. . . . These patients are often subjected to the painful, forced administration of sedatives, antipsychotics, and other mind-altering drugs.

Several demonstrators suffered psychiatric confinements in 1987. Igor Baryl'nik of the Group to Establish Trust Between East and West was placed in a psychiatric hospital September 11, apparently to prevent him from participating in a September 13 demonstration on behalf of Matthias Rust, the young West German who landed his small plane in Moscow's Red Square. He remained there until October. Serafim Yevsukov was placed in a mental hospital February 27 after demonstrating for permission to emigrate. Yuriy Makhov has been placed in mental institutions four times because of his desire to emigrate to the United States—the last time from September 24 to October 17.

Armenian human rights activist Sirvard Avagyan, a former political prisoner who has twice been confined to mental hospitals, was again forcibly confined in a mental institution outside Yerevan in April or May. In a tape played at a Moscow human rights activists' press conference October 20, Avagyan described forced drug treatments and beatings. . . .

The official press has begun to devote attention to the problem of psychiatric abuse, with a major article in Izvestiya in July, another important "expose" in Moscow News in October, and a third in Komsomol'skaya Pravda in November. The relationship between psychiatric abuse and control of political dissidence is, however, a subject that is still not discussed openly. . . .

In 1987 the Soviets released over 300 political prisoners; a number of them, however, had already completed their terms. A substantial number of the best-known prisoners were forced to emigrate, with the implicit or explicit understanding that the alternative was an eventual return to the labor camps or mental institutions from which they had just been released. With few exceptions, all were forced to leave on exit visas to Israel, which meant they were deprived of Soviet citizenship. . . .

Harassment of religious Jews decreased in 1987. A ritual bath in

Moscow's one Hasidic synagogue was restored by government authorities who had destroyed it in 1987. Chairman of the Council on Religious Affairs Konstantin Kharchev told U.S. Rabbi David Hollander in May that six young Soviet Jews would be permitted to study at rabbinical seminaries in the United States, although this has not yet taken place. Small numbers of Hebrew Bibles and prayer books provided by Western donors appear to have reached Moscow in 1987. In general, however, it remained next to impossible for religious Jews to obtain Hebrew prayer books and other religious items. Although there were reports toward year's end that Hebrew classes in the locality were being tolerated, the teaching of Hebrew remained illegal.

Although only a small number of mosques are open for use in the Muslim regions of Central Asia and Azerbaijan, Islam appears to retain a strong hold on the population. Unofficial mullahs, who function without government permission, are the subject of nearly constant pressure.... According to reliable Soviet dissident sources, there are at least 17 Muslims imprisoned on religious grounds. At the end of 1986 or beginning of 1987, a number of Muslims were sentenced to prison terms.... Very small religious groups were not immune to severe pressure. Harassment, arrests, and trials of Hare Krishna followers ... continued.

Northern Ireland

The Police (Northern Ireland) Order of 1987, which was approved by [British] Parliament in May 1987, provides for reform of police complaints procedures in Northern Ireland broadly in line with changes which were introduced in England and Wales in 1985. The new procedures are expected to go into effect in 1988 with the establishment of the Independent Commission for Police Complaints. The new commission will have powers to approve officers, including those drawn from other police forces in the United Kingdom, to investigate complaints. In 1987 there were no substantiated charges of mistreatment of arrestees during interrogation in Northern Ireland.

The Government acknowledges that some old British prisons are unsatisfactory and that many prisoners live in cramped, unhygienic cells. To improve conditions, the Government has embarked on a program to build 20 new prisons and to refurbish existing ones.

In Northern Ireland, where 60 percent of the prisoners are jailed for terrorist activities, prison conditions differ in some respects from those in Great Britain. All prisons in the province, except for the two centers for young offenders, are maximum-security institutions. This often forces low-risk common criminals in Northern Ireland to serve their sentences under maximum-security conditions....

Complaints continue about "strip searching," particularly of women, in Northern Ireland prisons, and Amnesty International, in its 1987 Report covering 1986, urged the Government to reconsider its policy. These searches involve a visual inspection conducted in special cubicles by female officers. Body cavity searches are not performed....

British law gives the police broad discretionary powers to make arrests without warrant based on reasonable cause. Procedures for bail, judicial determination of the legality of detention, and suits for false imprisonment are routinely utilized. . . .

British common law allows for the restriction of personal liberties by the Government in an emergency situation, subject to review by Parliament. Acting on the premise that the fundamental "right to life" has been in serious jeopardy due to the violence in Northern Ireland, the Government has adopted the Northern Ireland (Emergency Provisions) Acts of 1978 and 1987, which are applicable only to Northern Ireland; and the Prevention of Terrorism (Temporary Provisions) Act of 1984 (originally enacted in 1976), almost all of which is applicable to the entire United Kingdom. Although both these acts permit the restriction of personal liberties, they are subject to parliamentary review and to mandatory renewal at frequent intervals. In addition, Lord Colville was appointed in 1987 to provide Parliament with an annual independent assessment of the operation of the acts.

The 1984 Prevention of Terrorism Act allows the police to arrest without warrant persons anywhere in the United Kingdom whom they reasonably suspect to be involved in terrorism. Such persons may be detained for up to 48 hours without judicial review and up to a further 5 days on the authority of the Home Secretary. In recent years, the powers of the Act have been used when persons were suspected of acts of terrorism related to Northern Ireland, India, and the Middle East.

In September 1987, the European Commission on Human Rights recommended that, in the case of two men detained in 1984 under the Prevention of Terrorism Act's 7-day maximum detention period, the British Government respond to charges it had violated the requirement contained in the European Convention on Human Rights that a person should be brought "promptly to court." The Government quickly announced its intention to contest the Commission's findings before the European Court of Human Rights.

Israel

. . . As in the past, the most significant human rights problems for Israel in 1987 derived from the strained relations between the Israeli authorities and some Israelis on the one hand and the Arab inhabitants of the occupied territories on the other hand. These problems were again exacerbated in 1987 by attacks against Israelis in those areas and by acts of provocation or violence by Jewish settlers. The number of attacks on Israelis and acts of violence by settlers increased somewhat in 1987. . . .

In the course of the war of June 1967, Israel occupied the West Bank, East Jerusalem, the Golan Heights, the Gaza Strip and the Sinai Peninsula. As a result of the peace treaty between Egypt and Israel, the Sinai Peninsula was restored to Egypt. No peace treaty, however, has been concluded between Israel and its other neighboring countries. The West Bank and Gaza remain under military government. Israel unilaterally annexed East Jerusalem and regards the Golan Heights as subject to Israeli law, jurisdiction, and administration.

The United States recognizes Israel as an occupying power in all of these territories and therefore considers Israeli administration to be subject to the Hague Regulations of 1907 and the 1949 Fourth Geneva Convention concerning the protection of civilian populations under military occupation.

Israel denies the applicability of the Fourth Geneva Convention to the West Bank and Gaza, although it states that it observes many of the Convention's provisions in these areas. Israel enforces Jordanian law in the West Bank and British Mandate regulations in the Gaza Strip, although it has issued military orders significantly altering or overriding substantial portions of many of these laws.

Since 1967 approximately 60,000 Israeli citizens have taken up residence in the West Bank and Gaza, most of them in suburban enclaves. Their presence has resulted in a dual system wherein Palestinians are subject to laws and regulations in effect before the 1967 war, as amended by Israeli military authorities, while Israeli residents are subject to laws and regulations applicable to Israeli nationals living in Israel.

The complex human rights situation in the occupied territories arises from the absence of a peace settlement; the territories remain under military administration, and communal conflict continues between occupation authorities, Israeli settlers, and the Palestinian population. . . .

For many years, the situation in the occupied territories has fluctuated between periods of calm and periods of unrest, but tensions have been chronic and increasing, especially in the refugee camps and among younger Palestinians. Beginning in early December 1987, there were several weeks of violent confrontation, involving demonstrations and provocations by Palestinians and harsh reprisals by Israeli occupation authorities to restore security, which resulted in 22 Palestinian deaths and numerous less serious casualties on both sides by the end of the calendar year. . . .

Incidents of violence by Israeli settlers increased during the year, including the shooting death of one Palestinian youth, the use of unauthorized armed patrols, physical harassment, disruption of legally authorized political meetings, attacks on refugee camps, and running of IDF roadblocks. Occupation authorities stated they would take legal action against the settlers, and several were arrested. However, Palestinians assert that the authorities are generally lenient with Israeli settlers who violate security regulations. . . .

Palestinians and international human rights organizations complain of widespread and systematic mistreatment of prisoners. Amnesty International reports that confessions are extracted from suspects by severe interrogation and that security prisoners are subject to beatings, extended solitary confinement, hooding, and cold showers. Nearly all convictions in security cases are based on confessions. Attorneys are normally not allowed to see clients until after the suspects have confessed. The International Committee of the Red Cross is also denied access to prisoners for a prescribed period, resulting in frequent charges of physical mistreatment that are difficult to corroborate or disprove. Most interrogations are carried out by the General Security Service (Shin Bet). In 1987 a special judicial commission headed by former Israeli Supreme Court President Moshe Landau issued a report on Shin Bet practices since 1971. The commission found that Shin Bet officials for many years had used physical and psychological pressure to obtain confessions, and that they had routinely perjured themselves by denying in court that such mistreatment had occurred. . . .

Under occupation regulations, military authorities may enter private homes and institutions without prior judicial approval in pursuit of security objectives. An existing military order, for example, permits soldiers to search persons or premises on the West Bank without warrant on the suspicion that a person or organization may possess a proscribed publication.

In the West Bank and Gaza during 1987, at least 6 Arab houses were demolished and 13 sealed after their occupants or relatives of the occupants were accused of involvement in security incidents. Twenty-six individual rooms were also sealed. Such actions were usually taken before the suspects were tried.

Most Palestinians and other observers believe that mail and telephone services in the West Bank and Gaza are monitored. Individuals are questioned on their political views by security officials. Such inquiries have in some cases involved overnight detention. . . .

. . . Military orders also forbid the printing or publishing of politically significant material without a license. Political significance is not defined in the orders. During 1987 Israeli authorities closed one Jerusalem press agency for 6 months and one West Bank agency for 2 years. Another West Bank publishing company was closed for 6 months.

A permit is required for publications imported into the occupied territories. Arabic educational materials, periodicals, and books originating outside Israel are censored and may be banned for anti-Semitic or anti-Israeli content, or for encouraging Palestinian nationalism. In the past several years, the number of titles banned by Israel has declined significantly. Possession of banned materials by West Bank or Gaza Arabs is a criminal offense. Usually, however, possession of illegal publications is one of a series of charges levied against persons accused of security offenses.

At some point in 1987, Israeli authorities closed every university, as well as a number of vocational, secondary, and elementary schools, in the West Bank and Gaza on security grounds. The schools were closed for periods ranging from 1 day to 4 months, and some were subject to repeated closures. Military authorities also accused some Palestinian students of being agitators and expelled them from the occupied territories in violation of the Fourth Geneva Convention.

PRESIDENT'S ECONOMIC REPORT, ECONOMIC ADVISERS' REPORT

February 16, 1988

Containing unusual criticism of operations of the Federal Reserve Board, President Ronald Reagan's economic reports were presented to Congress February 16. The Economic Report of the President and the Annual Report of the Council of Economic Advisers also celebrated the economic achievements of his administration.

In his message, Reagan said that the prospects for economic growth in the immediate future had been "diminished somewhat by last year's plunge in the stock market, as well as by the increase in interest rates and tightening of monetary policy during 1987." And the economic advisers, though praising the performance of the Federal Reserve Board in the days immediately following the October 1987 market dive, said that the board's return to a "tight" monetary policy in late 1987 "may have underestimated the risks to adequate economic growth."

Pointing to his administration's economic accomplishments, Reagan said the prevailing attitude toward the economy in the early 1980s "could best be described as despair." But the past five years, he said, had "marked an outstanding period of economic growth in the United States." The president also said that his administration's economic policies had "spurred and sustained a record economic expansion—the longest in U.S. peacetime."

The three members of the Council of Economic Advisers—Chairman Beryl Sprinkel, Michael L. Mussa, and Thomas Gale Moore—all subscribed to the "monetarist" theory that steady growth of the nation's money supply is essential to economic growth. In contrast, the Federal Reserve Board, which actually sets monetary policy, relied on a wide range of economic indicators rather than using a monetarist approach. In its report, the council was critical of the Federal Reserve Board's operations that led to higher interest rates before the stock market collapse in October 1987. (Brady Commission report on the stock market crash, p. 9)

The advisers wrote, "Rising interest rates certainly were a factor in the stock market's decline." However, they praised as "exemplary" the operations of the Federal Reserve Board after the crash. They said it "was in the right place at the right time, supporting the financial system with ample liquidity."

Job Gains and Protectionism

Addressing "misconceptions" about trends in employment, productivity, and income growth, the president's advisers said that employment gains in the 1980s had been "largest in higher-paid occupations." They said that about half the increase in full-time employment between 1983 and 1986 had been in occupations "with real median earnings of at least $20,000 per year." They also said that in the current economic expansion employment of youths had risen relatively slowly, reflecting slower population growth among ages sixteen to nineteen. But, in a surprise to many, they said that job gains for black teenagers had been "among the strongest of all demographic groups."

The council warned against protectionist trade legislation, saying it would "increase protectionist activity in the rest of the world, poison the international climate for trade diplomacy in general, and slow the process of liberalization for years to come." In a discussion of the nation's large trade deficit, the economists tied that deficit to the low rate of national savings and to the federal budget deficit.

Praising the results of the deregulation of the airline industry, the council discussed ways to alleviate "short-term" congestion problems. One approach, the economists said, would set a price for takeoffs and landings "that adequately reflects direct and indirect costs." The other approach, they continued, would restrict the number of landings and takeoffs during peak periods and permit airlines to buy or sell "slots."

Council Forecasts

The council predicted that the rate of economic expansion would slow in 1988 from the "rapid pace set in 1987," and that the inflation rate would "move gradually downward" from the 4 percent range "toward the long-term goal of price stability." It predicted that real gross national product (GNP) would rise 2.4 percent from the fourth quarter of 1987 to the fourth quarter of 1988. In the previous year, the rise in GNP was 3.8 percent.

Following are the text of the Economic Report of the President and excerpts from the Annual Report of the Council of Economic Advisers, issued February 16, 1988:

ECONOMIC REPORT OF THE PRESIDENT

To the Congress of the United States:

My first *Economic Report*, issued in 1982 after a year in office, could look only to the future for encouraging economic news. The task of rebuilding the economy was just beginning, and hard choices were being made. Inflation had begun to come down from double-digit rates, but America was mired in recession, its second in as many years. Today, however, we can point to real, solid economic progress. The policies of this Administration have spurred and sustained a record economic expansion—the longest in U.S. peacetime. Fifteen million new jobs have been created during this expansion, with strong gains widespread across industries and demographic groups. Real gross national product (GNP) has risen nearly 23 percent during these 5 years of growth.

And the accomplishments are not all in the past. Our policies will continue to contribute to rising standards of living in the years ahead. By enhancing private incentives and opportunities for work, investment, and entrepreneurship, we have laid the groundwork for growth far into the future. To ensure that the renewed energy of the private sector remains a force for growth, we must continue our efforts to bring down the Federal deficit through restraint on spending, to resist the siren song of protectionism, to support policies that foster noninflationary economic growth, and to rein in government when it threatens to make our markets less open, our industries less responsive, or our economy less flexible.

The Economic Expansion

Since November 1982, the U.S. economy has grown without interruption and without a resurgence of inflation. Only twice before in our Nation's history—but never during peacetime—has recorded economic growth continued for so long. During the current expansion a strong increase in employment, combined with low rates of inflation and higher productivity growth, have meant rising standards of living for the American people.

Employment has increased dramatically, and all demographic groups have benefited. While overall employment has risen about 15 percent since November 1982, employment of blacks has increased by more than 25 percent and employment of Hispanics by more than 40 percent. Correspondingly, unemployment rates—especially among minorities—have fallen rapidly, although those rates are still unacceptably high. I believe that all who want jobs should be able to obtain employment commensurate with their skills and abilities.

As the unemployment rate has declined by almost one-half, some have claimed that the new jobs are low-quality, dead-end positions, while others have argued that booming employment has put us on the verge of another round of inflation. Neither view is accurate. The facts show that the strongest job growth has been in the higher paid, high-skill occupations. The bulk of the new jobs created have been full-time positions in occupations that pay well. While it is true that the number of jobs in manufacturing has risen more slowly than in the service-producing sector of the economy, this is a reflection of the innovation of American business and the skill of American workers, not a sign that the United States is "deindustrializing." The share of manufacturing output in total output actually has risen over the course of the expansion, and it is now above its postwar average. However, rapid increases in manufacturing productivity have meant slower growth in employment in this sector. This strong productivity growth, in combination with the downward adjustment of the dollar's exchange rate, has lifted the competitiveness of our products on world markets. Around the globe, products "Made in the U.S.A." are becoming more common and more sought after.

Moreover, I do not believe that our economy has yet reached its full potential, or that our economic growth threatens price stability. Growth can and should continue. With sound and stable economic policies, saving and investment will be encouraged, and the Nation's productive capacity will continue to expand. I remain committed to the goal of price level stability, and I view the decline in inflation during my Administration as a major accomplishment. I would not take lightly the prospect of a resurgence of inflation. But economic growth itself will not lead to a spiral of worsening inflation; only irresponsible economic policies would do that.

Our economic projections show inflation slowing during the coming years, even as output grows at a robust average annual rate of 3.2 percent. But continued economic progress requires that policy-makers adhere to forward-looking principles, pursuing the long-term best interests of the Nation through a sustained commitment to growth and stability. The prospects for growth in the immediate future have been diminished somewhat by last year's plunge in the stock market, as well as by the increase in interest rates and tightening of monetary policy during 1987. Nevertheless, I anticipate that the U.S. economy will continue to post gains in 1988, as the expansion moves through its 6th year.

The past 5 years have marked an outstanding period of economic growth in the United States. It has been unusual in its longevity, unusual for the fact that inflation has remained subdued, and unusual relative to the performance of other industrial economies. Between 1982 and 1986, American businesses, large and small, created two and one-half times as many new jobs as Japan and the major industrial countries of Europe combined. In 1987 this trend appears to have continued, as the U.S. economy again generated new jobs at a remarkable rate. The U.S. unemployment rate has fallen 5 percentage points, and now stands well below those in most other major industrialized countries, where unemployment rates have yet to recover fully from the last recession. Overall, we have not lost jobs because of foreign trade. Instead, growth-oriented policies of lower and fairer taxes, reduced interference by government, and free and open international trade have been a source of strength for the economy. Indeed, the U.S. economy has flourished, and the outlook is full of promise.

Role of Government in the Economy

It is hard to believe that at the beginning of the 1980s the prevailing attitude toward the economy could best be described as despair. Inflation and interest rates had ratcheted higher with each successive business cycle, and, as the economy suffered through its second recession in 2 years, the goal of sustainable growth appeared increasingly elusive. Amid double-digit inflation and unemployment rates, there were calls for the Federal Government to do more and more, thereby compounding the failed policies of the past. Instead, I took government policy back to the basics, and the last 5 years of economic growth testify to the vitality of free markets and the productivity of the American people. Government intrusions in the Nation's economic life have been reduced, and the private sector has responded with an explosion of activity, creating new products and new jobs at a very rapid rate.

The Federal Government has an important role to play in the Nation's economy, but it is a limited role. As a general proposition, economic decisions should be left to the private sector, which has been our economy's strength throughout its history, or to State and local governments when the issues cannot be handled satisfactorily by the private sector. Only in issues truly national in scope is there a role for the Federal Government.

We have made efforts to restrain Federal spending, to limit it to only the government's vital functions, and those efforts have borne fruit. Last fiscal year, for the first time in 14 years, Federal outlays, after adjustment for inflation, declined. Government spending on goods and services absorbs resources that might be used better by the private sector, and any Federal outlay must be financed eventually by inflation or taxes. Because there is no free lunch, we must make the hard choices, funding only those programs that are in the best interest of the Nation, not those that happen to have the most influential lobbyists. For example, while a strong national defense is rightly the responsibility of the Federal Government, a continued proliferation of pork-barrel projects is not. America's sense of fair play is violated when hard-earned tax dollars are needlessly turned over to powerful special interests.

In the conduct of macroeconomic policies, we have turned away from the stop-and-go policies of the past. My Administration has adopted a long-term view that fiscal policy determines the division of economic activity between the public and private sectors and is not meant to respond to every rise and fall in the economic data. Similarly, monetary policy should provide adequate liquidity for sustained noninflationary growth. Together, these policies create a stable environment in which individuals and businesses can plan for the future and make the most of their economic opportunities.

For too long the Federal Government has interfered unnecessarily in private economic decisions. There is a legitimate, although limited, role for the Federal Government in certain industries—for example, in ensuring the safety and soundness of the Nation's banking and payments systems. But many government regulations impede the operation of markets, inhibit competition, or impose costs on firms and raise the prices faced by consumers, without providing commensurate benefits. Regulations that interfere with the efficient use of labor, investment, and raw materials ultimately reduce our productive potential, making this country worse off.

While my Administration has been successful in reducing many regulations and intrusions into markets, much remains to be done. We must lessen remaining disincentives to work, diminish the burden of Federal regulations, and dismantle government programs that needlessly subsidize inefficient producers. In particular, we must release financial institutions from outdated legal restraints, eliminate the remaining controls on interstate trucking, deregulate natural gas, and repeal mileage standards for new automobiles. We must resist appeals for even more government intervention that would introduce additional inefficiencies, such as requiring advance notification of layoffs and plant closings. With few exceptions, the private sector is best able to allocate resources to their most highly valued uses, and it should be allowed to do so without excessive paperwork and restrictions. That is why privatization, deregulation, and private sector initiatives have been important elements of my economic program. I believe in the inherent dynamism of the private sector, and I believe that the most constructive thing government usually can do is simply get out of the way.

The International Environment

This Administration has been a force for economic change in the United States and, by our example, in the world at large. Our proven market-oriented policies are being adopted in more and more countries around the globe, as they recognize the high costs of government and the harmful effects of stifling the entrepreneurial spirit.

In order to enhance growth and economic opportunity, many nations have followed our lead, undertaking reductions in sky-high tax rates that diminish incentives to work, save, and produce. In addition, tax reform is becoming a worldwide movement. Just as in the United States, tax reform abroad promises to end many distortions and inefficiencies, allowing businesses and individuals to make decisions about production and investment in order to increase their economic well-being, rather than simply to reduce their tax bills.

From continent to continent, the benefits of privatization and deregulation are becoming appreciated. Even China, and perhaps now even the Soviet Union, appear to be edging toward freer economic systems. Instead of viewing private enterprise as the adversary, many governments now see it as their best hope for progress and prosperity. Developing as well as industrialized nations are reducing market rigidities and interferences, thereby expanding economic freedom and opportunity for their citizens.

In those developing countries that encourage investment and private enterprise, the ensuing economic growth should contribute to lessening their debt problems. The debt burden carried by developing countries is not just their problem; we all have a vital interest in finding solutions that promote growth and protect open international financial markets. And we will continue to work with all who display a real determination to deal with this difficult issue.

The United States has been a constructive force in the world economy, not only by demonstrating the benefits of private enterprise, but also by our commitment to free trade and international economic cooperation. In addition, this Nation's strong demands for imports helped support output growth abroad during much of this decade. The world economy has become increasingly interdependent, as trade has multiplied and financial markets have become essentially global.

To continue to reap the benefits of an open international trading system, we are committed to reducing further the barriers that interfere with the free flow of goods, services, and capital. To this end, the United States has entered into, and will continue to seek out, bilateral and multilateral agreements to lower impediments to international commerce. The Free-Trade Agreement recently negotiated with Canada is an historic accomplishment. Once the necessary implementing legislation is passed, it will establish the largest international free-trade area in the world. At the same time, in the Uruguay Round of the multilateral negotiations under the General Agreement on Tariffs and Trade, we have been working to lower trade barriers worldwide. In that forum, we have placed special emphasis on eliminating spiraling subsidies to agricultural production and harmful barriers to agricultural imports, on establishing and enforcing adequate protections for intellectual property, on liberalizing trade in services, and on ensuring evenhanded treatment of foreign investment. Through these avenues and others, we will continue to pursue the goal of free and fair trade, which can only expand opportunity and prosperity both at home and abroad.

The Challenges Ahead

The American poeple elected me to this office with a vision of a reinvigorated economy, and I have watched that vision become reality. The resurgence of America has confirmed my optimism. The accomplishments of the last 7 years should inspire us, but not blind us to the important challenges that remain.

Foremost among our challenges is the continued high level of Federal spending and the budget deficit. Federal receipts last year were $255 billion above their level in 1981; nevertheless, the deficit has nearly doubled since then, bloated by a $326 billion increase in outlays. Although we have succeeded recently in slowing the growth of spending, and the deficit declined by $71 billion in the last fiscal year, the deficit is still too large.

Recent progress in controlling Federal outlays notwithstanding, as a percent of GNP, outlays remain well above the postwar average. The government continues to spend too much, absorbing resources that could be put to better use by the private sector. There are several essential functions of the Federal Government, such as providing a strong national defense and ensuring an appropriate safety net for those in need. But in many areas the government's presence is oppressive and unnecessary.

Tax increases are not the key to eliminating the deficit. Some taxes are unavoidable—the necessary functions of the Federal Government must be paid for. But tax reform and the cuts that have been instituted in income tax rates represent successful efforts to find less distorting, less burdensome, and more equitable means of financing government. Undoing tax reform through tax increases would affect economic activity adversely by raising uncertainty about government policy and reducing incentives to work and produce. Rather, in coming years we should look to ways to enhance incentives for investment in future productive capacity, including reducing the tax rate on capital gains.

The Gramm-Rudman-Hollings law and our recent agreement with the Congress on a 2-year budget-trimming package have charted the course for additional deficit reduction. Those are steps in the right direction. But the budget process itself remains a major obstacle to eliminating the deficit. And I am not the only one to have noticed that the budget process is a disaster; a recent survey of Members of Congress identified it as a major source of frustration. The process is not working and it must be reformed: discipline and responsibility must be restored.

Current budget practice is to deliver a pair of mammoth bills that must be passed and signed in a matter of hours—or the government has to shut down. This is not responsible government, and I will not sign another of these behemoths. This budget process does not serve the best interests of the Nation, it does not allow sufficient review of spending priorities, and it undermines the checks and balances established by the Constitution.

So that such massive appropriations bills do not have to be an all-or-nothing proposition, I have asked for the line-item veto, a power that 43 State Governors already have. With a line-item veto, future Presidents could pare away waste and enforce budget discipline. In addition, expanded rescission powers would allow the Executive to cut unnecessary spending on programs that, in many cases, have outlived their usefulness. Finally, to ensure that balanced budgets become a permanent feature of our fiscal landscape, the legislatures of 32 States have asked for—and I endorse— a constitutional amendment to force the Federal Government to live within its means. These steps must be taken, because the current budget process is impeding budget progress. By its very nature, the democratic process is often messy and unfocused. But we know that democracy works and that tough decisions can be made. We must rise to the challenge again and prove that we can craft sound budgets through a sensible process.

We also must resist efforts to push the Nation into protectionism. Our foreign trade deficit is very large, but it has turned the corner in real terms. Last year foreign trade contributed significantly to our economic growth. Moreover, further improvements are on the way. At this point especially, it would be a tragic mistake to attempt to close the trade gap by closing our markets. Isolating U.S. markets could only lead to a global downward spiral in trade and economic activity.

My Administration is committed to working diligently with the Congress to draft responsible trade legislation, but if that legislation is not free of harmful protectionist measures, I will veto it. Our goal is to see the trade deficit reduced in an environment of sustained economic growth and low inflation. To this end, we are working with the other major industrial countries to coordinate economic policies that sustain noninflationary economic growth, encourage an orderly reduction of international imbalances, and thereby foster stability of exchange rates.

We must maintain the confidence of foreigners and our citizens alike in the ability of the United States to generate profitable investment opportunities and to follow responsible economic policies. The vitality of free and open markets, full of opportunity and promise, is the best foundation for investment. We must see to it that our tax structures and regulations do not discourage saving and investing. We must encourage investment not only in plant and equipment, but also in the American people themselves. Education, skills, research and development—these are some of the most fruitful areas for investment; expanded knowledge enhances the productive potential of our most valuable resource, our people.

Conclusion

America is blessed with great gifts—abundant land and natural resources, a diverse and hard-working people, an unshakable tradition of democratic values. My confidence in America has been shown to be well-founded over these past few years. The economy has been revitalized, and the record peacetime economic expansion has brought with it renewed opportunities and enhanced well-being. We set ourselves a formidable task: to reduce and to rationalize the role of government in the economy. That effort has been richly rewarded. During our watch, the U.S. economy again has shown its strength.

But our job is not finished. The Federal budget must be controlled in order to build a solid foundation for future economic growth. And I will not be satisfied until all Americans share in this prosperity; there are still too many enmeshed in poverty and without jobs. We must rise to our remaining challenges, heartened by our triumphs and inspired by the resilience of a resurgent America.

THE ANNUAL REPORT OF THE
COUNCIL OF ECONOMIC ADVISERS

U.S. Economy: Performance and Prospects

The longest peacetime expansion in the history of the U.S. economy entered its sixth year in 1987. Growth was vigorous, with the economy's real output rising by nearly 4 percent last year. Three million additional jobs were created in 1987, beyond the 12 million generated earlier in the expansion. The unemployment rate dropped almost a percentage point to its lowest level in 8 years. Significant improvement in the real trade deficit contributed importantly to growth of output and employment, for the first time since 1980. The inflation rate remained in the 4 percent range that has characterized most of the expansion—well down from the double-digit rates at the start of the decade. Dramatic progress was made in reducing the Federal budget deficit. Judged by these accomplishments, leaving aside the extraordinary events in financial markets, the U.S. economy enjoyed a good year in 1987. . . .

The past 5 years of sustained and vigorous growth in production, income, and employment did not occur by accident. It was [sic] shaped by government policies explicitly directed toward fostering the inherent dynamism of the private sector. In reviewing the record of the current expansion and looking to the future, this *Report* highlights the appropriate role for government in the economy—its macroeconomic responsibilities, such as fiscal and monetary policy, as well as its microeconomic responsibilities, which concern particular markets and industries. This chapter begins with a summary of the *Report*. . . .

Nineteen eighty-seven was a year of robust economic growth, strong increases in employment, and—despite a temporary acceleration early in the year—continued moderate inflation. The composition of demand changed in a welcome direction, as the foreign trade sector contributed to overall growth. But late in the year, the plunge in the stock market and a sharp buildup in inventories raised questions about the outlook. With appropriate economic policies, however, growth should continue through 1988—albeit at a more moderate rate than in 1987. A more balanced and sustainable pattern of growth in 1988 then will set the stage for a resumption of more rapid growth in the future, together with gradual reductions in both the unemployment and inflation rates. . . .

U.S. Economy in 1987

U.S. economic growth strengthened in 1987, and the sources of growth shifted markedly. Starting in the fourth quarter of 1986, real gross national product (GNP) growth began to exceed domestic demand growth, as—for the first time in 7 years—the foreign trade sector contributed on a sustained basis to economic growth in the United States. On the inflation front, the increase in consumer prices moved up into the 5 percent range early in 1987, spurred largely by the rebound in world petroleum prices.

Non-oil import prices, which had tended to restrain inflation during the first half of the 1980s, also contributed upward pressure on consumer prices. But this acceleration, which largely reflected a one-time shift in relative prices, proved short-lived, and inflation in the second half of the year fell back to the 4 percent rate that has characterized most of the current economic expansion. . . .

The economic expansion continued through 1987, and in October it claimed the record as the longest period of uninterrupted growth that the United States has experienced in peacetime. Ironically, the record was set just as the stock market's optimism was shaken, and the Dow Jones Industrial Average dropped more than 20 percent in a single day. Clearly, some stresses and imbalances had emerged during the expansion, but data on the real economy indicated that favorable adjustments were occurring, and that they were occurring within a context of continued growth. The trade deficit was narrowing in real terms, the Federal budget deficit had dropped by one-third, and business fixed investment was rebounding from its 1986 decline.

Real GNP grew 3.8 percent from the fourth quarter of 1986 through the fourth quarter of 1987, rising more than half again as fast as in the preceding year. But this acceleration was by no means uniform across components of demand. In fact, the largest component, personal consumption expenditures, slowed almost to a standstill, posting just a 0.6 percent rise after 4 consecutive years of 4-plus percent increases. . . . Similarly, investment in housing declined for the first time since 1981. While the growth of government purchases picked up slightly last year to 3.0 percent, the primary source of the acceleration in GNP was the rebound in three components that had been a drag on growth in 1986: net exports, business fixed investment, and inventories. . . .

The consumer price index (CPI) rose at more than a 5 percent annual rate during each of the first 4 months of 1987, but this initial acceleration did not herald a sustained resurgence of inflation. Last year the economy had to contend with significant increases in the prices of imports and energy—two categories that earlier in the economic expansion had tended to act as restraining influences on inflation. In addition, aided in part by the accommodative monetary policy of 1985-86, the economy was moving through a fifth year of growth, capacity utilization was rising, and the unemployment rate was continuing to fall. In similar circumstances in the 1970s, inflation had accelerated. But in 1987 most broad measures of inflation, although up from 1986 when oil prices had dropped sharply, remained close to their averages for the first 3 years of the current expansion. For example, the GNP fixed-weighted price index rose 4.0 percent, compared with an average of 3.7 percent during 1983-85.

In 1986 crude oil prices had fluctuated wildly, dropping from more than $25 per barrel for West Texas Intermediate at the beginning of the year to a low of less than half that in July, then climbing back up to more than $18 per barrel around the end of the year. During 1987 the price of oil was less volatile, ending the year only a little below its level at the beginning of the year. The deflationary impact of the earlier drop in oil prices was completed at the retail level during 1986, as the energy component of the CPI declined almost 20 percent over the year. The inflationary effect of the subsequent rebound in oil prices, however, was strongest during the first 3 months of 1987, when the energy component of the CPI rose at a 26 percent annual rate. Thereafter, the energy component increased at about the same rate as the aggregate CPI.

In early 1987 the higher relative price of oil gave a one-time boost to the aggregate price level, with no apparent effect on the economy's underlying inflation rate. Similarly, the rising import prices of recent quarters are a relative price adjustment which should produce only transitory upward pressure on inflation. But, in the case of imports, the relative price adjustment is likely to be a more drawn-out process. Prices of non-oil imports have been rising more rapidly than overall inflation since the end of 1985, and they likely will continue to do so for several more quarters as the dollar's drop on foreign exchange markets gradually affects prices. A fixed-weighted index of non-oil import prices has increased at a 9 percent annual rate during the last 2 years.

Although the passthrough effects of the lower dollar can be expected to take some time, rising import prices nevertheless represent a one-time change in relative prices and are a necessary factor in reducing the Nation's trade deficit. Only if macroeconomic policies are unduly expansionary, and wage increases fully reflect the increases in import prices, will the increased relative price of imports turn into a sustained higher rate of inflation. . . .

Macroeconomic Policies

Both fiscal and monetary policy turned toward restraint last year. The Federal deficit narrowed by one-third in fiscal 1987, and even on a cyclically adjusted basis—that is, abstracting from the deficit-reducing effect of faster economic growth—the restraint was clear. Moreover, measured either in real terms or as a share of GNP, Federal outlays fell below the level of the previous fiscal year. At the same time, rising interest rates and sharply lower money growth rates indicated a tightening of monetary policy during much of 1987.

In fiscal 1987 the reduction in the Federal budget deficit was remarkable. The deficit was cut $71 billion, or 1.9 percent of GNP, in a single year. This salutary development reduced the government's demands on credit markets, while restraint on Federal spending released more resources for use by the private sector and, by holding down growth of domestic demand, contributed to the improvement in the Nation's real trade gap. Despite the contradictory impulse from fiscal policy last year— equivalent on a cyclically adjusted basis to roughly 1 percent of GNP— economic growth did not slow. The economy performed well in 1987, supported in part by the monetary stimulus of the preceding years and in part by the strong export growth that stemmed from a lower dollar. . . .

The fiscal 1987 deficit of $150 billion came close to the $144 billion target specified in the original Gramm-Rudman-Hollings (GRH) legislation passed during 1985. After the method of imposing automatic spending cuts in that law was found to be unconstitutional, amendments to GRH, with new enforcement mechanisms and new deficit targets, were signed into law in September 1987. The amendments extended the deadline for a balanced budget by 2 years to 1993, and they eased the deficit reduction requirements for fiscal 1988 and 1989 by providing "safe harbors" in the form of caps on the amount of cuts mandated. For fiscal 1988 the amendments exchanged a $108 billion target, as specified in the original act, for a new $144 billion target with a maximum automatic cut of $23 billion. . . .

During 1987 the Federal Reserve continued the eclectic approach that has characterized decisionmaking within the Nation's central bank in recent years. The creation of new deposit instruments, wide fluctuations in market interest rates, the deregulation of deposit rates, and the accelerated process of general financial innovation had raised questions about how movements in money and credit aggregates should be interpreted. As the 1980s progressed, the Federal Reserve had watched the historical relationships between money and income and interest rates apparently break down in response to these influences, and it came to rely less on the monetary aggregates and more on a wide range of economic and financial variables as indicators of emerging trends. Finally, in 1987 the Federal Reserve refrained from specifying an annual growth range for M1, the measure of money which in the past had been related most closely and reliably to income growth. Thus, for the first time since 1975—when the Federal Reserve began to set money targets publicly—neither a target nor a monitoring range for M1 was announced. And while target ranges for M2 and M3 (broader measures of money) were specified, the Federal Reserve's midyear report to the Congress explicitly recognized that "[in certain circumstances] some shortfall, from the annual ranges might well be appropriate." . . .

Federal Reserve Actions in 1987

. . . Evaluating financial and economic indicators and predicting the precise effects of policy moves remain inexact sciences. On the domestic front, financial markets indicated that inflation expectations may have surged at times, although inflation itself exceeded the 4 percent range only briefly, early in the year. And on the international front, the value of the dollar came under pressure several times. Throughout the year, however, U.S. economic activity remained robust, and the unemployment rate dropped nearly a percentage point.

As 1987 began, the deciphering of economic and financial market trends was complicated by a year-end surge of transactions prompted by a change in tax laws. Because many provisions of the Tax Reform Act were to take effect at the turn of the year, individuals and businesses rushed to complete real estate transactions, mergers, sales of equities, car purchases, etc., before the end of 1986. In the process they generated huge demands for money and credit; for example, M1 rose at a 30.5 percent annual rate in December 1986, and business loans increased at a 36 percent rate.

In view of the difficulty in separating tax effects from underlying economic trends during this period, the Federal Open Market Committee (FOMC), the Federal Reserve's principal monetary policymaking body, chose not to make any substantive changes in its instructions to the Open Market Desk, which implements policy on a day-to-day basis. Thus the thrust of the directive that had been in place since the last discount rate cut in August 1986 remained in force. At the same time, however, the FOMC indicated its bias toward future tightening and noted that, at least with regard to M1, money growth would have to slow from the 1986 pace in order to sustain progress toward price stability.

As the year-end bulge in the monetary aggregates dissipated and the economy continued to grow at a moderate pace, the Federal Reserve made no explicit changes in monetary policy until late April. Then, in April and again in May, the market for bank reserves was tightened as policymakers responded to downward pressure on the dollar in exchange markets and a perceived ratcheting upward of inflation expectations. News on the real economy was generally good: growth was maintained, and the unemployment rate was dropping substantially. But the rebound in energy prices, with some help from higher import prices, had boosted the inflation rate above 5 percent, and expectations of inflation were heating up. While oil prices had roughly stabilized, broad indexes of commodity prices rose sharply in April and early May, as did the price of gold. Long-term interest rates also appeared to reflect an increase in inflation expectations: the rate on 30-year Treasury bonds increased 1½ percentage points in 2 months, to a peak of 9.0 percent.... The dollar also told a similar story about expectations during this period, losing nearly 5 percent of its value on a trade-weighted basis in those 2 months.

The Federal Reserve actions, complemented by measures taken abroad to ease policy, generally were successful in reassuring the domestic financial and foreign exchange markets. The dollar appreciated through mid-August, and interest rates remained below their highs of the spring. Meanwhile, the economy showed signs of additional strength, inflation dropped back from the elevated levels of early in the year, and wage increases remained subdued.

Under the influence of higher interest rates and tighter Federal Reserve policy, growth of the monetary aggregates continued to weaken. M1 rose at just a 2.7 percent annual rate in the 6 months through July, and M1A fell slightly, while M2 growth remained well below, and M3 just below, their 5½ to 8½ percent target ranges. To some, this sharp slowdown in money growth raised concerns about potential economic weakness.

In early September the Federal Reserve again tightened policy, both by restricting reserve availability further—which it did "in light of the potential for greater inflation, associated in part with weakness in the dollar"—and by raising the discount rate one-half percentage point to 6 percent. In the preceding 3 weeks the dollar had dropped nearly 5 percent on a trade-weighted basis, and interest rates had begun to move up very steeply in the last few days of August. Once again, foreign exchange markets apparently were reassured by the Federal Reserve's actions. The dollar stabilized, but this time interest rates continued to climb.

The spur for the dollar's drop and the bond market's weakness appears to have been the release in mid-August of the June foreign trade figures, which showed a $15.7 billion deficit—substantially worse than the markets had expected. With the trade deficit thus narrowing more slowly than anticipated, the financial markets surmised that further adjustments were required—either a lower dollar, reduced demand in the United States, or increased demand in our major trading partners. Against a background of rising interest rates abroad, and with little additional action expected to be taken to reduce the U.S. budget deficit or to augment demand abroad, attention focused on the foreign exchange market and U.S. interest rates. Specifically, a rise in U.S. interest rates appeared increasingly likely, perhaps reflecting expectations that further dollar depreciation would add to inflationary pressures. Higher rates would also have been expected to result from an effort to dampen business investment and consumer spending—and thereby U.S. imports, which would reduce the extent of the needed dollar decline.

The trade figures for the next 2 months also were worse than generally expected, and financial markets reacted adversely. On October 14, when the August data were released, the Dow Jones Industrial Average posted a 1-day drop of 3.8 percent, and the rate on 30-year Treasury bonds rose 20 basis points (0.20 percentage points). The dollar also declined, but by less than 1 percent. On balance between September 4 (when the discount rate was increased) and October 16, the trade-weighted value of the dollar remained unchanged, the Dow Jones Industrial Average dropped 12 percent, and interest rates rose 50-150 basis points.

The extent of Federal Reserve tightening through mid-October was most dramatic as measured by the sharp deceleration of money and reserve growth. In view of the relative looseness of money-GNP relationships in recent years, however, other indicators provide additional evidence on the stance of Federal Reserve policy. Judging by the level of the Federal funds rate in early October, the progressive tightening of monetary policy had effectively reversed most of the easing that had occurred during 1986. . . .

There is little question that a turn toward some restraint in 1987 was desirable; continued growth of money at the high rates experienced in 1985 and 1986 would have had inevitable inflationary consequences. With output growth apparently well-maintained and inflation expectations building at times, the Federal Reserve acted to forestall a resurgence of deep-rooted inflation and to retain hard-won gains toward price stability. As always . . . the tightening of policy last year had implications for future growth and price performance.

Break in the Stock Market

As the third quarter ended, preliminary evidence suggested—and data later confirmed—that the U.S. economy was growing strongly. The unemployment rate continued to edge down, reaching its lowest level since late 1979, and the index of leading indicators pointed to sustained economic growth. However, the outlook for further substantial improvement in the Federal deficit was clouded by an apparent deadlock between the Congress and the Administration over the budget for fiscal 1988, which began October 1. In financial markets, the Federal Reserve had tightened monetary policy in September. Interest rates, both short- and long-term, rose further in the first weeks of October.

The Crash

In mid-October the stock market posted a string of large declines, culminating in a 1-day plunge of unprecedented magnitude. The stock market had soared more than 40 percent in value from the start of the year through its August peak, but, by the close of business on October 16, nearly half of that gain had been erased. And the following Monday, October 19, after stock markets elsewhere in the world had posted sharp declines, the Dow Jones Industrial Average lost 22.6 percent in a single day. Trading volume was enormous, the markets were chaotic, many stocks opened very late, and the word "panic" aptly described the atmosphere. It was a worldwide phenomenon with potentially worldwide consequences.

On that 1 day, the total value of the stock market dropped by roughly half a trillion dollars. The next day, again amid an enormous volume of transactions, market conditions worsened. Trading in many stocks and index futures halted for a time, but the market managed to recover and closed higher. In subsequent days and weeks, investors remained nervous, but they drew reassurance from the Federal Reserve's prompt provision of liquidity and the large number of corporations announcing stock buybacks. During the remainder of the year, the market settled into a trading range that left the Dow at the end of 1987 quite close to its year-earlier level.

A wide range of explanations for the crash has been offered, and many factors may have contributed. However, no political or economic event occurred between the market's close on Friday and on Monday that appears capable of explaining such a huge revaluation of the net worth of U.S. corporations. To an extent, the stock market appeared to be reacting simply to itself; in increasingly heavy trading on the preceding Wednesday, Thursday, and Friday, the Dow had lost a total of 261 points, and on October 19, as more individuals and institutions became aware of the deepening plunge in stocks that day and tried to sell, the decline cumulated. . . .

Rising interest rates certainly were a factor in the stock market's decline. As noted above, rates had risen sharply in the weeks preceding the crash, and one major bank had announced another half percentage point hike in its prime rate on the Thursday before the plunge. Moreover, the outlook for even higher interest rates had been bolstered by the lack of improvement in the monthly U.S. trade figures. The slower-than-expected turnaround in the trade deficit implied to some that further adjustments— either to exchange rates or to foreign or domestic fiscal or monetary policies—would be necessary to stimulate U.S. exports and reduce U.S. import growth. . . .

Economic Implications

The damage to the financial system as a direct result of the stock market break was remarkably minor. Several brokerage firms closed their doors or merged with larger, better capitalized companies, a number of Wall Street firms announced layoffs, and the demand for portfolio insurance—which was supposed to provide a hedge against declining stocks—dropped off amid evidence that such insurance had failed to perform as expected.

Recent studies have provided much useful information concerning the events surrounding October 19. These studies deserve, and will receive, serious and careful attention. In response to the crash, however, it is important to avoid precipitous actions that might make financial markets less efficient and less flexible. The resilience of the financial system in the face of the unprecedented dive in stock prices can be read as eloquent testimony to the general adequacy of government regulations in this area. Regulatory authorities and market participants worked together effectively to ensure that, despite the large declines in stock prices, the financial system continued to function.

The implications of the market break for the economy, however, are harder to gauge and may ultimately be more serious, requiring a careful balance of macroeconomic policies to avoid the threat of an economic downturn. The stock market is a good, but not infallible, predictor of economic trends. While it is sufficiently reliable to be included in the Department of Commerce's index of leading indicators, it represents only 1 of 11 components in that index. The stock market tends to be overly pessimistic, erroneously predicting several additional recessions in the postwar period. But in those circumstances when a stock drop has not been followed by an economic downturn, it is often because economic policies have shifted direction, effectively preempting a recession. For example, in 1966, after the stock market had declined more than 20 percent, the Federal Reserve did an about-face, reversing much of its earlier tightening. The economy responded to the support, and a recession was avoided. . . .

Policy Response

In the days and weeks following October 19, U.S. macroeconomic policies were reassessed. The Federal Reserve reacted promptly, indicating by word and deed that ample liquidity would be provided to help the financial system and the economy weather the stresses associated with the market break. The fiscal policy response required more negotiation and more time, but 1 month after the plunge in stock prices, the Administration and the Congress concluded an agreement to continue efforts in the direction of restraint by cutting the fiscal 1988 and 1989 budget deficits by $30 billion and $46 billion, respectively, from a specified baseline.

Deficit reduction through Federal spending restraint was, and is, a high priority of the Administration. The stock market drop added urgency to Administration and congressional efforts to forge a 1988 budget that consolidated and built upon the deficit reduction progress made in fiscal 1987. At the "budget summit" set up in the wake of the stock market drop, participants agreed to a 2-year $76 billion deficit reduction package; the resulting legislation rendered GRH automatic spending cuts unnecessary for fiscal 1988. The spending cuts and revenue increases enacted preserve the progress on the deficit made in fiscal 1987 and set the stage for further gains.

While deficit reduction is a very important objective, it is not paramount. For example, GRH wisely allows for suspending the targets should the economy weaken markedly. In current circumstances, with the deflationary impact of the stock market decline not yet clear, progress on the fiscal deficit should continue to be made, but cautiously. The Federal Government's budget has the attractive property of providing the economy with automatic stabilizers, moving in the direction of deficit when the economy sinks and in the direction of surplus when it soars. These stabilizers should not be overridden in the pursuit of deficit reduction. Nor should the deficit reduction imperative run roughshod over considerations of economic efficiency by raising taxes that undo the benefits of tax reform and reduce incentives to work, produce, and invest.

Without question, in the long run the potential for growth in this country will be enhanced by moving toward a balanced Federal budget. Over the medium term, a tighter fiscal policy would play a major role in improving the balance between income and spending in the United States. As the government significantly reduces its demands on resources, there is an increased likelihood that the external imbalance can be righted without impairing the growth of private sector investment expenditures. If, instead, investment expenditures were to be stunted by a combination of loose fiscal policy and tight money, America's potential for future growth might be jeopardized by an increasingly outdated capital stock....

The stock market crash required—and received—an immediate monetary policy response. By the end of the day on October 19, billions of dollars of financial wealth had been lost, and fears of a possible collapse of the financial system and, ultimately, of the economy were palpable. The Federal Reserve responded promptly and unequivocally to these threats by issuing a brief statement the next day that emphasized its willingness to support the system with adequate liquidity. This statement was buttressed by open market operations that satisfied increased demands for liquidity and eased money market conditions. In the 2 weeks immediately following the crash, borrowing from the Federal Reserve declined to a level not seen since the initial tightening of policy in the spring, excess reserves soared to nearly double their usual amount, and the Federal funds rate dropped back to the 6¾ percent range that prevailed during the summer.

The stock market plunge changed the circumstances faced by monetary policymakers in an important way. The market break caused an abrupt loss of wealth and consumer confidence, removing some of the impetus for higher growth and higher prices. The balance of risks shifted as the possibility of recession increased, and the general level of uncertainty about the outlook was heightened enormously. In these circumstances, it was appropriate for the Federal Reserve to respond by making reserves freely available.

After its initial response, however, monetary policy began to take a more cautious tack. Amid signs that the economy had strong momentum going into the fourth quarter, and with few clear indications of economic retrenchment in reaction to the crash, the Federal Reserve took no further moves to ease policy, keeping the discount rate at 6 percent. Most monetary and reserve aggregates weakened over the balance of the year. M1, M1A, and total reserves each ended the year below their pre-crash levels, and M2 remained well below its target growth range, rising at just a 4 percent rate for the year as a whole.

Immediately following the 508-point drop in the Dow, the Federal Reserve's operations were exemplary. It was in the right place at the right time, supporting the financial system with ample liquidity. While it was appropriate for the conduct of policy to change subsequently (once constant reassurances to the markets were no longer needed), the stance of monetary policy at the end of 1987 may have underestimated the risks to adequate economic growth. At the end of the year, interest rates were down from their October highs, but they remained above the levels of January through August, while monetary aggregate growth remained weak. More recently, declining interest rates and increased money growth suggest that the Federal Reserve has been more supportive of economic growth.

The Economic Outlook

The Administration's economic forecast anticipates that the rate of economic expansion will slow this year from the rapid pace set in 1987. Subsequently, growth is projected to resume at a rate that more fully reflects the economy's long-term potential and that promises further reductions in unemployment. Improvement in the U.S. real trade balance is expected to contribute to output and employment growth in coming years, as it did in 1987; this contribution will play an especially important role in 1988. Increases in the working-age population, in labor force participation rates, and in the education, skill, and experience of the work force, together with an expanding capital stock and improving technology, are projected to sustain growth of the economy's output at a rate sufficient to meet rising domestic and international demand. The inflation rate is

projected to move gradually downward from the 4 percent range characteristic of the current expansion toward the long-term goal of price
stability. Underlying this outlook are economic policies that are assumed
to support these developments.

Forecast for 1988

Real GNP is forecast to rise 2.4 percent from the fourth quarter of 1987
to the fourth quarter of 1988, somewhat slower than the 3.8 percent
increase in 1987. Nevertheless, output growth in 1988 is expected to
generate employment growth sufficient to match increases in the labor
force and to keep the unemployment rate at about its current level. As a
result, the average unemployment rate during 1988 is likely to be the
lowest in 13 years.

The expected slowing of real GNP growth in 1988, also widely anticipated by private forecasters, reflects economic developments during 1987,
especially those during the last quarter of the year. The low rate of
personal saving and the slow growth of real disposable income through the
third quarter of last year already suggested some prospective slowing of
growth in consumer spending—even before the stock market crash lowered
household wealth and consumer confidence. Interest rates declined significantly after the market break, but they remained above their levels at the
beginning of the year. Slow growth of monetary aggregates throughout
1987 points to some possible weakening of economic growth in 1988. The
buildup of inventories at the end of 1987 also indicates a likely need to reduce production growth relative to final sales growth in the new year.
Weighing on the other side, gains in disposable income at the end of 1987
and tax rate reductions taking effect in January 1988 are likely to support
consumer spending. Declines in mortgage interest rates promise a future
boost for residential construction. Perhaps most important, prospects for
continued strong growth of U.S. exports look excellent. All told, however,
real GNP growth in 1988 appears likely to lag behind the rapid pace of
1987.

Probably the most immediate concern is the fast pace of inventory
accumulation during the fourth quarter of 1987. In particular, nonfarm
inventories appeared to rise at an unsustainable rate. To correct this
situation, production will have to decrease relative to final sales. Final
sales are expected to show renewed growth in 1988, after being essentially
flat in the final quarter of 1987. Consequently, an outright decline in
production can be avoided. The inventory adjustment can be achieved
through slower production growth relative to final sales growth. This
essentially reverses the situation in 1987. As discussed earlier, inventory
building accounted for one-half of overall economic growth last year, more
than offsetting deceleration in other domestic components of GNP. In
1988 inventories are expected to accumulate at a slower and more
sustainable pace. This slowdown will have a negative impact on real GNP
growth, possibly with much of the effect felt in the first half of the year.

Modest gains for most other domestic components of demand and strong gains for the U.S. trade sector are expected to keep real GNP growing.

Real net exports will be one of the main sources of growth in the economy in 1988, providing nearly half of overall output growth. Rapid productivity gains in manufacturing, moderate wage increases, and the effects of past exchange-rate adjustments will continue to help U.S. businesses expand exports in foreign markets and compete against imports at home. In addition, anticipated slow growth of final demand within the U.S. economy and the possible effect of the inventory correction on imports are expected to restrain growth of imports and to contribute to net export gains.

In 1987 growth of real consumption slowed to a 0.6 percent rate from the rapid pace set earlier in the expansion, and it actually fell at a 3.8 percent annual rate in the fourth quarter. The personal saving rate finished the year 1.3 percentage points above the year-earlier rate, due entirely to the drop in consumer spending and a strong gain in disposable income during the last quarter of the year. Given the high rate of auto purchases in the third quarter of 1987, the low personal saving rate for most of the year, and the likely effects of October's stock market decline, it was widely anticipated late last year that there would be some downward adjustment in consumer spending. It appears that much of that adjustment occurred in the fourth quarter. Accordingly, . . . real consumption spending is forecast to rise at a modest 1.9 percent rate during 1988, slightly below the projected growth rate of real disposable income, and substantially below the 4½ percent annual growth rate of real consumer spending during the first 4 years of the current expansion.

Despite slower growth of aggregate output this year, fixed investment is expected to accelerate somewhat. . . . [N]onresidential fixed investment is forecast to increase 4.4 percent during the current year, up from 3.7 percent last year. The improving trade picture, which is lifting capacity utilization rates in many manufacturing industries, will provide much of the motivation for increased investment. The need for additional capacity to meet demands both for exports and for import substitutes should continue to stimulate investment in equipment and nonresidential structures. Lower interest rates in 1988, partly as a result of slower economic growth and lower expected inflation, should strengthen housing demand. Residential investment, after falling in 1987, is forecast to increase 3.4 percent in 1988. . . .

The deficit reduction agreement concluded by the Congress and the Administration, together with earlier efforts to control Federal spending, will contribute to a decline in real Federal purchases in the current year. Increases in State and local spending are expected to offset much of this decline, leaving a small negative contribution to GNP growth from the government sector as a whole.

As discussed in Chapter 2, the United States has been notable among industrialized nations in its ability to create jobs both to meet the needs of an expanding labor force and to reduce unemployment. During the current expansion 15 million jobs have been created. Between the fourth quarter of 1986 and the fourth quarter of 1987, when real GNP rose 3.8 percent, 3 million new jobs were created, and the unemployment rate dropped from 6.8 percent to 5.8 percent. Even though slower real growth in the current year is not expected to bring further immediate reductions in the unemployment rate, it is anticipated that some 1½ million new jobs will be created as employment growth keeps pace with an expanding labor force.

Higher oil prices and higher import prices increased the 1987 inflation rate (as measured by the CPI) above the very low rate recorded in 1986. Higher import prices also are expected to contribute to consumer price inflation in 1988. However, after a year of slow growth of monetary aggregates, and in view of the expected slowing of real GNP growth, acceleration of inflation is not seen as a likely danger in 1988. On a fourth-quarter to fourth-quarter basis, the CPI is forecast to rise 4.3 percent in 1988, a small decline from the rise in 1987. The GNP deflator, which is not affected directly by import prices, is forecast to rise 3.9 percent in 1988. The increase from 1987 primarily reflects a shifting of weights attached to different component prices used to calculate the deflator. It does not signify an acceleration of inflation.

The Administration's forecast for 1988 takes account of the favorable effects of tax reform, i.e., full implementation in January 1988 of the reduced marginal tax rates mandated by the Tax Reform Act of 1986 and continued confidence in the preservation of tax reform's incentives for growth and efficiency. Embodied in the forecast is the expectation that the budget compromise agreed to by the Administration and the Congress will be followed, and that rates of demand growth in other industrial countries will be sufficient to sustain world output growth while the U.S. trade deficit is being reduced. Also critical for the forecast is the assumption that monetary authorities will provide sufficient liquidity to support real growth without fueling an acceleration of inflation. . . .

The Administration's medium-term projections show real GNP growth strengthening after 1988, with growth averaging 3.3 percent annually for the period 1989 through 1993. This projection is based on the assessment that recent events in financial markets and slower growth in 1988 will not materially alter the longer run growth potential of the U.S. economy. . . .

Implicit in the Administration's medium-term projections are important economic policy assumptions similar to those underlying the forecast for 1988. First, tax increases that would dull incentives to work, invest, and produce and that would impair the efficient allocation of resources are avoided, and the benefits of tax reform are preserved. Second, continued progress is made in reducing the Federal deficit, primarily by restraining the growth of Federal spending while allowing Federal revenues to rise with the growth of the economy. Third, government regulation continues to be directed toward legitimate interests of public policy and does not again become an excessive and unnecessary burden to enterprise and growth. Fourth, monetary authorities supply adequate liquidity to sustain economic expansion while fostering progress toward the long-run goal of price level stability. Fifth, protectionist pressures, which could provoke retaliation and hamper U.S. access to foreign markets, continue to be resisted successfully. This last assumption is especially important in view of the contribution that an improving U.S. trade balance is projected to make to overall U.S. economic growth in the medium term. It is crucial that American businesses be permitted to compete in markets that are as free as possible from the distorting effects of trade barriers. . . .

Rising Employment, Productivity, and Income

"Maximum employment, production, and purchasing power" are the fundamental goals of economic policy established by the Employment Act of 1946. These goals are among the most important criteria by which the success of the Administration's economic policies must be assessed. The overall record of the last 7 years is good. Since the longest peacetime expansion began in November 1982, 15 million new jobs have been created; production, as measured by real gross national product (GNP), has increased by almost 23 percent; living standards, as measured by real GNP per capita, have grown at an average annual rate of 3.2 percent; and inflation is down from double digits to a 4 percent annual rate.

Despite these accomplishments questions have been raised about the breadth of U.S. economic growth, the strength of the industrial base, and the rate at which incomes and productivity are rising. And as the unemployment rate recently approached its lowest levels in 15 years, people have wondered if further reductions in unemployment will accelerate inflation, as has happened in the past.

Many of these concerns are based on misconceptions about recent trends in employment, productivity, and income growth. These trends indicate that (1) most major demographic groups have shared in the employment and income gains realized during the current expansion; (2) employment growth has been strong particularly in high-paying occupations; (3) the U.S. industrial base remains strong and has not lost ground to other sectors of the economy; (4) incomes and productivity have rebounded after a period of slow growth in the 1970s; and (5) as U.S. economic growth continues, further reductions in the unemployment rate can be sustained without the damaging effects of accelerated wage and price inflation. . . .

Employment and Output

Strong employment growth is one of the outstanding features of the current expansion. Since the expansion began in November 1982, total employment has increased by 15 million, and the unemployment rate has fallen by 4.9 percentage points to 5.7 percent. By December 1987 the proportion of the working-age population employed reached a record 62.3 percent, and the unemployment rate stood at its lowest level since July

1979, and within 0.2 percentage point of its lowest level since 1974. . . .

Increases in employment and reductions in unemployment during the current expansion have affected all major demographic groups and virtually all areas of the country. During the current expansion unemployment rates for men and women have fallen by 5.4 and 4.3 percentage points, respectively, recording their largest declines of any expansion in the postwar era. This progress reflects both the depth of the 1981-82 recession, and the durability of the current expansion. Moreover, during this expansion, the unemployment rate for women has fallen to nearly the same level as the unemployment rate for men, in contrast to earlier periods when the rates for women were significantly higher than those for men.

Gains in employment and reductions in unemployment rates have been particularly large for minority groups. Employment of black workers has risen by 2.4 million since November 1982, with black female employment rising by 1.3 million and black male employment rising by 1.1 million. . . . [T]hese employment gains are significantly larger than those for other workers. As employment has risen, unemployment rates for black males and black females have fallen by 9.9 and 6.1 percentage points, respectively. Both the gains in employment and reductions in unemployment rates are substantially larger than those recorded during the 1975-80 expansion. . . .

Civilian employment of Hispanic workers has risen 2.3 million since the expansion began. In percentage terms the employment of Hispanics has risen much faster than the rest of the work force, although more slowly than the rapid pace set during the late 1970s. The rapid pace of Hispanic employment growth during the 1970s was partially due to rapid growth in the Hispanic labor force, which between 1973 and 1980 grew by 8.6 percent per year. Since 1982 the rate of Hispanic labor force growth has fallen by about one-third, and this slowdown accounts for the difference in employment growth during these two expansions. In recent years the pace of Hispanic employment growth has exceeded the rate of growth in their labor force, thus allowing their unemployment rate to fall by 7.1 percentage points.

Youth employment has risen relatively slowly during the current expansion, reflecting slower growth of the population between 16 and 19 years of age than during the 1970s. Yet employment gains for black youths have been among the strongest of all demographic groups. During 1987 alone employment of black teenagers increased by nearly the same amount as it did during the entire 1975-80 expansion. At the same time unemployment rates, especially for black youths, have declined dramatically. For all youths the unemployment rate declined by 8.0 percentage points between November 1982 and December 1987 to reach its lowest level in 8 years. For black youths the unemployment rate declined by 16.1 percentage points to reach its lowest level in 13 years. Unemployment among black youths is, however, still unacceptably high.

Gains in employment and reductions in unemployment rates also have been widespread geographically. Between November 1982 and November 1987, total employment increased in all but three States. . . .

Employment gains during the current expansion have been largest in higher paying occupations. Nearly two-thirds of the new employment growth has been in managerial, professional, technical, sales, or precision production occupations. Within these broadly defined occupational categories, employment growth has been strong for a wide variety of jobs. It has been less vigorous in lower paying, low-skilled occupations and in part-time work.

For full-time workers, data recently available on employment and earnings in nearly 500 occupations show that about 50 percent of the increase in full-time employment between 1983 and 1986 occurred in occupations with real median earnings of at least $20,000 per year. The median earnings of these occupations were at least 10 percent above the median earnings of all full-time workers. Managerial and administrative jobs, which tend to pay the highest wages and salaries and employ the most educated workers, accounted for 21 percent of the gains in employment, even though these occupations accounted for only 11 percent of all existing jobs in 1983.

In contrast, in low-paying occupations such as food preparation and services, janitorial services, and retail sales, where new job growth is commonly thought to be strong, the share of new employment growth was almost the same as the share of existing jobs. Employment growth was smallest, relative to its share of all jobs, for machine operators and other semiskilled blue-collar occupations.

Moreover, studies have indicated that the share of total full-time employment accounted for by the lowest paying occupations declined during the 1970s and has continued to fall during the current expansion, while the share accounted for by mid- and high-paying occupations has increased. Thus the growth in employment during the current expansion has not occurred solely in higher or lower paying occupations with fewer employed in the occupations in between.

The shift in employment toward higher paying occupations among full-time workers does not mask a shift from full-time to part-time employment. . . . For those employees who work part time, the vast majority, nearly 80 percent, work part time voluntarily, according to surveys conducted by the Bureau of Labor Statistics (BLS). . . .

During the current expansion real manufacturing output has increased more rapidly than real GNP, offsetting the effects of the recession and pushing the share of manufacturing output in real GNP very close to its peak for the postwar period. The share of final goods (as distinct from services and structures) has also risen and approached its highest level since 1960. In fact, except for business cycle movements, the shares of real manufacturing output and real final goods output have been remarkably stable for 25 years. In contrast, there has been a long and relatively steady decline in the fraction of all workers who are employed in manufacturing or in goods-producing industries, and a constant upward trend of the fraction employed in service-producing industries. More rapid gains in productivity in manufacturing and in goods-producing industries than in the rest of the economy have allowed declining shares of workers in these sectors to produce roughly constant shares of real GNP. . . .

Income and Productivity

By the broadest available measure, American living standards have resumed a steady rate of increase during the 1980s, after a period of sluggish growth in the 1970s. To a large extent, these gains reflect improved productivity growth. During the 1970s, gains in real GNP per capita resulted primarily from an increasing proportion of working-age persons in the population and signified little gain for individual workers. During the 1980s, by contrast, improved productivity growth has allowed more rapid growth in compensation per worker. These gains in labor compensation are broad-based, benefiting all major demographic groups. Furthermore, the upswing in productivity growth will sustain gains in both per capita income and labor compensation in the coming years. . . .

The broadest measure of the economy's ability to support the living standards of the American people is the real value of all goods and services produced in the economy each year, divided by the total population, i.e., real GNP per capita. . . . [R]eal GNP per capita has grown at an annual rate of 1.8 percent since the last business cycle peak in 1981. This rate of growth has approached the rapid rate recorded between 1948 and 1973, has exceeded the rate experienced between the business cycle peaks in 1973 and 1981, and has equaled the average rate achieved in the United States since 1900. . . .

. . . . Real income for the median family, measured in 1986 dollars, declined from $29,730 in 1973 to $26,990 in 1981, and rose to only $29,460 in 1986. As with measures of real earnings for workers, measures of real family incomes suffer from the bias in the CPI, which overestimates inflation during the 1970s. After correcting for this bias by using the CPI-U-X1, real family income still shows a $790 decline between 1973 and 1981. However, the adjusted real median family income in 1986 was the highest in U.S. history, and $1,430 higher than in 1973. . . .

Expanding Trade and Avoiding Protectionism

Twice in this century the United States has taken the lead in setting a new course for the world's trading system. The first time was in 1930 with the passage of the Smoot-Hawley Act, which led to global protectionism and contributed to the Great Depression. The second time was after World War II with the process of trade liberalization brought about through the General Agreement on Tariffs and Trade (GATT). The result was more rapid recovery from the destruction of war, the unprecedented expansion of world commerce, and increased prosperity in the industrialized and developing countries.

The Smoot-Hawley Act and GATT both taught that the United States has a large influence on the world economy, for better or worse. Likewise, the actions taken in the coming months regarding American trade policy have the potential to influence the course of international trade for years to come. . . .

The concerns and frustrations over trade felt today by the Congress, the President, and the American public stem from the large trade deficits which the United States has been running since 1982. . . . [T]he macroeconomic cause of the trade deficit is related to the tremendous growth in Federal spending (22.8 percent of gross national product (GNP) in 1987 versus 20.6 percent in 1979) relative to the also substantial growth in taxes (19.4 percent of GNP in 1987 versus 18.9 in 1979) and the harmful effect of the resulting Federal deficit on the savings-investment balance in the United States. . . .

The lesson from Smoot-Hawley is that passage of protectionist trade legislation by the United States will increase protectionist activity in the rest of the world, poison the international climate for trade diplomacy in general, and slow the process of trade liberalization for years to come. Since the United States is a major trading nation, it could suffer major economic losses in the event of increased global protectionism. . . .

Two of the most protected industries in the United States today are textiles and apparel. The costs which this protection places on the American family and consumer are enormous, running in the range of $200 to $400 per year per household.

In a major protectionist effort, the House of Representatives passed in 1987 the Textile and Apparel Trade Act which would raise the wall of protection even higher, adding another $280 to $420 in costs per household over the first 5 years. Similar textile legislation was passed by the Congress in 1986 and vetoed by the President. The current bill would set a 1 percent annual growth limit on U.S. global imports of textiles and apparel, freeze shoe imports at 1986 levels, and for the first time, restrict imports from Canada and the European Community. . . .

The most threatening proposal being considered by the Congress is the Omnibus Trade and Competitiveness Act of 1987, the House and Senate versions of which amount to about 1,000 pages. The bill, which now must be considered in conference committee, includes many features which have only a tangential relationship to trade policy or which are inconsistent with U.S. policy in GATT. Among these are sections dealing with education grants, plant closing restrictions, . . . subsidies to agricultural programs, changes to domestic tax laws, and investment screening regulations. With so many provisions grouped together in one bill, the President is given little opportunity to consider them on their separate merits. Furthermore, the Administration is on record stating that many of the provisions are unwise and damaging to U.S. interests.

Although the trade bill would include tariffs and trade barriers, as Smoot-Hawley did, it represents a fundamentally different kind of protectionism. In the area of trade policy, the legislation would change the rules for administering U.S. trade law and for granting protection to U.S. producers. . . .

In the area of trade policy, the United States today faces a choice. It can continue its commitment to foster an environment of trade liberalization, or it can turn to protectionism. The choice will be determined by how the Nation shapes domestic law and how it deals with its trade partners in the international forum, rather than by public statements of intentions. . . .

Airline Deregulation:
Maintaining the Momentum

During the last decade there have been dramatic changes in the way America's transportation sector is regulated. The railroad, bus, trucking, and airline industries all have become more efficient as a result. Since virtually all aspects of the economy depend on the transportation system, gains in this sector help the overall economy, thereby improving U.S. competitiveness. The principal force underlying these changes in productivity has been a deregulatory environment that allowed greater price flexibility for businesses while reducing government interference. . . .

While deregulation substantially improved productivity and efficiency in the transportation sector, the Airline Deregulation Act of 1978 has had the greatest immediate impact on the public. The benefits to travelers from airline deregulation have been estimated to exceed $11 billion per year.

The deregulation of the airline industry has permitted greater competition which, in turn, has led to a dramatic restructuring of the airline industry. The industry has become more streamlined. Fares generally are much lower than they would have been under regulation, and a wider menu of travel options is available to the consumer. Although there had been concern about air service to small communities following deregulation, such service, as measured by the frequency of flights and flight length, has improved.

Despite the economic gains from deregulation, complaints about a possible decline in the level of safety and an increase in flight delays have increased. It is sometimes argued that regulation should be restored. These concerns must be examined in the context of the evolution of the airline industry since deregulation. While airline safety is a serious public concern, the record indicates that safety has not deteriorated under deregulation; in fact, it appears to have improved. Moreover, while airport and airspace congestion has worsened, this is a direct result of the *success* of deregulation. More people are flying now than ever before, but the local and Federal authorities charged with managing the airports and airspace have been unable to adjust to the dramatic growth in demand. Congestion is a natural consequence of the fact that growth in demand for air travel has exceeded the supply of airport and airspace services. . . .

Results of Deregulation

Several factors have affected the performance of the airline industry over the last decade. Deregulation, while important, must not be given undue credit or unjust blame for the recent performance of the industry. Technical innovation, for example, has contributed to improvements in fuel efficiency and safety. The performance of the domestic economy also is linked to the overall health of the domestic airline industry, because more people travel when the economy is doing well. Since 1982 the United States has enjoyed its longest post-war peacetime economic expansion. Thus it is important to differentiate between the gains resulting from economic expansion and those resulting from deregulation. Even controlling for such changes in the economy, however, it is clear that deregulation has had a substantial positive effect.

The most important economic benefits that have resulted from U.S. airline deregulation are decreases in fares and increases in the frequency of service. The use of discount fares, which offer reductions from the standard coach fare, has increased dramatically. In 1976, 15 percent of travelers enjoyed discount fares; by 1987 this number had grown to 90 percent. The substantial rise in the availability of discount fares has been accompanied by a 15 percent decrease in these fares, adjusting for inflation. . . .

The route structure that evolved under regulation has undergone major changes as a result of increased competition. Free entry into city-pair markets has permitted the airlines to develop much more efficient routing patterns than under regulation. The most significant change has been the growth of a "hub-and-spoke" delivery system. As the name suggests, airlines have developed a series of networks analogous to a bicycle wheel. The hub represents the center of the network; the spokes link different origin and destination points. For example, a flight from Hartford to San Diego may be routed through a hub at Chicago. . . .

Managing the Increased Demand for Airspace

Deregulation has given rise to the highest levels of commercial air travel ever experienced in the world. If not managed properly, increased air traffic could lead to greater congestion, and in some situations could raise safety concerns. The deregulated environment has been quite effective in maintaining air safety. The growth of air traffic, however, has raised some important issues concerning the compatibility of airline deregulation with continued government management of airspace and airport services. If the benefits of deregulation are to be enhanced, market forces should be introduced to reform those elements of the air transport industry that are still regulated by the government. . . .

One feature not addressed by airline deregulation was the management of delays. Delays occur when the demand for system capacity exceeds the available supply. Delays usually are caused by congestion. Just as highways often become congested during rush hours, so do airports and airspace. Most delays occur at crowded airports during peak periods, just as most highway delays occur during rush hour traffic jams around major cities. In 1987, for example, 85 percent of total recorded delays were associated with only 22 airports.

The primary responsibility for managing the U.S. airspace continues to lie with the FAA. The policies adopted by the FAA have an important effect on the amount and distribution of delays. To understand appropriate remedies for problems related to delays, it is useful to have some understanding of how the air traffic control system works.

In the United States, more than 600 airport control towers clear planes for takeoff and landing. To help regulate traffic between airports, there are 20 domestic en route air traffic control centers which span the continental United States. These facilities help manage more than 40 million flights per year. To simplify this task, the airspace is divided into a number of sectors. Each sector corresponds to a parcel of airspace within which a controller is responsible for the safe passage of aircraft. Of the 47,000 people employed by the FAA, about 15,000 are air traffic controllers.. . .

The FAA and DOT have taken a variety of actions to address concerns about air traffic congestion. After the strike by air traffic controllers in 1981, the FAA adopted a new policy to minimize the number of aircraft that the system must track at any one time without reducing the overall volume of daily flight activity. When congestion is anticipated at the destination airport, the FAA requires that a plane wait on the ground. This policy, while perhaps addressing safety, actually may have introduced significant delays. If planes were allowed to circle in the vicinity of destination airports, waiting for weather or congestion to clear, unnecessary delays could be avoided.

To help ease the delay problem, the FAA has undertaken a major restructuring of the airspace along the east coast. The FAA significantly expanded air traffic capabilities through an improvement in routing procedures. This change required only a very small addition of personnel and equipment. The airspace reorganization is analogous to reducing traffic jams by increasing the number of lanes on a roadway and improving the timing of stoplights. The creation of additional departure routes and airways was accomplished primarily through better charting, efficient realignment of existing paths, and increased coordination among air traffic facilities. Similar plans for restructuring airways along the west coast are under development.

The Department of Transportation periodically has attempted to enlist the help of the airlines in sorting out scheduling problems. In 1984 and again in 1987, the DOT brought the airlines together to engage in scheduling discussions aimed at reducing delays. The DOT believes that these meetings have helped to reduce excessive bunching of departures at peak periods.

Since pricing mechanisms are not used to allocate takeoffs and landings at the most desirable times, the airlines have little incentive to transfer some of their peak traffic to off-peak periods. Reliance upon DOT meetings to deal with scheduling issues arises at least in part because pricing of airport usage does not reflect congestion costs. . . .

Because traffic volume has risen since deregulation, it has become increasingly difficult for the supply of airspace services to keep up with the demands imposed upon the system. Part of the problem is the way the system currently is financed. Instead of paying for services actually rendered by the air traffic control system, operators and travelers pay taxes only indirectly related to costs. The primary source of funding for the system is an 8 percent tax on each airline ticket sold. In 1987 the ticket tax yielded $2.7 billion in revenues, accounting for 88 percent of the revenues collected from users. The remaining revenues come from a tax on aviation fuel, a 5 percent tax on cargo, and a $3 passenger tax on international departures. These revenues flow into the Airport and Airway Trust Fund, out of which part of the Federal spending related to air transportation is financed. . . .

Virtually none of the measures developed by Federal authorities to address the short-term congestion problem incorporates economic approaches. Because of the way the system currently is managed, airlines have very little incentive to consider the costs they impose on others when flying at peak periods. Charges to aircraft operators do not reflect the full costs of using the airspace and airport facilities at these times. For example, if a plane lands at a congested airport during a peak period, all other planes waiting to land are delayed. Similarly, if a plane takes off during a peak period, planes waiting in line behind it are delayed. Operators will not take these costs into account unless a system is implemented in which they are charged for them.

There are two basic approaches that would help alleviate the congestion problem during peak periods while at the same time promote a more efficient use of available capacity. One would set a price for takeoffs and landings that adequately reflects direct and indirect costs. Direct costs include normal operating and maintenance costs, while indirect costs include the costs of congestion. The other approach would limit the quantity of takeoff and landing slots during peak periods and allow these slots to be bought and sold. Both the fee system and the slot system would allow passengers who value peak-period travel the most highly to have access to airports during these periods. Those passengers who have greater flexibility could elect to take flights during off-peak periods and, thus, take advantage of the lower fares that would be offered then.

The best way to strike an appropriate balance between the costs and benefits of congestion is to introduce tradable slots or variable fees that reflect the costs that each individual imposes on other travelers at peak times. These economic approaches would ensure that operators and customers take congestion costs into account in their travel decisions. Reducing the level of congestion at airports would increase the value of peak-period flights and would promote economic efficiency. . . .

An alternative to peak-period fees is a restriction on the number of landing and takeoff slots available during peak periods. At most airports there are no restrictions on landings and takeoffs other than those imposed by air traffic controllers. Planes typically are handled on a first-come, first-served basis. At O'Hare, La Guardia, Kennedy, and National Airports, however, the FAA has limited the number of takeoff and landing slots available. The FAA, in consultation with the airlines, has allocated slots to the carriers by criteria related to historical usage. The FAA can change this allocation and require one airline to transfer slots to another.

Beginning in April 1986, the FAA authorized the purchase and sale of slots at the four "slot-constrained" airports. . . .

Allowing purchases and sales of slots is a major improvement over the previous system, which allocated slots by committee. The committee process did not allocate slots on the basis of their most highly valued use. In contrast, the slot market allows firms that have a better product to expand their operations by buying slots from other firms. Since the exchange is voluntary, both the buyer and the seller are better off. In addition, consumers generally will be better off, since the airlines have more flexibility to respond to the demands of travelers with different valuations of time. Thus the tradable slot system is similar to the fee system in that it tends to reduce delays while increasing efficiency. . . .

PRESIDENT REAGAN'S
BUDGET MESSAGE
February 18, 1988

President Ronald Reagan submitted to Congress on February 18 a trillion-dollar federal budget for fiscal 1989, which would run eight months beyond his presidency. If tradition held, his successor, whether a Democrat or Republican, could be expected to try to revise the budget soon after taking office on January 20, 1989. However, the next president's budgetary flexibility would be greatly circumscribed—just as Reagan's was in preparing the 1989 budget—by mounting deficits, and defense and welfare commitments.

In presenting to Congress the projected $1.094 trillion budget for 1989, the Reagan administration estimated it would produce a deficit of $129.5 billion, adding to a national debt that already was in excess of $2 trillion. The White House calculated that the payment of interest on the debt would cost $151.8 billion in 1989, making debt service the third-biggest single item in the budget—after defense and Social Security expenditures.

Reagan gained much of what he wanted during his first years in office, partly through the budget-making process. He lowered taxes, increased defense spending, and had the political advantage of forcing opposition Democrats in Congress to make painful spending choices. But by 1987 he was caught in a trap of his own making. Opposed to raising taxes, he virtually abandoned his efforts to boost defense spending because the nation no longer could pay for it. Forced into a compromise with congressional leaders on the fiscal 1988 and 1989 budgets, he lost his dominance over economic policy making.

On November 20, 1987, the White House and congressional leaders agreed to a plan for reducing the deficit by $76 billion during 1988 and 1989, cementing the main spending and revenue levels for both fiscal years. Thus for the first time since Reagan took office in January 1981, the White House and Congress began the budget-making exercise with a common goal.

Unlike Reagan's first budgets, which were sharply focused political instruments defining an entirely new arrangement of government spending priorities, the 1989 budget was essentially a passive document— predetermined except in details by the necessity of trying to meet a congressionally mandated deficit-reduction goal. The administration's $299.5 billion request for defense was only 3 percent above the prevailing level of spending for the armed forces. That represented the smallest yearly increase during the Reagan presidency. It was not expected to keep pace with inflation, which was officially forecast at 3.8 percent.

While defense spending leveled off, the cost of domestic programs continued to grow. Reagan estimated a need of $511.5 billion in 1989—$20 billion more than in 1988—for welfare-related entitlements and other mandatory programs that are controlled by eligibility criteria and benefit formulas. He requested $148.1 billion in new budget authority for domestic programs that are funded by Congress on a year-to-year basis. Big increases were requested for drug enforcement, prison construction, space and science projects, and modernization of the air-traffic control system. Reagan requested $5 billion for Pell higher-education grants for low-income students, twice as much as he had previously, and his request for $2 billion for AIDS research was 40 percent more than before. At the same time, he proposed—as he had in previous years—to eliminate or severely reduce spending for the Legal Services Corporation, Urban Development Action Grants, and the Rural Electrification Administration.

As previously, the president put forward a "privatization" package, asking Congress to sell some of the government's physical assets, including Amtrak, the national passenger railroad system; the Naval Petroleum Reserves at Elk Hills, California, and Teapot Dome, Wyoming; and the Alaska Power Administration. But Reagan backed off from highly controversial ideas to privatize the Postal Service and the in-house research laboratories of the National Institutes of Health. He suggested instead that these ideas be studied during the next two years.

Following is the text of President Ronald Reagan's annual budget message to Congress, released February 18, 1988, with the fiscal 1989 budget:

To the Congress of the United States:

As we consider the state of our Nation today, we have much cause for satisfaction. Thanks to sound policies, steadfastly pursued during the past 7 years, America is at peace, and our people are enjoying the longest peacetime economic expansion in our Nation's history.

By reordering priorities so that we spend more on national security and less on wasteful or unnecessary Federal programs, we have made freedom more secure around the world and have been able to negotiate with our adversaries from a position of strength. By pursuing market-oriented economic policies, we have uncorked the genie of American enterprise and created new businesses, more jobs, improved production, and widespread prosperity. And we have done all this without neglecting the poor, the elderly, the infirm, and the unfortunate among us.

Seven Years of Accomplishment

Let me note a few of the highlights from our Administration's record of accomplishment:

- The current expansion, now in its sixty-third month, has outlasted all previous peacetime expansions in U.S. history. Business investment and exports are rising in real terms, foreshadowing continued economic growth this year and next.
- Since this expansion began, 15 million new jobs have been created, while the unemployment rate has fallen by 5 percentage points—to 5.7 percent, the lowest level in nearly a decade. By comparison, employment in other developed countries has not grown significantly, and their unemployment rates have remained high.
- Inflation, which averaged 10.4 percent annually during the 4 years before I came to office, has averaged less than a third of that during the past 5 years.
- The prime interest rate was 21.5 percent just before I came into office; it is now 8.5 percent; the mortgage rate, which was 14.9 percent, is now down to 10.2 percent.
- Since 1981, the amount of time spent by the public filling out forms required by the Federal Government has been cut by hundreds of millions of hours annually, and the number of pages of regulations published annually in the *Federal Register* has been reduced by over 45 percent.
- Between 1981 and 1987, changes in the Federal tax code, including a complete overhaul in 1986, have made the tax laws more equitable, significantly lowered earned income tax rates for many individuals and corporations, and eliminated the need for 4.3 million low-income individuals or families to file tax forms.
- At the same time, real after-tax personal income has risen 15 percent during the past 5 years, increasing our overall standard of living.
- The outburst of spending for means-tested entitlement programs that occurred in the 1970s has been curbed. Eligibility rules have been

tightened to retarget benefits to the truly needy, and significant progress has been made in improving the efficiency and effectiveness of these programs.

- We have begun the process of putting other entitlement programs on a more rational basis. This includes medicare, which was converted from cost-plus financing to a system that encourages competition and holds down costs.
- Federal spending for domestic programs other than entitlements has been held essentially flat over the past 5 years, while basic benefits for the poor, the elderly, and others in need of Federal assistance have been maintained. This is a dramatic improvement over the unsustainably rapid annual growth of these programs that prevailed before 1981.
- The social security system has been rescued from the threat of insolvency.
- Our defense capabilities have been strengthened. Weapons systems have been modernized and upgraded. We are recruiting and retaining higher caliber personnel. The readiness, training, and morale of our troops have been improved significantly. Because we are stronger, enormous progress has been achieved in arms reduction negotiations with the Soviet Union.
- Federal agencies have undertaken a major management improvement program called "Reform '88." This program has two main objectives: to operate Federal agencies in a more business-like manner, and to reduce waste, fraud, and abuse in government programs.
- Some functions of the Federal Government—such as financing waste treatment plants—are being transferred back to State and local governments. In other instances—such as water projects—State and local governments are bearing a larger share of costs, leading to more rational decision-making in these areas.
- Finally, we have made real progress in privatizing Federal activities that are more appropriate for the private sector than government. Notable examples include the sale of Conrail, the long-term lease of National and Dulles Airports, and the auction of billions of dollars in loan portfolios.
- Related to this shift away from the Federal budget are our achievements on cost sharing and user fees, shifting the cost of projects and programs where appropriate to non-Federal sources.

While we have reason to be proud of this record of achievement, we must be vigilant in addressing threats to continued prosperity. One major threat is the Federal deficit.

Deficit Reduction, the Agreement, and G-R-H

If the deficit is not curbed by limiting the appetite of government, we put in jeopardy what we have worked so hard to achieve. Larger deficits brought on by excessive spending could precipitate rising inflation, interest rates, and unemployment. We cannot permit this to happen, and we will not.

The Congress acknowledged the pressing need to reduce the deficit when, in December 1985, it enacted the Balanced Budget and Emergency Deficit Control Act, commonly known for its principal sponsors as the Gramm-Rudman-Hollings (G-R-H) Act. This Act committed both the President and the Congress to a fixed schedule of progress toward balancing the budget.

In 1987, the budget deficit was $150 billion—down $71 billion from the record level of $221 billion reached in 1986. This was also a record decline in the deficit. To some extent, however, this improvement represented one-time factors, such as a high level of receipts in the transitional year of tax reform. Economic forecasters predicted that without action the 1988 and 1989 deficits would be higher than the 1987 level. In order to prevent this, and to preserve and build upon the 1987 deficit-reduction progress in a realistic fashion, last fall the Congress modified the G-R-H Act. Specifically, it required that the 1988 deficit target be $144 billion and the target for 1989 be $136 billion.

Last year, members of my Administration worked with the Leaders of Congress to develop a 2-year plan of deficit reduction—the Bipartisan Budget Agreement. One of the major objectives of the budget I am submitting today is to comply with that agreement—in order to help assure a steady reduction in the deficit until budget balance is achieved.

The Bipartisan Budget Agreement reflects give and take on all sides. I agreed to some $29 billion in additional revenues and $13 billion less than I had requested in defense funding over 2 years. However, because of a willingness of all sides to compromise, an agreement was reached that pared $30 billion from the deficit projected for 1988 and $46 billion from that projected for 1989.

In submitting this budget, I am adhering to the Bipartisan Budget Agreement and keeping my part of the bargain. I ask the Congress to do the same. This budget does not fully reflect my priorities, nor, presumably, those of any particular Member of Congress. But the goal of deficit reduction through spending reduction must be paramount. Abandoning the deficit reduction compromise would threaten our economic progress and burden future generations.

This budget shows that a gradual elimination of the deficit is possible without abandoning tax reform, without cutting into legitimate social programs, without devastating defense, and without neglecting other national priorities.

Under the Bipartisan Budget Agreement, progress toward a steadily smaller deficit and eventual budget balance will continue, but this projected decline rests on two assumptions: continued economic growth, and implementation of the Agreement. If the economy performs as expected, and if the Bipartisan Budget Agreement reflected in this budget is adhered to, the deficit should decline to less than 3 percent of GNP in 1989. For the first time in several years, the national debt as a proportion of GNP will actually fall. Reducing the deficit and the debt in this manner would bring our goal of a balanced budget and a reduced burden on future generations much closer to realization.

Moreover, adherence to the Agreement, as reflected in this budget, will ensure the achievement of additional deficit reductions in future years, because in many cases the savings from a given action this year will generate deficit savings in subsequent years. Given the good start made in 1987, we have an opportunity this year to put the worst of the deficit problem behind us.

Meeting National Priorities

In formulating this budget, I have endeavored to meet national priorities while keeping to the terms of the Bipartisan Budget Agreement and the G-R-H Act. In essence, the Agreement limits the 1988-to-1989 increase in domestic discretionary program budget authority to 2 percent. To address urgent national priorities insofar as possible within this overall 2 percent limit, my budget proposes that some programs—such as those for education, drug enforcement, and technology development—receive larger funding increases, while others are reduced, reformed, or, in some cases, terminated.

High-priority programs must be funded adequately. One of our highest priorities is to foster individual success through greater educational and training opportunities. For example:

- I propose an increase of $656 million over the $16.2 billion appropriated for 1988 for discretionary programs of the Department of Education. Although State and local governments fund most education activity, Federal programs provide crucial aid for the poor, the handicapped, and the educationally disadvantaged.
- I have proposed reform of our overcentralized welfare system through State experimentation with innovative alternatives. In addition, my initiative would overhaul current employment and training programs for welfare recipients, and strengthen our national child support enforcement system.
- By emphasizing housing vouchers, I would provide housing assistance to 135,500 additional low-income households in 1989—8 percent more than the 125,000 additional households receiving housing subsidies in 1988.
- Ineffective programs to assist dislocated workers would be replaced by an expanded $1 billion worker readjustment program (WRAP) carefully designed to help those displaced from their jobs move quickly into new careers.

In addition, I am proposing funds to strengthen U.S. technology and make America more competitive. For example:

- I propose a continued increase in federally supported basic research aimed at longer-term improvements in the Nation's productivity and global competitiveness. This budget would double National Science Foundation support for academic basic research, increase support for training future scientists and engineers, and expedite technology transfer of Government-funded research to industry.
- I would provide $11.5 billion for space programs, including: essential funding for continued development of America's first permanently manned Space Station; increased support for improving the performance and reliability of the space shuttle; a major new initiative, the Advanced X-ray Astrophysics Facility, for space science; further support to encourage the commercial development of space; and a new technology effort, Project Pathfinder, designed to develop technologies to support future decisions on the expansion of human presence and activity beyond Earth's orbit, into the solar system.
- I also recommend $363 million in 1989 to initiate construction of the Superconducting Super Collider (SSC), including $283 million for construction and $60 million for supporting research and development. The SSC as currently envisaged will be the largest pure science project ever undertaken. It will help keep this country on the cutting edge of high energy physics research until well into the next century.

This budget also reflects my belief that the health of all our citizens must remain one of our top priorities:

- I continue to urge enactment of an affordable self-financing insurance program through medicare to protect families from economic devastation caused by catastrophic illness.
- To attack the scourge of AIDS, I propose $2 billion for additional research, education, and treatment in 1989—a 38 percent increase over the 1988 level and more than double the Federal Government's effort in 1987. This includes $1.3 billion in funding for the Public Health Service.
- Building upon the Nation's preeminence in basic biomedical research, I seek a 5.1 percent increase for non-AIDS research at the National Institutes of Health.

Our fight against drug abuse must continue, as well as our efforts to protect the individual against crime:

- For expanded law enforcement, including efforts targeted at white collar crime, organized crime, terrorism and public corruption, I propose $4.5 billion—an increase of 6 percent over 1988.
- For drug law enforcement, prevention, and treatment programs, I propose $3.9 billion in 1989, a 13 percent increase over the 1988 level.
- To relieve prison overcrowding and adequately house a growing inmate population, I would provide $437 million—more than double the $202 million devoted to Federal prison construction in 1988.

Other areas of Federal responsibility receive priority funding in this budget.

- For the Federal Aviation Administration to continue its multi-year program to modernize the Nation's air traffic control systems, I would provide $1.6 billion—a 44 percent increase over the level of 1988.
- To improve coordination of Federal rural development programs and to redirect funding toward needy rural areas and program recipients, I propose a rural development initiative to be coordinated by the Secretary of Agriculture.
- To carry out the joint recommendations of the U.S. and Canadian Special Envoys on Acid Rain, I recommend total funding of $2.5 billion for innovative clean coal technology demonstration projects over the period 1988 through 1992.
- I also recommend an expansion of hazardous waste cleanup efforts, with an increase in Superfund outlays of some $430 million in 1989.
- To continue filling the Strategic Petroleum Reserve (SPR) at the current rate of 50,000 barrels per day, I would provide $334 million in 1989. Contingent upon the enactment of legislation authorizing the sale of the Naval Petroleum Reserves (NPR), I would provide an additional $477 million to bring the fill rate up to 100,000 barrels per day, and an additional $208 million to establish a separate 10 million barrel defense petroleum inventory to offset the disposition of the NPR.
- To improve the speed and accuracy of tax processing and expand information services provided to taxpayers, I would provide a $241 million increase for the Internal Revenue Service. These funds are designed to assure smooth implementation of the 1986 tax reforms.

Maintaining peace in a troubled world is the most important responsibility of government. Fortunately, during the past 7 years, our defense capabilities have been restored toward levels more consistent with meeting our responsibility to provide an environment safe and secure from aggression. Specifically, combat readiness has been improved, and our forces have been modernized.

The proposals for national security contained in this budget represent an essential minimum program for keeping America safe and honoring our commitments to our friends and allies. Anything less would jeopardize not only our security—and that of our friends and allies—but also would dim the prospects for further negotiated agreements with our adversaries.

As called for in the Bipartisan Budget Agreement, my budget requests defense funding of $299.5 billion in budget authority and $294.0 billion in outlays for 1989. It also provides for about 2 percent real growth in these programs in future years. Also, as called for in the Agreement, my budget requests $18.1 billion in budget authority for discretionary spending for international affairs. This includes $8.3 billion in security assistance to allied and friendly countries where the United States has special security concerns.

Needed Programmatic Reforms

Incentives.—It is essential to continue to change the incentive structure for many domestic Federal programs to promote greater efficiency and cost-effectiveness. This budget proposes to create such needed incentives.

Many Federal programs offer payments without sufficient regard for how well taxpayers' money is being spent. For example, farm price support programs, under the Food Security Act of 1985, are much too costly. I plan to continue pushing for the elimination of artificially high price supports, thereby reducing the need for export subsidies. In particular, I plan to propose amendments to the Act to modify the counterproductive sugar price support program that currently poses significant problems in the areas of trade policy, foreign policy, and agricultural policy. The importance of agricultural trade to the economic health of the farm sector and the Nation as a whole mandates increased reliance on free markets, not government largess.

The budget proposes certain reforms in the medicare program in order to achieve the savings agreed to in the Bipartisan Budget Agreement. First, as justified by the results of several independent studies, I propose to reduce the add-on payment for teaching hospitals under the prospective payment system (PPS) for indirect medical education from 7.70 percent to 4.05 percent, the best estimate of the added costs incurred historically by teaching hospitals. Second, I propose to limit medicare overhead payments for graduate medical education and make consistent varying secondary payor enforcement mechanisms. To reduce escalating supplementary medical insurance costs and help slow future increases in beneficiary premiums, I propose to limit payments for certain overpriced physician procedures, limit payments for durable medical equipment and supplies, and eliminate a loophole in the payment process for kidney dialysis. In total, these reforms would reduce spending for medicare by $1.2 billion from the level that would occur if current law were continued. Spending for the medicare program would still increase by 7 percent from 1988 to 1989.

Although the provision of needed legal services for those who cannot afford them is an important goal in our society, the current system earmarks a large portion of the funding to "National and State Support Centers" that have been criticized for political involvement. I urge Congress to disallow use of Federal funds for such "think tanks" and limit the use of funds to the *direct* assistance of the poor in need of legal aid.

The Government often continues programs at the Federal level that are no longer needed. This is the case with rural housing programs, the Economic Development Administration, urban mass transit discretionary grants, urban development action grants, sewage treatment, Small Business Administration direct loans, housing development action grants, the housing rehabilitation loan program, and economic development programs of the Tennessee Valley Authority. Efforts to reverse this situation have been undertaken by prior administrations as well as my own, but the limited results to date indicate the difficulty of curbing excessive government involvement in these areas.

Regulatory Relief.—For 7 years I have worked to reduce the excess burdens of government regulation for all Americans—working men and women, consumers, businesses, and State and local governments. As a result, various departments and agencies have reduced the scope and costs of Federal regulation. Federal approval of experimental drugs has been expedited, making them available to treat serious or life-threatening diseases when other treatments do not work. Excessive burdens on State and local governments are being lifted. Access to goods and services has been made easier, and at less cost. Federal reporting requirements on individuals and businesses have been eased, as well as the paperwork burden on those who wish to compete for contracts with the Federal Government. Under the leadership of the Presidential Task Force on Regulatory Relief, headed by the Vice President, the Administration will continue these and other efforts to lessen the burden of excessive government regulation.

As a case in point, my budget proposes termination of the Interstate Commerce Commission, contingent upon enactment of legislation that completes deregulation of the motor carrier industry. There is no justification for continued economic (as opposed to safety) regulation of surface transportation, and there is a substantial argument against it. As a result of economic deregulation of trucking and railroads, consumers have tens of billions of dollars each year, and the industry is healthier, more innovative, and better able to adapt to changing economic circumstances. This is no time to turn back the clock.

Privatization.—The government and the private sector should do what each does best. The Federal Government should not be involved in providing goods and services where private enterprise can do the jobs cheaper and/or better. In some cases, the fact that no private provider exists is a reflection of government policy to prohibit competition—as with first class mail service. In other cases, an absence of private providers reflects a government policy of providing large subsidies—as with uranium enrichment. Invariably, the taxpayer ends up paying more for less.

Accordingly, my budget proposes that a number of Federal enterprises be transferred back to the private sector, through public offerings or outright sales. Following our successful sale of Conrail and auctioning of $5 billion in selected loan portfolios, I am proposing the sale not only of the Naval Petroleum Reserves, but also of the Alaska Power Administration, the Federal Government's helium program, excess real property, and a further $12 billion in loan portfolios. In addition, I have proposed legislation to authorize a study of possible divestiture of the Southeastern Power Administration, and plan to study possible privatization of our uranium enrichment facilities, as well as ways of making the U.S. Postal

Service more efficient through greater reliance on the private sector. Such "privatization" efforts continue to be a high priority of this Administration, and I look forward to acting on the final recommendations of the Privatization Commission, which I established last September.

Privatization does not necessarily imply abrogation of government responsibility for these services. Rather, it recognizes that what matters is the service provided, not who provides it. Government has an inherent tendency to become too big, unwieldy, and inefficient; and to enter into unfair competition with the private sector.

The Federal Government should also depend more on the private sector to provide ancillary and support services for activities that remain in Federal hands. Therefore, I am proposing the development of a private mediating institution to reduce the backlog of cases before the U.S. Tax Court. I propose that the private sector be relied upon for booking functions for concessional food programs. I also encourage the complete privatization of wastewater treatment plants, certain mass transit projects, the Department of Agriculture's National Finance Center, and the Rural Telephone Bank.

In addition, our Administration plans to initiate privatization and commercialization efforts involving Federal prison industries, relying on a private space facility for microgravity research opportunities in the early 1990's, commercial cargo inspection, military commissaries, Coast Guard buoy maintenance, and the management of undeveloped Federal land. Moreover, my budget proposes that the work associated with certain Federal employment positions be reviewed for the feasibility of contracting their responsibilities out to the private sector as yet another way to increase productivity, reduce costs, and improve services.

One of the best ways to test the worth of a governmental program or a particular project is to shift some of the cost of that program or project to the direct beneficiaries. We have done that, for example, with water resources development projects. As a result, local sponsors and users choose to proceed only on the projects that are most important and most cost effective.

Management Improvements.—As we all know, the Federal Government has a major effect upon our daily lives through the direct delivery of services, the payment of financial assistance through various entitlement programs, the collection of taxes and fees, and the regulation of commercial enterprises. As the 21st century approaches, the Federal Government must adapt its role in our society to meet changing demands arising from changing needs and requirements. At the turn of the century, the U.S. population will exceed 268 million, with a greater proportion of elderly requiring more specialized services. The Nation will operate at a much faster pace as changes in technology and communication link the world's economies, trade, capital flows, and travel as never before.

I have asked the Office of Domestic Affairs and the Office of Management and Budget to work with the President's Council on Management

Improvement to conduct an in-depth review and recommend to me by this August what further adjustments in the Federal role should be made to prepare for the challenge of government in the 21st century. This summer I will receive their report, "Government of the Future." I also intend to complete the "Reform '88" management improvement program I started 6 years ago to overhaul the administrative, financial, and credit systems in our Federal Government; to implement productivity and quality plans in each agency; and to examine the needs of the Federal work force of the future. I want to leave a legacy of good management of today's programs, with plans in place to handle tomorrow's challenges.

Efforts to improve the management of the Federal Government must be continued. We have all heard stories of the horrible waste that occurs in the Federal Government. Some of it is obvious—like the billions of dollars in unneeded projects that were included in the thousand-page 1988 spending bill that was dropped on my desk last December. Some are not obvious—like the billion dollars in unnecessary interest expense the government paid, year after year, because it lacked a cash management system, or the billions of dollars lost annually for lack of a credit management process to ensure collection of the trillion dollars in loans owed the Federal Government.

In July 1980, I promised the American people: "I will not accept the excuse that the Federal Government has grown ... beyond the control of any President, Administration or Congress ... we are going to put an end to the notion that the American taxpayer exists to fund the Federal Government. The Federal Government exists to serve the American people ... I pledge my Administration will do that." I have delivered on that promise.

The first step was taken within months after my inauguration when I formed the President's Council on Integrity and Efficiency, composed of the agency Inspectors General. By the time I leave office, they will have delivered savings of over $110 billion in reduced waste, fraud, and abuse to the American people.

Then, in March 1982, I initiated the world's largest management improvement program with these words: "With Reform '88 we're going to streamline and reorganize the processes that control the money, information, personnel and property of the Federal bureaucracy." I told my Cabinet at that time that "we have six years to change what it took twenty or thirty to create—and we came to Washington to make changes!" I have followed up on that commitment. The President's Council on Management Improvement has overseen this effort, and is generating significant results.

These efforts are described in greater detail in my *Management Report,* which is being submitted concurrently. They can succeed only if all Federal managers and employees work together. Therefore, I propose in this budget a new approach to paying Federal employees who increase their productivity. I ask the Congress to modify the current system of virtually automatic "within-grade" pay increases for the roughly 40 percent of employees eligible each year to one that is based on employee performance. This will give Federal employees stronger incentives to improve service delivery and reduce costs to the taxpayer.

The Budget Process

As I have stressed on numerous occasions, the current budget process is clearly unworkable and desperately needs a drastic overhaul. Last year, as in the year before, the Congress did not complete action on a budget until well past the beginning of the fiscal year. The Congress missed every deadline it had set for itself just 9 months earlier. In the end, the Congress passed a year-long, 1,057-page omnibus $605 billion appropriations bill with an accompanying conference report of 1,053 pages and a reconciliation bill 1,186 pages long. Members of Congress had only 3 hours to consider all three items. Congress should not pass another massive continuing resolution—and as I said in the State of the Union address, if they do I will not sign it.

I am asking for a constitutional amendment that mandates a balanced budget and forces the Federal Government to live within its means. A constitutional amendment to balance the Federal budget—and a provision requiring a super-majority vote in the Congress to increase taxes—would impose some much-needed discipline on the congressional budget process. Ninety-nine percent of Americans live in States that require a balanced State budget, and a total of 32 States already have passed resolutions calling for a convention for the purpose of proposing a balanced budget amendment to the U.S. Constitution.

Also, I am asking the Congress for a line-item veto, so that my successors could reach into massive appropriation bills such as the last one, cut out the waste, and enforce budget discipline. Forty-three State Governors have a line-item veto; the President should have this power as well. As Governor of the State of California (1967-1975), I used the line-item veto 943 times. The California State legislature upheld each of these vetos, even though both Houses were controlled by the opposition party.

In addition, I propose the following further reforms to the budget process:

(1) *Joint budget resolution.* The budget process has so degenerated in recent years that the presidential budget is routinely discarded and the congressional budget resolution is regularly disregarded. As a remedy, I propose that henceforth the Congress and the Executive collaborate on a joint resolution that sets out spending priorities within the receipts available. The requirement of a Presidential signature would force both branches of government to resolve policy differences before appropriations measures must be formulated. The budget process could be further improved by including in the budget law allocations by committee as well as by budget function.

(2) *Individual transmittal of appropriation bills.* The current practice of transmitting full-year continuing resolutions skirts appropriations com-

mittee-subcommittee jurisdictions. More importantly, it does not permit the Legislative and Executive branches to exercise proper scrutiny of Federal spending. Therefore, I propose a requirement that appropriations bills be transmitted individually to the President.

(3) *Strict observance of allocations.* During the 1980s, an unacceptable budget practice evolved within the Congress of disregarding congressionally approved function allocations. Funds regularly were shifted from defense or international affairs to domestic spending. I strongly urge that each fiscal year separate national security and domestic allocations be made and enforced through a point of order provision in the Budget Act.

(4) *Enhanced rescission authority.* Under current law, the President may propose rescissions of budget authority, but both Houses of Congress must act "favorably" for the rescission to take effect. In 1987, not a single rescission was enacted, or even voted on, before expiration of the 45-day deadline. I propose a change of law that would require the Congress to vote "up or down" on any presidentially proposed rescission, thereby preventing the Congress from ducking the issue by simply ignoring the proposed rescission and avoiding a recorded vote.

(5) *Biennial budgeting.* The current budget process consumes too much time and energy. A 2-year budget cycle offers several advantages—among them, a reduction in repetitive annual budget tasks, more time for consideration of key spending decisions in reconciliation, and less scope for gimmicks such as shifting spending from one year to the next. I call on the Congress to adopt biennial budgeting.

(6) *Truth in Federal spending.* As part of my Economic Bill of Rights, I will shortly transmit legislation that will require any future legislation creating new Federal programs to be deficit-neutral. In addition to requiring the concurrent enactment of equal amounts of program reductions or revenue increases, my proposal would require that all future legislation and regulations be accompanied by financial impact statements, including the effect on State and local governments.

Adoption of these reforms should enable the Federal Government to make informed decisions in a deliberate fashion that fosters rational priorities. The American people deserve no less from their elected representatives.

Conclusion

Looking back over the past 7 years we can feel a sense of pride in our accomplishments. Important tasks remain, however. The large and stubbornly persistent budget deficit has been a major source of frustration. It threatens our prosperity and our hopes for lessening the burden on future generations.

Two years ago, the Legislative and Executive branches of government responded to this threat by enacting the G-R-H Act, which mandated gradual, orderly progress toward a balanced budget over the next several years. My budget achieves the 1989 target of the amended Act while preserving legitimate programs for the aged and needy, providing for adequate national security, devoting more resources to other high-priority activities, and doing so without raising taxes.

My budget also embodies the Bipartisan Budget Agreement reached last November. In presenting this budget, I am keeping my end of the bargain. I call upon the Congress to uphold its end—by ensuring that appropriations and other legislation are in full accord with the Agreement. By exercising this measure of restraint and self-discipline, we can secure great benefits for the Nation: a lower budget deficit, reduced demand on credit markets, more stable financial markets, a steadily declining trade deficit, and continued prosperity with non-inflationary growth. And, by reforming the budget process, the Congress can improve its decisionmaking and garner the thanks of a grateful public. Surely, these are small prices for what is at stake.

PAPAL ENCYCLICAL
ON SOCIAL CONCERNS
February 19, 1988

In his encyclical letter Sollicitudo Rei Socialis *("Social Concerns of the Church"), Pope John Paul II looked at global economic development with deep pessimism, condemning Marxism and capitalism with equal vigor. The leader of the Catholic church, issuing his 20,000-word teaching document in Rome on February 19, asserted that both systems were "in need of radical correction." He portrayed them as overwhelming the poor nations of the Third World economically, politically, and culturally.*

An encyclical is the highest form of papal teaching, and Sollicitudo Rei Socialis *was the seventh to be issued by John Paul since his election to the papacy in October 1978. This encyclical, as others, was addressed not only to Catholics throughout the world but also to "all people of good will." According to the Vatican, the words were the pope's own, although much of the research for the encyclical was gathered by others. It looked back to a more optimistic one that Pope Paul VI issued twenty years earlier. In that 1968 document,* Populorum Progressio, *translated into English as "On the Development of Peoples," Pope Paul described development as "the new name for peace." But times had changed in the intervening twenty years, declared the current pontiff, and not for the better. "The first negative observation to make," wrote John Paul II, "is the persistence and often the widening gap between the areas of the so-called developed North and the developing South."*

"This is one of the reasons," he said, "why the church's social doctrine adopts a critical attitude toward both liberal capitalism and Marxist collectivism." The have-not countries of the South, the pope continued,

become caught up in the political, economic, and cultural rivalry between the East and West "instead of becoming autonomous nations concerned with their own progress toward a just sharing in the goods and services meant for all."

He did not offer a plan of action, saying that the church's social doctrine was not a "third way" between capitalism and collectivism. "Its main aim," he said, "is to interpret these realities, determine their conformity with or divergence from the lines of the Gospel teaching on man and his vocation . . . and to guide Christian behavior." Nevertheless, the pope did offer specific recommendations for changing the international systems of trade and finance, and he called for a better means of enabling poor countries to acquire needed technology.

Before assuming the papacy, John Paul II had led the church in Poland, as Cardinal Wojtyla. In his native Poland, as in Rome, he was perceived as strongly anticommunist. Thus his condemnation of Marxism came as no surprise. However, the document surprised some Western commentators by its plague-upon-both-houses tenor. The Economist, *the London-based international magazine, commented that the pope's thesis about both Marxism and capitalism being "structures of sin" was "a little hard on capitalism." William Buckley, publisher of* National Review *magazine and a prominent American Catholic layman, said the pope had overlooked the "spectacular rise from poverty" of Japan, Taiwan, Hong Kong, Singapore, and countries in the West as they "encouraged the exercise of capitalism" in the postwar years.*

Following are excerpts from the papal encyclical "Social Concerns of the Church," issued by John Paul II on February 19, 1988:

[Parts I and II omitted]

III. Survey of the Contemporary World

In its own time the fundamental teaching of the encyclical [of Pope Paul VI] *Populorum Progressio* received great acclaim for its novel character. The social context in which we live today cannot be said to be completely identical to that of 20 years ago. . . . The first fact to note is that the hopes for development, at that time so lively, today appear very far from being realized. . . .

It cannot be said that these various religious, human, economic and technical initiatives have been in vain, for they have succeeded in achieving certain results. But in general, taking into account the various factors, one cannot deny that the present situation of the world, from the point of view of development, offers a rather negative impression.

For this reason, I wish to call attention to a number of general indicators, without excluding other specific ones. Without going into an analysis of figures and statistics, it is sufficient to face squarely the reality of an innumerable multitude of people—children, adults and the elderly—in other words, real and unique human persons who are suffering under the intolerable burden of poverty. There are many millions who are deprived of hope due to the fact that in many parts of the world their situation has noticeably worsened. . . .

The first negative observation to make is the persistence and often the widening of the gap between the areas of the so-called developed North and the developing South. This geographical terminology is only indicative, since one cannot ignore the fact that the frontiers of wealth and poverty intersect within the societies themselves, whether developed or developing. In fact, just as social inequalities down to the level of poverty exist in rich countries, so in parallel fashion in the less developed countries one often sees manifestations of selfishness and a flaunting of wealth which is as disconcerting as it is scandalous. . . .

We should add here that in today's world there are many other forms of poverty. For are there not certain privations or deprivations which deserve this name? The denial or the limitation of human rights—as for example the right to religious freedom, the right to share in the building of society, the freedom to organize and to form unions or to take initiatives in economic matters—do these not impoverish the human person as much as, if not more than, the deprivation of material goods? And is development which does not take into account the full affirmation of these rights really development on the human level?

In brief, modern underdevelopment is not only economic, but also cultural, political and simply human as was indicated 20 years ago by the encyclical *Populorum Progressio*. Hence at this point we have to ask ourselves if the sad reality of today might not be, at least in part, the result of a too narrow idea of development, that is, a mainly economic one. . . .

Responsibility for this deterioration is due to various causes. Notable among them are undoubtedly grave instances of omissions on the part of the developing nations themselves and especially on the part of those holding economic and political power. Nor can we pretend not to see the responsibility of the developed nations, which have the duty to help countries separated from the affluent world to which they themselves belong.

Moreover, one must denounce the existence of economic, financial and social mechanisms which, although they are manipulated by people, often function almost automatically, thus accentuating the situation of wealth for some and poverty for the rest. These mechanisms, which are maneuvered directly or indirectly by the more developed countries, by their very functioning favor the interests of the people manipulating them. But in the end they suffocate or condition the economies of the less-developed countries. Later on these mechanisms will have to be subjected to a careful analysis under the ethical-moral aspect. . . .

Among the specific signs of underdevelopment which increasingly affect the developed countries also, there are two in particular that reveal a tragic situation. The first is the housing crisis. . . .

The lack of housing is being experienced universally and is due in large measure to the growing phenomenon of urbanization. Even the most highly developed peoples present the sad spectacle of individuals and families literally struggling to survive without a roof over their heads or with a roof so inadequate as to constitute no roof at all.

The lack of housing, an extremely serious problem in itself, should be seen as a sign and summing up of a whole series of shortcomings, economic, social, cultural or simply human in nature. Given the extent of the problem, we should need little convincing of how far we are from an authentic development of peoples.

Another indicator common to the vast majority of nations is the phenomenon of unemployment and underemployment. . . . This phenomenon too, with its series of negative consequences for individuals and for society, ranging from humiliation to the loss of that self-respect which every man and woman should have, prompts us to question seriously the type of development which has been followed over the past 20 years. . . .

A third phenomenon, likewise characteristic of the most recent period even though it is not met with everywhere, is without doubt equally indicative of the interdependence between developed and less-developed countries. . . .

Circumstances having changed both within the debtor nations and in the international financial market, the instrument chosen to make a contribution to development has turned into a counterproductive mechanism. This is because the debtor nations, in order to service their debt, find themselves obliged to export the capital needed for improving or at least maintaining their standard of living. It is also because, for the same reason, they are unable to obtain new and equally essential financing.

Through this mechanism the means intended for the development of peoples has turned into a brake upon development instead, and indeed in some cases has even aggravated underdevelopment. . . .

Faced with a combination of factors which are undoubtedly complex, we cannot hope to achieve a comprehensive analysis here. However, we cannot ignore a striking fact about the political picture since World War II, a fact which has considerable impact on the forward movement of the development of peoples.

I am referring to the existence of two opposing blocs, commonly known as the East and the West. The reason for this description is not purely political but is also, as the expression goes, geopolitical. Each of the two blocs tends to assimilate or gather around it other countries or groups of countries, to different degrees of adherence or participation.

The opposition is first of all political, inasmuch as each bloc identifies itself with a system of organizing society and exercising power which presents itself as an alternative to the other. The political opposition, in turn, takes its origin from a deeper opposition, which is ideological in nature.

In the West there exists a system which is historically inspired by the principles of the liberal capitalism which developed with industrialization during the last century. In the East there exists a system inspired by the Marxist collectivism which sprang from an interpretation of the condition of the proletarian classes made in the light of a particular reading of history. Each of the two ideologies, on the basis of two very different visions of man and of his freedom and social role, has proposed and still promotes on the economic level antithetical forms of the organization of labor and of the structures of ownership, especially with regard to the so-called means of production.

It was inevitable that by developing antagonistic systems and centers of power, each with its own forms of propaganda and indoctrination, the ideological opposition should evolve into a growing military opposition and give rise to two blocs of armed forces, each suspicious and fearful of the other's domination. . . . This opposition is transferred to the developing countries themselves and thus helps to widen the gap already existing on the economic level between North and South and which results from the distance between the two worlds: the more-developed one and the less-developed one.

This is one of the reasons why the church's social doctrine adopts a critical attitude toward both liberal capitalism and Marxist collectivism. . . .

The developing countries, instead of becoming autonomous nations concerned with their own progress toward a just sharing in the goods and services meant for all, become parts of a machine, cogs on a gigantic wheel. This is often true also in the field of social communications, which, being run by centers mostly in the Northern Hemisphere, do not always give due consideration to the priorities and problems of such countries or respect their cultural makeup. They frequently impose a distorted vision of life and of man, and thus fail to respond to the demands of true development.

Each of the two blocs harbors in its own way a tendency toward imperialism, as it is usually called, or toward forms of neo-colonialism: an easy temptation to which they frequently succumb as history, including recent history, teaches.

It is this abnormal situation, the result of a war and of an unacceptably exaggerated concern for security, which deadens the impulse toward united cooperation by all for the common good of the human race, to the detriment especially of peaceful peoples who are impeded from their rightful access to the goods meant for all. . . .

When the West gives the impression of abandoning itself to forms of growing and selfish isolation and the East in its turn seems to ignore for questionable reasons its duty to cooperate in the task of alleviating human misery, then we are up against not only a betrayal of humanity's legitimate expectations—a betrayal that is a harbinger of unforeseeable consequences—but also a real desertion of a moral obligation. . . .

One cannot deny the existence, especially in the Southern Hemisphere, of a demographic problem which creates difficulties for development. One must immediately add that in the Northern Hemisphere the nature of this problem is reversed: Here the cause for concern is the drop in the birthrate, with repercussions on the aging of the population, unable even to renew itself biologically. In itself, this is a phenomenon capable of hindering development. Just as it is incorrect to say that such difficulties stem solely from demographic growth, neither is it proved that all demographic growth is incompatible with orderly development.

On the other hand, it is very alarming to see governments in many countries launching systematic campaigns against birth, contrary not only to the cultural and religious identity of the countries themselves but also contrary to the nature of true development. It often happens that these campaigns are the result of pressure and financing coming from abroad, and in some cases they are made a condition for the granting of financial and economic aid and assistance. In any event, there is an absolute lack of respect for the freedom of choice of the parties involved, men and women often subjected to intolerable pressures, including economic ones, in order to force them to submit to this new form of oppression. It is the poorest populations which suffer such mistreatment, and this sometimes leads to a tendency toward a form of racism or the promotion of certain equally racist forms of eugenics. . . .

This mainly negative overview of the actual situation of development in the contemporary world would be incomplete without a mention of the coexistence of positive aspects.

The first positive note is the full awareness among large numbers of men and women of their own dignity and of that of every human being. This awareness is expressed, for example, in the more lively concern that human rights should be respected, and in the more vigorous rejection of their violation. One sign of this is the number of recently established private associations, some worldwide in membership, almost all of them devoted to monitoring with great care and commendable objectivity what is happening internationally in this sensitive field.

At this level one must acknowledge the influence exercised by the Universal Declaration of Human Rights promulgated some 40 years ago by the United Nations. Its very existence and gradual acceptance by the international community are signs of a growing awareness. The same is to be said, still in the field of human rights, of other juridical instruments issued by the United Nations or other international organizations. . . .

. . . Today, perhaps more than in the past, people are realizing that they are linked together by a common destiny which is to be constructed together if catastrophe for all is to be avoided. From the depth of anguish, fear and escapist phenomena like drugs, typical of the contemporary world, the idea is slowly emerging that the good to which we are all called and the happiness to which we aspire cannot be obtained without an effort and commitment on the part of all, nobody excluded, and the consequent renouncing of personal selfishness.

Also to be mentioned here, as a sign of respect for life—despite all the temptations to destroy it by abortion and euthanasia—is a concomitant concern for peace, together with an awareness that peace is indivisible. It is either for all or for none. It demands an ever greater degree of rigorous respect for justice and consequently a fair distribution of the results of true development. . . .

IV. Authentic Human Development

The examination which the encyclical invites us to make of the contemporary world leads us to note in the first place that development is not a straightforward process, as it were automatic and in itself limitless, as though, given certain conditions, the human race were able to progress rapidly toward an undefined perfection of some kind.

Such an idea—linked to a notion of "progress" with philosophical connotations deriving from the Enlightenment rather than to the notion of "development" which is used in a specifically economic and social sense—now seems to be seriously called into doubt, particularly since the tragic experience of the two world wars, the planned and partly achieved destruction of whole peoples and the looming atomic peril. A naive mechanistic optimism has been replaced by a well-founded anxiety for the fate of humanity.

At the same time, however, the "economic" concept itself, linked to the world *development,* has entered into crisis. In fact there is a better understanding today that the mere accumulation of goods and services, even for the benefit of the majority, is not enough for the realization of human happiness. . . .

All of us experience firsthand the sad effects of this blind submission to pure consumerism: in the first place a crass materialism, and at the same time a radical dissatisfaction because one quickly learns—unless one is shielded from the flood of publicity and ceaseless and tempting offers of products—that the more one possesses the more one wants, while deeper aspirations remain unsatisfied and perhaps even stifled. . . .

The danger of the misuse of material goods and the appearance of artificial needs should in no way hinder the regard we have for the new goods and resources placed at our disposal and the use we make of them. On the contrary, we must see them as a gift from God and as a response to the human vocation, which is fully realized in Christ. . . .

The story of the human race described by Sacred Scripture is, even after the fall into sin, a story of constant achievements which, although always called into question and threatened by sin, are nonetheless repeated, increased and extended in response to the divine vocation given from the beginning to man and to woman and inscribed in the image which they received.

It is logical to conclude, at least on the part of those who believe in the word of God, that today's "development" is to be seen as a moment in the story which began at creation, a story which is constantly endangered by reason of infidelity to the Creator's will and especially by the temptation to idolatry. But this "development" fundamentally corresponds to the first premises. Anyone wishing to renounce the difficult yet noble task of improving the lot of man in his totality, and of all people, with the excuse that the struggle is difficult and that constant effort is required, or simply because of the experience of defeat and the need to begin again, that person would be betraying the will of God, the creator.

Furthermore, the concept of faith makes quite clear the reasons which impel the church to concern herself with the problems of development, to consider them a duty of her pastoral ministry and to urge all to think about the nature and characteristics of authentic human development. Through her commitment she desires, on the one hand, to place herself at the service of the divine plan which is meant to order all things to the fullness which dwells in Christ and which he communicated to his body; and on the other hand she desires to respond to her fundamental vocation of being a "sacrament," that is to say, "a sign and instrument of intimate union with God and of the unity of the whole human race...."

Thus, part of the teaching and most ancient practice of the church is her conviction that she is obliged by her vocation—she herself, her ministers and each of her members—to relieve the misery of the suffering, both far and near, not only out of her "abundance" but also out of her "necessities." Faced by cases of need, one cannot ignore them in favor of superfluous church ornaments and costly furnishings for divine worship; on the contrary it could be obligatory to sell these goods in order to provide food, drink, clothing and shelter for those who lack these things. As has been already noted, here we are shown a "hierarchy of values"—in the framework of the right to property—between "having" and "being," especially when the "having" of a few can be to the detriment of the "being" of many others....

V. A Theological Reading of Modern Problems

... "Sin" and "structures of sin" are categories which are seldom applied to the situation of the contemporary world. However, one cannot easily gain a profound understanding of the reality that confronts us unless we give a name to the root of the evils which afflict us....

One can certainly speak of "selfishness" and of "shortsightedness," of "mistaken political calculations" and "imprudent economic decisions." And in each of these evaluations one hears an echo of an ethical and moral nature. Man's condition is such that a more profound analysis of individuals' actions and omissions cannot be achieved without implying, in one way or another, judgments or references of an ethical nature.

This evaluation is in itself positive, especially if it is completely consistent and if it is based on faith in God and on his law, which commands what is good and forbids evil....

This general analysis, which is religious in nature, can be supplemented by a number of particular considerations to demonstrate that among the actions and attitudes opposed to the will of God, the good of neighbor and the "structures" created by them, two are very typical: on the one hand, the all-consuming desire for profit, and on the other, the thirst for power, with the intention of imposing one's will upon others. In order to characterize better each of these attitudes, one can add the expression: "at any price." In other words, we are faced with the absolutizing of human attitudes with all its possible consequences.

Since these attitudes can exist independently of each other, they can be separated; however, in today's world both are indissolubly united, with one or the other predominating.

Obviously, not only individuals fall victim to this double attitude of sin; nations and blocs can do so too. And this favors even more the introduction of the "structures of sin" of which I have spoken. If certain forms of modern "imperialism" were considered in the light of these moral criteria, we would see that hidden behind certain decisions, apparently inspired only by economics or politics, are real forms of idolatry: of money, ideology, class, technology.

I have wished to introduce this type of analysis above all in order to point out the true nature of the evil which faces us with respect to the development of peoples: It is a question of a moral evil, the fruit of many sins which lead to "structures of sin." To diagnose the evil in this way is to identify precisely, on the level of human conduct, the path to be followed in order to overcome it. . . .

In the context of these reflections, the decision to set out or to continue the journey involves, above all, a moral value which men and women of faith recognize as a demand of God's will, the only true foundation of an absolutely binding ethic.

One would hope that also men and women without an explicit faith would be convinced that the obstacles to integral development are not only economic but rest on more profound attitudes which human beings can make into absolute values. . . .

For Christians, as for all who recognize the precise theological meaning of the word *sin*, a change of behavior or mentality or mode of existence is called *conversion*, to use the language of the Bible (cf. Mk. 13:3, 5; Is. 30:15). This conversion specifically entails a relationship to God, to the sin committed, to its consequences and hence to one's neighbor, either an individual or a community. . . .

VI. Some Particular Guidelines

The church does not have technical solutions to offer for the problem of underdevelopment as such, as Pope Paul VI already affirmed in his encyclical. For the church does not propose economic and political systems or programs nor does she show preference for one or the other, provided that human dignity is properly respected and promoted, and provided she herself is allowed the room she needs to exercise her ministry in the world.

But the church is an "expert in humanity," and this leads her necessarily to extend her religious mission to the various fields in which men and women expend their efforts in search of the always relative happiness which is possible in this world, in line with their dignity as persons....

It will thus be seen at once that the questions facing us are above all moral questions; and that neither the analysis of the problem of development as such nor the means to overcome the present difficulties can ignore this essential dimension.

The church's social doctrine is not a "third way" between liberal capitalism and Marxist collectivism nor even a possible alternative to other solutions less radically opposed to one another: Rather, it constitutes a category of its own. Nor is it an ideology, but rather the accurate formulation of the results of a careful reflection on the complex realities of human existence, in society and in the international order, in the light of faith and of the church's tradition. Its main aim is to interpret these realities, determining their conformity with or divergence from the lines of the Gospel teaching on man and his vocation, a vocation which is at once earthly and transcendent; its aim is thus to guide Christian behavior. It therefore belongs to the field, not of ideology, but of theology and particularly of moral theology....

The motivating concern for the poor—who are, in the very meaningful term, "the Lord's poor"—must be translated at all levels into concrete actions, until it decisively attains a series of necessary reforms. Each local situation will show what reforms are most urgent and how they can be achieved. But those demanded by the situation of international imbalance, as already described, must not be forgotten....

VII. Conclusion

... I wish to appeal with simplicity and humility to everyone, to all men and women without exception. I wish to ask them to be convinced of the seriousness of the present moment and of each one's individual responsibility, and to implement—by the way they live as individuals and as families, by the use of their resources, by their civic activity, by contributing to economic and political decisions and by personal commitment to national and international undertakings—the measures inspired by solidarity and love of preference for the poor. This is what is demanded by the present moment and above all by the very dignity of the human person, the indestructible image of God the Creator, which is identical in each one of us....

The church well knows that no temporal achievement is to be identified with the kingdom of God, but that all such achievements simply reflect and in a sense anticipate the glory of the kingdom, the kingdom which we await at the end of history when the Lord will come again. But that expectation can never be an excuse for lack of concern for people in their concrete personal situations and in their social, national and international life, since the former is conditioned by the latter, especially today.

COURT ON PRESS FREEDOM
February 24, 1988

The Supreme Court, in an 8-0 ruling on February 24, greatly extended free-speech rights in the realm of satire and criticism. The unanimous decision in Hustler Magazine, Inc., et al. v. Falwell reversed a lower court's $200,000 award to the Rev. Jerry Falwell for "emotional distress" resulting from a parody of him that appeared in the magazine. Falwell, a nationally prominent television evangelist and founder of the politically conservative Moral Majority organization, was portrayed as an alcoholic who committed incest with his mother in an outhouse. Even "outrageous" and offensive satire of public figures merited First Amendment protection, the unanimous Court declared in a sweeping opinion written by Chief Justice William H. Rehnquist.

The decision drew praise from journalists and civil libertarians, who saw it providing protection especially for editorial cartoonists, commentators, and others who employ caricature in drawings or the printed word. Never before in cases before the Supreme Court had the ideologically conservative chief justice so emphatically championed First Amendment protections. For a decade or more, many of the Court's decisions had narrowed rather than expanded those protections, and Rehnquist often voted for the narrower view. In a 1986 libel case that handed the news media an important victory, Rehnquist joined in the dissent. In that case, Philadelphia Newspapers v. Hepps, the Court's majority held that private persons who sue for libel must prove the challenged information false before they can recover damages. In so ruling, it overturned a Pennsylvania law placing the burden of proving the truth of the information with *the defendant.* (Court on media libel of private figures, Historic Documents of 1986, p. 355)

First Amendment advocates considered the ruling a victory that reinforced and built upon an earlier Court's landmark libel ruling. That was the 1964 case of New York Times v. Sullivan. *A Court then led by Chief Justice Earl Warren established the so-called* Sullivan *standard. For a public figure to be libeled, according to that standard, the statement about him or her must be not only false but also made with "actual malice"—with knowledge of its falsity or in reckless disregard of the truth.*

Falwell expressed his displeasure at the Court's ruling in his case, saying that "no sleaze merchant like [Hustler publisher and codefendant] Larry Flynt should be able to use the First Amendment as an excuse for maliciously and dishonestly attacking public figures." While saying that he respected the Court's "deep concern . . . for the sacredness of the First Amendment," Falwell contended that the decision "has given the green light to Larry Flynt and his ilk to print what they wish about any public figure at any time with no fear of reprisal."

The Hustler Case

Hustler's *portrayal of Falwell appeared in the magazine's November 1983 issue in a parody of Campari Liqueur advertisements. Typically, such ads featured prominent persons discussing their "first time"—which turned out to be the first time they drank Campari.* Hustler *pictured Falwell in a bogus Campari ad, which included his fictional responses to interview questions. In small print at the bottom of the ad was the line, "ad parody—not to be taken seriously." Falwell was not amused and sued Flynt and his magazine for invasion of privacy, libel, and "intentional infliction of emotional distress." The first charge was disallowed when the case went to trial in federal district court in Virginia, and the jury held he had not been libeled because the parody could not "reasonably be understood as describing actual facts" about him or actual events. However, it awarded Falwell damages for "emotional distress" under a separate tort law.*

On appeal, a divided federal appeals court at Richmond upheld the award, rejecting Flynt's argument that the trial court had erred by not forcing Falwell to prove "actual malice" in making the emotional-distress award. The Supreme Court accepted the case for review, and oral arguments followed on December 2, 1987. Flynt's attorney, Alton F. Isaacman, presented the case to the eight justices (Justice Anthony M. Kennedy had not yet joined the Court and thus did not vote in the decision) as more than a dispute between Hustler *and Falwell. He said its outcome would greatly affect the country's tradition of satirical commentary. Falwell's counsel, Norman Roy Grutman, said the satire was so outrageous that no civilized person reasonably could be expected to bear it, and thus the parody should be subject to legal remedies.*

In his formal opinion, Chief Justice Rehnquist said that if a "principled standard" could be devised separating the "outrageous" from other satirical material that abets a "robust" exchange in the marketplace of ideas, "public discourse would probably suffer no harm." But, he added, "we doubt that there is any such standard, and we are quite sure that the pejorative description 'outrageous' does not supply one."

Then, saying that the Sullivan *standard of "actual malice" should have been applied, the Court overturned the jury's award to Falwell. The chief justice said he and his colleagues were not merely making a "blind application" of the* Sullivan *standard, but, rather, it was "our considered judgment" that the freedoms protected by the First Amendment needed "breathing space." Justice Byron R. White, in a separate concurring opinion, disagreed about the relevance of* New York Times v. Sullivan *to this case. "But I agree with the Court that the [lower court's] ... judgment cannot be squared with the First Amendment."*

Following are excerpts from the Supreme Court's opinion, February 24, 1988, on Hustler Magazine, Inc., et al. v. Falwell, *ruling that satire—even if "outrageous"—enjoys First Amendment protection; and from the concurrence of Justice Byron R. White:*

No. 86-1278

Hustler Magazine and Larry C. Flynt, Petitioners *v.* Jerry Falwell	On writ of certiorari to the United States Court of Appeals for the Fourth Circuit

[February 24, 1988]

CHIEF JUSTICE REHNQUIST delivered the opinion of the Court.

Petitioner Hustler Magazine, Inc., is a magazine of nationwide circulation. Respondent Jerry Falwell, a nationally known minister who has been active as a commentator on politics and public affairs, sued petitioner and its publisher, petitioner Larry Flynt, to recover damages for invasion of privacy, libel, and intentional infliction of emotional distress. The District Court directed a verdict against respondent on the privacy claim, and submitted the other two claims to a jury. The jury found for petitioners on the defamation claim, but found for respondent on the claim for intentional infliction of emotional distress and awarded damages. We now consider whether this award is consistent with the First and Fourteenth Amendments of the United States Constitution.

The inside front cover of the November 1983 issue of Hustler Magazine featured a "parody" of an advertisement for Campari Liqueur that contained the name and picture of respondent and was entitled "Jerry Falwell talks about his first time." This parody was modeled after actual Campari ads that included interviews with various celebrities about their "first times." Although it was apparent by the end of each interview that this meant the first time they sampled Campari, the ads clearly played on the sexual double entendre of the general subject of "first times." Copying the form and layout of these Campari ads, Hustler's editors chose respondent as the featured celebrity and drafted an alleged "interview" with him in which he stated that his "first time" was during a drunken incestuous rendezvous with his mother in an outhouse. The Hustler parody portrays respondent and his mother as drunk and immoral, and suggests that respondent is a hypocrite who preaches only when he is drunk. In small print at the bottom of the page, the ad contains the disclaimer, "ad parody—not to be taken seriously." The magazine's table of contents also lists the ad as "Fiction; Ad and Personality Parody."

Soon after the November issue of Hustler became available to the public, respondent brought this diversity action in the United States District Court for the Western District of Virginia against Hustler Magazine, Inc., Larry C. Flynt, and Flynt Distributing Co. Respondent stated in his complaint that publication of the ad parody in Hustler entitled him to recover damages for libel, invasion of privacy, and intentional infliction of emotional distress. The case proceeded to trial. At the close of the evidence, the District Court granted a directed verdict for petitioners on the invasion of privacy claim. The jury then found against respondent on the libel claim, specifically finding that the ad parody could not "reasonably be understood as describing actual facts about [respondent] or actual events in which [he] participated." The jury ruled for respondent on the intentional infliction of emotional distress claim, however, and stated that he should be awarded $100,000 in compensatory damages, as well as $50,000 each in punitive damages from petitioners. Petitioners' motion for judgment notwithstanding the verdict was denied.

On appeal, the United States Court of Appeals for the Fourth Circuit affirmed the judgment against petitioners. The court rejected petitioners' argument that the "actual malice" standard of *New York Times Co.* v. *Sullivan* must be met before respondent can recover for emotional distress. The court agreed that because respondent is concededly a public figure, petitioners are "entitled to the same level of first amendment protection in the claim for intentional infliction of emotional distress that they received in [respondent's] claim for libel." But this does not mean that a literal application of the actual malice rule is appropriate in the context of an emotional distress claim. In the court's view, the *New York Times* decision emphasized the constitutional importance not of the falsity of the statement or the defendant's disregard for the truth, but of the heightened level of culpability embodied in the requirement of "knowing ... or reckless" conduct. Here, the *New York Times* standard is satisfied by the state-law requirement, and the jury's finding, that the defendants have acted intentionally or recklessly. The Court of Appeals then went on to reject the contention that because the jury found that the ad parody did not describe actual facts about respondent, the ad was an opinion that is protected by the First Amendment. As the court put it, this was "irrelevant," as the issue is "whether [the ad's] publication was sufficiently outrageous to constitute intentional infliction of emotional distress." Petitioners then filed a petition for rehearing en banc, but this was denied by a divided court. Given the importance of the constitutional issues involved, we granted certiorari.

This case presents us with a novel question involving First Amendment limitations upon a State's authority to protect its citizens from the intentional infliction of emotional distress. We must decide whether a public figure may recover damages for emotional harm caused by the publication of an ad parody offensive to him, and doubtless gross and repugnant in the eyes of most. Respondent would have us find that a State's interest in protecting public figures from emotional distress is sufficient to deny First Amendment protection to speech that is patently offensive and is intended to inflict emotional injury, even when that speech could not reasonably have been interpreted as stating actual facts about the public figure involved. This we decline to do.

At the heart of the First Amendment is the recognition of the fundamental importance of the free flow of ideas and opinions on matters of public interest and concern. "[T]he freedom to speak one's mind is not only an aspect of individual liberty—and thus a good unto itself—but also is essential to the common quest for truth and the vitality of society as a whole." *Bose Corp.* v. *Consumers Union of United States, Inc.* (1984). We have therefore been particularly vigilant to ensure that individual expressions of ideas remain free from governmentally imposed sanctions. The First Amendment recognizes no such thing as a "false" idea. *Gertz* v. *Robert Welch, Inc.* (1974). As Justice Holmes wrote [in dissent in *Abrams* v. *United States* (1919)], ... "the best test of truth is the power of the thought to get itself accepted in the competition of the market. ..."

The sort of robust political debate encouraged by the First Amendment is bound to produce speech that is critical of those who hold public office or those public figures who are "intimately involved in the resolution of important public questions or, by reason of their fame, shape events in areas of concern to society at large." *Associated Press* v. *Walker,* decided with *Curtis Publishing Co.* v. *Butts* (1967). Justice Frankfurter put it succinctly in *Baumgartner* v. *United States* (1944), when he said that "[o]ne of the prerogatives of American citizenship is the right to criticize public men and measures." Such criticism, inevitably, will not always be reasoned or moderate. ...

Of course, this does not mean that *any* speech about a public figure is immune from sanction in the form of damages. Since *New York Times Co.* v. *Sullivan*, . . . we have consistently ruled that a public figure may hold a speaker liable for the damage to reputation caused by the publication of a defamatory falsehood, but only if the statement was made "with knowledge that it was false or with reckless disregard of whether it was false or not." . . . But even though falsehoods have little value in and of themselves, they are "nevertheless inevitable in free debate," and a rule that would impose strict liability on a publisher for false factual assertions would have an undoubted "chilling" effect on speech relating to public figures that does have constitutional value. "Freedoms of expression require 'breathing space.'" *Philadelphia Newspapers, Inc.* v. *Hepps* (1986). This breathing space is provided by a constitutional rule that allows public figures to recover for libel or defamation only when they can prove *both* that the statement was false and that the statement was made with the requisite level of culpability.

Respondent argues, however, that a different standard should apply in this case because here the State seeks to prevent not reputational damage, but the severe emotional distress suffered by the person who is the subject of an offensive publication. . . . In respondent's view, and in the view of the Court of Appeals, so long as the utterance was intended to inflict emotional distress, was outrageous, and did in fact inflict serious emotional distress, it is of no constitutional import whether the statement was a fact or an opinion, or whether it was true or false. It is the intent to cause injury that is the gravamen of the tort, and the State's interest in preventing emotional harm simply outweighs whatever interest a speaker may have in speech of this type.

Generally speaking the law does not regard the intent to inflict emotional distress as one which should receive much solicitude, and it is quite understandable that most if not all jurisdictions have chosen to make it civilly culpable where the conduct in question is sufficiently "outrageous." But in the world of debate about public affairs, many things done with motives that are less than admirable are protected by the First Amendment. In *Garrison* v. *Louisiana* (1964), we held that even when a speaker or writer is motivated by hatred or ill-will his expression was protected by the First Amendment:

> "Debate on public issues will not be uninhibited if the speaker must run the risk that it will be proved in court that he spoke out of hatred; even if he did speak out of hatred, utterances honestly believed contribute to the free interchange of ideas and the ascertainment of truth."

Thus while such a bad motive may be deemed controlling for purposes of tort liability in other areas of the law, we think the First Amendment prohibits such a result in the area of public debate about public figures.

Were we to hold otherwise, there can be little doubt that political cartoonists and satirists would be subjected to damages awards without any showing that their work falsely defamed its subject. . . . The appeal of the political cartoon or caricature is often based on exploration of unfortunate physical traits or politically embarrassing events—an exploration often calculated to injure the feelings of the subject of the portrayal. The art of the cartoonist is often not reasoned or evenhanded, but slashing and one-sided. . . .

Despite their sometimes caustic nature, from the early cartoon portraying George Washington as an ass down to the present day, graphic depictions and satirical cartoons have played a prominent role in public and political debate. . . . Lincoln's tall, gangling posture, Teddy Roosevelt's glasses and teeth, and Franklin D. Roosevelt's jutting jaw and cigarette holder have been memorialized by political cartoons with an effect that could not have been obtained by the photographer or the portrait artist. From the viewpoint of history it is clear that our political discourse would have been considerably poorer without them.

Respondent contends, however, that the caricature in question here was so "outrageous" as to distinguish it from more traditional political cartoons. There is no doubt that the caricature of respondent and his mother published in Hustler is at best a distant cousin of the political cartoons described above, and a rather poor relation at that. If it were possible by laying down a principled standard to separate the one from the other, public discourse would probably suffer little or no harm. But we doubt that there is any such standard, and we are quite sure that the pejorative description "outrageous" does not supply one. "Outrageousness" in the area of political and social discourse has an inherent subjectiveness about it which would allow a jury to impose liability on the basis of the jurors' tastes or views, or perhaps on the basis of their dislike of a particular expression. An "outrageousness" standard thus runs afoul of our longstanding refusal to allow damages to be awarded because the speech in question may have an adverse emotional impact on the audience. . . .

Admittedly, these oft-repeated First Amendment principles, like other principles, are subject to limitations. We recognized in *Pacifica Foundation,* that speech that is " 'vulgar,' 'offensive,' and 'shocking,' " is "not entitled to absolute constitutional protection under all circumstances." In *Chaplinsky* v. *New Hampshire* (1942), we held that a state could lawfully punish an individual for the use of insulting " 'fighting' words—those which by their very utterance inflict injury or tend to incite an immediate breach of the peace." These limitations are but recognition of the observation in *Dun & Bradstreet, Inc.* v. *Greenmoss Builders, Inc.* (1985), that this Court has "long recognized that not all speech is of equal First Amendment importance." But the sort of expression involved in this case does not seem to us to be governed by any exception to the general First Amendment principles stated above.

We conclude that public figures and public officials may not recover for the tort of intentional infliction of emotional distress by reason of publications such as the one here at issue without showing in addition that the publication contains a false statement of fact which was made with "actual malice," *i.e.*, with knowledge that the statement was false or with reckless disregard as to whether or not it was true. This is not merely a "blind application" of the *New York Times* standard, ... it reflects our considered judgment that such a standard is necessary to give adequate "breathing space" to the freedoms protected by the First Amendment.

Here it is clear that respondent Falwell is a "public figure" for purposes of First Amendment law. The jury found against respondent on his libel claim when it decided that the Hustler ad parody could not "reasonably be understood as describing actual facts about [respondent] or actual events in which [he] participated." The Court of Appeals interpreted the jury's finding to be that the ad parody "was not reasonably believable," and in accordance with our custom we accept this finding. Respondent is thus relegated to his claim for damages awarded by the jury for the intentional infliction of emotional distress by "outrageous" conduct. But for reasons heretofore stated this claim cannot, consistently with the First Amendment, form a basis for the award of damages when the conduct in question is the publication of a caricature such as the ad parody involved here. The judgment of the Court of Appeals is accordingly

Reversed.

JUSTICE KENNEDY took no part in the consideration or decision of this case.

JUSTICE WHITE, concurring in the judgment.

As I see it, the decision in *New York Times* v. *Sullivan* (1964) has little to do with this case, for here the jury found that the ad contained no assertion of fact. But I agree with the Court that the judgment below, which penalized the publication of the parody, cannot be squared with the First Amendment.

March

Kerner Report Update 185

Carnegie Report on Urban Schools 195

Scientists' Report on Ozone Depletion 221

Report on Privatization 229

Central American Cease-Fire 241

KERNER REPORT UPDATE
March 1, 1988

In 1968 the Kerner Commission issued its widely quoted report, warning: "Our nation is moving toward two societies, one black, one white—separate and unequal." That dire prediction is "coming true," said another report released exactly twenty years later and titled "The Kerner Report Updated." It was issued March 1 by the "citizen-organized" 1988 Commission on the Cities.

The commission detected in America's central cities "quiet riots" of unemployment, poverty, social disorganization, segregation, family disintegration, housing and school disintegration, and crime among blacks and Hispanics. These "quiet riots," the commission said, "are even more destructive to human life than the violent riots of twenty years ago."

In the summer of 1967, as racially inspired riots occurred in one city after another, President Lyndon B. Johnson appointed the National Advisory Commission on Civil Disorders to investigate the source of the unrest and report its findings to the nation. His group of appointees soon became known as the Kerner Commission, assuming the name of its chairman, Gov. Otto Kerner of Illinois. The following March 1 the commission made its report, expressing its central conclusion in the quotation above.

The concern that this prophecy was being fulfilled was expressed in 1988 not only by the Commission on the Cities but also by the National Urban League and the Commission on Minority Participation in Education and American Life. All three groups issued reports contending that racial progress had been stalled during Ronald Reagan's presidency, and they urged that it should be pushed forward again.

The Kerner report "update" was based on the findings of fourteen urban affairs specialists and the eight-member Commission on the Cities, led by former senator Fred R. Harris, D-Okla., who had been a member of the Kerner Commission, and Roger Wilkins, a civil rights leader. The findings were presented at a conference in Racine, Wisconsin, sponsored by the Institute for Public Policy at the University of New Mexico and the Johnson Foundation.

Income gaps were widening between rich and poor and between whites and minorities, said the follow-up report. It traced the development of "a large and growing underclass" in America—principally inner-city blacks and Hispanics—to economic trends that caused job losses among blue-collar workers in central cities and to cuts in government programs such as education, housing, job training, and affirmative action.

Political Gains Noted

The Commission on the Cities noted that minorities had made legal and political gains, such as the rise in the number of elected black officials from 200 in 1965 to 6,500 in 1986. It also noted the growth of the black middle class and of minority "inroads" into the media, law enforcement, business, and the professions. But the commission contended that such progress has slowed.

The movement of middle-class blacks out of the inner city left the ghetto poor even more concentrated and isolated than twenty years earlier, the report said. Wilkins observed: "We've done the easy part—we have made opportunity for the blacks for whom it was easy to provide opportunities. We haven't come close to dealing with the problems of the most burdened legatees of our racist past, the poor and the unemployed." To address these problems, the report proposed an agenda for jobs, welfare, desegregation, affirmative action, health care, and education.

Other Reports

The National Urban League, in its ninety-page report on "Black Americans and Public Policy," saw a "momentous crossroad" for black America as the nation decides on policy directions in the post-Reagan era. The report included essays on civil rights and social justice, employment and training, education, welfare reform, and black economic development.

In presenting the report at a news conference on May 5, Urban League President John Jacob urged blacks to take advantage of the election year to bring social problems to "center stage."

The Commission on Minority Participation in Education and American Life said in a separate report, "America is moving backward—not forward—in its efforts to achieve full participation of minority citizens in the life and prosperity of the nation." Established by the American Council on Education and the Education Commission of the States, and funded by the Ford Foundation, the commission on May 23 released a report entitled "One-Third of a Nation"—echoing President Franklin D. Roosevelt's observation during the 1930s Depression that one-third of the nation was "ill-housed, ill-clad, and ill-nourished." The report said that by the year 2000 one-third of all school-age children in America will be members of minority groups.

Frank H. T. Rhodes, president of Cornell University, was chairman of the thirty-seven-member panel. Former presidents Gerald R. Ford and Jimmy Carter served as honorary cochairmen. Two commission members, John Ashcroft, Republican governor of Missouri, and former secretary of state William P. Rogers, refused to sign the report. They said it focused too heavily on problems, rather than achievements, in minority status.

All three reports reflected a concern that, in the words of the 1988 Commission on the Cities, "because we made progress for a time, most Americans—as well as American policymakers—likely think that we are still making progress or that most inequalities have disappeared. This is not true." The purpose of the "update" report, therefore, was to "bring the problems of race, unemployment, and poverty back into the public agenda."

> *Following is the text, except for the summary, of "The Kerner Report Updated: Race and Poverty in the United States Today," issued March 1, 1988, by the 1988 Commission on the Cities:*

Poverty Is Worse and More Persistent

For a time following the Kerner Report, America made progress on all fronts—from the late 1960s through the mid-1970s. Then came a series of severe economic shocks that hit the most vulnerable hardest. Poverty is worse now for black Americans, Hispanic Americans, American Indians, and other minorities. But not just for them. The rise in unemployment and poverty has cut across racial and ethnic lines—and affects both blacks and other minorities and whites. (More whites than minority people are poor.)

Severe Economic Shocks

There were a series of recessions—most often precipitated or accentuated by a restrictive monetary policy and high interest rates—culminating in an economic crisis as bad as any since the 1930s.

The closing of manufacturing plants and the removal of blue-collar jobs to the suburbs, as well as the loss of blue-collar jobs altogether—trends the Kerner Report had called attention to—accelerated. These were the very jobs upon which central city residents had been most dependent.

The movement of the unemployment rates through the last twenty years have [sic] tracked the poverty rates very closely.

Fast-food and other retail service jobs replaced some of this lost employment, but at much lower pay. The higher-pay new service jobs which came to the cities—accounting, finance, professional, and others— were those least available to the workers left in the inner cities.

Efforts to break unions were successful. Wage "givebacks" were common. The federal minimum wage, which had been raised four times between 1978 and 1981 (during which time, employment rose nine percent), was not raised again after 1981.

Poverty increased. Census figures show that in 1986, 32.4 million Americans were poor (compared with 24.1 million in 1969). This included about 22 million whites, nearly 9 million blacks, and about 5 million Hispanics.

In 1986, according to the Census, two million Americans were poor even though they were working full-time and year-round—52 percent more than in 1975, 22 percent more than in 1980. Another 6.9 million people were working part-time, or full-time for a part of the year, and still could not earn enough to get above the poverty line.

From 1980 through June of last year, average weekly earnings increased from $235 to $305, but, adjusted for inflation, this represented, in fact, a drop in real wages—down to $227. (This was true, even though productivity had risen at an impressive average of four percent a year from 1981 to 1985 and had increased in 1986 by 3.5 percent—better than either Japan or Germany.)

Nearly six percent of Americans—nearly eight million people—are officially unemployed. They are actively searching for work without success. Another one million "discouraged" workers have given up and stopped looking for jobs.

Cuts in Social Programs

Efforts to cut education, housing, job training, and other social programs became more determined. These efforts were largely successful.

Today, less than one percent of the federal budget is spent for education, down from two percent in 1980. Job training and job subsidization programs were cut nearly 70 percent—from $9 billion in 1981 to only $4 billion. Less than one percent of the federal budget is now spent on training and job programs. Yet, that part of the federal budget spent on the military has increased from 35 percent in 1980 to 41 percent today.

Job training funds peaked in 1978. Not only have they gone down since then, but the declining funds are mainly used, now, for the least disadvantaged, leaving very little for the highschool dropouts and the less skilled.

A quarter of a million young people—25 percent of the total when President Reagan took office—have been cut from the Summer Youth Employment Program.

Federal spending for non-insurance social programs, as a percentage of Gross National Product, has gone down from 4.2 percent in 1980 to 3.7 percent last year, while defense expenditures have increased during the same period from 5.2 percent to 6.9 percent.

With inflation, the real income of welfare recipients has been reduced nationally by approximately one-third since 1970; in Chicago, for example, the value of AFDC (Aid to Families with Dependent Children) has been halved during that time.

Poverty Worsened and Deepened

The gap between the rich and poor widened. In 1986, the top one-fifth of American households received 46.1 percent of total income, up from 43.3 percent in 1970, while the income share of the middle three-fifths declined from 52.7 percent to 50.2 percent and that of the poorest one-fifth of households went down from 4.1 percent to 3.8 percent.

Census figures also show that poverty has become more prevalent in America's central cities. There, the poverty rates rose by half from 1969 to 1985—increasing from 12.7 percent to 19 percent, a much steeper rise than for those outside.

Poverty has deepened. Typical poor people of the 1980s living in big cities are farther below the poverty line than their unfortunate counterparts of the 1960s. There was a sharp increase between 1970 and 1982 in the percentage of poor people with incomes less than 75 percent of the poverty line.

Urban poverty has become more persistent. According to Professor Greg J. Duncan of the University of Michigan's Survey Research Center, "the chances a poor person in a highly urbanized county would escape his poverty have fallen substantially since the 1970s," after some improvement between the late 1960s and mid-1970s, and are now well below the levels of twenty years ago.

"The increased persistence of urban poverty is alarming," Professor Duncan said. "Persistently inadequate living standards not only make life miserable for the families involved, but also reduce the chances that children will succeed in school and jobs when they grow up."

A Growing American "Underclass"

Blacks and other minorities have made important progress, legally and politically. The black middle class has grown. There were only 200 black elected officials in 1965; by 1986, that figure had mushroomed to 6500. Blacks and other minorities have made significant inroads into the media, law enforcement, business, and the professions. But progress has slowed, and the Reagan Administration has tried to turn the clock back.

Lack of Vigorous Affirmative Action

Though the Supreme Court has several times recently upheld affirmative action in hiring and promotions, the Reagan Administration has been hostile to affirmative action efforts and to the vigorous enforcement of civil rights laws.

Ralph G. Neas, Executive Director of the Leadership Conference on Civil Rights, has declared: "EEOC [Equal Employment Opportunity Commission] has become less vigorous in enforcing the law and has abandoned many of the civil rights remedies employed by previous Republican and Democratic administrations."

Cutbacks in affirmative action enforcement have been unfortunate, especially because earlier such efforts had been successful in increasing jobs and influence for blacks and in recruiting more blacks into higher education. Affirmative action worked.

Incentives for integrated housing have been ended by the Reagan Administration, incentives for subsidized housing have all but been eliminated, and civil rights enforcement in the Community Development Block Grant program has stopped.

The Kerner Commission recommended an open housing law. But the Fair Housing Law actually adopted in 1968 has proved to be too weak and without adequate enforcement machinery. All the secretaries of HUD have recommended its strengthening, but Congress has, so far, refused to toughen it.

More "Separate Societies"

The Kerner Report warning is coming true: America is again becoming two separate societies, one black (and, today, we can add Hispanic), one white—separate and unequal.

While there are few all-white neighborhoods, and there is some integration even in black neighborhoods, segregation by race still sharply divides America's cities—in both housing and schools for blacks, and especially in schools for Hispanics. This despite increases in suburbanization and the numbers of blacks and other minorities who have entered the middle class.

For the big cities studied by the Kerner Commission, housing segregation has changed little, if any, and is worse in terms of housing costs for blacks, who are more likely than whites to be renters. Segregation is not just a matter of income: it still cuts across income and education levels. Studies show continued discrimination in housing sales and rentals and in mortgage financing for blacks and Hispanics.

Segregation breeds further inequality for blacks and other minorities— including lessened opportunities for work and the greater likelihood of inferior education.

Segregated housing produces segregated schools, and these are most often worse schools than those available to the children of whites.

From 1968 to 1984, the number of white students in the public schools dropped by 19 percent, while the number of black students increased by 2 percent. Hispanic student numbers skyrocketed, up 80 percent.

Public schools are becoming more segregated. There has been no national school desegregation progress since the last favorable Supreme Court decision in this field in 1972. After declining from 1968 to 1976, the number of black students enrolled in predominantly minority schools increased from 62.9 percent in 1980 to 63.5 percent in 1984. The percentage for Hispanic students enrolled in minority schools has climbed steadily from 54.8 percent to 70.6 percent during the same period.

University of Chicago political scientist Gary Orfield has found that "a great many black students, and very rapidly growing numbers of Hispanic students, are trapped in schools where more than half of the students drop out, where the average achievement level of those who remain is so low that there is little serious pre-collegiate instruction, where pre-collegiate courses and counselors are much less available, and which only prepare students for the least competitive colleges." There have been severe cuts in federal student assistance funds.

The American Council on Education has said that, today, the gap between black and white college-going rates is the largest it has been in more than a quarter of a century.

The highschool graduation rate for black students rose to 75.6 percent in 1985, but the percentage of these students going on to college has been declining since 1976, dropping to 26.1 percent in 1985. Similarly, the highschool graduation rate for Hispanic students was 62.5 percent in 1985, but the percentage of them who enrolled in college had been on a four-year decline by that year and fell to only 26.9 percent in 1985. The college-going rate for American Indian students is also on the decline.

Greater Racial Contrast

Non-white unemployment in 1968 was 6.7 percent, compared to 3.2 percent for whites. Today, overall unemployment has doubled, and black unemployment is more than double white unemployment.

Median black family income, as a percentage of median white family income, dropped from 60 percent in 1968 to 57.1 percent in 1986. Those who would be classified as "working poor," if they were white—those with annual incomes between $9,941 and $18,700—are the middle class for black families; that is the present range of median black family income.

From these facts of black and Hispanic segregation and inequality, Professor Orfield has concluded that the ghettos and barrios of America's cities are "separate and deteriorating societies, with separate economies, increasingly divergent family structures and basic institutions, and even growing linguistic separation. The physical separation by race, class, and economic situation is much greater than it was in the 1960s, the level of impoverishment, joblessness, educational inequality, and housing even more severe."

The Urban Underclass

The result is a persistent, large, and growing American urban underclass.

Poverty is both urban and rural, both white and minority. But the great majority of the nation's poor people—70.4 percent in 1985—live in metropolitan areas. From 1974 to 1983, over 33 percent of highly urban population (those living in the nation's 56 most highly urban counties) was poor at least once, and 5.2 percent was poor at least 80 percent of the time. During the same period, 60 percent of blacks in these areas were poor at least once, and 21.1 percent were poor at least 80 percent of the time.

Central-city poverty has become more concentrated. From 1974 to 1985, in central-city poverty tracts with a poverty rate of 20 percent or more, the numbers of people living in poverty nearly doubled—from 4.1 million to 7.8 million. In areas of extreme poverty—more than 40 percent—the numbers of white families living in poverty went up 44 percent, the numbers of black families 104 percent, and the numbers of Hispanic families 300 percent.

University of Chicago sociologist William Julius Wilson has found a resulting "rapid social deterioration" in the inner-city neighborhoods since the Kerner Report, with "sharp increases in social dislocation and the massive breakdown of social institutions in ghetto areas."

Concentrated poverty is "one of the legacies of racial and class oppression," Professor Wilson has stated, and it has produced what he has termed "concentration effects"—the "added constraints and severe restrictions of opportunities associated with living in a neighborhood in which the population is overwhelmingly socially disadvantaged—constraints and opportunities with regard to access to jobs, good schools and other public services, and availability of marriageable partners." The result in these concentrated, central-city areas, he has said, is "sharp increases in joblessness, poverty, and the related problems of single-parent households, welfare dependency, housing deterioration, educational failure, and crime."

National Security Requires New Human Investment

"Quiet riots" are taking place in America's major cities: unemployment, poverty, social disorganization, segregation, family disintegration, housing and school deterioration, and crime.

These "quiet riots" may not be as alarming or as noticeable to outsiders—unless they are among the high proportion of Americans who are victimized by crime—but they are even more destructive of human life than the violent riots of twenty years ago.

This destruction of our human capital is a serious threat to America's national security. The Kerner Report said: "It is time to make good the promises of American democracy to all citizens—urban and rural, white and black, Spanish-surname, American Indian, and every minority group."

Such a recommitment now to that kind of human investment could begin to move us once again toward becoming a more stable and secure society of self-esteem.

As former Assistant Attorney General, now Clarence Robinson Professor of History at George Mason University, Roger W. Wilkins has said, "The problem is not a problem of defective people; the problem is a problem of a defective system."

The resistance of the system to change, its inflexibility, is nowhere better illustrated than in the failure of the federal government to fully implement Indian tribal self-determination and self-government; there have been little visible effects from two initiatives toward that end—a presidential one in 1968 and a congressional one in 1975.

We know what should be done.

Jobs. Jobs are the greatest need. Full employment is the best anti-poverty program. An economic policy of stabilization, greater spending for targeted social programs, low interest rates, and greater growth are essential. (A one percent decline in unemployment could reduce the federal deficit by $30 billion.)

We need a strong public jobs program; there is plenty of infrastructure work that needs doing. The minimum wage must be raised. The tax laws should be changed further to see that the working poor get to keep more of their earnings. Increased training for jobs, as well as a sound national day care program for mothers who want to work, must be provided.

Welfare. We should provide better income for those who cannot work or find work. There should be national standards for AFDC.

Desegregation. A stronger fair housing law should be passed, and it and other affirmative action laws vigorously enforced. More large-scale desegregation of schools is needed; where such actions have been tried, they have worked and produced stability over long periods of time. A majority of Americans under thirty, as well as a majority of college students as a group, support such desegregation. So do two-thirds of the families whose children have actually been bussed for desegregation purposes.

Affirmative Action. Vigorous enforcement of equal employment opportunity and affirmative action laws is vital. Where public funds or subsidies are used, there must be strict requirements for affirmative action and contract compliance.

Health. We need to extend national health insurance to more Americans, including the requirement of health insurance as a part of job benefits. This is important if we are to change our present two-tiered system, composed of those covered by health insurance and those who are not.

General. Childhood development is basically important; we know that programs like Head Start work, and they now are advocated by corporate leaders like those on the Committee for Economic Development. So does the Job Corps. We should give these programs added support. We should replicate successes in inner-city schools like those in Minneapolis.

These things are do-able. And we have the means. Doubling the percentage of the federal budget that now goes for job training, education, and community development, for example, would still only be roughly equal to the percentage increase in military spending since 1980.

The numbers of people in the underclass are relatively small. Improving their chances and their lives is increasingly in the self-interest of whites as whites become a declining proportion of America's population. Further, the fact that the labor force is shrinking as a percentage of total population should be seen as an increasing opportunity for finding work for the chronically unemployed.

We must find the will. A majority of Americans support increased spending for social programs (and believe that the military budget is the best place for cuts). They support the idea that more should be done to give a hand to black people and other minorities.

The problem is that, because we made progress for a time, most Americans—as well as American policymakers—likely think that we are still making progress or that most inequalities have disappeared. This is not true.

We must bring the problems of race, unemployment, and poverty back into the public consciousness, put them back on the public agenda.

That is our purpose in making this new report.

CARNEGIE REPORT
ON URBAN SCHOOLS
March 15, 1988

The Carnegie Foundation for the Advancement of Teaching announced March 15 a new master plan for salvaging schools in the nation's largest cities. Urban schools had been sadly neglected, the foundation's trustees charged, during the reform movement that followed publication of A Nation at Risk, *a much-heralded prescription for improving the schools produced by the National Commission on Excellence in Education in 1983* (Historic Documents of 1983, p. 413). *Visits to schools in six large cities had convinced foundation representatives that the outlook was deeply discouraging.*

The Reform Movement

In the years since the 1983 report, education had changed for the better in much of the country. It had become a high priority for many state governors, teachers' salaries had been raised, and students' scores on measures such as the Scholastic Aptitude Test were creeping upward. But the reforms had bypassed schools attended by many of the country's poorest and most educationally disadvantaged students, the Carnegie trustees asserted. "In almost every big city, dropout rates are high, morale is low, facilities often are old and unattractive, and school leadership is crippled by a web of regulations," they declared. "There is, in short, a disturbing gap betwen reform rhetoric and results."

To correct serious problems that seemed endemic to these schools, the Carnegie report, An Imperiled Generation: Saving Urban Schools, *called for a large-scale, coordinated crusade by local, state, and federal govern-*

ments. *"This nation must see the urban school crisis for what it is: a major failure of social policy, a piecemeal approach to a problem that requires a unified response," the trustees said.*

In some of its recommendations, the Carnegie report echoed A Nation at Risk. *Both documents urged that teachers expect more from students, that students master a central core of learning, and that schools spend less time on paperwork. Both said that schools should be held responsible for producing good—or bad—educational results.*

In contrast to the earlier reformers, however, the Carnegie trustees envisioned a large-scale federal rescue effort for urban schools, with more money for child nutrition, Head Start, and programs funded by Chapter One of the Education Consolidation and Improvement Act—programs that help pay for educating poor and minority-group students. The Carnegie trustees also proposed a new program of federal loans to rebuild rundown city schools. Although the report does not suggest how much should be spent on this effort, it does say that the new buildings could cost as much as $30 billion. Most of the money would be reserved for schools in the hundred largest cities in the country.

The Carnegie Recommendations

To tackle the city school crisis, the Carnegie trustees urged America to commit itself to a crusade to educate all students, including those who usually ended up in nonacademic tracks. The effort should begin as soon as children entered school; the trustees called for creation of ungraded "basic schools" during the primary years, where teachers would concentrate on giving children a good command of English. During visits to schools, Carnegie representatives repeatedly encountered high school classrooms where students could not read well enough to do normal grade-level work.

For older children, there would be substantial changes in the way schools were organized. To correct problems of student alienation and apathy, the trustees advocated breaking large high schools down into smaller "clusters," where students would have a greater sense of belonging and be less apt to cut class or drop out. The final two years of high school would become a "transition school," in which students could rearrange their class schedules to make room for outside obligations such as part-time work or parenthood.

For schools that failed to measure up, the trustees recommended outside intervention in the form of evaluation teams appointed by state and local education officials. The teams would work with schools, recommending changes in educational techniques, financing, or personnel. As a last resort, the team could recommend closing down a school.

The proposal to give outsiders such wide-ranging authority seemed likely to stir controversy among local school officials, since it challenged the tradition of local control over education. A few states, however, already had moved in that direction, passing laws that gave state officials power to evaluate schools and, if necessary, restructure or close them.

In a statement accompanying the report's release, foundation president Ernest L. Boyer, a former U.S. commissioner of education, called for a national forum on urban schools, a meeting of influential leaders that would become a permanent organization to lead the reform drive. The report itself advocated closer cooperation between city schools and other institutions, such as business and colleges.

One indication that the foundation attached great importance to the urban education issue was the fact that the Carnegie trustees themselves signed the report, an unusual practice for the organization. The trustees included Terrel H. Bell, the former U.S. secretary of education who had appointed the excellence commission. The Carnegie Foundation had been an influential voice in educational policy making for eighty years and had produced several other reports during the reform movement of the 1980s.

Following are excerpts from An Imperiled Generation: Saving Urban Schools, *the report of the Carnegie Foundation for the Advancement of Teaching, released March 15, 1988:*

A Generation Imperiled

Without good schools none of America's hopes can be fulfilled. The quality of our education will determine the strength of our democracy, the vitality of our economy, and the promise of our ideals. It is through the schools that this nation has chosen to pursue enlightened ends for all its people. And it is here that the battle for the future of America will be won or lost.

Since 1983, school reform has been at the top of the national agenda. Educators, governors, and even corporate leaders have played starring roles in this impressive drama. The curriculum has been enriched, graduation standards raised, teacher salaries improved, certification procedures tightened, and preschool education has received vigorous support.

We, as trustees of The Carnegie Foundation for the Advancement of Teaching, welcome this sustained push for school renewal. We applaud the progress. Still, we are deeply troubled that a reform movement launched to upgrade the education of *all* students is irrelevant to many children— largely black and Hispanic—in our urban schools. In almost every big city, dropout rates are high, morale is low, facilities often are old and unattractive, and school leadership is crippled by a web of regulations. There is, in short, a disturbing gap between reform rhetoric and results.

The failure to educate adequately urban children is a shortcoming of such magnitude that many people have simply written off city schools as little more than human storehouses to keep young people off the streets.

We find it disgraceful that in the most affluent country in the world so many of our children are so poorly served.

There are exceptions, to be sure. In preparing this report Foundation representatives traveled to some of the nation's largest cities. We found outstanding principals who have turned failing schools around. One junior high school principal in New York City's South Bronx, for example, has built a reputation of excellence that even attracts recruiters from elite private high schools. . . .

We met gifted teachers who believe in students and conduct their classes with the expectation that learning will occur. In one sixth grade class, we found a group of thirty students eagerly discussing Charles Dickens' *Oliver Twist*. They knew the good guys from the bad guys and were cheering for little Oliver who, like them, was trying to survive in a hostile climate. This teacher brought nineteenth century London to the classroom and related great literature to the realities of students' lives. Educators such as these are the unsung heroes of the nation.

But excellence in education ultimately must be judged by what happens to the least advantaged students. And, thus far, the harsh truth is that the reform movement has largely bypassed our most deeply troubled schools. Urban renewal has breathed fresh life into vast stretches of the nation's cities. Ramshackle structures have been razed, glass towers have risen, and city blocks have been beautified with plants, parks, and walking spaces. Cities have spacious convention centers, new hotels, and banks that look like great cathedrals. But what about the schools?

If urban America, regardless of its gleaming high rises and impressive skylines, is a place where education is neglected, then the glittering signs of "progress" remain a shameful facade.

One high school in Cleveland is near a once bustling intersection of commerce, but so many surrounding buildings have been razed that now the vacant land makes the school look like a forgotten outpost in an underdeveloped country. A sprawling playground is rendered useless by a carpet of glass. Inside, lavatories for students have no light bulbs, the stalls have no doors and there is no toilet paper in the dispensers. There is an atmosphere of hopelessness among students, mirroring the outside world.

In Cleveland, recently, only one public high school student was a semifinalist in the National Merit Scholarship competition, out of the 15,000 so recognized nationwide. At a Chicago high school, only 10 percent of the entering tenth graders were able to read effectively. In New Orleans, the average high school senior was reading at a level exceeded by 80 percent of the students in the country. In a Houston elementary school, half the students had to repeat a grade because of unsatisfactory academic progress.

During school visits, we found that 75 percent of the high school freshmen in Chicago had reading test scores below the national average, and only five of that city's sixty-four public high schools had averages approaching national reading norms. Only 229 of the 1,918 students at one

Los Angeles high school scored at grade level in reading.

A particularly sobering appraisal was offered by the City-wide Educational Coalition in Boston, which concluded: "Not only do 44 percent of (Boston's) high school students drop out before they reach 12th grade, but over 40 percent of those who do reach 12th grade score below the 30th percentile on a standardized reading test. They may graduate, but they are functionally illiterate."

In New York City, at academic high schools geared to prepare students for college, we found that one of every five students was absent on any given day. And in four of those schools, the absence rate approached one in three. "I made guest appearances when I was enrolled," said a student who transferred to an alternative high school. "The environment there was not one in which the kids wanted to learn. They just wanted to hang out on the streets."

There is, in fact, a widespread "culture of cutting" in many inner city schools. Evidence of this could be seen one Monday last spring in a high school where 11 of 28 students had shown up for a course called "High School Mathematics" and 7 of 18 for a biology course. Students selectively skipped classes, most often those early in the morning, or at the end of the day. In Boston, a study of middle schools showed that the portion of students absent at least 15 percent of the time increased in 14 of the 22 schools in just one year.

Such truancy is often a prelude to leaving school altogether. Each year almost 700,000 students call it quits, forming a group that exceeds the populations of all but the nation's largest cities. In New York, at least one of every three students drops out. At one high school in Los Angeles, because of their mobility and academic failure, seven out of ten students leave between the ninth and twelfth grades.

In large urban schools, we found an anonymity among students, an atmosphere in which young people are unknown and unsupported by adults. Teenagers in these schools are often socially unattached and feel unconnected to the larger world. For these students dropping out is easy. Alienated youth, for whom schools have barely made a difference, are flooding into communities where they confront unemployment lines, welfare checks, homelessness, and even jails.

Urban communities often are unsafe for children. They are places where the family is frequently a more troubled institution than the school. Poverty makes it difficult for parents, despite their caring and concern, to be helpful in their children's education. A startling 70 percent of teachers in urban schools say lack of parental support is a serious problem.

Thus, a devastating instability and divisiveness in cities undermines the effectiveness of schools. And America continues to face the very real possibility of the two separate societies envisioned by the Kerner Commission two decades ago. In its prophetic statement, the Commission warned of a social and economic division in the nation "so deep that it would be almost impossible to unite."

Here then is our conclusion: America must confront, with urgency, the crisis in urban schools. Bold, aggressive action is needed now to avoid leaving a huge and growing segment of the nation's youth civically unprepared and economically unempowered. This nation must see the urban school crisis for what it is: a major failure of social policy, a piecemeal approach to a problem that requires a unified response.

Improving schools cannot solve all our problems. Still, public education is the key to bringing hope to children, renewal to our cities, and vitality to the nation. Therefore, in this report we propose a *comprehensive* program, one that puts together, as a single strategy, the best practices we observed. Specifically, our plan includes the following: commitment to educate *all* children, new governance procedures, an educational renewal program for the local school and partnerships that link the school to a network of local, state, and federal support. Urban schools cannot do the job alone. . . .

The Mandate: Excellence for All

We begin with one essential declaration: an urban school will be successful only as teachers, administrators, and community leaders have confidence that all students can succeed. Different approaches to learning are required, but all students, regardless of background, should be given the tools and encouragement they need to be socially and economically empowered.

It is unacceptable that, year after year, about one out of every three urban students leaves school before completing the program or receiving a diploma. While the dropout rate among nonwhites has slowed, academic failure rates continue to be considerably higher for minority students than for whites. This gap persists precisely at a time when black and Hispanic students represent a growing proportion of the population.

During school visits we were struck by the frequency with which many students were described as "failures." While still in school they were, it seems, only marking time. It is significant, we believe, that 21 percent of today's teachers believe schools cannot expect to graduate more than 75 percent of those enrolled. Still more sobering, about 30 percent of urban high school teachers feel this way.

Teacher expectations vary dramatically from class to class. A social studies teacher in a Los Angeles high school confided somewhat sheepishly that her students were using a book written on a third-grade level because that was "all they could handle." "It's a game we play," said a teacher in Houston. "If we held them all back, the system would get clogged up. So we water down the curriculum and move them along."

At another high school, this one in Chicago, an English teacher told us, "the majority of students will try at the beginning of the year, but they get a few pages into the work and find that it's too hard. So they give up. The best of them, even though they can read the words, can't understand much beyond the basic plot and are unable to read for any kind of deeper meaning." . . .

Urban students are often academically restricted by the curriculum itself which is divided between the academic, vocational, and general programs. But putting students into boxes can no longer be defended. To call some students "academic" and others "nonacademic" has a devastating impact on how teachers think about students and how students think about themselves. The message to some is, you are the intellectual leaders; you will go on to further education. To others it is: you are not academic. You are not smart enough to do this work. Students are divided between those who think and those who work, when, if fact, life for all of us is a blend of both.

Clearly there are schools that make a difference, places where expectations for all students are high. At Bret Harte in Los Angeles, all seventh graders are taught the same lesson in mathematics. They then break into small groups and work at different levels, moving up as they demonstrate mastery of the material.

Locke High School, a large urban school, is pushing to raise the expectation levels of all students. It offers Advanced Placement courses in biology, chemistry, French, Latin, calculus, English and U.S. history.....

Equality of opportunity, along with the support to make it real and not merely rhetorical, must be seen as the unfinished agenda for the nation's schools. To expand access without upgrading urban schools is simply to perpetuate discrimination in a more subtle form. But to push for excellence in ways that ignore the needs of less privileged students is to undermine the future of the nation.....

Governance: A New Structure

The governance structure of urban schools must be radically overhauled. Basic education policy should be shaped at state and district levels, but day-to-day decision-making should shift to the local school. Principals and teachers must be given more authority. They must be freed from a system of red tape that causes them to scrounge for chalk and paper clips while bombarding them with a steady flow of procedural directives.

But, granting more autonomy to the local school, while essential, is insufficient. Such authority must be accompanied by accountability and also by procedures for intervention in the event a school fails to educate its students.

School-based Leadership

During school visits, we heard the word *bureaucracy* used derisively, time and time again. We often found a nightmare of regulation and frustration. Government agencies impose on schools a tangled web of mandates that cover attendance quotas, requirements for graduation, teacher certification, the nature of state aid, the selection of textbooks, the structure of curriculum and dozens of recordkeeping forms.

Principals and teachers, in many cities, are caught in a governmental system more preoccupied with paperwork, it seems, than with learning.

While tight control by public agencies is rooted in the call for accountability, the reality is that principals are often held responsible for the bureaucratic rather than the educational aspects of their work.

By mandating, in detail, how schools must be run, the professionalism of the staff is undermined and individual teachers are robbed of authority to act. . . .

Teachers in urban schools also have too little control over their work. They are three times as likely as their counterparts in non-urban districts to feel uninvolved in setting goals or selecting books and materials. They are twice as apt to feel they have no control over how classroom time is used or course content selected. . . .

Urban high school teachers frequently have no permanent classroom, or even a desk of their own. They have no pleasant place to take a break or to lunch with colleagues. Even access to a telephone is limited. In some schools, floors are dirty, windows grimy, rest room facilities a disaster, and even teaching materials are in short supply. Here is how one teacher described it:

> I sometimes wonder how we're able to teach at all. A lot of times there aren't enough textbooks to go around; the library here is totally inadequate; and the science teachers complain that the labs aren't equipped and are out-of-date. We're always running short on supplies. Last year we were out of mimeograph paper for a month, and once we even ran out of chalk. After a while you learn to be resourceful. But it's still frustrating to try to teach under these conditions. I mean, talk about teaching the basics! We don't even have the basics to teach with.

In the most troubled schools, teachers, with good reason, do not feel safe in the halls, in the parking lots, or even in the classrooms. Violence levels are high and assaults against teachers are not uncommon. A Carnegie Foundation poll of teachers nationwide revealed that over half the teachers in urban schools consider vandalism and disruptive class behavior a problem in their school.

Every school should have not only high expectations for academic achievement but high expectations for conduct, too. Standards of discipline must be consistently and sensitively enforced throughout the school. Education and civility are linked.

Further, the working conditions for teachers must improve. This nation cannot expect teachers to exhibit a high degree of professional competence when they are accorded a low degree of professional support. Nor can we attract the most thoughtful and intellectually capable students into teaching when, for twelve years, they have observed first-hand the frustrations and petty humiliations that many teachers must endure.

Here again, school-based management is the key. Principals and teachers—those closest to the students—should be given more authority to run the schools and the confidence between teachers, principals, and district and state education leaders must be strengthened. Our national survey revealed that the majority of teachers give good marks to their principals. However, this support is less strong in urban schools where teachers are more likely to rate the principal "below average" in supporting their work and communicating with them.

Even as we focus on the importance of the local schools, however, we acknowledge the key role of the central office and those who must coordinate the work of a complicated system.

Thus, we found it especially disturbing that only 18 percent of urban school teachers rank state and local education officials "above average." We recognize that issues of financing and equity, as well as court mandates, have placed heavy burdens on the central administration of urban schools. But boards and superintendents must think of themselves primarily as providing services and resources to enable teachers and principals and parents to be successful. Among the fundamental responsibilities of the school board, we emphasize three:

Finances: The district board should obtain—from local, state and federal sources—adequate financial support for schools and make resources available in ways that are minimally restrictive.

Personnel: The school board should ensure that the ablest and best qualified people are employed to lead and teach in the system's schools. This must begin with the selection of a thoughtful and knowledgeable superintendent.

Coordination: The school board should build a bridge between the school and those groups and agencies, including state and local governments, that seek to enrich school programs, doing so with due regard for both the integrity of the individual school and the legitimate expectations of those beyond its walls.

How can school leadership be strengthened? We recommend that the principal and teachers at each school have authority to allocate funds within guidelines set by the district office. Further, the district should provide each principal with a discretionary school improvement grant for program materials, special seminars, and staff retreats. . . .

We also recommend that the principal, acting in consultation with colleagues, be given responsibility for the final selection of teachers for the school. School boards and unions must be willing to set aside some of their controls over school assignments to make this work. In too many schools, principals are not consulted when the district decides which teachers should be assigned to which school. . . .

Accountability: A School Report Card

The debate about governance, in many cities, is whether to "centralize" or "decentralize" the public schools. On the one hand, tight district control promises accountability, but risks rigidity in a faceless system. On the other hand, granting autonomy offers the possibility of community participation, but with the risk that, without oversight, such freedom might be abused. Since governing boards often cannot agree on educational outcomes, they attempt to achieve accountability and control through bureaucratic regulations, not educational results.

What is often missing in the "control-no control" debate is a careful consideration of the middle ground. Teachers and principals must be given greater freedom to make decisions. But school empowerment is only a means to a larger end. The public deserves to see results. In calling for greater school authority, we acknowledge a parallel and absolutely essential need for evaluation.

We conclude that holding local schools accountable is perhaps the most important and least effective part of urban education. What is needed is a school report card, one that includes a wide range of measures to evaluate school goals and procedures as well as student progress. We recommend, therefore, that each school be asked to demonstrate, at regular intervals—perhaps on an annual or bi-annual basis—the educational effectiveness of its program. Such a strategy might include reports that respond to the following questions:

- Does the school have clearly defined goals?
- Does the school evaluate the language proficiency of each student? What evidence is there that students are developing their ability to communicate in both the written and spoken word?
- What are the number and types of books being read by students?
- Does the school have a core curriculum for all students? What is the general knowledge of students in such fields as history, geography, science, mathematics, literature, and the arts? Is such knowledge appropriately assessed?
- What is the enrollment pattern among the various educational programs at the school? Specifically, what is the distribution between remedial and academic courses?
- Is the school organized into small units to overcome anonymity among students and provide a close relationship between each student and a mentor?
- Are there flexible scheduling arrangements at the school?
- Is there a program that encourages students to take responsibility for helping each other learn and helps make the school a friendly and orderly place? How well is it succeeding?
- What teaching innovations have been introduced during the preceding academic year? Are there programs to reward teachers who exercise leadership?
- Does the school have a well developed plan of renewal for teachers and administrators?
- Is the school clean, attractive, and well equipped? Does it have adequate learning resources such as computers and a basic library? Can the school document that these resources are used by students and teachers to support effective learning?
- Are parents active in the school and kept informed about the progress of their children? Are there parent consultation sessions? How many

parents participate in such programs?

- Does the school have connections with community institutions and outside agencies to enrich the learning possibilities of students?
- What are daily attendance and graduation rates at the school?
- What changes have occurred in the drop-out rate and in students seeking postsecondary education and in getting jobs after graduation? What is being done to improve performance in these areas?

What we envision is an evaluation program in which the school systematically collects information and reports on *student and school progress,* not simply on *institutional procedures.* There is both input *and* output in the assessment, with a focus not just on means, but ends. For the school, the emphasis should be on a well-planned program, with flexibility, and a climate that supports a community of learning. For the student, the focus should be on language skills, acquisition of general knowledge, and on the capacity to think clearly and integrate ideas. Attention also should be given to the books the students read, the service activities they perform, and the uses they make of resources in the school and beyond.

The school report card we propose would be submitted to the district office and the state. Such reports should be accompanied by an overall evaluation prepared by the principal, teachers and parents who identify improvements as well as problems. A judgment of progress, or lack of progress, should be made—not against some arbitrary standard—but against the school's own performance in preceding years. Further, when the report card is submitted, the school should also set priorities for the subsequent year.

A Strategy for Intervention

... If the school, after a reasonable period, is not able to provide evidence of quality education for its students, if the accountability reports do not reveal satisfactory progress, there must be outside intervention.

... It is our deep conviction that when schools fail, swift changes must be made. No other crisis—a flood, a health epidemic, a garbage strike or even snow removal—would be as calmly accepted without full-scale emergency intervention.

Therefore, we propose that the state and local district be authorized to appoint a School Evaluation Team, made up of education officials, along with parents, teachers, and college faculty members, to review a school where unsatisfactory progress is reported. The evaluation team, in its assessment, would have access to school records in addition to the official report. On-site visits would be scheduled. Team members would observe classes and conduct interviews with the principal, teachers, students, and parents.

Upon completion of its site visit, the evaluation team would identify strengths and weaknesses and prepare a specific plan for school improvement. It would outline steps that the state, the district board, and the local school should take. A range of options would be available.

- First, the evaluation team might outline a list of emergency steps to be taken by the school itself with the understanding that another mid-year assessment would be scheduled.
- Second, the team could recommend a continuing review arrangement, citing problems that bear watching. Under this procedure, on-site consultation would be provided by a senior advisor who would spend time working with teachers, counselors, and administrators. An analog for this person might be the "School Inspector" in the English system who plays the role of prodder, coach, and advocate.
- Third, the evaluation team might also conclude that the school was failing because of a fiscal crisis. It could then recommend that a special state fund be established to provide emergency aid to the school, proposing also how the additional resources should be spent.
- Fourth, the team might conclude that poor leadership is the problem. In this case, it may well recommend removing the principal. This means that the practice of tenure for principals should be ended. Principals should continue in office only so long as they are able effectively to lead the school.
- Finally, the problems may be so great and so intractable that the school, as organized, cannot be improved. In such a case, the evaluation committee could recommend closing the school, providing new educational arrangements for the students....

... [L]ocal school control is crucial, but it is insufficient. In the end, students must be served and there may be times when the school, for whatever reason, is unable to provide the conditions for effective education. In such circumstances, public officials have both a legal and moral obligation to intervene.

Excellence: Priorities for Renewal

High expectations and good governance are the first steps in renewal; but the final test is what happens within the school itself. During our visits, we saw, in all too many cases, a fragmented approach to school improvement. We found isolated examples of good practices, but there was no overall design. We conclude that the time has come for a comprehensive program of renewal to be introduced in every school in every city. The exceptional example of excellence must become the rule.

In this chapter, we set forth a five-part plan for school renewal. We suggest that every school give priority to the early years; have a clearly defined curriculum; be flexible in its scheduling arrangements; provide a program of coordinated services; and be a safe, attractive place with good equipment and adequate resources for learning. The program we propose also calls for partnerships and additional state and federal support.

The Early Years: A Good Beginning

Poverty and schooling are connected, and a student's poor educational performance may relate to events that precede schooling—and even birth itself. The growing fetus requires a diet rich in protein, vitamins, and minerals. And yet, most mothers in poverty do not have adequate nutrition. Further, the human grows most rapidly during the first year of life. But for more than 20 percent of America's children, undernourishment is common. Malnutrition affects almost a half-million children in this nation. . . .

We realize that to talk about babies and poor health may appear to be far off the school reform agenda. Yet, the evidence is overwhelming. Educational problems cannot be divorced from poverty in the inner city. Poor health in the early years inhibits the physical and intellectual growth of children. It affects their ability to succeed in school. Mothers and young children must have good nutrition if good education is our goal.

Most urban teachers understand how learning is crippled if children are nutritionally or emotionally deprived. Half the urban secondary school teachers we surveyed said neglected children are a problem. Thirty-seven percent of these teachers described poor nourishment as a serious matter, and over 30 percent say "poor health" among children is a problem.

We conclude that federal child nutrition programs should be more adequately funded. Further, community health projects should be established with public and private funding to provide support and early intervention for poor mothers and their children. . . .

Another point of great concern: many poor children are not educationally stimulated in the early years or introduced to the richness of language. "Kids grow up with little interest in school," said Everett J. Williams, the school superintendent in New Orleans. "They come to school not able to count to ten, not knowing their colors, not knowing where they live, and some not even knowing their names. At the beginning of their careers in school they are already students at risk."

We conclude that every eligible child should receive the benefit of Head Start or an alternative preschool program. Head Start, which today serves fewer than 20 percent of those eligible, has proven to be especially successful in helping children overcome many social, health, nutritional, and learning difficulties in the early years. Specifically, we propose an annual incremental expansion of Head Start so the program can serve all eligible children before the year 2000. We also strongly recommend that funding for Chapter One of the *Education Consolidation and Improvement Act* be increased at least 5 percent each year until all of the nation's eligible children are served. These federal programs have demonstrated their value in offsetting the educational disadvantages of poor children. The investment we propose is small when compared with the cost of wasted lives.

This brings us to the school itself, where priority in the early years should be on helping each child become proficient in the written and the spoken word. Specifically, we recommend that the early years—kindergarten through grade 4—be reorganized into an ungraded *Basic School*. Such a school, with relatively small classes, would give priority to language. The goal would be to assure that every child completing the basic school could read with understanding, write with clarity, and effectively speak and listen. Children of different ages and achievement levels would be in classes together. Each student could work at his or her own performance level.

Children in the Basic School would, from the first, be speaking, writing, reading, and talking about words, listening to stories, become linguistically empowered in an environment that the foreign language people like to call the "saturation method." No child should leave fourth grade without good command of English.

An increasing number of urban children come from non-English speaking homes. It is estimated that the parents of about 10 percent of the nation's students do not speak English. . . .

The issue of how best to teach non-English speaking students is mired in a debate over bilingual education—a conflict that often has as much to do with politics as education. Advocates defend bilingual programs as the only way to be certain that students can keep up in their studies and maintain a positive view of their heritage while learning English; critics argue that the programs undermine the child's need for proficiency in English.

Research suggests that bilingual education succeeds in schools that are themselves effective. Typically, programs that fail are in schools that are ineffective in curriculum, classroom conditions, and social environment. In other words, good bilingual education, like every other kind of education, depends on clear goals and quality instruction. . . .

Small Schools: A Sense of Belonging

Most city schools are too big, and anonymity among students is a pervasive problem. There is a feeling of isolation among teenagers at the very time their need for belonging is most intense. . . .

Today, thousands of students, especially those in the upper grades, crowd into dilapidated buildings and drift unrecognized from class to class. There is a disturbing climate of impersonality in the urban school, a feeling among students of being unknown, unwanted, and unconnected to the world. Young people are cut off from the community and have few significant relationships with adults. They are not linked to a teacher who knows them on a personal level. . . .

This rootlessness is exacerbated by families that move from place to place. There is, for the children, little continuity to education. A high school in Los Angeles that began the school year with an enrollment of 2,028, had 1,790 students enter and withdraw during the academic year—a chaotic whirlwind that kept students faceless and unknown. . . .

The successful schools we visited were true communities of learning, places where students are known and have ongoing contact with their teachers. They belong. Therefore, we conclude that large schools should be divided into clusters with no more than 450 students each so that all students can be well known to each other, and to teachers. For example, a large school could have separate "schools-within-schools," with one on each floor or wing of the building. Every small school unit should have its own director and counselors who work with students and its own team of teachers assigned exclusively to that one cluster. Each unit would build its own traditions and sense of community.

Some old, unsafe schools should be closed, and smaller facilities should be leased or built. These new facilities could easily be located in residential or commercial buildings close to where students live or parents work. A new network of dispersed, "cluster schools" would have the added advantage of bringing young people more frequently into contact with adults. The goal must be to have within each urban school—regardless of its location and physical arrangement—a spirit of community, with a sense of bonding so that anonymity is overcome. . . .

Overcoming anonymity—creating a setting in which every student is known personally by an adult—is one of the most compelling obligations urban schools confront. Young people who have few constructive relationships with adults need a sense of belonging. They need positive encounters with older people who serve as mentors and role models for both educational and social growth. Building community must be a top priority if students in urban schools are to academically and socially succeed.

The Core Curriculum: Coherence and Connections

Students in the inner city, just as students elsewhere, should become proficient in English, have a broad, general education, and develop the ability to observe, weigh evidence, organize their thoughts, reach conclusions, and use knowledge wisely. To expect less is to underestimate the capacity of disadvantaged students and diminish their prospects for success. Further, students who do not have these important abilities and skills cannot reach their full potential, personally, socially, or economically. They will be unable to find satisfying work or participate in building their communities and the nation.

Too many urban students are just marking time, unable to see schooling as related to their lives. While living in the nation's largest and most dynamic cities, they are, paradoxically, cut off from the mainstream of American life and see little connection between the classroom and the reality of their world. They do not understand how the work they are asked to do in school will help them cope today or be successful tomorrow. Urban students rarely come in contact with anyone other than low-achieving peers and frequently do not have a realistic view of their own academic performance or potential. . . .

We are suggesting, quite simply, that inner city students must be no less informed and no less richly educated than their counterparts in the suburbs. And yet we found that, in many urban schools, peer pressure against academic achievement is strong, especially among young males. . . .

What, then, do we see as the basic curriculum for all students? Broadly defined, we propose a core of study based on those consequential ideas, experiences, and traditions common to all by virtue of our membership in the human family at a particular moment in history. These shared experiences include: written, verbal, and computational language; a heritage that reveals who we are and how we evolved; memberships in groups and institutions; an interdependent relationship to nature; the need for health and well-being; the urge to be creative; and the expression of our deepest feelings through participation in the arts. These common experiences would be explored through studies in English, history, mathematics, science, and the arts.

Further, there is the related need to prepare students for productive work. With a high school diploma, job prospects are enhanced. But the vocational programs offered in urban schools—those most directly related to entry level employment and the promotion of constructive attitudes toward work—are often disappointing. During our visits, we heard repeatedly that "voc-ed" is the place to send less capable students, those who are "able to work with their hands rather than their heads."...

We conclude that career-related courses have an important part to play in the curriculum of urban schools. They can be enriching and highly motivating for the students. What we would eliminate, however, is the tracking pattern that puts some students in what is thought of as a "nonacademic" program, one that reduces options and assumes "voc-ed" students need no further education. We would also eliminate the narrow "marketable" skills courses that have little intellectual substance and give students "hands-on" experience while denying them a decent education.

What then is appropriate vocational preparation? All students, in preparing for work, should have a command of English and a core of common learning, should develop good work habits, be introduced to job options, and be counseled regarding career choices. Extensive job training should occur in postsecondary education or in the work place under apprenticeship arrangements. Thus, the challenge for urban schools is not to lower educational expectations. The vocational and academic programs should have meaning and make a connection between the curriculum, the student's interest, and life beyond the classroom.

One of the more successful efforts to achieve this aim is the so-called magnet school. Whether it is health careers, performing arts, business education or the humanities, students—through a magnet school—get an opportunity to link classroom experiences to their interests. Magnet schools have resulted in improved academic achievement, higher attendance, and lower dropout rates.

Since many inner city students are not impressed by the long term payoff of education—going to college, getting a better job—there is a current move to give prizes for good performance. We applaud this practice, providing it does not trivialize learning or demean the enduring benefits of education. Recently, businessman Eugene Lang promised a free college education for all sixth graders in one Harlem school who continued to attend school and graduated. The key to Mr. Lang's success was not just the scholarship idea, but the quality of the relationship he, as a special counselor, established with those students. The payoff was both immediate *and* long term.

The Boston Compact, an organization of businesses, has promised jobs to all students who stay in school and graduate. In Los Angeles, there is a plan to guarantee jobs after graduation to students who maintain at least a C+ average and a 95 percent attendance record. The Cleveland public schools have a program to pay the college costs of students with high grades. Programs such as these give tangible evidence that success in school means success in life.

In the end, however, the rewards of learning are best found in the classroom, stirred by an inspiring teacher. . . .

We believe that all students, not just those who are college bound, should complete a core of common learning. The curriculum should help students meet their social and civic obligations and also give them the tools they need for productive work and further education. . . .

Flexible Arrangements: More Time, More Options

Flexible calendar arrangements are essential. The school calendar and daily schedule, as now constituted, often do not mesh with student needs. During our study we found young people who planned to drop out of school, not because they were failing, but because they had other obligations to fulfill. Students who may need to work part-time or care for a young baby are caught in a rigid lock step. An inflexible course sequence is squeezed into a predetermined block of time. But why cling to the anachronistic notion that high school must be completed in four years, particularly by those whose circumstances differ so greatly from the norm?

To achieve more flexibility we propose that the last two years of high school become a *Transition School*. The purpose is not to provide less academic content, but to arrange learning in a more manageable format. In the transition school, the daily class schedule would be more flexibly arranged. Class work could be stretched over five or six years. Students could scale down the number of courses they take, mixing work and study, possibly pursuing no courses for a semester without being considered a drop out.

The Transition School—with its attendant counseling and guidance—is, we believe, an idea whose time has come. It would give students the flexibility many of them need. . . . [N]etworks of learning could be established outside the school, blending school with college study. . . .

During our study, we saw many programs in which students broke out of the rigid lock step and, as young adults, extended the campus, enriched their learning and combined schooling with other obligations. City-As-School is a New York City alternative program with hundreds of learning experiences throughout the community. . . .

Flexibility depends heavily on good counseling. The school is, for many urban youth, the one institution that provides stability in a disintegrating community and, by operating in close alliance with other social service and health agencies, the urban school can help at-risk students confront problems that go beyond the academic. We do not suggest that the school itself do everything. What we do say is that services for many urban youth are a confusing maze of competing jurisdictions. Clearly, coordination is required.

One of the best known models of coordinated services is a national project called *Cities in Schools*. This program has, for years, helped at risk students stay in school by good counseling and by helping them with jobs, health, and family problems. . . .

Teen-age pregnancy and the general need for better health care for children who live in poverty are two of the most dramatic illustrations of how the social and educational needs of students interact. Pregnancy is, in fact, the primary reason young women leave school. More than a million teen-agers a year get pregnant and half of them, usually the poorest, have babies. And it is estimated that from 25 to 40 percent of the females who drop out are pregnant or already are mothers. . . .

In New York City, there are child-care facilities for young mothers at 24 of the 110 high schools. At one of the high schools we visited in Cleveland, a day care center was located acoss the corridor from the main office. It is the first room a visitor sees upon entering the school. This spacious, carpeted room with 12 cribs usually receives 10 to 15 children a day, ranging in age from three months to three years. Mothers are expected to spend the day in classes. . . .

Good Facilities: Places That Work

We visited urban schools where peeling paint, cracked plaster, torn window shades, and broken furniture are so common no one even seems to notice. In New York, for example, we saw schools that were filthy because the budget allowed for sweeping the floors only every other day. And at one school, two drinking fountains were in working order for its 2,000 students. In another, translucent plastic has replaced window glass. . . . We observed that George Washington High School—alma mater of Henry Kissinger, Jacob Javits, Kenneth Clark and William Schuman—had a biology laboratory that consisted of two tables for the teacher to demonstrate experiments. There were no laboratory benches for the students. Each time a microscope slide was prepared, it had to be passed through the flame of an alcohol lamp, posing a constant hazard. The school building was last painted 25 years ago.

At other schools, test tubes were broken and burners did not work. Dusty periodic table charts hung at odd angles on the walls. Text books were outdated. We found schools where the roofs leaked so badly that wastebaskets were used to catch the drips during rain storms. Students at Intermediate School 88 in Harlem walked around the charred remains of a fire that had occurred months before.

Half of New York City's 1,050 school buildings are at least 50 years old. The facilities are so dilapidated that the board of education said it would take $4.2 billion over the next 10 years to refurbish the physical plant. Nationally, it has been estimated that about $30 billion will be needed to refurbish public schools.

We were also disturbed by the neglect of libraries in many schools. And yet, in many inner city schools, funds are not available to purchase books and the library staff has been cut back or abolished all together. In many schools we visited, the library is used more as a detention center than for learning. Learning is enormously enhanced when students have books to read, library equipment that is up-to-date, and a setting where reading is encouraged.

Nationally, about half the teachers we surveyed rated the physical plant, security, and cleanliness at their school below average. In every category, these negative ratings were higher in urban schools than those in suburban and rural districts.

Another problem: many urban schools are often targets of vandalism, and an added burden is on those who would like to make the facilities a source of pride. Splattered by graffiti, windows shattered, and entrances padlocked in ways resembling prisons, inner-city schools frequently do not reflect a hopeful image. The general appearance speaks of an uncaring place.

The atmosphere of neglect reflects itself in the carelessness of students. In many urban classrooms, students routinely arrive after the bell has rung, slamming the door behind them, walking in front of the teacher, disrupting the lesson. . . .

Maintaining discipline is, in fact, a major issue in large inner-city schools. Statistics tell the story. In New York City there were 1,629 assaults and 410 robberies in the 1,000 public schools in the 1985-1986 year. This marked a 19 percent improvement in safety over the previous year. . . .

In our national survey we found that urban teachers were twice as likely as other teachers to rate vandalism as a problem and four times as likely to rate racial discord as a problem. Urban teachers also were more concerned about violence, absenteeism and student apathy. . . .

A good building does not necessarily make a good school. But the tacit message of the physical indignities in many urban schools is not lost on students. It bespeaks neglect, and students' conduct seems simply an extension of the physical environment that surrounds them. City leaders who take pride in the office towers that house banks, hotels, and shops are content to send children to decaying buildings.

Students cannot learn if there is chaos in the corridors and disruption in the classrooms. Teachers cannot be effective if they are physically threatened. But orderliness is only a means to a larger end, and the school will be tested, ultimately, by the degree to which the principal and teachers are empowered to make the school a safer place where learning can occur. . . .

We conclude that urban schools must be refurbished and that learning resources—libraries and laboratories—must be provided for effective learning. But for this to be accomplished, federal leadership is required. It will be impossible for school districts to find the billion dollar budgets required to overhaul the buildings. We propose, therefore, a federally-financed *School Facilities Program* for the nation's urban schools. The Higher Education Facilities Act of the 1960s was responsible for providing facilities to house this country's major growth in college and university attendance after World War II. Further, our invaluable network of community colleges would not have been available without such legislation. Why isn't this a precedent for urban schools?

The School Facilities Program we propose would provide low interest loans for the renovation and construction of school buildings. Such funds would be linked to educational renewal. Thus, the federal funds would not only provide attractive, safe places for students, they also would encourage use of the decentralized school model, breaking large schools into smaller units and encouraging some schools to relocate. Specifically, we suggest that loans be available only to districts that agree to reorganize the school into small learning units. Further, such loans would be available only if states can assure existence of an efficient construction process that is unencumbered by bureaucratic stalls and political intervention. . . .

Partnerships: Support Beyond the School

Whether a school succeeds or fails in its mission depends on the degree of support received from the community it serves, both locally and nationally. How we, as citizens, regard our urban schools determines the morale of the people who work in them and helps students gauge their expectations. In this section, we examine commitment to urban education as seen first from the home, then from college and the corporate community, and, finally, from the state government. Only by building a network of support beyond the school can urban schools improve.

Parents as Teachers

. . . We observed, time and time again, how important it is for parents to be involved in the education of their children. Schools, we conclude, have an obligation to view parents as co-teachers—not just as adults who sign report cards or show up for open house. And to the extent that school can enlist parents in the search for improvement, the greater the potential for success. . . .

Farren Elementary School in Chicago has a special program of parent participation. The goal is to prepare parents for the General Equivalency Diploma, making the school as much a place for parents to grow as it is for children. . . .

We recognize that the ideal of the parent as teacher is enormously difficult to achieve when work and school schedules overlap and when parents have neither the time nor energy to focus on the school. Still, schools have the obligation to create a climate and a schedule that conveniently involves parents. Some urban schools we visited do have evening and weekend appointment time for parent consultations. Others have parent advisory committees that give parents an important voice in school practices. There should be more neighborhood meetings in which school people meet with parents in homes, churches, or other convenient locations. Regardless of the structure, parents must feel empowered, confidently viewing the school as responsive to their interests and hopes for their children.

To strengthen the link between home and school we propose that parents spend at least one day each term with their child at school. To achieve this goal, employers need to get involved. Specifically, we recommend that parents be given released time from work to participate in teacher conferences. If society sees value in release from work to serve on juries and to vote, then surely allowing parents time periodically to visit their children's schools is in the public interest.

School-College Connections

Urban schools also should maintain close contact with higher education. Links between the two sectors must be strengthened. Students, after all, arrive at college after having attended elementary and secondary schools. School teachers are trained on college campuses. And yet, in one city we visited, the campuses of two universities could be seen from the local high school. Even though the institutions were within easy walking distance from each other, the principal reported that the school lived in isolation. He said they had no programs of any sort involving either institution.

One strategy is for colleges to work with a network of junior high schools, focusing on high risk students. College students, faculty, and staff can form one-to-one relationships with urban youngsters. The personal bonds that result from a mentoring relationship can dispel the hopelessness that robs many urban youths of motivation, and help disadvantaged students complete successfully their academic programs.

We are intrigued by the plan of the Abel Foundation in Baltimore to work with seven agencies, including two higher education institutions, to assist students in the city's junior high schools. Each of the seven participating agencies will be assigned 60 students for whom they are responsible for providing mentors. . . .

Milwaukee Area Technical College has joined forces with the city's public schools on Project Second Chance, which is designed to bring 16- to 18-year-old dropouts back into school. Returning students can take advantage of a range of alternative offerings at the college, including adult vocational courses, general education, rehabilitative and guidance services, and career counseling. Also available are a variety of coordinated services made possible by partnerships between educational institutions, community and social agencies, and the criminal justice system. A job placement service at Milwaukee Area Technical College connects students to a network of potential employers. . . .

Teacher recruitment is a special obligation of higher education. And priority should be given to attracting more blacks and Hispanics into the profession through scholarships. At a time when the needs for minority teachers are growing rapidly, minority teacher populations are declining. A crisis is unfolding. In addition, colleges should have summer and year-long institutes for teachers, following the Yale-New Haven Teachers Institute model which asks the teachers themselves to shape the content of the program.

The jurisdictional boundaries separating schools and colleges are crossed successfully only when institutions on both sides of the line are amenable. It is not easy to build incentives for cooperation if one institution considers itself the winner and the other sees itself as the loser. In all of this, a special burden falls on higher education. The nation's colleges and universities must, in tangible ways, affirm the essentialness of the nation's urban schools. . . .

Corporate Collaborations

Industry and business must be partners, too. Traditionally, corporate America has stood aloof from public schools. While complaining about the quality of education, it has failed to get involved. Today, however, collaboration is increasing. But what, specifically, can business do to enrich public education?

First, businesses can work with students who are educationally disadvantaged. In Chicago, a natural gas firm, People's Energy, sends tutors to the schools. Twenty employees tutor students in reading and math at Tilden High School for one and one-half hours twice weekly. In Houston the program that Tenneco first launched now sends twenty-five employees to primarily Hispanic inner-city schools, again providing tutorial help to students with language difficulties.

Hughes Tool in Houston sends Hispanic and Vietnamese workers to tutor high school students in the same ethnic groups. These tutors serve as role models, and place special emphasis on communication skills. . . .

Businesses also can help gifted students, especially in science and mathematics, and the new technologies. Shell Development, for example, sends high-level technical and computing staff to Houston's Jones High School Vanguard Program for the Gifted. . . .

Perhaps the most promising role for corporations is the renewal of the teacher. McDonnell-Douglas Corporation has opened its Employee Voluntary Improvement Program to the staff at nearby Central High School—at no charge. Under this program, high school administrators take management seminars and teachers take courses in computer science, algebra and trigonometry. Moreover, the head of the business department at Central went through the McDonnell-Douglas Secretarial School and, as a result, made major changes in the curriculum to better prepare students for vocations. . . .

Business also can help urban students take the step from school to work.

Before the name Adopt-a-School came along, General Electric donated a $5 million plant for use by the Cleveland Board of Education. That facility, located in the heart of a high unemployment district, became the Woodland Job Center. Students at Woodland work on various assembly lines, and are paid for their work....

Business and industry also can serve administrators, particularly by aiding principals in their capacities as both managers and leaders....

The State: Meeting the Mandates

Constitutionally, responsibility for education in America resides in the states. In fulfilling this obligation, each state should establish the general standards by which the educational mission is to be accomplished. State education laws should answer a few basic questions: What is a school? Who must attend it, and until what age? What are the statewide requirements and standards for entering high school? What is the state prepared to pay for, and on what terms? What are the requirements for becoming a public school teacher in the state?

None of these questions needs a long answer. Indeed, we caution state education agencies (and their boards) against tedious regulations in the interpretation of the statutes. Academic requirements should be defined in terms of general skills and bodies of knowledge, not course labels, periods of time spent on a subject, or Carnegie units accumulated. The Education Commission of the States has developed model legislation that may be especially helpful in drafting and revising the education laws. The fundamental goal must be the achievement of both quality and equality in the process.

If these twin objectives are to be met, greater equity in financing is critical. Today many inner city schools are starved for lack of funds while districts with less critical needs are well-financed. In the 1970s, a flurry of court cases gave promise of wiping out inequities in the funding of school districts. It appeared that, finally, the enormous differences in property wealth would no longer allow one school system to be well funded while others are impoverished. But that promise is sadly unfulfilled, and though adjustments have been made in some states, a child's place of residence can still determine the adequacy of his or her education.

A state with a relatively high per capita income that leaves support for the education of its children to the chance distribution of property values in local districts is selling its children short and failing to meet its obligations to the less fortunate....

Money alone will not make a better school. Still, it is foolish to suggest that money does not matter. Urban schools can not be run only on good will and inspiration; they must have the tools to do the job.

We strongly urge that states fulfill their legal and moral obligations by achieving greater equity in the financing of urban schools. The goal should be *at least* to equalize funds necessary to achieve a particular standard expenditure. Unless big city schools are given more support, much of what we propose in this report will remain a hollow promise.

A Nation Responds:
The Urban Schools Program

The entire country has a stake in the future of our urban schools, and if the crisis is to be resolved, greater federal leadership is essential. When the nation is at risk, the nation must respond. Specifically, we propose a new *National Urban Schools Program*. Such a program—similar in spirit to the Rural Extension Act that was enacted years ago to help farmers— would make it unmistakably clear that the federal government intends to be a partner in addressing one of today's most compelling social problems—the renewal of urban schools. The National Urban Schools Program would pull together pieces of existing legislation and introduce carefully selected new projects:

- First, we recommend that the funding of Head Start be incrementally increased so that all eligible children are served by the year 2000.
- Second, the appropriation for federal child nutrition programs should be increased.
- Third, we propose a 5 percent increase in the funding of Chapter One of the Education Consolidation and Improvement Act each year until all children eligible are provided service. Further, Chapter One should continue to focus on basic skills, but the rigid regulations regarding the supplemental support provisions should be loosened.
- Fourth, a new provision should be added to the Education Consolidation and Improvement Act to make it possible for parents living in poverty to place their children in afternoon and summer enrichment programs of their choice.
- Fifth, the National Urban Schools Program should contain a provision on teacher renewal, an updated version of the National Defense Education Act, to make summer fellowships available for teachers. This program also would expand the Christa McAuliffe Fellowship program and reinstitute the Teacher Center program, encouraging teacher teams at the local school to institute their own program of continuing education.
- Sixth, we propose an Urban School Facilities provision. Such legislation would make available to school districts low interest loans to demolish or refurbish old buildings and create more attractive, smaller units, or make it possible, where necessary, to relocate in residential or commercial buildings, or shopping centers. Loans also would be available to rebuild science laboratories and secure technology such as computers for more effective learning.
- Seventh, The National Urban Schools Program should have a school innovation provision, a fund that would encourage schools to introduce new curriculum or new scheduling arrangements.
- Finally, the new program should provide incentives for community colleges and four-year institutions in urban areas to maintain special relationships with schools, to enrich teachers, recruit minority stu-

dents, train more minority teachers, and help schools in the design of flexible school models. In this sense, higher education would play a role in urban schools analogous to the land grant mission.

Most funds appropriated under the National Urban Schools Program would be spent in behalf of school districts serving the nation's 100 largest cities. Recognizing that states without big cities also have urgent needs, we propose that 15 percent of the federal allocation of funds be set aside for students in these states whose pockets of disadvantaged children must also be served.

A comprehensive federal program such as the one we have just proposed would in no way signify a lessening of the belief that public education is primarily the responsibility of states and local districts. However, it would be a recognition of the enormity of the task and a declaration that a local, state and federal partnership is required. A federal government that can aid localities to build highways, provide for environmental protection and construct hospitals surely can find a way to play a larger part in securing the future of urban education.

Everyone's future is imperiled if disadvantaged young people are not economically and civically prepared. So long as failure is accepted, the lives of millions of children clustered in our big city school systems will be blighted. But still more is at stake. If urban education continues to fail, frustration will result, prospects for renewal will decline and the nation's future will be threatened.

What we offer in this report are not easy answers. Still, we are persuaded that students in our large cities can succeed if the nation's response is as urgent as the problem. We found, in every city, school administrators and teachers with a clear vision, high expectations, and dedication to the task. As a nation we must build on these heroic efforts and proceed, not only with urgency, but with confidence and hope.

SCIENTISTS' REPORT
ON OZONE DEPLETION
March 15, 1988

A study released March 15 by the National Aeronautics and Space Administration (NASA) warned that depletion of the protective ozone layer in the earth's upper atmosphere (stratosphere) was more severe than previous reports had indicated. The study, undertaken by a group known as the Ozone Trends Panel, involved more than one hundred scientists from the United States and several United Nations agencies. It provided further evidence of a worldwide depletion of the ozone layer, which filters out about 90 percent of the sun's harmful ultraviolet rays. The scientists concluded in their report that ozone had decreased by as much as 3 percent over densely populated areas in the Northern Hemisphere between 1969 and 1986. "Things are worse than we thought," said Robert T. Watson, a NASA scientist who was chairman of the group.

The report was made public one day after the Senate unanimously (83-0) approved a treaty, known as the Montreal Protocol on Substances That Deplete the Ozone Layer, limiting the use of chemicals that destroy ozone. The treaty, signed by thirty nations on September 16, 1987, would require a 50 percent cut in the production and consumption of chlorofluorocarbons (CFCs) and halons by 1999 (Treaty signing, Historic Documents of 1987, p. 745). CFCs are used primarily in refrigeration, air conditioning, insulation, and aerosol sprays, while halons are mainly used in fire extinguishers. Both emit long-lasting gases that react chemically with ozone molecules high above the earth, turning the ozone into oxygen.

Scientific studies have suggested that as the ozone layer thins, there will be a significant increase in the incidence of skin cancer and possibly an increase in global temperatures. Several scientists have advanced a theory that an apparent warming trend in recent years has been caused or aggravated by a "greenhouse effect." This theory holds that waste gases in the atmosphere—including CFCs—trap heat that would otherwise escape into space. James E. Hanson, director of NASA's Institute for Space Studies, told the Senate Energy and Natural Resources Committee on June 23 that "we can ascribe with a high degree of confidence a cause and effect relationship between the greenhouse effect and the observed warming."

Study Warnings

Loss of ozone in some latitudes reached 6.2 percent in winter—a greater loss than had previously been suggested—the Ozone Trends Panel reported. Its findings were based on data measurements that were more refined than previous ones. The loss of ozone over Antarctica—first observed in the 1970s and occurring particularly during that continent's spring—was affecting much of the Southern Hemisphere, the study reported. Between 1979 and 1986, ozone had decreased by 5 percent or more annually in latitudes below 60 degrees south, reaching its lowest amount in 1987.

"The observed [ozone] changes may be due wholly, or in part, to the increased atmospheric abundance of trace gases, primarily chlorofluorocarbons," the report concluded. Although total ozone was expected to increase in response to solar activity between 1985 and 1991, the increase would be offset after 1991 with the decline of solar output and the increasing concentrations of man-produced gases (CFCs, halons, methane, nitrous oxide, and carbon dioxide) that destroy ozone and remain in the stratosphere for approximately one hundred years after their release.

"For the first time, we have a really definitive answer that ozone has decreased," said John Gille, a member of the panel and a scientist with the National Center for Atmospheric Research. "We understand what is going on and we can predict it will be much more severe in the future."

That prediction was shared by officials from the U.S. Environmental Protection Agency (EPA), as well as several members of Congress. One reason was that CFCs are gradually released in the atmosphere over a long period of time, so that ozone depletion could continue for decades after the freeze on their production. "My own view is that we are seeing severe damage now and we know it is going to get worse because more chlorine is on its way" into the atmosphere, said F. Sherwood Rowland, a scientist at the University of California at Irvine, a member of the panel.

Countering Ozone Depletion

The treaty would require developed nations to freeze consumption and production of CFC compounds at 1986 levels seven months after the treaty became effective. Thirty months later, levels for halon compounds would be frozen. Industrialized nations would have until July 1, 1994, to reduce production and consumption of CFC compounds by 20 percent and until July 1, 1999, to bring them down to the 50 percent level. Developing nations, which make and use fewer CFC compounds, would have to reduce production and consumption by a smaller percentage. At least eleven countries that accounted for two-thirds of all CFC consumption and production worldwide would have to ratify the treaty for it to go into effect as scheduled on January 1, 1989.

A 95 percent reduction in CFC production had been sought by the EPA, but the agency's administrator, Lee M. Thomas, said the proposal was too severe to gain world acceptance. However, on September 26, Thomas issued a press release urging that the treaty be amended to eliminate the chemicals totally. He said a new EPA analysis of recent scientific information about CFCs "paints an alarming picture of present and future ozone levels."

Industry groups, notably the National Association of Manufacturers and the Alliance for Responsible CFC Policy, an association of companies that use or produce chemicals, supported the treaty but vigorously opposed making U.S. restrictions more stringent. According to the alliance, about 2.1 billion pounds of CFCs, valued at $2.2 billion, were produced annually throughout the world. The United States accounted for approximately 29 percent of production and sales. Shortly after the Ozone Trends Panel made public its findings, E. I. du Pont de Nemours & Company announced it would phase out its production of CFCs, which accounted for about 25 percent of the world's total.

Following are excerpts from the March 15, 1988, Executive Summary of the Ozone Trends Panel report, substantiating depletion of the earth's protective ozone layer:

Introduction

In 1985 two important reports of changes in atmospheric ozone were released. The first report was of a large, sudden, and unanticipated decrease in the abundance of springtime Antarctic ozone over the last decade. The second report, based on satellite data, was of large global-scale decreases since 1979 in both the total column content of ozone and in its concentration near 50 km [31 miles] altitude. In October of 1986, the National Aeronautics and Space Administration (NASA), in collaboration with the National Oceanic and Atmospheric Administration (NOAA), the Federal Aviation Administration (FAA), the World Meteorological Organization (WMO), and the United Nations Environment Program (UNEP), formed an Ozone Trends Panel, that involved over one hundred scientists, to study the question of whether carefully re-evaluated ground-based and satellite data would support these findings. This report critically assesses our present knowledge of whether the chemical composition and physical structure of the stratosphere has changed over the last few decades and whether our current understanding of the influence of natural phenomena and human activities is consistent with any observed change. This report is different from most previous national and international scientific reviews in that we did not simply review the published literature, but performed a critical reanalysis and interpretation of nearly all ground-based and satellite data for total column and vertical profiles of ozone....

Key Findings

Source and Trace Gases

There is undisputed observational evidence that the atmospheric concentrations of source gases important in controlling stratospheric ozone levels (chlorofluorocarbons, halons, methane, nitrous oxide, and carbon dioxide) continue to increase on a global scale because of human activities.

Global Ozone

Calculations using two-dimensional photochemical models predict that increasing atmospheric concentrations of trace gases would have caused a small decrease in ozone globally between 1969 and 1986. Predicted decreases between 30 and 60 degrees latitude in the northern hemisphere for this period ranged from 0.5 to 1.0% in summer and 0.8 to 2.0% in winter, where the range reflects the results from most models.

Analysis of data from ground-based Dobson instruments, after allowing for the effects of natural geophysical variability (solar cycle and the quasi-biennial oscillation (QBO)) shows measurable decreases from 1969 to 1986 in the annual average of total column ozone ranging from 1.7 to 3.0%, at latitudes between 30 and 64 degrees in the northern hemisphere. The decreases are most pronounced, and ranged from 2.3 to 6.2%, during the winter months....

The observed changes may be due wholly, or in part, to the increased atmospheric abundance of trace gases, primarily chlorofluorocarbons (CFCs).

Satellite instruments on Nimbus 7 (Solar Backscatter Ultraviolet (SBUV) and Total Ozone Mapping Spectrometer (TOMS)) have provided continuous global records of total column ozone since October 1978. Unfortunately, they suffer from instrumental degradation on the diffuser plate, the rate of which cannot be uniquely determined. Thus, the data archived as of 1987 cannot be used alone to derive reliable trends in global ozone....

Theoretical calculations predict that the total column ozone would decrease from solar maximum to solar minimum by an amount varying between 0.7 and 2% depending upon the model assumed for solar ultraviolet variability. Thus, the observed decrease in ozone from the satellite data between late 1978 and late 1985 is predicted to have a significant contribution from the decrease in solar activity during this period.

... [T]his assessment does not support the previous reports ... of large global decreases since 1979 in the total column of ozone (about 1% per year) or in the ozone concentration near 50 km altitude (about 3% per year). These reports used data archived as of 1987, and the trends obtained were erroneously large because of unjustified and incorrect assumptions about the degradation of the diffuser plate common to both the SBUV and TOMS satellite instruments.

Antarctic Ozone

There has been a large, sudden, and unexpected decrease in the abundance of spring-time Antarctic ozone over the last decade. Ozone decreases of more than 50% in the total column, and 95% locally between 15 and 20 km altitude have been observed.

The total column of ozone in the Austral spring of 1987 at all latitudes south of 60 degrees south, was the lowest since measurements began 30 years ago.

In 1987 a region of low column ozone over Antarctica lasted until late November-early December, which is the longest since the region of low ozone was first detected.

The weight of evidence strongly indicates that man-made chlorine species are primarily responsible for the observed decrease in ozone within the polar vortex.

Source and Trace Gases

There is undisputed observational evidence that the atmospheric concentrations of a number of the gases that are important in controlling atmospheric ozone and climate are increasing at a rapid rate on a global scale because of human activities. Such gases include nitrous oxide (N_2O), methane (CH_4), carbon tetrachloride (CCl_4), methyl chloroform (CH_3CCl_3), and several chlorofluorocarbons (CFCs) and halons (bromine-containing compounds, e.g. $CBrF_3$, $CBrClF_2$). These gases are important sources of the stratospheric nitrogen, hydrogen, chlorine, and bromine species that are predicted to photochemically control the abundance of ozone. The increasing atmospheric concentration of carbon dioxide (CO_2) is also predicted to affect the abundance of stratospheric ozone, but indirectly, by modifying the temperature structure of the atmosphere and hence the rates of ozone destruction.

Ground-based measurements of hydrochloric acid (HCl) and hydrofluoric acid (HF) indicate that, between 1976 and 1987, their column abundances increased annually by rates of 2-3% for HCl and 5-10% for HF. Within the limits of experimental uncertainty, these rates are consistent with those expected from the increased tropospheric abundances of their source gases that contain chlorine and fluorine. There are currently an insufficient number of measurements of the chlorine monoxide radical

(ClO) to determine an accurate trend in this key stratospheric ozone-altering species.

A critical analysis of all nitrogen dioxide (NO_2) data from ground-based, aircraft and satellite instruments indicates that, if there has been any increase in NO_2 at all since 1979, it is less than 20%. Therefore, this assessment cannot support the recent report of an approximately 60% increase in the stratospheric abundance of NO_2 between 1979 and 1986.

Total Column Ozone

Total column ozone measurements have been made for more than 30 years at many locations around the world using ground-based Dobson spectrophotometers. Satellite measurements suitable for detecting long-term changes began only in the late 1970s. Hence, at present, long-term changes and trends over decades can only be assessed using ground-based data. However, changes since late 1978 may be examined using both ground-based and satellite data. This assessment found that all of the ground-based and satellite data had to be critically reanalyzed before being used for the accurate determination of trends. The Dobson data were reanalyzed taking more fully into account instrument calibration changes. Furthermore, data from certain stations were deemed unusable because of questionable quality. The accuracy of the reevaluated data from a "good" Dobson station is estimated to be better than 0.7% per decade.

The quantity and quality of ground-based observations in the tropics and subtropics are such that the determination of trends is far less precise there than for northern midlatitudes. In addition, reliable data are sparse in the southern hemisphere outside of Antarctica. Thus, the Dobson data are not adequate to determine total column ozone changes in the tropics, subtropics, or southern hemisphere. The satellite data, while providing global coverage, are affected by long-term drifts in instrument calibration. The ground-based stations furnish these needed calibration standards for assuring stable performance in the satellite assessment of contemporary global changes in total column ozone. In this report, the determination of such changes since 1979 was made using satellite data normalized against the Dobson data. . . .

The next maximum in the solar sunspot cycle is expected in 1991, and theoretical calculations predict that the natural response of ozone to this cycle will be to increase toward a maximum at that time. During the 1986-1991 time period, this natural response to the solar cycle may offset or even reverse the predicted decrease in total column ozone that would be due to the increasing abundances of atmospheric trace gases alone. With the possible exception of high latitude winter, where decreases may continue to be evident, total column ozone is predicted to exhibit very little change or small increases up to 1991. After 1991, when the solar ultraviolet output begins to decline, the total column ozone is again predicted to decrease.

Comparison of the normalized TOMS satellite data . . . suggests that total column ozone, as predicted, has not continued to decrease in the northern hemisphere since passing the solar minimum in 1986 and the very intensive QBO of 1985. However, the rate of change of total column ozone averaged over the southern hemisphere appears to have remained more constant through 1987, possibly because of the additional ozone losses associated with the Antarctic ozone hole phenomenon, especially in high latitudes in the southern hemisphere. . . .

Vertical Distribution of Ozone

The vertical distribution of ozone has been measured globally using several instruments including the Nimbus 7 SBUV instrument, the Stratospheric Aerosol and Gas Experiment (SAGE) I and II visible spectrometers, and the Solar Mesospheric Explorer (SME) infra-red and ultra-violet spectrometers. Long-term ground-based measurements of ozone up to altitudes of 50 km are restricted to just a few locations around the world using the Umkehr technique at Dobson Stations. As in the case of the total column ozone data, the vertical ozone profile data had to be fully reanalyzed before using them to assess changes or derive small trends. These reanalyzed data were used to evaluate changes in the vertical distribution of ozone since the late 1970's and were compared to the model simulations of the period 1979-1986. . . .

Our analysis of the different satellite data sets suggest[s] that the determination of changes in the vertical distribution of ozone currently obtained using SAGE I and SAGE II data are [sic] the least sensitive to changes in the performance of the instruments over time. . . .

. . . [P]redicted changes in the vertical distribution of ozone over the period 1979-1985 indicate a maximum depletion near 40 km. Ozone near 40 km is predicted to have decreased by 5-12%: a 4-9% decrease in response to the increased abundances of the trace gases, and a 1-3% decrease in response to the reduced solar ultraviolet output over the time period. These ranges represent the decreases predicted from the different models for the latitude belt 30° to 60° N for all seasons. According to the theoretical models, the dominant effect due to trace gases over this period comes from the increase in the atmospheric abundance of CFCs. These predicted changes in ozone are consistent with the observations, although somewhat greater than the mean value obtained using SAGE I and SAGE II data. In particular, the overall shape of the predicted changes in the vertical distribution is consistent with the SAGE data.

Unambiguous separation of the impact upon the vertical distribution of ozone by the two major perturbations, solar cycle and trace gases, awaits continued observation over the remainder of this solar cycle and perhaps beyond. Model forecasts for the period 1985-1991, as we approach the next solar maximum, predict that ozone near 40 km will continue to decrease as a result of increases in stratospheric chlorine, despite the rise in solar ultraviolet output, which by itself would lead to an increase in ozone amounts.

Antarctic Ozone Phenomenon

Ground-based and satellite data have shown conclusively that the spring-time Antarctic column ozone decreased rapidly after the late 1970's. The high degree of interannual variability and the lack of satellite based ozone measurements precludes an accurate assessment of the magnitude of any ozone decreases prior to the late 1970's. The Antarctic ozone hole develops primarily during September, and the rate of loss of ozone within a given year appears to be increasing. Total column ozone (at all latitudes south of 60 degrees) was lower in the Antarctic springtime in 1987 than in any previous year since satellite measurements began (late 1978). In October 1987, the monthly zonal mean amount of total ozone at latitudes 60, 70, and 80 degrees south was about 20%, 40%, and 50% lower, respectively, than in October 1979. In 1987, a region of low ozone over Antarctica lasted until late November/early December, which is the longest since the region of low ozone was first detected. . . .

Postscript

The conclusions of this report regarding global ozone trends would have been aided if the NOAA National Environmental Satellite and Data Information Service (NESDIS) had been able to provide any validated data from the SBUV-2 instrument launched in late 1984. Reliable SBUV-2 data should enable an improved recalibration of the Nimbus 7 SBUV data and provide a system for determining future changes in ozone that does not rely so critically on the long-term stability of the absolute calibration of the Dobson network. There is an urgent need for NOAA NESDIS to increase the priority given for the timely processing and validation of SBUV-2 ozone data if the United States is to have a viable national program for monitoring ozone. Validated SBUV-2 data are absolutely necessary for the international scientific assessment scheduled for 1989 in preparation for the 1990 policy review in accordance with the Montreal Protocol. . . .

NASA must vigorously pursue the new insights into the Nimbus 7 SBUV and TOMS instruments in order to develop the best model of diffuser plate degradation and the associated uncertainties. Once sufficient improvement has been made, the SBUV and TOMS data sets should be reprocessed using the new model of the degradation of the diffuser plate and the data archived for additional scientific studies required by the 1989 international assessment. SAGE II data should be used as an independent measurement of changes in the vertical distribution of ozone to compare with and support this reanalysis.

The re-evaluation and interpretation of both ground-based and satellite ozone data must, in the near future, be given higher priority, and involve a broader cross section of the scientific community than in previous years.

REPORT ON PRIVATIZATION

March 18, 1988

Recommending the gradual transfer of many federal programs and services to the private sector, the President's Commission on Privatization submitted its report to President Ronald Reagan on March 18, 1988. In the 278-page report, Privatization: Toward More Effective Government, *the commission heartily endorsed the Reagan administration's efforts to promote privatization as a means of reducing the scope of the federal government. The report was viewed as going beyond earlier privatization proposals advanced by the administration.*

Speaking at a news conference when the report was issued, David L. Linowes, chairman of the twelve-member commission, said that the government "should reach out by opening its operations to the creative talents and drive of entrepreneurs." The privatization campaign stemmed from Reagan's firmly held ideas favoring free markets and small government. But the thrust of the commission's report was that the transfer of government programs to the private sector would result in improvements in efficiency and service.

The bipartisan panel was appointed in September 1977. Besides Linowes, a Democrat and professor of political economy and public policy at the University of Illinois, the commission included Melvin R. Laird, secretary of defense in the Nixon administration, James McIntyre, Jr., director of the Office of Management and Budget in the Carter administration, and Walter B. Wriston, retired chairman of Citicorp.

The report traced the concept of privatization in the United States to a reaction against an emphasis on government growth that sprang from the

Progressive movement at the turn of the century. In a real sense, however, privatization is as old as the country itself. Canals and toll roads, and later the railroads, were built and operated by private capital during the nation's formative years. Even some of the subway lines in New York City were privately operated as recently as the 1940s.

Recommendations

The commission's report recommended seventy-eight specific undertakings to promote privatization. Linowes said it was unlikely any of the panel's recommendations would be acted on before the end of the Reagan administration. A number of the proposals had been made before, and some of them had been soundly rejected by Congress.

The report identified the "techniques" of privatization as (1) the sale of government assets, (2) the use of voucher systems, and (3) "contracting out." The recommendations were highlighted by a plan for gradually ending the U.S. Postal Service monopoly on the delivery of letters, and by another proposal to sell the federal portfolio of housing, business, and agricultural loans.

Among other recommended actions were the use of vouchers to offer parents a wider choice of schools for their children, and an expansion of the voucher system for low-cost public housing. The report additionally proposed that the government contract with private enterprise for the operation of prisons, military commissaries, and air traffic control towers at the nation's airports.

Privatization Abroad

In Britain, privatization has been pushed as a national policy since Margaret Thatcher became prime minister in 1979. Many Americans first became familiar with the word—spelled privatisation by the British— through news coverage of her efforts to roll back decades of nationalization. Beginning with the Labour Party's election at the close of World War II, much of Britain's basic industry was removed from private hands and placed under government control. Thatcher, a conservative, sought to return much of it to private ownership—to "privatise" it. France, too, has engaged in privatization in recent years, even under the Socialist-led government of President François Mitterrand.

Opposition

The commission's report pointed to the U.S. government's $1.6 billion sale of the Consolidated Rail Corporation (Conrail) by the government in March 1987 as the first major privatization initiative in the United States "to come to fruition." But press accounts at the time of the sale stressed the great difficulties the government encountered in winning the support of Wall Street and overcoming resistance to the sale by unions, segments of industry, and members of Congress. Fortune *magazine* *reported soon after the sale that the problems it created might "herald the end" of the move toward privatizing big projects. Conrail had been pieced together by the government nine years earlier from the bankrupt Penn Central Railroad and other lines in the Northeast.*

Among the leading opponents of privatization were the American Federation of State, County, and Municipal Employees (AFSCME) and other public-employee unions. Many of the privatization moves had been undertaken by state and local governments—to have garbage collected, streets repaired, bus lines operated, and, in a few instances, jail inmates supervised.

The Grace Commission, in its January 1984 report to President Reagan, said the federal government could save $5.9 billion that year by contracting with private enterprise to do more of its work. But the General Accounting Office and the Congressional Budget Office said the figures were greatly exaggerated, and envisioned problems as well as benefits in the privatization that the commission recommended. The commission, known by the name of its chairman, industrialist J. Peter Grace, was formally the President's Private Sector Survey on Cost Control. President Reagan set up the commission in 1982 and its findings, comprising forty-seven volumes, were issued in January 1984. (CBO/GAO on Grace Commission, Historic Documents of 1984, p. 169)

> *Following are excerpts from* Privatization: Toward More Effective Government, *issued by the President's Commission on Privatization, March 18, 1988:*

Executive Summary

The President's Commission on Privatization was established on September 2, 1987, "to review the appropriate division of responsibilities between the federal government and the private sector," and to identify those government programs that are not properly the responsibility of the federal government or that can be performed more efficiently by the private sector.

The Commission reviewed a broad spectrum of government activities:

- Low-Income Housing
- Housing Finance
- Federal Loan Programs
- Air Traffic Control and other FAA Functions
- Educational Choice
- Postal Service
- Contracting Out: Military Commissaries; Prisons
- Federal Asset Sales: Amtrak; Naval Petroleum Reserves
- Other Programs. . . .

The following are summaries of the Commission's findings and recommendations in each area:

Low-Income Housing

Rather than financing new public housing construction, the government should provide housing subsidies to eligible low-income households in the form of vouchers enabling them to rent acceptable housing in the private marketplace. To the greatest extent possible existing public housing should either be sold to or managed by the residents. By giving residents a larger stake in their own housing by selling it to them, contracting with them to manage it, or by allowing them discretion in choosing it through a voucher program, the long-term quality of their housing will be improved at a lower cost per household.

Housing Finance

The federal government should assume a more neutral position with respect to direct housing finance programs (Farmers Home Administration, Government National Mortgage Association, Federal Home Loan Mortgage Corporation, Federal National Mortgage Association, Federal Housing Administration, and Veterans Administration). In addition, the federal government should refocus the mortgage insurance activity of the Federal Housing Administration so that it does not compete as directly with private mortgage insurers. Rather, it should direct its efforts, as originally intended, toward home buyers who have been turned down by private insurers. Similarly, the Federal National Mortgage Association and, by extension, the Federal Home Loan Mortgage Corporation, should not be allowed to compete on an unfair basis, and thus should be fully privatized, including the elimination of all federal benefits and limitations.

Federal Loan Programs

The federal government should phase in a loan asset sale program in order to avoid large uncertain liabilities in the future. Moreover, federal loans should not be sold with any type of recourse that would create a future liability for the government. When federal loan assets are sold, the legal and contractual rights of the borrowers should be protected and the private sector owners should be required to abide by the stated collection policies that are used by the agency that makes the loan.

The federal government also needs to implement better accounting methods and introduce better incentives to make the budget accurately reflect the impact of the various types of loans it makes. In particular, a market valuation method of identifying the subsidy cost of its credit programs would enable policymakers to more accurately weigh the costs and benefits of direct loan and loan guarantee programs. In order to reveal hidden subsidies, the federal government should phase in a policy of purchasing reinsurance for all loans it guarantees, and the agencies should be required to obtain annual appropriations to pay for reinsurance.

Air Traffic Control and Other FAA Functions

The FAA should continue to regulate the national airspace system for the foreseeable future for reasons of safety, public service, and efficiency. However, portions of that system can and should be considered for private operation or for contracting, when such options would improve air commerce. In this regard, the federal government should reduce its direct role in the development of airports, by encouraging each airport to develop its own sources of funding from the full range of beneficiaries of aviation services. In particular, the portion of national airport and airway expenditures borne by users should be increased. Airport operators should be allowed to charge peak-hour takeoff and landing fees to alleviate congestion, and to charge passenger facility fees as a means of generating revenues. The FAA should retain authority over the en route centers, but some center activities should be subject to contracting out. In addition, the FAA should move incrementally to a system of private airport traffic control towers, and should privatize its system of flight service stations and system maintenance service.

Educational Choice

The federal government should foster choice options, including the use of vouchers, to achieve the nation's full range of educational goals. Congress should adopt policies to increase parental choice in education at the elementary and secondary levels, just as it now fosters choice in higher education through GI Bill payments and Pell Grants. Private schools should be able to participate in federal programs providing educational choice to parents, but the federal government should remain sensitive to retaining the values represented by the public schools and should ensure that the full range of civil rights guaranteed by the Constitution is protected.

The federal government should encourage choice programs targeted to individuals in the lower percentiles of the current elementary and secondary student population. The schools are failing these children now, and alternatives beyond current programs should be explored. Finally, the Secretary of Education should use discretionary resources to conduct additional research on educational choice initiatives that might expand the range of educational options for children.

Postal Service

The private express statutes, which mandate the postal monopoly, should be repealed to allow competition in the provision of any and all postal services. The benefits conferred by competition, in terms of quality of service, cost efficiency, and the incentives for innovation, clearly outweigh the costs of transition to a free market. However, there must be a gradual phase-in period and compensation of postal employees for possible loss of benefits or earnings. The U.S. Postal Service should seek private sector involvement, with consideration given to selling it as an Employee

Stock Ownership plan. As part of the phase-in process, the monopoly restrictions on the carriage of third-class mail and on rural delivery should be lifted immediately. Similarly, the restrictions on private delivery of urgent mail should be loosened and the prohibition on private use of letter boxes should be repealed immediately. At the same time, the Postal Service should more actively pursue contracting out opportunities in all its functions and ensure highest and best use of all its assets.

Contracting Out

The federal government should not compete with the private sector in the provision of commercially available goods and services. Contracting out through the competitive bidding process should be pursued more aggressively through the Executive Branch as a means to procure the same or better level of service at a reduced cost. This process should include appropriate in-house competition and adequate safeguards against employee displacement. Employee Stock Ownership Plans (ESOPs) can also be devices for furthering competition and contracting. Although Fed CO-OP is still a demonstration program, it, and other ESOP options, should be pursued by the federal government. Public policy goals and the operational needs of government should not be threatened if proper attention is devoted to developing work specifications and administering contracts.

Military Commissaries. Private sector businesses should participate in managing and operating military commissaries in the United States in order to achieve greater efficiency through competitive stimulus.

Prisons. Contracting the administration of jails and prisons at the federal, state, and local levels could lead to improved, more efficient operation. Problems of liability and accountability should not be seen as posing insurmountable obstacles to contracting for the operation of confinement facilities, although Constitutional and legal requirements apply. Contracted facilities may also be required to meet American Correctional Association standards.

The Bureau of Prisons and the Immigration and Naturalization Service (INS), in cooperation with the appropriate government agencies, should prepare cost studies, following the guidelines of OMB Circular A-76, comparing the cost of contracting with total government costs for administering existing facilities. In addition, the Bureau of Prisons and the INS should be encouraged and authorized to pursue lease-purchase arrangements for the addition of new facilities and the Department of Justice should continue to give high priority to research on private sector involvement in corrections.

Federal Asset Sales

Divestiture of federal assets should be pursued either where federal ownership is unnecessary for achieving public policy goals or where private ownership, in combination with covenants, regulations, or other projections, could better achieve these goals. Statutory prohibitions on studying divestiture of federal assets cannot be justified. Without adequate study, there is insufficient evidence to determine whether public or private ownership would best serve public policy goals.

Amtrak. Private sector initiative in the provision of intercity passenger rail service should be encouraged. The federal government should adopt a multi-year plan to move Amtrak or major portions of its operations to the private sector, in conjunction with repealing Amtrak's exclusive rights to provide intercity rail service. As part of the multi-year plan, federal subsidies should be incrementally reduced, and a deadline should be set for the Department of Transportation to decide whether Amtrak or portions of its operations should be continued. Capital needs should be funded by the federal government only if the purchase can be justified as a means to reduce the federal subsidy and to facilitate the eventual transfer of Amtrak to the private sector with no additional commitment of federal funds, including government loan guarantees. At the same time, Amtrak should contract out operations wherever the level of service can be performed at an equal or improved level and cost savings would result— taking into consideration the interest of employees. It should charge states and other users the full costs associated with providing rail service and trackage rights.

Naval Petroleum Reserves. The federal government should begin immediately to divest itself fully of the Elk Hills, California, and Teapot Dome, Wyoming, reserves. The military purposes for which they were acquired can now be better met through alternative means. In developing the sale, some level of access to light Elk Hills crude oil for smaller refiners and producers, as well as structuring the sale to maximize the number of potential bidders, should be considered.

Other Programs

Medicare. Private sector competition, by means of vouchers, in the provision of health care financing (health insurance or HMOs) for the elderly can impart critically needed cost-containment incentives in this market and offer a broader choice of health plan options. The government should act to increase competition and private sector participation in health care financing under Medicare by encouraging the use of vouchers or capitated payments to purchase private health care financing. Since the private sector is naturally reluctant to assume greater risk without compensating benefits, some risk-sharing plan, such as the use of risk-corridors, should be considered in the implementation of any voucher system.

International Development Programs. Developing countries, for a variety of reasons, often have extensive state ownership of business enterprises. In many cases, these enterprises could be made more efficient and innovative if turned over to the private sector. The Agency for International Development (AID) should increase its support of privatization in developing countries by channeling its funds and expertise as much as possible toward the private sector or by aiding host governments in converting state-owned enterprises to private entities. AID should support employee stock ownership plans and debt-equity swaps as means of facilitating privatization efforts in developing countries, and should encourage multilateral financial institutions and regional banks to act more decisively in private sector lending and divestiture in less developed countries.

Urban Mass Transit. Various means of increasing private sector participation in the provision of urban mass transit, including contracting out, employee stock ownership plans, and stimulating competition, can result in improved service in many areas. The federal government should administer its grant programs so as to foster public-private partnerships and healthy competition among public and private providers of mass transit service. At the same time, the limitations and requirements of Section 13(c) of the Urban Mass Transportation Act should be interpreted and amended so as to grant transit authorities the ability to achieve economies through privatization. UMTA should allow grantees to sell UMTA-funded equipment to private operations where service is being permanently contracted out or reduced, and UMTA should be reimbursed only for the federal share percentage of the proceeds.

The Commission believes that increased private sector participation in activities currently performed by the public sector has great potential for increasing the efficiency, quality, and constructive innovation in providing goods and services for the benefit of all the people.

Introduction

The United States is experiencing a renewed interest in the systematic examination of the boundary between public and private delivery of goods and services. The interest has been stimulated in part by concern that the federal government has become too large, too expensive, and too intrusive in our lives. The interest also reflects a belief that new arrangements between the government and the private sector might improve efficiency while offering new opportunities and greater satisfaction for the people served. The President's Commission on Privatization was created to assess the range of activities that might properly be transferred to the private sector and to investigate methods by which such a shift could be accomplished.

There are essentially three techniques for the privatization of service delivery. The first method is simply selling the government's assets. The sale of Conrail in 1987 is an example of the sale of an enterprise as a functioning unit, in this case, through a public stock offering. Instead of selling an enterprise, the government could also sell assets piecemeal; examples are the sale of obsolete military bases, loan portfolios, or surplus equipment. . . .

The second technique is contracting out, whereby the government enters into contracts with private firms to provide goods and services used by the government or demanded by the public. Contracting usually results in cost savings because the process is opened to competition among vendors. . . .

Contracting out is widespread and increasing in popularity at the state and local levels. Included in contracting is franchising, under which the government awards an exclusive right to deliver a public service to a private contractor, who then is paid by consumers rather than by the government. Franchising is commonly used for services such as water, electricity, gas, telephone, and cable television.

The third main form of privatization is the use of vouchers, under which the government distributes purchasing power to eligible consumers, who then must spend the funds received on designated goods or services. For example, housing vouchers provide low-income families with the means to obtain better housing in the rental market. Food stamps provide purchasing power to lower income families, enabling them to buy more or better food than their income otherwise would allow. The GI Bill following World War II provided education vouchers that could be used at a wide range of schools at the individual veteran's discretion.

User fees have been classified as a method of privatization, although they do not involve the transfer of government functions, but resemble privatization in that they place the burden of paying for the public service on those who benefit from it, rather than on taxpayers in general. The fees charged to barge operators to use government locks and canals are one example. When user fees are insufficient to cover the true cost of the government service (as is often the case), taxpayers must subsidize the shortfall.

Also considered privatization, deregulation of industry has been one of the most important forms of curbing government and relying more heavily on the private sector. Deregulation in some cases results in competition between private suppliers and the government for the consumer's dollar. For example, since 1979, when the Postal Service began to allow private carriage of urgent mail, private express couriers have grown dramatically, to the point where the Postal Service share of the express mail market is only 12 percent. Under the private express statutes, however, private services are still prohibited from delivering first-class mail.

State and Local Privatization

Contracting out in the United States has been employed most widely at the state and local levels. From coast to coast, government bodies, principally in response to pressures from taxpayers for greater efficiency, have been relying increasingly on the private sector to get the job done.

Since 1932 San Francisco has franchised garbage collection to private companies. Today, drivers own their trucks and are responsible for collections. In 1975, a study showed that San Franciscans were paying $40 a year for the private service, whereas New Yorkers in two comparable neighborhoods were paying $297 a year for municipal collection. . . .

Since 1899, Vermont law has allowed school boards of towns with no public or union district high school to pay for the tuition of the town's high school students at any approved (nonparochial) secondary school "within or without the state," up to an amount (for nonpublic schools) equal to the average tuition rate for a union district high school. In 1985, 95 Vermont towns containing 24.2 percent of the state's high-school-age population used this education voucher system, and surveys have shown strong parental acceptance and satisfaction with it. . . .

Privatization at the Federal Level

In the fiscal 1988 budget, the Office of Management and Budget proposed a number of privatization initiatives. These included the sale of the five power-marketing administrations, two oilfields owned by the Department of Energy, excess real property owned by the General Services Administration, the Federal Housing Administration's rural housing insurance fund, auction of the unassigned radio frequency spectrum, termination of federal crop insurance, sale of federal helium equipment assets, sale of Export-Import Bank loans, and Amtrak. The budget also included proposals for additional contracting out by the federal government.

One innovative proposal, advanced by the Office of Personnel Management, is called "Fed CO-OP." It proposes to spin off government entities as independent, for-profit companies with the current government employees as shareholders. By offering employees an ownership stake in the privatized activity, the plan seeks to build support within a group normally opposed to proposals to reduce the federal role. To date, however, no entity has been spun off under the Fed CO-OP plans.

The 1987 sale of Conrail marked the first major privatization initiative to come to fruition. This was followed later in the year by the sale of loans by the Department of Education and the Farmers Home Administration. Even during the period when no highly visible privatization initiative surfaced, use was being made of the contracting out procedures, most notably by the Department of Defense. . . .

Privatization Worldwide

A worldwide trend toward privatization has accelerated dramatically in the past few years. It has encompassed governments of all political persuasions, including some in Communist countries, which are coming to appreciate the large gains in efficiency that involving the private sector can achieve.

The . . . champion for sweeping privatization is Britain. Prime Minister Margaret Thatcher's government has made the sale of government commercial entities one of the principal themes of her administration. . . .

In Japan, former Prime Minister Yasuhiro Nakasone had initiated the partial privatization of some of Japan's worst money-losing government enterprises, notably Japanese National Railways (JNR). In 1983, JNR was losing $25 million a day and had accumulated $120 billion in debts. Steps to sell part of the giant Nippon Telegraph and Telephone are also proceeding.

Privatization in France has been a top priority since March 1986, when Jacques Chirac became Prime Minister. . . .

The Italian state holding company, IRI, has begun selling many of its commercial assets. In Spain, part of the state-owned auto manufacturer was sold off to Volkswagen, and a state-owned ball-bearing factory will follow. The government bus and truck company has been sold to General Motors.

In the People's Republic of China, workers are being allowed to buy shares in their enterprises, which are slowly being freed from state and party control. Free markets are springing up in cities such as Guangzhou, Shanghai, and Chengdu. A stock market has been allowed to open in Shenyang, and extensive agricultural privatization has dramatically improved China's capacity to feed its people.

Even the Soviet Union is moving cautiously in the same direction. In November 1986 the Supreme Soviet issued a decree allowing a range of private sector activities. . . .

In Latin America, where inefficient state-owned corporations have been major recipients of foreign bank loans, numerous governments are moving to transfer their holdings to the private sector. Costa Rica has been one of the most enthusiastic. With help from the U.S. Agency for International Development, a trust fund has been established to buy companies now owned by the state holding company and to sell them to private investors. Costa Rica has converted a key agricultural complex into a 200,000-member agricultural cooperative.

Even in Africa, where socialized economies are almost taken for granted, the movement is gaining a foothold. All the government enterprises in Togo are for sale. . . .

Summary

The Commission has approached each of the areas of government activity addressed in this report with a firm commitment to improve services to the American people. The Commission received extensive evidence of difficulties in the current delivery of services, heard testimony that more effective alternatives are available through the private sector, and found convincing evidence that some government actions impede development of private alternatives (and obstruct improvements in public services). In many of these cases the Commission recommends a renewed reliance on the talents and ingenuity of private citizens to develop better ways to accomplish what is now government's business.

CENTRAL AMERICAN CEASE-FIRE
March 23, 1988

After seven years of civil war in Nicaragua, representatives of the Sandinista government and its foe, the National Resistance—a guerrilla force better known as the contras—agreed on March 23 to a sixty-day cease-fire, effective April 1. This set the stage for negotiations aimed at permanently ending the strife, which by some estimates had caused 25,000 deaths. The truce was one of seven points in an agreement signed in Sapoá, Nicaragua.

Less than a month before the signing, the United States had cut off military aid to the contras. The dominant mood in Congress, refusing President Ronald Reagan's request for more contra arms and equipment, was to "give peace a chance"—a phrase used by several leading Democrats that reflected a desire to await the results of a Central American peace plan initiated the previous year by President Oscar Arias Sánchez of Costa Rica. (Central American Peace Agreement, Historic Documents of 1987, p. 637)

Arias enlisted the backing of other Central American presidents, including Daniel Ortega Saavedra of Nicaragua, at a meeting in Guatemala City, August 7, 1987. He persuaded his colleagues from Guatemala, Honduras, Nicaragua, and El Salvador to join him in signing the peace plan, thereby pledging to work toward specific goals for ending hostilities, bringing about national reconciliation, and instituting democratic reforms in their region. Arias's plan gained further prestige when he was awarded the 1987 Nobel Peace Prize. (Arias Nobel Peace Prize Speech, Historic Documents of 1987, p. 1007)

The pledge to bring about democratic reforms, including free elections and a free press, seemed a direct challenge to the leftist Nicaraguan government, which is controlled by Sandinistas—a movement that takes its name from a martyred revolutionary hero, César Sandino. Ortega's acceptance of those terms was greeted by skepticism in the Reagan administration, which portrayed him not only as a Communist but also as an opportunist seeking to influence Congress to terminate U.S. military aid to the contras.

Steps to Sapoá

Whatever Ortega's motive may have been, his government soon made a number of gestures toward compliance with the peace plan. It allowed the opposition daily La Prensa *in Managua to publish again, appointed the Sandinista's leading critic in the Catholic church, Cardinal Miguel Obando y Bravo, to head the Nicaraguan Reconciliation Committee, and asked him to serve as intermediary for talks with the contra leaders.*

These efforts led to the meeting at Sapoá, a small town on the Costa Rican border. There, in a Nicaraguan customs house, Defense Minister Humberto Ortega Saavedra, the president's brother, and contra representatives came to terms on the agreement. In addition to the truce and promise of further negotiations, the agreement called for the government to grant amnesty to political prisoners and for the contras to forgo military aid—they could accept only "humanitarian aid channeled through neutral organizations." The final two points were pledges by the government to let Nicaraguan exiles return to their homeland without punishment and to permit free elections. Two other signers of the agreement were Cardinal Obando and João Clemente Baena Soares, secretary general of the Organization of American States, who together would verify compliance with its provisions.

Washington reacted gingerly. Secretary of State George P. Shultz called it an "important step forward," but White House spokesman Marlin Fitzwater said the Reagan administration remained "skeptical" about the aims of the Sandinistas. Alfredo César, a contra leader, indicated that the aid cutoff caused him to sign the document. An interviewer quoted him as saying that the United States had "no political will to continue supporting the war," and thus "we weren't going to win in that situation." President Ortega, projecting a different mood, said the parties to the accord were "determined to bury the ax of war and raise the olive branch of peace."

Unsuccessful Negotiations

Government and contra representatives held four rounds of negotiations in Managua, Nicaragua's capital, beginning April 16, ten days later than the Sapoá pact requested. After three days this initial meeting ended without agreement, as did the second round April 28-30. However, both sides agreed to extend the cease-fire through June and to resume their talks May 26. Contra negotiators opened that round with an offer to lay down their arms if the Sandinistas would make sweeping reforms, to be negotiated during a sixty-day period, and declare a general amnesty.

The government appeared conciliatory, but in the fourth round of talks, June 7-9, the contras added new demands to a "final proposal." The Sandinistas balked, accusing a new member of the negotiating team, Col. Enrique Bermúdez, the contra military commander, with hardening the demands in an effort to sabotage the negotiations. At this stage, the negotiations broke off, although the cease-fire was kept in effect.

Arias, too, attributed most of the blame to the contras and offered to try to get the talks started again. This task was soon made more difficult by events in Managua. Just a month after the talks collapsed, the Sandinista regime launched its harshest attack in more than a year on its domestic opponents. The police used brute force to break up a demonstration in Managua; the government closed anti-Sandinista media outlets and threw opposition leaders in jail. La Prensa was permitted to resume publication on July 27, after a two-week hiatus, but the government showed no other signs of easing its crackdown. Nicaragua expelled the American ambassador and seven of his colleagues, and the United States retaliated by expelling eight Nicaraguan diplomats.

Secretary Shultz reported to Congress on July 7, after a trip to Central America, that the "[National] Resistance stressed that it sincerely wants to achieve a negotiated settlement, but has been weakened by deficiencies in the current U.S. assistance program to the point where it has little leverage in the talks." His words and the Sandinistas' crackdown added pressure on Congress to renew military aid to the contras. However, the question was not pressed by President Reagan. Rep. Mickey Edwards, R-Okla., surmised that Vice President George Bush believed that a bruising contra-aid fight in Congress would not benefit his presidential candidacy. For fiscal year 1989, Congress approved $27.1 million in "humanitarian" aid and set up a procedure to let the president seek $16.5 million in previously appropriated but unspent military aid.

Following is the text of the agreement signed March 23, 1988, in Sapoá, Nicaragua, calling for a cease-fire and other measures to end the civil war in Nicaragua (translated from Spanish by the State Department):

The Constitutional Government of the Republic of Nicaragua and the Nicaraguan Resistance, meeting at Sapoa, Nicaragua, on March 21, 22, and 23, 1988, with the aim of contributing to national reconciliation within the framework of the Esquipulas II Agreements [the Arias peace plan] and in the presence of the witnesses, His Eminence Cardinal Miguel Obando y Bravo, President of the Episcopal Conference of Nicaragua, and His Excellency Ambassador Joao Clemente Baena Soares, Secretary General of the Organization of American States (OAS), have arrived at the following agreement:

1. Offensive military operations shall cease throughout the national territory for a period of 60 days beginning on April 1, 1988. During this period a process of comprehensive negotiation shall be conducted for the definitive cease-fire, the actual execution of which shall occur jointly with the other commitments contemplated in Esquipulas II, in order to end the war.

Both parties agree to meet at the highest level in Managua next April 6 in order to continue the negotiations for the definitive cease-fire.

2. During the first 15 days, the resistance forces shall situate themselves in zones whose location, size, and modus operandi shall be mutually agreed upon through special commissions in a meeting at Sapoa to begin on Monday, March 28.

3. The Government of Nicaragua shall decree a general amnesty for persons prosecuted for and convicted of violations of the Law for Maintenance of Order and Public Security, and for members of the former regime's army prosecuted for and convicted of crimes committed prior to July 19, 1979. In the case of the first group, the amnesty shall be a gradual one. In view of the religious feelings of the Nicaraguan people on the occasion of Holy Week, the release of the first 100 prisoners shall begin on Palm Sunday. Subsequently, when the entrance of the Nicaraguan Resistance Forces into the mutually agreed zones is verified, 50 percent of the prisoners shall be released. The remaining 50 percent shall be set free on a date following the signing of the definitive cease-fire to be agreed upon at the April 6 meeting at Managua.

In the case of the prisoners covered by the last part of the first paragraph of this section, their release shall begin upon signature of the definitive cease-fire, subject to a report of the OAS Inter-American Human Rights Commission.

The OAS Secretary General shall be guarantor and depositary of the implementation of this amnesty.

4. For the purpose of guaranteeing food and basic supplies for the irregular forces, steps shall be taken to obtain exclusively humanitarian aid and only such aid shall be accepted, in accordance with section 5 of the Esquipulas II Agreements. That aid shall be channeled through neutral organizations.

5. The Government of Nicaragua shall guarantee unrestricted freedom of expression, as provided for in the Esquipulas II Agreement.

6. Once the Nicaraguan Resistance Forces are gathered in the mutually agreed zones, they shall send to the national dialogue as many delegates as there are political organizations within the Resistance, up to a maximum of eight. The national dialogue shall address, among other topics, the issue of military service.

7. A guarantee is hereby given that all persons who have left the country for political or any other reasons, may return to Nicaragua and become part of the political, economic, and social processes with no type of

conditions other than those established in the laws of the Republic. They shall not be tried, sanctioned, or prosecuted for any political-military activities in which they might have been involved.

8. The Government of Nicaragua confirms that persons who have been reincorporated into peaceful life may participate under equal conditions and guarantees in elections for the Central American Parliament, and in municipal elections, on the dates established for them, as well as in national general elections on the dates established in the constitution.

9. For purposes of verifying compliance with this agreement, a verification commission shall be created composed of his Eminence Cardinal Miguel Obando y Bravo, President of the Episcopal Conference of Nicaragua, and His Excellency Ambassador Joao Clemente Baena Soares, Secretary General of the OAS.

Technical assistance and the necessary services for this Commission that would permit and expedite compliance with the follow-up and verification of this Agreement shall be requested from and entrusted to the OAS Secretary General.

Both Parties agree to extend until April 1, 1988, the cessation of offensive military operations that they agreed to on March 21, 1988.

In witness whereof, we, the undersigned, hereby sign this Agreement in four copies, all equally authentic, at Sapoa, Rivas, Nicaragua on March 23, 1988.

For the government of Nicaragua: General Humberto Ortega Saavedra, Minister of Defense

Hans Jurgen Wischnewski, Adviser; Paul Richler, Adviser

For the Nicaraguan Resistance: Dr. Adolfo Calero Portocarrero, Director; Alfredo Cesar Aguirre, Director; Dr. Aristides Sanchez Herdocia, Director

Cease-fire Commission for the Nicaraguan Resistance: Jaime Morales Carazo, Chief Negotiator; Roberto Urroz Castillo, Dr. Fernando Aguero Rocha, Walter Calderon Lopez, Commandante Tono, Diogenes Hernandez Membreno, Commandante Fernando, Arturo Salazar Barberena, Commandante Omar, Osorno Coleman, Commandante Blas, Adm. Ramon Emilio Jimenez, Adviser

Witnesses: Cardinal Miguel Obando y Bravo, Ambassador Joao Clemente Baena Soares

April

Impeachment and Conviction
of Arizona Governor Mecham 249

Agreements on Afghanistan 257

Report on Aviation Safety 267

Court on Alcoholism and
Veterans' Benefits 277

Reparations for Japanese-American
Internees 287

Assessing American Education 297

IMPEACHMENT AND CONVICTION OF ARIZONA GOVERNOR MECHAM

April 4, 1988

For the first time in almost sixty years, a state legislature impeached and convicted a sitting governor. On April 4 the Arizona state Senate voted 21-9—one more than the two-thirds majority required—to convict Gov. Evan Mecham of trying to obstruct an investigation of an alleged death threat. This was the first of three articles of impeachment issued against him. That vote removed Mecham from office.

The Senate subsequently voted 26-4 to convict him on a charge of misusing $80,000 from a fund to pay for state events by lending the money to his auto dealership. The Senate declined to consider the third article of impeachment (alleging that Mecham had concealed a $350,000 campaign loan) to avoid prejudicing a criminal trial connected with the loan. The vote to dismiss that charge was 16-12.

Mecham became the fifth governor to be impeached, convicted, and removed from office in this century. He was the first since 1929 when Henry S. Johnston lost the governorship of Oklahoma for involvement with the Ku Klux Klan. In all, seventeen U.S. governors have been impeached and convicted.

Mecham, a staunchly conservative Republican, was elected in a three-way race in 1986 with 40 percent of the vote. He attracted national attention within a few days of taking office by canceling a state holiday that had been decreed by his predecessor in honor of the birthday of Martin Luther King, Jr., the late civil rights leader. Other controversies arose over his appointments and blunt comments. He squabbled with blacks, feminists, homosexuals, Jews, Catholics, Hispanics, Japanese-Americans, and others. He also alienated some potential allies in the Republican-controlled legislature by trying to appoint a liquor commissioner suspected of involvement in a slaying in Mexico and a tax commissioner who had not paid his state taxes. By the end of 1987, Mecham was being urged to resign by Republicans and Democrats, including former senator Barry Goldwater, the patriarch of Arizona Republicans.

Impeachment and Conviction

As the potential for long-term damage to the party increased, Republican legislators initiated impeachment proceedings, beginning with a decision to hire a special counsel to investigate allegations against the governor. Mecham denied he was guilty of any wrongdoing and vowed to fight demands that he resign. "I cannot do that," he announced on February 1. "I have a duty and responsibility to those voters who believe in my integrity. And I will not let them be disenfranchised by the vote of a few."

Nonetheless, the Arizona House of Representatives voted 46-14 on February 5 to impeach Mecham, filing twenty-three charges against him, ranging from concealing the $350,000 campaign loan to impeding the investigation of a death threat to a state employee. The Senate opened its trial February 22. Mecham testified March 15, again denying guilt, and recalling that his campaign theme had been to "rid the state of corruption."

After the House vote, Secretary of State Rose Mofford, a Democrat, became acting governor. Mofford—folksy and plain spoken—had worked in the state government for forty-seven years, for the past decade as secretary of state. "I was thrust into this, " she said on becoming acting governor. "I have done nothing to hurt this governor [Mecham], nothing." When the Senate convicted Mecham, Mofford became the state's first woman governor. She was sworn into office April 5.

Mecham, meanwhile, had been indicted on six criminal charges in connection with the campaign loan; his brother, William (who had served as campaign treasurer), had been indicted on three counts. They pleaded not guilty January 22; both subsequently refused to take the stand in the trial that followed in Phoenix. On June 16, after seven days of testimony and after deliberating six and one-half hours, a jury acquitted the two men on all counts.

Recall Issue

A complicating factor during the impeachment proceedings was the prospect of a recall election for Mecham's removal from office. On January 25, 1988, Secretary of State Mofford verified that enough signatures had been filed to force a recall election. Insisting that he would not resign, Mecham contended that the recall effort was a

Democratic-led conspiracy. But a number of Republicans also called on him to resign.

After Mecham was forced out of office through impeachment, the state Supreme Court had to determine whether the recall election, scheduled for May 17, should proceed. Mecham's ouster appeared to render the question moot. But the state's attorney general ruled that because Mecham did not resign during a five-day period in January (when enough signatures were validated to warrant a recall election), the state constitution dictated that the election must be held. However, on April 12, the court ruled that the election was no longer necessary. The decision meant that Mofford would serve out Mecham's term through 1990.

Following is the text of the three articles of impeachment against Arizona Gov. Evan Mecham, which the state House filed on February 8, 1988, and on which the state Senate voted April 1, 1988:

Articles of Impeachment

The duly elected Board of Managers of the House of Representatives of the Thirty-Eighth Legislature of the State of Arizona, by the authority of the Arizona Constitution and House Resolution 2002, presents these Articles of Impeachment to the Senate of the State of Arizona:

Evan Mecham has served as Governor of the State of Arizona since January 5, 1987. To qualify as Governor, he took and subscribed to the oath of office required by Arizona Revised Statutes ("A.R.S.") Section 38-231, and thereby swore to support the Constitution of the United States and the Constitution and laws of the State of Arizona, and to faithfully and impartially discharge the duties of the Office of Governor.

Evan Mecham, while acting in his official capacity, has violated the high duties imposed upon him by the Office of Governor and by his solemn oath, and has committed high crimes, misdemeanors or malfeasance in office in the State of Arizona, as set forth in the following Articles:

Article I
(Obstruction of Justice)

A. On or about November 15, 1987, Evan Mecham, while acting in his official capacity as Governor of the State of Arizona, knowingly attempted, by means of misrepresentation or intimidation, to obstruct, delay or prevent the communication of information or testimony relating to a violation of a criminal statute to the Arizona Attorney General by ordering the Director of the Arizona Department of Public Safety, Colonel Ralph Milstead, not to cooperate with the Attorney General's investigation into allegations concerning a threat by Lee Watkins directed against Donna Carlson and/or by transferring Lieutenant Beau Johnson from the Governor's security force, all in violation of A.R.S. Section 13-2409;

B. On or about November 15, 1987, Evan Mecham, while acting in his official capacity as Governor of the State of Arizona, attempted to influence a witness by threatening Department of Public Safety Director Colonel Ralph Milstead with the intent to influence the testimony of Colonel Milstead, Officer Frank Martinez and/or Lieutenant Beau Johnson and/or by ordering the transfer of Lieutenant Johnson from the Governor's security force and/or by ordering Colonel Milstead and his officers to refrain from giving information or to give false information to the Arizona Attorney General's office in the Attorney General's investigation regarding a threat made by Lee Watkins directed against Donna Carlson, all in violation of A.R.S. Sections 13-2802 and 13-1001;

C. On or about November 15, 1987, Evan Mecham, while acting in his official capacity as Governor of the State of Arizona, attempted to tamper with a witness by knowingly inducing Colonel Ralph Milstead, Officer Frank Martinez and/or Lieutenant Beau Johnson, who were witnesses in an Attorney General's investigation, or who Governor Mecham believed might be called as witnesses, to unlawfully withhold testimony or to testify falsely when he ordered Colonel Milstead, Officer Martinez and/or Lieutenant Johnson not to cooperate with the Attorney General's investigation, or to give false information to the Attorney General in connection with that investigation, all in violation of A.R.S. Sections 13-2804 and 13-1001;

D. On or about November 15, 1987, Evan Mecham, while acting in his official capacity as Governor of the State of Arizona, knowingly, and with the intent to hinder the apprehension, prosecution, conviction or punishment of Lee Watkins, attempted to obstruct Colonel Ralph Milstead, Officer Frank Martinez and/or Lieutenant Beau Johnson, by means of intimidation or deception, from cooperating with the Arizona Attorney General's investigation of a threat made by Lee Watkins directed against Donna Carlson, all in violation of A.R.S. Sections 13-2512 and 13-1001;

E. On or about November 15, 1987, Evan Mecham, while acting in his official capacity as Governor of the State of Arizona, knowingly, and with the intent to promote or facilitate the commission of a felony or misdemeanor, commanded, encouraged, requested or solicited Colonel Ralph Milstead to engage in specific conduct in violation of A.R.S. Sections 13-2804 and 13-2802 by ordering Colonel Ralph Milstead to prevent other Department of Public Safety Officers from testifying or cooperating in an investigation regarding a threat made by Lee Watkins directed against Donna Carlson, all in violation of A.R.S. Section 13-1002;

F. On or about November 15, 1987, Evan Mecham, while acting in his official capacity as Governor of the State of Arizona, engaged in a prohibited personnel practice under A.R.S. Section 38-532 by knowingly ordering the transfer or reassignment of Lieutenant Beau Johnson from Governor Mecham's security detail as a reprisal against Lieutenant Johnson for disclosing information regarding an event that Lieutenant Johnson reasonably believed to be a violation of law or an abuse of authority;

G. By undertaking each of the acts set forth in this Article, Evan

Mecham disregarded and thereby violated the solemn oath of the office of Governor that he took pursuant to A.R.S. Section 38-231; or

H. Each of the acts set forth in this Article were undertaken by Evan Mecham without lawful authority and were positively wrong or unlawful, or constituted an abuse of official power, neglect of duty, corruption and/or obstruction of justice.

Article II
(False Sworn Statements Relating to Official Filings Made While in Office)

A. On or about April 1, 1987, Evan Mecham, while serving as Governor of the State of Arizona, signed and caused to be filed an amended statement of contributions and expenditures (the "Amended December 5 Statement of Contributions and Expenditures"), which related to an earlier statement of Contributions and Expenditures filed December 5, 1986 (the "December 5, 1986 Statement"). The December 5, 1986 Statement falsely stated that Evan Mecham contributed $465,000.00 to the Mecham for Governor Campaign, thereby concealing and failing to name Barry Wolfson as the lender of the sum of $350,000.00 to the Mecham for Governor Campaign and/or failing to list the individual promissory notes given in connection therewith. The Amended December 5 Statement of Contributions and Expenditures ratified, confirmed and contained a false sworn statement in regard to a material issue, which Evan Mecham believed to be false, all in violation of A.R.S. Sections 16-912, 16-915, 13-2701, 13-2702 and 13-2703;

B. On or about April 1, 1987, Evan Mecham, while serving as Governor of the State of Arizona, signed and caused to be filed with the Secretary of State's office the Amended December 5 Statement of Contributions and Expenditures which related to the December 5, 1986 Statement. The December 5, 1986 Statement falsely identified Evan Mecham as a contributor of $465,000.00 to the Mecham for Governor Campaign, and thereby falsified, concealed and/or covered up the material fact that Barry Wolfson loaned $350,000.00 to the Mecham for Governor Campaign and/or failed to list the individual promissory notes given in connection therewith. The Amended December Statement ratified, confirmed and failed to state facts relating to the December 5, 1986 Statement. In signing and causing to be filed the Amended December 5 Statement of Contributions and Expenditures, Evan Mecham concealed a material fact by a trick, scheme or device or made or used a false writing or document knowing such writing or document contained a false or fraudulent statement or entry, all in violation of A.R.S. Section 13-2311;

C. On or about April 1, 1987, Evan Mecham, while serving as Governor of the State of Arizona, signed and caused to be filed the Amended December 5 Statement of Contributions and Expenditures, which he knew failed to disclose under the Financial Statement required thereunder, a $600,000.00 line of credit provided by Barry Wolfson and/or Hugh Gregan to the Mecham for Governor Campaign, and a $350,000.00 loan made by

Barry Wolfson to the Mecham for Governor Campaign, all in violation of A.R.S. Section 16-912;

D. On or about April 1, 1987, Evan Mecham, while serving as Governor of the State of Arizona, signed and caused to be filed a Statement of Contributions and Expenditures (the "April 1 Statement of Contributions and Expenditures"), which falsely represented that Evan Mecham had been repaid the sum of $315,674.04 by the Mecham for Governor Campaign, and thereby concealed and failed to state that Barry Wolfson had been repaid the sum of $125,000.00 from the Mecham for Governor Campaign, and thereby made a false sworn statement in regard to a material issue that he believed to be false, all in violation of A.R.S. Sections 16-912, 16-915, 13-2701, 13-2702 and 13-2703;

E. On or about April 1, 1987, Evan Mecham, while serving as Governor of the State of Arizona, signed and caused to be filed with the Secretary of State's office the April 1 Statement of Contributions and Expenditures, which falsely listed a repayment to Evan Mecham of $315,674.04 from the Mecham for Governor Campaign, thereby falsifying, concealing and/or covering up the material fact that Barry Wolfson had been repaid the sum of $125,000.00 from the Mecham for Governor Campaign. In signing and causing to be filed the April 1, 1986 Statement of Contributions and Expenditures, Evan Mecham concealed a material fact by a trick, scheme or device or made or used a false writing or document knowing such writing or document contained a false or fraudulent statement or entry, all in violation of A.R.S. Section 13-2311;

F. On or about April 1, 1987, Evan Mecham, while serving as Governor of the State of Arizona, signed and caused to be filed the April 1 Statement of Contributions and Expenditures which he knew failed to fully disclose under the Financial Statement required thereunder, a $350,000.00 loan made by Barry Wolfson to the Mecham for Governor Campaign which is believed to have had a balance of $225,000.00 on April 1, 1987, all in violation of A.R.S. Section 16-912;

G. On or about October 25, 1986, Evan Mecham signed and caused to be filed a Statement of Contributions and Expenditures for the period from September 20, 1986 through October 15, 1986 in connection with the Mecham for Governor Campaign, which he knew failed to disclose a $600,000.00 line of credit provided by Barry Wolfson and/or Hugh Gregan to the Mecham for Governor Campaign and/or failed to list the individual promissory notes given in connection therewith, and thereby made a false sworn statement regarding a material issue that he believed to be false, all in violation of A.R.S. Sections 16-912, 16-915, 13-2701, 13-2702 and 13-2703, which false sworn statement Evan Mecham failed to correct while remaining as Governor of Arizona;

H. On or about February 2, 1987, and on or about February 6, 1987, Evan Mecham, while acting in his official capacity as Governor of the State of Arizona, made a false sworn statement in regard to a material issue, believing it to be false, by signing and causing to be filed a Financial Disclosure Statement for 1986 and an Amended Financial Disclosure

Statement for 1986, both of which falsely represented that reportable "Personal Debts of Over $1,000.00" owed by Evan Mecham included only those listed, when in fact Evan Mecham also personally owed money in 1986 in connection with a $350,000.00 loan to the Mecham for Governor Campaign, including but not limited to two $50,000.00 promissory notes signed by Evan Mecham payable to Barry Wolfson, all in violation of A.R.S. Sections 13-2701, 13-2702, 13-2703, 38-542, 38-543 and 38-544.

I. On or about February 2, 1987, and on or about February 6, 1987, Evan Mecham, while acting in his official capacity as Governor of the State of Arizona, signed and caused to be filed with the Secretary of State a 1986 Financial Disclosure Statement and an Amended 1986 Financial Disclosure Statement, both of which falsely represented that reported "Personal Debts Over $1,000.00" owed by Evan Mecham included only those listed, when in fact Evan Mecham had falsified, concealed and/or covered up the material fact that he personally owed money in 1986 in connection with a $350,000.00 loan to the Mecham for Governor Campaign, including but not limited to two $50,000.00 promissory notes signed by Evan Mecham payable to Barry Wolfson, which conduct on the part of Evan Mecham was pursuant to a scheme or artifice to defraud or deceive, knowingly falsify, conceal or cover up a material fact by a scheme or device or a false writing or document which Evan Mecham knew contained a false, fictitious or fraudulent statement or entry, all in violation of A.R.S. Sections 13-2311, 38-542, 38-543 and 38-544;

J. By undertaking each of the acts set forth in this Article, Evan Mecham disregarded and thereby violated the solemn oath of the Office of Governor that he took pursuant to A.R.S. Section 38-231; or

K. Each of the acts set forth in this Article were undertaken by Evan Mecham without lawful authority and were positively wrong or unlawful, or constituted an abuse of official power, neglect of duty, corruption and/or betrayal of public trust.

Article III
(Misuse of Funds)

A. On or about May 27, 1987, the Mecham Inaugural Committee transferred the sum of $92,910.35 to the Office of the Governor. On or about July 16, 1987, Evan Mecham, while acting in his official capacity as Governor of the State of Arizona, personally and knowingly directed and/or authorized James Colter, the Governor's Chief of Staff, to make a loan of $80,000.00 out of funds held by the Office of the Governor pursuant to A.R.S. Section 41-1105, to Mecham Pontiac Corporation, the stock of which was owned by Evan Mecham and his wife. The loan to Mecham Pontiac Corporation was without lawful authority and was a knowing unauthorized use, for an unauthorized term, of property of another, which property had been entrusted to the Office of the Governor or placed in the possession of the Office of the Governor for a limited authorized use. When the loan was made, it was not made for the purpose of promoting the interests of the State or to promote and encourage citizen public service to the State pursuant to A.R.S. Section 41-1105, and furthermore was made in violation of A.R.S. Sections 13-1802 and 35-301;

B. The monies loaned to Mecham Pontiac Corporation referred to in Article III(A) were obtained by the Office of the Governor pursuant to a settlement with the Maricopa County Attorney's Office in which the Maricopa County Attorney agreed not to charge Evan Mecham's Inaugural Committee with a violation of A.R.S. Section 16-905 if the monies remaining in the Mecham Inaugural Committee account were transferred to the Office of the Governor to be held and expended pursuant to A.R.S. Section 41-1105. If the loan to Mecham Pontiac Corporation was not made from monies held by the Office of the Governor pursuant to A.R.S. Section 41-1105 and/or the monies were not public monies, the monies were obtained by Evan Mecham in violation of A.R.S. Sections 16-905, 13-2310 and 13-2311, and/or said loan was made in violation of A.R.S. Sections 16-905 and 13-1802;

C. By undertaking each of the acts set forth in this Article, Evan Mecham disregarded and thereby violated the solemn oath of the Office of Governor that he took pursuant to A.R.S. Section 38-231; or

D. Each of the acts set forth in this Article were undertaken by Evan Mecham without lawful authority, and were positively wrong or unlawful, or constituted an abuse of official power, neglect of duty, corruption, obstruction of justice, betrayal of public trust, misapplication of funds and/or were in breach of his trust and fiduciary responsibilities.

* * *

As set forth in the foregoing Articles, Evan Mecham has committed high crimes, misdemeanors or malfeasance in office, and thus has acted in a manner contrary to public trust and his oath as Governor, and in violation of and contrary to the Constitution and laws of the State of Arizona, all to the great prejudice of the cause of law and justice, and to the manifest injury to the people of the State of Arizona.

Signed this 8th day of February, 1988, by the duly elected Board of Managers of the House of Representatives of the Thirty-Eighth Legislature of the State of Arizona.

Representative Heinz R. Hink,
Chairman

Representative Henry Evans,
Member

Representative Benjamin Hanley,
Member

Representative Chris Herstam,
Member

Representative Jim Miller,
Member

AGREEMENTS ON AFGHANISTAN
April 14, 1988

After nearly six years of negotiations, Afghanistan, Pakistan, the Soviet Union, and the United States signed agreements April 14 in Geneva providing for the withdrawal of Soviet troops from Afghanistan. Although the pacts imparted a negotiated solution to the eight-year Soviet occupation, they did not arrange a cease-fire in the fighting between guerrilla and Soviet-backed government forces in Afghanistan. Nor did the documents ensure a peaceful transition once the Soviet troops were removed.

Acknowledging those defects of the settlement, the chief United Nations mediator, Diego Cordovez, said on the eve of the signing that the accords reflected "the reality of the situation." The combination of stepped-up military activity by the Afghan Mujaheddin guerrillas and a general effort by Soviet leader Mikhail S. Gorbachev to remold the Soviet image led to the negotiated settlement. The first troops pulled out May 15. By agreeing to a U.S. provision calling for the early departure of most of the Soviet troops and not making the withdrawal contingent upon who will control the future Afghan government, Gorbachev suddenly breathed new life into the negotiations that had appeared deadlocked at the end of 1987. But on February 8 he said in a televised statement: "By now documents covering all aspects of a settlement have been almost fully worked out at the Geneva negotiations.... All of this creates the necessary conditions for signing the settlement agreement in the very near future."

In his closing remarks, Gorbachev said that "implementing a political settlement in Afghanistan will be an important rupture in the chain of regional conflicts." By withdrawing from Afghanistan, the Soviet Union would comply with the first of three demands made by China as conditions for closer Sino-Soviet relations. The other two involved the reduction of Soviet troops on the Sino-Soviet border and the evacuation of Soviet-backed Vietnamese forces in Cambodia.

UN Negotiations

As the final round of UN-mediated talks got under way in Geneva on March 4, debate continued over arms being supplied to the separate sides by the Soviet Union and United States, and also over a Pakistani demand for an "interim" government in Afghanistan. However, Secretary of State George P. Shultz and Soviet Foreign Minister Eduard Shevardnadze, meeting on March 22-23 to plan the Moscow summit in May (Reagan-Gorbachev Summit, p. 353), *came to an agreement on military aid and the course of Soviet troop withdrawals. Shortly thereafter, Pakistan dropped its demand for a coalition government in Afghanistan.*

Afghan guerrillas were denied a voice in the negotiations. Consequently, leaders of all seven Mujaheddin factions rejected the accord, and vowed to replace the existing Soviet-backed government. But rivalries among the guerrilla factions kept them from agreeing on the formation of a new government.

Treaty Provisions

The Geneva settlement, consisting of four agreements, ensured non-interference by Pakistan and Afghanistan in each other's internal affairs, U.S.-Soviet support of the Afghan-Pakistan agreement, "voluntary and unimpeded" return of Afghan refugees to their homeland, and the Soviet withdrawal of 100,000 to 120,000 troops from Afghanistan by the end of 1988.

In a war that has claimed the lives of an estimated one million Afghans and displaced five million others—three million to Pakistan and two million to Iran—the accords provided for the "voluntary and unimpeded" return to Afghanistan of refugees living in Pakistan. After a period of eighteen months, the signatories were directed to make "additional arrangements" for the repatriation of refugees if the present guidelines proved inadequate.

Of the four agreements, however, the issue of Soviet occupation demanded the most immediate attention. According to an agreed upon timetable, Soviet troops would begin leaving May 15, and by August 15 one-half of them would be gone. The last would leave by February 15, 1989. Both Shultz and Shevardnadze signed the agreement as guarantors "who have signified their consent with its provisions." But the terms of withdrawal limited the process to a bilateral arrangement between

Moscow and the Soviet-backed regime in Kabul, with little third-party oversight of the evacuation. In addition, the departure of Soviet forces referred only to "uniformed" Soviet troops: thousands of nonuniformed Soviet personnel in Afghanistan were not mentioned.

Before the signing ceremony, Shultz submitted a statement to UN Secretary General Javier Pérez de Cuéllar, stressing the importance of Soviet adherence to the withdrawal timetable. A Soviet breach of agreement, Shultz said, would allow the United States "to provide military assistance to parties in Afghanistan." Shultz added that "should the Soviet Union exercise restraint in providing military assistance to parties in Afghanistan, the U.S. similarly will exercise restraint."

Following are main portions of the documents comprising the negotiated settlement regarding Afghanistan, signed April 14, 1988:

BILATERAL AGREEMENT ON PRINCIPLES OF MUTUAL RELATIONS

The Republic of Afghanistan and the Islamic Republic of Pakistan, hereinafter referred to as the High Contracting Parties,

Desiring to normalize relations and promote good-neighbourliness and co-operation as well as to strengthen international peace and security in the region . . . ,

Have agreed as follows:

Article I

Relations between the High Contracting Parties shall be conducted in strict compliance with the principle of non-interference and non-intervention by States in the affairs of other States.

Article II

For the purpose of implementing the principles of non-interference and non-intervention each High Contracting Party undertakes to comply with the following obligations:

1. to respect the sovereignty, political independence, territorial integrity, national unity, security and non-alignment of the other High Contracting Party, as well as the national identity and cultural heritage of its people;
2. to respect the sovereign and inalienable right of the other High Contracting Party freely to determine its own political, economic, cultural and social systems, to develop its international relations and to exercise permanent sovereignty over its natural resources, in accordance with the will of its people, and without outside interven-

tion, interference, subversion, coercion or threat in any form whatsoever;

3. to refrain from the threat or use of force in any form whatsoever so as to not to violate the boundaries of each other, to disrupt the political, social or economic order of the other High Contracting Party, to overthrow or change the political system of the other High Contracting Party or its Government, or to cause tension between the High Contracting Parties;

4. to ensure that its territory is not used in any manner which would violate the sovereignty, political independence, territorial integrity and national unity or disrupt the political, economic and social stability of the other High Contracting Party;

5. to refrain from armed intervention, subversion, military occupation or any other form of intervention and interference, overt or covert, directed at the other High Contracting Party, or any act of military, political or economic interference in the internal affairs of the other High Contracting Party, including acts of reprisal involving the use of force;

6. to refrain from any action or attempt in whatever form or under whatever pretext to destabilize or to undermine the stability of the other High Contracting Party or any of its institutions;

7. to refrain from the promotion, encouragement or support, direct or indirect, of rebellious or secessionist activities against the other High Contracting Party, under any pretext whatsoever, or from any other action which seeks to disrupt the unity or to undermine or subvert the political order of the other High Contracting Party;

8. to prevent within its territory the training, equipping, financing and recruitment of mercenaries from whatever origin for the purpose of hostile activities against the other High Contracting Party, or the sending of such mercenaries into the territory of the other High Contracting Party and accordingly to deny facilities, including financing for the training, equipping and transit of such mercenaries;

9. to refrain from making any agreements or arrangements with other States designed to intervene or interfere in the internal and external affairs of the other High Contracting Party;

10. to abstain from any defamatory campaign, vilification or hostile propaganda for the purpose of intervening or interfering in the internal affairs of the other High Contracting Party;

11. to prevent any assistance to or use of or tolerance of terrorist groups, saboteurs or subversive agents against the other High Contracting Party;

12. to prevent within its Territory the presence, harbouring, in camps and bases or otherwise, organizing, training, financing, equipping and arming of individuals and political, ethnic and any other groups for the purpose of creating subversion, disorder or unrest in the

territory of the other High Contracting Party and accordingly also to prevent the use of mass media and the transportation of arms, ammunition and equipment by such individuals and groups;

13. not to resort to or to allow any other action that could be considered as interference or intervention.

Article III

The present Agreement shall enter into force on 15 May 1988.

Article IV

Any steps that may be required in order to enable the High Contracting Parties to comply with the provisions of Article II of this Agreement shall be completed by the date on which this Agreement enters into force.

Article V

This Agreement is drawn up in the English, Pashtu and Urdu languages, all texts being equally authentic. In case of any divergence of interpretation, the English text shall prevail. . . .

(Signed by Afghanistan and Pakistan)

DECLARATION ON INTERNATIONAL GUARANTEES

The Governments of the Union of Soviet Socialist Republics and of the United States of America,

Expressing support that the Republic of Afghanistan and the Islamic Republic of Pakistan have concluded a negotiated political settlement designed to normalize relations and promote good-neighbourliness between the two countries as well as to strengthen international peace and security in the region;

Wishing in turn to contribute to the achievement of the objectives that the Republic of Afghanistan and the Islamic Republic of Pakistan have set themselves, and with a view to ensuring respect for their sovereignty, independence, territorial integrity and non-alignment;

Undertake to invariably refrain from any form of interference and intervention in the internal affairs of the Republic of Afghanistan and the Islamic Republic of Pakistan and to respect the commitments contained in the bilateral agreement between the Republic of Afghanistan and the Islamic Republic of Pakistan on the Principles of Mutual Relations, in particular on Non-Interference and Non-Intervention;

Urge all States to do likewise.

The present Declaration shall enter into force on 15 May 1988. . . .

(Signed by the USSR and the USA)

BILATERAL AGREEMENT ON THE
VOLUNTARY RETURN OF REFUGEES

The Republic of Afghanistan and the Islamic Republic of Pakistan, hereinafter referred to as the High Contracting Parties . . . ,

Convinced that voluntary and unimpeded repatriation constitutes the most appropriate solution for the problem of Afghan refugees present in the Islamic Republic of Pakistan and having ascertained that the arrangements for the return of the Afghan refugees are satisfactory to them,

Have agreed as follows:

Article I

All Afghan refugees temporarily present in the territory of the Islamic Republic of Pakistan shall be given the opportunity to return voluntarily to their homeland in accordance with the arrangements and conditions set out in the present Agreement.

Article II

The Government of the Republic of Afghanistan shall take all necessary measures to ensure the following conditions for the voluntary return of Afghan refugees to their homeland:

(a) All refugees shall be allowed to return in freedom to their homeland;

(b) All returnees shall enjoy the free choice of domicile and freedom of movement within the Republic of Afghanistan;

(c) All returnees shall enjoy the right to work, to adequate living conditions and to share in the welfare of the State;

(d) All returnees shall enjoy the right to participate on an equal basis in the civic affairs of the Republic of Afghanistan. They shall be ensured equal benefits from the solution of the land question on the basis of the Land and Water Reform;

(e) All returnees shall enjoy the same rights and privileges, including freedom of religion, and have the same obligations and responsibilities as any other citizens of the Republic of Afghanistan without discrimination.

The Government of the Republic of Afghanistan undertakes to implement these measures and to provide, within its possibilities, all necessary assistance in the process of repatriation.

Article III

The Government of the Islamic Republic of Pakistan shall facilitate the voluntary, orderly and peaceful repatriation of all Afghan refugees staying within its territory and undertakes to provide, within its possibilities, all necessary assistance in the process of repatriation.

Article IV

For the purpose of organizing, co-ordinating and supervising the operations which should effect the voluntary, orderly and peaceful repatriation of Afghan refugees, there shall be set up mixed commissions in accordance with the established international practice. For the performance of their functions the members of the commissions and their staff shall be accorded the necessary facilities, and have access to the relevant areas within the territories of the High Contracting Parties.

Article V

With a view to the orderly movement of the returnees, the commissions shall determine frontier crossing points and establish necessary transit centres. They shall also establish all other modalities for the phased return of refugees, including registration and communication to the country of return of the names of refugees who express the wish to return.

Article VI

At the request of the Governments concerned, the United Nations High Commissioner for Refugees will co-operate and provide assistance in the process of voluntary repatriation of refugees in accordance with the present Agreement. Special agreements may be concluded for this purpose between UNHCR and the High Contracting Parties.

Article VII

The present Agreement shall enter into force on 15 May 1988. At that time the mixed commissions provided in Article IV shall be established and the operations for the voluntary return of refugees under this Agreement shall commence.

The arrangements set out in Articles IV and V above shall remain in effect for a period of eighteen months. After that period the High Contracting Parties shall review the results of the repatriation and, if necessary, consider any further arrangements that may be called for.

Article VIII

This Agreement is drawn up in the English, Pashtu and Urdu languages, all texts being equally authentic. In case of any divergence of interpretation, the English text shall prevail. ...

(Signed by Afghanistan and Pakistan)

AGREEMENT ON INTERRELATIONSHIPS

[Articles 1 through 6 omitted]

7. To consider alleged violations and to work out ... solutions to questions that may arise in the implementation of the instruments

comprising the settlement representatives of the Republic of Afghanistan and the Islamic Republic of Pakistan shall meet whenever required.

A representative of the Secretary-General of the United Nations shall lend his good offices to the Parties and in that context he will assist in the organization of the meetings and participate in them. He may submit to the Parties for their consideration and approval suggestions and recommendations for prompt, faithful and complete observance of the provisions of the instruments.

In order to enable him to fulfil his tasks, the representative shall be assisted by such personnel under his authority as required. . . . Any report submitted by the representative to the two Governments shall be considered in a meeting of the Parties no later than forty-eight hours after it has been submitted.

The modalities and logistical arrangements for the work of the representative and the personnel under his authority as agreed upon with the Parties are set out in the Memorandum of Understanding which is annexed to and is part of this Agreement. . . .

[Article 8 omitted]

(Signed by Afghanistan and Pakistan)

In witness thereof, the representatives of the States-Guarantors affixed their signatures hereunder:

(Signed by the USSR and USA)

Annex

Memorandum of Understanding

[Parts I and II omitted]

III. Modus Operandi and Personnel Organization

The Secretary-General will appoint a senior military officer as Deputy to the Representative who will be stationed in the area, as head of two small headquarters units, one in Kabul and the other in Islamabad, each comprising five military officers, drawn from existing United Nations operations, and a small civilian auxiliary staff.

The Deputy to the Representative of the Secretary-General will act on behalf of the Representative and be in contact with the Parties through the Liaison Officer each Party will designate for this purpose.

The two headquarters units will be organized into two Inspection Teams to ascertain on the ground any violation of the instruments comprising the settlement. Whenever considered necessary by the Representative of the Secretary-General or his Deputy, up to 40 additional military officers (some 10 additional Inspection Teams) will be redeployed from existing operations within the shortest possible time (normally around 48 hours).

The nationalities of all the Officers will be determined in consultation with the Parties.

Whenever necessary the Representative of the Secretary-General, who will periodically visit the area for consultations with the Parties and to review the work of his personnel, will also assign to the area members of his own Office and other civilian personnel from the United Nations Secretariat as may be needed. His Deputy will alternate between the two Headquarters units and will remain at all times in close communication with him. . . .

[Part IV omitted]

V. Duration

The Deputy to the Representative of the Secretary-General and the other personnel will be established in the area not later than twenty days before the entry into force of the instruments. The arrangements will cease to exist two months after the completion of all time-frames envisaged for the implementation of the instruments.

VI. Financing

The cost of all facilities and services to be provided by the Parties will be borne by the respective Governments. The salaries and travel expenses of the personnel to and from the area, as well as the costs of the local personnel assigned to the headquarters units, will be defrayed by the United Nations.

U.S. STATEMENT

The United States has agreed to act as a guarantor of the political settlement of the situation relating to Afghanistan. We believe this settlement is a major step forward in restoring peace to Afghanistan, in ending the bloodshed in that unfortunate country, and in enabling millions of Afghan refugees to return to their homes.

In agreeing to act as a guarantor, the United States states the following:

(1) The troop withdrawal obligations set out in paragraphs 5 and 6 of the Instrument on Interrelationships are central to the entire settlement. Compliance with those obligations is essential to achievement of the settlement's purposes, namely, the ending of foreign intervention in Afghanistan and the restoration of the rights of the Afghan people through the exercise of self determination as called for by the United Nations Charter and the United Nations General Assembly resolutions on Afghanistan.

(2) The obligations undertaken by the guarantors are symmetrical. In this regard, the United States has advised the Soviet Union that, if the USSR undertakes, as consistent with its obligations as guarantor, to provide military assistance to parties in Afghanistan, the U.S.

retains the right, as consistent with its own obligations as guarantor, likewise effectively to provide such assistance.

(3) By acting as a guarantor of the settlement, the United States does not intend to imply in any respect recognition of the present regime in Kabul as the lawful Government of Afghanistan.

REPORT ON AVIATION SAFETY
April 18, 1988

Recommending changes in the way the federal government regulates aviation safety, a presidential commission said in its report of April 18 that the current regulatory system was "inadequate to deal with future growth and technological change." The seven-member Aviation Safety Commission also proposed that the Federal Aviation Administration (FAA) be removed from the Department of Transportation and returned to independent status under a new name, the Federal Aviation Authority. An official of the proposed agency would be given broad powers as director of aviation safety—a position sometimes referred to as "safety czar."

President Ronald Reagan appointed the commission ten months earlier in response to rising concerns over safety in the air. The commission's chairman, John M. Albertine, said in a speech when the report was issued that "the nation's air transportation system is safe, for now." Albertine also said that safety was being maintained to an increasing extent through delays in flight departures and arrivals and through "the heroic efforts of air traffic controllers, airways facilities technicians, safety inspectors, and other FAA personnel."

The Aviation Safety Commission was established by a provision in a 1986 law (PL 99-591) that mandated a broad inquiry into federal air-safety responsibilities. As required by the law, a majority of the commission's members were from outside the aviation industry.

Besides Albertine, vice chairman of Farley Industries, other commis-

sion members were S. John Byington, a lawyer; Joseph P. Kalt, a professor at the John F. Kennedy School of Government, Harvard University; Michael E. Levine, a professor at the Yale School of Organization and Management; Russell W. Myer, Jr., chairman of the Cessna Aircraft Company; John E. Robson, dean of the School of Business Administration at Emory University; and Thomas W. Wathen, president of CPP Pinkerton, Inc.

Background

The Federal Aviation Administration, created in 1958 as an independent agency, became part of the Department of Transportation eight years later. The FAA operated the air-traffic control system, inspected aircraft for safety, and wrote and enforced rules on a wide range of aviation topics. The agency was also charged with promoting the growth of air commerce.

When the Professional Air Traffic Controllers Organization (PATCO) illegally went out on strike in August 1981, Reagan ordered the strikers to return to work in forty-eight hours or lose their jobs. When they did not return, the administration fired 11,400 controllers and kept the FAA from rehiring any of them. (Air Controllers Strike, Historic Documents of 1981, p. 621)

The agency also had found itself at the center of vast changes in aviation brought about by the Airline Deregulation Act of 1978. In the wake of economic deregulation, airline competition became intense. Fares declined on many routes and passenger traffic increased markedly. The number of airlines at first expanded as new carriers entered the market, but several fell on hard times and were merged with a diminishing number of remaining companies.

A public perception that airway safety was deteriorating seemed to be associated with deregulation and the dismissal of the air traffic controllers. The General Accounting Office, the investigative arm of Congress, surveyed the air traffic work force and issued a report in March 1986 recommending restrictions on air traffic. The FAA opposed the recommendations and Congress was not expected to act on them before 1989.

The uneasiness over safety continued. On April 13, just five days before the Aviation Safety Commission issued its report, the FAA proposed to fine Eastern Airlines $863,000 for alleged safety violations and initiated an aircraft-by-aircraft safety inspection of Eastern and its sister airline, Continental, both owned by Texas Air Corporation. At a news conference on June 2, Transportation Secretary James H. Burnley IV said Eastern and Continental flights were found to be operating safely during the course of the inspection.

However, the findings that Burnley announced also noted "an increased risk" that labor-management discord at Eastern "will, at some *time, either through inattention or design, have an adverse impact on public safety." On May 6, Texas Air brought a $1.3 billion lawsuit against two unions, the Air Line Pilots Association and the International Association of Machinists, charging that they had illegally conspired to destroy Eastern. The safety findings did not erase the FAA's proposal that Eastern be fined for infractions allegedly occurring before the inspection period. Ordinarily, such allegations are turned over to the Justice Department for legal action if the airline challenges them and the resulting negotiations fail.*

Recommendations

Burnley told a congressional subcommittee on March 23 that he was "dismayed at the institutional resistance [at the FAA] to improving safety regulations," which he attributed to the agency's close dealings with the aviation industry. The idea of a "powerful" safety director was viewed as an attempt to bypass that kind of situation. At a hearing before the Senate Commerce Subcommittee on Aviation on April 20, former FAA administrator Donald D. Engen challenged that view. He portrayed his ex-boss as a foot-dragger on safety rules.

In addition to creating the new position of safety director, the report recommended that the FAA be allowed to establish its own personnel and procurement rules. Freed from civil service rules, according to the report's authors, FAA air traffic controllers could be transferred more readily. Moreover, freed from government procurement rules, the FAA could modernize the nation's air traffic control system more rapidly. Finally, the report also urged tighter rules for commuter aviation lines, greater use of altitude-reporting equipment in small planes, and more surprise inspections.

The commission insisted that airline safety had not deteriorated since deregulation began. The report stressed that what took place in 1978 was economic deregulation and that the 1978 law "did not in any way change the scope or intent of air safety laws and regulations."

"While there seems to be a widespread perception of a growing safety problem," the report said, "a review of the post-deregulation accident record reveals a much different picture." The report also said that rates for accidents caused by air traffic control error, which had never been high, had "actually declined . . . during 1979 to 1985."

Reaction

Congress tended to look favorably on the commission's report. Drawing the most criticism among the recommendations was the provision for a "safety czar." Within the Reagan administration, Burnley argued that the authority should remain in his department. The secretary's office, Burnley said, had played a helpful role in promoting aviation safety.

Sen. Wendell H. Ford, D-Ky., chairman of the Commerce Subcommittee on Aviation, said, "I'd like to move as quickly as possible." But Ford raised questions about the division of responsibilities between the FAA administrator and a new safety director. Rep. Norman Y. Mineta, D-Calif., chairman of the House Public Works and Transportation Subcommittee on Aviation, planned to open hearings on air-safety responsibilities. Before the report was issued, Mineta had expressed apprehension that as an independent authority the FAA might be unable to obtain sufficient funding. Sen. Ernest F. Hollings, D-S.C., expressed concern that an independent FAA might be dominated by the aviation industry.

Following are excerpts from the final report and recommendations of the Aviation Safety Commission, issued April 18, 1988:

Executive Summary

After months of study, hearings, meetings around the country, and staff reports, the Aviation Safety Commission unanimously concludes that the nation's air transportation system is safe. However, safety is being maintained to an increasing extent through delays and other inconveniences.

Air transportation has changed during the past decade. Economic regulations that had shaped the industry since the 1920s were replaced by airline deregulation. The resulting increased competition has lowered fares, expanded service, and brought air travel to millions who had not previously been able to afford to fly. It has also made the FAA's job much more difficult.

The Aviation Safety Commission concludes that the present safety regulatory structure designed to ensure aviation safety is inadequate to deal with future growth and technological change. Now is the time to equip the regulatory system to accommodate changes in the numbers and kinds of aircraft, to take advantage of new technology in aircraft design and manufacture, to respond to heightened sensitivity on the part of the public to aviation safety, and to act on the backlog of potentially worthwhile safety improvements that have been languishing because of diffused authority and accountability. In short, *now* is the time for decisive action by Congress and the Executive Branch.

The Aviation Safety Commission believes that the Federal government must continue to play the central role in ensuring safe operation of the U.S. aviation system. We also share the common perception that, while the system is safe for now, the present governmental structure is not working effectively enough to ensure its safety in the future. Therefore, we agree unanimously that a major structural overhaul is essential. We believe that the regulatory process must remain governmental in character and should not be taken out of the Federal government or removed from public accountability. . . .

Specifically, the Aviation Safety Commission recommends that FAA be transferred from the Department of Transportation and be established as a user-funded authority which is:

- overseen by a nine-member Board of Governors appointed by the President and confirmed by the Senate;
- managed by an Administrator who is appointed and confirmed for a term of seven years;
- subject to agency-wide regulatory oversight by a Director of Aviation Safety who is appointed and confirmed for a term of seven years;
- freed from the constraints of the federal civil service and procurement systems.

The Director of Aviation Safety has the authority to initiate rulemaking as well as disapprove regulations promulgated by the Administrator, and also has the authority to enforce compliance by the Administrator of existing rules and regulations. Decisions by the Administrator and the Director of Aviation Safety are appealable to a Safety Committee of the Board of Governors composed of the Administrator, the Director of Aviation Safety, the Secretary of Transportation, the Secretary of Defense and a public member, and hence are not subjected to OMB review.

The Aviation Safety Commission also recommends the following agenda for improving aviation safety:

Safety Inspection Programs

- national rather than regional certification programs for major and national jet carriers;
- establishment of a nationwide inspection program for all size carriers with a combination of regular, in-depth, and surprise inspections;
- separation of certifications and surveillance functions in the new Authority;
- priority inspections for carriers undergoing major change;
- increasing the inspector workforce to accommodate these changes.

Regional Airline Safety

- reducing differences in equipment standards between regional and national carriers, with all aircraft providing scheduled service being required eventually to meet Air Transport Category Aircraft (Part 25) standards;
- reducing differences in operating practices between regional and national carriers, with all carriers eventually being required to meet Part 121 operations requirments.

General Aviation in the Air Traffic Control System

- requiring all aircraft to be equipped with a Mode C transponder in buffer zones around all large, medium, and small hubs;
- stronger enforcement against buffer zone violators with a separate

radar position dedicated to tracking and notifying violators in each buffer zone.

FAA Rulemaking

• process must be streamlined and restructured to include clear and unambiguous responsibility and accountability.

Airport Safety and Capacity

• base airport certification on passenger volume rather than type of equipment;
• review of existing policies and requirements with particular emphasis on signage, directional indicators, and taxiway and intersection markings.

Use of Operations Research

• need to enhance operations research capabilities for better utilization in problem solving.

Aviation Safety
and Airline Deregulation

The air transportation system has changed dramatically over the past 60 years. Throughout the first 50 of these years, the most significant changes were technological, as the airline industry progressed from piston-engine, propeller aircraft to widebodied fanjet aircraft. For the last ten years, the most important changes have been institutional, as the extensive system of government economic regulation that had shaped the industry since 1938 was dismantled by the Airline Deregulation Act of 1978, leaving market forces in its place.

These market forces led to an expansion in the number of airlines immediately after deregulation and then, more recently, to consolidation through an unprecedented wave of mergers and acquisitions. Route systems have changed, with routes radiating from approximately 25 connection centers or "hubs" replacing the linear routes that were a vestige of the limited nonstop range of the early propeller aircraft. For many smaller cities, infrequent scheduled service in jet aircraft has been replaced by more frequent service in smaller commuter aircraft.

Competition has been intense since deregulation. Fares have decreased in most markets, with some discount fares dropping to remarkably low levels. Traffic has expanded rapidly in response to increased service and reduced fares. In the process, aircraft fleet size and operations have grown as well. Competition, coupled with rapid growth, put pressure on the airlines by forcing them simultaneously to grow, to adapt their route systems and services to the free marketplace, to make their labor arrangements more efficient, to accommodate mergers, and, in many cases, to do all this while changing management, as managers whose skills were attuned to marketing and cost control replaced those whose focus had been operating in a regulated economic environment. . . .

Yet, even as this record has been compiled, the public, the Congress, and the Administration have expressed heightened concern over aviation safety. Well-publicized aviation accidents in the past three years have fueled these concerns. . . .

While there seems to be a widespread perception of a growing safety problem, a review of the post-deregulation accident record reveals a much different picture. . . . The number of passengers has grown from just under 254 million in 1978 to over 400 million in 1987. Total aircraft departures have increased 29 percent over the same period.

Despite a 26.5 percent increase in aircraft departures since 1978, the number of airline accidents (including jet and commuter carriers) fell from a total of 427 in the 1970 to 1978 period to 317 between 1979 and 1987. Similarly, despite a 55 percent increase in passenger enplanements, the number of passenger fatalities decreased from 1137 in 1970 to 1978 to 1067 in 1979 to 1987. . . . Measured in terms of rates (per million departures for accidents and per million enplanements for fatalities and injuries):

- Fatal accidents were down 51 percent.
- Serious injury accidents were down 56 percent.
- Minor accidents were down 55 percent.
- Passenger fatalities were down 45 percent.
- Serious passenger injuries were down 84 percent.

The post-deregulation record among commuter carriers exhibited much the same pattern, with passenger fatality rates dropping 42 percent and passenger injury rates dropping 49 percent. . . .

Assessing Deregulation's Effects on Safety

The Airline Deregulation Act did not in any way change the scope or intent of air safety laws and regulations. In some areas, notably the commuter airlines, safety regulations have become more stringent since 1978. However, deregulation has altered the nature of competition in the airline industry and has given rise to fears that the risk of specific types of accidents might increase. For example, one concern was that competitive pressures to reduce costs might lead some carriers to skimp or take shortcuts on maintenance with a resulting increased risk of equipment failure. An examination of the record, however, shows that the concern is thus far unfounded. For jet carriers, the post-deregulation rate for accidents precipitated by equipment failure has fallen from 1.49 accidents per million aircraft departures during 1970 to 1978 to 0.43 accidents per million departures between 1979 and 1985, a 67 percent decrease. For commuter carriers, the rate of accidents involving equipment failure is 71 percent lower in the post-deregulation period. . . .

Another concern was that deregulation might contribute to more pilot and crew error. Deregulation has stimulated increased pressure on airline labor for less restrictive work rules. Pilots and cabin attendants are flying more hours per month and ground crews typically are performing a wider variety of tasks than prior to deregulation. In addition, the rapid post-deregulation expansion of the industry may have reduced the average experience level of airline employees. Despite these apparent pressures, the rates for accidents caused by pilot error have declined from 0.54 accidents per million aircraft departures in 1970 to 1978 to 0.21 accidents per million departures between 1979 and 1985. Similarly, the rate for injuries caused by a failure to fasten the seatbelt has also declined by 54 percent suggesting that, if anything, cabin attendants have been more effective in making sure that passengers fasten their seatbelts when turbulence is expected.

Another concern is that safety has been reduced because of increased pressure on the air traffic control system from the combination of changes in routes and schedules in the wake of deregulation coupled with the aftermath of the 1981 dismissal of the striking PATCO controllers. The rates for accidents caused by air traffic control error have never been high and actually declined from 0.26 accidents per million aircraft departures prior to deregulation to 0.11 accidents per million departures during 1979 to 1985. Thus, in terms of accidents, there is no evidence that the air traffic control system has functioned less safely after deregulation than before. Similarly, the rate of airline accidents involving general aviation aircraft has not increased since deregulation. Thus despite the added pressure on the air traffic control system and on the airspace surrounding large airports because of the bunching of flights due to intensified hub and spoke operations, the rates for the sorts of accidents that some had feared might increase have, in fact, gone down. . . .

The Margin of Safety

Despite improving accident rates, some continue to argue that safety in the industry has deteriorated and that accident rates are not adequate measures of safety. Accidents are held to be the result of safety degradation; therefore accident rates possess no predictive power. It has been suggested that pre-accident indicators, which would capture deterioration in safety before accidents occurred, be developed. These pre-accident indicators would be used to track the margin of safety in the industry—the cushion which allows failures to occur in components of the nation's air transportation system (mechanical, human, and technological) without resulting injury to person or damage to property.

While the margin of safety is an intuitively appealing concept, it has not yet been defined in a way that allows measurement. . . .

Airport Congestion and Safety

. . . The air traffic control system as it currently operates converts excess demand on the system into delay to maintain safety margins. Thus, the system delays which have lately caused so much comment are not themselves dangerous. Rather, delays are a result of flow controls and other FAA measures to assure safe operations. But these delays and the resulting public comment create temptations to accommodate more traffic and avoid pressure by eroding margins of safety. The Commission has no basis for believing that such an erosion has yet occurred. But it is concerned that rising demand be accommodated in ways which ensure that even a subtle temptation to erode safety margins is avoided. . . .

A New Organizational Approach to Aviation Safety

. . . The current aviation safety rulemaking process has grown unnecessarily complex and as a result has become slow and unresponsive. The rulemaking process, from petition for rulemaking to the final rule, includes well over 200 separate steps when all parties agree on the rule. Without disagreement, it typically takes over two years to get a final rule. With disagreement, the process becomes even longer with some issues still unresolved after more than 15 years.

There appears to be no single cause for these delays. The blame does not lie with one party, such as the FAA, the Department of Transportation, or the Office of Management and Budget, but rather with a process involving all of them. The rulemaking process includes multiple reviews and yet does not contain clear responsibility and accountability. The Aviation Safety Commission could find few instances where the reviews outside of FAA changed even minor aspects of the technical content of the proposed rules. The result is a process that seeks public accountability but instead generates considerable disagreement and delay. Responsibility has become diffused to the point where decisive action is difficult to achieve except in the wake of an accident. . . .

Aviation Safety Commission Recommendations

The Aviation Safety Commission recommends that the functions of the FAA be transferred from the Department of Transportation to an independent, self-financing Federal Aviation Authority composed of a nine-member Board of Governors, an Administrator, who shall also chair the Board, a Director of Aviation Safety, and a Safety Committee of the Board. The Administrator has responsibility for the operation of the air traffic control system and regulatory authority. Both the Administrator and the Director of Aviation Safety would be appointed by the President and confirmed by the Senate for seven-year terms.

The Aviation Safety Commission recommends that the Authority be empowered to establish its own personnel and procurement systems and that its regulations would not be subject to OMB's regulatory review program. It would be financed by user charges, set by the Board after hearings by a User Fee Counsel. General fund revenues would be appropriated only to cover a statutorily-prescribed portion of the budget to cover the share of costs attributable to use of the air traffic control system by the Defense Department or other public agencies.

The Aviation Safety Commission recommends that the Director of Aviation Safety would have responsibility for inspecting, monitoring, and reviewing the system to ensure that the FAA is discharging both its regulatory and operational responsibilities safely. The Director of Aviation Safety would have the power to initiate or disapprove proposed regulations of the Authority affecting aircraft, aircrews, air carriers, or the air traffic control system, including the provision of navigational aids. Regulatory decisions of either the Administrator or the Director of Aviation Safety would be subject to appellate review by a five-member Safety Committee of the Board. The Safety Committee would be composed of four ex officio members of the Board, namely the Administrator, the Director of Aviation Safety, the Secretary of Transportation, and the Secretary of Defense, together with one public member. That public member and four other members would be appointed by the President and confirmed by the Senate to four-year overlapping terms. . . .

The Aviation Safety Commission believes that the Federal Government must continue to play the central role in ensuring the safe operation of the United States aviation system. The Commission shares the common perception that while the system is safe for now, the present governmental structure is not working very well to ensure its safety for the future. The Commission strongly believes that a major structural overhaul is essential to ensure the future safety of the system.

The Aviation Safety Commission believes that the regulatory process must remain governmental in character and cannot be taken out of the Federal government or removed from public accountability. . . .

COURT ON ALCOHOLISM AND VETERANS' BENEFITS

April 20, 1988

In a 4-3 decision handed down April 20, the Supreme Court narrowly upheld the authority of the Veterans Administration to categorize any alcoholism not connected with psychiatric illness as a problem that essentially was the veteran's own fault. The decision allowed the VA to continue denying educational benefits to many veterans disabled by drinking.

The ruling involved two cases, Traynor v. Turnage *and* McKelvey v. Turnage. *Eugene Traynor and James P. McKelvey were honorably discharged veterans who recovered from alcoholism during the 1970s and applied to the VA for educational benefits granted by the G.I. Bill of Rights. They asked the agency to extend the usual ten-year period during which veterans could draw benefits after leaving active duty. During most of that time, they said, they had been disabled by alcoholism and could not take advantage of the G.I. Bill's provisions.*

In 1977, Congress said the time period could be extended for veterans who had been unable to use their benefits because of "a physical or mental disorder which was not the result of [their] own willful misconduct." The VA, however, said that any alcoholism that was not associated with psychiatric problems fell into the "willful misconduct" category. According to the American Medical Association (AMA), 20 to 30 percent of alcoholism has a psychiatric connection.

VA officials used the term "secondary alcoholism" to describe drinking associated with mental illnesses and beyond the victims' control; all other alcoholism, in their view, was "primary"—meaning that drinking itself was the main problem—and the willful-misconduct provision applied. Primary alcoholics were not eligible for disability compensation, although the VA did pay for treating their alcoholism.

Traynor's and McKelvey's requests for additional time to use their educational benefits were denied because they had no psychiatric problems. The two veterans brought suit separately, arguing that the VA's action conflicted with the Rehabilitation Act of 1973. The act was amended in 1978 to prohibit any federal agency from discriminating against handicapped persons solely on the basis of a handicap. Alcoholism was accepted as a legitimate handicap by the officials who administered the act.

The plaintiffs contended that, to comply with the Rehabilitation Act, the VA should have reviewed their cases on an individual basis to determine whether their alcoholism actually stemmed from voluntary misbehavior. By lumping all primary alcoholics into the same category, they charged, the agency was discriminating against the handicapped.

Whether the courts had jurisdiction over veterans' benefit claims also was at issue in the case. Judicial review of VA decisions was specifically prohibited in laws spelling out benefit-distribution formulas.

Traynor's case originated in a District of Columbia federal court, while McKelvey brought suit in New York federal court. The lower courts upheld their petitions, but the appeals courts were less favorable. In New York, a court of appeals determined that it had no jurisdiction over McKelvey's claim; in the District of Columbia, appellate judges ruled that, while they had the authority to review the case, they supported the VA's position.

Alcoholism as a Disease

The case touched on a subject hotly debated by medical and psychiatric authorities—whether alcoholism is a physical disease or chiefly a matter of moral irresponsibility. Some researchers had produced evidence indicating that alcoholism had a genetic basis and tended to run in families. In 1956 the AMA endorsed the disease concept, and most treatment for problem drinkers was based on that premise. Proponents hoped that the Supreme Court would, for the first time, place the theory on a solid legal footing when it ruled on the veterans' petitions.

Experts on alcoholism were by no means united behind the disease concept, however, and critics of that approach were outspoken as the cases came before the Court. Spokesmen opposing the disease theory contended that alcoholism was rooted in psychological problems or a lack of moral values.

The issue also had proved nettlesome for Congress. The Senate repeatedly had passed legislation to extend the time limit in which veterans disabled by alcohol or drug dependence could receive educational benefits, but the House had blocked the measures. The Veterans Administration firmly opposed the benefit extension because it feared that the step would lead to disability compensation for primary alcoholics.

By some estimates, this nation's alcoholic population ran as high as ten million, one million of whom were likely to seek treatment during a given year. Supporters of Traynor and McKelvey—including the AMA and the National Association of Addiction Treatment Providers—were concerned that the Court's ruling might encourage insurers to curtail coverage for alcoholism treatment programs.

The Court's Decision

The Court declined to take a stand on the disease theory. "The litigation does not require the Court to decide whether alcoholism is a disease whose course its victims cannot control," said Justice Byron R. White, writing for the majority. "It is not our role to resolve this medical issue on which the authorities remain sharply divided."

Instead, the majority confined its ruling to a narrower and apparently conflicting issue—what precisely Congress meant in two vaguely worded statutes. They were the amended Rehabilitation Act and the law granting educational benefits to veterans, last changed in 1977. The majority concluded that Congress intended to support the VA's position linking primary alcoholism and willful misconduct, and that the two laws were not in conflict.

The majority did reject the VA's argument that the courts could never review its decisions about veterans' benefit decisions. This case, the majority found, involved the Rehabilitation Act, an area where the VA had no special expertise; consequently, judicial review was not prohibited.

The Dissent

Justice Harry A. Blackmun vigorously disputed the majority's conclusion that supported the VA's view of primary alcoholism. The fact that both veterans had begun drinking at an early age, Blackmun argued, raised doubts as to whether their consequent drinking problems had been willfully incurred. Justices William J. Brennan, Jr., and Thurgood Marshall joined Blackmun in the dissent. Justices Antonin Scalia and Anthony M. Kennedy took no part in the deliberations.

Following are excerpts from the Supreme Court's decision, issued April 20, 1988, in Traynor v. Turnage and McKelvey v. Turnage, upholding the Veterans Administration's authority to characterize any alcoholism not connected with

279

psychiatric illness as a problem that was essentially the veteran's own fault; and from the dissent of Justice Harry A. Blackmun:

Nos. 86-622 and 86-737

Eugene Traynor, Petitioner

v.

Thomas K. Turnage, Administrator, Veterans' Administration and the Veterans' Administration

On writ of Certiorari to the United States Court of Appeals for the Second Circuit

James P. McKelvey, Petitioner

v.

Thomas K. Turnage, Administrator of Veterans' Affairs, et al.

On writ of Certiorari to the United States Court of Appeals for the District of Columbia Circuit

[April 20, 1988]

JUSTICE WHITE delivered the opinion of the Court.

These cases arise from the Veterans' Administration's refusal to grant two recovered alcoholics extensions of time in which to use their veterans' educational benefits. We must decide whether the Veterans' Administration's decision is subject to judicial review and, if so, whether that decision violates § 504 of the Rehabilitation Act of 1973, which requires that federal programs not discriminate against handicapped individuals solely because of their handicap.

I

Veterans who have been honorably discharged from the United States Armed Forces are entitled to receive educational assistance benefits under the G.I. Bill to facilitate their readjustment to civilian life. These benefits generally must be used within 10 years following discharge or release from active duty. Veterans may obtain an extension of the 10-year delimiting period, however, if they were prevented from using their benefits earlier by "a physical or mental disability which was not the result of . . . [their] own willful misconduct."

Petitioners are honorably discharged veterans who did not exhaust their educational benefits during the decade following their military service. They sought to continue to receive benefits after the expiration of the 10-year delimiting period on the ground that they had been disabled by alcoholism during much of that period. The Veterans' Administration determined that petitioners' alcoholism constituted "willful misconduct"

... and accordingly denied the requested extensions.

Petitioner Traynor sought review of the Veterans' Administration's decision in the United States District Court for the Southern District of New York. The District Court held that it was not foreclosed from exercising jurisdiction over the case by ... [a provision of law, 38 U.S.C. § 211(a)], which bars judicial review of "the decisions of the Administrator on any question of law or fact under any law administered by the Veterans' Administration providing benefits for veterans," because the complaint "requires us to examine constitutional and statutory questions and not merely issues of VA policy." The court rejected Traynor's claim that the Veterans' Administration's refusal to extend his delimiting period violated the Due Process Clause and the equal protection component of the Fifth Amendment. However, the court concluded that alcoholism is a handicap within the meaning of the Rehabilitation Act, and that the Veterans' Administration therefore had engaged in the sort of discrimination on the basis of handicap that is forbidden by that Act.

A divided panel of the Court of Appeals for the Second Circuit reversed on the ground that § 211(a) barred judicial review of the Rehabilitation Act claim. The Court reasoned that, while "many veterans have in the service of our country suffered injuries that qualify them as 'handicapped individual[s]' for purposes of [the Rehabilitation Act]," Congress evinced no intent in enacting that statute "to grant to 'handicapped' veterans the judicial review traditionally denied all other veterans" under § 211(a).

Meanwhile, petitioner McKelvey sought review of the Veterans' Administration's decision in the District Court for the District of Columbia. The District Court exercised jurisdiction over McKelvey's claims on the ground that § 211(a) permits judicial review of decisions rejecting claims that Veterans' Administration regulations of general applicability violate a federal statute that is "completely independent of the complex statutory and regulatory scheme for dispersing veterans' benefits." The court then invalidated [the regulations] as contrary to the Rehabilitation Act. The court ordered the Veterans' Administration to determine without resort to the regulation whether McKelvey had suffered a disability attributable to his own misconduct.

On appeal, the Court of Appeals for the District of Columbia Circuit agreed that judicial review was not foreclosed.... On the merits, however, the Court of Appeals reversed, holding that the Veterans' Administration could consistently with the Rehabilitation Act distinguish between veterans who are at least to some extent responsible for their disabilities and veterans who are not. With respect to alcoholism, ... said the court, ... the Veterans' Administration could reasonably conclude that alcoholism is a "willfully caused handicap" unless attributable to an underlying psychiatric disorder....

We granted certiorari to resolve the conflicts between the Courts of Appeals as to whether Veterans' Administration decisions challenged under the Rehabilitation Act are subject to judicial review and, if so, whether that Act bars the Veterans' Administration from characterizing petitioners' alcoholism as "willful misconduct.". . .

II

. . . We have repeatedly acknowledged "the strong presumption that Congress intends judicial review of administrative action." The presumption in favor of judicial review may be overcome "only upon a showing of 'clear and convincing evidence' of a contrary legislative intent.". . .

The text and legislative history of § 211(a) likewise provide no clear and convincing evidence of any congressional intent to preclude a suit claiming that § 504 of the Rehabilitation Act, a statute applicable to all federal agencies, has invalidated an otherwise valid regulation issued by the Veterans' Administration and purporting to have the force of law. . . .

Accordingly, we conclude that the question whether a Veterans' Administration regulation violates the Rehabilitation Act is not foreclosed from judicial review by § 311(a). We therefore turn to the merits of petitioners' Rehabilitation Act claim.

III

Congress historically has imposed time limitations on the use of G.I. Bill educational benefits. Veterans of World War II were required to use their benefits within nine years after their discharge from military service, while Korean Conflict veterans had eight years. . . . The delimiting period under the current G.I. Bill was raised from 8 years to 10 years in 1974. In 1977, Congress created an exception to this 10-year delimiting period for veterans who delayed their education because of "a physical or mental disability which was not the result of [their] own willful misconduct."

Congress did not use the term "willful misconduct" inadvertently. . . . The same term had long been used in other veterans' benefits statutes. For example, veterans are denied compensation for service-connected disabilities that are "the result of the veteran's own willful misconduct.". . .

. . . The legislative history confirms that Congress intended that the Veterans' Administration apply the same test of "willful misconduct" in granting extensions of time under . . . [the 1977 law] as the agency already was applying in granting disability compensation. . . .

It is thus clear that the 1977 legislation precluded an extension of time to a veteran who had not pursued his education because of primary alcoholism. . . . Nor did Congress anywhere in the language or legislative history of the 1978 amendments expressly disavow its 1977 determination that primary alcoholism is not the sort of disability that warrants an exemption from the time constraints. . . .

Accordingly, petitioners can prevail under their Rehabilitation Act claim only if the 1978 legislation can be deemed to have implicitly repealed the "willful misconduct" provision of the 1977 legislation or forbade the Veterans' Administration to classify primary alcoholism as willful misconduct.

... [T]he "willful misconduct" provision does not undermine the central purpose of § 504, which is to assure that handicapped individuals receive "evenhanded treatment" in relation to nonhandicapped individuals. This litigation does not involve a program or activity that is alleged to treat handicapped persons less favorably than nonhandicapped persons. . . .

There is nothing in the Rehabilitation Act that requires that any benefit extended to one category of handicapped persons also be extended to all other categories of handicapped persons. Hence, the regulations promulgated by the Department of Health, Education, and Welfare in 1977 with regard to the application of § 504 to federally-funded programs provide that "exclusion of a specific class of handicapped persons from a program limited by Federal statute or executive order to a different class of handicapped persons" is not prohibited. It is therefore not inconsistent with the Rehabilitation Act for only those veterans whose disabilities are not attributable to their own "willful misconduct" to be granted extensions of the 10-year delimiting period applicable to all other veterans. . . .

Furthermore, [the VA] does not deny extensions of the delimiting period to all alcoholics but only to those whose drinking was not attributable to an underlying psychiatric disorder. . . .

Petitioners, however, perceive an inconsistency between § 504 and the conclusive presumption that alcoholism not motivated by mental illness is necessarily "willful." They contend that § 504 mandates an individualized determination of "willfulness" with respect to each veteran who claims to have been disabled by alcoholism. It would arguably be inconsistent with § 504 for Congress to distinguish between categories of disabled veterans according to generalized determinations that lack any substantial basis. If primary alcoholism is not always "willful," as that term has been defined by Congress and the Veterans' Administration, some veterans denied benefits may well be excluded solely on the basis of their disability. We are unable to conclude that Congress failed to act in accordance with § 504 in this instance, however, given what the District of Columbia Circuit accurately characterized as "a substantial body of medical literature that even contests the proposition that alcoholism is a disease, much less that it is a disease for which the victim bears no responsibility." . . . As we see it, § 504 does not demand inquiry into whether factors other than mental illness rendered an individual veteran's drinking so entirely beyond his control as to negate any degree of "willfulness" where Congress and the Veterans' Administration have reasonably determined for purposes of the veterans' benefits statutes that no such factors exist. . . .

IV

This litigation does not require the Court to decide whether alcoholism is a disease whose course its victims cannot control. It is not our role to resolve this medical issue on which the authorities remain sharply divided. Our task is to decide whether Congress intended, in enacting § 504 of the Rehabilitation Act, to reject the position taken on the issue by the

Veterans' Administration and by Congress itself only one year earlier. In our view, it is by no means clear that § 504 and the characterization of primary alcoholism as a willfully incurred disability are in irreconcilable conflict. If petitioners and their proponents continue to believe that this position is erroneous, their arguments are better presented to Congress than to the courts.

The judgment of the Court of Appeals for the District of Columbia Circuit in 86-737 is affirmed. The judgment of the Court of Appeals for the Second Circuit in 86-622 is reversed, and the case is remanded for further proceedings consistent with this opinion.

It is so ordered.

JUSTICE BLACKMUN, with whom JUSTICE BRENNAN and JUSTICE MARSHALL join, concurring in part and dissenting in part.

I join Parts I and II of the Court's opinion, for I agree that, under § 504 of the Rehabilitation Act of 1973, as amended, the "final and conclusive" language of 38 U.S.C. § 211(a) does not bar judicial review of petitioners' claims. Similarly, I acknowledge the legality (a) of the 10-year delimiting period imposed ... upon veterans' educational assistance, and (b) of that statute's alleviation of the delimiting period in cases of disability except where that disability is the result of a veteran's "own willful misconduct."

My dispute with the Court centers in its upholding of the regulation, whereby the Veterans' Administration (VA) presumes, *irrebuttably,* that primary alcoholism always is the result of the veteran's "own willful misconduct." This is the very kind of broad social generalization that § 504 of the Rehabilitation Act is intended to eliminate. The petitioners in these cases ask only that their situations be given individualized evaluation. Because I think this is what the Rehabilitation Act clearly requires, I dissent from the Court's conclusion to the contrary.

I

Petitioner Eugene Traynor began drinking when he was eight or nine years old. He drank with increasing frequency throughout his teenage years, and was suffering alcohol-related seizures by the time he was on active military duty in Vietnam. During the four years following his honorable discharge in 1969, Mr. Traynor was hospitalized repeatedly for alcoholism and related illnesses.

By the end of 1974, however, petitioner Traynor had conquered his drinking problem. He attended college part-time beginning in 1977, and continued working toward his degree until the 10-year period for using his veteran's educational benefits expired for him in 1979. ...

Petitioner James P. McKelvey also started drinking as a child. He was 13 when he began to develop the alcohol dependency that was common among members of his family. His drinking problem plagued him while he was in the Army, and he was hospitalized frequently during the nine years that followed his honorable discharge in 1966. Despite his disability, however, McKelvey managed, between hospital stays to attend two educational institutions under the veterans' educational-benefit program. . . .

II

The VA's reliance on its irrebuttable presumption that all primary alcoholism is attributable to willful misconduct cannot be squared with the mandate against discrimination contained in § 504 of the Rehabilitation Act. Just last year, in *School Bd. of Nassau County v. Arline,* this Court explained in no uncertain terms that § 504 bars the generic treatment of any group of individuals with handicaps based on archaic or simplistic stereotypes about attributes associated with their disabling conditions. Instead, § 504 requires an individualized assessment of each person's qualification, based on "reasoned and medically sound judgments." In sanctioning the VA's irrebuttable presumption that any veteran suffering from primary alcoholism brought the ailment upon himself through willful misconduct, the Court ignores the lesson of *Arline,* and the clear dictate of the Rehabilitation Act. . . .

Respondent argues, however, that a case-by-case assessment of whether a claimant's alcoholism was the result of willful misconduct is not necessary for two reasons. First, respondent contends that Congress, in enacting the 1977 amendment (the extension-of-time provision, see 91 Stat. 1439) to § 1662(a), mandated a conclusive presumption that primary alcoholism is caused by willful misconduct. Second, respondent contends that the VA's determination that primary alcoholism always is due to willful misconduct is reasonable, and that therefore the presumption is not based on the kind of stereotyping that § 504 forbids. The Court today finds each of these arguments persuasive. In my view, each patently is without merit.

III

The Court explains:

> "As we see it, § 504 does not demand inquiry into whether factors other than mental illness rendered an individual veteran's drinking so entirely beyond his control as to negate any degree of 'willfulness' where Congress and the Veterans' Administration have reasonably determined for purposes of the veterans' benefits statutes that no such factors exist."

As I see it, § 504 demands precisely the inquiry the Court says is unnecessary. While Congress certainly has the authority to determine that primary alcoholism always should be attributed to willful misconduct, I find no support whatever for the Court's conclusion that Congress made that determination when it amended . . . [the 1977 law].

REPARATIONS FOR
JAPANESE-AMERICAN INTERNEES
April 20, 1988

After an intense and at times emotional debate, the Senate April 20, 1988, approved by a 69-27 vote a measure providing for apologies and reparations to be made to 60,000 Japanese-Americans who were interned in U.S. relocation camps during World War II. The Japanese-Americans had been forcibly removed from their homes on the West Coast and placed in inland camps early in 1942 in response to Japan's attack on U.S. naval and military bases in Hawaii, December 7, 1941, which triggered America's entry into the war.

The legislation provided for the payment of $20,000 to each of the survivors from among 120,000 Japanese-Americans held during the war and also for about 900 Aleuts who were evacuated from Alaska's Pribilof Islands after the 1942 Japanese seizure of two islands in the Aleutian chain some two thousand miles away. The House had passed a similar measure September 17, 1987. After both chambers approved a conference report, President Ronald Reagan signed the measure into law on August 10, 1988, to "right a grave wrong."

The law sets up a trust fund of ultimately $1.25 billion to pay the reparations over a period of ten years. The first payments are due to go to former internees who are now elderly. All who receive the payments must agree to drop any legal claims resulting from their internment. Although the legislation provides money, it was widely viewed as a mainly symbolic move to redress what many Americans regarded as a woeful injustice. In Senate debate, Pete Wilson, R-Calif., called the wartime internment of the Japanese-Americans "one of the great travesties of our history."

President Reagan said at the White House ceremony: "Yes, the nation was then at war struggling for its survival. And it's not for us today to pass judgment upon those who made mistakes in that great struggle. Yet we must recognize that the internment of Japanese-Americans was just that, a mistake."

Background

Most of the internees were U.S. citizens; the others held the status of resident aliens. Once taken from their homes, they were sent to assembly centers and eventually to the relocation camps, as was required by an executive order President Franklin D. Roosevelt issued February 19, 1942. Through another executive order, issued about a month later, Roosevelt authorized the creation of a War Relocation Authority to administer the operation.

So sudden was the evacuation that many of the Japanese-Americans were forced to sell or lease their homes or businesses at substantial losses. Even though Japanese-Americans living in Hawaii were never detained, the internment in the continental United States continued through the war. Wilson told the Senate that "having made that mistake, we persisted in it for four long years." There was never any evidence of disloyalty to the United States on the part of the Japanese-Americans.

West Coast Fears

The evacuation of the Japanese-Americans took place during a time of great unease on the West Coast. The bombing of Pearl Harbor was followed quickly by Japanese military victories in the Pacific, creating fear that the U.S. mainland was in danger of attack. Ted Stevens, R-Alaska, recalled during Senate debate that as a young boy living in Los Angeles he heard antiaircraft guns "shooting at the moon, literally," because someone had falsely reported a Japanese attack. Many West Coast residents and military officials feared that the Japanese-Americans might communicate with Japanese ships offshore and assist in an invasion.

At relocation centers in six western states and Arkansas, the Japanese-Americans were jammed into tar-papered barracks in bleak surroundings. There was little regard for privacy. Sen. Alan Simpson, R-Wyo., remembered Heart Mountain Relocation Center—with 15,000 people the third largest community in his home state—as a place enclosed by barbed wire and guard towers. Among its occupants, he discovered to his surprise, were Boy Scouts working on merit badges just as he was.

Commission Report

Generally, the legislation implemented recommendations made by the Commission on Wartime Relocation and Internment of Civilians in its reports of February 24 and June 16, 1983. The nine-member, nonpartisan commission had been established by Congress in 1980. The commission estimated that the interned Japanese-Americans lost income and property worth up to $2 billion in terms of the dollar value in 1983. The panel proposed that each surviving internee be awarded a payment of $20,000, together with official apologies. (Report on Internment of Japanese-Americans, Historic Documents of 1983, p. 211)

The commission found that President Roosevelt was advised to intern the Japanese-Americans by Army Lt. Gen. John L. DeWitt, commander of West Coast defense, and Secretary of War Henry L. Stimson. Without cabinet discussion, Roosevelt issued his order. For a brief time Milton Eisenhower, a brother of President Dwight D. Eisenhower and many years later president of Johns Hopkins University, headed the War Relocation Authority. He took the job reluctantly and in later years described the internment as "an inhuman mistake."

Earl Warren, the attorney general of California and later the chief justice of the United States, backed the detainment when it occurred. When he was appointed to the Supreme Court, Warren said that he "deeply regretted the removal and my own testimony [to a congressional committee] advocating it...."

Congressional Action

Barney Frank, D-Mass., the chief sponsor of the reparations measure in the House, told his colleagues that the payments to the internees were not intended as compensation but as a "symbolic gesture." He also said, "We have an obligation to act as people in charge of the government today." Two Japanese-American members of the House who had themselves been interned, Norman Y. Mineta and Robert T. Matsui, both California Democrats, pushed hard for passage of the measure. The House passed the bill 343-141.

In the Senate, the measure's principal advocate was Spark M. Matsunaga, D-Hawaii. Matsunaga had persuaded authorities to let him join the U.S. Army during World War II. With other Japanese-American volunteers, he served in a special regiment that engaged in bitter fighting in the Italian campaign. He was wounded twice. His fellow senator from Hawaii, Daniel K. Inouye, served in the same unit and lost his right arm in combat. "A stigma has haunted Japanese-Americans for forty-five years," Matsunaga told his Senate colleagues. He urged their support of the legislation to remove the cloud "over their heads."

Sen. Jesse Helms, R-N.C., an opponent of the legislation, said he "could not buy this business of kicking our government around at a time when horrible destruction had occurred at Pearl Harbor, unprovoked.... It is all very well on Monday morning to replay the game of Saturday. But the president ... had a responsibility to protect this country as best he could based on the information available to him." Senator Simpson said that while the internment was "the gravest of injustices," giving money to the victims was not the proper way to make an apology.

Writing in the New York Times *August 11, 1988, Kathleen Bishop said that leaders of organizations that had pushed for the legislation reacted to its enactment "with a collective sigh of relief." Bishop quoted Ben Takeshita, a spokesman for the Japanese American Citizens League, as saying that while the payments could not "begin" to compensate a person for "lost freedom, property, livelihood or for the stigma of disloyalty," it showed that the government's apology was "sincere."*

Following are Congressional Record *excerpts from Senate debate April 20, 1988, on reparations for interned Japanese-Americans:*

Mr. [Daniel K.] INOUYE [D-Hawaii]. . . . The measure before us is the source of much anguish and much controversy. Because of the commitment and dedication of Senator [Spark M.] Matsunaga [D-Hawaii], he has been able to convince 72 of his colleagues to join him in this endeavor.

Many fellow Americans, including my colleague from Nevada, have asked: "Why should Japanese-Americans be compensated?" During times of war, especially in times of fear, all people suffer. That is a very common argument made against this measure.

[W]hile it is true that all people of this Nation suffer during wartime, the Japanese-American internment experience is unprecedented in the history of American civil rights deprivation. I think we should recall, even if painful, that Americans of Japanese ancestry were determined by our Government to be security risks without any formal allegations or charges of disloyalty or espionage. They were arbitrarily branded disloyal solely on the grounds of racial ancestry.

No similar mass internment was deemed necessary for Americans of German or Italian ancestries, and I think we should recall and remind ourselves that in World War II, the Japanese were not our only enemies.

These Japanese-Americans who were interned could not confront their accusers or bring their case before a court. These are basic rights of all Americans. They were incarcerated, forced to live in public communities with no privacy, and stripped of their freedom to move about as others could.

Japanese-Americans wishing to fight for this country were initially declared ineligible. However, once allowed to volunteer, they volunteered in great numbers. In fact, proportionately and percentagewise, more Japanese-Americans put on the uniform of this country during World War II, more were wounded and more were killed, even if they were restricted to serving in ethnically-restricted military units.

The individual payments acknowledge the unjust deprivation of liberty, the infliction of mental and physical suffering, and the stigma of being branded disloyal, losses not compensable under the Japanese Evacuation Claims Act of 1948. . . .

The Presidentially appointed Commission on Wartime Relocation and

Internment of Civilians found no documented acts of espionage, sabotage, or fifth column activity by any, Mr. President, by any identifiable American citizen of Japanese ancestry or resident Japanese aliens on the west coast.

This was supposed to have been the rationale for this mass evacuation and mass incarceration, that these Americans were not to be trusted, that these Americans were agents of an enemy country, that these Americans would spy and carry out espionage, and this Presidentially appointed Commission, which incidentally was made up of leading citizens throughout this land—and only one member of that Commission was of Japanese ancestry—declared that there were no acts of espionage whatsoever. And sadly, the Commission in its 1983 report concluded that internment was motivated by racial prejudice, war hysteria, and a failure of political leadership. . . .

[T]he goal of S. 1009 is to benefit all citizens of our Nation by educating our citizens to preclude this event from occurring again to any other ethnic or religious group or any person suspected of being less than a loyal citizen. This bill reinforces the strength of our Constitution by reaffirming our commitment to upholding the constitutional rights of all our citizens. So, respectfully, I strongly urge its passage and in so doing once again commend and congratulate my distinguished colleague from Hawaii. . . .

Mr. MATSUNAGA. I congratulate the senior Senator from Hawaii for his excellent statement. Coming from one who served in the 442d Regimental Combat Team, the most highly decorated military unit in the entire history of the United States, and having been highly decorated with the second highest award, the Distinguished Service Cross, and having sacrificed an arm in that war, I believe what the senior Senator from Hawaii has to say should be taken most seriously. . . .

Mr. [Ted] STEVENS [R-Alaska]. . . . As recounted yesterday what happened when the United States military removed 900 American citizens—Aleuts, who lived on the Aleutian chain and the Pribilof Islands—from their homes and took them to abandoned canneries and gold mining camps in southeastern Alaska

Not many people understand the distances in our State. Attu and Kiska, which the Japanese invaded, are the most western islands in the Aleutian chain. The military saw fit to remove all Aleuts from all of the islands. Alaskans believed they did that because they wanted to occupy the islands and just did not want any local people in their way.

The Pribilof Islands were over 1,000 miles from the two islands the Japanese had taken. The Japanese never attempted to move further up along the Aleutian chain. They made an invasion of those two islands and fortified them. But there was really no necessity to remove these people. . . . Let us assume that the Japanese came to Baltimore. The action of the United States military removing the Aleuts would be like going to Chicago and then going west from Chicago about 1,000 miles and taking everyone between Chicago and Denver and moving them out of harm's way.

The record is clear that in terms of this internment—and it was an internment—was for the convenience of the Government. And these people, because they were of native descent, were taken and interned. They were kept for 2 to 3 years in those camps. In those days, Alaska was a territory, under wartime conditions, and it was not possible to travel.

I related yesterday how one of my friends, Flore Lekanoff, was taken from one of those camps in southeastern Alaska back to the Pribilof Islands to hunt for seals for the military. He was never paid for that. He was never recognized as being in the service of the Government. None of these people were treated as though they were in the service of the Government. They were literally just shoved aside. . . .

They have waited a long, long time. Most of them never recovered financially, particularly the people I represent in the Aleutian chain. Many are still destitute. This settlement is the final act to close this chapter of history and try to make restitution for that period of hysteria.

The people who made those decisions were good Americans. They were defending the country. They made mistakes. . . .

Mr. [Daniel J.] EVANS [D-Wash.]. . . . As a Senator from the State of Washington, I have a special interest in this legislation. The first group of Japanese citizens to be removed from their homes under President Roosevelt's Executive Order were from Bainbridge Island, WA. They were the first of nearly 13,000 Japanese-Americans from the State of Washington to be funneled into assembly centers and eventually into relocation facilities.

Victims of Executive Order 9066 were given very short notice that they would be sent to relocation facilities. Most were granted just a few days to abandon their homes and belongings. As a result they were forced to sell or lease their property and businesses at prices reflecting only a fraction of their worth. Substantial economic losses were incurred. Once they arrived at the relocation centers they found a quality of life which was atrocious. They were overcrowded and families suffered from an acute lack of privacy with no borders or walls to separate them from others.

Opponents of this legislation choose to ignore raw, racial prejudice woven in what was supposed to be legitimate national security justification for internment. The evacuees, however, were guilty of no crime other than the apparent crime of being of Japanese ancestry. Japanese-Americans left their homes in an atmosphere of racial prejudice and returned to the same.

What is perhaps most alarming about the Japanese internment is that it took place in the United States of America. This is the same country which has prided itself on freedom, justice, and the preservation and protection of individual rights.

Thirty-four years after the last citizens were released from captivity, Congress established the Commission on the Wartime Relocation and Internment of Japanese-American Citizens to assess the decision to intern and relocate Japanese-Americans. Two years after its inception, the Commission issued certain factual findings and subsequent recommendations. I have cosponsored legislation to implement these recommendations throughout my tenure in the U.S. Senate.

The $20,000 compensation that would be allotted to each victim, and the educational fund established by this legislation are a modest attempt to redress wrongs against loyal Americans. Although we cannot restore completely what already has been lost, the legislation would serve as a symbol to all that the United States can come to terms with its own tragic mistake. . . .

Mr. [Jesse A.] HELMS [R-N.C.]. . . . Nobody is, in retrospect, proud of the relocation of the Japanese-Americans during World War II, but as I said earlier, we lived in a time of terror in this country immediately after the attack on Pearl Harbor. Nobody knew what was coming next. . . . We had just been attacked by a totalitarian regime which had enjoyed a virtually unbroken string of military successes, both before and immediately after the Government of Japan attacked the United States of America. . . .

I think it is only fair to look back to that time, and recall the fact that our intelligence community told the then President of the United States, Franklin Delano Roosevelt, that there was great risk. Now we can see that it was a mistake.

I have no vision problem with respect to that. We will have 20-20 vision by hindsight, and I am perfectly willing for this Senate and this Congress to declare that this kind of thing must never happen again.

But the Senate has just voted to give the priority emphasis to money, $1.3 billion. So I think we ought to look at our priorities. . . .

. . . [T]he U.S. Government, contrary to suggestions otherwise, has not ignored the suffering that occurred as a result of the relocation and internment during the war. The Government has officially recognized that much unjustified personal hardship was, in fact, caused. Previous Congresses, Presidents and Attorneys General have taken steps to acknowledge and compensate Japanese-Americans for the injuries they suffered.

For example, in 1948, Congress enacted the American Japanese Claims Act, which authorized compensation for "any claim" for damages to or loss of real or personal property "as a reasonable consequence of the evacuation or exclusion of" persons of Japanese ancestry as a result of governmental action during World War II.

I might add that this act of 1948 was subsequently amended to liberalize its compensation provisions.

Under the amended act, the Justice Department received claims seeking approximately $147 million. Ultimately, 26,568 settlements were achieved. . . . True enough, the American Japanese Claims Act did not include every item of damage that was or could have been suggested. It did, however, address the hardships visited upon persons of Japanese ancestry in a comprehensive, considered manner taking into account individual needs and losses, and this effort to correct injustice to individuals was in keeping with our Nation's best tradition of individual rather than collective response, and it was far more contemporaneous with the injuries to the claimants than would be any payments at this late date. . . .

Mr. [Alan K.] SIMPSON [R-Wyo.]. It has been a very interesting debate for me. I have been paying attention to it on the monitor. It has made me recall some most interesting and memorable parts of my own life because I was a young boy in Cody, WY, in 1941 when the war started. I was 10 then.

Two years later, at the age of 12, somewhere between the years of 12 and 13, the third largest community in Wyoming was constructed between the communities of Powell and Cody, WY, a city of 15,000 people which really literally went up overnight. And the name of it, of course, was Heart Mountain War Relocation Center, known to the people of the area simply as the "Jap Camp," a term which may be hard for us to believe now but that is what it was referred to then; swiftly built by those who had not been drafted into the war, or older men in their 40's who were not able to be taken into the war effort.

And so came into being Heart Mountain, WY, War Relocation Center. There was barbed wire around it. There were guard towers at the edges of it. It was a very imposing area.... I remember one night very distinctly when the scoutmaster—I was a Boy Scout, a rather nominal one, but I enjoyed the activities of the group. And he said, "We are going to go out to the War Relocation Center and have a scout meeting." I said, "Well, I mean, are there any of them out there?"... He said, "Yes, yes, these are American citizens, you see." And that put a new twist on it because we thought of them as something else—as aliens; we thought of them as spies; we thought of them as people who were behind wire because they were trying to do in our country.

So I shall not forget going to the Boy Scout meeting and meeting Boy Scouts from California, most of them, I recall, same merit badges, same scout sashes, same clothing.

And why not? Some of them were second- or third-generation American citizens.... I also remember those other nights we would go into the compound—which it was in every sense, with searchlights and with wire—visiting with some of the older people. There were very few young men there from the ages of 17 through 28, because many of them were in the armed services of the United States. But I do remember visiting with the older people and there were many of them there.

The younger and the older were there. Those were the principal inhabitants. I remember a woman, a very old woman to me at that age, said "Do you have grandparents?"

I said, "Yes, I do."

She said, "Where do they live?"

I said, "In Cody, down the road there."

She said, "Well, what kind of a house do they have?"

I thought, well, that is interesting to ask. I described it.

"What do they do?"

And then I remember she showed me pictures of her family.

She said, "This is my son. He is in Italy now fighting for this country, the United States of America."

Then we would go downtown in Cody, WY, and there would be a sign on the restaurant that said, "No Japs allowed here." And then you would go down to another place of business, it might be a sign that said, "My son was killed at Iwo Jima. How do you think I feel?"

And the trustees would come into town. They were remarkable people. Usually the best and the brightest. Maybe those who had been involved in agriculture and whose lands had been taken from them—confiscated.

So I really had a lot of trouble sorting that all out at the age of 13. I maybe have some of the same kind of trouble sorting it all out at the age of 56. But let me just say that I preserve it as a very formative part of my life. . . . There is no question about it being the gravest of injustices. And it may be hardly a repayable one. How do you ever really repay these people for the wages, the property, the opportunity, the education, the part of their lives lost during this period? And this taxpayer expenditure is a troubling part of the bill for me.

I have trouble with the money. An apology may be long overdue and may be so appropriate. But, coupled with money, it takes away some of the sincerity of the apology, somehow. If you did that with a friend, a lovely friend, and you said: I am sorry for what I did. I know that was very harmful to you and hurtful. But I am sorry and I apologize and I want to give you some money.

I think that that somehow is unbecoming. It may not be to some. It is a troubling aspect of it to me. . . . So we will conclude this, and I think probably we will revisit this issue again, not with this situation but in other populations of our country, and we best know indeed, that will likely take place.

There is not one of us here today with what we have been through with our civil rights activities in 1964 and Selma that probably thinks: "How could this have ever occurred?" And yet at the time it occurred, it seemed at that time of our lives to be the most important step that could be taken.

That decision was made by people with much greater wisdom than I had at the age of 13 in Cody, WY.

Hopefully, we will conclude this debate shortly and move on to other issues of the day because this is an old and sad and very painful thing that we have reopened here in this debate. The sooner we close that wound and suture it with love and understanding and affection, we will be better off. And suturing it with money does not seem like the best way to conclude the issue.

ASSESSING AMERICAN EDUCATION
April 26, 1988

William J. Bennett, U.S. secretary of education, produced a report on April 26 that appraised progress toward correcting the educational problems outlined five years earlier in A Nation at Risk, *the scathing critique of American education prepared by the National Commission on Excellence in Education* (Education Report, Historic Documents of 1983, p. 413). *Bennett's study,* American Education: Making It Work, *found that the situation had improved somewhat: state funding of education had risen 40 percent since 1980; students' scores on the Scholastic Aptitude Test had climbed sixteen points during the 1980s, reversing a seventeen-year slump; teachers' salaries were rising; and students were spending more time in courses such as English, mathematics, science, and social studies.*

But the nation was still at risk, Bennett warned, pointing to a large number of high school graduates who read at the junior high level and to a worrisome high school dropout rate. Overall, 25 percent of the nation's high school students were not destined to graduate; for black and Hispanic youths, the figures were 35 percent and 45 percent, respectively. Tests such as the National Assessment of Educational Progress (NAEP) continued to turn up embarrassing data—for example, that more than two-thirds of the seventeen-year-olds tested in 1986 did not know when the Civil War occurred.

International tests also had produced disquieting results, especially in science and mathematics, subjects in which American students trailed youths from several countries, including Japan, a major economic com-

petitor. "We are certainly not doing well enough, and we are not doing well enough fast enough," Bennett wrote. "The absolute level at which our improvements are taking place is unacceptably low. Too many students do not graduate from our high schools, and too many of those who do graduate have been poorly educated."

Bennett's report was published as consternation was growing about literacy problems among American workers. The Education and Labor departments had raised doubts about whether schools were turning out a sufficient supply of future workers who could read, write, and calculate well enough to perform increasingly technological jobs. A document issued jointly by the two departments on March 28, entitled The Bottom Line: Basic Skills in the Workplace, *cited predictions that by the end of the century the nation would face a growing mismatch between job requirements and the skills that potential workers possessed.*

By then, for the first time in the nation's history, most new jobs would call for some education beyond high school education, the report said. "As a consequence of smaller growth in the labor force and a diminishing pool of qualified workers, employers may face serious skill shortages not experienced since World War II," it continued. "The emphasis on school improvement alone will not be an adequate response between now and the year 2000."

Coping with Semiliteracy

To produce a more literate workforce, The Bottom Line *urged the business community to take upon itself a part of the task of educating workers through in-house programs of continuing education.*

Although the literacy level of the country was clearly rising—a 1986 NAEP study found that only 5 percent of Americans between the ages of twenty-one and twenty-five could not read at the fourth-grade level— literacy requirements were climbing as well. The NAEP concluded that about 10 million adults in the United States were truly illiterate; other estimates have run as high as 25 million.

Furthermore, the NAEP projected that 20 percent of the young adults in the nation could not read better than the average eighth-grader and that almost 40 percent read below average for the eleventh grade (even though most of those tested said that they were high school graduates). NAEP investigators concluded that the United States needed educational programs not only for illiterates but also for those who fell into the middle ranges on the reading tests—youths who were not literate enough for a technologically advanced society.

Recommendations for Change

Secretary Bennett proposed solutions for educational problems that by and large reiterated the prescriptions of A Nation at Risk: *schools should* expect more from students and enforce order and discipline; states should open teaching jobs to persons who lacked traditional education credits (but were otherwise qualified to teach); public school principals should provide better leadership; schools should be held accountable for good teaching; and the best teachers should get higher pay. In addition, schools should place more stress on moral values and keep a close eye on the actual content of coursework—students should not only take courses with academic-sounding names but also face truly rigorous subject matter.

"We know what needs to be done," Bennett declared. "We must exert the will and demonstrate the resolve to overcome the obstacles that block reform." Among the chief obstacles, according to Bennett, was the "narrow, self-interested exercise of political power in statehouse corridors and local school board meetings" practiced by "those with a vested interest in the educational status quo," including teachers' union members who opposed competency tests and merit-pay plans for their colleagues.

Leaders of teachers' organizations and other educational groups greeted Bennett's charges with allegations of their own. Mary Hatwood Futrell, president of the influential National Education Association, charged that the Reagan administration had thwarted reform by refusing to recognize that "excellence costs"; Albert Shanker, head of the American Federation of Teachers, said that Bennett had failed to grasp the fact that "we do not yet know how to educate the overwhelming majority of kids." Bennett proposed no major new federally funded education programs and accused his critics of practicing "opposition by extortion" when they claimed the administration had short-changed the reform movement.

Congressional Initiatives

Congress in the meantime had launched several new programs to address literacy problems. It passed an education act April 26 authorizing a $50 million dropout-prevention program, a $200 million initiative to help students develop basic literacy skills, and an experimental venture to combine preschool and adult basic education. Low-income parents would be taught to read and would, in turn, be able to help their children learn to read. No federal money had been reserved specifically for dropout prevention since the late 1960s.

Another of the bill's provisions seemed to endorse some of the ideas in the Bennett report. It required states to set aside some of their educational block grant money for measures that presumably would make schools more effective: setting clear educational goals, establishing an orderly environment, providing strong administrative leadership, raising expectations for students, and testing students regularly.

Following are excerpts from American Education: Making it
Work, *by Secretary of Education William J. Bennett, released April 26, 1988:*

... Five years ago, *A Nation At Risk,* the landmark report of the
National Commission on Excellence in Education, gave eloquent voice to
the growing public sense of crisis about our children and their schools.

This report evaluates the state of American education today, five years
later. It assesses what we have learned and accomplished in our efforts to
restore purpose and quality to our schools. And it is a guide to the critical
task that remains: putting our knowledge and experience together, applying it to each and every one of our schools, and once again making
American education work.

Where We Stand Today

American education has made some undeniable progress in the last few
years. The precipitous downward slide of previous decades has been
arrested, and we have begun the long climb back to reasonable standards.
Our students have made modest gains in achievement. They are taking
more classes in basic subjects. And the performance of our schools is
slightly improved. This is the good and welcome news: we are doing better
than we were in 1983.

But we are certainly not doing well enough, and we are not doing well
enough fast enough. We are still at risk. The absolute level at which our
improvements are taking place is unacceptably low. Too many students do
not graduate from our high schools, and too many of those who do
graduate have been poorly educated. Our students know too little, and
their command of essential skills is too slight. Our schools still teach
curricula of widely varying quality. Good schools for disadvantaged and
minority children are much too rare, and the dropout rate among black
and Hispanic youth in many of our inner cities is perilously high. An ethos
of success is missing from too many American schools. Our teachers and
principals are too often hired and promoted in ways that make excellence a
matter of chance, not design. And the entire project of American education—at every level—remains insufficiently accountable for the result that
matters most: student learning. ...

Scattered across the landscape of American education are hundreds—
even thousands—of good examples: fine schools, outstanding teachers,
courageous principals, committed governors and legislators, and eager and
accomplished students of every color, class, and background. Visiting 97
elementary and secondary schools, meeting students and educators, seeing
them learn and work, has been the most gratifying experience of my three
years as Secretary of Education. The success of many American schools is
reason for hope and optimism. And their success should be a model and
foundation for the future of education reform in America. Extending and
applying the lessons of what works—to every school in every community

and state in the nation—is the task that lies ahead. . . .

But needed reforms, however popular, will not take place overnight. Even those changes that are underway will take time to show results. And future reforms face serious obstacles. We have more than 100,000 elementary and secondary schools, and the sheer magnitude of the system creates a bureaucratic inertia that is difficult to overcome.

Above all, sound education reforms are threatened by the determined opposition they elicit. That opposition has taken various forms over the years. Early on it appeared as a form of denial—as a claim that things were not so bad as they seemed in our schools. A little later, the opposition to reform took a different tack, admitting that things might be bad, but insisting that they could not be fixed in the schools—that first "society" or "the system" must be altered. Today we tend to hear what might be called opposition by extortion, the false claim that to fix our schools will first require a fortune in new funding.

But more and more the opposition to school reform is now manifested in the narrow, self-interested exercise of political power in statehouse corridors and local school board meetings. Almost without fail, wherever a worthwhile school proposal or legislative initiative is under consideration, those with a vested interest in the educational status quo will use political muscle to block reform. And too often the anti-reformers succeed. . . .

How Far Have We Come?

Shortly after *A Nation At Risk* appeared, the Education Commission of the States counted no fewer than 275 state and local task forces at work on education issues. Within twelve months, 35 states had strengthened their high school graduation requirements. At the same time, the country saw a wave of reports and studies further evaluating the troubled state of our schools. . . .

By and large, governors and state legislators have responded conscientiously, sometimes admirably. A notable example is *Time For Results,* the August 1986 report of the National Governors' Association, which put the governors on record in support of basic reforms such as higher quality teaching, better school leadership, and increased parental choice. It also promised yearly assessments of state reform efforts and continued gubernatorial leadership.

That leadership has been, in part, fiscal. In recent years most states have spent generously in an effort to improve their schools. Between 1981 and 1986, per capita state spending for elementary and secondary education increased nationally by more than 40 percent. In fact, education is now the single largest budget item in all but two of the 50 states.

But more important than the size of education budgets has been state-level commitment to reform and improvement. Many of the most significant ideas advanced by the education reform movement are currently being put into practice—singly or in combination, by one state or another—with successful and promising results. New Jersey, for example, has conclusively demonstrated that we can and should look beyond teacher colleges when recruiting able instructors for our schools. Utah has shown that it is possible to reward teachers with salaries and professional status based on excellent performance, not mere length of service. Indiana has installed a new performance-based system of school accreditation. South Carolina is now in the third year of its incentive reward program, which provides monetary awards to individual schools based on annual assessments of student achievement. Minnesota has instituted an open enrollment plan under which almost 100 school districts are offering parents and students their choice of attendance among local public schools....

What Our Students Know

A sharp drop in SAT scores was noted in *A Nation At Risk:* between 1963 and 1980, combined average SAT scores fell 90 points. That plunge focused the American public's attention on a grave decline in student achievement. Since 1980, combined average SAT scores have recovered 16 points, though they have stalled for the last three years at an average score of 906....

On the ACT examination, which measures knowledge of English, mathematics, social studies, and the natural sciences, scores were relatively flat between 1978 and 1983, rose half a point over the next three years, and dropped one-tenth of a point between 1986 and 1987.

Test data show that black and Hispanic children are performing better. Minority participation in Advanced Placement exams has doubled since 1980. Minority participation in the SAT test also has increased. These test-taking gains are themselves a good sign, but minority test scores are up, too. Between 1985 and 1987, ACT scores of black students gained nine-tenths of a point on the 36-point ACT scale and those of Hispanics gained eight-tenths of a point, while those of white students increased just two-tenths of a point. The performance of minority students on the SAT has also been improving for the past decade, though scores for white students have declined slightly....

Mathematics. Math performance by American students has begun to recover a bit from declines in the 1970s.... But the absolute level at which these welcome gains are occurring remains low.... American students consistently rate at or near the bottom of most international comparisons of math performance....

Science. Recent years have produced some gains in science achievement by American students. The pervasive downward trend apparent through much of the 1970s appears to have been arrested....

Again, it is important to remember that these improvements are taking place within a general range of achievement that is very low. A new assessment places American science students in rough international perspective. Our 10-year-olds seem about average, scoring in 8th place among 15 countries tested. But our 14-year-olds are far behind their peers around the world, placing 14th out of 17 countries, tied with Singapore and

Thailand. Advanced American science students (seniors in their second year of study in given disciplines) fare even more poorly: 9th place out of 13 countries in physics, 11th of 13 in chemistry, and last in biology.

History. In 1987, the Education for Democracy Project—a joint venture of the American Federation of Teachers, Freedom House, and the Educational Excellence Network—issued a statement of alarm about young Americans' knowledge of history. "Many students," it concluded, "are unaware of prominent people and seminal ideas and events that have shaped our past and created our present."

. . . More than one-fifth of the students could not identify George Washington as the commander of colonial forces during the Revolution. Almost one in three did not know that Lincoln was the author of the Emancipation Proclamation. And nearly half failed to recognize Patrick Henry as the man who said "Give me liberty or give me death."

Questions requiring somewhat deeper understanding of American history produced still more discouraging results. . . .

What Our Students Study

Whether students succeed academically depends in large part on what they study. . . . It comes as no surprise that a serious deterioration in the rigor of American elementary and secondary curricula accompanied the precipitous declines in student achievement already noted.

A Nation At Risk had especially harsh words for high school curricula, which over the years had become "homogenized, diluted, and diffused to the point that they no longer have a central purpose." In 1983, the report concluded that "we have a cafeteria-style curriculum in which the appetizers and desserts can easily be mistaken for the main courses." Its authors were distressed to find that 25 percent of credits earned by "general track" students were in "physical and health education, work experience outside the school, remedial English and mathematics, and personal service and development courses, such as training for adulthood and marriage."

To replace this smorgasbord of incoherent classwork, *A Nation At Risk* proposed a reinvigorated core curriculum for American secondary schools, one organized around a set of "New Basics": four years of English; three years each of mathematics, science, and social studies; one-half year of computer science; and, for those students planning to attend college, two years of a foreign language.

Today, five years after these recommendations were issued, we are still a long way from providing every American student with a solid academic curriculum. But there are now grounds for hope, and if visible improvements at the high school level are complemented by similar changes in the earlier grades—and are given a full chance to work—we may begin to see substantial benefits in learning.

As part of its research for this report, the Department of Education undertook a national study comparing the transcripts of 15,000 1987 high school graduates with those of a comparable group of 1982 graduates. The news is encouraging. Less than 2 percent of the 1982 sample had completed the academic program suggested in *A Nation At Risk;* in 1987, 12.7 percent of graduating students had done so. When foreign language and computer science classes are omitted from the tally, improvement is more dramatic—from 13.4 percent of 1982 graduates to nearly 30 percent in the 1987 sample.

These figures mark a welcome break from a trend much lamented by *A Nation At Risk:* a 15-year migration of American high school students from solid academic work into vague "general track" courses. The proportion of students in the "general track" dropped from 35 percent in 1982 to 17 percent in 1987. Nearly all of this change reflects movement back into a more rigorous academic curriculum. . . .

In another sign of improvement, the proportion of American high school graduates who have taken Advanced Placement (AP) exams has more than doubled, from 4.7 percent to 9.7 percent. . . .

Yet we still have much room for improvement; curricular foolishness has not been eliminated from American high schools and not all students have shared equally in the national trend toward stronger curricula. Compared with public high schools, private and parochial schools still do a somewhat better job of ensuring that their students take the "New Basics" recommended in *A Nation At Risk.* At the same task, suburban schools do a better job than either rural or urban schools. More Asian students (26 percent) take all the "New Basics" than do either whites (13 percent) or blacks (9 percent), though racial differences in course-taking have narrowed since 1982. Most discouragingly, students remaining in the vocational track are still taking far too few courses in the core disciplines. . . .

How Our Schools Perform

Time for Instruction. *A Nation At Risk* expressed concern that many American schools make inefficient use of the class time at their disposal. School and classroom management varies widely ... but the National Commission on Excellence in Education reported that schools were devoting, on average, only 22 hours of a 30-hour week to academic instruction—and some schools were spending as few as 17 hours. . . .

A Nation At Risk also noted that it is not unusual for high school students in other industrialized countries to spend eight hours a day at school, 220 days each year. In the United States, by contrast, a typical school day lasts six hours, and the school year runs 175 to 180 days. *A Nation At Risk* recommended that school districts and state legislatures consider increasing instructional time by implementing a seven-hour school day and a 200- to 220-day school year, a recommendation that has been largely ignored.

American teachers prefer their current nine- or ten-month contracts, and their union leaders have opposed most legislative efforts to lengthen the school day or year. Since 1983, such proposals have been considered in 37 states. But a longer school year has been adopted in only nine of them—

and all of those states merely extended their unusually short calendars to the more common 180-day standard. Only five states have lengthened the school days—none to more than six-and-a-half hours. . . .

The high school completion rate among blacks ages 18 to 19 is 10 percent lower than the national average of 75 percent; the completion rate for Hispanic youths of the same age is . . . only 55 percent. . . .

In short, student achievement and school performance earn a mixed grade for progress during the past five years. Despite encouraging improvements in patterns of course-taking, gains in student learning are slight and the average level of student skill and knowledge remains unacceptably low. . . .

What We Need to Do

. . . Replacing the cafeteria curriculum with a well-balanced academic menu has been an overriding goal of the education reform movement since then. Without the right curriculum, efforts to improve teaching, governance and school accountability will make little difference. The transmission of knowledge and skills is, after all, what we aim to hold schools accountable *for*. If we allow schools to avoid or be diverted from this task, we cannot legitimately complain if student achievement remains low. School time is limited—it will either be spent on important subjects, or it will be frittered away. . . .

Some argue that our nation's cultural and ethnic diversity makes it impossible to construct a core curriculum appropriate for all students and schools. They may concede that curricular deterioration is a problem, but they resist the obvious solution, believing instead that our sprawling, heterogeneous culture defies any attempt to codify an American "canon" of essential learning.

This view is unduly pessimistic and it is at odds with a basic tradition of American education. Our pluralism has always posed formidable challenges to our schools. But our history demonstrates that for more than two centuries American education has welcomed, accommodated, and celebrated diversity while joining our students in a cooperative undertaking. Today, still, every American child has an equal claim to a common future under common laws, enjoying common rights and charged with common responsibilities. There follows the need for common education, now and in the future. In fact, a general American consensus does exist about the most compelling ideas and books and authors our students should know. . . .

Order and Discipline

By themselves, committed school professionals and strong curricula are insufficient means of communicating character and inspiring achievement. Students must first understand that they are in school to learn and that a structure of school authority and order is necessary for them to do it. Articulating and securing that structure should be the first priority for schools seeking real improvement. . . .

A large part of any school's ethos derives simply from its physical tone. A school with broken window panes, graffiti on its walls, and littered floors is, strictly speaking, a school without order. The character of an environment can sink deep into the souls of those whom it surrounds, and a disorderly school environment is bound to affect student character and attitudes toward learning.

Even more basic to the establishment of a positive school ethos is student discipline. Regular and prompt attendance, respect for teachers, and good conduct go hand in hand with academic success. . . .

Behavior is learned, of course, a habit that comes of rules and the routines that reinforce them. Students must be given clear standards of conduct; they must know what is expected of them. . . .

Some forms of misconduct—the use or sale of drugs during school hours or on school grounds, for example—should not be tolerated. Lesser violations of a school code, like class disruptions or attendance problems, should incur carefully articulated and logical penalties. Punishment that inadvertently rewards misbehavior—responding to student absenteeism with suspension from school, for instance—ought to be avoided. And all disciplinary actions should seek to involve the parents. Parents need to know when their children are breaking rules. For some students, the knowledge that their parents may be brought into school will itself help to deter misbehavior.

Parents can and should help in more active ways as well. Students bring to school habits and attitudes they learn at home. Not all teachers are parents, but every parent is a teacher—the child's first and all-but-indispensable teacher. Many parents can do more than they are accustomed to doing today. According to one recent survey, majorities of both parents and teachers think that "most parents fail to motivate their children so that they want to learn in school." Half of teachers and nearly 60 percent of parents believe that "many or most parents fail to discipline their children." Parents have a responsibility to contribute to a good school ethos by sending to school children who are respectful, self-disciplined, and prepared to work hard and to learn.

Hard Work

To be sure, student discipline is not the end of education. It is only a means. Schools must insist on order in and near their buildings, not pay for it by abandoning what ought to be their ultimate goals: good teaching and effective learning. Yet too often a quiet but insidious "deal" is struck in American classrooms—minimal demand from teachers in exchange for minimal disruption by students. . . .

There is a simple explanation for the fact that virtually all international studies show American students being outperformed by their foreign counterparts: children in many other countries spend more time in class and their teachers use that time more efficiently. In other words, both teachers and students in other countries *do more work*. . . .

May

Report on Nicotine Addiction 309

Science Board Panel
on Strategic Missile Defense 323

Public Health Service Report
on Length of Hospitalization 333

Trade Bill Vetoes 339

Sweden's Pioneer Law on
Farm-Animal Rights 347

Reagan-Gorbachev Summit 353

REPORT ON
NICOTINE ADDICTION
May 16, 1988

In a report to Congress released May 16, U.S. Surgeon General C. Everett Koop likened nicotine's addictive qualities to those of heroin and cocaine. It was the latest in a series of annual reports that Congress has required since 1969 from the Public Health Service, which the surgeon general heads, on the consequences of tobacco use. "This report addresses why people continue to smoke despite the known health hazards," Koop said at a press conference announcing the report. "The short answer is that cigarettes are addicting."

Although the number of Americans who smoke had declined steadily for more than a decade, there were still some 50 million smokers in 1987. The record amount of $33.3 billion was spent in the United States that year on cigarettes. "An extensive body of research has shown that nicotine is the drug in tobacco that causes addiction," Koop wrote in the preface to the 618-page report. "Moreover, the processes that determine tobacco addiction are similar to those that determine addictions to drugs such as heroin and cocaine." The report, compiled by fifty scientists, drew its conclusions from more than 2,000 research papers.

Nicotine's effects on the brain and other parts of the nervous system were prominently cited in the report's evidence of addiction. Nicotine produces mood alterations, reduces stress, relaxes skeletal muscles, and alters the workings of the heart, blood vessels, and hormonal system. As explained by the report, nicotine addicts use tobacco compulsively and develop a tolerance to it, and then suffer withdrawal symptoms when they try to stop smoking.

The first report detailing the links between cigarette smoking and lung cancer, issued in 1964 by Surgeon General Luther L. Terry, is credited with providing the impetus for the first congressionally required warning labels on cigarette packages. Koop's report in 1986, pointing to smoke as a health hazard to nonsmokers, prompted Congress to ban smoking on airplane flights of less than two hours. (Surgeon General's Report on Involuntary Smoking, Historic Documents of 1986, p. 1079)

"Our nation has mobilized enormous resources to wage a war on drugs," Koop said in releasing the report. "We should also give priority to the one addiction—tobacco addiction—that is killing more than 300,000 Americans each year." Saying that Congress was "on a roll and doing the right thing about tobacco," Koop recounted the report's proposals for additional measures to curb smoking. It proposed that health-warning labels on tobacco products also carry a notice that they contain an addictive substance, and that insurers should pay for treatment programs to help smokers quit. Koop also suggested in his press conference that Congress increase the excise tax on cigarettes above the prevailing rate of sixteen cents per pack. Previous efforts to increase that rate have been rebuffed.

In addition, the report said that children should be taught in school about the risks of smoking, and state laws banning tobacco sales to minors should be more strictly enforced. At his press conference, Koop showed a public-service television spot for children featuring the slogan, "Don't be a butt-head." He called for a ban on vending machine sales of cigarettes and stricter regulation of free cigarette samples. "Shouldn't we treat tobacco sales at least as seriously as the sale of alcoholic beverages, for which a specific license is required and revoked for repeated sales to minors?" he asked.

Congressional, Industry Reaction

Sen. Bill Bradley, D-N.J., used the occasion of the report's release to introduce legislation to require an addiction warning on all tobacco products and advertisements. The label would say "WARNING: Smoking is addictive. Once you start, you may not be able to stop." The same day, three members of the House Energy and Commerce Committee, which has jurisdiction over most of the health and advertising issues related to tobacco, appeared at a press conference called by the Coalition on Smoking OR Health to discuss the legislative implications of the report. Noting that the tobacco industry spends more than $2 billion in advertising and promotion each year, Mike Synar, D-Okla., said, "We intend to continue to stretch their resources" by making the industry fight "brush fires" on several different bills, rather than letting them pour resources into seeking defeat of one omnibus measure.

"Claims that smokers are 'addicts' defy common sense," said the Tobacco Institute, which represented tobacco manufacturers, in a statement issued after the surgeon general's report was released. "Smoking is

truly a personal choice which can be stopped if and when a person decides to do so."

Members of Congress from tobacco-producing states took offense as well. "In the middle of a supposed war on drugs, the surgeon general has mistaken the enemy," said Sen. Terry Sanford, D-N.C. "In comparing tobacco—a legitimate and legal substance—to insidious narcotics such as heroin and cocaine, he has directed 'friendly fire' at American farmers and businessmen."

Antismoking groups predicted the report would help former smokers who sue tobacco companies for health damages. Since 1954 more than 300 such lawsuits had been filed, but no tobacco company had lost even a single claim or paid anything in damages. Most of the suits had been dismissed or withdrawn.

Then, less than a month after Koop's report was released, a federal jury in Newark, N.J., found the Liggett Group, a cigarette manufacturer, partially liable in the lung cancer death of a New Jersey woman. The jury ruled in the much-publicized case that the company had failed to warn of the health risks of smoking before warnings were required on cigarette packs in 1966, and had misled the public by suggesting that smoking was safe. The jury awarded $400,000 in damages to Antonio Cipollone, the husband of the woman, Rose Cipollone.

However, the jury's decision was such that both sides could claim victory. Liggett and two other defending companies, Lorillard and Philip Morris, were found not guilty of fraudulently misrepresenting the risks of smoking and conspiring to misrepresent facts. The jury said that Mrs. Cipollone, who had smoked a pack and a half of cigarettes a day for forty years, ignoring warning labels after they appeared, was primarily responsible for her death in 1984.

Defense attorneys said the verdict would have a favorable effect on the industry. "If anything, it will close the floodgates on this kind of litigation," said Alan Naar, one of Liggett's lawyers. "It is clear that the jury ruled in favor of personal choice and personal responsibility and that they refused to find any fraud, misrepresentation, or conspiracy." But consumer advocate Ralph Nader predicted that the extensive documents obtained in the case "will assure the Cipollone case will be a rallying point" against the industry. The documents were "pretty important enlargements of tobacco industry history," he said.

On June 29 the Canadian Parliament passed some of the world's strongest antismoking measures, among them a ban on all forms of cigarette advertising and a requirement that every pack contain a leaflet warning of health hazards. The laws also restricted smoking to designated rooms in all federally regulated workplaces, prohibited the use of tobacco brand names in connection with cultural and sporting events,

311

*and banned point-of-sale advertising (for example, placards in stores).
The penalty for violating the laws could run as high as $245,000.*

*According to the World Health Organization, about twenty other
nations prohibited tobacco advertising, and forty-three nations—including the United States—required health warnings on cigarette packages.*

Following are excerpts from The Health Consequences of
Smoking: Nicotine Addiction, *a report of the surgeon general, released May 16, 1988:*

This Report of the Surgeon General is the U.S. Public Health Service's
20th Report on the health consequences of tobacco use and the 7th issued
during my tenure as Surgeon General. Eighteen Reports have been
released previously as part of the health consequences of smoking series; a
report on the health consequences of using smokeless tobacco was released
in 1986.

Previous Reports have reviewed the medical and scientific evidence
establishing the health effects of cigarette smoking and other forms of
tobacco use. Tens of thousands of studies have documented that smoking
causes lung cancer, other cancers, chronic obstructive lung disease, heart
disease, complications of pregnancy, and several other adverse health
effects.

Epidemiologic studies have shown that cigarette smoking is responsible
for more than 300,000 deaths each year in the United States. As I stated in
the Preface to the 1982 Surgeon General's Report, smoking is the chief
avoidable cause of death in our society.

From 1964 through 1979, each Surgeon General's Report addressed the
major health effects of smoking. The 1979 Report provided the most
comprehensive review of these effects. Following the 1979 Report, each
subsequent Report has focused on specific populations (women in 1980,
workers in 1985), specific diseases (cancer in 1982, cardiovascular disease
in 1983, chronic obstructive lung disease in 1984), and specific topics (low-
tar, low-nicotine cigarettes in 1981, involuntary smoking in 1986).

This Report explores in great detail another specific topic: nicotine
addiction. Careful examination of the data makes it clear that cigarettes
and other forms of tobacco are addicting. An extensive body of research
has shown that nicotine is the drug in tobacco that causes addiction.
Moreover, the processes that determine tobacco addiction are similar to
those that determine addiction to drugs such as heroin and cocaine.

Actions of Nicotine

All tobacco products contain substantial amounts of nicotine. Nicotine is
absorbed readily from tobacco smoke in the lungs and from smokeless
tobacco in the mouth or nose. Levels of nicotine in the blood are similar in
magnitude in people using different forms of tobacco. Once in the blood
stream, nicotine is rapidly distributed throughout the body.

Nicotine is a powerful pharmacologic agent that acts in a variety of ways at different sites in the body. After reaching the blood stream, nicotine enters the brain, interacts with specific receptors in brain tissue, and initiates metabolic and electrical activity in the brain. In addition, nicotine causes skeletal muscle relaxation and has cardiovascular and endocrine (i.e., hormonal) effects.

Human and animal studies have shown that nicotine is the agent in tobacco that leads to addiction. The diversity and strength of its actions on the body are consistent with its role in causing addiction.

Tobacco Use as an Addiction

Standard definitions of drug addiction have been adopted by various organizations including the World Health Organization and the American Psychiatric Association. Although these definitions are not identical, they have in common several criteria for establishing a drug as addicting.

The central element among all forms of drug addiction is that the user's behavior is largely controlled by a psychoactive substance (i.e., a substance that produces transient alterations in mood that are primarily mediated by effects in the brain). There is often compulsive use of the drug despite damage to the individual or to society, and drug-seeking behavior can take precedence over other important priorities. The drug is "reinforcing"— that is, the pharmacologic activity of the drug is sufficiently rewarding to maintain self-administration. "Tolerance" is another aspect of drug addiction whereby a given dose of a drug produces less effect or increasing doses are required to achieve a specified intensity of response. Physical dependence on the drug can also occur, and is characterized by a withdrawal syndrome that usually accompanies drug abstinence. After cessation of drug use, there is a strong tendency to relapse.

This Report demonstrates in detail that tobacco use and nicotine in particular meet all these criteria. The evidence for these findings is derived from animal studies as well as human observations. Leading national and international organizations, including the World Health Organization and the American Psychiatric Association, have recognized chronic tobacco use as a drug addiction.

Some people may have difficulty in accepting the notion that tobacco is addicting because it is a legal product. The word "addiction" is strongly associated with illegal drugs such as cocaine and heroin. However, as this Report shows, the processes that determine tobacco addiction are similar to those that determine addiction to other drugs, including illegal drugs.

In addition, some smokers may not believe that tobacco is addicting because of a reluctance to admit that one's behavior is largely controlled by a drug. On the other hand, most smokers admit that they would like to quit but have been unable to do so. Smokers who have repeatedly failed in their attempts to quit probably realize that smoking is more than just a simple habit.

Many smokers have quit on their own ("spontaneous remission") and some smokers smoke only occasionally. However, spontaneous remission and occasional use also occur with the illicit drugs of addiction, and in no way disqualify a drug from being classified as addicting. Most narcotics users, for example, never progress beyond occasional use, and of those who do, approximately 30 percent spontaneously remit. Moreover, it seems plausible that spontaneous remitters are largely those who have either learned to deliver effective treatments to themselves or for whom environmental circumstances have fortuitously changed in such a way as to support drug cessation and abstinence.

Treatment

Like other addictions, tobacco use can be effectively treated. A wide variety of behavioral interventions have been used for many years, including aversion procedures (e.g., satiation, rapid smoking), relaxation training, coping skills training, stimulus control, and nicotine fading. In recognition of the important role that nicotine plays in maintaining tobacco use, nicotine replacement therapy is now available. Nicotine polacrilex gum has been shown in controlled trials to relieve withdrawal symptoms. In addition, some (but not all) studies have shown that nicotine gum, as an adjunct to behavioral interventions, increases smoking abstinence rates. In recent years, multicomponent interventions have been applied successfully to the treatment of tobacco addiction.

Public Health Strategies

The conclusion that cigarettes and other forms of tobacco are addicting has important implications for health professionals, educators, and policymakers. In treating the tobacco user, health professionals must address the tenacious hold that nicotine has on the body. More effective interventions must be developed to counteract both the psychological and pharmacologic addictions that accompany tobacco use. More research is needed to evaluate how best to treat those with the strongest dependence on the drug. Treatment of tobacco addiction should be more widely available and should be considered at least as favorably by third-party payors as treatment of alcoholism and illicit drug addiction.

The challenge to health professionals is complicated by the array of new nicotine delivery systems that are being developed and introduced in the marketplace. Some of these products are produced by tobacco manufacturers; others may be marketed as devices to aid in smoking cessation. These new products may be more toxic and more addicting than the products currently on the market. New nicotine delivery systems should be evaluated for their toxic and addictive effects; products intended for use in smoking cessation also should be evaluated for efficacy.

Public information campaigns should be developed to increase community awareness of the addictive nature of tobacco use. A health warning on addiction should be rotated with the other warnings now required on cigarette and smokeless tobacco packages and advertisements. Prevention of tobacco use should be included along with prevention of illicit drug use in comprehensive school health education curricula. Many children and adolescents who are experimenting with cigarettes and other forms of tobacco state that they do not intend to use tobacco in later years. They are unaware of, or underestimate, the strength of tobacco addiction. Because this addiction almost always begins during childhood or adolescence, children need to be warned as early as possible, and repeatedly warned through their teenage years, about the dangers of exposing themselves to nicotine.

This Report shows conclusively that cigarettes and other forms of tobacco are addicting in the same sense as are drugs such as heroin and cocaine. Most adults view illegal drugs with scorn and express disapproval (if not outrage) at their sale and use. This Nation has mobilized enormous resources to wage a war on drugs—illicit drugs. We should also give priority to the one addiction that is killing more than 300,000 Americans each year.

We as citizens, in concert with our elected officials, civic leaders, and public health officers, should establish appropriate public policies for how tobacco products are sold and distributed in our society. With the evidence that tobacco is addicting, is it appropriate for tobacco products to be sold through vending machines, which are easily accessible to children? Is it appropriate for free samples of tobacco products to be sent through the mail or distributed on public property, where verification of age is difficult if not impossible? Should the sale of tobacco be treated less seriously than the sale of alcoholic beverages, for which a specific license is required (and revoked for repeated sales to minors)?

In the face of overwhelming evidence that tobacco is addicting, policymakers should address these questions without delay. To achieve our goal of a smoke-free society, we must give this problem the serious attention it deserves. . . .

Introduction [Chapter 1]

This Report was developed by the Office on Smoking and Health, Center for Health Promotion and Education, Centers for Disease Control, Public Health Service of the U.S. Department of Health and Human Services as part of the Department's responsibility, under Public Law 91-222, to report new and current information on smoking and health to the United States Congress.

The scientific content of this Report reflects the contributions of more than 50 scientists representing a wide variety of relevant disciplines. These experts, known for their understanding of and work in specific content areas, prepared manuscripts for incorporation into this Report. The Office on Smoking and Health and its consultants edited and consolidated the individual manuscripts into appropriate chapters. These draft chapters were subjected to an extensive outside peer review ... whereby each chapter was reviewed by up to 11 experts. Based on the comments of these

315

reviewers, the chapters were revised and the entire volume was assembled. This revised edition of the Report was resubjected to review by 20 distinguished scientists inside and outside the Federal Government, both in this country and abroad. Parallel to this review, the entire Report was also submitted for review to 12 institutes and agencies within the U.S. Public Health Service. The comments from the senior scientific reviewers and the agencies were used to prepare the final volume of this Report. . . .

This Report topic is particularly timely because of recent advances and extensive data gathered in the 1980s relevant to the issue of tobacco addiction. Since the early 1900s scientific literature and historic anecdotes have provided evidence that tobacco use is a form of drug addiction. In the 1970s, however, research efforts increased considerably on various aspects of tobacco addiction, including nicotine pharmacokinetics, pharmacody-namics, self-administration, withdrawal, dependence, and tolerance. In addition, advances in the neurosciences have begun to reveal effects of nicotine in the brain and body that may help to explain why tobacco use is reinforcing and difficult to give up. These issues are addressed in this Report. Finally, recent developments in the use of nicotine replacement in smoking cessation emphasize the importance of pharmacologic aspects of cigarette smoking. . . .

The main conclusions of the Report are based upon concepts of drug dependence that have been developed by expert committees of the World Health Organization, as well as in publications of NIDA and the American Psychiatric Association. These concepts were used to develop a set of criteria to determine whether tobacco-delivered nicotine is addicting. The criteria for drug dependence include primary and additional indices and are summarized below.

Criteria for Drug Dependence

Primary Criteria

- Highly controlled or compulsive use
- Psychoactive effect
- Drug-reinforced behavior

Additional Criteria

- Addictive behavior often involves:
  - stereotypic patterns of use
  - use despite harmful effects
  - relapse following abstinence
  - recurrent drug cravings
- Dependence-producing drugs often produce:
  - tolerance
  - physical dependence
  - pleasant (euphoriant) effects

The primary criteria listed above are sufficient to define drug dependence. Highly controlled or compulsive use indicates that drug-seeking and drug-taking behavior is driven by strong, often irresistible urges. It can persist despite a desire to quit or even repeated attempts to quit. Such behavior is also referred to as "habitual" behavior. To distinguish drug dependence from habitual behaviors not involving drugs, it must be demonstrated that a drug with psychoactive (mood-altering) effects in the brain enters the blood stream. Furthermore, drug dependence is defined by the occurrence of drug-motivated behavior; therefore, the psychoactive chemical must be capable of functioning as a reinforcer that can directly strengthen behavior leading to further drug ingestion. . . .

. . . A summary of the main findings of the Report follows.

Major Conclusions

1. Cigarettes and other forms of tobacco are addicting.
2. Nicotine is the drug in tobacco that causes addiction.
3. The pharmacologic and behavioral processes that determine tobacco addiction are similar to those that determine addiction to drugs such as heroin and cocaine.

Brief History Relevant to this Report

. . . While the health-promoting and health-damaging effects of tobacco products were being debated throughout the 17th and 18th centuries, scientists were trying to determine the chief active ingredient in tobacco. In the early 1800s the oily essence of tobacco was discovered by Cerioli and by Vauquelin. This active substance was named "Nicotianine," after Jean Nicot, who sent tobacco seeds from Portugal to the French court at the end of the 16th century. In 1828, Posselt and Reimann at the University of Heidelberg isolated the pure form of Nicotianine and renamed it "Nikotin." The chemical's empirical formula, $C_{10}H_{14}N_2$, was determined in the 1840s, and "nicotine" was synthesized in the 1890s.

Since the late 1800s, research on the pharmacologic actions of nicotine has contributed substantially to basic information about the nervous system. The classic work by [J. N.] Langley and [W. L.] Dickinson (1889) on nicotine's effects in autonomic ganglia led to the postulates that chemicals transmit information between neurons and that there are receptors on cells that respond functionally to stimulation by specific chemicals. As early as the 1920s and 1930s, some investigators were concluding that nicotine was responsible for the compulsive use of tobacco products. [L. M.] Johnston (1942) concluded that, "smoking tobacco is essentially a means of administering nicotine, just as smoking opium is a means of administering morphine."

Throughout the 20th century, research has continued to investigate the role of nicotine in tobacco use. . . . There was no question at the time of the 1964 Report that nicotine was the critical pharmacologic agent for tobacco use, but its role was then considered to be more similar to cocaine and amphetamines than to opiates and barbiturates. Later in 1964 the World

Health Organization dropped this semantic distinction between habituating and addicting drugs . . . . In an effort to shift the focus to dependent patterns of behavior and away from moral and social issues associated with the term addiction, the term dependence was recommended. . . .

In the late 1950s, the U.S. Public Health Service, the National Cancer Institute, the National Heart Institute, the American Cancer Society, and the American Heart Association appointed a study group to examine the available evidence on smoking and health. This study group concluded that excessive cigarette smoking is a causative factor in lung cancer.

In 1962, Surgeon General Luther Terry established an advisory committee on smoking and health. This committee released its Report on January 11, 1964, concluding that cigarette smoking is a cause of lung cancer in men and a suspected cause of lung cancer in women, and increased the risk of dying from pulmonary emphysema. The next Report was issued in 1967 and stated that "the case for cigarette smoking as the principal cause of lung cancer is overwhelming.". . .

The 1968 and 1969 Reports strengthened the conclusions reached in 1967. The 1971 Report provided a detailed review of the evidence to date regarding health consequences of smoking. The subsequent reports continued to review the increasing evidence associating cigarette smoking with many health hazards. The 1972 Report also discussed involuntary or passive smoking. The 1973 Report included some data on the health hazards of smoking pipes and cigars. The 1975 Report updated information on the health effects of involuntary or passive smoking. The combined 1977-78 Report discussed smoking-related problems unique to women.

At the time of its release, the 1979 Report was the most comprehensive review by a Surgeon General's Report of the health consequences of smoking, smoking behavior, and smoking control. In addition to providing a thorough review of the health consequences of smoking, the 1979 Report discussed the health consequences of using forms of tobacco other than cigarettes (pipes, cigars, and smokeless tobacco). Moreover, the 1979 Report expanded the scope of the previous reports and examined behavioral, pharmacologic, and social factors influencing the initiation, maintenance, and cessation of cigarette smoking. Relevant to the topic of the present Report, the 1979 Report concluded that "it is no exaggeration to say that smoking is the prototypical substance-abuse dependency and that improved knowledge of this process holds great promise for prevention of risk." Since the release of the 1979 Report, each subsequent Report has focused on a specific population or setting (women in 1980, the workplace in 1985), a specific topic (health effects of low-tar and low-nicotine cigarettes in 1981, involuntary smoking in 1986), or a specific disease (cancer in 1982, cardiovascular disease in 1983, chronic obstructive lung disease in 1984).

In addition to the previous Surgeon General's Reports, several other developments and publications provide relevant background for the present Report. For example, numerous monographs prepared in the 1970s by the National Institute on Drug Abuse (NIDA) considered tobacco use as a form of drug dependence. In 1980, the American Psychiatric Association, in its Diagnostic and Statistical Manual of Mental Disorders, included tobacco dependence as a substance abuse disorder and tobacco withdrawal as an organic mental disorder. The 1987 revised edition of this manual, in recognition of the role of nicotine, changed "tobacco withdrawal" to "nicotine withdrawal." In 1982, the Director of NIDA testified to Congress that the position of NIDA was that tobacco use could lead to dependence and that nicotine was a prototypic dependence-producing drug. In a 1983 publication, "Why People Smoke Cigarettes," the U.S. Public Health Service supported this position of NIDA regarding tobacco and nicotine. In the 1984 NIDA Triennial Report to Congress, nicotine was labeled a prototypic dependence-producing drug and the role of nicotine in tobacco use was considered to be analogous to the roles of morphine, cocaine, and ethanol, in the use of opium, coca-derived products, and alcoholic beverages, respectively. In 1986, a consensus conference of the National Institutes of Health and the Report of the Advisory Committee to the Surgeon General on the health consequences of using smokeless tobacco concluded that smokeless tobacco can be addicting and that nicotine is a dependence-producing (i.e., addicting) drug. . . .

The deleterious effects of cigarette smoking are now well known. Therefore, this Report focuses on pharmacological information to help understand why people smoke. Such information will assist health professionals in developing effective strategies to prevent initiation and to promote cessation. The literature reviewed in this Report indicates that tobacco use is an addictive behavior. It is the purpose of this Report to thoroughly review the relevant literature. . . .

These points are listed under the appropriate Chapter and Appendix headings.

Chapter II: Nicotine: Pharmacokinetics, Metabolism, and Pharmacodynamics

1. All tobacco products contain substantial amounts of nicotine and other alkaloids. Tobaccos from low-yield and high-yield cigarettes contain similar amounts of nicotine.
2. Nicotine is absorbed readily from tobacco smoke in the lungs and from smokeless tobacco in the mouth or nose. Levels of nicotine in the blood are similar in magnitude in people using different forms of tobacco. With regular use, levels of nicotine accumulate in the body during the day and persist overnight. Thus, daily tobacco users are exposed to the effects of nicotine for 24 hr each day.
3. Nicotine that enters the blood is rapidly distributed to the brain. As a result, effects of nicotine on the central nervous system occur rapidly after a puff of cigarette smoke or after absorption of nicotine from other routes of administration.
4. Acute and chronic tolerance develops to many effects of nicotine.

Such tolerance is consistent with reports that initial use of tobacco products, such as in adolescents first beginning to smoke, is usually accompanied by a number of unpleasant symptoms which disappear following chronic tobacco use.

Chapter III: Nicotine: Sites and Mechanisms of Actions

1. Nicotine is a powerful pharmacologic agent that acts in the brain and throughout the body. Actions include electrocortical activation, skeletal muscle relaxation, and cardiovascular and endocrine effects. The many biochemical and electrocortical effects of nicotine may act in concert to reinforce tobacco use.
2. Nicotine acts on specific binding sites or receptors throughout the nervous system. Nicotine readily crosses the blood-brain barrier and accumulates in the brain shortly after it enters the body. Once in the brain, it interacts with specific receptors and alters brain energy metabolism in a pattern consistent with the distribution of specific binding sites for the drug.
3. Nicotine and smoking exert effects on nearly all components of the endocrine and neuroendocrine systems (including catecholamines, serotonin, corticosteroids, pituitary hormones). Some of these endocrine effects are mediated by actions of nicotine on brain neurotransmitter systems (e.g., hypothalamic-pituitary axis). In addition, nicotine has direct peripherally mediated effects (e.g., on the adrenal medulla and the adrenal cortex).

Chapter IV: Tobacco Use as Drug Dependence

1. Cigarettes and other forms of tobacco are addicting. Patterns o tobacco use are regular and compulsive, and a withdrawal syndrome usually accompanies tobacco abstinence.
2. Nicotine is the drug in tobacco that causes addiction. Specifically nicotine is psychoactive ("mood altering") and can provide pleasur able effects. Nicotine can serve as a reinforcer to motivate tobacco seeking and tobacco-using behavior. Tolerance develops to actions o nicotine such that repeated use results in diminished effects and ca be accompanied by increased intake. Nicotine also causes physica dependence characterized by a withdrawal syndrome that usuall accompanies nicotine abstinence.
3. The physical characteristics of nicotine delivery systems can affec their toxicity and addictiveness. Therefore, new nicotine deliver systems should be evaluated for their toxic and addictive effects.

Chapter V: Tobacco Use Compared to Other Drug Dependencies

1. The pharmacologic and behavioral processes that determine tobacc addiction are similar to those that determine addiction to drugs suc as heroin and cocaine.

2. Environmental factors including drug-associated stimuli and social pressure are important influences of initiation, patterns of use, quitting, and relapse to use of opioids, alcohol, nicotine, and other addicting drugs.
3. Many persons dependent upon opioids, alcohol, nicotine, or other drugs are able to give up their drug use outside the context of treatment programs; other persons, however, require the assistance of formal cessation programs to achieve lasting drug abstinence.
4. Relapse to drug use often occurs among persons who have achieved abstinence from opioids, alcohol, nicotine, or other drugs.
5. Behavioral and pharmacologic intervention techniques with demonstrated efficacy are available for the treatment of addiction to opioids, alcohol, nicotine, and other drugs.

Chapter VI: Effects of Nicotine
That May Promote Tobacco Dependence

1. After smoking cigarettes or receiving nicotine, smokers perform better on some cognitive tasks (including sustained attention and selective attention) than they do when deprived of cigarettes or nicotine. However, smoking and nicotine do not improve general learning.
2. Stress increases cigarette consumption among smokers. Further, stress has been identified as a risk factor for the initiation of smoking in adolescence.
3. In general, cigarette smokers weigh less (approximately 7 lb less on average) than nonsmokers. Many smokers who quit smoking gain weight.
4. Food intake and probably metabolic factors are involved in the inverse relationship between smoking and body weight. There is evidence that nicotine plays an important role in the relationship between smoking and body weight.

Chapter VII: Treatment of Tobacco Dependence

1. Tobacco dependence can be treated successfully.
2. Effective interventions include behavioral approaches alone and behavioral approaches with adjunctive pharmacologic treatment.
3. Behavioral interventions are most effective when they include multiple components (procedures such as aversive smoking, skills training, group support, and self-reward). Inclusion of too many treatment procedures can lead to less successful outcome.
4. Nicotine replacement can reduce tobacco withdrawal symptoms and may enhance the efficacy of behavioral treatment.

Appendix A: Trends in Tobacco Use in the United States

1. An estimated 32.7 percent of men and 28.3 percent of women smoked cigarettes regularly in 1985. The overall prevalence of smoking in the

United States decreased from 36.7 percent in 1976 (52.4 million adults) to 30.4 percent in 1985 (51.1 million adults).

2. In 1985, the mean reported number of cigarettes smoked per day was 21.8 for male smokers and 18.1 for female smokers.

3. Smoking is more common in lower socioeconomic categories (blue-collar workers or unemployed persons, less educated persons, and lower income groups) than in higher socioeconomic categories. For example, the prevalence of smoking in 1985 among persons without a high school diploma was 35.4 percent, compared with 16.5 percent among persons with postgraduate college education.

4. An estimated 18.7 percent of high school seniors reported daily use of cigarettes in 1986. The prevalence of daily use of one or more cigarettes among high school seniors declined between 1975 and 1986 by approximately 35 percent. Most of the decline occurred between 1977 and 1981. Since 1976, the smoking prevalence among females has consistently been slightly higher than among males.

5. The use of cigars and pipes has declined 80 percent since 1964.

6. Smokeless tobacco use has increased substantially among young men and has declined among older men since 1975. An estimated 8.2 percent of 17- to 19-year-old men were users of smokeless tobacco products in 1986.

Appendix B: Toxicity of Nicotine

1. At high exposure levels, nicotine is a potent and potentially lethal poison. Human poisonings occur primarily as a result of accidental ingestion or skin contact with nicotine-containing insecticides or, in children, after ingestion of tobacco or tobacco juices.

2. Mild nicotine intoxication occurs in first-time smokers, non-smoking workers who harvest tobacco leaves and people who chew excessive amounts of nicotine polacrilex gum. Tolerance to these effects develops rapidly.

3. Nicotine exposure in long-term tobacco users is substantial, affecting many organ systems (Chapters II and III). Pharmacologic actions of nicotine may contribute to the pathogenesis of smoking-related diseases, although direct causation has not yet been determined. Of particular concern are cardiovascular disease, complications of hypertension, reproductive disorders, cancer, and gastrointestinal disorders, including peptic ulcer disease and gastroesophageal reflux.

4. The risks of short-term nicotine replacement therapy as an aid to smoking cessation in healthy people are acceptable and substantially outweighed by the risks of cigarette smoking.

SCIENCE BOARD PANEL
ON STRATEGIC MISSILE DEFENSE
May 20, 1988

The SDI Milestone Panel, a senior Defense Department advisory group, on May 20 recommended changing the focus of the Strategic Defense Initiative (SDI) antiballistic missile defense program. In a report issued that day, the panel advocated a step-by-step approach to the creation of a U.S. missile defense. First to be developed would be a ground-based system capable of being deployed in a few years—a goal more modest than the space-based system envisioned by President Ronald Reagan.

From the time he announced the SDI, or "Star Wars," program in a nationally televised address March 23, 1983, the president had spoken in terms of a U.S. defense system capable of destroying all incoming enemy missiles in flight. In announcing SDI, he challenged scientists to develop the technology that would render nuclear weapons "impotent and obsolete." (Reagan on Defense in Space, Historic Documents of 1983, p. 305)

Reagan enlisted support in Congress, which during the next five years appropriated $12 billion for SDI research and development. By 1988, however, the future of SDI was uncertain. Enormous federal budget deficits forced spending cuts in many defense programs, including SDI. Progress in arms control with the Soviets eased fears of the Soviet nuclear threat, undermining support for SDI. Finally, many members of Congress were skeptical that a space-based missile defense could be deployed in the coming decade, as the Pentagon planned to do. The purpose of the SDI Milestone Panel was to review SDI's progress and make recommendations concerning its current objectives.

The nine-member panel, formally the Defense Science Board Task Force Subgroup on Strategic Air Defense, was headed by Robert R. Everett, chairman of the Defense Science Board and retired president of the Mitre Corporation. Other members included scientists, defense industry executives, and retired Air Force generals.

Debate over SDI Goals

Despite President Reagan's confidence in the scientific community's ability to develop a leakproof "astrodome" missile defense, few scientists were willing to say that this was a realistic objective. Critics of Reagan's vision portrayed its potential cost in the hundreds of billions of dollars. They said the Soviet Union could be expected to develop countermeasures, and that an enormous number of technological breakthroughs would be required to build, control, and defend a multilayered, space-based missile defense.

While Reagan continued to talk about his dream of making the United States invulnerable to ballistic missile attack, Pentagon scientists and officials in charge of SDI explored more modest goals they hoped to attain by the end of the twentieth century.

In September 1987 the Defense Department announced that SDI would focus on developing by the late 1990s a space-based system capable of destroying about 30 percent of the Soviet warheads that might be launched in an attack before they ever reached American soil. A system that could intercept that many warheads, the Pentagon maintained, would deter an attack because Kremlin leaders would doubt that a first strike could cripple the United States' ability to retaliate.

This system, known as Phase I, would probably consist of hundreds of heat-seeking missiles housed in "garages" orbiting in space. The Pentagon emphasized, however, that Phase I was not the final goal of SDI, but only a stage of development toward achieving the president's objective of a leakproof missile defense.

The Phase I plan proved to be almost as controversial as President Reagan's original proposal. Some SDI opponents, notably the Union of Concerned Scientists, contended that Phase I was intended primarily to develop a constituency among defense contractors who would lobby Congress to maintain SDI funding. Others were worried that the Phase I system could not be deployed during the 1990s at an affordable cost. Even some SDI supporters expressed concern that Phase I would draw research dollars away from other SDI technologies that might be more effective.

Report Findings

The Milestone Panel attempted to take account of not only technological and strategic factors, but also current political and economic realities.

The panel agreed with SDI planners that the program should proceed in steps, but it disagreed that the Phase I system was the proper initial objective. Instead the report advocated that SDI efforts initially be directed at developing a ground-based defense consisting of no more than one hundred missiles.

Such a system, it said, could complicate Soviet attack plans, guard against an accidental launch, and deter an attack by a minor nuclear power. The panel suggested a second step would be to improve the nation's early warning surveillance capabilities. Later steps could include deployment of a system similar to Phase I, and eventually the integration of directed energy weapons such as lasers into the missile defense systems.

The panel favored the step-by-step approach because the promise of short-term achievements—"each of which should provide some capability and have some value in itself"—would reduce SDI's technological and political problems. It asserted that the first two steps could be accomplished without violating the 1972 Antiballistic Missile (ABM) Treaty between the United States and the Soviet Union. The treaty outlaws antiballistic missile defenses except for one system, containing up to one hundred missiles, on each side.

SDI's Political Future

The SDI Milestone Panel's advocacy of a limited ground-based missile defense echoed a proposal by Sen. Sam Nunn, D-Ga., chairman of the Senate Armed Services Committee. Nunn suggested in a speech to the Arms Control Association on January 19, 1988, that the Defense Department should explore the feasibility of a ground-based missile system capable of stopping accidentally launched missiles. He emphasized that before any ABM system is deployed its effectiveness, affordability, and contribution to stability should be proven.

Members of the panel acknowledged to reporters that Nunn's proposal influenced their conclusions. They reasoned that, with Congress searching for ways to cut the budget, a less expensive first step such as Senator Nunn proposed might offer a way to sustain SDI funding.

The Defense Department gave no immediate indication that it would act on the panel's recommendation. Secretary of Defense Frank C. Carlucci praised the panel's work but denied that the report signaled a change in the department's strategy. However, congressional opposition to Phase I increased the chances that the Pentagon would eventually embrace the concept of a step-by-step SDI program beginning with a limited ground-based defense.

One week after the department released the panel's report, a House Democratic study group announced its opposition to deployment of the Phase I system. The group, which included most of the House Democratic leaders, declared that it favored prudent long-term SDI research and encouraged the Pentagon to study the possibility of ground-based defenses against "the threat of accidental and unauthorized missile attacks."

Later in the summer, Congress directly challenged the Pentagon's Phase I plan by passing a defense bill for fiscal year 1989 that authorized only $85 million of the $350 million that the president requested for development of space-based missiles. Reagan vetoed the bill, citing the funding cuts. The amount was restored in a revised bill that Congress subsequently passed and sent to him. He signed it September 29. Congress appropriated for all SDI purposes a total of just over $4 billion in various bills, about $900 million less than the amount the president had requested.

In the meanwhile, the Pentagon announced that Air Force Lt. Gen. James A. Abrahamson had resigned as director of the SDI program, which he had headed for four years. In his letter of resignation, Abrahamson said: "[A] new administration will undoubtedly have different ideas or approaches to SDI. Therefore, I reluctantly have concluded that the program will best be served by allowing new leadership to represent new policy and direction." Indicating what lay ahead, Pentagon officials said at a joint hearing of the House and Senate Armed Services Committees on October 6 that they proposed to halve the number of space-based weapons to be used initially, reducing the estimated cost of deployment from $115 billion to $69 billion. Their announcement, though stopping short of embracing the SDI Milestone Panel's recommendations, nevertheless was interpreted as the Defense Department's recognition that for the program to survive, it had be be made less costly.

> *Following are excerpts from the "Report of the Defense Board Task Force Subgroup on Strategic Air Defense" (SDI Milestone Panel), released May 20, 1988:*

Summary

1. In view of the technical, budgetary, political, and arms control uncertainties surrounding the ballistic missile defense program, the Panel recommends planning a number of steps in the technical development and deployment of a system to meet the JCS [Joint Chiefs of Staff] requirements rather than a single major action.

2. From a development point of view, priority should be given to the sensors, processing and communications necessary to provide an adequate assessment of what is actually going on, the nature and extent of the attack, and the detection and tracking of boosters and reentry vehicles. This framework is needed whatever weapons are actually used, and the

research, development, and experimentation required to provide it involves most of the critical technologies. This surveillance system should evolve as the supporting technology becomes available, allowing the inclusion of whatever weapons are available and wanted. This restructuring would help assure priority attention to critical technical problems despite budget uncertainties.

3. Deployment should be in steps, each of which should provide some capability and have some value in itself. One possible set of steps is as follows:

First—A limited, treaty compliant, deployment of 100 fixed ground-based long range interceptors cued from existing warning sensors. Such a system falls within our present demonstrated technical capabilities. It would be a limited deployment and as such would have limited capabilities, but it would provide some preferential defense as well as some protection against accidental or third country attacks or blackmail attempts.

Second—A treaty compliant deployment of the next generation of space surveillance systems to improve our early warning detection and assessment of a ballistic missile attack and to lay the foundation for subsequent steps that can deal with larger and more sophisticated attacks.

Third—A deployment to protect the NCA [National Command Authority] against decapitation by ballistic missiles, including those from submarines. This would require the emplacement of shorter range interceptors.

Fourth—Further expansion, including additional bases and ground-based interceptors and improved sensors to cope with countermeasures.

Fifth—The addition of space-based interceptors for boost and post-boost attack to fully meet the JCS requirement. This step might begin before step 4 was completed.

Sixth—The addition of space-based or ground-based directed energy weapons.

For each step the deployment decision would entail a separate and discrete act.

4. The first two deployment steps as well as the continued development of improved weapons up to the point of prototype demonstration could all reasonably be judged to be allowable under the narrow definition of the ABM Treaty. The third step may be achievable within the Treaty depending on the characteristics of the systems deployed. Subsequent deployment steps would require renegotiation of or withdrawal from the Treaty. The continued evolution of the surveillance system as described above does not appear to be constrained by the Treaty.

5. This approach would allow for more confident decisions and more flexibility in the face of uncertainties and would probably not require any more time in the long run.

6. The JCS have not addressed the utility of deployments short of the full Phase I deployment. Their views on the utility of possible phased deployments and the desirability of proceeding with them should be explored.

7. The Panel understands that the SDIO [Strategic Defense Initiative Organization] is evaluating this concept and is developing alternative plans for a stepped deployment.

8. We believe very strongly that capable long term engineering support for the SDIO is essential to carry out this large complex program. The existing limitations on such support should be removed as a part of any agreement on the future of ballistic missile defenses.

Introduction

The Strategic Defense Milestone panel was reconvened at the request of the Secretary of Defense to review the current plans for the Strategic Defense Initiative. . . .

In general, we believe that the concerns we expressed last year are being addressed in a forceful manner but many concerns are yet to be satisfactorily resolved. This is not surprising since many of the problems facing the SDI are of substantial difficulty and require a great deal of work to solve. Although the plans for attacking these problems appear reasonable in themselves, we are concerned about the larger problems that result from the financial and political uncertainties that surround the program. These uncertainties lead to unrealistic schedules and to a wasteful process of replanning as funding changes. Varying interpretations of the constraints imposed by the ABM Treaty lead to confusion in the testing process.

About a year ago, a decision was made to develop the SDI system in phases. . . . Because of the complexity and cost of the Phase One concept, the time required to deploy it and the political sensitivity of issues related to the ABM Treaty, we believe that SDIO should plan the Phase One deployment as a sequence of steps, each accomplishing a useful mission. Such a sequential program, which pays for itself with incremental benefits as it goes, will be more likely to achieve support than one which contributes little or nothing until the completion of Phase One.

Typically, large complex systems whether military or commercial, have not been created all at once. Rather they have all evolved over a period of time with each new step built on the foundations of technology, management, and public acceptance previously established. . . .

Development

. . . Once a surveillance system exists it can be used to provide information to whatever weapon systems are available. . . . A limited surveillance system now exists, consisting of the warning satellites and radars. This system should evolve as better sensors, better information on objects and backgrounds, and better processing and communications are developed and deployed.

This way of looking at ballistic missile defenses should help to enforce an orderly set of priorities on the development program. It will continually emphasize the need for system design, for a measurement program, and for a close tie between ballistic missile defenses and the other deterrent forces.

Emphasis on a surveillance system will not, of course, remove or even weaken the need for weapons and their associated fire control. However, it will make possible an evolutionary approach to weapons development and procurement. The several types now under development could then be deployed when and if they make sense in themselves. Each element will not be hostage to the successful development and deployment of the others. A ballistic missile defense system will, in fact, exist at all times. The process is one of improving that system in ways and at rates which are both positive and acceptable.

Deployment

There are a number of possible ways in which a ballistic missile defense system might be deployed in steps. It is neither necessary nor possible to lay out a fixed plan for all steps at this time because the actual steps to be taken depend on technical advances, international relations, and public acceptance. The first step or two must be defined, however, and subsequent steps outlined as possibilities. The purpose is to provide a set of options for future decision makers.

While the Panel is in no position to specify a plan in detail, we suggest the following possible directions for a stepped deployment plan.

First—A limited deployment of long range ground based interceptors.... They would be something like ERIS [Exoatmospheric Reentry System Interceptors] but would probably be somewhat larger, both to provide greater performance margins and to permit deployment before the final high quantity production version of the interceptor is complete. The earlier version should have adequate performance margins to provide, from a single deployment site, a very thin area defense for much of CONUS [the continential United States]. If such an interceptor deployment were sited at Grand Forks or in the national capitol region it would be Treaty-compliant so long as the number of interceptors remained below 100....

The choice of an initial site involves political judgments and is beyond the scope of our Panel. We note that the Grand Forks site currently exists and would provide coverage over most of CONUS while a deployment in the national capitol region would provide a beginning for an NCA defense. We note also that a decision to switch our permitted deployment from Grand Forks to the national capital region would have to be announced by October 1988, the end of the current 5-year ABM Treaty review period....

Second—Begin to update and improve our surveillance, in particular by deploying an improved satellite Early Warning System (EWS). Better space surveillance is needed to provide better warning and better attack assessment through better counting and tracking, whatever happens in active defense....

Improvements to other surveillance systems should be investigated as well....

Third—Install shorter range interceptors in the Washington area to protect the NCA against decapitation by ballistic missiles, including those from submarines. . . .

Fourth—Further expansion, including additional bases and interceptors, to cover other parts of the country and cope with larger attacks and improved sensors to cope with countermeasures.

Fifth—The addition of space-based interceptors for boost and post boost attack. The deployment of this step would probably meet the JCS requirement.

Sixth—The addition of space- or ground-based directional energy weapons.

The development of these or equivalent steps would be carried to the point of decision but would not be deployed unless actually wanted at the time. Each step would build upon the previous steps, most of which would continue to coexist.

The ABM Treaty

. . . The Treaty limits the number of effective ABM interceptors each country can have by placing a limit of 100 on launchers, requiring that they be fixed, restricting them to limited areas, and prohibiting rapid reload and MIRVing [multiple warheads]. The Treaty says nothing about the size, range, velocity, or guidance of the interceptors. The Treaty limits the radars to the vicinity of the launchers but permits warning radars around the periphery of the country. It says nothing about and therefore places no limits on warning satellites.

We believe that the first two deployment steps, plus the follow-on development of weapons up to the point of prototype demonstration, could be judged to be allowable under the Treaty. The third step may be achievable within the Treaty depending on the characteristics of the systems deployed. Subsequent deployment steps would require renegotiation of or withdrawal from the Treaty. The continued evolution of the surveillance system as previously described does not appear to be constrained by the Treaty.

We also believe step one to be treaty compliant by comparison with the existing Soviet ABM deployment. The step one system is very similar in general terms, contains only elements already in the existing Soviet system, and has capabilities which are similar to and may be less than the Soviet system. The differences are largely technical details which are not even mentioned let alone limited by the Treaty.

We do not see that the Treaty limits tactical warning and attack assessment . . . so step two should not violate the treaty.

Step three may or may not violate the Treaty depending on what is actually done. . . .

Schedule

A stepped process such as we have described would appear to lengthen the schedule by increasing the number of deployments and requiring money for earlier deployment. The current schedules are very uncertain, however, not only because of technical uncertainties but because of funding uncertainties. If the present program enjoyed stable funding and support, it might go faster without intermediate steps. We believe, however, that the difficulty of supporting such a large decision all at once and of bringing all system elements to a satisfactory stage at the same time make the all-at-once plan very risky. The stepped plan allows much more confident decisions and much more flexibility in the face of uncertainties. Furthermore it allows decoupling the schedules of many of the system elements. We think a stepped plan will eventually lead to shorter schedules and lower costs than the current Phase 1 plan.

Requirements

The JCS requirement for Phase I was very important in placing a foundation under the SDI program. A stepped program such as described above would not meet the current requirement until something like the fifth step. The JCS have not addressed the utility of deployments short of the full Phase I. Their views on this matter need to be explored and the military utility of various steps agreed upon.

System Engineering Support

The Panel was pleased to learn that the ad hoc system engineering team under discussion last year has been established. . . . We believe this is an important advance but are still concerned about the need for long term support. We think that a stepped deployment increases this need if the steps are to be properly planned and integrated.

The SDIO's need for responsive, long term systems engineering and technical assistance is very evident to the Panel: we think this need must be satisfied if we are to achieve an effective ballistic missile defense. The Systems Engineering and Integration contractor, although needed to meet other demands, is not a substitute. We recommend strongly that the Secretary of Defense make such support available to the Director, SDIO. . . .

PUBLIC HEALTH SERVICE REPORT ON LENGTH OF HOSPITALIZATION
May 24, 1988

"Relatively fewer patients are being admitted to hospitals and those patients who are admitted are staying shorter periods of time." Those were the major findings of a report issued May 24 by the National Center for Health Services Research and Health Care Technology Assessment, a unit of the U.S. Public Health Service. The report, based on a nationwide survey of about 400 hospitals, determined that a patient's average length of hospitalization on each admission fell 22 percent during a five-year period, from 7.3 days in 1980 to 5.7 days in 1985. The shorter time spent in hospitals was a key factor in dropping the overall hospital occupancy rate to 56.6 percent in mid-decade, down from 69.7 percent at the start.

"Patients are both entering hospitals closer to the time of their [surgical] procedure and leaving sooner after its completion," the report noted. The shortened hospital stays applied almost equally to all patients regardless of who paid the bill. The drop was 20 percent for privately insured patients, 22 percent for those covered by Medicaid, and 26 percent for those covered by Medicare. Medicaid, covering the poor, and Medicare, covering the elderly, together accounted for 40 percent of all hospital admissions.

The report attributed the shorter stays—and the accompanying reduced bed-use rate—to advances in medical technology, greater use of outpatient services, and new restrictions by the government, health-maintenance organizations, and insurance companies. They all "have strong incentives to reduce the use of hospital services," and thus have emphasized outpatient care.

"Unless these [hospitalization use] trends are reversed, hospital beds will either be closed or converted to other uses," the report said, noting that occupancy rates of about 50 percent cannot be sustained for long. Dean E. Farley, author of the report, said when it was released: "There was a lot of fat in this industry, and that's being burned out. We have reached the point where we're getting down to the bone and muscle." In fact, preliminary data reported by the American Hospital Association suggested that the trend toward low occupancy has been halted and perhaps reversed in 1986 and 1987.

All the while, the cost of hospitalization continued to rise. In 1987 a patient's bill averaged $697 a day, compared with about $400 a day in 1980, according to Blue Cross/Blue Shield. In an attempt to deal with the situation of costs outracing coverage, Congress completed action in its 1988 session on "catastrophic health insurance" legislation, which was signed into law (PL 100-360) July 1 by President Ronald Reagan. It expanded Medicare coverage to provide for unlimited hospital stays for the treatment of acute illnesses.

The law also set a ceiling of a patient's out-of-pocket expenses for Medicare-related services and medicines, including prescription drugs, in any given year. However, it did not underwrite long-term home care, a provision pushed by Rep. Claude Pepper, D-Fla., a congressional champion of the aging. However, Congress did establish a commission to study methods of providing long-term care.

> *Following are excerpts from the National Center for Health Services Research and Health Care Technology Assessment report, "Trends in Hospital Average Lengths of Stay, Casemix, and Discharge Rates, 1980-85," issued May 24, 1988:*

From 1980 to 1985, the average occupancy rate of community hospitals in the United States declined nearly 20 percent—from 69.7 to 56.6 percent. . . . [T]his measure of overall hospital utilization has been affected by changes in its two components: mean discharge rate (MDR) and average length of stay (ALOS). Mean discharge rate, which is the ratio of total discharges in a year to number of beds, measures the flow of patients through a hospital. . . . MDR declined nearly 10 percent from 1980 to 1985. Average length of stay measures how long the typical patient occupies a hospital bed. It fell 12 percent over the same period. Clearly, both components have contributed to declines in hospital occupancy; relatively fewer patients are being admitted to hospitals and those patients who are admitted are staying shorter periods of time.

. . . [A]ll of the declines . . . accelerated sharply from 1983 to 1985, the period during which the Medicare prospective payment system (PPS) was implemented. . . .

Declines in utilization of the magnitude that have occurred since 1980 have potentially profound implications for the hospital industry. Unless these trends are reversed, hospital beds will either be closed or converted to other uses. Some hospitals may face serious financial problems because reductions in volume could also reduce their cash flow and operating surpluses. Paradoxically, smaller surpluses may limit the ability of hospitals to eliminate excess capacity. Hospitals that experience financial difficulties may find it difficult to obtain the financial resources they need to convert beds to alternative uses and otherwise restructure physical plants.

On a policy level, the question of how to deal with excess hospital capacity must be addressed. Who should pay for the renovations needed to eliminate beds or to convert them to other uses? One possible position is that this is a governmental responsibility since many public programs now provide incentives to reduce lengths of stay and unnecessary hospitalization to achieve more efficient provision of hospital services. Such objectives are fundamental to the Medicare PPS, recent changes in State Medicaid policies, and utilization review programs such as professional review organizations (PROs). Alternatively, it can be argued that these financial burdens should be shared more broadly, since private-sector initiatives have contributed to the problem through mandatory second opinions, capitated insurance arrangements, and restructured copayment provisions that encourage the use of outpatient services when possible. A third option is for hospitals to bear the primary responsibility for dealing with excess capacity. In this case, the ultimate financial burden would vary across hospitals based on institutional objectives and market forces. . . .

Although reductions in average lengths of stay and mean discharge rates have both contributed to recent declines in occupancy rates, the reduction in ALOS is especially interesting. ALOS is determined largely by factors beyond the immediate control of hospitals, unlike discharge rates which hospitals can stabilize by altering staffed beds in response to changes in the number of admissions. In general, ALOS is determined by physicians as they decide who should be admitted to hospitals and how such patients should be treated. Recent declines in ALOS may reflect fundamental changes in the role of acute care facilities and the relationship between physicians and their patients. . . .

. . . Between 1980 and 1985 Medicare beneficiaries, who have relatively long hospital stays, had the largest absolute decline in ALOS, 2.16 days. They also had the greatest relative decline in average length of stay, more than 20 percent. Medicaid patients had a 17.7 percent decline in ALOS during the same period, followed by a residual group of payers using "other sources" with a 16.1 percent decline and private insured patients (either commercial insurance or Blue Cross) with an 11.5 percent decline in ALOS. . . . For all payers, the decline in ALOS accelerated from 1983 to 1985. For Medicare, Medicaid, and privately insured patients, approximately 60 percent of the decline from 1980 to 1985 occurred after 1983. . . .

. . . The increase in Medicare expected ALOS is consistent with the incentives created by the Medicare PPS. Under PPS, hospitals benefit from recording diagnoses accurately and from completing discharge abstracts so that patients are assigned to DRGs with higher weights. They also have an incentive to shift patients out of inpatient settings into ambulatory care, which continues to be reimbursed under Part B on a retrospective cost basis. In general, these incentives increase expected length of stay. On the other hand, PPS-related behavior is not a satisfactory explanation for increases in Medicaid and privately insured casemix. Both groups had substantial increases in expected ALOS that predate both PPS and the Tax Equity and Fiscal Responsibility Act of 1982 (TEFRA). In the case of Medicaid, the increase may be due to more restrictive eligibility requirements and other efforts to limit Medicaid expenditures. For privately insured patients, possible explanations include increased enrollment in health maintenance organizations (HMOs), the growth of preferred provider organizations (PPOs), increased cost sharing, and mandatory second-opinion programs for elective surgery....

... Since 1980, there has been a substantial change in the mix of payers among hospital patients. Privately insured patients, who generally have relatively short stays, accounted for more than one-half of all hospital admissions in 1980. By 1985, they represented only 45 percent. In contrast, the proportion of patients covered by Medicare increased from 26.2 percent in 1980 to 30.6 percent in 1985....

In summary, then, the dramatic decline in hospital occupancy since 1980 is primarily the result of substantial reductions in average length of stay....

To assess the causes and implications of declining average lengths of stay, one must know what portions of the hospital stay have been most affected. If reductions have occurred primarily at the end of stays, after patients have been evaluated and treatment begun, one might argue that the responsibility for providing care during later stages of a typical hospital stay is being shifted onto subacute care facilities and into the home. Alternatively, if most of the reduction has occurred at the "front end" of hospital stays, it might indicate that hospitals have been more efficiently scheduling and performing basic diagnostic and prescriptive functions.

The timing of diagnosis, treatment, and recuperation is most evident for patients receiving a medical/surgical procedure during their hospitalization....

... [R]eductions in preoperative stays were proportionately larger than the overall decline in ALOS from 1980 to 1985. Preoperative stays fell more than 18 percent during this period, compared to an overall decline in ALOS of 13.5 percent. Yet, on an absolute basis, the decline in postoperative stays appears to have been larger. On average, the principal procedure now occurs more than a third of a day earlier in a typical hospital stay but the average postoperative stay has declined more than half a day.... Patients are both entering hospitals closer to the time of their procedure and leaving sooner after its completion....

A variety of incentives exist to shorten inhospital stays prior to scheduled procedures. If routine examinations and tests can be performed on an outpatient basis prior to admission, their costs can be billed separately under insurance provisions applicable to outpatient hospital care. For example, preadmission testing of Medicare beneficiaries allows a hospital to reduce the costs it incurs under Part A, now covered by PPS, and to increase the costs for which it is reimbursed under Part B. Similarly, more efficient scheduling of surgery reduces costs associated with preoperative stays. To the extent that a hospital's revenues are not based directly on its costs, it will have an incentive to take advantage of such cost savings. . . .

. . . [T]he growth of arthroscopic surgery appears to have had a major impact on discharge rates for knee procedures. . . . In addition, several factors have combined to bring about a decline in hospital discharges for certain medical conditions as patients have moved from inpatient to outpatient settings. These factors include a growing acceptance of outpatient treatment by the medical profession, greater scrutiny by third parties of decisions to treat patients on an inpatient basis, and changes in financial incentives inherent in reimbursement systems. . . .

. . . [C]hanging practice patterns and technology per se are not satisfactory explanations for such developments. These factors may describe the mechanisms by which changes in utilization trends have occurred but they do not address the question of why such changes have taken place.

The answer to this second, more fundamental question probably involves a number of separate considerations. The more commonly mentioned factors include: (1) changing financial incentives as a result of the Medicare PPS, new State initiatives affecting Medicaid programs, and restructuring of private insurance packages; (2) pressure from utilization review programs to prevent unnecessary admissions and to shorten hospital stays when possible; (3) growth in the proportion of insured individuals enrolled in HMO or PPO arrangements, which have strong incentives to reduce the use of hospital services; and (4) a general reorientation of hospital markets away from nonprice competition, in which hospitals attempt to attract patients and physicians by offering services and resources that increase costs, to more price-oriented competition, in which hospitals attempt to offer more value per dollar of expenditure. . . .

TRADE BILL VETOES

May 24, 1988

As the end of President Ronald Reagan's second term approached, international trade issues increasingly troubled his relations with the Democratic-controlled Congress. The controversy was highlighted in 1988 by the president's veto of two trade bills—the first on May 24 and the second on September 28.

Congress revised the first of the two bills, the Omnibus Trade and Competitiveness Act of 1988, more to Reagan's liking, and he subsequently signed it into law. The other veto applied to a bill to give the domestic textile and footwear industries protection from lower-priced imports. The president's congressional opponents tried to override both vetoes but fell short of mustering the required two-thirds majority.

Reagan's vetoes underscored the sharp differences between his administration and the majority Democrats in Congress over the best way of correcting the nation's huge international trade imbalances. Organized labor, along with businesses that were losing out to foreign competitors, pushed for quotas on the amount of foreign goods that could be imported. Congressional Democrats generally—and some Republicans—were receptive to their demands.

In contrast, administration officials argued that the best answer to the trade problem was to make U.S. industries more competitive, even if some workers lost their jobs as a result. Long an advocate of free trade, Reagan preferred negotiating with foreign leaders in an effort to open markets overseas, rather than taking retaliatory steps. He and others in the administration expressed fear that other countries might impose harsh trade barriers against American goods in response to U.S. protectionism.

Omnibus Trade Bill

Thus the stage was set for the first of two confrontations between Congress and the White House. The omnibus trade bill, as it finally cleared Congress by sizable majorities despite Reagan's veto threat, represented nearly two years of legislative tugging and pulling and compromise. The 1,100-page document touched on trade policy and negotiations, import relief, "intellectual" property such as patents and computer programming, export controls, and a long list of other trade-related issues. In one of its most important features, the bill sought to strengthen the Office of the U.S. Trade Representative, the office responsible for carrying on international trade negotiations, and to make it more responsive to Congress.

The bill also directed the president to intervene more actively to help businesses that were hard hit by foreign competition. In addition, it spelled out ways to handle countries that "dumped" their goods on American markets, selling them at artificially low prices to gain a foothold in those markets. Another provision removed the "windfall" profits tax on oil, which was enacted in the 1970s when oil prices were skyrocketing.

In his May 24 veto message, Reagan objected to several features of the trade bill. He reserved his greatest disapproval for a provision that had less to do with international trade than with domestic political considerations. It would have required companies with one hundred or more employees to give workers sixty days' notice of any plan to close the plant or lay them off. Businesses had lobbied hard against that provision, and labor had fought hard to retain it.

Reagan said that while he believed in voluntarily giving workers advance notice of closings or layoffs, "I object to the idea that the Federal Government would arbitrarily mandate, for all conditions and under all circumstances, exactly when and in what form the notification should take place."

Only a few hours after the announcement of Reagan's veto officially reached the House of Representatives, that body voted overwhelmingly to override it. The 308-113 vote came about when sixty Republicans broke with their party's position and voted with the Democratic majority. Only one Democrat, Rep. Robert J. Mrazek of New York, voted to uphold the veto. Some observers attributed the lopsided vote to the belief of many House members that the plant-closing provision had strong popular support. Indeed, Democratic leaders in Congress believed that their party would reap rewards in the presidential and congressional elections because of its backing the provision.

In the Senate, where the Democratic majority was smaller than in the House, the attempt to override the veto fell short of the necessary two-thirds majority. The override failure, however, did not erase strong support for the passage of a trade bill. During the summer the bill's backers worked out a compromise with the White House that dropped the plant-closing feature but retained some mildly protectionist elements. The president, saying that the revised bill would facilitate trade in the long run, signed it into law on August 23. Meanwhile, the Democratic leadership in Congress wrote the plant-closing provision into a separate bill and won passage in both houses by veto-proof majorities. Reagan let it become law without his signature.

Textile and Footwear Protection

All the while, the bill to limit textile and shoe imports had been moving through Congress and reached the president's desk in September. Although both chambers passed it by large margins, neither could muster the votes to overcome his September 28 veto. Reagan had vetoed a similar measure three years earlier, and his veto message on the new bill indicated that his views had not changed. The bill would "have disastrous effects on the U.S. economy," he said. "It would impose needless costs on American consumers, threaten jobs in our export industries, jeopardize our overseas farm sales, and undermine our efforts to obtain a more open trading system for U.S. exports."

"This bill," he continued, "represents protectionism at its worst. Protectionism does not save jobs. Only improved competitiveness can truly protect jobs, yet there is nothing in this bill that would encourage domestic industries to become more competitive." Democrats sought, apparently without much success, to exploit the veto during the fall election campaigns in the South, where the American textile industry is concentrated. At the time the veto was cast, several Republicans expressed fear that it was a political blunder.

> Following are the texts of President Reagan's messages informing the House of Representatives on May 24, 1988, of his veto of the Omnibus Trade and Competitiveness Act of 1988, and on September 28, 1988, of his veto of the Textile Apparel and Footwear Trade Act of 1988:

OMNIBUS TRADE BILL VETO

TO THE HOUSE OF REPRESENTATIVES:

It is with sincere regret that today I must disapprove and return HR 3, the Omnibus Trade and Competitiveness Act of 1988. We worked long and hard to produce legislation that would enhance our country's ability to meet foreign competition head-on — to strengthen our trade laws and remove restrictions on America's great economic engine. And we came very close to developing such a bill. Unfortunately, as the process came to a close, provisions were included that simply make this bill, on balance, bad for America — particularly working men and women. The criteria I used in reaching this decision were whether this legislation will create jobs and help sustain our economic growth. I am convinced this bill will cost jobs and damage our economic growth.

During this Administration the American economy has created 16 million new jobs. Our unemployment rate is the lowest in 14 years with more Americans working than ever before in our history. And we are experiencing the longest peacetime expansion this country has ever seen.

While this has been going on at home, many of our trading partners have had a different economic situation. Perhaps the most compelling and important comparison is that over the past decade, the United States has created more than twice as many jobs as Europe and Japan combined.

The United States economy, which foreign leaders have dubbed the "American Miracle," is not a freak accident or a statistical curiosity. It is the result of 7 years of consistent policies: lower tax rates, reduced regulation, control returned to State and local governments. The Washington tendency to have government be all things to all people has been reversed, and we have gotten government off the backs of the American people. In contrast, many foreign countries remain hamstrung by archaic policies and are now trying to remove these impediments, to reform tax systems, to make labor markets more flexible, and to encourage entrepreneurs.

That is not to say that we cannot do more here at home — we can. That is why I forwarded proposals to improve our competitive strength and why we worked hard with the Congress to try to achieve a positive, forward-looking bill. Unfortunately, that is not the bill the Congress passed and sent to my desk.

The issue receiving the most attention in this bill is the mandatory requirement for businesses to give advance notice of closings or layoffs. I support voluntarily giving workers and communities as much advance warning as possible when a layoff or closing becomes necessary. It allows the workers, the employer, the community, time to adjust to the dislocation. It is the humane thing to do.

But I object to the idea that the Federal Government would arbitrarily mandate, for all conditions and under all circumstances, exactly when and in what form that notification should take place. There are many circumstances under which such mandatory notification would actually force a faltering business to close — by driving away creditors, suppliers, customers, and — in the process destroying jobs. While the legislation attempts to mitigate this outcome, its "faltering business" exemption is too ambiguous to be workable and invites untold litigation.

These concerns are real, not simply philosophical or theoretical. The experience of the Caterpillar company in the early 1980's, for example, is indicative of the need to be flexible to meet foreign competition and indeed to survive. They had to utilize layoffs and temporary plant closings to respond to competitive developments. And, as one executive of that company stated, they did not have the luxury then, nor do they now, of knowing with certainty what business conditions would be like 60 days in the future. Without the ability to be agile and responsive, they might have closed their doors permanently.

Caterpillar's experience is repeated many times over throughout our economy. One independent analysis shows that if this law had been in place between 1982 and 1986, the United States would have produced almost one-half million fewer jobs. And that is what this debate is about — creating jobs and keeping them — not losing jobs by the straightjacket of regulations.

Over a year ago, I submitted legislation that would provide assistance to workers, employers, and communities in the event of a layoff or closing. The program would serve virtually every dislocated worker who needs it with training, education, and assistance in securing a new job and provide an incentive for giving advance notice of layoffs and closings. Ironically, the one piece of that package that the Congress rejected was a direct incentive for business to give advance notices of closing and layoffs. We need labor laws that fit the flexible, fast-paced economy of the 1990's, not restrictive leftovers from the 1930's agenda. And I encourage the Congress in any subsequent trade bill to include a program that provides incentives for such notice.

There are other provisions in the legislation that provide disincentives to our sustained economic growth or serve some narrow special interests:

- New restrictions on the export, transportation, and even utilization of Alaskan oil further complicate the overbearing regulatory scheme that already impedes the development of Alaskan oil fields. It is the wrong policy. We need to provide incentives, not restrictions, for the production of oil in the United States so that we can reduce our dependence on foreign suppliers. Further, as the Congress has now recognized, it amounts to an unconstitutional discrimination against a single State.
- A mistaken effort to revive discredited industrial policy planning through a so-called Council on Competitiveness that will open even more venues for special pleaders.
- A requirement to negotiate a new centralized international institution to arrange the forgiveness of billions of dollars of debt around the world — all supposedly without increasing U.S. taxes or adding to *our* debt.
- Expanded ethanol imports that could harm U.S. grain producers.
- An amendment to the Trading with the Enemy Act that prevents the President from moving swiftly to block blatant enemy propaganda material from entering the United States *even during wartime.*

While the Congress did a remarkable job in watering down or eliminating the most protectionist provisions, there remain sections of the bill that push us in the direction of protectionism. Closing our borders is not the solution to opening foreign markets. We need to demand to be treated fairly and take a strong stand against barriers abroad. In short, we need to open markets, not close them.

While there are objectionable portions of the bill, there are also desirable provisions. There is negotiating authority so that the next President will have congressional support to continue to seek agreements that open markets abroad. That, coupled with new trade law tools to strengthen the hand of America in international trade negotiations, will mean that this country can enter the next decade with new agreements that reduce barriers and encourage trade. There are strengthened protections for intellectual property, such as copyrights, and a reduction in various handicaps to U.S. exporters. Finally, the bill would remove a major impediment to U.S. oil production by repealing the windfall profits tax.

That is why I want a trade bill, and why I like much of this bill. But I regret that the addition of a few counterproductive and costly measures outweighs the positive features of this particular legislation. I will continue to work vigorously to secure sound legislation this year.

Let me reiterate what I have said on a number of occasions. I am committed to enactment of a responsible trade bill this year. I have heard some say that there is not time to send me a second bill after my veto is sustained; my response is that there are many months left in 1988 — time enough to set aside partisanship and finish the job. I want to sign a trade bill this year. I urge prompt action on a second bill immediately after the Congress sustains my veto.

RONALD REAGAN

TEXTILE BILL VETO

TO THE HOUSE OF REPRESENTATIVES:

I am returning without my approval H.R. 1154, the "Textile Apparel and Footwear Trade Act of 1988," a bill that would have disastrous effects on the U.S. economy. It would impose needless costs on American consumers, threaten jobs in our export industries, jeopardize our overseas farm sales, and undermine our efforts to obtain a more open trading system for U.S. exports.

This bill represents protectionism at its worst. The supposed benefits of the bill would be temporary at best. Protectionism does not save jobs. Only improved competitiveness can truly protect jobs, yet there is nothing in this bill that would encourage domestic industries to become more competitive. At a time when American exports are booming, the United States must not embark on a course that would diminish our trade opportunities.

Moreover, there is no economic justification for the bill. Fibers consumed by U.S. mills were at record levels in 1987. Domestic textile and apparel production, profits, and exports all posted sharp gains in 1986 and 1987, and this trend is continuing in 1988. Capacity utilization in this industry remains well above the national average. Consumer apparel prices, which rose sharply in the first half of this year, would be forced up even faster by the bill. This would break the clothing budgets of many American families.

When I vetoed an earlier version of the textile bill 3 years ago, I directed the Office of the U.S. Trade Representative to renegotiate the Multi-Fiber Arrangement—the multilateral agreement that sets the rules for trade in textiles—in order to strengthen our ability to control textile and apparel imports. That task was accomplished on August 1, 1986. Under this Arrangement, we have negotiated tough, new agreements with our largest textile trading partners. Nearly 1,500 quotas, in addition to textile and apparel tariffs averaging almost 18 percent, make this industry the most protected sector of our economy. Indeed, textile and apparel imports increased only 2 percent in 1987 and have decreased almost 10 percent during the first 7 months of 1988. There is no need for further protection from imports.

At the same time I am sensitive to the difficulties that families and communities face because of internal restructuring in the textile, apparel, and footwear industries. This bill would not stop these trends. They are the inevitable result of a dynamic, expanding economy. The best way to help displaced workers is to retrain them for new jobs. Thanks to dislocated workers assistance, Trade Adjustment Assistance, and the Worker Readjustment Assistance Program I proposed, many services are now available for workers who must shift jobs as the economy adjusts to competitive challenges. Our goal must be to retrain and move dislocated workers into the industries of the future, not to maintain them in noncompetitive and inefficient facilities at all costs.

Our free and fair trade policies have created 17 million new jobs in the past 6 years. The percentage of the working-age population now employed is the highest in our Nation's history. Exports are running at record levels, and our manufacturing industries are stronger and more competitive than they have been in a decade. H.R. 1154 would threaten these gains by setting off a dangerous chain reaction of retaliation and counter-retaliation in the international trade system.

Three years ago I announced an aggressive, growth-oriented trade strategy aimed at opening markets currently closed to American exporters. Since then we have challenged unfair trade practices around the world and negotiated trade agreements that have created significant export opportunities for American firms. In August I signed into law the "Omnibus Trade and Competitiveness Act of 1988," which provides additional tools for prying open closed foreign markets. And today I am approving legislation to implement the U.S.-Canada Free Trade Agreement, a historic trade pact that will create the world's largest free trade area. The protectionism of H.R. 1154 is the antithesis of the free trade principles of these two laws.

America's export opportunities have never been brighter and our prospects for continued economic growth have never been better. Increased trade means more jobs and a better standard of living. It would be a tragic mistake to change course now that American businesses have regained their competitive edge and are winning sales around the globe. Accordingly, I am disapproving H.R. 1154.

RONALD REAGAN

SWEDEN'S PIONEER LAW
ON FARM-ANIMAL RIGHTS
May 27, 1988

Sweden, a pioneer in social-welfare legislation, enacted a law in 1988 that amounted to a bill of rights for farm animals. The new legislation, setting standards and conditions for the animals' care, outlawed many practices common to "farm factories." The big operations typically employed assembly-line techniques to achieve huge yields from milk cows or laying hens, and to fatten large numbers of domestic animals for slaughter in the most efficient and least costly ways possible.

Such techniques usually resulted in the animals being confined to cramped spaces. In tight confinement they do not lose extra pounds in unnecessary movement, and they can easily be fed and controlled in large numbers. As passed by the Swedish Parliament on May 27, the law required cattle, hogs, and chickens to be freed from crowded conditions, and it decreed that slaughtering must be done as humanely as possible.

The law went on the books July 1, although many of its provisions were to be phased in gradually over several years. It greatly extended the scope of an existing animal-rights law dating from 1944 and made violators subject to fines or, in some instances, up to a year in prison. The old law provided only for fines. Madelaine Emmervall, first secretary in the Swedish Ministry of Agriculture, said the law made her country a leader among nations in the matter of animal rights.

Model for U.S. Animal-Rights Groups

In the United States, animal-rights groups praised Sweden's new law. "It has set a shining example for the rest of the civilized world," said Alex

Hershaft, president of the Farm Animal Reform Movement (FARM), an organization founded in 1981 and based in Washington, D.C. Hershaft said FARM sought to have similar legislation enacted in this country.

Over the years, American animal-rights groups often had come to public attention through their efforts to protect animals from cruelty in medical experimentation. What happened on the farm appeared to command less attention, at least until farm factories increasingly replaced small, family-operated holdings.

In these mechanized and specialized farming operations, chickens ceased to roam the barnyard. Straight from the hatchery, the chicks would be confined to long, windowless sheds until they were of an age and weight to slaughter as "broilers" or be moved to similar quarters as "layers" (laying hens). They were fed vitamin D to replace sunlight and were given commercial feed laced with vitamins and minerals to replace the insects, green grass, and other nutrients no longer available to them outdoors. With hogs and cattle, similarly, the feed lot replaced the pasture and range for their fattening.

The farm industry has argued that the public benefits far outweigh any suffering by the animals in confinement. Agricultural experts insist that by confining large numbers of chickens, hogs, and cattle, farmers can bring about a larger production of eggs and meat per animal at lower cost—an efficient way to feed the millions of people who depend on those products for daily sustenance. As reported by the Council on Agricultural Science and Technology, an industry research group based at Ames, Iowa, "Such efficiency is effected by the large volume of animals, often located near available feed supplies, that can be handled by a few workers."

A Swedish Woman's Crusade

In Sweden, an elderly woman writer of children's books saw the matter in a different light. The writer, Astrid Lindgren, undertook a campaign in 1985 to persuade the government to ensure that farm animals would not be mistreated. She wrote stories in Sweden's leading publications from the animals' point of view and won a sizable following in her legal-reform movement. Moreover, she caught the attention of prominent politicians who remembered her influence on the elections in 1976. That year the Social Democratic party was voted out of office after more than half a century of holding power. The defeat was partly attributed to satirical articles Lindgren had written attacking a tax rate, which one year had amounted to 102 percent of her income.

When Parliament passed the Animal Protection Act, over the opposition of farm groups, Prime Minister Ingvar Carlsson visited Lindgren, then age eighty-one, at her home in Stockholm. He took along a copy of the law to show her that her concerns had been met.

Following are excerpts from a press release by the Swedish Ministry of Agriculture, in English translation, explaining the Animal Protection Act passed by Sweden's Parliament on May 27, 1988:

... The new Act will place on the statute book greater powers for the prevention of cruelty to animals in a number of different respects:

- All cattle are to be entitled to be put out to graze.
- Poultry are to be let [out] of cramped battery cages.
- Sows are no longer to be tethered. They are to have sufficient room to move. Separate bedding, feeding and voiding places are to be provided.
- Cows and pigs are to have access to straw and litter in stalls and boxes.
- Technology must be adapted to the animals, not the reverse. As a result, it must be possible to test new technology from the animal safety and protection viewpoint before being put into practice.
- All slaughtering must be as humane as possible.
- In future, the government is empowered to forbid the use of genetic engineering and growth hormones which may mutate our domestic animals.
- Permission will now be necessary for pelt and fur farms.
- Doping of animals for competitions and events is prohibited. ...

The basic concept of the new Animal Protection Act is that technology must adapt to meet the needs of the animals, not the reverse.

This naturally implies that animals' natural behavior must be paramount. The emphasis of animal husbandry must be to keep the animals healthy and contented.

Particular attention is given to the management of domestic animals in the new Act. This is because of the economic interests which are inherent in animal husbandry. As a result, the importance of not overlooking the animals themselves in any form of production has been given prominence.

Proposals

Cattle shall be entitled to be put out to graze.

Today, most milk cows are tethered in stalls. However, the cattle sheds which have been built in recent years are better adapted to allow freedom of movement. The new proposal on freedom to graze applies to both tethered cattle and free grazing cattle.

This proposal relates to all animals in new production. For animals in existing cattle sheds, the new proposal is to take effect as soon as it may be practical. In turn, this relates to such matters as the availability of suitable grazing pasture. One alternative could be to allow the animals to graze in outdoor paddocks. When the cows are housed indoors, they are to have bedding in the stall, to protect them from injury.

Poultry are to be let out of cramped battery cages.

Hens for egg production are currently battery caged. Four hens are cramped together in a cage which allows each hen a floorspace of roughly the size of a school exercise book. The cages fail to meet even the most basic requirements of the hens—for moving, scratching, flapping, bathing and preening—and for laying.

Such a system is unacceptable and must, therefore, be finally phased-out over the next ten year period. In future, no form of animal husbandry which is so insensitive to the needs of the animals will be permitted.

At present, no viable alternative system has been developed. Research in this area is currently underway, above all in Switzerland.

Before a new system can be introduced, the environment in the cages must be improved, for example by reducing the number of caged birds from four to three per cage. Perches and stones should be provided in the cage.

Sows are not to be tethered. They are to have sufficient room to move.

The system of tethering sows is to be discontinued, since it is counter to the principle of answering to the natural behaviour of the animal.

It is also important that the sows' stalls be designed in such a manner that the animals have access to separate spaces for bedding, eating and voiding.

It is important to provide large space for pigs for slaughter, so as to avoid aggressive behaviour. The environment in the stalls must also be improved. Access to straw is vital to the wellbeing of the pigs.

Technology must be adapted to the animals, not the reverse. As a result, it must be possible to test new technology from the viewpoint of animal safety and protection before being put into practice.

Animals are entitled to be reared in environments in which production has been adapted to them and their needs. Methods of production which injure or exploit the animals, such as in so-called animal factories, are unacceptable.

A suitable stall or pen environment and appropriate management methods are indispensible for contented animals. With this in mind, all animal stalls and pens are already subject to inspection before a certificate of worthiness can be issued.

In future, all new technology is to be subject to prior testing before approval. This prior testing forms the basis of an appraisal of the new technology in terms of animal health and animal protection, before it can be put into practice.

All slaughtering must be as humane as possible.

The new Animal Protection Act includes a specific stipulation to the effect that animals are to be spared suffering while being led to slaughter and during slaughter.

In future, the government is empowered to forbid the use of genetic engineering and growth hormones which may mutate our domestic animals.

There are no laws currently in force which govern how genetic engineering may be applied to our domestic animals, with the exception of the rules on ethical examination of animal experiments.

Genetic engineering has yet to be applied within the field of domestic animal management. However, legislation must encompass the powers to meet with such an eventuality. As a result, the government will be enabled to forbid the use of genetic engineering on animals, or the administration of hormones or other substances which may affect animals, other than for veterinary purposes.

Permission will now be necessary for pelt and fur farms.

Pelt and fur farming entails that animals are held captive under extreme conditions for the animals themselves. The mink and the fox, both predators by their very nature, are most generally the animals involved and ... need to be able to move freely.... Statutory permission is now required for anyone breeding pelt and fur animals on a professional or semi-professional scale.

Doping of animals for competitions and events is prohibited.

Recent years have seen the introduction of measures to improve or hamstring the performance of competition horses—doping.

Doping in all its forms and names is a serious problem for animal protection, and, as a result, every such operation has now been outlawed by the new Animal Protection Act.

Permission must be obtained for all those engaged in animal experiments.

Such institutions as departments of advanced technology and hospitals have hitherto been exempt from applying for permission to conduct animal experiments. The new Act will require that permission be sought by all. In addition, a legally liable head of operations must be named in the application.

Stiffer punishments for breaches of the law.

Anyone found to have been in breach of the new Animal Protection Act may be punishable by fines or inprisonment of up to one year. This raises the level of sanctions in comparison with the Act of 1944, under which the maximum penalty was a fine. ...

REAGAN-GORBACHEV SUMMIT
May 29-31, June 1, 1988

The fourth summit meeting between President Ronald Reagan and Soviet leader Mikhail S. Gorbachev, held in Moscow May 29-June 2, was noteworthy more for its cordial atmosphere than for policy break-throughs. The highlight of the summit was the exchange of documents of ratification for the intermediate-range nuclear-forces (INF) treaty, which entered into force on June 1. The treaty had been signed by Reagan and Gorbachev at their December 1987 meeting in Washington, D.C. The U.S. Senate and the Supreme Soviet Presidium approved the treaty only days before the Moscow summit. (U.S.-Soviet INF Treaty, Historic Documents of 1987, p. 945; Reagan-Gorbachev Summit, Historic Documents of 1987, p. 991)

The two leaders made only slight progress toward their primary goal— a strategic arms reduction treaty (START)—or toward resolving any of the world conflicts on which the two superpowers differed. Both men, however, declared that the meeting helped improve U.S.-Soviet relations. Gorbachev said it had "dealt a blow at the foundations of the Cold War." Both leaders talked about the possibility of a fifth meeting before the end of Reagan's presidency in January 1989, and Reagan said such a meeting could occur even if a START agreement was not ready for signing.

Whatever its shortcomings as a substantive event, the summit was a theatrical success. Throughout his five days in Moscow, Reagan portrayed himself to Soviet audiences as a friendly antagonist enchanted by local people and customs, and who shared a dislike of government "bureaucracy." For Americans back home, he tried to use the Moscow forum to claim victory for his foreign policies and to establish himself as a man of peace and a strong proponent of human rights. Gorbachev, who upstaged Reagan at the previous summit in Washington, seemed willing to let the president hold center stage in Moscow. But he also got into the spirit of showmanship on June 1 by holding the first press conference a Soviet leader ever conducted at home.

At the Kremlin on May 31, Reagan backed away from his declaration that the Soviet Union was an "evil empire." Asked about that statement, made March 8, 1983, Reagan said, "I was talking about another time, another era." The president denied he had changed his mind about the Soviet Union. What had changed, he said, was that Gorbachev was "different than previous Soviet leaders have been." Whether flattered or amused, Gorbachev said the president's remarks demonstrated "a sense of realism."

INF Treaty and START

The INF treaty was the first between the two nations to ban an entire class of nuclear weapons. The treaty prohibited the production and flight testing of ground-launched missiles that have ranges of 300 to 3,400 miles. The pact also called for the destruction of existing intermediate-range missiles—some 1,762 Soviet missiles and 859 U.S. missiles. It was the first arms control accord ratified since 1972, when the strategic arms limitation (SALT I) and the antiballistic missile (ABM) treaties were approved. Although U.S. and Soviet leaders signed the SALT II treaty in 1979, it died in the Senate. (SALT II Treaty, Historic Documents of 1979, p. 413)

On May 27, in a race with the summit calendar, the Senate cut through a thicket of procedural obstacles and ratified the pact by a 93-5 vote. But first, the senators adopted an amendment, on a 72-27 vote pushed by Senate Democrats, that had the effect of restoring an interpretation of SALT I—that space testing of Reagan's cherished strategic defense initiative (SDI or "Star Wars") would violate the treaty.

In Moscow, Reagan called the treaty "the first step toward a brighter future, a safer world," and Gorbachev said its approval "means that the era of nuclear disarmament has begun." Appearing to respond to charges by American conservatives that the Soviets would cheat on the treaty, Gorbachev said it was "a matter of honor" for both countries that "each letter in that treaty, each comma, be observed and complied with and implemented."

In their communiqué, the leaders reaffirmed the goal of a treaty limiting each country to 1,600 strategic delivery systems and 6,000 warheads; they ordered their Geneva negotiators to resume work July 12 on a START treaty cutting arsenals of long-range nuclear weapons by 30 to 50 percent.

Reagan and Gorbachev both held out hope that a treaty could be signed in 1988, but Reagan said he would not accept an agreement just to have one by the end of his term. "I am dead set against deadlines," the president said. Senate leaders Robert C. Byrd, D-W.Va., and Robert Dole, R-Kan., in Moscow for the INF ratification ceremony, also urged caution. The two senators also agreed that the Senate probably could not approve a START treaty by the end of Reagan's presidency even if one were signed.

The greatest obstacle to START had been the Soviet Union's objection to the strategic defense initiative, which Reagan envisioned as an umbrella against ballistic missiles but which the Soviets portrayed as a catalyst for a new arms race. As in previous summits, Reagan and Gorbachev skirted the issue of SDI testing, thereby postponing a decision that would have to be made before a new treaty could be signed. Little progress could be detected on another major START issue, that of monitoring cruise missiles launched from ships and submarines, or on the related matter of establishing a "balance" of NATO and Warsaw Pact conventional forces.

Human Rights Remarks

During his first two days in Moscow, Reagan used practically every occasion to chastise the Soviets for human rights violations. He cited in particular the government's extreme reluctance to allow Jews, other minorities, and dissidents to emigrate; he gave Gorbachev lists of people who had been waiting for years for permission to leave. In a dramatic gesture denounced by the Soviet press, Reagan on May 30 met with ninety-eight Soviet citizens, including many well-known "refusniks" who wanted to emigrate.

Shortly before, he had traveled to the renovated Danilov Monastery, Moscow's oldest, to address a group of Russian Orthodox monks and church leaders. Noting the church was celebrating the thousandth year of Christianity's introduction into Russia, the president said Americans "hope with you that soon all the many Soviet religious communities ... will be able to practice their religion freely...." In an indirect reference to Gorbachev's new tolerance, indicated by the reopening of many places of worship and plans for an elaborate celebration of the church's millennium, the president said, "We don't know if this first thaw will be followed by a resurgent spring of religious liberty ... but we may hope."

After Gorbachev expressed irritation, the president eased up on his high-profile criticism and blamed the Soviet "bureaucracy" for rights abuses. In a speech to students at Moscow State University on May 31, Reagan said the bureaucracy was responsible for emigration restrictions, rather than the Soviet people or their leaders. By the end of his visit, the president was citing a "sizable improvement" in human rights observance in the Soviet Union.

In spite of Reagan's efforts to clear government leaders of responsibility, Gorbachev on June 1 complained about the president's "attempts at scoring points through such propaganda ploys" as the meeting with dissidents. After Reagan left, the Soviet leader said, "We do not need anyone else's model. We do not need anyone else's values."

Regional and Bilateral Issues

The most important regional issue in previous summits, the Soviet occupation of Afghanistan, had been defused by the international agreement of April 14, 1988, setting a timetable for a phased withdrawal of Soviet troops. (Agreements on Afghanistan, p. 257)

As for the civil war in Angola, where the Soviet Union and Cuba supported the government and the United States aided a guerrilla movement, a U.S. official said the two sides set a deadline of September 29 for concluding an international agreement providing for the withdrawal of some 30,000 to 40,000 Cuban forces from Angola in return for a South Africa pullout from neighboring Namibia. On that day in 1978, the United Nations Security Council adopted Resolution 435 calling for the independence of Namibia.

Gorbachev said he and Reagan agreed that an international conference was the starting point for talks between Israel and its Arab neighbors, but the Soviet leader made it clear that differences remained over the role of that conference. The two sides remained apart on the U.S. demand for a mandatory arms embargo against Iran. They also failed to resolve their dispute over Communist support of the Sandinista government in Nicaragua and U.S. assistance to the contra guerrillas there.

Progress was made on bilateral cooperation. The two governments signed or extended several agreements, including those on cultural exchanges; operation of fishing fleets and radio navigation systems; and cooperation in joint outer space exploration, peaceful uses of nuclear energy, transportation research and technology, and search and rescue missions on the high seas.

> *Following are excerpts from remarks by President Ronald Reagan and Soviet leader Mikhail S. Gorbachev at the opening ceremony of the U.S.-Soviet summit in Moscow, May 29, 1988; from Reagan's remarks to religious leaders at the Danilov Monastery, May 30; from Reagan's remarks to Soviet dissidents at Spaso House, the U.S. ambassador's residence, May 30; from Reagan's and Gorbachev's toasts at the state dinner, May 30; from Reagan's remarks and a question-and-answer session with the students and faculty at Moscow State University, May 31; from toasts by the two leaders at a dinner hosted by Reagan at Spaso House, May 31; from remarks by Reagan and Gorbachev at the exchange*

of ratification instruments for the INF treaty, June 1; from the joint U.S.-Soviet communiqué, June 1; and from the president's news conference at Spaso House at the close of the summit, June 1:

REMARKS AT THE OPENING CEREMONY

The General Secretary. Esteemed Mr. Ronald Reagan, President of the United States of America; esteemed Mrs. Nancy Reagan, on behalf of the people and Government of the Soviet Union, I extend to you my sincere greetings on the occasion of your visit. Welcome....

... The peoples of the world and, in the first place, the Soviet and the American people welcome the emerging positive changes in our relationship and hope that your visit and talks here will be productive....

You and I are conscious of our two peoples' longing for mutual understanding, cooperation, and a safe and stable world. This makes it incumbent upon us to discuss constructively the main aspects of disarmament: the set of issues related to 50-percent cuts in strategic offensive arms, while preserving the 1972 ABM treaty; problems of eliminating chemical weapons; reductions in armed forces and conventional armaments in Europe; cessation of nuclear testing....

Our previous meetings have shown that constructive Soviet-U.S. relations are possible. The treaty on intermediate- and shorter-range missiles is the most impressive symbol of that. But even more complex and important tasks lie ahead. And so, Mr. President, you and I still have a lot of work to do. And it is good when there is a lot of work to be done and people need that work. We are ready to do our utmost in these coming days in Moscow....

The President. Mr. General Secretary, thank you for those kind words of welcome. We've traveled a long road together to reach this moment—from our first meeting in Geneva in November, 1985, when I invited you to visit me in Washington and you invited me to Moscow. It was cold that day in Geneva, and even colder in Reykjavik when we met the following year to work on the preparations for our exchange of visits. We've faced great obstacles; but by the time of your visit to Washington last December ... we had achieved impressive progress in all the areas of our common agenda—human rights, regional issues, arms reduction, and our bilateral relations.

We signed a treaty that will reduce the level of nuclear arms for the first time in history by eliminating an entire class of U.S. and Soviet independent-range missiles. We agreed on the main points of a treaty that will cut in half our arsenals of strategic offensive nuclear arms. We agreed to conduct a joint experiment that would allow us to develop effective ways to verify limits on nuclear testing. We held full and frank discussions that planted the seeds for future progress.

It is almost summer; and some of those seeds are beginning to bear fruit.... We have signed the Geneva accords, providing for the withdrawal of all Soviet troops from Afghanistan, and the first withdrawals have begun. We and our allies have completed technical arrangements necessary to begin implementing the INF treaty as soon as it enters into force....

I could go on; the list of accomplishments goes far beyond what many anticipated. But I think the message is clear: Despite clear and fundamental differences, and despite the inevitable frustrations that we have encountered, our work has begun to produce results....

REAGAN REMARKS AT MONASTERY

It's a very great pleasure to visit this beautiful monastery and to have a chance to meet some of the people who have helped make its return to the Russian Orthodox Church a reality. I am also addressing in spirit the 35 million believers whose personal contributions made this magnificent restoration possible.

... Like the saints and martyrs depicted in these icons, the faith of your people has been tested and tempered in the crucible of hardship. But in that suffering, it has grown strong, ready now to embrace with new hope the beginnings of a second Christian millennium.

We in our country share this hope for a new age of religious freedom in the Soviet Union. We share the hope that this monastery is not an end in itself but the symbol of a new policy of religious tolerance that will extend to all peoples of all faiths. We pray that the return of this monastery signals a willingness to return to believers the thousands of other houses of worship which are now closed, boarded up, or used for secular purposes.

There are many ties of faith that bind your country and mine. We have in America many churches, many creeds that feel a special kinship with their fellow believers here—Protestant, Catholic, Jewish, Orthodox, and Islamic. They are united with believers in this country in many ways, especially in prayer. Our people feel it keenly when religious freedom is denied to anyone anywhere and hope with you that soon all the many Soviet religious communities that are now prevented from registering, or are banned altogether, including the Ukranian Catholic and Orthodox Churches, will soon be able to practice their religion freely and openly and instruct their children in and outside the home in the fundamentals of their faith.

We don't know if this first thaw will be followed by a resurgent spring of religious liberty—we don't know, but we may hope. We may hope that *perestroika* will be accompanied by a deeper restructuring, a deeper conversion, a *mentanoya*, a change in heart, and that *glasnost*, which means giving voice, will also let loose a new chorus of belief, singing praise to the God that gave us life.

There is a beautiful passage that I'd just like to read, if I may. It's from one of this country's great writers and believers Aleksandr Solzhenitsyn, about the faith that is as elemental to this land as the dark and fertile soil. He wrote: "When you travel the byroads of central Russia, you begin to understand the secret of the pacifying Russian countryside. It is in the churches. They lift their belltowers—graceful, shapely, all different—high over mundane timber and thatch. From villages that are cut off and invisible to each other, they soar to the same heaven. People who are always selfish and often unkind—but the evening chimes used to ring out, floating over the villages, fields, and woods, reminding men that they must abandon trivial concerns of this world and give time and thought to eternity."

In our prayers we may keep that image in mind: the thought that the bells may ring again, sounding throughout Moscow and across the countryside, clamoring for joy in their newfound freedom.

Well, I've talked long enough. I'm sure you have many questions and many things on your minds, and I'm anxious to hear what you have to say.

REAGAN REMARKS
TO SOVIET DISSIDENTS

In one capacity, of course, I speak as a head of government. The United States views human rights as absolutely fundamental to our relationship with the Soviet Union and all nations. From the outset of our administration, we've stressed that an essential element in improving relations between the United States and the Soviet Union is human rights and Soviet compliance with international covenants on human rights. There have been hopeful signs; indeed, I believe this a hopeful time for your nation. Over the past 3 years more than 300 political and religious prisoners have been released from labor camps. Fewer dissidents and believers have been put in prisons and mental hospitals. And in recent months, more people have been permitted to emigrate or reunite with their families. The United States applauds these changes, yet the basic standards that the Soviet Union agreed to almost 13 years ago in the Helsinki accords, or a generation ago in the Universal Declaration of Human Rights, still need to be met. . . .

In particular, I've noted in my talks here the many who have been denied the right to emigrate on the grounds that they held secret knowledge, even though their secret work had ended years before and their so-called secrets had long since either become public knowledge or obsolete. Such cases must be rationally reviewed.

And finally, institutional changes to make progress permanent.

I've come to Moscow with this human rights agenda because, as I suggested, it is our belief that this is a moment of hope. The new Soviet leaders appear to grasp the connection between certain freedoms and economic growth. The freedom to keep the fruits of one's own labor, for example, is a freedom that the present reforms seem to be enlarging. We hope that one freedom will lead to another and another; that the Soviet Government will understand that it is the individual who is always the source of economic creativity, the inquiring mind that produces a technical breakthrough, the imagination that conceives of new products and markets; and that in order for the individual to create, he must have a sense of just that—his own individuality, his own self-worth. He must sense that others respect him and, yes, that his nation respects him—respects him enough to grant him all his human rights. This, as I said, is our hope; yet whatever the future may bring, the commitment of the United States will nevertheless remain unshakeable on human rights. On the fundamental dignity of the human person, there can be no relenting, for now we must work for more, always more. . . .

Thank you all, and God bless you.

TOASTS BY REAGAN AND GORBACHEV

The General Secretary. . . . [W]e wish to emphasize the importance of the newly discovered truth that it is no longer possible to settle international disputes by force of arms. Our awareness of the realities of the present-day world has led us to that conclusion. I like the notion of realism, and I also like the fact that you, Mr. President, have lately been uttering it more and more often. . . .

I recall the words you once spoke, Mr. President, and I quote: "The only way to resolve differences is to understand them." How very true. Let me just add that seeking to resolve differences should not mean an end to being different. The diversity of the world is a powerful wellspring of mutual enrichment, both spiritual and material.

Ladies and gentlemen, comrades, the word *perestroika* does not sound anachronistic, even within these ancient walls [of the Kremlin], for renewal of society, humanization of life, and elevated ideals are at all times and everywhere in the interests of the people and of each individual. And when this happens, especially in a great country, it is important to understand the meaning of what it is going through. It is this desire to understand the Soviet Union that we are now seeing abroad. And we regard this as a good sign because we do want to be understood correctly. This is also important for civilized international relations. Everyone who wants to do business with us will find it useful to know how Soviet people see themselves.

We see ourselves even more convinced that our Socialist choice was correct, and we cannot conceive of our country developing without socialism based on any other fundamental values. Our program is more democracy, more *glasnost,* more social justice with full prosperity and high moral standards. Our goal is maximum freedom for man, for the individual, and for society. Internationally, we see ourselves as part of an integral civilization, where each has the right to a social and political choice, to a worthy and equal place within the community of nations. . . .

Mr. President, this meeting, while taking stock of a fundamentally important period in Soviet-American relations, has to consolidate our achievements and give new impetus for the future. Never before have nuclear missiles been destroyed. Now we have an unprecedented treaty, and our two countries will be performing for the first time ever this overture of nuclear disarmament. The performance has to be flawless.

The Soviet Union and the United States are acting as guarantors of the Afghan political settlement. This, too, is a precedent of tremendous importance. As guarantors, our two countries face a very responsible period, and we hope they both will go through it in a befitting manner. The whole world is watching to see how we are going to act in this situation. . . .

To cooperation between the Soviet Union and the United States of America, to their better mutual knowledge and mutual understanding. I wish good health and happiness to you, Mr. President, to Mrs. Nancy Reagan, and to all our distinguished guests.

The President. I want to thank you again for the hospitality that we've encountered this evening and at every turn since our arrival in Moscow. We appreciate deeply the personal effort that you, Mrs. Gorbachev, and all of your associates have expended on our behalf. . . .

. . . The American and Soviet peoples are getting to know each other better, but not well enough. Mr. General Secretary, you and I are meeting now for the fourth time in 3 years—a good deal more often than our predecessors. And this has allowed our relationship to differ from theirs in more than a quantitative state or sense.

We have established the kind of working relationship I think we both had in mind when we first met in Geneva. We've been candid about our differences, but sincere in sharing a common objective and working hard together to draw closer to it. It's easy to disagree and much harder to find areas where we can agree. We and our two governments have both gotten into the habit of looking for those areas. We found more than we expected. . . .

REMARKS AND QUESTIONS
AT MOSCOW STATE UNIVERSITY

The President. . . . Let me say it's also a great pleasure to once again have this opportunity to speak directly to the people of the Soviet Union. Before I left Washington, I received many heartfelt letters and telegrams asking me to carry here a simple message, perhaps, but also some of the most important business of this summit: It is a message of peace and good will and hope for a growing friendship and closeness between our two peoples.

As you know, I've come to Moscow to meet with one of your most distinguished graduates. In this, our fourth summit, General Secretary

Gorbachev and I have spent many hours together, and I feel that we're getting to know each other well. Our discussions, of course, have been focused primarily on many of the important issues of the day, issues I want to touch on with you in a few moments. But first I want to take a little time to talk to you much as I would to any group of university students in the United States. I want to talk not just of the realities of today but of the possibilities of tomorrow.

Standing here before a mural of your revolution, I want to talk about a very different revolution that is taking place right now, quietly sweeping the globe without bloodshed or conflict. Its effects are peaceful, but they will fundamentally alter our world, shatter old assumptions, and reshape our lives. It's easy to underestimate because it's not accompanied by banners or fanfare. It's been called the technological or information revolution, and as its emblem, one might take the tiny silicon chip, no bigger than a fingerprint. One of these chips has more computing power than a roomful of old-style computers. . . .

Like a chrysalis, we're emerging from the economy of the Industrial Revolution—an economy confined to and limited by the Earth's physical resources—into, as one economist titled his book, "The Economy in Mind," in which there are no bounds on human imagination and the freedom to create is the most precious natural resource. . . .

But progress is not foreordained. The key is freedom—freedom of thought, freedom of information, freedom of communication. . . .

We are seeing the power of economic freedom spreading around the world. Places such as the Republic of Korea, Singapore, Taiwan have vaulted into the technological era, barely pausing in the industrial age along the way. Low-tax agricultural policies in the sub-continent mean that in some years India is now a net exporter of food. Perhaps most exciting are the winds of change that are blowing over the People's Republic of China, where one-quarter of the world's population is now getting its first taste of economic freedom. At the same time, the growth of democracy has become one of the most powerful political movements of our age. In Latin America in the 1970's, only a third of the population lived under democratic government; today over 90 percent does. In the Philippines, in the Republic of Korea, free, contested, democratic elections are the order of the day. Throughout the world, free markets are the model for growth. Democracy is the standard by which governments are measured.

We Americans make no secret of our belief in freedom. In fact, it's something of a national pastime. Every 4 years the American people choose a new President, and 1988 is one of those years. . . . But freedom doesn't begin or end with elections. Go to any American town, to take just an example, and you'll see dozens of churches, representing many different beliefs—in many places, synagogues and mosques—and you'll see families of every conceivable nationality worshiping together. Go into any school room, and there you will see children being taught the Declaration of Independence, that they are endowed by their Creator with certain unalienable rights—among them life, liberty, and the pursuit of happiness—that no government can justly deny; the guarantees in their Constitution for freedom of speech, freedom of assembly, and freedom of religion.

Go into any courtroom, and there will preside an independent judge, beholden to no government power. There every defendant has the right to a trial by a jury of his peers, usually 12 men and women—common citizens; they are the ones, the only ones, who weigh the evidence and decide on guilt or innocence. In that court, the accused is innocent until proven guilty, and the word of a policeman or any official has no greater legal standing than the word of the accused.

Go to any university campus, and there you'll find an open, sometimes heated discussion of the problems in American society and what can be done to correct them. . . .

Today the world looks expectantly to signs of change, steps toward greater freedom in the Soviet Union. We watch and we hope as we see positive changes taking place. . . . Such change will lead to new understandings, new opportunities, to a broader future in which the tradition is not supplanted but finds its full flowering. That is the future beckoning to your generation. . . .

Your generation is living in one of the most exciting, hopeful times in Soviet history. It is a time when the first breath of freedom stirs the air and the heart beats to the accelerated rhythm of hope, when the accumulated spiritual energies of a long silence yearn to break free. . . .

We do not know what the conclusion will be of this journey, but we're hopeful that the promise of reform will be fulfilled. In this Moscow spring, this May 1988, we may be allowed that hope: that freedom, like the fresh green sapling planted over Tolstoi's grave, will blossom forth at last in the rich fertile soil of your people and culture. . . .

Thank you all very much, and *da blagoslovit vas gospod*—God bless you.

Mr. [Anatoliy Alekseyevich] Logunov [rector of Moscow State University]. Dear friends, Mr. President has kindly agreed to answer your questions. But since he doesn't have too much time, only 15 minutes—so, those who have questions, please ask them.

Q. And this is a student from the history faculty, and he says that he's happy to welcome you on behalf of the students of the university. And the first question is that the improvement in the relations between the two countries has come about during your tenure as President, and in this regard he would like to ask the following questions. . . . Do you think that it will be possible for you and the General Secretary to get a treaty on the limitation of strategic arms during the time that you are still President?

The President. . . . We are both hopeful that it [the START treaty] can be finished before I leave office, which is in the coming January, but I assure you that if it isn't—I assure you that I will have impressed on my successor that we must carry on until it is signed. My dream has always been that once we've started down this road, we can look forward to a day, you can look forward to a day, when there will be no more nuclear weapons in the world at all.

Q. The question is: The universities influence public opinion, and the student wonders how the youths have changed since the days when you were a student up until now?

The President. Well, wait a minute. How you have changed since the era of my own youth?

Q. How just students have changed, the youth have changed. You were a student. [Laughter] At your time there were one type. How they have changed?

The President. Well, I know there was a period in our country when there was a very great change for the worst. When I was Governor of California, I could start a riot just by going to a campus. But that has all changed, and I could be looking out at an American student body as well as I'm looking out here and would not be able to tell the difference between you.

I think that back in our day—I did happen to go to school, get my college education in a unique time; it was the time of the Great Depression, when, in a country like our own, there was 25-percent unemployment and the bottom seemed to have fallen out of everything. But we had—I think what maybe I should be telling you from my point here, because I graduated in 1932, that I should tell you that when you get to be my age, you're going to be surprised how much you recall the feelings you had in these days here and how easy it is to understand the young people because of your own having been young once. You know an awful lot more about being young than you do about being old. [Laughter]. . . .

Twenty-five years after I graduated, my alma mater brought me back to the school and gave me an honorary degree. And I had to tell them they compounded a sense of guilt I had nursed for 25 years because I always felt the first degree they gave me was honorary. [Laughter] You're great. Carry on. . . .

Q. The reservation of the inalienable rights of citizens guaranteed by the Constitution faced certain problems; for example, the right of people to have arms, or for example, the problem appears, an evil appears whether spread of pornography or narcotics is compatible with these rights. Do you believe that these problems are just unavoidable problems connected with democracy, or they could be avoided?

The President. Well, if I understand you correctly, this is a question about the inalienable rights of the people—does that include the right to do criminal acts—for example, in the use of drugs and so forth? No. [Applause] No, we have a set of laws. I think what is significant and different about our system is that every country has a constitution, and most constitutions or practically all of the constitutions in the world are documents in which the government tells the people what the people can do. Our Constitution is different, and the difference is in three words; it almost escapes everyone. The three worlds are, "We the people." Our Constitution is a document in which we the people tell the government what its powers are. . . .

Q. Mr. President, from history 1 know that people who have been connected with great power, with big posts, say goodbye, leave these posts with great difficulty. Since your term of office is coming to an end, what sentiments do you experience and whether you feel like, if, hypothetically, you can just stay for another term? [Laughter]

The President. Well, I'll tell you something. I think it was a kind of revenge against Franklin Delano Roosevelt, who was elected four times— the only President. There had kind of grown a tradition in our country about two terms. . . . And then Roosevelt ran the four times—died very early in his fourth term. And suddenly, in the atmosphere at that time, they added an amendment to the Constitution that Presidents could only serve two terms.

When I get out of office—I can't do this while I'm in office, because it will look as I'm selfishly doing it for myself—when I get out of office, I'm going to travel around, what I call the mashed-potato circuit—that is the after dinner speaking and the speaking to luncheon groups and so forth— I'm going to travel around and try to convince the people of our country that they should wipe out that amendment to the Constitution because it was an interference with the democratic rights of the people. . . .

Q. Mr. President, I've heard that a group of American Indians have come here because they couldn't meet you in the United States of America. If you fail to meet them here, will you be able to correct it and to meet them back in the United States?

The President. I didn't know that they had asked to see me. If they've come here or whether to see them there—[laughter]—I'd be very happy to see them.

Let me tell you just a little something about the American Indian in our land. We have provided millions of acres of land for what are called preservations—or reservations, I should say. They, from the beginning, announced that they wanted to maintain their way of life, as they had always lived there in the desert and the plains and so forth. And we set up these reservations so they could, and have a Bureau of Indian Affairs to help take care of them. At the same time, we provide education for them— schools on the reservations. And they're free also to leave the reservations and be American citizens among the rest of us, and many do. Some still prefer, however, that way—that early way of life. And we've done everything we can to meet their demands as to how they want to live. Maybe we made a mistake. Maybe we should not have humored them in that wanting to stay in that kind of primitive lifestyle. Maybe we should have said, no, come join us; be citizens along with the rest of us. As I say, many have; many have been very successful. . . . Some of them became very wealthy because some of those reservations were overlaying great pools of oil, and you can get very rich pumping oil. And so, I don't know what their complaint might be. . . .

TOASTS AT SPASO HOUSE DINNER

The President. . . .It's a particular pleasure to be able to welcome you to Spaso House—a house of considerable beauty in its own right—the residence of our Ambassadors to the Soviet Union. During the 55 years of diplomatic relations between our two nations, Spaso House has served as one of the principal settings for exchanges between us—exchanges formal and informal alike. . . .

Mr. General Secretary, we know that on matters of great importance we will continue to differ profoundly, and yet you and I have met four times now, more often than any previous President and General Secretary. While our discussions have sometimes been pointed or contentious, we possess an enlarged understanding of each other and of each other's country. On specific matters of policy, we have made progress, often historic progress. And perhaps most important, we have committed our nations to continuing to work together, agreeing that silence must never again be permitted to fall between us. . . .

The General Secretary. . . .The visit by a President of the United States to the Soviet Union is an occasion for a glance at the past and a look into the future. The history of relations between our two countries has known all kinds of things, good and bad. Of the good things, we remember particularly the Soviet-American comradeship in arms in World War II. Those grim years saw the emergence of the first shoots of Soviet-American friendship. And there was not one single Soviet citizen who did not feel bitter when that glorious page in the history of our relations gave way to cold war. That was a hard test for our peoples. The world found itself in a dangerous situation. We all felt the breath of impending catastrophe. Even today, we're sometimes chilled by cold winds.

But world developments in their main tendency are turning toward a search for political solutions, toward cooperation and peace. We are, all of us, witnesses to momentous changes, though a lot still has to be done to achieve irreversible change.

. . . We have seriously studied the economic system in developing nations, and I am convinced that a way out is possible along the lines of a radical restructuring of the entire system of world economic relations, without any discrimination for political reasons. This would promote a political settlement of regional conflicts which not only impede progress in that part of the world but also cause turmoil in the entire world situation. . . .

Soviet and American people want to live in peace and communicate in all areas in which they have a mutual interest. The interest is there, and it is growing. We feel no fear. We are not prejudiced. We believe in the value of communication. I see a future in which the Soviet Union and the United States base their relations on disarmament and a balance of interest, and comprehensive cooperation. . . .

May the years to come bring a healthier international environment. May life be triumphant. To the very good health of the President, to the very good health of Mrs. Nancy Reagan, to cooperation between our two peoples.

EXCHANGE OF INF TREATY
RATIFICATION PAPERS

The General Secretary. . . .The President and I have summed up the results of a dialog between our two countries at the highest level. We have discussed both the immediate and longer term prospects for Soviet-U.S. relations. We have signed documents which record what has been achieved and provide guidelines for the future. Among them, an historic place will belong to the ratification documents which give effect to the treaty on intermediate- and shorter-range missiles. The exchange a few minutes ago of the Instruments of Ratification means that the era of nuclear disarmament has begun. . . .

Thank you.

The President. . . .[T]oday, on this table before us, we see the fruits of how, evidence of what candor and realism can accomplish. We have dared to hope, Mr. General Secretary, and we have been rewarded.

For the first time in history, an entire class of U.S.-Soviet nuclear missiles is eliminated. In addition, this treaty provides for the most stringent verification in history. And for the first time, inspection teams are actually in residence in our respective countries. . . . This we have done today, a first step toward a brighter future, a safer world. . . .

JOINT U.S.-SOVIET STATEMENT

. . . The President and the General Secretary view the Moscow summit as an important step in the process of putting U.S.-Soviet relations on a more productive and sustainable basis. Their comprehensive and detailed discussions covered the full agenda of issues to which the two leaders agreed during their initial meeting in Geneva in November, 1985—an agenda encompassing arms control, human rights and humanitarian matters, settlement of regional conflicts, and bilateral relations. Serious differences remain on important issues; the frank dialogue which has developed between the two countries remains critical to surmounting these differences.

The talks took place in a constructive atmosphere which provided ample opportunity for candid exchange. As a result, the sides achieved a better understanding of each other's positions. The two leaders welcomed the progress achieved in various areas of U.S.-Soviet relations since their last meeting in Washington, notwithstanding the difficulty and complexity of the issues. They noted with satisfaction numerous concrete agreements which have been achieved, and expressed their determination to redouble efforts in the months ahead in areas where work remains to be done. They praised the creative and intensive efforts made by representatives of both sides in recent months to resolve outstanding differences.

Assessing the state of U.S.-Soviet relations, the President and the General Secretary underscored the historic importance of their meetings in Geneva, Reykjavik, Washington, and Moscow in laying the foundation for a realistic approach to the problems of strengthening stability and reducing the risk of conflict. They reaffirmed their solemn conviction that a nuclear war cannot be won and must never be fought, their determination to prevent any war between the United States and Soviet Union, whether nuclear or conventional, and their disavowal of any intention to achieve military superiority.

The two leaders are convinced that the expanding political dialogue they have established represents an increasingly effective means of resolving issues of mutual interest and concern. They do not minimize the real differences of history, tradition and ideology which will continue to characterize the U.S.-Soviet relationship. But they believe that the dialogue will endure, because it is based on realism and focused on the achievement of concrete results. It can serve as a constructive basis for addressing not only the problems of the present, but of tomorrow and the next century. It is a process which the President and the General Secretary believe serves the best interests of the peoples of the United States and the Soviet Union, and can contribute to a more stable, more peaceful and safer world.

I. Arms Control

The President and the General Secretary, having expressed the commitment of their two countries to build on progress to date in arms control, determined objectives and next steps on a wide range of issues in this area. These will guide the efforts of the two governments in the months ahead as they work with each other and with other states toward equitable, verifiable agreements that strengthen international stability and security.

INF

The President and the General Secretary signed the protocol on the exchange of instruments of ratification of the Treaty between the United States of America and the Union of Soviet Socialist Republics on the Elimination of Their Intermediate-Range and Shorter-Range Missiles. The two leaders welcomed the entry into force of this historic agreement, which for the first time will eliminate an entire class of U.S. and Soviet nuclear arms, and which sets new standards for arms control. The leaders are determined to achieve the full implementation of all the provisions and understandings of the Treaty, viewing joint and successful work in this respect as an important precedent for future arms control efforts.

Nuclear and Space Talks

The two leaders noted that a Joint Draft Text of a Treaty on Reduction and Limitation of Strategic Offensive Arms has been elaborated. Through this process, the sides have been able to record in the Joint Draft Text extensive and significant areas of agreement and also to detail positions on remaining areas of disagreement. While important additional work is required before this Treaty is ready for signature, many key provisions are recorded in the Joint Draft Text and are considered to be agreed, subject to the completion and ratification of the Treaty.

Taking into account a Treaty on Strategic Offensive Arms, the sides have continued negotiations to achieve a separate agreement concerning the ABM Treaty building on the language of the Washington Summit Joint Statement dated December 10, 1987. . . .

The Joint Draft Treaty on Reduction and Limitation of Strategic Offensive Arms reflects the earlier understanding on establishing ceilings of no more than 1600 strategic offensive delivery systems and 6000 warheads as well as agreement on subceilings of 4900 on the aggregate of ICBM and SLBM warheads and 1540 warheads on 154 heavy missiles.

The Draft Treaty also records the sides' agreement that as a result of the reductions the aggregate throw-weight of the Soviet Union's ICBMs and SLBMs will be reduced to a level approximately 50 percent below the existing level and this level will not be exceeded.

During the negotiations the two sides have also achieved understanding that in future work on the Treaty they will act on the understanding that on deployed ICBMs and SLBMs of existing types the counting rule will include the number of warheads referred to in the Joint Statement of December 19, 1987, and the number of warheads which will be attributed to each new type of ballistic missile will be subject to negotiation.

In addition, the sides agreed on a counting rule for heavy bomber armaments according to which heavy bombers equipped only for nuclear gravity bombs and SRAMs will count as one delivery vehicle against the 1600 limit and one warhead against the 6000 limit. . . .

Guided by this fundamental agreement, the U.S. President and the General Secretary of the Central Committee of the CPSU agreed to continue their efforts in this area energetically and purposefully. The Delegations of the two countries have been instructed to return to Geneva on July 12, 1988. It has been agreed as a matter of principle that, once the remaining problems are solved and the Treaty and its associated documents are agreed, they will be signed without delay.

Ballistic Missile Launch Notifications

The agreement between the U.S. and the USSR on notifications of launches of Intercontinental Ballistic Missiles and Submarine-Launched Ballistic Missiles, signed during the Moscow summit, is a practical new step, reflecting the desire of the sides to reduce the risk of outbreak of nuclear war, in particular as a result of misinterpretation, miscalculation or accident.

Nuclear Testing

The leaders reaffirmed the commitment of the two sides to conduct in a single forum full-scale, stage-by-stage negotiations on the issues relating to nuclear testing. In these negotiations the sides as the first step will agree upon effective verification measures which will make it possible to ratify the U.S.-USSR Threshold Test Ban Treaty of 1974 and Peaceful Nuclear Explosions Treaty of 1976, and proceed to negotiating further intermediate limitations on nuclear testing leading to the ultimate objective of the complete cessation of nuclear testing as part of an effective disarmament process. This process, among other things, would pursue, as the first priority, the goal of the reduction of nuclear weapons and, ultimately, their elimination. In implementing the first objective of these negotiations, agreement upon effective verification measures for the U.S.-USSR Threshold Test Ban Treaty of 1974, the sides agreed to design and conduct a Joint Verification Experiment at each other's test sites.

The leaders therefore noted with satisfaction the signing of the Joint Verification Experiment Agreement.... They also noted the substantial progress on a new Protocol to the Peaceful Nuclear Explosions Treaty and urged continuing constructive negotiations on effective verification measures for the Threshold Test Ban Treaty....

Chemical Weapons

The leaders reviewed the status of on-going multilateral negotiations and bilateral U.S.-Soviet consultations toward a comprehensive, effectively verifiable, and truly global ban on chemical weapons, encompassing all chemical weapons-capable states. They also expressed concern over the growing problem of chemical weapons proliferation and use....

Conference on Security and Cooperation in Europe

They expressed their commitment to further development of the CSCE process. The U.S. and USSR will continue to work with the other 33 participants to bring the Vienna CSCE follow-up meeting to a successful conclusion....

II. Human Rights and Humanitarian Concerns

... [T]hey discussed the possible establishment of a forum which, meeting regularly, would bring together participants from across the range of their two societies. They noted steps already taken to establish the exchange of information and contacts between legislative bodies of both countries, as well as discussion between legal experts, physicians and representatives of other professions directly involved in matters pertaining to human rights, and between representatives of non-governmental organizations.

[Part III omitted]

IV. Bilateral Affairs

Cultural and People-to-People Exchanges

Noting the expansion of exchanges in the areas of education, science, culture and sports under the General Exchanges Agreement, the two leaders welcomed the signing of a new implementing program for 1989-91 under the Agreement and expressed their intention to continue expansion of such exchanges. . . .

Global Climate and Environmental Change Initiative

The two leaders expressed their satisfaction with activities since the Washington summit in expanding cooperation with respect to global climate and environmental change, including in areas of mutual concern relating to environmental protection, such as protection and conservation of stratospheric ozone and a possible global warming trend. They emphasized their desire to make more active use of the unique opportunities afforded by the space programs of the two countries to conduct global monitoring of the environment and the ecology of the Earth's land, oceans and atmosphere. . . .

Arctic Contacts and Cooperation

... [T]hey expressed their support for increased people-to-people contacts between the native peoples of Alaska and the Soviet North.

The President and the General Secretary noted the positive role played by the multilateral Antarctic Treaty and emphasized the importance of U.S.-Soviet scientific and environmental cooperation in that region. . . .

V. Future Meetings

The President and the General Secretary, recognizing the importance of their personal involvement in the development of relations in the months ahead, instructed Secretary of State Schultz and Foreign Minister Shevardnadze to meet as necessary and to report to them on ways to ensure continued practical progress across the full range of issues. Expert-level contacts will also continue on an intensified basis.

SPASO HOUSE NEWS CONFERENCE

The President. . . . This is my fourth summit. For some in our governments and some of you in the media, the number is higher. But a good deal of important work has been accomplished here in Moscow. And the relationship between Mr. Gorbachev and me, and the various members of our respective delegations, has continued to deepen and improve. . . .

. . . [P]ermit me to go back for just a moment to our first summit meeting at Geneva. There we agreed on certain fundamental realities that would govern our relations: that a nuclear war cannot be won and must never be fought, that the United States and the Soviet Union bear special responsibilities for avoiding the risk of war, that neither side should seek military superiority over the other. We affirmed our determination to prevent war, whether nuclear or conventional, and our resolve to contribute in every way possible, along with other nations, to a safer world. . . .

For the past 3 years, General Secretary Gorbachev and I have worked to build a relationship of greater trust. . . . Each of our summit meetings moved us farther toward an INF treaty, capped by today's exchange of ratification instruments, which now makes it a reality. . . .

We've moved forward in other areas as well, including agreements on an experiment to improve the verification of existing nuclear testing treaties and on notification of strategic ballistic missile launches.

Finally, let me say how deeply moving I have found my discussions with various citizens of the Soviet Union. The monks of Danilov, the dissidents and refuseniks, the writers and artists, the students and young people have shown once again that spiritual values are cherished in this nation. It's my fervent hope that those values will attain even fuller expression.

And now I will be happy to take your questions. . . .

Q. Mr. President . . . at your first news conference in 1981, you said that the Soviets lie and cheat and pursue their ends of world domination. What has really changed your mind? Can the American people really trust the Russians now? And I'd like to follow up.

The President. . . . I cited some of the leaders of the Communist movement in the Soviet Union that said that the only immorality was anything that slowed the growth of socialism and that there was no immorality in lying or cheating or doing anything of that kind, as long as it advanced the cause of socialism. Now, that was my answer. So, it wasn't an opinion. I was quoting what their leaders themselves—the beginners of that particular system—had said. . . .

Q. Mr. President, on the START treaty, what are the areas of progress, and what's the specific progress that you achieved here? And why do you think that you can conclude a treaty this year, when Senate leaders are urging you to go slow, and this summit, with all its momentum, wasn't able to break the impasse?

The President. Well, the Senate leaders themselves brought the verification—or the ratification papers here that we just received today on the INF treaty. It meant changing their own schedules a great deal and speeding up the ratification process. I think that we could count on them to feel the same if we are coming to final agreement of a START treaty.

But I want to remind you of one thing that we've said over and over again. The START treaty is infinitely more complex than the INF treaty, and therefore, there is going to be continued negotiation on a number of points. . . .

We can hope. I would hope that before the year is out that we could eliminate the differences that still exist. But if not, I would hope that my successor would continue because here we are getting at, I think, the most important reduction that should take place in nuclear weapons. The most destabilizing are the intercontinental ballistic missiles in which someone pushes a button and minutes later a part of the Earth blows up. . . .

Q. Mr. President, what have you learned about the Soviet Union? What have you learned in your first trip to Moscow?

The President. I'm going to do one answer because I've wanted to say this. And I say it anytime I get a chance. I think that one of the most wonderful forces for stability and good that I have seen in the Soviet Union are the Russian women.

June

Reports on Math and Science Education 377

Toronto Economic Summit 391

Court on Private Clubs 399

Pope John Paul's Visit to Austria 405

Presidential Commission Report on AIDS ... 415

Soviet Party Conference 447

Court on Independent Counsel 465

U.S. District Court Order
   to Bar Closing of PLO Office 479

REPORTS ON MATH
AND SCIENCE EDUCATION
June 7, 1988

American students' proficiency in math is "dismal," according to a report the National Assessment of Educational Progress (NAEP) released June 7. It was one of a series issued by the NAEP, a project authorized by Congress to study achievement every two years in several subjects and prepared by the Educational Testing Service at Princeton, New Jersey, under contract to the Department of Education. On September 22, the NAEP issued a report that said American schools did not adequately educate children in the sciences. The 142-page math report, entitled "The Mathematics Report Card: Are We Measuring Up?" was based on a 1986 study of 10,945 students in third grade, 12,185 students in seventh grade, and 11,850 students in eleventh grade. The math assessment was the fourth that the NAEP had conducted since 1973.

"Too many students leave high school without the mathematical understanding that will allow them to participate fully as workers and citizens in contemporary society," the report said. About half of the seventeen-year-olds tested could not perform "moderately complex" procedures, and only 6 percent were able to solve multistep problems. The NAEP found that the discrepancy between what students were expected to know and what they could demonstrate they knew widened as they grew older. By the time they reached eleventh grade, only half of the students tested had mastered junior-high-school-level skills.

"Translated into population figures, nearly 1.5 million 17-year-old students across the nation appear scarcely able to perform the kind of numerical applications that will be required of them in future life and

work settings," the study asserted. The fact that the students performed well only on simple math topics might be due to schools' emphasis on basic skills, which had become "a ceiling rather than a floor" for many students, Ann P. Kahn, former president of the National Parent-Teacher Association, told the publication Education Week.

Math Gains by Minorities

The study results were in line with a 1982 international mathematics assessment that placed American students far behind those in other industrialized nations. On the other hand, the report noted some "encouraging" trends that included significant gains in math scores for blacks and Hispanics, although overall their scores still were lower than those of white students. It was also noted that more students were taking advanced-level math courses.

In a news conference after the report's release, Assistant Secretary of Education Chester E. Finn, Jr., said it would take some "reaching to find a silver lining in this particular cloud." He added, "We are climbing the cellar steps to get up to the ground floor."

Low Science Achievement Levels

The science study, entitled "Science Report Card: Elements of Risk and Recovery," concluded that American students displayed "distressingly low"' levels of achievement in science, ranking lowest in an assessment conducted in seventeen countries. The findings were similar to those of the math survey: elementary and secondary students lacked a basic foundation in concepts, teaching practices were outmoded, and there was a general perception that the subject was of peripheral use to those who were not in an educated "elite" group. As in its math study, however, the NAEP reported that minorities scored higher in 1986 than in 1982.

Tests of third, seventh, and eleventh graders conducted between 1970 and 1986 showed a drop in science proficiency until 1982 and slight gains after that. The gains did not offset the previous losses, however. The report suggested that the gains "were largely the result of students' increased knowledge about [report's emphasis] science, rather than increased skills in scientific reasoning." Almost all students had a grasp of everyday science, but only slightly more than half of the thirteen-year-olds could apply that basic science information. The fact that only a very small group of high school students could perform at the highest level— integrating specialized scientific information—was "particularly troublesome," the report said. Students at that level "are likely to represent the pool from which future scientists are drawn," but their numbers were "substantially smaller than that needed for the future workplace."

The NAEP found that the quality of instruction generally did not enhance student aptitudes in science. "Many students [in all grades surveyed] appear to be unenthusiastic about the value and personal relevance of their science learning, and their attitudes seem to decline as they progress through school," the report stated. However, some positive signs in instruction were noted. One was that most science teachers in junior and senior high school held the highest certification available for their grade level, and almost all considered themselves "adequately prepared" to teach science.

"The data in this report present a situation that can only be described as a national disgrace," said Bassam Z. Shakhashiri, director of the science- and engineering-education directorate of the National Science Foundation, at a press conference soon after its release. "Excellent grades on future national report cards in science are more central to our national security than half a dozen strategic weapons systems," astronomer-author Carl Sagan was quoted as saying. "I think the conclusion to draw from the NAEP results is that there is something fundamentally wrong with the way we approach science in our schools," said Albert Shanker, president of the American Federation of Teachers, in a statement his organization issued.

Following are excerpts from "The Mathematics Report Card: Are We Measuring Up?" and "The Science Report Card: Elements of Risk and Recovery," issued June 7 and September 22, 1988, respectively, by the National Assessment of Educational Progress:

THE MATHEMATICS REPORT CARD

Overview

Why Mathematics Counts

The skills and expertise of a country's workforce are the foundation of its economic success. Lately, in our country, this foundation appears too fragile to withstand the challenges of the 21st century.

- The most recent international mathematics study reported that average Japanese students exhibited higher levels of achievement than the top 5 percent of American students enrolled in college preparatory mathematics courses. As a case in point, a Japanese semiconductor company recently opening a plant in the Southeastern United States had to use college students at the graduate level to perform statistical quality control functions; the same jobs were performed by high-school graduates in Japan.
- One out of three major corporations already provides new workers with basic reading, writing, and arithmetic courses. If current demographic and economic trends continue, American businesses will hire a million

new people a year who can't read, write, or count. Teaching them how, and absorbing the lost productivity while they are learning, will cost industry $25 billion a year for as long as it takes—and nobody seems to know how long that will be.

- American colleges have reported a 10- to 30-percent rise in demand over the past several years for remedial coursework in mathematics for incoming freshmen. As diagnosed in one study, these young people are not defined as at-risk, yet they are not workforce ready. For the at-risk populations, the mismatch between workplace needs and workforce skills is even greater.
- Looking toward the year 2000, the fastest-growing occupations require employees to have much higher math, language, and reasoning capabilities than do current occupations.

Too many students leave high school without the mathematical understanding that will allow them to participate fully as workers and citizens in contemporary society. As these young people enter universities and businesses, American college faculty and employers must anticipate additional burdens. As long as the supply of adequately prepared precollegiate students remains substandard, it will be difficult for these institutions to assume the dual responsibility of remedial and specialized training; and without highly trained personnel, the United States risks forfeiting its competitive edge in world and domestic markets.

Even for those working in less scientifically specialized areas, technological innovations require the ability to learn and adapt to new conditions. Studies of technological change have reached differing conclusions as to the nature and extent of its impact on job skill requirements, but it is certain that the current generation of students will need to work with increasingly large and complex bodies of information in performing even basic tasks. From the basic computational skills required to organize and track large-scale shipments of merchandise to the higher-level expertise necessary to make technological discoveries, it is clear that mathematical abilities will be critical to our nation's continued economic success.

Highlights from NAEP's Mathematics Assessments

NAEP's 1986 mathematics assessment provides a timely account of student achievement in this vital subject, and the results highlight the need for even greater commitment to school mathematics programs. Trends across four assessments since 1973 offer a comprehensive view of achievement patterns for students at ages 9, 13, and 17.

- Recent national trends in mathematics performance are somewhat encouraging, particularly for students at ages 9 and 17. Subpopulations of students who performed comparatively poorly in past assessments have shown significant improvement in average proficiency since 1978: at all three ages, Black and Hispanic students made appreciable gains, as did students living in the Southeast.

- While average performance has improved since 1978, the gains have been confined primarily to lower-order skills. The highest level of performance attained by any substantial proportion of students in 1986 reflects only moderately complex skills and understandings. Most students, even at age 17, do not possess the breadth and depth of mathematics proficiency needed for advanced study in secondary school mathematics.

While we may be recovering from the doldrums of poor performance that characterized the 1970s, it is crucial that we do even better to reach expected or hoped-for levels of achievement. Improvements are needed, not only in average proficiency, but also in the number of students who reach the upper levels of performance.

Other Findings

- Discrepancies between the level of mathematics commonly taught in elementary, middle, and high schools and what students know and can do in the subject appear to increase over the school years, especially for Black and Hispanic students. Only about half of all the 17-year-olds in the 1986 assessment reached a level of proficiency associated with material taught in junior high school mathematics.
- Mathematics instruction in 1986, as in previous years, continues to be dominated by teacher explanations, chalkboard presentations, and reliance on textbooks and workbooks. More innovative forms of instruction—such as those involving small group activities, laboratory work, and special projects—remain disappointingly rare.
- Students reported more homework and testing in mathematics in 1986 than in previous assessments, perhaps indicating a growth in academic expectations in schools.
- Students appear to gain basic mathematics knowledge and skills in numbers and operations between grades 3 and 7, while higher-level applications in numbers and operations develop steadily across the three grade levels. Females outperformed males in the area of basic knowledge and skills, while males had the advantage in higher-level applications.
- Although the role of technology in the mathematics classroom appears to be changing, the benefits of using computers and calculators seem to be available primarily to small proportions of students who are in the upper range of ability or in the upper grades.
- Although more high school students in 1986 than in previous years reported taking higher-level mathematics courses, including Algebra II, Geometry, and Calculus, the overall percentage of students taking these advanced courses remains disappointingly low.
- High school students whose parents encourage mathematics course-taking and have higher levels of education tend to exhibit higher mathematics proficiency than those who lack this home support.

● Students who enjoy mathematics and perceive its relevance to every-day life tend to have higher proficiency scores than students with more negative perspectives. At the same time, students' enjoyment of and confidence in mathematics appear to wane as they progress through their schooling. Most perceive that the subject is composed mainly of rule memorization, and expect to have little use for mathematic skills in their future work lives. . . .

Reflections

The assessment findings show both encouraging and discouraging trends for mathematics education in the United States. It is encouraging to see improvements in performance occurring across such a wide segment of the student population, especially among Black and Hispanic students and those in the Southeast. However, this good news must be tempered by continuing concern over the generally low levels of performance exhibited by most high school students and by the fact that the majority of improvement shown resulted from increased performance in low-level skills.

Evidence concerning the nature of mathematics education suggests that the curriculum continues to be dominated by paper-and-pencil drills on basic computation. Little evidence appears of any widespread use of calculators, computers, or mathematics projects. This picture reflects classrooms more concerned with students' rote use of procedures than with their understanding of concepts and development of higher-order thinking skills. The continuance of such a pattern offers little hope that the mathematics education of our children will achieve the goals being set by the recent educational excellence movement.

Findings from the 1986 assessment, however, indicate that recent reforms directed toward increasing requirements in high school mathematics education, and schooling in general, may be beginning to have some effect in raising the overall performance of our students.

Achieving a higher-quality mathematics curriculum across schools in the United States will require new materials, effective instructional methods, and improved means of evaluating student performance. There are many well-qualified and dedicated teachers in our classrooms capable of promoting improved ways of learning. In order to do so, our teachers will need the support of administrators, parents, and the public at large. No longer can society afford to view mathematics as a subject for a chosen few or as a domain solely composed of arithmetic skills. Students must come to see it as a way of thinking, communicating, and resolving problems. Until American schools move toward these more ambitious goals in mathematics instruction, there is little hope that current levels of achievement will show any appreciable gain.

THE SCIENCE REPORT CARD

Interpretive Overview

The State of Science Learning

It is widely believed that the condition of science education in this country needs improvement, and the results of NAEP's 1986 science assessment do not assuage this concern. In 1983, the National Science Board's Commission on Precollege Education in Mathematics, Science, and Technology described the implications of neglecting science education:

> Alarming numbers of young Americans are ill-equipped to work in, contribute to, profit from and enjoy our increasingly technological society. Far too many emerge from the nation's elementary and secondary schools with an inadequate grounding in mathematics, science and technology. As a result, they lack sufficient knowledge to acquire the training, skills and understanding that are needed today and will be even more critically needed in the 21st century.

Since this statement was made, as many as 100 national reports have been issued calling for greater rigor in science education and suggesting numerous reforms. The nation has responded by updating standards for school science programs, strengthening teacher preparation, increasing the use of assessments, stiffening graduation requirements, and implementing a wide variety of research efforts to deepen our understanding of science teaching and learning. Despite these efforts, average science proficiency across the grades remains distressingly low.

Trends for 9-, 13-, and 17-year-olds across five national science assessments conducted by NAEP from 1969 to 1986 reveal a pattern of initial declines followed by subsequent recovery at all three age groups. To date, however, the recoveries have not matched the declines. . . .

National expectations are high. Students are expected to complete their high-school studies with sufficient science understanding for assuming their responsibilities as voters and as efficient contributors in the workplace. In addition, school science is expected to prepare adequately for postsecondary science courses those students who are continuing their formal education. Unfortunately, these expectations have not been met. An examination of NAEP trends in science proficiency suggests that a majority of 17-year-olds are poorly equipped for informed citizenship and productive performance in the workplace, let alone postsecondary studies in science.

- More than half of the nation's 17-year-olds appear to be inadequately prepared either to perform competently jobs that require technical skills or to benefit substantially from specialized on-the-job training. The thinking skills and science knowledge possessed by these high-school students also seem to be inadequate for informed participation in the nation's civic affairs.
- Only 7 percent of the nation's 17-year-olds have the prerequisite knowledge and skills thought to be needed to perform well in college-

level science courses. Since high-school science proficiency is a good predictor of whether or not a young person will elect to pursue post-secondary studies in science, the probability that many more students will embark on future careers in science is very low.

These NAEP findings are reinforced by results from the second international science assessment, which revealed that students from the United States—particularly students completing high school—are among the lowest achievers of all participating countries.

- At grade 5, the U.S. ranked in the middle in science achievement relative to 14 other participating countries.
- At grade 9, U.S. students ranked next to last.
- In the upper grades of secondary school, "advanced science students" in the U.S. ranked last in Biology and performed behind students from most countries in Chemistry and Physics.

Given evidence from both the NAEP and international results that our students' deficits increase across the grades, projections for the future do not appear to be bright. The further students progress in school, the greater the discrepancies in their performance relative both to students in other countries and to expectations within this country. Because elementary science instruction tends to be weak, many students—especially those in less affluent schools—are inadequately prepared for middle-school science. The failure they experience in middle school may convince these young people that they are incapable of learning science, thus contributing to the low enrollments observed in high-school science courses. Unless conditions in the nation's schools change radically, it is unlikely that today's 9- and 13-year-olds will perform much better as the 17-year-olds of tomorrow.

The Status of Science Learning for "At-Risk" Populations

Students do not all arrive at the kindergarten door with equal opportunities and aspirations. Social and economic realities have begun to have an impact long before that time, and schooling does not serve to eradicate these inequities. . . .

Since a higher proportion of Black and Hispanic children than White children come from homes of lower socioeconomic status, disparities in performance attributed to race/ethnicity may be due in large part to differences in such factors as parents' education levels and access to reading and reference materials in the home. In fact, recent research on mathematics achievement shows that when other school and home factors are controlled, students' socioeconomic status accounts for a large part of the performance gap. Economically disadvantaged students are likely to enter school at an educational disadvantage, because they appear to be behind their peers and are therefore placed in remedial classes. The consequence of this early tracking is that many of these students are poorly prepared to pursue higher-level science and mathematics coursework when they get to high school.

In the case of performance disparities between male and female students, there is growing evidence of differential treatment and opportunities in science instruction. Teachers have higher expectations for boys than girls, and ask them higher-level questions. Textbooks may also send the message that most of the notable accomplishments in science are attributable to White males. Because there are still relatively few female and minority scientists, students are unlikely to encounter them as role models.

While one would expect in-school experiences to contribute to students' participation and achievement in science, the NAEP data also suggest that some of the factors underlying performance differences may originate outside of the school. This appears to be particularly true for the performance gap by gender. In the 1986 assessment, females were substantially less likely than males to report science-related activities or experiences.

While the NAEP data cannot tell us what causes these differences, there is evidence from other sources that sex- and race-role stereotyping are often major deterrents to the participation of female and minority students in science and science-related activities. For example, parents, peers, the media, teachers, counselors, and curriculum materials may give females and minority students the idea that only certain roles are appropriate for them. Within- and out-of-school experiences appear to reinforce one another in creating and perpetuating differences in achievement.

Research on teaching and learning indicates some approaches that appear promising for improving the participation of females and minorities in science. For example, to counteract the aversion toward physical science that girls seem to develop even before they enter school, elementary science should include an abundance of hands-on activities related to concepts in electricity, magnetism, and other areas, structured so that girls play an active rather than a passive role. In addition, appropriate role models should be provided through interactions with both male and female scientists of various racial/ethnic backgrounds, both in person and through textbooks, films, and other instructional materials.

Teacher education, both pre-service and in-service, should make teachers aware of the more subtle behaviors that communicate low expectations to particular students, and give them assistance in implementing instructional techniques that are effective with female and minority students, as well as White males. Finally, alternative mechanisms need to be developed to foster the skills that will prepare students for academic sequences in high school rather than curtail their opportunities.

Opportunity to Learn Science

Two distinct aspects of an opportunity to learn are the amount of time spent on instruction and the quality of that time. The first is a necessary but insufficient condition for the second; however, results from the 1986

NAEP science assessment suggest that *neither* condition of the opportunity to learn science is afforded our nation's youth.

- More than two-thirds of the third-grade teachers responding to NAEP's 1986 teacher questionnaire reported spending 2 hours or less each week on science instruction; many spent more than that amount of time maintaining order and disciplining students in the classroom.
- Eleven percent of the third graders assessed in 1986 reported having no science instruction at the time of the assessment; in addition, one-third of the elementary students who were receiving instruction reported spending no time on science homework.
- All but 6 percent of the seventh graders reported taking some type of science course in 1986, but enrollment dropped substantially by grade 11. Only 58 percent of the eleventh-grade students were taking a science course at the time of the assessment.
- Approximately half of the teachers in grades 7 and 11 reported spending three hours or less providing science instruction each week.
- Of the seventh- and eleventh-grade students taking a science class in 1986, 12 to 16 percent reported spending no time on science homework each week.

These findings are corroborated by recent literature in which teachers reported spending only an average of 18 minutes per day on science at grades K-3 and only about 29 minutes per day at grades 4-6. Across these grades, the amount of time spent was greatest for reading, followed by mathematics, then social studies and science—a ranking which had not changed since 1977. . . .

In addition, very few students in this country take advanced science courses. Preliminary results of a follow-up transcript study of eleventh-grade students participating in the 1986 assessment indicate that while 90 percent of these graduating students had studied at least one year of Biology, only 45 percent had studied one year or more of Chemistry, and 20 percent that amount of Physics. Although these findings represent increases in science course-taking since 1982, enrollments generally remain low from an international perspective. Only about 6 percent of all high-school students in this country take advanced courses in Biology, compared with 45 percent of the students in Finland and 28 percent of the students in English-speaking Canada. Similarly, students studying advanced Chemistry and Physics represent a very small percentage of the total U.S. student population; by comparison, in other countries these students represent as much as one-sixth to one-fourth of the total student population.

The Relationship Between Amount of Science Instruction and Proficiency

A recent report issued by the National Academy of Science Committee on Indicators of Precollege Science and Mathematics Education reviewed the research literature linking instructional time and student learning; it concluded that at both the elementary- and secondary-school levels, the amount of time given to studying a subject is correlated with student performance as measured by achievement tests. The report also found that the amount of time spent on homework is correlated with student achievement, and that teachers' attention to homework affects its contribution to performance.

These conclusions are further reinforced by NAEP findings from the 1986 assessment, which suggest positive associations between science proficiency and the amount of time spent in science learning (i.e., through course-taking and homework), particularly among eleventh-grade students. It may be, however, that highly proficient students choose to take more courses or select more challenging courses that require more homework. Further, as previously noted, time spent in science classes *per se* cannot guarantee the quality of that instructional time. Although both common sense and empirical findings indicate that more time spent in science instruction will improve science learning—thus supporting reforms that are targeted toward reducing absenteeism, increasing science course-taking requirements, and assigning more homework—great care also must be taken to address the quality of that instructional time.

Because educational reforms implemented in the 1980s cannot be expected to have immediate impact and their full effects may not be noticeable for some time, the slight progress evidenced in the NAEP results may portend improvements for the future. It must be recognized, however, that improvements in average performance seen in the 1986 assessment were largely the result of students' increased knowledge *about* science rather than increased skills in scientific reasoning. This finding, coupled with the disappointing state of science education, suggests that current reforms tend to be aimed primarily at the symptoms rather than the disease. What has traditionally been taught in science may be neither sufficient nor appropriate for the demands of the future, necessitating reforms that go beyond increasing students' exposure to science and that center on implementing new goals for improving curriculum and instruction.

Science Learning in the "Spirit of Science"

Embarking on fundamental reforms of science curriculum and instruction requires a reexamination of the conceptual underpinnings of science education. Science educators have maintained that hands-on and laboratory experiences should be an integral part of science instruction, explaining that it is appropriate for science teaching and learning to parallel the methods of investigation used by scientists to understand the natural world.

Results from the 1986 science assessment do indicate a positive relationship between students' use of scientific equipment and their proficiency in the subject, particularly at the eleventh-grade level, but cause-and-effect relationships cannot be addressed by NAEP data. Schools with laboratory facilities and other scientific equipment may be the wealthier schools, populated by advantaged students who tend to perform better in academic assessments. Disciplined research is needed to substantiate the impact of hands-on activities on science proficiency, and the appropriate role of these activities in science instruction.

Findings from the NAEP assessment also suggest positive associations between participatory classroom activities and science proficiency, and between attitudes toward science and students' proficiency in the subject. Again, while the NAEP data are suggestive, they by themselves do not permit the conclusion that more participatory activities or efforts to improve students' views of science will necessarily raise achievement levels for any given student population. Decisions to strengthen science education that may be suggested by the NAEP data must be firmly based on relevant research and experience.

Given these caveats, some aspects of science practice can be used to analyze the nation's science education program and reflect on NAEP findings. What are the features of the scientific enterprise that our science education system might emulate?

Activities. Procedures of investigation—such as observation, measurement, experimentation, and communication—allow the scientist to gain an understanding of natural phenomena. In addition, mental processes such as hypothesizing, using inductive and deductive reasoning, extrapolating, synthesizing, and evaluating information are necessary to scientific investigation, as are the less well defined but no less important skills of speculation, intuition, and insight. An effective science learning system would provide students with opportunities to engage in these activities, and encourage science teachers to model them in their classrooms.

Beliefs and Assumptions. Scientists appear to operate in accordance with a set of beliefs about the natural world that guide their methods of inquiry and the knowledge yielded by these methods. For example, scientists believe a real world exists that can be understood; they assume that nature is not capricious and that events in nature have causes.

Implementing the methods of scientific inquiry yields knowledge about the natural world, contained in the form of facts, concepts, hypotheses, theories, and laws. These structures are characterized in part by scientists' beliefs, making it possible to communicate scientific knowledge, give it logical coherence, offer explanations, and make predictions. Yet another key aspect of the knowledge of science is its tentativeness: Scientists view findings not as final statements but rather as reasonable assertions about some distant, but seldom reached, truth.

Characteristics of Scientists. Certain personality traits seem to characterize successful scientists, and these may provide additional guidance for determining the features of an effective science education program. Among the salient traits of successful scientists are curiosity, creativity, and dedication. Scientists ask questions about and are sensitive to the world around them. The critical nature of the profession requires a strong belief in one's ability to learn, and an ability to distinguish between productive and unproductive ideas. The joy of discovery is a driving force in scientists' professional lives; they are hungry for knowledge and recognition, and strive to achieve both. . . .

Elements of the Model
in Light of NAEP Findings

. . . A classroom environment that emulates the "spirit" of science is characterized by collaboration between teachers and students to test knowledge that is gained and a willingness to modify this knowledge in light of new evidence. This setting encourages students to wonder about the world around them and actively seek to understand it. It builds their thirst for knowledge and strengthens their sense of responsibility to learn. Teachers provide role models for students and stimulate their curiosity. Yet numerous studies of the last few years—for example, John Goodlad's *A Place Called School*—have indicated that most teaching, including science teaching, is instead dreadfully dull.

For the classroom to mirror the real-world practice of science, the teacher should be an active model, spending less time lecturing and more time engaging students in hands-on activities and asking open-ended questions than do teachers in general. In contrast, students in the 1986 NAEP science assessment reported few opportunities to explore natural phenomena directly or engage in discussions about the limited experiences that they did have. They revealed a preponderance of class time spent listening to teachers' lectures; in addition, limited information on school curriculum suggests that scientific content appears to be largely textbook- and workbook-driven, reflecting little—or not at all—the recent technological advances in the domain of science.

Science Curriculum

To provide curriculum, instruction, and facilities appropriate to the demands of science teaching and learning, it is clear that a number of substantial changes are needed. The need for greater availability of classroom laboratory facilities is undeniable. The 1985-86 National Survey of Science and Mathematics Education found that while most teachers believed that laboratory classes were more effective than non-laboratory classes, lectures were reported as their primary teaching technique. However, this paradox may be partially explained by the fact that a substantial percentage of teachers do not have access to adequate laboratories, science equipment, supplies, and other resources needed for teaching science.

Perhaps even more crucial than greater access to laboratory facilities are the more fundamental, but less obvious, changes associated with teaching and curriculum. Cross-cultural studies shed some light on the direction that is needed, revealing significant differences between science curricula in this country and those in Japan, China, East and West Germany, and the Soviet Union. In these five countries, science content is more closely linked to the requirements of modern industrial society, and the instructional approach is to teach an array of disciplines over a period of years, maintaining continuity across the grades. In comparison, the prevailing practice for public school students in the United States is to take one science subject for one academic year and then move to another discipline the following year—sometimes referred to as the "layer-cake curriculum". . . .

Conclusion

Evidence from NAEP and other sources indicates that both the content and structure of our school science curricula are generally incongruent with the ideals of the scientific enterprise. By neglecting the kinds of instructional activities that make purposeful connections between the study and practice of science, we fail to help students understand the true spirit of science, as described in these pages.

In limiting opportunities for true science learning, our nation is producing a generation of students who lack the intellectual skills necessary to assess the validity of evidence or the logic of arguments, and who are misinformed about the nature of scientific endeavors. The NAEP data support a growing body of literature urging fundamental reforms in science education—reforms in which students learn to use the tools of science to better understand the world that surrounds them.

TORONTO ECONOMIC SUMMIT
June 19-21, 1988

A congratulatory mood dominated the fourteenth annual summit meeting of the leaders of the seven biggest industrial countries. At the conference in Toronto, Canada, held June 19-21, the leaders of Britain, France, West Germany, Italy, Japan, Canada, and the United States praised the performance of their economies and projected an optimistic outlook for the world economy. For President Ronald Reagan, who was attending his eighth and last summit, the conference echoed with expressions of affection and praise.

In their concluding statement, the leaders said that since the 1987 Economic Summit in Venice, Italy, their national economies had "kept up the momentum of growth" (Venice Economic Summit, Historic Documents of 1987, p. 525). *"Employment has continued to expand generally, inflation has been restrained, and progress has been made toward the correction of major external imbalances," the statement added.*

However, a darker side of the world economy was implicitly acknowledged in the main accomplishment of the conference—a broad agreement to ease the debt burden of about thirty "poorest of the poor" countries, most of them in sub-Saharan Africa. The debt of those countries, amounting to about $110 billion, represented only a small part of a growing and worrisome world debt. The combined debt of Mexico and Brazil was twice that of the thirty countries destined to be aided by the summit plan.

Turning from economics, the summit members approvingly noted that "changes" had taken place in Western relations with the Soviet Union "since last we met." In a Political Declaration, issued June 20, they said "this evolution" in Soviet-Western relations "has come about because the industrialized democracies have been strong and united."

Reagan's Farewell

In addition to Reagan, other leaders in attendance were Prime Minister Margaret Thatcher of Britain, President François Mitterand of France, Prime Minister Ciriaco De Mita of Italy, Prime Minister Noboru Takeshita of Japan, Chancellor Helmut Kohl of West Germany, and Prime Minister Brian Mulroney of Canada. Occupying an eighth seat at the summit was Jacques Delors, president of the European Community Commission. De Mita and Takeshita were attending their first economic summit.

In closing ceremonies at Roy Thomson Hall in Toronto, Reagan heard a chorus of praise for his leadership at the economic summits he had attended since 1981. The president also had the satisfaction of being told throughout the conference that the current prosperity in the West resulted from the kind of economic policies his administration had pursued: free markets, tax cuts, and deregulation.

Reagan's staunchest friend abroad, Prime Minister Thatcher, spoke of her "wholehearted support and affection for President Reagan." Mulroney, the host prime minister, said of the president: "We shall all miss his warmth and wisdom." Reagan, in turn, was lavish in his praise of Mulroney, leader of Canada's Progressive Conservative party, who was facing strong opposition in his country to a free-trade agreement between Canada and the United States that he and Reagan had signed in January. (Trade Pact with Canada, p. 571)

Writing from Toronto, Washington Post *reporter Lou Cannon said that as Reagan neared the end of his presidency, he was "on the whole far more popular with foreign leaders than he was seven years ago."*

Debt Relief Plan

The debt relief plan for the world's poorest countries called for lending governments to offer better loan terms, including longer repayment schedules, partial loan write-offs, and interest rate concessions. The agreement, seen at the summit as primarily a humanitarian gesture, represented a change in policy for the Reagan administration. Previously, it had opposed all forms of debt relief, depending instead on the so-called Baker Plan of encouraging private lending in return for economic reforms.

James A. Baker III, author of the plan in 1985 when he was secretary of the treasury, told reporters that the new position marked "a rather significant change in attitudes as far as the poorest of the poor are concerned." But Baker added, "These countries have no reasonable prospect of ever getting back on their feet." The United States was expected to do its share in the agreement by offering longer maturities. U.S. law prevented the government from writing off foreign loans.

Farm Subsidies

Reagan was unable to persuade the other leaders to agree to a plan for ending farm subsidies by the year 2000. While acknowledging that the subsidies distorted food prices worldwide and severely damaged the economies of poorer food-exporting countries, they balked at the prospect of eliminating aid to farmers.

Farm politics are viewed as even stronger in Western Europe and Japan than in the United States. A communiqué issued at the end of the summit merely called for reducing the subsidies and making the farm sector "more responsive to market signals."

Other Issues

Having rebuffed Reagan on agricultural subsidies, the six other national leaders supported him on his proposal to establish a special international task force to deal with the narcotics trade. United States officials said that one of the priorities of the task force would be to reduce "money-laundering" operations used by drug lords.

The leaders also endorsed Prime Minister Thatcher's plea that nations everywhere refuse hijacked aircraft permission to take off except when there was a clear threat to life.

Following are excerpts from the Political Declaration, issued June 20, 1988, and the Economic Declaration, issued June 21, 1988, at the Toronto Economic Summit:

POLITICAL DECLARATION

East-West

... In several important respects changes have taken place in relations between Western countries and the Soviet Union since we last met. For our part this evolution has come about because the industrialized democracies have been strong and united. In the Soviet Union greater freedom and openness will offer opportunities to reduce mistrust and build confidence. Each of us will respond positively to any such developments.

We welcome the beginning of the Soviet withdrawal of its occupation troops from Afghanistan. It must be total and apply to the entire country. The Afghan people must be able to choose their government freely. Each of us confirms our willingness to make our full contribution to the efforts of the international community to ensure the return of the refugees to their homeland, their resettlement, and the reconstruction of their country. We now look to the Soviet Union to make a constructive contribution to resolving other regional conflicts as well.

Since our last meeting, progress has been made between the United States and the Soviet Union in agreeing to reduce nuclear weapons in a manner which accords fully with the security interests of each of our countries. The INF Treaty, the direct result of Western firmness and unity, is the first treaty ever actually to reduce nuclear arms. It sets vitally important precedents for future arms control agreements: asymmetrical reductions and intrusive verification arrangements. We now look for deep cuts in U.S. and Soviet strategic offensive arms. . . .

Nonetheless, the massive presence of Soviet conventional forces in Eastern Europe, the ensuing conventional superiority of the Warsaw Pact, and its capacity to launch surprise attacks and large scale offensive operations, lie at the core of the security problem in Europe. The Soviet military buildup in the Far East is equally a major source of instability in Asia. . . .

Genuine peace cannot be established solely by arms control. It must be firmly based on respect for fundamental human rights. We urge the Soviet Union to move forward in ensuring human dignity and freedoms and to implement fully and strengthen substantially its commitments under the Helsinki process. Recent progress must be enshrined in law and practice, the painful barriers that divide people must come down, and the obstacles to emigration must be removed. . . .

We take positive note of Eastern countries' growing interest in ending their economic isolation, for example in the establishment and development of relations with the European Community. . . .

Terrorism

We strongly reaffirm our condemnation of terrorism in all its forms, including the taking of hostages. We renew our commitment to policies and measures agreed at previous Summits, in particular those against state-sponsored terrorism. . . .

We express support for work currently under way in the International Civil Aviation Organization aimed at strengthening international protection against hijackings. We welcome the most recent declaration adopted by the ICAO Council which endorses the principle that hijacked aircraft should not be allowed to take off once they have landed, except in circumstances as specified in the ICAO declaration.

We welcome the adoption this year in Montreal and Rome of two international agreements on aviation and maritime security to enhance the safety of travelers. . . .

Narcotics

. . . There is an urgent need for improved international cooperation in all appropriate fora on programs to counter all facets of the illicit drug problem, in particular production, trafficking, and financing of the drug trade. The complexity of the problem requires additional international cooperation, in particular to trace, freeze and confiscate the proceeds of drug traffickers, and to curb money laundering. . . .

We supported the initiative of the Government of the United States for a special task force to be convened to propose methods of improving cooperation in all areas including national, bilateral and multilateral efforts in the fight against narcotics.

ECONOMIC DECLARATION

. . . We observed a sharp contrast between the 1970s and 1980s. The former was a decade of high and rising inflation, declining productivity growth, policies dominated by short-term considerations, and frequently inadequate international policy cooperation. In the 1980s inflation has been brought under control, laying the basis for sustained strong growth and improved productivity. The result has been the longest period of economic growth in post-war history. However, the 1980s have seen the emergence of large external imbalances in the major industrial economies, greater exchange rate volatility, and debt-servicing difficulties in a number of developing countries. Our response to these developments has been an increased commitment to international cooperation, resulting in the intensified process of policy coordination adopted at the 1986 Tokyo Summit and further strengthened at the [1987] Venice Summit and in the Group of Seven [the seven summit members]. . . .

Since we last met, our economies have kept up the momentum of growth. Employment has continued to expand generally, inflation has been restrained, and progress has been made toward the correction of major external imbalances. These encouraging developments are cause for optimism, but not for complacency. To sustain non-inflationary growth will require a commitment to enhanced cooperation. This is the key to credibility and confidence. . . .

Macroeconomic Policies and Exchange

The Tokyo and Venice Summits have developed and strengthened the process of coordination of our economic policies. Developments in the wake of the financial strains last October demonstrate the effectiveness and resilience of the arrangements that have emerged. The policies, the short-term prospects, and the medium-term objectives and projections of our economies are being discussed regularly in the Group of Seven. The policies and performance are assessed on the basis of economic indicators. We welcome the progress made in refining the analytical use of indicators, as well as the addition to the existing indicators of a commodity-price indicator. The progress in coordination is contributing to the process of further improving the functioning of the international monetary system. . . .

The exchange rate changes in the past three years, especially the depreciation of the U.S. dollar against the Japanese yen and the major European currencies, have placed a major role in the adjustment of real trade balances. We endorse the Group of Seven's conclusion that either excessive fluctuation of exchange rates, a further decline of the dollar, or a rise in the dollar to an extent that becomes destabilizing to the adjustment process, could be counterproductive by damaging growth prospects in the world economy.

Structural Reforms

International cooperation involves more than coordination of macroeconomic policies. . . . We will continue to pursue structural reforms by removing barriers, unnecessary controls and regulations; increasing competition, while mitigating adverse effects on social groups or regions; removing disincentives to work, save, and invest, such as through tax reform; and by improving education and training. . . .

One of the major structural problems in both developed and developing countries is in the field of agricultural policies. . . . More market-oriented agricultural policies should assist in the achievement of important objectives such as preserving rural areas and family farming, raising quality standards and protecting the environment. . . .

. . . Countries must continue to resist protectionism and the temptation to adopt unilateral measures outside the framework of GATT [General Agreement on Tariffs and Trade] rules. In order to preserve a favourable negotiating climate, the participants should conscientiously implement the commitments to standstill and rollback that they have taken at Punta del Este and subsequent international meetings.

We strongly welcome the Free Trade Agreement between Canada and the USA, and the steady progress towards the target of the European Community to complete the internal market by 1992. It is our policy that these developments, together with other moves toward regional cooperation in which our countries are involved, should support the open, multilateral trading system and catalyze the liberalizing impact of the Uruguay Round [of world trade talks].

. . . It is vital that the GATT become a more dynamic and effective organization, particularly in regard to the surveillance of trade policies and dispute settlement procedures, with greater Ministerial involvement, and strengthened linkages with other international organizations. GATT disciplines must be improved so that members accept their obligations and ensure that disputes are resolved speedily, effectively and equitably. . . .

Debt of the Poorest

An increase in concessional resource flows is necessary to help the poorest developing countries resume sustained growth, especially in cases where it is extremely difficult for them to service their debts. Since Venice, progress in dealing with the debt burden of these countries has been encouraging. Paris Club creditors are rescheduling debt at extended grace and repayment periods. In addition, the recent enhancement of the IMF's Structural Adjustment Facility; the World Bank and Official Development Assistance (ODA) agencies' enhanced program of co-financing; and the fifth replenishment of the African Development Fund will mobilize a total of more than US $18 billion in favour of the poorest and most indebted countries undertaking adjustment efforts over the period 1988/90. Out of this total, US $15 billion will be channelled to sub-Saharan African countries.

We welcome proposals made by several of us to ease further the debt service burdens of the poorest countries that are undertaking internationally-approved adjustment programs. We have achieved consensus on rescheduling official debt of these countries within a framework of comparability that allows official creditors to choose among concessional interest rates usually on shorter maturities, longer repayment periods at commercial rates, partial write-offs of debt service obligations during the consolidation period, or a combination of these options. This approach allows official creditors to choose options consistent with their legal or budgetary constraints. . . .

Environment

. . . Threats to the environment recognize no boundaries. Their urgent nature requires strengthened international cooperation among all countries. Significant progress has been achieved in a number of environmental areas. The Montreal Protocol on Substances that Deplete the Ozone Layer is a milestone. All countries are encouraged to sign and ratify it.

Further action is needed. Global climate change, air, sea, and fresh water pollution, acid rain, hazardous substances, deforestation, and endangered species require priority attention. It is, therefore, timely that negotiations on a protocol on emissions of nitrogen oxides within the framework of the Geneva Convention on Long-range Transboundary Air Pollution be pursued energetically. The efforts of the United Nations Environment Program (UNEP) for an agreement on the transfrontier shipment of hazardous wastes should also be encouraged as well as the establishment of an intergovernmental panel on global climate change under the auspices of UNEP and the World Meteorological Organization (WMO). We also recognize the potential impact of agriculture on the environment, whether negative through over-intensive use of resources or positive in preventing desertification. . . .

COURT ON PRIVATE CLUBS
June 20, 1988

The Supreme Court on June 20 unanimously upheld the constitutionality of a New York City ordinance that outlawed discrimination against
women and minorities by large private clubs. The local law had been
challenged by a group of private clubs as an infringement on the
constitutional rights of association and equal protection.

The Court rejected these arguments on both technical and substantive
grounds, finding that the law had not affected the fundamental interests
of the private clubs in any significant way. The Court's otherwise
unanimous opinion did not apply to the analysis of the equal protection
issue. Justice Antonin Scalia disagreed with the majority's reasoning but
concurred in the result. A concurring opinion by Justice Sandra Day
O'Connor emphasized that the ruling did not extend the reach of
antidiscriminatory laws to all types of private clubs.

This ruling was the Court's third in recent years on the criteria local
and state authorities may exercise in prohibiting discrimination by
private organizations. In 1984 the Court held 7-0 that an all-male local
Jaycees' (Junior Chamber of Commerce) organization could be required
to accept women members under a Minnesota law that barred discrimination in "public accommodation." In 1987, in another 7-0 decision, the
Court ruled that California could apply its public accommodation law to
prohibit sex discrimination by Rotary Clubs. In all three cases it made it
clear that there were limits to the rights of free association guaranteed by
the First Amendment.

In this case, New York State Club Association v. City of New York, *the Court accepted the argument that because large, all-male clubs often were places where business deals were transacted, local authorities had a legitimate interest in seeing that women and minorities were not excluded arbitrarily.*

In 1965, shortly after national civil rights legislation was enacted, New York City prohibited discrimination in public places such as hotels, stores, theaters, and on public transportation. But that law permitted discrimination by institutions, clubs, and places of accommodation that could prove they were distinctly private. In 1984 the City Council extended the law's antidiscrimination provisions to include clubs having more than 400 members, providing regular meal service, and regularly receiving payment from nonmembers who use club facilities "for furtherance of trade or business." However, clubs established under the benevolent orders' law or under the religious corporation statutes were exempt and could continue to be considered distinctly private.

As soon as the new law became effective, and before it had been enforced, the New York State Club Association challenged it on constitutional grounds. The association argued that the mere existence of the statute—quite aside from its application—violated member rights to free association and to equal protection. The nature of the legal challenge proved to be important.

The Court held that in order to argue that a law is invalid on its face, it must be shown either that the law could never be applied in a valid manner, or that it was so broad that it would affect the rights of others even though it may have been applied appropriately to the party bringing suit. The Court found that the association had not met either test.

The second main issue was whether a law that applied to some private clubs but not to benevolent and religious associations violated the Constitution's equal protection clause. The law, for example, did not apply to some private groups, such as the American Legion, Loyal Order of Moose, Catholic War Veterans, and Veterans of Foreign Wars. They were excluded primarily because the City Council had made a legislative finding that neither benevolent associations nor religious groups were the source of the discriminatory problem it was trying to correct. As legislative classifications are presumed valid, the ordinance was upheld.

Justice Scalia's difference with the majority on this issue centered on the extent of the logical connection between the legislative classification and the purpose of the law. However, he agreed that the association had not established that the connection was unreasonable and thus reached the same result as the majority.

While the Court upheld the law, it did not strike down sex discrimina-

tion at private clubs. It also left open many issues concerning the extent of the right to associate privately.

Following are excerpts from the majority opinion of Justice Byron R. White in the case of New York State Club Association, Inc. v. City of New York et al., *decided June 20, 1988, and from the concurring opinions of Justice Sandra Day O'Connor and Justice Antonin Scalia:*

No. 86-1836

New York State Club Association, Inc., Appellant *v.* City of New York et al.	On appeal from the Court of Appeals of New York

[June 20, 1988]

JUSTICE WHITE delivered the opinion of the Court.

New York City has adopted a local law that forbids discrimination by certain private clubs. The New York Court of Appeals rejected a facial challenge to this law based on the First and Fourteenth Amendments. We sit in review of that judgment.

I

In 1965, New York City adopted a Human Rights Law that prohibits discrimination by any "place of public accommodation, resort or amusement." This term is defined broadly in the Law to cover such various places as hotels, restaurants, retail stores, hospitals, laundries, theatres, parks, public conveyances, and public halls, in addition to numerous other places that are specifically listed. Yet the Law also exempted from its coverage various public educational facilities and "any institution, club or place of accommodation which proves that it is in its nature distinctly private." The city adopted this Law soon after the Federal Government adopted civil rights legislation to bar discrimination in places of public accommodation, Civil Rights Act of 1964. . . .

In 1984, New York City amended its Human Rights Law . . . to prohibit discrimination in certain private clubs that are determined to be sufficiently "public" in nature that they do not fit properly within the exemption for "any institution, club or place of accommodation which is in its nature distinctly private." As the City Council stated at greater length:

> . . . One barrier to the advancement of women and minorities in the business and professional life of the city is the discriminatory practices of certain membership organizations where business deals are often made

and personal contacts valuable for business purposes, employment and professional advancement are formed. While such organizations may avowedly be organized for social, cultural, civic or educational purposes, and while many perform valuable services to the community, the commercial nature of some of the activities occurring therein and the prejudicial impact of these activities on business, professional and employment opportunities of minorities and women cannot be ignored.

For these reasons, the City Council found that "the public interest in equal opportunity" outweighs "the interest in private association asserted by club members." It cautioned, however, that it did not purpose "to interfere in club activities or subject club operations to scrutiny beyond what is necessary in good faith to enforce the human rights law"....

[II omitted]

III

New York City's Human Rights Law authorizes the city's Human Rights Commission or any aggrieved individual to initiate a complaint against any "place of public accommodation, resort or amusement" that is alleged to have discriminated in violation of the Law. The Commission investigates the complaint and determines whether probable cause exists to find a violation. When probable cause is found, the Commission may settle the matter by conciliatory measures, if possible; if the matter is not settled, the Commission schedules a hearing in which the defending party may present evidence and answer the charges against it. After the hearing is concluded, the Commission states its findings of fact and either dismisses the complaint or issues a cease-and-desist order. Any person aggrieved by an order of the commission is entitled to seek judicial review of the order, and the Commission may seek enforcement of its orders in judicial proceedings.

None of these procedures has come into play in this case, however, for appellant brought this suit challenging the constitutionality of the statute on its face before any enforcement proceedings were initiated against any of its member associations. Although such facial challenges are sometimes permissible and often have been entertained, especially when speech protected by the First Amendment is at stake, to prevail on a facial attack the plaintiff must demonstrate that the challenged law either "could never be applied in a valid manner" or that even though it may be validly applied to the plaintiff and others, it nevertheless is so broad that it "may inhibit the constitutionally protected speech of third parties."...

We are unpersuaded that appellant is entitled to make either one of these two distinct facial challenges....

... The City Council explained that it limited the Law's coverage to large clubs and excluded smaller clubs, benevolent orders, and religious corporations because the latter associations "have not been identified in testimony before the Council as places where business activity is prevalent." ... The Court rejected a claim that the statute violated the Equal

Protection Clause, finding on the evidence before it that the legislative distinction was justified because benevolent orders were judged not to pose the same dangers as other groups that were required to file the documents. In addition, New York state law indicates that benevolent orders and religious corporations are unique and thus that a rational basis exists for their exemption here. For well over a century, the State has extended special treatment in the law to these associations, and each continues to be treated in a separate body of legislation. . . .

The City Council's explantion for exempting benevolent orders and religious corporations from the Law's coverage reflects a view that these associations are different in kind, at least in the crucial respect of whether business activity is prevalent among them, from the associations on whose behalf appellant has brought suit. Appellant has the burden of showing that this view is erroneous and that the issue is not truly debatable, a burden that appellant has failed to carry. . . .

We therefore affirm the judgment below.

So ordered.

JUSTICE O'CONNOR, with whom JUSTICE KENNEDY joins, concurring.

I agree with the Court's conclusion that the facial challenge to Local Law 63 must fail. I write separately only to note that nothing in the Court's opinion in any way undermines or denigrates the importance of any associational interests at stake. . . .

In a city as large and diverse as New York City, there surely will be organizations that fall within the potential reach of Local Law 63 and yet are deserving of constitutional protection. For example, in such a large city a club with over 400 members may still be relatively intimate in nature, so that a constitutional right to control membership takes precedence. Similarly, there may well be organizations whose expressive purposes would be substantially undermined if they were unable to confine their membership to those of the same sex, race, religion, or ethnic background, or who share some other such common bond. The associational rights of such organizations must be respected. . . .

JUSTICE SCALIA, concurring in part and concurring in the judgment. . . .

With respect to the equal protection issue discussed in Part IV of the opinion, I do not believe that the mere fact that benevolent orders "are unique," suffices to establish that a rational basis exists for their exemption. As forgiving as the rational basis test is, it does not go that far. There must at least be some plausible connection between the respect in which they are unique and the purpose of the law. . . .

POPE JOHN PAUL'S
VISIT TO AUSTRIA
June 23-27, 1988

Pope John Paul II encountered the "Waldheim problem" on a visit to Austria, June 23-27, and it overshadowed all other events on his five-day journey. The problem, as presented in the Western press and some Catholic church publications, was how to deal with Kurt Waldheim, Austria's president and a former secretary general of the United Nations (1972-1982), who long concealed his service in a unit of Hitler's army that engaged in war crimes.

The disclosure about Waldheim's service in World War II was made by the World Jewish Congress in 1986, but it did not prevent him from being elected president of Austria later that year. Although the Austrian president's duties are mostly ceremonial, Waldheim's prominence was sufficient to focus international attention on his—and his country's—role in the Nazi atrocities.

Facing the "Waldheim Problem"

In 1987 Waldheim became the first head of a friendly nation to be barred from the United States. The U.S. Justice Department, acting under terms of a law that excludes several categories of unwanted foreigners, said it had evidence that Waldheim, while serving as a lieutenant in the German army in 1942-1945, was involved in shipping civilians from occupied Greece and Yugoslavia to Nazi concentration camps.

Upon disclosure of his past activities, Waldheim was shunned by most foreign leaders, who declined to pay official visits to Austria or invite him abroad. Despite objections from many quarters, particularly Jewish groups, Pope John Paul permitted Waldheim to come to the Vatican in 1987 as a visiting head of state. At the time, papal authorities said Waldheim the officeholder, not the individual, was being received.

The "Waldheim problem" flared up again early in 1988. On February 9, an international commission of historians appointed by the Austrian government concluded that while it had no evidence that Waldheim himself committed war crimes, he must have known about his military unit's involvement in them and that he later attempted to cover up his war record. In his autobiography, for instance, Waldheim said he was drafted into the German army, wounded on the Russian front, and discharged in 1941, when he began the study of law. After his real military service became known, Waldheim insisted that he was but a junior officer with no knowledge of wartime atrocities.

A Vatican spokesman said John Paul's visit to Austria—the thirty-eighth foreign journey in his ten-year papacy and the second trip to Austria—was pastoral and not political, being made at the request of the bishops in that predominantly Catholic country. The timing of the papal visit nearly coincided with the fiftieth anniversary of Germany's takeover of Austria in March 1938—reviving an old argument of whether Austria was Hitler's "first victim," as Austrians tend to claim, or a willing accomplice. Promptly upon arriving in Vienna on June 23, John Paul indicated that he saw Austria as the victim. "In this year of 1988," he said, "I should like to particularly recall the great trials and cruel tyranny that Austria, along with other nations, had to suffer in the not too distant past."

Waldheim greeted John Paul in the president's offices at the Hofsburg Palace. Soon afterward, when the pope went to say mass at the Cathedral of St. Stephen in the heart of Vienna's historic central area, protesting American Jews displayed banners that read "Nazi Waldheim" and "Don't Meet Waldheim." In New York, the World Jewish Congress released a statement saying: "The Pope's meeting with his flock in Austria is not what troubles the Jewish community. It is the deliberate inclusion of meetings with Kurt Waldheim on his itinerary."

Criticism over Death Camp Omission

The next day John Paul went to Mauthausen, the site of a death camp the Nazis operated in Austria from 1938 until the end of the war in 1945, and he also met in Vienna with Austrian Jewish leaders. Some 6,000 Jews remain in Austria from a pre-1938 population of more than 200,000. At Mauthausen, he spoke of the suffering caused by "an insane ideology" and called for efforts to make certain it would never happen again.

At the Vienna meeting, the pope was welcomed by Paul Grosz, president of the Austrian Jewish Community, who observed that events of the previous two years—an allusion to Waldheim's election—demonstrated that "many Austrians have still not come to terms with their past." Grosz then asked the pontiff to say publicly that they should acknowledge their country's participation in the Nazi era. John Paul did not respond directly to that request, although on other occasions in Austria he mentioned the country's "burdensome legacy of the past."

Pope John Paul told Jewish leaders he was "deeply moved by your words" and had "deeply engraved in my soul" the "intolerable pain" Austrian Jews suffered in the Nazi era. The meeting did not still the criticism that he was insensitive to the Jewish need to keep alive the memory of the Holocaust, however. At Mauthausen, where John Paul spoke emotionally of human suffering and invoked the names of three Catholics who suffered martyrdom in Nazi camps, he made no mention of Jews—who there, as in most other Nazi death camps, were the principal victims. A critic commented afterward in the American liberal Catholic magazine Commonweal: *"The Mauthausen stop, if intended, even in part, to neutralize the objections of meeting with Waldheim, actually aggravated an already difficult situation."*

Despite these difficulties, the pope was greeted by large and enthusiastic crowds at many of his twenty public appearances in Austria. At Eisenstadt, near the Hungarian border, he celebrated what was described as the first East-West mass. Some 50,000 Hungarians took advantage of a recent easing of travel restrictions to attend, as did 13,000 Croatian Catholics from Yugoslavia. They were joined, according to police estimates, by 17,000 Austrians.

Waldheim traveled to Innsbruck to bid the pope farewell before his departure for Rome on June 27. The pontiff greeted the president warmly at an outdoor mass on the site of the 1964 and 1976 winter Olympic games. In his homily, the pope warned against "bitter confrontations among Christians themselves" and "cynical criticism of the church even in the church's own publications."

Following are excerpts from the remarks of Pope John Paul II at the former Mauthausen concentration camp and to the leaders of the Austrian Jewish Community in Vienna, and from the welcoming remarks of Paul Grosz on the Jewish Community's behalf, all made on June 24, 1988 (translated from the German by National Catholic News Service):

REMARKS AT MAUTHAUSEN

... From this, one of the most terrifying experiences in its history, Europe emerges defeated ... defeated in what seemed to be its inheritance and mission.... "Its ways are blocked." The burden of doubt has come down hard on the history of people, nations and continents.

Are the questions of our own conscience strong enough? Are the pangs of conscience that have remained in us strong enough?

You people who have experienced fearful tortures—how worthy you are of the Lamentations of Jeremiah!

What is your last word? Your word after so many years which separate our generation from the sufferings in the Mauthausen concentration camp and in many others?

You people of yesterday, and you people of today, if the system of extermination camps continues somewhere in the world even today, tell us, what message can our century convey to the next?

Tell us, in our great hurry, haven't we forgotten your hell? Aren't we extinguishing traces of great crimes in our memories and consciousness?

Tell us, what direction should Europe and humanity follow "after Auschwitz" . . . and "after Mauthausen"? Is the direction we are following away from those past dreadful experiences the right one?

Tell us, how should today's person be and how should this generation of humanity live in the wake of the great defeat of the human being? How must that person be? How much should he require of himself?

Tell us, how must nations and societies be? How must Europe go on living?

Speak, you have the right to do so—you who have suffered and lost your lives. We have the duty to listen to your testimony.

Hasn't humanity and the system established by humanity aroused the anger of God with the abuses they have created?

Hasn't humanity darkened the image of God with the abuses they have created?

Nevertheless, the prophet calls out with the words of Lamentations: "The favors of the Lord are not exhausted, his mercies are not spent. They are renewed each morning, so great is his faithfulness" (Lam 3:22-23).

Yes. Faithfulness. There is only one "man of suffering" who has been true to all people of suffering, here in Mauthausen and wherever in the world they endure or have endured an inhuman system of contempt.

There was such a man of suffering, and such a person continues to exist. His cross remains ever present in world history.

Should we turn away from the cross? Can we pass it by in the future? Europe, can you pass it by?

Must you not at least stand by it, even if the generations of your sons and daughters move away from it, and the past vanishes?

Christ! The Christ of so many human sufferings, humiliations and devastation. Christ, crucified and resurrected. In this place, one of so many, which cannot be erased from the history of this century.

I, the bishop of Rome and the successor to Peter the apostle, beg you fervently: Remain!

Remain and live on in our future!

Remain and live on!

Where should we go? You have the word of life that has been covered up neither by death nor by destruction. . . . You have the words of eternal life (cf Jn. 6:68).

Blessed Marcel Callo, martyr of Mauthausen; and Blessed Sister Teresa Benedicta of the Cross, Edith Stein; and St. Maximilian Kolbe, honored and venerated martyrs of Auschwitz: Pray for all those who were tortured and martyred in these places! Pray for all the victims of unjust power in both the present and past—pray, too, for their executioners!

Jesus Christ, the lamb of God, have mercy on them all, have mercy on us all!

MEETING WITH JEWISH LEADERS
Address by Paul Grosz

The representatives of the Jewish communities in Austria extend to the spiritual leader of the 850 million Roman Catholic Christians, our brother in God, Pope John Paul II, our greeting of peace: Shalom.

Your Holiness, we are very pleased that, on your second pastoral visit to Austria, the occasion for this meeting arose. As we are all aware, we live in times when a fraternal rapprochement—and a brotherly dialogue among religions—have become imperatives to peace. Our common task is to uphold everywhere the God-given values intrinsic to the miracle and the dignity of life. But we are only human and even our utmost efforts are often wrought with paradox.

There is a story about a rabbi, whose disciples say to their revered teacher: "I love you." The wise teacher replies to his students with a question: "Do you know what hurts me?" Surprised and shocked by the response, the students responded by asking how they could know. To which the rabbi said: "If you do not know what hurts me, then how can you say you love me?"

The second ecumenical council became a turning point in the painful 2,000-year-old relationship between Jews and Christians: the church definitely removed from Christian doctrine the teaching of contempt and the accusation of deicide against the Jewish people.

We regard our meeting today as a continuation of the fruitful dialogue initiated by the second ecumenical council, based on the dignity and equality of both partners. Several of the post-ecumenical council documents, your visit to the Rome synagogue and your many heartfelt statements on the Shoah have greatly contributed to bringing us closer.

Of late, there have been some encounters of historical significance between representatives of the church and the Jewish community in Austria. The courageous stance taken by the bishop of Innsbruck must be stressed. In particular his efforts to eradicate the cult of Rinn (based on the legend of ritual murder) has [sic] not gone unnoticed.

The moral impact of such an authoritative voice as that of the Roman Catholic Church can contribute to impeding a repetition of that deterioration of moral values that led to Hitler's murderous campaign directed toward the annihilation of European Jewry.

To have been a victim of this drama of human failure is no merit in itself. Nonetheless, as survivors of the Shoah, we are obliged to preserve the memory of the millions of our brothers and sisters thus killed; moreover, to claim respect for and deference to the sanctity of their martyrdom.

To achieve this end, we must contest all endeavors to make banal the unique tragedy of the Jews in the Shoah or to equate it with other events of this evil period.

We cannot forget and we must not forget. It is indispensable for us to preserve the knowledge of the Shoah, to pass it on from generation to generation. Only in this way will we ensure that such a conscience is born, that will become a safeguard against future atrocities. For whoever forgets his own past is condemned to relive it.

The representatives of the decimated Jewish community in Austria, which now numbers only a few thousand, bear the great burden of a thousand-year-old history laden with depressing and abominable, yet monotonously repetitive events, such as dispossession and oppression, expulsion and persecution.

And yet, we have always preserved our faith in God; we have remained true to our Torah and endeavored to fulfill our prophetic mission to become light unto the nations.

The occurrences in Austria in the past two years have shown—and a fact which became particularly evident at the time of the president's visit to the Vatican—that many Austrians have still not come to terms with their past. It is considered patriotic to remain silent about the matter; unpatriotic to speak out. One prefers to hold foreigners or Jews responsible for any problems that crop up.

With deep regret, we missed a public statement from Your Holiness, similar to the one made in Cologne, concerning the nation's relationship to its past.

We would like to ask Your Holiness to make use, this time, of the authority that surrounds your person and of the love that the Austrian people hold for you, to stress the significance of conscientiously and consciously examining their own history.

The Austrian Jewish community also sets high hopes for another aspect of your pastoral visit.

There are still too many areas where the teachings of the Second Vatican Council have not yet penetrated. We hope that the words of Your Holiness will find their way to the hearts of the Austrian people, thus enabling the contributions of the ecumenical council to take root.

Last, Your Holiness, permit me to refer to Israel.

Owing to the special relationship with the state of Israel, we sincerely regret that full diplomatic relations between Israel and the Holy See have not yet been established.

As the Holy See has interests in this region too, it is in a position to make considerable contributions toward the peace efforts in the Middle East. To us, this appears to be practicable only when the Vatican will have established normal diplomatic relations with all the countries concerned; therefore also the state of Israel.

The diplomatic recognition of Israel would represent a clear rejection of Palestinian terrorism, whose declared intention it is to destroy Israel. In addition, the normalization of diplomatic relations between the two states would help to delegitimize that brand of anti-Semitism that is disguised as anti-Zionism.

Your Holiness, as the heir of St. Peter, you have always called for peace and justice, as well as condemning both terrorism and anti-Semitism. Let us seek a way to solve the problem of the Middle East together! Ultimately, in the quest to bring tranquility to this troubled part of the world—to Jews, Christians and Moslems alike.

We have shared with you our grief, in the spirit of the introductory Hassidic tale. Let us set out as brothers, to seek the truth, to apprehend the complexities from which we descend and with which we must come to terms; let us speak and listen tirelessly, if hand in hand we wish to create a better future.

Your Holiness, we wish you shalom and may you be blessed in your coming and in your going.

ADDRESS TO JEWISH COMMUNITY

Honorable president of the Jewish communities, distinguished chief rabbi, ladies and gentlemen:

The prophet Jeremiah (31, 15f) says: "In Ramah is heard the sound of moaning, of bitter weeping! Rachel mourns her children.... Because her children are no more."

Such weeping has also been the keynote of the words of welcome which you, on behalf of the Jewish communities in Austria, have just addressed to me. I am deeply moved by your words. I return your greeting in a spirit of love and respect, and I assure you that this love is acutely aware of the grief you feel. Fifty years ago the synagogues in the city were burning. Thousands of people were sent from here to their deaths, countless are those who were driven to flight. Their intolerable pain, their suffering and their tears are before my eyes and have become deeply engraved in my soul. Truly one can only love those whom he knows.

I am filled with joy that in the course of my pastoral visit I have also been given the opportunity to meet with you. May this meeting be taken as a sign of mutual respect and may it testify to our willingness to learn more about each other, to overcome deeply rooted fears, to share our experiences and learn to trust one another.

"Shalom," "Peace be with you"—this religious word of welcome is a call to peace. Peace is of central importance to our meeting this morning, the morning before the Sabbath; it is of central importance also to us

Christians, as it was the word said by our Lord to the apostles in the hall of the Last Supper after his resurrection. *Peace* in this sense means an opportunity to forgive and be forgiven, to show and be shown mercy—forgiveness and mercy, the most eminent qualities of our God, of the God of the covenant. You have this assurance, you celebrate this assurance in your faith when you observe in a festive manner Yom Kippur, the great Day of Atonement.

We Christians contemplate this mystery of atonement in the heart of Christ who—pierced by our sins and the sins of the whole world—died for us on the cross. This means the utmost solidarity and brotherliness born of mercy. Hatred is wiped out; hatred vanishes. The covenant of love is renewed. This is the covenant the church lives in faith; in it is rooted its deep and mysterious union, in love and faith, with the Jewish people. No historic event, however painful it may be, can be so dominant that it might contradict this reality, which is part of God's plan for our salvation and our fraternal reconciliation.

The relationship between Jews and Christians has much changed and improved since the Second Vatican Council and its solemn declaration *Nostra Aetate.* ... In the meantime, we have moved forward on the road to reconciliation, one symbol of which my visit to the synagogue in Rome was meant to be.

Still, you and we are weighed down by memories of Shoah, the murder of millions of Jews in camps of destruction. It would be unjust and wrong to attribute these unspeakable crimes to Christianity. Much to the contrary, these events show us the horrifying face of a world without God, of a world even inimical to God, of a world whose stated intent it was to destroy not only the Jewish people but also the faith of those who venerate the Redeemer of the world in the Jew Jesus of Nazareth. Solemn protests and appeals on the part of a few individuals only served to nurture this fanaticism.

An adequate consideration of the suffering and the martyrdom of the Jewish people is impossible without relating it in its deepest dimension to the experience of faith that has characterized its history, from the faith of Abraham to the exodus from the bondage of Egypt to the covenant on Mount Sinai. It is a constant progression in faith and obedience in response to the loving call of God. As I said last year before representatives of the Jewish community in Warsaw, from these cruel sufferings may rise even deeper hope, a warning call to all humanity that may serve to save us all. Remembering Shoah means hoping that it will never happen again, and working to ensure that it does not.

Faced with this immeasurable suffering we cannot remain cold; but faith teaches us that God never forsakes those who suffer persecution but reveals himself to them and enlightens through them all peoples on the road to salvation. This is what the holy Scripture teaches us, this is what was revealed to us by the prophets, by Isaiah and Jeremiah. It is in faith, the common heritage of Jews and Christians, that the history of Europe has its roots. For us Christians all human suffering finds its ultimate meaning in the cross of Jesus Christ. This does not prevent us from feeling solidarity with the deep wounds that have been inflicted on the Jewish people by persecution, especially in this century, by contemporary anti-Semitism; on the contrary, it makes this solidarity a bounden duty.

We must do all we can to continue the process of full reconciliation between Jews and Christians, at all levels of the relationship between our communities. Cooperation and joint studies should be undertaken in order to inquire into the significance of the Shoah. We have to trace, and wherever possible, eliminate, the causes of anti-Semitism or, more generally, of "religious warfare." Seeing what has already been achieved by ecumenism, I trust that it will be possible to speak frankly with one another about rivalries, radicalism and conflicts of the past. We must try to see them in their historical context and to overcome them in a common effort for peace, for a coherent testimony to faith and for the fostering of moral values to guide individuals and nations. . . .

Catholics in Austria, bishops and the faithful, as well as a variety of associations, have for many years been actively engaged in this extensive program of action, to which we invite Jews, Christians and all people of good will. Only recently, some fruitful encounters with members of the Jewish community have taken place in Vienna.

Harmony and unity among the different groups in a nation are also an essential prerequisite for an effective contribution to the promotion of peace and understanding among peoples, as the history of Austria has shown over the last few decades. The cause of peace is dear to the hearts of us all, in particular in the Holy Land, in Israel, Lebanon, in the Middle East. With these regions we are linked by deep biblical, historical, religious and cultural roots. According to the prophets of Israel, peace is the fruit of law and justice and at the same time an undeserved gift of the messianic era. It is for this reason that violence of any sort has to be done away with in this area, violence which repeats old mistakes and in this way engenders hatred, fanaticism and religious integralism, attitudes which are inimical to harmony among people. It is for everyone to search his conscience in accordance with their responsibility and competence. Above all, however, it is imperative that we promote constructive discussions between Jews, Christians and Moslems so that our common testimony to our faith in the "God of Abraham, the God of Isaac and the God of Jacob" (Ex. 3:6) become fruitful in our search for mutual understanding and fraternal living together without detriment to the rights of any person or group.

It is in this spirit that any initiative of the Holy See should be seen when it endeavors to seek recognition of the same dignity for the Jewish people in the state of Israel and for the Palestinian people. As I stressed last year before representatives of Jewish communities in the United States, the Jewish people has a right to a country of its own, as any other nation has under international law.

The same, however, holds for the Palestinian people, many of whom have become homeless and are refugees. Through mutual understanding and compromise, solutions will finally have to be found which result in just, comprehensive and permanent peace in the region. If only forgiveness and love are abundantly sown, the tares of hatred will no longer be able to grow; they will be choked. To remember Shoah also means to stand up against the seed of violence and to protect and nurture, patiently and persistently, any tender shoot of peace and freedom.

In the spirit of Christian reconciliation I return your shalom from the bottom of my heart and ask of the Lord the gift of fraternal unity and the blessing of the almighty and all-bountiful God of Abraham, your Father and ours in faith.

PRESIDENTIAL COMMISSION REPORT ON AIDS

June 24, 1988

In a report issued June 24, a presidential advisory commission recommended measures to protect the public from the human immunodeficiency virus (HIV)—which causes AIDS (acquired immune deficiency syndrome), assist in finding a cure, and provide care for those already afflicted. President Ronald Reagan had created the commission by executive order exactly one year earlier in response to complaints that his administration had failed to provide strong leadership in the nation's fight against the epidemic. In his order, the president instructed the commission to report on "the public health dangers including the medical, legal, ethical, social, and economic impact, from the spread of the HIV and resulting illnesses."

The commission was controversial from its inception. The thirteen members named to the commission by the White House were criticized by AIDS activists and many in the research and public health community as lacking in experience with the disease and having a conservative ideological bias. Only reluctantly did the administration name a homosexual representative to the commission, geneticist Frank Lilly, even though homosexuals comprised the largest group affected by AIDS.

For the first three months of its existence, the commission seemed to bear out the critics. That period was, in the words of an internal commission document, "disastrous." Persistent reports of ideological infighting, lack of focus, weak leadership, and nonexistent White House support culminated in October 1987 in the resignations of the chairman, Dr. W. Eugene Mayberry, chief executive of the Mayo Clinic, and his executive assistant, Dr. Woodrow A. Myers, Jr., health commissioner of Indiana.

James D. Watkins, a retired admiral who had been chief of naval operations, was chosen to replace Mayberry and was credited with quickly bringing leadership and direction to the faltering commission. He hired a large, professional staff, divided the commission's task into manageable subjects, and scheduled more than forty hearings throughout the country. In these hearings, the commission heard the testimony of more than 600 witnesses on all aspects of the AIDS epidemic. An interim report, issued February 24, 1988, helped convince skeptics that the commission was taking its mandate seriously. The report emphasized that needle-sharing among drug users was a key means of spreading the disease, and it proposed a $2 billion expansion of drug treatment facilities to provide "treatment on demand" to intravenous (IV) drug abusers.

Report's Wide-Ranging Recommendations

The final report was both wide ranging and specific, setting forth almost 600 recommendations in its 201 pages. In what was widely regarded as the central recommendation of the report, the commission directly challenged administration policy by calling for federal legislation to prevent discrimination against victims: "HIV-related discrimination is impairing this nation's ability to limit the spread of the epidemic.... Public health officials will not be able to gain the confidence and cooperation of infected individuals or those at high risk for infection if such individuals fear that they will be unable to retain their jobs and their housing.... This fear ... will undermine our efforts to contain the HIV epidemic, and will leave HIV-infected individuals isolated and alone." The report recommended laws to protect the confidentiality of HIV test results.

The commission urged states to apply criminal penalties to persons who knowingly transmit the HIV virus, and state boards of education to require AIDS instruction in schools, beginning in the elementary grades. The commission strongly endorsed voluntary testing as the best means of monitoring and interrupting the spread of the virus. It favored mandatory testing only for prisoners who were sex offenders.

In October 1987 the American Medical Association had rejected any expansion of mandatory AIDS testing, advocated frankness in educational material, and called for legislation to protect the civil rights of the AIDS victims and people being tested for exposure to HIV. (AMA Report on AIDS, Historic Documents of 1987, p. 817)

Response and Plan of Action

The report received widespread praise, even from those who had originally been critical of the commission. "I am very much surprised," said Mathilde Krim, president of the American Foundation for AIDS Research. "The big difference was made by Admiral Watkins and his total lack of prejudice and preconceived ideas." Rep. Henry A. Waxman, D-Calif., a leading voice in the House on health affairs, called the report "a major contribution to AIDS policy."

Many political conservatives, however, disagreed with the commission's stand on confidentiality and antibias legislation. Some considered such legislation as a protection of homosexuals and drug addicts, and thus morally offensive. Others championed the administration's view that discrimination problems are better handled through state rather than federal laws.

The White House reception of the report was low-key and lukewarm. President Reagan forwarded it to Dr. Donald Ian MacDonald, his special adviser on drug policy, for review. On August 2, the administration responded by outlining its "AIDS action plan." It ordered all federal agencies to adopt AIDS employment policies based on guidelines issued in March 1988 by the Office of Personnel Management. Those guidelines called for federal employees infected with HIV to be allowed to continue working as long as they were performing competently and did not pose a safety or health threat to themselves or others. A number of issues were referred to federal agencies for further study. The Justice Department was ordered to determine the need for antidiscrimination legislation.

Following are excerpts from the "Report of the Presidential Commission on the Human Immunodeficiency Virus Epidemic," issued June 24, 1988:

Executive Summary

The Human Immunodeficiency Virus (HIV) epidemic will be a challenging factor in American life for years to come and should be a concern to all Americans. Recent estimates suggest that almost 500,000 Americans will have died or progressed to later stages of the disease by 1992.

Even this incredible number, however, does not reflect the current gravity of the problem. One to 1.5 million Americans are believed to be infected with the human immunodeficiency virus but are not yet ill enough to realize it.

The recommendations of the Commission seek to strike a proper balance between our obligation as a society toward those members of society who have HIV and those members of society who do not have the virus. To slow or stop the spread of the virus, to provide proper medical care for those who have contracted the virus, and to protect the rights of both infected and non-infected persons requires a careful balancing of interests in a highly complex society.

Knowledge is a critical weapon against HIV—knowledge about the virus and how it is transmitted, knowledge of how to maintain one's health, knowledge of one's own infection status. It is critical too that knowledge lead to responsibility toward oneself and others. It is the responsibility of all Americans to become educated about HIV. It is the responsibility of those infected not to infect others. It is the responsibility of all citizens to treat those infected with HIV with respect and compassion. All individuals should be responsible for their actions and the consequences of those actions. . . .

Chapter One: Incidence and Prevalence

Late in 1980, small numbers of patients in several widely separated locations sought treatment for an unusual pattern of disease symptoms. In all cases their physicians found that even the most aggressive treatment proved ineffective in controlling the unusually virulent infections. When conferring with colleagues across the country, the physicians treating these persons found that similar patients were appearing elsewhere, often in small patient clusters, with identical patterns of disease and patient histories. Many patients had Kaposi's sarcoma, a skin lesion usually benign, but in these patients aggressively malignant. Others had *Pneumocystis carinii* pneumonia, a rare lung infection. Many patients had both, and all were unresponsive to treatment and rapidly died.

Because so many of these patients also had sexually transmitted diseases, including parasitic and fungal infections, and had histories of multiple other conditions, such as hepatitis or drug use, it was difficult to isolate what was making them critically ill. As time passed and the patient population increased, medical researchers suggested that the cause was a specific combination of several infectious diseases. Those who thought the cause was a single agent suggested cytomegalovirus, a new form of syphilis, or a rarely seen parasite that irreversibly damaged the immune system. Still others felt that this disease might be the result of an organism never before seen: a new virus.

Modeling AIDS

As the first cases of acquired immune deficiency syndrome (AIDS) were identified, nationwide surveillance activities were initiated to monitor the spread of the disease. . . .

The case definition of AIDS has undergone revisions, and in September 1987, the new definition was expanded to include wasting syndrome and central nervous system manifestations, increasing the number of reportable cases. As of June 6, 1988, 64,506 cases of AIDS have been reported to CDC [Center for Disease Control]. . . .

Modeling HIV Infection

Disease surveillance began early in the epidemic, before the human immunodeficiency virus (HIV) had been identified or isolated, and before it was known that there could be a lengthy period of infection prior to illness. Because at that time it was possible to identify only those individuals in whom disease was far enough advanced to be symptomatic, monitoring the epidemic meant monitoring disease, rather than monitoring infection. The early concentration on the clinical manifestation of AIDS has had the unintended effect of misleading the public as to the extent of the infection in the population, from initial infection to seroconversion, to an antibody positive asymptomatic stage to initial indicative symptoms to full-blown AIDS. Continued emphasis on AIDS has also impeded long-term planning efforts necessary to effectively allocate resources for prevention and health care. Decisions on who will receive care, and whose costs will be covered, focused only on those most seriously ill. Continuing to use only the term "AIDS" to make treatment, reimbursement, or prevention program decisions is anachronistic and a policy we can no longer afford.

While it is of value to continue monitoring diagnosed AIDS cases, public policy and prevention efforts should be based on an understanding of the extent and distribution of HIV in the population and on the rate at which new infections occur. This is especially critical in dealing with HIV, for which the average length of time between infection and diagnosis is at least eight years, according to the Institute of Medicine.

In 1986, during a Public Health Service conference in Coolfont, West Virginia, public health experts, using limited data, estimated the number of persons in the United States infected with HIV from one million to 1.5 million. Since that time, additional data have become available, particularly on the size of certain population groups and the HIV prevalence in populations at higher risk of infection.

Current knowledge of HIV prevalence is limited by the relatively small proportion of the potentially infected population who have been tested, either as part of specially organized research/surveillance studies or as individuals concerned about their own possible infection. It is also limited by a lack of uniformity in reporting procedures, specifically, from physicians and laboratories to states, and from states to CDC. It is critical that CDC begin now to collect HIV infection data from the states, not just case reports. . . .

At President Reagan's persistent direction, CDC has undertaken a massive project of HIV surveillance and data collection. The family of surveys and studies that are components of this project are urgently needed and are designed to gather a variety of data from a cross section of geographical locations and population groups. These surveys include testing of voluntary participants from specified settings either on a confidential or anonymous basis and, in a sentinel hospital survey, testing of unidentified blood samples from groups of interest. Pilot studies for a proposed nationwide household infection prevalence survey are a major part of this project. However, the complete results of these studies will not be available until 1991. Apart from this extraordinary effort, much will be learned from ongoing state, local, and private testing when CDC institutes HIV infection data collection from the states instead of limiting its surveillance to diagnosed AIDS cases. . . .

Chapter Two: Patient Care

Treatment Needs

... Although HIV infection is not curable at this time, many of its manifestations are treatable. Early diagnosis of both HIV and its clinical consequences results in more appropriate and effective care and management. A careful history, physical examination, and laboratory diagnosis are critical and should be regularly employed in diagnosing HIV infection and related diseases.

Early diagnosis of HIV infection can also assist the infected person to take precautions because of his or her suppressed immune system. The HIV-infected person must strive to avoid becoming infected with other diseases, both opportunistic infections and secondary infections, in order to lengthen life and enhance its quality. Definitive early diagnosis can assist in motivating the adoption of healthful behaviors....

Opportunistic Infections

Infections seen in AIDS parallel infections seen in other immunosuppressed patients, such as those with cancer. When people in the United States with normal immune systems die of infection, their deaths are caused by the usual spectrum of bacterial and viral diseases that have killed mankind for ages (i.e., infections with staphylococci, pneumococci, gram negative bacteria, and common viruses such as influenza, among others). Although as susceptible to these infections as any other person, immunosuppressed patients also suffer from infections— "opportunistic infections"—only rarely seen in people with normal host responses. They get critical and fatal infections from organisms that much of the normal population carries more or less with impunity....

It should be added that the antibiotics used for these unusual infections are frequently very expensive and, as noted, not readily available. It is common for the person with symptomatic HIV infection to lack insurance or the funds to pay several hundred dollars a day for these drugs. Financial considerations are serious and are particularly critical for our hospital system, both public and private. The hospitals are rarely adequately reimbursed for this level of care, especially for indigents. Many voluntary hospitals attempt to divert these patients into the local municipal hospital system. This is becoming a fiscal challenge for our cities, where most of these patients are found....

Psychosocial Needs

As in other fatal diseases, persons with HIV infection and their loved ones suffer high levels of distress, depression, and anxiety due to the great degree of uncertainty associated with the diagnosis. Often, there is an overwhelming task of sorting through changing medical and scientific information in order to make accurate decisions regarding health care and life planning. Much anxiety is created by the many questions about HIV infection which remain unanswered. In addition, many people with HIV infection and its various manifestations feel the need to hide their condition from friends, co-workers, employers, and even family members in order to prevent social isolation and ostracism. This contributes greatly to their psychological stress at a time when they are coping with a devastating illness.

Many people with HIV infection, especially those who are active intravenous drug users, are unemployed and without adequate financial resources. Other persons with HIV infection may lose their jobs because of discrimination or inability to work, also becoming financially needy. Some people with HIV infection are without homes or lose their homes. All of these factors contribute to the stress and anxiety experienced by someone who is seriously ill.

For the family of the person with HIV infection who is being cared for at home, there is considerable stress since at least one member of the family often must be available for full-time nursing care. A significant proportion of people with HIV infection do not have the support of family or close friends. For all of these reasons, the person with HIV and his supporting care givers require access to sensitive psychosocial support services. These include training in the bedside care of the patients, counseling, support groups, differential diagnosis, antidepressant medications, financial assistance, and social support services.

HIV-Infected Children

A population which poses unique challenges to the health care system are children with HIV infection. According to a report by the National Commission on Infant Mortality, by 1991, there will be an estimated 10,000 to 20,000 cases of symptomatic HIV infection in children in the United States. Most cases of AIDS in children (77 percent) are a result of perinatal transmission from infected mothers. These infants can be infected either through maternal blood *in utero,* by exposure to maternal blood and other body fluids during birth, or through breast milk. . . .

Most of these children die of HIV-related diseases before the age of three. A few children have lived as long as nine years. The course of their illness is often stormy, with multiple and severe infections, presenting problems not usually seen on general pediatric wards. . . .

Experimental therapies for pediatric patients have lagged behind trials for adults due to the small number of patients available for study, and the cultural and ethical issues surrounding such treatment. Funds for additional pediatric trials are not currently available at NIH.

Thirteen percent of the children with HIV infection in the United States acquired the virus by means of transfusion, and six percent are hemophiliacs. These children are subject to the same range of secondary infections as perinatally exposed children, but are sometimes older, and therefore suffer the additional burden of having their otherwise normal lives severely altered by this new disease and the discrimination that often attends it.

Parents of these children, while not necessarily indigent, may require financial assistance to care for their children, as costs can be catastrophic. Parents of all HIV-infected children may also have to deal with problems of their child's isolation or sense of abandonment, if relationships with friends and schoolmates change. . . .

Homosexual Men

. . . .The health care provider must care for the homosexual man with awareness and sensitivity. A careful sexual, psychological, and family history must be obtained in an effective and non-judgmental manner. The provider should look for and evaluate Kaposi's sarcoma, which in HIV infection occurs almost exclusively in homosexual men. There should be a careful examination for bowel infections, bowel trauma, STDs, and other co-factors.

Some homosexual men experience societal and personal rejection, loneliness, guilt, self-hatred, and a loss of self-worth. Family abandonment is not uncommon. Meaningful relationships that exist with friends and the nontraditional family of the homosexual man must be recognized, so that these individuals may be included in care decisions if the patient so requests. Friction with relatives can occur and must be handled with care.

Heterosexual Adults

Although at present, the incidence of HIV infection is believed to be low in the general heterosexual population, there are distinct segments with much higher incidence of infection. Drug addicts and their sexual partners are at high risk and represent the principal mode of spread into the non-homosexual, non-intravenous drug-using population. Another risk is a history of prior blood transfusion. The risk of spread from bisexual men to their unsuspecting female partners is particularly worrisome because the magnitude of the risk is unknown. The estimated number of men who have had more than one casual homosexual experience, varies from 10 to 30 percent. An accurate assessment of this problem is currently lacking, but if 10 percent of the men in the United States are active bisexuals, this would represent the very distinct possibility of a large number of potentially HIV-infected women, many of whom have no knowledge at all about their sexual partner's homosexual activity. Almost by definition, the homosexual lives of bisexuals, especially those who are married, are clandestine, with transient, and possibly anonymous contacts, thereby exposing them to greater risk of HIV infection.

As is true for all sexually transmitted diseases, an increased number of partners represents increased risk and any person with multiple partners must be advised to reduce the number of sexual partners. Any health care provider must underline to everyone he or she counsels that the "window" between infection and a positive antibody test, although usually between six weeks and three months, may be as long as three years or more, and therefore an initial negative test may be misleading. (Testing methods currently under development are expected to greatly reduce this problem.) For freedom from exposure to HIV, long-term mutual monogamy remains the best prevention short of abstinence.

Because the epidemic has predominantly been confined to people participating in behaviors such as homosexual sex and intravenous drug abuse, health care practitioners are less likely to consider a diagnosis of HIV positivity or AIDS in an individual apparently not at high risk, such as a white heterosexual non-intravenous drug-using female who is not aware that her sole male partner is infected. In the past, this situation has extended the length of time from onset of symptoms to diagnosis of such individuals. One compelling witness before the Commission revealed that she had gone to doctors for nearly two years with mild to severe problems before anyone thought to do any antibody test. Because no one associated her with high-risk behaviors, no one suspected that she might be HIV-infected. She now has AIDS.

Minorities

The impact of HIV infection on black and Hispanic communities has been felt very strongly; individuals from these groups comprise about 40 percent of all persons with symptomatic HIV infection. Similar to the non-Hispanic white population, the major category of transmission for blacks and Hispanics is homosexual/bisexual behavior. However, blacks and Hispanics who engage in these behaviors are less likely to obtain services from organizations which are perceived as homosexually-related and more likely to seek information and guidance from those community-based organizations which have traditionally served their respective communities. Of great concern is that intravenous drug use is a much greater method of transmission for blacks and Hispanics than it is for non-Hispanic whites. The incidence of HIV infection among inner city drug users is growing more rapidly than the incidence in the homosexual population. Most of these patients have no private health insurance and must rely on Medicaid. It is only recently that black and Hispanic community-based organizations have been able to obtain funds so that they could also use their diverse expertise and credibility to address the HIV epidemic. . . .

Large numbers of minorities are uninsured or underinsured and, consequently, turn to public health care systems, creating high levels of demand for services from public clinics and hospitals, community health centers, and migrant health centers.

Inpatient Hospitalization

. . . The costs of caring for persons with HIV infection are extremely high. Estimates from recent studies calculate the AIDS-related hospital bill for 1985 at $380 million, and economists project costs greater than $8.5 billion for AIDS-related medical care by 1991. Financing of care is complex, coming primarily from private insurance, Medicaid, and other state, local, and private monies. Increasingly, the cost burden of providing care to persons with symptomatic HIV infection is falling to the public hospitals, the state and local public assistance programs, and Medicaid. . . .

Out-of-Hospital Care

. . . The availability of care settings staffed by practitioners knowledgeable in the care of HIV-infected persons is an essential alternative to hospital-based care. There is a vital need for replicating the coordinated system developed in San Francisco, and for reimbursement systems to respond by supporting high quality and cost-effective care in out-of-hospital settings.

Home care should be made available, particularly for the indigent, covering the range from high-tech intravenous therapies to chronic care by attendants. The average cost of home health care is $15,000 per year, while the average year cost for nursing homes ranges from $24,000 to $60,000, depending on geographic location. Hospice care should be available, as well as nursing home beds or residential facilities for those who cannot be adequately cared for in their homes. Currently, there are few nursing homes that will accept patients with advanced HIV illness; this situation must be resolved, and additional alternative settings sought. In some areas, small group homes and nursing services may be a feasible approach. Reimbursement and funding for these services should be available from a variety of sources. Homeless persons with AIDS often remain in the hospital because they have no home address to which they can be discharged. Nowhere is this more evident than with the hospitalized infants and children with HIV infection, the so-called "boarder babies." The cost of maintaining a child in a municipal hospital pediatric ward for one year is in excess of $250,000. Congregate living facilities have been identified as a potential alternative to hospital-based care, and are often able to provide a quality home environment for $60 to $100 per day, versus $500 to $1,000 per hospital day. Some private sector institutions have begun to provide a quality home environment for $60 to $100 per day, versus $500 to $1,000 per hospital day. Some private sector institutions have begun to provide high quality, cost-effective, and compassionate care for homeless persons with AIDS and their families. . . .

Community-based organizations (CBOs) have played an enormous role in providing health care and psychosocial services for persons with HIV infection. The prototypes for these organizations were developed within homosexual communities nationwide and illustrate, through their diversity and numbers, a self-reliant and vigorous response in coping with the HIV epidemic. . . .

Chapter Three: Health Care Providers

. . . A well-educated, skilled, and concerned health care community is not only vital to the task of caring for those who are ill, but during this critical time when fear and misunderstanding about the HIV epidemic exist within our population, the leadership established by providers of health care to persons with HIV infection is crucial to fostering a sense of compassion and rationality among all our citizens. When health care professionals care for all patients who need their help, regardless of HIV infection status, and do so without reservation or trepidation using time-tested infection control methods, they communicate to all people that calmness and reason can prevail over panic and anxiety as we confront this epidemic.

There is clearly a need for more knowledge about HIV among many health care providers—an issue that was repeatedly raised by expert witnesses at the hearings on care....

Policies for Prevention of Transmission of HIV

CDC has developed basic policy recommendations for prevention of HIV transmission in the health care setting. These recommendations, which call for the use of Universal Precautions, are designed to emphasize the need for all health care workers to consider the blood and blood-contaminated body fluids of *all* patients as potentially infected with HIV and/or other blood-borne pathogens and to adhere rigorously to infection control precautions for minimizing the risk of exposure to blood and body fluids of all patients.

This represents a major difference in the way body substance precautions were taken in the past. Under the old system the health care worker was required to identify the patient and the specific infection in order to implement appropriate infection control procedures.

It is generally felt at this time that dependence on HIV blood testing as an infection control procedure or to screen all patients for the purpose of preventing occupational transmission of HIV is not effective and in fact may interfere with other means of preventing occupational transmission. However, the use of testing for the early diagnosis, medical management, care, and understanding of the patient is appropriate....

Chapter Four: Basic Research, Vaccine, and Drug Development

Basic biomedical research continues to make vast and unprecedented advances in key scientific areas directly applicable to the HIV epidemic. However, significant obstacles confront both the scientist seeking a cure, and the individual with HIV infection seeking treatment. Our national system of research programming and funding is not equipped to reorganize rapidly in response to an emergency. The process of individual initiatives by scientists, followed by peer review, while essential, produces results at a rate too slow to be understood or accepted by a country at risk. Innovative initiatives are urgently needed that will both maintain scientific integrity and shorten the time from discovery to trial, and from trial to safe and effective treatment use....

Facilities

HIV has added an increased burden to our already overstrained research facilities. Many scientists believe that our research efforts have been slowed because of outdated and antiquated facilities. Work with viruses, viral concentrations, genetically altered and virus-infected animals must be done in highly controlled settings. The model developed for expanding such research includes construction of containment laboratories with a P-3 level of biosafety or modification of existing labs. At the beginning of the epidemic, very few of these facilities were in existence.

In the research community outside NIH, few universities and research institutions have funds immediately available to create or convert facilities for HIV-related work. The cost of upgrading existing laboratories to P-3 level is approximately $250,000 per laboratory. Many laboratories now exist around the country that could be upgraded in this manner, providing space for additional HIV-related research. This diverse pluralistic distribution of research space was highly recommended by several witnesses as offering the greatest potential for discovery.

Testimony suggested to the Commission that federal funding be supplied to establish regional centers for basic and applied research in retroviral diseases. These centers would be located in a university or a research institute where a critical mass of expertise already exists, and the existing research team would be organized and expanded for maximum interaction under the leadership of an appropriate investigator. The enlarged facility would be optimally equipped for this work. It would provide an appropriate environment for training of graduate students and postdoctoral fellows, and would ideally be able to share a portion of its facilities with qualified visiting researchers from outside the parent institution who lacked facilities to advance their own research. Such centers would have a great impact by providing opportunity to young researchers. . . .

Administrative Processes

HIV was isolated in 1983 and because the disease known as AIDS was then determined to be a virus-induced infectious disease, NIH designated NIAID [National Institute for Allergy and Infectious Diseases] as the administrator for HIV-related federal research management. . . .

. . . The Commission's examination of HIV research programs has revealed that despite NIAID's commitment to rapid response, limitations in the federal system must be addressed if this nation's goal of controlling the epidemic is to be realized. One of the greatest obstacles cited by NIH administrators is the inflexibility of Office of Management and Budget (OMB) regulation of internal resource allocation and program development. Currently, OMB acts as a surrogate Secretary of HHS [Health and Human Services], in effect, micromanaging research on the institute level within NIH. The Commission favors allocating pools of resources (funds and personnel) to NIH and allowing the Director greater discretionary powers to make subsequent personnel and funding allocations to each institute. NIH witnesses have repeatedly indicated their desire to be held accountable for results and asked for greater flexibility to employ innovative methods through which to achieve those results. . . .

Obstacles to Progress

Testimony before the Commission reported results of the Institute of Medicine's (IOM) "Conference on the Development of Vaccines against HIV and AIDS" on December 14 and 15, 1987. . . .

The IOM conference presented a variety of methods currently under exploration for vaccine development and gave an overall status report. The tenor of the conference indicated that it may be many years before a vaccine that is proven safe and effective is developed. . . . The conference concluded that prevention remains the greatest single means by which to curtail extension of the epidemic.

Ethics

Vaccine trials pose exceptionally difficult ethical questions for both researchers and participants. Essential to any blinded trial is the equal exposure to risk of disease by both the vaccinated group and the placebo group, yet medical ethics mandate counseling all patient participants to avoid the very behaviors that may put them at risk. Successfully avoiding risk delays confirmatory trial results. Vaccination causes an individual to produce antibodies to the virus, and the presence of these antibodies is currently the basis for a diagnosis of active HIV infection, thus potentially subjecting the vaccinated person to discrimination or stigma. To achieve results most rapidly, trials would be done in populations in which HIV is endemic. These are often third world or minority populations, or intravenous drug users in certain cities, raising the issue of exploitation. Because of the "window" of antibody response, an individual who tests negative at the beginning of a trial may in fact be infected, and vaccination could conceivably be injurious to his health. Vaccine trials in pediatric populations are even more ethically and emotionally complicated. All of these issues present the research and patient communities with as yet unresolved obstacles.

Liability

One of the few obstacles to vaccine development which may be more easily answered is liability, which could be addressed by legislation. Testimony before the Commission indicated substantial differences of opinion on the need for liability protection. One witness stated that only 25 to 30 vaccine liability cases have actually come to court in the past 20 years, and that the manufacturers won the majority of those cases. However, it was noted by another witness that for every case that actually reaches trial stage, there may be dozens or hundreds that are resolved earlier but that require substantial litigation time and investment on the

427

part of manufacturers. Testimony indicated that several manufacturers were currently working on HIV vaccines, and that the threat of liability did not seem to be a great deterrent. A spokesman for one manufacturer, however, stated that unless the liability problem, real or perceived, was resolved, few if any of the manufacturers now developing HIV vaccines would be eager to bring them to market. . . .

. . . These small companies licensed their products to larger companies that possibly had hundreds of products on the market and could therefore spread the liability risk.

The question was raised as to whether, given the cost of development, production, and trial, it would be possible to produce a vaccine that was affordable in developing nations. It was suggested that if manufacturers could or would not be willing to make the long-term investment, the government should. Having the science and technology to produce a vaccine that would save lives, and declining to do so, would seem to be ethically unacceptable. . . .

Using a process known as rational drug modeling, it is theoretically possible to design new drugs that will have HIV-specific activity, such as interfering with viral replication. In theory, it should also be possible to design a drug that is easy to take (oral) and can cross the "blood-brain" barrier and eliminate virus in the central nervous system. This process, however, can be slow.

Within NIH, NCI has a long established history of research excellence associated with drug development. Faced with this new medical emergency, NCI geared up its off-the-shelf drug screening program, and made it available to all pharmaceutical companies, biotechnology firms, and universities for products they had already produced and had in stock. Compounds that universities or corporations felt might be effective against HIV were submitted to NCI for *in vitro* (test tube) screening. This effort resulted in the demonstration of the antiviral properties of azidothymidine (AZT), a compound submitted for screening to NCI by the Burroughs Wellcome Co.

The high level of anti-HIV activity discovered in AZT indicated that a product might be quickly developed that had the potential to stop the progression of disease in people who were already infected. When it appeared that Burroughs Wellcome lacked sufficient amounts of a key ingredient to produce enough AZT for trials, NCI, in the belief that AZT represented an extraordinary opportunity in HIV treatment, provided the ingredient at no cost.

Because no product-patent application could be filed by NIH, Burroughs Wellcome retained full market control of the compound. Many witnesses have criticized Burroughs Wellcome for the high price of the drug and NIH for contributing so greatly without retaining some control over the final cost to patients. The company indicated that its development costs were substantial, but lowered the wholesale price by 20 percent. Procedures have been instituted at NIH so that patent applications are routinely filed for all new compounds that NIH originates, as well as filing use-patents when appropriate.

By understanding how the virus works, what its physical properties are, and how virus-infected cells behave, drugs can be developed that interact with the virus at various points in its life cycle. Some witnesses indicate that enough has been learned through basic research to re-emphasize drug development through rational drug modeling, the traditional approach.

Private Sector Collaborative Research and Development

The pharmaceutical industry is playing a significant role in the development of vaccines and therapeutic agents. Hundreds of millions of dollars have been committed to such research. The private sector has a long tradition of excellent drug and vaccine development.

In times of serious medical emergency, the competition that normally fuels progress in the private sector can actually slow down the production and marketing of potentially beneficial substances. If several companies are working separately on a potential therapy that is costly and difficult to develop, they may all relinquish their efforts if the ultimate return on investment will be too low. In theory, had private companies been able and willing to pool resources and collaborate on the project, they would have eliminated the duplicated efforts, reduced cost and development time, and been able to share profits. In reality, a complex set of antitrust laws prohibit this type of collaboration.

The Food and Drug Administration

The Food and Drug Administration (FDA) is the principal consumer protection agency of the federal government. Its primary responsibility with respect to HIV is to ensure that drugs, biological products (such as vaccines and blood components), and medical devices are safe and effective. . . .

In spite of the best efforts of the Commissioner of FDA, with respect to newly developed anti-viral drugs or immunomodulators, the treatment IND program is not meeting the needs of persons with AIDS or advanced HIV-related illness. Treatment INDs were designed to offer some hope of access to experimental drugs to those with life-threatening disease. They allow the release of the drug on a non-clinical-trial use basis even before the end of Phase II efficacy testing, based on the FDA Commissioner's recommendation, and after safety and some degree of efficacy have been demonstrated. Although the program is well-intentioned, and does work for antibiotics and other types of drugs for HIV-infected persons, and for persons needing drugs for other diseases, the fact remains that for antivirals and immunomodulators for HIV, the system is not working. Reasons for its failure to date include the following:

- some pharmaceutical companies are unwilling to allow their drugs to be used in this program, even when they are sought after by physicians and desperately ill patients;

- there is no information system that allows the patient or physician population to know what is available;
- methods of obtaining drugs that *are* available through this program are poorly understood and seem unnecessarily complicated; and
- some physicians are reluctant to prescribe treatment IND drugs because liability limits are not clearly defined. . . .

Physicians indicated an unwillingness to order the drugs even if they were available because they feared that their patients would be receiving inadequately tested therapies and because of potential malpractice litigation.

The underutilization of this program is of concern to the Commission. We have received many calls and letters from concerned patients, their friends, and families seeking help. They were unable to find answers to the simplest questions about the availability of drugs. There was no centralized information network, and no one to help them through the FDA maze. If and when they did reach the right individual at FDA, they were referred to the drug companies, who, in some cases, just said no. Individuals who qualify for this program are by definition desperately or terminally ill, and it is unacceptable that this situation has languished this long without resolution. . . .

Community-based Trials

Many witnesses before the Commission testified that there was a need for greater access by a broader spectrum of the infected population to clinical trials, specifically women, hemophiliacs, children, and transfusion-exposed individuals. Concern was expressed by many of these witnesses that drugs were being tested on one segment of the population and may be licensed for use in other segments without having been intensively tested in them. As these populations may represent the future of the epidemic (e.g., children and intravenous drug abusers), the immediate implementation of more broadly available therapeutic protocols is essential.

The Community Research Initiative (CRI) offers the possibility to combine the technical expertise of the research community with the outreach potential of community health clinics and physicians in community practice. This outreach effort to minority populations, drug users, and women may increase the access of these populations to experimental treatment. The Commission is hopeful that greater access by a broader based community will also increase the information gathered on co-factors and increase knowledge of disease manifestation and progression. In addition, as many "underground" drugs are being used by the HIV-infected population, community-based efforts may offer the added possibility of increasing our knowledge of the effectiveness of these substances, and how they interact with other medications. Such "observational trials" can also provide valuable information about "patterns of care" in community settings. . . .

Behavioral and Social Science Research

HIV transmission is linked to specific and potentially changeable patterns of behavior. For individuals currently engaging in those behaviors, prevention of transmission depends on implementing effective behavioral change programs which seek to reduce or eliminate exposure to the virus. Research on sexual and drug-abusing behavior must, therefore, be an integral part of all HIV intervention efforts. . . .

To date, most of the efforts used to stop the spread of HIV have been informational mass communications, such as pamphlets, public service announcements, advertisements in magazines, and—to a limited extent—television commercials. However, some behavioral research indicates that simply providing information may increase awareness about HIV, but does not necessarily lead to change in risk behavior. . . .

Transmission of HIV can occur in any sexual behavior (from female to male, from male to female, and between two partners of the same sex) in which there is an exposure of HIV-infected body fluids to cells which can be infected. For this reason, research on sexual behavior is particularly relevant for designing and implementing appropriate and effective prevention programs. In addition, research indicates that sexual behavior and attitude vary somewhat as a function of ethnicity and culture. In order to be effective, educational efforts must be sensitive to these differences. . . .

Currently, researchers in the field of adult sexual behavior must continue to refer to data collected by Kinsey over 40 years ago. There is an urgent need to update the information base. Data collected in the future should include not only prevalence of behaviors, but also attitudes and beliefs about sex. . . .

There is reason to be optimistic about projects aimed at reducing high-risk behaviors. Results from a behavioral research study in San Francisco shows that the incidence of detected HIV infection in a group of over 800 homosexual and bisexual men is approaching zero. From 1984 through 1986, the prevalence of HIV-infection in this group of homosexual and bisexual men was stable at approximately 50 percent. Not surprisingly, this is concomitant with substantial reductions in self-reported high-risk activities. The study results may show effectiveness in both behavior modification efforts and community-based HIV educational programs.

There are some researchers who believe that the San Francisco study sample is not representative of all homosexual and bisexual men. Therefore, further studies must be targeted on this population. . . .

[Chapter Five omitted]

Chapter Six: Prevention

Although the HIV epidemic has presented the public health system with a new set of challenges, the prevention of disease has been the primary mission of that system since its inception. Prevention refers to any action that interrupts or halts the progressive path of a disease. Effective preventive interventions which can be applied to the HIV epidemic include the implementation of widespread testing and counseling, partner notification, the pre-donation screening of potential blood and semen donors, the testing of donated blood and organs, restrictive measures, and the implementation of general and targeted education programs. . . .

. . . Only a limited number of individuals potentially infected with HIV have been counseled and tested, and only a limited percentage (approximately five percent) of those infected with HIV have laboratory confirmation of their infection due to a lack of information, fears of testing, or limited access to voluntary testing and counseling services.

Testing provides an opportunity for effective education and counseling and, for some, the initiation of behavior modification. When a person has volunteered to be tested, or when his or her physician has determined with the individual's consent that an HIV antibody test is appropriate, the tested person's interest is elevated; in short, he or she is more likely at this point to pay attention than in merely receiving impersonal educational messages. The type and intensity of education and counseling linked to testing ought to be guided by two factors—the test results and the reason the person offers for being tested. If the test result is negative, a simple brochure accompanying the result could, in some cases, suffice.

If a person expresses concern that his or her own behavior has led to the test or appears agitated at the time the blood is drawn, person-to-person counseling is appropriate both before and after the administration of the test. Particularly, counseling should be available for these persons between the time the test is administered and the result is known. The person who has participated in high-risk behavior but has a negative test result should receive counseling in an effort to ensure that he or she remains uninfected.

If the test result is confirmed positive, intensive counseling at the time the result is given is needed. Because of the significance of that result and the natural tendency for the infected person to block out much of the information given at the initial session while concentrating on the result itself, it is imperative that the initial counseling session include the presentation in writing of the implications of the test result and of the opportunity for further testing and for further counseling, which may be by referral. An effort should be made at the initial counseling session to link the infected individual with a primary care provider if that link does not already exist. Consideration should be given to providing take-home materials, such as brochures or audiotapes, so that the infected person can review the information at home if he or she so chooses.

Counseling of infected persons should also include the means to and the responsibility to avoid transmitting the virus to others, the responsibility and benefits of telling one's sexual or drug-using contacts about the test result, and the availability of public health services to inform those partners should the person be unable or unwilling to do so. . . .

Both public health practice and case law makes clear that persons put at risk of exposure to an infectious disease should be alerted to their exposure. The Commission believes that there should be a process in place in every state by which the official state health agency is responsible for assuring that those persons put unsuspectingly at risk for HIV infection are notified of that exposure. Such a process will enable that agency to work with the infected individual and the patient's primary health care provider to assure that contacts are notified of their exposure and urged to take advantage of the opportunity for testing and counseling. . . .

In keeping with the long tradition of the public health profession in respecting, in a confidential manner, both data and affected persons, the need to report identities should not be a bar to partner notification or to persons coming forward for testing. It is critical, however, that in proposing and implementing partner notification, the public health authorities involved must stress the confidential nature of the process and build confidence in those affected. Furthermore, there would be no purpose in public health authorities informing the notified partner of the identity of the person who disclosed the partner's name; this standard operating policy of traditional partner notification procedures should be followed also with respect to HIV. . . .

The primary focus in developing a comprehensive public health strategy to control HIV infection should be placed on those public health measures that are based on voluntary cooperation in risk-reducing behavior change: focused education; voluntary testing; counseling; partner notification; and treatment for drug abuse. However, these prevention measures even vigorously applied will be unsuccessful in persuading some small number of individuals to alter their behavior. When an individual poses a health risk to others by remaining noncompliant with recommended behavior change, appropriate control measures should be employed to achieve the public health objective of controlling the spread of HIV. . . .

As of June 6, 1988, 2,399 of the people diagnosed with AIDS had acquired the infection through transfusions of blood, blood products, or the clotting factors used to treat hemophilia. The initial response of the nation's blood banking industry to the possibility of contamination of the nation's blood by a new infectious agent was unnecessarily slow. However, important lesions were learned from this chapter of our blood banking history which cannot be dismissed as we face further problems. The Commission believes strongly that the blood banks should not delay any longer the screening for another blood-borne virus, HTLV-1, which is believed to be the cause of adult T-cell leukemia/lymphoma and a severe neurological disease known as tropical spastic paraparesis (TSP). . . .

Chapter Seven: Education

. . . During the last year, there has been a great deal of sometimes acrimonious debate over the content of HIV education. The Commission is concerned that, in the promotion of the personal moral and political values of those from both ends of the political spectrum, the consistent distribution of clear, factual information about HIV transmission has suffered.

HIV education programs for example, should discourage promiscuous sexual activity and recognize the benefits of abstinence and monogamy; however, they need to be explicit in nature so that there is no confusion about how to avoid acquiring or transmitting the virus. The Commission firmly believes that it is possible to develop educational materials and programs that clearly convey an explicit message without promoting high-risk behaviors. All HIV education programs should emphasize personal responsibility for one's actions. Actions have consequences.

No citizen of our nation is exempt from the need to be educated about the HIV epidemic. The real challenge lies in matching the appropriate educational approach with the people to be educated. It is not the role of the federal government to dictate to local communities their values, and too much time has been wasted on this debate when educational materials are needed which clearly present the facts about AIDS and HIV transmission. In a similar vein, those who seek to use HIV education programs to further their own ideology of whichever stripe cannot expect federal funds for this purpose. In short, the federal, state, and local governments should convey the current medical and scientific facts to the American public and they, in turn, will build curricula suited to their own community value systems. When these curricula are constructed well, with all responsible local entities working in a collaborative way to help ensure their efficacy, the educational response of one region of the country can be expected to differ from that of another. Both responses should be applauded.

The Commission believes that several education initiatives are of such vital importance to the effective preventive management of the HIV epidemic that they must be implemented immediately. . . .

A two-part response to the epidemic is required from the nation's elementary and secondary school system. The first part must happen in the short term. It is the opinion of the Commission that the provision of HIV education in our schools is of vital importance and must be introduced across the nation immediately. Some states have already ensured that this is happening; the rest must follow their lead. The decisions about appropriate content and methods of instruction should be determined at the local level; however, both elementary and secondary school students should receive such education. Students must be provided with current and accurate information about the HIV epidemic that is appropriate for age so that they can make informed decisions about their behavior and avoid those actions that put them at risk for HIV infection. School-based education should highlight the benefits of character development, abstinence, and monogamy. By ensuring that appropriate education about the virus is provided in the elementary and secondary school system, we can help our younger generation avoid the tragedy we are witnessing today.

The second part is the long-term response, which will have a far greater pay-off when fully implemented; that is the introduction of a comprehensive health education curriculum for all grades K through 12. . . .

Chapter Eight: Societal Issues

As the Commission looked at patterns of HIV infection and particularly their correlation to intravenous drug abuse, the relationship between the spread of HIV and longstanding societal problems became apparent. It is imperative that this nation recognize and address the context in which the epidemic is occurring. It is occurring disproportionately within the underclass, the largely minority population of the inner city poor....

Witnesses before the Commission presented considerable evidence that the occurrence of drug abuse, particularly intravenous heroin abuse, is frequently found in communities where poverty and crime are endemic. It has been noted that persistent poverty in the midst of an affluent society engenders hopelessness and despair which can lead to heroin abuse and related high rates of crime.

In HIV prevalence studies of homosexual men, intravenous drug users, and patients at sexually transmitted disease clinics, inner city areas consistently report the highest prevalence rates, with minorities overrepresented among this population. In addition, witnesses testified that neighborhoods characterized by high rates of teenage pregnancy, high school dropouts, crime (particularly drug-related crime), welfare dependency, males who are jobless, and female-headed households (which represent over 90 percent of households in some urban housing projects) have suffered a high rate of heterosexual transmission.

Heterosexual transmission is occurring particularly in communities where prostitution and drug abuse are prevalent, and where HIV infection is correspondingly high (as high as 70 percent among intravenous heroin users in some areas). In this setting, the disease has dispersed rapidly into the heterosexual community through the sexual partners of those infected. As many as five percent of mothers delivering babies in some inner city hospitals are now infected, a frightening statistic, especially when we consider the social and financial ramifications of a rapidly increasing incidence of pediatric HIV infection. Some of our public city hospitals are already overwhelmed, and we have only seen the beginning of the acceleration of this pediatric HIV crisis....

Drug Abuse and the HIV Epidemic

Our nation's ability to control the course of the HIV epidemic depends greatly on our ability to control the problem of intravenous drug abuse. Intravenous and other drug abuse is a substantial carrier for infection, a major port of entry for the virus into the larger population. Although intravenous drug abusers constitute only 25 percent of AIDS cases in the United States, 70 percent of all heterosexually transmitted cases in native-born citizens comes from contact with this group. In addition, 70 percent of perinatally transmitted AIDS cases are the children of those who abuse intravenous drugs or whose sexual partners abuse intravenous drugs. And the situation is rapidly worsening as the number of infected drug abusers grows daily.

Among the more tragic manifestations of this epidemic are the infected infants of intravenous drug abusers. Most of these children die in their first few years of life. Many never leave the hospital. Their time on this earth begins with a few months of drug withdrawal in an isolation unit and ends after a series of painful illnesses. Because few have visitors in the hospital, the nurses, physicians, social workers, and volunteers who staff our pediatric acute care units become father, mother, and friend to these children. By 1991 there are expected to be 10,000 to 20,000 cases of AIDS among infants and children.

But they represent only the beginning of the tragedy if this nation does not move to address its entire drug abuse problem. The Commission recognizes that alcohol and drug abuse in all their manifestations represent a threat since the use of alcohol or any drug which impairs judgment may lead to the sexual transmission of HIV. The United States continues to have the highest rate of illicit drug use among young people of any country in the industrialized world. Our drug problem pervades all elements of society. A recent study has demonstrated that drug abuse is a problem for both suburbs and inner cities, for all races, and at all income levels. Without a coordinated and sustained response, America as a whole faces a bleak future. . . .

The Commission believes it is imperative to curb drug abuse, especially intravenous drug abuse, by means of treatment in order to slow the HIV epidemic. Because a clear federal, state, and local government policy is needed, the Commission recommends a national policy of providing "treatment on demand" for intravenous drug abusers.

This policy would need to be a long-term commitment, and the funding should come from a 50 percent federal and 50 percent state-and-local matching program. The spending should be accompanied by the institution of a national campaign to promote community acceptance of treatment programs.

Given the fact that temporarily alleviating the health effects of symptomatic HIV infection can cost as much as $100,000 per person and that imprisonment costs an average of $14,500 per person per year, and even without considering the previously cited astronomical costs of drug abuse to the nation, the investment necessary to provide for intravenous drug abuse "treatment on demand" is sound public policy. Current treatment modes for intravenous drug abusers, including methadone maintenance and drug-free residential communities, reduce illicit drug use, improve employment among addicts, reduce crime rates, and improve social functioning.

Infants and Children with HIV Infection

There has been a recent, disturbing rise in pediatric AIDS cases, with 85 percent of the total cases reported since 1985. Through June 6, 1988, of the total of 64,506 cases of AIDS reported to CDC, 1,013 have been infants and children under the age of 13 at the time of diagnosis. According to the Report of the Surgeon General's Workshop on Children with HIV Infection and Their Families, over 75 percent of babies born with AIDS are black or Hispanic. Public health experts predict a substantial increase in pediatric AIDS cases by 1991, ranging from 3,000 cases estimated by the Public Health Service to 10,000 to 20,000 AIDS cases predicted by the National Commission to Prevent Infant Mortality.

CDC categorizes pediatric AIDS cases as children of a parent with or at risk of AIDS, hemophiliacs, or children who became infected through a blood transfusion. For a large majority, epidemiologic data suggests perinatal transmission from a mother who uses intravenous drugs or is the sexual partner of an intravenous drug user. Most pediatric AIDS cases that are being diagnosed now fall within this category, as transmission to hemophiliacs and through blood transfusions have been largely prevented with new blood screening methods.

Hospitals serving pediatric HIV cases, especially urban hospitals in areas with a high incidence of drug abusers, report a growing problem with children with HIV infection who must remain in the hospital when it is no longer medically necessary for them to be there simply because there is no one to care for them at home. In some cases the parents are drug addicts, are themselves ill with HIV infection, or have previously died from HIV-related diseases and the child has been abandoned. In other cases, the family may be homeless, or the parents are ill and there is no extended family able to take care of the child.

As a result, these children must live in a hospital setting, receiving intermittent attention from a variety of attendants, rather than experiencing the stimulation and bonding with a constant care giver that occurs in a home atmosphere. In addition, they unnecessarily occupy costly hospital beds and stretch hospital budgets when a less expensive, community-based setting would better meet their needs.

While hospitals and service agencies are stretched to their limits in some areas with a high incidence of pediatric HIV infection, other areas have yet to face the problem. While a serious problem now, care of an increasing number of HIV-infected children may overwhelm hospital budgets in the future unless a plan is developed to place these children in more appropriate settings, either with their own families or, where that is not possible, in a foster home or small group home....

The Workplace and HIV Infection

Policies concerning the HIV-infected worker involve critical issues for the United States workplace. The impact of HIV will be felt both in terms of the personal suffering of the HIV-infected individual, especially as an employee becomes too ill to work, as well as the reaction of coworkers and members of the public with whom the individual comes in contact. Education about HIV infection and employment policies for infected workers is imperative to enable employers to minimize disruptions in worker productivity, maintain employee morale, and avoid litigation for noncompliance with worker safety procedures or discrimination against HIV-infected employees.

Some employers in both the public and private sectors have established exemplary HIV-related workplace programs and should be commended for their participation in national, state, and local coalitions which have brought issues related to HIV and HIV disease to the attention of the business community. A few employee unions have also been active in both protecting the rights of employees with HIV infection and protecting the health and safety of workers, especially those in occupations where workers might be exposed directly to the blood of individuals infected with HIV. . . .

In March 1988, the Office of Personnel Management (OPM) issued comprehensive guidelines which outline employment policies for federal workers who are HIV-infected. The Commission commends OPM for developing these guidelines, which offer a compassionate approach to a delicate human situation and provide excellent advice based on open communication, comprehensive education, and sound legal principles. Employers should refer to these guidelines when developing policies for their employees with HIV.

However, the majority of employers in both the public and private sectors have yet to develop programs or guidelines to address this issue. Small businesses in particular remain unaware, for the most part, of the challenges of HIV, although they may be significantly affected because of the size of their work forces, their small profit margins, and their inability to absorb major increases in health insurance costs for an employee with HIV-related diseases.

Regardless of the size of the business, it is the responsibility of every employer to provide a safe environment for his or her work force. Employers should implement HIV-related policies or guidelines *before* a case occurs to give everyone sufficient time to understand the procedures and to demonstrate management's support for protecting the rights of all their employees. . . .

The Commission believes that HIV-infected individuals, including those with symptomatic HIV infection, should continue their self-sufficiency through employment as long as possible. Every effort should be made to keep disabled individuals, including those with HIV infection, gainfully employed.

Employers are encouraged to provide the same reasonable accommodations, including alternative work schedules and job modifications for employees with HIV-related problems that are offered employees with other illnesses or disabilities. Because HIV is not transmitted in the type of casual contact that generally takes place in the workplace, there is no justification for fear of transmission of the virus in the vast majority of workplace and public settings. In occupations where there is a risk of exposure to HIV, such as police officers, fire fighters, sanitation workers, and hospital workers, it is the employer's responsibility to provide health and safety protection and training for the workers, as was discussed in the chapter on health care providers.

Chapter Nine: Legal and Ethical Issues

Discrimination

Throughout our investigation of the spread of HIV in the United States, the Commission has been confronted with the problem of discrimination against individuals with HIV seropositivity and all stages of HIV infection, including AIDS. At virtually every Commission hearing, witnesses have attested to discrimination's occurrence and its serious repercussions for both the individual who experiences it and for this nation's efforts to control the epidemic. Many witnesses have indicated that addressing discrimination is the first critical step in the nation's response to the epidemic.

HIV-related discrimination is impairing this nation's ability to limit the spread of the epidemic. Crucial to this effort are epidemiological studies to track the epidemic as well as the education, testing, and counseling of those who have been exposed to the virus. Public health officials will not be able to gain the confidence and cooperation of infected individuals or those at high risk for infection if such individuals fear that they will be unable to retain their jobs and their housing, and that they will be unable to obtain the medical and support services they need because of discrimination based on a positive HIV antibody test.

As long as discrimination occurs, and no strong national policy with rapid and effective remedies against discrimination is established, individuals ... infected with HIV will be reluctant to come forward for testing, counseling, and care. This fear of potential discrimination will limit the public's willingness to comply with the collection of epidemiological data and other public health strategies, will undermine our efforts to contain the HIV epidemic, and will leave HIV-infected individuals isolated and alone.

In general, because HIV is blood-borne and sexually transmitted, there is no need to treat those infected with HIV in a manner different from those not infected in such settings as the workplace, housing, and the schools. In the vast majority of workplace and public settings there is virtually no risk of the direct exposure to body fluids which could result in HIV transmission. Detailed Centers for Disease Control (CDC) guidelines have been issued for dealing with HIV infection in those cases which require special handling, such as health care workers and other workers who might be exposed to blood or those schoolchildren who lack control of their body secretions.

Therefore, discrimination against persons with HIV infection in the workplace setting, or in the areas of housing, schools, and public accommodations, is unwarranted because it has no public health basis. Nor is there any basis to discriminate against those who care for or associate with such individuals.

It is illegal to discriminate against persons with AIDS in those local jurisdictions with AIDS-specific anti-discrimination statutes, in those states which include AIDS as a protected handicap under their disability anti-discrimination laws, and in programs which receive federal funds. Section 504 of the Rehabilitation Act of 1973 is the federal anti-discrimination statute which prohibits discrimination against otherwise qualified persons with disabilities (including persons subject to a range of AIDS-related discrimination) in any program or activity receiving federal funds.

Nevertheless, complaints of HIV-related discrimination persist and their number is increasing. For example, HIV-related cases handled by the New York City Commission on Human Rights have risen from three in 1983, to more than 300 in 1986, to almost 600 in 1987. Similarly, the Office of Civil Rights which enforces federal disability discrimination law in programs funded by the Department of Health and Human Services reports a rise in complaints related to HIV infection in the past few years. AIDS advocacy groups and civil rights organizations nationwide also are experiencing an increase in HIV-related discrimination cases.

As a witness at the Commission's hearing on discrimination explained, individuals infected with HIV face two fights: the fight against the virus and the fight against discrimination. Just as the HIV-infected must have society's support in their fight against the virus, these individuals must have society's support in their fight against discrimination and must have assurances that policies will be implemented to prevent discrimination from occurring in the future.

One of the primary causes of discriminatory responses to an individual with HIV infection is fear, based on ignorance or misinformation about the transmission of the virus. We cannot afford to let such ignorance and misinformation persist. Each publicized incidence of discrimination, such as the picketing of a school that has admitted a child with HIV infection, perpetuates this ignorance and sows doubts in the minds of those who hear of it. This undermines current and future HIV education programs as well as rational HIV policies.

Furthermore, each act of discrimination, whether publicized or not, diminishes our society's adherence to the principles of justice and equality. Our leaders at all levels—national, state, and local—should speak out against ignorance and injustice, and make clear to the American people that discrimination against persons with HIV infection will not be tolerated. . . .

The Commission believes that persons with HIV infection should be considered members of the group of persons with disabilities, not as a separate group unto themselves. Persons with HIV infection deserve the same protections as all other persons with disabilities, including those with cancer, cerebral palsy and epilepsy. The Commission rejected the notion of providing anti-discrimination protection only for persons with HIV infection, outside of the context of other disabilities.

For the long term, federal legislation which clearly provides comprehensive anti-discrimination protection for all persons with disabilities, including those with HIV infection, is needed. As a critical first step towards passage and enforcement of such federal legislation, the Commission recommends that the federal government take the following immediate, affirmative steps to articulate a strong national policy against discrimination and thereby lay the groundwork for such legislation:

> The President should issue an executive order banning discrimination on the basis of handicap, with HIV infection included as a handicapping condition. This executive order would reinforce existing Section 504 regulations and clarify that all persons with HIV infection are covered by Section 504. Such an executive order would reaffirm existing federal anti-discrimination law which prohibits discrimination on the basis of handicap and would be a powerful message from the leadership of the nation. . . .

The Commission believes that federal disability anti-discrimination law should be expanded to cover the private as well as the public sector. Specifically, the Commission recommends:

> Comprehensive federal anti-discrimination legislation which prohibits discrimination against persons with disabilities in the public and private sectors, including employment, housing, public accommodations, and participation in government programs, should be enacted. All persons with symptomatic or asymptomatic HIV infection should be clearly included as persons with disabilities who are covered by the anti-discrimination protections of this legislation.

Confidentiality

Rigorous maintenance of confidentiality is considered critical to the success of the public health endeavor to prevent the transmission and spread of HIV infection. Current public health strategies for fighting the spread of HIV infection are entirely dependent on voluntary cooperation. To encourage individuals to come forward voluntarily for necessary testing, counseling, and treatment, our health care system must be viewed with confidence and trust by those in need of its services. Individuals entering the system must be convinced that information about their health will be kept confidential by those in the system. Aside from the illness itself, it is discrimination that is most feared by the HIV-infected. An effective guarantee of confidentiality is the major bulwark against that fear. A federal statute that carefully balances the need for confidentiality of HIV information against the protection of the public health is a necessary and appropriate response to confidentiality concerns.

To confirm our commitment to the principle of confidentiality in this epidemic and to ensure national uniformity in confidentiality protection policies, it is important for the federal government through legislation to take a leadership role in assuring the confidentiality of HIV-related records, while defining those situations in which information must be shared. In addition, state model confidentiality legislation must be developed and passed as reinforcement to federal confidentiality protection. . . .

Criminalization of HIV Transmission

Extending criminal liability to those who knowingly engage in behavior which is likely to transmit HIV is consistent with the criminal law's concern with punishing those whose behavior results in harmful acts. Just as other individuals in society are held responsible for their actions outside the criminal law's established parameters of acceptable behavior, HIV-infected individuals who knowingly conduct themselves in ways that pose a significant risk of transmission to others must be held accountable for their actions. Establishing criminal penalties for failure to comply with clearly set standards of conduct can also deter HIV-infected individuals from engaging in high-risk behaviors, thus protecting society against the spread of the disease....

Ethical Issues

... The current generation of health care workers had not confronted an infectious disease that posed such a serious threat. In recent years, most patients requiring care were those with chronic diseases presumably caused by environmental or lifestyle factors, not by microorganisms. But now there is HIV infection, which poses the danger of infection with a blood-borne virus. Health care workers, by virtue of their exposure to blood and body fluids, are at some risk of acquiring an HIV infection while caring for infected patients. In many areas, despite the low risk, health care workers, including physicians, nurses, emergency medical technicians, and others, have been plagued with a fear of this disease that sometimes interferes with their ability and/or willingness to care for infected persons.

In addition to the actual risk—and the perceived risk—of infection, some health care workers have expressed disapproval of the lifestyles and behaviors of some of the people who have acquired HIV infection (homosexual men, intravenous drug users, and prostitutes). Some have allowed this disapproval, and a feeling that "they got what they deserved," to interfere with the care they provide to infected persons. Fortunately, this is a minority view, and there are large numbers of health care workers who tirelessly provide quality care to HIV-infected persons in a compassionate and sensitive manner.

The ethical principle of beneficence (do not harm and promote good), amplified by the role of promoter of health and provider of care to which the health professional is committed and licensed to practice, serves as a solid rationale for the provision of care to all who need it. Health care providers also have an obligation to plan for and provide optimal treatment and care to every patient. This necessitates knowledge of and employment of all available technologies to achieve early diagnosis and treatment.

In addition, codes of ethics and statements from the various professional associations provide guidance for health professionals. The Commission applauds these groups for clear statements of obligation. A few examples:

"A physician may not ethically refuse to treat a patient whose condition is within the physician's current realm of competence solely because the patient is infected with HIV." —*American Medical Association*

"The nurse provides services with respect for human dignity and the uniqueness of the client, unrestricted by considerations of social or economic status, personal attributes, or the nature of the health problem." —*American Nurses' Association*

Chapter Ten: Financing Health Care

Equitable financing of the HIV epidemic has been one of the greatest challenges placed before our health care delivery system. This epidemic has magnified flaws in the methods and mechanisms of the health care financing system in this country and magnified the impact on the delivery of quality care and services.

The Commission believes that the financing issue is one of the most difficult problems of the HIV epidemic. It is not easy to answer the questions about treating AIDS and HIV infection apart from other devastating sicknesses and diseases. If we can make changes in our financing system, do we do it only for those with HIV or do we do it for everyone? Allocating limited health care resources when the needs are so great presents a significant challenge.

The catastrophic financial impact that HIV infection has had on the personal lives of many was shared with the Commission during four days of public hearings. Persons with symptomatic HIV infection testified on the obstacles they must overcome when becoming ill as a result of HIV: the constant fear of losing a job and thereby a means of paying for health insurance; a daunting number of forms to be filed for various assistance programs and, very often, a long waiting period before receiving benefits, if at all; and the painful process of "spending down"—using up most resources on medical bills if insurance is unavailable and income and assets are too high—in order to qualify for Medicaid benefits. The obstacles faced by these persons point out the limited access to quality care, as well as the limitations of financing illness care in general across the nation. . . .

Financing Comprehensive Care

In the public hearings on finance, the Commission addressed the problems of equitable financing of care for persons with HIV infection and discovered linkages with the broader issues of financing our health care system. The issues brought to the surface by the HIV epidemic have been part of our health care financing system for a long time: the impact of catastrophic illnesses; increasing costs of inpatient services (including funds for recruitment and retention of nurses); lack of alternatives to hospital care; and inadequate reimbursement mechanisms. . . .

Costs of Care

The costs of inpatient care for a person with AIDS are high, but are comparable to other high-cost medical conditions or illnesses. Current estimates of lifetime hospital costs for a person with AIDS are under $100,000 and annual treatment costs are approximately $40,000. In comparison, the estimated costs of a liver transplant are $175,000, of end-stage renal disease $158,000, and of a heart transplant $83,000. . . .

Reimbursement for Care

Both public and private health insurance reimbursement is based on the expected costs of a service. If the individual has no health insurance or inadequate coverage, the unreimbursed costs must be paid out-of-pocket or the hospital and other patients incur the cost for provision of service. Unreimbursed care in public hospitals must eventually be compensated by the community through general revenues.

While reimbursement has been inadequate from both public and private payers to hospitals for the costs of treating persons with HIV infection and AIDS, the problem is felt most acutely in the public hospital systems, particularly in the South. The average national inpatient cost of caring for a patient with AIDS has been estimated at about $630 per day. The Medicaid reimbursement rate in the South, however, averages about $282 per day and in other regions of the country about $500 per day. . . .

Provision of Services

A major problem in the provision of services for persons with AIDS is that public and private payers set limits on the extent of services that are covered and in many instances the excluded services are those that are most relevant in the care of persons with AIDS. . . .

In order to encourage more innovation in providing health care for persons with AIDS, several states have activated additional options under their Medicaid programs. New Jersey and New Mexico were the first two states in the country to use a waiver authorized under Section 2176 of the Omnibus Budget Reconciliation Act of 1981. This waiver allows states to provide cost-effective home and community-based care for persons with AIDS. . . .

States should continue to explore the set of options at their disposal under the Medicaid waiver program to provide appropriate, cost-effective services to persons with AIDS and extend those services to all persons with symptomatic HIV infection. We have heard testimony, however, indicating that significant administrative problems exist in obtaining approval for these waivers. The waiver review process is burdensome and includes administrative requirements, which may be unnecessary.

Another problem in the provision of services is a scarcity of resources available for dealing with HIV infection in both the inpatient setting and in providing community-based, out-of-hospital care, particularly in areas that are disproportionately affected by HIV. While there are excess hospital beds in many parts of the country, New York City is currently experiencing a shortage of beds, and it projects a need for approximately 1,300 to 1,500 beds by 1991 to care for AIDS patients. In these hard-hit areas, there is an inadequate provision of long-term care, a lack of capital funding to provide facilities, and/or a lack of treatment facilities for intravenous drug abusers. . . .

While the Commission recognizes that some suggested major adjustments will not happen in the near future, the current situation calls for immediate action to provide funding necessary to help the hardest hit areas and provide care for people in desperate need of assistance. This would mean providing targeted assistance in the form of block grants to the hardest hit areas and encouraging cost-effective care through enhanced reimbursement from the federal government. . . .

Financing Health Insurance Coverage

Access to adequate health care has been hindered by a lack of health insurance in general. As many as 35 million Americans may be without health insurance coverage. In one public hospital . . . with a large proportion of AIDS patients, fully 75 percent of its patients had no health insurance.

The lack of adequate health insurance among persons with AIDS is an even greater problem. The uninsured make up a larger proportion of persons with AIDS than among the general population (20 percent vs. 16 percent) and persons with AIDS have a much greater reliance on Medicaid than the general population (40 percent vs. 9 percent). Private health insurance and Medicaid cover about the same proportion of funding for individuals with AIDS (40 percent), but private insurance coverage among the general population is much higher (62 percent). This situation will become worse as the proportion of intravenous drug abusers among persons with AIDS continues to rise and if private insurance limits coverage for persons with AIDS. . . .

State uninsurable risk pools, now operating in 15 states and under consideration in 13 others, have provided a partial solution to comprehensive coverage of the uninsurable, but they face several problems. Experts have testified that the deficits in most of these pools are disproportionately financed by the small and medium-sized firms paying for group health insurance since many of the larger companies are self-insured and thereby exempt from contributing to high-risk pools. In addition, high premiums and coinsurance charges preclude many of the individuals in need of this health coverage from participating. On the other hand, such programs in some states are threatening to strain state budgets.

A reinforcement of the current pluralistic system, while adjustments are made and existing gaps in coverage are filled, should enable all persons to gain access to necessary care.

[Chapter Eleven omitted]

Chapter Twelve: Guidance for the Future

Over the past year, the Commission has heard testimony from over 100 officials of the federal government representing virtually every agency which has been significantly involved in responding to the epidemic. In addition, Commission staff has met with congressional offices and reviewed voluminous documents which describe policies, programs and legislative initiatives designed to respond to the HIV epidemic. Hundreds of others, including persons infected with HIV, representatives of state and local governments, the private sector and community-based organizations have offered the Commission their reflections about what the response of the federal government has been and what the response should be.

Additionally, no comprehensive legislation addressing the HIV epidemic has been enacted by the Congress. While appropriations for HIV-related research and activities have steadily increased since 1982, no comprehensive substantive legislation has emerged. Congress has spent considerable time examining the HIV epidemic via committee hearings in both the House and Senate and in floor debate when various provisions were addressed. Several pieces of comprehensive HIV legislation have been introduced and considered, but none has yet been endorsed by both houses.

As a result of the aforementioned, all Commissioners believe we have now arrived at a key milestone for placing this epidemic under closer management control than heretofore practicable. With a national strategy in hand, Commissioners believe that some special management oversight entity is needed at this early juncture in the epidemic to see that an action plan to carry out the strategy is aggressively followed. The goal of this entity should be to help bring the existing institutional process up to an acceptable level of efficiency in the near term and to remain in being until demonstrated management control over the epidemic is assured.

SOVIET PARTY CONFERENCE
June 28, 1988

"Our country is going through profound revolutionary reforms of historic significance," the Central Committee of the Soviet Union's Communist party said in its published "theses" for a party conference. The convening of the conference was part of Soviet leader Mikhail S. Gorbachev's orchestrated campaign for perestroika, a restructuring of the nation's political and economic life.

The conduct of the party's nineteenth All-Union Conference, held in Moscow June 28 to July 1, was as remarkable as the reforms it adopted. The numbing show of consensus characterizing past party gatherings was replaced by sharp debates among the 4,991 delegates and by the first openly divided votes since the 1920s. Much of this drama was broadcast on national television to an astonished Soviet public.

As the conference progressed, the New York Times reported July 2 that the delegates "seemed to undergo a transformation ... discarding their jackets, leaning forward in their seats, applauding, shouting out questions and criticism as they were swept up in the heady atmosphere of openness and unbridled discourse." The public, closely following the debates, argued among themselves "with the same fervor as the delegates."

The conference approved seven resolutions endorsing Gorbachev's blueprint for change. But it also revealed the continuing strength of party officials hesitant or hostile toward the reforms. The reforms included political changes intended to weaken the influence of the party *bureaucracy, stir up grass-roots participation, and strengthen Gorbachev's position.*

The conference approved plans to convert the largely ceremonial office of president into a position of real power. This was accomplished October 1 when the Supreme Soviet, the nominal parliament, named Gorbachev to the post, replacing the seventy-nine-year-old Andrei A. Gromyko, who resigned. Three veteran members of the Politburo had been dismissed the previous day by the party's Central Committee, which had hastily been called into session by Gorbachev. Foreign analysts concluded that Gorbachev consolidated his power to overcome internal opposition to his reforms. The enactment of these reforms into law appeared likely, leading to the election of a new national legislature in 1989.

In contrast to the June meetings, those in October "took place in time-honored Soviet style of no debate," the New York Times *reported from Moscow. It observed that the more Gorbachev "tries to disperse power, the more he finds it necessary to concentrate power in his own hands." Some Russians were left wondering, the paper added, whether his "growing power was compatible with his programs."*

Gorbachev's Appeal to the Conference

The basic question at the June conference, Gorbachev said in his opening address, was how to further "revolutionary restructuring" and to make it "irreversible." The "crucial" issue he said, was to reform the political system so that those who hesitated to support perestroika could be confident it would not be reversed like previous reform movements. Gorbachev saw glasnost—*open debate of controversial issues—as a way to build popular pressure for changing the political system.*

The need to revitalize the Soviet economy was used repeatedly by Gorbachev to justify greater political freedoms. Such freedoms, he insisted, were needed to motivate hitherto alienated Soviet citizens and thus lift the economy from years of "stagnation" under the Leonid I. Brezhnev regime (1967-1982). To make his reforms legitimate in the eyes of the party faithful, Gorbachev traced their roots to policies of Lenin that Stalin had abandoned in the late 1920s. The conference, endorsing Gorbachev's interpretation of Soviet history, approved plans for a monument to victims of Stalin's repression.

Gorbachev sought to stimulate the economy by limiting party interference in economic matters, by giving more autonomy and accountability to management, and by introducing incentives for increased productivity. He admitted that many of the hoped-for economic rewards had not been achieved, and he referred to stubborn food and housing shortages. Implicit in his concern was a belief that shortages of consumer goods could undermine popular support for perestroika. Gorbachev appealed to fears of the Soviet economy's falling behind other countries—especially in high technology—as a means of gaining support for a more open, and therefore more innovative, society.

The Central Committee theses stated that "the international position of the Soviet Union has markedly improved, and through heightened trust in our country rather than an increase in might." In his address, Gorbachev expressed regret that "we allowed ourselves to be drawn into an arms race," which he said affected the country's socioeconomic development and international standing.

Without losing their "class character," he said, referring to the Marxist framework for analyzing world politics, international relations are "increasingly coming to be precisely relations between nations." This shift from the diplomacy of global class conflict to acceptance of national "freedom of choice," Gorbachev said, means that "the imposition of a social system, way of life, or policies from outside by any means, let alone military, are dangerous trappings of the past period."

Challenging Established Ideology

Such tolerance for different social systems abroad, like the tolerance of different opinions at home, challenged established Soviet ideology and habits. "We still lack the habit to engage in debate, to dissent, to practice free competition," Gorbachev observed. His own stirring pleas for open debate and individual freedoms were often hedged with warnings against "abuses of democratisation," and he maintained that society needs "effective means of influencing anti-social elements, re-educating them and returning them to a normal working life."

While Gorbachev sought to soothe fears that a more open society might turn away from the basic values of the 1917 Russian Revolution, the Western press saw the conference as a profound challenge to Communist orthodoxy. The Economist compared Gorbachev's perestroika to the Protestant Reformation wrought by Martin Luther and John Calvin. The British magazine noted that the Soviet people were in a "state of shock" from a "sweeping reassessment of the communist creed."

The New York Times, while cautioning that the "concrete effect" of the conference remained to be seen, said it had "clearly altered the political climate." More than any event since Gorbachev took office in March 1985, the newspaper said, "the conference shattered the stifling political customs of the Soviet system, making candor, pointed debate, even public confrontation between party leaders acceptable."

Following are excerpts from the report by Mikhail Gorbachev, as general secretary of the Central Committee, to the nineteenth All-Union Party Conference, June 28, 1988, at the Kremlin Palace of Congresses in Moscow (as translated into English by Novosti Press Agency, Moscow):

Comrade delegates,

The basic question facing us, delegates to the 19th All-Union Party Conference, is how to further the revolutionary restructuring launched in our country on the initiative and under the leadership of the Party, and to make it irreversible. . . .

The past three years of our life may be quite legitimately described as a radical turn. The Party and the working people have managed to halt the country's drift towards an economic, social and spiritual crisis. Society is now more aware of its past, present, and future. The perestroika policy, as translated into concrete socio-economic programmes, is becoming the practical business of millions of people. . . .

We can see how society has rallied. The country's spiritual life has become more diverse, more interesting, and richer. Many ideas of Karl Marx and Vladimir Lenin previously treated one-sidedly, or totally hushed up, are being rethought. The creative nature of scientific and humane socialism is being revived in the struggle against dogmatism.

People have become aware of their responsibility, and are shaking off apathy and estrangement. The winds of change are improving the moral health of the people. Democratisation has released a powerful flood of thoughts, emotions and initiatives. Assertion of the truth and glasnost, is purifying the social atmosphere, giving people wings, emancipating the consciousness, and stimulating activity. . . .

In short, the main political result of the post-April 1985 period has been a change in the entire social climate, a beginning of the materialisation of the ideas of renewal, and the Soviet people's mounting support for the Party's perestroika policy.

But does this mean that changes for the better are under way everywhere, that they are going on in full gear, and that the revolutionary transformations have become irreversible?

No, it does not. If we want to be realists, comrades, we must admit that this has not yet occurred. We have not yet coped with the underlying reasons for the retarding factors, we have not yet everywhere set in motion mechanisms of renewal, and in some spheres have not even worked out any such mechanisms. The capability of a large number of Party organisations is no match as yet for the tasks of perestroika. What we need are new, qualitative changes in our development, and that calls for cardinal solutions and for vigorous and imaginative action.

We are facing many intricate questions. But which one of them is the crucial one? As the CPSU [Communist Party of the Soviet Union] Central Committee sees it, the crucial one is that of reforming our political system.

The Central Committee has expounded its platform in the Theses for the Conference. We did not intend to give ready-made answers to all matters. We figured that new ideas and proposals would arise in the course of the discussion, and that the Conference take them into account. Its decisions then will really be a collective achievement of the whole Party and people.

It follows that the political objective of our Conference is to examine the period after the April 1985 CC [Central Committee] Plenum and the 27th Congress of the CPSU comprehensively and critically, to enrich the strategy and specify the tactics of our changes, and define the ways, means and methods that would assure the steady advancement and irreversibility of our perestroika, and to do so in the spirit of Lenin's traditions and with reference to available experience.

I. To Develop and Deepen Perestroika

1. To Assess Achievements Self-Critically

... The economy is gradually gaining pace. Last year, for the first time, the entire accretion of the national income was obtained by increasing the productivity of labour. People's per capita real incomes have begun to grow again: they have gone up 4.6 percent in the past two years of the current five-year plan.

Fifteen million square metres more housing is being opened for tenancy each year as compared with the previous, eleventh, five-year period. We are reorganising public education and health in all earnest. The birth rate has gone up while the death rate has dropped. This is related to no small extent to the war we have declared on hard drinking and alcoholism.

This year, too, the socio-economic situation has been improving steadily. The national income is growing more rapidly than planned, while the number of those employed in material production has been going down in absolute terms. The output of consumer goods is rising at priority rates, which has made it possible to fulfill commodity turnover target for the first five months of this year. Sales of food products and other goods have risen 5.9 percent as compared with the same period last year, and the volume of consumer services has increased 13.5 percent.

House-building and construction of community projects has been going on at a faster rate. Construction of flats and cottages has increased six percent, that of secondary schools 22 percent, of nurseries and kindergartens, clubhouses and cultural centres some 30 percent, and hospitals as much as 100 percent.

Those are tangible fruits of perestroika. But, comrades, we have got to be self-critical; we must see clearly that despite all the positive things, the state of affairs in the economy is changing too slowly, especially if we judge by the end result, that is, the people's standard of living.

What are the reasons for this?

Frankly speaking, comrades, we have underestimated the extent and gravity of the deformations and the stagnation of the preceding period. There was a lot we simply did not know and did not see until now: the neglect in various fields of the economy turned out to be more serious than we had initially thought.

How serious the situation is, may be judged, among other things, by the country's financial situation. For many years, state budget expenditures grew more rapidly than the revenue. The budget deficit is pressing down upon the market, undermining the stability of the rouble and of monetary circulation as a whole, and giving rise to inflationary processes....

Let me begin with the food problem, which is probably the most painful and the most acute problem in the life of our society.

Some advances are on hand. But they cannot satisfy us. In substance, the increase we have achieved in food output has largely been used to cover the demand connected with the growth of the population. And that, comrades, means that we need other, still higher rates of building up food resources. We have neither the moral nor the political right to tolerate the delay in resolving the food problem.

A legitimate question: why are we taking so long to make headway here? There is no denying that many of the reasons go far back to the past when the principles of agricultural development had been gravely undermined. But this does not in the least justify the present faults. It would appear that all the knots have been untied. The collective and state farms, the districts, regions, and republics have been granted the broadest possible rights for increasing the output of crop and animal farming. Yet so far the desired result is out of reach. What is more, many of the recent decisions are not understood; they encounter procrastination and all sorts of bureaucratic hindrances, and, all too often, plain reluctance to work in a new way....

And a few words about another important problem. Whatever resources we put into agriculture, they will not yield the desired results if no concern is shown for the individual, for his conditions of work and life. I should like to say a few words specifically about social development in the countryside. Here society has accrued a considerable debt. Housing, social and cultural conditions, and medical services are of a low standard in many districts. And add to this the unsatisfactory amenities in village homes, irregular power supplies, difficulties in using domestic appliances, and the poor state of roads....

In short, comrades, the substance of the current agrarian policy is to change the relations of production on the farms. We must restore the economic balance between town and countryside, and release to the utmost the potential of collective and state farms by promoting diverse contractual and lease arrangements. We must overcome the estrangement between farmer and soil. We must make the farmer sovereign master, protect him against command methods, and cardinally change the conditions of life in villages. That is the only way to rapidly heighten the efficiency of the agro-industrial sector, and to secure a radical improvement in food supplies across the country.

A few words about the housing problem. We have tackled a most important task, that of providing practically every family with a separate flat or a cottage by the year 2000. To accomplish this, as you know, we shall have to build more than 35 million flats and cottages. Though the situation in house-building has begun to change for the better, it is still fairly tense because people have been waiting for flats for years.

We have therefore adopted extraordinary decisions, and substantially increased the volume of state-funded house-building, while cutting back on investments in industrial construction. We are also letting work collectives that have gone over to khozraschot [self-managing and self-financing] build their own housing. Tangible steps have also been taken to promote the building of condominiums and individual cottages. The idea here is to meet people's wishes to have a cooperative flat or their own cottage. Hence, all bans and restrictions have been lifted as to the size and height of the buildings. Since people are spending their earnings on it, let them build what they may need at present or in the future. The many proposals on letting people pay the state the cost of their flats so as to be able to leave them to their heirs, seem to be reasonable as well. . . .

Finally, a few words about meeting consumer demand and building up trade and services. The changes that are seen here have failed to solve the main problem: the supply of goods and services is still lagging behind people's increasing purchasing capacity, which is due largely to the neglected state of that field and to the attitude towards it. . . .

We must create a powerful up-to-date consumer industry as soon as possible. This applies not only to light industries, but also to defence factories and enterprises of the heavy industry whose contribution to the production and supply of consumer goods has got to be visibly enhanced. Not only as concerns quantity, but also quality.

Local government bodies bear a special responsibility for supplying goods and services. No few models of real initiative and enterprise are to be found in the republics and regions in saturating the market with locally-made commodities. But all too many regions tend to rely too much on others, trying to secure delivery of goods that could quite easily be produced on the spot. This approach is now unforgivable, for extensive opportunities have been created for the development of cooperatives and self-employment. Tangible results have been achieved wherever this was promptly understood and requisite conditions were provided, with new types of goods and services appearing on the market. And this can only be welcomed.

In short, the attitude towards the matter which concerns the vital interests of people, has got to be changed radically, both at the centre and locally.

2. To Consistently Carry Forward the Radical Economic Reform

Comrades, examining the progress of perestroika, we should specifically single out the progress of the radical economic reform.

The conversion of enterprises to khozraschot . . . is letting the personnel really feel their new rights, and also an uneasy burden of responsibility. And though the reform has only just begun, and the new methods of management are only just being introduced, this is already having a positive effect on many production and social problems, and the situation at enterprises as a whole.

During the current year, enterprises operating along new lines have not only reached their output targets, but have also visibly improved their economic results. This is highly important.

But the main thing today is to draw lessons from the difficulties of the initial stage of the reform.... Difficulties arose largely due to the tenacity of managerial stereotypes, to a striving to conserve familiar command methods of economic management, to the resistance of a part of the managerial personnel. In some cases, indeed, we are running into undisguised attempts at perverting the essence of the reform, at filling the new managerial forms with the old content....

And what is most intolerable is that enterprises are being compelled by means of state orders to manufacture goods that are not in demand, compelled for the simple reason that they want to attain the notorious "gross output" targets....

Considering the different starting potentials of various work collectives embarking on khozraschot and cost-effectiveness, such redistribution is probably justifiable to some extent. But the main purpose of norm-setting is to directly dovetail incomes with the end results, so that any improvement in the collective's work would be encouraged by higher incomes. We cannot tolerate any form of scrounging, be it overt or covert, and any opportunity to lead an untroubled life while doing poor work. Wage-levelling, I am sorry to say, has impressed itself much too strongly on our psychology and economic practices. We keep chasing it out of the door, as the saying goes, but it climbs back through the window.

We are running into the same problem in the reform of wages and salaries. The first results, it would appear, are promising. Collectives that have gone over to the new terms, have pushed up their productivity of labour, with payments for it also going up. But even here wage-levelling is not yielding ground. Enterprises that have been given the right to reward their more efficient workers and cut down the incomes of those who are lazy, wasteful, and idle, are using it much too timidly in fear of offending anyone....

To put it plainly, the reform will not work, will not yield the results we expect, if it does not affect the personal interests of literally every person, if it fails to become every person's vital affair....

3. To Activate the Intellectual and Spiritual Potential of Society

... When perestroika was just beginning, we formulated the task of radically altering priorities, enhancing the role of the spiritual sphere, and overcoming its underestimation. Here, too, much has changed. A new socio-political atmosphere has arisen—an atmosphere of openness, freedom of creativity and discussion, of objective, unbiassed research, criticism and self-criticism. A genuine revolution in thinking is under way, without which a new life cannot be created.

The Party attaches great significance to the contribution of our scientists to perestroika. In the Central Committee's Theses it is emphasised that the Party's economic and social strategy is to accelerate scientific and technological progress, and, above all, to master the achievements of its present-day stage, which involves advances in high technologies: in microelectronics, robotics, information science, biotechnology, etc.

There are signs of favourable changes in the development of science and technology, the attitude to the technical standards of products is more exacting, and the results emerging from research organisations are being put to use more quickly. Big steps have been taken to change the systems of planning and funding research and development, providing them with the necessary materials, making faster practical use of scientific advances, and encouraging scientific work. These measures have had a favourable effect, although as yet it has not been possible to alter the situation radically.

The situation is particularly complex in basic research, which shapes the prospects of science, and of scientific and technological progress. Many inhibiting factors still make themselves felt, factors inherited from the days when command methods of management prevailed and when science was not infrequently saddled with research areas that did not follow from the logic of its own development. And, conversely, many promising new areas of research failed to receive timely support or were even banned.

... What is most disturbing is that in the years of stagnation science in the Soviet Union fell behind in several key areas and the prevailing mode of its development became geared to "catching up with" others. It is abnormal that the academic sector of science, which does the bulk of the basic research, receives a mere 6.8 percent of the total funding of scientific work.

That is why it is not enough today merely to rectify all these errors and omissions in science policy. We are talking about a profound restructuring, about breaking down many established structures of the economic mechanism, and about improving internal relationships within science. . . .

Special attention must be given to developing the social sciences. It is they that suffered the most from the personality cult, from bureaucratic methods of management, from dogmatism and incompetent meddling. Following the 20th Congress of the CPSU there was, as is known, a noticeable increase in activity in the social sciences. New scientific areas and a new generation of scholars appeared, capable of doing things in a new way. But soon there was a resurgence of the voluntaristic approach to formulating problems in the social sciences, of dogmatic methods of solving them.

In the environment of perestroika, society is acutely in need of research in the social sciences. What we need is a genuine advancement of the social sciences on a Marxist-Leninist philosophical and methodological footing. There must be objective scientific studies of such problems of perestroika as the economic reform, the restructuring of the political system, democratisation, a humanitarian revival, interethnic relations, new political thinking, and many others. . . .

In the past three years the Party and society have seen a vigorous process of realising the enormous role of education as one of the fundamental factors in economic and social progress and spiritual rejuvenation. We have critically assessed the situation in this sphere, too, and have drawn up a programme of changes in education. Large additional funds are being channelled into this sphere. Much headway is being made in computerising the process of instruction, and the pay of teachers has been increased.

Certainly the expenditures on education and scientific research are high, but their lagging behind is immeasurably costlier. Without high standards of education, scientific research, general culture and proficiency on the job the objectives of perestroika cannot be achieved. . . .

In our political writings, literary and scientific publications there is now a discussion of unprecedented scope, frankness, and intellectual vigour concerning the ways of rejuvenating socialism, concerning history and the present day. This is a fine thing. The Party highly appreciates the growing contribution of the intelligentsia to perestroika. . . .

By and large, the processes in the cultural sphere are thus developing on a sound basis. But we would not be objective, we would be sinning against the truth, if we said that they were proceeding without contradictions and without costs, which sometimes overstep the boundaries of socialist values. Both in society as a whole and among the intelligentsia there are instances of conservatism and the rejection of the new, there is a superficiality in evaluating current events and even irresponsibility in dealing with complex problems in our development.

Unfortunately, one sometimes observes that even in this crucial time for the country's destiny some comrades just cannot give up internal strife, group obsessions, and personal ambitions. There are also quite a number of people who react with annoyance to creative quests and who see mounting diversity as a departure from the principles of socialist art. This is understandable: for much too long uniformity, monotonous conformity, and mediocrity were made out to be the hallmarks of progress. We still lack the habit to engage in debate, to dissent, to practise free competition. . . .

4. Democratising International Relations

. . . In response to the nuclear challenge to us and to the entire socialist world it was necessary to achieve strategic parity with the USA. And this was accomplished. But, while concentrating enormous funds and attention on the military aspect of countering imperialism, we did not always make use of the political opportunities opened up by the fundamental changes in the world in our efforts to assure the security of our state, to scale down tensions, and promote mutual understanding between nations. As a result, we allowed ourselves to be drawn into an arms race, which could not but affect the country's socio-economic development and its international standing.

As the arms race approached a critical point, our traditional political and social activities for peace and disarmament began, against this background, to lose their power of conviction. To put it even more bluntly, without overturning the logic of this course, we could actually have found ourselves on the brink of a military confrontation.

Hence, what was needed was not just a refinement of foreign policy, but its determined reshaping.

This called for new political thinking. The foundations of that thinking were formulated by the April 1985 Plenary Meeting of the Central Committee and the 27th Party Congress....

As we analysed the contemporary world, we realised more clearly that international relations, without losing their class character, are increasingly coming to be precisely relations between nations. We noted the enhanced role in world affairs of peoples, nations, and emerging new national entities. And this implies that there is no ignoring the diversity of interests in international affairs. Consideration for these interests is an important element of the new political thinking....

These include the programme for the step-by-step elimination of nuclear weapons by the year 2000, the system of universal security, a freedom of choice, a balance of interests, our "common European home," the restructuring of relations in the Asian and Pacific region, defence sufficiency and the non-offensive doctrine, the scaling down of arms levels as a means of strengthening national and regional security, the recall of forces from foreign territories and dismantling of bases there, confidence-building measures, international economic security, and the idea of directly projecting the authority of science into world political affairs....

A key factor in the new thinking is the concept of freedom of choice. We are convinced that this is a universal principle for international relations at a time when the very survival of civilisation has become the principal problem of the world, its common denominator.

This concept stems from the unprecedented and mounting diversity of the world. We are witnessing such a phenomenon as the active involvement in world history of millions upon millions of people who for centuries remained outside its pale. These millions are taking to the arena of independent history-making in entirely new conditions. In an environment of a universally growing national awareness they will yet have their say in taking the road of their own choice.

In this situation the imposition of a social system, way of life, or policies from outside by any means, let alone military, are dangerous trappings of the past period. Sovereignty and independence, equal rights and non-interference are becoming universally recognised rules of international relations, which is in itself a major achievement of the 20th century. To oppose freedom of choice is to come out against the objective tide of history itself. That is why power politics in all their forms and manifestations are historically obsolescent. . . .

II. Reform of the Political System: Principal Guarantee of Irreversibility of Perestroika

[Paragraph deleted]

1. Why a Reform of the Political System Is Necessary

. . . [A] . . . serious shortcoming of the political system that had taken shape was the excessive governmentalisation of public life. To be sure, the tasks and functions of the state under socialism are much bigger in scope than under capitalism. But, as conceived by the founders of Marxism-Leninism, management functions should be expanded not by strengthening power resting upon high-handed administration and compulsion, but above all by increasing the role of the democratic factor and involving broad sections of the people in administration.

Let us recall Lenin's well-known definition of the socialist state as one "which is *no longer* a state in the proper sense of the term" or even a "half-state," which gradually develops into social self-government. Unfortunately, after Lenin's death, the prevailing approach to the state in theory—and, for that matter, in practice too—became one of treating the state in the "full," that is old, meaning of the term. State regulation was extended to an inordinately broad sphere of public activities. The tendency to encompass every nook of life with detailed centralised planning and control literally straitjacketed society and became a serious brake on the initiative of people, civic organisations, and collectives. This gave rise, among other things, to a "shadow" economy and culture, which thrive as parasites on the inability of state bodies to provide timely and adequate satisfaction of the population's material and spiritual requirements. . . .

The price paid for such methods was a heavy one: indifference, a reduction in the people's social activity, and the alienation of the working man from public ownership and management. It is this ossified system of government, with its command-and-pressure mechanism, that is the cause of the fundamental problems of perestroika: the economic reform, the development of the socio-cultural sphere, and the inculcation in people of a proprietary interest in everything that goes on in the country.

. . . A new economic mechanism is gradually being whipped into shape. The character of social relations is changing. The legal basis of perestroika is being consolidated. We are learning democracy and glasnost, learning to argue and conduct a debate, to tell one another the truth. These are certainly not small things.

But the processes of democratisation—centrally and locally—are developing slowly. Today we must have the courage to admit that if the political system remains immobile and unchanged, we will not cope with the tasks of perestroika. . . .

2. Perestroika and Human Rights

... Perestroika has brought the question of people's political rights into focus. Their implementation was affected particularly painfully by the command methods of administration and associated restriction of democracy. All this retarded and inhibited the process of overcoming the people's alienation from government and from politics, a process that began with the October Revolution.

The draft political reform that is being submitted ... for discussion is aimed precisely at speeding the process of the broad involvement of the people in running the country's affairs. This, naturally, requires the establishment of realistic conditions: a modification of the electoral system, a structural reorganisation of the bodies of authority and management, and an overhaul of legislation. This, of course, also presupposes corresponding changes in the consciousness of millions ... of people.

Just now it is often being said and written by people in various localities that perestroika has not reached them; they ask when this will happen. But perestroika is not manna from the skies—instead of waiting for it to be brought in from somewhere, it has to be brought about by the people themselves in their town or village, in their work collective. What is needed today more than ever are deeds, actions, not talk about perestroika. Much here depends on our personnel, on leaders at the district, town, regional, republican and Union level....

I would like to dwell particularly on the political freedoms that enable a person to express his opinion on any matter. The implementation of these freedoms is a real guarantee that any problem of public interest will be discussed from every angle, and all the pros and cons will be weighed, and that this will help to find optimal solutions with due consideration for all the diverse opinions and actual possibilities. In short, comrades, what we are talking about is a new role of public opinion in the country. And there is no need to fear the novel, unconventional character of some opinions, there is no need to overreact and lapse into extremes at every turn of the debates.

I also want to touch upon such a fundamental matter as freedom of conscience, which is very much in the public eye just now in connection with the millennium of the introduction of Christianity in Russia. We do not conceal our attitude to the religious outlook as being non-materialistic and unscientific. But this is no reason for a disrespectful attitude to the spiritual-mindedness of the believer, still less for applying any administrative pressure to assert materialistic views.

Lenin's decree on the separation of the church from the state and schools from the church, adopted seventy years ago, provided a new basis for the relations between them. It is known that these relations have not always developed normally. But the course of events, history united believers and non-believers as Soviet citizens and patriots in the years of the ordeal of the Great Patriotic War, in building up our socialist society, and in the struggle for peace.

All believers, irrespective of the religion they profess, are full-fledged citizens of the USSR. The overwhelming majority of them take an active part in our industrial and civic life, in solving the problems of perestroika. The law on freedom of conscience now being drafted is based on Lenin's principles and takes into consideration all the realities of the present day.

Now about the personal rights of citizens. Here, too, there is a need for more precise legislative regulation. Something has already been accomplished. There was deep satisfaction at the decision not to consider unsigned poison-pen letters, at the establishment of criminal liability for victimising people for criticism, at the procedure for taking officials to court for illegal actions and compensation for damages caused by such actions, and at measures providing greater protection of the rights of the mentally ill. Our entire legal system is designed to guarantee strict observance of the rights of citizens to the inviolability of their private life, home, the secrecy of telephone communication, postal and telegraph correspondence. The law must reliably protect a person's dignity.

But while in every way protecting and guaranteeing people's rights and freedoms, we cannot divorce them from civil duties. Democracy presupposes a rational social order, without which, actually, there can be no personal freedom. Our legislation has the purpose of firmly protecting society from all kinds of money-grubbers, scroungers, pilferers, hooligans, slanderers, and boors. Society must have at its disposal effective means of influencing anti-social elements, re-educating and returning them to a normal working life.

One more problem. The assertion of personal rights and freedoms, and the expansion of democracy and glasnost in general, must proceed hand-in-hand with the reinforcement of legality and the inculcation of an absolute respect for the law. Democracy is incompatible either with wantonness, or with irresponsibility, or with permissiveness.

As you know, we have lately more than once encountered attempts to use democratic rights for undemocratic purposes. There are some who think that in this way any problems can be solved—from redrawing boundaries to setting up opposition parties. The CPSU Central Committee considers that such abuses of democratisation are fundamentally at variance with the aims of perestroika and run counter to the people's interests. . . .

3. Perfecting the Organisation of Government

. . . Many suggested that we turn to the record of the first post-revolutionary decades with their system of Congresses of Soviets. Those were broad and plenipotentiary people's assemblies, and in between the necessary work was performed by the central executive committees which enjoyed sufficiently extensive powers. Mass representation was combined with constant legislative, administrative and monitoring work. In the course of the discussion it was also suggested that our public organisations be directly represented on our country's supreme government body.

Summing up these views, the CPSU Central Committee is submitting the following proposals for consideration by the Conference.

First, that representation of the working people in the top echelon of government be extended considerably.

With this end in view, direct representation of the public organisations incorporated into our political system should be added to the currently existing territorial representation of the entire population on the Soviet of the Union and the representation of our nations and nationalities on the Soviet of Nationalities. Thus 1,500 deputies would be elected, as they are now, from the territorial and national districts, and approximately another 750 deputies would be elected at the congresses or at plenary sessions of the governing bodies of Party, trade union, cooperative, youth, women's, veterans', academic, writers', artists', and other organisations. The list of these organisations and the quotas of their representation could be incorporated into the Constitution.

All these deputies, elected for a five-year term, would comprise a new representative supreme government body—the Congress of the USSR People's Deputies. It would be convened annually to decide on ... constitutional, political and socio-economic issues.

The Congress of People's Deputies would elect from among its members a relatively small (say, 400- to 450-strong) bicameral USSR Supreme Soviet which would consider and decide all legislative, administrative and monitoring questions and direct the activities of the bodies accountable to it and of the lower-level Soviets. It would be a standing supreme government body reporting to the Congress of People's Deputies. In this way, all legislative and monitoring work would be concentrated directly within the Supreme Soviet and its commissions. That would be a new step forward in the democratisation of the highest structures of government. We can also consider a periodic renewal of part of the USSR Supreme Soviet.

Second, the work of the chambers of the USSR Supreme Soviet should be stepped up and their current functional anonymity ended.

Naturally, draft legislation and other matters of key importance to the country should, as before, be considered and decided by the members of both chambers of the Supreme Soviet.

At the same time, the Soviet of Nationalities which represents all of the country's national entities—Union and Autonomous republics and Autonomous regions and areas—could consider issues of their economic and social development, interethnic relations, observance of relevant legislation, monitoring the activities performed by USSR ministries and agencies and affecting the interests of republics or autonomous entities, etc.

For its part, the Soviet of the Union, which represents the interests of all the people, of all classes and social groups, could focus on the drafting of major socio-economic programmes and plans and on policy issues concerning prices, taxation, labour relations, protection of civil rights, the strengthening of national defence, the ratification of international treaties and the like.

Here at this Conference we should agree in general terms on the division of the chambers' functions. All this should be specified in the USSR Constitution and other legislative instruments. . . .

In the opinion of the CPSU Central Committee, establishing the post of President of the USSR Supreme Soviet would be in line with enhancing the role played by the supreme representative bodies and by the entire system of the Soviets of People's Deputies, strengthening the rule-of-law basis of government and improving the representation of the Soviet Union in world affairs. It should be ruled that the President shall be elected and recalled by secret ballot by, and be fully answerable and accountable to, the Congress of the USSR People's Deputies. Given the overall strengthening of the role played by representative bodies, the President of the USSR Supreme Soviet should be granted sufficiently broad state authority powers. Specifically, the President could exercise overall guidance in the drafting of legislation and of major socio-economic programmes, decide on the key issues of foreign policy, defence and national security, chair the Defence Council, submit proposals on nominating the Chairman of the USSR Council of Ministers, and discharge several other duties traditionally connected with the Presidency.

We also believe that the government structure at top level should comprise a Presidium of the USSR Supreme Soviet which would be guided in its work by the President of the Supreme Soviet. Serving on the Presidium could be two senior Vice-Presidents (one being the Chairman of the USSR People's Control Committee), fifteen Vice-Presidents (one from each Union republic), and the chairmen of the chambers, standing commissions and committees of the Supreme Soviet. The Presidium would convene sessions, coordinate the work of the commissions and deputies of the Supreme Soviet, and discharge certain representative and other functions.

It would be useful to enhance the status of the standing commissions to be established by the supreme government body and comprising members of the Supreme Soviet and of the Congress of People's Deputies. These bodies could be established by the chambers both separately and jointly (joint committees).

In view of their new tasks, the commissions and committees should be granted much broader powers. Specifically, a provision could be adopted stating that decisions on major issues of domestic and foreign policy and on the appointment of heads of ministries and departments and other officials could be taken only after a preliminary discussion of these matters in the commissions and committees. It would be advisable to expand the practice of open hearings in the commissions and committees and to set up special groups of deputies to study questions of acute public interest.

There is also the issue of establishing, within the structure of supreme authority, a Constitutional Review Committee to be elected by the Congress of the USSR People's Deputies. It would verify the constitutionality of our legislation and other legal instruments and have sufficient powers to do it. Incidentally, this committee would be an additional guarantee of democratic control over the activities of all officials, including those in top-level posts.

Third, the new forms of organisation of supreme authority do not by themselves guarantee its efficiency. This objective calls for a radical change in the very character and style of the work performed by the Supreme Soviet. Its sessions should do away with long-winded speeches, with statements in which the speaker reports on his own accomplishments, with excessive and formalistic organisational procedures. The sessions should become lively and demanding; they should compare different suggestions and discuss amendments, additions and objections. It would be worthwhile to designate dates on which the government would reply to questions from deputies and to expand the practice of deputies' inquiries. . . .

[Sections 4-7 omitted]

III. Democratisation of the Leading Role and Internal Activity of the CPSU

. . . The Central Committee has spoken in favour of sociopolitical certification procedures for Communists, and we have felt that this proposal is, in principle, approved of.

However, apprehensions, too, have been expressed, two apprehensions, in fact. Some insist that such certification will be of no use, that the Party should be purged and relieved of the dead wood. We in the Central Committee consider this approach incorrect in the conditions of perestroika and democratisation. I will tell you why. Many of these who only recently were regarded inactive and had lost contact with the Party branch, who had been regarded as dead wood, are now trying to find their place in life. Comrades in the Party should be treated with utmost respect. . . .

. . . By proposing the idea of the Party's self-purification we expect that certification would be conducted in keeping with the Party Rules, in the framework of a normal democratic process, at open Party meetings, and not by commissions of three or five persons, nor through discussion behind the scenes, nor by issuing testimonials which are not to be made public. The very certification process should be a school of educating Communists, from which they would emerge closely united by the bonds of Party comradeship, by the common goals and tasks set by perestroika for all of us.

The next question, and a very significant one, concerns admittance to the Party. We should not hesitate to get rid of all kinds of quotas and bureaucratic approaches to this question which is so vital to the Party. The main criterion of appraising the merits of a person applying for Party membership is his stance and the part he really plays in perestroika. . . .

We see socialism as a system of the true equality of all nations and nationalities, a system in which they are assured social and spiritual advancement and mutual enrichment, in which there is no room for any strife between nations, for nationalist and chauvinist prejudices, and in which internationalism and the fraternity of nations rule supreme. . . .

We are convinced in the vitality of the Marxist-Leninist teaching which has scientifically substantiated the possibility of building a society of social justice and a civilisation of free and equal people. That is what guides us in our revolutionary perestroika. And that is how we shall act in its new and crucial stage that is being ushered in by our Party Conference!

Comrades, as I conclude my report, I should like to refer in general outline to the discussion that preceded the Conference and that was especially active after the Theses of the Central Committee were published.

It is a long time since our Party and society had so broad, so impassioned and fruitful a discussion, with vital thinking, a large number of proposals, and an often sharp collision of opinions. At its centre were the essential chief issues of perestroika and the democratisation of public and inner-Party life. In effect, it concerned just one thing: how to do the job better. . . .

COURT ON
INDEPENDENT COUNSEL
June 29, 1988

In a constitutionally significant decision, the Supreme Court on June 29 upheld the legality of a 1978 law that permits the appointment of an independent counsel—a special prosecutor—to investigate claims of wrongdoing by government officials. The central issue was whether the law violated the Constitution's separation-of-powers doctrine by encroaching on executive branch prerogatives.

The decisive 7-1 ruling in the case of Morrison v. Olson *was a defeat for President Ronald Reagan, who opposed the law. The defeat was sharpened by the fact that the decision was delivered by William H. Rehnquist, whom Reagan had elevated to chief justice in 1986 in the apparent belief that as fellow political conservatives they shared essentially the same ideology.*

Speaking for the Court's majority, Rehnquist undercut a key defense argument of Theodore B. Olson, a former assistant attorney general accused of falsely testifying before Congress in its 1983 investigation of the "superfund" toxic waste-disposal program. Olson had challenged the May 1986 appointment of Alexia Morrison as special prosecutor, arguing that the appointment of special prosecutors was unlawful. A federal district court rejected his argument, but an appeals court agreed with him, holding that the law was unconstitutional. Morrison then took the case to the Supreme Court.

By declaring the special prosecutor law valid, the Supreme Court in effect upheld the convictions of former Reagan aides Michael K. Deaver and Lyn (Franklyn C.) Nofziger and permitted special prosecutor investigations of other former administration officials to continue. Those officials included Lt. Col. Oliver North, Rear Adm. John M. Poindexter, Maj. Gen. Richard V. Secord, and Albert Hakim, all of whom awaited trial on charges of conspiring to defraud the United States and trying to thwart congressional inquiries into the funding of Nicaragua's contra rebels. The charges grew out of an investigation, headed by independent counsel Lawrence E. Walsh, into the use of proceeds from the secret sale of arms to Iran to finance the insurgency in Nicaragua. (Iran-Contra Reports, Historic Documents of 1987, p. 891)

Deaver was the first person convicted under the special prosecutor law. On December 16, 1987, he was found guilty by a federal district court of commiting perjury during an investigation of his lobbying activities after he left the White House.

Nofziger was convicted February 11, 1988, of illegal lobbying. Still another independent counsel's investigation focused on Attorney General Edwin Meese III. The counsel, James C. McKay, issued a report July 5, 1988, saying that Meese "probably" had violated federal tax and conflict-of-interest laws, but McKay declined to prosecute the attorney general. That same day, Meese, saying that he had been cleared of wrongdoing, announced his resignation as the nation's chief law enforcement officer. (Ethics Investigation of Edwin Meese III, p. 495)

The use of special prosecutors to look into government corruption predates the 1978 law by more than a century. A special prosecutor was first used to determine whether President Ulysses S. Grant's personal secretary was involved with a ring of tax-evading whiskey distillers. In this century, special prosecutors investigated the Teapot Dome scandal in Warren G. Harding's administration, allegations of tax-fixing during Harry S Truman's presidency, and the illegal Watergate-related activities that forced President Richard Nixon to resign from office in 1974. During the Watergate investigation, Nixon fired Special Prosecutor Archibald Cox, causing Attorney General Elliot L. Richardson and Deputy Attorney General William Ruckelshaus to resign in protest. From the events of that time, Congress determined the need for a law detailing what authority, responsibility, and protection from firing should be accorded a special prosecutor—who by then was being called an independent counsel.

The provisions of the independent counsel law, enacted as Title VI of the 1978 Ethics in Government Act, were distilled from numerous proposals citing the need for an independent investigator to handle politically sensitive cases. The objective was to eliminate having the attorney general, a political appointee, investigate the president, the attorney general, or other high officials in the executive branch of government.

Background to the Suit

The Morrison v. Olson *case involved a dispute between Congress and the Environmental Protection Agency. Two congressional subcommittees sought to obtain documents relating to the agency's administration of the superfund law, which created a special fund for cleaning up toxic waste sites. On advice from Olson, the president cited executive privilege and directed the agency's administrator to withhold the documents. The House Judiciary Committee subsequently suggested in a formal report that Olson had given false and misleading testimony to Congress, and that he and two other Justice Department officials—Edward Schmults and Carol Dinkins—had wrongfully withheld documents from the committee, thus obstructing its investigation. Committee chairman Peter W. Rodino, Jr., D-N.J., requested that Meese set in motion the procedure for the appointment of an independent counsel to look into the allegations. Counsels are appointed by a special three-judge panel upon request of the attorney general.*

Morrison was appointed to that position May 29, 1986, and she requested Meese to allow her to investigate Schmults and Dinkins as well as Olson. He refused, and she appealed to a special three-judge panel. It similarly refused, holding that the attorney general's decision was final and unreviewable under the statute.

The question of the law's constitutionality drew a "yes" ruling July 20, 1987, in District of Columbia federal court. However, on January 22, 1988, the U.S. Court of Appeals for the District of Columbia concluded by a 2-1 majority that the law encroached on presidential prerogatives and gave the judiciary inappropriate powers. Morrison then appealed to the Supreme Court.

Majority Ruling and Dissent

Rehnquist's majority opinion rejected the encroachment view. The argument turned essentially on the question of whether the independent counsel was an "inferior" or "principal" judicial officer under terms of the Constitution's "Appointments Clause" (Article II, Section 2). An inferior officer could be appointed by congressionally crafted procedure—as was set forth in the 1978 law—but a principal officer had to be nominated by the president and confirmed by the Senate. Acknowledging that the line between inferior and principal officers was "far from clear," Rehnquist concluded that the special prosecutor "clearly falls on the 'inferior officer' side of that line."

The law did not "unduly interfere" with the executive branch, he concluded. The case did "not involve an attempt by Congress to increase its own powers at the expense of the Executive Branch.... Congress retained for itself no powers of control or supervision over an independent counsel."

The lone dissenter, Justice Antonin Scalia (Justice Anthony M. Kennedy did not participate in the ruling), characterized the majority opinion as a misguided interpretation of the Constitution and the special prosecutor statute. In an impassioned dissent that was as lengthy as the thirty-eight page majority opinion, Scalia challenged the notion that the independent counsel's authority was limited and that the position was "inferior." Scalia argued that the statute had "an intimidating effect" on the president and his aides. He contended that the majority opinion was "ad hoc" and "standardless"—essentially the subjective view of the majority, who determined that the power taken from the president by the independent counsel was not "too" much.

Impact of the Ruling

"The decision is not a green light for Congress to go and run federal programs of any kind," said Alan B. Morrison, head of the Public Citizen Litigation Group. But, he added, "I think this opinion could be read as saying that Congress, when it acts to limit presidential power, has got some authority." A former Justice Department official, Richard K. Willard, said the Court's decision was so "vague and imprecise" that it was hard to predict future application. "The Court doesn't establish any bright line" for resolving disputes, he said. The decision, however, meant that investigations of several past Reagan administration officials would continue. Walsh, independent counsel in the Iran-contra investigation, said he was "gratified" that the Court upheld the law. He said it "provides a workable solution to a difficult problem."

Following are excerpts from the Supreme Court's 7-1 ruling in Morrison v. Olson, *June 29, 1988, upholding the constitutionality of the law providing for the appointment of a special prosecutor, or independent counsel, to investigate alleged wrongdoing by high executive branch officials, and from the dissent by Justice Antonin Scalia:*

<u>No. 87-1279</u>

Alexia Morrison, Independent
Counsel, Appellant
v.
Theodore B. Olson, Edward C.
Schmults, and Carol E. Dinkins

On appeal from the United States Court of Appeals for the District of Columbia Circuit

[June 29, 1988]

CHIEF JUSTICE REHNQUIST delivered the opinion of the Court. This case presents us with a challenge to the independent counsel provisions of the Ethics in Government Act of 1978. We hold today that these provisions of the Act do not violate the Appointments Clause of the Constitution, Art. II, § 2, cl. 2, or the limitations of Article III, nor do they impermissibly interfere with the President's authority under Article II in violation of the constitutional principle of separation of powers.

I

Briefly stated, Title VI of the Ethics of Government Act (Title VI or the Act), allows for the appointment of an "independent counsel" to investigate and, if appropriate, prosecute certain high ranking government officials for violations of federal criminal laws. The Act requires the Attorney General, upon receipt of information that he determines is "sufficient to constitute grounds to investigate whether any person [covered by the Act] may have violated any Federal criminal law," to conduct a preliminary investigation of the matter. When the Attorney General has completed this investigation, or 90 days has elapsed, he is required to report to a special court (the Special Division) created by the Act "for the purpose of appointing independent counsels." If the Attorney General determines that "there are no reasonable grounds to believe that further investigation is warranted," then he must notify the Special Division of this result. In such a case, "the division of the court shall have no power to appoint an independent counsel." If, however, the Attorney General has determined that there are "reasonable grounds to believe that further investigation or prosecution is warranted," then he "shall apply to the division of the court for the appointment of an independent counsel." The Attorney General's application to the court "shall contain sufficient information to assist the [court] in selecting an independent counsel and in defining that independent counsel's prosecutorial jurisdiction." Upon receiving this application, the Special Division "shall appoint an appropriate independent counsel and shall define that independent counsel's prosecutorial jurisdiction."

With respect to all matters within the independent counsel's jurisdiction, the Act grants the counsel "full power and independent authority to exercise all investigative and prosecutorial functions and powers of the Department of Justice, the Attorney General, and any other officer or employee of the Department of Justice." The functions of the independent counsel include conducting grand jury proceedings and other investigations, participating in civil and criminal court proceedings and litigation, and appealing any decision in any case in which the counsel participates in an official capacity. ... [T]he counsel's powers include "initiating and conducting prosecutions in any court of competent jurisdiction, framing and signing indictments, filing informations, and handling all aspects of any case, in the name of the United States.". . .

Two statutory provisions govern the length of an independent counsel's tenure in office. The first defines the procedure for removing an independent counsel. Section 596(a)(1) provides:

"An independent counsel ... may be removed from office, other than by impeachment and conviction, only by the personal action of the Attorney General and only for good cause, physical disability, mental incapacity, or any other condition that substantially impairs the performance of such independent counsel's duties."

If an independent counsel is removed pursuant to this section, the Attorney General is required to submit a report to both the Special Division and the Judiciary Committees of the Senate and the House "specifying the facts found and the ultimate grounds for such removal." ... [A]n independent counsel can obtain judicial review of the Attorney General's action by filing a civil action in the United States District Court for the District of Columbia....

The other provision ... defines the procedures for "terminating" the counsel's office. Under § 596(b)(1), the office of an independent counsel terminates when he notifies the Attorney General that he has completed or substantially completed any investigations or prosecutions undertaken pursuant to the Act. In addition, the Special Division, acting either on its own or on the suggestion of the Attorney General, may terminate the office of an independent counsel at any time if it finds that "the investigation of all matters within the prosecutorial jurisdiction of such independent counsel ... have been completed or so substantially completed that it would be appropriate for the Department of Justice to complete such investigations and prosecutions."

Finally, the Act provides for Congressional oversight of the activities of independent counsels. An independent counsel may from time to time send Congress statements or reports on his activities. The "appropriate committees of the Congress" are given oversight jurisdiction in regard to the official conduct of an independent counsel, and the counsel is required by the Act to cooperate with Congress in the exercise of this jurisdiction....

II

Before we get to the merits, we first must deal with appellant's contention that the constitutional issues addressed by the Court of Appeals cannot be reviewed on this appeal from the District Court's contempt judgment. Appellant relies on *Blair* v. *United States* (1919), in which this Court limited rather sharply the issues that may be raised by an individual who has been subpoenaed as a grand jury witness and has been held in contempt for failure to comply with the subpoena. On the facts of this case, however, we find it unnecessary to consider whether *Blair* has since been narrowed by our more recent decisions, as appellees contend and the Court of Appeals found in another related case, *In re Sealed Case* (1987). Appellant herself admits that she failed to object to the District Court's consideration of the merits of appellees' constitutional claims, and as a result, the Court of Appeals ruled that she had waived her opportunity to contend on appeal that review of those claims was barred by *Blair*. We see no reason why the Court of Appeals was not entitled to conclude that the failure of appellant to object on this ground in the District Court was a sufficient reason for refusing to consider it, and we likewise decline to consider it. . . .

III

The Appointments Clause of Article II reads as follows:

"[The President] shall nominate, and by and with the Advice and Consent of the Senate, shall appoint Ambassadors, other public Ministers and Consuls, Judges of the supreme Court, and all other Officers of the United States, whose Appointments are not herein otherwise provided for, and which shall be established by Law: but the Congress may by Law vest the Appointment of such inferior Officers, as they think proper, in the President alone, in the Courts of Law, or in the Heads of Departments."

. . . The initial question is, accordingly, whether appellant is an "inferior" or a "principal" officer. If she is the latter, as the Court of Appeals concluded, then the Act is in violation of the Appointments Clause.

The line between "inferior" and "principal" officers is one that is far from clear, and the Framers provided little guidance into where it should be drawn. . . . We need not attempt here to decide exactly where the line falls between the two types of officers, because in our view appellant clearly falls on the "inferior officer" side of that line. Several factors lead to this conclusion.

First, appellant is subject to removal by a higher Executive Branch official. Although appellant may not be "subordinate" to the Attorney General (and the President) insofar as she possesses a degree of independent discretion to exercise the powers delegated to her under the Act, the fact that she can be removed by the Attorney General indicates that she is to some degree "inferior" in rank and authority. Second, appellant is empowered by the Act to perform only certain, limited duties. An independent counsel's role is restricted primarily to investigation and, if appropriate, prosecution for certain federal crimes. Admittedly, the Act delegates to appellant "full power and independent authority to exercise all investigative and prosecutorial functions and powers of the Department of Justice," but this grant of authority does not include any authority to formulate policy for the Government or the Executive Branch, nor does it give appellant any administrative duties outside of those necessary to operate her office. The Act specifically provides that in policy matters appellant is to comply to the extent possible with the policies of the Department.

Third, appellant's office is limited in jurisdiction. Not only is the Act itself restricted in applicability to certain federal officials suspected of certain serious federal crimes, but an independent counsel can only act within the scope of the jurisdiction that has been granted by the Special Division pursuant to a request by the Attorney General. Finally, appellant's office is limited in tenure. There is concededly no time limit on the appointment of a particular counsel. Nonetheless, the office of independent counsel is "temporary" in the sense that an independent counsel is appointed essentially to accomplish a single task, and when that task is over the office is terminated, either by the counsel herself or by action of the Special Division. Unlike other prosecutors, appellant has no ongoing responsibilities that extend beyond the accomplishment of the mission that she was appointed for and authorized by the Special Division to undertake. In our view, these factors are sufficient to establish that appellant is an "inferior" officer in the constitutional sense.

This conclusion is consistent with our few previous decisions that considered the question of whether a particular government official is a "principal" or an "inferior" officer. In *United States* v. *Eaton* (1898), for example, we approved Department of State regulations that allowed executive officials to appoint a "vice-consul" during the temporary absence of the consul, terming the "vice-consul" a "subordinate officer" notwithstanding the Appointment Clause's specific reference to "Consuls" as principal officers. As we stated, "Because the subordinate officer is charged with the performance of the duty of the superior for a limited time and under special and temporary conditions he is not thereby transformed into the superior and permanent official." In *Ex parte Siebold* (1880), the Court found that federal "supervisor[s] of elections," who were charged with various duties involving oversight of local congressional elections were inferior officers for purposes of the Clause....

This does not, however, end our inquiry under the Appointments Clause. Appellees argue that even if appellant is an "inferior" officer, the Clause does not empower Congress to place the power to appoint such an officer outside the Executive Branch. They contend that the Clause does not contemplate congressional authorization of "interbranch appointments," in which an officer of one branch is appointed by officers of another branch. The relevant language of the Appointments Clause is worth repeating. It reads: "... but the Congress may by Law vest the Appointment of such inferior Officers, as they think proper, in the President alone, in the courts of Law, or in the Heads of Departments." On its face, the language of this "excepting clause" admits of no limitation on interbranch appointments. Indeed, the inclusion of "as they think proper" seems clearly to give Congress significant discretion to determine whether it is "proper" to vest the appointment of, for example, executive officials in the "courts of Law." We recognized as much in one of our few decisions in this area, *Ex parte Siebold*....

We also note that the history of the clause provides no support for appellees' position.... [T]here was little or no debate [in the Constitutional Convention] on the question of whether the Clause empowers Congress to provide for interbranch appointments, and there is nothing to suggest that the Framers intended to prevent Congress from having that power.

We do not mean to say that Congress' power to provide for interbranch appointments of "inferior officers" is unlimited. In addition to separation of powers concerns, which would arise if such provisions for appointment had the potential to impair the constitutional functions assigned to one of the branches, *Siebold* itself suggested that Congress' decision to vest the appointment power in the courts would be improper if there was some "incongruity" between the functions normally performed by the courts and the peformance of their duty to appoint. . . . In this case, however, we do not think it impermissible for Congress to vest the power to appoint independent counsels in a specially created federal court. We thus disagree with the Court of Appeals' conclusion that there is an inherent incongruity about a court having the power to appoint prosecutorial officers. . . . Congress of course was concerned when it created the office of independent counsel with the conflicts of interest that could arise in situations when the Executive Branch is called upon to investigate its own high-ranking officers. If it were to remove the appointing authority from the Executive Branch, the most logical place to put it was in the Judicial Branch. In the light of the Act's provision making the judges of the Special Division ineligible to participate in any matters relating to an independent counsel they have appointed, we do not think that appointment of the independent counsels by the court runs afoul of the constitutional limitation on "incongruous" interbranch appointments.

IV

Appellees next contend that the powers vested in the Special Division by the Act conflict with Article III of the Constitution. We have long recognized that by the express provision of Article III, the judicial power of the United States is limited to "Cases" and "Controversies." See *Muskrat v. United States* (1911). As a general rule, we have broadly stated that "executive or administrative duties of a nonjudicial nature may not be imposed on judges holding office under Art. III of the Constitution." *Buckley* [1976]. The purpose of this limitation is to help ensure the independence of the Judicial Branch and to prevent the judiciary from encroaching into areas reserved for the other branches. . . .

[T]he Act vests in the Special Division the power to choose who will serve as independent counsel and the power to define his or her jurisdiction. Clearly, once it is accepted that the Appointments Clause gives Congress the power to vest the appointment of officials such as the independent counsel in the "courts of Law," there can be no Article II objection to the Special Division's exercise of that power, as the power itself derives from the Appointments Clause, a source of authority for judicial action that is independent of Article III. Appellees contend, however, that the Division's Appointments Clause powers do not encompass the power to define the independent counsel's jurisdiction. We disagree. In our view, Congress' power under the Clause to vest the "Appointment" of inferior officers in the courts may, in certain circumstances, allow Congress to give the courts some discretion in defining the nature and scope of the appointed official's authority. Particularly when, as here, Congress creates a temporary "office" the nature and duties of which will by necessity vary with the factual circumstances giving rise to the need for an appointment in the first place, it may vest the power to define the scope of the office in the court as an incident to the appointment of the officer pursuant to the Appointments Clause. This said, we do not think that Congress may give the Division *unlimited* discretion to determine the independent counsel's jurisdiction. In order for the Division's definition of the counsel's jurisdiction to be truly "incidental" to its power to appoint, the jurisdiction that the court decides upon must be demonstrably related to the factual circumstances that gave rise to the Attorney General's investigation and request for the appointment of the independent counsel in the particular case....

The Act also vests in the Special Division various powers and duties in relation to the independent counsel that, because they do not involve appointing the counsel or defining her jurisdiction, cannot be said to derive from the Division's Appointments Clause authority. These duties include granting extensions for the Attorney General's preliminary investigation; receiving the report of the Attorney General at the conclusion of his preliminary investigation; referring matters to the counsel upon request; receiving reports from the counsel regarding expenses incurred; receiving a report from the Attorney General following the removal of an independent counsel; granting attorney's fees upon request to individuals who were investigated but not indicted by an independent counsel; receiving a final report from the counsel; deciding whether to release the counsel's final report to Congress or the public and determining whether any protective orders should be issued; and terminating an independent counsel when his task is completed.

Leaving aside for the moment the Division's power to terminate an independent counsel, we do not think that Article III absolutely prevents Congress from vesting these other miscellaneous powers in the Special Division pursuant to the Act....

We are more doubtful about the Special Division's power to terminate the office of the independent counsel.... As appellees suggest, the power to terminate, especially when exercised by the Division on its own motion, is "administrative" to the extent that it requires the Special Division to monitor the progress of proceedings of the independent counsel and come to a decision as to whether the counsel's job is "completed." It also is not a power that could be considered typically "judicial," as it has few analogues among the court's more traditional powers. Nonetheless, we do not, as did the Court of Appeals, view this provision as a significant judicial encroachment upon executive power or upon the prosecutorial discretion of the independent counsel.

We think that the Court of Appeals overstated the matter when it described the power to terminate as a "broadsword and ... rapier" that enables the court to "control the pace and depth of the independent counsel's activities." The provision has not been tested in practice, and we do not mean to say that an adventurous special court could not reasonably construe the provision as did the Court of Appeals; but it is the duty of federal courts to construe a statute in order to save it from constitutional infirmities, and to that end we think a narrow construction is appropriate here. . . .

Nor do we believe . . . that the Special Division's exercise of the various powers specifically granted to it under the act poses any threat to the "impartial and independent federal adjudication of claims within the judicial power of the United States." We reach this conclusion for two reasons. First, the Act as it currently stands gives the Special Division itself no power to review any of the actions of the independent counsel or any of the actions of the Attorney General with regard to the counsel. Accordingly, there is no risk of partisan or biased adjudication of claims regarding the independent counsel by that court. Second, the Act prevents members of the Special Division from participating in "*any* judicial proceeding concerning a matter which involves such independent counsel while such independent counsel is serving in that office or which involves the exercise of such independent counsel's official duties, regardless of whether such independent counsel is still serving in that office." . . . We think both the special court and its judges are sufficiently isolated by these statutory provisions from the review of the activities of the independent counsel so as to avoid any taint of the independence of the judiciary such as would render the Act invalid under Article III.

We emphasize, nevertheless, that the Special Division has *no* authority to take any action or undertake any duties that are not specifically authorized by the Act. . . .

V

We now turn to consider whether the Act is invalid under the constitutional principle of separation of powers. Two related issues must be addressed: The first is whether the provision of the Act restricting the Attorney General's power to remove the independent counsel to only those instances in which he can show "good cause," taken by itself, impermissibly interferes with the President's exercise of his constitutionally appointed functions. The second is whether, taken as a whole, the Act violates the separation of powers by reducing the President's ability to control the prosecutorial powers wielded by the independent counsel.

A

Two Terms ago we had occasion to consider whether it was consistent with the separation of powers for Congress to pass a statute that authorized a government official who is removable only by Congress to participate in what we found to be "executive powers." *Bowsher* v. *Synar* (1986). We held in *Bowsher* that "Congress cannot reserve for itself the power of removal of an officer charged with the execution of the laws except by impeachment." A primary antecedent for this ruling was our

1925 decision in *Myers* v. *United States* (1926). *Myers* had considered the propriety of a federal statute by which certain postmasters of the United States could be removed by the President only "by and with the advice and consent of the Senate." There too, Congress' attempt to involve itself in the removal of an executive official was found to be sufficient grounds to render the statute invalid....

Unlike both *Bowsher* and *Myers,* this case does not involve an attempt by Congress itself to gain a role in the removal of executive officials other than its established powers of impeachment and conviction. The Act instead puts the removal power squarely in the hands of the Executive Branch; an independent counsel may be removed from office, "only by the personal action of the Attorney General, and only for good cause." There is no requirement of congressional approval of the Attorney General's removal decision, though the decision is subject to judicial review....

... [T]he real question is whether the removal restrictions are of such a nature that they impede the President's ability to perform his constitutional duty....

... Although the counsel exercises no small amount of discretion and judgment in deciding how to carry out her duties under the Act, we simply do not see how the President's need to control the exercise of that discretion is so central to the functioning of the Executive Branch as to require as a matter of constitutional law that the counsel be terminable at will by the President.

Nor do we think that the "good cause" removal provision ... impermissibly burdens the President's power to control or supervise the independent counsel, as an executive official, in the execution of her duties under the Act. This is not a case in which the power to remove an executive official has been completely stripped from the President.... Rather, because the independent counsel may be terminated for "good cause," the Executive, through the Attorney General, retains ample authority to assure that the counsel is competently performing her statutory responsibilities....

B

The final question to be addressed is whether the Act, taken as a whole, violates the principle of separation of powers by unduly interfering with the role of the Executive Branch....

We observe first that this case does not involve an attempt by Congress to increase its own powers at the expense of the Executive Branch.... The Act does empower certain members of Congress to request the Attorney General to apply for the appointment of an independent counsel, but the Attorney General has no duty to comply with the request, although he must respond within a certain time limit. Other than that, Congress' role under the Act is limited to receiving reports or other information and oversight of independent counsel's activities....

Similarly, we do not think that the Act works any *judicial* usurpation of properly executive functions....

VI

In sum, we conclude today that it does not violate the Appointments Clause for Congress to vest the appointment of independent counsels in the Special Division; that the powers exercised by the Special Division under the Act do not violate Article III; and that the Act does not violate the separation of powers principle by impermissibly interfering with the functions of the Executive Branch. The decision of the Court of Appeals is therefore

Reversed.

JUSTICE KENNEDY took no part in the consideration or decision of this case.

JUSTICE SCALIA, dissenting.

I

. . . [T]he Act before us here requires the Attorney General to apply for the appointment of an independent counsel within 90 days after receiving a request to do so, unless he determines within that period that "there are no reasonable grounds to believe that further investigation or prosecution is warranted." As a practical matter, it would be surprising if the Attorney General had any choice (assuming this statute is constitutional) but to seek appointment of an independent counsel to pursue the charges against the principal object of the congressional request, Mr. Olson. Merely the political consequences (to him and the President) of seeming to break the law by refusing to do so would have been substantial. . . . But the Act establishes more than just practical compulsion. Although the Court's opinion asserts that the Attorney General had "no duty to comply with the [congressional] request," that is not entirely accurate. He *had* a duty to comply unless he could conclude that there were *"no reasonable grounds to believe,"* not that prosecution was warranted, but merely that *"further investigation"* was warranted (emphasis added), after a 90-day investigation in which he was prohibited from using such routine investigative techniques as grand juries, plea bargaining, grants of immunity or even subpoenas. The Court also makes much of the fact that "the courts are specifically prevented from reviewing the Attorney General's decision not to seek appointment. Yes, but *Congress* is not prevented from reviewing it. The context of this statute is acrid with the smell of threatened impeachment. . . .

Thus, by the application of this statute in the present case, Congress has effectively compelled a criminal investigation of a high-level appointee of the President in connection with his actions arising out of a bitter power dispute between the President and the Legislative Branch. Mr. Olson may or may not be guilty of a crime; we do not know. But we do know that the investigation of him has been commenced, not necessarily because the President or his authorized subordinates believe it is in the interest of the

United States ... but only because the Attorney General cannot affirm, as Congress demands, that there are *no reasonable grounds to believe* that further investigation is warranted....

II

If to describe this case is not to decide it, the concept of a government of separate and coordinate powers no longer has meaning. The Court devotes most of its attention to such relatively technical details as the Appointments Clause and the removal power, addressing briefly and only at the end of its opinion the separation of powers....

To repeat, Art. II, § 1, cl. 1 of the Constitution provides:

"The executive Power shall be vested in a President of the United States."

As I described at the outset of this opinion, this does not mean *some of* the executive power, but *all of* the executive power. It seems to me, therefore, that the decision of the Court of Appeals invalidating the present statute must be upheld on fundamental separation-of-powers principles if the following two questions are answered affirmatively: (1) Is the conduct of a criminal prosecution (and of an investigation to decide whether to prosecute) the exercise of purely executive power? (2) Does the statute deprive the President of the United States of exclusive control over the exercise of that power? Surprising to say, the Court appears to concede an affirmative answer to both questions, but seeks to avoid the inevitable conclusion that since the statute vests some purely executive power in a person who is not the President of the United States it is void.

... [The] President's constitutionally assigned duties include *complete* control over investigation and prosecution of violations of the law, and that the inexorable command of Article II is clear and definite: the executive power must be vested in the President of the United States.

It is unthinkable that the President should have such exclusive power, even when alleged crimes by him or his close associates are at issue? No more so than that Congress should have the exclusive power of legislation, even when what is at issue is its own exemption from the burdens of certain laws....

The Court has, nonetheless, replaced the clear constitutional prescription that the executive power belongs to the President with a "balancing test." What are the standards to determine how the balance is to be struck, that is, how much removal of presidential power is too much? ... Once we depart from the text of the Constitution, just where short of that do we stop? The most amazing feature of the Court's opinion is that it does not even purport to give an answer....

U.S. DISTRICT COURT ORDER TO BAR CLOSING OF PLO OFFICE

June 29, 1988

In the final days of the 1987 session of Congress, the Senate declared the Palestine Liberation Organization (PLO) a "terrorist" organization, requiring the federal government to close the PLO's quasi-diplomatic offices in Washington and New York. This action set in motion a chain of events that divided the Reagan administration, embroiled the United States in a diplomatic wrangle with the United Nations, and created court cases at home and abroad.

The declaration came in the form of amendments to a bill authorizing funds for the State Department. Offered by Sen. Charles E. Grassley, R-Iowa, they were quickly approved by voice vote in the Senate and became known as the Grassley amendments or formally as the Anti-Terrorism Act of 1987. The House approved the amendments as part of a legislative package that compromised House-Senate differences over the bill.

No problem arose over closing the PLO's Washington office, but the New York office was the organization's mission to the United Nations. The United Nations and many individual countries—including most of America's European allies—argued that to close the office would violate a treaty in which the United States guaranteed the rights of UN diplomats to maintain offices in New York.

The PLO observer mission to the United Nations was established in 1974. That November 22 the General Assembly passed resolution 3237 inviting the PLO to "participate in the sessions and the work of the General Assembly in the capacity of observer." The United States, as the host country, was obligated, by a treaty known as the Headquarters Agreement, to allow PLO personnel to "enter and remain in the United States to carry out their official functions at the United Nations."

At issue was the validity of the Anti-Terrorism Act. On December 27, 1987, President Ronald Reagan signed into law the authorization bill, though objecting to office-closing provisions. The law took effect March 21, 1988.

The General Assembly had meanwhile met in emergency session on March 2 and approved resolutions declaring that the closing would violate international law and asking for a ruling from the International Court of Justice (World Court) as to whether the United States should be required to submit the issue to arbitration. One-hundred forty-three nations voted for each resolution. Israel cast the only vote against the first resolution, and did not vote on the second. The United States listed itself as a nonvoting participant.

The World Court issued an advisory opinion April 26 stating that the United States was obligated, "in accordance with section 21 [of the Headquarters Agreement], to enter arbitration for the settlement of the dispute between itself and the United Nations."

Three of the four justices who heard the case wrote in their separate concurring opinions that little disagreement existed between the United Nations and the United States over the meaning of the Headquarters Agreement. Citing statements by Secretary of State George P. Shultz, the justices acknowledged that the administration wanted to honor the Headquarters Agreement and to reconcile domestic law with the treaty obligations.

This reconciliation was left to the determination of U.S. District Court Judge Edmund Palmieri in New York City. The day the law took effect, the Justice Department petitioned his court in Manhattan to grant an injunction ordering the PLO office to be closed. The PLO challenged the law's validity.

On June 29, Palmieri ruled that the Anti-Terrorist Act did not override the Headquarters Agreement. Palmieri interpreted the law as "inapplicable to the PLO Mission to the United Nations." "The Agreement, along with longstanding practice," he said, "leaves no doubt that it places an obligation upon the United States to refrain from impairing the function of the PLO observer mission."

President Reagan, supported by the State Department, was reported to have intervened with the Justice Department and requested that it not appeal the judge's ruling. The Justice Department announced on August 29 that the case would be dropped. Its announcement said the administration's "decision was based on a determination that, on balance, the interests of the United States" would not be served by an appeal.

Following are excerpts of the order and opinion issued by Judge Edmund L. Palmieri in U.S. District Court, Southern District of New York, June 29, 1988, allowing the PLO mission to the United Nations to remain open:

The Anti-terrorism Act of 1987 (the "ATA"), is the focal point of this lawsuit. At the center of controversy is the right of the Palestine Liberation Organization (the "PLO") to maintain its office in conjunction with its work as a Permanent Observer to the United Nations. The case comes before the court on the government's motion for an injunction closing this office and on the defendants' motions to dismiss.

I

Background

The United Nations' Headquarters in New York were established as an international enclave by the *Agreement Between the United States and the United Nations Regarding the Headquarters of the United Nations* (the "Headquarters Agreement"). This agreement followed an invitation extended to the United Nations by the United States, one of its principal founders, to establish its seat within the United States. . . . Today, 159 of the United Nations' members maintain missions to the U.N. in New York. . . . In addition, the United Nations has, from its incipiency, welcomed various non-member observers to participate in its proceedings. . . . Of these, several non-member nations, intergovernmental organizations, and other organizations currently maintain "Permanent Observer Missions" in New York.

The PLO falls into the last of these categories and is present at the United Nations as its invitee. . . . The PLO has none of the usual attributes of sovereignty. It is not accredited to the United States and does not have the benefits of diplomatic immunity. There is no recognized state it claims to govern. It purports to serve as the sole political representative of the Palestinian people. . . . The PLO nevertheless considers itself to be the representative of a state, entitled to recognition in its relations with other governments, and is said to have diplomatic relations with approximately one hundred countries throughout the world. . . .

II

The Anti-Terrorism Act

In October 1986, members of Congress requested the United States Department of State to close the PLO offices located in the United States. That request proved unsuccessful, and proponents of the request introduced legislation with the explicit purpose of doing so.

The result was the ATA. It is of a unique nature. We have been unable to find any comparable statute in the long history of Congressional enactments. The PLO is stated to be "a terrorist organization and a threat

481

to the interests of the United States, its allies, and to international law and should not benefit from operating in the United States." The ATA was added, without committee hearings, as a rider to the Foreign Relations Authorization Act for Fiscal Years 1988-89, which provided funds for the operation of the State Department, including the operation of the United States Mission to the United Nations. The bill also authorized payments to the United Nations for maintenance and operation.

The ATA, which became effective on March 21, 1988, forbids the establishment or maintenance of "an office, headquarters, premises, or other facilities or establishments within the jurisdiction of the United States at the behest or direction of, or with funds provided by" the PLO. . . .

Ten days before the effective date, the Attorney General wrote the Chief of the PLO Observer Mission to the United Nations that "maintaining a PLO Observer Mission to the United Nations will be unlawful," and advised him that upon failure of compliance, the Department of Justice would take action in federal court. . . .

The United States commenced this lawsuit the day the ATA took effect, seeking injunctive relief to accomplish the closure of the Mission. The United States Attorney for this District [Southern New York] has personally represented that no action would be taken to enforce the ATA pending resolution of the litigation in this court.

There are now four individual defendants in addition to the PLO itself. Defendant Zuhdi Labib Terzi, who possesses an Algerian passport but whose citizenship is not divulged, has served as the Permanent Observer of the PLO to the United Nations since 1975. Defendant Riyad H. Mansour, a citizen of the United States, has been the Deputy Permanent Observer of the PLO to the United Nations since 1983. Defendant Nasser Al-Kidwa, a citizen of Iraq, is the Alternate Permanent Observer of the PLO to the United Nations. And defendant Veronica Kanaan Pugh, a citizen of Great Britain, is charged with administrative duties at the Observer Mission. These defendants contend that this court may not adjudicate the ATA's applicability to the Mission because such an adjudication would violate the United States' obligation under Section 21 of the Headquarters Agreement to arbitrate any dispute with the United Nations. Apart from that, they argue, application of the ATA to the PLO Mission would violate the United States' commitments under the Headquarters Agreement. They assert that the court lacks subject matter and personal jurisdiction over them and that they lack the capacity to be sued. Defendant Riyad H. Mansour additionally moves to dismiss for failure to state a claim upon which relief can be granted. Plaintiff, the United States, moves for summary judgment.

III

Personal Jurisdiction over the Defendants

. . . The PLO does not argue that it or its employees are the beneficiaries of any diplomatic immunity due to its presence as an invitee of the United

Nations. We have no difficulty in concluding that the court has personal jurisdiction over the PLO and the individual defendants.

IV

The Duty to Arbitrate

Counsel for the PLO and for the United Nations and the Association of the Bar of the City of New York, as *amici curiae,* have suggested that the court defer to an advisory opinion of the International Court of Justice. That decision holds that the United States is bound by Section 21 of the Headquarters Agreement to submit to binding arbitration of a dispute precipitated by the passage of the ATA. Indeed, it is the PLO's position that this alleged duty to arbitrate deprives the court of subject matter jurisdiction over this litigation.

In June 1947, the United States subscribed to the Headquarters Agreement, defining the privileges and immunities of the United Nations' Headquarters in New York City, thereby becoming the "Host Country".... Section 21(a) of the Headquarters Agreement ... provides for arbitration in the case of any dispute between the United Nations and the United States concerning the interpretation or application of the Headquarters Agreement. Because interpretation of the ATA requires an interpretation of the Headquarters Argreement, they argue, this court must await the decision of an arbitral tribunal yet to be appointed before making its decision.

... Because these proceedings are not in any way directed to settling any dispute, ripe or not, between the United Nations and the United States, Section 21, is, by its terms, inapplicable. The fact that the Headquarters Agreement was adopted by a majority of both Houses of Congress and approved by the President, might lead to the conclusion that it provides a rule of decision requiring arbitration any time the interpretation of the Headquarters Agreement is at issue in the United States Courts. That conclusion would be wrong for two reasons.

First, this court cannot direct the United States to submit to arbitration without exceeding the scope of its Article III powers. What sets this case apart from the usual situation in which two parties have agreed to binding arbitration for the settlement of any future disputes, requiring the court to stay its proceedings, is that we are here involved with matters of international policy. This is an area in which the courts are generally unable to participate. These questions do not lend themselves to resolution by adjudication under our jurisprudence. ... [It] is a question of policy not for the courts but for the political branches to decide. ... It would not be consonant with the court's duties for it to await the interpretation of the Headquarters Agreement by an arbitral tribunal, not yet constituted, before undertaking the limited task of interpreting the ATA with a view to resolving the actual dispute before it.

In view of the foregoing, the court finds that it is not deprived of subject matter jurisdiction by Section 21 of the Headquarters Agreement and that any interpretation of the Headquarters Agreement incident to an interpretation of the ATA must be done by the court.

V

The Anti-Terrorism Act
and the Headquarters Agreement

If the ATA were construed as the government suggests, it would be tantamount to a direction to the PLO Observer Mission at the United Nations that it close its doors and cease its operations *instanter*. Such an interpretation would fly in the face of the Headquarters Agreement, a prior treaty between the United Nations and the United States, and would abruptly terminate the functions the Mission has performed for many years. This conflict requires the court to seek out a reconciliation between the two.

Under our constitutional system, statutes and treaties are both the supreme law of the land, and the Constitution sets forth no order of precedence to differentiate between them. Wherever possible, both are to be given effect. Only where a treaty is irreconcilable with a later enacted statute and Congress has clearly evinced an intent to supersede a treaty by enacting a statute does the later enacted statute take precedence....

The long standing and well-established position of the Mission at the United Nations, sustained by international agreement, when considered along with the text of the ATA and its legislative history, fails to disclose any clear legislative intent that Congress was directing the Attorney General, the State Department or this Court to act in contravention of the Headquarters Agreement. This court acknowledges the validity of the government's position that Congress *has the power* to enact statutes abrogating prior treaties or international obligations entered into by the United States. However, unless this power is clearly and unequivocally exercised, this court is under a duty to interpret statutes in a manner consonant with existing treaty obligations. This is a rule of statutory construction sustained by an unbroken line of authority for over a century and a half....

We believe the ATA and the Headquarters Agreement cannot be reconciled except by finding the ATA inapplicable to the PLO Observer Mission....

... The United States has, for fourteen years, acted in a manner consistent with a recognition of the PLO's rights in the Headquarters Agreement. This course of conduct under the Headquarters Agreement is important evidence of its meaning....

It seemed clear to those in the executive branch that closing the PLO mission would be a departure from the United States' practice in regard to observer missions, and they made their views known to members of Congress who were instrumental in the passage of the ATA. In addition,

United States representatives to the United Nations made repeated efforts to allay the concerns of the U.N. Secretariat by reiterating and reaffirming the obligations of the United States under the Headquarters Agreement. . . .

. . . [T]he language, application and interpretation of the Headquarters Agreement lead us to the conclusion that it requires the United States to refrain from interference with the PLO Observer Mission in the discharge of its functions at the United Nations. . . .

We have interpreted the ATA as inapplicable to the PLO Mission to the United Nations. The statute remains a valid enactment of general application. It is a wide gauged restriction of PLO activity within the United States and, depending on the nature of its enforcement, could effectively curtail any PLO activities in the United States, aside from the Mission to the United Nations. We do not accept the suggestion of counsel that the ATA be struck down. The federal courts are constrained to avoid a decision regarding unconstitutionality except where strictly necessary. . . .

VI

Conclusions

The Anti-Terrorism Act does not require the closure of the PLO Permanent Observer Mission to the United Nations nor do the act's provisions impair the continued exercise of its appropriate functions as a Permanent Observer at the United Nations. The PLO Mission to the United Nations is an invitee of the United Nations under the Headquarters Agreement and its status is protected by that agreement. The Headquarters Agreement remains a valid and outstanding treaty obligation of the United States. It has not been superceded by the Anti-Terrorism Act, which is a valid enactment of general application. . . .

The motion of the defendants to dismiss for lack of personal jurisdiction is denied.

The motion of the defendants to dismiss for lack of subject matter jurisdiction is denied.

The motion of the defendants to dismiss for lack of capacity, which was not briefed, is denied.

Mansour's motion to dismiss for failure to state a claim upon which relief may be granted is treated, pursuant to Rule 12(b) of the Federal Rules of Civil Procedure, as a motion for summary judgment, Fed. R. Civ. P. 56, and is granted.

The motion of the United States for summary judgment is denied, and summary judgment is entered for the defendants, dismissing this action with prejudice.

SO ORDERED:

Edmund L. Palmieri
United States District Judge

July

Excommunication of Archbishop Lefebvre ... 489

Ethics Investigation of Edwin Meese III 495

Endowment Report
on the State of the Humanities 517

Iran-Iraq Truce 529

Democratic National Convention 533

Democratic Party Platform 557

Trade Pact with Canada 571

King Hussein's Speech
Severing West Bank Ties 579

EXCOMMUNICATION OF ARCHBISHOP LEFEBVRE

July 1, 1988

After two decades of arguments with French Archbishop Marcel Lefebvre, the Vatican excommunicated him on July 1—and announced it July 11—bringing about the Catholic church's first official schism since the Polish National Church of America broke away from Rome at the turn of the century. Before that, none had occurred since groups of Catholics in Austria, Germany, and Switzerland (subsequently called Old Catholics) split off over the first Vatican Council's adoption of the dogma of papal infallibility in 1870.

The 1988 schism resulted from the refusal of Archbishop Lefebvre and his followers to abide by changes in church practice and doctrine that were initiated by the second Vatican Council (Vatican II). Ever since the council closed in 1965, the archbishop had been outspoken in his opposition to its stated aim of "updating" the church. Lefebvre especially abhorred catholicism's attempts to bring about reconciliation with other churches and religions, and the church's new forms of worship—especially the abandonment of the Latin mass in favor of the parishioner's native tongue. He repeatedly denounced "modernism, socialism, and Zionism" in the church.

The eighty-two-year-old archbishop drew the excommunication, however, not for his divergent views but for his defiance of Pope John Paul II, who had refused him permission to consecrate four priests as bishops to carry on his work. Protracted negotiations with Rome collapsed and Lefebvre proceeded with his long-announced plans to carry out the consecrations. This he did on June 30, in a tent-church at the Swiss village of Econe, near Geneva, where he formed the Fraternity of St. Pius X in 1969. The following year, he established a seminary there to train future priests in traditionalist values. Lefebvre defied the Bishop of Rome, he said, to save the "true church" from apostasy. He said the excommunication, formally casting him out of the church, was "null and void"—something imposed by the "anti-Christs" in the Vatican.

This was not the first "Econe affair" with which the Holy See had had to contend. In 1975 the Vatican withdrew its approval of the Fraternity of St. Pius X, but it continued functioning. The next year Pope Paul VI suspended the archbishop's priestly functions, prohibiting him from celebrating the mass and giving sacraments. It was Lefebvre's punishment for ordaining some of his seminarians as priests without proper authority. He ignored the penalty and kept ordaining.

However, without other bishops among his followers, no one could continue to ordain priests if Lefebvre died. So to try to ensure his movement's survival, the archbishop announced in June 1987 that he was preparing to elevate four priests to bishop. From that time until almost the eve of their consecration at Econe, Vatican officials had sought his acceptance of compromise agreements.

The two sides reached a tentative accord on May 5 by which the Vatican would recognize the Fraternity of St. Pius X as legitimate and Lefebvre would nominate a candidate for bishop, subject to the pope's approval. Vatican officials accused him of reneging on the agreement; Lefebvre said it broke down because liberal bishops complained that Rome had yielded too much. Further efforts failed. The Vatican released an exchange of letters between Pope John Paul and his dissident archbishop in which, on June 2, Lefebvre said the consecration would go on as scheduled. He added: "We shall continue to pray that modern Rome, infested by modernism, will once again become Catholic Rome and will once again find its 2,000-year-old tradition." The pope wrote him on June 9: "I exhort you, venerable brother, to give up your project . . . [and] invite you to return, in humility, to full obedience to the vicar of Christ." The next missive from Rome about the matter, as released by the Vatican, was the notice of excommunication.

All four newly consecrated bishops were also excommunicated. They were Bernard Tissier de Mallerais, 43, a Frenchman serving as secretary general of the Fraternity of St. Pius X; Bernard Fellay, 30, a Swiss ranked as the order's top administrator; Alfonso de Galarreta, 31, a Spaniard in charge of its seminary in Argentina; and Richard William- son, 48, an Englishman in charge of St. Thomas Aquinas Seminary in Ridgefield, Connecticut.

The size of the movement they represent is uncertain. Vatican officials credited it with no more than 60,000 to 100,000 followers and said it would probably shrink as a result of the excommunications. Other estimates had run as high as 500,000 believers in thirty countries, principally France, Switzerland, and the United States. After the excommunications, a commission was created and entrusted with the mission of bringing back into the church about 250 priests who were said to be Lefebvre supporters. Some success was reported.

Following are the texts of the Vatican document announcing Archbishop Lefebvre's excommunication, dated July 1, and of a papal letter to the archbishop's followers, dated July 2, as translated from Latin and published in the English-language edition of the official newspaper L'Osservatore Romano, *upon their release to the public on July 11:*

EXCOMMUNICATION TEXT

Msgr. Marcel Lefebvre, archbishop-bishop emeritus of Tulle, notwithstanding the formal canonical warning of last June 17 and the repeated appeals to desist from his intention, has performed a schismatical act by the episcopal consecration of four priests, without pontifical mandate and contrary to the will of the supreme pontiff, and has therefore incurred the penalty envisaged by Canon 1364, Paragraph 1 and Canon 1382 of the Code of Canon Law.

Having taken account of all the juridical effects, I declare that the above-mentioned Msgr. Marcel Lefebvre and Bernard Fellay, Bernard Tissier de Mallerais, Richard Williamson and Alfonso de Galarreta have incurred "ipso facto" excommunication "latae sententiae" reserved to the Apostolic See.

Moreover, I declare that Msgr. Antonio de Castro Mayer, bishop emeritus of Campos, since he took part directly in the liturgical celebration as co-consecrator and adhered publicly to the schismatical act, has incurred excommunication "latae sententiae" as envisaged by Canon 1364, Paragraph 1.

The priests and faithful are warned not to support the schism of Msgr. Lefebvre, otherwise they shall incur "ipso facto" the very grave penalty of excommunication.

From the office of the Congregation for Bishops, July 1, 1988,

Cardinal Bernardin Gantin, prefect of the Congregation for Bishops.

PAPAL LETTER

1. With great affliction the church has learned of the unlawful episcopal ordination conferred on June 30 by Archbishop Marcel Lefebvre, which has frustrated all the efforts made during the previous years to ensure the

full communion with the church of the Priestly Society of St. Pius X, founded by the same Msgr. Lefebvre. These efforts, especially intense during recent months, in which the Apostolic See has shown comprehension to the limits of the possible, were all to no avail.

2. This affliction was particularly felt by the successor of Peter to whom in the first place pertains the guardianship of the unity of the church, even though the number of persons directly involved in these events might be few, since every person is loved by God on his own account and has been redeemed by the blood of Christ shed on the cross for the salvation of all.

The particular circumstances, both objective and subjective, in which Archbishop Lefebvre acted provide everyone with an occasion for profound reflection and for a renewed pledge of fidelity to Christ and to his church.

3. In itself, this act was one of disobedience to the Roman pontiff in a very grave matter and of supreme importance for the unity of the church, such as is the ordination of bishops whereby the apostolic succession is sacramentally perpetuated. Hence such disobedience—which implies in practice the rejection of the Roman primacy—constitutes a schismatic act. In performing such an act, notwithstanding the formal canonical warning sent to them by the cardinal prefect of the Congregation for Bishops on June 17, Msgr. Lefebvre and the priests Bernard Fellay, Bernard Tissier de Mallerais, Richard Williamson and Alfonso de Galarreta, have incurred the grave penalty of excommunication envisaged by ecclesiastical law.

4. The root of this schismatic act can be discerned in an incomplete and contradictory notion of tradition. Incomplete, because it does not take sufficiently into account the living character of tradition, which, as the Second Vatican Council clearly taught, "comes from the apostles and progresses in the church with the help of the Holy Spirit. There is a growth in insight into the realities and words that are being passed on. This comes about in various ways. It comes through the contemplation and study of believers who ponder these things in their hearts. It comes from the intimate sense of spiritual realities which they experience. And it comes from the preaching of those who have received, along with their right of succession in the spiscopate, the sure charism of truth."

But especially contradictory is a notion of tradition which opposes the universal magisterium of the church possessed by the bishop of Rome and the body of bishops. It is impossible to remain faithful to the tradition while breaking the ecclesial bond with him to whom, in the person of the apostle Peter, Christ himself entrusted the ministry of unity in his church.

5. Faced with the situation that has arisen, I deem it my duty to inform all the Catholic faithful of some aspects which this sad event has highlighted.

A) The outcome of the movement promoted by Msgr. Lefebvre can and must be, for all the Catholic faithful, a motive for sincere reflection concerning their own fidelity to the church's tradition, authentically interpreted by the ecclesiastical magisterium, ordinary and extraordinary, especially in the ecumenical councils from Nicaea to Vatican II. From this reflection all should draw a renewed and efficacious conviction of the necessity of strengthening still more their fidelity by rejecting erroneous interpretations and arbitrary and unauthorized applications in matters of doctrine, liturgy and discipline.

To the bishops especially it pertains, by reason of their pastoral mission, to exercise the important duty of a clear-sighted vigilance full of charity and firmness, so that this fidelity may be everywhere safeguarded.

However, it is necessary that all the pastors and the other faithful have a new awareness, not only of the lawfulness but also of the richness for the church of a diversity of charisms, traditions of spirituality and apostolate, which also constitutes the beauty of unity in variety: of that blended "harmony" which the earthly church raises up to heaven under the impulse of the Holy Spirit.

B) Moreover, I should like to remind theologians and other experts in the ecclesiastical sciences that they should feel called upon to answer in the present circumstances. Indeed, the extent and depth of the teaching of the Second Vatican Council call for a renewed commitment to deeper study in order to reveal clearly the council's continuity with tradition, especially in points of doctrine which, perhaps because they are new, have not yet been well understood by some sections of the church.

C) In the present circumstances I wish especially to make an appeal, both solemn and heartfelt, paternal and fraternal, to all those who until now have been linked in various ways to the movement of Archbishop Lefebvre, that they may fulfill the grave duty of remaining united to the vicar of Christ in the unity of the Catholic Church, and of ceasing their support in any way for that movement.

Everyone should be aware that formal adherence to the schism is a grave offense against God and carries the penalty of excommunication decreed by the church's law.

To all those Catholic faithful who feel attached to some previous liturgical and disciplinary forms of the Latin tradition, I wish to manifest my will to facilitate their ecclesial communion by means of the necessary measures to guarantee respect for their rightful aspirations. In this matter I ask for the support of the bishops and of all those engaged in the pastoral ministry in the church.

6. Taking account of the importance and complexity of the problems referred to in this document, by virtue of my apostolic authority I decree the following:

A) A commission is instituted whose task it will be to collaborate with the bishops, with the departments of their Roman Curia and with the circles concerned, for the purpose of facilitating full ecclesial communion of priests, seminarians, religious communities or individuals until now linked in various ways to the fraternity founded by Msgr. Lefebvre, who may wish to remain united to the successor of Peter in the Catholic Church, while preserving their spiritual and liturgical traditions, in the light of the protocol signed on May 5 by Cardinal [Joseph] Ratzinger and Msgr. Lefebvre.

B) This commission is composed of a cardinal-president and other members of the Roman Curia, in a number that will be deemed opportune according to circumstances.

C) Moreover, respect must everywhere be shown for the feelings of all those who are attached to the Latin liturgical tradition, by a wide and generous application of the directives already issued some time ago by the Apostolic See, for the use of the Roman missal according to the typical edition of 1962.

7. As this year specially dedicated to the Blessed Virgin is now drawing to a close, I wish to exhort all to join in unceasing prayer which the vicar of Christ, through the intercession of the Mother of the Church, addresses to the Father in the very words of the Son: "That they all may be one!"

Given at Rome, at St. Peter's, July 2, 1988, the 10th year of the pontificate,

John Paul II

ETHICS INVESTIGATION
OF EDWIN MEESE III
July 5, 1988

While stating that Attorney General Edwin Meese III had "probably violated the criminal law" in certain instances "but that no prosecution is warranted," Independent Counsel James C. McKay concluded an investigation of the nation's top law-enforcement officer. Meese, a confidant of President Ronald Reagan, long had been troubled by personal legal and ethical questions. After serving as the presidential counselor during Reagan's first term, he was nominated by Reagan in 1984 to become attorney general. But it took thirteen months for the Senate to confirm his appointment, and the final vote (63-31), on February 23, 1985, came only after another independent counsel had investigated allegations of improprieties involving Meese's personal financial dealings and found no evidence that he had broken the law.

McKay's inquiry into Meese's activities began in May 1987 as the outgrowth of an investigation he was conducting as an independent counsel (special prosecutor) into the dealings of Lyn (Franklyn C.) Nofziger, another of Reagan's former presidential assistants. The special prosecutor set forth a detailed account of his findings and conclusions in a 518-page report, "In Re Edwin Meese III," filed July 5 with a special three-member panel of federal appellate judges in Washington, D.C. The panel was set up under terms of the 1978 Ethics in Government Act, which provides the legal mechanisms for independent investigations in government in instances when the Justice Department's own inquiries might create conflicts of interest. The legality of investigations by independent counsels had been challenged by the Reagan administration and remained in question until it was upheld by the Supreme Court on June 29. (Court on Independent Counsel, p. 465)

McKay and his staff investigated allegations that Meese (1) assisted Wedtech Corporation, a Bronx, New York, defense contracting company, on behalf of a friend who helped him financially; (2) willfully filed a false income tax return; (3) failed to pay capital gains taxes when they were due; and (4) twice ran afoul of conflict-of-interest laws by participating in regulatory matters involving the telephone industry when he had financial interests at stake.

When the report was publicly released July 18, McKay told a news conference that he had decided not to prosecute Meese because "it came down to the question, 'If this were an ordinary person, would he be prosecuted?' And we concluded that he probably would not be." When the still-secret report was submitted to the judiciary panel, Meese declared that he had been "completely vindicated." He explained: "When he [McKay] decided to file a report rather than file an indictment, he has completed his task, and that is vindication. He has fulfilled his duty in a way that indicates that the allegations that were made are false."

Upon the report's public release, Meese told a news conference he was indignant at its suggestions that he had broken the law. "The assertion is absolutely false.... I have always acted legally, ethically and properly," he said. His lawyers filed a 104-page response to the report, contending that many erroneous conclusions had been drawn from the factual information.

Meese had informed Reagan when the report was filed on July 5 that he intended to resign later that summer, though without specifying a departure date. The president promptly issued a statement saying: "I accept with regret Attorney General Meese's determination to step down." Reagan added that his "good friend and close adviser" of more than two decades "has served the American people loyally and well." Meese remained in office until his successor, Richard L. Thornburgh, was sworn into office on August 12. Thornburgh, a Republican former governor of Pennsylvania, had little difficulty in winning the Senate's approval of his nomination. It voted unanimously (85-0) for his confirmation.

For Meese's detractors, particularly those in Congress, the report confirmed their contention that he had not met the ethical demands of his office. The Justice Department's Office of Professional Responsibility reported to Thornburgh in October that Meese had "engaged in conduct which should not be tolerated of any government employee," the Washington Post reported January 17, 1979. The report had not been publicly released at that time.

For several months Meese's continued presence in office had been *regarded as an embarrassment to the Reagan administration and a liability to Vice President George Bush's presidential candidacy. Deputy Attorney General Arnold Burns, who together with another ranking Justice Department official abruptly resigned in March, later testified before Congress that life in the Justice Department under Meese had become bizarre—"a world of Alice in Wonderland . . . of illusion in which up was down . . . in was out . . . rain was sunshine." Burns said, "Meese still clings to the thought that he committed no crime . . . no wrong . . . no act or impropriety . . . no ethical violation . . . nor error of bad taste or bad judgment."*

Meese's Personal Finances

During his 1985 confirmation hearings as attorney general, Meese promised members of the Senate Judiciary Committee that he would sell his securities, including stock in the American Telephone & Telegraph Company (AT&T) and in regional operating companies of the Bell telephone system, the so-called "Baby Bells." The securities were not sold until September 1987. McKay said in his report that Meese, meanwhile, in October 1985, gave then-Assistant Attorney General Douglas H. Ginsburg approval to seek court action to loosen restrictions on the regional companies.

Both of these acts, the prosecutor said, constituted "personal and substantial participation" by Meese within the meaning of conflict-of-interest laws. But McKay said he decided not to prosecute because there was no evidence that "Meese acted from motivation for personal gain" and because his intervention did not alter the Justice Department's policy in regard to the Baby Bells.

The tax allegations stemmed from Meese's 1985 federal income-tax return, filed October 15, 1986. McKay said Meese did not declare certain capital gains from the sale of securities in 1985 and did not pay $3,579 in taxes on those capital gains. The prosecutor said this appeared to be an isolated case of a tax violation and that the attorney general "never intended permanently" to deprive the government of revenue. He eventually paid the taxes.

Wedtech Bribery Allegations

Meese's alleged improprieties in the Wedtech matter occurred in 1981 and 1982, when he was still in the White House. According to McKay's report, businessman E. Robert Wallach, who was later indicted for alleged irregularities in his dealings with Wedtech, enlisted Meese's help in obtaining a contract to build small engines for the United States Army. However, "there is no substantial evidence" that Meese acted for reasons other than friendship, McKay determined.

Related allegations involved Meese's 1985 assistance to Wallach to build an oil pipeline from Iraq to the port of Aqaba in Jordan. McKay said that at Wallach's urging Meese asked Robert C. McFarlane, then presidential assistant for national security affairs, to meet with Wallach about United States participation in a financial guarantee for the pipeline. Meese then asked Assistant Attorney General Allan Gerson to prepare a memo supporting the legality of such a financial guarantee.

The special prosecutor pointed out "some notable coincidences in the timing of Mr. Meese's acceptance of things of value from Mr. Wallach and some of the official acts done by Mr. Meese that benefited Mr. Wallach." Those "things of value," McKay said, included Wallach's paying for social functions Meese attended, facilitating an $80,000 personal loan for Meese, providing Meese free legal services, and trying to arrange employment for Meese's wife. But McKay concluded that "there is nothing inherent in any of the things of value ... or in the circumstances of Mr. Meese's acceptance of them, that constitutes sufficient evidence to determine that they were accepted as unlawful gratuities."

McKay noted that his investigation was hampered by his not being able to obtain sworn testimony from Wallach and several other persons both in the United States and Israel, including former prime minister Shimon Peres. Wallach purportedly sought assurance that Israel would not disrupt the proposed pipeline. According to McKay, Wallach had informed Meese "orally and in writing" of a plan that included a "covert payment of some kind from profits generated by the Aqaba project" to Israel's Labor party, which Peres led. Despite Wallach's "startling language" about a payoff to the Labor party, the prosecutor said "available evidence does not meet the requisite standard of proof" to conclude that Meese violated the foreign bribery statute.

Wedtech's Biaggi Connection

Fate was not so kind to Rep. Mario Biaggi, another figure in the Wedtech investigation. Biaggi, a Democratic House member from the Bronx, who had assisted the company with its contract, was convicted August 4 of fifteen counts of racketeering, conspiracy, extortion, and bribe-taking. Biaggi's pretrial popularity in his district had won him reelection endorsements from both the local Democratic and Republican parties. Facing expulsion from Congress and sentencing in November, Biaggi resigned his seat before New York's September 15 primary elections to pursue legal appeals. Because of a fluke in the election rules, his name remained on ballots in the primary elections and on the Republican ticket in the November 8 general election—but he was not reelected.

On November 18, Biaggi was sentenced to eight years in prison and fined $242,000. Four other defendants in the Wedtech scandal drew lesser prison sentences and fines. They were Biaggi's son Richard, former Bronx borough president Stanley Simon, Wedtech cofounder John Mariotta, and Peter Neglia, former regional administrator of the federal Small

Business Administration. At their sentencing by Judge Constance Baker Motley in U.S. District Court in Manhattan, Biaggi continued to assert his innocence. In a tearful address to Judge Motley, he said, "I am still of the belief, I always have been, that I am innocent." The eight-year sentence, due to begin January 9, 1989, would run concurrently with a two-and-a-half-year sentence he drew in an unrelated case in September 1987 for obstructing justice and accepting an illegal gratuity.

Two days after Biaggi's sentencing, another member of Congress from the Bronx, Democrat Robert Garcia, was indicted in connection with the Wedtech investigation. The indictment charged that Garcia and his wife, Jane Lee Garcia, operated a bribery and extortion scheme to obtain more than $170,000 from the defense-manufacturing company. James M. Fox, head of the FBI's New York City office, said Garcia took payments "to obtain favorable, lucrative defense contracts for Wedtech." Garcia issued a statement proclaiming his innocence.

McKay's investigation of Meese had its origins in a Wedtech inquiry that was being conducted by the United States attorney's office in Manhattan. The link between the Manhattan and Washington investigations was Nofziger, the former presidential assistant. McKay was appointed independent counsel on February 27, 1987, to determine if Nofziger had violated a federal criminal law by lobbying his former colleagues in the White House within a year of his departure from the government. Nofziger was accused and later convicted of doing so—on behalf of Wedtech. During interviews that New York investigators conducted with former officers of the company, McKay reported, they learned of allegations against Wallach "that possibly implicated Meese." This information was referred to the independent counsel, through the Public Integrity Section of the Justice Department, on May 11, 1987. On the following August 27, the judicial panel enlarged McKay's scope of investigation to include Meese's activities.

Following are excerpts from the "Report of Independent Counsel: In Re Edwin Meese III," filed by James C. McKay and others with a three-judge panel of the United States Court of Appeals for the District of Columbia, July 5, 1988:

Summary of Facts and Conclusions

I. Mr. Meese's Assistance to the Welbilt/Wedtech Corporation

In April 1981, three months after becoming Counselor to the newly elected President, Edwin Meese III was approached by his close friend, E. Robert Wallach. Mr. Meese and Mr. Wallach had been friends for 24 years since they were law school classmates at the University of California at Berkeley. Mr. Wallach, a successful California personal injury lawyer, asked Mr. Meese to use his influence to help a private corporation, Welbilt

Electronic Die Corporation (Welbilt/Wedtech), obtain a government contract. Mr. Meese obliged his friend and, through his deputies at the White House, assisted Welbilt in procuring the contract.

Over the next 17 months, Mr. Wallach repeatedly sought and obtained Mr. Meese's intervention to support Welbilt's efforts to be awarded the government contract. Welbilt, a minority-owned company in New York's South Bronx, was seeking in 1981 to obtain a non-competitive contract from the Department of the Army to manufacture military standard engines under a Small Business Administration (SBA) pilot program designed to help minority-owned enterprises.

In April 1981, Welbilt [later renamed Wedtech] reached an impasse in price negotiations with the Army. The Army wanted to withdraw the contract from the SBA pilot program and proceed with a competitive procurement. The SBA supported Welbilt, and opposed the Army's effort to withdraw the contract.

Welbilt's founder and President, John Mariotta, learned that Mr. Wallach was Mr. Meese's close friend. Mr. Mariotta solicited Mr. Wallach's assistance—not in negotiating as a lawyer for the company with the Army—but in using his friendship with Mr. Meese to help Welbilt obtain the contract.

Franklyn C. Nofziger, another friend of Mr. Meese's and the former Assistant to the President for Political Affairs, also successfully solicited Mr. Meese's assistance in the Welbilt contract dispute. Mr. Meese did nothing to discourage or dissuade Mr. Nofziger from lobbying him on behalf of Welbilt. This contact by Mr. Nofziger occurred while he was barred by the Ethics in Government Act from lobbying his former agency, the White House. Mr. Nofziger was prosecuted by the independent counsel for that contact and other illegal contacts with the White House, and was found guilty by a jury on February 11, 1988, of three counts of violating 18 U.S.C. § 207(c).

Mr. Meese did not directly intervene in response to these solicitations, but delegated the task to his deputies, first Edwin Thomas and later James E. Jenkins. These officials, cognizant of the close friendship between Messrs. Wallach and Meese, acted with Mr. Meese's knowledge and approval. The combined efforts of Mr. Meese and his staff were instrumental in persuading the Army to reverse its decision to withdraw the contract from the pilot program. The Army awarded the engine contract to Welbilt on September 28, 1982.

In July 1983, Mr. Meese at Mr. Wallach's request also interceded in connection with Welbilt's efforts to secure the Economic Development Administration's approval of private financing arrangements which Welbilt needed to avoid bankruptcy.

The independent counsel investigated Welbilt/Wedtech contacts with Mr. Meese to determine whether Mr. Meese violated the gratuities provisions of 18 U.S.C. § 201. Part of the independent counsel's investigation focused on Mr. Wallach's relationship with and compensation by

Welbilt/Wedtech. The gratuities provision makes it a crime for a public official to receive anything of value for or because of any official act performed or to be performed by him. In summary, the investigation revealed the following:

Mr. Meese and his staff, with Mr. Meese's approval, took steps to assist Welbilt in obtaining the engine contract after Mr. Wallach began his requests for assistance in May 1981. A member of Mr. Meese's staff contacted the SBA about the contract on at least two occasions during the summer of 1981. Mr. Meese facilitated and was responsive to Mr. Nofziger's illegal lobbying for the contract in April 1982. Mr. Meese's deputy, Mr. Jenkins, made several contacts with the SBA about the contract from April through June 1982. Mr. Jenkins arranged and conducted a May 19, 1982 White House meeting for Welbilt with Army and SBA officials. At the meeting he insisted that steps be taken by the Army and SBA representatives to ensure that Welbilt be awarded the engine contract.

In 1981, when Mr. Wallach was first contacted by Welbilt, he refused to accept any compensation for his efforts. He received only reimbursement of his out-of-pocket expenses. His stated motivation was that the White House could use the company's success as an example of the Administration's commitment to revitalize economically blighted areas.

In December 1982, three months after Welbilt was awarded the engine contract, Mr. Wallach proposed a consulting agreement whereby Welbilt would pay him $200,000, in part retroactively, for services rendered from October 1, 1982, through December 31, 1983. Mr. Wallach specified that the fees would compensate him for his services as a legal and policy adviser.

Welbilt officers informed Mr. Wallach that the company was unable to finalize the consulting agreement due to its financial straits. However, in an agreement dated January 1, 1983, Welbilt promised Mr. Wallach that he would receive one percent of the company's common stock as compensation. The company officers predicted Mr. Wallach's shares would have a value of as much as $1,000,000, if Welbilt could remedy its financial problems sufficiently to complete a public stock offering. Mr. Wallach was fully aware that Welbilt would have to solve these problems before he could realize the potential value of his stock.

Mr. Wallach used his contacts with Mr. Meese to try to assist Welbilt in solving its financial problems and to enable the company to make a public offering in August 1983 under its new name, Wedtech Corporation. Specifically, at Mr. Wallach's request, Mr. Meese telephoned Secretary of Commerce Malcolm Baldridge about an important Welbilt application pending before the Department of Commerce. For such efforts, and for his prior assistance to the company in 1981 and 1982, Mr. Wallach received from Wedtech more than $125,000 in fees in September 1983, common stock (subject to restrictions) with a market value of $720,000 in August 1983, and options to buy 50,000 shares of Wedtech common stock.

Five months after the public offering, and several days after Mr. Meese's nomination on January 23, 1984, to be Attorney General, Mr. Wallach advised the Wedtech officers of his willingness to continue to assist Welbilt through his friendship with Mr. Meese. However, Mr. Wallach told the Wedtech officers that he would require advance payment for his services because he anticipated obtaining a position at the Department of Justice. Mr. Wallach added that he intended to continue to help the company, but he could not receive compensation from Wedtech while he was employed by the Department. On February 3, 1984, Wedtech paid Mr. Wallach a fee of $150,000 for services to be performed in 1984.

Mr. Wallach assisted Mr. Meese in connection with his confirmation hearings. However, the hearings were recessed in March 1984, when allegations were made of irregularities and possible improprieties in Mr. Meese's financial relationships with various individuals. An independent counsel was appointed under the Ethics in Government Act to investigate those allegations.

Mr. Wallach represented Mr. Meese in connection with that independent counsel's investigation until its completion in September 1984. During this six-month period, Mr. Wallach received no compensation from Mr. Meese. His retainer agreement with Mr. Meese, consistent with the Ethics in Government Act, provided for compensation by the court if no indictment was returned against Mr. Meese at the completion of the independent counsel's inquiry. There was no indictment, and Mr. Wallach sought compensation from the court in a process that proved to be protracted.

In September 1984, when the independent counsel's investigation was nearly completed, Mr. Wallach informed the Wedtech officers that he had been representing Mr. Meese without compensation and therefore needed another advance fee payment. He requested $500,000 for future services to the company. Mr. Wallach emphasized that his representation of Mr. Meese gave him greater access to Mr. Meese and to the Administration as a whole. Mr. Wallach reiterated his expectation that he would soon be assuming a top post at the Department of Justice upon Mr. Meese's confirmation as Attorney General; from this post, he predicted he could continue to assist Wedtech.

The Wedtech officers persuaded Mr. Wallach to accept a reduced amount, $300,000, as an advance payment for 1985 and 1986. On October 26, 1984, Wedtech paid Mr. Wallach the agreed sum. The Wedtech officers told the office of independent counsel that they regarded the additional advance payment, in part, to cover Mr. Wallach's loss of income from his representation of Mr. Meese. In 1984, Mr. Wallach received a total of $450,000 in advance payments for services Wedtech expected him to perform over a three-year period for the company primarily through his friendship with Mr. Meese.

Mr. Wallach allegedly received an additional $100,000 from Wedtech through payments at the end of 1985 and the beginning of 1986. He was awarded additional stock options in 1985.

Mr. Meese became Attorney General on February 23, 1985. Although Mr. Meese wanted Mr. Wallach to join him at the Department of Justice, Mr. Wallach was not so employed because Mr. Meese was advised against hiring a lawyer to whom he owed a debt. (The legal fees incurred during the independent counsel investigation had not yet been resolved.) In addition, Mr. Meese understood from Mr. Wallach that a Department of Justice position would not provide him with an adequate income.

Mr. Meese told the office of independent counsel that he did not know what income Mr. Wallach was receiving from Wedtech, and knew nothing about any of the statements Mr. Wallach allegedly made to Wedtech officials to the effect that he (1) required additional payments from Wedtech because he was representing Mr. Meese without compensation, and (2) required advance fee payments because he anticipated obtaining a Department of Justice job.

There is no evidence, apart from Mr. Wallach's unsubstantiated claims to Wedtech officers, that Mr. Wallach used his access to Mr. Meese to assist Wedtech after July 1983. Nor was any evidence discovered that Mr. Meese, at any time, knowingly received any money or thing of value from anyone in return for or on account of any official act he performed which benefited the company.

The independent counsel's investigation of the Wedtech matter is incomplete because four key witnesses have asserted their constitutional privilege against self-incrimination: Mr. Wallach, John Mariotta, W. Franklyn Chinn, who was a Wedtech director and money manager for Messrs. Meese and Wallach, and Dr. Rusty Kent London, who was an associate of Mr. Chinn and financial consultant to Wedtech. However, the independent counsel has determined that the currently available evidence does not show any criminal wrongdoing by Mr. Meese in relation to Welbilt/Wedtech.

II. Benefits to Mr. Meese from Mr. Chinn's Management of Meese Partners from 1985 through 1987

In April 1985, Mr. Wallach referred Mr. Meese to Mr. Chinn, a San Francisco money manager. At Mr. Wallach's urging, Mr. Chinn became Mr. Meese's money manager in May 1985. In encouraging Mr. Meese to use Mr. Chinn's services, Mr. Wallach told Mr. Meese that Mr. Chinn had obtained a return on Mr. Wallach's investments in excess of 20 percent. Mr. and Mrs. Meese understood that Mr. Chinn was taking them on as customers as a favor to Mr. Wallach.

Mr. Wallach referred Mr. Meese to Mr. Chinn shortly after Mr. Meese became the Attorney General. At that time, Mr. Meese was endeavoring to fulfill his confirmation commitment to sell certain securities. In partial fulfillment of that commitment, Mr. Meese sent almost all of his and Mrs. Meese's holdings to Mr. Chinn in May 1985. Mr. Chinn established brokerage accounts for the Meeses, and sold their securities for $54,581.

The proceeds from the sale of securities were transferred into new accounts and invested by Mr. Chinn in the name of a new investment partnership, Meese Partners.

The Meeses formed Meese Partners with Mr. Chinn effective May 23, 1985. Mr. and Mrs. Meese were limited partners; Financial Management International, Inc., a company wholly owned by Mr. Chinn, was the general partner. The general partner did not have a financial interest in the partnership. Except for language added to make the arrangement "blind," the Meese Partners agreement was identical to Mr. Chinn's agreement with Mr. Wallach of December 1984. The Meese Partners agreement expressly provided that Mr. Chinn could use "aggressive" investment and trading techniques.

Mr. and Mrs. Meese's assets were invested through Meese Partners from July 10, 1985, through June 30, 1987. The partnership had a net return of $30,943, with an overall annual rate of return of approximately 24.8 percent.

Mr. Chinn invested his customers' assets, including the assets of Meese Partners, in money market funds with the brokerage firm and bank that he used to process all of his securities transactions. He actively purchased new issues of securities from underwriters for all of his customers, and sold those securities on the day of their purchase. As a result of his trading strategy, Mr. Chinn had discretion to allocate transactions among his customers after the results of the transactions were known.

The independent counsel learned of unusual transactions engaged in by Mr. Chinn which resulted in the transfer of money to Hong Kong and to England. To the extent that it was possible, the independent counsel fully explored those arrangements, and determined that Mr. Chinn's questionable activities did not provide any improper benefit to Mr. Meese.

The independent counsel also investigated the investment relationship between Messrs. Chinn and Meese, and Mr. Chinn's investment strategy on behalf of Meese Partners to determine whether, in light of Mr. Chinn's management discretion, Mr. Meese improperly received anything of value, directly or indirectly, through Meese Partners. Mr. Chinn and Mr. Wallach asserted their fifth amendment privileges not to be compelled to be witnesses against themselves. Consequently, their critical testimony on this matter is currently unavailable. Moreover, Mr. Chinn's failure to maintain certain routine business records further handicapped the independent counsel's investigation. In spite of these obstacles, the independent counsel has reconstructed what is believed to be reasonably complete information relating to Mr. Chinn's handling of customer accounts from early 1985 through May of 1987.

The evidence shows that Meese Partners did not receive a better overall net return on its investments than Mr. Chinn's other comparable customer, MPVC Partners. It does appear, however, that Meese Partners may have received slightly preferential handling over the course of its day-to-day management, through a consistent allocation of profitable trades in desirable hot issues. The independent counsel did not obtain any evidence that Mr. Meese had any knowledge of the management of Meese Partners or of Mr. Chinn's questionable trading practices.

The independent counsel has determined that, while Mr. Chinn's services to Mr. Meese may have been unusual, there is no substantial evidence to conclude that any benefit that was accepted in this regard by Mr. Meese from Mr. Chinn, or from Mr. Wallach, was an unlawful gratuity under 18 U.S.C. § 201.

III. Mr. Meese's Participation in Telecommunications Matters Before the Department of Justice

During Mr. Meese's confirmation hearings in January 1985, he stated that over the course of four years in Washington, D.C., he had learned a great deal "about how people view things, or how people might view things." He added:

> And I can assure you that I have a much higher level of sensitivity to these matters now than I did when I arrived in Washington. And I can assure you that I would take great pains to avoid any kind of a situation or circumstance that might give rise to a misunderstanding or a misinterpretation of my acts or what I intended.

Mr. Meese promised the Senators, among other things, that he would sell certain securities, including AT&T and regional Bell operating company (RBOC) stock, and that he would advise the Office of Legal Counsel and the Office of Professional Responsibility in the Department of Justice of all his financial holdings.

When Mr. Meese sent the securities to Mr. Chinn in 1985, Mr. Meese was unable to locate the RBOC stock certificates. On May 23, 1985, he and Mrs. Meese executed a Transfer of Property document which purported to transfer to Mr. Chinn all of Mr. and Mrs. Meese's right, title and interest in the RBOC stocks. However, as a matter of law, the Transfer of Property document was insufficient to transfer ownership of the stock, and Mr. and Mrs. Meese continued to retain both equitable and legal title in the securities. Mr. and Mrs. Meese's continued ownership of the RBOC stock was evidenced by their receipt of quarterly and annual reports, as well as dividend checks, which they did not cash until the securities were sold in September 1987.

Mr. Meese, knowing that he had a financial interest in the RBOCs, nevertheless personally and substantially participated in two particular telecommunications matters as Attorney General before he belatedly sought and received from the White House in January 1987 a prospective statutory waiver of the prohibition against participation in RBOC matters in which he had a financial interest.

On October 17, 1985, Assistant Attorney General for Antitrust, Douglas H. Ginsburg, sought and received Attorney General Meese's approval of a plan for the formulation of a report to the Court in connection with the Court's triennial review of the AT&T consent decree.

In late May 1986, Mr. Ginsburg sought and received Attorney General Meese's approval of proposed telecommunications legislation. The proposed legislation was designed to shift from the Court and the Department of Justice to the Federal Communications Commission the responsibility for administration of the consent decree.

There was a real possibility that the market value of the RBOC stock would be affected by the outcome of each of these two matters. Moreover, the evidence supports the conclusion that Mr. Meese knew of his financial interest in each matter. After a full investigation, the independent counsel has determined that a trier of fact would probably conclude beyond a reasonable doubt that the approvals constituted personal and substantial participation by Mr. Meese in two particular matters in which, to his knowledge, he had a financial interest, in violation of 18 U.S.C. § 208. The independent counsel has determined, however, that a criminal prosecution of Mr. Meese for those violations is not warranted under the particular facts of this case.

IV. Mr. Meese's Failure to Disclose the Sale of Securities on His 1985 Federal Income Tax Return

As indicated above, Mr. Meese transferred most of his securities to Mr. Chinn in May 1985, and Mr. Chinn sold the securities in May and June, 1985 for $54,581.

In 1986, when Mr. Meese was required to report the sales transactions and resulting capital gains on his 1985 federal income tax return, Mr. Meese obtained two extensions of the filing deadline. When he filed his 1985 income tax return on October 15, 1986, he failed to report any capital gain from the sale of securities or to make any reference to the securities sales. Over fifteen months later, on February 6, 1988, the Meeses filed an amended 1985 income tax return in which they reported a capital gain of $14,606 and paid a tax of $2,454, plus interest, on the 1985 sale of securities. Through an accounting error, the amended return incorrectly reported the amount of capital gains and taxes. The amount of capital gain reported should have been $20,706, resulting in taxes of $3,479.

In summary, the independent counsel's investigation of the circumstances surrounding the preparation and filing of the 1985 income tax return revealed the following:

On or about October 7, 1986, approximately one week before the final October 15, 1986 filing deadline, Mr. Meese, for the first time, informed his accountant of the May and June 1985 securities sales. He also informed his accountant that he had not obtained the information needed to report these transactions, and discussed with his accountant how to proceed with the filing of his tax return. Mr. Meese and his accountant decided that, if the information was unavailable by the filing deadline, the return would be filed without any reference to the sales transactions, and that an amended return would be filed when Mr. Meese furnished the information.

On October 13, 1986, Mr. and Mrs. Meese signed and sent to their accountant a blank federal income tax return, together with the data needed for completing the return except for the information relating to the securities sales.

Mr. Meese knew that October 15, 1986, was the filing deadline, and was the date on which his reporting and payment obligations had to be satisfied. He also knew that his return as filed would omit material facts, and would not be accompanied by any payment of taxes attributable to the securities sales. That was how the return was actually filed.

Mr. Meese did not collect and provide his accountant with complete information, from which he could calculate Mr. Meese's tax obligation on the capital gains, until late 1987, more than one year later, despite repeated efforts by his accountant to obtain that information from him.

The independent counsel has determined form the available evidence that a trier of fact would probably conclude beyond a reasonable doubt that Mr. Meese violated 26 U.S.C. § 7206(1) by willfully filing a materially false tax return, and that Mr. Meese violated 26 U.S.C. § 7203 by willfully failing to pay his income tax when due. Nevertheless, for the reasons set forth in the legal analysis, the independent counsel has concluded that these violations do not warrant prosecution.

V. The Bender Foundation's Funding of a Job at a Charitable Organization for Mrs. Meese at Mr. Wallach's Request

The independent counsel investigated an arrangement by Mr. Wallach and Howard M. Bender, a Washington, D.C. businessman, whereby Mrs. Meese's salary at the National Capital Chapter of the Multiple Sclerosis Society (the Chapter) was funded by Mr. Bender's charitable organization, the Bender Foundation. Because Mrs. Meese's salary was deposited into Mr. and Mrs. Meese's joint checking account, the independent counsel considered whether this job opportunity constituted an unlawful gratuity accepted by Mr. Meese in violation of 18 U.S.C. § 201.

In December 1985, Mrs. Meese obtained a $40,000-per-year position with the Chapter. Prior to her obtaining that position, she had been an active and productive volunteer for the Chapter since 1981. Funds earmarked for Mrs. Meese's salary were provided by a grant to the Chapter by the Bender Foundation.

Mr. Bender, Chairman of the Board of Blake Construction Co. Inc. (Blake Construction), was also a principal in real estate partnerships which purchased, managed, and sold buildings in the Washington, D.C., metropolitan area. In December 1984, one of Mr. Bender's partnerships purchased the Chester Arthur Building; Blake Construction was the managing and leasing agent for the partnership.

On September 30, 1985, Blake Construction learned of a problem with one of the Chester Arthur Building's major tenants, the Department of Justice. The Department of Justice was seriously considering not renewing a 10 year lease due to expire in March 1986. This development caused serious concerns for Mr. Bender's representatives because a refusal by the

Department of Justice to renew the lease on favorable terms would likely have serious financial repercussions for Mr. Bender and Blake Construction.

In late June 1985, Mr. Wallach first discussed Mrs. Meese's need for a new job with his friends Howard and Sondra Bender. At that time the Benders suggested to Mr. Wallach that Mrs. Meese might host public interest programs on a Washington, D.C. radio station owned by the Benders. Although Mr. Bender said he would arrange a meeting between Mrs. Meese and the radio station manager, those arrangements were not made until early October, 1985.

The independent counsel investigated whether there was any connection between the renewal of the Department of Justice lease with Blake Construction and Mr. Bender's decision, at Mr. Wallach's request, first to offer Mrs. Meese a job at his radio station, and later to donate $40,000 in payment of her salary through the Bender Foundation. In summary, the investigation revealed the following:

In early October 1985, Mr. Bender telephoned the station manager and asked him to interview Mrs. Meese. The station manager informed the office of independent counsel that Mr. Bender rarely became involved with the radio station operations.

Mrs. Meese, accompanied by Mr. Wallach, was interviewed by the station manager. She later decided not to accept employment at the station.

In mid-October 1985, Mrs. Meese and the Executive Director of the Chapter decided to suggest to the Benders that the Bender Foundation fund the salary of a position for Mrs. Meese at the Chapter.

After Mrs. Meese informed Mr. Wallach of this suggestion, Mr. Wallach urged the Benders to fund Mrs. Meese's salary, and recommended a grant in the amount of her current financial need for an annual salary of $40,000, which was the salary she had earned in her prior job.

The Benders agreed that the Bender Foundation would make a grant of $40,000 to the Chapter for the purpose of funding Mrs. Meese's salary. The Bender Foundation in prior years had made grants to the Chapter of between $1,000 and $4,000, but it had ignored a solicitation from the Chapter for $10,000 in April 1985.

In December 1985, Mrs. Meese asked for and received a salary advance of $15,000 from the Chapter to pay year-end expenses, and deposited that money (and future salary checks) in a joint bank account she maintained with Mr. Meese.

At the time Mr. Wallach was arranging for the Benders to fund a job for Mrs. Meese, he introduced Mr. Jenkins, Mr. Meese's former deputy at the White House, to Mr. Bender with the suggestion that Mr. Jenkins could, among other things, work on Mr. Bender's lease renewal problems with the Department of Justice.

Mr. Bender himself hired Mr. Jenkins as a consultant to Blake Construction for one year beginning in December of 1985. Mr. Jenkins, through an associate, made unproductive inquiries of the General Services Administration about the status of the Chester Arthur Building lease.

In late December 1985, the Department of Justice agreed that the lease with the Bender partnership would be renewed.

There is no evidence that Mr. Jenkins or any other representative of Mr. Bender had any contacts with Mr. Meese or with the Office of the Attorney General relating to the lease renewal. There also is no evidence that Mr. Meese or the Office of the Attorney General was in any way involved in the lease renewal.

Although Mr. Wallach and Mr. Bender may have had ulterior motives in taking the actions described above, the available evidence obtained by the independent counsel does not support a conclusion that Mr. Meese was aware of such motives. The independent counsel also has determined that Mr. Meese did not perform any official act for the benefit of Mr. Bender or any of his business entities in violation of any federal criminal law.

VI. Investigation of Mr. Meese's Finances

The independent counsel reviewed Mr. Meese's financial disclosure forms and related actions taken by him to fulfill his obligations under the Ethics in Government Act. Although the financial disclosure forms and related documents submitted by Mr. Meese contained certain inaccuracies, Mr. Meese's actions in this respect did not rise to the level of criminal conduct.

A full investigation of financial transactions of Mr. and Mrs. Meese since 1980 was conducted by Internal Revenue Service agents assigned to the staff of the independent counsel. A complete set of records of the financial affairs of the Meeses was assembled and thoroughly examined by the independent counsel. The financial records of Mr. and Mrs. Meese did not evidence any unexplained income or expenditure, unusual asset, concealed transaction or any other unexplained improvement in their financial condition since 1980.

After a less extensive analyses [sic] of currently available financial records for the transactions of Mr. Wallach, Mr. Chinn and Dr. London, the independent counsel has determined that there is no evidence of any payments directly or indirectly to Mr. Meese. However, complete information could not be obtained from Messrs. Wallach, Chinn and London as a result, in part, of their assertion of the privilege against self-incrimination.

VII. Benefits Given and Received by Mr. Meese and Mr. Wallach

The independent counsel also developed information of benefits provided by Mr. Wallach to Mr. Meese and by Mr. Meese to Mr. Wallach during the relevant period of time for the purpose of determining whether or not Mr. Meese performed any official act on behalf of Mr. Wallach in violation of 18 U.S.C. § 201 or 18 U.S.C. § 211.

Some of the actions taken by Mr. Wallach that benefited Mr. Meese have previously been mentioned. They included: Mr. Wallach's introduction of Mr. Meese to Mr. Chinn; Mr. Wallach's role in obtaining the funding by the Bender Foundation of Mrs. Meese's position with the Multiple Sclerosis Chapter; and Mr. Wallach's representation of Mr. Meese in connection with Mr. Stein's independent counsel investigation for a court-awarded fee which was less than Mr. Wallach claimed for his services.

The independent counsel also discovered evidence of other actions taken by Mr. Wallach that benefited Mr. Meese. There is evidence that Mr. Wallach assisted Mr. Meese in securing two bank loans at conventional terms: one loan for $80,000, obtained within the space of one day, September 14, 1983; the other, a $260,000 mortgage loan on Mr. and Mrs. Meese's residence obtained on July 2, 1986.

There also is evidence that Mr. Wallach provided gifts, meals, entertainment and other favors to Mr. and Mrs. Meese during the relevant period of time. The amount of money involved was not insubstantial; however, it was not extraordinary in the context of the longstanding friendship between Mr. Meese and Mr. Wallach.

Several official acts peformed by Mr. Meese were directly or indirectly beneficial to Wedtech or to Mr. Wallach. They included the assistance provided Welbilt in 1981 and 1982 in its efforts to obtain the small engine contract; the intercession by Mr. Meese with Secretary Baldridge in connection with Welbilt's efforts to persuade the EDA to subordinate its interests to those of a private lender; and the actions taken by Mr. Meese to further the Aqaba pipeline project, which is discussed below.

Evidence discovered by the office of independent counsel also shows that Mr. Meese arranged for the nomination of Mr. Wallach by the President to a position on the United States Advisory Commission on Public Diplomacy, a prestigious post which Mr. Wallach held from 1982 through January 1988.

In addition, Mr. Meese was instrumental in Mr. Wallach's presidential appointment first as the alternate United States Delegate to the United Nations Human Rights Commission in January 1986, and later, in October 1986, as the Representative of the United States on the Commission.

After thoroughly examining all of the evidence pertaining to benefits given and received by Mr. Meese and Mr. Wallach, the independent counsel has determined that the evidence is insufficient to conclude that any of the official acts performed by Mr. Meese that directly or indirectly benefited Mr. Wallach violated 18 U.S.C. §§ 201, 211 or any other federal criminal law.

VIII. Mr. Meese's Involvement in the Aqaba Pipeline Project

In the course of obtaining documents from the Office of the Attorney General, the independent counsel learned that Mr. Wallach and Mr. Meese were involved during 1985 in the Aqaba pipeline project. The independent counsel investigated the question whether their conduct violated the Foreign Corrupt Practices Act, and whether certain official acts Mr. Meese performed in connection with the project were rewarded by unlawful gratuities from Mr. Wallach.

Bechtel Great Britain, Ltd., one of the Bechtel Group of companies (Bechtel), proposed to Iraq and Jordan in 1983 that a pipeline be constructed from Kirkuk, Iraq, to the Jordanian port of Aqaba. Both Iraq and Jordan were receptive to the proposal; however, Iraq expressed fears that Israel might attack the pipeline.

Iraq's fear increased as negotiations on the proposed pipeline progressed. By mid-1984, Iraq was insisting that prospective lending agencies agree in advance to forgive Iraq's construction financing obligations during any interruption of the pipeline's construction or operation caused by an Israeli hostile act. Bechtel determined that this was an impossible demand to satisfy and, by November 1984, concluded that the project would never succeed.

Bruce Rappaport, a wealthy Swiss industrialist and financier, learned of Bechtel's problem and approached the company with a solution. In January 1985, Mr. Rappaport proposed to Bechtel that he obtain from his friend, Prime Minister of Israel Shimon Peres, a written guarantee of pipeline security. In addition, he asserted that he would assemble a fund to insure the debt service for the pipeline during any interruption caused by Israeli aggression.

Mr. Rappaport insisted in his discussions with Bechtel that the Government of Israel would require a *quid pro quo* for a written security guarantee. Mr. Rappaport then negotiated with Bechtel an exclusive oil lift agreement including a 10 percent discount. The agreement would generate substantial profits for him, a portion of which he intended to pay to Israel in satisfaction of the *quid pro quo*.

In February 1985, Mr. Rappaport obtained a letter from Prime Minister Peres in which Mr. Peres indicated a willingness to consider providing a security guarantee in the future.

After it became apparent that he could not obtain a financial commitment from Israel to guarantee payment of the pipeline financing, Mr. Rappaport decided to come to the United States to seek United States government support for the project, and to develop an insurance fund with such government support.

Mr. Wallach was recommended to Mr. Rappaport as someone who could assist Mr. Rappaport in obtaining support from the United States government. In May 1985, Mr. Rappaport first met Mr. Wallach in Washington, D.C., and retained him to assist on the project. Within hours of that first meeting, Mr. Wallach contacted Attorney General Meese and sought his assistance in obtaining United States government support for financing a political-risk insurance fund to support an Israeli pipeline security guarantee.

The independent counsel investigated Mr. Meese's actions in response to this and later contacts by Mr. Wallach, as well as his response to others in connection with the Aqaba pipeline project. The investigation was hampered by several circumstances. Mr. Wallach asserted his privilege under the fifth amendment not to be a witness against himself. Mr. Rappaport was willing to give an unsworn preliminary interview in return for full immunity. Later, however, after entering into a cooperation agreement with the independent counsel, Mr. Rappaport was unwilling to answer questions under oath or agree to any additional interviews unless the independent counsel first agreed that he could not and would not be prosecuted for obstructing justice or willfully giving false statements during any interview. The independent counsel refused to grant Mr. Rappaport the requested blanket immunity, and terminated the cooperation agreement. The investigation was further hampered by the unavailability of the testimony of key Israeli government officials, including current Foreign Minister Shimon Peres.

In summary, the independent counsel's investigation of the Aqaba pipeline project revealed the following:

In late May or early June, 1985, Mr. Meese, knowing that Mr. Wallach was retained by Mr. Rappaport to assist him in connection with an overseas commercial enterprise, contacted National Security Advisor Robert C. McFarlane and requested that he meet with Mr. Wallach about the pipeline matter.

At the time of this first contact, the question of Mr. Meese's debt to Mr. Wallach for legal fees arising from Mr. Wallach's representation of Mr. Meese in an independent counsel investigation had not been resolved by the court.

It was highly unusual for a Cabinet officer to request Mr. McFarlane to meet with the Cabinet officer's friend about a matter of commercial interest to the friend. Mr. McFarlane regarded Mr. Meese as his superior and obliged Mr. Meese by agreeing to meet with Mr. Wallach.

Mr. McFarlane met with Mr. Wallach and Mr. Rappaport in June 1985, and gave his assurances that he and his staff at the National Security Council (NSC) would assist them in efforts to fund the insurance package.

Mr. McFarlane immediately assigned a senior staff member, Roger J. Robinson, Jr., to oversee the NSC efforts to obtain the requisite funding. Mr. Robinson worked diligently with the Overseas Private Investment Corporation (OPIC), a federal agency, and with Mr. Wallach in this endeavor. Mr. Rappaport and Mr. Wallach took it upon themselves to assemble a "salvage package" for the insurance fund. The salvage package was to be a readily available fund of money from which OPIC and another co-insurer could obtain reimbursement in the event Israel broke its commitment and damaged the pipeline.

Mr. Wallach kept Mr. Meese informed throughout the summer and fall of 1985 of the progress in assembling the political risk insurance package and a salvage package for the insurers. In promoting the project during this time period, Mr. Wallach met with Mr. Rappaport, United States government officials, Jordanian government officials, private lending institutions, and others.

In mid-August 1985, Mr. Wallach received a fee of $150,000 for his services to Mr. Rappaport. At Mr. Wallach's specific request, Mr. Rappaport wired the $150,000 to Mr. Chinn's bank.

In mid-September 1985, Mr. Rappaport obtained from Prime Minister Peres a hand-written letter from the Prime Minister addressed to Attorney General Meese. Mr. Rappaport summoned Mr. Wallach to Geneva to relate the circumstances of his receipt of the letter and to give Mr. Wallach the letter for delivery to Mr. Meese.

Mr. Peres told Mr. Meese in the letter that he was "following with great interest the projected pipeline from Iraq to Jordan as a possible additive to introduce economic consideration to this troubled land." He indicated that he "would go a long way to help [the pipeline project] out." The Prime Minister requested that Mr. Meese arrange a contact on the pipeline matter with the appropriate United States official. He ended by noting that he had "asked my friends Bruce and Bob to let you know the whole story," and would "depend on [Mr. Meese's] judgment about the best way to handle this matter."

Mr. Wallach personally delivered the letter to Mr. Meese on or about September 25, 1985, along with two memoranda from Mr. Wallach to Mr. Meese of that date. The memoranda reiterated the history of the United States government involvement in the pipeline project since May of 1985. In the memoranda, Mr. Wallach explained the purported significance of, and sensitivities involved in, the Israeli security guarantee issue, and urged a direct United States commitment to the funding of the salvage package.

In one of the memoranda which was labeled "Personal and Confidential—FOR YOUR EYES ONLY," Mr. Wallach emphasized Mr. Rappaport's ties to the Israeli Labor Party, and spoke in positive terms of the United States' interests in a strong Israeli Labor Party. Mr. Wallach wrote:

> B.R. has been financing private polls for quite a long time in Israel on behalf of labor-Peres. They demonstrate an increasing strength for labor and the high probability of elections, no later than March 1986.
>
> He confirmed the arrangement with Peres to the effect that Israel will receive somewhere between $65-70 million a year for ten years out of the conclusion of the project. What was also indicated to me, and which would be denied everywhere, is that a portion of those funds will go directly to Labor.

In the second memorandum of September 25, 1985, Mr. Wallach told Mr. Meese of a "never-to-be-stated but fully understood *quid pro quo* which helped to produce the commitment by the friendly country [Israel]" to the security package.

Upon receiving the Prime Minister's letter and Mr. Wallach's memoranda, Mr. Meese sought Mr. McFarlane's advice as to how to respond to Mr. Peres. Mr. Meese did not inform Mr. McFarlane of the alleged secret arrangement to provide the Israeli Labor Party with a portion of the oil pipeline profits.

After consulting with Mr. McFarlane, Mr. Meese sent a handwritten letter to Mr. Peres in which he suggested that Mr. Peres discuss the pipeline project with Mr. McFarlane. This exchange of correspondence and the second contact by Mr. Meese with Mr. McFarlane on this subject sparked renewed interest and activity by Mr. McFarlane and the NSC staff, despite reports from intelligence sources at the time that the Government of Iraq had lost interest in the Aqaba pipeline project and was developing, instead, two other pipeline projects.

NSC staff member David G. Wigg, Mr. Robinson's successor, accompanied Mr. Wallach to a meeting with the President of OPIC, Craig A. Nalen, at which Mr. Wallach made a new proposal for dealing with the salvage fund problem. Mr. Wallach proposed a novel plan whereby Israel would agree to assign to OPIC and the private co-insurer, Citibank, its "right" to future United States government foreign aid funds, if Israel disrupted the pipeline.

OPIC General Counsel Robert G. Shanks prepared a letter seeking a legal opinion on the matter from the Department of Justice. Mr. Wallach insisted that the letter be addressed only to the attention of Mr. Meese. When Mr. Shanks explained that the Department of Justice procedure was to route a request for a legal opinion to the Office of Legal Counsel, Mr. Wallach continued to insist, nevertheless, that the letter be addressed and sent only to Mr. Meese.

Meanwhile, Mr. Wallach solicited the assistance of Allan Gerson, Deputy Assistant Attorney General for the Office of Legal Counsel, whom Mr. Wallach had recommended Mr. Meese hire for that position. Mr. Wallach informed Mr. Gerson that OPIC would be sending a request for a legal opinion to the Attorney General, and that Mr. Gerson was to prepare a positive response to the request. Mr. Wallach advised Mr. Gerson that this was an extremely sensitive matter of importance to the Prime Minister of Israel, and that the project had the full backing of the NSC and of Mr. Meese. Mr. Wallach also cautioned Mr. Gerson that no one else except Mr. Wallach and the Attorney General should know that Mr. Gerson would be preparing the legal opinion for OPIC.

When Mr. Gerson informed Mr. Meese that he was working with Mr. Wallach on the legal opinion, Mr. Meese expressed awareness of the matter and sanctioned Mr. Gerson's actions.

Thereafter, Mr. Gerson drafted a memorandum of law responding to the request for a legal opinion. The Attorney General recalled that he may have shown the memorandum to Mr. Wallach. However, after Messrs. Gerson, Wallach and Meese learned that OPIC General Counsel Shanks had sent a blind copy of the request for the legal opinion to the Office of Legal Counsel, Mr. Wallach abandoned his foreign aid assignment proposal.

During this same time period, in mid-October 1985, Prime Minister Peres visited Washington, D.C., and New York City. During a reception at the Embassy of Israel in Washington, Messrs. Meese and Wallach together and separately engaged in private conversations with Mr. Peres in which the Prime Minister reiterated his personal interest in the pipeline project and his willingness to supply his government's guarantees on the security issue.

Within a week of the reception, Mr. Wallach and Mr. Wigg traveled to New York City and met privately with Prime Minister Peres. They presented him with a proposed letter of guarantee for his signature. This letter was redrafted by associates of Mr. Peres in consultation with Mr. Rappaport. Thereafter, on November 20, 1985, Prime Minister Peres sent a letter to Mr. McFarlane, in which he stated that his government was prepared to give the agreed guarantees with respect to the security of the Aqaba pipeline.

After the failure to obtain a favorable opinion from the Department of Justice for the use of United States foreign aid funds, Messrs. Wallach and Wigg decided to explore an alternative plan which also would have involved funding the insurance salvage package with United States government funds. From late October through mid-December, 1985, Mr. Wigg worked with two Department of Defense lawyers outside of regular channels to devise a novel plan whereby Israel would receive an additional appropriation of $375 million in Foreign Military Sales (FMS) Assistance funds from the United States, and Israel would place the funds in an offshore escrow account. If Israel took no hostile acts against the pipeline, it could retain the $375 million; if Israel damaged the pipeline by hostile action, the insurers could obtain reimbursement from the escrow account. The plan ultimately took the form of a proposed National Security Decision Directive (NSDD) for the signature of the President of the United States.

The proposed plan eventually was rejected by the new National Security Advisor, Admiral John Poindexter, upon the advice of a former National Security Advisor, Judge William P. Clark. Judge Clark characterized the Israeli security guarantee arrangements and the proposed NSDD as a "protection racket."

Mr. Wallach reported to Mr. Rappaport in December 1985 and February 1986 that "his friend"—Mr. Meese—would continue to support them on the project, despite "transition events (the departure of Mr. McFarlane in December 1985 as National Security Advisor), holidays, and other priorities. . . ." In December 1985, Mr. Wallach wrote that "I have assurance from my friend that if necessary, he will engage [a] new person on project." In February 1986, Mr. Wallach wrote to Mr. Rappaport that he "met with my friend, who will personally contact J. P. [John Poindexter] to arrange [a] meeting for me, if it is necessary to obtain signature of his superior [President Reagan]" on the NSDD for the FMS plan.

Mr. Meese told the office of independent counsel that he did not recall contacting Mr. Poindexter on the matter, but that he may have told Mr. Wallach that he would make an introductory telephone call for him.

Although Mr. Meese told the office of independent counsel that he has no recollection of the specifics of any conversation with Mr. Wallach concerning the Aqaba pipeline project or of any of the details of Mr. Wallach's efforts in connection with the project, he has a general recollection of Mr. Wallach's telling him through the winter of 1985, about his activities in connection with the pipeline matter.

The NSDD apparently was never presented to the President. The Aqaba pipeline was never built. When it became obvious in January and February, 1986, that Mr. Wallach could no longer deliver the necessary NSC support, Mr. Rappaport dispensed with his services.

The evidence developed by the independent counsel shows that Mr. Meese, upon learning from Mr. Wallach of Mr. Rappaport's statements about a promised covert payment to the Israeli Labor party, took no action to terminate United States government involvement in the Aqaba pipeline project or even to notify other United States government authorities of the possible existence of an illegal scheme. Instead, he took acts to further the commercial enterprise. Thus, if an illegal bribery scheme actually was afoot, as the Wallach memoranda suggested, Mr. Meese's actions would have furthered the scheme.

There is no direct evidence, apart from Mr. Wallach's September 25, 1985 memoranda, that a bribe was or would be offered to any official of the Israeli Labor Party. The independent counsel has determined that the available admissible evidence is insufficient to conclude that Mr. Meese's activities in furtherance of the pipeline project violated the Foreign Corrupt Practices Act.

ENDOWMENT REPORT ON THE STATE OF THE HUMANITIES

July 8, 1988

The National Endowment for the Humanities, in its first biennial report on the state of the humanities in America, was a study of contrasts. It determined that while the public's interest in the humanities was broadening, academic interest seemed to be shrinking. Criticism of the "academy" was a major thrust of the sixty-two-page report, issued July 8 under the authorship of the Endowment's chairman, Lynne V. Cheney, and titled "Humanities in America: A Report to the President, the Congress, and the American People."

It contended that colleges and universities rewarded research over teaching, prompting narrow specialization that increasingly left scholars unable to communicate with others. "The very attempt to address a large audience," Cheney wrote, "is often viewed with suspicion, labeled 'journalism,' or 'entertainment,' rather than scholarship." Paradoxically, she said, this trend was occurring at the same time people outside academia were turning to literary, historical, and philosophical study to enrich themselves and society. She wrote of the growth in book buying even though people were spending more time watching television, and of the growing popularity of museums.

The report was the first on this subject that the Endowment is required to publish every two years under terms of legislation Congress passed in 1985. To help prepare the report, Cheney convened three advisory groups of scholars, administrators, and others with ties to the humanities to discuss three topics, "the scholar and society," "the word and the image," and "the public and the humanities." Opinions of the three groups, as well as other scholars, were reflected in the report.

The report also dealt with a longstanding controversy over curriculum development—should college students today be required to know about the development of Western civilization and the American society that has grown out of it? Yes, said a sizable body of scholarly opinion, whose advocacy had been carried beyond the campus in two best-selling books, The Closing of the American Mind, *by Allan Bloom, and* Cultural Literacy, *by E. D. Hirsch. Others had argued that the emphasis on Western culture was too confining, at best devoid of Eastern values and at worst irrelevant to many people.*

A survey by the National Endowment determined that in 1988 students could graduate from almost 80 percent of the nation's four-year colleges and universities without taking a course in the history of Western civilization or in American history. The survey also found it possible to earn a bachelor's degree in 1988-1989 at 45 percent of those institutions without taking American or English literature, at 62 percent without taking philosophy, and at 77 percent without taking a foreign language.

Cheney came down squarely on the side of the traditionalists. Because society's laws and institutions are based on Western civilization, she wrote, it should be obvious that "education should ground the upcoming generation in the Western tradition." It should also be obvious, she added, that students should learn about the texts that had formed the foundation of Western society. "History, literature, and philosophy are crucial to teaching the humanities," Cheney specified. "The humanities are about more than politics, about more than social power. What gives them their abiding worth are truths that pass beyond time and circumstance—truths that, transcending accidents of class, race, and gender, speak to us all."

Reaction to the report was mixed, the Chronicle of Higher Education *reported. Paul J. Oscamp, president of Bowling Green State University and a member of the National Council of the Humanities, agreed with Cheney's assertion that students were not adequately educated in the humanities, but he disagreed with her contention that faculty research was adversely affecting the teaching of humanities or was causing it to be overly specialized. Carol Schneider, executive vice president of the Association of American Colleges, said it was "unfortunate" that the report had been so critical of the efforts of colleges to revise and update their curricula.*

Following are excerpts from the text of "Humanities in America: A Report to the President, the Congress, and the American People," issued by the National Endowment for the Humanities, July 8, 1988:

... Ten years ago, philosopher Charles Frankel suggested that when we talk about the place of the humanities in American life, we are really asking a series of questions:

> What images of human possibility will American society put before its members? What standards will it suggest to them as befitting the dignity of the human spirit? What decent balance among human employments will it exhibit? Will it speak to them only of success and celebrity and the quick fix that makes them happy, or will it find a place for grace, elegance, nobility, and a sense of connection with the human adventure?

In 1988 it is possible to answer that our society has made progress in expanding images of human possibility for its members, in increasing awareness of what human excellence can mean, in developing insight into the past and all it has to tell us of triumph and disappointment, of choices made and not made and their consequences. Much remains to be done, but the task, in terms of the general public, has been well begun.

It is not possible to make such a positive assessment when one looks at our colleges and universities. At the same time that public interest in the humanities has grown, study of these disciplines has declined among formally enrolled students. Between 1966 and 1986, a period in which the number of bachelor's degrees awarded increased by 88 percent, the number of bachelor's degrees awarded in the humanities declined by 33 percent. Foreign language majors dropped by 29 percent; English majors, by 33 percent; philosophy majors, by 35 percent; and history majors, by 43 percent.

The most recent statistics, for both majors and enrollments, seem to show a bottoming out of this long downward slide and even slight movement upward; nevertheless, the loss remains dramatic. In 1965-66, one of every six college students was majoring in the humanities. In 1985-86, the figure was one in sixteen; one in every four students, by contrast, was majoring in business.

Today's college students have a strong vocational orientation, and the high cost of higher education may offer one explanation. As students become concerned about being able to pay for college, they may well be attracted to courses that promise direct vocational benefit. Although there are studies showing that liberal arts majors do very well in the business world, the reasons for that are not obvious. The judgment and perspective that can come from studying history, for example, while of great value both professionally and personally, are, nonetheless, intangibles that students— and parents—may not consider when facing tens of thousands of dollars in tuition bills....

Concern about the humanities on our nation's campuses reaches beyond students and curricula to the disciplines themselves and the way they have developed in the academic setting. Since 1982 when Harvard professor Walter Jackson Bate declared the humanities were "plunging into their worst state of crisis since the modern university was formed a century ago," many observers and participants have offered similar descriptions.

They have written of disarray and isolation, of rupture and distrust. They have written of a lost sense of meaning in academic humanities. And they have made these observations, paradoxically enough, at the same time that people outside the academy are increasingly turning to literary, historical, and philosophical study, are increasingly finding in the "good arts" a source of enrichment for themselves and their society.

The Scholar and Society

... In college and university classrooms across the nation, humanities scholars teach with thoughtful attention to enduring concerns. In libraries and archives, they work with care and precision to recover and interpret the past so as to enlarge general understanding. But in the academy, the humanities have also become arcane in ways that many find deeply troubling. . . .

Specialization

The modern academy in the United States owes much of its character to an event that occurred in 1876. With the founding that year of Johns Hopkins University, a model was established that came to dominate higher education. Based on a scientific view, it emphasized discovery of knowledge and encouraged narrowly focused research rather than broad learning. . . .

Sometimes the scientific model has suited the humanities, encouraging careful procedures and a respect for evidence that has resulted in meticulous and enlightening work. But sometimes the fit between scientific approach and humanistic content has been painful. As specialization becomes ever narrower, the humanities tend to lose their significance and centrality. The large matters they address can disappear in a welter of detail. . . .

The difficulties following from specialization have become acute in recent years. In the rapid expansion of higher education that occurred between the late 1950s and the mid-1970s, the number of humanities Ph.D.'s nearly quadrupled. As more and more scholars set about producing what Daniel Coit Gilman [founding president of Johns Hopkins] thought of as building blocks for the temple of knowledge, specialties narrowed and deepened; and the sudden collapse of the academic job market in the 1970s accelerated the trend. As competition for positions and tenure became increasingly fierce, fewer and fewer scholars could risk straying from the prescribed path of advancement by taking a general view rather than a specialized one.

And so the building blocks have piled up, many of them elegantly formed, many of great interest in their own right. But what is the shape of the temple? . . .

Overspecialization frequently makes the academy a target for outsiders. It is scarcely possible any longer for a professional group like the Modern Language Association to hold a convention without the titles of such papers as "Written Discourse as Dialogic Interaction" or "Abduction, Transference, and the Reading Stage" being held up as examples of how trivial academic study of the humanities has become. Such criticism is often dismissed as anti-intellectual; but scholars themselves lament the splintering of their disciplines and the increasing diminishment of the audiences they address. . . .

In recent years, the methods of scholars, like the subjects they deal with, have become highly specialized. New methodological approaches—ranging from cliometrics in history to various forms of poststructuralism in literature and other disciplines—have, in the view of some, revitalized both scholarship and teaching. Observed Paul Alpers at a forum at the University of California at Berkeley, "The new questions being asked have made things a lot more interesting and lively. They have been a bracing wind that has raised intellectual self-awareness."

Others argue that the new theoretical approaches have further isolated scholars, making it difficult even for colleagues in the same discipline to understand one another. Jaime O'Neill, an English professor at Butte College in Oroville, California, pointed to a long, theoretical article in a well-known scholarly journal. . . . The article was incomprehensible, in O'Neill's view, even though its subject—how to teach English—is one in which he is immersed professionally.

Almost thirty years ago, C. P. Snow expressed concern about the division between the "two cultures" of science and literature. At an advisory group meeting in Washington, D.C., historian Gertrude Himmelfarb expressed concern about a newer chasm, equally deep and troubling. Scholarship in the humanities is frequently so arcane, she said, that now the "two cultures" are the academy and society.

Teaching and Publishing

When Daniel Coit Gilman laid out his plans for a university, it was graduated education in which he was chiefly interested; in fact, he agreed to establish an undergraduate college at Johns Hopkins only after his board of trustees insisted. The teaching of undergraduates, an afterthought in his mind, has often seemed an afterthought in the institutions that his thinking has influenced.

This is not because faculty members dislike teaching. To the contrary, on a recent survey, 63 percent declared that their interest lies more in teaching than in research. But since the founding of the modern university, teaching has typically not been valued as highly as publication of the results of specialized research. When tenure and promotion decisions have been made, achievements in the classroom have counted less than scholarly monographs and articles in professional journals.

There have been recent—and laudable—efforts to redress the balance. . . . But it will require sustained and thoughtful commitment to make teaching as valued as it should be, because the reasons it has been devalued are systemic. . . . Neither reputation nor financial reward is typically linked to teaching, and this is true for institutions as well as for individuals. Examining the higher-education spectrum—from community colleges and four-year colleges through comprehensive institutions to research universities—one sees a clear pattern: as teaching responsibilities decrease, faculty salaries increase. . . .

There ought to be faculty members devoted to research; there ought to be institutions that have research as a primary mission. But a system that so favors research drives everyone in the same direction. . . . [T]he demands of publication come all too easily to dominate the classroom. "Teaching is all too often filling empty vessels with information *about,* rather than initiating the young into thinking and feeling *with,* the books they read," Professor Leon Kass of the University of Chicago observed in a letter. "Students are drawn into second-order scholarly concerns even before they have directly experienced the texts and the *human concerns* that moved authors to write them."

The kind of teaching that will bring students to a love for the humanities is difficult to evaluate. It is much easier to count publications than to credit the engagement that good teachers have with texts, much easier to judge whether a faculty member has written a sufficient number of articles than whether he or she reveals to students by example and thorough questioning how and why it is that learning matters to life.

But difficult as it is, finding ways to place value on good teaching is essential. Good teaching is the surest method for bringing students to understand the worth of the humanities, the surest method for encouraging lifelong exploration of what Alexis de Tocqueville called "the empire of the mind."

Politics and the Curriculum

. . . Debates about curriculum today often concentrate on the teaching of Western culture. Should students be required to know about the Old Testament and the New, about the classical works of Greece and Rome, about Shakespeare and Cervantes, about Hobbes and Locke and Freud and Darwin? Since Western civilization forms the basis for our society's laws and institutions, it might seem obvious that education should ground the upcoming generation in the Western tradition. It might seem obvious that all students should be knowledgeable about texts that have formed the foundations of the society in which they live. But opponents argue that those works, mostly written by a privileged group of white males, are elitist, racist, and sexist. If students are to be taught works by writers like Plato and Rousseau at all, it should be to expose and refute their biases. Teaching becomes a form of political activism, with texts used to encourage students, in the words of one professor, to "work against the political horrors of one's time."

Several doubtful assumptions lie behind such an approach, the first having to do with the nature of Western civilization and the American society that has grown out of it. Are they productive mainly of "political horrors" or have they not also seen splendid achievements, persistent self-examination, and decided progress toward the goal of recognizing the dignity of every human being? To focus only on error, though surely that needs to be recognized, is to focus on partial truth, and not even the most important part. In what other civilization have women and ethnic minorities advanced farther? In what other society has social mobility so mitigated the effect of class? In what other culture has debate about these issues been so prolonged and intense?

The Western tradition *is* a debate, though those who oppose its teaching seem to assume that it imposes consensus. What is the nature of human beings? One finds very different answers in Plato and Hobbes, or Hume and Voltaire. What is the relation of human beings to God? Milton and Nietzsche certainly do not agree. "Far from leading to a glorification of the *status quo*," philosopher Sidney Hook has written, ". . . the knowledge imparted by [Western civilization] courses, properly taught, is essential to understanding the world of our own experience, whether one seeks to alter or preserve it. . . . It would hardly be an exaggeration to say that of all cultures of which we have knowledge, Western culture has been the most critical of itself." . . .

The Western tradition is a continuing one, and students should understand this. Any course in the American experience should make clear how men and women of diverse origins have shaped and enriched this nation's Western inheritance. Students also gain from learning about other civilizations, about their values, their successes, their failures. . . .

The Word and the Image

. . . Those who worry about the future of the book in the age of the image have powerful reasons for their concern. There are, to begin with, the statistics that show our national obsession with television. The average adult watches television more than thirty hours a week. Children between ages two and eleven watch almost twenty-four hours a week. By the time a young person graduates from high school, he or she will have spent almost 20,000 hours watching television—as compared to 12,500 hours in the classroom. As a result, our common culture seems increasingly a product of what we watch rather than what we read. A professor at Wright State University reported not long ago that after the students in his class had read about Adam Smith, only 29 percent could identify the eighteenth-century philosopher. Ninety-five percent, on the other hand, could identify Spuds MacKenzie, the dog used in television advertising for light beer. . . .

With the end in sight almost as soon as the beginning credits roll, television has little use for the tangential, for the side trips with which great writers immensely enrich the longer journey. One thinks of the chapter, "The Whiteness of the Whale," in Herman Melville's *Moby Dick* in which Ismael ponders why absence of color heightens terror. "Is it," he asks, "that by its indefiniteness it shadows forth the heartless voids and immensities of the universe, and thus stabs us from behind with the thought of annihilation?" The precise moral and philosophical dimensions that Melville's words propel us into, video images can only intimate. But in another way, television is very specific. It shows us exactly what Hester Prynne or Tom Sawyer looks like rather than forcing us to the active and imaginative task of using Hawthorne's or Twain's words to make our own pictures. We become, in Professor Wayne Booth's words, "passive receivers" as opposed to "active creators."

Although aware of these concerns, the group that gathered at the National Endowment for the Humanities to discuss "The Word and the Image" repeatedly pointed out positive aspects to television. While the kind of knowledge television offers is different from that offered by reading, it is, as philosopher Michael Novak pointed out, valuable in its own way: Specificity of image, for example, can be enormously important to understanding contemporary issues. "When I teach a class I find my students' imaginations are much more fully stocked with vivid images of the rest of the world than mine was when I was young," Novak observed. "When I say 'armed guerrilla,' they have a mental picture of an armed guerrilla and know just how heavily armed they are. Students don't learn that from newspapers." ...

Various members of the group also pointed out that advancing technology expands the possibilities of television. Cable television—now in 51 percent of the nation's households—increases our choices, offering, as does public television, ballet, drama, opera, documentaries. Videocassette recorders—now in 58 percent of the nation's households—allow further choice and add a dimension of control. Being able to stop action and to repeat filmed sequences, publisher Ellendea Proffer pointed out, enhances possibilities for reflection. "I simply reject the idea," she said, "that only reading is good in an intellectual sense."

The Fate of the Book

The most recent study of American reading habits shows that half of all Americans read some part of a book within a six-month period. One might well lament this statistic, particularly since a study done five years earlier showed a 55 percent figure. But author Daniel Boorstin warned against "quantitative obsession"—being too absorbed with numbers, particularly when they are based on descriptions people offer about their reading. "The only more unreliable descriptions you could ask them to give," he said, "would be about their sexual activities or their political affiliations." Indeed, statistics about book sales in the years since television has become a central part of our national lives paint a very different picture. In 1947 when less than one-half of one percent of U.S. households had television sets, 487 million books were sold. By 1985 when 98 percent of the homes in the United States had television, books sales were more than two *billion*— 400 percent of their 1947 level. ...

Anyone who has spent time in a bookstore recently knows that many of the books available are what some have called "non-books"—collections of statistics or cartoons, for example, that one dips into here and there, but seldom reads sequentially. It is also obvious that the print medium is as capable of producing trash as the video medium is. But in the vast outpouring of books that has occurred in the television age, there is also much of quality. Classics are amazingly easy to obtain. In neighborhood bookstores, one can find volumes of Aeschylus and Sophocles, Dickens and Shakespeare selling for under five dollars. Observed Michael Novak, "The very best books ever produced in the history of the human race are available for many times less than a pair of basketball shoes."

Time and again, television has led to dramatic increases in sales of good books:

- Before PBS aired "Brideshead Revisited," Little, Brown & Company was selling fewer than 10,000 copies a year of Evelyn Waugh's book. When the series aired in 1982, sales shot up to nearly 200,000.
- Before Bill Moyers's six-part PBS program of conversations with Professor Joseph Campbell, Penguin, publishers of Professor Campbell's *The Masks of God*, was selling 300 copies of the book a week. With one-half the series broadcast, sales were averaging 1,700 per week. . . .

The Future of the Image

Important as moving images can be for leading us to the word, it must be remembered that they compose a medium quite distinct from print, one that communicates differently, one that achieves excellence differently. While a successful film adaptation of a book or story will aim at fidelity to the original, it will not be—cannot be—a slavish rendering. . . .

Historical documentaries and docudramas present the past differently from the way books do. When these documentaries and dramas are well done, they aim, nonetheless, not only at the spirit of the times, but at truth. It sometimes happens, however, that the facts of the past are sacrificed in the name of dramatic interest. Mrs. Lincoln will appear in places she never was. Peter the Great will talk with Isaac Newton, though the two never met. Having scholars work with filmmakers on humanities projects is an important way to be sure that television educates rather than misinforms. Sometimes the collaboration is difficult, as scholars realize that not every detail can be used and as filmmakers realize that even an inspired idea, if it is inaccurate, should not be used. . . .

The Public and the Humanities

The remarkable blossoming of the humanities in the public sphere is one of the least noted, though most important, cultural developments of the last few decades. It may be that the sheer variety of activities has kept us from recognizing the phenomenon as a whole. Or it may be that we have become so accustomed to thinking of ourselves—indeed, priding ourselves—on being a practical people that we have been slow to recognize our interest in what Tocqueville called "the pleasures of the mind."

It is also true that when we evaluate our culture, we tend to focus on how far we have to go before all Americans know as much as they should. We are fascinated by surveys showing lack of knowledge of the U.S. Constitution or world geography, and our interest is a positive trait, doubtless a spur to learning. But concentrating on what we do not know does obscure the fact that millions of adults are anxious to learn; indeed, that they are learning every day in a multitude of ways.

In preparing this report, I talked with many people who spoke thoughtfully about the reasons for growing public interest in the kind of knowledge the humanities provide. Carl Raschke, a philosophy professor from the University of Denver, pointed to similarities between our own time and the late 1870s, the period that saw the growth of the original Chautauqua movement. It was a time of expansion in the economy, he observed, and of rapid social change as the country moved from an agrarian base to an industrial one, from isolated existence to integration with the rest of the world. "We were then, as we are now, about fifteen years after a devastating war that had divided the country," Raschke noted. "The American people seemed to have been emerging out of a kind of cynicism and slumber and dispiritedness with a hunger for a new vitality and vision. There was a hunger to reappropriate and to understand anew values, traditions, and history that had been set aside during the period of conflict." . . .

New Skills, New Attitudes, New Scholars

. . . New skills to promote public learning are developing; there are new attitudes toward the importance of encouraging it; and there is a new group of people now involved in cultural organizations who are interested in providing humanities programming that is intellectually rigorous. Many of those who received humanities Ph.D.'s in the 1960s and 1970s when the academic job market was tight, now work in public humanities institutions; and while they frequently join in efforts with academic scholars, they do not see themselves merely as brokers, bringing the knowledge of others to the public. They see themselves as scholar-educators—and wish others to see them that way also. Said Harold Skramstad, director of the Henry Ford Museum & Greenfield Village, "We have to get away from the sense that public humanities institutions like libraries, museums, and heritage centers are bridge institutions that take revealed truths of academic humanities and deliver them in popularized form, when, in fact, those organizations are fundamental humanities institutions in their own right."

Robert Bergman, director of the Walters Art Gallery in Baltimore, said, "In the case of our institution, we define our professional staff as a faculty, and we define our classroom as our city." Bergman also noted the important scholarly work occurring in museums, pointing to a catalogue that accompanied a Walters exhibition on Byzantine silver that won the distinguished Schlumberger prize for its scholarship. . . .

A Parallel School

Public programming in the humanities is now so substantial and extensive that it has become a kind of parallel school, one that has grown up outside established institutions of education. Including a wide variety of programs and projects—from reading groups through exhibitions to educational television, the parallel school has much to commend it, not least of which is its diversity. There are projects in Western culture and programs focusing on the way Western culture has evolved in the United States. There are projects in non-Western history and in the ways different cultures have interacted. The humanities council in Oregon, for example, recently helped fund a conference on Islam and Judaism.

Public programming in the humanities is seldom subject to a curriculum. Indeed, it is almost impossible for it to be, given the variety of institutions and people involved. The unrestrained diversity that is one of its greatest attributes is also a reason why the parallel school is not an alternative school. The parallel school cannot provide the coherence plan of study, the overarching vision of connectedness, that our schools and colleges can. All too often, schools and colleges fail to provide that vision, but it is in them that the potential for it exists. . . .

IRAN-IRAQ TRUCE
July 18, 1988

"Taking this decision was more deadly for me than taking poison," said Ayatollah Ruhollah Khomeini. "I submitted myself to God's will and drank this drink for his satisfaction." In those words from a brief statement read by an announcer on Tehran radio July 20, the aged religious leader and ruler spoke of Iran's acceptance, two days earlier, of a cease-fire in the eight-year war with Iraq.

The ayatollah's rhetoric was as alien to the West as the reasons behind the brutal war that had left a million dead, by some estimates. But the apparently senseless slaughter expressed the depth of pain of a conflict at the heart of modern Islam.

The Iranian revolution led by Khomeini sought to destroy the influence of Western civilization in the Moslem world. Above all, the revolution rejected the secularism of the West and sought to replace it with a society guided by its understanding of the purpose of God. Khomeini had understood God's will as including the destruction of the government of Iraq—a secular regime that epitomized for him the corruption of Islam by Western values. But when years of sacrifice led only to Iran's exhaustion, he "submitted" to a new understanding of God's will, expressed, evidently, in Resolution 598 of the United Nations Security Council.

The Security Council adopted Resolution 598 on July 20, 1987, as part of international diplomatic efforts to end the war between Iran and Iraq. The Iraqi government of President Saddam Hussein had welcomed the resolution when it was adopted, but the Iranians rejected all peace initiatives until, in an announcement that surprised the world, it accepted Resolution 598 on July 18, 1988. (UN Resolution, Historic Documents of 1987, p. 609)

The ten-point resolution called for an immediate cease-fire, withdrawal of armies to "internationally recognized boundaries," exchange of prisoners, and negotiation of a "comprehensive, just and honorable settlement." The resolution also proposed, as frequently demanded by Iran, that an impartial body investigate "responsibility" for the conflict.

Origins of Conflict

The war began September 20, 1980, when Iraq bombed Tehran airport and invaded Iran. Two weeks earlier, Saddam Hussein had abrogated a 1975 treaty with the shah of Iran and claimed full sovereignty over the Shatt-al-Arab, a waterway between the two countries at the head of the Persian Gulf.

The revolutionary regime established in Iran after the flight of Shah Mohammed Reza Pahlavi in January 1979 had vowed to export its revolution. Neighboring Iraq, a majority of whose population share Iran's Shi'ite version of Islam, was a prime target. The secular Ba'ath Party government of Saddam Hussein (a Sunni Moslem) was particularly odious to Khomeini because in 1978 it had, at the request of the shah, expelled him from Iraq, to which he had been exiled in 1963. Khomeini had continued to inspire the revolution from Paris and returned to Iran in triumph on the heels of the fleeing shah. (Iran Crisis, Historic Documents of 1978, p. 699)

Provoked by revolutionary Iran's propaganda, and fearful of the spread of its revolution, Saddam Hussein was also tempted to seize the opportunity and invade Iran. Although Iraq's population was only one-third that of Iran's—16 million compared with 46 million—Saddam Hussein believed that the confusion in Iran, and the demoralization of its armed forces, which had been a pillar of the shah's regime, would ensure his forces a quick and easy victory. The victory, he thought, would place Iraq in the leading position in the Middle East.

Underlying the immediate causes of war were thousands of years of conflict between the peoples of the Iranian plateau and those of the Tigris and Euphrates lowlands, centuries of conflicts between Iranians and Arabs, and the twentieth-century struggle within Islam to respond to the power, wealth, science, technology, and freedoms of the West. The rapid westernization of Iran under the shah, especially in the boom years following the 1973 upsurge in oil prices, had produced feelings of spiritual poverty beneath the heady pleasures of material wealth. To free Iran of this "westoxication," Khomeini called upon Iranians to return to a simpler, purer life centered on spiritual rather than worldly values.

The War

The Iranian army and volunteer "Revolutionary Guards" halted Iraqi forces after a twenty-mile advance across the border, and the world was appalled by the "human-wave" attacks with which Iran gradually turned the tide of war. Appealing to Shi'ite traditions of martyrdom, Iran's clergy recruited young boys and sent them into minefields assured that their sacrifice would serve God and transport them to heaven.

At terrible cost Iran pushed the Iraqis from the territory, entered Iraq in February 1984, and, two years later, occupied the Faw Peninsula and the port of Faw. The territorial gain was small, but conservative Arab governments and Western nations feared that Saddam Hussein's government might collapse and open the way to a tide of revolution in the Middle East. Although Iraq, in an effort to hurt the Iranian economy by curtailing its oil exports, was the first to attack neutral shipping in the Persian Gulf, U.S. naval forces committed to the gulf in 1987 were seen as "tilting" toward Iraq.

The failure of an Iranian offensive against Basra, Iraq's second-largest city, was apparently a turning point in the war. Launched on December 24, 1986, the offensive had been planned for a year and publicized as the final blow that would topple Saddam Hussein's regime. When two months of human-wave assaults produced only huge losses, Iran's psychology, according to a U.S. intelligence officer quoted July 19, 1987, in the New York Times, *"changed dramatically." The Iranians were, he said, "militarily bankrupt and demoralized."*

An independent team of experts appointed soon afterward by the United Nations reported that Iraq had used chemical weapons on an "intense and frequent scale" against Iran, while Iran had employed such weapons on a smaller scale. When Iraqi forces began driving back Iranian troops in the late spring and early summer of 1988, diplomatic observers speculated that chemical warfare may have demoralized the Iranian troops. Iranian civilians had also been demoralized by recent missile exchanges between Baghdad and Tehran, a "war of the cities" in which Iraq had launched seven times as many missiles as Iran.

Sensing that the enthusiasm and faith with which the revolution began was exhausted, Iran's leaders finally accepted a stalemate in the war. Iranian President Ali Khamenei, in a July 18 letter to UN Secretary General Javier Pérez de Cuéllar, accepted Resolution 598. Ayatollah Khomeini, in his July 20 statement, called acceptance of the UN resolution "truly a very bitter and tragic issue for everyone, particularly for me."

Iraq was at first suspicious of the Iranian decision, fearing that Iran wanted a cease-fire only to rebuild its forces and renew the war. But Iraq yielded to international pressure and agreed to a cease-fire, which went

into effect August 20. UN-mediated talks between the two countries'
foreign ministers opened in Geneva August 25. The first round of
negotiations quickly stalled over Iraq's refusal to carry out the peace
plan outlined in Resolution 598 unless Iran first guaranteed freedom of
navigation for Iraqi shipping in the Persian Gulf and agreed to reopen
the Shatt-al-Arab to shipping. Twice more the negotiations were resumed
and recessed during the fall without reaching agreement.

Following is the text of President Ali Khamenei's letter of
July 18, 1988, to UN Secretary General Javier Pérez de
Cuéllar accepting UN Resolution 598 on behalf of Iran:

In the name of God, the Compassionate, the Merciful.

Excellency,

Please accept my warm greetings with best wishes for Your Excellency's
success in efforts to establish peace and justice.

As you are well aware, the fire of the war which was started by the Iraqi
regime on 22 September 1980 through an aggression against the territorial
integrity of the Islamic Republic of Iran has now gained unprecedented
dimensions, bringing other countries into the war and even engulfing
innocent civilians.

The killing of 290 innocent human beings, caused by the shooting down
of an Airbus aircraft of the Islamic Republic of Iran by one of America's
warships in the Persian Gulf is a clear manifestation of this contention.

Under these circumstances, Your Excellency's effort for the implementation of Resolution 598 is of particular importance. The Islamic Republic
of Iran has always provided you with its assistance and support to achieve
this objective. In this context, we have decided to officially declare that the
Islamic Republic of Iran—because of the importance it attaches to saving
the lives of human beings and the establishment of justice and regional
and international peace and security—accepts Security Council Resolution
598.

We hope that the official declaration of this position by the Islamic
Republic of Iran would assist you in continuing your efforts, which has
always received our support and appreciation.

DEMOCRATIC NATIONAL
CONVENTION
July 18-21, 1988

The Democratic party's quest for unity—and victory in November—dominated its 1988 national convention in Atlanta on July 18-21. With a few notable exceptions, intraparty disputes were cast aside or smoothed over in the interest of unifying the Democrats to accomplish a goal that had eluded them for most of the past two decades. This pronounced interest in unity reflected a belief that divisions within the party and voter defections among its followers ("Reagan Democrats") were responsible for eight years of Republican control of the White House. The convention site itself was considered part of the plan to "call home" wayward Democrats and appeal anew to the South, a former Democratic bastion that within a generation had turned almost solidly Republican in its presidential voting. The 1988 Democratic convention was the first held in the South since Miami Beach in 1972.

One strand of the Democratic southern strategy was displayed in presidential nominee Michael S. Dukakis's choice of Sen. Lloyd Bentsen of Texas as his running mate. Bentsen's selection by the Massachusetts governor recalled John F. Kennedy's successful 1960 strategy of sharing the ticket with Texan Lyndon B. Johnson—enabling Kennedy to win the Texas electoral votes and the presidency. In 1960, as in 1988, the vice presidential candidate from Texas was a congressional veteran, a political leader in his state, and was perceived as considerably more conservative politically than the presidential candidate. At the convention and afterward, Dukakis sought to shun ideological labels, refusing until the final stage of the autumn election campaign to accept the "liberal" label that his Republican counterpart, Vice President George Bush, persistently tried to pin on him. "[T]his election isn't about ideology," Dukakis told the convention in his speech accepting the party's nomination. "It's about competence." He sought to depict his competence as governor as being far greater than the competence shown by the Reagan administration, in which Bush served. Dukakis spoke of "the next American frontier," envisioning a well-run country providing "good jobs at good wages" for all its citizens, regardless of race or ethnic background. He thus alluded to Democratic charges that under President Ronald Reagan the well-to-do had prospered at the expense of the poor.

Visions of Victory

In muting their differences and showing a marked disinclination to engage in verbal blood-lettings, the delegates and their leaders created a convention mood that sometimes bordered on euphoria and produced repeated predictions of a Democratic presidency in 1989. Dukakis himself asserted to the cheering throng in Atlanta's Omni Coliseum and to a nationwide television audience, "We're going to win in November." At that time, the opinion polls suggested that his prophecy might be fulfilled. Immediately before and after the Democratic convention, Dukakis drew more favorable voter support in the opinion polls than Bush did. But by late August, after the Republicans had held their convention, Bush began to outpoll Dukakis and never lost the lead.

As Dukakis's popularity initially moved up in the polling charts at the convention's conclusion, commentators attributed much of these gains to his acceptance speech. Some described it as the most effective one he had made all year in projecting "warmth" and overcoming a platform manner that tended to be cerebral, cold, and austere.

As a speaker, it was said, he would rather quote statistics than illustrate his point with a colorful anecdote. During his acceptance speech, Dukakis spoke about "old-fashioned values" and family, introducing his own family and emphasizing his immigrant heritage—of the "dream" that brought his parents to this country from their native Greece, and of "the American dream" that "belongs to . . . all of us." He closed by reciting the pledge ancient Greece required of its marathon runners to "never bring disgrace on this, our country," and to fight for its ideals.

Dukakis's twin images as an effective manager and uninspiring speaker had been borne out in the long Democratic primary campaign that preceded the convention. In state Democratic primaries, caucuses, and conventions during the previous weeks and months, the governor amassed nearly twice as many delegate votes as his nearest rival, Jesse L. Jackson. From among the original Democratic candidates, only Jackson remained to challenge Dukakis in the convention—although the challenge was often more symbolic than real.

Promoting Harmony with Jackson

Dukakis and his operatives at the convention concentrated on minimizing the potential for a floor fight with Jackson over ideology or major issues. To achieve this, they made concessions to Jackson's forces by permitting a few sections of the party's generally centrist, though vaguely worded, platform to be amended to reflect Jackson's stronger, more liberal bent (Democratic Party Platform, p. 557). Moreover, Jackson was alloted prime television time to address the convention and later appeared prominently and repeatedly with Dukakis and Bentsen.

When Dukakis initially selected Bentsen as his running-mate—a selection whose ratification by the convention was a mere formality—he not only bypassed Jackson but did not inform him before the selection was publicly announced. Jackson did little to disguise his chagrin. "I'm too mature to be angry," he told news reporters upon learning of Bentsen's selection. But on the night of Jackson's convention address, July 19—"Jesse's night"—he cast himself in the role of team player.

Jackson's speech, laying out a vision of a better America in which the poor and downtrodden might realize their dreams, electrified the convention. He struck notes for party and national unity, which he suggested—in an echo of his own campaign theme—could be achieved through a "rainbow" coalition of Americans of various skin colors and ethnic and religious backgrounds. Coming from the country's most prominent black leader, Jackson's appeal to black voters for Dukakis was considered critical to the nominee's campaign. This was forthcoming. "Tonight I salute Gov. Michael Dukakis," Jackson said. "I have watched a good mind fast at work, with steel nerves, guiding his campaign out of the crowded field [of Democratic candidates] without appeal to the worst in us. I have watched his perspective grow as his environment has expanded. I have seen his toughness and tenacity close up, and I know his commitment to public service."

Bentsen, in his acceptance speech, sought to assist the Dukakis candidacy from another direction. He spoke of farmers in Iowa, oil field workers in Oklahoma and Louisiana, and factory workers in Ohio who had not shared in the prosperity "the Reagan-Bush administration likes to talk about."

Following are speeches at the Democratic national convention in Atlanta as delivered by Michael S. Dukakis and Lloyd Bentsen accepting the Democratic party's nominations for president and vice president, respectively, July 21, 1988, and by former presidential candidate Jesse L. Jackson on July 19, 1988. (The bracketed headings have been added by Congressional Quarterly to highlight the organization of the text.):

DUKAKIS ACCEPTANCE SPEECH

A few months ago, when Olympia Dukakis, in front of about a billion and a half television viewers all over the world, raised that Oscar over her head and said, "OK, Michael, let's go," she wasn't kidding.

Kitty and I are grateful to her for that wonderful introduction and grateful to all of you for making this possible.

This is a wonderful evening for us and we thank you from the bottom of our hearts.

My fellow Democrats, my fellow Americans, sixteen months ago, when I announced my candidacy for the presidency of the United States, I said this campaign would be a marathon.

Tonight, with the wind at our backs, with friends at our sides, and with courage in our hearts, the race to the finish line begins.

And we're going to win this race. We're going to win because we are the party that believes in the American dream.

A dream so powerful that no distance of ground, no expanse of ocean, no barrier of language, no distinction of race or creed or color can weaken its hold on the human heart.

And I know, because, my friends, I'm a product of that dream, and I'm proud of it.

A dream that brought my father to this country 76 years ago; that brought my mother and her family here one year later—poor, unable to speak English; but with a burning desire to succeed in their new land of opportunity.

And tonight, in the presence of that marvelous woman who is my mother and who came here seventy-five years ago; with the memory in my heart of the young man who arrived at Ellis Island with only $25 in his pocket, but with a deep and abiding faith in the promise of America—and how I wish he was here tonight. He would be very proud of his son.

And he'd be very proud of his adopted country, I can assure you.

Tonight, as a son of immigrants with a wonderful wife and now, with Lisa, our lovely daughter-in-law, four terrific children; and as a proud public servant who has cherished every minute of the last sixteen months on the campaign trail, I accept your nomination for the presidency of the United States.

My friends, the dream that carried me to this platform is alive tonight in every part of this country—and it's what the Democratic party is all about.

[San Antonio Mayor] Henry Cisneros of Texas, [Rep.] Bob Matsui of California, [Sen.] Barbara Mikulski of Maryland, [Gov.] Mario Cuomo of New York, [Rep.] Claude Pepper of Florida, and Jesse Louis Jackson.

A man who has lifted so many hearts with the dignity and the hope of his message throughout this campaign; a man whose very candidacy has said to every child—aim high; to every citizen—you count; to every voter— you can make a difference; to every American—you are a full shareholder in our dream.

[The Reagan Era Is Over]

And, my friends, if anyone tells you that the American dream belongs to the privileged few and not to all of us; you tell them that the Reagan era is over and a new era is about to begin.

Because it's time to raise our sights—to look beyond the cramped ideals and limited ambitions of the past eight years—to recapture the spirit of energy and of confidence and of idealism that John Kennedy and Lyndon Johnson inspired a generation ago.

It's time to meet the challenge of the next American frontier—the challenge of building an economic future for our country that will create good jobs at good wages for every citizen in this land, no matter who they are or where they come from or what the color of their skin.

It's time to rekindle the American spirit of invention and daring; to exchange voodoo economics for can-do economics; to build the best America by bringing out the best in every American.

It's time to wake up to the new challenges that face the American family.

Time to see that young families in this country are never again forced to choose between the jobs they need and the children they love; time to be sure that parents are never again told that no matter how long they work or how hard their child tries, a college education is a right they can't afford.

It's time to ask why it is that we have run up more debt in this country in the last eight years than we did in the previous two hundred; and to make sure it never happens again.

It's time to understand that the greatest threat to our national security in this hemisphere is not the [Nicaraguan] Sandinistas—it's the avalanche of drugs that is pouring into this country and poisoning our kids.

[Competence and Opportunity]

I don't think I have to tell any of you how much we Americans expect of ourselves.

Or how much we have a right to expect from those we elect to public office.

Because this election isn't about ideology. It's about competence.

It's not about overthrowing governments in Central America; it's about creating good jobs in middle America. That's what this election is all about.

It's not about insider trading on Wall Street; it's about creating opportunity on Main Street.

And it's not about meaningless labels. It's about American values. Old-fashioned values like accountability and responsibility and respect for the truth.

And just as we Democrats believe that there are no limits to what each citizen can do; so we believe there are no limits to what America can do.

And, yes, I know, this fall, we're going to be hearing a lot of Republican talk about how well some neighborhoods and some regions of this country are doing; about how easy it is for some families to buy a home or to find child care or to pay their doctor's bills or to send their children to college.

But, my friends, maintaining the status quo—running in place standing still—isn't good enough for America. Opportunity for some isn't good enough for America.

My friends, we're going to forge a new era of greatness for America.

We're going to take America's genius out of cold storage and challenge our youngsters; we're going to make our schools and universities and laboratories the finest in the world; and we're going to make teaching a valued and honored profession once again in this country.

We're going to light fires of innovation and enterprise from coast to coast and we're going to give those on welfare the chance to lift themselves out of poverty; to get the child care and the training they need; the chance to step out into the bright sunshine of opportunity and of hope and of dignity.

We're going to invest in our urban neighborhoods; and we're going to work to revitalize small town and rural America. We're going to give our farm families a price they can live on, and farm communities a future they can count on.

We're going to build the kind of America that Lloyd Bentsen has been fighting for for forty years; the kind of America where hard work is rewarded; where American goods and American workmanship are the best in the world, the kind of America that provides American workers and their families with at least 60 days' notice when a factory or a plant shuts down.

Now, I know, I have a reputation for being a somewhat frugal man. But let me state for the record that that snow blower is still in good working order, even if it sits in our garage. In nine years, I've balanced nine more budgets than this administration has and I've just balanced a tenth. And I've worked with the citizens of my state—worked hard to create hundreds of thousands of new jobs—and I mean good jobs, jobs you can raise a family on, jobs you can build a future on, jobs you can count on.

And I'm very proud of our progress, but I'm even prouder of the way we've made that progress—by working together, by excluding no one and including everyone: business and labor, educators and community leaders and just plain citizens—sharing responsibility, exchanging ideas, building confidence about the future.

[A Sense of Community]

And, my friends, what we have done reflects a simple but very profound idea—an idea as powerful as any in human history. It is the idea of community. The kind of community that binds us here tonight.

It is the idea that we are in this together; that regardless of who we are or where we come from or how much money we have—each of us counts. And that by working together to create opportunity and a good life for all—all of us are enriched—not just in economic terms, but as citizens and as human beings.

The idea of community—an idea that was planted in the New World by the first governor of Massachusetts.

"We must," said John Winthrop, "love one another with a pure heart fervently. We must delight in each other, make each other's condition our own, rejoice together, mourn together, and suffer together . . . . We must," he said, "be knit together as one."

Now, John Winthrop wasn't talking about material success. He was talking about a country where each of us asks not only what's in it for some of us, but what's good and what's right for all of us.

When a young mother named Dawn Lawson leaves seven years of welfare to become a personnel specialist in a Fortune 500 company in Worcester, Massachusetts—we are all enriched and ennobled.

When a Catholic priest named Bill Kraus helps homeless families in Denver not just by giving them shelter, but by helping them to find the jobs they need to get back on their feet, we are all enriched and ennobled.

When a high school principal named George McKenna and his dedicated staff of teachers and counselors create an environment for learning at the George Washington Preparatory High School in Los Angeles, a high school in Los Angeles that is 90 percent black and 10 percent Hispanic and has 80 percent of its graduates accepted to college, we are all enriched and ennobled.

When a dedicated new management team and a fine union in Milwaukee work together to turn Harley-Davidson around and help it come back to life and save 1,200 good jobs, we are all enriched and ennobled.

And when a man named Willie Velasquez—Y cuando un Willie Velasquez—can register thousands of his fellow citizens as voters—puede inscribir decena de miles de sus conciudadanos para votar—and when Willie Velasquez can bring new energy and new ideas and new people—brindando así nuevas energías, nuevas ideas, nuevas personas—into court houses and city halls and state capitals of the Southwest—a los gobiernos municipales y estatales del suroeste—my friends, we are all enriched and ennobled—mis amigos, todos nos enriquecemos y enoblecemos.

My friends, as president, I'm going to be setting goals for our country; not goals for our government working alone; I mean goals for our people working together.

I want businesses in this country to be wise enough and innovative enough to retrain their workers, to retool their factories, and to help rebuild their communities.

I want students and office workers and retired teachers to share with a neighbor the precious gift of literacy.

I want those of you who are bricklayers and carpenters and developers and housing advocates to work with us to help create decent and affordable housing for every family in America, so that we can once and for all end the shame of homelessness in the United States of America.

I want our young scientists to dedicate their great gifts not to the destruction of life, but to its preservation; I want them to wage war on hunger and pollution and infant mortality; and I want them to work with us to win the war against AIDS, the greatest public health emergency of our lifetimes, and a disease that must be conquered.

I want a new attorney general. I want a new attorney general to work with me and with law enforcement officials all over America to reclaim our streets and neighborhoods from those who commit violent crime.

And I want the members of the Congress to work with me—and I'm going to work with them—so that, at long last, we can make good on Harry Truman's commitment to basic health insurance for every family in America.

[The Defense of Freedom]

My friends, the dream that began in Philadelphia two hundred years ago; the spirit that survived that terrible winter at Valley Forge and triumphed on the beach at Normandy; the courage that looked Khrushchev in the eye during the Cuban missile crisis—is as strong and as vibrant today as it has ever been.

We must be—we are—and we will be—militarily strong.

But we must back that military strength with economic strength; we must give the men and women of our armed forces weapons that work; we must have a secretary of defense who will manage—and not be managed by—the Pentagon; and we must have a foreign policy that reflects the decency and the principles and the values of the American people.

President Reagan has set the stage for deep cuts in nuclear arms—and I salute him for that.

He has said that we should judge the Soviet Union not by what it says, but by what it does—and I agree with that.

But we can do a lot more to stop the spread of nuclear and chemical arms in this world. We can do a lot more to bring peace to Central America and the Middle East. And we can and we will do a lot more to end apartheid in South Africa.

John Kennedy once said that America "leads the ... world, not just because we are the richest or the strongest or the most powerful, but because we exert that leadership for the cause of freedom around the globe ... and ... because," in his words, "we are moving on the road to peace."

Yes, we must always be prepared to defend our freedom.

But we must always remember that our greatest strength comes not from what we possess, but from what we believe; not from what we have, but from who we are.

You know, I've been asked many times over the past sixteen months if I have one very special goal for these next four years—something that reflects everything I stand for and believe in as an American.

And the answer to that question is yes, I do.

[A Government with High Standards]

My friends, four years from now, when our citizens walk along Pennsylvania Avenue in Washington, D.C., or when they see a picture of the White House on television, I want them to be proud of their government. I want them to be proud of a government that sets high standards not just for the American people, but high standards for itself.

We're going to have a Justice Department that isn't the laughingstock of the nation. We're going to have a Justice Department that understands what the word "justice" means.

We're going to have nominees to the federal bench who are men and women of integrity and intelligence and who understand the Constitution of the United States.

We're going to have an Environmental Protection Agency that is more interested in stopping pollution than in protecting the polluters.

We're going to have a real war, not a phony war, against drugs; and my friends, we won't be doing business with drug-running Panamanian dictators any more.

We're going to have a vice president who won't sit silently by when somebody at the National Security Council comes up with the cockamamie idea that we should trade arms to the ayatollah [Ruhollah Khomeini of Iran] for hostages.

We're going to have a vice president named Lloyd Bentsen who will walk into the Oval Office and say, "Mr. President, this is outrageous and it's got to stop." That's the kind of vice president we're going to have.

My friends, in the Dukakis White House, as in the Dukakis Statehouse, if you accept the privilege of public service, you had better understand the responsibilities of public service. If you violate that trust, you'll be fired. If you violate the law, you'll be prosecuted. And if you sell arms to the ayatollah, don't expect a pardon from the president of the United States.

[An Era of Greatness]

Monday night, like millions of Americans, I laughed and was moved by the wit and wisdom of Ann Richards. And Tuesday night, along with millions of other Americans, I was inspired, as you were, by the powerful words of Jesse Jackson.

But what stirred me most on Monday was a grandmother talking about her "nearly perfect" granddaughter; and what stirred me most on Tuesday were those handsome and proud and articulate Jackson children—those Jackson children talking about their hopes for the future of this country.

You know, young Jackie Jackson goes to school in my state. And last month, she visited with me in the Statehouse in Boston. She's a remarkable young woman, and I know her parents are very, very proud of her.

My thoughts tonight—and my dreams for America—are about Ann Richards' granddaughter Lily; about young Jackie Jackson; and about the baby that's going to be born to our son John and his wife Lisa in January. As a matter of fact the baby is due on or about January 20.

God willing, our first grandchild will reach the age that Jackie Jackson is now at the beginning of a new century. And we pray that he or she will reach that age with eyes as filled with the sparkle of life and of pride and of optimism as that young woman we watched together two nights ago.

Yes, my friends, it's a time for wonderful new beginnings.

A little baby.

A new administration.

A new era of greatness for America.

And when we leave here tonight, we will leave to build that future together.

To build that future so that when our children and our grandchildren look back in their time on what we did in our time; they will say that we had the wisdom to carry on the dreams of those who came before us; the courage to make our own dreams come true and the foresight to blaze a trail for generations yet to come.

And as I accept your nomination tonight, I can't help recalling that the first marathon was run in ancient Greece, and that on important occasions like this one, the people of Athens would complete their ceremonies by taking a pledge.

That pledge, that covenant, is as eloquent and as timely today as it was two thousand years ago.

"We will never bring disgrace to this, our country—We will never bring disgrace to this, our country, by any act of dishonesty or of cowardice. We will fight for the ideals of this, our country. We will revere and obey the law. We will strive to quicken our sense of civic duty. Thus, in all these ways, we will transmit this country greater, stronger, prouder and more beautiful than it was transmitted to us."

That is my pledge to you, my fellow Democrats.

And that is my pledge to you, my fellow Americans.

Thank you all very, very much.

BENTSEN ACCEPTANCE SPEECH

Thank you very much.

[Ohio Sen.] John Glenn is one of the most talented, respected figures in America. And I thank him for a very gracious introduction.

And [Illinois Rep.] Danny Rostenkowski, [South Dakota Sen.] Tom Daschle, [former Texas Rep.] Barbara Jordan, [Texas Rep.] Mickey Leland, what great friends you are.

Thank you very much.

And I thank you, my fellow Democrats, for this high honor.

I am proud and pleased to accept your nomination for vice president of the United States of America.

In four months America will elect a new president. And his name will be Michael Dukakis. His theme will be economic opportunity for all. His values will be honesty, integrity, and fairness. And his party will be a united Democratic Party.

Twenty-eight years ago, our party nominated a president from Massachusetts and a vice president from Texas. The Texan on that ticket was Lyndon Baines Johnson. Lyndon Johnson knew then what you and I know so well today. The equality of opportunity is the ultimate civil right.

His vision and his victories paved the way for Democratic leaders like Reverend Jesse Jackson whose eloquence, whose leadership and achievements transcend pride of party and inspire a nation.

[Tackle the Tough Problems]

Tonight the hopes of a nation—the incredible energy and diversity of America—are focused on Atlanta. This convention reflects that energy and diversity.

We are a mirror of America.

We Democrats don't march in lockstep behind some narrow, rigid ideology of indifference. We are not gray grains of oatmeal in a bland porridge of privilege.

Our way, the Democratic way, is to tackle the tough problems. Our way is to search out the honest answers and stand by our principles.

Of course, we have differences of opinion. But on the basic issues of justice and opportunity, we stand united.

Democrats agree that a good job at a fair wage is the passport to opportunity in America.

Democrats agree that America needs a trade policy based on the simple premise of fairness. We demand that nations selling goods freely into our country—that we have full access to their markets.

Democrats agree that the economic, trade, and energy policies of the Reagan-Bush administration have devastated vast areas of America. We see an agricultural economy that has been driven to its knees. We see the energy economy reeling in crisis. We see the loss of more than one million high-paying jobs in manufacturing.

Democrats agree that the American worker who has struggled for twenty years to support his or her family has earned sixty days' notice when that management closes down a plant.

But the Reagan-Bush administration insists a pink slip in the mail is notice enough. That's their notion of fairness. That's their message to the working men and women of America.

Democrats want a strong national defense, and we will pay the price to defend freedom. But we also demand a careful accounting of our hard-earned dollars. And we will not tolerate the corruption and greed that threatens to undermine our military might.

Democrats agree that decent housing, a clean environment, a good education, and quality health care should be the birthright of every American citizen and not the private domain of a privileged few.

So make no mistake about it. We are united in our commitment to do better for America.

[An Eight-Year Coma]

My friends, America has just passed through the ultimate epoch of illusion: An eight year coma in which slogans were confused with solutions and rhetoric passed for reality; a time when America tried to borrow its way to prosperity and became the largest debtor nation in the history of mankind; when the Reagan-Bush administration gave lip service to progress while fighting a frantic, losing battle to turn back the clock on civil rights and equal opportunity; a time of tough talk on foreign policy and strange tales of double-dealing Swiss bank accounts, and a botched campaign against a drug-running, tin-horn dictator [Panamanian strongman Manuel Antonio Noriega].

The Reagan-Bush administration likes to talk about prosperity. But the farmers in Iowa don't hear them. The oil field workers in Texas and Oklahoma and Louisiana don't hear them. The factory workers in John Glenn's Ohio don't hear them.

My fellow Democrats, it is easy enough to create an illusion of prosperity. All you have to do is write hot checks for $200 billion a year. That's what the Reagan-Bush administration has done. That's how they doubled our national debt in just seven years.

At long last the epoch of illusion is drawing to a close. America is ready for the honest, proven, hands-on, real-world leadership of Michael Dukakis backed by the power of a united, committed Democratic party.

[Land of Opportunity]

For two hundred years America has worked better than any society in history. A major reason for our success is that every generation of Americans has accepted responsibility to expand the frontiers of individual opportunity. We have expanded that opportunity through universal education, the Homestead Act, land-grant colleges, women's suffrage, Social Security, the GI bill, civil rights, and health care.

Taken together and placed in the context of the free enterprise system, these progressive actions made America the land of opportunity. They created a magnet that drew millions of people from around the world—people like Michael Dukakis' father from Greece, like my grandfather from Denmark, like your relatives who came here willing to accept enormous risks and dangers in return for the chance to take a step up in life.

Recently, it has become more difficult for working Americans to take that step up. Oh, I see the charts and numbers that suggest prosperity. But I also talk with those people and I hear what they say.

I know that if you are a teacher, or a factory worker, or if you are just starting a family, it's almost impossible to buy a house—no matter how hard you work or how carefully you save.

A college education is slipping beyond the reach of millions of hard working Americans. If you have a child that's born today, plan on having $60,000 in the bank when that child reaches the age of eighteen in the hopes of sending that child to a public university. And if the Republicans have their way, you won't have any college loan program to help work it out for you.

[Effective Leadership]

When Michael Dukakis talks about the economics of opportunity, he is talking about making our country work again. He's talking about putting the American dream back in the reach of all the American people. He is talking sense—and America is listening.

Michael Dukakis understands the reality of America. But even more important, he understands the potential of America. He turned around the economy of Massachusetts, not by writing hot checks, but by careful planning, careful management of the taxpayers' dollar, and a healthy respect for the entrepreneurial system.

When the nation's governors were asked: Who among you is the most effective leader, the answer was Michael Dukakis of Massachusetts. When millions of Democrats went to the polls this year to choose the leader who will blaze America's path during the twenty-first century, they chose Michael Dukakis of Massachusetts.

Michael Dukakis has an uncanny ability to bring forth the very best in America. He knows that government can't solve all our problems. But he also understands that government has an obligation to lead.

Michael Dukakis and I will lead a government that cares about people, about jobs, about all regions of America, about housing and the homeless, about the defense of freedom, about education and health care, about justice and opportunity for all Americans.

We believe America deserves an administration that will obey the law, tell the truth, and insist that all who serve it do the same.

We believe the best way to lead America is by force of character and personal integrity.

[The Chance for a Step Up]

This convention has been a triumph for Michael Dukakis and the Democratic party. It has certainly been a proud moment for me and for my family. My wife, B. A., my sons, my daughter and their families are here tonight to share this honor with me.

My father is also here. He is ninety-four years old, proud of his country, and proud of his son.

Dad, you have been telling the reporters stories about me lately, so let me tell one about you. My father is a symbol of what people of courage and vision and daring can achieve in America.

He has lived the American dream—the dream we want to come true for our children.

Talk about risk-takers. His family came to this country across the ocean, across the prairie, and homesteaded on the plains of South Dakota when the government would bet you 160 acres that you couldn't make it through the winter.

They built a sod house, and when that first blizzard blew in, they took turns staying awake for 36 hours, burning bundles of straw so they wouldn't freeze to death.

But like your ancestors, they made it through the storm. They made it through the winter. They planted and harvested and eventually they prospered.

They made their way in America.

My father made his way to Texas. And I've made my way to Atlanta with Michael Dukakis to stand before my family, before a united Democratic party, before the American people, to accept your nomination as vice president of the United States of America.

Now, that's the American dream we have nourished and protected for two hundred years—the dream of freedom and opportunity, the chance for a step up in life.

I want to help Michael Dukakis protect that dream for the next generation. And I want to help Michael Dukakis maintain freedom as the most powerful and persuasive force on earth. And I want to thank all of you for the opportunity to serve America.

Thank you very much.

ADDRESS BY JACKSON

Tonight we pause and give praise and honor to God for being good enough to allow us to be at this place at this time. When I look out at this convention, I see the face of America, red, yellow, brown, black and white, we're all precious in God's sight—the real rainbow coalition. All of us, all of us who are here and think that we are seated. But we're really standing on someone's shoulders. Ladies and gentlemen, Mrs. Rosa Parks. The mother of the civil rights movement.

I want to express my deep love and appreciation for the support my family has given me over these past months. They have endured pain, anxiety, threat and fear.

But they have been strengthened and made secure by a faith in God, in America and in you.

Your love has protected us and made us strong.

To my wife Jackie, the foundation of our family; to our five children whom you met tonight; to my mother Mrs. Helen Jackson, who is present tonight; and to my grandmother, Mrs. Matilda Burns; my brother Chuck and his family; my mother-in-law, Mrs. Gertrude Brown, who just last month at age 61 graduated from Hampton Institute, a marvelous achievement; I offer my appreciation to [Atlanta] Mayor Andrew Young who has provided such gracious hospitality to all of us this week.

And a special salute to President Jimmy Carter. President Carter restored honor to the White House after Watergate. He gave many of us a special opportunity to grow. For his kind words, for his unwavering commitment to peace in the world and the voters that came from his family, every member of his family, led by Billy and Amy, I offer him my special thanks, special thanks to the Carter family.

My right and my privilege to stand here before you has been won—in my lifetime—by the blood and the sweat of the innocent.

Twenty-four years ago, the late Fanny Lou Hamer and Aaron Henry—who sits here tonight from Mississippi—were locked out on the streets of Atlantic City, the head of the Mississippi Freedom Democratic Party.

But tonight, a black and white delegation from Mississippi is headed by [state party Chairman] Ed Cole, a black man, from Mississippi, 24 years later.

Many were lost in the struggle for the right to vote. Jimmy Lee Jackson, a young student, gave his life. Viola Liuzzo, a white mother from Detroit, called nigger lover, and brains blown out at point blank range.

[Michael] Schwerner, [Andrew] Goodman and [James] Chaney—two Jews and a black—found in a common grave, bodies riddled with bullets in Mississippi. The four darling little girls in the church in Birmingham, Ala. They died so that we might have a right to live.

Dr. Martin Luther King Jr. lies only a few miles from us tonight.

Tonight he must feel good as he looks down upon us. We sit here together, a rainbow, a coalition—the sons and daughters of slave masters and the sons and daughters of slaves sitting together around a common table, to decide the direction of our party and our country. His heart would be full tonight.

As a testament to the struggles of those who have gone before; as a legacy for those who will come after; as a tribute to the endurance, the patience, the courage of our forefathers and mothers; as an assurance that their prayers are being answered, their work has not been in vain, and hope is eternal; tomorrow night my name will go into nomination for the presidency of the United States of America.

[Common Ground at a Crossroads]

We meet tonight at a crossroads, a point of decision.

Shall we expand, be inclusive, find unity and power; or suffer division and impotence?

We come to Atlanta, the cradle of the old South, the crucible of the new South.

Tonight there is a sense of celebration because we have moved, fundamentally moved, from racial battlegrounds by law, to economic common ground. Tomorrow we will challenge to move to higher ground. Common ground!

Think of Jerusalem—the intersection where many trails met. A small village that became the birthplace for three great religions—Judaism, Christianity and Islam.

Why was this village so blessed? Because it provided a crossroads where different people met, different cultures, and different civilizations could meet and find common ground.

When people come together, flowers always flourish and the air is rich with the aroma of a new spring.

Take New York, the dynamic metropolis. What makes New York so special? It is the invitation of the Statue of Liberty—give me your tired, your poor, your huddled masses who yearn to breathe free.

Not restricted to English only.

Many people, many cultures, many languages—with one thing in common, they yearn to breathe free. Common ground!

Tonight in Atlanta, for the first time in this century we convene in the South. A state where governors once stood in school house doors. Where [former Georgia state Sen.] Julian Bond was denied his seat in the state legislature because of his conscientious objection to the Vietnam War. A city that, through its five black universities, has graduated more black students than any city in the world. Atlanta, now a modern intersection of the new South. Common ground!

That is the challenge to our party tonight.

Left wing. Right wing. Progress will not come through boundless liberalism nor static conservatism, but at the critical mass of mutual survival. It takes two wings to fly.

Whether you're a hawk or a dove, you're just a bird living in the same environment, in the same world.

The Bible teaches that when lions and lambs lie down together, none will be afraid and there will be peace in the valley. It sounds impossible. Lions eat lambs. Lambs sensibly flee from lions. But even lions and lambs find common ground. Why?

Because neither lions nor lambs want the forest to catch on fire. Neither lions nor lambs want acid rain to fall. Neither lions nor lambs can survive nuclear war. If lions and lambs can find common ground, surely, we can as well, as civilized people.

The only time that we win is when we come together. In 1960, John Kennedy, the late John Kennedy, beat Richard Nixon by only 112,000 votes—less than one vote per precinct. He won by the margin of our hope. He brought us together. He reached out. He had the courage to defy his advisors and inquire about Dr. King's jailing in Albany, Georgia. We won by the margin of our hope, inspired by courageous leadership.

In 1964, Lyndon Johnson brought both wings together. The thesis, the antithesis and to create a synthesis and together we won.

In 1976, Jimmy Carter unified us again and we won. When we do not come together, we never win.

In 1968, division and despair in July led to our defeat in November.

In 1980, rancor in the spring and the summer led to [President Ronald] Reagan in the fall.

When we divide, we cannot win. We must find common ground as a basis for survival and development and change and growth.

Today when we debated, differed, deliberated, agreed to agree, agreed to disagree, when we had the good judgment to argue our case and then not self-destruct, George Bush was just a little further away from the White House and a little closer to private life.

Tonight, I salute Governor Michael Dukakis. He has run a well-managed and a dignified campaign. No matter how tired or how tried, he always resisted the temptation to stoop to demagoguery.

I've watched a good mind fast at work, with steel nerves, guiding his campaign out of the crowded field without appeal to the worst in us. I've watched his perspective grow as his environment has expanded. I've seen his toughness and tenacity close up. I know his commitment to public service.

Mike Dukakis' parents were a doctor and a teacher; my parents, a maid, a beautician and a janitor. There's a great gap between Brookline, Massachusetts, and Haney Street, the Fieldcrest Village housing projects in Greenville, South Carolina.

He studied law; I studied theology. There are differences of religion, region, and race; differences in experiences and perspectives. But the genius of America is that out of the many, we become one.

Providence has enabled our paths to intersect. His foreparents came to America on immigrant ships; my foreparents came to America on slave ships. But whatever the original ships, we're in the same boat tonight.

Our ships could pass in the night if we have a false sense of independence, or they could collide and crash. We would lose our passengers. But we can seek a higher reality and a greater good apart. We can drift on the broken pieces of Reaganomics, satisfy our baser instincts, and exploit the fears of our people. At our highest, we can call upon noble instincts and navigate this vessel to safety. The greater good is the common good.

[Expansion and Inclusion]

As Jesus said, "Not my will, but thine be done." It was his way of saying there's higher good beyond personal comfort or position.

The good of our nation is at stake—its commitment to working men and women, to the poor and the vulnerable, to the many in the world. With so many guided missiles, and so much misguided leadership, the stakes are exceedingly high. Our choice, full participation in a Democratic government, or more abandonment and neglect. And so this night, we choose not a false sense of independence, not our capacity to survive and endure.

Tonight we choose interdependency in our capacity to act and unite for the greater good. The common good is finding commitment to new priorities, to expansion and inclusion. A commitment to expanded participation in the Democratic Party at every level. A commitment to a shared national campaign strategy and involvement at every level. A commitment to new priorities that ensure that hope will be kept alive. A common ground commitment for a legislative agenda by empowerment for the [Michigan Rep.] John Conyers bill, universal, on-site, same-day registration everywhere—and commitment to D.C. statehood and empowerment— D.C. deserves statehood. A commitment to economic set-asides, a commitment to the [California Rep. Ronald V.] Dellums bill for comprehensive sanctions against South Africa, a shared commitment to a common direction.

Common ground. Easier said than done. Where do you find common ground at the point of challenge? This campaign has shown that politics need not be marketed by politicians, packaged by pollsters and pundits. Politics can be a marvelous arena where people come together, define common ground.

We find common ground at the plant gate that closes on workers without notice. We find common ground at the farm auction where a good farmer loses his or her land to bad loans or diminishing markets. Common ground at the schoolyard where teachers cannot get adequate pay, and students cannot get a scholarship and can't make a loan. Common ground at the hospital admitting room where somebody tonight is dying because they cannot afford to go upstairs to a bed that's empty, waiting for someone with insurance to get sick. We are a better nation than that. We must do better.

Common ground. What is leadership if not present help in a time of crisis? And so I met you at the point of challenge in Jay, Maine, where paper workers were striking for fair wages; in Greenfield, Iowa, where family farmers struggle for a fair price; in Cleveland, Ohio, where working women seek comparable worth; in McFarland, Calif., where the children of Hispanic farm workers may be dying from poison land, dying in clusters with cancer; in the AIDS hospice in Houston, Texas, where the sick support one another, too often rejected by their own parents and friends. Common ground.

[A Quilt of Unity]

America's not a blanket woven from one thread, one color, one cloth. When I was a child growing up in Greenville, S.C., and grandmother could not afford a blanket, she didn't complain and we did not freeze. Instead, she took pieces of old cloth—patches, wool, silk, gabardine, crockersack on the patches—barely good enough to wipe off your shoes with.

But they didn't stay that way very long. With sturdy hands and strong cord, she sewed them together into a quilt, a thing of beauty and power and culture.

Now, Democrats, we must build such a quilt. Farmers, you seek fair prices and you are right, but you cannot stand alone. Your patch is not big enough. Workers, you fight for fair wages. You are right. But your patch labor is not big enough. Women, you seek comparable worth and pay equity. You are right. But your patch is not big enough. Women, mothers, who seek Head Start and day care and prenatal care on the front side of life, rather than jail care and welfare on the back side of life, you're right, but your patch is not big enough.

Students, you seek scholarships. You are right. But your patch is not big enough. Blacks and Hispanics, when we fight for civil rights, we are right, but our patch is not big enough. Gays and lesbians, when you fight against discrimination and a cure for AIDS, you are right, but your patch is not big enough. Conservatives and progressives, when you fight for what you believe, right-wing, left-wing, hawk, dove—you are right, from your point of view, but your point of view is not enough.

But don't despair. Be as wise as my grandmama. Pool the patches and the pieces together, bound by a common thread. When we form a great quilt of unity and common ground we'll have the power to bring about health care and housing and jobs and education and hope to our nation.

[Reagan: "Reverse Robin Hood"]

We the people can win. We stand at the end of a long dark night of reaction. We stand tonight united in a commitment to a new direction. For almost eight years, we've been led by those who view social good coming from private interest, who viewed public life as a means to increase private wealth. They have been prepared to sacrifice the common good of the many to satisfy the private interest and the wealth of a few. We believe in a government that's a tool of our democracy in service to the public, not an instrument of the aristocracy in search of private wealth.

We believe in government with the consent of the governed of, for, and by the people. We must emerge into a new day with a new direction. Reaganomics, based on the belief that the rich had too much money—too little money, and the poor had too much.

That's classic Reaganomics. It believes that the poor had too much money and the rich had too little money.

So, they engaged in reverse Robin Hood—took from the poor, gave to the rich, paid for by the middle class. We cannot stand four more years of Reaganomics in any version, in any disguise.

How do I document that case? Seven years later, the richest 1 percent of our society pays 20 percent less in taxes; the poorest 10 percent pay 20 percent more. Reaganomics.

Reagan gave the rich and the powerful a multibillion-dollar party. Now, the party is over. He expects the people to pay for the damage. I take this principled position—convention, let us not raise taxes on the poor and the middle class, but those who had the party, the rich and the powerful, must pay for the party!

I just want to take common sense to high places. We're spending $150 billion a year defending Europe and Japan 43 years after the war is over. We have more troops in Europe tonight than we had seven years ago, yet the threat of war is ever more remote. Germany and Japan are now creditor nations—that means they've got a surplus. We are a debtor nation—it means we are in debt.

Let them share more of the burden of their own defense—use some of that money to build decent housing!

Use some of that money to educate our children!

Use some of that money for long-term health care!

Use some of that money to wipe out these slums and put America back to work!

I just want to take common sense to high places. If we can bail out

Europe and Japan, if we can bail out Continental Bank and Chrysler—and Mr. Iacocca makes $8,000 an hour—we can bail out the family farmer.

I just want to make common sense. It does not make sense to close down 650,000 family farms in this country while importing food from abroad subsidized by the U.S. government.

Let's make sense. It does not make sense to be escorting oil tankers up and down the Persian Gulf paying $2.50 for every $1.00 worth of oil we bring out while oil wells are capped in Texas, Oklahoma and Louisiana. I just want to make sense.

Leadership must meet the moral challenge of its day. What's the moral challenge of our day? We have public accommodations. We have the right to vote. We have open housing.

[End Economic Violence]

What's the fundamental challenge of our day? It is to end economic violence. Plant closing without notice, economic violence. Even the greedy do not profit long from greed. Economic violence. Most poor people are not lazy. They're not black. They're not brown. They're mostly white, and female and young.

But whether white, black or brown, the hungry baby's belly turned inside out is the same color. Call it pain. Call it hurt. Call it agony. Most poor people are not on welfare.

Some of them are illiterate and can't read the want-ad sections. And when they can, they can't find a job that matches their address. They work hard every day, I know. I live amongst them. I'm one of them.

I know they work. I'm a witness. They catch the early bus. They work every day. They raise other people's children. They work every day. They clean the streets. They work every day. They drive vans with cabs. They work every day. They change the beds you slept in these hotels last night and can't get a union contract. They work every day.

No more. They're not lazy. Someone must defend them because it's right, and they cannot speak for themselves. They work in hospitals. I know they do. They wipe the bodies of those who are sick with fever and pain. They empty their bedpans. They clean out their commode. No job is beneath them, and yet when they get sick, they cannot lie in the bed they made up every day. America, that is not right. We are a better nation than that. We are a better nation than that.

[War on Drugs]

We need a real war on drugs. You can't just say no. It's deeper than that. You can't just get a palm reader or an astrologer; it's more profound than that. We're spending $150 billion on drugs a year. We've gone from ignoring it to focusing on the children. Children cannot buy $150 billion worth of drugs a year. A few high profile athletes—athletes are not laundering $150 billion a year—bankers are.

I met the children in Watts who are unfortunate in their despair. Their grapes of hope have become raisins of despair, and they're turning to each other and they're self-destructing—but I stayed with them all night long. I wanted to hear their case. They said, "Jesse Jackson, as you challenge us to say no to drugs, you're right. And to not sell them, you're right. And to not use these guns, you're right."

And, by the way, the promise of CETA [Comprehensive Employment and Training Act]—they displaced CETA. They did not replace CETA. We have neither jobs nor houses nor services nor training—no way out. Some of us take drugs as anesthesia for our pain. Some take drugs as a way of pleasure—both short-term pleasure and long-term pain. Some sell drugs to make money. It's wrong, we know. But you need to know that we know. We can go and buy the drugs by the boxes at the port. If we can buy the drugs at the port, don't you believe the federal government can stop it if they want to?

They say, "We don't have Saturday night specials any more." They say, "We buy AK-47s and Uzis, the latest lethal weapons. We buy them across the counter on Long Beach Boulevard." You cannot fight a war on drugs unless and until you are going to challenge the bankers and the gun sellers and those who grow them. Don't just focus on the children, let's stop drugs at the level of supply and demand. We must end the scourge on the American culture.

[Leadership in Pursuit of Peace]

Leadership. What difference will we make? Leadership cannot just go along to get along. We must do more than change presidents. We must change direction. Leadership must face the moral challenge of our day. The nuclear war build-up is irrational. Strong leadership cannot desire to look tough, and let that stand in the way of the pursuit of peace. Leadership must reverse the arms race.

At least we should pledge no first use. Why? Because first use begat first retaliation, and that's mutual annihilation. That's not a rational way out. No use at all—let's think it out, and not fight it out, because it's an unwinnable fight. Why hold a card that you can never drop? Let's give peace a chance.

Leadership—we now have this marvelous opportunity to have a break-through with the Soviets. Last year, 200,000 Americans visited the Soviet Union. There's a chance for joint ventures into space, not Star Wars and the war arms escalation, but a space defense initiative. Let's build in space together, and demilitarize the heavens. There's a way out.

America, let us expand. When Mr. Reagan and Mr. [Mikhail S.] Gorbachev met, there was a big meeting. They represented together one-eighth of the human race. Seven-eighths of the human race was locked out of that room. Most people in the world tonight—half are Asian, one-half of them are Chinese. There are 22 nations in the Middle East. There's Europe; 40 million Latin Americans next door to us; the Caribbean; Africa—a half-billion people. Most people in the world today are yellow or brown or black, non-Christian, poor, female, young, and don't speak English—in the real world.

This generation must offer leadership to the real world. We're losing ground in Latin America, the Middle East, South Africa, because we're not focusing on the real world, that real world. We must use basic principles, support international law. We stand the most to gain from it. Support human rights; we believe in that. Support self-determination; we'll build on that. Support economic development; you know it's right. Be consistent, and gain our moral authority in the world.

I challenge you tonight, my friends, let's be bigger and better as a nation and as a party. We have basic challenges. Freedom in South Africa—we've already agreed as Democrats to declare South Africa to be a terrorist state. But don't just stop there. Get South Africa out of Angola. Free Namibia. Support the front-line states. We must have a new, humane human rights assistance policy in Africa.

[To Hope and to Dream]

I'm often asked, "Jesse, why do you take on these tough issues? They're not very political. We can't win that way."

If an issue is morally right, it will eventually be political. It may be political and never be right. Fannie Lou Hamer didn't have the most votes in Atlantic City, but her principles have outlasted every delegate who voted to lock her out. Rosa Parks did not have the most votes, but she was morally right. Dr. King didn't have the most votes about the Vietnam war, but he was morally right. If we're principled first, our politics will fall in place.

"Jesse, why did you take these big bold initiatives?" A poem by an unknown author went something like this: We mastered the air, we've conquered the sea, and annihilated distance and prolonged life, we were not wise enough to live on this earth without war and without hate.

As for Jesse Jackson, I'm tired of sailing my little boat, far inside the harbor bar. I want to go out where the big ships float, out on the deep where the great ones are. And should my frail craft prove too slight, the waves that sweep those billows o'er, I'd rather go down in a stirring fight than drown to death in the sheltered shore.

We've got to go out, my friends, where the big boats are.

And then, for our children, young America, hold your head high now. We can win. We must not lose you to drugs and violence, premature pregnancy, suicide, cynicism, pessimism and despair. We can win.

Wherever you are tonight, I challenge you to hope and to dream. Don't submerge your dreams. Exercise above all else, even on drugs, dream of the day you're drug-free. Even in the gutter, dream of the day that you'll be upon your feet again. You must never stop dreaming. Face reality, yes. But don't stop with the way things are; dream of things as they ought to be. Dream. Face pain, but love, hope, faith, and dreams will help you rise above the pain.

Use hope and imagination as weapons of survival and progress, but you keep on dreaming, young America. Dream of peace. Peace is rational and reasonable. War is irrational in this age and unwinnable.

Dream of teachers who teach for life and not for living. Dream of doctors who are concerned more about public health than private wealth. Dream of lawyers more concerned about justice than a judgeship. Dream of preachers who are concerned more about prophecy than profiteering. Dream on the high road of sound values.

["Don't Surrender"]

And in America, as we go forth to September, October and November and then beyond, America must never surrender to a high moral challenge.

Do not surrender to drugs. The best drug policy is a no first use. Don't surrender with needles and cynicism. Let's have no first use on the one hand, or clinics on the other. Never surrender, young America.

Go forward. America must never surrender to malnutrition. We can feed the hungry and clothe the naked. We must never surrender. We must go forward. We must never surrender to illiteracy. Invest in our children. Never surrender; and go forward.

We must never surrender to inequality. Women cannot compromise ERA [Equal Rights Amendment] or comparable worth. Women are making 60 cents on the dollar to what a man makes. Women cannot buy milk cheaper. Women deserve to get paid for the work that you do. It's right and it's fair.

Don't surrender, my friends. Those who have AIDS tonight, you deserve our compassion. Even with AIDS you must not surrender in your wheelchairs. I see you sitting here tonight in those wheelchairs. I've stayed with you. I've reached out to you across our nation. Don't you give up. I know it's tough sometimes. People look down on you. It took you a little more effort to get here tonight.

And no one should look down on you, but sometimes mean people do. The only justification we have for looking down on someone is that we're going to stop and pick them up. But even in your wheelchairs, don't you give up. We cannot forget 50 years ago when our backs were against the wall, [Franklin D.] Roosevelt was in a wheelchair. I would rather have Roosevelt in a wheelchair than Reagan and [George] Bush on a horse. Don't you surrender and don't you give up.

Don't surrender and don't give up. Why can I challenge you this way? "Jesse Jackson, you don't understand my situation. You be on television. You don't understand. I see you with the big people. You don't understand my situation." I understand. You're seeing me on TV but you don't know the me that makes me, me. They wonder why does Jesse run, because they see me running for the White House. They don't see the house I'm running from.

I have a story. I wasn't always on television. Writers were not always outside my door. When I was born late one afternoon, October 8th, in

Greenville, S.C., no writers asked my mother her name. Nobody chose to write down her address. My mama was not supposed to make it. And I was not supposed to make it. You see, I was born to a teen-age mother who was born to a teen-age mother.

I understand. I know abandonment and people being mean to you, and saying you're nothing and nobody, and can never be anything. I understand. Jesse Jackson is my third name. I'm adopted. When I had no name, my grandmother gave me her name. My name was Jesse Burns until I was 12. So I wouldn't have a blank space, she gave me a name to hold me over. I understand when nobody knows your name. I understand when you have no name. I understand.

I wasn't born in the hospital. Mama didn't have insurance. I was born in the bed at the house. I really do understand. Born in a three-room house, bathroom in the backyard, slop jar by the bed, no hot and cold running water. I understand. Wallpaper used for decoration? No. For a windbreaker. I understand. I'm a working person's person, that's why I understand you whether you're black or white.

I understand work. I was not born with a silver spoon in my mouth. I had a shovel programmed for my hand. My mother, a working woman. So many days she went to work with runs in her stockings. She knew better, but she wore runs in her stockings so that my brother and I could have matching socks and not be laughed at at school.

I understand. At 3 o'clock on Thanksgiving Day we couldn't eat turkey because mama was preparing someone else's turkey at 3 o'clock. We had to play football to entertain ourselves and then around 6 o'clock she would get off the Alta Vista bus when we would bring up the leftovers and eat our turkey—leftovers, the carcass, the cranberries around 8 o'clock at night. I really do understand.

Every one of these funny labels they put on you, those of you who are watching this broadcast tonight in the projects, on the corners, I understand. Call you outcast, low down, you can't make it, you're nothing, you're from nobody, subclass, underclass—when you see Jesse Jackson, when my name goes in nomination, your name goes in nomination.

I was born in the slum, but the slum was not born in me. And it wasn't born in you, and you can make it. Wherever you are tonight you can make it. Hold your head high, stick your chest out. You can make it. It gets dark sometimes, but the morning comes. Don't you surrender. Suffering breeds character. Character breeds faith. In the end faith will not disappoint.

You must not surrender. You may or may not get there, but just know that you're qualified and you hold on and hold out. We must never surrender. America will get better and better. Keep hope alive. Keep hope alive. Keep hope alive. On tomorrow night and beyond, keep hope alive.

I love you very much. I love you very much.

DEMOCRATIC PARTY PLATFORM
July 19, 1988

Democrats broke with their party's recent practice and adopted a 1988 platform noted for brevity and generalization. It was handcrafted largely by operatives of the party's presidential nominee, Massachusetts governor Michael S. Dukakis. The document ran about 4,500 words—approximately one-tenth the length of the 1984 platform. That platform, characterized by its specificity and planks intended to appeal to broad and diverse groups of Americans, made the 1984 Democratic nominee, former vice president Walter F. Mondale, vulnerable to Republican charges that the Democratic party was pleading for special interests. Four years later, the Democrats drew up a statement of their beliefs and goals for governing the United States. This platform was adopted July 19 at the Democratic national convention in Atlanta after only a flurry of dissent from the supporters of Dukakis's chief rival for the nomination, Jesse L. Jackson. (Democratic National Convention, p. 533)

"Common-sense politics has given us a short statement of principle all Democrats can run on," said Paul G. Kirk, Jr., chairman of the Democratic National Committee, at the conclusion of the platform's final preconvention meeting in Denver on June 29. "Brevity is the soul of victory," said Theodore C. Sorensen, the committee's vice chairman and principal draftsman. A generation earlier, as President John F. Kennedy's chief speechwriter, Sorensen was credited with the authorship of some of Kennedy's best-known phrases.

In contrast to Kirk's opinion, his Republican counterpart, Frank J. Fahrenkopf, called the platform "a facade without an interior, drafted by politicians who have chosen to avoid the issues of this election." As if to emphasize the point, when the Republican party held its convention the following month, it drafted a detailed, 40,000-word platform. (Republican Party Platform, p. 615)

Jackson supporters had argued that the Democratic platform should be more explicit. At Denver, and in previous drafting sessions elsewhere, they pressed for stark and clearly stated alternatives to the policies of Ronald Reagan's presidency. Dukakis supporters resisted and instead opted for a document that would soften ideological edges, lessen intraparty friction, and appeal to lapsed Democrats. The 1988 nominee wanted especially to "call home" the "Reagan Democrats" who helped elect a Republican president in 1980 and reelect him in 1984.

The Jackson "Compromises"

To minimize controversy at the Atlanta convention, where party unity was the dominant theme, the Dukakis forces met with Jackson's strategists and agreed to compromises in the wording of several planks. The convention delegates approved nine amendments that Jackson advocated. His backers forced a floor debate on three proposed planks—tax increases on the wealthy, a "no first use" of nuclear weapons pledge by the United States, and a Middle East policy that called for Palestinian self-determination. The first two proposals were rejected by margins of more than two to one. By prior agreement, the Palestinian plank was withdrawn before it came to a vote.

Without debate, the delegates adopted a package of nine amendments that Jackson had pressed. These included a denunciation of aid to "irregular" forces in Central America and called for a national health program, higher spending for education, a moratorium on missile flight-testing, and restraint on Pentagon spending. Despite the compromise language inserted at Jackson's insistence, the overall platform debate represented a victory for Dukakis. "We got almost 100 percent of what we wanted," said former representative Michael D. Barnes of Maryland, Dukakis's chief representative at the platform-drafting sessions. "It was one of the elements that created the atmosphere in Atlanta that we were unified and going to win."

Criticism of the Platform

The Washington Post *editorially pronounced the platform a "Dukakis document" and criticized it for being silent about "the fundamental problem of the next presidency"—that of "paying Ronald Reagan's bills," an allusion to large yearly deficits. The new president "will not be truly free to embark on programs of his own until he reduces the deficit," the* Post *said. It observed that the platform did not attach price tags to the things it committed the party to support. These included full employment, an indexed minimum wage, portable pensions, an expansion of*

*preschool education for the poor, more aid to higher education, increased
federal funds for local school districts, aid for the arts and humanities,
more federal housing, more health programs for the poor, and long-term
care for the elderly.*

*Republican partisans called the platform vague and evasive. These
colorations made it difficult for Dukakis to criticize his Republican foe,
Vice President George Bush, when Bush recoiled from substantive issues.
Moreover, the platform did not shield Dukakis from Bush's attacks on his
positions on gun control, the death penalty, the Pledge of Allegiance, and
prison furloughs. Nevertheless, Democratic congressional candidates
were able to interpret the platform more broadly than in the past and
thus were freed from provocative platform positions, which Republicans
had often used to attack them.*

*Following is the text of the 1988 Democratic party platform,
entitled "The Restoration of Competence and the Revival of
Hope," adopted July 19, 1988, by delegates to the Demo
cratic party convention in Atlanta:*

WE THE PEOPLE OF THE DEMOCRATIC PARTY OF THE UNITED STATES OF AMERICA,

In order to initiate the changes necessary to keep America strong and
make America better, in order to restore competence, caring and in-
corruptibility to the Federal Executive Branch and get it working again
fairly for all Americans, and in order to secure for our children a future of
liberty and opportunity,

Hereby pledge our Party, our leaders, our elected officials and our every
individual effort to fulfilling the following fundamental principles for all
members of the American family.

WE BELIEVE that all Americans have a fundamental right to economic
justice in a stronger, surer national economy, an economy that must grow
steadily without inflation, that can generate a rising standard of living for
all and fulfill the desire of all to work in dignity up to their full potential in
good health with good jobs at good wages, an economy that is prosperous
in every region, from coast to coast, including our rural towns and our
older industrial communities, our mining towns, our energy producing
areas and the urban areas that have been neglected for the past seven
years. We believe that, as a first-rate world power moving into the 21st
century, we can have a first-rate full employment economy, with an
indexed minimum wage that can help lift and keep families out of poverty,
with training and employment programs—including child care and health
care—that can help people move from welfare to work, with portable
pensions and an adequate Social Security System, safeguarded against
emasculation and privatization, that can help assure a comfortable and
fulfilling old age, with opportunities for voluntary national public service,

above and beyond current services, that can enrich our communities, and with all workers assured the protection of an effective law that guarantees their rights to organize, join the union of their choice, and bargain collectively with their employer, free from anti-union tactics.

WE BELIEVE that the time has come for America to take charge once again of its economic future, to reverse seven years of "voodoo economics," "trickle down" policies, fiscal irresponsibility, and economic violence against poor and working people that have converted this proud country into the world's largest debtor nation, mortgaged our children's future by tripling our national debt, placed home ownership out of reach for most young families, permitted the rise of poverty and homelessness on the streets of America, reduced the buying power of working men and women, and witnessed the decline of our industrial, natural resource and mining base, the unending tragedy of family farm foreclosures, an unhealthy dependence on foreign energy and foreign capital, and the increasing foreign ownership of our land and natural resources.

WE BELIEVE that it is time for America to meet the challenge to change priorities after eight years of devastating Republican policies, to reverse direction and reassert progressive values, to reinvest in its people within a strong commitment to fiscal responsibility. If we are to seriously pursue our commitments to build a secure economic future for all Americans we must provide the resources to care for our newborns, educate our children, house the homeless, heal the sick, wage total war on drugs and protect the environment. Investing in America and reducing the deficit requires that the wealthy and corporations pay their fair share and that we restrain Pentagon spending. We further believe that we must invest in new priorities, in life-long education and training, in targeted economic development, in a healthy small business community and in retooled American industry; that it is time for the broad revitalization of home town America, involving financial institutions in the provision of crucial credit by encouraging special commitments in exchange for bailing out those that are failing, reforming and expanding community reinvestment laws, and reversing the trend of financial concentration and deregulation, all combining to reverse the insecurity that has increasingly troubled our workers and their families in this rapidly changing society that has left some communities and regions behind. There is no good reason why the nation we love, the greatest and richest nation on earth, should rank first among the industrialized nations in output per person but nearly last in infant mortality, first in the percentage of total expenditures devoted to defense but nearly last in the percentage devoted to education and housing.

WE BELIEVE that Government should set the standard in recognizing that worker productivity is enhanced by the principle of pay equity for working women and no substandard wage competition for public contracts; by family leave policies that no longer force employees to choose between their jobs and their children or ailing parents; by safe and healthy work places, now jeopardized by seven callous years of lowered and unenforced occupational safety standards for American workers; and by major increases in assistance making child care more available and affordable to low and middle income families, helping states build a strong child care infrastructure, setting minimum standards for health, safety, and quality, and thereby enabling parents to work and their children to get an early start on their education and personal fulfillment. We believe that the strength of our families is enhanced by programs to prevent abuse and malnutrition among children, crime, dropouts and pregnancy among teenagers and violence in the family; by aggressive child support enforcement; and by emphasizing family preservation and quality foster care. We further believe that our nation faces a crisis of under-investment in our children, particularly in the early years of life. Strong, healthy babies with early opportunities that foster intellectual, emotional and physical growth begin school with an enhanced foundation for learning. There are few better investments for this country than prenatal care, infant nutrition and preschool eduction, and there are few more successful programs than WIC [Women, Infants and Children supplemental food program], Head Start, and prenatal care. We know what works; yet these successful programs have been starved for funds. The Democratic Party pledges to meet this urgent need by providing the funding necessary to reach those unserved children who are—and must be—our national priority.

WE BELIEVE that America needs more trade, fair trade, an administration willing to use all the tools available to better manage our trade in order to export more American goods and fewer American jobs, an administration willing to recognize in the formulation and enforcement of our trade laws that workers' rights are important human rights abroad as well as at home, and that advance notice of plant closings and major layoffs is not only fundamentally right but also economically sound. We believe that we can and must improve our competitiveness in the world economy, using our best minds to create the most advanced technology in the world through a greater commitment to civilian research and development and to science, engineering and mathematics training, through more public-private and business-labor cooperation and mutual respect, through more intergovernmental partnerships, and through a better balance between fiscal and monetary policy and between military and civilian research and development. We further believe in halting such irresponsible corporate conduct as unproductive takeovers, monopolistic mergers, insider trading, and golden parachutes for executives by reinvigorating our anti-trust and securities laws, reviewing large mergers, and discouraging short-term speculation taking place at the expense of long-term investment.

WE BELIEVE that the education of our citizens, from Head Start to institutions of higher learning, deserves our highest priority; and that history will judge the next administration less by its success in building new weapons of war than by its success in improving young minds. We now spend only two cents of every federal dollar for education. We pledge to better balance our national priorities by significantly increasing federal funding for education. We believe that this nation needs to invest in its children on the front side of life by expanding the availability of pre-school education for children at risk; to invest in its teachers through training and enrichment programs, including a National Teacher Corps to recruit teachers for tomorrow, especially minorities, with scholarships today; to commit itself for the first time to the principle that no one should be denied the opportunity to attend college for financial reasons; to ensure equal access to education by providing incentives and mechanisms for the equalization of financing among local school districts within each state; to reverse cuts made in compensatory reading, math and enrichment services to low income children; and to expand support for bilingual education, historically Black and Hispanic institutions, the education of those with special needs, the arts and humanities, and an aggressive campaign to end illiteracy.

WE BELIEVE that illegal drugs pose a direct threat to the security of our nation from coast to coast, invading our neighborhoods, classrooms, homes and communities large and small; that every arm and agency of government at every federal, state and local level — including every useful diplomatic, military, educational, medical and law enforcement effort necessary — should at long last be mobilized and coordinated with private efforts under the direction of a National Drug "Czar" to halt both the international supply and the domestic demand for illegal drugs now ravaging our country; and that the legalization of illicit drugs would represent a tragic surrender in a war we intend to win. We believe that this effort should include comprehensive programs to educate our children at the earliest ages on the dangers of alcohol and drug abuse, readily available treatment and counseling for those who seek to address their dependency, the strengthening of vital interdiction agencies such as the U.S. Coast Guard and Customs, a summit of Western Hemispheric nations to coordinate efforts to cut off drugs at the source, and foreign development assistance to reform drug-based economies by promoting crop substitution.

WE BELIEVE that the federal government should provide increased assistance to local criminal justice agencies, enforce a ban on "cop killer" bullets that have no purpose other than the killing and maiming of law enforcement officers, reinforce our commitment to help crime victims, and assume a leadership role in securing the safety of our neighborhoods and homes. We further believe that the repeated toleration in Washington of unethical and unlawful greed among too many of those who have been governing our nation, procuring our weapons and polluting our environment has made far more difficult the daily work of the local policemen, teachers and parents who must convey to our children respect for justice and authority.

WE BELIEVE that we honor our multicultural heritage by assuring equal access to government services, employment, housing, business enterprise and education to every citizen regardless of race, sex, national origin, religion, age, handicapping condition or sexual orientation; that these rights are without exception too precious to be jeopardized by Federal Judges and Justice Department officials chosen during the past seven years — by a political party increasingly monolithic both racially and culturally — more for their unenlightened ideological views than for their respect for the rule of law. We further believe that we must work for the adoption of the Equal Rights Amendment to the Constitution; that the fundamental right of reproductive choice should be guaranteed regardless of ability to pay; that our machinery for civil rights enforcement and legal services to the poor should be rebuilt and vigorously utilized; and that our immigration policy should be reformed to promote fairness, non-discrimination and family reunification and to reflect our constitutional freedoms of speech, association and travel. We further believe that the voting rights of all minorities should be protected, the recent surge in hate violence and negative stereotyping combatted, the discriminatory English-only pressure groups resisted, our treaty commitments with Native Americans enforced by culturally sensitive officials, and the lingering effects of past discrimination eliminated by affirmative action, including goals, timetables, and procurement set-asides.

WE BELIEVE that the housing crisis of the 1980s must be halted — a crisis that has left this country battered by a rising tide of homelessness unprecedented since the Great Depression, by a tightening squeeze on low and moderate income families that is projected to leave seven million people without affordable housing by 1993, and by a bleak outlook for young working families who cannot afford to buy their first home. We believe that steps should be taken to ensure a decent place to live for every American. We believe that homelessness — a national shame — should be ended in America; that the supply of affordable housing should be expanded in order to avoid the projected shortfall; that employer-assisted housing and development by community based non-profit organizations should be encouraged; that the inventory of public and subsidized housing should be renovated, preserved and increased; that foreclosed government property should be restored to productive use; and that first-time home buyers should be assisted.

WE BELIEVE that we can rebuild America, creating jobs at good wages through a national reinvestment strategy to construct new housing, repair our sewers, rebuild our roads and replace our bridges. We believe that we must pursue needed investment through innovative partnerships and creative financing mechanisms such as a voluntary program to invest a portion of public and private pension funds as a steady source of investment capital by guaranteeing security and a fair rate of return and assuring sound project management.

WE BELIEVE that all Americans should enjoy access to affordable, comprehensive health services for both the physically and mentally ill, from prenatal care for pregnant women at risk to more adequate care for our Vietnam and other veterans, from well-baby care to childhood immunization to Medicare; that a national health program providing federal coordination and leadership is necessary to restrain health care costs while assuring quality care and advanced medical research; that quality, affordable, long-term home and health care should be available to all senior and disabled citizens, allowing them to live with dignity in the most appropriate setting; that an important first step toward comprehensive health services is to ensure that every family should have the security of basic health insurance; and that the HIV/AIDS crisis now threatening our public health and safety requires increased support for expedited research on treatments and vaccines, comprehensive education and prevention, compassionate patient care, adoption of the public health community consensus on voluntary and confidential testing and counseling, and protection of the civil rights of those suffering from AIDS or AIDS-Related Complex or testing positive for the HIV antibody.

WE BELIEVE that the last seven years have witnessed an unprecedented assault on our national interest and national security through the poisoning of our air with acid rain, the dumping of toxic wastes into our water, and the destruction of our parks and shores; that pollution must be stopped at the source by shifting to new, environmentally sound manufacturing and farming technologies; that the federal government must promote recycling as the best, least costly way to solve the trash crisis, aggressively enforce toxic waste laws and require polluters to be responsible for future clean-up costs; that this nation must redouble its efforts to provide clean waterways, sound water management and safe drinkable ground water throughout the country; that our national parks, forests, wildlife refuges and coastal zones must be protected and used only in an environmentally sound manner; that all offshore oil drilling in environmentally sensitive areas should be opposed; and that regular world environmental summits should be convened by the United States to address the depletion of the ozone layer, the "greenhouse effect," the destruction of tropical forests and other global threats and to create a global action plan for environmental restoration.

WE BELIEVE that all Americans, producers and consumers alike, benefit when food and fiber are produced not by a few large corporations and conglomerates but by hundreds of thousands of family farmers obtaining a fair price for their product; that the disastrous farm policies of the last seven years, despite record federal spending, have forced hundreds of thousands of families from their farms while others are struggling to survive; and that a workable agricultural policy should include supply management, reasonable price supports, soil conservation and protection of rural water quality, credit and foreclosure relief, the return of federally held foreclosed lands to minority, beginning and restarting farmers, the development of new uses and markets for American farm products, improved disaster relief, and the revitalization of rural America through new sources of capital for rural business and new federal support for rural health care, housing, education, water supply and infrastructure. We further believe that no person should go to bed hungry and that we must renew the fight against hunger at home and abroad, make food available to those nations who need it and want it, and convene an international conference of food producing nations.

WE BELIEVE that a balanced, coherent energy policy, based on dependable supplies at reasonable prices, is necessary to protect our national security, ensure a clean environment, and promote stable economic growth and prosperity, both nationally and in our energy producing regions; that the inevitable transition from our present, nearly total dependence on increasingly scarce and environmentally damaging non-renewable sources to renewable sources should begin now; that such a policy includes increased cooperation with our hemispheric neighbors, filling the Strategic Petroleum Reserve, promoting the use of natural gas, methanol and ethanol as alternative transportation fuels, encouraging the use of our vast natural gas and coal reserves while aggressively developing clean coal technology to combat acid rain, and providing targeted new incentives for new oil and gas drilling and development, for the development of renewable and alternative sources of energy, and for promotion of energy conservation. We believe that with these changes the country could reduce its reliance on nuclear power while insisting that all plants are safe, environmentally sound, and assured of safe waste disposal.

WE BELIEVE that this country's democratic processes must be revitalized: by securing universal, same day and mail-in voter registration as well as registration on the premises of appropriate government agencies; by preventing the misuse of at-large elections, the abuse of election day challenges and registration roll purges, any undercounting in the national census, and any dilution of the one-person, one-vote principle; by ending discrimination against public employees who are denied the right to full political participation; by supporting statehood for the District of Columbia; by treating the offshore territories under our flag equitably and sensitively under federal policies, assisting their economic and social development and respecting their right to decide their future in their relationship with the United States; by empowering the commonwealth of Puerto Rico with greater autonomy within its relationship with the United States to achieve the economic, social and political goals of its people, and by giving it just and fair participation in federal programs; by assuring and pledging the full and equal access of women and minorities to elective office and party endorsement; and by minimizing the domination and distortion of our elections by moneyed interests.

WE BELIEVE in a stronger America ready to make the tough choices of leadership in an ever-dangerous world: **militarily** stronger in our overall defense and anti-terrorist capabilities and in the cohesion of our military alliances; **economically** stronger at home and in the global marketplace; **intellectually** stronger in the advances of our schools, science and technology; and **spiritually** stronger in the principles we exemplify to the world.

WE BELIEVE in a clear-headed, tough-minded, decisive American foreign policy that will reflect the changing nature of threats to our security and respond to them in a way that reflects our values and the support of our people, a foreign policy that will respect our Constitution, our Congress and our traditional democratic principles and will in turn be respected for its quiet strength, its bipartisan goals, and its steadfast attention to the concerns and contributions of our allies and international organizations. We believe that we must reassume a role of responsible active international leadership based upon our commitment to democracy, human rights and a more secure world; that this nation, as the world power with the broadest global interests and concerns, has a greater stake than any in building a world at peace and governed by law; that we can neither police the world nor retreat from it; and that to have reliable allies we must be a reliable ally.

WE BELIEVE that our national strength has been sapped by a defense establishment wasting money on duplicative and dubious new weapons instead of investing more in readiness and mobility; that our national strength will be enhanced by more stable defense budgets and by a commitment from our allies to assume a greater share of the costs and responsibilities required to maintain peace and liberty; and that as military spending and priorities change, government should encourage the conversion of affected military facilities and the retraining of workers to facilitate the creation of new forms of communication, space development and new peacetime growth and productivity.

WE BELIEVE in an America that will promote peace and prevent war—not by trading weapons for hostages, not by sending brave Americans to undefined missions in Lebanon and Honduras, not by relaxing our vigilance on the assumption that long-range Soviet interests have permanently changed, not by toasting a tyrant like Marcos as a disciple of democracy, but by maintaining a stable nuclear deterrent sufficient to counter any Soviet threat, by standing up to any American adversary whenever necessary and sitting down with him whenever possible, by making clear our readiness to use force when force is required to protect our essential security commitments, by testing the intentions of the new Soviet leaders about arms control, emigration, human rights and other issues, and by matching them not merely in rhetoric but in reciprocal initiatives and innovation, which takes advantage of what may be the greatest opportunity of our lifetime to establish a new, mutually beneficial relationship with the Soviet Union, in which we engage in joint efforts to combat environmental threats, explore peaceful uses of space and eradicate disease and poverty in the developing world, and in a mutual effort to transform the arms race that neither side can win into a contest for people's minds, a contest we know our side will win.

WE BELIEVE in following up the INF [intermediate-range nuclear-force] Treaty, a commendable first step, with mutual, verifiable and enforceable agreements that will make significant reductions in strategic weapons in a way that diminishes the risk of nuclear attack by either superpower; reduce conventional forces to lower and equivalent levels in Europe, requiring deeper cuts on the Warsaw Pact side; ban chemical and space weapons in their entirety; promptly initiate a mutual moratorium on missile flight testing and halt all nuclear weapons testing while strengthening our efforts to prevent the spread of these weapons to other nations before the nightmare of nuclear terrorism engulfs us all.

WE BELIEVE in an America that recognizes not only the realities of East-West relations, but the challenges and opportunities of the developing world; that will support and strengthen international law and institutions, promote human and political rights and measure them by one yardstick, and work for economic growth and development. We believe that we must provide leadership, compassion and economic assistance to those nations stunted by overwhelming debt, deprivation and austerity, and that we must work to promote active agreements between developing and industrial countries, and the major public and commercial lenders, to provide debt relief and rekindle and sustain economic growth and democracy in Latin America, Asia, and the poorest continent, Africa, which deserves special attention. We further believe that we must enlist the trade surplus nations to join with us in supporting new aid initiatives to fuel growth in developing countries that, though economically depressed, are rich in human and natural potential.

WE BELIEVE this country should work harder to stop the supplies of arms, from both East and West, that fuel conflict in regions such as the Persian Gulf and Angola. Deeply disturbed that the current administration has too long abandoned the peace process in the Middle East and consistently undermined it in Central America, we believe that this country, maintaining the special relationship with Israel founded upon mutually shared values and strategic interests, should provide new leadership to deliver the promise of peace and security through negotiations that has been held out to Israel and its neighbors by the Camp David Accords. We support the sovereignty, independence, and territorial integrity of Lebanon with a central government strong enough to unite its people, maintain order and live in peace in the region. We are committed to Persian Gulf security and freedom of navigation of international waters, and to an end to the Iran-Iraq war by promoting United Nations efforts to achieve a ceasefire and a negotiated settlement, through an arms embargo on the combatants. We further believe that the United States must fully support the Arias Peace Plan, which calls for an end to the fighting, national reconciliation, guarantees of justice, freedom, human rights, and democracy, an end to support for irregular forces, and a commitment by the Central American governments to prevent the use of their territory to destabilize others in the region. Instead of the current emphasis on military solutions we will use negotiations and incentives to encourage free and fair elections and security for all nations in the region. We will cease dealing with drug smugglers and seek to reconcile our differences with countries in Central America, enabling the United States and other nations to focus on the pressing social and economic needs of the people of that region. We further believe in pursuing a policy of economic cooperation instead of confrontation with Mexico and our other hemispheric friends; in helping all developing countries build their own peaceful democratic institutions free from foreign troops, subversion and domination and free from domestic dictators and aggressors; in honoring our treaty obligations; and in using all the tools at our disposal, including diplomacy, trade, aid, food, ideas, and ideals, to defend and enlarge the horizons of freedom on this planet.

WE BELIEVE in an America that will promote human rights, human dignity and human opportunity in every country on earth; that will fight discrimination, encourage free speech and association and decry oppression in nations friendly and unfriendly, communist and non-communist; that will encourage our European friends to respect human rights and resolve their long-standing differences over Northern Ireland and Cyprus; that will encourage wherever possible the forces of pluralism and democracy in Eastern Europe and that will support the struggle for human rights in Asia.

WE BELIEVE the apartheid regime in South Africa to be a uniquely repressive regime, ruthlessly deciding every aspect of public and private life by skin color, engaging in unrelenting violence against its citizens at home and promoting naked aggression against its neighbors in Africa. We believe the time has come to end all vestiges of the failed policy of constructive engagement, to declare South Africa a terrorist state, to impose comprehensive sanctions upon its economy, to lead the international community in participation in these actions, and to determine a date certain by which United States corporations must leave South Africa. We further believe that to achieve regional security in Southern Africa, we must press forcefully for Namibia's independence by calling for the end of South Africa's illegal occupation, a cease fire and elections, must end our counterproductive policy in Angola and must offer support and further assistance to Mozambique and other frontline states.

IN SUM, WE BELIEVE it is time for America to change and move forward again in the interest of all its families — to turn away from an era in which too many of America's children have been homeless or hungry and invest in a new era of hope and progress, an era of secure families in a secure America in a secure world.

WE BELIEVE the American dream of opportunity for every citizen can be a reality for all Americans willing to meet their own responsibilities to help make it come true. We believe that the governments at the national, state and local level, in partnerships between those levels and in partnership with the private sector, exist to help us solve our problems instead of adding to them. We believe in competent, pragmatic governments, accountable to the people, led by men and women dedicated not to self interest but to service, motivated not by ideology but by American ideals, governing not in a spirit of power and privilege but with a sense of compassion and community. For many years, in state and local capitals across this nation, Democrats have been successfully solving problems and helping people with exactly this kind of innovative government.

THEREFORE, THE DEMOCRATIC PARTY in Convention assembled and united, the Party of hope and change and fairness for all, hereby declares its readiness to end the stalemate in Washington by challenging, encouraging and inviting the American people — challenging them to do their patriotic best to meet their community responsibilities, encouraging them to protect and preserve their families, our most precious assets, and inviting them to join with us in leading the land we love to a brighter and still greater future of opportunity and justice for all.

TRADE PACT WITH CANADA
July 25 and September 28, 1988

Throughout most of 1988, Canada was engaged in a spirited debate of historic proportions over a free-trade agreement with the United States. Prime Minister Brian Mulroney had signed the pact January 2, but its acceptance by Canada was not assured until Mulroney's Progressive Conservative party retained control of the House of Commons in a November 21 national election. The election amounted to a referendum on the trade question. In the United States the agreement stirred some opposition in industries fearful of Canadian competition, especially in lumbering and fishing. But the debate did not approach the intensity of Canada's. The agreement easily won approval in Congress after President Ronald Reagan formally submitted it July 25. He had signed it at the same time Mulroney did.

Through their agreement, Canada and the United States pledged that in the ten years beginning January 1, 1989, they would phase out virtually all remaining tariffs and other barriers in their voluminous cross-border trade. Free-trade backers in both countries envisioned the creation of a single North American market rivaling in size the European Economic Community.

Each country was the other's biggest trading partner, producing a 1987 trade amounting to $136 billion, measured in American dollars. Besides providing an unimpeded flow of most goods, services, and financial transactions across the border, the pact guaranteed U.S. access to Canada's abundant supplies of oil, gas, and uranium. It would also create new procedures for resolving trade disputes between the two countries.

Approval Fight in Canada

Canadian foes argued that the prevailing trade situation should not be changed. For several years, Canada's trade balance with the United States had been favorable. In 1987, for instance, its exports to the American market ran to $74 billion, some $12 billion ahead of its imports from the United States. Eighty percent of the goods already moved across the border duty-free as a result of numerous prior agreements on specific matters. If the remaining duties were eliminated, the foes contended, Canada would be the loser because those it applied to American imports were higher (averaging 9 percent) than those the United States applied (averaging 4 percent) to Canadian exports. Traditionally, Canada had relied on tariff barriers to protect its industries from bigger U.S. competitors.

The pact's foes drew on widespread Canadian fears—as expressed in the press and opinion polls—that the agreement had the potential for overwhelming their country's smaller economy and chipping away its separate cultural identity. As measured by gross national product (GNP), the Canadian economy was less than one-sixth the size of the U.S. economy. In population, the disparity was even greater: 26 million Canadians and 244 million Americans. The "Americanization" of Canada, long a troublesome issue in Canadian thought and politics, arose with vigor in the 1988 election campaign.

"Keep Canada Canadian" became the slogan of Liberal party leader John Turner. His fierce opposition to the trade pact was matched by Edward Broadbent, leader of the populist New Democrats, who formed a sizable third party. Mulroney, the Conservative leader, had staked his political fortunes on winning ratification of the document.

The House of Commons, where the Conservatives had held a strong majority since the last national election in September 1984, readily approved the agreement. But the Senate, a bastion of Liberal sentiment, withheld its approval, blocking ratification. Mulroney then called for the new election—ten months before it was due—putting the fate of his government and the trade pact in the hands of the voters. The trade question was so central to the campaign that a vote for the Conservatives was understood to be a vote for ratification.

In a nationally televised political debate, Turner accused Mulroney of "selling out" Canada to the United States and of being "dishonest" in his representation of the agreement to the public. For the first time in many years, violence erupted in a Canadian election rally; in Montreal, Turner's supporters attacked free-trade demonstrators who had interrupted his speech with cries of "Liar!"

Mulroney, for his part, campaigned across Canada defending the pact as a means of ensuring the country's future prosperity. He contended that it was not a surrender of the "Canadian soul" to Yankee interests but a commercial agreement that could be canceled "on six months' notice," if either country wanted to pull out. Also important to Mulroney's campaign was a concern among many Canadians that a protectionist mood in Congress could result in new U.S. barriers against their country's exports. A free-trade agreement would keep such barriers from being erected.

Until late in the sixty-day election campaign, opinion polls indicated that the Conservatives were headed for defeat. But when the ballots were cast, Mulroney's party won 170 seats in the House of Commons, against 82 for the Liberals and 43 for the New Democrats. It was the first time since 1953 that any party had won a majority in Commons in successive elections.

"The Canadian people have given us a clear mandate to implement the free-trade agreement," Mulroney jubilantly told reporters the day after the election. "We intend to do so." Soon afterward he called a special session of Parliament to open December 12 and predicted approval of the agreement before January 1, 1989.

Action in Congress

Reagan administration officials were elated by the outcome of the Canadian election. The president, who had made the pact the cornerstone of his trade policy, promptly sent his congratulations to Mulroney. The two had announced they would seek the agreement after their St. Patrick's Day meeting in 1984 in Quebec. However, as early as 1979, when he first announced for president, Reagan said he envisioned a free-trade zone encompassing the United States, Canada, and Mexico. Although the United States and Mexico lowered or eliminated many trade barriers, their agreements were not so sweeping as the one with Canada. Only one other country, Israel, had entered into a free-trade arrangement with the United States. That arrangement began in 1985.

The House of Representatives August 9 voted 366-40 to make the U.S.-Canada agreement part of American law and bring statutes into conformity. Senate approval followed on September 19, also by a large majority (83-9) and after little debate. The measure was protected in both chambers from amendment or filibuster by special expedited status reserved for trade pacts. Moreover, the Reagan administration smoothed over the members' complaints in lengthy negotiations that preceded the bill's formal introduction.

The critics focused particularly on Canadian subsidies left in place by the agreement. Rep. Olympia J. Snowe, R-Maine, cited "government-modernized sawmills located right over the border in Quebec," and fifty-five government subsidy programs for Canadian fishermen as providing unfair competition for Maine's lumber and fishing industries.

Senate action cleared the bill for the president's signature. At a September 28 White House signing ceremony, Reagan said the U.S.-Canada trade agreement was "a model" for global trade. It was seen strengthening the hand of U.S. negotiators in the so-called Uruguay round of international trade talks, which began there in September 1986. The talks were the eighth set of trade-liberalization talks conducted under terms of the forty-year-old General Agreement on Tariffs and Trade (GATT). Its rules applied to member nations of the organization—ninety-six in 1988. The United States has hinted it would negotiate agreements similar to the Canadian accord with other countries if the GATT negotiations did not progress to America's liking.

Following are the texts of a letter from President Reagan to the Speaker of the House and president of the Senate transmitting the Canada-United States Free Trade Agreement to Congress, July 25, 1988, and of the president's remarks at White House ceremonies, September 28, 1988, at which he signed legislation implementing the agreement:

LETTER OF TRANSMITTAL

Pursuant to section 102 of the Trade Act of 1974, I herewith transmit the final legal text of the United States-Canada Free-Trade Agreement, which Prime Minister Brian Mulroney and I entered into on behalf of our Governments on January 2, 1988.

With this truly historic agreement, I am submitting the proposed United States-Canada Free-Trade Agreement Implementation Act of 1988, which will revise domestic law as required or appropriate to implement this Agreement and fulfill our international obligations. Further, in accordance with section 102 of the Trade Act of 1974, I am submitting a Statement of Administrative Action that:

- outlines proposed administrative actions to implement the Agreement;
- explains how the implementing bill and proposed administrative actions change or affect existing law; and
- provides reasons as to why the implementing bill and proposed administrative actions are required or appropriate to carry out the Agreement.

Finally, I am submitting a statement of reasons as to how the Agreement serves the interests of U.S. commerce.

With this Agreement and its implementing bill, we set a new standard for exemplary teamwork between the Congress and the Executive branch. The Administration and many congressional committees have cooperated closely in drafting the bill I am submitting today. No one branch of our government has dictated the terms of this bill; rather, we have all cooperated for the greater good of the Agreement, which so manifestly serves our national economic interests. I compliment and thank the Congress for its substantial contributions to this process, and particularly for the timeliness of its efforts in this regard. I believe this cooperation fully reflects the responsible way in which "fast track" legislative procedures for trade agreements were intended to be used.

The United States-Canada Free-Trade Agreement is one of the most comprehensive agreements on trade ever negotiated between two nations. It provides for the elimination of all tariffs, reduces many non-tariff barriers, liberalizes investment practices, and covers trade in services. For example, the Agreement:

- significantly liberalizes Canada's foreign investment regime;
- provides secure, nondiscriminatory access to Canadian energy supplies, even in times of shortages;
- establishes the critical principle of national treatment with respect to trade in over 150 services, which will ensure nondiscriminatory treatment of U.S. services providers under future Canadian laws and regulations;
- removes essentially all existing Canadian discrimination faced by U.S. financial institutions operating in Canada;
- facilitates the temporary entry of U.S. business persons and professionals into Canada;
- freezes coverage of the United States-Canada "Auto Pact" and limits future Pact-like provisions;
- eliminates Canadian duty remission programs linked to performance requirements;
- removes the current Canadian embargo on imports of used motor vehicles and aircraft;
- expands opportunities to sell U.S. goods to the Canadian Government by extending the coverage of the GATT Government Procurement Code bilaterally to purchases between $25,000 and the Code threshold (currently about $156,000);
- provides that owners of U.S. television programs should be compensated for the retransmission of their programs in Canada;
- eliminates Canadian export subsidies on agricultural trade to the United States;
- prohibits Canadian Government and public entity sales for export to the United States of agricultural goods at prices below cost;
- generally exempts meat products of one country from the other country's meat import quota laws;
- increases Canadian poultry and egg minimum import quotas;
- sets conditions for the removal of Canadian import licensing of wheat, barley, and oats;
- establishes a forum for discussing the possible harmonization of technical regulations on agricultural trade;
- facilitates the recognition by one party of the other's testing facilities and certification bodies in the area of technical standards; and

• removes barriers to the sale of U.S.-produced wine and distilled spirits in Canada.

While I have highlighted here major benefits for the United States, the Agreement of course provides reciprocal benefits for Canada. Thus, the Agreement is a win-win situation for both countries. It will create more jobs and lower prices for consumers on both sides of the border. The overall result will be increased competitiveness and a higher standard of living in both countries.

Moreover, the Agreement looks to the future by providing a concrete example of the kind of market-opening steps the entire world should be pursuing. It thus supports U.S. efforts at trade liberalization in the Uruguay Round of multilateral trade negotiations.

With this Agreement and the free-trade area it establishes, we are poised to make a great leap of progress. Already Canada and the United States generate the world's largest volume of trade. Canada is by far our largest trading partner. The United States exports more to the Province of Ontario alone than to the entire country of Japan. United States citizens are by far the principal foreign investors in Canada, and Canadians, on a per capita basis, are even greater investors in this country. This two-way traffic in trade and investment has helped to create more than a million jobs, expand opportunity for both our peoples, and augment the prosperity of both nations.

With this Agreement, we are tearing down the tariff walls that block the flow of trade and generally eliminating the tangle of restrictions and regulations that inhibit our commerce and economic cooperation. As this Agreement takes effect, Americans and Canadians will be more able to conduct business, invest, and trade where they like. Two proud, independent, and sovereign nations—Canada and the United States—will pull together, as partners, toward a future of economic growth and prosperity.

With this Agreement, we reject "beggar-thy-neighbor" policies in order to build with our neighbors; we put aside special interests in favor of the common interest; we break free from limitations of the past not only to enhance our prosperity today, but also to build a better tomorrow for the generations to come in the 21st century.

With this Agreement, both the United States and Canada will be better prepared to compete in the global marketplace of the 21st century. Therefore, in the interest of strengthening our economy, creating jobs, reducing consumer burdens, and advancing U.S. efforts in multilateral trade negotiations, I urge prompt approval and implementation of the United States-Canada Free-Trade Agreement by the Congress.

Sincerely,

Ronald Reagan

REMARKS AT PACT SIGNING

This is a moment future historians will cite as a landmark, a turning point in the forward march of trade, commerce, and even civilization itself. That's a dramatic statement, I know, but I think everyone here is aware of the historical import of what we do today. Today, September 28, 1988, I am signing into law the United States-Canada Free Trade Agreement Implementation Act of 1988.

This agreement brings down the tariff walls between our two nations and, in so doing, creates the world's largest free-trade area. Businesses and consumers in both our countries will have unprecedented freedom to choose among a staggering array of goods and services. It'll mean lower prices for consumers, jobs galore for workers, and new markets for producers. It'll stimulate investment in both economies, which will mean the rapid advancement of new technologies. It means a stronger and freer marketplace for the United States and Canada. There'll be a rich flow of agriculture and energy resources from one country to the other in a way that will profit both. We also deal with the service sectors of our economies, providing for the first time an explicit assurance that in such areas as accounting, tourism, insurance, and engineering our peoples will be free to choose their suppliers.

The U.S.-Canada Free Trade Agreement, which recognizes the similarities between our economies and our political systems, also respects our different histories, aspirations, and densities—the reality that Canada and the United States are two distinct variations of a common theme of freedom, democracy, and human rights. As leaders of the free world, Canada and the United States are pointing the way toward the future. Canada's visionary Prime Minister, Brian Mulroney, and its able Ambassador, Allan Gotlieb, understand well that free trade is an idea whose time has come. One of the signs of this change is the very passage of this bill. We must make sure the freedoms we enjoy include the freedom to choose at home and the freedom to be chosen abroad. This nation, which was born to nurture human freedoms, must take the lead in establishing the principle that one of the most important human freedoms is free exchange.

That principle was the animating force behind the sterling work of Ambassador Clayton Yeutter [U.S. Trade Representative] and former Treasury Secretary James Baker. The cooperation among them, the administration, and Members of Congress on both sides of the aisle was decisive. The congressional leadership promised and delivered prompt action, and the result was overwhelming approval by both Houses. They deserve the Nation's thanks for a job well done.

This legislation reflects overwhelming support for the elimination of barriers to trade between the United States and Canada. It reflects the sound economic principles of free trade that benefit American businesses and workers. The bill is a hallmark of free trade, in marked contrast to the damaging protectionist textiles bills that I vetoed earlier today.

What the United States and Canada are accomplishing on a bilateral basis is an example of what we can and must achieve multilaterally. That is why we look forward to continuing the midterm review of the Uruguay round negotiations [multilateral trade negotiations] in Montreal later this year. This agreement is a model for those talks to follow. Just as the pessimists were wrong about this agreement, so will the pessimists be wrong about the Uruguay round. Today we not only commemorate this legislation as the happpy conclusion of a bilateral pact but pledge our commitment to the successful completion of the Uruguay round by 1990. The midterm review will be the most important trade matter in the last months of this administration, and I urge our trading partners to be ready to do business in December. We sure will be.

Let the 5,000-mile border between Canada and the United States stand as a symbol for the future. No soldier stands guard to protect it. Barbed wire does not deface it. And no invisible barrier of economic suspicion and fear will extend it. Let it forever be not a point of division but a meeting place between our great and true friends. This bill is the product of the vision of the American and Canadian people who are leading the way toward a new era of freedom. Now, I thank you. May God bless all of you. And I shall now sign this agreement.

KING HUSSEIN'S SPEECH SEVERING WEST BANK TIES

July 31, 1988

Forty years after his grandfather's army moved into the West Bank of the Jordan River to confront the new state of Israel, King Hussein of Jordan renounced his government's claims to that territory on July 31. In a televised speech in Amman, the Jordanian capital, Hussein said the Palestine Liberation Organization (PLO) was "the sole legitimate representative of the Palestine people." With the renunciation, he severed legal and administrative links that Jordan had maintained in the West Bank, a portion of Palestine annexed by Jordan in 1950 and occupied by Israel since 1967.

His words jolted the Palestinians, worried the Israelis, and jeopardized U.S. peacemaking efforts. But some observers suspected that the king's action was a tactical maneuver to expose the PLO's weakness and thereby restore his influence. Hussein insisted, however, that his decision was taken only in response to the wish of the PLO and "the prevailing Arab conviction that such measures will contribute to the struggle of the Palestinian people and their glorious uprising." The "uprising"—rioting in Gaza and the West Bank that began in December 1987—greatly influenced his decision. He noted a "general conviction" that Jordanian links with the West Bank "hamper the Palestinian struggle to gain international support for the Palestinian cause."

Even after Israel occupied the West Bank in the June 1967 war, Jordan had continued to pay salaries to roughly 21,000 civil servants, including teachers, health workers, municipal officials, and Moslem clergy. Building deeds, housing loans, professional licenses, and school diplomas were granted from Jordan, and Jordanian dinars were the accepted currency in the territory. West Bank residents were granted Jordanian passports.

Hussein said on August 4 that Jordanian passports would remain in the hands of Palestinian residents of the West Bank and Gaza unless and until they could obtain passports from an independent Palestinian state. Jordanian officials said these passports would henceforth be marked to indicate that a resident of the occupied territories was no longer a Jordanian citizen. Except for clergy and pensioners, Jordanian salaries to West Bank employees were terminated on August 16.

On the day before his speech, Hussein dissolved the lower house of the Jordanian parliament, half of whose sixty delegates were Palestinians from the West Bank. Two days earlier on July 28 he had cancelled a plan for spending $1.3 billion on housing, health, education, and cultural projects in the West Bank. This plan, backed by the United States, had been widely viewed as an effort to create a conservative alternative to the PLO on the West Bank that Israel would welcome.

Palestinian Identity

The West Bank uprising strengthened the determination of Palestinians and other Arabs to leave Israel no choice but to negotiate with the PLO—which it long had refused to do. Hussein said his decision to withdraw from the West Bank was in response to a growing pressure for "highlighting the Palestinian identity in a complete manner."

Palestinian identity had been the subject of much controversy. The Arabs of Palestine were simultaneously Arabs and Palestinians, a double identity that seemed anomalous in an age of nation-states. The identity controversy was entangled with the question of who had the right to govern the West Bank. Palestinian nationalists rejected not only Israel's claims to the territory but also the claims of their brother Arabs, notably Hussein.

As a youth, Hussein had seen his grandfather, King Abdullah, assassinated by Palestinian foes on the steps of a Jerusalem mosque. In 1970 radical Palestinian factions living in Jordan tried to overthrow Hussein in the bloody "Black September" civil war. In 1974 Arab leaders meeting in Rabat, Morocco, designated the PLO the sole legitimate representative of the Palestinian people, forcing a reluctant Hussein to yield any claim to that role. And in May 1988 Hussein was upset when Arab leaders at a summit meeting in Algiers decided to channel funds to the West Bank uprising solely through the PLO and not, as in the past, through a joint PLO-Jordanian committee.

Hussein's disengagement speech reiterated Jordan's public policy of support for an independent Palestinian state in the West Bank, but many observers were skeptical that he wanted a PLO-controlled state on Jordan's border. Nadav Safran, a professor of Middle East studies at

Harvard, observed that "such a state would be helpless against Israel, but deadly for Hussein, because it would arouse the nationalistic feelings of the Palestinians on the East Bank, who constitute a majority of the population there." In announcing Jordan's withdrawal from the West Bank, Hussein explained that Palestinians on the East Bank retained all the rights and obligations of Jordanian citizens.

American officials estimated that Palestinians accounted for 65 to 70 percent of Jordan's 2.8 million people. Hussein, in a news conference August 7, said such estimates were inaccurate. He said the notion that most Jordanians were of Palestinian origin was promoted by Israel and its supporters in the United States to foster the belief "that Palestinians can form their state elsewhere, and that that 'elsewhere' obviously has been, in their minds, Jordan."

Origins of the Controversy

Both Palestine and Jordan were part of Arab territories governed for centuries by Turkey's Ottoman Empire. When the Ottomans, together with their German and Austro-Hungarian allies, were defeated in World War I, victorious Britain and France divided the Arab lands between them. The League of Nations recognized their rule as "mandates" to prepare the populations for eventual self-government. Britain governed through its wartime allies of the Hashemite clan, establishing King Abdullah in Transjordan (later Jordan). Britain directly administered the territory west of the Jordan River and the Dead Sea as "Palestine."

Transjordan obtained its independence in 1948, the same year Israel did. Jewish immigration into Palestine, which began with the birth of Zionism at the end of the nineteenth century, increased during the Nazi persecution of the 1930s and swelled with the flight of refugees after World War II. Caught in the middle of conflicts between Palestine's Jews and Arabs, war-weary Britain abandoned its mandate. The United Nations, under international pressure to fulfill Jewish aspirations for a homeland, in 1947 partitioned Palestine against the wishes of its Arab majority, granting 55 percent of the land to the Jews.

In armed hostilities, Jewish forces secured control of most of the areas accorded them in the partition plan. When Israel declared its independence in May 1948, the armies of neighboring Arab states attacked the new nation. The resulting war ended in 1949 with an armistice leaving Israel with more territory than in the partition plan (about 8,000 of Palestine's 10,000 square miles), Egypt in control of the small Gaza strip, and Jordan's army—the Arab Legion—holding what is now called the West Bank. Jordan annexed the West Bank in 1950.

Embittered and humiliated by Israel's victory, Arab nationalists from Iraq to Morocco dreamed of a unity that proved elusive. Increasingly disillusioned by the military and diplomatic failures of the Arab govern-

ments, the Arabs of Palestine developed a passionate nationalism of their own. Palestinian nationalism came to rival Zionism in its zeal for a homeland.

Israelis continued to reject Palestinian claims to a homeland in their native territory by continuing to view Palestinians not as a separate people, but as part of a larger Arab nation. According to the dominant Israeli view, the Palestinians could satisfy their aspirations for a homeland in Arab lands outside the West Bank. This view was directly challenged by Hussein's withdrawal from the West Bank. Jordan has long been Israel's candidate for an alternative to an independent Palestinian state. Such a state, Israelis feared, would aspire to recover all of the original territory of Palestine, and, thus, to eliminate Israel as a Jewish state. On the other hand, Jordan, in the Israeli view, shared Israel's interest in limiting Palestinian aspirations.

Israel's Labor party had long sought an understanding with Hussein by which territory on the West Bank would be traded for some form of Jordanian responsibility to maintain stability there. Hussein had been unwilling to provoke Palestinian wrath by making a deal with the Israelis, but his continuing ties to the West Bank kept alive the Labor party's hopes for a "Jordanian option." Hussein's severing of West Bank ties dealt a blow to those hopes and boosted the determination of the rival Likud political coalition in Israel never to negotiate any Israeli withdrawal from occupied territory.

Hussein's speech cast a shadow on flagging American peace efforts. When President Ronald Reagan first described his administration's Middle East peace plan in 1982, he said, "Self-government by the Palestinians of the West Bank and Gaza in association with Jordan offers the best chance for durable, just and lasting peace." (Reagan Peace Plan, Historic Documents of 1982, p. 753)

The United States refused to deal directly with the PLO, insisting that the organization must first renounce terrorism, recognize Israel's right to exist, and accept United Nations Security Council resolutions establishing a framework for peace in the Middle East. Secretary of State George P. Shultz responded to Hussein's speech by observing that the king "has to be a partner" in any future peace talks with Israel because "Jordan has the longest border with Israel of any Arab state."

Hussein's withdrawal left the PLO the only Arab power in the West Bank. But it also left the organization in a quandary over how to exercise its responsibility. Unless the PLO declared—and demonstrated—peaceful intent toward Israel, there appeared little chance that Israel would permit it to take over the West Bank functions Hussein abandoned. If the PLO failed, it was speculated, West Bank residents might clamor for the king to resume his former role. Whether or not it ultimately fails, the situation already had been changed drastically.

Following are excerpts from the text of King Hussein's
speech, July 31, 1988, as translated into English by the
Jordanian government:

In the name of God, the compassionate, the merciful
and peace be upon his faithful Arab messenger

Brother citizens. . . . [W]e have initiated, after seeking God's assistance, and in light of a thorough and extensive study, a series of measures with the aim of enhancing the Palestinian national orientation, and highlighting the Palestinian identity. Our objective is the benefit of the Palestinian cause and the Arab Palestinian people.

Our decision, as you know, comes after thirty-eight years of the unity of the two banks, and fourteen years after the Rabat Summit Resolution, designating the Palestine Liberation Organization (PLO) as the sole legitimate representative of the Palestinian people. It also comes six years after the Fez [Morocco] Summit Resolution of an independent Palestinian state in the occupied West Bank and the Gaza Strip. . . .

The considerations leading to the search to identify the relationship between the West Bank and the Hashemite Kingdom of Jordan, against the background of the PLO's call for the establishment of an independent Palestinian state, are twofold:

  I. The principle of Arab unity, this being a national objective to which all the Arab peoples aspire, and which they all seek to realize.
 II. The political reality of the scope of benefit to the Palestinian struggle that accrues from maintaining the legal relationship between the two banks of the kingdom. . . .

. . . We respect the wish of the PLO, the sole legitimate representative of the Palestinian people, to secede from us in an independent Palestinian state. We say this in all understanding. Nevertheless, Jordan will remain the proud bearer of the message of the great Arab revolt; faithful to its principles; believing in the common Arab destiny; and committed to joint Arab action.

Regarding the political factor, it has been our belief, since the Israeli aggression of June 1967, that our first priority should be to liberate the land and holy places from Israeli occupation.

Accordingly, as is well known, we have concentrated all our efforts during the twenty-one years since the occupation towards this goal. We had never imagined that the preservation of the legal and administrative links between the two banks could constitute an obstacle to the liberation of the occupied Palestinian land. . . .

Lately, it has transpired that there is a general Palestinian and Arab orientation towards highlighting the Palestinian identity in a complete manner. . . . It is also viewed that these [Jordanian-West Bank] links hamper the Palestinian struggle to gain international support for the

Palestinian cause, as the national cause of a people struggling against foreign occupation. . . .

. . . [T]here is a general conviction that the struggle to liberate the occupied Palestinian land could be enhanced by dismantling the legal and administrative links between the two banks, we have to fulfill our duty, and do what is required of us. At the Rabat Summit of 1974 we responded to the Arab leaders' appeal to us to continue our interaction with the occupied West Bank through the Jordanian institutions, to support the steadfastness of our brothers there. Today we respond to the wish of the Palestine Liberation Organization, the sole legitimate representative of the Palestinian people, and to the Arab orientation to affirm the Palestinian identity in all its aspects. . . .

Brother citizens. . . . We cannot continue in this state of suspension, which can neither serve Jordan nor the Palestinian cause. We had to leave the labyrinth of fears and doubts, towards clearer horizons where mutual trust, understanding, and cooperation can prevail, to the benefit of the Palestinian cause and Arab unity. This unity will remain a goal which all the Arab peoples cherish and seek to realize.

At the same time, it has to be understood in all clarity, and without any ambiguity or equivocation, that our measures regarding the West Bank, concern only the occupied Palestinian land and its people. They naturally do not relate in any way to the Jordanian citizens of Palestinian origin in the Hashemite Kingdom of Jordan. They all have the full rights of citizenship and all its obligations, the same as any other citizen irrespective of his origin. They are an integral part of the Jordanian state. They belong to it, they live on its land, and they participate in its life and all its activities. Jordan is not Palestine; and the independent Palestinian state will be established on the occupied Palestinian land after its liberation, God willing. There the Palestinian identity will be embodied, and there the Palestinian struggle shall come to fruition, as confirmed by the glorious uprising of the Palestinian people under occupation.

National unity is precious in any country; but in Jordan it is more than that. It is the basis of our stability, and the springboard of our development and prosperity. It is the foundation of our national security and the source of our faith in the future. It is the living embodiment of the principles of the great Arab revolt, which we inherited, and whose banner we proudly bear. It is a living example of constructive plurality, and a sound nucleus for wider Arab unity.

Based on that, safeguarding national unity is a sacred duty that will not be compromised. Any attempt to undermine it, under any pretext, would only help the enemy carry out his policy of expansion at the expense of Palestine and Jordan alike. Consequently, true nationalism lies in bolstering and fortifying national unity. Moreover, the responsibility to safeguard it falls on every one of you, leaving no place in our midst for sedition or treachery. With God's help, we shall be as always, a united cohesive family, whose members are joined by bonds of brotherhood, affection, awareness, and common national objectives. . . .

The constructive plurality which Jordan has lived since its foundation, and through which it has witnessed progress and prosperity in all aspects of life, emanates not only from our faith in the sanctity of national unity, but also in the importance of Jordan's Pan-Arab role. Jordan presents itself as the living example of the merger of various Arab groups on its soil, within the framework of good citizenship, and one Jordanian people. This paradigm that we live on our soil gives us faith in the inevitability of attaining Arab unity, God willing. . . .

Citizens, Palestinian brothers in the occupied Palestinian lands, to dispel any doubts that may arise out of our measures, we assure you that these measures do not mean the abandonment of our national duty, either towards the Arab-Israeli conflict, or towards the Palestinian cause. . . . Jordan will continue its support for the steadfastness of the Palestinian people, and their courageous uprising in the occupied Palestinian land, within its capabilities. I have to mention, that when we decided to cancel the Jordanian Development Plan in the occupied territories, we contacted, at the same time, various friendly governments and international institutions, which had expressed their wish to contribute to the plan, urging them to continue financing development projects in the occupied Palestinian lands, through the relevant Palestinian quarters.

. . . No one outside Palestine has had, nor can have, an attachment to Palestine, or its cause, firmer than that of Jordan or of my family. Moreover, Jordan is a confrontation state, whose borders with Israel are longer than those of any other Arab state, longer even than the combined borders of the West Bank and Gaza with Israel.

In addition, Jordan will not give up its commitment to take part in the peace process. We have contributed to the peace process until it reached the stage of a consensus to convene an international peace conference on the Middle East. The purpose of the conference would be to achieve a just and comprehensive peace settlement to the Arab-Israeli conflict, and the settlement of the Palestinian problem in all its aspects. . . .

Jordan, dear brothers, is a principal party to the Arab-Israeli conflict, and to the peace process. It shoulders its national responsibilities on that basis.

I thank you and salute you, and reiterate my heartfelt wishes to you, praying God the almighty to grant us assistance and guidance, and to grant our Palestinian brothers victory and success.

May God's peace, mercy, and blessings be upon you.

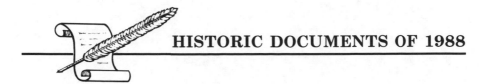

August

Republican National Convention 589

Republican Party Platform 615

Report on the Downing
of an Iranian Airliner 703

REPUBLICAN NATIONAL CONVENTION
August 15-18, 1988

As George Bush and family members watched on television from a nearby hotel in New Orleans, the Republican convention celebrated the culmination of his long pursuit of the party's presidential nomination. The nomination came at 11:08 p.m. CDT, August 17, when the nominee's son, George, announced the Texas delegation votes that put his father over the top.

The result was preordained. Bush had been assured of the nomination since his victories in the March 8 Super Tuesday primary elections, and his win in Illinois the next week. With little suspense over the proceedings of the four-day convention held August 15-18, the national media turned their attention to fleshing out the record of Dan Quayle, the little-known Indiana senator Bush had unexpectedly selected to be his running mate.

The scene at the Superdome on the evening of August 15 was familiar. Ronald and Nancy Reagan stood atop the Republican convention podium, waving to throngs of adoring delegates and visitors. They cheered enthusiastically at his applause lines, as red, white, and blue balloons floated from the rafters. But the mood was tempered by the poignancy of the moment—a realization that Reagan was making his last convention speech as leader of his party and his country.

Reagan Praises Bush

For his part, Reagan was firm if slightly subdued in a speech that centered on the accomplishments of his administration and the role of

Vice President Bush in those achievements. The president offered again his optimistic vision of America as a place with no twilight, where it was "sunrise every day," with "fresh new opportunities and dreams to build." He hit a sentimental note early in the speech, thanking the convention for its tribute to Nancy Reagan, who had delivered her own farewell. The president took some predictable jabs at his Democratic critics. He accused them of "inflated rhetoric" at their convention in Atlanta in July, adding, "But, then, inflation is their speciality." (Democratic National Convention, p. 533)

The most pertinent symbol of Reagan's role in the 1988 campaign was his strong praise of Bush as a key player in his administration. Reagan's promise of campaign assistance and his call for Bush to "win one for the Gipper" was a lift for Bush supporters, who had been disturbed by Reagan's pallid endorsement of their candidate in May.

The Republicans had plenty of theater scheduled for August 16, with an agenda that included New Jersey Gov. Thomas H. Kean's keynote address and speeches by Pat Robertson, the television evangelist who had also sought the presidential nomination; Jeane J. Kirkpatrick, former representative to the United Nations; and former president Gerald R. Ford. But Bush himself stole the show with his midafternoon announcement that he had selected Quayle as his running mate.

Bush's aides had said the candidate would not announce his choice until August 18, to maintain some suspense and keep the television-viewing public focused on the convention. But after being greeted by the departing Reagan at the Belle Chasse Naval Air Station near New Orleans, Bush told reporters that he had settled on his choice. He made the selection public at a welcoming ceremony on the New Orleans riverfront. Bush praised Quayle, who at forty-one was twenty-three years his junior, as "a man of the future." The selection was apparently intended to appeal to younger voters and also to party conservatives, but it had the unintended effect of drawing severe criticism and calling Bush's judgment into question.

With Bush trailing his Democratic foe Michael Dukakis in public opinion polls at the time of the convention, media commentators and Bush supporters alike said he had to make the "speech of his life" in his formal acceptance of the nomination August 18. Bush did not waste the opportunity. Seemingly unfazed by the controversy over Quayle, Bush presented an assertive and sometimes commanding persona in an acceptance speech that stirred the Republican delegates.

"I mean to run hard, to fight hard, to stand on the issues—and I mean to win," Bush said early in his speech. Near his conclusion, he said his experience as vice president had made him the candidate who was prepared to deal with the critical issues that come across the president's desk. "I am that man," Bush said emphatically, as the crowd roared its approval.

The Quayle Controversy

With his performance, Bush rescued himself from a day that had the ingredients for a political disaster. Quayle's muddled answers to questions about how and why he came to serve in the Indiana National Guard during the Vietnam War fueled what was becoming a full-blown controversy. The network newscasts on August 17 led with inquiries into whether Quayle, a scion of the Pulliam publishing empire, had used family connections to get into the guard in 1969.

But if Quayle was burdened with concerns over the military service issue, he checked those emotions backstage before giving his acceptance speech. The youthful-looking senator tackled his first appearance on the national stage with the cheerleader-like élan for which he was known in Indiana. Stating that "the future under George Bush means peace and economic opportunity," Quayle lumped Dukakis in with other Democratic figures who were frequent targets of GOP criticism. "We do not need the future the Democratic party sees, the party of George McGovern, Jimmy Carter, Walter Mondale ... Ted Kennedy, and his buddy, Michael Dukakis," Quayle said, as the delegates lustily booed each name. Elucidating his own record, Quayle took credit for writing the 1982 Job Training Partnership Act and discussed his membership on the Senate Armed Services Committee.

Bush, in his acceptance speech, acknowledged the necessity of establishing his own identity. "Ronald Reagan asked for, and received, my candor; he never asked for, but he did receive, my loyalty," Bush said. "But now you must see me for what I am: the Republican candidate for president. . . . And now I turn to the American people to share my hopes and intentions, and why and where I wish to lead."

Bush praised the Pledge of Allegiance, the death penalty, voluntary school prayer, and gun ownership, and opposed abortion and prison furloughs—issues of conservative appeal that had been raised by speaker after speaker during the convention and would form the basis of his attacks on Dukakis in the campaign that followed.

Like Reagan, who ended his 1980 acceptance speech with a moment of silent prayer, Bush finished with a flourish. He led the convention in the Pledge of Allegiance, highlighting his criticism of Dukakis for vetoing a Massachusetts law requiring school teachers to lead the pledge.

> *Following are speeches at the Republican national convention in New Orleans as delivered by President Reagan on August 15, by Sen. Dan Quayle of Indiana accepting the vice presidential nomination August 18, and by Vice President George Bush accepting the presidential nomination August 18. (The bracketed headings have been added by Congressional Quarterly to highlight the organization of the text.):*

ADDRESS BY PRESIDENT REAGAN

Thank you. Thank you, thank you all.

Madam chairman, delegates to this convention and fellow citizens, thank you for that warm and generous welcome.

Nancy and I have been enjoying the finest of Southern hospitality since we arrived here yesterday.

And believe me, after that reception, I don't think the Big Easy has ever been bigger than it is tonight.

And with all due respect to Cajun cuisine, cooking, and New Orleans jazz, nothing could be hotter than the spirit of the delegates in this hall, except maybe a victory celebration on November 8.

In that spirit, I think we could be forgiven if we give ourselves a little pat on the back for having made "Republican" a proud word once again. And, America a proud nation again.

Nancy and I are so honored to be your guests tonight—to share a little of your special time. And we thank you.

Now I want to invoke executive privilege to talk for a moment about a very special lady who has been selfless, not just for our party but for the entire nation.

She is a strong, courageous and compassionate woman, and wherever she's gone, here in the United States as well as abroad, whether with young or old, or comforting the grieving or supporting the youngsters who are fighting the scourge of drugs, she makes us proud. I've been proud of her for a long time, but never more so than in these last eight years. With your tribute to Nancy today, you warmed my heart as well as hers—and believe me, she deserved your tribute.

I am deeply grateful to you for what you have done.

When people tell me that I became president on January 20, 1981, I feel I have to correct them.

You don't become president of the United States. You are given temporary custody of an institution called the presidency, which belongs to our people.

Having temporary custody of this office has been for me a sacred trust and an honor beyond words or measure. That trust began with many of you in this room many conventions ago.

Many's the time that I've said a prayer of thanks to all Americans who placed this trust in my hands, and tonight, please accept again our heartfelt gratitude, Nancy's and mine, for this special time that you've given in our lives.

Just a moment ago, you multiplied the honor with a moving tribute. And being only human, there's a part of me that would like to take credit for what we have achieved.

But tonight, before we do anything else, let us remember, that tribute really belongs to 245 million citizens who make up the greatest—and the first—three words in the Constitution: We the people.

It is the American people who endured the great challenge of lifting us from the depths of national calamity, renewing our mighty economic strength and leading the way to restoring our respect in the world. They are an extraordinary breed we call Americans.

So if there is any salute deserved tonight—it's to the heroes everywhere in this land who make up the doers, the dreamers, and the life-builders without which our glorious experiment in democracy would have failed.

[A Look Back]

So, this, this convention brings back so many memories for a fellow like me. I can still remember my first Republican convention: Abraham Lincoln giving a speech that sent tingles down my spine. No, I have to confess, I wasn't actually there. The truth is, way back when I belonged to the other party.

But surely we can remember another convention. Eight years ago, we gathered in Detroit in a troubled time for our beloved country.

And we gathered solemnly to share our dreams.

And, when I look back, I wonder if we dared to be so bold to take in those burdens.

But in that same city of Detroit, when the 20th century was only in its second year, another great Republican, Teddy Roosevelt, told Americans not to hold back from dangers ahead, but to rejoice: "... our hearts lifted with the faith that to us and to our children ... it shall be given to make this republic the mightiest among the peoples of mankind." Teddy said those, years ago.

In 1980, we needed every bit of that kind of faith.

That year, it was our dream that together we could rescue America and make a new beginning—to create anew that shining city on a hill. The dream we shared was to reclaim our government—to transform it from one that was consuming our prosperity into one that would get out of the way of those who created prosperity.

It was a dream of again making our nation strong enough to preserve world peace and freedom and to recapture our national destiny.

We made a determination that our dream would not be built on a foundation of sand—something called "Trust Me Government"—but we would trust, instead, the American spirit.

And, yes, we were unashamed in believing that this dream was driven by a community of shared values of family, work, neighborhood, peace, and freedom.

And on the night of July 17, 1980, we left with a mutual pledge to conduct a national crusade to make America great again.

We had faith, because the heroes in our midst had never failed us before. Tom Paine knew what these Americans with character of steel could do when he wrote: "... the harder the conflict, the more glorious the triumph."

And my fellow citizens, while our triumph is not yet complete, the road has been glorious, indeed. Eight years ago, we met at a time when America was in economic chaos—and today, we meet in a time of economic promise. We met then in international distress and today with global hope.

[Pre-Reagan Years]

Now, I think we can be forgiven if we engage in a little review of that history tonight.

As the saying goes—"Just a friendly reminder." I've been doing a little remembering of my own because of all that inflated rhetoric by our friends in Atlanta last month. But then, inflation is their specialty.

Before we came to Washington, Americans had just suffered the two worst back-to-back years of inflation in 60 years. Those are the facts.

And as John Adams said: "Facts are stubborn things."

Interest rates had jumped to over 21 percent—the highest in 120 years—more than doubling the average monthly mortgage payments for working families—our families.

When they sat around the kitchen table, it was not to plan summer vacations, it was to plan economic survival.

Facts are stubborn things.

Industrial production was down, and productivity was down for two consecutive years. The average—missed me [Reagan responded to a balloon that had just popped]—the average weekly wage plunged 9 percent.

Median family income fell 5½ percent. Facts are stubborn things.

Our friends on the other side had actually passed the single highest tax bill in the 200-year history of the United States. Auto loans, because of their policies, went up to 17 percent—so our great factories began shutting down. Fuel costs jumped through the atmosphere—more than doubling. Then people waited in gas lines as well as unemployment lines.

Facts are stupid things—stubborn things, I should say.

And then there was the misery index. That was an election year gimmick they designed for the 1976 campaign—they added the unemployment and inflation rates. And it came to 13.4 percent in 1976, and they declared that our candidate, Jerry Ford, had no right to seek re-election with that kind of misery index.

But four years later, in the 1980 campaign, they didn't mention the misery index. Do you suppose it was because it was no longer 13.4 percent? In those four years it had become almost 21 percent.

And last month, in Atlanta at their convention, there was again no mention of the misery index. Why? Because, right now, it's less than 9.2 percent.

Facts are stubborn things.

When we met in Detroit in that summer of 1980—it was a summer of discontent for America around the world. Our national defense had been so weakened, the Soviet Union had begun to engage in reckless aggression, including the invasion and occupation of Afghanistan.

The U.S. response to that was to forbid our athletes to participate in the 1980 Olympics and to try to pull the rug out from under our farmers with a grain and soybean embargo.

And in those years, on any given day, we had military aircraft that couldn't fly for lack of spare parts, and ships that couldn't leave port for the same reason or for lack of a crew. Our embassy in Pakistan was burned to the ground, and the one in Iran was stormed and occupied with all Americans taken as hostages. The world began to question the constancy and resolve of the United States. Our leaders answered, not that there was something wrong with our government, but that our people were at fault because of some malaise.

Well, facts are stubborn things.

When our friends last month talked of unemployment, despair, hopelessness, economic weakness—I wondered why on Earth they were talking about 1978 instead of 1988.

[The Past Seven Years]

Now, now we hear talk that it's time for a change. Well, ladies and gentlemen, another friendly reminder: We are the change.

We rolled up our sleeves and went to work in January of 1981; we focused on hope, not despair. We challenged the failed policies of the past, because we believed that a society is great, not because of promises made by its government, but only because of progress made by its people. And that was our change.

We said something shocking: Taxes ought to be reduced, not raised. We cut the tax rates for the working folks of America. We indexed taxes, and that stopped a bracket creep which kicked average wage-earners into higher tax brackets when they'd only received a cost-of-living pay raise. And we initiated reform of the unfairness in our tax system. And what do you know—the top 5 percent of earners are paying a higher percentage of the total tax revenue at the lower rates than they ever had before, and millions of earners at the bottom of the scale have been freed from paying any income tax at all.

That was our change.

So together we pulled out of a tailspin and created 17½ million good jobs. That's more than a quarter of a million new jobs a month—every month—for 68 consecutive months. America is working again. Just, and just since our 1984 convention, we have created over 11 million of those new jobs. Now, just why would our friends on the other side want to change that? Why do they think putting you out of work is better than putting you to work?

New homes are being built. New car sales reached record levels. Exports are starting to climb again. Factory capacity is approaching maximum use. You know, I've noticed they don't call it "Reaganomics" anymore.

As, as for inflation—well, that, too, has changed. We changed it from the time it hit 18 percent in 1980—down to between 3½ and 4 percent.

Interest rates are less than half of what they were. In fact, nearly half of all mortgages taken out on family homes in 1986 and more than a third of those in 1987 were actually old loans being refinanced at the new, lower rates. Young families have finally been able to get some relief.

These, too, were our changes.

We rebuilt our armed forces. We liberated Grenada from the Communists and helped return that island to democracy. We, we struck a firm blow against Libyan terrorism. We've seen the growth of democracy in 90 percent of Latin America. The Soviets have begun to pull out of Afghanistan. The bloody Iran-Iraq war is coming to an end. And for the first time in eight years we have the prospects of peace in southwest Africa and the removal of Cuban and other foreign forces from the region. And in the 2,765 days of our administration, not one inch of ground has fallen to the Communists.

Today—today we have the first treaty in world history to eliminate an entire class of U.S. and Soviet nuclear missiles. We're working on the Strategic Defense Initiative to defend ourselves and our allies against nuclear terror, and American and Soviet relations are the best they've ever been since World War II.

And virtually all this change occurred—and continues to occur—in spite of the resistance of those liberal elites who loudly proclaim that it's time for a change.

They resisted our defense buildup; they resisted our tax cuts; they resisted cutting the fat out of government; and they resisted our appointments of judges committed to the law and the Constitution.

And it's time for some more straight talk. This time it's about the budget deficit. Yes, it's much too high. But the president doesn't vote for a budget, and the president can't spend a dime. Only the Congress can do that. They blame, they blame the defense increases for the deficit, yet defense spending today, in real dollars, is almost exactly what it was six years ago. In a six-year period, Congress cut defense spending authority by over $125 billion. And for every $1 reduction in defense outlays, they added $2 to domestic spending. Now, if they had passed my first budget, my first spending plan in 1982, the cumulative outlays and deficits would have been $207 billion lower by 1986.

Every single year I've been in office, I have supported and called for a balanced budget amendment to the Constitution, and the liberals have said no every year.

I've called for the line-item veto, which 43 governors have, to cut fat in the budget, and the liberals have said no.

Every year, I have attempted to limit their wild spending sprees, and they've said no.

They would have us believe that runaway budget deficits began in 1981 when we took office. Well, let me tell you something—the fact is, when they began their war on poverty in the middle '60s, from 1965 through 1980—in just those fifteen years—the budgets increased to five times what they had been, and the deficits went up to 52 times what they had been before their war on poverty.

Now, don't we know that, if they're elected, their answer will be the one they have relied on in the past—and that is higher taxes.

The other party has controlled the House of Representatives for fifty-two out of the last fifty-six years. They've controlled the Senate also for 46 of those years. Where we really need a change is to elect Republican majorities in both houses.

Then, George Bush can have a team that will protect your tax cuts, keep America strong, hold down inflation and interest rates, appoint judges to preserve your rights, and, yes, reduce the budget deficit.

Early in the first term, we set out to reduce federal regulations that had been imposed on the people, on business, and on local and state governments. Today, I'm proud to say, that we have eliminated so many unnecessary regulations that government-required paperwork imposed on citizens, businesses, and other levels of government has been reduced by an estimated 600 million man-hours of paperwork a year.

And George was there.

No. You haven't heard it all yet. George Bush headed up that task force that eliminated those regulations.

In 1980 and before, it took seven weeks to get a Social Security card. Now it takes ten days. It only takes ten days to get a passport. It used to take forty-three days. It took seventy-five days to get an export license; now it's only seventeen days, and for some countries, only five. It took over one-hundred days to process a claim for a Department of Housing and Urban Development Title I loan—one-hundred days. It now takes less than one-fourth of that—twenty-two days.

I think these specifics suggest there is a new level of competent management in the departments of our government.

George played a major role in everything that we have accomplished in these eight years.

Now, early on, we had a foreign policy problem. Our NATO allies were under the threat of Soviet intermediate-range missiles, and NATO had no equivalent deterrent. Our effort to provide a deterrent—Pershing and ground-launched cruise missiles on the NATO line—resulted in political problems for our NATO allies.

There was objection on the part of many of their people to deployment of our missiles. George represented us in Brussels with the heads of the NATO countries, and they agreed when he finished to take the missiles. This subsequently persuaded the Soviets to sign the INF [Intermediate-Range Nuclear-Force] Treaty and begin removing their SS-20s.

None of our achievements happened by accident, but only because we overcame liberal opposition to put our programs in place. And without George Bush to build on those policies, everything we've achieved will be at risk. All the work, sacrifice and effort of the American people could end in the very same disaster that we inherited in 1981.

[Bush Is the Right Man]

Because I feel so strongly about the work that must continue and the need to protect our gains for the American family and for national security, I want to share with you the qualities we should seek in the next president.

We need someone who's big enough and experienced enough to handle tough and demanding negotiations with Mr. [Mikhail S.] Gorbachev—because this is no time to gamble with on-the-job training. We need someone who's prepared to be president and who has the commitment to stand up for you against massive new taxes and who will keep alive the hope and promise that keeps our economy strong.

But it takes somebody who sees this office from the inside, who senses the danger points, will be cool under fire and knows the range of answers when the tough questions come.

Well, that's the George Bush that I've seen up close—when the staff and Cabinet members have closed the door and when the two of us are alone. Someone who is not afraid to speak his mind and who can cut to the core of an issue. Someone who never runs away from a fight, never backs away from his beliefs, and never makes excuses.

This office is not mine to give—only you, the people, can do that. But I love America too much and care too much about where we will be in the next few years. I care that we give custody of this office to someone who will build on our changes, not retreat to the past—someone who will continue the change all of us fought for. To preserve what we have and not risk losing it all—America needs George Bush—and Barbara Bush as first lady.

All right.

With George Bush, I'll know, as we approach the new millenium, our children will have a future secure with a nation at peace and protected against aggression; we'll have a prosperity that spreads the blessings of our abundance and opportunity across all America; we'll have safe and active neighborhoods; drug-free schools that send our children soaring in the atmosphere of great ideas and deep values; and a nation confidently willing to take its leadership into the uncharted reaches of a new age.

So, George, I'm in your corner. I'm ready to volunteer a little advice now and then, and offer a pointer or two on strategy, if asked. I'll help keep the facts straight or just stand back and cheer. But George, just one personal request: Go out there and win one for the Gipper.

[Republican Principles]

As you can imagine, I'm sorely tempted to spend the rest of this evening telling the truth about our friends who met in Atlanta—but, then, why should I have all the fun?

So, for the next few moments, let's talk about the future.

This is the last Republican convention I will address as president. Maybe you'll see your way to inviting me back sometime.

But like so many of us, as I said earlier, I started out in the other party. But 40 years ago, I cast my last vote as a Democrat. It was a party in which Franklin Delano Roosevelt promised the return of power to the states. It was a party where Harry Truman committed a strong and resolute America to preserving freedom. F.D.R. had run on a platform of eliminating useless boards and commissions and returning autonomy and authority to local governments and states.

That party changed—and it will never be the same. They left me; I didn't leave them.

So, it was our Republican Party that gave me a political home. When I signed up for duty, I didn't have to check my principles at the door. And I soon found out that the desire for victory did not overcome our devotion to ideals.

And what ideals those have been.

Our party speaks for human freedom—for the sweep of liberties that are at the core of our existence. We do not shirk from our duties to preserve freedom so it can unfold across the world for yearning millions.

We believe that lasting peace comes only through strength and not through the good will of our adversaries.

We have a healthy skepticism of government—checking its excesses at the same time we are willing to harness its energy when it helps improve the lives of our citizens.

We have pretty strong notions that higher tax receipts are no inherent right of the federal government. We don't think that inflation and high interest rates show compassion for the poor, the young, and the elderly.

We respect the values that bind us together as families and as a nation.

For our children—we don't think it's wrong to have them committed to pledging each day to the "one nation, under God, indivisible, with liberty and justice for all."

And we have so many requirements in their classrooms, why can't we at least have one thing that is voluntary—and that is allow our kids to repair quietly to their faith to say a prayer to start the day as Congress does.

For the unborn—quite simply—shouldn't they be able to live to become children in those classrooms?

Those, those are some of our principles. You in this room, and millions like you watching and listening tonight, are selfless and dedicated to a better world based on these principles.

[Land of Freedom]

You aren't quitters. You walk not just precincts, but for a cause. You stand for something—the finest warriors for free government that I have known. Nancy and I thank you for letting us be a part of your tireless determination to leave a better world for our children.

And that's why we're here, isn't it? A better world.

I know I've said this before, but I believe that God put this land between the two great oceans to be found by special people from every corner of the world who had that extra love of freedom that prompted them to leave their homeland and come to this land to make it a brilliant light beam of freedom to the world.

It's our gift to have visions, and I want to share that of a young boy who wrote to me shortly after I took office. In his letter he said, "I love America because you can join Cub Scouts if you want to. You have a right to worship as you please. If you have the ability, you can try to be anything you want to be. And I also like America because we have about 200 flavors of ice cream."

Truth, truth through the eyes of a child. Freedom of association. Freedom of worship. Freedom of hope and opportunity. And the pursuit of happiness—in this case, choosing among 200 flavors of ice cream.

That's America. Everyone with his or her vision of the American promise. That's why we're a magnet for the world—for those who dodged bullets and gave their lives coming over the Berlin Wall and others, only a few of whom avoided death, coming in tiny boats on turbulent oceans.

This land, its people, the dreams that unfold here and the freedom to bring it all together—well, those are what make America soar—up where you can see hope billowing in those freedom winds.

When our children turn the pages of our lives, I hope they'll see that we had a vision to pass forward a nation as nearly perfect as we could. Where there's decency, tolerance, generosity, honesty, courage, common sense, fairness, and piety.

This is my vision, and I'm grateful to God for blessing me with a good life and a long one. But when I pack up my bags in Washington, don't expect me to be happy to hear all this talk about the twilight of my life.

Twilight? Twilight? Not in America.

Here, it's a sunrise every day. Fresh new opportunities. Dreams to build.

Twilight? That's not possible, because I confess there are times when I feel like I'm still little Dutch Reagan racing my brother down the hill to the swimming hole under the railroad bridge over the Rock River.

You see, there's no sweeter day than each new one because here in our country, it means something wonderful can happen to you.

And something wonderful happened to me.

We lit a prairie fire a few years back. Those flames were fed by passionate ideas and convictions, and we were determined to make them run, burn I should say, all across America.

And what times we've had. Together we've fought for causes we loved. But we can never let the fire go out or quit the fight, because the battle is never over. Our freedom must be defended over and over again. And then again.

There's still a lot of brush to clear out at the ranch, fences that need repair, and horses to ride.

But I want you to know that if the fires ever dim, I'll leave my phone number and address behind just in case you need a foot soldier. Just let me know, and I'll be there—as long as words don't leave me and as long as this sweet country strives to be special during its shining moment on Earth.

Twilight, you say?

Listen to H. G. Wells. H. G. Wells says: "The past is but the beginning of a beginning, and all that is and has been is but the twilight of the dawn."

Well, that's a new day—our sunlit new day—to keep alive the fire so that when we look back at the time of choosing, we can say that we did all that could be done.

Never less.

Thank you, good night. God bless you and God bless America.

QUAYLE ACCEPTANCE SPEECH

Thank you. Thank you very much.

You're great.

Boy, I can see we're going to have a lot of fun in this campaign.

Thank you very much.

Mr. Chairman, Mr. Chairman, fellow Republicans, I accept your nomination for vice president of the United States of America.

Just, just think, 82 days from now, George Bush and I are going to win one for you, win one for America's future, and, yes, win one for the Gipper.

My friends, I am standing here tonight because of the decision made by a great man and a great leader, George Bush.

Two days ago, he asked me if I would join him as his running mate. I am deeply grateful for George's confidence in me, and I am humbled by the task ahead.

I would like to add a very personal note. I am also standing here tonight because of the decision my wife, Marilyn, and I made nearly 16 years ago to be married. Marilyn and our children, Tucker, Benjamin and Corinne, are my strength, my pride, my joy, my love. They are and always will be my total life.

["One Humble Hoosier"]

Many this week have asked, who is Dan Quayle?

The people of Indiana know me and now the nation will.

Since 1980, I have been a United States senator from Indiana—and very proud of it. Before that, I was a member of the United States House of Representatives—and proud of it. And, as a young man, I served six years in the National Guard, and, like millions of Americans who have served in the Guard and who serve today—and I am proud of that.

In Indiana, in Indiana they call us Hoosiers, and if you saw the movie *Hoosiers* you have a feeling of what life is like in small towns of our state.

My hometown of Huntington is a little bigger than the town in the movie, and the high school I graduated from is a little bigger than the one that fielded the basketball team in the film.

Still, I identify with that movie, *Hoosiers,* because it reflects the values I grew up with in our small town. We believe very strongly in hard work, in getting an education, in offering an opportunity to our families. Yes, we love basketball, we love underdogs, but most important, we love our country.

So tonight, so tonight, I am one humble Hoosier, whose efforts to devote part of his life to public service have led him here.

I would have been quite happy spending my life in Huntington, in the newspaper business, watching my kids grow, seeing a community with plenty of opportunity to go around. But I looked around me in the mid-70s and I saw threats to the future of my family and to the values that could once be taken for granted in our country.

Beyond my town, there were communities torn by crime and drugs, and there were neighborhoods where the very word "opportunity" didn't exist because there were no jobs.

[Trying to Change Things]

I decided to try to change these things: to make opportunity replace despair, and to make the future just as good as the past for the families of the many Huntingtons of our great land.

That was in 1976, when I was first elected to the House of Representatives. But [with] both houses of Congress and the White House in the hands of liberal Democrats, it was a lot tougher than I ever imagined to turn my determination into reality.

In those Jimmy Carter years, the people running things thought government was the answer, instead of part of the problem. They thought high taxes and big spending would solve anything. I think you know the rest. None of their policies worked and the American people knew it.

In 1980, they voted for a bold new course for the country; a course that brought us more jobs for working Americans, more security for a peace-loving people, more respect from friends and foes around the globe, more opportunity for women and minorities, and a renewed belief that America is a land where you can make your dreams come true.

The Reagan-Bush revolution has already been written on the pages of history. Now, George Bush and Dan Quayle are going to add several bold new chapters to the story of the greatest nation God ever put on this Earth.

["Freedom, Family and Future"]

When I think, when I think of America under the leadership of George Bush, three words come to mind: Freedom. Family. And future.

Freedom first, because without it, nothing else is possible.

When I was a boy, my grandfather used to say to me—and I say it to you here tonight—that America is the greatest nation on Earth because America is free. This is true today and it will always be true.

Next, family. George Bush understands, you understand, I understand, that the family has always been the very heart of civilization. We know the importance of the family to a child growing up. We know the help a family can be to a kid out of school, out of hope, out of luck. And we know the importance of family where one generation helps take care of another, young and old.

And then, there is the future. That word symbolizes hope and opportunity. To make sure hope and opportunity are always there, we need a strong economy so there will be good jobs for all who seek them.

We need an investment in our national defense that brings us long-term security in the world.

We do not need the future the Democratic Party sees, the party of George McGovern, Jimmy Carter, Walter Mondale, just wait, it gets better—Ted Kennedy and now, his buddy, Michael Dukakis. That future has America in retreat. That future has higher taxes and a guaranteed loss of job opportunities. And that future has more government intervention in the lives of all of us.

The future under George Bush means peace and economic opportunity for all.

And, I can tell you, you have George Bush's track record to go on. The tax cuts the Republicans have brought America have resulted in 17 million new jobs being created.

Let me tell you something: George Bush will not raise your taxes, period.

And let me tell you something else: Michael Dukakis will. He has a track record, too, and that is what it tells us: higher taxes.

[Job-Training Program]

As the new jobs opened up during our current economic expansion, not everyone had the necessary skills for them. Some had lost their jobs and others could not find their first one.

In 1982, the Job Training Partnership Act [JTPA] became law. I was the author of that legislation, and I am proud of it. It established a nationwide training program that has a partnership of government and the private sector. Today, because of the Job Training Partnership Act, hundreds of thousands of graduates of these programs have jobs with a future.

One of them is Pam Snyder-La Rue of Roy, Utah. A single parent with four children, she was a high school dropout, and on welfare. She joined a JTPA program. First, she earned her high school equivalency credential. Then she earned an accounting certificate. Today, she is a staff accountant at a vocational center. She is off welfare, and proud to be making it on her own. She now has a future.

[Peace, Freedom and Opportunity]

We could not have a secure economy at home if we [did] not have a peaceful and secure world. As a member of the Senate Armed Services Committee, I know well that it is rebuilding our defense that persuaded the Soviet Union to return to the negotiating table to get us a treaty that, for the first time, actually reduces nuclear arms.

Today, our relationship with the Soviet Union is the best it has been since the end of World War II. George Bush will keep it that way, and I will be right there with him.

Freedom is the most precious commodity our nation has. Let me say again, all else rests on it. We have worked hard for more than 200 years to preserve freedom. In the Soviet Union, people are trying to get out. In the United States, people are trying to get in. Our freedom is the beacon that draws them.

A great American novelist, the late Thomas Wolfe, once wrote, "This is a fabulous country—the only fabulous country. The one where miracles not only happen, they happen all the time."

Miracles do happen all the time in America because we live in freedom and because the energy and imagination of our people makes their dreams come true every day.

I am privileged to be the first person of my generation to be on a national ticket. I don't presume to talk for everyone of my generation, but I know that a great many will agree with me when I express my thanks to the generation of George Bush for bringing us to an era of peace and freedom and opportunity.

My generation has a profound debt to them. We will pay it by making sure that our children and the generations that follow will have the same freedom, the same family values and a future bright with opportunity for all.

Thank you very much. Good night. God bless you. Let's go on to victory.

BUSH ACCEPTANCE SPEECH

Thank you ladies and gentlemen, thank you very, very much.

I have many friends to thank tonight. I thank the voters who supported me. I thank the gallant men who entered the contest for this presidency this year, and who've honored me with their support. And, for their kind and stirring words, I thank Governor Tom Kean of New Jersey, Senator, Senator Phil Gramm of Texas, President Gerald Ford—and my friend, and my friend, President Ronald Reagan.

I accept your nomination for president. I mean to run hard, to fight hard, to stand on the issues—and I mean to win.

There are a lot, there are a lot of great stories in politics about the underdog winning—and this is going to be one of them.

And we're going to win with the help of Senator Dan Quayle of Indiana—a young leader who has become a forceful voice in preparing America's workers for the labor force of the future. What a superb job he did here tonight.

Born in the middle of the century, in the middle of America, and holding the promise of the future—I'm proud to have Dan Quayle at my side.

Many of you have asked, many of you have asked, "When will this campaign really begin?" Well, I've come to this hall to tell you, and to tell America: Tonight is the night.

For seven and a half years I've helped the president conduct the most difficult job on Earth. Ronald Reagan asked for, and received, my candor. He never asked for, but he did receive, my loyalty. And those of you who saw the president's speech last week, and listened to the simple truth of his words, will understand my loyalty all these years.

And now, now you must see me for what I am: the Republican candidate for president of the United States. And now I turn to the American people to share my hopes and intentions, and why and where I wish to lead.

And so tonight is for big things. But I'll try to be fair to the other side. I'll try to hold my charisma in check.

I reject the temptation to engage in personal references. My approach this evening is, as Sergeant Joe Friday used to say, "Just the facts, ma'am."

And after all, after all, the facts are on our side.

[Build a Better America]

I seek the presidency for a single purpose, a purpose that has motivated millions of Americans across the years and the ocean voyages. I seek the presidency to build a better America. It's that simple—and that big.

I'm a man who sees life in terms of missions—missions defined and missions completed.

And when I was a torpedo bomber pilot they defined the mission for us. And before we took off, we all understood that no matter what, you try to reach the target. And there have been other missions for me—Congress, and China, the CIA. But I'm here tonight, and I am your candidate, because the most important work of my life is to complete the mission we started in 1980. And how, and how do we complete it? We build on it.

The stakes are high this year and the choice is crucial, for the differences between the two candidates are as deep and wide as they have ever been in our long history.

Not only two very different men, but two very different ideas of the future will be voted on this Election Day.

And what it all comes down to is this: My opponent's view of the world sees a long slow decline for our country, an inevitable fall mandated by impersonal historical forces.

But America is not in decline. America is a rising nation.

He sees, he sees America as another pleasant country on the U.N. [United Nations] roll call, somewhere between Albania and Zimbabwe. And I see America as the leader—a unique nation with a special role in the world.

And this has been called the American century, because in it we were the dominant force for good in the world. We saved Europe, cured polio, went to the moon, and lit the world with our culture. And now we are on the

605

verge of a new century, and what country's name will it bear? I say it will be another American century.

Our work is not done, our force is not spent.

["We Can Deliver"]

There are those, there are those who say there isn't much of a difference this year. But America, don't let 'em fool ya.

Two parties this year ask for your support. Both will speak of growth and peace. But only one has proved it can deliver. Two parties this year ask for your trust, but only one has earned it.

Eight years ago, eight years ago, I stood here with Ronald Reagan and we promised, together, to break with the past and return America to her greatness.

Eight years later, look at what the American people have produced: the highest level of economic growth in our entire history—and the lowest level of world tensions in more than 50 years.

You know, some say this isn't an election about ideology, but it's an election about competence. Well, it's nice of them to want to play on our field. But this election isn't only about competence, for competence is a narrow ideal.

Competence makes the trains run on time but doesn't know where they're going. Competence, competence is the creed of the technocrat who makes sure the gears mesh but doesn't for a second understand the magic of the machine.

The truth is, the truth is, this election is about the beliefs we share, the values we honor and the principles we hold dear.

But, but since someone brought up competence ...

Consider the size of our triumph: A record number of Americans at work, a record high percentage of our people with jobs, a record high of new businesses, a high rate of new businesses, a record high rate of real personal income.

These are facts.

And one way, and one way we know our opponents know the facts is that to attack our record they have to misrepresent it. They call it a Swiss cheese economy. Well, that's the way it may look to the three blind mice.

But, but when they were in charge it was all holes and no cheese.

Inflation—you know the litany—inflation was 13 percent when we came in. We got it down to four. Interest rates, interest rates were more than 21. We cut them in half. Unemployment, unemployment was up and climbing, and now it's the lowest in 14 years.

My friends, eight years ago this economy was flat on its back—intensive care. And we came in and gave it emergency treatment: Got the temperature down by lowering regulation, and got the blood pressure down when we lowered taxes.

And pretty soon the patient was up, back on his feet, and stronger than ever.

And now who do we hear knocking on the door but the same doctors who made him sick. And they're telling us to put them in charge of the case again? My friends, they're lucky we don't hit 'em with a malpractice suit!

We've created 17 million new jobs [in] the past five years—more than twice as many as Europe and Japan combined. And they're good jobs. The majority of them created in the past six years paid an average—average—of more than $22,000 a year. And someone better take a message to Michael: Tell him, tell him that we have been creating good jobs at good wages. The fact is, they talk and we deliver.

They promise and we perform.

And there are millions of young Americans in their 20s who barely remember, who barely remember the days of gas lines and unemployment lines. And now they're marrying and starting careers. To those young people I say, "You have the opportunity you deserve, and I'm not going to let them take it away from you."

The leaders, the leaders of the expansion have been the women of America who helped create the new jobs, and filled two out of every three of them. And to the women of America I say, "You know better than anyone that equality begins with economic empowerment. You're gaining economic power, and I'm not going to let them take it away from you."

There are millions, there are millions of older Americans who were brutalized by inflation. We arrested it—and we're not going to let it out on furlough.

We're going, and we're going to keep the Social Security trust fund sound, and out of reach of the big spenders. To America's elderly I say. "Once again you have the security that is your right, and I'm not going to let them take it away from you."

I know the liberal Democrats are worried about the economy. They're worried it's going to remain strong. And they're right, it is—with the right leadership it will remain strong.

But let's be frank. Things aren't perfect in this country. There are people who haven't tasted the fruits of the expansion. I've talked to farmers about the bills they can't pay and I've been to the factories that feel the strain of change. And I've seen the urban children who play amidst the shattered glass and the shattered lives. And, you know, there are the homeless. And you know, it doesn't do any good to debate endlessly which policy mistake of the '70s is responsible. They're there, and we have to help them.

But what we must remember if we're to be responsible and compassionate is that economic growth is the key to our endeavors.

I want growth that stays, that broadens, and that touches, finally, all Americans, from the hollows of Kentucky to the sunlit streets of Denver, from the suburbs of Chicago to the broad avenues of New York, and from the oil fields of Oklahoma to the farms of the Great Plains.

And can we do it? Of course we can. We know how. We've done it. If we, if we continue to grow at our current rate, we will be able to produce 30 million jobs in the next eight years.

And we will do it—by maintaining our commitment to free and fair trade, by keeping government spending down, and by keeping taxes down.

[Peace Through Strength]

Our economic life is not the only test of our success. One issue overwhelms all the others, and that is the issue of peace.

Look at the world on this bright August night. The spirit of democracy is sweeping the Pacific rim. China feels the winds of change. New democracies assert themselves in South America. And one by one the unfree places fall, not to the force of arms but to the force of an idea: freedom works.

And we, we have a new relationship with the Soviet Union. The INF [intermediate-range nuclear-force] treaty, the beginning of the Soviet withdrawal from Afghanistan, the beginning of the end of the Soviet proxy war in Angola, and with it the independence of Namibia. Iran and Iraq move toward peace.

It's a watershed. It is no accident.

It happened when we acted on the ancient knowledge that strength and clarity lead to peace—weakness and ambivalence lead to war. You see, you see, weakness tempts aggressors. Strength stops them. I will not allow this country to be made weak again—never.

The tremors in the Soviet world continue. The hard earth there has not yet settled. Perhaps what is happening will change our world forever. And perhaps not. A prudent skepticism is in order. And so is hope.

But either way, we're in an unprecedented position to change the nature of our relationship. Not by preemptive concession, but by keeping our strength. Not by yielding up defense systems with nothing won in return, but by hard, cool engagement in the tug and pull of diplomacy.

My life, my life has been lived in the shadow of war—I almost lost my life in one. And I hate war. Love peace.

And we have peace.

And I am not going to let anyone take it away from us.

Our economy is stronger but not invulnerable, and the peace is broad but can be broken. And now we must decide. We will surely have change this year, but will it be change that moves us forward? Or change that risks retreat?

In 1940, when I was barely more than a boy, Franklin Roosevelt said we shouldn't change horses in midstream.

My friends, these days the world moves even more quickly, and now, after two great terms, a switch will be made. But when you have to change horses in midstream, doesn't it make sense to switch to one who's going the same way?

[Family and Community]

An election that is about ideas and values is also about philosophy. And I have one.

At the bright center is the individual. And radiating out from him or her is the family, the essential unit of closeness and of love. For it is the family that communicates to our children—to the 21st century—our culture, our religious faith, our traditions and history.

From the individual to the family to the community, and then on out to the town, the church and the school, and, still echoing out, to the county, the state, and the nation—each doing only what it does well, and no more. And I believe that power must always be kept close to the individual, close to the hands that raise the family and run the home.

I am guided by certain traditions. One is that there is a God and he is good, and his love, while free, has a self-imposed cost: We must be good to one another.

I believe in another tradition that is, by now, imbedded in the national soul. It is that learning is good in and of itself. You know, the mothers of the Jewish ghettoes of the east would pour honey on a book so the children would know that learning is sweet. And the parents who settled hungry Kansas would take their children in from the fields when a teacher came. That is our history.

And there is another tradition. And that is the idea of community—a beautiful word with a big meaning. Though liberal Democrats have an odd view of it. They see "community" as a limited cluster of interest groups, locked in odd conformity. And in this view, the country waits passive while Washington sets the rules.

But that's not what community means—not to me.

For we are a nation of communities, of thousands and tens of thousands of ethnic, religious, social, business, labor union, neighborhood, regional and other organizations—all of them varied, voluntary and unique.

This is America: the Knights of Columbus, the Grange, Hadassah, the Disabled American Veterans, the Order of AHEPA [American Hellenic Educational Progressive Association], the Business and Professional Women of America, the union hall, the Bible study group, LULAC [League of United Latin American Citizens], "Holy Name"—a brilliant diversity spread like stars, like a thousand points of light in a broad and peaceful sky.

Does government have a place? Yes. Government is part of the nation of communities—not the whole, just a part.

And I don't hate government. A government that remembers that the people are its master is a good and needed thing.

["Old-Fashioned Common Sense"]

I respect old-fashioned common sense, and have no great love, and I have no great love for the imaginings of the social planners. You see, I like what's been tested and found to be true.

For instance.

Should public school teachers be required to lead our children in the pledge of allegiance? My opponent says no—and I say yes.

Should society be allowed to impose the death penalty on those who commit crimes of extraordinary cruelty and violence? My opponent says no—but I say yes.

And should our children, should our children have the right to say a voluntary prayer, or even observe a moment of silence in the schools? My opponent says no—but I say yes.

And should free men and women have the right to own a gun to protect their home? My opponent says no—but I say yes.

And is it right to believe in the sanctity of life and protect the lives of innocent children? My opponent says no—but I say yes.

You see, we must, we must change, we've got to change from abortion to adoption. And let me tell you this: Barbara and I have an adopted granddaughter. And the day of her christening we wept with joy. I thank God that her parents chose life.

I'm the one who believes it is a scandal to give a weekend furlough to a hardened first-degree killer who hasn't even served enough time to be eligible for parole.

I'm the one who says a drug dealer who is responsible for the death of a policeman should be subject to capital punishment.

[Policies for the Future]

And I'm the one who will not raise taxes. My opponent now says, my opponent now says he'll raise them as a last resort, or a third resort. Well, when a politician talks like that, you know that's one resort he'll be checking into. And, my opponent won't rule out raising taxes. But I will.

And the Congress will push me to raise taxes, and I'll say no, and they'll push, and I'll say no, and they'll push again. And I'll say to them: Read my lips. No new taxes.

Let me tell you more—let me tell you more, let me just tell you more about the mission.

On jobs, my mission is: 30 in 8. Thirty million jobs in the next eight years.

Every one of our children deserves a first-rate school. The liberal Democrats want power in the hands of the federal government. And I want power in the hands of the parents. And, I will—and I will, I will encourage merit schools. I will give more kids a head start. And I'll make it easier to save for college.

I want a drug-free America—and this will not be easy to achieve. But I want to enlist the help of some people who are rarely included. Tonight I challenge the young people of our country to shut down the drug dealers around the world. Unite with us, work with us.

"Zero tolerance" isn't just a policy, it's an attitude. Tell them what you think of people who underwrite the dealers who put poison in our society. And while you're doing that, my administration will be telling the dealers: Whatever we have to do we'll do, but your day is over, you're history.

I am going to do whatever it takes to make sure the disabled are included in the mainstream. For too long they've been left out. But they're not going to be left out anymore.

And I am going to stop ocean dumping. Our beaches should not be garbage dumps and our harbors should not be cesspools.

And I am going to have the FBI trace the medical wastes and we are going to punish the people who dump those infected needles into our oceans, lakes and rivers. And we must clean the air. We must reduce the harm done by acid rain.

And I will put incentives back into the domestic energy industry, for I know from personal experience there is no security for the United States in further dependence on foreign oil.

In foreign affairs I will continue our policy of peace through strength. I will move toward further cuts in strategic and conventional arsenals of both the United States and the Soviet Union and the Eastern Bloc and NATO. I will modernize and preserve our technological edge and that includes strategic defense.

And a priority, a priority: Ban chemical and biological weapons from the face of the Earth. That will be a priority with me.

And I intend to speak for freedom, stand for freedom, be a patient friend to anyone, East or West, who will fight for freedom.

[A New Harmony]

It seems to me the presidency provides an incomparable opportunity for "gentle persuasion."

And I hope to stand for a new harmony, a greater tolerance. We've come far, but I think we need a new harmony among the races in our country. And we're on a journey into a new century, and we've got to leave that tired old baggage of bigotry behind.

Some people who are enjoying our prosperity have forgotten what it's for. But they diminish our triumph when they act as if wealth is an end in itself.

And there are those who have dropped their standards along the way, as if ethics were too heavy and slowed their rise to the top. There's graft in city hall, and there's greed on Wall Street; there's influence peddling in Washington, and the small corruptions of everyday ambition.

But you see, I believe public service is honorable. And every time I hear that someone has breached the public trust it breaks my heart.

And I wonder sometimes if we have forgotten who we are. But we're the people who sundered a nation rather than allow a sin called slavery—and we're the people who rose from the ghettoes and the deserts.

And we weren't saints, but we lived by standards. We celebrated the individual, but we weren't self-centered. We were practical, but we didn't live only for material things. We believed in getting ahead, but blind ambition wasn't our way.

The fact is prosperity has a purpose. It is to allow us to pursue "the better angels," to give us time to think and grow. Prosperity with a purpose means taking your idealism and making it concrete by certain acts of goodness.

It means helping a child from an unhappy home learn how to read—and I thank my wife Barbara for all her work in helping people to read and all her work for literacy in this country.

It means teaching troubled children through your presence that there is such a thing as reliable love. Some would say it's soft and insufficiently tough to care about these things. But where is it written that we must act as if we do not care, as if we are not moved?

Well, I am moved. I want a kinder and gentler nation.

["Quiet Man"]

Two men this year ask for your support. And you must know us.

As for me, I have held high office and done the work of democracy day by day. Yes, my parents were prosperous; and their children sure were lucky. But there were lessons we had to learn about life.

John Kennedy discovered poverty when he campaigned in West Virginia; there were children who had no milk. And young Teddy Roosevelt met the new America when he roamed the immigrant streets of New York. And I learned a few things about life in a place called Texas.

And when I—and when I was, when I was working on this part of the speech, Barbara came in and asked what I was doing. And I looked up, and I said I'm working hard. And she said: "Oh dear, don't worry, relax, sit back, take off your shoes and put up your silver foot."

Now, we moved to West Texas 40 years ago—40 years ago this year. The war was over, and we wanted to get out and make it on our own. Those were exciting days. We lived in a little shotgun house, one room for the three of us. Worked in the oil business, and then started my own.

And in time we had six children. Moved from the shotgun to a duplex apartment to a house. And lived the dream—high school football on Friday nights, Little League, neighborhood barbecue.

People don't see their own experience as symbolic of an era—but of course we were.

And so was everyone else who was taking a chance and pushing into unknown territory with kids and a dog and a car.

But the big thing I learned is the satisfaction of creating jobs, which meant creating opportunity, which meant happy families, who in turn could do more to help others and enhance their own lives.

I learned that the good done by a single good job can be felt in ways you can't imagine.

It's been said that I'm not the most compelling speaker, and there are actually those who claim that I don't always communicate in the clearest, most concise way. But I dare them to keep it up—go ahead: Make my 24-hour time period!

Well, I—I may be, may not be the most eloquent, but I learned that, early on, that eloquence won't draw oil from the ground.

And I may sometimes be a little awkward. But there's nothing self-conscious in my love of country.

And I am a quiet man, but—I am a quiet man, but I hear the quiet people others don't. The ones who raise the family, pay the taxes, meet the mortgages.

And I hear them and I am moved, and their concerns are mine.

[Man with a Mission]

A president must be many things.

He must be a shrewd protector of America's interests; and he must be an idealist who leads those who move for a freer and more democratic planet.

And he must see to it that government intrudes as little as possible in the lives of the people; and yet remember that it is right and proper that a nation's leader take an interest in the nation's character.

And he must be able to define—and lead—a mission.

For 7½ years, I have worked with a great president—I have seen what crosses that big desk. I have seen the unexpected crisis that arrives in a cable in a young aide's hand. And I have seen problems that simmer on for decades and suddenly demand resolution. And I have seen modest decisions made with anguish, and crucial decisions made with dispatch.

And so I know that what it all comes down to, this election—what it all comes down to, after all the shouting and the cheers—is the man at the desk. And who should sit at that desk.

My friends, I am that man.

I say it, I say it without boast or bravado.

I've fought for my country, I've served, I've built—and I will go from the hills to the hollows, from the cities to the suburbs to the loneliest town on the quietest street to take our message of hope and growth for every American to every American.

I will keep America moving forward, always forward, for a better America, for an endless enduring dream and a thousand points of light.

This is my mission. And I will complete it.

Thank you.

You know, you know it is customary to end an address with a pledge or a saying that holds a special meaning. And I've chosen one that we all know by heart. One that we all learned in school. And I ask everyone in this great hall to stand and join me in this—we all know it.

I pledge allegiance to the flag of the United States of America and to the republic for which it stands, one nation under God, indivisible, with liberty and justice for all.

Thank you.

REPUBLICAN PARTY PLATFORM

August 16, 1988

Amplifying its 1984 themes, the Republican party adopted at its 1988 convention in New Orleans a lengthy and detailed platform that sought to accommodate all factions. The document expressed the will of conservatives on taxes, abortion, school prayer, defense spending, and strategic defense, but the platform drafters allowed a few carefully circumscribed sentences on issues such as AIDS, education, and child care for the benefit of a small group of moderates. The 107-member platform committee issued no minority reports—for which twenty-seven votes were required. The platform was formally approved by the committee on August 15, and by the convention delegates the next day—on both occasions by voice vote and virtually without dissent.

The platform's overall approach diffused confrontation between moderate and conservative Republicans, and conveyed an impression of party harmony even where the divisions were the deepest and presidential nominee George Bush had chosen not to express his own views.

While the Democratic party, meeting in Atlanta in July, had shortened its platform to about 4,500 words, roughly one-tenth the length of the party's 1984 document, the Republican platform moved in the opposite direction. The 1984 Republican platform of about 30,000 words was succeeded in 1988 by a version of about 40,000. (Democratic Party Platform, p. 557)

Although wordy, the platform was credited with helping Bush— considered a moderate by many Republicans—subdue his detractors on the right. It also enabled Republicans to boast during the presidential campaign that their agenda was substantive and issue-oriented.

Major Features of the Platform

The platform, entitled "An American Vision: For Our Children and Our Future," praised President Ronald Reagan's first-term reversal of the policies of his Democratic predecessor, Jimmy Carter. It lauded Reagan's military buildup and explicitly called for an expansion of defense spending, while also supporting mutually verifiable reductions in nuclear weapons.

Among the platform's major planks were:

- *a pledge not to raise taxes, coupled with support for instituting lower, less graduated tax rates; tax credits for child care; and major reductions in the tax rate on capital gains (all major themes of the Bush campaign)*
- *opposition to gun control legislation*
- *opposition to federal regulation of business*
- *support for right-to-work laws (which curtailed union influence in the workplace)*
- *support for voluntary school prayer*
- *support for an earned income tax credit for the working poor "as an alternative to inflationary—and job-destroying—increases in the minimum wage"*
- *an outright ban on abortion (the rights of a fetus "cannot be infringed" under any circumstances)*

The platform also opposed energy price controls and supported the development of nuclear power. It called for toxic-waste cleanups but also for cost-effectiveness in all environmental programs. It came down squarely for lowering tariff barriers to free trade. The platform also addressed the federal deficit issue by blending Reagan's longstanding faith in private-sector economic growth, the line-item veto (which would allow the president to strike out specific items in a bill), and a balanced budget amendment to the Constitution—all in combination with Bush's call for a "flexible freeze" (which would allow some new spending for priority programs while cutting others). Denial of prison furloughs for murderers, and death penalties for major drug dealers—destined to become prominent campaign issues for Bush—were also on the agenda.

Defense and foreign policy planks attributed the Soviet retreat from the cold war to Reagan's defense buildup. On superpower relations, it warned against "naive inexperience or overly enthusiastic endorsement of current Soviet rhetoric" and called on the Soviet Union to release political prisoners and open its borders. In sharp contrast to the Democratic platform, the Republican document advocated military aid to insurgents in Nicaragua, Angola, Afghanistan, and elsewhere, hailing the

"Reagan doctrine" for encouraging anticommunist guerrillas in the Third World.

The platform urged "our representatives in all multilateral organizations such as the World Bank to support conditionality with all loans to encourage democracy, private sector development, and individual enterprise. . . . [W]e remain opposed to U.S. funding for organizations involved in abortion." The Republicans also rejected the concept of a Palestinian state on the West Bank. On defense, the platform called for modernizing land, sea, and air nuclear arms; "rapid and certain" deployment of strategic defense not subject to negotiation; a 600-ship navy with two new aircraft carriers; and updated chemical weapons.

Negotiations Strike Alliance

The Bush forces prevailed throughout the platform proceedings. Although during the presidential campaign, Bush favored permitting abortions in the cases of rape or incest and backed public funding of abortions if the mother's life was endangered, the candidate appeared to accept the platform plank calling for a total ban on abortions.

Efforts by moderates to lighten the plank's social conservatism were generally rebuffed by a platform committee that reflected the conservatism of the convention. Sen. Lowell P. Weicker and Rep. Nancy L. Johnson, two platform members from Connecticut, tried to restore the party's former support for the Equal Rights Amendment (ERA), but their proposal was shouted down. On AIDS, the platform accepted sympathetic language but repeatedly stressed abstinence from drugs and extramarital sex as the best prevention.

The Republican platform, like its Democratic counterpart, gave no substantive answers on how to reduce the massive federal deficit; how to pay for the new social programs it advocated without raising taxes; how to deal with U.S. hostages in the Middle East and international terrorism, how to grapple with Third World debt; and how to cope with failing savings and loan institutions.

Following is the text of the Republican party platform, entitled "An American Vision: For Our Children and Our Future," adopted August 16, 1988, by delegates to the Republican party convention in New Orleans:

Preamble

An election is about the future, about change. But it is also about the values we will carry with us as we journey into tomorrow and about continuity with the best from our past.

On the threshold of a new century, we live in a time of unprecedented technological, social, and cultural development, and a rapidly emerging global economy. This election will bring change. The question is: Will it be change and progress with the Republicans or change and chaos with the Democrats?

Americans want leadership to direct the forces of change, on America's terms, guided by American values. The next stage of the American experiment will be a new dynamic partnership in which people direct government and government empowers people to solve their own problems and to have more choices in their lives.

In 1984, we said, "From freedom comes opportunity; from opportunity comes growth; from growth comes progress."

In 1988, we reaffirm that truth. *Freedom works*. This is not sloganeering, but a verifiable fact. It has been abundantly documented during the Reagan-Bush Administration in terms of real jobs and real progress for individuals, families and communities urban and rural. Our platform reflects on every page our continuing faith in the creative power of human freedom.

Defending and expanding freedom is our first priority. During the last eight years, the American people joined with the Reagan-Bush Administration in advancing the cause of freedom at home and around the world. Our platform reflects George Bush's belief that military strength, diplomatic resoluteness, and firm leadership are necessary to keep our country and our allies free.

Republicans know the United States is a nation of communities— churches, neighborhoods, social and charitable organizations, professional groups, unions and private and voluntary organizations in city, suburb, and countryside. It is We, the people, building the future in freedom. It is from these innumerable American communities, made up of people with good heads and good hearts, that innovation, creativity, and the works of social justice and mercy naturally flow and flourish. This is why George Bush and all Republicans believe in empowering people and not bureaucracies.

At the very heart of this platform is our belief that the strength of America is its people: free men and women, with faith in God, working for themselves and their families, believing in the inestimable value of every human being from the very young to the very old, building and sustaining communities, quietly performing those "little, nameless, unremembered acts of kindness and love" that make up the best portion of our lives, defending freedom, proud of their diverse heritage. They are still eager to grasp the future, to seize the life's challenges and, through faith and love and work, to transform them into the valuable, the useful, and the beautiful.

This is what the American people do, quietly, patiently, without headlines, as a nation of communities, every day. This is the continuing American revolution of continuity and change.

This is the American people's true miracle of freedom. It is to them that we dedicate this platform.

Jobs, Growth, and Opportunity for All

America again leads the world, confident of our abilities, proud of our products, sure of our future, the pacesetter for all mankind. Moving toward the threshold of the 21st century, the American people are poised to fulfill their dreams to a degree unparalleled in human history.

Our nation of communities is prosperous and free. In the sixth year of unprecedented economic expansion, more people are working than ever before; real family income has risen; inflation is tamed. By almost any measure, Americans are better off than they were eight years ago. The Reagan Revolution has become a Republican renaissance. Our country's back—back in business and back on top again.

Government didn't work this economic wonder. The people did. Republicans got government out of the way, off the backs of households and entrepreneurs, so the people could take charge. Once again our people have the freedom to grow. From that freedom come prosperity and security.

From freedom comes opportunity; from opportunity comes growth; from growth comes progress.

Freedom is not an abstract concept. No, freedom is the inescapable essence of the American spirit, the driving force which makes Americans different from any other people on the face of the globe.

The restoration of our country's tradition of democratic capitalism has ushered in a new age of optimistic expansion. Based on free enterprise, free markets, and limited government, that tradition regards people as a resource, not a problem. And it works.

On every continent, governments are beginning to follow some degree of America's formula to cut tax rates, loosen regulation, free the private sector, and trust the people.

Remember the Carter-Mondale years:

- Taxes skyrocketed every year as the Democrats' inflation pushed everyone into higher brackets.
- Prices spiraled, financially strangling those people least able to keep up. This was heightened by the spending mania of a Democrat-controlled Congress. Savings plunged as prices rose. A dollar saved in 1977 was worth only half by 1981.
- 21.5 percent interest rates—levels not seen before or since—placed the basic needs of life beyond the means of many American families.
- The Democrats threatened workers, investors, and consumers with "industrial policies" that centralized economic planning.
- Joblessness eroded the earnings and dignity of millions under the Democrat Administration.
- The number of poor households grew dramatically during the Democrats' years in power.
- Economic stagnation caused by the Democrats' policies made it harder to find a job, get a promotion, buy a home, raise a family, or plan for old age.

In addition to all of these problems, the Democrats were telling us that there was something wrong with America and something wrong with its people.

Something *was* terribly wrong, but not with the people. A half-century of destructive policies, pitting Americans against one another for the benefit of the Democrats' political machine, had come to a dead end. The Democrats couldn't find a way out, so the voters showed them the door.

Now the ideological heirs of [Jimmy] Carter and [Walter F.] Mondale are trying again to sell the public a false bill of goods. These liberals call America's prosperity an illusion. They fantasize our economy is declining. They claim our future is in the hands of other nations. They aren't operating in the real world.

They can't build the future on fear. Americans know that and are constructing their futures on the solid foundation Republicans have already set in place:

- We are in the midst of the longest peacetime expansion in our country's history. Where once we measured new businesses in the thousands, we now count millions. These small businesses have helped create 17 million well-paying, high-quality new jobs, more than twice the number of jobs that were created during that time in Japan, Canada and Western Europe combined! Small business has accounted for 80 percent of the jobs created during the recovery. Who says America has lost its competitive edge?
- More Americans are working than ever before. Because of Republican pro-growth policies, the unemployment rate has plunged to its lowest level in 14 years.
- Since 1983, 3 million people have risen above the government poverty level. The poverty rate is down for the third consecutive year. The Republican economic program has been the most successful war on poverty.
- Under a Republican Administration, family incomes are growing at the fastest pace recorded in 15 years.
- Under Republican leadership, tax reform removed 6 million low-income people from the income tax rolls and brought financial relief to tens of millions more.
- The typical family is now paying almost $2,000 less per year in income taxes than it would if the Democrats' antiquated income tax system of the 1970s were still in place.
- The Carter "misery index"—the sum of the inflation and unemployment rates—is half of what it was in 1980. Republican economic policies have turned it into a "prosperity index."
- Republicans reduced inflation to one-third of its 1980 level, helping not only average Americans but also low-income Americans and elderly Americans on fixed incomes, who spend most of their income on necessities.

- Interest rates are lower by nearly two-thirds than under the Democrats in 1980.
- Exports are booming. World sales create local jobs!
- Productivity is rising three times as fast under Republican policies as it did during the late 1970s.
- Industrial output increased by one-third during the current expansion.
- Business investment is increasing 20 percent faster, in real terms, than before the Republican economic resurgence.
- The manufacturing sector is now accounting for 23 percent of GNP [gross national product]. U.S. manufacturing jobs have increased overall since 1982. The Democrats are wrong about America losing its industrial base, except in Massachusetts, where the Democratic governor of that State has presided over a net decline of 94,000 manufacturing jobs.

This is not a portrait of a people in decline. It is the profile of a can-do country, hopeful and compassionate, on the move. It is America resurgent, renewed, revitalized by an idea: the belief that free men and women, caring for families and supporting voluntary institutions in a nation of communities, constitute the most powerful force for human progress.

In 1980, Ronald Reagan and George Bush called upon us all to recover from a failed political system the power rightly belonging to the people. Now we call upon our fellow citizens, at the bicentennial of our Constitution, in the words of its preamble, to "secure the blessings of liberty to ourselves and our posterity" by opening new vistas of opportunity.

These "blessings of liberty"—the chance to make a decent living, provide for the family, buy a home, give children a superior education, build a secure retirement, help a new generation reach farther and build higher than we were able to—these are the goals that George Bush and the Republican Party seek for every American.

But this prosperity is not an end in itself. It is a beginning. It frees us to grow and be better than we are, to develop things of the spirit and heart. This is the direction in which George Bush will lead our country. It is prosperity with a purpose.

Jobs

The Republican Party puts the creation of jobs and opportunity first. In our 1980 and 1984 platforms, we promised to put Americans back to work by restoring economic growth without inflation. We delivered on our promise:

- Small business entrepreneurs have led the way in creating new job opportunities, particularly for women, minorities, and youths.
- Over 17 million new jobs have been created.
- More than 60% of these new jobs since 1982 are held by women.
- More Americans are working now than at any time in our history.
- The unemployment rate is at its lowest level in 14 years.

- Statistics show that the great majority of the jobs we have created are full-time, quality jobs, paying more than $20,000 per year.

Job growth for minority and ethnic Americans has been even more impressive:

- Minority workers have been finding jobs twice as fast as others.
- Black unemployment has been cut almost in half since 1982. Black Americans gained 2.3 million new jobs in the last few years.
- Black teen unemployment is at its lowest level in 15 years.
- Sales from the top 100 Black firms rose 15 percent between 1982 and 1986. The 7.9 percent growth rate for all Black businesses compares to an overall rate of 5 percent for all business.
- Family incomes of Asian-Americans rank among the highest of all ethnic groups in the United States.
- Hispanic employment increased nearly three times as fast as for all civilian workers. More Hispanics are at work now than at any time since record-keeping began.

We will use new technologies, such as computer data bases and telecommunications, to strengthen and streamline job banks matching people who want work with available jobs.

We advocate incentives for educating, training, and retraining workers for new and better jobs—through programs like the Job Training Partnership Act, which provides for a public/private partnership—as our country surges ahead.

The best jobs program—the one that created 17 million jobs since 1982—is lower taxes on people. We believe that every person who wants a job should have the opportunity to get a job. We reject the notion that putting more Americans to work causes inflation. The failure of government make-work programs proves that jobs are created by people in a free market.

Opportunity for All

With its message of economic growth and opportunity, the GOP is the natural champion of blacks, minorities, women and ethnic Americans. We urge Republican candidates and officials at all levels to extend to minority Americans everywhere the historic invitation for full participation in our party.

A free economy helps defeat discrimination by fostering opportunity for all. That's why real income for Black families has risen 14 percent since 1982. It's why members of minority groups have been gaining jobs in the Republican recovery twice as fast as everyone else. Upward mobility for all Americans has come back strong.

We are the party of real social progress. Republicans welcome the millions of forward-looking Americans who want an "opportunity society," not a welfare state. We believe our country's greatest resource is its people —all its people. Their ingenuity and imagination are needed to make the most of our common future. So we will remove disincentives that keep the less fortunate out of the productive economy:

- Families struggling near the poverty line are always hurt most by tax increases. Six million poor have been removed from the tax rolls in the 1986 Tax Reform Act—the largest income transfer to lower-income Americans since the early 1970s. We will continue to reduce their burden.
- We advocate a youth training wage to expand opportunities and enable unskilled young people to enter the work force.
- As an alternative to inflationary—and job-destroying—increases in the minimum wage, we will work to boost the incomes of the working poor through the Earned Income Tax Credit, especially for earners who support children. This will mean higher take-home pay for millions of working families.
- We will reform welfare to encourage work as the ticket that guarantees full participation in American life.
- We will undertake a long overdue reform of the unemployment insurance program to reward workers who find new jobs quickly.
- We insist upon the right of Americans to work at home. The Home Work Rule, banning sale of certain items made at home, must go. It idles willing workers, prevents mothers from working and caring for their children in their own homes, limits the country's output, and penalizes innocent persons to please special interests.
- We will fight to end the Social Security earnings limitation for the elderly. It discourages older persons from reentering or remaining in the work force, where their experience and wisdom are increasingly needed. As a first step, we will remove the earnings limitation for those whose income is from child care.

We will continue our efforts, already marked with success, to revitalize our cities. We support, on the federal, State and local levels, enterprise zones to promote investment and job creation in beleaguered neighborhoods.

Entrepreneurship

Our country's 18 million small business entrepreneurs are the superstars of job creation. In the past decade, they created two out of three new jobs. When they are free to invest and innovate, everyone is better off. They are today's pathfinders, the explorers of America's economic future.

Republicans encourage the women and men in small businesses to think big. To help them create jobs, we will cut to 15% the current counter-productive capital gains tax. This will foster investment in new and untried ventures, which often are the cutting edge of constructive change. It will also build the retirement value of workers' pension funds and raise revenues for the federal government.

We will increase, strengthen, and reinvigorate minority business development efforts to afford socially and economically disadvantaged individuals the opportunity for full participation in our free enterprise system.

Workplace benefits should be freely negotiated by employee-employer bargaining. We oppose government requirements that shrink workers' paychecks by diverting money away from wages to pay for federal requirements. These hidden taxes add to labor costs without paying those who labor. That is the liberals' way of replacing collective bargaining with congressional edicts about what's good for employees. It reduces the number of jobs and dishonestly imposes on others the costs of programs the Congress can't afford.

We call for a reasonable state and federal product liability standard that will be fair to small businesses, including professional and amateur sports, and to all who are in liability contests. We propose to return the fault based standard to the civil justice system. Jobs are being lost, useful and sometimes life-saving products are being discontinued, and America's ability to compete is being adversely affected. Reform will lower costs for all and will return fairness to the system for the benefit of everyone. Republicans recognize the basic right of all Americans to seek redress in the courts; however, we strongly oppose frivolous litigation. In addition, we support enactment of fair and balanced reforms of the tort system at the State level.

The remarkable resurgence of small business under the Republican renaissance of the 1980s highlights the key to the future: plant openings, thousands of them in every part of this land, as small businesses lead the way toward yet another decade of compassionate prosperity.

Reducing the Burden of Taxes

The Republican Party restates the unequivocal promise we made in 1984: *We oppose any attempts to increase taxes.* Tax increases harm the economic expansion and reverse the trend to restoring control of the economy to individual Americans.

We reject calls for higher taxes from all quarters—including "bipartisan commissions." The decisions of our government should not be left to a body of unelected officials.

The American people deserve to know, *before the election,* where all candidates stand on the question of tax increases. Republicans unequivocally reiterate the no-tax pledge we have proudly taken. While we wouldn't believe the Democrats even if they took the pledge, they haven't taken it.

The crowning economic achievement of the Republican Party under Ronald Reagan and George Bush has been the dramatic reduction in personal income taxes. The Reagan-Bush Administration has cut the top marginal tax rate from 70 percent to 28 percent. We got government's heavy hand out of the wallets and purses of all our people. That single step has sparked the longest peacetime expansion in our history.

We not only lowered tax rates for all. We tied them to the cost of living so congressional Democrats couldn't secretly boost taxes by pushing people into higher brackets through inflation. We took millions of low-income families off the tax rolls and we doubled the personal exemption for all.

As a result, by 1986 the income tax bill of a typical middle-income family had declined by one-quarter. If the Democrats had defeated our economic recovery program, that family would have paid nearly $6,000 more in taxes between 1982 and 1987. Meanwhile, average Americans and the working poor carry substantially less of the burden. Upper income Americans now pay a larger share of federal taxes than they did in 1980.

Our policies have become the model for much of the world. Through the power of capitalism, governments are rushing to reduce tax rates to save their stagnating economies. This is good for America, for their recovery will make them better trading partners for our own exuberant economy.

Many economists advising the Democrat Party have publicly called for a national sales tax or European-style Value-Added Tax (VAT) which would take billions of dollars out of the hands of American consumers. Such a tax has been imposed on many nations in Europe and has resulted in higher prices, fewer jobs, and higher levels of government spending. We reject the idea of putting a VAT on the backs of the American people.

Republicans know that sustaining the American economic miracle requires a growing pool of private savings. From bank accounts, small stock purchases, and piggy banks, the streams of thrift must flow together and form a mighty tide of capital. That rushing force pushes our society ahead, lifting everyone as it goes. To keep it going:

- We support incentives for private savings, such as our deductibility for IRA contributions.
- We oppose tax withholding on savings.
- To protect savings by ensuring the soundness of our financial system, the federal government must continue to play an active role through its regulatory responsibilities and supervisory duties. We demand stern punishment for those persons, whether in financial institutions or in Congress, whose wheeling and dealing have betrayed the public trust.
- We will reduce to 15 percent the tax rates for long-term capital gains to promote investment in jobs and to raise revenue for the federal government by touching off another surge of economic expansion. In 1978, we cut the capital gains tax from 49.1 percent to 28 percent; in 1981, it was slashed again to 20 percent. The cuts injected a new vitality into the economy, with the result that revenues from this tax rose 184 percent from 1978 to 1985.
- We call for a taxpayers' bill of rights to give everyone simple and inexpensive means to resolve disputes with government. Democrats, using the Massachusetts Revenue Department as a model, intend to squeeze more out of the public by making the IRS [Internal Revenue Service] more intrusive. Republicans will not tolerate tax cheating by anyone, but we know most Americans responsibly pay their fair share.

By restoring their confidence in frugal, limited government, we will enhance compliance with tax laws that are simple and fair.

Beating Inflation

Today, the dollar is sound again. The Republican economic program brought inflation under control and lowered interest rates. Ten million more American families have bought homes for the first time. Inflation has been forced down from over 13 percent to 4 percent. Interest rates are only half of what they were at the end of the Carter years.

If the Democrats' inflation rates had continued all these years, a family of four would now be paying an average of $200 a month more for food and over $300 a month more for housing. That's the real cost of the Democrats' bad policies.

The Democrats would drag us back to those dreadful years when inflation was robbing workers of their earnings, consumers of their spending power, and families of their savings. Skyrocketing interest rates were stalling the economy and pushing decent housing out of reach for millions.

We can't let them do it again. To sustain the country's economic expansion, confidence in American monetary policy is vital. The possibility of imprudent action by government breeds fear, and that fear can shake the stock and commodity markets worldwide. To keep markets on an even keel, we urge objective Federal Reserve policies to achieve long-run price stability.

Regulatory Reform

This is a success story for the entire nation. Eight years ago, the country was strangling in red tape. Decades of rules and regulations from official Washington smothered enterprise, hindered job creation, and crippled small businesses. Even worse, the federal bureaucracy was spreading its intrusion into schools, religious institutions, and neighborhoods.

At the outset of his Administration, President Reagan asked Vice President Bush to take charge of an unprecedented exercise in liberty: relieving Americans from oppressive and unnecessary regulations and controls. With George Bush's leadership, Republicans turned the tables on the regulators.

We saved consumers tens of billions of dollars in needless regulatory costs that had been added to the price of virtually every product and service.

- In banking, we ensured that savers would get a fair return on their savings through market interest rates in place of artificially low rates capped by government.
- In energy, transportation, telecommunications, and financial services, we made fundamental changes in the way Americans could do business. We trusted them. We hacked away at artificial rules that stifled

innovation, thwarted competition, and drove up consumer prices. Indeed, telecommunications and computer technology innovations have improved economic performance in nearly every American industry and business.

- In education, housing, and health care, we reduced the chilling effect of regulation upon the private sector and communities. Despite opposition from liberals in the Congress, we have at least slowed the expansion of federal control.
- We turned dozens of narrow programs, full of strings attached, into a few block grants with leeway for State and local administration.

The job isn't over yet. We will resist the calls of Democrats to turn back or eliminate the benefits that reducing regulations have brought to Americans from every walk of life in transportation, finance, energy and many other areas. We want to reduce further the intrusion of government into the lives of our citizens. Consistent with the maintenance of a competitive market place, we are committed to breaking down unnecessary barriers to entry created by regulations, statutes and judicial decisions, to free up capital for productive investment. Let Democrats trust the federal bureaucracy. Republicans trust the creative energy of workers and investors in a free market.

We are committed to further return power from the federal government to state and local governments, which are more responsive to the public and better able to administer critical public services.

Competition in Public Services

Republicans recognize that the American people, in their families, places of work, and voluntary associations, solve problems better and faster than government. That's why the Republican Party trusts people to deal with the needs of individuals and communities, as they have done for centuries.

In recent decades, however, big government elbowed aside the private sector. In the process, it made public services both expensive and inefficient. The federal government should follow the lead of those cities and States which are contracting out for a wide range of activities.

We resolve to defederalize, denationalize, and decentralize government monopolies that poorly serve the public and waste the taxpayer's dollars. To that end, we will foster competition wherever possible.

We advocate privatizing those government assets which would be more productive and better maintained in private ownership. This is especially true of those public properties that have deteriorated under government control, and public housing, where residents should have the option of managing their own project. In other areas as well, citizens and employees should be able to become stockholders and managers of government enterprises that would be more efficiently operated by private enterprise. We will not initiate production of goods and delivery of services by the federal government if they can be procured from the private sector.

Housing

The best housing policy is sound economic policy. Low interest rates, low inflation rates, and the availability of a job with a good paycheck that makes a mortgage affordable are the best housing programs of all.

That has been the key to the rebirth of housing during the Reagan-Bush Administration. If things had continued the way they were in 1980, the average family today would have to pay over $300 more for housing every month. Instead, we curbed inflation, pulled down interest rates, and made housing affordable to more Americans than ever before. We promoted home ownership by stoking the engines of economic growth. The results have been spectacular.

- Mortgage rates have fallen from 17.5 percent to single digits today.
- Home ownership has become affordable for more than 10 million additional families.
- Our regulatory reform campaign, in cooperation with local government and the housing industry, has pointed the way to lower housing through removal of needless rules that inflate prices.

That's only the beginning. We want to foster greater choice in housing for all:

- First and foremost, Republicans stand united in defense of the homeowner's deduction for mortgage interest. That separates us from the Democrats who are already planning to raise taxes by limiting its deductibility.
- We will continue our successful drive for lower interest rates.
- We support the efforts of those in the States who fight to lower property taxes that strike hardest at the poor, the elderly, large families, and family farmers.
- We support programs to allow low-income families to earn possession of their homes through urban and rural homesteading, cooperative ventures in construction and rehabilitation, and other pioneering projects that demonstrate the vitality of the private sector and individual initiative.
- We support the FHA [Federal Housing Administration] mortgage insurance program, the Government National Mortgage Association, the VA [Veterans Administration] guarantee program, and other programs that enhance housing choices for all Americans.
- We pledge to continue to expand opportunities for home ownership and to maintain the strength of savings institutions, including thrifts.
- We call on the Departments of Treasury, Housing and Urban Development, Agriculture, and the Federal Home Loan Bank Board to develop incentives for the private sector to bring housing stock foreclosed on by federal agencies back into service for low and moderate income citizens.
- We call for repeal of rent control laws, which always cause a shortage of

decent housing by favoring the affluent with low rents, denying persons with modest incomes access to the housing market.

In public housing, we have turned away from the disasters of the past, when whole neighborhoods became instant slums through federal meddling. We are determined to replace hand-out housing with vouchers that will make low-income families neighbors in communities, not strangers in projects. We have promoted a long-range program of tenant management with encouraging results already. We pledge to continue that drive and to move toward resident ownership of public housing units, which was initiated under Ronald Reagan and George Bush.

To ensure that federal housing funds assist communities, rather than disrupt them, we advocate merging programs into a block grant at the disposal of States and localities for a wide range of needs.

We reaffirm our commitment to open housing as an essential part of the opportunity we seek for all. The Reagan-Bush Administration sponsored a major strengthening of the federal fair housing law. We will enforce it vigorously and will not allow its distortion into quotas or controls.

Controlling Federal Spending

The Reagan-Bush policies of economic growth have finally turned around the deficit problem. Through Republican-initiated constraints on spending, the federal budget deficit dropped by over 25 percent last year. With the help of the Gramm-Rudman law and a flexible budget freeze, a balanced budget can be expected by 1993.

But the relentless spending of congressional Democrats can undo our best efforts. No president can cause deficits; Congress votes to spend money. The American people must prevent big-spending congressional Democrats from bringing back big budget deficits; we must return both the Senate and the House of Representatives to Republican control for the first time in 36 years.

In 1981, we inherited a federal spending machine that was out of control. During the Carter-Mondale years, spending grew by 13.6 percent annually. We cut that growth rate in half, but the cancer still expands, as it has in some States such as Massachusetts where the budget has increased more than twice as fast as the federal budget. We will not be content until government establishes a balanced budget and reduces its demands upon the productivity and earnings of the American people.

We categorically reject the notion that Congress knows how to spend money better than the American people do. Tax hikes are like addictive drugs. Every shot makes Congress want to spend more. Even with the Republican tax cuts of 1981, revenues have increased by about $50 billion every year. But congressional spending has increased even more! For every $1.00 Congress takes in in new taxes, it spends $1.25.

That's why congressional Democrats have sabotaged the Republican program to control the federal budget. They refuse to put any reasonable restraints on appropriations. They smuggle through pork barrel deals in huge "continuing resolutions" larded for the special interests. They oppose the balanced budget amendment and all reforms in the bankrupt process. They mock the restraints legally mandated by our Gramm-Rudman budget plan.

Enough is enough. It's time to push through the Republican agenda for budget reform to teach the Congress the kind of financial responsibility that characterizes the American family:

- We call for structural changes to control government waste, including a two-year budget cycle, a super-majority requirement for raising taxes, a legislatively enacted line-item veto, individual transmission of spending bills, greater rescission authority for the chief executive and other reforms.
- We call for a flexible freeze on current government spending. We insist on the discipline to provide stable funding for important government programs, increasing spending only for true national priorities. We oppose any increase in taxes, so that the economy will continue to expand and revenues from a growing tax base will reduce the deficit.
- We believe the Grace Commission report to eliminate waste, inefficiency, and mismanagement in the federal government must be re-examined; its recommendations should be given a high profile by public policy officials.
- We call for a balanced budget amendment to the Constitution. If congressional Democrats continue to block it, we urge the States to renew their calls for a constitutional convention limited to consideration of such an amendment.
- We will use all constitutional authority to control congressional spending. This will include consideration of the inherent line-item veto power of the president.

Opening Markets Abroad

America's best years lie ahead. Because Republicans have faith in individuals, we welcome the challenge of world competition with confidence in our country's ability to out-produce, out-manage, out-think, and out-sell anyone.

This is the voters' choice in 1988: compete or retreat. The American people and the Republican party are not about to retreat.

To make the 1990s America's decade in international trade, Republicans will advance trade through strength. We will not accept the loss of American jobs to nationalized, subsidized, protected foreign industries and will continue to negotiate assertively the destruction of trade barriers:

- We negotiated a sweeping free trade agreement with Canada, our largest trading partner. Under this agreement, Americans will now be able to trade, invest, and prosper, with no barriers to competition and economic growth.

- We have sought enforcement of U.S. international trade rights more vigorously than any previous administration. The Reagan-Bush Administration was the first to self-initiate formal trade actions against unfair foreign market barriers.
- We launched the "Uruguay Round" of trade talks to promote a more open trading system and address new trade problems that stifle world economic progress.
- We negotiated long and hard to beat back the most protectionist provisions in trade legislation and produced a bill that focuses on opening markets around the world.
- We support multilateral actions to open up foreign markets to U.S. products through the General Agreement on Tariffs and Trade [GATT]. We will use GATT as well to deal with problems involving agricultural subsidies, trade in services, intellectual property rights, and economic relations with countries that mismanage their economies by suppressing market forces.

We will not tolerate unfair trade and will use free trade as a weapon against it. To ensure that rapid progress is forthcoming from our work through GATT, we stand ready to pursue special arrangements with nations which share our commitment to free trade. We have begun with the U.S.-Israel and U.S.-Canada free trade agreements. These agreements should be used as a model by the entire Western Hemisphere as it moves toward becoming a free trade zone, a powerhouse of productivity that can spur economic growth throughout the continents. We are prepared to negotiate free trade agreements with partners like the Republic of China on Taiwan and the Association of Southeast Asian Nations (ASEAN) countries if they are willing to open their markets to U.S. products.

The emerging global economy has required American workers and consumers to adapt to far-reaching transformations on every continent. These changes will accelerate in the years ahead as nations with free economic systems rush toward a future of incredible promise. International trade among market economies is the driving force behind an unprecedented expansion of opportunity and income.

Unfortunately, international markets are still restricted by antiquated policies: protective tariffs, quotas, and subsidies. These hinder world trade and hurt everyone, producers and consumers alike. It is the politicians and special interests who use protectionism to cover up their failures and enrich themselves at the expense of the country as a whole.

We propose that the General Accounting Office be required to issue regular statistics on the costs of U.S. trade restrictions to American workers, consumers and businesses.

The bosses of the Democratic party have thrown in the towel and abandoned the American worker and producer. They have begun a full-scale retreat into protectionism, an economic narcotic that saps the life out of commerce, closes foreign markets to U.S. producers and growers, and costs American consumers billions of dollars. The Democrats' plans would endanger 200,000 jobs and $8 billion in economic activity in agriculture alone! Over the past year, U.S. exports have expanded by 30 percent. The Democrats would reverse that growth by cowering behind trade barriers.

The bottom line in international trade must be American excellence. Every part of our economy is challenged to renew its commitment to quality. We must redouble our efforts to cut regulation, keep taxes low, and promote capital formation to sustain the advance of science and technology. Changes in both the managing of business and our approach to work, together with a new emphasis on quality and pleasing the customer, are creating a new workplace ethic in our country. We will meet the challenges of international competition by know-how and cooperation, enterprise and daring, and trust in a well trained workforce to achieve more than government can even attempt.

International Economic Policy

Eight years ago, Ronald Reagan and George Bush offered visionary leadership to make a clean break with the failed past of international economics.

Our economic success is now acknowledged worldwide. Countries all over the world, even the Soviet Union, are abandoning worn out industrial policy planning by government in favor of the market-oriented policies underlying what foreign leaders call the "American Miracle."

We encouraged the major economic powers to draw greater guidance for their monetary policies from commodity prices. This was an important step toward ensuring price stability, eliminating volatility of exchange rates, and removing excessive trade imbalances.

We support the Administration's efforts to improve coordination among the industrialized nations regarding their basic economic policies as a means of sustaining non-inflationary growth. It is important that we continue and refine efforts to dampen the volatility of exchange rate fluctuations, which have at times impeded improvements in investment and trade. Further, it is important to guard against the possibility of inflation in all currencies by comparing them with a basket of commodities, including gold.

International price stability will set the stage for developing countries to participate in the transforming process of economic growth. We will not turn our backs on the Third World, where Soviet imperialism preys upon stagnation and poverty. The massive debt of some emerging nations not only cripples their progress but also disrupts world trade and finance.

We will use U.S. economic aid, whether bilateral or through international organizations, to promote free market reforms: lower marginal tax rates, less regulation, reduced trade barriers. We will work with developing nations to make their economies attractive to private investment—both domestic and foreign—the only lasting way to ensure that these nations can secure capital for growth. We support innovations to facilitate repayment of loans, including "debt for equity" swaps. We urge our representatives in all multilateral organizations such as the World Bank to support conditionality with all loans to encourage democracy, private sector development, and individual enterprise. As part of our commitment to the family as the building block of economic progress, we believe decisions on family size should be made freely by each family and remain opposed to U.S. funding for organizations involved in abortion.

To dig their way out of debt, those nations must do more than take out additional loans. They need America's greatest export: capitalism. While sharing the pie of prosperity with others, we will teach its recipe. It is this simple: Where democracy and free markets take root, people live better. Where people live better, they produce and trade more. As capitalism spreads throughout the world, more nations are prospering, international commerce is booming, and U.S. trade is breaking records.

But even more important than economic progress is the advance of freedom. Republicans want not only a better life for the people of developing lands; we want a freer and more peaceful future for them too. Those goals are inextricably linked. It is a case of all or nothing, and we believe that free people can have it all.

From all over the world, capital flows into the United States because of confidence in our future. Direct investment in America creates important economy wide benefits: jobs, growth, and lower interest rates. We oppose shortsighted attempts to restrict or overly regulate this investment in America that helps our people work, earn, and live better.

Most important, we will lead by example. We will keep the United States a shining model of individual freedom and economic liberty to encourage other peoples of the world to assert their own economic rights and secure opportunity for all.

Strong Families and Strong Communities

Strong families build strong communities. They make us a confident, caring society by fostering the values and character—integrity, responsibility, and altruism—essential for the survival of democracy. America's place in the 21st Century will be determined by the family's place in public policy today.

Republicans believe, as did the framers of the Constitution, that the God-given rights of the family come before those of government. That separates us from liberal Democrats. We seek to strengthen the family. Democrats try to supplant it. In the 1960s and 1970s, the family bore the brunt of liberal attacks on everything the American people cherished. Our whole society paid dearly.

It's time to put things together again. Republicans have started this critical task:

- We brought fairness to the tax code, removed millions of low income families from the rolls, and cut tax rates dramatically.
- We reestablished a pro-family tax system. We doubled the exemption for dependents and protected families from backdoor tax hikes by

linking the exemption to inflation.

- We tamed inflation to lower interest rates, protect the savings of the elderly, and make housing more affordable for millions of households.
- We fought to reverse crime rates and launched the nation's first all-out war on drug abuse, though there is still much more to do.
- We appointed judges who respect family rights, family values, and the rights of victims of crime.
- We brought education back to basics, back to parents, and strengthened the principle of local control.
- Through President Reagan's historic executive order on the family, we set standards in law for determining whether policies help or hurt the American family.

Republicans have brought hope to families on the front lines of America's social reconstruction. We pledge to fulfill that hope and to keep the family at its proper place at the center of public policy.

Caring for Children

The family's most important function is to raise the next generation of Americans, handing on to them the Judeo-Christian values of western civilization and our ideals of liberty. More than anything else, the ability of America's families to accomplish those goals will determine the course our country takes in the century ahead.

Our society is in an era of sweeping change. In this era of unprecedented opportunity, more women than ever before have entered the work force. As a result, many households depend upon some form of non-parental care for their youngsters. Relatives, neighbors, churches and synagogues, employers and others in the private sector, are helping to meet the demand for quality care. In the process, we are learning more about the needs of children and about the impact of various forms of care. That knowledge should guide public policy and private options on many issues affecting the way we work and raise our families.

Republicans affirm these commonsense principles of child care:

- The more options families have in child care, the better. Government must not constrain their decisions. Individual choice should determine child care arrangements for the family.
- The best care for most children, especially in the early years, is parental. Government must never hinder it.
- Public policy must acknowledge the full range of family situations. Mothers or fathers who stay at home, who work part-time, or who work full-time, should all receive the same respect and consideration in public policy.
- Child care by close relatives, religious organizations, and other community groups should never be inhibited by government programs or policies.

In sum, this is a perfect example of the difference between the two parties. Republicans want to empower individuals, not bureaucrats. We seek to minimize the financial burdens imposed by government upon families, ensure their options and preserve the role of our traditional voluntary institutions. Democrats propose a new federal program that negates parental choice and disdains religious participation. Republicans would never bar aid to any family for choosing child care that includes a simple prayer.

In returning to our traditional commitment to children, the Republican Party proposes a radically different approach:

- Establish a toddler tax credit for pre-school children as proposed by Vice President Bush, available to all families of modest means, to help them support and care for their children in a manner best suited to their families' values and traditions.
- Establishment of a plan that does not discriminate against single-earner families with one parent in the home.
- Continue to reverse the Democrats' 30-year erosion of the dependent tax exemption. That exemption has been doubled under Republican leadership. This will empower parents to care for their families in a way that public services can never do.
- Make the dependent care tax credit available to low-income families for young children.
- Eliminate disincentives for grandparents and other seniors to care for children by repealing the earnings limitation for Social Security recipients.
- Encourage States to promote child care programs which allow teen-age mothers to remain in school.
- Promote in-home child care—preferred by almost all parents—by allowing annual, instead of quarterly, payments of income taxes by employees and withholding taxes by employers.
- Encourage employers, including government agencies, to voluntarily address their employees' child care needs and use more flexible work schedules and job sharing to recognize the household demands for their workforce.
- Reform the tort liability system to prevent excessive litigation that discourages child care by groups who stand ready to meet the needs of working parents.
- Reform Federal Home Mortgage Association rules to retain mortgage eligibility for homeowners who offer family child care.

Adoption

Adoption is a special form of caring for children. We recognize the tremendous contributions of adoptive parents and foster parents. The Reagan-Bush Administration has given unprecedented attention to adoption through a presidential task force, whose recommendations point the way toward vastly expanding opportunities for children in need.

Republicans are determined to cut through red tape to facilitate the adoption process for those who can offer strong family life based on traditional values. Trapping minority and special needs children in the foster care system, when there are families ready to adopt these young-sters, is a national disgrace. We urge States to remove obstacles to the permanent placement of foster children and to reform antiquated regula-tions that make adoption needlessly difficult.

Pornography

America's children deserve a future free from pornography. We applaud Republicans in the 100th Congress who took the lead to ban interstate dial-a-porn. We endorse legislative and regulatory efforts to anchor more securely a standard of decency in telecommunications and to prohibit the sale of sexually explicit materials in outlets operated on federal property. We commend those who refuse to sell pornographic material. We support the rigorous enforcement of "community standards" against pornography.

Health

Americans are accustomed to miracles in health care. The relentless advance of science, boosted by space age technology, has transformed the quality of health care and broadened the exercise of our compassion. By the year 2000, more than 100,000 Americans will be more than 100 years old. Yesterday's science fiction regularly becomes today's medical routine.

The American people almost lost all that in the 1960s and 1970s, when political demagogues offered quack cures for the ills of our health care system. They tried to impose here the nationalized medicine that was disastrous in other countries.

Republicans believe in reduced government control of health care while maintaining an unequivocal commitment to quality health care:

- We fostered competition and consumer choice as the only way to hold down the medical price spiral generated by government's open-ended spending on health programs.
- We gave the hospice movement its important role in federal programs.
- We launched a national campaign to ensure quality treatment and to prevent abuse in nursing homes.
- We led the way to enacting landmark legislation for catastrophic health insurance under Medicare.
- We speeded up the regulatory process for experimental drugs for life-threatening illness and loosened import controls to allow greater choice by patients.
- We promoted home health care through pilot projects in the states. We took extraordinary steps to ensure health care so that chronically ill children under Medicaid would not have to stay in the hospital.

Republicans will continue the recovery of America's health care system from the Democrats' mistakes of the past:

- We will promote continuing innovation to ensure that tomorrow's miracles are affordable and accessible to all. We are encouraged by advances in communications which enable small or isolated facilities to tap the resources of the world's greatest centers of healing. Many breakthroughs in recent years have dramatically reduced the incidence of surgery and replaced lengthy hospital stays with out-patient treatment.

- We will work for continuing progress in providing the most cost-effective, high-quality care.
- We will lead the fight for reform of medical malpractice laws to stop the intolerable escalation of malpractice insurance. It has artificially boosted costs for patients, driven many good doctors out of fields such as obstetrics, and made care unavailable for many patients.
- We are opposed to the establishment of government mandated professional practice fees and services requirements as a condition of professional licensure or license renewal.
- We are committed to avoiding the kind of medical crisis facing Massachusetts—a State the American Medical Association has labelled the "Beirut of medicine" where the delivery of quality health care has deteriorated.
- We will continue to seek opportunities for private and public cooperation in support of hospices.
- We are committed to improving the quality and financing of long term care. We will remove regulatory and tax burdens to encourage private health insurance policies for acute or long term care. We will work for convertibility of savings, IRAs [Individual Retirement Accounts], life insurance, and pensions to pay for long term care.
- We will encourage the trend in the private sector to expand opportunities for home health care to protect the integrity of the family and to provide a less expensive alternative to hospital stays. We want to ensure flexibility for both Medicare and Medicaid in the provision of services to those who need them at home or elsewhere.
- We will foster employee choice in selecting health plans to promote personal responsibility for wellness.
- Recognizing that medical catastrophes can strike regardless of age, we empathize with the plight of the thousands of American families with catastrophically ill children and will work toward making catastrophic health care coverage available to our youngest citizens.
- Recognizing that inequities may exist in the current treatment of health insurance costs for those who are self employed, including farmers, we will study ways to more appropriately balance such costs.
- We will continue to promote alternative forms of group health care that foster competition and lower costs.
- We will make special provision for relief of rural hospitals and health care providers who have been unduly burdened by federal cost control efforts. The availability of health services, especially during a crisis like the current drought, is essential for rural America.

- We will continue generous funding for the National Institutes of Health.
- We will hold down Medicaid costs by promoting State pilot programs to give low-income persons the opportunity to secure health insurance. We demand tough penalties against providers who defraud this and other health programs.
- We will work to assure access to health care for all Americans through public and private initiatives.
- We will promote wellness, especially for the nation's youth. Personal responsibility in behavior and diet will dramatically reduce the incidence of avoidable disease and curb health costs in decades ahead.
- We will call on the Food and Drug Administration to accelerate its certification of technically sound alternatives to animal testing of drugs and cosmetics when considering data regarding product safety and efficacy.

AIDS

Those who suffer from AIDS, their families, and the men and women of medicine who care for the afflicted deserve our compassion and help. The Reagan-Bush Administration launched the nation's fight against AIDS, committing more than $5 billion in the last five years. For 1989, the President's budget recommends a 42 percent increase in current funding.

We will vigorously fight against AIDS, recognizing that the enemy is one of the deadliest diseases to challenge medical research. Continued research on the virus is vital. We will continue as well to provide experimental drugs that may prolong life. We will establish within the Food and Drug Administration a process for expedited review of drugs which may benefit AIDS patients. We will allow supervised usage of experimental treatments.

We must not only marshal our scientific resources against AIDS, but must also protect those who do not have the disease. In this regard, education plays a critical role. AIDS education should emphasize that abstinence from drug abuse and sexual activity outside of marriage is the safest way to avoid infection with the AIDS virus. It is extremely important that testing and contact tracing measures be carried out and be appropriately confidential, as is the case with the long-standing public health measures to control other communicable diseases that are less dangerous than AIDS.

We will remove barriers to making use of one's own (autologous) blood or blood from a designated donor, and we call for penalties for knowingly donating tainted blood or otherwise deliberately endangering others.

The latency period between infection with the virus and onset of AIDS can be lengthy. People should be encouraged to seek early diagnosis and to remain on the job or in school as long as they are functionally capable.

Healthy Children, Healthy Families

As we strengthen the American family, we improve the health of the nation. From prenatal care to old age, strong family life is the linchpin of wellness and compassion.

This is especially important with regard to babies. We have reduced infant mortality, but it remains a serious problem in areas where alcohol, drugs, and neglect take a fearful toll on newborns. We will target federal health programs to help mothers and infants get a good start in life. We will assist neighborhood institutions, including religious groups, in reaching out to those on the margins of society to save their children, especially from fetal alcohol syndrome, the major cause of birth defects in this country. Inadequate prenatal care for expectant mothers is the cause of untold numbers of premature and low birth-weight babies. These newborns start life at severe disadvantage and often require massive health care investments to have a chance for normal childhood. We continue to endorse the provision of adequate prenatal care for all expectant mothers, especially the poor and young.

We hail the way fetal medicine is revolutionizing care of children and dramatically expanding our knowledge of human development. Accordingly, we call for fetal protection, both in the work place and in scientific research.

Most of the health problems of young people today stem from moral confusion and family disruption. Republicans are ready to address the root causes of today's youth crisis:

- We will assert absolutes of right and wrong concerning drug abuse and other forms of self-destructive behavior.
- We will require parental consent for unemancipated minors to receive contraceptives from federally funded family planning clinics.
- We support efforts like the Adolescent Family Life program to teach teens the traditional values of restraint, respect, and the sanctity of marriage.
- We urge all branches of the entertainment industry to exercise greater responsibility in addressing the youth market.

To prepare for tomorrow's expanding opportunities, today's young Americans must be challenged by high values with the support that comes from strong families. That is the surest way to guide them to their own affirmation of life.

Older Americans

Older Americans are both our bridge to all that is precious in our history and the enduring foundation on which we build the future. Young Americans see most clearly when they stand on the shoulders of the past.

After eight years of President Reagan's youthful leadership, older Americans are safer and more secure. In 1980, we promised to put Social Security back on a sound financial footing. We delivered. We established the national commission that developed the plan to restore the system and led the way in enacting its recommendations into law.

Now that Social Security is in healthy shape, congressional Democrats are plotting ways to use its short-term revenue surplus for their own purposes. We make this promise: They shall not do so. We pledge to preserve the integrity of the Social Security trust funds. We encourage public officials at all levels to safeguard the integrity of public and private pension funds against raiding by anyone, in labor, business, or government, such as in Massachusetts where the current Democrat governor has raided $29 million from the State pension reserves to fund his enormous deficit in the State budget.

We will not allow liberal Democrats to imperil the other gains the elderly have made during the Reagan-Bush Administration:

- Inflation, the despoiler of household budgets for the aged, has been reduced to less than one-third of its peak rate under the last Democrat Administration.
- Passage of our anti-crime legislation has helped target resources to fight crime against the elderly, many of whom have been prisoners in their own homes.
- As a result of the Republican economic program, the poverty rate for older Americans has declined by 20 percent during the Republican Administration. When the value of non-cash benefits is counted, the poverty rate is the lowest in history: 3 percent.
- We dramatically cut estate taxes so surviving spouses will not have to sell off the property they worked a lifetime to enjoy just to pay the IRS.
- President Reagan led the Congress in expanding Medicare coverage to include catastrophic health costs.
- Effective spending on Medicare has more than doubled. We have, however, saved money for both taxpayers and beneficiaries through reforms in Medicare procedures.
- Congressional Republicans have supported reauthorization of the broad range of programs under the Older Americans Act.
- The Republican Party reaffirms its long-standing opposition to the earnings test for Social Security recipients. Industrious older persons should not be penalized for continuing to contribute their skills and experience to society.

The 1990s should be the best decade ever for America's older worker. Older Americans will be our natural teachers. In a civilization headed for the stars, they will help us keep our feet on the ground.

The Homeless

Republicans are determined to help the homeless as a matter of ethical commitment, as well as sound public policy. The Reagan-Bush Administration has been at the forefront of the effort:

- In 1987, President Reagan signed a $1 billion aid package to help local governments aid the homeless.
- In 1988, the federal government will spend $400 million on emergency

shelters and medical care alone. Today, a total of 45 federally assisted programs are potentially available to the homeless.

- In 1983, we launched an Emergency Food and Shelter Program under the Federal Emergency Management Administration.
- The General Services Administration has donated both buildings and equipment for shelters.
- In 1985, the Department of Housing and Urban Development [HUD] began to lease single family homes at a nominal rent for use as shelters.
- The Department of Agriculture has provided hundreds of millions of dollars worth of surplus food—more than 1.1 billion pounds to soup kitchens and shelters.
- The Alcohol, Drug Abuse and Mental Health Administration gives the States about a half-billion dollars a year to offset the lack of outpatient services.

Homelessness demonstrates the failure of liberalism. It is the result of Democratic policies in the 1960s and 1970s that disrupted mental health care, family stability, low-cost housing, and the authority of towns and cities to deal with people in need. Republicans are ready to deal with the root causes of the problem:

- Our top priority must be homeless families. As part of an overall emphasis on family responsibility, we will strongly enforce child support laws. We call for development of a model divorce reform law that will adequately safeguard the economic and social interests of mothers and children while securing fairness to fathers in decisions concerning child custody and support.
- We will improve safety in federally assisted shelters for the good of all, particularly families.
- We will work with State and local governments to ensure that education is available to homeless children. All appropriate federal education and health programs must make provision for the special needs of these youngsters.
- We will create, as a national emergency effort, a regulatory reform task force drawn from all levels of government to break through the restrictions that keep 1.7 million housing units unrehabilitated and out of use. We will explore incentives for the private sector to put these housing units back into service.
- As detailed elsewhere in this platform, we will advance tenant management and resident ownership of public housing as a proven means of upgrading the living environment of low-income families.
- We favor expanding Community Development Block Grants for acquiring or rehabilitating buildings for shelters. We urge work requirements, no matter how modest, for shelter residents so they can retain skills and a sense of responsibility for their future.
- Rent controls promise housing below its market cost, but inevitably

result in a shortage of decent homes. Our people should not have to underwrite any community which erodes its own housing supply by rent control.

We call upon the courts to cooperate with local officials and police departments in arranging for treatment for persons whose actions disrupt the community or endanger their own or others' safety.

Constitutional Government and Individual Rights

Equal Rights

Since its inception, the Republican Party has stood for the worth of every person. On that ground, we support the pluralism and diversity that have been part of our country's greatness. "Deep in our hearts, we do believe":

- That bigotry has no place in American life. We denounce those persons, organizations, publications and movements which practice or promote racism, anti-Semitism or religious intolerance.
- That the Pledge of Allegiance should be recited daily in schools in all States. Students who learn we are "one nation, under God, with liberty and justice for all" will shun the politics of fear.
- In equal rights for all. The Reagan-Bush Administration has taken to court a record number of civil rights and employment discrimination cases. We will continue our vigorous enforcement of statutes to prevent illegal discrimination on account of sex, race, creed, or national origin.
- In guaranteeing opportunity, not dictating the results of fair competition. We will resist efforts to replace equal rights with discriminatory quota systems and preferential treatment. Quotas are the most insidious form of reverse discrimination against the innocent.
- In defending religious freedom. Mindful of our religious diversity, we firmly support the right of students to engage in voluntary prayer in schools. We call for full enforcement of the Republican legislation that now guarantees equal access to school facilities by student religious groups.
- That the unborn child has a fundamental right to life which cannot be infringed. We therefore reaffirm our support for a human life amendment to the Constitution, and we endorse legislation to make clear that the Fourteenth Amendment's protections apply to unborn children. We oppose the use of public revenues for abortion and will eliminate funding for organizations which advocate or support abortion. We commend the efforts of those individuals and religious and private organizations that are providing positive alternatives to abortion by meeting the physical, emotional, and financial needs of pregnant women and offering adoption services where needed.
- We applaud President Reagan's fine record of judicial appointments, and we reaffirm our support for the appointment of judges at all levels

of the judiciary who respect traditional family values and the sanctity of innocent human life.

- That churches, religious schools and any other religious institution should not be taxed. We reject as wrong, bigoted, and a massive violation of the First Amendment the current attempt by the ACLU [American Civil Liberties Union] to tax the Roman Catholic Church or any other religious institutions they target in the future.

Private Property

We believe the right of private property is the cornerstone of liberty. It safeguards for citizens everything of value, including their right to contract to produce and sell goods and services. We want to expand ownership to all Americans, for that is the key for individuals to control their own future.

To advance private stewardship of natural resources, we call for a reduction in the amount of land controlled by government, especially in our western States. Private ownership is best for our economy, best for our environment, and best for our communities. We likewise consider water rights a State issue, not a federal one.

Women's Rights

We renew our historic commitment to equal rights for women. The Republican Party pioneered the right of women to vote and initiated the rights now embodied in the Equal Pay Act, requiring equal pay for equal work. But legal rights mean nothing without opportunity, and that has been the hallmark of Republican policy. In government, the Reagan-Bush team has broken all records for the advancement of women to the most important positions: 28 percent of the top policy-level appointments went to women. But far more important than what we've done in government is what women have accomplished with the economic freedom and incentives our policies have provided them.

We must remove remaining obstacles to women's achieving their full potential and full reward. That does not include the notion of federally mandated comparable worth, which would substitute the decisions of bureaucrats for the judgment of individuals. It does include equal rights for women who work for the Congress. We call upon the Democratic leadership of House and Senate to join Republican Members in applying to Congress the civil rights laws that apply to the rest of the nation. Women should not be second-class citizens anywhere in our country, but least of all beneath the dome of the Capitol.

Recognizing that women represent less than 5 percent of the U.S. Congress, only 12 percent of the nation's statewide offices, plus 15 percent of State legislative positions, the Republican Party strongly supports the achievements of women in seeking an equal role in the governing of our country and is committed to the vigorous recruitment, training, and campaign support of women candidates at all levels.

Americans with Disabilities

One measure of our country's greatness is the way it treats its disabled citizens.

Our citizens are the nation's most precious resource. As Republicans, we are committed to ensuring increased opportunities for every individual to reach his or her maximum potential. This commitment includes providing opportunities for individuals with disabilities. The 1980s have been a revolution, a declaration of independence for persons with disabilities, and Republicans have initiated policies which remove barriers so that such persons are more independent.

The most effective way to increase opportunities for such persons is to remove intentional and unintentional barriers to education, employment, housing, transportation, health care, and other basic services. Republicans have played an important role in removing such barriers:

- Republicans supported the creation of a new program to provide early intervention services to infants and toddlers with disabilities.
- Republicans initiated a supported employment program that allows individuals with severe disabilities to earn competitive wages in integrated work settings, thus, in many instances, creating first-time taxpayers.
- Republicans initiated changes in the Social Security Act that now permit individuals with disabilities to work without losing health insurance coverage.
- Republicans developed legislation to increase the availability of technology-related assistance for individuals with disabilities, thereby increasing their ability to do things for themselves, others, and their communities.
- Republicans have made a sustained commitment to policies that create opportunities for individuals with disabilities to lead productive and creative lives.

Republicans will continue to support such policies:

- We recognize the great potential of disabled persons and support efforts to remove artificial barriers that inhibit them from reaching their potential, and making their contributions, in education, employment and recreation. This includes the removal, insofar as practicable, of architectural, transportation, communication and attitudinal barriers.
- We support efforts to provide disabled voters full access to the polls and opportunity to participate in all aspects of the political process.
- By promoting vigorous economic growth, we want to provide incentives for the scientific and technological research that may reverse or compensate for many disabilities.
- We pledge to fight discrimination in health care. Following the example of President Reagan, we insist upon full treatment for

disabled infants. We find no basis, whether in law or medicine or ethics, for denying care or treatment to any medically dependent or disabled person because of handicap, age, or infirmity.

- We will strongly enforce statutory prohibitions barring discrimination because of handicap in any program receiving federal financial assistance.
- We will protect the rights established under the Education for All Handicapped Children Act, Section 504 of the Rehabilitation Act of 1973, and the Civil Rights of Institutionalized Persons Act. We will balance those rights against the public's right to be protected against diseases and conditions which threaten the health and safety of others.
- We recognize the need to procedural due process rights of persons with disabilities both to prevent their placement into inappropriate programs or settings and to ensure that their rights are represented by guardians or other advocates when necessary.

We endorse policies that give individuals with disabilities the right to participate in decisions related to their education, the right to affect how and where they live and the right to choose or change a job or career.

To further promote the independence and productivity of people with disabilities and their integration into the mainstream of life, the Republican Party supports legislation to remove the bias in the Medicaid program toward serving disabled individuals in isolated institutional settings and ensure that appropriate, community-based services are reimbursable through Medicaid.

Native Americans

We support self-determination for Indian Tribes in managing their own affairs and resources. Recognizing the government-to-government trust responsibility, we will work to end dependency fostered by federal controls. Reservations should be free to become enterprise zones so their people can fully share in America's prosperity. We will work with tribal governments to improve environmental conditions and will ensure equitable participation by Native Americans in federal programs in health, housing, job training and education.

We endorse efforts to preserve the culture of native Hawaiians and to ensure their equitable participation in federal programs that can recognize their unique place in the life of our nation.

The Right of Gun Ownership

Republicans defend the constitutional right to keep and bear arms. When this right is abused by an individual who uses a gun in the commission of a crime, we call for stiff, mandatory penalties.

The Rights of Workers

We affirm the right of all freely to form, join or assist labor organizations to bargain collectively, consistent with state laws. Labor relations must be based on fairness and mutual respect. We renew our long-standing support for the right of states to enact "Right-to-Work" laws. To protect the political rights of every worker, we oppose the use of compulsory dues or fees for partisan purposes. Workers should not have to pay for political activity they oppose, and no worker should be coerced by violence or intimidation by any party to a labor dispute.

The Republican Party supports legislation to amend the Hobbs Act, so that union officials, like all other Americans, are once again subject to the law's prohibition against extortion and violence in labor disputes.

We also support amendments to the National Labor Relations Act to provide greater protection from labor violence for workers who choose to work during strikes.

The Right to Political Participation

Republicans want to broaden involvement in the political process. We oppose government controls that make it harder for average citizens to be politically active. We especially condemn the congressional Democrats' scheme to force taxpayer funding of campaigns.

Because we support citizen participation in politics, we continue to favor whatever legislation may be necessary to permit American citizens residing in Guam, the Virgin Islands, American Samoa, the Northern Mariana Islands, and Puerto Rico to vote for president and vice president in national elections and permit their elected federal delegate to have the rights and privileges—except for voting on the floor—of other Members of Congress.

Puerto Rico has been a territory of the United States since 1898. The Republican Party vigorously supports the right of the United States citizens of Puerto Rico to be admitted into the Union as a fully sovereign State after they freely so determine. Therefore, we support the establishment of a presidential task force to prepare the necessary legislation to ensure that the people of Puerto Rico have the opportunity to exercise at the earliest possible date their right to apply for admission into the Union.

We also pledge that a decision of the people of Puerto Rico in favor of statehood will be implemented through an admission bill that would provide for a smooth fiscal transition, recognize the concept of a multicultural society for its citizens, and ensure the right to retain their Spanish language and traditions.

We recognize that the people of Guam have voted for a closer relationship with the United States of America, and we reaffirm our support of their right to improve their political relationship through a commonwealth status.

The Republican Party welcomes, as the newest member of the American family, the people of the Commonwealth of the Northern Marianas Islands, who became U.S. citizens with President Reagan's 1986 presidential proclamation.

Immigration

We welcome those from other lands who bring to America their ideals and industry. At the same time, we insist upon our country's absolute right to control its borders. We call upon our allies to join us in the responsibility shared by all democratic nations for resettlement of refugees, especially those fleeing Communism in Southeast Asia.

Restoring the Constitution

We reassert adherence to the Tenth Amendment, reserving to the States and to the people all powers not expressly delegated to the national government.

Our Constitution provides for a separation of powers among the three branches of government. In that system, judicial power must be exercised with deference towards State and local authority; it must not expand at the expense of our representative institutions. When the courts try to reorder the priorities of the American people, they undermine the stature of the judiciary and erode respect for the rule of law. That is why we commend the Reagan-Bush team for naming to the federal courts distinguished women and men committed to judicial restraint, the rights of law-abiding citizens, and traditional family values. We pledge to continue their record. Where appropriate, we support congressional use of Article III, section 2 of the Constitution to restrict the jurisdiction of federal courts.

Government Ethics and Congressional Reform

As the United States celebrates the bicentennial of the U.S. Congress, many Americans are becoming painfully aware that they are being disenfranchised and inadequately represented by their elected officials.

Indeed, the process of government has broken down on Capitol Hill. The Founding Fathers of the United States Constitution would be shocked by congressional behavior:

- The Democrat congressional leaders exempt themselves from the laws they impose on the people in areas like health, safety and civil rights.
- Salaries and staff keep growing. Lavish free mailing privileges and other power perks help most incumbents hold onto their offices, election after election.
- Out of 91 appropriations bills in the past seven years, only seven made it to the president's desk on time.
- A catch-all bill to fund the government for 1988 was 2,100 pages long, lumping together 13 money bills that should have been separately subject to presidential review.
- $44 billion is currently being spent for programs not authorized by legislation.
- Special interest spending and pork barrel deals are larded throughout massive bills passed in chaotic late-night sessions.
- Vetoed bills are not dealt with directly by the Congress but are buried in other pending legislation.

- Phony numbers are used to estimate budgets and to cover up the true costs of legislation.

Even worse, outright offenses against ethical standards and public laws are treated lightly. National security leaks go unpunished. In the House of Representatives, the Ethics Committee has become a shield for Democrats who get caught but don't get punished.

After 36 years of one-party rule, the House of Representatives is no longer the people's branch of government. It is the broken branch. It is an arrogant oligarchy that has subverted the Constitution. The Democrat congressional leaders:

- Stole a congressional seat from the people of Indiana by barring a duly elected, and officially certified, Republican Member.
- Flagrantly abuse every standard of accepted procedure by adjourning and, contrary to 200 years of House tradition, immediately reconvening in order to create a "new day" and pass legislation previously defeated.
- Deny the century-old right of the minority party to offer its final alternatives to bills.
- Change House rules to prevent debate and thwart the offering of amendments.
- Rig adoption of substantive legislation on mere procedural votes, so their followers won't be accountable on controversial votes to the people back home.
- Protect their cronies charged with personal misconduct or criminal activities.
- Refuse to allow the House to vote on issues of tremendous concern to the American people and viciously penalize independent Democrats who vote their conscience.
- Rig the subcommittee system to give themselves artificial majorities and additional staff members.

Republicans want to hold accountable to the people, the Congress and every other element of government. We will:

- Extend the independent counsel law to Congress.
- Apply health and safety laws and civil rights statutes to the Congress.
- Give to whistleblowers on Capitol Hill the same legal protection they have in the executive branch, to encourage employees to report illegalities, corruption and sexual harassment.
- Implement the budget reform agenda outlined elsewhere in this platform—a balanced budget amendment, line-item veto, and other steps—to restore accountability, order, and truth in government to the way Congress spends the people's money.
- Support citizen efforts in the Senate to defeat the gerrymanders that steal seats for Democrat congressmen by denying fair representation to the voters.

- Force democracy into the committee system of the House so that committees and staffs reflect the overall composition of the House.
- We favor a constitutional amendment which would place some restriction on the number of consecutive terms a man or woman may serve in the U.S. House of Representatives or the U.S. Senate.

Educating for the Future

Republican leadership has launched a new era in American education. Our vision of excellence has brought education back to parents, back to basics, and back on a track of excellence leading to a brighter and stronger future for America.

Because education is the key to opportunity, we must make America a nation of learners, ready to compete in the rapidly changing world of the future. Our goal is to combine traditional values and enduring truths with the most modern techniques and technology for teaching and learning.

This challenge will be immense. For two decades before 1981, poor public policies had led to an alarming decline in performance in our schools. Unfocused federal spending seemed to worsen the situation, hamstringing education with regulations and wasting resources in faddish programs top-heavy with administrative overhead.

Then President Reagan and Vice President Bush rallied our "nation at risk." The response was in the best traditions of the American people. In every state, indeed, in every community, individuals and organizations have launched a neighborhood movement for education reform. It has brought together Americans of every race and creed in a crusade for our children's future. Since 1980, average salaries for elementary and secondary teachers have increased to over $28,000, an increase of 20 percent after inflation. We can enhance this record of accomplishment by committing ourselves to these principles:

- Parents have the primary right and responsibility for education. Private institutions, communities, States, and the federal government must support and stimulate that parental role. We support the right of parents to educate their children at home.
- Choice and competition in education foster quality and protect consumers' rights.
- Accountability and evaluation of performance at all levels of education is the key to continuing reform in education. We must reward excellence in learning, in teaching and in administration.
- Values are the core of good education. A free society needs a moral foundation for its learning. We oppose any programs in public schools which provide birth control or abortion services or referrals. Our "first line of defense" to protect our youth from contracting AIDS and other sexually communicable diseases, from teen pregnancy, and from illegal drug use must be abstinence education.
- Quality in education should be available to all our children within the

communities and neighborhoods. Federal policy should empower low-income families to choose quality and demand accountability in their children's schooling.

- Throughout all levels of education we must initiate action to reduce the deplorable dropout rate which deprives young people of their full potential.
- Federal programs must focus on students at special risk, especially those with physical disabilities or language deficits, to increase their chance at a productive future in the mainstream of American life.
- Because America's future will require increasingly competent leadership in all walks of life, national policy should emphasize the need to provide our most talented students with special programs to challenge their abilities.

Based on these principles, the Republican agenda for better education looks first to home and family, then to communities and States. In States and localities, we support practical, down-to-earth reforms that have made a proven difference in actual operation:

- Choice in education, especially for poor families, fosters the parental involvement that is essential for student success, and States should consider enacting voucher systems or other means of encouraging competition among public schools.
- Performance testing, both for students and teachers, measures progress, assures accountability to parents and the public, and keeps standards high.
- Merit pay, career ladders, or other rewards for superior teachers acknowledge our esteem for them and encourage others to follow their example of dedication to a profession that is critical to our nation's future.
- Making use of volunteerism from the private sector and providing opportunity for accelerated accreditation for those with needed expertise broadens the classroom experience and encourages excellence.
- Expansions of curriculum to include the teaching of the history, culture, geography and, particularly, the languages of key nations of the world is a necessity. To compete successfully throughout the world, we must acquire the ability to speak the languages of our customers.
- Excellence in the teaching of geography is essential to equipping our people with the ability to capture new markets in all parts of the world.
- Discipline is a prerequisite for learning. Our schools must be models of order and decorum, not jungles of drugs and violence.

On the federal level, Republicans have worked to facilitate State and local reform movements:

- We kept the spotlight on the reform movement through White House leadership, and we refocused the Department of Education to recognize and foster excellence.
- We enacted legislation to ensure equal access to schools for student

religious groups and led Congressional efforts to restore voluntary school prayer.

- We led a national crusade against illiteracy, following the example of Barbara Bush.
- We put into law protection for pupils in federally funded programs, to shield students and their families from intrusive research and offensive psychological testing.
- We strengthened education programs by proposing to replace federal aid to schools with direct assistance that would give choice to low-income parents.
- We broke new ground in early childhood development programs, such as Even Start, that emphasize the involvement of parents in the learning process and address adult illiteracy and school readiness education holistically.
- We intervened in court cases to defend the right of students to learn in a safe, drug-free environment.

We will continue to advance that agenda and to expand horizons for learning, teaching, and mastering the future:

- We will protect the Pledge of Allegiance in all schools as a reminder of the values which must be at the core of learning for a free society.
- We will use federal programs to foster excellence, rewarding "Merit Schools" which significantly improve education for their students.
- We will urge our local school districts to recognize the value of kindergarten and pre-kindergarten programs.
- We will direct federal matching funds to promote magnet schools that turn students toward the challenges of the future rather than the failures of the past.
- We will support laboratories of educational excellence in every State by refocusing federal funds for educational research.
- We will increase funding for the Head Start program to help children get a fair chance at learning, right from the beginning.
- We will work with local schools and the private sector to develop models for evaluating teachers and other school officials.
- We will continue to support tuition tax credits for parents who choose to educate their children in private educational institutions.
- We would establish a public-private partnership using the Department of Labor's Job Training Partnership Act funds to encourage youth to stay in school and graduate. The Labor Department funds would be made available to local employers and business groups to hire high school students after school and during the summer with the requirement that they keep their grades at a "C" average or above until graduation.

In higher education, Republicans want to promote both opportunity and responsibility:

- We will keep resources focused on low-income students and address the barriers that discourage minority students from entering and succeeding in institutions of higher education.

- We are determined to reverse the intolerable rates of default in the guaranteed student loan program to make more money available to those who really need to borrow it.
- We will keep the spotlight of public attention on the college cost spiral—running far ahead of inflation overall—and challenge administrators to exercise more fiscal responsibility.
- We will create a College Savings Bond program, with tax-exempt interest, to help families save for their children's higher education.
- We will condition federal aid to post-secondary institutions upon their good faith effort to maintain safe and drug-free campuses.
- We will insist freedom of speech is not only a fundamental right, it is one of the first lines of education. This freedom should be afforded to all speakers with a minimum of harassment.
- We will continue education benefits for veterans of military service and advance the principle that those who serve their country in the armed forces have first call on federal education assistance.
- We will continue the Reagan-Bush policy of emphasizing vocational-technical education. A large number of jobs in our society require secondary and post-secondary vocational-technical education. Federal programs and policies must recognize and enhance vocational-technical students.
- We will support educational programs in federal prisons that will allow prisoners the opportunity to become literate and to learn an employable skill. We encourage similar programs at the state level.

To compete globally, our society must prepare our children for the world of work. We cannot allow one of every eight 17-year-olds to remain functionally illiterate. We cannot allow 1 million students to drop out of high school every year, most of them without basic skills; therefore, we must teach them reading, writing and mathematics. We must re-establish their obligation to learn.

Education for the future means more than formal schooling in classrooms. About 75 percent of our current workforce will need some degree of retraining by the year 2000. More than half of all jobs we will create in the 1990s will require some education beyond high school, and much of that will be obtained outside of regular educational institutions. Unprecedented flexibility in working arrangements, career changes, and a stampede of technological advances are ushering us into an era of lifelong learning. Therefore, we support employment training programs at all levels of government such as the Job Training Partnership Act and the recently restructured Worker Adjustment Program for dislocated workers. The placement success of these programs can be directly traced to their public/private sector partnerships and local involvement in their program development and implementation.

In the 1960s and 1970s, we learned what doesn't solve the problems of education: federal financing and regimentation of our schools. In the 1980s, we asserted what works: parental responsibility, community support and local control, good teachers and determined administrators, and a return to the basic values and content of western civilization. That combination gave generations of Americans the world's greatest opportunities for learning. It can guarantee the same for future generations.

Arts and Humanities

Republicans consider the resurgence of the arts and humanities a vital part of getting back to basics in education. Our young people must acquire more than information and skills. They must learn to reason and to appreciate the intellectual achievements that express the enduring values of our civilization. To that end, we will:

- Continue the Republican economic renaissance which has made possible a tremendous outpouring of support for arts and humanities.
- Support full deductibility for donations to tax-exempt cultural institutions in order to encourage the private support of arts and humanities.
- Support the National Endowments for the Arts and Humanities and the Institute of Museum Services in their effort to support America's cultural institutions, artists, and scholars.
- Guard against the misuse of governmental grants by those who attack or derogate any race or creed and oppose the politicization of the National Endowments for the Arts and Humanities.

While recognizing the diversity of our people, we encourage educational institutions to emphasize in the arts and humanities those ideas and cultural accomplishments that address the ethical foundations of our culture.

Science and Technology

Our nation's continuing progress depends on scientific and technological innovation. It is America's economic fountain of youth. Republicans advocate a creative partnership between government and the private sector to ensure the dynamism and creativity of scientific research and technology:

- We recognize that excellence in education, and especially scientific literacy, is a precondition for progress, and that economic growth makes possible the nation's continuing advancement in scientific research.
- We consider a key priority in any increased funding for the National Science Foundation the retooling of science and engineering labs at colleges and universities.
- We endorse major national projects like the superconducting Super Collider.
- We will ensure that tax policy gives optimum incentive for the private sector to fund a high level of advanced research. Toward that end, we

will make permanent the current tax credit for research and development and extend it to cooperative research ventures.

- We will strengthen the role of science and engineering in national policy by reinforcing the Office of the President's Science Advisor with the addition of a Science Advisory Council.
- We will encourage exchange of scientific information, especially between business and academic institutions, to speed up the application of research to benefit the public.
- We will improve the acquisition of scientific and technical information from other countries through expedited translation services and more aggressive outreach by federal agencies.
- We will include international technology flows as part of U.S. trade negotiations to ensure that the benefits of foreign advances are available to Americans.
- We will encourage innovation by strengthening protection for intellectual property at home and abroad. We will promote the public benefits that come from commercialization of research conducted under federal sponsorship by allowing private ownership of intellectual property developed in that manner.
- We will oppose regulation which stifles competition and hinders breakthroughs that can transform life for the better in areas like biotechnology.

That is an agenda for more than science and technology. It will broaden economic opportunity, sustain our ability to compete globally, and enhance the quality of life for all.

Space

The Republican Party will re-establish U.S. preeminence in space. It is our nation's frontier, our manifest destiny. President Reagan has set ambitious goals for a space comeback. We are determined to meet them and move on to even greater challenges.

We support further development of the space station, the National Aerospace Plane, Project Pathfinder, a replacement shuttle, and the development of alternate launch vehicles. We endorse Mission to Planet Earth for space science to advance our understanding of environmental and climatic forces.

A resurgent America, renewed economically and in spirit, must get on with its business of greatness. We must commit to manned flight to Mars around the year 2000 and to continued exploration of the Moon.

These goals will be achievable only with full participation by private initiative. We welcome the Reagan-Bush initiative to increase the role of the private sector in transport, particularly in the launch of commercial satellites. The Reagan-Bush Administration's proposed space station will allow the private sector additional opportunities in the area of research and manufacturing.

Our program for freedom in space will allow millions of American investors to put their money on the future. That's one of the ways to lift the conquest of space out of the congressional budget logjam. Republicans believe that America must have a clear vision for the future of the space program, well defined goals, and streamlined implementation, as we reach for the stars.

Strong Communities and Neighborhoods

Crime

Republicans want a free and open society for every American. That means more than economic advancement alone. It requires the safety and security of persons and their property. It demands an end to crime.

Republicans stand with the men and women who put their lives on the line every day, in State and local police forces and in federal law enforcement agencies. We are determined to re-establish safety in the streets of those communities where the poor, the hard-working, and the elderly now live in fear. Despite opposition from liberal Democrats, we've made a start:

- The rate of violent crimes has fallen 20 percent since 1981. Personal thefts fell 21 percent, robberies fell 31 percent, assaults fell 17 percent, and household burglaries fell 30 percent.
- In 1986, crimes against individuals reached their lowest level in 14 years.
- The Reagan-Bush Administration has crusaded for victims' rights in trials and sentencing procedures and has advocated restitution by felons to their victims.
- We have been tough on white-collar crime, too. We have filed more criminal antitrust cases than the previous Administration.
- We pushed an historic reform of toughened sentencing procedures for federal courts to make the punishment fit the crime.
- We appointed to the courts judges who have been sensitive to the rights of victims and law-abiding citizens.

We will forge ahead with the Republican anti-crime agenda:

- We must never allow the presidency and the Department of Justice to fall into the hands of those who coddle hardened criminals. Republicans oppose furloughs for those criminals convicted of first degree murder and others who are serving a life sentence without possibility of parole. We believe that victims' rights should not be accorded less importance than those of convicted felons.
- We will re-establish the federal death penalty.
- We will reform the exclusionary rule, to prevent the release of guilty felons on technicalities.
- We will reform cumbersome habeas corpus procedures, used to delay cases and prevent punishment of the guilty.
- We support State laws implementing preventive detention to allow

courts to deny bail to those considered dangerous and likely to commit additional crimes.

The election of 1988 will determine which way our country deals with crime. A Republican President and a Republican Congress can lay the foundation for a safer future.

Drug-Free America

The Republican Party is committed to a drug-free America. Our policy is strict accountability, for users of illegal drugs as well as for those who profit by that usage.

The drug epidemic didn't just happen. It was fueled by the liberal attitudes of the 1960s and 1970s that tolerated drug usage. Drug abuse directly threatens the fabric of our society. It is part of a worldwide narcotics empire whose $300 billion business makes it one of the largest industries on earth.

The Reagan-Bush Administration has set out to destroy it. In the past six years, federal drug arrests have increased by two-thirds. Compared with 1980, two and a half times as many drug offenders were sent to prison in 1987. Federal spending for drug enforcement programs more than tripled in the last seven years. And we have broken new ground by enlisting U.S. intelligence agencies in the fight against drug trafficking.

Drug usage in our armed forces has plummeted as a direct result of an aggressive education and random testing program. In 1983, we instituted random drug testing in the Coast Guard. At that time, 10.3 percent of the tests showed positive drug usage. As a result of this testing program, the positive usage rate fell dramatically to 2.9 percent in 1987. The Reagan-Bush Administration has also undertaken efforts to insure that all those in safety related positions in our transportation system are covered by similar drug testing requirements. We commend this effort.

We are determined to finish the job.

- The Republican Party unequivocally opposes legalizing or decriminalizing any illicit drug.
- We support strong penalties, including the death penalty for major drug traffickers.
- User accountability for drug usage is long overdue. Conviction for any drug crime should make the offender ineligible for discretionary federal assistance, grants, loans and contracts for a period of time.
- To impress young Americans with the seriousness of our fight against drugs, we urge States to suspend eligibility for a driver's license to anyone convicted of a drug offense.
- We urge school districts to get tough on illegal drug use by notifying parents and police whenever it is discovered.
- We will encourage tougher penalties for those who use children in illegal narcotics operations.
- We will require federal contractors and grantees to establish a drug-

free workplace with the goal that no American will have to work around drug abuse.

- We will suspend passports from those convicted of major drug offenses.
- To protect residents of public housing, we will evict persons dealing in drugs. We will foster resident review committees to screen out drug abusers and dealers. We will promote tenant management as the surest cure for the drug plague in public projects.
- We will strengthen interdiction of foreign drugs and expand the military's role in stopping traffickers.
- We will work with foreign governments to eradicate drug crops in their countries.
- In a summit of Western Hemisphere nations, we will seek total cooperation from other governments in wiping out the international drug empire.
- In addition to our enforcement activities, we encourage drug education in our schools. These programs should begin as early as the elementary school years, before children are subjected to peer pressure to experiment with drugs, and should continue through high school. Cutting down on the demand for drugs will be of great assistance as we increase our enforcement efforts to reduce drug supply.
- We will encourage seizure and forfeiture programs by the Department of the Treasury and each State to take the profits out of illicit drug sales.

We commend our fellow citizens who are actively joining the war against drugs. Drug dealers are domestic terrorists, and we salute the heroic residents of poor neighborhoods who have boldly shut down crack houses and run traffickers out of their communities.

We recognize the need to improve the availability of drug rehabilitation and treatment.

There's a bright side to the picture. We know the most powerful deterrent to drug abuse: strong, stable family life, along with the absolute approach summed up in "Just Say No." Nancy Reagan has made that phrase the battle-cry of the war against drugs, and it is echoed by more than 10,000 Just Say No clubs. We salute her for pointing the way to our nation's drug-free future.

Opportunity and Assistance

Our country's economic miracle of the last eight years has been the most successful assault on poverty in our era. Millions of families have worked their way into the mainstream of national life. The poverty rate continues to decline. However, many remain in poverty, and we pledge to help them in their struggle for self-sufficiency and independence.

For most of our country's history, helping those less fortunate was a community responsibility. Strong families pulled together, and strong communities cared for those in need. That is more than a description of

the past. It is a prescription for the future, pointing the way toward real reform of today's welfare mess through these Republican principles:

- We support the maintenance of income assistance programs for those
  who cannot work. In particular, we recognize our responsibility to
  ensure a decent standard of living for the aged, the disabled, and
  children dependent upon the community.
- Poverty can be addressed by income assistance or in-kind services.
  Dependency, on the other hand, requires a comprehensive strategy to
  change patterns of attitude and behavior. We will work to address both
  poverty and dependency.
- Work is an essential component of welfare reform, and education is an
  essential component of employability. Welfare reform must require
  participation in education and work, and provide day care assistance
  and continued access to Medicaid during the transition to full
  independence.
- Fathers of welfare dependent children must be held accountable by
  mandating paternity determinations and requiring the participation of
  unemployed fathers in education and work programs.
- State and local administration of education, work, and welfare programs is best for both the taxpayers and those in need.
- State and local pilot programs in welfare are the cutting edge of
  welfare reform. States should be granted the authority by the federal
  government to pursue innovative programs which return teen mothers
  to school and welfare recipients to work. Congressional Democrats are
  blocking the expansion of this vital process. A Republican Congress
  will give the States authority to meet local needs.
- Welfare fraud is an offense against both the taxpayers and the poor.
  Whether perpetrated by participants or providers of services, its
  eradication is an essential component of a compassionate welfare
  policy.

We are committed to assisting those in need. We are equally committed
to addressing the root causes of poverty. Divorce, desertion, and illegiti-
macy have been responsible for almost all the increase in child poverty in
the last 15 years. Because strong family life is the most remarkable anti-
poverty force in history, Republicans will make the reinforcement of
family rights and responsibilities an essential component of public policy.
Stronger enforcement of child support laws must be an important part of
that effort, along with revision of State laws which have left many women
and children vulnerable to economic distress.

Children in poverty deserve our strongest support. We are committed to
safer neighborhoods and full prosecution for child abuse and exploitation.
We will reach out to these children through Head Start and targeted
education, basic health and nutrition assistance, local community efforts
and individual concern. But something more is required to fulfill the hope
for self-sufficiency: a job in an expanding economy. The most compassion-

ate policy for children in need is the chance for families to stand on their own feet in a society filled with opportunity.

Fighting poverty means much more than distributing cash. It includes education and work programs. It means reducing illiteracy, the single greatest indicator of life-long poverty. It involves combating crime so that the homes and earnings of the poor are secure. It includes Republican reforms in public housing, like resident management and ownership. It requires regulatory reforms to open up opportunities for those on the margins of the work force. It means streamlining adoption rules and ensuring poor parents a real say in their children's educations. Above all, it means maintaining a strong, healthy economy that creates jobs.

Urban Revitalization

Urban America is center stage of our country's future. That is why we address its problems and potential throughout this platform, rather than limiting our concern to a particular section. In doing so, Republicans follow three broad principles:

- Economic growth is the most important urban program. Because we cut taxes, a new prosperity has transformed many towns and cities. Because we forced down inflation, cities pay much lower bond rates. Because we created 17.5 million new jobs through a thriving economy, millions of urban residents have seized the opportunity to escape welfare and unemployment. Because we slashed regulatory burdens, enterprise is transforming areas untouched by government programs of past years.
- Local control is the best form of administration. That's why we merged federal programs into block grants for community development and housing.
- Citizen choice is the key to successful government. Options in education empower parents and attract new residents. Options in public housing transform slums into real communities, bustling with enterprise and hope.

Building on those principles, Republicans will advance our urban agenda which is to:

- Enterprise zones, where tax incentives and regulatory reforms open the way for creating jobs and rebuilding neighborhoods from the ground up which have been blocked by the Democrats in Congress.
- Resident control—both management and ownership—of public housing, with a goal of transferring one-third of the country's public housing space to tenants by 1995.
- Urban homesteading and other programs to ensure affordable housing opportunities in our cities.
- Emergency waiver of Davis-Bacon wage requirements for cities with severe deterioration of the public infrastructure.
- Contract out public services to workers in the private sector.

- Education assistance directed to low-income households instead of aid to institutions that fail to meet their needs.
- Continued reduction in crime rates, especially street crime and the violence that destroys community life.
- Unrelenting war on drugs.
- Greater control by local government in federally assisted programs, especially transportation and housing.
- Steady environmental progress to ensure clean air and clean water to our cities and assist local governments in solving their solid waste disposal problems in order to make our cities safe and healthy places to live.
- Special attention to urban residents in the national census, to ensure that cities are not shortchanged in federal representation or in federal programs based upon population.

Rural Community Development and the Family Farm

Introduction

Republicans see a robust future for American agriculture. Rural America is our country's heartland and pillar of economic and moral strength. From its small towns and communities comes more than the world's greatest bounty of food. From them also comes a commitment to the land by a proud and independent people.

For much of this century, the first line of defense against world hunger has been the American farmer and rancher. In the future as in the past, the enterprise of rural Americans will be crucial to the progress of our country and of mankind. The entire nation—and indeed, the world—benefits from their unsurpassed productivity.

When farmers and ranchers face adversity, the communities that depend on them do, too. When farmers' income falls, the earnings of others follow. When agriculture suffers, the tax base and public services of whole regions decline.

That is why the current drought is an emergency for our entire country. It will affect every American: the way we live, the food we eat, the land we cherish. We cannot promise to bring rain, but we can bend every arm of government to provide for the expeditious relief of farmers and ranchers in trouble. We pledge to do so. We will focus assistance on those most seriously hurt by the drought. With strong Republican support in the House and Senate, a major relief bill has been signed by President Reagan.

The Record

Some disasters are man-made. In the late 1970s, American agriculture bore the brunt of bad public policy. Long thereafter, farmers suffered the consequences of those four years of devastating Democrat mismanagement. Inflation drove production costs and farm debt to their highest levels in history. To top it off, the Democrats' embargo of grain and other agricultural products dealt a blow to the nation's heartland from which many farmers never recovered.

NEVER AGAIN!

For eight years, Ronald Reagan and George Bush have provided the leadership to turn that situation around. Despite strong Democrat opposition, Republicans have made a good beginning. Because of Republican policies, America's farm and rural sector is coming alive again:

- Inflation, unemployment, and interest rates are at their lowest levels in years. Our dollar exchange rate is more competitive.
- Land values, the best indicator of farm prospects, have stabilized and are rising in many areas.
- Farm credit institutions, both public and private, are back on their feet.
- Farm debt has been reduced from $193 billion in 1983 to a projected $137 billion in 1988.
- Net farm income increased to its highest level ever in 1987, reaching $46 billion, while net cash income was also a record at $57 billion.
- We have reduced price-depressing surpluses to their lowest levels in many years. Total grain surpluses have been cut in half from their high in 1986.

In summary, increased agricultural exports, higher commodity and livestock prices, increased profits and land values, declining farm debt and surpluses, all these point to a healthier outlook for the rural economy.

The recovery is no accident. Republicans have acted decisively in the interest of rural America. Look at the record:

- In 1981, we immediately halted the Democrats' embargo on grain and other agricultural products and kept our pledge always to be a reliable supplier. We now reaffirm our promise never to use food as a weapon as was done by the last Democrat Administration.
- We have successfully opened more markets for our agricultural commodities and value-added products around the world through competitive pricing, aggressive use of the Export Enhancement Program, the Targeted Export Assistance Program, marketing loans, and generic commodity certificates.
- Through tough trade negotiations, we have opened markets abroad including the Japanese beef and citrus markets. Numerous markets for specialty products have also been opened.
- We ended the notorious "widow's tax" so surviving spouses don't have to sell family farms and ranches to meet inheritance taxes. We also reduced other burdensome inheritance taxes for farm and ranch families.
- In 1985, President Reagan signed one of the most successful farm bills in modern history. The dual goals of protecting farm income while gaining back our lost markets are being achieved.

- We have given farmers the opportunity to profitably retire millions of acres of erodible and generally less productive land through the Conservation Reserve Program, and we enacted legislation to ensure that taxpayers' dollars will not be used to subsidize soil erosion or otherwise damage the environment that makes rural America a place where people want to live.

The Democrats offer nothing for the future of farming. Their plan for mandatory production controls would make productive and efficient American farmers beat a full-scale retreat from the world market:

- It would be a boon to family farms — in Argentina, Brazil, Canada, the European Community, Australia, and other competitor nations.
- It would pull the plug on rural Americans. It would sound a death-knell for rural towns and cities as land is taken from production. According to a United States Department of Agriculture study, it would reduce Gross National Product by $64 billion and wipe out 2.1 million jobs in the private sector.

In short, Democrats want to put farmers on welfare while Republicans want to look after the welfare of all rural Americans.

Our Global Economy

Better than most people, agriculturists know we live in a global economy. America's farmers, ranchers, foresters, and fishermen can compete against anyone in the world if trade rules are fair.

We recognize the historical contribution of agricultural exports to a positive national trade balance and will work on all fronts to improve agricultural trade.

Republicans will aggressively pursue fair and free trade for all U.S. products:

- We will insist that production-, consumption-, and trade-distorting agricultural subsidies of the European Economic Community and others be phased out simultaneously with the phasing out of our farm and export assistance programs.
- We will continue to put free and fair trade for farmers and ranchers on the agenda of every international conference on trade.
- We will use free trade agreements with good trading partners as leverage to open markets elsewhere.
- We will be a reliable supplier of agricultural products to world markets and will not use food as a weapon of foreign policy.

In short, instead of retreat, Republicans promise a full-scale assault on foreign markets.

The Future

Republicans will work to improve agricultural income through market returns at home and abroad, not government controls and subsidies:

- We pledge early action to renew and improve the successful farm programs set to expire in 1990.
- We pledge to continue international food assistance, including programs through the Eisenhower Food for Peace program, to feed the world's hungry and develop markets abroad.
- We will continue to provide leadership in the effort to improve standards of quality for grain and other agricultural products in order to meet international competition.
- We call for greater planting flexibility in federal programs to allow more diversity in farming and more freedom for farmers to grow what they want to grow and to sell their products to whoever will buy them.
- We recognize the need for appropriate multiple-use policy on federal range lands and retention of a fair and equitable grazing fee policy as has been established by the Reagan Administration.
- We support a State's review of the adequacy of crop irrigation capacity under severe water shortage conditions, such as the 1988 drought, to identify areas of potential need and development.
- Water use policy formulation belongs to the States without federal interference; we recognize traditional State supremacy in water law, which is the best bulwark against future water crises.
- We resolve to lower tax rates for long-term capital gains and to work for fairer preproductive expense capitalization laws, including the so-called "heifer tax" as just one example, to promote investment in the production of food and fiber.
- We stand with the nation's foresters and the communities that depend on the forest products industry in supporting an annual timber harvest and multiple-use policy that meets national needs both for a sustained yield of wood products and for sound environmental management.
- We will continue our strong support for agricultural research, including increased emphasis on developing new uses for farm products, such as alternative fuels, food, non-food and industrial products. The agricultural industry is, and always has been, on the leading edge of the technological revolution, and it must continue this tradition in order to be internationally competitive.
- We will encourage public and private research and technical assistance to ensure that the resource base of American agriculture is preserved. Sound stewardship of our land and water resources is important for this and future generations. The soil and water resources of our nation must provide profit for farmers and ranchers and a safe and wholesome food supply. Our Land Grant institutions, working with the private sector, can provide more environmentally safe and biodegradable agrichemicals and improved farming techniques that will help preserve the quality of our underground and surface water supplies.
- We pledge that State farm home exemption and redemption rights shall remain inviolate from federal interference.

Rural Economic Development

Republicans realize that rural communities face challenges that go beyond agricultural concerns. Rural economic development is about more than jobs; it is also about the quality of life. We are ready to address the needs of rural America with creativity and compassion:

- The best jobs program for rural Americans is a good farm program.
- The key to rural development is effective local leadership working in partnership with private businesses and federal, State, and local governments. We will advance, in Congress and at the State level, rural enterprise zones to attract investment and create jobs geared to the opportunities of the century ahead.
- Education is the crucial element to ensuring that rural Americans will be in the mainstream of our national future. We must assure rural youngsters quality education and good schools.
- The roads, bridges, schools, sewer and water systems, and other public works of many rural communities have deteriorated. We will ensure that those communities receive their fair share of aid under federal assistance programs.
- Discrimination against rural hospitals and medical practices in federal reimbursement of health care costs has contributed to reduced medical services in rural America. We pledge to help rural Americans meet their health care needs and will ensure fair treatment for their health care institutions under federal health programs.
- To have full participation in our country's unbounded future, rural people will need access to modern telecommunications and satellite communications systems including commercial decryption devices. Adequate supplies of reasonably priced electric power are also a necessity. We continue to support a strong rural electrification and telephone program. We believe the network of local rural electric and telephone cooperatives that provide these services represents a vital public/private partnership necessary to assure growth and development of the rural economy.
- We will energetically use the Job Training Partnership Act and a newly enacted worker retraining program to ensure that rural workers are fully integrated into the work force of the future.
- We will continue to support programs that enhance housing, business, and industry opportunities for rural Americans; and we will adapt urban homesteading programs to rural communities.
- Sound agricultural policy for rural America demands sound economic policy for all America. We will continue to stabilize fiscal and monetary policies in order to keep inflation in check and interest rates stable. This foundation of economic stability must underly all rural initiatives by all levels of government.

This is our pledge for the continuing renewal of a prosperous rural America.

Energy for the Future

To make real their vision for the future, the American people need adequate, safe, and reliable supplies of energy. Both the security of our nation and the prosperity of our households will depend upon clean and affordable power to light the way ahead and speed a daring society toward its goals. We recognize that energy is a security issue as well as an economic issue. We cannot have a strong nation if we are not energy independent.

We are part way there. In 1981, Republican leadership replaced the Democrats' energy crisis with energy consensus. We rejected scarcity, fostered growth, and set course for an expansive future. We left behind the days of gasoline lines, building temperature controls, the multi-billion dollar boondoggle of Synfuels Corporation, and the cancellation of night baseball games.

The Carter-Mondale years of crippling regulation and exorbitant costs are a thing of the past. We returned the country to policies that encourage rather than discourage domestic production of energy. With a free, more competitive system of producing and marketing energy, American consumers gained a wider range of energy choices at lower prices.

During the Reagan-Bush years, we loosened OPEC's [Organization of Petroleum Exporting Countries] hold on the world's petroleum markets. The United States built up its Strategic Petroleum Reserve and persuaded its allies to increase their emergency petroleum stocks as both a deterrent and a cushion against supply disruptions. When President Reagan and Vice President Bush took office, the Strategic Petroleum Reserve held only 79 million barrels. Now it contains almost 550 million, a three-month cushion in the event of a crisis.

Conservation and energy efficiency, stimulated by the oil shocks of the 1970s, made impressive gains. The nation now consumes less oil, and no more energy in total, than it did in 1977, despite the remarkable growth in our economy under the Reagan-Bush Administration.

Despite these gains, much hard work remains. A strong energy policy is required to assure that the needs of our society are met. Because of low oil prices, domestic oil and gas production has declined significantly. New initiatives will be required to halt the erosion of the domestic oil reserve base, to restore the vitality of the domestic oil and gas industry, to slow the rise in oil imports, and to prevent a return to the vulnerabilities of the 1970s. We must maintain the progress made in conservation and rely more heavily on secure American fuels: domestic oil, natural gas, coal, nuclear energy, alternative sources and renewables.

Oil

The United States is heavily dependent on oil, which represents 40 percent of our total energy consumption. We must have a healthy domestic industry to assure the availability of this fuel to meet our needs. The decline in oil prices has brought exploratory drilling in the country to a virtual standstill, and continuing low prices threaten the hundreds of thousands of small wells that make up the most of U.S. production.

We will set an energy policy for the United States to maintain a viable core industry and to ensure greater energy self sufficiency through private initiatives. We will adopt forceful initiatives to reverse the decline of our domestic oil production. Republicans support:

- Repeal of the counterproductive Windfall Profits Tax.
- Maintenance of our schedule for filling the Strategic Petroleum Reserve to reach 750 million barrels by 1993 and encouragement of our allies to maintain similar reserves.
- Tax incentives to save marginal wells, to encourage exploration for new oil, and to improve the recovery of oil still in place.
- Repeal of the Transfer Rule prohibiting independent producers from using certain tax provisions on acquired properties.
- Elimination of 80 percent of intangible drilling costs as an alternative minimum tax preference item.
- Exploration and development in promising areas, including federal lands and waters, particularly in the Arctic, in a manner that is protective of our environment and is in the best national interest.

Such continued exploration and development of new domestic oil and gas reserves are essential to keep our nation from becoming more dependent on foreign energy sources. Indeed, tax incentives can make our investment in U.S. oil and gas exploration competitive with other countries. They can stimulate drilling, put people back to work, and help maintain our leadership in oilfield technology and services. Incentives and opportunities for increased domestic exploration can also help limit the rise in imports, discourage oil price shocks and enhance energy security.

Natural Gas

Natural gas is a clean, abundant, and reasonably priced fuel secure within the borders of the nation. Increased reliance on natural gas can have significant national security and environmental benefits. While U.S. gas resources are plentiful and recoverable at competitive prices, regulatory burdens and price controls still impede development.

More progress must be made in deregulation of natural gas:

- We support fully decontrolling prices and providing more open access to transportation.
- We also support the flexible use of natural gas to fuel automobiles and boilers.

Over the longer term, natural gas as an alternative fuel could significantly reduce overdependence on imported oil, while also improving air quality. We should support cost effective development and greater use of this fuel.

Coal

The United States enjoys a rich national endowment of enormous supplies of coal which can provide a secure source of energy for hundreds of years.

- We should aggressively pursue the clean coal technology initiative successfully launched by the Reagan-Bush Administration as part of the solution to coal's environmental problem.
- A major effort should be made to encourage coal exports, which could improve the trade balance, put Americans to work, and provide reliable energy supplies to our allies.

Nuclear Power

We must preserve nuclear power as a safe and economic option to meet future electricity needs. It generates 20 percent of our electricity, and we anticipate the continued expansion of renewable energy and environmentally safe nuclear power. We will promote the adoption of standardized, cost-effective, and environmentally safe nuclear plant designs. We should enhance our efforts to manage nuclear waste and will insist on the highest standards of safety.

Technology, Alternatives, Conservation and Regulation

Technology is America's competitive edge, and it should be encouraged in finding new solutions to our energy problems. Energy efficiency improvements such as more efficient cars, better insulated homes, and more efficient industrial processes, have resulted in substantial savings, making the U.S. economy more competitive.

- We support funding for research and development, particularly where current market economics preclude private initiative.
- We will set priorities and, where cost effective, support research and development for alternative fuels such as ethanol, methanol, and compressed natural gas, particularly for use in transportation.
- We will also support research and development for energy efficiency, conservation, renewables, fusion and superconductivity.
- We encourage the improvement of our national electricity transportation network, to achieve the economic and environmental efficiencies and reliability of linking electricity-exporting regions with importers.

Substantial progress has been made in eliminating the intrusive and costly regulatory functions of the Department of Energy and should be continued. Efforts should be made to streamline the department's functions and evaluate its long-term institutional role in setting national energy policy, in discouraging a return to regulation, and in promoting long-term scientific research.

We believe continued economic progress requires an adequate and secure supply of electricity from every possible source in addition to energy conservation. Conservation alone cannot meet the energy needs of a growing economy. Witness the case of Massachusetts, where the State government's energy policy of stopping construction of any significant electric generating plants of all kinds has caused a dangerous shortage.

Preserving and Protecting the Environment

The Republican Party has a long and honored tradition of preserving and protecting our nation's natural resources and environment. We recognize that the preservation, conservation, and protection of our environment contribute to our health and well-being and that, as citizens, we all share in the responsibility to safeguard our God-given resources. A great Republican President, Teddy Roosevelt, once characterized our environmental challenge as "the great central task of leaving this land even a better land for our descendants than it is for us." Satisfying this imperative requires dedication and a commitment both to the protection of our environment and to the development of economic opportunities for all through a growing economy.

Republicans have led the efforts to protect the environment.

- We have dramatically reduced airborne lead contamination. This reduction has been perhaps the most important contribution to the health of Americans living in urban areas.
- By almost any measure, the air is vastly improved from the 1970s. Carbon monoxide, sulphur dioxide, ozone, nitrogen dioxide, and other emissions have declined substantially.
- We brought record numbers of enforcement cases against toxic polluters based on the principle that polluters should pay for the damages they cause.
- We pioneered an international accord for the protection of the stratospheric ozone layer, the first such international agreement.
- Dramatic progress has been made in protecting coastal barrier islands, in reducing coastal erosion, and in protecting estuaries.
- We have led the fight to clean up our Great Lakes and the Chesapeake and Narragansett Bays, some of the most unique and productive ecosystems on earth.
- We encouraged agricultural conservation, enhanced our wetlands, and preserved and restored our national parks, which had suffered tragic neglect in the years preceding the Reagan-Bush Administration.
- Under Republican leadership, the most important soil conservation measure of the last half-century became law as the Conservation Title of the 1985 Farm Bill.
- We established 34 national wildlife refuges in 21 States and territories.
- We reformed U.S. and international aid programs to assist developing nations to assure environmental protection.

Republicans look to the environmental future with confidence in the

American people and with a renewed commitment to world leadership in environmental protection. We recognize the necessary role of the federal government only in matters that cannot be managed by regional cooperation or by levels of government closer to the people. Cooperative action by all is needed to advance the nation's agenda for a cleaner, safer environment.

The toughest challenges lie ahead of us. Republicans propose the following program for the environment in the 1990s:

- We will work for further reductions in air and water pollution and effective actions against the threats posed by acid rain. These goals can and must be achieved without harmful economic dislocation.
- We are committed to minimizing the release of toxins into the environment.
- We will continue to lead the effort to develop new clean-coal technologies and to remove the barriers that prevent cleaner, alternative fuels from being used.
- We support a comprehensive plan of action to fight coastal erosion and to protect and restore the nation's beaches, coral reefs, bodies of water, wetlands and estuaries such as the Louisiana coast, Chesapeake Bay, the Great Lakes, San Francisco Bay, Puget Sound, Narragansett Bay, and other environmentally sensitive areas. The restoration of these areas will continue to be a priority.
- A top priority of our country must be the continued improvement of our National Parks and wildlife areas. We must upgrade our recreation, fisheries, and wildlife programs in parks, wildlife refuges, forests, and other public lands. We support efforts, including innovative public-private partnerships, to restore declining waterfowl populations and enhance recreational fisheries.
- We will fight to protect endangered species and to sustain biological diversity worldwide.
- We support federal, State, and local policies, including tax code provisions, which lead to the renewal and revitalization of our environment through restoration and which encourage scenic easements designed to preserve farmland and open spaces.
- We will protect the productive capacity of our lands by minimizing erosion.
- We believe public lands should not be transferred to any special group in a manner inconsistent with current Reagan-Bush Administration policy. To the extent possible, consistent with current policy, we should keep public lands open and accessible.
- We are committed to the historic preservation of our American heritage, including our architectural, archaeological, and maritime resoures.
- We support strong enforcement of our environmental laws and are committed to accelerating the pace of our national effort to clean up hazardous waste sites and to protect our groundwater. We will promote

proper use of fertilizers and pesticides to minimize pollution of groundwater.

● Republicans recognize that toxic and hazardous waste production is increasing. Therefore, we will utilize the nation's scientific community to develop solutions to this waste disposal dilemma as an alternative to the continued burying and ocean dumping of these dangerous substances, as they are no more than stop-gap measures with extremely tragic potential.

● We are committed to solving our country's increasing problem of waste disposal. By 1995, half of our existing landfills will be closed, and municipalities will have increased difficulty finding new sites. This is an issue which will require the dedication and resolve of our local communities, the private sector, and all of us as citizens. Resource recovery, recycling, and waste minimalization are critical elements of our solution, and we will work to ensure that innovative approaches to the problem are encouraged.

● We are determined to prevent dumping off our coasts and in international waters. Ocean dumping poses a hazard not only to marine life, but also to those who live along our coasts and to those who use them for recreation. Where federal laws have been violated, we will prosecute polluters to the full extent of the law, including adherence to the 1991 federal ban on ocean dumping of sewage sludge. Where laws need to be strengthened, we will work at the federal, State, and local levels to do so.

● We will support all serious efforts to cope with the special problems of illegal dumping of hospital and medical waste. We pledge close cooperation by the Environmental Protection Agency with States and industry groups to develop new approaches to the most cost-effective means for the safe disposal by responsible medical facilities. Those who continue to dump illegally threaten the very life and health of our communities, and we call for enactment by the States of tough new felony laws that will permit swift prosecution of these criminals.

● We will require that federal departments and agencies meet or exceed the environmental standards set for citizens in the private sector.

Many of the most serious environmental problems that will confront us in the years ahead are global in scope. For example, degradation of the stratospheric ozone layer poses a health hazard not only to Americans, but to all peoples around the globe. The Reagan-Bush Administration successfully pioneered an agreement to attack this problem through worldwide action. In addition, we will continue to lead this effort by promoting private sector initiatives to develop new technologies and adopt processes which protect the ozone layer. A similar ability to develop international agreements to solve complex global problems such as tropical forest destruction, ocean dumping, climate change, and earthquakes will be increasingly vital in the years ahead. All of these efforts will require strong and experienced leadership to lead the other nations of the world in a common effort to combat ecological dangers that threaten all peoples. The Republican Party believes that, toward this end, the National Oceanic and Atmospheric Administration should be joined with the Environmental Protection Agency.

We all have a stake in maintaining the environmental balance and ecological health of our planet and our country. As Republicans, we hold that it is of critical importance to preserve our national heritage. We must assure that programs for economic growth and opportunity sustain the natural abundance of our land and waters and protect the health and well-being of our citizens. As a nation, we should take pride in our accomplishments and look forward to fulfilling our obligation of leaving this land an even better place for our children and future generations.

Transportation for America

Republican leadership has revitalized America's transportation system. Through regulatory reform, we increased efficiency in all major modes of transportation. By making our national transportation system safer, more convenient, and less expensive, we have both strengthened our economy and served the interests of all the American people:

- Aviation deregulation now saves consumers $11 billion annually through improved productivity and lower air fares. Millions more Americans can now afford to fly. Even though more people are flying, the overall safety record for commercial aviation during the past four years has been the best in history.
- The National Airspace System (NAS) Plan is upgrading virtually all the equipment in the air traffic control system to meet safety and capacity needs into the next century.
- Rail freight service has been rescued from the brink of insolvency and revitalized. Railroads have lowered rates for many shippers, helping to keep the transportation cost of coal-generated electric power down and making America's farmers more competitive abroad.
- The creation of regional and short-line railroads has been encouraged by the Reagan-Bush Administration. The development of these small businesses has been a welcome alternative to railroad abandonments, and we will continue to encourage their growth.
- The Reagan-Bush Administration achieved new rail safety legislation which expands federal jurisdiction over drug, alcohol, and safety violations.
- America's trucking industry has also been improved. The number of motor carriers has more than doubled since regulatory barriers to competition were removed. Many of these new carriers are small or minority-owned businesses. Private enterprise has thus been able to restructure routes, reduce empty backhauls, and simplify rates. Reduced regulation saves the American consumer $37 billion annually in lower freight bills, making businesses in every part of America more competitive.

- The successful sale of Conrail through a public offering recouped nearly $2 billion dollars of the taxpayers' investment in bankrupt railroads from the 1970s.
- The Reagan-Bush Administration has undertaken a comprehensive program to upgrade federal interstate highways and bridges.
- Through highway improvements, education, and federal encouragement of tougher State laws against drunk driving, highway safety has vastly improved.

As we look to the future, the Republican Party will continue to press for improved transportation safety, reduced costs, and greater availability and convenience of transportation through more open markets and other mechanisms. The Republican Party believes that:

- Americans demand that those entrusted with their safety while operating commercial motor vehicles, railroads, or aircraft will not use drugs or alcohol. While we will protect individual rights, the Republican Party supports comprehensive efforts to curb drug and alcohol abuse in transportation, including drug and alcohol testing of all those in safety-related positions.
- Our transportation system is based upon a vast public and private investment in infrastructure, which must continue to grow and to be maintained to meet America's needs. We advocate greater local autonomy in decision-making concerning the Highway Trust Fund and the Airport and Airway Trust Fund, and we oppose diversion of their resources to other purposes.
- Research should be developed for new technologies to deal with urban gridlock and congested highways.
- The travel and tourism industry is a positive force in enhancing cultural understanding and sustaining economic prosperity. We recognize its important contributions and should work to encourage its continued growth.
- The federal government and local communities must work together to develop additional airport capacity of all types. At the same time, we support timely completion of the National Airspace System plan and continuing augmentation of air traffic control and aircraft inspection personnel.
- We will further increase American jobs and trade opportunities by assuring that American air carriers are afforded full and fair access to international route authorities.
- We will not abandon the economic flexibility that has so enormously strengthened the health of our railroads and so powerfully benefited the American economy.
- Development of high speed rail systems to meet the needs for intercity travel should be encouraged.
- Year by year since 1981, Amtrak operations have shown improvement. Amtrak's ratio of revenues to costs stood at 48 percent in 1981. Last

year, 65 percent of the costs were covered by revenues. Fiscal year 1988 will see the ratio pushing 70 percent. We recognize that intercity rail passenger service plays an important role in our transportation system. At the same time, we support continued reduction in public subsidies.

- A new spirit of competitive enterprise in transportation throughout all levels of government should be encouraged. We will encourage both States and cities to utilize private companies, where effective, to operate commuter bus and transit services at substantial savings over what publicly funded systems cost.
- The engines of innovation powered by regulatory reform have brought forth exciting advances in the technology of trucking, rail, and shipping, particularly as they work together as an integrated system for the movement of goods domestically and abroad. Alternative fuels, that are clean and efficient, will both improve air quality and reduce our dependence on imported oil in meeting transportation needs. These technological approaches are far preferable to outmoded regulation, such as the current design of corporate average fuel economy (CAFE) standards, which create substantial advantages for foreign auto manufacturers and actually promote the export of U.S. jobs.
- We consider a privately owned merchant fleet and domestic shipbuilding capacity necessary to carry our nation's commerce in peace and to support our defense responsibilities. We will support programs to give the American maritime industry greater flexibility and freedom in meeting foreign competition.
- We are committed to continuing the Reagan-Bush Administration efforts to stop foreign protectionism that inhibits U.S. flag vessels from fairly competing abroad.
- Maritime safety, search and rescue, military preparedness, environmental and fisheries enforcement, and drug interdiction have long been the responsibility of the U.S. Coast Guard. The Republican Party supports all of these vital roles, and we will support funding and manpower adequate to enable the Coast Guard to carry out its responsibilities.

America Leading the World

Under the leadership of President Ronald Reagan and Vice President George Bush, America has led the world through eight years of peace and prosperity.

In the years since 1980, our nation has become in fact what it has always been in principle, "the last best hope of mankind on earth."

Republicans know that free nations are peace loving and do not threaten other democracies. To the extent, therefore, that democracies are established in the world, America will be safer. Consequently, our nation has a compelling interest to encourage and help actively to build the conditions of democracy wherever people strive for freedom.

In 1961, President John Kennedy said, "We shall pay any price, bear any burden, meet any hardship, support any friend, oppose any foe to assure the survival and success of liberty." Seeds sown by the Reagan-Bush Administration to make good on that promise are now bearing fruit.

Today's Republican Party has the only legitimate claim to this legacy, for our opposition to totalitarianism is resolute. For those Democrats who came of age politically under the party of [Harry S.] Truman and Kennedy, the message is clear: The old Democrat world view of realistic anti-communism, with real freedom as its goal, has been abandoned by today's national Democrat Party.

In the tradition of the Republican Party, we have long-term foreign-policy goals and objectives which provide vision and leadership. We also have a *realistic,* long-term strategy to match those goals. The primary objectives of foreign policy must be defending the United States of America and its people; protecting America's vital national interests abroad; and, fostering peace, stability and security throughout the world through democratic self-determination and economic prosperity.

To accomplish these goals, we believe our policies must be built upon three basic pillars: strength, realism, and dialogue.

Republican foreign policy, based on a peace preserved by steadfastly providing for our own security, brought us the INF [Intermediate-Range Nuclear-Force] treaty, which eliminated an entire class of nuclear weapons. America's determination and will, coupled with our European allies' staunch cooperation, brought the Soviets to the bargaining table and won meaningful reductions in nuclear weapons. The INF treaty was not won by unilateral concessions or the unilateral canceling of weapons programs.

Today's Republican foreign policy has been tested and validated. Our formula for success is based on a realistic assessment of the world as it is, not as some would like it to be. The Soviet retreat from Afghanistan is not the result of luck or the need of the Kremlin to save a few rubles. It is a direct result of a Republican policy known as the Reagan Doctrine: our determination to provide meaningful aid to people who would rather die on their feet than live on their knees under the yoke of Soviet-supported oppression. Support for freedom-fighters, coupled with an openness to negotiate, will be the model for our resistance to Marxist expansionism elsewhere.

The world expects the United States to lead. Republicans believe it is in our country's best interest to continue to do so. For this reason, we will engage both our adversaries and friends. We share a common interest in survival and peaceful competition. However, the Reagan-Bush Administration has shown that dialogue and engagement can be successful only if undertaken from a position of strength. We know something the national Democrats seem to have forgotten: If a foreign policy is based upon weakness or unrealistic assumptions about the world, it is doomed to failure. If it is based upon naivete, it will be doomed to disaster.

Under our constitutional system, the execution of foreign policy is the prime responsibility of the executive branch. We therefore denounce the excessive interference in this function by the current Democrat majority in the Congress, as it creates the appearance of weakness and confusion and endangers the successful conduct of American foreign policy.

The world in 1988 shows the success of peace through strength and the Reagan Doctrine advancing America's national interests. Our relations with the Soviets are now based on these determined and realistic policies. Results such as the INF treaty are a concrete example of the soundness of this approach:

- The Afghan people are on the verge of ridding their country of Soviet occupation, and with our continued support they can secure true liberty.
- In Southeast Asia, our policies of isolation toward Vietnam and our support for the Cambodian resistance have contributed to Vietnam's decision to get out of Cambodia.
- In southern Africa, Cuban troops may soon be leaving Angola; Namibia may soon enjoy independence.
- The Iran-Iraq war is closer to a settlement due to the strong leadership of the Reagan-Bush Administration in the United Nations and the American presence in the Persian Gulf.

The party Abraham Lincoln helped to establish—the party of Teddy Roosevelt, Dwight Eisenhower, Ronald Reagan, and George Bush—today offers the United States of America continued leadership, strong and effective. The President of the United States must be a good Commander-in-Chief; the Oval Office is no place for on-the-job training. The Republican Party, tempered by real-world experience, accustomed to making tough choices, is prepared to lead America forward into the 1990s.

The Americas

Our future is intimately tied to the future of the Americas. Family, language, culture, environment and trade link us closely with both Canada and Mexico. Our relations with both of these friends will be based upon continuing cooperation and our mutually shared interests. Our attention to trade and environmental issues will contribute to strong economic growth and prosperity throughout the Americas.

Today, more Latin Americans than ever before live free because of their partnership with the United States to promote self-determination, democracy, and an end to subversion. The Republican party reaffirms its strong support of the Monroe Doctrine as the foundation for our policy throughout the Hemisphere, and pledges to conduct foreign policy in accord with its principles. We therefore seek not only to provide for our own security, but also to create a climate for democracy and self-determination throughout the Americas.

Central America has always been a region of strategic importance for the United States. There, Nicaragua has become a Soviet client state like Cuba. Democratic progress in the region is threatened directly by the

Sandinista military machine and armed subversion exported from Nicaragua, Cuba, and the Soviet Union. The Sandinistas are now equipped with Soviet arms which, in quality and quantity, are far in excess of their own defense requirements.

The people of Nicaragua are denied basic human, religious, and political rights by the Sandinista junta. Today, thousands of Nicaraguans are united in a struggle to free their homeland from a totalitarian regime. The Republican Party stands shoulder to shoulder with them with both humanitarian and military aid. Peace without freedom for the Nicaraguan people is not good enough.

If democracy does not prevail, if Nicaragua remains a communist dictatorship dedicated to exporting revolution, the fragile democracies in Central America will be jeopardized. The Republican Party stands with them in their struggle for peace, freedom, and economic growth. We express our emphatic support for the people and government of El Salvador, a target of foreign-directed insurgency. Under Republican leadership, the United States will respond to requests from our Central American neighbors for security assistance to protect their emerging democracies against insurgencies sponsored by the Soviets, Cuba, or others.

Democracy continues to prosper in El Salvador, Guatemala, Honduras, and in Costa Rica, the region's oldest democracy. However, economic growth in these countries has not matched their political progress. The United States must take the lead in strengthening democratic institutions through economic development based on free market principles. We pledge our continued support to the peoples of the Americas who embrace and sustain democratic principles in their self-government.

A Republican Administration will continue to promote policy reforms to free the private sector, such as deregulation of enterprise and privatization of government corporations. We will assist friendly democracies in reviving the institutions of regional economic cooperation and integration, and will allow Nicaragua to participate when it enjoys a free, pluralist society and respects free-market principles.

The growth of democracy and freedom throughout Latin America is one of the most positive foreign policy developments of the 1980s. Republican leadership has created the environment necessary for this growth. Over the past decade, Latin Americans have moved boldly toward democracy, with 26 of 33 nations now democratic or in transition toward democracy. Mexico has a special strategic and economic importance to the United States, and we encourage close cooperation across a wide variety of fronts in order to strengthen further this critical relationship.

We believe the governments of Latin America must band together to defeat the drug trade which now flourishes in the region. We must pledge our full cooperation and support for efforts to induce producers of illicit drug crops to substitute other methods of generating income.

Republicans will continue to oppose any normalization of relations with the government of Cuba as long as Fidel Castro continues to oppress the Cuban people at home and to support international terrorism and drug trafficking abroad. We will vigorously continue our support for establishment of a genuinely representative government directly elected by the Cuban people. We reiterate our support of Radio Marti and urge the creation of TV Marti to better reach the oppressed people of Cuba.

Panama now poses a different challenge to the regional progress made over the past eight years. Our policy must be as firm with respect to military authoritarianism and narco-terrorism as it is with communist tyranny and guerrilla subversion. That policy must include a determined effort to bring to justice any identified narco-terrorist or drug dealer within his or her country of residence or in the courts of the United States of America. Republicans view the Panama Canal as a critical, strategic artery connecting the Atlantic and Pacific. We believe that U.S. access to the Panama Canal must remain free and unencumbered consistent with the foremost principle of the Canal Treaty. We acknowledge, however, the historical partnership and friendship between the American and Panamanian people.

Republicans believe that an active, engaged America, clear of purpose and steady in action, is essential to continued progress in Latin America. Passivity and neglect are a sure prescription for the reversal of freedom and peace in Latin America.

The Soviet Union: New Challenges and Enduring Realities

Steady American leadership is needed now more than ever to deal with the challenges posed by a rapidly changing Soviet Union. Americans cannot afford a future administration which eagerly attempts to embrace perceived, but as yet unproven, changes in Soviet policy. Nor can we indulge naive inexperience or an overly enthusiastic endorsement of current Soviet rhetoric.

The current leaders in the Soviet Union came to power while the United States was undergoing an unsurpassed political, economic, and military resurgence. The Reagan-Bush success story—new jobs and unprecedented economic growth combined with reasserted leadership of the free world—was not lost on the new Soviet regime. It had inherited a bankrupt economy, a society with a Third World standard of living, and military power based upon the sweat of the Soviet workers. Confronted by the failure of their system, the new Soviet leaders have been forced to search for new solutions.

Republicans are proud that it was a Republican President who extended freedom's hand and message to the Soviet Union. It will be a new Republican President who can best build on that progress, ever cautious of communism's long history of expansionism and false promises. We are prepared to embrace real reform, but we will not leave America unprepared should reform prove illusory.

Soviet calls for global peace and harmony ring hollow when compared with ongoing Soviet support for communist guerrillas and governments throughout the Third World. Even in Afghanistan, the Soviet Union is in retreat not as a result of a more benevolent Soviet world view, but because of the courage of determined Mujaheddin freedom fighters fully supported by the United States.

The Soviet military continues to grow. Tanks and aircraft continue to roll off Soviet production lines at a rate two to three times that of the United States.

Soviet military doctrine remains offensive in nature, as illustrated by the intimidating presence of massed Soviet tank divisions in Eastern Europe. This is the reality of Soviet military posture.

With a realistic view of the Soviet Union and the appropriate role of arms reductions in the U.S.-Soviet relationship, the Reagan-Bush Administration concluded the historic INF agreement with the Soviet Union. Ongoing negotiations with the Soviet Union to reduce strategic nuclear weapons by 50 percent are possible because the American people trust Republican leadership. The American people know that, for Republicans, no agreement is better than an agreement detrimental to the security of the free world. To pursue arms control for its own sake or at any cost is naive and dangerous.

Republicans will continue to work with the new Soviet leadership. But the terms of the relationship will be based upon persistent and steady attention to certain fundamental principles:

- Human and religious rights in the Soviet Union.
- Economic reform in the Soviet Union.
- Cessation of Soviet support for communist regimes, radical groups, and terrorists.
- Verified full compliance with all arms control agreements.
- The right of free emigration for all Soviet citizens.
- Reduction in the Soviets' massive offensive strategic and conventional capability. In other words, Soviet military doctrine must match its rhetoric.
- An end to untied credits, particularly general purpose loans which provide the Soviet Union with desperately needed hard currency to bolster its weak economy and facilitate illicit Soviet purchase of U.S. technology.

Republicans proudly reaffirm the Reagan Doctrine: America's commitment to aid freedom-fighters against the communist oppression which destroys freedom and the human spirit. We salute the liberation of Grenada. We affirm our support for the heroic fighters in the Afghan resistance and pledge to see them through to the end of their struggle. We pledge political and material support to democratic liberation movements around the world.

Republicans believe human rights are advanced most where freedom is advanced first. We call on the Soviet government to release political prisoners, allow free emigration for "refuseniks" and others, and introduce full religious tolerance. Soviet Jews, Christians, and other ethnic and religious groups are systematically persecuted, denied the right to emigrate, and prevented from freely practicing their religious beliefs. This situation is intolerable, and Republicans demand an end to all of these discriminatory practices.

We support the desire for freedom and self-determination of all those living in Captive Nations. The Republican Party denounces the oppression of the national free will of Poles, Hungarians, Czechoslovakians, East Germans, Bulgarians, Romanians, and Albanians. We support the desire for freedom of Estonians, Latvians, Lithuanians, Ukrainians, the people of the Caucasus, and other peoples held captive in the Soviet Union. We support the Solidarity free trade union movement in Poland.

We find the violation of human rights on the basis of religion or culture to be morally repugnant to the values we hold. Historical tragedies—like the Holocaust or the terrible persecution suffered by the Armenian people—vividly remind us of the need for vigilance in protecting and promoting human rights. We and others must ensure that such tragedies occur never again.

The Republican Party commends the Reagan-Bush Administration for its far-sighted efforts to modernize our electronic tools of public diplomacy to reach the Captive Nations. The Voice of America, Worldnet, Radio Free Europe and Radio Liberty are on the leading edge of our public diplomacy efforts. These electronic means of communication are force-multipliers of truth. They attack one of the darkest pillars of totalitarianism: the oppression of people through the control of information. We urge the further use of advanced technologies such as Direct Broadcast Satellites and videotape, as well as continuing use of television and radio broadcasting, to articulate the values of individual liberty throughout the world.

Combatting Narcotics: Defending Our Children

By eradication at the source, interdiction in transit, education and deterrence against use, prompt extradition of drug kingpins, or rehabilitation, America must be drug free. No nation can remain free when its children are enslaved by drugs. We consider drugs a major national security threat to the United States.

We urge all nations to unite against this evil. Although we salute our hemispheric neighbors who are fighting the war on drugs, we expect all nations to help stop this deadly commerce. We pledge aggressive interdiction and eradication, with strong penalties against countries which shield or condone the narcotics traffic.

Republicans are proud of the fact that we have dramatically increased the interdiction of dangerous drugs. For example, over the past 6 years, our annual seizure of cocaine has increased by over 1,500 percent. While much has been accomplished in eradicating drugs at the source and in transit, much more remains to be done.

We will use our armed forces in the war on drugs to the maximum extent practical. We must emphasize their special capabilities in surveillance and command and control for interdiction and in special operations for eradication of drugs at the source.

To fight international drug trade, we will stress the swift extradition of traffickers. We support a comprehensive use of America's resources to apprehend and convict drug dealers. To enforce anti-drug policy, we pledge to enhance eradication efforts with increased herbicide use; regulate exports of "precursor chemicals" used in the manufacture of illicit drugs; train and equip cooperating government law-enforcement agencies; emphasize a strategy to "choke off" drug supply routes; and impose the death penalty for drug kingpins and those who kill federal law enforcement agents.

Europe and the
Defense of the West

The United States and Europe share a wide array of political, economic, and military relationships, all vitally important to the United States. Together they represent a growing, multifaceted bond between America and the European democracies.

Culturally, as well as militarily, we share common goals with Western Europe. The preservation of liberty is first among these. We will not allow the cultural, economic, or political domination of Western Europe by the Soviet Union. Our own national security requires it, for our democracy cannot flourish in isolation. The United States, led by the Reagan-Bush Administration, and our European allies have successfully reasserted democracy's ideological appeal. This formula is without equal for political and economic progress.

Republicans believe that the continued growth of trade between Europe and the United States is in the best interest of both the American people and their European friends. However, this economic relationship must be based upon the principle of free and fair trade. Protectionism and other barriers to American products will not be tolerated. The American people demand economic fair play in U.S.-European trade.

The recently signed INF treaty has proven that NATO's dual track policy of improving NATO nuclear forces in Europe, while negotiating arms reductions with the Soviet Union, was the only way to make the Soviet leadership accept meaningful nuclear arms reductions. NATO's cohesion as an alliance, when assaulted by Soviet propaganda attacks during the 1980s, proved its resilience. Bolstered by the strong leadership of the United States, Europe stood firm in opposing Soviet demands for a nuclear freeze and unilateral disarmament.

American aid and European industriousness have restored West Europe to a position of global strength. In accord with this, the Republican Party believes that all members of NATO should bear their fair share of the defense burden.

Republicans consider consultation and cooperation with our allies and friends to stop the proliferation of ballistic missile technology is a crucial allied goal. We believe that continued support for the Strategic Defense Initiative will yield the type of defensive insurance policy the American people want for themselves and their allies.

We share a deep concern for peace and justice in Northern Ireland and condemn all violence and terrorism in that strife-torn land. We support the process of peace and reconciliation established by the Anglo-Irish Agreement, and we encourage new investment and economic reconstruction in Northern Ireland on the basis of strict equality of opportunity and non-discrimination in employment.

The Republican Party strongly encourages the peaceful settlement of the long-standing dispute on Cyprus.

The future of U.S. relations with Europe is one of endless opportunity and potential. Increased cooperation and consultation will necessarily lead to greater economic, political and military integration, thus strengthening the natural bonds between the democratic peoples on both sides of the Atlantic. This will require a seasoned American leadership, able to build on the achievements of the Reagan-Bush Administration and prepared to lead the alliance into the 1990s and beyond.

Asia and the Pacific

Democratic capitalism is transforming Asia. Nations of the Pacific Rim have become colleagues in the enterprise of freedom. They have shown a strong capacity for economic growth and capital development.

The Asia-Pacific arena continues to be a vital strategic interest for the U.S. and is an area of increased military, economic, and diplomatic activity for the Soviet Union.

Japan has assumed the role earned by her people as a world economic power. The GOP believes that our relations can only be strengthened by attacking trade barriers, both tariff and nontariff, which not only hurt the U.S. now but also will eventually distort Japan's own economy. We believe that it is time for Japan to assume a greater role in this region and elsewhere. This should include a greater commitment to its own defense, commitment to leading the way in alleviating Third World debt, and fostering economic growth in fragile democracies.

Today, democracy is renewed on Taiwan, the Philippines, and South Korea and is emerging elsewhere in the area. We pledge full cooperation in mutual defense of the Philippines and South Korea and the maintenance of our troops and bases vital for deterring aggression. The United States, with its friends and allies, will strengthen democratic institutions in the Philippines by assisting in its economic development and growth. We reaffirm our commitment to the security of Taiwan and other key friends and allies in the region. We regard any attempt to alter Taiwan's status by force as a threat to the entire region. We adhere to the Taiwan Relations Act, the basis for our continuing cooperation with those who have loyally stood with us, and fought at our side, for half a century.

Today, the communist regime of the People's Republic of China looks to free market practices to salvage its future from stagnant Marxism. We welcome this development. As we draw closer in our relationship, the Republican Party believes that we must continue to encourage the abandonment of political repression in the People's Republic of China and movement toward a free market. We also look toward continued improvement in mutually beneficial trade between our two nations.

We recognize the significant progress made by the Reagan-Bush Administration to assure the end of the Soviet occupation of Afghanistan. We will continue to press for self-determination and the establishment of a genuinely representative government directly elected by the Afghan people. We pledge to continue full military and humanitarian support and supplies for the resistance until complete Soviet withdrawal is realized.

We commend the government of Pakistan for its opposition to the Soviet occupation of Afghanistan and its support of the Afghan people, particularly its refugees. We reaffirm our friendship and will continue the strong security assistance relationship between the United States and Pakistan.

We will press for the withdrawal of Vietnamese occupation of Laos and Cambodia and will continue support for the efforts of the non-Communist resistance.

Republicans insist that Vietnam, Laos, and Cambodia must provide adequate information on American POWs and MIAs. The grief of the POW and MIA families is a constant reminder to all Americans of the patriotic sacrifice made by their missing loved ones. Republicans will not rest until we know the fate of those missing in Indochina. We will continue to press relentlessly for a full accounting of America's POWs and MIAs. We put the government of Vietnam on notice that there will be no improvement in U.S.-Vietnam relations until such a satisfactory full accounting has been provided by the government of Vietnam.

Republicans are committed to providing assistance for refugees fleeing Vietnam, Laos, and Cambodia. Republicans strongly believe that the promise of asylum for these refugees must be met by adequate resources and vigorous administration of refugee programs. We will increase efforts to resettle Vietnamese refugees under the orderly departure program. We are particularly committed to assisting the resettlement of Amerasian children against whom brutal discrimination is practiced.

We recognize the close and special ties we have maintained with Thailand since the days of Abraham Lincoln. Thailand stands tall against the imperialist aggression of Vietnam and the Soviet Union in Southeast Asia.

Republicans strongly support our traditional close bilateral relations with our ally Australia. We also look forward to a rejuvenation of the

ANZUS [Australia, New Zealand and the United States] alliance with its benefits and responsibilities to all partners.

The Middle East

The foundation of our policy in the Middle East has been and must remain the promotion of a stable and lasting peace, recognizing our moral and strategic relationship with Israel. More than any of its predecessors, the Reagan-Bush Administration solidified this partnership. As a result, the relations between the United States and Israel are closer than ever before.

We will continue to maintain Israel's qualitative advantage over any adversary or coalition of adversaries.

We will continue to solidify our strategic relationship with Israel by taking additional concrete steps to further institutionalize our partnership. This will include maintaining adequate levels of security and economic assistance; continuing our meetings on military, political and economic cooperation and coordination; prepositioning military equipment; developing joint contingency plans; and increasing joint naval and air exercises. The growth of the Soviets' military presence in the Eastern Mediterranean and along NATO's southern flank has demonstrated the importance of developing and expanding the U.S.-Israel strategic relationship.

We oppose the creation of an independent Palestinian state; its establishment is inimical to the security interests of Israel, Jordan and the U.S. We will not support the creation of any Palestinian entity that could place Israel's security in jeopardy.

Republicans will build upon the efforts of the Reagan-Bush Administration and work for peace between Israel and her Arab neighbors based upon the following principles:

- A just and lasting peace is essential, urgent, and can be reached only through direct negotiations between Israel and the Arab nations.
- Peace treaties must be reached through direct negotiations and must never be imposed upon unwilling partners.
- The PLO should have no role in the peace process unless it recognizes Israel's right to exist, accepts United Nations Security Council resolutions 242 and 338, renounces terrorism, and removes language from its charter demanding Israel's destruction.

Under Republican leadership, the United States will explore every opportunity to move forward the peace process toward direct negotiations as long as the security of Israel is not compromised. Much work remains to establish a climate in the Middle East where the legitimate rights of all parties, including the Palestinians, can be equitably addressed.

We recognize that Israel votes with the United States at the United Nations more frequently than any other nation. The Reagan-Bush Administration supported legislation mandating that if the U.N. and its agencies were to deny Israel's right to participate, the United States would withhold financial support and withdraw from those bodies until their action was rectified. The Republican Party reaffirms its support for the rescission of U.N. Resolution 3379, which equates Zionism with racism. Failure to repeal that resolution will justify attenuation of our support for the U.N.

We believe that Jerusalem should remain an undivided city, with free and unimpeded access to all holy places by people of all faiths.

Republicans see Egypt as a catalyst in the Arab world for advancing the cause of regional peace and security. For this reason, we believe that the United States has a significant stake in Egypt's continuing economic development and growth. As the only Arab nation to have formally made peace with Israel, it is reaping the benefits. Egypt's support of the Camp David Accords demonstrates that an Arab nation can make peace with Israel, be an ally of the U.S., and remain in good standing in the Arab world. Republicans support the Reagan-Bush Administration's formal designation of Egypt as a major non-NATO ally.

Our continued support of Egypt and other pro-Western Arab states is an essential component of Republican policy. In support of that policy, we deployed a naval task force to join with allies to keep the sea lanes open during the Iran-Iraq war. We also recognize the important role the moderate Arab states play in supporting U.S. security interests.

Republicans will continue to build on the Reagan-Bush achievement of increased security cooperation with the pro-Western Arab states. We recognize that these Arab nations maintain friendly relations with the United States in the face of potential retaliation attempts by radical elements in the Middle East.

Continuing strife in Lebanon is not in the interest of the U.S. Until order is established, Lebanon will be a source of international terrorism and regional instability. To re-establish normalcy in Lebanon, the U.S. must strengthen the hand of the overwhelming majority of Lebanese, who are committed to an independent, peaceful, and democratic Lebanon.

In order to achieve this goal, we will base the policy of the United States on the principles of the unity of Lebanon; the withdrawal of all foreign forces; the territorial integrity of Lebanon; the re-establishment of its government's authority; and the reassertion of Lebanese sovereignty throughout the nation, with recognition that its safekeeping must be the responsibility of the Lebanese government. We will strive to help Lebanon restore its society so that, in the future as in the past, religious groups will live in harmony, international commerce will flourish and international terrorism will not exist.

For nearly four decades, U.S. policy in the Persian Gulf has reflected American strategic, economic, and political interests in the area. Republican policy has three fundamental objectives:

- Maintaining the free flow of oil.
- Preventing the expansion of Soviet influence.
- Supporting the independence and stability of the states in the region.

By pursuing those goals, we have created the political leverage to begin the process of ending the Iran-Iraq war. Our re-flagging of Kuwaiti ships limited the expansion of both Iranian and Soviet influence in the region.

Africa

Republicans have three priorities in our country's relations with Africa. The first is to oppose the forces of Marxist imperialism, which sustain the march of tyranny in Africa. This priority includes giving strong assistance to groups which oppose Soviet and Cuban-sponsored oppression in Africa.

Our second priority is the need to develop and sustain democracies in Africa. Democrats have often taken the view that democracy is unattainable because of Africa's economic condition, yet at the same time they refuse to promote the conditions in which democracies can flourish. Economic freedom and market-based economies are the key to the development of democracy throughout Africa.

Our third area of concern is humanitarian assistance, especially food aid, to African nations. The Reagan-Bush Administration has always provided it.

Republicans salute the Reagan-Bush Administration for responding with characteristic American compassion to famine conditions in Africa by providing record amounts of food, medical supplies, and other life-saving assistance. In spite of our efforts, the people of Africa continue to suffer. Republicans condemn the cynical Marxist governments, especially in Ethiopia, which use planned starvation as a weapon of war and a tool for forced migration.

The recent African drought and resulting famine were not just natural disasters. They were made worse by poorly conceived development projects which stripped lands of their productive capacity. Republicans recognize that protecting the natural resource base of developing nations is essential to protecting future economic opportunities and assuring stable societies. We are leading the fight worldwide to require sound environmental planning as part of foreign development programs.

We believe that peace in southern Africa can best be achieved by the withdrawal of all foreign forces from Angola, complete independence and self-determination for the people of Namibia, a rapid process of internal reconciliation, and free and fair elections in both places. The Reagan-Bush Administration has worked tirelessly to achieve this outcome; and while obstacles remain, we are closer than ever to a comprehensive settlement of these interrelated conflicts. America's strong support for Angolan freedom-fighters has helped make this progress possible. We also oppose the maintenance of communist forces and influence in Mozambique.

Republicans deplore the apartheid system of South Africa and consider it morally repugnant. All who value human liberty understand the evil of apartheid, and we will not rest until apartheid is eliminated from South Africa. That will remain our goal. Republicans call for an effective and coordinated policy that will promote equal rights and a peaceful transition to a truly representative constitutional form of government for all South Africans and the citizens of all nations throughout Africa. We deplore violence employed against innocent blacks and whites from whatever source.

We believe firmly that one element in the evolution of black political progress must be black economic progress; actions designed to pressure the government of South Africa must not have the effect of adversely affecting the rising aspirations and achievements of black South African entrepreneurs and workers and their families. We should also encourage the development of strong democratic black political institutions to aid in the peaceful transition to majority rule. Republicans believe that it is wrong to punish innocent black South Africans for the policies of the apartheid government of South Africa.

Child Survival Program

The health of children in the developing countries of Asia, Africa, the Near East, Latin America and the Caribbean has been a priority of the Reagan-Bush Administration. Republicans have designated the Child Survival Program as one of our highest foreign assistance priorities. With the creation of the Child Survival Fund in early 1985, we have helped to ensure that children in developing countries worldwide get a decent start in life.

Our commitment to the Child Survival Program is more than a compassionate response to this challenge. It is in part an indication of the success of the program. Child Survival funding has been put to good use, and it is making a difference. Experience has shown that a few dollars go a long way in saving a child's life.

Republican efforts have seen results. The pilot studies begun by the Reagan-Bush Administration a few years ago have resulted in child survival programs that today are reaching hundreds of thousands of women and children in the developing world. Policies are in place, health workers are trained, and host governments throughout the world are committed to child survival programs.

Republicans are committed to continuing our contribution to this vital program. As we look forward to the 1990s, many countries will have achieved what only a few years ago seemed like unattainable goals. Those countries need to find ways to sustain those achievements. It will not be easy. For other countries, the road to these goals will be longer as they strive to give every child what should be his or her birthright, a chance to thrive.

We can help them. We can provide leadership and support. We are committed to sustaining this effort to save and improve the lives of the world's children.

We commend the Reagan-Bush Administration for its courageous defense of human life in population programs around the world. We support its refusal to fund international organizations involved in abortion.

Stopping International Terrorism and
Dealing with Low-Intensity Conflict

The nature of warfare itself has changed. Terrorism is a unique form of warfare that attacks and threatens security and stability around the world. Ranging from the attempted assassination of the Pope and car-bomb attacks on American USO clubs, to narco-subversion in the nations of the West, terrorism seeks to silence freedom as an inalienable right of Man.

The world of totalitarianism and anti-Western fanatics have joined forces in this campaign of terror. The goals of their undeclared war against the democracies are the withdrawal of our presence internationally and the retraction of our freedoms domestically.

The Republican Party believes that, in order to prevent terrorist attacks, the United States must maintain an unsurpassed intelligence capability. In cases of terrorism where prevention and deterrence are not enough, we believe that the United States must be prepared to use an appropriate mix of diplomatic, political, and military pressure and action to defeat the terrorist attack. The United States must continue to push for a Western commitment to a "no-concessions" policy on terrorism.

The Republican Party understands that many problems facing our country are centered on "Low Intensity Conflicts." These include insurgencies, organized terrorism, paramilitary actions, sabotage, and other forms of violence in the gray area between peace and declared conventional warfare. Unlike the Democrat Party, Republicans understand that the threat against the vital interests of the United States covers a broad spectrum of conflict. We are committed to defending the people of the United States at all levels. To implement that commitment, we will rely on the planning and strategy of the U.S. Special Operations Command and other Department of Defense offices.

We commend the Reagan-Bush Administration for its willingness to provide a measured response to terrorists such as Libya's Colonel Qadhafi. We affirm our determination to continue isolating his outlaw regime. We applaud the Reagan-Bush Administration's dispatch in implementing the Omnibus Diplomatic Security and Anti Terrorism Act of 1986. We are strongly committed to obtaining the freedom of all Americans held captive by terrorist elements in the Middle East. Where possible, we will hold accountable those responsible for such heinous acts. We also support foreign military assistance that enables friendly nations to provide for their own defense, including defense against terrorism.

We recognize the increasing threat of terrorism to our overall national security. We will pursue a forward-leaning posture toward terrorism, and are prepared to act in concert with other nations or unilaterally, as necessary, to prevent or respond to terrorist attacks. Our policy will emphasize preemptive anti-terrorist measures; allied and international cooperation; negotiation toward an international agreement to facilitate pre-emptive and proactive measures against terrorists and narco-terrorists; and creation of a multi-national strike force, on the authority granted in a multi-national agreement, specializing in counterterrorism, intelligence and narcotics control.

Republicans believe that, when necessary, our own armed forces must have the capability to meet terrorist crises. Our support for defense forces specifically equipped and trained to conduct unconventional warfare has resulted in important improvements in this critical area. Under the Reagan-Bush Administration, major improvements have been made in the special operations force's readiness, manning, and modernization.

The Republican Party is strongly committed to increased support for unconventional forces by streamlining the bureaucracy which supports them, building the weapons and platforms which are a minimal requirement for their success, and funding the research and development needed for their future vigor. We wholeheartedly support greater international cooperation to counter terrorism and to ensure the safety of innocent citizens travelling abroad.

State Department Organization

The United States depends upon effective diplomacy to protect and advance its interests abroad. Modern diplomacy requires an institution capable of integrating the international dimension of our national values and concerns into a coherent foreign policy. That institution must be made fully responsive to the guidance and direction provided by our country's political leadership.

This requires a truly hierarchical decision-making structure in the Department of State to assure that issues not directly decided by the Secretary of State are not out of reach of politically accountable authority.

Republicans commend the efforts initiated by the Reagan Administration, and in particular the Secretary of State, to restructure and streamline management of the department in order to provide for greater flexibility, efficiency and accountability.

We will continue these efforts in the areas of organization, personnel, and responsiveness as part of a long-term program to make the Department of State more immediately responsive to a complex and changing world.

Peace Through Strength—A Proven Policy

Peace through strength is now a proven policy. We have modernized our forces, revitalized our military infrastructure, recruited and trained the most capable fighting force in American history. And we have used these tools with care, responsibility, and restraint.

The Reagan-Bush national security program has restored America's credibility in the world. Our security and that of our allies have been dramatically enhanced; the opportunities for the United States to be a positive force for freedom and democracy throughout the world have expanded, and the chances for new breakthroughs for peace have risen dramatically.

Republicans will build upon this record and advance the cause of world freedom and world peace by using our military credibility as a vehicle for security at home and peace abroad.

These new opportunities for peace and world freedom pose new challenges to America.

The INF Treaty, the first treaty to actually reduce the number of nuclear weapons, was made possible by our commitment to peace through strength. It will impose new demands on our armed forces. We will redouble our commitment to correct a dangerous imbalance of conventional forces both through negotiation and through force improvements.

The Carter Administration left our armed forces in a dangerously weakened position. Ten of the Army's 16 divisions were rated as "not combat ready" due to shortages of skilled manpower, spare parts, fuel, ammunition, and training. For the same reasons, more than 40 percent of the U.S. Air Force and Navy combat aircraft were not fully mission-capable.

The vacillating, ineffectual defense policies of the Democratic presidential nominee would similarly weaken our national security. His ideas about strategic weapons are not only out of step with the thinking of the vast majority of Americans, but also in direct conflict with those of his vice presidential running mate and most of the leading Democrats on the Senate and House Armed Services Committees.

Republicans will support U.S. defense capabilities by keeping our economy strong and inflation rates low. Continued economic growth will allow more dollars to be available for defense without consuming a larger portion of the GNP or the federal budget; continued efficiency and economy will assure those dollars are well-spent.

Even as we engage in dialogue with our adversaries to reduce the risks of war, we must continue to rely on nuclear weapons as our chief form of deterrence. This reliance will, however, move toward non-nuclear defensive weapon systems as we deploy the Strategic Defense System. We will greatly enhance security by making the transition from an all-offensive balance of nuclear terror to a deterrent that emphasizes non-nuclear defense against attack.

We must improve conventional deterrence that would prevent our adversaries from being able to advance successfully into allied territory. We stand in unity with our European allies in the conviction that neither a nuclear war nor a conventional war should be fought. Nonetheless, we must stay on the cutting edge of weapon system development and deployment to deter Soviet aggression in Europe and throughout the free world.

Only by maintaining our strength and resolve can we secure peace in the years ahead. Republicans will provide the steady leadership needed to move our nation effectively into the 21st century.

America Defended

We have begun a historic transition from an American threatened by nuclear weapons to an America defended against the possibility of a devastating nuclear atack.

We understand the ominous implications of the proliferation of ballistic missile technology in the Third World. The Reagan-Bush Administration has succeeded in negotiating an agreement among the seven leading industrial countries to stop the spread of this technology. This underscores the need for deployment of the Strategic Defense System commonly known as SDI. SDI represents America's single most important defense program and is the most significant investment we can make in our nation's future security.

SDI is already working for America. It brought the Soviets back to the bargaining table, and it has energized and challenged our research and technology community as never before. It has started to reverse the trend of unmatched heavy Soviet investment. Republicans insist it is unacceptable that today the citizens of Moscow are protected against ballistic missile attack while Americans have no such protections.

The SDI program has been structured to facilitate a smooth transition to a safer world. It emphasizes deployments based upon the following objectives:

- Providing protection against an accidental or unauthorized launch of a nuclear missile or an attack by a rogue nation.
- Changing the emphasis on our deterrent from nuclear offense to non-nuclear defensive weapons and providing the only real safeguard against cheating on offensive arms control agreements.
- Ultimately, providing a comprehensive defense against all ballistic missile attacks.

We are committed to rapid and certain deployment of SDI as technologies permit, and we will determine the exact architecture of the system as technologies are tested and proven.

In response to the dangerous proliferation of ballistic missiles, a joint U.S.-Israeli effort is now underway to produce the free world's first anti-tactical ballistic missile system, "Project Arrow." We will support this use of SDI research funds.

The Democrat nominee for president opposes deployment of any SDI system. He opposes deployment of even a limited ballistic missile defense system to protect Americans against missile attacks that might be launched accidentally or by an outlaw ruler with access to a few nuclear weapons. His position contradicts the sponsorship by certain Democrats in Congress of a system to protect Americans from such missile attacks.

Republicans want to begin with protection and add to deterrence. We applaud the leaders of the scientific community for their confidence in the ability of U.S. technology to enhance deterrence and to provide effective defenses. We urge the universities of our country to continue to cooperate with the government and the private sector in establishing the SDI system.

A Strategy for Deterrence

Republicans will implement a strategic modernization program, emphasizing offensive and defensive strategic forces that are affordable and credible and that provide for a more stable balance. In contrast with the Democrat nominee and his party, we will not jeopardize America's security and undermine the advances we have made for peace and freedom by permitting erosion of our nuclear deterrent.

Over the past 10 years, every administration—Democrat and Republican alike—has understood the importance of maintaining a strategic triad: a mix of ground, air and sea retaliatory forces. Republicans know our country needs a survivable land-based leg of the triad. The current Democrat leadership rejects this integral element of our strategic force posture. This will destroy the triad by neglecting necessary modernization and forgoing the strategic forces essential for preserving deterrence.

The most critical element in enabling the President to preserve peace is to assure his ability to communicate with foreign leaders and our armed forces under the most adverse circumstances. The Democrat nominee has acted to prevent a future President from having this ability by denying the federal government the needed approval to deploy key elements of the Ground Wave Emergency Network (GWEN) in Massachusetts. By doing so, he has demonstrated a shocking disregard for the security of all Americans. This nation cannot afford such irresponsible leadership from one who aspires to be our Commander-in-Chief.

To end our historic reliance on massive nuclear retaliation, we need to develop a comprehensive strategic defense system. This system will deter and protect us against deliberate or accidental ballistic missile attack, from whatever source.

In the conventional area, we need to ensure that our ground, naval, and air forces are outfitted with the finest equipment and weapons that modern technology can provide; we must also assure that they are fully capable of meeting any threats they may face. We put special emphasis on integrating the guard and reserves into effective combat forces. We must sustain and accelerate the progress we have already made to ensure that all of our forces are prepared for special operations warfare. In addition, advances in conventional weapons technology, specifically, "smart," highly accurate weaponry, must be accelerated. These new weapons will deter our adversaries by threatening significant targets with very precise conventional weapons. We must provide sealift and airlift capability needed to project and support U.S. forces anywhere in the world.

We must also deal with the reality of chemical and biological weapons. We must have a deterrent capability; that requires modernization of our own chemical weapons. But we must also strengthen our efforts to achieve a verifiable agreement to eliminate all chemical and biological weapons.

Getting a completely verifiable agreement will be difficult, requiring for tough, on-site, on-demand verification. It is, however, essential that we press ahead, particularly given the growing proclivity in some quarters to use chemical and biological weapons.

In recognition of our responsibility to provide optimum protection for the American people from terrorists, accidents and—should deterrence fail—from war, we also believe that a high priority should be given to Civil Defense.

In each aspect of our deterrent forces, Republicans propose to foster and take advantage of our technology and our democratic alliance systems to develop competing strategies for most effectively defending freedom around the world.

An Arms Reduction Strategy

Arms reduction can be an important aspect of our national policy only when agreements enhance the security of the United States and its allies. This is the Reagan-Bush legacy: true arms reductions as a means to improve U.S. security, not just the perception of East-West detente. Clear objectives, steady purpose, and tough negotiating, backed up by the Republican defense program, produced the INF Treaty. This is the first real nuclear arms reduction treaty in history. Until 1981, we had accepted arms "control" as simply a "managed" arms build-up, always waiting for the next agreement to reverse the trend. Republicans insist on mutual arms reductions. We have proven that there are no barriers to mutual reductions except the will and strength to safely achieve them.

We cannot afford to return to failed Democrat approaches to arms control. Democrats treat arms control as an end in itself, over-emphasizing the atmospherics of East-West relations, making unilateral concessions, and reneging on the traditional U.S. commitment to those forces essential to U.S. and allied security. Notwithstanding their stated intentions, the Democrats' approach—particularly a nuclear freeze—would make nuclear war more, not less, likely.

Republicans are committed to completing the work the Reagan-Bush Administration has begun on an unprecedented 50 percent cut in strategic nuclear weapons. We will achieve verifiable and stable reductions by implementing the Republican agenda for a secure America:

- We will consistently undertake necessary improvements in our forces to maintain the effectiveness of our deterrent.
- We will not negotiate in areas which jeopardize our security. In particular, we will not compromise plans for the research, testing, or the rapid and certain deployment of SDI.
- We will insist on effective verification of compliance with any and all treaties and will take proportional, compensatory actions in cases of non-compliance. Specifically, the Soviet ABM [Anti-Ballistic Missile] radar at Krasnoyarsk poses a clear violation of the ABM Treaty and, if not corrected, would constitute a "material breach" of the Treaty.

- We will place special emphasis on negotiating asymmetrical Soviet cutbacks in those areas where a dangerous imbalance exists. For example, during the three-year reign of Mikhail Gorbachev, the Soviet military has added more new conventional weapons than currently exist in the entire armed forces of France and West Germany.
- We will reject naive and dangerous proposals such as those offered by the Democrat nominee to ban the testing of weapons and delivery systems. Those simplistic and destabilizing proposals are designed only for domestic political appeal and would actually jeopardize achievement of stable arms reductions. The accuracies and efficiencies achieved by testing have in fact resulted in 25 percent fewer warheads and 75 percent less megatonnage than 20 years ago. Our more accurate weapons of today enhance stability.

We must always remember—and ever remind our fellow citizens—that, when the future of our country is at stake, no treaty at all is preferable to a bad treaty.

The Space Challenge

The Republican Party is determined to lead our country and the world into the 21st century with a revitalized space program. The American people have never turned back from a frontier.

Our exploration of space has kept this country on the leading edge of science, research, and technology. Our access to space is essential to our national security. In the coming decade, nations around the world will compete for the economic and military advantages afforded by space.

The free and unchallenged use of space offers to the free world, and the Soviet bloc as well, unprecedented strategic, scientific, and economic advantages. The Soviets openly seek these advantages, which must not be denied to the United States and other free nations. Our goal is for the United States to acquire the means to assure that we can enforce a stable and secure space environment for all peoples.

We must establish a permanent manned space station in orbit during the 1990s for a commercial and governmental space presence.

U.S. satellites currently act as the "eyes and ears" for our strategic forces. The survivability of U.S. space assets is vital to American interests.

We believe the U.S. needs an Anti-Satellite (ASAT) capability to protect our space assets from an operational Soviet threat, and we intend to deploy it rapidly. Furthermore, we encourage the responsible Democrat Members of Congress to join us in this effort. Our country's advance in space is essential to achieve the economic transformations which await us in the new century ahead.

Two powerful engines that can re-energize the space program will be competitive free enterprise and SDI. The United States must regain assured access to space through a balanced mix of space shuttles and unmanned vehicles. We must also expand the role—in investment, opera-

693

tion, and control—of the private sector. Republicans believe that this nation can and must develop a private sector capability to compete effectively in the world market place as a provider of launches and other services.

We applaud those who have pioneered America's rendezvous with the future. We salute those who have lifted the nation's spirit by raising its sights. We remember in special honor those who gave their lives to give our country a leading role in space.

America: A Strong Leader and Reliable Partner

NATO remains the United States' most important political and military alliance. Republican commitment to NATO is unwavering, reflecting shared political and democratic values which link Europe, Canada, and the United States. NATO pools our collective military resources and capabilities, stretching in Europe from Norway in the north to Turkey, our strategic friend and pillar in the south.

Our challenge is to assure that today's positive signals from the Soviets translate into a tangible reduction of their military threat tomorrow. Soviet conventional superiority remains a serious problem for NATO. Soviet-Warsaw Pact military doctrine continues to be predicated upon the Soviet Union's ability to mount a massive conventional offensive against the NATO allies. The NATO allies must strengthen their conventional forces, modernize their remaining nuclear systems, and promote rationalization, standardization and interoperability.

On the critical issues of defense burden sharing, Republicans reflect the belief of the American people that, although we must maintain a strong presence, the alliance has now evolved to a point where our European and Japanese allies, blessed with advanced economies and high standards of living, are capable of shouldering their fair share of our common defense burden.

We are commited to supporting the network of liberty through balanced regional or bilateral alliances with nations sharing our values in all parts of the world, especially our neighbors in Central America. The Republican Party reiterates its support of the people of Central America in their quest for freedom and democracy in their countries.

We are proud of the great economic and democratic progress throughout the world during the Reagan-Bush Administration, and we are committed to strengthening the defensive ties that have thwarted Soviet expansion in the past seven years.

Keeping the Sea Lanes Free

The United States has always been a maritime nation. We have rebuilt our Navy to permit continued freedom of the seas. Our focus has correctly been on the fighting ships our Navy would use in the event of a conflict. Our successful peace mission in the Persian Gulf is eloquent testimony to the benefits of a blue water Navy.

To protect American interests in remote areas of the world, we require a 600-ship Navy with 15 aircraft carrier battle groups. This number enables us to operate in areas where we lack the infrastructure of bases we enjoy in Western Europe and the western Pacific. A force of this size will enable us to meet both our security interests and commitments into the 21st century. Republicans are also committed to the strategic homeporting of our forces throughout the United States. Notwithstanding the Democrat nominee's claim to support conventional arms improvements, U.S. security interests are jeopardized by his proposal to cancel two aircraft carriers previously authorized and funded by Congress.

Providing new policies for the maritime industry is crucial to this nation's defense capability and its economic strength. These policies must include leadership to help make the industries competitive through reform of government programs, aggressive efforts to remove barriers to the U.S. flag merchant fleet, and a commitment to cooperate with the industries themselves to improve their efficiency, productivity, and competitive positions.

A national commitment to revitalize the commercial shipbuilding industry is needed in this country. Shipyards and the supplier base for marine equipment necessary to build and maintain a merchant marine must survive and prosper. Our merchant marine must be significantly enlarged and become more competitive in order to vastly increase the amount and proportion of our foreign trade it carries.

Sealift is needed to supply our troops and transport commercial cargo during a prolonged national emergency. As a nation, we must be willing to pay for the strategic sealift capability we require. We can do this by ensuring that the needed ships are built and by helping to sustain the ships and their crews in commercial operation. We must return this nation to its foremost place among the world maritime powers through a comprehensive maritime policy.

Last year Congress slashed the Administration's budget request for the Coast Guard. We urge Congress to adjust the budget process to protect the Coast Guard appropriation, thereby removing the temptation to siphon its funds and personnel into other programs and ensuring improved coordination of government agencies in our nations' war against drugs.

Our Nation's Technology Base

Science and technology are the keys to a better future for all. Many of the miracles we take for granted in everyday life originated in defense and space research. They have not only helped preserve the peace, but also have made America's standard of living the envy of the world.

Because of advances in science and technology, our defense budget today is actually one-third lower, as a fraction of the gross national product, than it was a generation ago.

Today, national security and technological superiority are increasingly linked by the relationship between technology and key strategies of credible and flexible deterrence, defenses against ballistic missiles, and space pre-eminence.

Investment in defense research and development must be maintained at a level commensurate with the Reagan-Bush years. This investment should be focused on efficient and effective areas such as ballistic missile defense, space, command and control, and "smart" munitions.

We support a defense budget with the necessary funds and incentives for industry to invest in new technologies and new plant and equipment. This is needed to preserve and expand our competitive edge, thereby assuring future opportunities for America's next generation in science, engineering, and manufacturing.

Our nation will benefit greatly from patent royalties and technological progress that will be developed through spinoffs, especially in the fields of micro-miniaturization and super-conductivity, which are vital in order for U.S. industry to compete in the world.

We regard the education of American students in the fields of science and technology as vital to our national security.

Our investment in militarily critical knowledge and technology must be safeguarded against transfer to the Soviet Union and other unfriendly countries.

Defense Acquisition

Americans are prepared to support defense spending adequate to meet the needs of our security. Americans have a right—and the government has a duty—to ensure that their hard-earned tax dollars are well-spent. We Republicans recognize that waste and fraud in the defense acquisition process cheat the American people and weaken our national security. Neither can be tolerated.

Those who loot national security funds must be prosecuted and punished. Mismanagement must also be rooted out. The planning and budgeting process must be improved, and the acquisition process reformed, recognizing that congressionally mandated waste contributes mightily to inefficiencies in the system.

We will sustain consistent necessary appropriations in the defense budget to avoid the destructive impact of wildly fluctuating and unpredictable annual funding.

The Packard Commission recommended a series of important reforms for improved defense management. We are committed to ensuring that these reforms are fully implemented—by Congress, the Defense Department and the defense industry. Most particularly we call for submission of a two-year budget for defense to help us meet these goals. Persons involved in the federal government procurement process must be subject to "revolving door" legislation.

Procurement today is constrained by an adversarial relationship between the Congress and the Defense Department. The result is micromanagement by Congress, which has resulted in thousands of regulations that add expensive and time consuming red tape without adding value. Republicans support a firm policy of cooperation, treating Members of Congress as full partners in the acquisition process. This will result in more efficiency and better weapons. An example of what can be accomplished with this partnership is the new base closing legislation.

To make real these reforms, we will once again depend on the professionalism, the diligence, and the patriotism of the men and women who comprise the vast majority of our defense establishment.

Armed Forces Personnel for the Nineties

A free society defends itself freely. That is why Republicans created an all-volunteer force of men and women in the 1970s, and why it has proven to be a tremendous success in the 1980s.

From Grenada to the Persian Gulf, the readiness of those in uniform has made America proud again. Despite a demographic decline in the number of those eligible for service, military recruitment and retention rates are at all time highs. Quality is outstanding, and all sectors of society are participating.

We will continue to make the military family a special priority, recognizing strong home life as an essential component in the morale and performance of the armed forces.

Republicans deplore and reject the efforts of those who would support either a numerical cap or a reduction in the number of military dependents able to accompany U.S. servicemen and women overseas. We recognize that a stable and happy family life is the most important prerequisite for retaining these dedicated men and women in the service of our country.

Republicans recognize that a secure national defense depends upon healthy military personnel. We commend the United States Armed Forces for their leadership in proving the utility of testing active duty personnel and applicants for disease and substance abuse.

Republicans will never take the military for granted. We support an all-volunteer force and we will continue to insist on fairness in pay and benefits for military personnel and their families, always striving to keep compensation in line with the civilian economy.

The National Guard and Reserve are essential to the integrated force concept of our armed services. Prior to 1981, the Guard and Reserve were deprived of both modern equipment and integration into the active forces. This policy has been changed to enable the Guard and Reserve to make their full contribution to our security. We recognize the major role played by the men and women of the Guard and Reserves in the total defense policy. These improvements will be sustained.

Veterans

Veterans have paid the price for the freedoms we enjoy. They have earned the benefits they receive, and we will be vigilant in protecting those programs of health care, education and housing.

We believe men and women veterans have earned the right to be heard at the highest levels of government. With the personal support of President Reagan, America's veterans will now have a seat in the president's Cabinet.

The health needs of our aging veterans are of special importance, and Republicans will not retreat from this national commitment. We encourage the new Secretary of the Veterans Department to work with the Federal Council on the Aging, and other agencies and organizations, to assure that the development of new facilities and treatment programs meet the special needs of our elderly veterans.

Republicans will provide adequate funding for the policy that, in all areas where there are no VA hospitals or long-term care facilities, veterans needing medical attention for service-connected disabilities should have the option of receiving medical care within their communities with adequate funding.

We must continue to address the unique readjustment problems of Vietnam veterans by continuing the store-front counseling, vocational training and job placement programs. We support veterans preference in federal employment and are vigilant about the serious problems associated with delayed stress reaction in combat veterans, particularly disabled and Vietnam veterans. An intense scientific effort must continue with respect to disabilities that may be related to exposure to ionizing radiation or herbicides.

The Republican Party supports sufficient funding to maintain the integrity of the VA hospital and medical care system and the entitlement and beneficiary system. We also support the efforts of the Department of Labor to properly meet the needs of unemployed veterans, particularly disabled and Vietnam veterans.

Our commitment to America's veterans extends to the men and women of all generations.

Intelligence: An Indispensable Resource at a Critical Time

A crucial part of the Reagan-Bush administration's rebuilding of a strong America has been the restoration of the nation's intelligence capabilities after years of neglect and down-grading by the Carter-Mondale Administration. This renewed emphasis has been essential in conducting diplomacy, supporting our armed forces, confronting terrorism, stopping narcotics traffic, battling Soviet subversion, and influencing events in support of other national policies. Our vital intelligence capability will continue to prevent tragedies and save lives.

In the years ahead, the United States will face a widening range of national security challenges and opportunities. Scores of foreign intelligence services will seek to uncover our secrets and steal our technology. But there will also be opportunities to advance U.S. interests, for freedom and democracy are on the march. Both the threats and the opportunities will place demands on our intelligence capabilities as never before.

The Republican Party endorses covert action as one method of implementing U.S. national security policy. We reject legislative measures that impinge on the President's constitutional prerogatives. Our country must be able to collect from both technical and human sources the vital information which is denied to us by closed societies in troubled regions of the world. Our senior national security officials must be informed about trends in foreign societies, opportunities to advance U.S. interests, and the vulnerabilities of those who seek to harm our interests. This information can then be used, through the proper chain of command, to support our national policies.

To strengthen the decision-making process and further limit access to classified information, we support the concept of a single joint congressional committee for intelligence, made up of appropriate congressional leaders and analogous to the former Joint Atomic Energy Committee.

We will continue to enhance the nation's capability for counter-intelligence. Congressional intrusion into the administration of counter-intelligence must be kept to a minimum.

Leaks of highly sensitive and classified national security information and materials have increased at an alarming rate in recent years. Such leaks often compromise matters critical to our defense and national security; they can result in the tragic loss of life. We advocate a law making it a felony for any present or former officer or employee of the federal government, including Members of Congress, to knowingly disclose classified information or material to a person not authorized to have access to it.

The U.S. must continue to provide political, military, and economic assistance to friends abroad and to those seeking to help us against our adversaries. These activities must always be in support of our national policy, and the U.S. has the right to expect reciprocity wherever possible.

To the extent the Congress requires the President to inform its Members of activities sensitive to national security, the President is entitled to require that Congress will respect that sensitivity.

National Security Strategy for the Future

We have set forth the foreign and defense policies of the Republican Party in the two preceding sections of this Platform. To implement those policies, we propose this integrated national security strategy for the future.

The long-term security of our nation is the most important responsibility of the U.S. government. The domestic well-being of the American people cannot be ensured unless our country is secure from external attack. To guard our borders, preserve our freedom, protect America from ballistic missile attack, foster a climate of international stability and tranquility—so that nations and individuals may develop, interact, and prosper free from the threat of war or intimidation—these are the most important goals of America's foreign and defense policy.

We dare not abandon to others our leadership in pursuit of those goals. International peace and stability require our country's engagement at many levels. While we cannot resolve all issues unilaterally, neither can we abdicate our responsibilities by retrenchment or by relying on the United Nations to secure our interests abroad. Those who advocate America's disengagement from the world forget the dangers that would be unleashed by America's retreat—dangers which inevitably increase the costs and risks of the necessary reassertion of U.S. power.

Republicans learned this lesson well as we implemented the most successful national security policy since World War II. In 1981, we had to deal with the consequences of the Democrats' retreat. We inherited an America in decline, with a crisis of confidence at home and the loss of respect abroad. Re-establishing America's strength, its belief in itself, and its leadership role was the first and most important task facing the Reagan-Bush Administration. We met that task. We repaired our defenses, modernized our strategic nuclear forces, improved our strategy for deterrence with our development of the Strategic Defense Initiative, deployed INF missiles in Europe, and restored pride in our nation's military services.

We also met that task by a policy of engagement. We worked with allies, not against them. We supported friends instead of accommodating foes. We fostered the achievement of genuine self-determination and democracy rather than merely preaching about human rights in the Third World.

The Reagan-Bush approach produced dramatic results. Our policy is proven: To foster peace while resolutely providing for the security of our country and its allies. We have significantly enhanced that security. We have expanded the opportunities for the United States to be a positive force for freedom and democracy throughout the world. The chances for new breakthroughs for peace have risen dramatically.

We secured the first arms reduction agreement, eliminating an entire class of soviet and U.S. nuclear weapons. We laid the basis in START [Strategic Arms Reduction Talks] for unprecedented, radical reductions in strategic nuclear arms.

In regional conflicts, a humiliating Soviet retreat from Afghanistan, made possible by our unyielding support for the Mujahadeen, helped to sober the Soviet rulers about the costs of their adventurism. Our protection of vital U.S. interests in the Persian Gulf against Iranian aggression led to the agreement to start resolving the Persian Gulf War. Our support for freedom fighters in Angola has resulted in the chance of a settlement there and elsewhere in southern Africa. Our isolation of Vietnam has led to the prospect of its withdrawal from Cambodia.

In human rights and the building of democracy, Republican leadership has turned the tide against terror in Central America, aided the restoration of democracy in the Philippines and South Korea, and liberated the island of Grenada from a Cuban-controlled dictatorship.

This is a remarkable record of achievement. It shows that our policies of achieving peace through strength have worked. By rebuilding American strength and restoring American self-confidence, Republicans achieved a remarkable series of foreign policy objectives critical to our country's security. The resurgence of American leadership has changed the world and is shaping the future, creating new opportunities not dreamt of eight years ago. This is the true measure of competence.

Although we have established a framework for the future, we cannot rest on our laurels. The young democracies we have helped to flourish may yet be overcome by authoritarian pressures. The Soviet Union can easily revert to past practices. Its current effort for internal restructuring could create a more powerful adversary with unchanged objectives. Arms reductions could again become an excuse for reducing our commitment to defense, thus creating dangerous instabilities. Economic competition could easily slip into protectionism and mercantilism. Both to meet those challenges and to build upon the opportunities created by our success, the U.S. must continue in the strong leadership role it has assumed over the past eight years.

As we face the opportunities and challenges of the future, our policies will be guided by realism, strength, dialogue, and engagement. We must be realistic about the Soviet Union and the world we face. Hostile forces remain in that world. Soviet military capabilities are still dangerous to us. It must be clear to all, except the leadership of the Democrat Party, that we are not beyond the era of threats to the security of the United States.

Our country must have all the military strength that is necessary to deter war and protect our vital interests abroad. Republicans will continue to improve our defense capabilities. We will carefully set priorities within a framework of fiscal conservatism, more stringent measures to increase productivity, and improved management of defense resources.

We will continue modernizing our strategic forces, emphasizing a mix of offensive and defensive forces, effective and survivable, employing unique U.S. technological advantages. We will redouble our commitment through force improvement to correct the dangerous imbalance that now exists in conventional forces.

At the same time, we will pursue negotiations designed to eliminate destabilizing asymmetries in strategic and conventional forces. Arms reductions can contribute to our national security only if they are designed to reduce the risk of war and result in greater stability. They must be part of a process of broader dialogue with the Soviet Union, as well as other nations, a process in which we explore possible opportunities to reduce tensions and to create more stable, predictable, and enduring relationships.

As we shape our foreign and defense policies, we must never lose sight of the unique leadership role the United States plays in the world community. No other nation can assume that role. Whether we are dealing with security challenges in the Persian Gulf or terrorism or the scourge of drugs, the willingness of other nations to act resolutely will depend on the readiness of America to lead, to remain vigorously engaged, and to shoulder its unique responsibilities in the world.

The American people and the Republican Party, in the tradition of Ronald Reagan and with the leadership of George Bush, are indeed ready to do so.

REPORT ON THE DOWNING
OF AN IRANIAN AIRLINER
August 19, 1988

The missile cruiser Vincennes, *part of a U.S. fleet stationed in the Persian Gulf to protect neutral shipping endangered by the Iran-Iraq War, on July 3 shot down an Iranian commercial airliner, killing all 290 persons on board. Although the $1 billion warship was equipped with advanced Aegis detection electronic equipment, its crew had mistaken the wide-body A300 Airbus for an American-built F-14 tomcat fighter.*

Department of Defense investigators issued a report August 19 that said the performance of the ship's computerized detection system was "excellent" and that the tragedy was attributable to a series of human errors. "Stress, task fixation, and unconscious distortion of data," the fifty-three page report said, "may have played a major role in this incident."

The Vincennes *was engaged in combat with Iranian speedboats when Iran Air Flight 655, on a scheduled flight across the gulf to Dubai, appeared as a blip on its computer screen. The report noted that the attention of the ship's commander, Capt. Will Rogers III, was necessarily devoted to the surface combat during the approximately three minutes and forty seconds between the time he was notified of the potential threat and his decision to fire the missiles that brought down the airliner. He had little time "to personally verify" information from his crew. That information was apparently distorted "in an unconscious attempt to make available evidence fit a preconceived scenario."*

Perceptions of danger to U.S. ships in the Persian Gulf had been influenced by an incident May 17, 1987. The American frigate Stark *was struck by two Iraqi missiles, killing thirty-seven of its crew. Iraq apologized for "pilot error," but the* Stark's *captain and senior officers, who had taken no action against a presumed "friendly" aircraft, were later dismissed from the U.S. Navy.* (Report on USS *Stark* Attack, Historic Documents of 1987, p. 791)

No disciplinary action was taken against the captain or crew of the Vincennes. *The six-man investigative team headed by Rear Adm. William M. Fogarty found that "based on the information used by the commanding officer ... the short time frame available to him in which to make his decision and his personal belief that his ship and the [nearby] USS* Montgomery *were being threatened, he acted in a prudent manner."*

First Reactions

President Ronald Reagan's immediate reaction to the downing of the airliner was to call it "a proper defensive action" and "a terrible human tragedy." His July 3 statement also extended "our sympathy and condolences" to the victims. He later announced that the United States would compensate the families of the victims but had not submitted a request for payment to Congress before its adjournment. Administration officials said the request awaited a confirmed passenger list, which Iran had not supplied. The United States had demanded from Iraq $800,000 compensation for each of the thirty-seven servicemen killed on the Stark.

Vice President George Bush told the United Nations Security Council July 14 that "the victims of Iran Air 655 were only the most recent victims of a brutal and senseless war that has brought immense pain and suffering to the people of both sides." He urged Iran to comply with the Security Council's Resolution 598, a call for a cease-fire and negotiation of a peace settlement with Iraq. (Iran-Iraq Truce, p. 529)

Iran at first accused the United States of a "barbaric massacre" and threatened revenge. Iranian television showed bodies of "martyred" victims floating amid the plane's wreckage, and Iranian protesters took to the streets. But official as well as popular protests were muted in comparison with past expressions of anti-American feeling.

The incident brought back to public attention the 1983 episode of a Soviet warplane shooting down Korean Airlines Flight 007 when it strayed off course into Soviet airspace. The Soviet government had said that the intruding plane could not have been identified as a civilian aircraft because it was flying at night without navigation lights and was not answering signals. On that occasion, President Reagan said "there is no way a pilot could mistake this for anything other than a civilian airliner." (Korean Airline Tragedy, Historic Documents of 1983, p. 775)

By contrast, the American mistake happened in a war zone during combat, the chairman of the U.S. Joint Chiefs of Staff, Adm. William J. Crowe, stressed at a July 3 news conference.

The Gulf War

Between 1984 and mid-1988 about 475 commercial vessels had been attacked in the Persian Gulf by Iraqi or Iranian forces, according to the Center for Defense Information, a private research group in Washington, D.C., that monitored military affairs. On November 1, 1986, Kuwait informed its fellow members of the Gulf Cooperation Council that it would seek international protection for its ships.

The Reagan administration, soon after learning that Kuwait had an offer of Soviet protection for its vessels, accepted a Kuwaiti request to register its ships under the American flag. The United States on March 7, 1987, offered to protect eleven Kuwaiti tankers, and on April 4 Secretary of Defense Caspar Weinberger ordered a stronger U.S. naval presence in the gulf.

A series of Iranian attacks on Kuwait-bound tankers had preceded the Iraqi attack on the Stark. *The administration April 22, 1988, informed Congress that the Navy would protect neutral ships from Iranian forces when assistance was requested at the scene of battle. The first such request was made July 2 by a Danish tanker fired on by Iranian boats. The Iranian boats fled after warning shots from the American frigate* Montgomery. *The next morning, the* Vincennes *was ordered to the area to investigate the* Montgomery's *reports of Iranian small boats preparing to attack another merchant ship.*

The Decision

Early on July 3, a helicopter from the Vincennes *was fired on by an Iranian boat. When the* Vincennes *and* Montgomery *approached the scene, two of the boats turned toward them. The* Vincennes *fired at them and was actively engaged in this surface combat from the time the Iranian airliner took off until the decision was made to fire at it.*

In reconstructing this decision, the investigative team found discrepancies between tapes that recorded electronic observations and the information relayed to the captain by his crew members. The Navy assigned a psychiatrist and a physiologist to join the investigative team in the Persian Gulf to determine whether "the dynamics of the situation" affected the crew's "ability to perceive and relay the data which was available to them."

In a news briefing presenting the investigative report, Secretary of Defense Frank C. Carlucci said he and Admiral Crowe had tried to reconstruct how the decision was made by replaying recording tapes at a mock-up of the Aegis system. Carlucci said the experience made clear "the sense of inexorability when you see that one target moving steadily at you" and "the number of things you have to concentrate on." He observed that the simulation could not replicate such things as "the number of voices coming at you over the ear phones" or the "actual environment" of the decision point, during which the ship was "heeling over at about a 32-degree angle and things were falling in the CIC [Combat Information Center], lights were flickering, and in the background guns were booming."

The report noted that the airliner had taken off from a combined military-civilian airfield—Bandar Abbas on the Iranian shore of the gulf—headed directly into a combat zone, moved rapidly toward the Vincennes, *and failed to respond to repeated warnings from the ship. But the report found that the crew had erred in several respects, including the following:*

- *The identification signals issued by the airliner were misidentified as military rather than civilian.*
- *The plane was incorrectly described as outside the commercial air corridor from Bandar Abbas to Dubai.*
- *The crew reported that the aircraft was descending, as if on an attack approach, when it was in fact ascending to a higher cruising altitude.*

At the news briefing presenting the report, Crowe said the mistakes, considered singly, "were not crucial to the fateful decision." Even taken cumulatively, he said, "they do not appear to change the picture in a decisive way." In his endorsement of the report, Crowe said: "Given the fact that the surface engagement was initiated by the Iranians, I believe that the actions of Iran were the proximate cause of this accident and would argue that Iran must bear the principal responsibility for the tragedy."

Crowe rejected a recommendation that a "non-punitive letter of censure" be issued to the ship's officer in charge of antiair warfare. The "unusual public attention" to the incident, Crowe said, would vitiate the purpose of such a letter, which is intended to "point out lessons to be learned" without becoming part of the officer's record or influencing his career prospects. Crowe said that "this regrettable accident, a byproduct of the Iran-Iraq war, was not the result of culpable conduct aboard the Vincennes.*"*

*President Reagan ruled out any compensation to the government of Iran but told reporters July 11 that "compassion" for the families of the victims justified his proposal to compensate them. An ABC/*Washington Post *opinion poll indicated strong public opposition to compensation, and some members of Congress argued that payment should be made conditional on release of American hostages held by pro-Iranian factions in Lebanon.*

> *Following are excerpts from the news briefing at the Pentagon, August 19, 1988, at which Secretary of Defense Frank*

C. Carlucci and Adm. William J. Crowe, Jr., chairman of the Joint Chiefs of Staff, presented the results of an investigation conducted by Adm. William M. Fogarty and five others into the circumstances of the missile firing from the U.S. Navy frigate Vincennes *that shot down an Iranian commercial airliner over the Persian Gulf, July 3, 1988:*

Secretary Carlucci: . . . [W]e are today issuing the report of the investigation conducted by Admiral Fogarty and his team on the circumstances surrounding the downing of Iranian Air Flight 655. In addition we will make available to you endorsements of this report by [Marine Corps] General [George B.] Crist, CENTCOM [U.S. Central Command] Commander; Admiral Crowe; and myself.

A copy of the report has been provided to the President. The President has been briefed on the findings and on the endorsements and concurs in them. . . . [I]n my judgment this has been a thorough investigation. I believe the facts to the extent they can be known are clearly presented in the report and I commend Admiral Fogarty and his team for a thorough job.

On the day that the incident occurred, Admiral Crowe appeared before you and made available virtually every scrap of information that we had in our possession. This was a deliberate decision. We chose not to withhold anything. Admiral Crowe stated repeatedly that our initial information, as is always the case, was sketchy, preliminary, and very likely to prove false in some instances. But nonetheless, we decided to go ahead with it, running the risk that there would subsequently be stories that the Pentagon had put out mistaken information, and indeed we've had some of those stories.

We now have a complete report which tells a very complex story and I hope you will help us convey to the public the very complexity of the situation. This tragedy occurred, of course, in the context of the long and bloody Iran-Iraq War. . . .

This week Admiral Crowe and I have spent hours going over this report. The other day I said to Admiral Crowe, it's very hard to get a sense of this report just reading the written word. Let's see if we can't get a mock-up. So yesterday Admiral Crowe and I and some others flew down to Wallops Point [Va.] where they have a mock-up of the Aegis System. We had the tapes replayed once in real time, once in slow motion so to speak, so we could go over every step of the incident.

A couple of things come through to you very clearly when you go through this process. One is the sense of inexorability when you see that one target moving steadily at you on a constant bearing, decreasing range, refusing to respond or not responding to all of the challenges and in total I think there were some 12 challenges between the VINCENNES and the [sister ship] SIDES.

The other thing that comes through is the number of things you have to concentrate on. The Captain, and in this case the Force Anti-Air Warfare Controller had before them two large display screens: the Captain with his screen on a larger scale working the surface situation, the surface combat that was underway; and the Anti-Air Warfare Controller worrying not just about this track but about an Iranian P3 over to the west, a couple of E2C's or an E2C taking off from a carrier, and worrying about communicating with Commander Task Force Middle East. Bear in mind that all of this is happening within, well a total of about seven minutes from the time the plane was first spotted and the actual decision process and the firing is closer to four minutes, the time that the Captain began to focus on it. So there were a tremendous number of things to do and a lot of distractions.

There are a couple of things that can't be replicated in a simulator. The number of voices coming at you over the ear phones being one. Or the actual environment in which they were operating. It's important to bear in mind that this ship was engaged in combat with Iranian Boghammers. There have been reports of sounds of metal hitting the side of the ship which we assumed and still assume today were bullets from the Boghammer. The ship had a foul mount, mount 51, and had to turn, a 30 degree turn. This turn took place just at the crucial decision point so it was heeling over at about a 32 degree angle and things were falling in the CIC [Combat Information Center aboard the *Vincennes*], lights were flickering, and in the background guns were booming. I dare say it would be hard to even have this press conference under those conditions, much less reach a crucial decision on a number of targets during a very short time frame. Nonetheless, the investigators found that the Captain acted prudently on the basis of the information available to him. Both Admiral Crowe and I and General Crist concurred in that judgment. Admiral Crowe has given me a clearly detailed presentation of his views, and I'll let him now summarize those for you.

Admiral Crowe: . . . Admiral Fogarty's investigation was conducted with complete independence from any pre-conceived notions of culpability or non-culpability. The investigation after four weeks of work submitted its findings of fact, opinions, and recommendations to Commander in Chief U.S. Central Command.

The main recommendation of the investigation was that no disciplinary action should be taken against any U.S. Naval personnel associated with this incident. I concurred, and so recommended to the Secretary.

Let me briefly touch on the highlights of my review. An examination of the events on 3 July leads quickly to the conclusion that Iran must share the responsibility of the tragedy and the investigation so found. By any measure, it was unconscionable to ignore the repeated warnings of the United States and to permit an airliner to take off from a joint military/civilian airfield and fly directly into the midst of the ongoing surface action in the Strait of Hormuz which the Iranians themselves had initiated.

The tragic events of July 3rd did not occur in a vacuum as the Secretary explained to you. They happened in an area where 37 American sailors on board the USS STARK has been killed by an air attack in May 1987 and where our military had been tested by fire time and again over the last year. The actions of Captain Rogers and the VINCENNES crew must be judged in that context.

The investigation paints in vivid terms the history of our commitment, the Iranian threats, intelligence reports, and the commanding officer's fundamental responsibility to protect his ship and his people. It also describes in detail the stress which surrounded events in VINCENNES on July 3.

During the critical seven minutes that Flight 655 was airborne, Captain Rogers and his CIC team were conducting a surface action, tracking a multitude of contacts, coordinating U.S. units, and trying to sort out friend from foe with spotty information. He had a genuine dilemma. In the midst of all this, the threatening air contact was closing at five to six miles a minute, and he felt if it continued to present a danger he should fire before it got much closer than ten miles.

The villains of the piece were six significant problems which plagued the Captain and which he could not control or discount. VINCENNES was engaged in intense surface action with Iranian gunboats. The unidentified assumed hostile contact had taken off from an airfield used by military aircraft. The flight was heading directly at VINCENNES and its range was relentlessly closing. The unknown aircraft radiated no definitive radar emissions. Seven VINCENNES warnings went unacknowledged and unanswered. The compression of time gave him an extremely short decision window, less than five minutes. It was only prudent for [Vincennes] Captain [Will] Rogers [III] to assume that the contact was related to his engagement with the Iranian boats until proven otherwise. The proof never came.

Given the time available, the commanding officer could hardly meet his obligation to protect his ship and crew and also clear up all of the possible anomalies or ambiguities. It is not unusual in combat to have to deal with uncertainties and conflicting information. Although it might not seem fair, commanding officers do not have the luxury of reconciling all such questions before committing themselves. They have to go with the weight of the evidence and their best judgment. These are the realities of combat. The commanding officer, if he is to be effective, must be given the latitude to deal with them.

Admiral Fogarty's investigation also revealed that mistakes were made on board VINCENNES that day. That in itself is not surprising to anyone who understands the stress of hostile action in a life or death situation. No military combat operation is flawless, even when there is a successful outcome. The more important question in this case was whether those mistakes were critical to the tragic result.

Our early Washington briefings of the accident were based on information received from the ship shortly after the action, some of which were found by the investigation to be incorrect. Let me comment on the significant items.

Admiral Fogarty's probing revealed the IFF [Identification Friend or Foe system] emission from Flight 655 was Mode 3 which a commercial aircraft normally uses. The VINCENNES also detected a contradictory Mode 2 military squawk and mistakenly concluded that it came from Flight 655. That detection did lead the CIC team to declare the contact an F14. Much has been made of that error. However, this decision must be understood in the total context. It was not a crucial element in Captain Roger's ultimate decision to fire. Military aircraft on attack runs can disguise their identity using civilian IFF signals, or on occasion, no IFF signal at all. For example, significantly Iranian F4's operating against U.S. units on 18 April were squawking only Mode 3, the civilian code.

Under standard procedures even if the F14 designation had not been made, the plane would have remained designated an unidentified assumed hostile and would have been treated as a potential threat by the captain and the crew. That was standard procedure.

Questions have been raised about the ship's initial report that the aircraft was outside of the air corridor. The report was wrong. Whether or not an aircraft is in a commercial air corridor is a peripheral point to a commanding officer engaged in hostile action, particularly when the corridor covers the engagement area. The Persian Gulf is blanketed by commercial air routes. They cover over 50 percent of the Gulf. Captain Rogers testified that in his experience commercial airliners tried hard to stay on the center line of the corridor. He did not focus on the fact that the corridor is 20 miles wide, but rather that the contact was three to four miles off the median. The CO [commanding officer] interpreted that as unusual.

Perhaps the most puzzling mistake was the ultimate call of Flight 655 as descending instead of climbing. The investigation concluded that the range in altitude information passed to the commanding officer was correct until the airbus reached a range of approximately 15 miles from VINCENNES. Captain Rogers had already received permission to fire from his immediate superior. One of the radar operators reported at 11 miles that the aircraft was no longer climbing and that the altitude had commenced to decrease, a report that was not supported by a subsequent review of the Aegis tapes. Two other reports of descending altitude may have been made at 10 and 9 miles. It is not altogether clear. The last report was apparently announced after the decision to fire had been made. In fact, the investigation concluded that the time between the initial report of decreasing altitude and the decision to fire was in the neighborhood of 20 to 30 seconds.

It is impossible to say with assurance how those two imputs bore on the commanding officer's final decision, but it is important to keep in mind that the CO had this information for only 20 to 30 seconds, and that during this interval he was involved in other things as well as preparations to fire. The investigation made the point clearly that this was only one consideration among the many in the CO's mind.

Singly, these errors or mistakes were not crucial to the fateful decision. Even cumulatively they do not appear to change the picture in a decisive way. The commanding officer never received the clear evidence that he felt he needed to establish that the Iranian aircraft had not come to participate in the ongoing surface action. Our past experience in the Gulf, the intelligence available to the ship, and the rules of engagement all supported such a judgment.

I believe that given the operating environment, Captain Rogers acted reasonably and did what his nation expected of him in the defense of his ship and crew. In all good conscious [sic] I concur with Admiral Fogarty's finding that there was no culpable conduct dispayed on board VINCENNES. This regrettable accident, and it was an accident, was a by-product of the Iran-Iraq War and saddened all Americans, most of all the crew of the VINCENNES.

Q: Mr. Secretary, you outlined a number of mistakes. You say none of them were crucial, but it raises the question of what they did right. What did the crew of the VINCENNES do right? And if all of these are understandable mistakes, is not the captain of the ship responsible for the training of his crew, shouldn't he have to take responsibility for the mistakes they make?

A: The question is not whether mistakes were made. Mistakes are made in virtually every combat situation. The question is whether the mistakes were made through negligence or whether there is culpability. The determination is that no, these mistakes were not due to negligence or culpability. . . .

The ship had undergone extensive training. The investigating team found that the training had been adequate. There were a number of things, to answer your question . . . that were done right including the engagement of the Boghammers, securing the helicopter. The principal responsibility of the commanding officer, and I can't emphasize this too strongly, under the rules of engagement is to protect his ship. The finding is that the captain behaved prudently and within the rules of engagement based on the information that he had received. . . .

Q: Admiral Crowe, did the investigation show how the operator misread whether the plane was descending or ascending? Isn't that a digital readout he would be looking at?

Sec. Carlucci: It is a digital readout, and we went over and went down the digital readout yesterday. The report talks a little bit about the possibility of a scenarial fulfillment syndrome which could have happened once the airplane was identified as F14. There is also the possibility that he or some of the listeners could have confused range and altitude. But once again, the fundamental point is what Admiral Crowe said, that this reading of descending altitude was made within 20 to 30 seconds of the time of firing, and it's really questionable whether a different reading would have affected the judgment at that point. It would have had to have been a negative decision by the captain at that point in time.

Adm. Crowe: The specific question you asked, it was never adequately reconciled.

Q: During the efforts to replicate this particular incident, were the tapes played through the VINCENNES or through the tape readers in an automatic mode, and did the VINCENNES on its own, without human involvement, elect to fire?

A: In replicating? I'm not sure...

Q: In trying to replicate the incident, the VINCENNES will operate in an automatic mode if you turn it on so it will automatically fire.

A: I'll have to defer to Admiral Fogarty or Admiral Crowe.

A: It was in manual that day, not automatic.

Q: Did you try it in automatic to see if it would replicate the incident?

A: No, we didn't need to because our investigation is based on the fact that it was in manual.

A: It would not make a decision itself to fire unless you had decided all these other parameters were right and you could fire the minute you got in the envelope.

Q: It could make a conclusion though, that you should fire, and then you make the decision.

A: But there's an awful lot of information involved in a firing decision that is not in the computer. The Iran-Iraq War, the Boghammers, the bullets impinging on it, the intelligence report, the experience of the last year, the computer doesn't sort them all out.

Q: Mr. Secretary, can you tell us were there any recommendations, or have any actions been taken in the nature of non-punitive punishment of the type that you don't normally discuss?

A: General Crist, in his endorsement, indicated that he was issuing a non-punitive letter of censure to Lieutenant Commander Lustig basically because of the failure of Lieutenant Commander Lustig to verify the data coming to him. By that I assume he means the designation of F14, although that would have been very difficult to verify, in fact impossible for him to verify; but more significantly, the range data that was received within the last 30 to 40 seconds prior to firing.

The investigators did not reach that kind of a determination. Admiral Crowe has recommended to me, and I have accepted his recommendation, that that letter be withdrawn.

First of all, let me emphasize that it is a non-punitive letter and the purpose of a non-punitive letter is to try to explain things and teach lessons. It is Admiral Crowe's judgment, and I share that judgment, that in the current circumstances with all the publicity surrounding this incident, there is no such thing as a non-punitive letter. Any letter that is sent is going to be punitive. Therefore, I have decided to withdraw the letter.

Q: Secretary Carlucci, you mentioned that the radar operator may have made a mistake reading the Mode 3, Mode 2, that particular crucial mistake because his range finder was still at the airport on the scope. Can you explain that mistake? And was not that mistake a crucial one mixed with the intelligence that F14's had been squawking different modes?

A: Well it is not crucial, as Admiral Crowe pointed out, in the sense that you still had these fundamental factors. You had an unidentified aircraft that had lifted off from a civilian airport that was on constant bearing, decreasing range, did not emit any radar signals, had refused to respond to seven warnings from the VINCENNES and five from the SIDES, and was closing rapidly. So even if it had not been designated an F14, they probably would have considered it a hostile aircraft.

Now the explanation, and this gets a bit technical and I'm perhaps not the best person qualified to do it and I'll defer to others in a minute, is that you have a spy radar which will do IFF, but you also have something called an RCI, a remote control indicator, which is a separate, manual IFF generally used for backup. There you have to put the ball or the range gate on the target. The radar operator apparently left his range gate on the target a little bit too long. It is possible that due to ducting in the Persian Gulf that that RCI picked up the Mode 2 squawk. That's speculation. We do know he had his range gate on the target on the airport, on the airfield for about 90 seconds. We cannot verify from tapes what he actually picked up. There is no Mode 2 squawk on the tapes.

A: I just wanted to add on the word crucial. The guidance advises the commanding officer not to put that as a single piece of information to make decisions on the base of it because we know the Iranians can and do play with the IFF in order to confuse our ships. It is supporting information, but it is not crucial in itself.

Q: You say these mistakes weren't crucial, but it seems to be the accumulation of mistakes that was crucial.

A: I don't know how you can say that.

Q: The misidentification on the squawking IFF; the descending report from the radar operator.

A: But he had a lot of other information.

Q: When you put all of these. . .

A: You've got to explain to me what you mean when you make that general statement, because I don't accept it.

A: The crucial facts are that you had an unidentified aircraft lifting off from a combined civilian/military airfield heading into a zone where there's a battle going on on a constant bearing, decreasing range, that did not acknowledge any of 12 challenges. Those are the crucial facts.

Q: What about the commercial airlines schedules? Was the VINCENNES unable to . . .

A: They did check the commercial airline schedule. That, too, is not a crucial element. Actually the plane was some 20 minutes behind schedule. . . .

Q: Mr. Secretary, what happened when they checked the schedule? Did they see the fact that Flight 655 was scheduled for that time period, or did they miss that also?

A: I'll have to defer to Admiral Fogarty.

A: He referred to the schedule and the plane took off 27 minutes late.

A: He identified 655 on the schedule. If your question is was it on the schedule that he had, the answer is yes.

Q: Did he call it to Captain Rogers' attention that there is a Flight 655 scheduled to take off from Bandar Abbas Airport heading for Dubai at about. . . .

A: There was one officer in the CIC that did say possible com air. Possible commercial air.

Q: Are you saying that these mistakes are in no way responsible for the downing of this airliner? You use the word crucial, but there is some responsibility here, and these mistakes are in no way responsible for that.

A: If your question is had these mistakes not been made would the events have unfolded in a different direction, obviously no one can say for sure. It is the judgment of those who have investigated this, and it is Admiral Crowe's judgment which I accept, that the errors were not crucial to the decision. That is to say the factors that I just listed, and the factors that Admiral Crowe has listed were fundamental to the decision and that these mistakes did not alter those fundamental factors.

Q: Did the investigation disclose any evidence that the pilot of the Iran air jet or the ground controllers in Iran were aware of the warnings? Secondly, did the ship make any effort to communicate with the tower at Bandar Abbas to determine whether this could have been a commercial aircraft?

A: We have no indications that the air controller was aware of the warnings, although I'll have to defer once again to the experts.

A: We tried to retrieve the black box and we were unsuccessful, so we did not confirm that the pilot heard the warnings or the tower.

Q: Was there any effort to communicate with the tower at Bandar Abbas to see whether this might be a commercial aircraft?

A: Not to my knowledge. I don't believe there was. But once again, you have to put yourself inside that CIC in a four minute time frame with a lot of things going on, the ship heeling over, 30 degree turn, firing at small boats, everybody focused on the small ship engagement. Now one can think of a thousand different things the captain might have done, but how many of those things are reasonable to do during that short time frame under the conditions that I just described?

Q: Are you going to make any changes in the operating procedures of the Aegis or any modifications to the Aegis equipment?

A: We've discussed that and the report does suggest a few things that I think are healthy. One is that there be some adjustment to the large screen display. . . .

A recommendation has been made that there be an additional talker, voice communicator, put in the CIC to help communicate with superior commands because that was being done by one of the officers.

Admiral Crowe has recommended that we look at the process for certain critical designations. That is to say designation of an aircraft as an F14, to see whether there shouldn't automatically be some checks on that process.

The report recommends that a psychological profile be developed for certain critical jobs in the Aegis system.

So there are a series of recommendations looking at what can be done to improve both the system and the people operating it.

Q: So the equipment itself and the procedures did contribute to the errors made.

A: No, the equipment functioned as designed. We cannot find any errors in the equipment.

Q: Then it wasn't designed correctly.

A: I'm not indicating it wasn't designed correctly. I am indicating that as you go through experience with any weapon you improve the design.

A: Particularly in combat....

Q: Mr. Secretary, you indicated that one officer in the CIC said that it was a possible commercial aircraft. Were you able to identify who that was and on what he based that, and to whom he communicated that?

A: It was the CIC officer, and he simply made the statement on Circuit 15, I assume, which was ...

A: He said it directly.

A: He was standing behind the commanding officer. His name is in the report.

Q: Mr. Secretary, the Iranians indicated, or made the point at the time this happened that the plane was in frequent radio communication with the control tower from the time the engines were turned on until shortly before it was shot down. They said this information should have been available to the VINCENNES and made it clear this was a commercial aircraft. Can you comment on that?

A: They certainly didn't make it available to the VINCENNES....

Q: Did the VINCENNES or any of the ships in the task force in the immediate area pick up any of the communications between the air bus and the control tower?

A: I do not believe so.

Q: Mr. Secretary, with the ceasefire going into effect tomorrow, have there been any changes in the force status in the Persian Gulf, or are you contemplating any?

A: No, there have been no changes in the force status in the Persian Gulf....

Q: One point of clarification. You both said that the failure of the air bus to emit clear radar signals was one of the elements that contributed to the decision that it was potentially hostile. Why is that? Had the plane been an F14 trying to search for a ship on the surface, trying to zero in, to fire on it, would it have been emitting radar signals?

A: Yes, it would have been distinguishing. In other words, if the F14 had been using the radar it normally does, it would have definitely identified it as an F14. If the air bus had had its air weather radar on and we'd picked it up it would definitely have identified it as a commercial aircraft. Incidentally, the commanding officer, that was the one thing he was really zeroing in on the last few seconds. He kept asking for readouts. In fact held up firing because of that. He wanted a readout on the radar, and he never got it. . . .

Q: Mr. Secretary, you said the investigating team said the training of the Aegis crew was adequate. Three weeks ago the General Accounting Office came out with a report on DoD's Operational Test and Evaluation [OT&E] Office. Within that report they said the training of the Aegis system was inadequate. Primarily they said the amount of stress placed on the crews in training was not adequate to simulate a combat situation. Will you be going back and looking at the training?

A: We will be responding to the GAO report. Unfortunately, as happens in many cases, the GAO did not ask our views before they issued that report.

Q: Actually they did. They did sit down with OT&E.

A: But they did not submit the report to us and ask for our views on that particular point, that's my recollection. But we will be responding.

Q: Mr. Secretary, does the report vindicate the Aegis weapon system?

A: I don't know what you mean. The Aegis weapon system was never on trial, so it's not a question of vindicating it. Did it work as designed? The answer is yes. It worked as designed.

Q: Mr. Secretary, there were several reports that came out that there was some difficulty in launching the standard missiles, that someone was having problems getting the missiles launched. Were there errors made? Were there problems getting those fired?

A: Lieutenant Zucker who was the Anti-Air Warfare Coordinator, but who had had his responsibilities somewhat reduced, did have some trouble; I guess that was trouble illuminating the aircraft. There was no trouble in firing the standard missile. . . .

Q: You said the Iranians are partially responsible. Do you have indications that the Bandar Abbas Airport was aware that there was fighting going on between the VINCENNES and Boghammers?

A: When we say Iranians we don't distinguish between the people at Bandar Abbas Airport and the people controlling the ships that are engaged in the fire fight. It's certainly not our job to make sure that the Iranian military communicates with Bandar Abbas Airport. I would hope they would have. But surely the Iranian Government bears some responsibility here.

Q: But they had to know there was fighting going on. You're talking about three small ships.

A: Who had to know? The Iranians?

Q: Yes.

A: I assume they knew. The fighting had been going on for about three hours, so they must have known there was fighting going on. . . .

Q: You're making the assumption that they work together on joint operations. Is that really the case?

A: Whether it's the case or not, the point is they were all Iranians. All we can do is hold the Iranians responsible for sending a civilian aircraft into a zone where they had initiated a fire fight. We think that obviously contributed to this incident. . . .

Q: Can Admiral Crowe go over the speed? That was the other crucial point.

A: There was a mention in a report right after the incident at 4:50 that was picked up by a note taker from one observer, one operator in the console. Those were not the speeds, however, they were working with and the speeds were all the way in the range, after it got really airborne, 300 right on up to, gradually increased right up to the time, the speed did. Consistently throughout it could be either a military or a commercial. It was in the envelope of either a military or a commercial aircraft, and the people in the fire control and the captain were dealing with correct speeds.

Q: Speeds of 300 to 350, would that have been consistent with an F14?

A: It would have been, yes. Our experience with it is yes. Unless it's in an air to air fight with a fighter. Then the final speed was 380. They wanted a speed that would distinguish and they couldn't get it.

September

Presidential Debates 721

Apostolic Letter on Women 785

PRESIDENTIAL DEBATES
September 25 and October 13, 1988

As the 1988 election campaign went into its final weeks, national television audiences watched two ninety-minute debates between presidential nominees George Bush and Michael S. Dukakis. Dukakis, the Democratic governor of Massachusetts, was widely regarded as the winner of the first debate, held September 25 at Wake Forest University, Winston-Salem, North Carolina. However, Vice President Bush, the Republican nominee, was generally judged the more "likable," and he was seen as the outright winner of the second debate, held at the University of California at Los Angeles, October 13.

The public's perception of the nominees turned not only on their answers to questions by a panel of print and broadcast journalists in each debate, but also on their warmth and "likability." Dukakis, who was sometimes portrayed in the press as a technocrat without political passion, found himself under pressure to exhibit warmth. Most analysts of the debates concluded that he failed to meet that goal, especially in the second debate—when it was considered critical to the success of his campaign. Indeed, David Broder, the veteran Washington Post *political reporter and columnist, called the second debate "close to a total mismatch in terms of the human dimension."*

First Debate

As the two candidates entered their first debate, Bush had erased Dukakis's midsummer lead in the opinion polls, but Bush's own lead was still narrow. As the debate was assessed by James M. Perry and David

Shribman of the Wall Street Journal, *Dukakis scored points and appeared "cool and confident," moving him into the final six weeks of the campaign "in contention and maybe even on a modest roll."*

On the other hand, Bush's repeated attempts to label his Democratic opponent as a "liberal" apparently planted seeds of doubt about Dukakis in the minds of many viewers. The term had lost much of its popularity in recent years, and Dukakis refused to accept it until later in the campaign. Bush called Dukakis a "strong liberal Democrat" and a "strong progressive liberal." As part of Bush's strategy to portray Dukakis as out of the political mainstream, he attacked the governor's membership in the American Civil Liberties Union (ACLU), invoking the phrase "card-carrying member." Bush also raised Dukakis's veto of a Massachusetts bill to require teachers to lead the Pledge of Allegiance in the state's public schools. "I'm not questioning his patriotism," the vice president insisted at one point. "Of course, the vice president is questioning my patriotism. . . . And I resent it," the governor shot back. But otherwise, Dukakis's defense of his position on those issues seemed inadequate to many viewers, according to subsequent polling.

On the other hand, Dukakis scored points with his attacks on Bush as an advocate of uncaring social policies during the Reagan presidency, for the administration's dealings with Manuel Noriega, the Panamanian strongman, and for its involvement in the secret Iran-contra arrangement for supplying arms to Iran and the Nicaraguan rebels. (Iran-Contra Reports, Historic Documents of 1987, p. 891)

Above all, Dukakis attempted to exploit the widely perceived weakness of Sen. Dan Quayle of Indiana, Bush's choice as a running mate (Vice Presidential Debate, p. 799). *The idea of Quayle as "President Quayle," Dukakis said in the debate, "is a very, very troubling notion."*

Bush seemed to trip on the issue of abortion when he said that he had not "sorted out" penalties that might be imposed if a constitutional amendment were passed banning most abortions. His staff later issued a clarification, which stated that after "thinking about it overnight" the Republican candidate believed that women undergoing abortions should not be penalized but that doctors peforming them should be.

Second Debate

The stakes were again much higher for Dukakis than for Bush in the second debate. Bush's lead in the polls had persisted after the first debate. The challenge for Dukakis was to show the public a warmer personality than in the first debate and generally in the course of the election campaign.

Dukakis responded to an early question about his personality by saying, "I think I'm a reasonably likable guy. . . . But I'm also a serious guy. I think the presidency of the United States is a very serious office."

Bush responded far less coolly, "I don't think it's a question of whether people like you or not to make you an effective leader. I think it's whether you share the broad dreams of the American people."

But the Dukakis response that elicited the most comment was to an opening question by the moderator, Bernard Shaw of Cable News Network. Shaw asked if Dukakis would favor an irrevocable death penalty if his wife, Kitty Dukakis, were "raped and murdered." Shaw's question was seriously described in the press as "brutal" and "tasteless." Dukakis merely answered that there was no evidence that the death penalty was a deterrent and that there were "better and more effective" ways to deal with violent crime. Bush, on the other hand, said that some crimes were "so heinous, so brutal, so outrageous ... those real brutal crimes, I do believe in the death penalty."

Broder wrote that Dukakis's face, as he heard Shaw's question, was "as impassive as if he had been asked the time." After the election, Robin Toner wrote in the New York Times that the Massachusetts governor had been sick on the day of the second debate and had slept most of the afternoon preceding the debate. "He was flat at a time when he could not afford to be flat," Toner said. Yet observers believed that Dukakis made a number of strong points in the debate. He pointed up the difference the election would make in appointments to the Supreme Court. He firmly stated that individual women should be the ones to decide whether to have an abortion. And he emphasized that he would give higher priority to domestic needs than to some weapons systems.

"Spin Control"

More conspicuously than ever before, the Bush-Dukakis encounters were given immediate interpretations by members of the candidates' campaign staffs. Almost before the applause for the nominees had died, representatives of the candidates appeared on television and fanned out among print reporters. By their interpretation of what had just occurred, the campaign representatives hoped to create an impression (or "spin") that would affect the public's perception of the debate.

Whatever the impact of the "spin doctors" or indeed of the debates themselves, Bush won the election with 54 percent of the popular vote and an electoral college vote of 426 to 111. Bush won in forty states; Dukakis won in the remaining ten states and the District of Columbia.

The questioners in the first debate were: Jim Lehrer of the "MacNeil-Lehrer News Hour," Anne Groer of the Orlando Sentinel, Peter Jennings of ABC News, and John Mashek of the Atlanta Journal-Constitution. The questioners in the second debate were: Bernard Shaw of Cable News Network, Ann Compton of ABC News, Andrea Mitchell of NBC News, and Margaret Warner of Newsweek. Both debates were sponsored by the Commission on Presidential Debates.

Following are texts of the presidential debates between George Bush and Michael S. Dukakis, held September 25 and October 13, 1988. (The bracketed headings have been added by Congressional Quarterly to highlight the organization of the text.):

FIRST PRESIDENTIAL DEBATE

MR. LEHRER: You have two minutes for an answer, sir.

The polls say the number one domestic issue to a majority of voters is drugs. What is there about these times that drives or draws so many Americans to use drugs?

VICE PRESIDENT BUSH: I think we've seen a deterioration of values. I think for a while, as a nation, we condoned those things we should have condemned. For a while, as I recall, it even seems to me that there was talk of legalizing or decriminalizing marijuana and other drugs, and I think that's all wrong.

So, we've seen a deterioration in values. And one of the things that I think we should do about it, in terms of cause, is to instill values into the young people in our schools. We got away—we got into this feeling that value-free education was the thing. And I don't believe that at all. I do believe there are fundamental rights and wrongs, as far as use.

And of course, as far as the—how we make it better—yes, we can do better on interdiction, but we've got to do a lot better on inter—we've got to do a lot better on education. And we have to do—be tougher on those who commit crimes. We've got to get after the users more. We have to change this whole culture.

You know, I saw a movie—*Crocodile Dundee.* And I saw the cocaine scene treated with humor, as though this was a humorous little incident. And it's bad. Everybody ought to be in this thing —[the] entertainment industry, people involved in the schools, education. And it isn't a Republican or Democrat or a liberal problem, but we have got to instill values in these young people.

And I have put forward a many-point drug program that includes what I would do as President of the United States in terms of doing better on interdiction, and in terms of doing better in the neighborhoods. But I think we're all in this together, and my plea to the American people is: values in the schools.

MR. LEHRER: Governor, you have one minute to respond.

GOV. DUKAKIS: I agree with Mr. Bush that values are important. But it's important that our leaders demonstrate those values from the top. That means those of us who are elected to positions of political leadership have to reflect those values ourselves. Here we are with a government that's been dealing with a drug-running Panamanian dictator. We've been dealing with him; he's been dealing drugs with our kids. And governors like me, and others, have been trying to deal with the consequences.

I remember being in a high school in my own state as we were organizing something we called the Governor's Alliance Against Drugs, and a young 16-year-old girl coming up to me, desperate, addicted, dependent, saying, "Governor, I need help." We're providing that young woman with help.

But I want to be a President of the United States who makes sure that we never again do business with a drug-running Panamanian dictator; that we never again funnel aid to the contras through convicted drug dealers.

Values begin at the top—in the White House. Those are the values I want to bring to the Presidency and to the White House beginning in January of 1989.

MR. LEHRER: Governor, a follow-up question; you have two minutes to answer it. Are you suggesting, sir, that President Reagan is one of the causes of the drug problem in this country?

MR. DUKAKIS: I'm saying that those of us who are elected to positions of political leadership, Jim, have a special responsibility, not only to come up with programs and I have outlined in detail a very important, very strong program of enforcement as well as drug education and prevention—and Mr. Bush is right, the two go hand-in-hand. But if our government itself is doing business with people who we know are engaging in drug profiteering and drug trafficking; if we don't understand that that sends out a very, very bad message to our young people. It's a little difficult for me to understand just how we can reach out to that youngster that I talked about and to young people like her all over the country and say to them, "We want to help you."

Now, I've outlined in great detail a program for being tough on enforcement at home and abroad: doubling the number of drug enforcement agents; having a hemispheric summit soon after the 20th of January when we bring our democratic neighbors and allies together here in this hemisphere and go to work together. But, we also have to take demand seriously. You know we have five percent of the world's population in this country. We're consuming 50 percent of the world's cocaine.

And, in my state, I'm proud to say we've organized a drug education prevention program which the Federal Drug Enforcement Administration says is a model for the country. We're helping youngsters. We're reaching out to them. And we're beginning with drug education and prevention beginning in the early elementary grades in every elementary school in our state and that's the kind of effort we need in every elementary school in the United States of America. And we've got to begin early—in the first, second, and third grade, before our youngsters begin to experiment with these very, very dangerous substances.

I guess the question I would ask of Mr. Bush is how we instill those values, how we create this environment for the drug free schools that we want in this country—if he or representatives of the administration are either dealing with and involving people like [Panamanian leader Manuel Antonio] Noriega in our foreign policy or don't pursue that connection in a way that makes it possible for us to cut it off and to be an example to our kids all over this country.

MR. LEHRER: A minute to rebut, Mr. Vice President.

MR. BUSH: The other day my opponent was given a briefing by the CIA. I asked for and received the same briefing. I am very careful in public life about dealing with classified information, and what I'm about to say is unclassified. Seven administrations were dealing with Mr. Noriega. It was the Reagan-Bush administration that brought this man to justice. And as the Governor of Massachusetts knows, there was no evidence that Mr. Noriega was involved in drugs, no hard evidence until we indicted him. And, so, I think, it's about time we get this Noriega matter in perspective. Panama is a friendly country. I went down there and talked to the President of Panama about cleaning up their money laundering, and Mr. Noriega was there, but there was no evidence at that time. And when the evidence was there, we indicted him, and we want to bring him to justice, and so, call off all those pickets out there that are trying to tear down seven different administrations.

MR. LEHRER: All right. The next question will be asked by John Mashek. It goes to Governor Dukakis, and you will have two minutes to answer.

[Budget Deficit]

MR. MASHEK: Governor Dukakis, another troublesome issue for voters this year is the bulging federal deficit. In a Dukakis administration, you say taxes will be raised only as a last resort. Would you identify for us then, please, three specific programs that you are willing to cut to bring that deficit down?

MR. DUKAKIS: Yes, I've been very specific about these, John, and let me lay out for you my own strategy for bringing that deficit down because as the chief executive that's balanced ten budgets in a row, I've had to make those tough decisions and those tough choices.

First, I have suggested that there are certain weapons systems which we don't need and we can't afford. Mr. Bush has been critical of me for that, but I think those are the kinds of test choices you have to make. I've also suggested that there are weapons systems that we should proceed on, and I've outlined those in detail.

Secondly, we've got to invest in economic growth in this country, in every part of this country. Building that kind of growth expands revenues and helps to bring down that deficit.

Thirdly, we have to bring interest rates down, and we will as we come up with a good solid plan with the Congress for bringing that deficit down.

And finally, we've got to go out there and collect billions and billions of dollars in taxes owed that aren't being paid in this country. It's very unfair to the average taxpayer who pays his taxes and pays them on time to permit those monies to go uncollected.

I've also suggested that on the domestic side there are areas where we can make some cuts. We ought to be able to come up with an agricultural policy in this country that gives our farm families a fair price and a decent future without spending $20 [billion] to $25 billion a year, which is what we've been doing under this administration. We can help people to live better lives, and at the same time save money by helping hundreds of thousands of families on welfare to get off of welfare, and to become productive citizens again.

The thing I don't understand about Mr. Bush's approach to this is how he could possibly be serious about bringing that deficit down given what he says he wants to do. He seems to want to spend a great deal of money on just about every weapon system, he says he's against new taxes although he's broken that pledge at least three times in the last year that I know of. He wants to give the wealthiest taxpayers in this country a five-year $40 billion tax break, and he also wants to spend a lot of money on additional programs. If he keeps this up he's going to be the Joe Isuzu of American politics. But I hope you won't take my five seconds away from me, but I will say this—

MR. LEHRER: Your two minutes is up, Governor.

MR. DUKAKIS: I will say this, if he's serious about what he's saying then the only place he can go to balance that budget is to raid the Social Security trust fund, and he tried that in 1985 and I think he's going to try that again.

MR. LEHRER: You have a minute to rebut.

MR. BUSH: Is this the time to unleash our one-liners? That answer was about as clear as Boston Harbor. Let me help the Governor. There's so many things there I don't quite know where to begin. When you cut capital gains you put people to work. John Kennedy proposed cutting capital gains. Paul Tsongas, a liberal Senator from Massachusetts, said, "The dumbest thing I did was to oppose the capital gains cut." It's not going to cost the government money, it's going to increase revenues to the federal government, and it's going to create jobs. So that's one of the things that I think makes a big difference between us.

Now Massachusetts doesn't have an enormous defense budget, but nevertheless the Governor raised taxes five different times. That happens to be a fact. And so let's kind of stay on the issue, and I have made a specific proposal for what I call a "Flexible Freeze." And it permits— economists on the East Coast and West think it's good—it permits the presidents to sort out the priorities, and we continue to grow because I will not raise taxes.

MR. LEHRER: Your time is up too. A follow-up, John.

MR. MASHEK: Mr. Vice President, you have vowed not to raise taxes of any kind during your administration. And at the same time, you've proposed this capital gains cut, you've proposed more incentive breaks for the oil industry, you've suggested new spending programs. And even some Republicans say [the] flexible freeze you just spoke about will hardly make a dent in the deficit. Is the deficit no longer really a concern of yours, the

Republican party, or the taxpayers?

MR. BUSH: I think it's the Republican party's and my concern to bring it down. And presidential leadership, that I want to provide in this area, will bring it down. But, we've got to get the Democrats' Congress under control. They do all the spending. They appropriate every dime and tell us how to spend every dime. I'd like to ask the Governor to join me in getting for the President what 43 governors have—the line-item veto. He has to operate in Massachusetts under a balanced budget proviso. I would like a balanced budget amendment. But, the dynamics of the economy— we cut the taxes and revenues are up by 25 percent in three years.

So the problem is, it's not that the working man is being taxed too little, or the person working—the woman working in some factory being taxed too little; it is that we are continuing to spend too much. So, my formula says grow at the rate of inflation, permit the President to set the priorities on where we do this spending, and remember, the federal deficit has come down $70 billion in one year, in 1987. And if we—and actually, this year, Congress is doing a little better in controlling the growth of spending. Spending was only up something like four percent.

So, it isn't that we're taking too little per taxpayer—we're spending too much still. And the formula I've given you works. We've put it through a good economic model. We've got good economists on the West Coast— Michael Boskin and [Martin] Feldstein up there, who's a very respected economist in the—Massachusetts—and they agree that if we can do what I've said, we can get it down without going and socking the American taxpayer once again.

And capital gains—one more point on that. Please, let's learn from history. A capital gains differential will increase jobs, increase risk taking, increase revenues to the federal government.

MR. LEHRER: Governor, you have a minute to rebut.

MR. DUKAKIS: Well, I hope all of those Americans out there who are watching us, listening to us, and trying to make up their minds about which one of us ought to be President of the United States—listen to the Vice President very carefully. What he's proposing, after over a trillion dollars in new debt which has been added to the federal debt, in the course the past eight years, an IOU that our children and grandchildren will be paying for years, is a tax cut for the wealthiest one percent of the people in this country. An average of about $30,000 that we're going to give to people making $200,000 a year. Why, that's more than the average teacher makes. We've had enough of that, ladies and gentlemen. We've run up more debt in the last eight years than under all of the presidents from George Washington to Jimmy Carter combined. It's time for a chief executive who can make tough choices, can work with the Congress, can get that deficit down and begin to build a strong fiscal foundation under this country.

MR. LEHRER: All right, the next question will be asked by Anne Groer, and it will go to the Vice President. You have two minutes to answer, sir.

[Health Insurance]

MS. GROER: Mr. Vice President, you've said you want a kinder, gentler presidency. One that helps the less fortunate. Today, 37 million Americans, including many working families with aging parents and young children, cannot afford any health insurance—but earn too much to qualify for Medicaid. What will you do to provide protection for them, and how will you pay for it?

MR. BUSH: One thing I will not do, is sock every business in the country, and thus, throw some people out of work. I want to keep this economic recovery going, more Americans at work today than at any time in history, a greater percentage of the workforce. What I will do, is permit people to buy into Medicaid. I believe that's the answer. I am proud to have been part of an administration that passed the first catastrophic health bill. And in that, there's some Medicaid provisions that will be very helpful to the kind of people we're talking about here. But, we've got to keep going forward without killing off the engine, and throwing people out of work. So, the answer lies, it seems to me, in full enforcement of the catastrophic program. It lies to me in flexibility in Medicaid, so people at the lowest end can buy in there, and get their needs covered, and then it—also, I do not want to see us mandate across the board that every company has to do this. Because I really think that marginal operators are going to go say, "We can't make it," and I think, then, you're going to see people are put out of work.

All of these programs, and the cost on his was—I saw an estimate—I'd love to know what he thinks $35, $40 billion, and it seems to me that somebody pays that. There isn't any such thing as something "free" out there. It either gets passed along as increased prices, or it gets passed along by people being put out of work so the business can continue to compete.

So, I think we ought to do it in the Medicaid system. I think we ought to do it by full enforcement of the Catastrophic Health Insurance. I think we ought to do it by everybody doing what they can do out of conscience. It's a terrible problem in terms of the—in terms of flexibility on private insurances. But, I just don't want to mandate it and risk putting this—setting recovery back.

MR. LEHRER: A rebuttal, Governor.

MR. DUKAKIS: But, George, that's no answer. You know, last—

MR. BUSH: You don't like the answer, but it was an answer.

MR. DUKAKIS: Well, no. It's no answer to those 37 million people, most of them members of working families who don't have a dime of health insurance, and don't know how to pay the bills if the kids get sick at night.

I was in Houston on Tuesday, meeting with a group of good citizens, working citizens, all of them with little or no health insurance. One of them was a father who had been laid off a few months ago and lost his health insurance. He has an 11-year-old son, and can't let that son compete in sports in Little League because he's afraid he's going to get hurt and he won't be able to provide health insurance to pay those bills.

My state just became the only state in the nation to provide for universal health care, and we did it with the support of the business community, and labor, and the health care community, and with virtually everybody in the state. The fact of the matter is that employers who today are insuring their employees are paying the freight, because they're paying for those who aren't. And I think it's time that when you get a job in this country it came with health insurance. That's the way we're going to provide basic health security for all of the citizens in this country of ours.

MR. LEHRER: Follow up, Anne.

[AIDS]

MS. GROER: Yes. Since your Massachusetts health plan has been attacked by the Vice President and you have defended it in this way, I'd like to move on to perhaps one of the most costly medical catastrophes facing Americans today and that is AIDS.

At the end of September, the—thousands of AIDS patients will lose their access to AZT, which is the only federally approved drug for treatment of the disease. Now, I'd like to know, sir, if—what your position is on extending that, and what it is that you think the government ought to be doing about making AZT and other drugs available to people who are suffering from this disease?

MR. DUKAKIS: Well, Anne, let me just say before I answer your question that I didn't know that the Vice President had attacked our program in Massachusetts; I hope he hasn't, because it has won the support of a great many people all over the state, and I think it's a model for what I hope we can do across the country.

But when I proposed my plan this past Tuesday, he, or one of his spokesman, called it socialized medicine. The last time the Vice President used that phrase, I suspect he remembers it—[to Vice President Bush] don't you? It was in 1964 and that's what he called Medicare. Well, he was wrong then and he's wrong now.

MR. LEHRER: If I may—

MR. DUKAKIS: Let me also—

MR. LEHRER: Excuse me, Governor. If I may interrupt at this point and caution the audience, as I did before we went on the air: please, hold it down. You're only taking time away from your candidate when you do that [the audience had applauded]. Governor, continue, please.

MR. DUKAKIS: Let me say this about AIDS; it's the single most important public health crisis, single most important public health emergency we've had in our lifetimes. And I think there are a number of things we have to do, including supporting legislation which is now moving through the Congress, which will commit this nation to the resources to find a cure, which will provide broad education and prevention, which will find sensitive and caring treatment for the victims of AIDS.

I think we have to demonstrate some flexibility, and I think the FDA [Food and Drug Administration] is attempting to do so now, in trying to make it possible for new and experimental drugs to be available to the people who are at risk [of contracting] AIDS. And I would hope that we could bring that kind of a policy to bear beginning in January. And I would encourage the current administration to proceed with that kind of flexibility where it's appropriate and where it's done carefully and responsibly. But we have not had the kind of leadership we should have had. In this particular area, I think the Vice President and I are in general agreement on what we have to do. The special federal commission made good, solid recommendations. I think we're both supportive of them. And I would strongly lead in that area, as I have in my state, as governor.

MR. LEHRER: Mr. Vice President, a minute rebuttal.

MR. BUSH: Well, we're on the right track. The NIH [National Institutes of Health] is doing a good job in research. The Surgeon General is doing a good job in encouraging the proper kind of education. I noticed that the Governor did not mention any testing, but we've got to have a knowledge base. Testing should be confidential, but we have to have a knowledge base. We can't simply stick our heads in the sands in terms of testing.

I'm Chairman of the President's Task Force on Regulatory Relief, and we are working with the FDA, and they have sped up bringing drugs to market that can help. And you've got to be careful here, because there's a safety factor. But I think these things—and then, also, I am one who believes we've got to go the extra mile in clean—being sure that the blood supply is—is pure. We cannot have a lack of confidence in the blood supply when it comes to operations and surgery and things of this nature. So, research, speeding the drugs to market, testing, blood supply, are very important elements of this.

MR. LEHRER: Next question will be asked by Peter Jennings. It goes to the Governor.

MR. JENNINGS: Good evening, Mr. Vice President, Governor.

MR. DUKAKIS: Peter.

[Dukakis Lacks Passion, Patriotism?]

MR. JENNINGS: Governor, one theme that—theme that keeps coming up about the way you govern—you have both mentioned leadership tonight, so I'd like to stay with that for a second. The theme that keeps coming up about the way you govern is: passionless, technocratic.

MR. DUKAKIS: Passionless?

MR. JENNINGS: Passionless, technocratic—the smartest clerk in the world. Your critics maintain that in the 1960s your public passion was not the War in Vietnam or Civil Rights, but no-fault auto insurance. They say that in the 1970s, you played virtually no role in the painful bussing crisis in Boston. Given the fact that a President must, sometimes, lead by sheer inspiration and passion, we need to know if this is a fair portrait of your governing, or is it a stereotype? And if it isn't fair, can you give us an example of where you have had that passion and leadership that sometimes a president needs?

MR. DUKAKIS: Peter, I care deeply about people, all people, working people, working families, people all over this country who in some cases are living from paycheck to paycheck, in other cases they're having a hard time opening up the door of college opportunity to their children, in other cases don't have basic health insurance which for most of us we accept as a matter of course, assuming we're going to have and we're going to pay the bills we incur when we get sick, and somebody who believes deeply in genuine opportunity for every single citizen in this country. And that's the kind of passion that I brought to my state.

I was a leader in the civil rights movement in my state and in my legislature. I cared very deeply about that war in Vietnam. I thought it was a mistake. I thought it was wrong, and I was one of the few legislators early in that war that took a stand against the war. I think it was the right stand at the time, and I think history has proved us to be correct.

But I have learned over time, I served one term, I was defeated as you know and defeat sometimes is an important lesson. I think I'm a much better governor today. I think I'm a much better person, a much better listener. I think I'll be a much better president for having gone through that experience. But the things that we've done in my state to bring opportunity to people on public assistance; over 50,000 families on welfare that we've helped to move from welfare to work and to become productive citizens; the universal health care bill that we've just talked about which will guarantee health care for all our citizens; the opening up of opportunities for minorities in my state, affirmative action, minority contracting; the fact that we have a 3 percent unemployment rate and more jobs than people to fill them, which gives us a tremendous opportunity to reach out to everybody and make them a part of this wonderful nation of ours with the opportunity that we create.

These are things that I believe in very, very deeply. I might be a little calmer than some about it. I may be a greater consensus-builder these days than I used to be and I think that's a good thing. But I'm running for the presidency of the United States. I've been in public service for 25 years, because I believe very deeply in American goals and values and the people of this country and that's the kind of president I want to be.

MR. LEHRER: Mr. Vice President, a rebuttal.

MR. BUSH: Well I don't question his passion. I question—and I don't question his concern about the war in Vietnam. He introduced and supported legislation back then that suggested that kids from Massachusetts should be exempt from going overseas in that war. Now, that's a certain passion, but in my view it's misguided passion. He—we have big differences on issues. You see, last year in the primary, he expressed his passion. He said, "I am a strong, liberal Democrat"—August, 1987. Then he said, "I am a card-carrying member of the ACLU [American Civil Liberties Union]." That was what he said. He is out there on out-of-the-mainstream. He is very passionate. My argument with the Governor is, do we want this country to go that far left? And I wish we had time to let me explain. But I salute him for his passion. We just have a big difference on where this country should be led, and in what direction it ought to go.

MR. LEHRER: Peter—Peter, a question—a question for the Vice President, Peter.

MR. JENNINGS: I'd just like to follow up, if I may, on this mention you have made of his card-carrying membership in the American Civil Liberties Union. Now, you've used the phrase "card-carrying" so many times, since Governor Dukakis first acknowledged that he was a card-carrying member of the ACLU, that some people—some people have come to believe that you have used it in—to brand him in some way, to identify him as people were identified in the 1950s, as less than patriotic. I'd like to know why you keep repeating the phrase. What's the important issue here? What is so wrong with the Governor being a member of an organization which has come to the defense of, among other people, Colonel Oliver North?

MR. BUSH: Nothing's wrong with it, but just take a look at the positions of the—just take a look at the positions of the ACLU. But Peter, please understand—the liberals do not like me talking about liberals. They do not like it when I say that he says he's a card-carrying member. Now, if that quote was wrong, he can repudiate it right here. I've seen it authoritatively written twice, and if I've done him an injustice, and he didn't say it, I'm very, very sorry. But I don't agree with a lot of the—most of the positions of the ACLU. I simply don't want to see the ratings on movies—I don't want my ten-year-old grandchild to go into an X-rated movie. I like those rating systems. I don't think they're right to try to take the tax exemption away from the Catholic church. I don't want to see their kiddie pornographic laws repealed. I don't want to see "under God" come out from our currency. Now, these are all positions of the ACLU. And I don't agree with them.

He has every right to exercise his passion as what he said: a strong, progressive liberal. I don't agree with that. I come from a very different point of view. And I think I'm more in touch with the mainstream of America. They raised the same thing with me on the Pledge of Allegiance. You see, I'd have found a way to sign that bill. Governor [James R.] Thompson of Illinois did. I'm not questioning his patriotism. He goes out and says, "The man is questioning my patriotism." And then all the liberal columnists join in. I am not. I am questioning his judgment on these matters. Or where he's coming from. He has every right to do it. But, I believe that's not what the American people want. And when he said—when he was moving away from his own record, from what his passion has been over the years. And that's—all I'm trying to do is put it in focus. And I hope people don't think that I'm questioning his patriotism when I say he—use his words to describe his participation in that organization.

MR. LEHRER: Governor, response?

MR. DUKAKIS: Well, I hope this is the first and last time I have to say this. Of course, the Vice President is questioning my patriotism. I don't think there's any question about that. And I resent it. My parents came to this country as immigrants. They taught me that this was the greatest country in the world. I'm in public service because I love this country. I believe in it. And nobody's going to question my patriotism as the Vice President has now repeatedly. The fact of the matter is that if the Pledge of Allegiance was the acid test of one's patriotism, the Vice President's been the presiding officer in the United States Senate for the past 7½ years. To the best of my knowledge, he's never once suggested that the session of the Senate begin with the Pledge of Allegiance.

Mr. Bush, I don't question your patriotism. When you were attacked for your military record, I immediately said that it was inappropriate. It had no place in this campaign and I rejected it. And I would hope that, from this point on, we get to the issues that affect the vast majority of Americans: jobs, schools, health care, housing, the environment. Those are the concerns of the people who are watching us tonight; not labels that we attach to each other, questions about each other's patriotism and loyalty.

MR. LEHRER: Time is up, Governor. Let's go now to John Mashek again—a question for the Vice President.

[Homelessness, Housing]

MR. MASHEK: Mr. Vice President, in the debate during the Republican primaries, you said most of the nation's homeless are suffering from mental illness—an assertion immediately challenged by one of your rivals. Estimates of the homeless range from a low of 250,000 by the government, to around three million, including working families and their children. What commitment are you willing to make tonight to this voiceless segment of our society?

MR. BUSH: I want to see the McKinney Act fully funded. I believe that that would help in terms of shelter. I want to see—when I talked at our—at our convention about a thousand points of light, I was talking about the enormous numbers of shelters and organizations that help. The Governor's wife [has] been very active [with] the homeless, and my—my campaign chairman, Secretary Jim Baker's wife. This isn't government—these are people that care, that are trying to give themselves. The government has a role. It is to fully fund the McKinney Act. There are certain army bases that the act calls for that can be used in certain cases to shelter people when it's rough.

And so, I think that we're on the right track. I don't see this incidentally as a Democrat or a Republican or a liberal or a conservative idea—I see an involvement by a thousand points of light. I see the funding that is required. And I hope the Congress will fully fund this bill. They gave it a great deal of conscience and a great deal of work. And we're on the right track on this one. But—and I—look, mental—that was a little overstating it. I'd say around 30 percent. And I think maybe we could look back over our shoulders and wonder whether it was right to let all of those mental patients out. Maybe we need to do a better job in mental clinics to help—

help them, because there is a major problem there. A lot of them are mentally sick, and we've got to attend to them.

But fully, my—my short-range answer is, fully fund that McKinney Act.

MR. LEHRER: Governor, a response.

MR. DUKAKIS: Well, this is another fundamental difference that I have with the Vice President, just as I do in the case of health care for 37 million members of working families in the country who don't have health insurance. The problem, Mr. Bush, is that you've cut back by 90 percent on our commitment to affordable housing for families of low and moderate income. And when you do that, you have homeless families. We didn't have two-and-a-half million or three million homeless people living on streets and in doorways in this country ten years ago. We've got to begin to get back to the business of building and rehabilitating housing for families of low and moderate income in this country. Housing for young families that they can look forward someday to buy. We've got communities in this country increasingly where our own kids can't afford to live in the communities they grew up in.

That's an essential commitment, and I think the housing community is ready. But it's going to take a president who's committed to housing, who's had experience in building and rehabilitating housing, who understands that affordable housing for families of low and moderate income, for young families, first time home buyers, is an essential part of the American dream. And while I'm all for the McKinney Bill, that by itself simply won't do. We've got to have a president that can lead on this issue, that can work with the Congress, and I'm prepared to do so. This is one of the most important priorities that face this country.

MR. LEHRER: John, a question for the Governor.

MR. MASHEK: All right. Governor, you've mentioned the American dream of home ownership, and it's certainly become an impossible one for many of the young people of our nation, who are caught up in this "economic squeeze of the middle class," as you've said so frequently during the campaign. And yet, in spite of your answer just a few minutes ago, what promise can you realistically hold out to these people that, with the costs of housing going up and with the limited help available from Washington—are we destined to become a nation of renters?

MR. DUKAKIS: Well, I certainly hope not, and it's all a question of what our priorities are. Mr. Bush talked about values; I agree with him. What are our values? Isn't providing housing for families of low and moderate income, isn't it making it possible for young families, first time home buyers, to own their own home someday, something that's part of the American dream? I think so.

You know, back after World War II, when we had hundreds of thousands of GIs who came back from the war, we didn't sit around, we went out and built housing. The government was very much involved, so was the housing industry, so was the banking industry, so were housing advocates, so were non-profit agencies, so were governors and mayors, and people all over this country who believed deeply in home ownership and affordable housing. Now, that's the kind of leadership that I want to provide as president of the United States. This isn't a question of a little charity to the homeless; this is a question of organizing the housing community. I've talked to bankers, and builders and developers, to housing advocates, to community development agencies, and they want leadership from Washington. Washington by itself can't do it all. We shouldn't expect that. But Governors are ready, mayors are ready, builders and community leaders are ready. It will require some funds, John, and we ought to be prepared to find those funds. But that, too, will require some choices. Mr. Bush wants to spend billions and trillions on "Star Wars." Well, that's a choice we have to make, isn't it? Do we spend money on that weapon system in the billions and trillions? Or is providing some decent and affordable housing for families of this country something that isn't at least as important, and probably more so because it's so essential to our economic strength and to our future?

Now that's the kind of presidency I believe in. And simply to say, "Well, the McKinney bill will do it" just doesn't do. We need a president who will lead on this issue, who's had experience on this issue. It's the kind of priority that will be at the top of our list beginning in January of 1989.

MR. LEHRER: A response, Mr. Vice President.

MR. BUSH: I think that the Governor is blurring housing and the homeless. Let's talk about housing, which the question was. When you talked to those bankers, did they discuss where interest rates were when your party controlled the White House? Ten days before I took the oath of office as President [*sic*] they were 21.5 percent. Now how does that grab you for increasing housing?

Housing is up. We are serving a million more families now. But we're not going to do it in that old Democratic liberal way of trying to build more bricks and mortars. Go out and take a look at St. Louis at some of that effort; it is wrong. I favor home ownership, I want to see more vouchers, I want to see tenant control of some of these projects, and I want to keep the interest rates down. They're half now of what they were when we came into office, and with my policy of getting this deficit under control, they'll be a lot less. But if we spend, and spend, and spend that is going to wrap up the housing market and we'll go right back to the days of the misery index and malaise that President Reagan and I have overcome, thank God for the United States on that one.

MR. LEHRER: All right, the next question is to the Governor. Anne Groer will ask it.

[Death Penalty, Abortion]

MS. GROER: Governor Dukakis, is there a conflict between your opposition to the death penalty and your support for abortion on demand, even though in the minds of many people that's also killing?

MR. DUKAKIS: No, I don't think there is. There are two very different issues here, and they've got to be dealt with separately. I'm opposed to the death penalty. I think everybody knows that. I'm also very tough on violent crime. And that's one of the reasons why my state has cut crime by more than any other industrial state in America. It's one of the reasons why we have the lowest murder rate of any industrial state in the country. It's one of the reasons why we have a drug education and prevention program that is reaching out and helping youngsters all over our state—the kind of thing I want to do as President of the United States.

You know, the Vice President says he wants to impose the death penalty on drug traffickers, and yet his administration has a federal furlough program which is one of the most permissive in the country, and which gave, last year, 7,000 furloughs to drug traffickers and drug pushers—the same people that he says he now wants to execute.

This issue of abortion is a very difficult issue, one that I think we all have to wrestle with, we have to come to terms with. I don't favor abortion. I don't think it's a good thing. I don't think most people do. The question is, who makes the decision. And I think it has to be the woman, in the exercise of her own conscience and religious beliefs, that makes that decision.

MR. LEHRER: A response, Mr. Vice President.

MR. BUSH: Well, the Massachusetts furlough program was unique. It was the only one in the nation that furloughed murderers who had not served enough time to be eligible for parole. The federal program doesn't do that—no other state programs do that. And therefore—and I—I favor the death penalty. I know it's tough, and honest people can disagree. But when a narcotics wrapped-up guy goes in and murders a police officer, I think they ought to pay with their life. And I do believe it would be inhibiting. And so, I am not going to furlough men like Willie Horton, and I would meet with the victims of his last escapade, the rape and the brutalization of the family down there in Maryland. Maryland would not extradite Willie Horton, the man who was furloughed, the murderer, because they didn't want him to be furloughed again. And so, we have a fundamental difference on this one. And I think most people know my position on the sanctity of life. I favor adoption—I do not favor abortion.

MR. LEHRER: Question for the Vice President, Anne?

MS. GROER: Yes, Mr. Vice President, I'd like to stay with abortion for just a moment if I might. Over the years you have expressed several positions, while opposing nearly all forms of government payment for it. You now say that you support abortion only in cases of rape, incest, or threat to a mother's life. And you also support a constitutional amendment that, if ratified, would outlaw most abortions. But, if abortions were to become illegal again, do you think that the women who defy the law, and have them anyway—as they did before it was okayed by the Supreme Court—and the doctors who performed them, should go to jail?

MR. BUSH: I—I haven't sorted out the penalties, but I do know—I do know that I oppose abortion, and I favor adoption. And if we can get this law changed, where everybody should make extraordinary effort to take these kids that are unwanted and sometimes aborted, take the—let them come to birth and then put them in a family where they'll be loved. And, you see, yes my position has evolved, and it's continuing to evolve and it's evolving in favor of life. And I had a couple of exceptions that I support— rape, incest, and the life of the mother. Sometimes, people feel a little uncomfortable talking about this. But, it's much clearer for me now. As I've seen, abortion is sometimes used as a birth control device, for heaven's sake—see the millions of these killings—accumulate. And this is one where you can have an honest difference of opinion. We certainly do. But, no, I'm for the sanctity of life. And once that illegality is established, then we can come to grips with the penalty side, and of course there's got to be some penalties to enforce the—enforce the law—whatever they may be.

MR. LEHRER: Governor?

MR. DUKAKIS: Well, I think what the Vice President is saying is that he's prepared to brand a woman a criminal for making this decision. It's as simple as that. I don't think it's enough to come before the American people, who are watching us tonight, and say, "Well, I haven't sorted it out." This is a very, very difficult and a fundamental decision that all of us have to make. And what he is saying, if I understand him correctly, is that he's prepared to brand a woman a criminal for making this choice.

MR. BUSH: I just said—

MR. DUKAKIS: No. Let me finish.

MR. BUSH: Yes. Sure.

MR. DUKAKIS: Let me simply say that I think it has to be the woman and the exercise of her own conscience and religious beliefs that makes that decision. And I think that's the right approach, the right decision and I would hope by this time that Mr. Bush had sorted out this issue, and come to terms with it as I have. I respect his right to disagree with me but I think it's important that we have a position and that we take it and we state it to the American people.

MR. LEHRER: Peter Jennings, a question for the Vice President.

[Domestic Programs]

MR. JENNINGS: Mr. Vice President, I'm struck by your discussion of women and the sanctity of life and it leads me to recall your own phrase that you are "haunted" by the lives which children in our inner cities live. Certainly the evidence is compelling, there's an explosion of single-parent families, and by any measure these single families—many with unwanted children—are the source of poverty, school dropouts, crime which many people in the inner city simply feel is out of control. If it haunts you so, why over the eight years of the Reagan-Bush Administration have so many programs to help the inner cities been eliminated or cut?

MR. BUSH: One of the reasons—and I first would like to know which programs you're talking about and then we could talk on the merits of the programs—but you see my fundamental philosophy is give local and state government as much control as possible. That might be the explanation if you tell me the program. I do strongly support the WIC [Women, Infants and Children Supplemental Food] program. I think it is good.

I think part of the answer to the haunting of these children that are out there and suffering lies in extension of Medicaid to challenge the states and maybe, maybe we're going to have to enforce more on the states in terms of Medicaid taking care of these. But, Peter, so much of it is—gets into a whole other phase of things. The neighborhood, the kind of environment people are growing up in and that leads me to the programs I'm talking about in terms of education. I think part of it is the crime-infested neighborhoods, and that's why I'm a strong believer in trying to control crimes in the neighborhood, why I was so pleased to be endorsed by the policemen on the beat—the Boston Police Department—the other day. I think they understand my commitment to helping them in the neighorhoods. And so, it's a combination of these things.

But do not erode out of the system the thousand points of light, the people that are out there trying to help these kids, the programs like Cities and Schools, the work that Barbara Bush is doing so people can learn to read in this country, and then go on and break this cycle of poverty. I'm for Head Start, moving that up, and I've already made a proposal. And yes, it'll cost some money, but I favor that. So these are the combination of things I want, and the fact that I don't think the federal government can endorse a $35 billion program does not mean I have less compassion than the person who endorses such a program.

MR. LEHRER: Governor.

MR. DUKAKIS: Well, I must have been living through [a] different eight years from the one that the Vice President's been living through, because this administration has cut and slashed and cut and slashed programs for children, for nutrition, for the kinds of things that can help these youngsters to live better lives. It's cut federal aid to education; it has cut Pell grants and loans to close the door to college opportunity on youngsters all over this country. And that, too, is a major difference between the Vice President and me.

Let me just give you one other example. We have a great many people— hundreds of thousands of people living on public assistance in this country. The 50 governors of this nation have proposed to the Congress that we help those families to get off of welfare, help those youngsters, help their mothers to become independent and self-sufficient. It's taken months and months and months to get Mr. Bush and the administration to support that legislation, and they're still resistant. Now, that's the way you help people. Being haunted—"a thousand points of light"—I don't know what that means. I know what strong political leadership is. I know what's happened over the course of the past eight years. These programs have been cut and slashed and butchered, and they've hurt kids all over this country.

MR. LEHRER: A question for the governor. Peter.

MR. JENNINGS: Governor, the crisis is no less a crisis for you if you were elected President. Where would you get the money to devote to the inner cities, which is clearly needed? And can you be specific about the programs not only you'd reinstate, but the more imaginative ones that you'd begin?

MR. DUKAKIS: Well, I said a few minutes ago, Peter, that you could improve the lives of families and youngsters and save money at the same time. Welfare reform is one way to do it. If we invest in job training, in child care for those youngsters, in some extended health benefits so that that mother and her kids won't lose their health benefits when she goes to work, we can help, literally, hundreds of thousands, if not millions, of families to get off of welfare, to become independent and self-sufficient, to be taxpaying citizens, and to improve their lives—the quality of lives, their futures, and the futures of those children. That's just one example of how you can save money and improve the quality of life at the same time.

In my state, for example, we now have that universal health care system, which the Vice President opposes—I think very unwisely. One of the greatest barriers to opportunity for a family and for those children is the threat that they may lose their health insurance. Think about that father down there in Houston who has to tell his youngster that he can't play Little League ball, that he can't go out on that ball field, because he's afraid he's going to get hurt. And, yet, Mr. Bush says, "Well, I don't think we ought to expect businesses to provide health insurance for their employees." When responsible employers—a majority of employers in this country do and are paying more for their insurance to reimburse hospitals for free care on account of people that are not employed—that are not insured that have to go to that hospital.

So, these are the ways that you help families, you help youngsters to live better lives and more decent lives. And we're ready to go to work at the state level, all of us. I know the private sector is—people are all over the country. But, it takes Presidential leadership. It takes a commitment to being involved and to leading. And that's the kind of Presidency I want to lead.

MR. LEHRER: Mr. Vice President.

MR. BUSH: What troubles me is that when I talk of the voluntary sector and a "thousand points of light" and a thousand different ways to help on these problems, the man has just said he doesn't understand what I'm talking about. And this is the problem I have with the big-spending liberals. They think the only way to do it is for the federal government to do it all. The fact happens to be—that education spending is up by the federal government. It is up, it is not down. The federal—but here's the point he misses. The federal government spends seven percent of the total money on education, and the rest of the state governments and local governments, and the "thousand points of light"—and I'm talking about private schools, and private church schools, and things of this nature—are putting up 93 percent. But the federal spending for education is up.

And I want to be the "education president," because I want to see us do better. We're putting more money per child into education, and we are not performing as we should. We've gotten away from the values and the fundamentals, and I would like to urge the school superintendents and the others around the country to stand up now and keep us moving forward on a path toward real excellence. And we can do it, but it's not going to be dictated by some federal bureaucracy in Washington, D.C.

MR. LEHRER: All right. Let's move now to some questions on foreign and national security policy. John Mashek will ask the first question of the Governor.

[Defense Policy]

MR. MASHEK: Governor, the Vice President continually refers to your lack of experience, weakness, naïveté on foreign policy and national security matters. He says you are prepared to eliminate weapons systems that will result in the unilateral disarmament of this country. Is that true?

MR. DUKAKIS: Of course not. Of course, that's a charge that's always made against any governor who runs for the presidency. I think it was one of the things that Mr. Bush said about Mr. Reagan back in 1980. Remember that, George? And yet, some of our finest presidents, some of our strongest international leaders were governors: Franklin Roosevelt, Woodrow Wilson, Theodore Roosevelt.

It's not the amount of time you've spent in Washington, it's not the length of your resume; it's your strength, it's your values, it's the quality of the people you pick, it's your understanding of the forces of change that are sweeping the world, and whether or not you're in a position to provide leadership to make those forces of change work for us and not against us.

The Vice President has a long resume, but it didn't stop him from endorsing the sales of arms to the Ayatollah. And we now know that he was not out of the loop—he was in meeting after meeting after meeting listening to Secretary [of State George P.] Shultz or Secretary [of Defense Caspar W.] Weinberger opposing that, and yet, he supported it. His experience didn't prevent him from participating or involving or in some way being involved [in] the relationship between this government and Mr. Noriega and the drug-trafficking in Panama. He went to the Philippines in the early 1980s and commended Ferdinand Marcos for his commitment to democracy. And he continues to support a failed policy in Central America which is getting worse and worse, and which has, in fact, increased Cuban and Soviet influence in that region.

So, I don't believe the fact that you've got that long resume or had that experience is the real question. The question is values. The question is strength. The question is your willingness to provide the kind of leadership that must be provided. I'm ready to provide that leadership. I want to be the commander in chief of this country. I think it takes fresh leadership now and an understanding of those forces of change to provide the kind of strength that we need. And perhaps the Vice President can explain what he was doing when he supported the trading of arms to a terrorist nation, and his involvement in Panama, and that endorsement of Mr. Marcos.

But, I don't think it's just experience that makes a difference—it's values.

MR. LEHRER: Mr. Vice President.

MR. BUSH: Well, I thought the question was about defense. The Governor was for a nuclear freeze that would have locked in a thousand Soviet intermediate nuclear force weapons and zero for the West. And because we didn't listen to the freeze advocates and strengthened the defenses of this country, we now have the first arms control agreement in the nuclear age. Now, we're sitting down and talking to the Soviets about strategic arms, and he wants to do away with the Midgetman and the MX, the modernization of our nuclear—nuclear capability—that is not the way you deal with the Soviets.

I've met Mr. Gorbachev. I met Mr. Shevardnadze and talked substance with him the other day. These people are tough. But, now we have a chance, if we have the experience to know how to handle it. But please, do not go back to the days when the military was as weak as they could be, when the morale was down, and we—when we were the laughingstock around the world. And now we are back, because we have strength in the defenses of this country. And believe me, I don't want to see us return to those days.

As to Ferdinand Marcos, he isn't there any more. It was under our administration that Mrs. [Corazon] Aquino came in. I'll tell you what I was thinking of. I flew a combat mission. My last one was over Manila, and he was down there fighting against imperialism—

MR. LEHRER: Vice President.

MR. BUSH: —and all of those things happened because the Philippines do crave democracy. And he [word inaudible] up—

MR. LEHRER: Mr. Vice President—

MR. BUSH: —out he goes.

MR. LEHRER: Mr. Vice President, your time is up. John, a question for the Vice President.

MR. MASHEK: Mr. Vice President, the Governor has suggested that you've never met a weapon system that you didn't like or want. Are you prepared to tell the voters one system, in this time of tight budgetary restraints and problems at the Pentagon, that you'd be willing to cut or even eliminate that wouldn't endanger national security?

MR. BUSH: I don't think it's a question of eliminating. I can tell him some I'm against: A-6F, for example, DIVAD [Division Air Defense], and I can go on and on—Minuteman II, penetrations systems. I mean, there's plenty of them that I oppose.

But what I am not going to do when we are negotiating with the Soviet Union, sitting down talking to Mr. Gorbachev about how we achieve a 50 percent reduction in our strategic weapons, I'm not going to give away a couple of aces in that very tough card game. I'm simply not going to do that.

And under me, when I lead this country, the Secretary of Defense is going to have [to] make the choices between how we keep—how we protect the survivability of our nuclear weapons. We are going to make some changes and some tough choices before we go to deployment on the Midgetman missile, or on the—on the Minuteman—whatever it is—we're going to have to—the MX—MX. We're going to have to do that. It's Christmas. It's Christmas. Wouldn't it be nice to be perfect; wouldn't it be nice to be the Ice Man so you never make a mistake?

MR. DUKAKIS: [Speaking at the same time Vice President Bush is speaking.] Well, if this is Christmas—I hope it's [inaudible] Christmas when you make that decision.

MR. BUSH: These are the—these are the—these are the—my answer is: do not make these unilateral cuts. And everybody now realizes that peace through strength works. And so this is where I have a big difference. Of course we're going to have to make some determination on this, and we're going to have to make it on conventional forces. But now, we've got a very good concept called competitive strategies. We will do what we do best. It's a strategy that we've been working on for a couple of years. It is going to take us to much a better advantage in conventional forces.

But look, let me sum it up. I want to be the president that gets conventional forces in balance. I want to be the one to banish chemical and biological weapons from the face of the earth. But you have to have a little bit of experience to know where to start, and I think I've had that.

MR. LEHRER: Governor?

MR. DUKAKIS: Well first, let me say with respect to the freeze, that back in the spring of 1982, Mr. Bush was a lot more sympathetic to the freeze than he seems to be today. As a matter of fact, he said it was not and should not be a subject of partisan demagoguery, because it was too important to the United States, or for the world.

I didn't hear, John, exactly where he was going to cut and what he was going to do, but I know this. We have serious financial problems in this country. We've piled up over $1 trillion in debt, and the next president of the United States is going to have to make some choices. Mr. Bush wants to spend billions on Star Wars. He apparently wants to spend billions on the MX on railroad cars, a weapons system we don't need and can't afford. I thought the administration was opposed to the Midgetman. I thought the administration was at the negotiating table in Geneva suggesting that we ban mobile missile systems entirely.

But those are the choices the next president of the United States is going to have to make. I am for the Stealth, I am for the D-5, I am for going ahead with the advanced cruise missile. But I don't think we need these other systems. I don't think we need them to remain strong. We've got to move ahead with the strategic arms negotiation process, with the comprehensive test-ban treaty, and—

MR. LEHRER: Governor?

MR. DUKAKIS: —with negotiations leading to conventional force reduction in Europe, with deeper cuts on the Soviet side. And Senator [Lloyd] Bentsen and I will pursue that policy.

MR. LEHRER: Anne Groer, a question for the Vice President.

[Dealing with the Soviets]

MS. GROER: Well, Mr. Vice President, you said you met with Secretary General Gorbachev, you have met with Mr. Shevardnadze. But for the last 40 years, Americans have been taught to regard the Soviet Union as the enemy. Yet, President Reagan has signed two arms control treaties, and he's promised to share Star Wars technology with the very country he once called the "evil empire." So, perhaps you could tell us this evening, should we be doing a lot to help the economics and the social development of a country that we have so long regarded as an adversary?

MR. BUSH: What I think we ought to do is take a look at perestroika and glasnost, welcome them, but keep our eyes open—be cautious— because the Soviet change is not fully established yet. Yes I think it's fine to do business with them, but I don't want to see us exporting our highly sensitive, national security oriented technology to the Soviet Union. I don't want to see us making unilateral cuts in our strategic systems while we are negotiating with them.

And so I'm encouraged by what I see when I talk to Mr.—what I hear when I talk to Mr. Gorbachev and Mr. Shevardnadze. But can they pull it off? And when they have deals that are good for us as China started to do—the changes in China since Barbara and I lived there is absolutely amazing in terms of incentive and partnerships and things of this nature. And now the Soviet Union seems to be walking down that same path. We should encourage that. We ought to say this is good.

But where I differ with my opponent is, I am not going to make unilateral cuts in our strategic defense systems or support some freeze when they have superiority. I'm not going to do that because I think the jury is still out on the Soviet experiment. And the interesting place, one of the things that fascinates me about this perestroika and glasnost is what's going to happen in eastern Europe. You see the turmoil in Poland today. And I think we have enormous opportunity for trade. I don't want to go back to the Carter grain embargo on the Soviets. We are once again reliable suppliers and I would never use food as a political tool like our predecessors did.

But this is an exciting time. But all I'm suggesting is, let's not be naive in dealing with the Soviets and make a lot of unilateral cuts hoping against hope that they will match our bid. Look at the INF [Intermediate Nuclear-Force] treaty. And if we haven't learned from the negotiating history on that we'll never learn. The freeze people were wrong. The Reagan Administration was right. Excuse me.

MR. LEHRER: Governor Dukakis.

MR. DUKAKIS: That was a very different George Bush who was talking much more sympathetically about the freeze in the spring of 1982 than he is today, and you were right then, George, when you said that it was no time for partisan demagoguery. Nobody is suggesting that we unilaterally disarm or somehow reduce our strength. Of course not. What we're talking about is a combination of a strong and effective and credible nuclear deterrent, strong, well equipped, well trained, well maintained conventional forces, and at the same time, a willingness to move forward steadily, thoughtfully, cautiously. We have serious differences with the Soviet Union. We have very fundamental differences about human rights, democracy, and in our basic system, our basic view of human beings and of what life is all about. But there are opportunities there now. Senator Bentsen and I have a plan for the 1990s and beyond; Mr. Bush and Mr. [Dan] Quayle do not. And we want to pursue that plan in a way which will bring down the level of nuclear armament, will build a more stable and more peaceful world, and we can do so while making choices here at home. Let's not forget that our national security and our economic security go hand in hand. We cannot be strong militarily when we're teeter-tottering on top of a mountain of debt which has been created in the past eight years. That's why we need a Democratic administration in Washington in 1989.

MR. LEHRER: Anne Groer, a question for the Governor.

[Strategic Defense Initiative]

MS. GROER: Yes. Governor Dukakis, speaking of seeming changes of position, you have gone from calling the Strategic Defense Initiative, or Star Wars, "a fantasy and a fraud" to saying recently you would continue SDI research, and might even deploy the system if Congress supported such a move. Why the change of heart?

MR. DUKAKIS: No, there's been no change of heart. I've said from the beginning that we ought to continue research into the strategic system at about the level it was at in 1983. That's about a billion dollars a year. But I don't know of any reputable scientists who believe that this system, at least as originally conceived, could possibly work—this notion of some kind of an astrodome over ourselves that could protect us from enemy attack—makes real sense. And as a matter of fact, the system that the administration's now talking about is very different from the one that was originally proposed in 1983. So, I am for continued research.

But I also want strong conventional forces. Now, the other day Mr. Bush said, "Well, if we continued with Star Wars, we'd have to cut some place." He hasn't told us where. We know where they're cutting. We know where you're cutting right now. You're cutting into the fiber and muscle of our conventional forces. You're cutting back on maintenance and equipment. There was an Air Force general, not too long ago, in Europe, who said that pretty soon we'd have airplanes without engines, tank commanders who can't drive their tanks more than three-quarters of a mile because they don't have enough fuel, Coast Guard cutters tied up at the dock this summer, not patrolling—they're supposed to be our first line of defense against drugs and the war against drugs—because they don't have enough fuel. You have to make choices. We're not making those choices, and to spend billions and billions as Mr. Bush apparently wants to—although he himself has been all over the lot on this issue lately—on "Star Wars," in my judgment, makes no sense at all. We need a strong, credible, effective nuclear deterrent. We have 13,000 strategic nuclear warheads right now. On land, on sea, and in the air, enough to blow up the Soviet Union—forty times over. They have about 12,000. So, we've got to move forward with those negotiations, get the level of strategic weapons down, but to continue to commit billions to this system makes no sense at all and I think Mr. Bush has been reconsidering his position over the course of the past few weeks—at least that's what I read. Maybe, he'll tell us where he stands tonight.

MR. LEHRER: Mr. Vice President.

MR. BUSH: I'm not reconsidering my position. Two questions—how do you deter nuclear attack without modernizing our nuclear forces, when the Soviets are modernizing? And, how come you spend—[are] willing to spend a dime on something that you consider a fantasy, and a fraud? Those are two, hypo-rhetorical questions. He is the man on conventional forces that wants to eliminate two carrier battlegroups. The armed forces—the conventional forces of the United States have never been more ready. Every single one of the Joint Chiefs [of Staff] will testify to the fact that readiness is at a historic high. And, secondly, in terms of the cutting of the Coast Guard, it was the Congress—the Democratic controlled Congress—so please help us with that, who cut 70 million dollars from the Coast Guard out of the interdiction effort on narcotics. He's got to get this thing more clear. Why do you spend a billion dollars on something you think is a fantasy, and a fraud? I will fully research it, go forward as fast as we can. We've sent up the levels of funding, and when it is deployable, I will deploy it. That's my position on SDI, and it's never wavered a bit.

MR. LEHRER: Peter Jennings. A question for Governor Dukakis?

[Dealing with Terrorists]

MR. JENNINGS: Well, Governor, and Vice President Bush, you both talked tonight about hard choices. Let me try to give you one. Somewhere in the Middle East tonight, nine Americans are being held hostage. If you are Commander in Chief, and Americans are held hostage, what will be more important to you—their individual fate—their individual fate—or the commitment that the United States government must never negotiate with terrorists. And, if any Americans are held hostage, and you become president, to what lengths would you go to rescue them?

MR. DUKAKIS: Peter, it's one of the most agonizing decisions a president has to make. These are American citizens. We care deeply about them. Their families care deeply about them, want them back, and understandably so, and we want to do everything we can to bring them back. But, if there's one thing we also understand it is that you cannot make concessions to terrorists, ever—ever. Because if you do, it's an open invitation to other terrorists to take hostages and to blackmail us. And that's the tragedy of the Iran-contra scandal.

As a matter of fact, Mr. Bush was the chairman of a task force on international terrorism, which issued a report shortly before that decision was made, and said—and rightly so—that we never, ever can make concessions to terrorists and hostage takers. And yet, after sitting through meeting after meeting, he endorsed that decision, endorsed the sale of arms to the Ayatollah in exchange for hostages, one of the most tragic, one of the most mistaken foreign policy decisions we've ever made in this country, and I dare say, encouraged others to take hostages, as we now know.

So, there can be no concessions under any circumstances, because if we do, it's an open invitation to others to do the same. We've got to be tough on international terrorism. We've got to treat it as international crime. We've got to attack it at all points. We've got to use undercover operations. We have to be prepared to use military force against terrorist base camps. We have to work closely with our allies to make sure that they're working with us and we with them. And we can give no quota when it comes to breaking the back of international terrorism.

Yes, we should make every effort to try help those hostages come home, but it can never be because we make concessions. That was a tragic mistake that we made—mistake that Mr. Bush made, and others made, and it should never, ever be made again.

MR. LEHRER: Mr. Vice President.

MR. BUSH: I wrote the Anti-Terrorist Report for this government. It is the best anti-terrorist report written. Yes, we shouldn't trade arms for hostages, but we made vast improvements in our anti-terrorism. Now, it's fine to say that sometimes you have to hit base camps, but when the President saw the state-sponsored fingerprints of Muammar Qaddafi on the loss of American life, he hit Libya. And my opponent was unwilling to support that action—

MR. DUKAKIS: That's not true. That's not true.

MR. BUSH: —terrorist action[s] against the United States citizens have gone down and I have long ago said I supported the President in this matter. And I've said mistakes were made—clearly, nobody's going to think the President started out thinking he was going to trade arms for hostages. That is a very serious charge against the President. And that has been thoroughly looked into. But, the point is, sometimes the action—has to be taken by the federal government. And, when we took action, it had a favorable response.

MR. LEHRER: A question for the Vice President, Peter?

[Bush as Vice President]

MR. JENNINGS: It seems, perhaps, a good subject on which to make the point that you've campaigned vigorously as part of a leadership team.

But, so far, you won't tell the American people in considerable measure what advice you gave the President on issues, including the sale of arms to Iran. And what should have been done about the hostages. To the best of my knowledge, there's no constitutional requirement which prevents you from doing so. Jimmy Carter urged his Vice President, Walter Mondale, to tell the American people. Would you now ask President Reagan for permission to tell the American people what advice you did give him? And, if you don't, how do we judge your judgment in the Oval Office in the last eight years?

MR. BUSH: You judge by the whole record. You judge by the entire record. Are we closer to peace? Are we doing better in anti-terrorism? Should we have listened to my opponent who wanted to send the UN into the Persian Gulf? Or, in spite of the mistakes of the past, are we doing better there? How is our credibility with the GCC [Gulf Cooperation Council] countries on the western side of the Gulf? Is Iran talking to Iraq about peace? You judge on the record. Are the Soviets coming out of Afghanistan? How does it look in a program he called phony, or some one of these marvelous Boston adjectives up there, about Angola? Now, we have a chance, now—several Bostonians don't like it but the rest of the country will understand—now, we have a chance. Now, we have a chance. And, so, I think that I'd leave it right there and say that you judge on the whole record.

And let me say this, all he can talk about—he goes around ranting about Noriega. Now, I've told you what the intelligence briefing he received said about that. He can talk about Iran-contra, and also—I'll make a deal with you. I will take all the blame for those two incidences if you give me half the credit for all of the good things that have happened in world peace since Ronald Reagan and I took over from the Carter Administration—. I still—I still have a—I still have a couple of minutes left. And there is a different principle here on—

MR. LEHRER: Sorry—sorry, Mr. Vice President.

MR. BUSH: Sorry, [it's only] on yellow out here—wait a minute—

MR. LEHRER: I'm sorry. I'm wrong. Go ahead. My apologies.

MR. BUSH: Jim.

MR. LEHRER: You said, nobody's perfect.

MR. BUSH: I said, I wasn't perfect, but I thought you were. Where was I?

MR. LEHRER: My apology.

MR. DUKAKIS: The 25th of December, Mr. Vice President.

MR. BUSH: I agree. I agree. Where was I?

MR. LEHRER: Governor.

MR. DUKAKIS: He can have another ten seconds if he wants to.

MR. LEHRER: Yes, sir. Go ahead.

MR. BUSH: Go ahead.

MR. LEHRER: All right. All right. Governor, you have a minute to respond.

MR. DUKAKIS: Well, the matter of judgment is very important, and I think it's important to understand what happened here. A report on international terrorism chaired by the Vice President was released, and made some very specific recommendations about how to deal with terrorism. They were ignored. The Vice President ignored them. It says mistakes were made—very serious mistakes in judgment were made. He says, "Well, let's concede that the administration has been doing business with Noriega," who's made him a part of our foreign policy and has been funneling aid to the contras through convicted drug dealers.

I think those are very, very serious questions of judgment, which those of you who are watching us here tonight have a right to judge and review. We're not going to make those kinds of mistakes. You cannot make concessions to terrorists. If you do, you invite the taking of more hostages—that's a basic principle. It was ignored in that case, and it was a very, very serious mistake in judgment.

MR. LEHRER: Go to a question from John Mashek—it goes to the Vice President.

[Quayle's Qualifications]

MR. MASHEK: Mr. Vice President, Democrats, and even some Republicans, are still expressing reservations about the qualifications and credentials of Senator Dan Quayle of Indiana, your chosen running mate, to be a heartbeat away from the presidency. What do you see in him that others do not?

MR. BUSH: I see a young man that was elected to the Senate twice, to the House of Representatives twice. I see a man who is young and I'm putting my confidence in a whole generation of people that are in their thirties and in their forties. I see a man that took the leadership in the Job Training Partnership Act, and that retrains people in this highly competitive changing society we're in so if a person loses his job, he is retrained for a benefit—for a work that will be productive and he won't have to go on one of these many programs that the liberals keep talking about.

I see a young man who is knowledgeable in the whole—in the race, knowledgeable in defense, and Dan Quayle is one of them, and I am one of them. And I believe that he will be outstanding. And he took a tremendous pounding, and everybody now knows that he took a very unfair pounding. And I'd like each person to say, did I jump to conclusions running down rumors that were so outrageous and so brutal. And he's kept his head up and he will do very, very well. And he has my full confidence and he'll have the confidence of people that are in their thirties and forties and more. So judge the man on his record, not on a lot of rumors and innuendo and trying to fool around with his name.

My opponent says, "J. Danforth Quayle." Do you know who J. Danforth was? He was a man that gave his life in World War II. So ridiculing a person's name is a little beneath this process and he'll do very well when we get into the debate.

MR. DUKAKIS: Well when it comes to ridicule, George, you win a gold medal. I think we can agree on that.

MR. BUSH: Just the facts.

MR. DUKAKIS: But did I sense a desire that maybe Lloyd Bentsen ought to be your running mate when you said that the three people on your ticket—

MR. BUSH: No. I think the debate ought to be—

MR. DUKAKIS: I think the American people have a right to judge us on this question, on how we picked a running mate, a person who is a heartbeat away from the presidency. I picked Lloyd Bentsen, a distinguished, strong, mature, leader in the Senate; somebody whose qualifications nobody has questioned. Mr. Bush picked Dan Quayle. I doubt very much that Dan Quayle was the best qualified person for that job. And as a matter of fact, I think for most people the notion of "President Quayle" is a very, very troubling notion tonight.

MR. LEHRER: All right. John will now ask a question of the Governor. It will be the last question, and then the Vice President will have a rebuttal. John?

MR. MASHEK: Well, Governor, you did select Lloyd Bentsen of Texas.

MR. DUKAKIS: Indeed.

[Bentsen/Dukakis Disagreements]

MR. MASHEK: And you have a lot of disagreement with him on fundamental issues, including the Reagan tax cuts, aid to the rebels in Nicaragua, the death penalty, gun control—who's right?

MR. DUKAKIS: Well, John, I'm a man who's been a chief executive for 10 years. I've picked a lot of people. I've picked cabinets, I've named judges. I know that the people you pick make an enormous difference in your ability to govern. And I set high standards, I try to meet them, and I insist that people who work for me meet them. And if they don't, they don't stick around very long. But, I didn't pick Lloyd Bentsen because he was a clone of Mike Dukakis. I picked him because he was somebody who would be a strong vice president, somebody who would be an active vice president—somebody who would come to me, if somebody came up with a crazy idea that we ought to trade arms to the Ayatollah for hostages, and say, "Mr. President, that's wrong. We shouldn't do that." That's the kind of vice president I want.

He himself has said, and rightly so, that he will be a strong vice president, but when the president makes a decision, that will be his decision. And I am very, very proud of that choice. And I didn't pick him because he agreed with me on everything.

You know, [House Speaker] Sam Rayburn once said that if two people agree on everything, then only one person is doing the thinking. The fact is that I've picked somebody who not only will be a great vice president, but if, God forbid, something happens to the president, could step into that office and do so with distinction and with strength and with leadership. I doubt very much—I doubt very much that Mr. Bush's selection for the vice presidency of the United States meets that test.

MR. LEHRER: Mr. Vice President.

MR. BUSH: We obviously have a difference. I believe it does meet the test. We'll have an opportunity to see the two of them in action in a friendly forum—wonderful, friendly fashion like this. I had hoped that this'd—I'd hoped this had been a little friendlier an evening. I'd wanted to hitch-hike a ride home in his tank with him, but—I think now we're— we've got the lines too carefully drawn here.

But you talk about judgment. I mean, what kind of judgment—I mean, jumping all over the President on his decision on one area of the foreign policy. What kind of judgment sense has your chief education advisor, now in jail in Massachusetts? I mean, I don't think this is a fair argument, but nevertheless, I support my nominee for Vice President, and he'll do an outstanding job.

MR. LEHRER: Gentlemen, I was given some bad word a moment ago. There is time for one more question. Getting it in my ear. And Ann Groer will ask it.

MS. GROER: To—Vice President Bush?

MR. LEHRER: To—to the Governor. Sorry.

[Agriculture, Third World Debt]

MS. GROER: Oh, I'm so sorry. Governor Dukakis, as many US farmers face or undergo foreclosure, the United States is considering the possibility of forgiving a certain percentage of debt owed by Latin American and Third World countries. Do you favor giving these countries a break in their loans? And if so, how do you explain that to the American farmers who are losing their land and livelihood?

MR. DUKAKIS: Well, I think we have to go to work on the problem of Third World debt, and we've got to assist those Third World countries in dealing with this massive debt which they currently—which they have incurred, and which is burdening them, and which, if we don't do something about it and assist them, along with other nations around the world, we'll destroy their economies, destroy their future, and at the same time, we'll destroy markets that are important to our farmers.

But I also believe that we need an agricultural policy which doesn't cost us the $15 [billion] to $20 [billion] to $25 billion a year that it's been costing us over the course of the past three or four years under this administration. I think it's going to require good, solid credit policies, and thanks to the Congress, we now have an agricultural credit bill which is helping, and improving the situation with at least some of our farmers. I think it's going to require a combination of supply management and reasonable price supports to make sure that our farmers get a decent price. And I think it also is going to require an administration that understands that there are tremendous opportunities out there for the development of new uses for agricultural products, new uses which can help us to clean up our environment at the same time: biodegradable plastic, gasohol, which the Vice President himself has been involved in, road de-icers made from corn products. I mean, there are enormous opportunities out there to expand markets and to build a strong future for our farmers.

But I don't think there is anything mutually exclusive or contradictory about building a strong farm economy in this country and assisting our family farms, and providing a good, strong future for rural communities and for rural America, and at the same time working on Third World debt. As a matter of fact, Mexico itself is one of our biggest agricultural customers. So, in the sense that we can work to help Mexico, we build and expand and deal with its very serious economic problems; we help our farmers at the same time.

MR. LEHRER: Mr. Vice President.

MR. BUSH: I oppose supply management and production controls. I support the Farm Bill, the 1985 Farm Bill, and its spending is moving in the right direction.

I want to expand our markets abroad, and that's why I'd like to call for that first economic summit to be on agriculture. I will not go back to the way the Democrats did it, and use food as a political weapon and throw a grain embargo on the farmers in this country. I want to see rural redevelopment, and I have been out front in favor of alternate sources of energy, and one of them is gasohol, and it comes from using your corn, and I think we can do better in terms of biodegradables, for a lot of products. So, I'm optimistic about the agricultural economy.

In terms of the Third World, I support the Baker Plan. I want to see market economies sprung up all around the world. And, to the degree they do, we are succeeding. And I don't want to see the banks let off the hook; I would oppose that. But I think we're on the right track in agriculture, and I am very, very encouraged. But let's not go back to—that's what they call "supply management" and "production control," that will simply price us out of the international market. Let's try to expand our markets abroad.

MR. LEHRER: All right. That really is the end. Now, let's go to closing statements. They will be two minutes each in duration by agreement. Vice President Bush goes first. Governor Dukakis second.

Mr. Vice President.

[Closing Statements]

MR. BUSH: I talked in New Orleans about a gentler and kinder nation, and I have made specific proposals on education, and the environment, on ethics, on energy, and on how we do better in battling crime in our country. But there are two main focal points of this election: opportunity and peace. I want to keep this expansion going. Yes, we want change, but we are the change, I am the change. I don't want to go back to malaise and misery index. And so opportunity—keep America at work. The best poverty program is a job with dignity in the private sector.

And in terms of peace, we are on the right track. We've achieved an arms control agreement that our critics thought was never possible. And I want to build on it; I want to see us finalize that START [Strategic Arms Reduction Talks] agreement; and I want to be the one to finally lead the world to banishing chemical and biological weapons. I want to see asymmetrical reductions in conventional forces.

And then it gets down to a question of values. We've had a chance to spell out our differences on the Pledge of Allegiance here tonight, and on tough sentencing of drug kingpins and this kind of thing. I do favor the death penalty. And we've got a wide array of differences on those.

But in the final analysis, in the final analysis, [when] the person goes into that voting booth they're going to say: Who has the values I believe in? Who has the experience that we trust? Who has the integrity and the stability to get the job done? My fellow Americans, I am that man and I ask for your support. Thank you very much.

MR. LEHRER: Governor. Governor Dukakis.

MR. DUKAKIS: This has been an extraordinary 18 months for Kitty and me, and our family. We've had an opportunity to campaign all over this country—to meet with so many of you in communities, states and regions, to get to know you.

I'm more optimistic today than I was when I began about this nation, providing we have the kind of leadership in Washington that can work with you, that can build partnerships, that can build jobs in every part of this country, not certain parts of this country.

You know, my friends, my parents came to this country as immigrants, like millions and millions of immigrants before them and since, seeking opportunity, seeking the American dream. They made sure their sons understood this is the greatest country in the world. That those of us, especially who were the sons and daughters of immigrants, had a special responsibility to give something back to the country that had opened up its arms to our parents and given so much to them. I believe in the American dream. I am a product of it. And I want to help that dream come true for every single citizen in this land—with a good job and good wages, with good schools in every part of this country and every community in this country. With decent and affordable housing that our people can buy and own and live in, so that we end the shame of homelessness in America. With decent and affordable health care for all working families. Yes, it's a tough problem, as Mr. Bush says, but it's not an insolvable problem. It's one that we will solve and must solve—with a clean and wholesome environment. And with a strong America, that's strong militarily and economically, as we must be. An America that provides strong, international leadership because we're true to our values. We have an opportunity, working together, to build that future. To build a better America, to build a best America. Because a best America doesn't hide, we compete. The best America doesn't waste, we invest. The best America doesn't leave some of its citizens behind, we leave—we bring everybody along. And the best America is not behind us, the best America is yet to come. Thank you very much for listening.

SECOND PRESIDENTIAL DEBATE

MR. SHAW: By agreement between the candidates, the first question goes to Governor Dukakis. You have two minutes to respond. Governor, if Kitty Dukakis were raped and murdered, would you favor an irrevocable death penalty for the killer?

MR. DUKAKIS: No, I don't, Bernard, and I think you know that I've opposed the death penalty during all of my life. I don't see any evidence that it's a deterrent, and I think there are better and more effective ways to deal with violent crime. We've done so in my own state, and it's one of the reasons why we have had the biggest drop in crime of any industrial state in America, why we have the lowest murder rate of any industrial state in America.

But we have work to do in this nation; we have work to do to fight a real war and not a phony war against drugs. And that's something that I want to lead, something we haven't had over the course of the past many years, even though the vice president has been, at least allegedly, in charge of that war. We have much to do to step up that war, to double the number of drug enforcement agents, to fight both here and abroad, to work with our neighbors in this hemisphere. And I want to call a hemispheric summit just as soon after the 20th of January as possible to fight that war.

But we also have to deal with drug education prevention here at home. And that's one of the things that I hope I can lead personally as the president of the United States. We've had great success in my own state, and we've reached out to young people and their families and been able to help them by beginning drug education and prevention in the early elementary grades.

So we can fight this war and we can win this war, and we can do so in a way that marshals our forces, that provides real support for state and local law enforcement officers who have not been getting that kind of support, do it in a way which will bring down violence in this nation, will help our youngsters to stay away from drugs, will stop this avalanche of drugs that's pouring into the country, and will make it possible for our kids and our families to grow up in safe and secure and decent neighborhoods.

MR. SHAW: Mr. Vice President, your one-minute rebuttal.

MR. BUSH: Well, a lot of what this campaign is about, it seems to me, Bernie, is to a question of values. And here, I do have, on this particular question, a big difference with my opponent.

You see, I do believe that some crimes are so heinous, so brutal, so outrageous—and I'd say particularly those that result in the death of a police officer—those real brutal crimes, I do believe in the death penalty. And I think it is a deterrent. And I believe we need it, and I'm glad that the Congress moved on this drug bill, and it finally called for that, related to these narcotics drug kingpins. And so, we just have an honest difference of opinion. I support it, and he doesn't.

[On the Vice Presidency]

MR. SHAW: Now, to you, Vice President Bush. I quote to you this from Article II of the 20th Amendment of the Constitution: Quote, "If, at the time fixed for the beginning of the term of the President, the President-elect shall have died, the Vice President-elect shall become President," meaning, if you are elected and die before Inauguration Day—

MR. BUSH: Bernie!

MR. SHAW: —automatically—automatically, Dan Quayle would become the 41st president of the United States. What have you to say about that possibility?

MR. BUSH: I'd have confidence in him, and I made a good selection. And I've never seen such a pounding, an unfair pounding, on a young senator in my entire life. And I've never seen a presidential campaign where the presidential nominee runs against my vice presidential nominee—never seen one before. You know, Lloyd Bentsen jumped on Dan Quayle when Dan Quayle said he's had roughly the same amount of experience. He had two terms in the Congress; he had two terms in the Senate, serving his second term.

He founded the—authored the Job Training Partnership Act that says to American working men and women that are thrown out of work for no fault of their own, that they're going to have jobs. We're moving into a new, competitive age, and we need that kind of thing. He, unlike my opponent, is an expert in national defense, helped amend the INF Treaty, so we got a good, sound treaty when these people over here were talking about a freeze. If we'd listened to them, we would never have had a treaty.

And so I have great confidence in him and he's—it's turning around. You know, the American people are fair. They don't like it when there's an unfair pounding and kind of hooting about people. They want to judge it on the record itself. And so I'm proud of my choice. And, you know, I don't think age is the only criterion. But, I'll tell you something, I'm proud that people that are 30 years old and 40 years old now have someone in their generation that is going to be vice president of the United States of America. I made a good selection. The American people are seeing it and I'm proud of it. That's what I'd say. And he could do the job.

MR. SHAW: Governor Dukakis, your one-minute rebuttal.

MR. DUKAKIS: Bernard, this was the first presidential decision that we, as nominees, were called upon to make and that's why people are so concerned because it was an opportunity for us to demonstrate what we were looking for in a running mate. More than that, it was the first national security decision that we had to make.

The vice president talks about national security. Three times since World War II, the vice president has had to suddenly become the president and commander in chief. I picked Lloyd Bentsen because I thought he was the best qualified person for the job. Mr. Bush picked Dan

Quayle and, before he did it, he said, "Watch my choice for vice president. It will tell all." And it sure did. It sure did.

MR. SHAW: Ann Compton for the vice president.

[Taxes and the Budget]

MS. COMPTON: Thank you, Bernie. Mr. Vice President, yes, we read your lips: "No new taxes." But, despite that same pledge from President Reagan, after income tax rates were cut, in each of the last five years, some federal taxes have gone up—on Social Security, cigarettes, liquor, even long-distance telephone calls. Now that's money straight out of people's wallets. Isn't the phrase "no new taxes" misleading the voters?

MR. BUSH: No, because that's—that I'm pledged to that. And, yes, some taxes have gone up. And the main point is taxes have been cut and yet income is up to the federal government by 25 percent in the last three years. And so, what I want to do is keep this expansion going. I don't want to kill it off by a tax increase.

More Americans [are] at work today than at any time in the history of this country and a greater percentage of the work force. And the way you kill expansions is to raise taxes. And I don't want to do that. And I won't do that. And what I have proposed is something much better. And it's going to take discipline of the executive branch. It's going to take discipline of the congressional branch—and that is what I call a flexible freeze that allows growth—about 4 percent or the rate of inflation—but does not permit the Congress just to add on spending.

I hear this talk about a blank check—the American people are pretty smart. They know who writes out the checks. And they know who appropriates the money. It is the United States Congress and by two to one, Congress is blamed for these deficits. And the answer is to discipline both the executive branch and the congressional branch by holding the line on taxes.

So I am pledged to do that. And those pessimists who say it can't be done, I'm sorry. I just have fundamental disagreement with them.

MR. SHAW: Governor Dukakis, your one-minute response.

MR. DUKAKIS: Ann, the vice president made that pledge; he's broken it three times in the past year already, so it isn't worth the paper it's printed on. And what I'm concerned about is that if we continue with the policies that Mr. Bush is talking about here this evening—flexible freeze—somebody described it the other day as a kind of economic Slurpee.

He wants to spend billions on virtually every weapons system around. He says he's not going to raise taxes, though he has broken that pledge repeatedly. He says he wants to give the wealthiest 1 percent in this country a five-year, $40 billion tax break, and we're going to pay for it. And he's been proposing all kinds of programs for new spending costing billions.

Now, if we continue with these policies, this trillion and a half dollars worth of new debt that's already been added on the backs of the American taxpayers is going to increase even more. If we continue with this for another four years, then I'm worried about the next generation, whether we can ever turn this situation around.

No, we need a chief executive who's prepared to lead, who won't blame the Congress, but will lead, will bring down that deficit, will make tough choices on spending, will go out and do the job that we expect of him and do with it the Congress of the United States.

MR. SHAW: And to Governor Dukakis.

MS. COMPTON: Governor, let me follow up on that by asking you, you've said it many times, that you have balanced 10 budgets in a row in Massachusetts. Are you promising the American people, here tonight, that within a four-year presidential term, you will balance the federal budget?

MR. DUKAKIS: No, I'm not sure I can promise that. I don't think either one of us can, really. There's no way of anticipating what may happen. I will say this, that we'll set as our goal a steady, gradual reduction of the deficit, which will require tough choices on spending. It will require a good strong rate of economic growth. It will require a plan that the president works out with the Congress—doesn't blame them, works it out with them—which brings that deficit down. It will require us to go out and collect billions and billions of dollars in taxes owed that aren't being paid in this country. And that's grossly unfair to the average American who's paying his taxes, and paying them on time, and doesn't have any alternative—it's taken out of his paycheck.

Mr. Bush says we're going to put the IRS on every taxpayer. That's not what we're going to do. I'm for the Taxpayer Bill of Rights. Well, I think it's unconscionable, Ann, that we should be talking or thinking about imposing new taxes on average Americans, when there are billions out there—over a hundred billion dollars in taxes owed that aren't being paid.

Now, I think if we work together on it, and if you have a president that will work with the Congress and the American people, we can bring that deficit down steadily, $20, 25, 30 billion a year, build economic growth, build a good strong future for America, invest in those things which we must invest in: economic development, good jobs, good schools for our kids, college opportunity for young people, decent health care and afford-able housing, and a clean and safe environment. We can do all of those things, and at the same time build a future in which we're standing on a good strong fiscal foundation.

Senator Bentsen said, as you recall at the debate with Senator Quayle, that if you give any of us $200 billion worth of hot checks a year, we can create an illusion of prosperity. But sooner or later, that credit card mentality isn't going to work. And I want to bring to the White House a sense of strength and fiscal responsibility which will build a good strong foundation under which this country, or above which this country can move, grow, invest and build the best America for its people and for our kids and our grand-kids.

MR. SHAW: Mr. Vice President? Your one-minute response.

MR. BUSH: The governor has to balance a budget in his state. He's required to by law. He's raised taxes several times. I wish he would join me, as a matter of fact, in appealing to the American people for the balanced-budget amendment for the federal government and for the line-item veto. I'd like to have that line-item veto for the president, because I think that would be extraordinarily helpful.

And I won't do one other thing that he's had to do—took $29 million out of his state pension fund. That's equivalent in the federal level of taking out of the Social Security Trust Fund. I'm not going to do that. I won't do that. And so I'm still a little unclear as to whether he's for or against a tax increase. I have been all for the Taxpayer's Bill of Rights all along. And this idea of unleashing a whole bunch, an army, a conventional force army of IRS agents into everybody's kitchen—I mean, he's against most defense matters, and now he wants to get an army of IRS auditors going out there. I'm against that. I oppose that.

MR. SHAW: I'm going to say this, and I'm going to say it once to every person in this auditorium. What these candidates are about is of utmost seriousness to the American voters. They should be heard, and you should be quiet. If you are not quiet, I'm going to implore the candidates to do something about prodding—or quieting their own partisans. But we cannot get through this program with these outbursts. Margaret Warner, for Governor Dukakis.

[Candidate Qualities]

MS. WARNER: Good evening, Governor, Mr. Vice President. Governor, you won the first debate on intellect, and yet you lost it on heart.

MR. BUSH: Just a minute.

MR. DUKAKIS: I don't know about the vice—

MS. WARNER: You'll get your turn. The American public—

MR. DUKAKIS: I don't know whether the vice president agrees with that.

MS. WARNER: The American public admired your performance, but didn't seem to like you much. Now Ronald Reagan has found his personal warmth to be a tremendous political asset. Do you think that a president has to be likable to be an effective leader?

MR. DUKAKIS: Margaret, may I go back and just say to the vice president that I didn't raid the pension fund in Massachusetts. You're dead wrong, George. We didn't do that. As a matter of fact, I'm the first governor in the history of my state to fund that pension system, and I'm very proud of that. And you just had your—

MR. BUSH: (Inaudible.)

MR. DUKAKIS: —You just have your information—no, we did not. No, we did not. I've been in politics for 25 years, Margaret. I've won a lot of elections; I've lost a few, as you know, and learned from those losses. I won the Democratic nomination in 51 separate contests. I think I'm a reasonably likable guy. I'm serious, though I think I'm a little more lovable these days than I used to be back in my youth when I began in my state legislature. But I'm also a serious guy. I think the presidency of the United States is a very serious office. And I think we have to address these issues in a very serious way.

So I hope and expect that I'll be liked by the people of this country as president of the United States. I certainly hope I'll be liked by them on the 8th of November. But I also think it's important to be somebody who's willing to make those tough choices. Now, we've just heard two or three times from the vice president that he's not going to raise taxes. I repeat, within days after you made that pledge, you broke it. You said, "Well, maybe as a last resort, we'll do it," and you supported legislation this year that's involved tax increases not once, but twice.

So that pledge isn't realistic, and I think the vice president knows it. I think the people of this country know it. The fact of the matter is that the next president of the United States is going to have to go to the White House seriously, he's going to have to work with the Congress seriously. He can't turn to the Congress and blame them for the fact that we don't have a balanced budget and that we have billions and billions of dollars in red ink.

And I'm going to be a president who is serious, I hope and expect will be liked by the American people. But more than that, will do the kind of job that I'm elected to do, will do it with as much good humor as I can, but at the same time, will do it in a way which will achieve the goals we want for ourselves and our people. And I think we know what they are—

MR. SHAW: Governor—

MR. DUKAKIS: —a good strong future, a future in which there—

MR. SHAW: Your time has run out, sir.

MR. DUKAKIS: is opportunity for all of our citizens.

MR. SHAW: One minute from the vice president.

MR. BUSH: I don't think it's a question of whether people like you or not to make you an effective leader. I think it's whether you share the broad dreams of the American people, whether you have confidence in the people's ability to get things done, or whether you think it all should be turned over, as many of the liberals do, to Washington, D.C. You see, I think it's a question of values, not likability or lovability.

It's a question in foreign affairs of experience, knowing world leaders, knowing how to build on a superb record of this administration in arms control because you'd know exactly how to begin. You have to learn from experience that making unilateral cuts in the defense system is not the way that you enhance the peace.

You've got to understand that it is only the United States that can stand for freedom and democracy around the world, and we can't turn it over to the United Nations or other multilateral organizations. It is, though, trying to understand the heartbeat of the country. And I know these campaigns get knocked a lot, but I think I'd be a better president now—

MR. SHAW: Mr. Vice President—

MR. BUSH: —for having had to travel to these communities and understand the family values and the importance of neighborhood.

MR. SHAW: Margaret Warner for the vice president.

MS. WARNER: I'd like to follow up on that, Mr. Vice President. The tenor of the campaign you've been running in terms of both the issues and your rhetoric has surprised even some of your friends. Senator Mark Hatfield has known your family a long time and who knew your father, the late Senator Prescott Bush, said, and I quote, "If his father were alive today I'm sure his father would see it as a shocking transformation."

Is Senator Hatfield right?

MR. BUSH: What was he referring to?

MS. WARNER: He was referring to your performance in the campaign.

MR. BUSH: Well I think my dad would be pretty proud of me, because I think we've come a long, long way. And I think, you know, three months ago, I remember some of the great publications in this country had written me off. And what I've had to do is to define not just my position, but to define his [Dukakis']. And I hope I've done it fairly. And the reason I've had to do that is that he ran on the left in the Democratic primary, ran firmly and ran with conviction, and ran on his record.

And then at the Democratic Convention they made a determination. And they said there ideology doesn't matter, just competence. And in the process the negatives began. It wasn't me that was there at that convention. Thank God, I was up with Jimmy Baker camping out and I didn't have to hear all of the personal attacks on me out of that Democratic convention. It was wonderful not to listen to it. And I'm not the one that compared the president of the United States of rotting like a dead fish from the head down; I didn't do that.

But I have defined the issues and I am not going to let Governor Dukakis go through this election without explaining some of these very liberal positions. He's the one that said, "I am a liberal—traditional liberal—progressive liberal Democrat." He's the one that brought up, to garner primary votes, the whole question of the ACLU. And I have enormous difference with the ACLU on their political agenda, not on their defending some minority opinion on the right or the left. I support that. But what I don't like is this left-wing political agenda, and therefore, I have to help define that. And if he's unwilling to do it, if he says ideology doesn't matter, I don't agree with him.

MR. SHAW: One minute, from Governor Dukakis.

MR. DUKAKIS: Well, Margaret, we've heard it again tonight, and I'm not surprised. The labels. I guess the vice president called me a liberal two or three times, said I was coming from the left. In 1980, President Reagan called you a liberal for voting for federal gun control. And this is something Republicans have used for a long time. They tried it with Franklin Roosevelt and Harry Truman and John Kennedy. It's not labels, it's our vision of America, and we have two fundamentally different visions of America.

The vice president is complacent, thinks we ought to stick with the status quo, doesn't think we ought to move ahead, thinks things are okay as they are. I don't. I think this is a great country because we've always wanted to do better, to make our country better, to make our lives better. We've always been a nation which was ambitious for America, and we move forward. And that's the kind of America I want; that's the kind of leadership I want to provide.

But I don't think these labels mean a thing, and I would hope that tonight, and in the course of the rest of this campaign, we can have our good, solid disagreements on issues; there's nothing the matter with that. But let's stop labeling each other and let's get to the heart of the matter, which is the future of this country.

MR. SHAW: Andrea Mitchell, for the Vice President.

[Weapons Systems]

MS. MITCHELL: Mr. Vice President, Governor. Mr. Vice President, let me return for a moment to the issue of the budget, because so much has already been put off limits in your campaign that most people do not believe that the flexible freeze alone will solve the problem of the deficit. So, let's turn to defense for a moment.

Pentagon officials tell us that there is not enough money in the budget to handle military readiness, preparedness, as well as new weapons systems that have been proposed, as well as those already in the pipeline. You were asked at the first debate what new weapons systems you would cut. You mentioned three that had already been canceled. Can you, tonight, share with us three new weapons systems that you would cut?

MR. BUSH: If I knew of three new weapons systems that I thought were purely waste, and weren't protected by the Congress, they wouldn't be in the budget. They would not be in the budget. But you want one now? I'll give you one. That HEMAT, that heavy truck, that's cost, what is it, $850 million and the Pentagon didn't request it and yet a member of Congress, a very powerful one, put it in the budget.

I think we can save money through this whole, very sophisticated concept, Andrea, that I know you do understand, of competitive strategies. It is new. And it is very, very different than what's happened. But it's not quite ready to be totally implemented. But it's very important. I think we can save through the Packard Commission report, and I'm very proud that David Packard, the originator of that report, is strongly supporting me. So it's not a question of saying our budget is full of a lot of waste. I don't believe that.

I do think this: We're in the serious stages of negotiation with the Soviet Union now on the strategic arms control talks. And we are protecting a couple of options in terms of modernizing our strategic forces. My secretary of defense is going to have to make a very difficult decision in which system to go forward with. But, we are protecting both of them. We're moving forward with negotiations. And, you see, I just think it

761

would be dumb negotiating policy with the Soviets, to cut out one or the other of the two options right now. The Soviets are modernizing. They continue to modernize. And we can't simply say, "We've got enough nuclear weapons. Let's freeze." We can't do that.

We have to have modernization. Especially if we achieve the 50 percent reduction in strategic weapons that our president is taking the leadership to attain. And so that's the way I'd reply to it. And I believe we can have the strongest and best defense possible if we modernize, if we go forward with competitive strategies, and if we do follow through on the Packard Commission report.

MR. SHAW: Governor Dukakis, one minute.

MR. DUKAKIS: Well, Andrea, we've just had another example of why the Vice President's mathematics just doesn't add up. I think you know, because you've covered these issues, that there's no way that we can build all of the weapons systems that the vice president says he wants to build within the existing defense budget. Everybody knows that, including the people at the Pentagon.

Now, my defense secretary is going to have a lot to do with some of those decisions, but it's going to be the president that's going to have to ultimately decide, before that budget goes to the Congress, what weapon systems are going to go and what are going to stay. We're not going to spend the billions and trillions that Mr. Bush wants to spend on Star Wars. We're not going to spend billions on MXs on railroad cars, which is a weapon system we don't need, can't afford, and won't help our defense posture at all. We're not going to spend hundreds of millions on a space plane from Washington to Tokyo.

Those are decisions that the chief executive has to make. Yes, we're going to have a strong and credible and effective nuclear deterrent. We're going to go forward with the Stealth, the D-5 and the advanced cruise missile and good conventional forces. But the next president of the United States will have to make some tough and difficult decisions. I'm prepared to make them—

MR. SHAW: Governor.

MR. DUKAKIS: —the Vice President is not.

MR. SHAW: Andrea has a question for you.

MS. MITCHELL: Governor, continuing on that subject then, you say that we have to do something about conventional forces. You have supported the submarine-launched missile, the D-5, you just referred to. Yet, from Jerry Ford to Jimmy Carter to Ronald Reagan, there has been a bipartisan consensus in favor of modernizing the land-based missiles. Now, you have ruled out the MX and the Midgetman. More recently, some of your aides have hinted at some flexibility that you might show about some other new form of missile. Can you tell us tonight why you have rejected the collected wisdom of people as diverse as Sam Nunn, Henry Kissinger, Al Gore, people in both parties, and what type of land-based missile would you consider?

MR. DUKAKIS: Well, Andrea, today we have 13,000 strategic nuclear warheads—on land, on air and the sea. That's an incredibly powerful nuclear deterrent. I don't rule out modernization and there are discussions going on now in the Congress and over at the Pentagon about a less expensive modernized land-based leg of the triad.

But there are limits to what we can spend. There are limits to this nation's ability to finance these weapons systems. And one of the things that the vice president either ignores or won't address is the fact that you can't divorce our military security from our economic security. How can we build a strong America militarily that's teeter-tottering on a mountain of debt?

And if we go forward with the kinds of policies that the vice president is suggesting tonight and have in the past, that debt is going to grow bigger and bigger and bigger. So military security and economic security go hand in hand. And we will have a strong and effective and credible nuclear deterrent. We're going to have conventional forces that are well maintained, well equipped, well trained, well supported. And we have serious problems with our conventional forces at the present time and they'll get worse unless we have a president who's willing to make some of these decisions.

And we also have important domestic priorities in education and housing and health care, in economic development and job training, in the environment. Now, all of these things are going to have to be addressed. That's why I say again to all of you out there who have to deal with your household budgets and know how difficult it is, that the next president has to do the same.

I want the men and women of our armed forces to have the support they need to defend us, the support they need when they risk our lives to keep us free and to keep this country free. But we cannot continue to live on a credit card. We cannot continue to tell the American people that we're going to build all of these systems, and at the same time invest in important things here at home, and be serious about building a strong and good America. And that's the kind of America I want to build.

MR. SHAW: One minute for the vice president.

MR. BUSH: I think the foremost—Can we start the clock over? I held off for the applause. Can I get—

MR. SHAW: You can proceed, sir.

MR. BUSH: I think the foremost responsibility of a president really gets down to the national security of this country. The governor talks about limits, what we can't do, opposes these two modernization systems, talks now about, "May, well, we'll develop some new kind of a missile." It takes eight years, 10 years to do that.

He talked about a nuclear freeze back at the time when I was in Europe, trying to convince European public opinion that we ought to go forward with the deployment of the INF weapons. And thank God the freeze people were not heard. They were wrong. And the result is we deployed and the Soviets kept deploying, and then we negotiated from strength. And now we have the first arms control agreement in the nuclear age to ban weapons. You just don't make unilateral cuts in the naive hope that the Soviets are going to behave themselves. World peace is important, and we have enhanced the peace. And I'm proud to have been a part of an administration that has done exactly that. Peace through strength works.

MR. SHAW: Ann Compton, for Governor Dukakis.

[Today's Heroes]

MS. COMPTON: Governor, today they may call them "role models," but they used to be called "heroes," the kind of public figure who could inspire a whole generation, someone who is larger than life. My question is not who your heroes were. My question instead is, who are the heroes who are there in American life today? Who are the ones that you would point out to young Americans as figures who should inspire this country?

MR. DUKAKIS: Well, I think—when I think of heroes, I think back, not presently, Ann, but there are many people who I admire in this country today. Some of them are in public life, in the Senate and the Congress— some of my fellow governors who are real heroes to me. I think of those young athletes who represented us at the Olympics, who were tremendously impressive. We were proud of them. We felt strongly about them and they did so well by us.

I can think of doctors and scientists—Jonas Salk who, for example, discovered a vaccine which cured one of the most dread diseases we ever had; and he's a hero. I think of classroom teachers—classroom teachers that I have had, classroom teachers that youngsters have today who are real heroes to our young people because they inspire them, they teach them, but more than that, they are role models. Members of the clergy who have done the same. Drug counselors out there in the street who are providing help to youngsters who come up to me and others and ask for help and want help and are doing the hard work, the heroic work which it takes to provide that kind of leadership, that kind of counseling, that kind of support.

I think of people in the law enforcement community who are taking their lives in their hands every day when they go up to one of those doors and kick it down and try to stop this flow of drugs into our communities and into our kids. So there are many, many heroes in this country today. These are people that give of themselves every day and every week and every month. In many cases they're people in the community who are examples and are role models.

And I would hope that one of the things that I could do as president is to recognize them, to give them the kind of recognition that they need and deserve so that more and more young people can themselves become the heroes of tomorrow, can go into public service, can go into teaching, can go into drug counseling, can go into law enforcement and be heroes themselves to generations yet to come.

MR. SHAW: One minute for Vice President Bush.

MR. BUSH: I think of a teacher right here—largely Hispanic school—Jamie Escalante, teaching calculus to young kids, 80 percent of them going on to college. I think of a young man now in this country named Valladeres who was released from a Cuban jail; came out and told the truth in this brilliant book, *Against All Hope,* about what is actually happening in Cuba.

I think of those people that took us back into space again—Rick Hauck and that crew—as people that are worthy of this. I agree with the governor on athletics. And there's nothing corny about having sports heroes, young people that are clean and honorable and out there setting a—setting the pace. I think of Dr. Fauci—probably never heard of him—you did? Ann heard of him. He's a very fine research, top doctor at the National Institute of Health, working hard doing something about research on this disease of AIDS.

But look, I also think we ought to give a litle credit to the President of the United States. He is the one that has gotten us that first arms control agreement and the cynics abounded—

MR. SHAW: Mr. Vice President—

MR. BUSH: — and he is leaving office with a popularity at an all-time high—

MR. SHAW: Mr. Vice President, your time has expired—

MR. BUSH: —because American people say, he is our hero.

MR. SHAW: Ann has a question for you, Mr. Vice President.

[Opponent Praise]

MS. COMPTON: Let's change the pace a little bit, Mr. Vice President. In this campaign, some hard and very bitter things have been spoken by each side, about each side. If you'd consider for a moment Governor Dukakis in his years of public service, is there anything nice you can say about him, anything you find admirable?

MR. BUSH: Hey, listen, you're stealing my close. I had something very nice to say in that.

MS. COMPTON: Somebody leaked my question to you?

MR. BUSH: No, look, I'll tell you what, no, let me tell you something about that. And Barbara and I were sitting there before that Democratic convention, and we saw the governor and his son on television the night before, and his family and his mother who was there. And I'm saying to Barbara, "You know, we've always kept family as a bit of an oasis for us." You all know me, and we've held it back a little. But we use that as a role model, the way he took understandable pride in his heritage, what his family means to him.

And we've got a strong family and we watched that and we said, "Hey, we've got to unleash the Bush kids." And so you saw 10 grandchildren there jumping all over their grandfather at the, at the convention. You see our five kids all over this country, and their spouses. And so I would say that the concept of the Dukakis family has my great respect. And I'd say, I don't know whether that's kind or not, it's just an objective statement. And I think the man, anybody that gets into this political arena and has to face you guys every day deserves a word of praise because it's gotten a little ugly out there, it's gotten a little nasty. It's not much fun sometimes.

And I would cite again Dan Quayle. I've been in politics a long time and I don't remember that kind of piling on, that kind of ugly rumor that never was true, printed. Now, come on. So some of it's unfair, but he's in the arena. Teddy Roosevelt used to talk about the "arena"—you know, daring to fail greatly or succeed. No matter, he's in there. So, I salute these things. I salute those who participate in the political process.

Sam Rayburn had a great expression on this. He said, "You know, I hear all of these intellectuals out there griping and complaining and saying it's negative coverage." Rayburn says, "Yeah, and that guy never ran for sheriff either." Michael Dukakis has run for sheriff, and so has George Bush.

MR. SHAW: Governor, a one-minute response, sir.

MR. DUKAKIS: I didn't hear the word "liberal" or "left" one time. I thank you for that.

MR. BUSH: That's not bad; that's true.

MR. DUKAKIS: And doesn't that prove the point, George, which is that values like family, and education, community—

MR. BUSH: That's where you want to take the country.

MR. DUKAKIS: —decent homes for young people—that family in Long Island I visited on Monday, where Lou and Betty Tulamo bought a house for some $19,000 back in 1962, have had seven children. They're all making good livings. They can't live in the community in which they grew up in. Those are basic American values. I believe in them, I think you believe in them. They're not left or right, they're decent American values.

I guess the one thing that concerns me about this, Ann, is this attempt to label things which all of us believe in. We may have different approaches, we may think that you deal with them in different ways, but they're basically American. I believe in them, George Bush believes in them, I think the vast majority of Americans believe in them, and I hope—

MR. SHAW: Governor.

MR. DUKAKIS: —the tone we've just heard might just be the tone we have for the rest of the campaign. I think the American people would appreciate that.

MR. SHAW: Margaret Warner, for the vice president.

[Abortion]

MS. WARNER: Vice President Bush, abortion remains with us as a very troubling issue, and I'd like to explore that for a minute with you. You have said that you regard abortion as murder, yet you would make exceptions in the cases of rape and incest. My question is, why should a woman who discovers through amniocentesis that her baby will be born with Tay-Sachs disease, for instance, that the baby will live at most two years, and those two years in incredible pain, be forced to carry the fetus to term, and yet a woman who becomes pregnant through incest would be allowed to abort her fetus?

MR. BUSH: Because you left out one other exception, the health of the mother. Let me answer your question, and I hope it doesn't get too personal, or maudlin. Bar and I lost a child, you know that. We lost a daughter, Robin. And we took—we were out—I was over running records in West Texas, and I got a call from her—"Come home." Went to the doctor. The doctor said—beautiful child—"Your child has a few weeks to live." And I said, "What can we do about it?" He said, "No, she has leukemia, acute leukemia, a few weeks to live." We took the child to New York. Thanks to the miraculous sacrifices of doctors and nurses, the child stayed alive for six months, and then died. If that child were here today, and I was told this same thing—my granddaughter Noel, for example— that child could stay alive for 10 or 15 years, or may for the rest of her life. And so, I don't think that you make an exception based on medical knowledge at the time. I think human life is very, very precious.

And look, this hasn't been an easy decision for me to make—work— meet. I know others disagree with it. But when I was in that little church across the river from Washington and saw our grandchild christened in our faith, I was very pleased indeed that the mother had not aborted that child, and put the child up for adoption. And so I just feel this is where I'm coming from. And it is personal. And I don't assail him on that issue or others on that issue. But that's the way I, George Bush, feel about it.

MR. SHAW: One minute for Governor Dukakis.

MR. DUKAKIS: Margaret, Kitty and I had very much the same kind of experience that the Bushes had. We lost a baby—lived about 20 minutes after it was born. But, isn't the real question that we have to answer, not how many exceptions we make—because the vice president himself is prepared to make exceptions—it's who makes the decision, who makes this very difficult, very wrenching decision.

And I think it has to be the woman, in the exercise of her own conscience and religious beliefs, that makes the decision. Who are we to say, "Well, under certain circumstances it's all right, but under other circumstances it isn't?" That's a decision that only a woman can make after consulting her conscience and consulting her religious principles. And I would hope that we would give to women in this country the right to make that decision, and to make it in the exercise of their conscience and religious beliefs.

MR. SHAW: Governor, Margaret has a question for you.

[The Defense Budget]

MS. WARNER: Governor, I'd like to return to the topic of the defense budget for a minute. You have said in this campaign, that you would maintain a stable defense budget. Yet, you are on the board—on the advisory—

MR. DUKAKIS: And incidentally, may I say that—that that's the decision of the Congress, and the president has concurred.

MS. WARNER: Yet you are on the board of a group called Jobs With Peace in Boston, that advocates a 25 percent cut in the defense budget, and the transfer of that money to the domestic economy. My question is: Do you share that goal, perhaps as a long-range goal? And if not, are you aware of, or why do you permit this group to continue to use your name on its letterhead for fund-raising?

MR. DUKAKIS: Well, I think I was on the advisory committee, Margaret. No, I don't happen to share that goal. It's an example of how oftentimes we may be associated with organizations, all of whose particular positions we don't support—even though we support in general the hope that over time, particularly if we can get those reductions in strategic weapons, if we can get a comprehensive test-ban treaty, if we can negotiate with the Soviet Union and bring down the level of conventional forces in Europe with deeper cuts in the Soviet side. Yes, at some point it may be possible to reduce defense outlays and use those for important things here at home, like jobs and job training and college opportunity and health and housing and the environment, and the things that all of us care about.

But I do think this: That the next president, even within a relatively stable budget—and that's what we're going to have for the foreseeable future—will have to make those tough choices that I was talking about and that Mr. Bush doesn't seem to want to make. And that really is going to be a challenge for the next president of the United States. I don't think there's any question about it.

But I also see a tremendous opportunity now to negotiate with the Soviet Union, to build on the progress that we've made with the INF Treaty—which I strongly supported, and most Democrats did—to get those reductions in strategic weapons, to get a test-ban treaty, and to really make progress on the reduction of conventional forces in Europe.

And if we can do that, and do it in a way that gets deeper cuts on the Soviet side, which is where they ought to come from—then I think we have an opportunity over the long haul to begin to move priorities that can provide college opportunity for that young woman whose mother wrote me from Texas just the other day, from Longview, Texas—two teachers, a mother and a father who have a child that's a freshman in college who's an electrical engineering major, a very bright student—and they can't afford to keep that child in college.

So I hope that we can begin to move those resources. It's not going to happen overnight. It certainly will have to happen on a step-by-step basis as we make progress in arms negotiation and arms control and arms reduction. But it certainly ought to be—

MR. SHAW: Governor—

MR. DUKAKIS: —a long-term goal of all Americans, and I think it is.

MR. SHAW: One minute for the vice president.

MR. BUSH: The defense budget today takes far less percentage of the gross national product than it did in President Kennedy's time. For example—moved tremendously—and you see, I think we're facing a real opportunity for world peace. This is a big question. And it's a question as to whether the United States will continue to lead for peace. See, I don't believe any other country can pick up the mantle.

I served at the U.N. I don't think we can turn over these kinds of decisions of the collective defense to the United Nations or anything else. So, what I'm saying is, we are going to have to make choices. I said I would have the secretary of defense sit down. But while the president is negotiating with the Soviet Union, I simply do not want to make these unilateral cuts.

And I think those that advocated the freeze missed the point that there was a better way and that better way has resulted in a principle— asymmetrical cuts. The Soviets take out more than we do and the principle of intrusive verification. And those two principles can now be applied to conventional forces, to strategic forces, provided—

MR. SHAW: Mr. Vice President—

MR. BUSH: —we don't give away our hand before we sit down at the head table.

MR. SHAW: Andrea Mitchell for Governor Dukakis.

[Taxes and Social Security]

MS. MITCHELL: Governor, you've said tonight that you set as a goal the steady reduction of the deficit. And you've talked about making tough choices, so perhaps I can get you to make one of those tough choices. No credible economist in either party accepts as realistic your plan to handle the deficit by tightening tax collection, investing in economic growth, bringing down interest rates, and cutting weapons systems ...

MR. DUKAKIS: And some domestic programs as well, Andrea.

MS. MITCHELL: And some domestic programs as well. So let's assume now, for argument purpose, that it is the spring of 1989 and you are President Dukakis, and you discover that all of those economists were right and you were wrong. You are now facing that dreaded last resort—increase taxes. Which tax do you decide is the least onerous?

MR. DUKAKIS: May I disagree with the premise of your question?

MS. MITCHELL: For the sake of argument, no.

MR. DUKAKIS: As a matter of reality, I'm going to have to because we have had not one but two detailed studies which indicate that there are billions and billions of dollars to be collected that are not being paid in. These are not taxes owed by average Americans. We don't have an alternative. We lose it when it's taken out of our paycheck before we even get it. But it's the Internal Revenue Service which estimates now that we aren't collecting $100 billion or more in taxes owed in this country. And that is just absolutely unfair to the vast majority of Americans who pay their taxes and pay them on time.

The Dorgan Task Force, which included two internal revenue commissioners, one a Republican—former internal revenue commissioners—one a Republican, one a Democrat. It was a bipartisan commission, a study by two respected economists, which indicated that we could collect some $40, 45, 50 billion of those funds. The point is you've got to have a president who's prepared to do this and to begin right away and, preferably, a president who as a governor of a state that's had very, very successful experience at doing this. In my own state, we did it. In other states, we've done it. Republican governors as well as Democratic governors. And we've had great success at revenue enforcement.

Now, the vice president will probably tell you that it's going to take an army of IRS collectors again. Well, his campaign manager, who used to be the secretary of the treasury, was taking great credit about a year ago and asking and receiving from the Congress substantial additional funds to hire internal revenue agents to go out and collect these funds and I'm happy to join Jim Baker in saying that we agree on this.

But, the fact of the matter is that this is something that we must begin, it's going to take at least the first year of the new administration. But the Dorgan Task Force, the bipartisan task force, estimated that we could collect about $35 billion in the fifth year, $105 billion over five years, the other study even more than that—

MR. SHAW: Governor.

MR. DUKAKIS: —and that's where you begin.

MR. SHAW: One minute response, Mr. Vice President.

MR. BUSH: Well, Andrea, you didn't predicate that lack of economist's support for what I call a flexible freeze 'cause some good, very good economists do support that concept. And I think where I differ with the governor of Massachusetts is, I am optimistic. They jumped on me yesterday for being a little optimistic about the United States. I am optimistic and I believe we can keep this longest expansion going.

I was not out there when that stock market dropped, wringing my hands and saying this was the end of the world, as some political leaders were— 'cause it isn't the end of the world. And what we have to do is restrain the growth of spending. And we are doing a better job of it. The Congress is doing a better job of it. And the dynamics work. But they don't work if you go raise taxes and then the Congress spends it, continues to spend that. The American working man and woman are not taxed too little, the federal government continues to spend too much. Hold it.

MR. SHAW: Mr. Vice President, Andrea has a question for you.

MS. MITCHELL: Mr. Vice President, you have flatly ruled out any change in Social Security benefits, even for the wealthy. Now, can you stand here tonight and look a whole generation of 18 to 34 year olds in the eye, the very people who are going to have to be financing that retirement, and tell them that they should be financing the retirement of people like yourself, like Governor Dukakis, or for that matter, people such as ourselves here on this panel?

MR. BUSH: More so you than me. But—

MS. MITCHELL: —We could argue about that.

MR. BUSH: —No, but, you've got to go back to what Social Security was when it was created. It wasn't created as a welfare program, it wasn't created—it was created as a whole retirement or health supplement to retirement program. It wasn't created as a welfare program. So here's what's happened. We came into office and the Social Security Trust Fund was in great jeopardy. And the President took the leadership, working with the Democrats and the Republicans in Congress. Some tough calls were made and the Social Security Trust Fund was put back into sound, solvent condition.

So I don't want to fool around with it. And there's several—there's a good political reason, because it's just about this time of year that the Democrats start saying: "The Republicans are going to take away your Social Security." It always works that way. I've seen it in precinct politics in Texas, and I've seen it at the national level.

We have made the Social Security Trust Fund sound, and it is going to be operating at surpluses. And I don't want the liberal Democratic Congress to spend out of that Social Security Trust Fund or go and take the money out for some other purpose. I don't want that. And I will not go in there and suggest changes in Social Security. I learned that the hard way.

And the Governor and I both supported slipping the COLAs for one year; he supported it at the National Governors' Conference, and I supported it in breaking a tie in a major compromise package. And we got assailed by the Democrats in the election over that. And I am going to keep that Social Security Trust Fund sound and keep our commitment to the elderly. And maybe down the line, maybe when you get two decades or one into the next century, you're going to have to take another look at it, but not now. We do not have to do it. Keep the trust with the older men and women of this country.

MR. SHAW: Governor, you have one minute, sir.

MR. DUKAKIS: Andrea, I don't know which George Bush I'm listening to. George Bush, a few years ago, said that the Social Security was basically a welfare system. And in 1985 he flew back from the West Coast to cut that COLA. I voted against that at the National Governors' Association. We won a majority; we didn't win the two-thirds that was necessary in order to pass that resolution, George, but everybody knew what we were doing, and I've opposed that.

The reason that we raised concerns not just in election years, but every year, is because Republicans, once they're elected, go in there and start cutting. You did it in 1985. The administration tried to do it repeatedly, repeatedly in '81, '82, and I'm sure you'll try to do it again because there's no way that you can finance what you want to spend, there's no way you can pay for that five-year, $40 billion tax cut for the rich and still buy all those weapon systems you want to buy, unless you raid the Social Security Trust Fund.

[Supreme Court Vacancies]

MR. SHAW: Ann Compton, for the vice president.

MS. COMPTON: Mr. Vice President, there are three justices of the Supreme Court who are in their eighties, and it's very likely the next president will get a chance to put a lasting mark on the Supreme Court. For the record, would your nominees to the Supreme Court have to pass something that has been called a kind of conservative ideological litmus test, and would you give us an idea of perhaps who two or three people on your short list are for the court?

MR. BUSH: Well, one, I don't have a list yet. I feel pretty confident tonight, but not that confident. And secondly—secondly, I don't have any litmus test. But, what I would do is appoint people to the federal bench that will not legislate from the bench, who will interpret the Constitution. I do not want to see us go to again—and I'm using this word advisedly—a liberal majority that is going to legislate from the bench.

They [Dukakis supporters] don't like the use of the word, but may I remind his strong supporters that only last year in the primary to capture that Democratic nomination, he said, "I am a progressive liberal Democratic." I won't support judges like that.

There is no litmus test on any issue. But, I will go out there and find men and women to interpret. And I don't have a list, but I think the appointments that the president has made to the bench have been outstanding, outstanding appointments—

MS. COMPTON: Including Bork, including Bork?

MR. BUSH: Yeah.

MR. SHAW: Governor—

MR. BUSH: —I supported him.

MR. SHAW: —you have a one-minute response time.

MR. DUKAKIS: If the Vice President of the United States thinks that Robert Bork was an outstanding appointment, that is a very good reason for voting for Mike Dukakis and Lloyd Bentsen on the 8th of November. And I think Mr. Bush supported the Bork nomination.

You know Mr. Bush has never appointed a judge. I've appointed over 130, so I have a record—and I'm very proud of it. I don't ask people whether they're Republicans or Democrats. I've appointed prosecutors, I've appointed defenders. I don't appoint people I think are liberal, or people who I think are conservative; I appoint people of independence and integrity and intelligence, people who will be a credit to the bench. And those are the standards that I will use in nominating people to the Supreme Court of the United States.

These appointments are for life—these appointments are for life, and when the vice president talks about liberals on the bench, I wonder who he's talking about? Is he talking about a former governor of the state of California, who was a former prosecutor—

MR. SHAW: Governor—

MR. DUKAKIS: —a Republican, named Earl Warren? Because I think Chief Justice Warren was an outstanding chief justice, and I think most Americans do too.

MR. SHAW: Anne Compton has a question for you, Governor Dukakis.

[On Entitlements]

MS. COMPTON: Governor, millions of Americans are entitled to some of the protections and benefits that the federal government provides, including Social Security, pensions, Medicare for the elderly, Medicaid for the poor. But in fact, there are so many millions of Americans who are eligible that government just can't continue to pay for all of those programs as they're currently constituted. A blue ribbon panel, shortly after the election, is likely to recommend that you go where the money is when you make budget cuts, and that means entitlements. Before the election, would you commit yourself to any of those hard choices, such as which one of those entitlements ought to be redrawn?

MR. DUKAKIS: Andrea, why do people who want to balance budgets, or bring the deficit down, always go to those programs which tend to benefit people of very modest means? You know, two-thirds of the people in this country who receive Social Security checks live entirely on that check, they have no other income. And yet, Mr. Bush tried to cut their cost-of-living increase in 1985.

Medicare is not getting less expensive; medical care for the elderly is getting more expensive, with greater deductibles, with fewer benefits, the kinds of things that we've had under this administration, that have cut and chopped and reduced the kinds of benefits that one gets under Medicare. Yes, we now have catastrophic health insurance, but it's going to cost. And that's going to be an additional burden on elderly citizens. It had bipartisan support; it should have had bipartisan support, but I suggest that we understand that those are going to be additional costs on senior citizens across this country.

So I'm not going to begin, and I'm not going to go to entitlements as a means for cutting that deficit, when we're spending billions on something like Star Wars, when we're spending billions on other weapon systems which apparently the vice president wants to keep in his back pocket, or someplace, but which, if we continue to spend billions on them, will force us to cut Social Security, to cut Medicare, to cut these basic entitlements to people of very, very modest means.

Now there are some things we can do to help people who currently do get entitlements to get off of public assistance. I talked in our first debate about the possibilities of helping millions and millions of welfare families to get off of welfare, and I'm proud to say that we finally have a welfare reform bill. And the Ruby Sampsons and Dawn Lawsons, hundreds of thousands of welfare mothers in this country and in my state and across the country who today are working and earning, are examples of what can happen when you provide training for those welfare mothers, some day care for their children so that those mothers can go into a training program and get a decent job.

MR. SHAW: Governor—

MR. DUKAKIS: That's the way you bring a deficit down, and help to improve the quality of life for people at the same time.

MR. SHAW: One minute for the vice president.

MR. BUSH: I think I've addressed it, but let me simply say for the record, I did not vote to cut COLAs. And I voted the same way that he did three months before in a National Governors' conference, and he said at that time, quote, and this is a paraphrase—A freeze, that's easy. So I don't believe that we need to do what you've suggested here, and I've said that I'm going to keep the Social Security entitlement, to keep that trust fund sound.

But I do think there are flexible ways to solve some of the pressing problems, particularly that affect our children. And I have made some good, sound proposals.

But again, we've got a big difference on child care, for example. You see, I want the families to have the choice. I want, I don't want to see the federal government licensing grandmothers. I don't want to see the federal government saying to communities, "Well, you can't do this anymore. We're going to tell you how to do it all."

I want flexibility. And I do, you know, these people laugh about the thousand points of life. You ought to go out and—light—you ought to go out and see around this country what's happening in the volunteer sector, American helping American. And I want to keep it alive in child care—

MR. SHAW: Mr. Vice President—

MR. BUSH: —and in other entitlements.

MR. SHAW: Margaret Warner, for Governor Dukakis.

MS. WARNER: Governor, I'm going to pass on the question I originally planned to ask you to follow up on your rebuttal to a question Andrea asked, and that involves Social Security. Now it is true, as you said, that originally you sought an exemption for Social Security COLAs in this National Governors' Association vote.

MR. DUKAKIS: Right.

MS. WARNER: But when you lost that vote, you then endorsed the overall freeze proposal. And what's more, you had great criticism of your fellow governors who wouldn't go along as political cowards. You said—"It takes guts, and it takes will."

MR. DUKAKIS: That is absolutely not true, Margaret. No, that is absolutely—that is absolutely not true. It had nothing to do with the debate on Social Security. It had to do with the discussion we had had the previous day on the overall question of reducing the budget.

MS. WARNER: My question is, aren't you demagoguing the Social Security issue?

MR. DUKAKIS: No, and I have to—I have to—I just have to correct the record. That simply isn't true. Now, we're not a parliamentary body— the National Governors' Association. We vote on resolutions. If you don't get a two-thirds, then your resolution doesn't pass. But everybody knew that those of us who voted against the freezing of COLAs did so—we did so emphatically and I never made that statement—never would.

The point is that as we look at this nation's future, and we have two very different visions of this future—I want to move ahead. The vice president talks about a thousand points of light. I'm interested in 240 million points of light. I'm interested in 240 million citizens in this country who—who share in the American dream—all of them, in every part of this country.

But, as we look at the decisions that the next president of the United States is going to have to make, I just don't believe the place you go first is those programs, those so-called entitlements which provide a basic floor of income and a modest amount of medical care for the elderly, for the disabled, for people who can't make their way on their own, and in many cases have given a great deal to this country.

The vice president did call Social Security a few years ago basically or largely a welfare program. It isn't. It's a contract between generations. It's something that we pay into now so that we will have a secure retirement, and our parents and grandparents will have secure retirement. It's a very sacred contract, and I believe in it. So that's not where we ought to go.

There are plenty of places to cut. There's lots we can do in the Pentagon where dishonest contractors have been lining their pockets at the expense of the American taxpayer. There are—we certainly ought to be able to give our farm families a decent income without spending 20 to 25 billion dollars a year in farm subsidies and I'm sure we can do that. That's where we ought to go and those are the programs that we ought to review first.

MR. SHAW: One minute for the vice president.

MR. BUSH: Well, let me take him up on this question of farm subsidies. We have a fundamental difference approach on agriculture. He favors this supply maintenance or production controls. He said that. He's been out in the states saying that in these Midwestern states. I don't. I think the farm bill that he criticizes was good legislation, outstanding legislation. And I believe the answer to the agricultural economy is not to get the government further involved, but to do what I'm suggesting.

First place, never go back to that Democratic grain embargo, that liberal Democrat grain embargo that knocked the markets right out from under us and made Mr. Gorbachev say to me, when he was here, "How do I know you're reliable suppliers?" We never should go back to that. And we ought to expand our markets abroad. We ought to have rural enterprise zones. We ought to move forward swiftly on my ideas of ethanol, which would use more corn and therefore make, create a bigger market for our agricultural products. But let's not go back and keep assailing a farm bill that passed with overwhelming Democrat and Republican support.

MR. SHAW: Mr. Vice President—

MR. BUSH: The farm payments are going down because the agricultural economy is coming back.

MR. SHAW: Margaret Warner has a question for you, Mr. Vice President.

[The Environment]

MS. WARNER: Mr. Vice President, I'd like to cover a subject that wasn't covered in the first debate. You have said in this campaign, "I am an environmentalist," and described yourself as having zero tolerance for polluters. And yet your record does seem to suggest otherwise.

When you were head of the President's Task Force of Regulatory Relief, you did urge EPA to relax regulations involving the elimination of lead from gasoline. I believe you urged suspension of rules requiring industries to treat toxic wastes before discharging them in sewers. And your group also urged OSHA to weaken the regulations requiring that workers be informed of dangerous chemicals at the worksite.

Finally, I believe you did support the President's veto of the Clean Water Act. And my question is, aren't you—how do you square your campaign rhetoric with this record?

MR. BUSH: Ninety percent reductions in lead since I chaired that regulatory task force—ninety percent. It's all—do you remember that expression—"Get the lead out"—it's almost out. Almost gone. Clean water—I'm for clean water—but what I'm not for, what I'm not for is measuring it the way the Democratic Congress does.

We sent up a good bill on clean water, a sound bill on clean water, but the only way you can express your love for clean water is to double the appropriations for clean water and then rant against the deficit. I am for clean water. I've been an outdoorsman and a sportsman all my life. I've been to these national parks. I led for the Earl-Wallop bill, or what formerly Dingell-Johnson. I headed the Task Force when I was a member of the Congress way back in the late '60s on these kinds of things on the Republican side. I led for that. And so I refuse to—to measure one's commitment as to whether you're going to double the spending. That is the same old argument that'd gotten us into the trouble on the deficit side.

So I'll just keep saying: I am one. I'm not going to go down there and try to dump the sludge from Massachusetts off the beaches off of New Jersey—I'm not going to do that. That boo was excessively loud. Can you add five seconds, Bernie, out of fairness? Come on! Give me five. I mean this guy—this is too much down there.

But I'm not gonna do that. I am an environmentalist. I believe in our parks; I believe in the President's Commission on Outdoors. And I'll do a good job because I am committed.

MR. SHAW: Governor Dukakis, you have one minute to respond.

MR. DUKAKIS: Bernard, I'm not sure I can get all of this in in one minute. George, we have supply management today under the 1985 bill, it's called "set asides." Secondly, if you were so opposed to the grain embargo, why did you ask the godfather of the grain embargo to be one of your top foreign policy advisers?

I'm against the grain embargo; it was a mistake. I'm also against the pipeline embargo which you folks attempted to impose; that was a mistake as well, and cost thousands of jobs for American workers in the Midwest and all over the United States of America.

Margaret, once again, I don't know which George Bush I'm talking about here, or looking at—the George Bush who was a charter member of the environmental wrecking crew that went to Washington in the early '80s and did a job on the EPA, or the one we've been seeing and listening to the past two or three months. But let me say this, because he spent millions and millions of dollars on advertising on the subject of Boston Harbor: George, Boston Harbor was polluted for 100 years. I'm the first Governor to clean it up. No thanks to you—no thanks to you. And we've been cleaning it up for four years—

MR. SHAW: Governor—

MR. DUKAKIS: —we passed landmark legislation in '84. No thanks to you. Did everything you could to kill the Clean Water Act and those grants—

MR. SHAW: Governor—

MR. DUKAKIS: —which make it possible for states and local communities to clean up rivers and harbors and streams.

MR. SHAW: Andrea Mitchell has a question for you, Mr. Vice President.

[The Campaign's Final Month]

MS. MITCHELL: Mr. Vice President, Jimmy Carter has called this the worst campaign ever. Richard Nixon has called it trivial, superficial and inane. Whoever started down this road first of negative campaigning, the American people, from all reports coming to us, are completely fed up. Now, do you have any solutions to suggest? Is there time left to fix it? There are 26 days left. For instance, would you agree to another debate before it's all over so that the American people, so that the American people would have another chance before Election Day to compare you two?

MR. BUSH: No, I will not agree to another debate. The American people are up to here with debates. They had 30 of them. We had seven of them. Now we got three of them. I am going to carry this election debate all across this country in the last, whatever remains of the last three and a half weeks or whatever we have. And the answer is no. I am not going to have any more debates. We don't need any more debates. I've spelled out my position.

In terms of negative campaigning, you know, I don't want to sound like a kid in a schoolyard—"He started it." But, take a look at the Democratic convention, take a look at it. Do you remember the senator from Boston chanting out there and the ridicule factor from that lady from Texas that was on there? I mean, come on. This was just outrageous. But, I'll try harder to keep it on a high plane.

But, let me, let me—if you could accept a little criticism. I went all across central Illinois and spoke about agricultural issues in about seven stops. We had some fun—Crystal Gayle and Loretta Lynn with us and they got up and sang. We went to little towns and I talked agriculture. And not one thing did I see, with respect, on your network about my views on agriculture and not one did I read in any newspaper. Why? 'Cause you're so interested in a poll that might have been coming out. Or because somebody had said something nasty about somebody else.

And, so, I don't know what the answer is. I don't—somebody hit me and said Barry Goldwater said you ought to talk on the issues more. How can Barry Goldwater, sitting in Arizona, know whether I'm talking on the issues or not, when we put out position paper after position paper, he puts out position paper after position paper, and we see this much about it because everyone else is fascinated with polls and who's up or down today and who's going to be up or down tomorrow.

So I think we can all share, with respect, in the fact that maybe these, the message is not getting out. But it's not getting out because there are too few debates. There will be no more debates.

MR. SHAW: Governor Dukakis, you have one minute to respond, sir.

MR. DUKAKIS: Well, I can understand, after the vice presidential debate why Mr. Bush would want no more debates. That's my five seconds, George. Andrea, I think we both have a responsibility to try to address the issues.

Yes, we have fundamental differences. I think a great many of them have come out today. And I think if we get rid of the labels and—I'm not keeping count, but I think Mr. Bush has used the label "liberal" at least 10 times. If I had a dollar, George, for every time you used that label, I'd qualify for one of those tax breaks for the rich that you want to give away.

Isn't that the point? Most Americans believe in basic values, we have differences about how to achieve them. I want to move forward. I want this nation to move forward. I'm concerned about the fact that 10 percent of our manufacturing and 20 percent of our banking and nearly half of the real estate in the city of Los Angeles are in the hands of foreign investors. I'm concerned about what that does to our future. I'm concerned about the fact that so many of our securities are in the hands of foreign banks because of these massive deficits. But, those are the issues on which we ought to be debating, and—

MR. SHAW: Governor.

MR. DUKAKIS: —if we'd just put away the flag factories and the balloons and those kinds of things and get on to a real discussion of these issues, I think we'll—

MR. SHAW: Andrea.

MR. DUKAKIS: —have a good 26 days.

MR. SHAW: Andrea Mitchell has a question for you, Governor Dukakis.

MR. DUKAKIS: I beg your pardon.

MR. SHAW: Andrea Mitchell has a question for you, sir.

[Defense and the Pentagon]

MS. MITCHELL: While we're talking about issues, so let's return to something you said earlier about the modernization of land-based missiles.

You said that you didn't rule it out but that there are limits to what we can spend. And then you went on to talk about a much more expensive part of our defense strategy, namely conventional forces. Do you somehow see conventional forces as a substitute for our strategic forces? And in not talking about the land-based missiles and not committing to modernizing, do you somehow believe that we can have a survivable nuclear force based on the air and sea legs of our triad?

MR. DUKAKIS: I think we ought to be looking at modernization. I think we ought to be exploring less expensive ways to get it on land, and we ought to make sure that we have an effective and strong and credible nuclear deterrent. But we also need well-equipped and well-trained and well-supported conventional forces. And every defense expert I know, including people in the Pentagon itself, will tell you that given the level of defense spending and the level of defense appropriations which the Congress has now approved and the president has signed, there's no way that you can do all of these things and do them well. That's why tough choices will be required, choices I'm prepared to make, Mr. Bush is not prepared to make.

But Andrea, I think we can go far beyond this as well because we have opportunities now, step by step, to bring down the level of strategic weapons and get a test ban treaty, negotiate those conventional force reductions. I would challenge Mr. Gorbachev to join with us in limiting and eliminating regional conflict in the Middle East, in Central America. Let's get him working on Syria, their client state, and see if we can't get them to join Israel and other Arab nations, if at all possible, and Arab leaders, in finally bringing peace to that troubled region. And I think that's one reason why we need fresh leadership in the White House that can make progress now in bringing peace to the Middle East.

Let's go to work and end this fiasco in Central America, a failed policy which has actually increased Cuban and Soviet influence. The democratic leaders of Central and Latin America want to work with us. I've met with them. I know them. I've spent time in South America. I speak the language; so does Senator Bentsen. We want to work with them and build a new relationship, and they with us. But not a one of those key democratic leaders support our policy in Central America. And we've got to work with them if we're going to create an environment for human rights and democracy for the people of this hemisphere, and go to work on our single most important problem, and that is the avalanche of drugs that is pouring into our country and virtually destroying those countries.

Those are the kinds of priorities, for national security and for foreign policy, that I want to pursue. Mr. Bush and I have major differences on these issues—

MR. SHAW: Governor—

MR. DUKAKIS: —and I hope very much to be president and pursue them.

MR. SHAW: Mr. Vice President, you have one minute.

MR. BUSH: In terms of regional tensions, we have now gotten the attention of the Soviet Union. And the reason we've gotten it is because they see us now as unwilling to make the very kinds of unilateral cuts that have been called for, and to go for the discredited freeze. My opponent had trouble, criticized us on our policy in Angola. It now looks, because of steady negotiation, that we may have an agreement that will remove the Cubans from Angola.

We see the Russians coming out of Afghanistan. That wouldn't have stopped if we hadn't been willing—wouldn't have even started, the Soviets coming out, if we hadn't even been willing to support the freedom fighters there. And the policy in Central America regrettably has failed because the Congress has been unwilling to support those who have been fighting for freedom. Those Sandinistas came in and betrayed the trust of the revolution. They said it was about democracy. And they have done nothing other than solidify their Marxist domination over that country.

MR. SHAW: Ann Compton for Governor Dukakis.

MS. COMPTON: Governor, nuclear weapons need nuclear material replenished on a regular basis. And just this week, yet another nuclear manufacturing plant was closed because of safety concerns. Some in the Pentagon fear that too much priority has been put on new weapons programs, not enough on current programs, and worry that the resulting shortage would be amounting to nothing less than unilateral nuclear disarmament.

Is that a priority that you feel has been ignored by this administration? Or are the Pentagon officials making too much of it?

MR. DUKAKIS: Well, its a great concern of mine, and I think of all Americans, and perhaps the vice president can tell us what's been going on. This is another example of misplaced priorities.

The administration, which wants to spend billions on weapons systems that we don't need and can't afford, and now confronts us with a very serious problem in plants that are supposed to be producing tritium and plutonium and providing the necessary materials for existing weapons.

Yes, if we don't do something about it, we may find ourselves unilaterally— if I may use that term—dismantling some of these weapons. What's been going on? Who's been in charge? Who's been managing this system? Why have there been these safety violations? Why are these plants being closed down? I don't know what the latest cost estimates are, but it's going to be in the range of $25, 50, 75, 100 billion. Now, somebody has to bear the responsibility for this.

Maybe the vice president has an answer, but I'm somebody who believes very strongly in taking care of the fundamentals first, before you start new stuff. And that's something which will be a priority of ours in the new administration, because without it we cannot have the effective and strong and credible nuclear deterrent we must have.

MR. SHAW: Mr. Vice President, you have one minute.

MR. BUSH: That is the closest I've ever heard the governor of Massachusetts come to support anything having to do with nuclear. That's about as close as I've ever heard him. Yes, this Savannah River plant needs to be made more safe. Will he join me in suggesting that we may need another plant, maybe in Idaho, to take care of the requirements—nuclear material requirements for our Defense Department? I hope he will.

This sounds like real progress here, because we've had a big difference on the safe use of nuclear power. I believe that we—the more dependent we become on foreign oil, the less our national security is enhanced. And, therefore, I've made some proposals to strengthen the domestic oil industry, by more incentive going in to look for and find and produce oil, made him some incentives in terms of secondary and tertiary production. But we're going to have to use more gas, more coal, and more safe nuclear power for our energy base. So, I am one who believes that we can and must—

MR. SHAW: Mr. Vice President—

MR. BUSH: —do what he's talking about now.

MR. SHAW: Ann Compton has a question for you.

[Government Ethics]

MS. COMPTON: Mr. Vice President, as many as 100 officials in this administration have left the government under an ethical cloud. Some have been indicted, some convicted. Many of the cases have involved undue influence once they are outside of government. If you become president, will you lock that revolving door that has allowed some men and women in the government to come back and lobby the very departments they once managed?

MR. BUSH: Yes, and I'll apply it to Congress too. I'll do both. I'll do both, because I think, you see, I am one who—I get kidded by being a little old fashioned on these things, but I do believe in public service. I believe that public service is honorable. And I don't think anybody has a, has a call on people and their administrations going astray. His chief education adviser is in jail. He's in jail because he betrayed the public trust. The head of education.

And yet, this man, the governor, equated the president to a rotting fish. He said that a fish rots from the head down, as he was going after Ed Meese. Look, we need the highest possible ethical standards. I will have an ethical office in the White House that will be under the president's personal concern. I will see that these standards apply to the United States Congress. I hope I will do a good job as one who has had a relatively clean record with no conflicts of interest in his own public life—as has the governor—to exhort young people to get into public service.

But, there is no corner on, on this sleaze factor, believe me. And it's a disgrace, and I will do my level best to clean it up, recognizing that you can't legislate morality. But, I do believe that with my record in Congress having led the new congressmen to a Code of Ethics through major, main emphasis on it in full disclosure, that I've got a good record. And there are more, if you want to talk about percentage appointments, more members of Congress who have been under investigation, percentage wise, than people in the executive branch. And so it isn't want—state governments have had a tough time. His. Some of his college presidents aren't exactly holier than thou. So let's not be throwing stones about it. Let's say, "This isn't Democrat or Republican, and it isn't liberal or conservative." Let's vow to work together to do something about it.

MR. SHAW: Governor, you have one minute to respond.

MR. DUKAKIS: Well, I would agree that integrity is not a Republican or a Democratic issue. It is an American issue. But, here again, I don't know which George Bush I'm listening to. Wasn't this the Mr. Bush that supported Mr. Meese? Called James Watt an excellent Secretary of Interior? Provided support for some of these people, supported the nomination of Robert Bork to the Supreme Court of the United States? We've had dozens, we've had dozens and dozens of officials in this administration, who have left under a cloud, who have left with a special prosecutor on their arm. They've been indicted, convicted.

This isn't the kind of administration we need and one of the reasons our selection of a running mate is so important and is such a test of the kinds of standards we'll set is because it tells the American people in advance of the election just what kind of people we're looking for. I picked Lloyd Bentsen. Mr. Bush picked Dan Quaid, Dan Quayle. I think that says a great deal to the American people about the standards we'll set and the quality of the people that we will pick to serve in our administration.

MR. SHAW: To each of you candidates, regrettably, I have to inform you that we have come to the end of our questions. That's a pity. Before I ask the candidates to make their closing remarks, on behalf of the Commission on Presidential Debates, I would like to thank all of you for joining us this evening. Governor Dukakis, yours is the first closing statement, sir.

[Closing Statements]

MR. DUKAKIS: Twenty-eight years ago, as a young man, just graduated from law school, I came to this city, came clear across the country to watch John Kennedy be nominated for the presidency of the United States, right here in Los Angeles.

I never dreamed that someday I would win that nomination and be my party's nominee for president. That's America. That's why I'm proud and grateful to be a citizen of this country.

Twenty-six days from today, you and millions of Americans will choose two people to lead us into the future as president and vice president of the United States. Our opponents say, "Things are okay. Don't rock the boat. Not to worry." They say we should be satisfied.

But I don't think we can be satisfied when we're spending $150 billion a year in interest alone on the national debt, much of it going to foreign bankers, or when 25 percent of our high school students are dropping out of school, or when we have two and a half million of our fellow citizens, a third of them veterans, who are homeless and living on streets and in doorways in this country, or when Mr. Bush's prescription for our economic future is another tax giveaway to the rich.

We can do better than that. Not working with government alone, but all of us working together. Lloyd Bentsen and I are optimists, and so are the American people. And we ask you for our hand—for your hands and your hearts and your votes on the 8th of November so we can move forward into the future. Kitty and I are very grateful to all of you for the warmth and the hospitality that you've given to us in your homes and communities all across this country. We love you, and we're grateful to you for everything that you've given to us. And we hope that we'll be serving you in the White House in January of 1989. Thank you, and God bless you.

MR. SHAW: Vice President Bush, your closing statement, sir.

MR. BUSH: Sometimes it does seem that a campaign generates more heat than light. And so let me repeat, I do have respect for my opponent, for his family, for the justifiable pride he takes in his heritage.

But we have enormous differences. I want to hold the line on taxes and keep this, the longest expansion in modern history, going until everybody in America benefits. I want to invest in our children, because I mean it when I say I want a kinder and gentler nation. And by that, I want to have child care where the families, the parents, have control.

I want to keep our neighborhoods much, much better in terms of anti-crime. And that's why I would appoint judges that have a little more sympathy for the victims of crime and a little less for the criminals. That's why I do feel if some police officer is gunned down that the death penalty is required. I want to help those with disabilities fit into the mainstream.

There is much to be done. This election is about big things, and perhaps the biggest is world peace. And I ask you to consider the experience I have had in working with a president who has revolutionized the situation around the world. America stands tall again and, as a result, we are credible and we have now achieved a historic arms control agreement.

I want to build on that. I'd love to be able to say to my grandchildren, four years after my first term, I'd like to say, "Your grandfather, working with the leaders of the Soviet Union, working with the leaders of Europe, was able to ban chemical and biological weapons from the face of the Earth."

Lincoln called this country the last, best hope of man on Earth. And he was right then, and we still are the last, best hope of man on Earth. And I ask for your support on November 8th, and I will be a good president. Working together we can do wonderful things for the United States and for the free world.

Thank you very, very much.

APOSTOLIC LETTER ON WOMEN
September 30, 1988

Pope John Paul II issued a theological response to the women's movement in the form of a lengthy apostolic letter to the church. It was dated August 15 and publicly released September 30. The letter, "On the Dignity and Vocation of Women," was presented to the Catholic church by the pope as a "meditation" based primarily on analyses of pertinent biblical passages.

As an apostolic letter, it did not bear the weight of a papal encyclical, nor did it claim to be infallible truth. Nevertheless, such a document is considered an important expression of the pope's teaching authority. The document set forth his views on issues that had often sorely vexed church authority in recent years—the concerns of women in society and their role in the church.

U.S. Bishops' Pastoral Letter

Women's concerns were the subject of a pastoral letter for American Catholics that a committee of U.S. bishops had drafted earlier in the year. It was issued April 11 for consideration by the National Conference of Catholic Bishops at its November 1989 meeting in Washington, D.C. A spokesman for the organization said there was "no doubt" that the American bishops would closely study the papal statement before they decided whether to modify, approve, or reject their 35,000-word draft document, titled "Partners in the Mystery of Redemption: A Pastoral Response to Women's Concerns." The bishops' document drew on the testimony of thousands of American Catholics who had appeared before diocesan commissions and other church-sponsored gatherings, including hearings conducted by the drafting committee.

The bishops condemned the "sin of sexism"—which they said included sexist attitudes that had colored the church's teaching for centuries. Furthermore, they found value in pursuing two troublesome matters that Pope John Paul appeared to view as closed to further consideration: ordaining women as priests and sanctioning the use of artificial contraceptives.

Mary as the Model

Both the bishops and the pope extolled Mary, the mother of Jesus, as the perfect model for Christian women in obedience to God. The bishops' draft letter said "contemporary portraits celebrate Mary's bond with ordinary women and reflect on her condition as wife, mother, widow; as refugee and displaced person; as woman of an oppressed people; as a mother of a prisoner and victim of persecution. Mary is thus not only a model to emulate but an 'active presence for the life of the church.'" John Paul, for his part, urged that Catholic women continue to regard the feminine role, exemplified in the veneration of Mary, as the ideal. He stressed the Marian theme by issuing his letter August 15, the day on which the church celebrates the doctrine of the Assumption of the Blessed Virgin Mary.

In the name of liberation from male domination, he said, "women must not appropriate to themselves characteristics contrary to their own feminine originality." Although the pontiff pleaded for adherence to a traditional view of the role of women, he pointed to scriptural evidence of equality between the sexes embedded in the foundations of Christian belief.

Response Among Catholics

At a news conference held in Rome when the letter was made available to the press, senior Vatican officials were quoted as predicting that the letter would have a long-term effect on the debate of the the role of women in the church and society. The reaction to his letter among American Catholics was decidedly mixed. Bishop Joseph L. Imesch of Joliet, Illinois, chairman of the American bishops' drafting committee, said the pope had come out "more strongly than ever on the equality and dignity of women."

Catholic scholars tended to applaud John Paul's rejection of a scriptural basis for inequality between the sexes. However, some Catholic women scholars were not pleased. Sister Sandra Schneiders, an associate professor of New Testament at the Graduate Theological Union in Berkeley, California, objected that the pope constructed a "static eternalized feminine archetype." Alice L. Laffey, head of the religious studies department at Holy Cross College, Worcester, Massachusetts, said: "I

*value motherhood and I value tradition, but what is happening is that we
are not facing the modern world."*

*Following are excerpts from the apostolic letter, "On the
Dignity and Vocation of Women," issued August 15, 1988, in
Rome by Pope John Paul II:*

[Chapters I and II Omitted]

III

The Image and Likeness of God

The Book of Genesis

Let us enter into the setting of the biblical "beginning." In it the
revealed truth concerning man as "the image and likeness" of God
constitutes the immutable *basis of all Christian anthropology.* "God
created man in his own image, in the image of God he created him; male
and female he created them" (*Gen* 1:27). This concise passage contains the
fundamental anthropological truths: man is the highpoint of the whole
order of creation in the visible world; the human race, which takes its
origin from the calling into existence of man and woman, crowns the whole
work of creation; *both man and woman are human beings to an equal
degree,* both are created *in God's image....*

The second description of the creation of man (cf *Gen* 2:18-25) makes
use of different language to express the truth about the creation of man,
and especially of woman. In a sense the language is less precise, and, one
might say, more descriptive and metaphorical, closer to the language of the
myths known at the time. Nevertheless, we find no essential contradiction
between the two texts....

In the description found in *Gen* 2:18-25, the woman is created by God
"from the rib" of the man and is placed at his side as another "I," as the
companion of the man, who is alone in the surrounding world of living
creatures and who finds in none of them a "helper" suitable for himself.
Called into existence in this way, the woman is immediately recognized by
the man as "flesh of his flesh and bone of his bones" (cf *Gen* 2:23) and for
this very reason she is called "woman." In biblical language this name
indicates her essential identity with regard to man—*'is-'issah*—something
which unfortunately modern languages in general are unable to express:
"She shall be called woman ('issah) because she was taken out of man ('is):
Gen 2:23.

The biblical text provides sufficient bases for recognizing the essential
equality of man and woman from the point of view of their humanity.
From the very beginning, both are persons, unlike other living beings in
the world about them. *The woman* is *another "I" in a common humanity....*

... Already in the Book of Genesis we can discern, in preliminary outline, the spousal character of the relationship between persons, which will serve as the basis for the subsequent development of the truth about motherhood, and about virginity, as two particular dimensions of the vocation of women in the light of divine Revelation. These two dimensions will find their loftiest expression at the "fullness of time" (cf *Gal* 4:4) in the "woman" of Nazareth: the Virgin-Mother. . . .

IV

Eve-Mary

The "Beginning" and the Sin

. . . The biblical description of original sin in the third chapter of Genesis in a certain way "distinguishes the roles" which the woman and the man had in it. This is also referred to later in certain passages of the Bible, for example, Paul's Letter to Timothy: "For Adam was formed first, then Eve; and Adam was not deceived, but the woman was deceived and became a transgressor" (1 *Tim* 2:13-14). But there is no doubt that, independent of this "distinction of roles" in the biblical description, *that first sin is the sin of man,* created by God as male and female. It is also *the sin of the "first parents,"* to which is connected its hereditary character. In this sense we call it "original sin". . . .

"He Shall Rule Over You"

The biblical description in the Book of Genesis outlines the truth about the consequences of man's sin, as it is shown by *the disturbance* of that original *relationship between man and woman* which corresponds to their individual dignity as persons. A human being, whether male or female, is a person, and therefore, "the only creature on earth which God willed for its own sake"; and at the same time this unique and unrepeatable creature "cannot fully find himself except through a sincere gift of self." Here begins the relationship of "communion" in which the "unity of the two" and the personal dignity of both man and woman find expression. Therefore when we read in the biblical description the words addressed to the woman: *"Your desire shall be for your husband, and he shall rule over you"* (*Gen* 3:16), we discover a break and a constant threat precisely in regard to this "unity of the two" which corresponds to the dignity of the image and likeness of God in both of them. But this threat is more serious for the woman, since domination takes the place of "being a sincere gift" and therefore living "for" the other: "he shall rule over you." This "domination" indicates the disturbance and *loss of the stability* of that *fundamental equality* which the man and the women possess in the "unity of the two": and this is especially to the disadvantage of the woman, whereas only the equality resulting from their dignity as persons can give to their mutual relationship the character of an authentic *"communio personarum."* While the violation of this equality, which is both a gift and a right deriving from God the Creator, involves an element to the disadvantage of the woman, at the same time it also diminishes the true dignity of the man. Here we touch upon *an extremely sensitive point in the dimension of that "ethos"* which was originally inscribed by the Creator in the very creation of both of them in his own image and likeness.

This statement in Genesis 3:16 is of great significance. It implies a reference to the mutual relationship of man and woman *in marriage*. It refers to the desire born in the atmosphere of spousal love whereby the woman's "sincere gift of self" is responded to and matched by a corresponding "gift" on the part of the husband. Only on the basis of this principle can both of them, and in particular the woman, "discover themselves" as a true "unity of the two" according to the dignity of the person. The matrimonial union requires respect for and a perfecting of the true personal subjectivity of both of them. *The woman cannot become the "object" of "domination" and male "possession."* But the words of the biblical text directly concern original sin and its lasting consequences in man and woman. Burdened by hereditary sinfulness, they bear within themselves the constant *"inclination to sin,"* the tendency to go against the moral order which corresponds to the rational nature and dignity of man and woman as persons. . . .

In our times the question of "women's rights" has taken on new significance in the broad context of the rights of the human person. *The biblical and evangelical message* sheds light on this cause, which is the object of much attention today, *by safeguarding the truth about the "unity" of the "two,"* that is to say the truth about that dignity and vocation that result from the specific diversity and personal originality of man and woman. Consequently, even the rightful opposition of women to what is expressed in the biblical words "He shall rule over you" (*Gen* 3:16) must not under any condition lead to the "masculinization" of women. In the name of liberation from male "domination," women must not appropriate to themselves male characteristics contrary to their own feminine "originality." There is a well-founded fear that if they take this path, women will not "reach fulfilment," but instead will *deform and lose what constitutes their essential richness*. It is indeed an enormous richness. In the biblical description, the words of the first man at the sight of the woman who had been created are words of admiration and enchantment, words which fill the whole history of man on earth.

The personal resources of feminity are certainly no less than the resources of masculinity: they are merely different. Hence a woman, as well as a man, must understand her "fulfilment" as a person, her dignity and vocation, on the basis of these resources, according to the richness of the feminity which she received on the day of creation and which she inherits as an expression of the "image and likeness of God" that is specifically hers. *The inheritance of sin* suggested by the words of the Bible—"Your desire shall be for your husband, and he shall rule over you"—*can be conquered* only by following this path. The overcoming of this evil inheritance is, generation after generation, the task of every human being, whether woman or man. For whenever man is responsible for offending a woman's personal dignity and vocation, he acts contrary to his own personal dignity and his own vocation. . . .

V

Jesus Christ

"They Marvelled That He Was Talking with a Woman"

. . . It is universally admitted—even by people with a critical attitude towards the Christian message—that *in the eyes of his contemporaries Christ became a promotor of women's true dignity* and of the *vocation* corresponding to this dignity. At times this caused wonder, surprise, often to the point of scandal: "They marvelled that he was talking with a woman" (*Jn* 4:27), because this behaviour differed from that of his contemporaries. Even Christ's own disciples "marvelled." The Pharisee to whose house the sinful woman went to anoint Jesus' feet with perfumed oil "said to himself, 'If this man were a prophet, *he would have known who and what sort of woman this is who is touching him, for she is a sinner'*" (*Lk* 7:39). Even greater dismay, or even "holy indignation," must have filled the self-satisfied hearers of Christ's words: "the tax collectors and the harlots go into the Kingdom of God before you" (*Mt* 21:31). . . .

VI

Motherhood-Virginity

Two Dimensions of Women's Vocation

We must now focus our meditation on virginity and motherhood as two particular dimensions of the fulfillment of the female personality. In the light of the Gospel, they acquire their full meaning and value in Mary, who as a Virgin became the Mother of the Son of God. These *two dimensions of the female vocation* were united in her in an exceptional manner, in such a way that one did not exclude the other but wonderfully complemented it. . . .

This *mutual gift of the person in marriage* opens to the gift of a new life, *a new human being,* who is also a person in the likeness of his parents. Motherhood implies from the beginning a special openness to the new person: and this is precisely the woman's "part." In this openness, in conceiving and giving birth to a child, the woman "discovers herself through a sincere gift of self." The gift of interior readiness to accept the child and bring it into the world is linked to the marriage union which—as mentioned earlier—should constitute a special moment in the mutual self-giving both by the woman and the man. . . .

Virginity for the Sake of the Kingdom

In the teaching of Christ, *motherhood is connected with virginity,* but also *distinct from it.* Fundamental to this is Jesus' statement in the conversation on the indissolubility of marriage. Having heard the answer given to the Pharisees, the disciples say to Christ: "If such is the case of a man with his wife, it is not expedient to marry" (*Mt* 19:10). Independently of the meaning which "it is not expedient" had at that time in the mind of the disciples, *Christ* takes their mistaken opinion as a starting point for instructing them *on the value of celibacy*. He distinguishes celibacy which results from natural defects—even though they may have been caused by man—from *"celibacy for the sake of the Kingdom of heaven."* ... Consequently, *celibacy for the kingdom of heaven* results not only from a free *choice* on the part of man, but also from a special *grace* on the part of God, who calls a particular person to live celibacy. ... Christ's answer, in itself, has a *value both for men and for women.* ...

VII

The Church—The Bride of Christ

The Eucharist

... Against the broad background of the "great mystery" expressed in the spousal relationship between Christ and the Church, it is possible to understand adequately the calling of the "Twelve." *In calling only men as his Apostles,* Christ acted *in a completely free and sovereign manner.* In doing so, he exercised the same freedom with which, in all his behaviour, he emphasized the dignity and the vocation of women, without conforming to the prevailing customs and to the traditions sanctioned by the legislation of the time. Consequently, the assumption that he called men to be apostles in order to conform with the widespread mentality of his times, does not at all correspond to Christ's way of acting. ...

Since Christ, in instituting the Eucharist, linked it in such an explicit way to the priestly service of the Apostles, it is legitimate to conclude that he thereby wished to express the relationship between man and woman, between what is "feminine" and what is "masculine." It is a relationship willed by God both in the mystery of creation and in the mystery of Redemption. It is *the Eucharist* above all that expresses *the redemptive act of Christ the Bridegroom towards the Church the Bride.* This is clear and unambiguous when the sacramental ministry of the Eucharist, in which the priest acts *"in persona Christi,"* is performed by a man. This explanation confirms the teaching of the Declaration *Inter Insigniores,* published at the behest of Paul VI in response to the question concerning the admission of women to the ministerial priesthood.

The Gift of the Bride

... In every age and in every country we find many "perfect" women (cf. *Prov.* 31:10) who, despite persecution, difficulties and discrimination, have shared in the Church's mission. It suffices to mention: Monica, the mother of Augustine, Macrina, Olga of Kiev, Matilda of Tuscany, Hedwig of Silesia, Jadwiga of Cracow, Elizabeth of Thuringia, Brigitta of Sweden,

Joan of Arc, Rose of Lima, Elizabeth Ann Seton and Mary Ward.

The witness and the achievements of Christian women have had a significant impact on the life of the Church as well as of society. Even in the face of serious social discrimination, holy women have acted "freely," strengthened by their union with Christ. Such union and freedom rooted in God explain, for example, the great work of Saint Catherine of Siena in the life of the Church, and the work of Saint Teresa of Jesus in the monastic life.

In our own days too the Church is constantly enriched by the witness of the many women who fulfil their vocation to holiness. Holy women are an incarnation of the feminine ideal; they are also a model for all Christians, a model of the *"sequela Christi,"* an example of how the Bride must respond with love to the love of the Bridegroom.

VIII

"The Greatest of These Is Love"

Awareness of a Mission

A woman's dignity is closely connected with the love which she receives by the very reason of her femininity; it is likewise connected *with the love which she gives in return.* The truth about the person and about love is thus confirmed. . . .

While the dignity of woman witnesses to the love which she receives in order to love in return, the biblical "exemplar" of the Woman also seems to reveal *the true order of love which constitutes woman's own vocation.* Vocation is meant here in its fundamental, and one may say universal significance, a significance which is then actualized and expressed in women's many different "vocations" in the Church and the world. . . .

In our own time, the successes of science and technology make it possible to attain material well-being to a degree hitherto unknown. While this favours some, it pushes others to the edges of society. In this way, unilateral progress can also lead to a gradual *loss of sensitivity for man, that is, for what is essentially human.* In this sense, our time in particular *awaits the manifestation* of that "genius" which belongs to women, and which can ensure sensitivity for human beings in every circumstance: because they are human!—and because "the greatest of these is love"(cf. 1 *Cor* 13:13) . . . .

October

Space Shuttle *Discovery*'s Tribute
 to *Challenger* Victims 795

Vice Presidential Debate 799

Peary's Polar Notes 831

Harvard Report
 on the Presidential Press Conference 835

Revision of the U.S. Welfare System 847

South Korean President's
 United Nations Address 853

EPA Report of "Greenhouse Effect"
 on America's Climate 861

Indictment of Ferdinand and
 Imelda Marcos 867

Creation of Department of
 Veterans Affairs 873

Study of Child Poverty
 in America and Abroad 877

SPACE SHUTTLE *DISCOVERY'S* TRIBUTE TO *CHALLENGER* VICTIMS

October 2, 1988

America's manned space program, grounded for thirty-two months after the Challenger *disaster, soared into orbit again on September 29. At Cape Canaveral, Florida, a throng of spectators cheered as the space shuttle* Discovery's *booster rockets dropped away without mishap. This signaled that the spacecraft was in orbit and had escaped* Challenger's *fate.*

From the same launch site on January 28, 1986, the space shuttle Challenger *roared skyward for seventy-three seconds and then exploded in view of aghast onlookers nearby and a national television audience. It plunged into the Atlantic Ocean, bringing death to its seven occupants and creating the worst disaster in the quarter-century of manned space flight.*

As Discovery *circled the globe on October 2, its next-to-last day aloft, the five crew members took turns reading a tribute to the memory of those who were aboard* Challenger. *These brief readings from space, monitored and broadcast to listeners on Earth, concluded with the words of Navy Capt. Frederick H. Hauck, the mission commander. "Dear friends," he said to his deceased colleagues, "we have resumed the journey ... for you.... Your spirit and dreams are still alive in our hearts."*

The Challenger *deaths had been especially heart-rending because they included not only the astronaut crew—Francis Scobee, Michael Smith, Judith Resnik, Elison Onizuka, Ronald McNair, and Gregory Jarvis—but also Christa McAuliffe, a New Hampshire schoolteacher who had been chosen from 11,000 applicants to represent her profession on the flight. The National Aeronautics and Space Administration (NASA) was then engaged in a highly publicized plan to select people from several walks of life for space journeys with the various astronaut crews. This plan was shelved after the* Challenger *disaster.*

After Discovery's *successful launching, President Ronald Reagan commented to a gathering in the White House Rose Garden, "America is back in space again." But he added, "I think I had my fingers crossed like everybody else." From the moment of liftoff at Cape Canaveral to its flawless landing at Edwards Air Force Base in California on October 3 before a crowd of 400,000 people, the shuttle's performance was marred by only slight problems. During their flight, the astronauts performed scientific experiments, tested the shuttle's equipment, and deployed a $100 million communications satellite. Rear Adm. Richard H. Truly, director of NASA's shuttle program, declared, "It's an absolute, stunning success."*

On hand to greet the returning astronauts was Vice President George Bush, who told them and assembled NASA employees: "Thank you for putting America back in space. Thank you for reminding us that's where we belong. Thank you for all the hard work."

Long Preparation

After the Challenger *disaster, NASA technicians and engineers redesigned the spaceship and made substantial improvements in technical support facilities at Cape Canaveral and Houston, Texas. "They went way beyond what we recommended," said Robert Hotz, a member of a panel that investigated the* Challenger *disaster. "[NASA] went with the spirit, not the letter, of what we recommended. This is the way the program should have been run from the very beginning." Among the thousands of components that were redesigned were the huge solid-fuel booster rockets whose failure had caused* Challenger *to explode. The changes were costly—estimated at nearly $2.4 billion by James H. Brier, a financial analyst at the space agency.* (Challenger Accident Commission Report, Historic Documents of 1986, p. 515)

Observers agreed that the success of Discovery—*followed by a four-day military mission completed December 6 by the shuttle* Atlantis—*did much to repair NASA's tarnished image. Nonetheless, questions remained about the future direction of the U.S. space program. Shortly after the* Discovery *mission, the agency signed an agreement with nine European nations, Canada, and Japan to build a permanent, manned station in space. But the achievements did not silence critics of manned space flight. They long had argued that using unmanned rockets to put communications and other satellites in orbit was less costly and without risk to human life.*

The Schedule Ahead

Whether NASA could keep to its schedule of seven shuttle flights in 1989 and ten in 1990 also was questioned. Shuttle testing and outfitting had become more time-consuming after the Challenger *disaster. The* Discovery *mission was postponed several times, and* Atlantis *did not hold firmly to schedule. The planned space missions in 1989 included separate unmanned flights to Venus and Jupiter. These would be the first interplanetary probes undertaken by the United States in almost a decade. Others had fallen victim to cost overruns and delays in the manned shuttle program.*

The triumph of Discovery *was tempered by a Soviet achievement in space. The Soviet's first reusable shuttle made a three and one-half hour flight November 15. The unmanned spacecraft* Buran *(Russian for snowstorm or blizzard) closely resembled the American shuttles in design. No problems were reported, although the flight had been delayed for several months. American engineers noted that a totally automated shuttle landing, as is required of an unmanned shuttle, was extremely difficult to devise. Computers control much of the American shuttle's operations, but astronauts take over during the final landing phase. The* Buran *launch came as two Soviet astronauts, Vladimir Titov and Musa Manarov, completed their 330th day in orbit in the* Mir *space station, setting a record for time in space.*

Following are the texts of tributes delivered in orbit October 2, 1988, by the five astronauts of the space shuttle Discovery *to the seven persons who died in the* Challenger *disaster January 28, 1986:*

Marine Corps Lt. Col. David C. Hilmers:

We'd like to take just a few moments today to share with you some of the sights that we have been so privileged to view over the past several days. As we watch along with you, many emotions well up in our hearts—joy, for America's return to space—gratitude, for our nation's support through difficult times—thanksgiving, for the safety of our crew—reverence, for those whose sacrifice made our journey possible.

Ex-Navy test pilot John M. Lounge:

Gazing outside we can understand why mankind has looked towards the heavens with awe and wonder since the dawn of human existence. We can comprehend why our countrymen have been driven to explore the vast expanse of space. And we are convinced that this is the road to the future—the road that Americans must travel if we are to maintain the dream of our Constitution—to "secure the blessings of liberty to ourselves and to our posterity."

Air Force Col. Harvey O. Covey, the pilot:

As we, the crew of *Discovery,* witness this earthly splendor from America's spacecraft, less than 200 miles separates us from the remainder of mankind; in a fraction of a second our words reach your ears. But lest we ever forget that these few miles represent a great gulf—that to ascend through this seemingly tranquil sea will always be fraught with danger— let us remember the *Challenger* crew whose voyage was so tragically short. With them we shared a common purpose; with them we shared a common goal.

Astronomer George D. Nelson:

At this moment our place in the heavens makes us feel closer to them than ever before. Those on *Challenger* who had flown before and had seen these sights, they would know the meaning of our thoughts. Those who had gone to view them for the first time, they would know why we have set forth. They were our fellow sojourners; they were our friends.

Navy Capt. Frederick H. Hauck, mission commander:

Today, up here where the blue sky turns to black, we can say at long last, to Dick, Mike, Judy, to Ron and El, and to Christa and to Greg: Dear friends, we have resumed the journey that we promised to continue for you; dear friends, your loss has meant that we could confidently begin anew; dear friends, your spirit and your dream are still alive in our hearts.

VICE PRESIDENTIAL DEBATE
October 5, 1988

Vice presidential candidates Dan Quayle and Lloyd Bentsen made their only joint appearance of the 1988 campaign in a ninety-minute nationally televised debate October 5 at Omaha, Nebraska. Questions that were directed to the two candidates by a panel of four journalists focused on Quayle's fitness for the office. And the line of questioning produced a dramatic clash between Democrat Bentsen, a sixty-seven-year-old senator from Texas, and Republican Quayle, a forty-one-year old senator from Indiana.

The exchange came when Quayle said he had as much experience in Congress "as Jack Kennedy did when he sought the presidency." In measured tones, Bentsen responded, "Senator, I served with Jack Kennedy. I knew Jack Kennedy. Jack Kennedy was a friend of mine. Senator, you're no Jack Kennedy."

Visibly wounded, Quayle interjected, "That was really uncalled for, senator." Bentsen replied: "... I think you're so far apart [from former president John F. Kennedy] in the objectives that you choose for your country that I did not think the comparison was well taken."

The clash was the highlight of an attempt in the debate by Bentsen to play on voters' doubts about Quayle's ability to step into the presidency if the president died or was disabled. Quayle experienced some difficulty in responding to questions about what he would do if he became president. After the debate, many observers decried the fact that Bentsen had not been asked the same questions.

There was broad agreement that Bentsen clearly had won the debate. A telephone poll by ABC News immediately after the encounter indicated that 51 percent of the people considered Bentsen the victor and only 27 percent thought Quayle had won. Editorial opinion generally concurred with that finding. For instance, Larry Eichel wrote in the Philadelphia Inquirer *the day after the debate that while Quayle had shown "a certain command of the issues," he was "anything but dazzling. As the debate wore on, his answers increasingly lacked focus and coherence."*

Quayle Controversy

Quayle had become an issue in the campaign almost from the moment presidential candidate George Bush selected him as a running mate. Immediately after Bush announced Quayle's selection to the Republican convention in New Orleans on August 16, the press reported Quayle's mediocre academic record in college and his apparent use of family influence to secure a place in the Indiana National Guard and avoid combat duty during the Vietnam War. (Republican Convention, p. 589)

Bentsen, chairman of the Senate Finance Committee and twenty-six years older than Quayle, had won favorable attention in the press and far higher ratings in the polls than his debate opponent. Therefore, the stakes in the debate were far higher for Quayle than for Bentsen, though expectations of his debate performance were lower.

The Debate

While the thrust of the debate was on Quayle's readiness for the office, the two candidates argued about a broad range of foreign and domestic issues. Quayle, a second-term senator with prior House experience, insisted that he was "prepared" to become president and called attention to his membership on the Senate Armed Services Committee, work on the Job Partnership Training Act, a major piece of legislation, and being the ranking Republican on a Senate Labor subcommittee. He also served on the Senate Budget Committee. "I have more experience than others that have sought the office. . . ," he said. Bentsen countered, "You have to look at maturity of judgment, the breadth of experience, and the leadership roles that person [a vice president] has played before the tragedy [of a president's death or disability] struck him."

Repeatedly attacking the Democratic presidential candidate, Michael S. Dukakis, Quayle sarcastically referred to "Tax Hike Mike," the governor of "Taxachusetts." The governor, he asserted, "has run up more debt than all the governors in the history of Massachusetts going back to the days of the Pilgrims."

Quayle attacked Bentsen for setting up a "breakfast club" to solicit funds from lobbyists for his reelection fund. (Bentsen was reelected senator even though the Dukakis-Bentsen presidential ticket was defeated.) Those who contributed $10,000 could meet with Bentsen at monthly breakfasts. He hurriedly disbanded the club in 1987 when critical stories began appearing in the press. Repeating what he had said before about the breakfast club, Bentsen told the debate viewers, "I don't make many mistakes, but that one was a real doozy."

Bentsen cited the huge increases in the national debt when asked why, with a generally healthy economy, voters would want to turn the Republicans out of the White House. "You know, if you let me write $200 billion worth of hot checks every year, I could give you an illusion of prosperity, too," he said. Bentsen acknowledged that he and Dukakis disagreed on the issue of aid to the contras in Nicaragua. "No question about that," he said. But he added that both Dukakis and he favored giving "peace a chance" in Central America.

Quayle criticized Dukakis for opposing the death penalty for "drug kingpins." He said, "We believe people convicted of that crime deserve the death penalty." Bentsen countered that Quayle had voted against a Senate resolution assuring that the United States would not make any deals with Gen. Manuel Antonio Noriega, the Panamanian leader who had been indicted by a grand jury in the United States on drug-trafficking charges. (Grand Jury Indictments of General Noriega, p. 81)

Campaign Impact

In the aftermath of the debate, Dukakis attempted to capitalize on Bentsen's popularity by campaigning with him and calling him the "star of the show." Dukakis told an audience, "Strong presidents look for strong vice presidents. Weak candidates look for something else." Bush stoutly stood by Quayle. "He did an outstanding job," Bush said, complaining that Quayle had been "unfairly pounded in the press." For the remainder of the campaign, the Bush campaign staff scheduled Quayle for speeches in smaller cities and before conservative and generally supportive audiences.

The questioners for the debate were moderator Judy Woodruff of the "MacNeil/Lehrer News Hour," Jon Margolis of the Chicago Tribune, Tom Brokaw of NBC News, and Brit Hume of ABC News.

> Following is the text of the 1988 vice presidential debate between Sen. Dan Quayle of Indiana, the Republican nominee, and Sen. Lloyd Bentsen of Texas, the Democratic nominee, October 5, 1988, at Omaha, Nebraska. (The bracketed headings have been added by Congressional Quarterly to highlight the organization of the text.):

MS. WOODRUFF: By prior agreement between the two candidates, the first question goes to Senator Quayle, and you have two minutes to respond.

Senator, you have been criticized, as we all know, for your decision to stay out of the Vietnam War, for your poor academic record. But more troubling to some are some of the comments that have been made by people in your own party. Just last week, former Secretary of State Haig said that your pick was the dumbest call George Bush could have made. Your leader in the Senate, your leader in the Senate, Bob Dole, said that a better qualified person could have been chosen. Other Republicans have been far more critical in private. Why do you think that you have not made a more substantial impression on some of these people who have been able to observe you up close?

MR. QUAYLE: The question goes to whether I am qualified to be vice president and, in the case of a tragedy, whether I'm qualified to be president. Qualifications for the office of vice president or president are not age alone. We must look at accomplishments, and we must look at experience. I have more experience than others that have sought the office of vice president. Now let's look at qualifications, and let's look at the three biggest issues that are going to be confronting America in the next presidency. Those three issues are national security and arms control, jobs and education, and the federal budget deficit. On each one of those issues I have more experience than does the governor of Massachusetts.

In national security and arms control you have to understand the relationship between a ballistic missile, a warhead, what throw-weight, what mega-tonnage is; you better understand about telemetry and encryption; and you better understand that you have to negotiate from a position of strength. These are important issues because we want to have more arms control and arms reductions.

In the area of jobs and education, I wrote the Job Training Partnership Act, a bipartisan bill—a bill that has trained and employed over three million economically disadvantaged youth and adults in this country. On the area of federal budget deficit, I have worked eight years on the Senate Budget Committee, and I wish that the Congress would give us the line-item veto, to help deal with that. And if qualifications alone are going to be the issue in this campaign, George Bush has more qualifications than Michael Dukakis and Lloyd Bentsen combined.

MS. WOODRUFF: Senator Bentsen, Senator Bentsen. I'm going to interrupt at this point and ask once again that the audience please keep your responses as quiet as possible. We know that many of you here are for one candidate or another, but you are simply taking time away from your candidate, and more likely than not, you'll be causing the partisans for the other candidate to react again on—when their candidates speaks—so please. Senator Bentsen, you have one minute to respond.

MR. BENTSEN: This debate tonight is not about the qualifications for the vice presidency. The debate is whether or not Dan Quayle and Lloyd Bentsen are qualified to be president of the United States. Because, Judy, just as you have said, that has happened too often in the past. And if that tragedy should occur, we have to step in there without any margin for error, without time for preparation, to take over the responsibility for the biggest job in the world—that of running this great country of ours. To take over the awesome responsibility for commanding the nuclear weaponry that this country has. No, the debate tonight is a debate about the presidency itself, and a presidential decision that has to be made by you. The stakes could not be higher.

[Bentsen vs. Dukakis]

MS. WOODRUFF: Senator Bentsen—a question for you, and you also have two minutes to respond. What—while this is not so much your qualifications, but your split on policy with Govenor Dukakis. He has said that he does not want a clone of himself, but you disagree with him on some major issues—aid to the Nicaraguan contras, the death penalty, gun control, among others. If you had to step in to the presidency, who's agenda would you pursue? Yours, or his?

MR. BENTSEN: Well, I'm delighted to respond to that question, because we agree on so many things, and the vast majority of the issues. We agree on the fact that we have to cut this deficit, and Governor Dukakis has been able to cut that deficit ten budgets in a row in the State of Masschusetts, while he lowered the tax burden on their people from one of the highest to one of the lower in the United States. That is a major sense of achievement, and I admire that. And I'm just delighted to be on the ticket with him. Governor Dukakis and I agree that we ought to have a trade policy for this country, that we've seen this administration more than double the national debt, that they've moved this country from the number one lender nation in the world to the number one debtor nation in the world under their administration, that they have not had a trade policy, that they've let trade be a handmaiden for the foreign policy objectives of the country, that this country has exported too many jobs and not enough products.

And as I worked to pass a trade bill through the United States Senate, they threw roadblocks in the way every step of the way, but we passed a trade bill that has this premise: that any country that has full access to our markets, we're entitled to full access to their markets. Now, that means that we're going to stand tough for America, and we're going to protect those jobs, and we're going to push American products, and we're going to open up markets around the world. We'll show leadership in that respect and turn this deficit in trade around. That's the sort of thing that Michael Dukakis and I will do to bring about a better America for all of our people.

MS. WOODRUFF: Senator Quayle, a minute to respond.

MR. QUAYLE: As you noticed, Senator Bentsen didn't tell you very much about what Governor Dukakis would do—Governor Dukakis, one of the most liberal governors in the United States of America. The one thing he tried to point out about Governor Dukakis is that he's cut taxes. The fact of the matter is, Senator Bentsen, he's raised taxes five times. He just raised taxes this year, and that's why a lot of people refer to him as "Tax Hike Mike." That's why they refer to the state of Massachusetts as

"Taxachusetts." Because every time there's a problem the liberal governor from Massachusetts raises taxes. I don't blame Senator Bentsen for not talking about Governor Michael Dukakis; he's talking more about his record. If I had to defend the liberal policies of Governor Michael Dukakis, I wouldn't talk about it either.

MS. WOODRUFF: Jon Margolis, a question for Senator Bentsen.

[Social Security]

MR. MARGOLIS: Senator Bentsen, you have claimed that Vice President Bush and the Republicans will raid the Social Security trust fund, and you have vowed to protect it, but as chairman of the Senate Finance Committee, you must know that there is something to the argument of your fellow Democrat, Bob Strauss, that some restraint on Social Security growth may be needed, or at least some decision to tax most Social Security benefits as regular income. In fact, you once voted for, and spoke for, a six-month delay on cost-of-living adjustment increases for Social Security. Senator, aren't you and Governor Dukakis using this issue politically, rather than dealing with it responsibly?

MR. BENTSEN: Well, I must say I hate to disappoint my good friend Bob Strauss, but we have a contract with the American people on Social Security, and Social Security is an issue where Senator Quayle voted eight times to cut the benefits on Social Security.

MR. QUAYLE: (interjecting) That's wrong.

MR. BENTSEN: (continuing) When this administration came in and tried to cut the benefits, the minimum benefits—$122 a month for widows, for retirees—tried to cut the benefits for 62-year-old retirees by 40 percent, tried to do an end-run on Social Security when they first came in after promising not to cut it, to cut it by some $20 billion. And while we were working together to reform the Social Security system and to be certain that that money was going to be there for people when they retired, at that point they tried a $40 billion end-run to cut Social Security. Now, the record is clear.

And we saw Vice President Bush fly back from the West Coast to break a tie in the United States Senate. He doesn't get to vote very often in the Senate, but he made a special trip to come back and vote against a cost-of-living increase. Now, when you talk about Social Security the people that are going to protect it are the Democrats who brought forth that program. And I think it's very important that we now see these kinds of end-runs by this administration. When they talk about the fact that they're going to continue to cut this budget, I know too well what their track record is. And we should be concerned about that kind of an effort once again after the election is over.

MS. WOODRUFF: Senator Quayle, your response.

MR. QUAYLE: Senator Bentsen, you know that I did not vote to cut Social Security benefits eight times. What I have voted for, and what Senator Bentsen has voted for, is to delay the cost-of-living adjustments.

Sen. Bentsen, two times in the United States Senate, voted to delay the cost-of-living adjustment. The governor of Massachusetts at a governors' conference supported a resolution to delay the cost-of-living adjustment.

And, Jon, you're right, they use this for political advantage. What they try to do time and time again is to scare the old people of this country. That's the politics of the past. In 1983, Republicans and Democrats dropped their political swords and, in a bipartisan effort, saved the Social Security system. Republicans and Democrats banded together because we know that this program is not a Republican program, it's not a Democrat program; it's a program for older Americans. And that program is actuarially sound to the turn of this century.

MS. WOODRUFF: Jon, a question for Senator Quayle.

[Environmental Issues]

MR. MARGOLIS: Senator, since coming to the Senate, you have voted against environmental protection legislation about two-thirds of the time. These include votes against pesticide controls, the toxic-waste Superfund, and health and safety protection from nuclear wastes. Senator, do you consider yourself an environmentalist? And, if you do, how do you reconcile that with your voting record?

MR. QUAYLE: I have a very strong record on the environment in the United States Senate. I have a record where I voted against my president on the override of the Clean Water Act. I have voted for the major pieces of environmental legislation that have come down and been voted on in the United States Senate. This administration, and I support this administration in its environmental effort, has moved in the area for the first time to deal with the ozone problem. We now have an international treaty, a treaty that is commonly referred to as the Montreal Treaty. For the first time we are talking about the impact of CO_2 to the ozone layer. That's progress for the environment. We are committed to the environment. I take my children hiking and fishing, walking in the woods, in the wilderness. Believe me, we have a commitment to preserving the environment.

If you bring up the environment, you can't help but think about the environmental policy of the governor of Massachusetts. He talks about being an environmentalist. Let me tell you about his environmental policy. The Boston Harbor, the Boston Harbor which is the dirtiest waterway in America. Tons of raw sewage go in there each and every day. What has the governor of Massachusetts done about that? Virtually nothing. Then he has the audacity to go down to New Jersey and tell the people in New Jersey that he's against ocean dumping. This is the same governor that applied for a license to dump Massachusetts sewage, waste off the coast of New Jersey. Who has the environmental record? Who has the environment interests? George Bush and I do.

MS. WOODRUFF: Senator Bentsen?

MR. BENTSEN: Well this late conversion is interesting to me. When they talk about Boston Harbor, and he says he hasn't done anything, the facts are he has a $6 billion program under way on waste treatment, and it was this administration, their administration, that cut out the money early on to be able to clean up water and made it impossible to move ahead at that time on Boston Harbor.

We're the authors, the Democratic Party, of Clean Air, of Clean Water, of the Superfund. I'm one who played a very major role in passing the Superfund legislation. And every environmental organization that I know, every major one has now endorsed the Dukakis-Bentsen ticket. And I'm one who has just received the environmental award in Texas for the work I've done to clean up the bays, to clean up the water off the coast of Texas. Now I think we know well who's going to help clean up this environment. The record is there, the history is there, and Dukakis and Bentsen will be committed to that.

MS. WOODRUFF: Tom Brokaw, a question for Senator Quayle.

[Family Assistance Programs]

MR. BROKAW: Thank you Judy. Senator Quayle, there's been a lot of talk during the course of this campaign about family; it was the principal theme as I recall it in your acceptance speech in New Orleans. Tonight I'd like to ask you about the 65 million American children who live with their families in poverty. I'd like for you to describe to the audience the last time that you may have visited with one of those families personally, and how you explain to that family your votes against the school breakfast program, the school lunch program and the expansion of the child immunization program.

MR. QUAYLE: I have met with those people, and I met with them in Fort Wayne, Indiana, at a food bank. And you may be surprised, Tom, they didn't ask me those questions on those votes because they were glad that I took time out of my schedule to go down and to talk about how we're going to get a food bank going and making sure that a food bank goes to Fort Wayne, Indiana. And I have a very good record and a commitment to the poor, to those that don't have a family, want to have a family. This administration and a George Bush administration will be committed to eradicating poverty. Poverty hasn't gone up in this administration. It hasn't gone down much either, and that means that we have a challenge ahead of us.

But let me tell you something, what we have done for the poor. What we have done for the poor is that we, in fact—the homeless bill—the McKinney Act, which is a major piece of legislation that deals with the homeless. Congress has cut the funding that the administration recommended.

The poor and poverty—the biggest thing that we have done for poverty in America is the Tax Simplification Act of 1986. Six million working poor families got off the payroll. Six million people are off the taxpaying payrolls because of that tax reform, and they're keeping the tax money there. To help the poor, we'll have a commitment to the programs, and those programs will go on. And we are spending more in poverty programs today than we were in 1981. That is a fact. The poverty program we are going to concentrate on is creating jobs and opportunities so that everyone will have the opportunities they want.

MS. WOODRUFF: Senator Bentsen, your response.

MR. BENTSEN: I find that very interesting, because he has been of no help at all when it comes to passing the most major welfare reform bill in the history of our country, one where we're working very hard to see that people can get off welfare, break that cycle, take a step up in life, doing the kinds of things that we did there to let them have Medicaid for a year. That's a positive thing that's done. What also frustrates me with the kind of report that I just heard here is the kind of votes he's cast against child nutrition programs, the fact that he has voted against money that we needed for further immunization, the denial of polio shots to kids where the parents couldn't afford to get that kind of a shot. Now I don't really believe that is identifying with the concerns of people in poverty.

MS. WOODRUFF: Tom, a question for Senator Bentsen.

[Contra Aid Qualms]

MR. BROKAW: Senator Bentsen, I'd like to take you back to the question that Judy asked you about your differences with Michael Dukakis on contra aid. After all, contra aid is one of the cutting issues of foreign policy of this country in the last eight years. You and Michael Dukakis seem to be diametrically opposed on that.

I have been told that in a closed session of the U.S. Senate, you made one of the most eloquent and statesmanlike speeches in behalf of contra aid that anyone had made in the eight years of the Reagan term; that, in fact, you alluded to the threat the Sandinista regime could pose to your own state of Texas. Governor Dukakis, on the other hand, has described the contra aid policy as "immoral and illegal." Is he wrong?

MR. BENTSEN: Governor Dukakis and I have disagreed on the contra program—no question about that. But my big difference with this administration is they look at the contra aid program as the only way to resolve that problem. They concentrate on that. And I really think we have to give peace a chance. And that's why I've been a strong supporter of the Arias plan, a plan that won the Nobel Prize for President Arias, the president of Costa Rica. I believe that you have to work with the leaders of those other Central American countries to try to bring about the democratization of Nicaragua by negotiation, by pressure, by counseling, by diplomatic pressure—that we ought to be trying that first.

But in concentrating so much just on the contras, this administration has not paid enough attention to the rest of Central America. The concern I have is that we have a country with 85 million people sharing a 2,000-mile border with us with half of those people under the age of 15, a country that has had its standard of living cut 50 percent in the last six years. Now, we ought to be concerned about that and we ought to be involved. I was born and reared on that Mexican border. I speak their language. I spent a good part of my life down there. Governor Dukakis speaks Spanish, too. He's spent a good deal of time in Central and South America.

And we believe that we ought to be working together with a new alliance for progress, bringing in other countries to help. Bring in Europeans, the Spanish, who have a real affinity for that area. Bringing in the Japanese, who have a great capital surplus now and [are] looking for places to invest it. Those are the policy things I think we could do to bring about peace in that area, to help raise that standard of living and give them the kind of stability where democracy can proceed and can prosper and bloom.

Those are the kinds of things that we'd be committed to in a Dukakis-Bentsen administration, to try to make this world a better place in which to live.

MS. WOODRUFF: Senator Quayle, your response.

MR. QUAYLE: There's no doubt, in a Dukakis administration that the aid would be cut off to the democratic resistance in Nicaragua and that is unfortunate. The reason it is unfortunate—because it is beyond me why it's okay for the Soviet Union to put in billions of dollars to prop up the communist Sandinistas, but somehow it's wrong for the United States to give a few dollars to the democratic resistance.

There's a thing called the Monroe Doctrine, something that the governor of Massachusetts has said has been superseded. I doubt if many Americans agree with that. I think they believe in the Monroe Doctrine. Sen. Bentsen talked about the entire Central America. There's another issue that Michael Dukakis is wrong on in Central America and that's Grenada. He criticized our rescue mission in Grenada, according to a UPI report—criticized that, yet 85 percent of the American people supported our rescue mission and we turned a communist country into a non-communist country. The governor of Massachusetts is simply out of step with mainstream American.

[PAC Money]

MS. WOODRUFF: Brit Hume, a question for Senator Bentsen.

MR. HUME: Good evening, Senator Bentsen, Senator Quayle. I'm sort of the clean-up man in this order, and I've been asked by my colleagues to try to deal with anything that's been left on base. Senator, I have a follow-up question for you, Senator Quayle. But Senator Bentsen, I first want to ask you a question about PAC money, something I'm sure you're prepared to talk about. Governor Dukakis has tried to make ethics a major issue in the campaign. And he has you as a running mate, a man who leads the league, at last count, in the receipt of PAC money—that being the money raised by the special-interest organizations. That is the kind of campaign financing which Governor Dukakis finds so distasteful that he has refused to accept any of it. Do you find that embarrassing, Senator?

MR. BENTSEN: No, I don't find it embarrassing at all because you have to remember that PAC money is the result of the last campaign reform bill, one that talks about employees having greater participation. And what I've done in PAC money is just what my opponent in my campaign has done in his campaign. He has, he's been raising PAC money, too. So what you have to do is comply with the laws as they are, whether you're paying taxes, or you're playing a football game; whether you like those laws or not you comply with them.

Now, I have been for campaign reform and have pushed it very hard. I believe that we have to do some things in that regard. But I've noticed that the Senator from Indiana has opposed that campaign reform and voted repeatedly against it. The things we have to do, I believe, that will cut back on "soft money," for example, which I look on as, frankly, one of those things that we have had to do because the Republicans have done it for so long, but I think it's a loophole, frankly.

But campaign reform, changing the rules of the game, is something we tried repeatedly in this session of the Congress, but only to have the Republicans lead the charge against us and defeat us. And I wish that Senator Quayle would change his mind on that particular piece of legislation and give us the kind of a campaign reform law that I think is needed in America.

MS. WOODRUFF: Senator Quayle, your response.

MR. QUAYLE: Senator Bentsen is the number one PAC raiser. As a matter of fact, he used to have a $10,000 Breakfast Club. A $10,000 Breakfast Club. It only cost high-paid lobbyist special interests in Washington to come down and have breakfast with the chairman of the Senate Finance Committee—the one that oversees all the tax loopholes in the tax code—$10,000. I'm sure they weren't paying to have Corn Flakes.

Well, I'll tell you the kind of campaign reform I'm supporting, Senator Bentsen. I think it's time that we get rid of PAC money. Support our legislation where we totally eliminate contributions by special interests and political action committees, and let's have the individual contribute and the political parties contribute. That's the kind of campaign reform that Republicans are for. They want to get rid of this special interest money and rely on the individuals, and also the political parties.

MS. WOODRUFF: Brit, your question for Senator Quayle. Once again, let me caution the audience: please, keep your reaction as quiet as possible. Brit.

[On Becoming President]

MR. HUME: Senator, I want to take you back, if I can, to the question Judy asked you about some of the apprehensions people may feel about your being a heartbeat away from the presidency. And let us assume, if we can, for the sake of this question, that you become vice president and the president is incapacitated for one reason or another and you have to take the reins of power. When that moment came, what would be the first steps that you'd take and why?

MR. QUAYLE: First I'd say a prayer for myself and for the country that I'm about to lead. And then I would assemble his people and talk. And I think this question keeps going back to qualifications and what kind of vice president and this hypothetical situation if I had to assume the responsibilities of the president what I would be. And, as I have said, age alone—although I can tell you, after the experience of these last few weeks on the campaign, I've added 10 years to my age—age alone is not the only qualification. You've got to look at experience, and you've got to look at accomplishments. And can you make a difference?

Have I made a difference in the United States Senate where I served for eight years? Yes, I have. Have I made a difference in the Congress that I served for twelve years? Yes, I have. As I said before, looking at the issue of qualifications, and I am delighted that it comes up, because on the three most important challenges facing America—arms control and national security, jobs and education, and budget deficit—I have more experience and accomplishments than does the governor of Massachusetts.

I have been in the Congress, and I have worked on these issues. And, believe me, when you look at arms control and trying to deal with the Soviet Union, you cannot come at it from a naive position. You have to understand the Soviet Union. You have to understand how they will respond. Sitting on that Senate Armed Services Committee for eight years has given me the experience to deal with the Soviet Union and how we can move forward. That is just one of the troubling issues that's going to be facing this nation. And I am prepared.

MR. HUME: Senator Bentsen?

MR. BENTSEN: Well, I can't leave something on the table that he's charged me with, so let's get to that one. When you talk about the "Breakfast Club," as you know, that was perfectly legal. And I formed it and I closed it down almost immediately, because I thought the perception was bad. But it's the same law. It's the same law that lets you invite high-priced lobbyists down to Williamsburg; and bring them down there and entertain them playing golf, playing tennis and bringing Republican senators down there, to have exchanged for that contributions to their campaign.

It's the same kind of law that lets you have honorariums, and you've collected over a quarter of a million dollars of honorariums now, speaking to various interest groups. And there's no control over what you do with that money. You can spend it on anything you want to. You can spend it on golf club dues, if you want to do that. Now that's what I've seen you do in this administration, and that's why we need campaign reform laws and why I support them and you, in turn, have voted against them time and time again.

MS. WOODRUFF: Jon Margolis, question for Senator Quayle.

[Workers' Rights]

MR. MARGOLIS: Senator Quayle, in recent years the Reagan administration has scaled back the activities of the Occupational Safety and

Health Administration, prompted in part by Vice President Bush's task force on regulatory relief. The budget for the agency has been cut by 20 percent, and the number of inspections at manufacturing plants have been reduced by 33 percent.

This has had a special effect in this area where many people work in the meat-packing industry, which has a far higher rate of serious injuries than almost any other injury, a rate which appears to have been rising, although we're not really sure because some of the largest companies have allegedly been falsifying their reports. Would you acknowledge to the hundreds of injured and maimed people in Nebraska, Iowa, and elsewhere in the Midwest that, in this case, deregulation may have gone too far and the government should reassert itself in protecting workers' rights?

MR. QUAYLE: The premise of your question, Jon, is that somehow this administration has been lax in enforcement of the OSHA regulations and I disagree with that, and I'll tell you why. If you want to ask some business people that I've talked to periodically, they complain about the tough enforcement of this administration.

And furthermore, let me tell you this for the record, when we have found violations in this administration there has not only been tough enforcement, but there have been the most severe penalties—the largest penalties in the history of the Department of Labor—have been levied when these violations have been found.

There is a commitment, and there will always be a commitment, to the safety of our working men and women. They deserve it, and we're committed to them. Now, the broader question goes to the whole issue of deregulation, and has deregulation worked or has deregulation not worked? In my judgment, deregulation has worked. We have a deregulated economy and we have produced through low taxes, not high taxes, through deregulation, the spirit of entrepreneurship, the individual going out and starting a business, the businessman or woman willing to go out and risk their investment and start up a business and hire people—we have produced 17 million jobs in this country since 1982.

Deregulation as a form of political philosophy is a good philosophy. It's one that our opponents disagree with. They want a centralized government. But we believe in the market; we believe in the people. And yes, there's a role of government and the role of government is to make sure that the safety and health and welfare of the people is taken care of. And we'll continue to do that.

MS. WOODRUFF: Senator Bentsen?

MR. BENTSEN: I think you see once again a piece of Democratic legislation that's been passed to try to protect the working men and women of America. And then you've seen an administration that came in and really didn't have its heart in that kind of an enforcement. A good example of that is the environmental protection laws that we were talking about a moment ago. This administration came in and put in a James Watt and Anne Gorsuch. Now that's the Bonnie and Clyde, really, of environmental protection. And that's why it's important that you have people that truly believe, and trying to represent the working men and women of America. Most employers do a good job of that, but some of them put their profits before people. And that's why you have to have OSHA, and that's why you have to have tough and good and fair enforcement of it. And that's what a Democratic administration would do to help make this working place a safer and a better place to be employed.

MS. WOODRUFF: Jon Margolis, another question for Senator Bentsen.

[Farm Policy]

MR. MARGOLIS: Senator Bentsen, since you have been in the Senate, the government has spent increasing amounts of money in an effort to protect the family farmer, but most of the subsidies seem to go, do go, to the largest and richest farmers, who presumably need it least, while it's the smaller farmers who are often forced to sell out, sometimes to their large farmer neighbor who's gotten more subsidies to begin with.

Despite the fact that I believe you, sir, are rather a large farmer yourself, do you believe it's time to uncouple the subsidy formula from the amount of land a farmer has and target federal money to the small- and medium-size farmer?

MR. BENTSEN: Well, I've supported that. I voted for the 50,000 limitation to get away from the million-dollar contributions to farmers. You know, of the four that are on this ticket, I'm the only one that was born and reared on a farm, and still involved in farming. So I think I understand their concerns and their problems. Now, I feel very strongly that we ought to be doing more for the American farmer, and what we've seen under this administration is neglect of that farmer.

We've seen them drive 220,000 farmers off the farm. They seem to think the answer is, "Move 'em to town." But we ought not to be doing that. What you have seen them do is cut farm assistance for the rural areas by over 50 percent. We're seeing rural hospitals close all over the country because of this kind of an administration. We've seen an administration that has lost much of our market abroad because they have not had a trade policy. We saw our market lost by some 40 percent. And that's one of the reasons that we've seen the cost of the farm program, which was only about $2.5 billion when they took office, now go to about $25 billion. Now we can bring that kind of a cost down and get more to market prices if we'll have a good trade policy.

I was, in January, visiting with Mr. Takeshita, the new prime minister of Japan. I said, "You're paying five times as much for beef as we pay for in our country—pay for it in our country—six times as much for rice. You have a $60 billion trade surplus with us. You could improve the standard of living of your people. You're spending 27 percent of your disposable income on food. We spent 14 or 15 percent. When you have that kind of a barrier up against us, that's not free and fair trade, and we don't believe that should continue."

We should be pushing very hard to open up those markets, and stand up for the American farmer. And see that we recapture those foreign markets, and I think we can do it with a Dukakis-Bentsen administration.

MS. WOODRUFF: Senator Quayle.

MR. QUAYLE: Senator Bentsen talks about recapturing the foreign markets. Well, I'll tell you one way that we're not going to recapture the foreign markets, and that is if, in fact, we have another Jimmy Carter grain embargo. Jimmy—Jimmy Carter grain embargo—Jimmy Carter grain embargo set the American farmer back. You know what the farmer is interested in? Net farm income. Every 1 percent of increase in interest rates—a billion dollars out of the farmer's pocket. Net farm income—increase inflation another billion dollars.

Another thing that a farmer's not interested in and that's supply management the Democratic platform talks about. But, the governor of Massachusetts, he had the farm program. He went to the farmers in the Midwest, and told them not to grow corn, not to grow soybeans, but to grow Belgium endive. That's what his—that's what he and his Harvard buddies think of the American farmers. Grow Belgium endive. To come in and to tell our farmers not to grow corn, not to grow soybeans, that's the kind of farm policy you'll get under a Dukakis administration, and one I think the American farmer rightfully will reject.

MS. WOODRUFF: Tom Brokaw, a question for Senator Bentsen?

[Current Economic Policies]

MR. BROKAW: Senator Bentsen, you were a businessman before you entered the U.S. Senate. Let me offer you an inventory, if I may: lower interest rates, lower unemployment, lower inflation, and an arms control deal with the Soviet Union. Now, two guys come through your door at your business, and say, "We'd like you to change," without offering a lot of specifics. Why would you accept their deal?

MR. BENTSEN: You know, if you let me write $200 billion worth of hot checks every year, I could give you an illusion of prosperity, too. This is an administration that has more than doubled the national debt, and they've done that in less than eight years. They have taken this country from the number one lender nation in the world to the number one debtor nation in the world. And the interest on that debt next year, on this Reagan-Bush debt of our nation, is going to be $640 for every man, woman and child in America, because of this kind of a credit card mentality. So, we go out and we try to sell our securities, every week, and hope that the foreigners will buy them. And they do buy them, but every time they do, we lose some of our economic independence for the future.

Now they've turned around and they've bought 10 percent of the manufacturing base of this country. They bought 20 percent of the banks. They own 46 percent of the commercial real estate in Los Angeles. They're buying America on the cheap. Now when we have other countries that can't manage their economy down in Central and South America, we send down the American ambassador. We send down the International Monetary Fund and we tell them what they can buy and what they can sell and how to run their economies. The ultimate irony would be to have that happen to us because foreigners finally quit buying our securities.

So what we need in this country is someone like Mike Dukakis who gave 10 balanced budgets in a row there and was able to do that, meet that kind of a commitment, set those tough priorities. We need an administration that will turn this trade policy around and open up those markets, stand tough with our trading partners to help keep the jobs at home and send the products abroad.

MS. WOODRUFF: Senator Quayle?

MR. QUAYLE: Senator Bentsen talks about running up the debt. Well the governor of Massachusetts has run up more debt than all the governors in the history of Massachusetts combined going back to the days of the Pilgrims. I don't believe that that's the kind of policy that we want. The question went to the heart of the matter, Tom. You asked the question that why would we change? Well we have changed since 1980. We've got interest rates down. We got inflation down. People are working again. America is held in respect once again around the world. But we're going to build on that change.

And as we made those positive change of lower interest rates, lower rate of inflation, the governor of Massachusetts fought us every step of the way. We are proud of the record of accomplishment and the opportunities and the hope for millions of Americans—hope and opportunity of these Americans is because of the policies that we have had for the last eight years and we want to build on that and change it for even the better.

MS. WOODRUFF: Tom, a question for Senator Quayle.

[The Military in the Drug War]

MR. BROKAW: Senator Quayle, as you mention here tonight, you actively supported the invasion of Grenada, which was the military operation to rescue some American medical students and to rescue an island from a Marxist takeover. If military force was necessary in that endeavor, why not use the military to go after the South American drug cartels and after General Noriega for that matter on a surgical strike, since drugs in the minds of most Americans pose a far greater danger to many more people?

MR. QUAYLE: You're absolutely right. You're absolutely right, the drug problem is the number one issue.

MR. BROKAW: But would you please address the military aspect of it?

MR. QUAYLE: I will address the military aspect if I may respond. The military aspect of the drug problem is being addressed. As a matter of fact, we are using the Department of Defense in a coordinated effort on reconnaissance, but I don't believe that we're going to turn the Department of Defense into a police organization. We are using our military assets in a prudent way to deal with interdiction. And we've made some success in this area. Seventy tons of cocaine have been stopped.

But, you know, when you look at the drug problem, and it is a tremendous problem and there are no easy solutions to it, it's a complicated problem. And it's heading up the effort to try to create a drug-free America, which is a challenge and a goal of all of us. Not only will we utilize national defense and the Department of Defense, but we've got to get on the demand side of the ledger. We've got to get to education, and education ought to begin at home, and it ought to be reinforced, reinforced in our schools.

And there's another thing that will be more important than the premise of this question on a hypothetical of using troops. We'll use military assets. We're not going to, we'll use military assets, but we need to focus on another part of this problem, and that problem is law enforcement. And here's where we have a major disagreement with the governor of Massachusetts. He is opposed to the death penalty for drug kingpins. We believe people convicted of that crime deserve the death penalty, as does the legislation that's in the Congress that's supported by a bipartisan group, including many Democrats of his party. He also was opposed to mandatory drug sentencing for drug dealers in the state of Massachusetts. You cannot have a war on drugs, you cannot be tough on drugs and weak on crime.

MS. WOODRUFF: Senator Bentsen.

MR. BENTSEN: It's interesting to see that the senator from Indiana, when we had a resolution on the floor of the United States Senate sponsored by Senator Dole, that this government would make no deal with Noriega, that the senator from Indiana was one of the dozen senators that voted against it. It's also interesting to see that one of his campaign managers that's trying to help him with his image, was also hired by Noriega to help him with his image in Panama.

What we have seen under this administration, we have seen them using eight Cabinet officers, 28 different agencies, all fighting over turf. And that's one thing we'd correct under the Dukakis-Bentsen administration. We'd put one person in charge in the war against drugs, and we'd commit the resources to get that job done. Now, Mike Dukakis has been able to do that type of thing in the state of Massachusetts by cutting the drug use in high schools while it's going up around the rest of the country, by putting in a drug educational program that the Drug Enforcement Agency said was a model for the country. We'd be doing that around the rest of the country. That's a positive attack against drugs.

MS. WOODRUFF: Brit Hume, a question for Senator Quayle.

[Assuming the Presidency]

MR. HUME: Senator, I want to take you back to the question that I asked you earlier about what would happen if you were to take over in an emergency and what you would do first and why. You said you'd say a prayer and you said something about a meeting. What would you do next?

MR. QUAYLE: I don't believe that it's proper for me to get into the specifics of a hypothetical situation like that. The situation is that if I was called upon to serve as the president of this country, or the responsibilities of the president of this country, would I be capable and qualified to do that? And I've tried to list the qualifications of 12 years in the United States Congress. I have served in the Congress for 12 years; I have served in the Congress and served eight years on the Senate Armed Services Committee.

I have traveled a number of times; I've been to Geneva many times to meet with our negotiators as we were hammering out the INF Treaty. I've met with the Western political leaders—Margaret Thatcher, Chancellor Kohl—I know them; they know me. I know what it takes to lead this country forward. And if that situation arises, yes, I will be prepared, and I'll be prepared to lead this country if that happens.

MR. HUME: Senator Bentsen.

MR. BENTSEN: Well, once again, I think what we're looking at here is someone that can step in at the presidency level at the moment, if that tragedy would occur. And if that's the case, again you have to look at maturity of judgment, and you have to look at breadth of experience. You have to see what kind of leadership roles that person has played in his life before that crisis struck him. And if you do that type of thing, then you'll arrive at a judgment that I think would be a wise one, and I hope that would mean that you say, "We're going to vote for Mike Dukakis and Lloyd Bentsen."

MS. WOODRUFF: Brit, a question for Senator Bentsen.

[Bentsen's Breakfast Club]

MR. HUME: Senator, I want to take you back, if I can, to the celebrated "Breakfast Club." When it was first revealed that you had a plan to have people pay $10,000 a plate to have breakfast with you, you handled it with disarming, not to say charming, candor. You said it was a mistake and you disbanded it and called the whole idea off, and you were widely praised for having handled it deftly.

The question I have is, if the *Washington Post* had not broken that story and other media picked up on it, what can you tell us tonight as to why we should not believe that you would still be having those breakfasts to this day?

MR. BENTSEN: (Laughs) Well, I must say, Brit, I don't make many mistakes, but that one was a real doozy. And I agree with that. And, as you know, I immediately disbanded it; it was perfectly legal. And you have all kinds of such clubs on the Hill, and you know that. And—but I still believe that the better way to go is to have a campaign reform law that takes care of that kind of a situation. Even though it's legal, the perception is bad. So I would push very strong to see that we reform the entire situation. I'd work for that end and that's what my friend from Indiana has opposed repeatedly, vote after vote.

MS. WOODRUFF: Senator Quayle?

MR. QUAYLE: He disbanded the club, but he's still got the money. He is the number one receiver of political action committee money. Now, Senator Bentsen's talked about reform. Well, let me tell you about the reform that we're pushing. Let's eliminate political action committees to special interest money. There's legislation before the Congress to do that. That way we won't have to worry about breakfast clubs or who's the number one PAC raiser. We can go back and get the contributions from the working men and women and the individuals of America. We can also strengthen our two-party system, and it needs strengthening, and rely more on the political parties than we have in the past. That's the kind of campaign reform that I'm for, and I hope the senator will join me.

MS. WOODRUFF: Jon Margolis, a question for Sen. Bentsen.

["Greenhouse Effect"]

MR. MARGOLIS: Senator, we've all just finished—most America has just finished one of the hottest summers it can remember, and apparently this year will be the fifth out of the last nine that are among the hottest on record. No one knows, but most scientists think that something we're doing, human beings are doing, are exacerbating this problem and that this could, in a couple of generations, threaten our descendants' comfort and health and perhaps even their existence.

As vice president, what would you urge our government to do to deal with this problem? And specifically, as a Texan, could you support a substantial reduction in the use of fossil fuel, which might be necessary down the road?

MR. BENTSEN: Well, I think what you can do in that one, and which would be very helpful, is to use a lot more natural gas, which burns a lot cleaner. And what Mike Dukakis has said is that he'll try to break down those regulatory roadblocks that you have in the regulatory agency that denies much of the passage of that natural gas to the Northeast, where you, in turn, can fight against acid rain, which is another threat because it's sterilizing our lakes, it's killing our fish.

And it's interesting to me to see in the résumé of Senator Quayle that he brags on the fact that he's been able to fight the acid rain legislation. I don't think that that's a proper objective in trying to clean up this environment. But the greenhouse effect is one that has to be a threat to all of us, and we have to look for alternative sources of fuel, and I've supported that very strongly.

The Department of Energy is one that has cut back substantially on the study of those alternative sources of fuel. We can use other things that'll help the farmer. We can convert corn to ethanol, and I would push for that very strong. So absolutely, I'll do these things that are necessary to put the environment of our country number one, because if we don't protect that, we'll destroy the future of our children, and we must be committed to trying to clean up the water, clean up the air, and do everything we can not only from a research standpoint, but also in the applied legislation to see that that's carried out.

MS. WOODRUFF: Senator Quayle?

MR. QUAYLE: Vice President George Bush has said that he will take on the environmental problem. He has said further that he will deal with the acid rain legislation and reduce millions of tons of the SO_2 content. That legislation won't get through the Congress this year, but it will get through in a George Bush administration, a George Bush administration that is committed to the environment. Now the greenhouse effect is an important environmental issue. It is important for us to get the data in, to see what alternatives we might have to the fossil fuels, to make sure that we know what we're doing. And there are some explorations and things that we can consider in this area. The drought highlighted the problem that we have. And, therefore, we need to get on with it. And in a George Bush administration, you can bet that we will.

MS. WOODRUFF: A question for Senator Quayle.

[U.S. Foreign Debt]

MR. MARGOLIS: Senator, as vice president, your most important contribution would be the advice you gave the president. One of the most troubling facts that's going to face the new administration is the fact that the United States has now become the world's largest debtor nation. In 1987, foreigners underwrote our debts to the tune of about $138 billion.

Last week, a top official of the Japanese Economic Planning Agency bragged that Japan now is in a position to influence the value of the dollar, of our interest rates, and even our stock prices, and he warned that one day maybe they'd do just that. If you were vice president of the United States and Japan did that, what would you tell the president to do?

MR. QUAYLE: When you look at dealing with this total problem—not just with the Japanese, but the underlying question on this total world debt problem—you have got to see why are we a debtor and what is attracting the foreign investment into our country today, whether it's the Japanese or others.

I would rather have people come over here and to make investments in this country rather than going elsewhere, because by coming over here and making investments in this country, we are seeing jobs. Do you realize that today we are producing Hondas and exporting Hondas to Japan? We are the envy of the world.

The United States—some of Senator Bentsen's supporters laugh at that. They laugh at that, because they don't believe that the United States of America is the envy of the world. Well, I can tell you, the American people think the United States of America is the envy of the world.

MS. WOODRUFF: Senator Bentsen—oh, I'm sorry, go ahead.

MR. QUAYLE: We are the greatest nation in this world and the greatest economic power. Now, there's been some talk in Congress about forgiveness of debt. Forgiveness of debt is wrong. Forgiveness of international debt would be counterproductive. And I'd like to see those that talk about forgiving debt, Senator Bentsen, to go out and talk about the farmer that's in debt that doesn't have his forgiven. That's not the kind of policy George Bush will have.

MS. WOODRUFF: Senator Bentsen.

MR. BENTSEN: Well, I've told you what I'd do about trade and trying to help turn that situation around. But [what] we also should do is get them to give us more burden-sharing when it comes to national defense. We have a situation today where on a per capita basis, people in western Europe are spending about one third as much as we are in our country. And then when you go to Japan, where we're spending 6½ percent on defense of the democracies, they're spending 1 percent.

I met with some of the Japanese business leaders, talking to them about it. And I said, "You know, we have 50,000 troops here in Japan, protecting the democracies of Asia. And it costs $3.5 billion a year. You're the number two economic power in the world. You ought to measure up to that responsibility and carry some of that cost."

I said, "If we were not doing what we're doing, we'd have a big budget surplus." And I said, "You'd have chaos, because you get 55 percent of your oil from the Persian Gulf and you wouldn't have the U.S. Navy down there to take care of that." Now, the senator from Indiana, when we passed a resolution in the United States Senate to ask for burden-sharing on that cost to keep those sea lanes open from the Japanese, he voted against that. I don't understand that.

MS. WOODRUFF: Tom Brokaw, a question for Senator Quayle.

[The Presidency]

MR. BROKAW: Senator Quayle, I don't mean to beat this drum until it has no more sound left in it, but to follow up on Brit Hume's question, when you said that it was a hypothetical situation, it is sir, after all, the reason that we're here tonight, because you are running not just for vice president. And if you cite the experience that you had in Congress, surely you must have some plan in mind about what you would do if it fell to you to become president of the United States as it has to so many vice presidents just in the last 25 years or so.

MR. QUAYLE: Let me try to answer the question one more time. I think this is the fourth time that I have had this question and—

MR. BROKAW: Third time.

MR. QUAYLE: Three times, that I've had this question and I'll try to answer it again for you as clearly as I can because the question you're asking is, "What kind of qualifications does Dan Quayle have to be president?" What kind of qualifications do I have and what would I do in this kind of a situation? And what would I do in this situation?

I would make sure that the people in the Cabinet and the people and advisers to the president are called. I'll talk to them and I'll work with them. And I will know them on a firsthand basis, because as vice president, I'll sit on the National Security Council and I'll know them on a firsthand basis because I'm going to be coordinating the drug effort. I'll know them on a firsthand basis because Vice President George Bush is going to recreate the Space Council and I'll be in charge of that. I will have day-to-day activities with all the people in government.

And then if that unfortunate situation happens, if that situation which would be very tragic happens, I will be prepared to carry out the responsibilities of the presidency of the United States of America. And I will be prepared to do that. I will be prepared not only because of my service in the Congress, but because of my ability to communicate and to lead. It is not just age, it's accomplishments, it's experience. I have far more experience than many others that sought the office of vice president of this country. I have as much experience in the Congress as Jack Kennedy did when he sought the presidency. I will be prepared to deal with the people in the Bush administration if that unfortunate event would ever occur.

MS. WOODRUFF: Senator Bentsen?

MR. BENTSEN: Senator, I served with Jack Kennedy. I knew Jack Kennedy. Jack Kennedy was a friend of mine. Senator, you're no Jack Kennedy. What has to be done in a situation like that, in a situation like that is to call in the joint—

MS. WOODRUFF: Please, please, once again you're only taking time away from your own candidates.

MR. QUAYLE: That was really uncalled for, Senator.

MR. BENTSEN: You're the one that was making the comparison, Senator, and I'm one who knew him well. And frankly, I think you're so far apart in the objectives you choose for your country that I did not think the comparison was well taken.

MS. WOODRUFF: Tom, a question for Senator Bentsen.

[Middle East Hostages]

MR. BROKAW: Since you seem to be taking no hostages on the stage, let me ask you a question about the American—nine still in brutal captivity in the Middle East. Senator Bentsen, you have been critical of the Iran-contra affair. But tell me, does the Dukakis-Bentsen ticket have any realistic plan for getting the American hostages being held in the Middle East released in any due time?

MR. BENTSEN: Tom, that's one of the toughest problems that any chief executive will face because you can't help but have the sympathy for that family and for those hostages in themselves. But the one thing we ought to have, know by now is that you can't go out and make secret deals with the Ayatollah. You can't trade arms for hostages. When you try to do that there's no question but what you just encourage more taking of hostages. And that's been the result by this dumb idea that was cooked out, cooked up in the White House basement.

And I want to tell you that George Bush, attending 17 of those meetings and having no record of what he said—if Lloyd Bentsen was in those meetings, you would certainly hear from him, and no one would be asking, "Where is Lloyd?" Because I would be making, I would be saying, "That's a dumb idea and now let's put an end to it." And I would speak up on that type of thing. So all you can do on that is to continue to push, use every bit of diplomatic pressure you can, what you can do in the way of economic pressure in addition to that. And that's what you strive to do to have a successful release, finally, of those hostages. But not to encourage more taking of hostages.

MS. WOODRUFF: Senator Quayle?

MR. QUAYLE: There's no doubt about it that arms for hostages is wrong, and it will never be repeated. We learn by our mistakes. But there have been a number of successes in foreign policy in this administration. But the question goes to a very difficult one: How do you do it? No one has the answer. If they did we'd, we'd certainly do it. But we won't keep trying, we'll keep trying, we'll keep the doors open. And hopefully some day Iran, and others who control those hostages, will want to return to civilized international community. And they can do that starting now by releasing those hostages that are held illegally.

MS. WOODRUFF: Brit Hume, a question for Senator Bentsen.

[Bentsen's Past Presidential Bid]

MR. HUME: Senator, much of the Dukakis and Bentsen campaign of late has been devoted to the notion that Senator Quayle isn't ready for the vice presidency and perhaps the presidency. And certainly nothing that you have said here tonight suggests that you think otherwise. I wonder if you think it's really fair for you to advance that view in light of the fact that you ran for the presidency, not the vice presidency, in 1976, having not yet completed one full term in the Senate and having previously served three terms in the House almost a quarter of a century earlier, when in fact your time in Washington was about equal to what he has now?

MR. BENTSEN: Well, I think what you have to look at is the record of a man who has served his country—served his country in war, headed up a squadron in combat, a man who built a business, knew what it was to meet a payroll, create jobs, and then serve in the United States Senate; and one who has been able to bring about some of the kinds of legislation that I've been able to bring about in my service there. I must say I didn't do a very good job of running for the presidency, and I'm well aware of that. But what we're looking at today is trying to judge, once again, the breadth of experience and the maturity of someone taking on this kind of task. That's the judgment that has to be exercised by the people of America. It's a presidential decision that you're facing, and it's a very important one, because we're talking about who's going to lead this country into its future, and you can't have a more important responsibility than that one.

MR. HUME: Senator Quayle?

MR. QUAYLE: When you look at qualifications, you look at accomplishments as well as experience. And one of the accomplishments that I'm proudest of is the authorship of the Job Training Partnership Act that has trained and educated and employed over 3 million young people and adults that are economically disadvantaged.

And we did it in a way that we got the private sector to involve itself with the public sector on Private Industry Councils throughout America that serve over the service delivery areas. We have 51 percent of that Private Industry Council that are businessmen and women; we have members of unions; we have community-based organizations; we have education leaders. And what we've been able to do is establish a program that's working, that's putting people back to work. That is an accomplishment, and that is an accomplishment that I will take with me into the White House.

MS. WOODRUFF: Brit, a question for Senator Quayle.

[Cultural Influences]

MR. HUME: Senator, I want to ask you a question, and it may be a little off the subject of politics, it's aimed to get more at the question of what sort of person you are. I hope that, Senator Bentsen, if you choose to, you might choose to answer the same question, in your rebuttal time. Senator, can you identify any work of literature or art, or even a film that you have seen or read or experienced anywhere in the last two years that has had a particularly strong effect on you, and tell us why?

MR. QUAYLE: In the last six months I think there are three very important books that I read that have had an impact. The three books are: one, Richard Nixon's *Victory in 1999*, Richard Lugar's—Senator Richard Lugar's *Letters to the Next President*, Bob Massey's *Alexandra—Nicholas and Alexandra*, which deals with the fall of the Russian empire and the coming of Leninism in 1917.

Those three books, which I read over the last spring vacation and early summer, had a very definite impact because what former President Nixon and Senator Richard Lugar were talking about was a foreign policy as we move toward the 21st century. And the historical book of the downfall of the Czar and the coming of Leninism—combining those three books together gave me a better appreciation of the challenges that we have ahead of us. In Senator Lugar's book he talks about the advancement of human rights around the world. He talked about his leadership effort in the Philippines and South Africa, where we now see human rights and advancement of the Reagan agenda.

Former President Nixon talked about what we're going to do after détente and arms control, and how we're going to pursue new arms control with the Soviet Union. He talked a little bit about how we deal with the Soviet Union. And this is one of the differences between George Bush and Michael Dukakis, because George Bush understands to deal with the Soviet Union and to get progress, you must deal from a position of strength. And the governor of Massachusetts doesn't understand that. I understand it, and a George Bush administration will pursue that policy.

MR. HUME: Senator Bentsen?

MR. BENTSEN: I think reading—pardon me—I think reading *Winds* *of War* and *Guns of August* back to back, I think that really shows you how we make the same mistakes too often, over and over again. And it seems to me that the senator from Indiana is beginning to do that one. As I look on the progress that's been made toward disarmament and cutting back on nuclear weapons, and see what Ronald Reagan has been able to do with the INF Treaty—and I think he deserves great credit for that one—I see a situation where the senator from Indiana has now jumped off the reservation when we talk about building on what Ronald Reagan has done, and opposes what Ronald Reagan wants to do, the Joint Chiefs of Staff and the secretary of defense, and says, "Let's go slow on doing further disarmament and trying to get to the next treaty." I think that's a mistake.

I think that you have to deal with the Russians from strength, and we have to understand that you have to have a strong modernized nuclear deterrent. But I think we can make substantial progress, and we ought to take advantage of it. I think he's arrived at a very dangerous judgment in the question of war and peace, and it concerns me very much, because I saw him also try to sabotage the INF Treaty when it was on the floor of the United States Senate, with what he was doing there. He's listening once again—

MS. WOODRUFF: Senator—

MR. BENTSEN: —to the winds of the radical right. My light was still on, Judy.

MS. WOODRUFF: Jon Margolis, a question for Senator Quayle.

[Character Questions]

MR. MARGOLIS: Senator Quayle, I want to go back to the matter of qualifications, which I think for most people is more than just—more than just your—how long you've been in the Senate—

MR. BENTSEN: Jon, we can't hear you.

MR. QUAYLE: I can hear you.

MR. MARGOLIS: You can hear now?

I want to go back to the question of qualifications, which I think for most people is more than just how long you've been in the Senate and how long you've been in public life. There's also a question of candor and of consistency. And several of the things you've said, both here and earlier, I think have raised some reasonable questions.

Each of them alone might seem rather trivial, but I think together they create a pattern that needs to be asked. You've talked a few times today about the Job Training Partnership Act, which you authored. In fact, I believe you co-authored it with another senator whom you almost never name. Earlier in the campaign, when you were asked why you got a very—a desk job in the National Guard, after being trained as a welder—you said, at the time, you had a very strong background in journalism, which at that time was summer jobs at your family-owned newspaper, which you have not been very forthcoming about what they were, as you have not been very forthcoming about your college record. Now, you'll have to say—you have, at least the males on this panel have earlier agreed that your record was probably comparable to ours.

But, nonetheless, these examples of sort of overstatement and exaggeration, and not being forthcoming, this is what has led a lot of people to question this part of your qualifications. Not your—not your experiences, but your character. Would you like to set some of these things straight now, as to what you did in your summer jobs in college, what your grades were like, and would you like to identify your cosponsor of the Job Training Partnership Act?

MR. QUAYLE: All in two minutes?

MR. MARGOLIS: Sure.

MR. QUAYLE: Let me—let me start with the underlying premise that somehow I haven't been straightforward, and I have, and let's go—right to the very first question: The Job Training Partnership Act. I was the author of that. The co-author in the United States Senate was Senator Kennedy. I was the chairman of the employment and productivity subcommittee— chairmen of the committee write that legislation. Chairmen of the commit- tee write the legislation, and then they go out and get cosponsorship. And when you are the chairman of the committee, and you sit down and you write the legislation, you are the author of that.

And I'm proud to have been the author of that, because you know what we had, we had a CETA program, that spent $50 billion—from about 1973 through 1982. And when we concluded that program—when we concluded that program, unemployment was higher than when it began. It was a program that didn't work, and the Job Training Partnership Act does work.

Now, the issue of releasing all of my grades. I am, and I stand before you tonight, as the most investigated person ever to seek public office. Thousands of journalists have asked every professor I've had, all my teachers, and they know—and I've never professed to be anything but an average student. I have never said that I was anything more than that, but it's not whether you're an average student, it's what are you going to do with your life? And what am I going to do with my life? I have committed it to public service since I was 29 years of age: Elected to the House of Rep- resentatives, elected to the United States Senate when I was 33, and now....

MS. WOODRUFF: Senator? Senator Bentsen?

MR. BENTSEN: I have absolutely no quarrel with Senator Quayle's military record, but I do strongly disagree with him on some of the issues. You make great patriotic speeches, and I enjoy them. But I don't understand your vote on veterans' issues. Senator Quayle has one of the worst voting records in the United States Senate on veterans' issues. And one of them that particularly bothers me, sponsoring legislation to put a tax on combat pay and disability pay for veterans, for fighting men and women of America—tax on disability pay when lying there in the hospital, people who have sacrificed for our country. I think you ought to explain that to the people of America, and you ought to explain it tonight.

MS. WOODRUFF: Jon, a question for Senator Bentsen.

[Domestic Budget Cuts]

MR. MARGOLIS: Senator, you're chairman of the Senate Finance Committee, and you're generally considered rather an orthodox conservative on fiscal matters, meaning someone who would be very concerned about the budget deficit. With everybody in politics afraid even to mention taxes or Social Security cuts or even very much restraint in defense spending, would you now list a few specific programs which would reduce or eliminate—which you would reduce or eliminate to cut the deficit by about $50 billion, the deficit which is expected to be about $135 billion this fiscal year?

MR. BENTSEN: One of them that I'd work on, and I do this as a farmer, I'd try to turn the situation around where we have seen the subsidy payments go from two and a half billion to 10 times that under this administration. And the way I would accomplish that was with a tough trade policy—opening up those markets, getting those prices back up to market prices. We can do that if we have an aggressive trade policy for our country, if we make trade a number one priority and not trade it off for some foreign policy objective of the moment. That means we have to stand up for the American farmers, and that cuts back on the regulation on American farmers.

That's a positive way to accomplish that. In addition to that, we'd do some of the things that I think have to be done insofar as doing a better job of procurement, particularly when we're talking about some of our military things that we should buy. I know that I've fought very hard to put in an independent inspector general for the Defense Department, but the senator from Indiana opposed me on that.

But we were finally able to put that into effect, and we saved over a quarter of a billion dollars this year—almost enough to buy a squadron of 716s. Those are the kinds of things that I'd work on, and one of the things I learned in business is that you can expect what you inspect. So we'd be doing a much tougher job of auditing to try to get rid of some of these kickbacks to consultants on military contracts, to be much more aggressive on that. In addition, those types of things would bring the interest rate down. I'd try to turn this trade deficit around and that too would help us and help us very substantially.

And I'd get rid of some things like these planes that you're going to have that the administration wants that will fly from New York to Tokyo and take those investment bankers over there in four hours. I don't think we can afford a piece of technological elegance like that. I'd strike that sort of thing from the ticket. I don't know how many people have ridden the Concorde. Not many. But I voted against it [and] said it would be a financial disaster, and it's been just that. So those are the types of things that I would work on.

MS. WOODRUFF: Senator Quayle.

MR. QUAYLE: The way we're going to reduce this budget deficit—and it is a challenge to make sure that it is reduced—is first to stick to the Gramm-Rudman targets. The Gramm-Rudman targets have worked. We've reduced the federal budget deficit $70 billion. Senator Bentsen voted against Gramm-Rudman—the very tool that has been used to bring the federal budget deficit down.

We're going to need all the tools possible to bring this federal budget deficit down. We need the tools of a line-item veto. A line-item veto that 43 governors in this country have, but not the president of the United States. The president of the United States needs to have a line-item veto when Congress goes ahead and puts into appropriations bills unrequested and unnecessary spending. Let the president put a line through that, send it back to the Congress, and then let the Congress vote on it again. Congress has got to help out in reducing this budget deficit as much as the executive branch.

MS. WOODRUFF: Tom Brokaw, a last question for Senator Bentsen.

[Democratic Differences]

MR. BROKAW: Senator Bentsen, I'd like to ask you about your split personality during this election year. You're running on a ticket with Michael Dukakis, a man who is opposed to the death penalty, a man who is in favor of gun control and at the same time, you're running for the United States Senate in the state of Texas where your position on many of those same issues is well-known and absolutely opposed to him. How do you explain to the people of Texas how you can be a social conservative on those cutting issues and still run with Michael Dukakis on the national ticket?

MR. BENTSEN: Michael Dukakis wasn't looking for a clone. I think it's part of the strength and the character of this man that he reaches out and that he wants someone that will speak up, and that I'll do. I've seen many chief executives come into my office and say, they're going over and tell the president of the United States off, they're going to pound the desk, and go into that office and turn to jello. Now, I dealt with many a president, and I don't hesitate for a minute to speak up.

But when you're talking about something like the death penalty, where Michael Dukakis and I do disagree, what you really ought to get to is what's being done against crime and what kind of progress he's been able to make. In the state of Massachusetts, he has the homicide rate down to the lowest of any industrial state. It's substantially ahead of the national average. He's been able to do that with an educated program for the people of that state by adding some 1,500 new police officers. He's done it in turn by the leadership that I think he will bring to the ticket when he becomes president of the United States. And fighting drugs, he's taken it down some 4 percent in the high schools of that state while it's gone up around the rest of the nation.

But you would see him as president of the United States being very aggressive in this fight against crime and having that kind of a successful result. And that's one of the reasons I'm delighted and proud to be on the ticket with him. Sure we have some differences, but overall we have so many things we agree on. This situation of a trade policy, of cutting back on the deficit, those are positive, plus things and major issues facing our nation.

MS. WOODRUFF: Senator Quayle?

MR. QUAYLE: One of the things that they don't agree on is in the area of national defense, national defense and how we're going to preserve the freedom in this country. Michael Dukakis is the most liberal national Democrat to seek the office of presidency since George McGovern.

He is for, he is against the MX missile, the Midgetman, cutting two aircraft carriers. He is opposed to many defense programs that are necessary to defend this country. That's why former Secretary of Defense and former Energy Secretary in the Carter administration Jim Schlesinger in an open letter to *Time* magazine asked Governor Dukakis, "Are you viscerally anti-military?" Jim Schlesinger never got an answer and the reason he didn't is because the governor of Massachusetts doesn't want to answer former Secretary Jim Schlesinger on that very important question.

MS. WOODRUFF: Tom, a last question for Senator Quayle.

[Life's Experiences]

MR. BROKAW: Senator Quayle, all of us in our lifetime encounter an experience that helps shape our adult philosophy in some form or another. Could you describe for this audience tonight what experience you may have had and how it shaped your political philosophy?

MR. QUAYLE: There are a lot of experiences that I've had that have shaped my adult philosophy, but the one that I keep coming back to time and time again, and I talk about at commencement addresses, I talk about it in the high schools, I talk about it when I visit the job training centers, and it's the advice that my maternal grandmother Martha Pulliam, who's 97 years old—we are a modern-day four-generation family. The informa—, the advice that she gave me when I was growing up is advice that I've given my children and I've given to a number of children, a number of people, and it's very simple, it's very common sense. And she says, "You can do anything you want to if you just set your mind to it and go to work."

Now the Dukakis supporters sneer at that, because it's common sense. They sneer at common sense advice, Midwestern advice, Midwestern advice from a grandmother to a grandson, important advice, something that we ought to talk about, because if you want to, you can make a difference. You, America, can make a difference. You're going to have that choice come this election. Everyone can make a difference if they want to.

MS. WOODRUFF: Senator Bentsen?

MR. BENTSEN: I think being born and reared on the Rio Grande, to have spent part of my life seeing some of the struggles that have taken place in one of the lowest per capita incomes in the United States, and that's one of the reasons I've worked so hard to try to assist on education. And when I found that the bankers in that area found that they could not handle the loans because of some of the detail and the expense, couldn't make a profit on it, I went down there and helped form a non-profit organization to buy up those loans from them and to manage them, and do it in a way where they'd continue to make those loans.

Now they have, and they've educated more than 20,000 of those students, loaned out over $100 million. And it hasn't cost the taxpayers of this country one cent. It's one of the reasons I've worked so hard to bring better health care to the people, because of what I've seen in the way of poverty down there in that area, and the lack of medical attention, and trying to see that that's turned around, why I worked so hard on the welfare reform bill, to give them a chance to break these cycles of poverty, the chance for a step up in life.

MS. WOODRUFF: Senator.

MR. BENTSEN: Judy, something's happened, but my light's still on.

MS. WOODRUFF: Your lights aren't working?

MR. BENTSEN: All right.

MS. WOODRUFF: We're sorry about that, if that's the case.

MR. BENTSEN: Okay.

MS. WOODRUFF: Thank you. Thank you, Senator Bentsen. Thank you, Senator Quayle. We have now come to the end of the questions. And before I ask the candidates to make their closing remarks, on behalf of the Commission on Presidential Debates, I'd like to thank all of you for joining us. Senator Quayle, yours is the first closing statement.

[Closing Statements]

MR. QUAYLE: Thank you. Tonight has been a very important evening. You have been able to see Dan Quayle as I really am, and how George Bush and I want to lead this country into the future. Thank you, America, for listening, and thank you for your fairness.

Now you will have a choice to make on election day. You will have a choice of whether America is going to choose the road of Michael Dukakis or the road of George Bush as we march toward the 21st century. The road of Michael Dukakis comes down to this: bigger government, higher taxes— they've always believed in higher taxes, they always have and they always will—cuts in national defense. Back to the old economics of high interest rates, high inflation and the old politics of high unemployment.

Now, the road of George Bush is the road to the future and it comes down to this: An America second to none, with visions of greatness, economic expansion, tough laws, tough judges, strong values, respect for the flag and our institutions. George Bush will lead us to the 21st century, a century that will be of hope and peace. Ronald Reagan and George Bush saved America from decline. We changed America. Michael Dukakis fought us every step of the way. It's not that they're not sympathetic. It's simply that they will take America backwards. George Bush has the experience, and with me, the future—a future committed to our family, a future committed to the freedom. Thank you, good night and God bless you.

MS. WOODRUFF: Senator Bentsen—Senator Bentsen, your closing statement.

MR. BENTSEN: In just 34 days America will elect new leadership for our country. It's a most important decision, because there's no bigger job than governing this great country of ours and leading it into its future. Mike Dukakis and Lloyd Bentsen offer you experienced, tempered, capable leadership to meet those challenges of the future. Our opposition says, "Lower your sights, rest on your laurels." Mike Dukakis and Lloyd Bentsen think America can do better. But America can't just coast into the future, clinging to the past. This race is too close. The competition is too tough. And the stakes are too high.

Michael Dukakis and Lloyd Bentsen think America must move into that future united in a commitment to make this country of ours the most powerful, the most prosperous nation in the world. As Americans we honor our past, and we should. But our children are going to live in the future. And Mike Dukakis says the best of America is yet to come. But that won't happen—taking care of our economy—just putting it on automatic pilot. It won't happen by accident, it's going to take leadership and it's going to take courage, and the commitment and a contribution by all of us to do that.

I've worked for the betterment of our country, both in war and peace, as a bomber pilot, as one who has been a businessman and a United States senator, working to make this nation the fairest and the strongest and the most powerful in the world. Help us bring America to a new era of greatness. The debate has been ours, but the decision is yours. God bless you.

MS. WOODRUFF: Thank you both. Thank you.

PEARY'S POLAR NOTES
October 12, 1988

An exploration of history may have changed the history of exploration. The discovery of a page from Robert E. Peary's notes challenged his claim to have discovered the North Pole. The navigational notes that Peary evidently wrote at the northernmost point of his 1909 arctic expedition indicated to Baltimore astronomer-historian Dennis Rawlins that Peary was 121 statute miles from the spot he claimed to have reached. Discovered and deciphered by Rawlins, and disclosed to the public October 12 by the Washington Post, *the slip of paper on which Peary had written sextant readings had been kept secret. Many years after Peary's death in 1920 the page of notes, with his other papers, was placed in the National Archives. There it was uncovered nearly eighty years after it had been written on the arctic ice.*

Peary had been hailed as a national hero at a time when polar exploration excited the popular imagination as space travel does today. But Rawlins, in a telephone interview reported in the October 13 New York Times, *called Peary's claim "one of the greatest scientific frauds of this century." Rawlins also called the episode "an awful tragedy," because in every other way Peary was "the best of the North Polar explorers, daring and able."*

Longstanding Controversy

Peary's claim had been controversial from the start because he had failed to provide even rudimentary evidence, such as sextant readings, to support it. Peary admitted to a 1910-1911 congressional investigation that he lacked the corroborative evidence normally expected to support such a claim, and insisted that his word was sufficient. Endorsed by the National Geographic Society, one of his financial backers, Peary secured from Congress official recognition of his achievement, promotion to rear admiral in the U.S. Navy, and a lifetime pension.

Although Peary's claim won wide acceptance, and brought him wealth through his writings and lectures, doubts never vanished. A rival claim by Frederick A. Cook, who insisted he had beaten Peary to the Pole in 1909, was supported by even less evidence and never widely credited but found enough adherents to fuel the controversy.

Document Discovered

Rawlins said he learned of the existence of the navigational notes by chance. While pursuing another matter at Johns Hopkins University's Eisenhower Library, Rawlins learned that a secret file of Peary's dealings with the university's former president, Isaiah Bowman, had recently been unsealed. In the file's documents, Rawlins found correspondence between Bowman and Peary's daughter, Marie.

Asked by Marie to help defend her father's claim against supporters of Cook, Bowman, who was head of the American Geographical Society, in 1935 examined Peary's papers, then kept in a safe at the family home on Eagle Island, Maine. Bowman was then told of another paper, kept in a safe deposit in Portland, Maine, by the explorer's wife, Jo. According to the correspondence, Peary had told her to "treasure it as her most precious possession and never let it out of her hands unless it was to silence 'that G-- d--- s-- of a b---- Cook'" [Bowman's dashes]. Marie made a copy of this document for Bowman. The copy was found by Rawlins among Bowman's papers in an envelope labeled in Jo Peary's handwriting, "Original Observations made by R. E. Peary U.S.N. at 90° N Lat. April 5 & 6, 1909."

As Rawlins reconstructed events, Bowman asked Harry Raymond, an astronomer at the Carnegie Institution of Washington, to help in deciphering the document's figures. Raymond recognized that the sextant readings showed that Peary must have been far from the Pole on the day he claimed to have been there. Bowman suppressed the document, and in his letters to Marie Peary spoke of sealing the papers for fifty years. Rawlins located the original document at the National Archives among papers unsealed by Peary's descendants in 1984, and he verified the accuracy of Bowman's copy.

Rawlins Challenged, Supported

The National Geographic Society asked Robert Lillestrand, a scientist and polar explorer, to examine Rawlins's methods and conclusions. Lillestrand concluded that Rawlins had pinned down Peary's location "to a very impressive accuracy."

Rawlins's challengers agreed that the readings could not have been taken at the Pole, but said the readings would prove nothing if they had been taken on another date. But Rawlins used standard navigational tables of the sort Peary was known to have used to show that the figures on the document could only have been recorded if he were taking his sextant readings on April 7—when Peary said he was at the Pole.

Another challenge arose over whether Peary's notes were actually related to his polar claim. Thomas D. Davies, a retired rear admiral and president of the Navigational Foundation, suggested that Peary's wife placed the wrong worksheet in the envelope. The final results of an in-depth study by the Navigational Foundation into this controversy are expected in 1989.

If Peary indeed never reached the North Pole, nor did Cook, the honor goes to Roald Amundsen of Norway, who flew over it in 1926. Amundsen in 1911 was also the first to reach the South Pole. The first to stand at the North Pole would be Joseph Fletcher, who flew there in 1952 aboard a U.S. Air Force plane. The first arrival over the surface would be credited to Ralph Plaisted, an American who traveled by snowmobile in 1968.

Following is a photographic reproduction of the page from Robert E. Peary's notes containing his sextant readings that presumably were written at the northernmost point of his 1909 arctic expedition, as discovered at the National Archives and disclosed October 12, 1988:

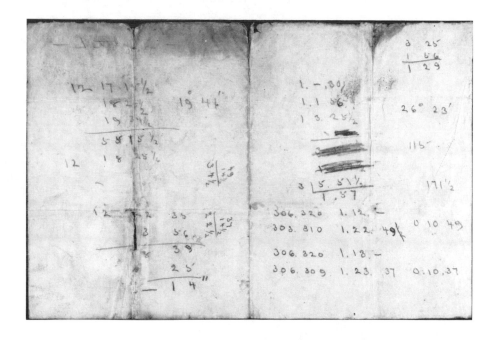

HARVARD REPORT ON THE PRESIDENTIAL PRESS CONFERENCE

October 12, 1988

Has the presidential press conference become obsolete? That question was the subject of a Harvard commission report released October 12. The third such study in less than fourteen years, the report agreed with earlier assessments that the institution of the press conference had fallen into "distressing disrepair" and had deteriorated into a staged, infrequent event in which reporters asked predictable questions and presidents gave predictable answers.

Furthermore, opinion polls indicated that fewer people cared. Only 61 percent of the prime-time audience kept their televisions tuned to Ronald Reagan's press conferences, compared with 77 percent for Jimmy Carter and 79 percent for Gerald Ford. "Press conferences no longer serve the presidency or the press," wrote Larry Speakes, a former White House press secretary, in Speaking Out: Inside the Reagan White House.

The twenty-one-member commission—made up of journalists, former White House officials, and academics—met three times, beginning in September 1987, under the auspices of the Joan Shorenstein Barone Center on Press, Politics, and Public Policy of the John F. Kennedy School of Government at Harvard University, and drafted the report. The principal authors were Marvin Kalb, the center's director, and Professor Frederick W. Mayer of Duke University.

A Flawed Institution

The commission determined that the press conference as currently conducted was seriously flawed, but that it still served the president and public. It was in the president's interest to maintain a healthy relationship with the press to help build support among the people for his policy agenda, the report said. As for the public's interest, it added, the press conference is a vehicle for presidential accountability.

The problem, according to the Harvard report, was not with the institution of the press conference, but its format. The growth of the White House press corps within two decades from a few dozen reporters to more than 200, the dominance of television, and the infrequency and location of these press conferences had turned them into an empty spectacle, the commission said. It concluded that the answer lay not in abandoning the press conference but in making it a routine, regular, and undramatic event.

Based on its study, the Harvard commission concluded that a president's problems were exacerbated when he avoided the press, giving the impression that he had something to hide. If President Reagan had been forced to monitor his administration to prepare for regular press conferences, for example, "there might have been no Iran-contra affair," wrote David R. Gergen, a former Reagan aide.

Devising a New Format

The main thrust of the commission's report was to find a way to revitalize the president's relationship with the press by providing an unthreatening, "unscripted forum for the president to meet the press." Specifically, the commission recommended that the president promise to hold two small news conferences each month. Attendance would be restricted to regular White House reporters and rotated among the rest on a lottery basis. These meetings would not necessarily be televised, but transcripts and tapes could be made available to other reporters. Further, six times a year the president would hold an open televised news conference in prime time, with focused lines of questioning.

Not surprisingly, the report generated controversy. Commission member Richard C. Darman, an adviser to George Bush during his presidential campaign, resigned in disagreement with the commission's assumption that the press conference was important to the president's communicating with the American people. Jody Powell, Carter's former White House press secretary, said it was unrealistic to expect the president to commit himself to a specific schedule.

Other media observers objected to the report's "elitism." They protested that restricting attendance at a press conference would create a royalty in a profession that had always taken pride in its egalitarian nature.

Some critics contended that the report gilded over the media's responsibility for the current lack of substance in the press conference. They noted that the pressures on news management had increased, as had the competition among all sectors of the press, for ratings or readers. Consequently, the line between news and entertainment became blurred.

Following are excerpts from the Harvard Commission on the Presidential Press Conference, "Reviving the Presidential News Conference," issued October 12, 1988:

Preface

This report represents the third time in 14 years that a prominent university has issued a report on the presidential news conference. In 1974, in the wake of Watergate, acute concern about the collapse of the presidential press conference as a key means of communication between the President and the public led the National News Council to commission the first major study. A group of scholars met at the Boston University School of Communication. Their report, written by Lewis Wolfson, Professor of Communication at American University, concluded that the presidential press conference was in a sad state. Six years later, the disappointments of the Carter press conferences led to a second study, by a commission chaired by former Virginia Governor Linwood Holton and former NBC White House correspondent Ray Scherer. The report of that commission, published in 1981 by the White Burkett Miller Center of Public Affairs at the University of Virginia, decried the "distressing disrepair" in which it found the press conference and called for changes that would revitalize the institution. Eight years later, the condition of the press conference has, if anything, even further deteriorated. Reports of its imminent demise have been circulating for many months.

Believing that the presidential press conference is an essential link between the President and the people, a number of columnists and Washington bureau chiefs urged us to look into the problem. It was an easy sell. The Joan Shorenstein Barone Center on the Press, Politics and Public Policy decided to sponsor a new commission, to look again at the state of the press conference and to make recommendations for its improvement. In September 1987, we started our deliberations. We convened a distinguished group of journalists, former White House officials, and academics, and solicited the views of former Presidents [Gerald] Ford and [Jimmy] Carter. We . . . drafted this report for release several weeks before the 1988 general election. The timing is deliberate: To encourage both major Presidential candidates to think seriously about the problem and pledge, when one is elected, to hold frequent news conferences in a routine and undramatic fashion. . . .

I. Introduction

The Presidential Press Conference is 75 years old, and it is not aging well. Once a forum for a vigorous exchange between the President and the press, the institution has withered. It is now in a serious state of disrepair. A recent NBC News report on the anniversary of the press conference reported that "[i]t has become spectacle from the star's entrance, to the critics, the reporters, ready to write their reviews, to the audience at home watching the performance. And there are few people in or out of the White House who are happy with what the presidential news conference has become." David Gergen, former adviser to President Reagan and a commission member, argued that "[t]he big presidential press conference, with 200 or so reporters, is increasingly obsolete and unnecessary. It does not serve anyone's purpose very well. They are theater for both sides; the press asks predictable questions and the president gives predictable answers." Former White House spokesman Larry Speakes writes in his recent book, "Press conferences no longer serve the presidency or the press, and are in danger of becoming obsolete." Yet the institution has a curious resilience about it, too. Despite repeated alarms about its imminent demise, this uniquely American institution staggers on.

Press conferences, of course, are but one of several ways that Presidents can interact with the press and the public. Perhaps, if they are not serving the interests of Presidents, press and public, we should simply abandon the institution and rely instead on other forms of Presidential communication—speeches, news releases, briefings by the press secretary, leaks, etc.—to link the President to the public. The commission considered this possibility. But our conclusion is just the opposite. The press conference as currently conducted is seriously flawed, but the answer lies not in abandoning it but in improving it. It is simply too important to our democratic system that there be some opportunity for the press to question the President, and for the public to witness this interaction. To some extent, our press conferences serve the same function as the British tradition of regular questioning of the Prime Minister by Members of Parliament.

Once regular and frequent occurrences, press conferences have become unusual and rare events. Franklin Roosevelt met with the press twice a week, on average, throughout his entire presidency. John Kennedy held nationally televised press conferences every two weeks. But Ronald Reagan has averaged only one conference every two months. Lest one think this is only a reflection of one presidency, however, we should note that the average since President Johnson is only one conference every month and a half. How we have come to this state of affairs and what can be done about it is the focus of this report. For now, however, it is worth discussing briefly the damaging consequences.

When press conferences are rare, each assumes disproportionate importance. Every conference becomes the focus of enormous attention, raising the stakes for both the President and the press. The President feels that he cannot afford to make any mistakes, or to demonstrate uncertainty in any answer. As a result, Presidents tend to spend days preparing for each conference and to await them with considerable anxiety. In Reagan's case, the President spends a weekend reading through a briefing book, then goes through two full dress rehearsals before "show time" and still, even for this seasoned performer, reports Larry Speakes, "[w]hen Jim Baker or Don Regan and I would go up to the White House living quarters to get the President a few minutes before a press conference began, there would be as much tension as there would be if he were getting ready to enter the ring for a prize fight."

Members of the White House press corps also experience the heightened tension of the prime time, East Room extravaganza. Because conferences are so rare, there are enormous pressures on reporters to ask their questions. And because reporters are also on stage in these events, the drama makes each somewhat self consciously a performer, perhaps less interested in obtaining information than in asking a question with style. [*Time* magazine correspondent] Larry Barrett says that he's always known when there's a press conference because the press office looks and smells different: the press primps for the performance.

The deterioration of the press conference has also affected other areas of the relationship between the President and the press. When reporters can't get the access they need to do their jobs, they become testy, frustrated. The unseemly scenes of the press shouting questions at the President as he and Mrs. Reagan head to a waiting helicopter—images that do more damage to the press than to the President—can be traced to the simple frustration of limited access. And it is almost inevitable that when access is denied, the press will become suspicious that something is being withheld, a suspicion that can degenerate into cold cynicism.

Some might argue that all of this is only a problem for the press, that the public neither cares nor should care whether the President meets with the press. It is the view of the commission that this is not the case. . . . [T]he press certainly has a strong stake in the matter, but the interests of the press and the public overlap more than they diverge. . . . There is, of course, another view, one that was advanced by Richard Darman before he withdrew from the Commission. It is that the press conference is not "of central importance" to the President's ability to communicate his views to the American people, that there are other, more effective ways. Most members of the Commission agreed that there are obviously other ways, but none more proven effective than the news conference. . . .

II. History

. . . By some accounts, the presidential press conference began on a generous impulse by Teddy Roosevelt, who took pity on reporters forced to wait in the rain outside the White House for their interviews. He invited them in and set aside a room for their use. The offer, once extended, proved difficult to withdraw, and although subsequent Presidents have been tempted to put the press back out on the street, none has been willing to pay the price to do it.

In retrospect, though, it might be more accurate, to credit Woodrow Wilson with the initiator's role. T. R.'s meetings with the press were not really in the spirit of a modern press conference. Roosevelt understood that the press could be a great asset to him and knew how to use it. . . . When reporters met with President Theodore Roosevelt, they were not around to ask questions and could not report what they heard; the reporters simply stood and listened while the President talked to them, often while being shaved by the White House barber. Furthermore, these encounters were only open to those whom T. R. chose.

William Howard Taft, Roosevelt's successor, felt no obligation to do even that much for the press, and chose not to meet with them at all. . . .

Wilson actually had the notion that the President should be obliged to answer questions, in the same manner as the Prime Minister in a Parliamentary system routinely fields questions from the opposition. He opened press conferences to all reporters and responded on-the-spot to their spoken questions. For the first two and a half years of his presidency, Wilson met with the press once or twice a week. Although he then switched gears and went a year without meeting the press and subsequently held conferences only irregularly. . . .

. . . The President, having lapsed into serious illness, barely performed the usual functions of his office. It was left to Wilson's successor, Warren Harding, to revive the press conference. He returned to the frequency of Wilson's first years, meeting with the press twice a week for most of his presidency. But . . . he required that the questions be written and submitted in advance. . . . Not only could Harding decide beforehand how he wanted to answer the questions, he could also decide which questions to answer. Calvin Coolidge retained the same format and frequency, but his relations with the press were considerably frostier than those of his predecessor. To show his disdain for the press, Coolidge on occasion would read a question, and then without answering, crumple it up and throw it away.

Herbert Hoover took office intent on improving relations with the press. In his first few months he met with the press more than twice a week. Questions were still written and submitted in advance, but his answers were more often on the record. After the 1929 stock market crash, however, the relationship soured. Hoover backed away from contact with the press. Contact only meant unanswerable questions—and trouble. He continued to hold press conferences, averaging more than one a week, but they were often very short and so uninformative that the institution again lost its bloom and purpose and appeared to be heading to a premature death.

By almost all accounts, the premodern press conference reached its high water mark, ironically, when the nation was in the depths of economic depression. Franklin Roosevelt entered the White House, and as part of a shrewd strategy aimed at revitalizing the nation, he gave the press conference a burst of life and unprecedented growth. During his tenure he met with the press nearly one thousand times, almost twice a week for 13 years. But it was not just the frequency of the meetings that distinguished them—Coolidge held them as frequently—but the skill with which he used them to help him govern.

Roosevelt found the press conference an effective way to influence the press and through them the American people. His conferences were intimate, private affairs, regardless of how many reporters filled the office (or bunched around his car in Warm Springs). Roosevelt would sit at his desk while reporters crowded around him and he would field all questions with spontaneity, wit, and charm. He could flatter reporters by taking them into his confidence, impress them with the breadth of his knowledge, and occasionally even bully them into toeing the line. (Once, Roosevelt forced a reporter who asked an objectionable question to wear a dunce cap and sit in the corner.) Roosevelt abandoned the requirement that questions be written, but retained the right to make statements on an off-the-record basis as he saw fit. For their part, reporters were quite cooperative. They felt as if they were being brought into the process of governance—and indeed they were. Few, if any, ever broke the ground rules. Indeed, so great was their deference that none ever reported on the President's physical disability.

By the end of the Roosevelt era, the press conference was clearly a permanent part of the Presidential landscape. . . . [B]eginning with [Harry S] Truman, and increasingly thereafter (especially with the introduction of television), press conferences became on-the-record, public affairs. . . .

Truman moved the press conference out of the Oval Office and into the Indian Treaty Room in the nearby Executive Office Building. The change reflected both the large post-war increase in the number of reporters covering the White House (the number had swollen from the 30-40 average of Roosevelt's time to nearly 150) and Truman's desire for a more formal atmosphere at the press conferences. The change also meant that the conferences were more public events, part of the record of an administration. Most of what Truman said in press conferences could be reported, and the consequences of a slip of the Presidential tongue could be profound. . . .

Beginning with Truman, too, expectations about the normal frequency of press conferences began to diminish. Rather than the norm of two a week that had operated from Wilson to Roosevelt, Truman averaged less than one a week. During crises he would hold even fewer. Truman's habits set the stage for the even more infrequent patterns of his successors.

Easily the biggest change in the institution came during the Eisenhower administration with the introduction of television cameras. . . . For the first time, the American people could see their President as he interacted with the press. And for the first time, reporters themselves became visible to the public as actors in the process. With television, too, the possibility of keeping remarks off the record or of censoring what the President said was virtually eliminated, although the Eisenhower administration retained the right to approve transcripts of the conference before they were actually released. Ike also cut the frequency of press conference in half again, to once every two weeks, a frequency that would be the norm until [Richard M.] Nixon.

The modern press conference reached full bloom during the Kennedy administration. Kennedy's performance became the standard against which subsequent Presidents would be judged—or judged themselves. Kennedy was the first President (and quite possibly the only one until Reagan) who understood fully how to use television to advance his policy agenda. He took the next—bold—step with television: his conferences were allowed to be broadcast live and unedited. Kennedy and his advisers were aware of the dangers of live television—the possibility of a slip or misstatement—but because they were confident of the positive impact he would have if Americans could see him directly, they were willing to take the risk. With live television, more time went into preparing the President for his performance. Kennedy not only had a briefing book prepared for him, but also had his staff throw questions at him so he could practice his answers.

With Kennedy, the press conference became an "event" in Washington: No one wanted to miss the young, articulate and witty President sparring with the press. The President was not alone in his appreciation of the dramatic possibilities; the press too became aware that their performance was also being judged. Indeed, criticism that the press was being too hard on the President may have contributed to the apparent softening of questions in the concluding months of his administration. Kennedy, like Eisenhower, tried to hold press conferences once every two weeks.

Kennedy's was a hard act to follow. Lyndon Johnson, nowhere near as comfortable with the cameras, struggled with the standard and expectations that had been established by Kennedy. Johnson had marveled at Kennedy's ability in press conferences. According to David Gergen, Johnson actually believed that all the questions had been prepared in advance by the White House staff, and given to the press. He thought that they were all planted questions. Shortly after LBJ became President, he asked George Reedy, his press secretary, when he was going to get the list. A stunned Reedy had to inform the President, no innocent politician, that this was not the way it worked, that Kennedy was just good at press conferences. . . .

Johnson's real problems with the press conference and with his capacity to govern began when the press and the public began to doubt his official version of events in Vietnam. What developed was a "credibility gap" between what Johnson said and what the press (and ultimately the public) believed. To avoid unpleasant questioning, Johnson took to making long statements at the beginning of his conferences, thereby limiting the time for questioning. One study found that more than a third of the time was taken up in the opening statements.

Yet despite his distaste for the encounters, Johnson continued to hold press conferences. Even as late as 1967, when press coverage had become quite negative, Johnson continued to hold conferences every other week. In all, he held 135 conferences, an average of more than two a month, the frequency that had been the norm for both Eisenhower and Kennedy.

With Richard Nixon, though, the frequency of press conferences dropped precipitously. The bi-weekly press conference became a bi-monthly press conference, on average, although the timing was considerably more irregular than that designation suggests. In his term and a half, he held only 37 news conferences in all, a little over six a year.

Nixon clearly found press conferences a chore, and avoided holding them. When he did hold them, he sometimes refused to engage in serious discussion. In his first press conference he argued that neither domestic nor foreign affairs should be addressed in "off-the-cuff responses in press conferences." Nixon's natural tendency toward secrecy and his belief that the press was "out to get him," growing suspicions about secret activities in Vietnam and Cambodia, and finally the revelations about dirty tricks and the Watergate burglary, all contributed to a gaping rift between Nixon and the press. Nixon took to holding fewer and fewer press conferences. . . .

Gerald Ford came to office wanting to re-establish good relations with the press, including holding more regular and frequent press conferences. . . . In his short tenure, Ford returned to nearly the frequency of the Johnson years, averaging a conference every three weeks. Compared with Nixon certainly, his press conferences were quite successful, but Ford still had difficulty dampening down the press cynicism that had developed during the Johnson and Nixon administrations.

Jimmy Carter said he wanted to run an "open presidency." In his first press conference he pledged to hold two conferences a month during his presidency. That pledge and the conference itself drew rave reviews. . . .

But what had started so well ended poorly. Carter kept to his two-a-month pledge for a year and a half, then cut back to once a month and then, as the Iran hostage crisis developed into a continuing obsession, to even less frequent meetings. In all, Carter held 59 conferences in 4 years, which although an improvement over Nixon, was still only an average of a little more than one a month. As he cut down on the number of conferences, he moved them from the afternoon to the evening. Carter had become frustrated with the way the nightly news shows would edit the conferences and report them, and felt that holding them in the evening would give him a more direct means of communication with the American people. Despite the frustrations at the time, in retrospect Carter said in his written comments to the commission that he does not "remember any occasion when a press conference was damaging to my interests or to the nation."

It is inevitable that the current presidency be the primary point of reference for a report of this kind. But as this quick survey of the history of the Presidential press conference suggests, the problems that have arisen during the Reagan administration are by no means new to it. The problems have simply become more acute during the Reagan presidency, and are now in even more urgent need of attention.

Like Carter, Reagan began by pledging to hold regular press conferences, indeed even embracing the recommendations of the Miller commission. But from the first, it was apparent that there were considerable differences between the two administrations in their approaches to press relations generally, and to the press conference in particular. Reagan and his team were much more concerned with public relations, with projecting positive images of the President on television, and were much more sophisticated in their ability to do so. . . .

Every morning, the President's team would meet to determine what images of the President they wanted to get on the nightly news. . . . As a means of getting a positive image on nightly television, press conferences were less pliable, less easy to control than other public activities. Reagan proved to be much better with a prepared script than he was at responding to reporters' questions at a press conference (despite the fact that most questions are anticipated and that Reagan had practice sessions). As a consequence, he and his aides chose not to meet with the press at anything approaching the original once a month plan. During the first seven and a half years of the Reagan presidency, the President has held 47 press conferences. It is true that he has spoken with members of the press in other settings—during photo opportunities or on his way to Camp David—but Reagan's frequency of press conferences has been as low as that of Richard Nixon. . . .

Paradoxically, as the press conference has become more open and public, it has also become less informative and spontaneous. In part this evolution reflects changes in the press—the growing influence of television and the increasing numbers of reporters covering the White House, in particular. With television and with large numbers of reporters, it has become virtually impossible to hold off-the-record conferences, for example. But the decline of the press conference is not just the result of inexorable technological trends or of the growing White House press corps. Part of what has happened . . . reflects choices that Presidents have made. . . .

. . . When press conferences are carried in the evening, more people see the conference live rather than in edited form on the nightly news. There is a lot of evidence to suggest that this too can be a mistake; the dynamics of a live prime-time event tend to work against substance and for drama. . . .

[Sections III and IV deleted]

V. Recommendations to the Next President

. . . It is our view that the President, the press, and the American public have not been well-served by the pattern of Presidential interaction with the press which we all have witnessed during the last few administrations. Occasional theatrical press conferences in the East Room, interspersed with questions shouted over helicopter engines, do not constitute a healthy relationship. We believe that all parties would benefit from restoring the habit of *frequent, routine,* and *undramatic* news conferences and from introducing a variety of alternative formats that are likely to stimulate better communication between the President and the public. To these ends we make the following recommendations.

Recommendation 1: The President should meet with the press on a regularly scheduled basis, *twice a month,* during *daytime* hours.

a. No less than once a month, the President should hold news conferences, open to television coverage, with the White House beat reporters. These sessions should be at least a half-hour long. They should be held in the White House Briefing Room or in a similar location. One seat should be guaranteed to each news organization that maintains a full-time White House reporter. A limited number of seats should be set aside by lottery for news organizations that do not maintain a full-time White House reporter.

b. The other daytime news conferences should be with smaller groups of journalists. These need not be televised "live," but transcripts and tapes from a pool camera should be made available afterwards to other reporters.

Recommendation 2: In addition to the daytime news conferences, the President should hold *a minimum of six televised news conferences a year during evening hours.* These news conferences perform the critically important role of allowing the American people to see their President at work in prime-time. At least three of these should be for the regular White House reporters. The President is encouraged to consider a variety of other formats with smaller groups of journalists that would allow prime time exploration of his views and policies in more detail....

REVISION OF THE
U.S. WELFARE SYSTEM
October 13, 1988

Congress in 1988 revised the nation's welfare system in an effort to move many of the recipients into paying jobs and off the welfare rolls. Signing the legislation into law at a White House ceremony October 13, President Ronald Reagan said it "responds to the call ... for real welfare reform—reform that will lead to lasting emancipation from welfare dependency."

Some others called it the biggest change in the welfare system since its beginnings in New Deal legislation of the 1930s. The new law, the Family Support Act of 1988, required states to prepare welfare mothers for the job market with education and training and then assist in their job search. It also guaranteed child care, transportation, and other support for the mothers to participate in the work program.

Aid to Families with Dependent Children (AFDC), the program addressed by the 1988 act, is the one most people mean when they speak of welfare. It was begun in an effort to assist widows with small children. These women were not expected to work outside the home. However, by the late 1950s it became apparent that most welfare mothers were not widows; many had never been married, and typically they were continuing to have more children. Welfare had become a way of life.

Legislative, administrative, and court decisions during the 1960s made AFDC more generous and less restrictive, and the rolls grew rapidly. Although the extent of chronic welfare dependency became a matter of definition and scholarly dispute, it was increasingly recognized as a

*problem. Many experts said it helped to perpetuate in society an
"underclass" that was often identified with black people in urban slums.*

*Much of the liberal thinking was reshaped by the prevalence of welfare
dependency and by a great increase of working women, which by the
1980s included half of the mothers with children under age three.
Conservatives, too, rethought the subject. They put new stress on the
impact of welfare dependency, not just the impact of welfare expenditures on government budgets.*

Action in Congress

*Liberals and conservatives alike entered the 100th Congress in January
1987 hoping they could succeed where past efforts had failed. Aside from
moving closer to a consensus on welfare revision, they were buoyed by
Reagan's vow in his 1986 State of the Union message to make welfare
reform a priority, and by the elevation of Daniel Patrick Moynihan, D-
N.Y., to the chairmanship of the Senate subcommittee with jurisdiction
over welfare—the Finance Committee's panel on Social Security and
Family Policy. Moynihan was a veteran of nearly every welfare reform
battle of the previous three decades.*

*Moreover, an activist bipartisan group of governors were eager for
federal assistance for education and training programs that some states
already operated in an effort—often experimental—to link welfare to
work. Indeed, the welfare revision legislation was initially devised at the
annual governors' conference in 1987.*

*It still took the lawmakers fifteen months to give their final approval,
on September 30, 1988. Agreement came during a September 26 meeting
of House, Senate, and White House negotiators. Sen. Lloyd Bentsen of
Texas, the Finance Committee chairman and Democratic vice presidential nominee, cancelled campaign appearances to participate. Thomas J.
Downey, D-N.Y., acting chairman of the House Ways and Means Subcommittee on Public Assistance and principal negotiator for the House,
said, "Everyone wanted a bill. There was a desire to do welfare reform."*

*During the presidential campaign, Vice President George Bush spoke
of the need to "break the cycle of poverty." Similarly, his Democratic foe,
Massachusetts Gov. Michael S. Dukakis, talked of helping families get off
of welfare. Advisers to Bush and Dukakis made it known to House-Senate
negotiators that both candidates wanted favorable action on a bill. When
Dukakis named Bentsen his running mate on July 12, he endorsed the
Senate bill that Bentsen had assisted in passing. That same day, Bush
also endorsed the bill.*

Long Road to Compromise

*The White House initially argued that the states should merely
experiment with existing programs, without requiring the allocation of*

any new federal funds. But in the closing days of the 1987 session of Congress, House Democrats succeeded in passing a bill to expand the benefits greatly at a cost estimated at more than $7 billion over a five-year period. Moynihan and Bentsen steered a far more modest $2.8 billion plan through the Senate in June 1988. The final bill bore a five-year cost estimated at $3.3 billion.

There was virtually no dispute over the basic aims of both bills—the creation and funding of a major education and training program for welfare recipients and more stringent enforcement of federal child-support laws. For the first time, child-support payments had to be deducted from an absent father's paycheck even if payment was not overdue.

But House-Senate negotiators bogged down on questions of whether welfare recipients should be required, rather than merely encouraged, to work for their benefits, and whether increased benefits promoted welfare dependency. Conservatives insisted on "workfare"—the first ever mandated in federal welfare legislation. It came in a requirement that one parent in two-parent welfare families must perform at least sixteen hours of unpaid community-service work per week if a paying job was not available. That provision was added by Robert Dole, the Senate Republican leader from Kansas, and Sen. William L. Armstrong, R-Colo. In a compromise with the House, the provision's implementation was postponed until 1994.

Liberals obtained a requirement that states offer benefits for at least six months a year to two-parent households, which made up about 5 percent of all welfare families. Such coverage for two-parent families in which the breadwinner was unemployed had been optional; twenty-three states did not offer it.

The new law required the states to set up education and training programs, called Job Opportunities and Basic Skills (JOBS), as a condition for receiving federal money for welfare. It also extended child care and medical benefits for a full year after recipients left the welfare rolls for jobs. Both the child care and medical transition benefits would begin April 1, 1990, and end September 30, 1998.

In 1988 there were an estimated 3.8 million welfare parents, 90 percent of whom were mothers without a husband in the home. Existing laws did not generally require welfare mothers with children under age six to participate in work-readiness and job-seeking programs, for which relatively little federal money was provided. The new law required the states to set up such programs by October 1, 1990; welfare mothers whose youngest child had reached the age of three (or, at state option, one) could be required to participate, to the extent financing was available, if the state provided day care.

Praise and Misgivings

It was Congress's third attempt in twenty years to restructure the welfare system. The two previous efforts foundered over philosophical differences about how best to reduce welfare dependency. Many of the same differences threatened to doom the 1988 legislation. "No issue is more divisive or difficult than welfare," said Dan Rostenkowski, D-Ill., chairman of the House Ways and Means Committee. "I've served in Congress a long time, and I have witnessed many welfare debates. I can tell my colleagues on the conference that a chance like this doesn't come along very often."

Many members had high praise for Moynihan, who, as a senator, and before that as a professor and an official in three administrations, had long studied and argued for welfare reform. Sen. David Pryor, D-Ark., said Moynihan "has literally raised this issue from the dead." According to Bob Packwood of Oregon, the ranking Republican on the Senate Finance Committee: "There's no guarantee that this bill will resolve the crisis facing our welfare system. But there's one certainty, and that's that the present system does not work and cannot work. And but for Pat Moynihan, we would not be trying to fix it at all."

Most members and outside groups participating in the negotiations rushed to embrace the compromise. "I'm very pleased. I think we've got a bill that's consistent with the policy we started with," said Gov. Bill Clinton of Arkansas, a Democrat who was involved in the congressional negotiations. Similarly, the American Public Welfare Association, which nearly withdrew its support for the measure when the Senate passed its version, said the compromise would "begin to make a real difference in the lives of America's poor children."

"We started from a much different position and we've come a long way," said White House policy adviser Charles D. Hobbs, one of the president's representatives at the negotiations. Hobbs was enthusiastic about the work rule. "The psychological effect of having a work requirement will go a long way towards reducing dependency, not because people will be afraid they'll have to go to work, but because they'll feel proud to," *he said.*

To some House Democrats, the final bill remained unacceptable. Augustus F. Hawkins, D-Calif., chairman of the House Education and Labor Committee, was a leader of that group. "I think we can do much better," he said, calling the work requirement "absurd and unrealistic."

> *Following are excerpts from President Ronald Reagan's remarks October 13, 1988, on signing the Family Support Act of 1988, revising the welfare system:*

I am pleased to sign into law today a major reform of our nation's welfare system, the Family Support Act. This bill, H.R. 1720, represents the culmination of more than 2 years of effort and responds to the call in my 1986 State of the Union Message for real welfare reform—reform that will lead to lasting emancipation from welfare dependency.

It is fitting that the word "family" figures prominently in the title of this legislation. For too long the Federal Government, with the best of intentions, has usurped responsibilities that appropriately lie with parents. . . . In so doing, it has reinforced dependency and separated welfare recipients from the mainstream of American society. The Family Support Act says to welfare parents, "We expect of you what we expect of ourselves and our own loved ones: that you will do your share in taking responsibility for your life and for the lives of the children you bring into this world."

Well, the Family Support Act focuses on the two primary areas in which individuals must assume this responsibility. First, the legislation improves our system for securing support from absent parents. Second, it creates a new emphasis on the importance of work for individuals in the welfare system.

Under this bill, one parent in a two-parent welfare family will be required to work in the public or private sector for at least 16 hours a week as a condition of receiving benefits. This important work requirement applies to families that come onto the welfare rolls as a result of the unemployment of the principal wage earner. It recognizes the need for a family's breadwinner to maintain the habits, skills, and pride achieved through work. This work requirement also allows us to expand coverage for two-parent families to all States without dangerously increasing welfare dependency. A key part of this bill is to make at least one of the parents in a welfare family participate in meaningful work while still getting a needed cash support.

Single parent families also share in the message of hope underlying this bill. They, too, will know that there is an alternative to a life on welfare. To ensure that they get a better start in life, young parents who have not completed high school will be required to stay in or return to school to complete the basic education so necessary to a productive life. Other parents will be offered a broad range of education, employment, and training activities designed to lead to work. . . .

The Family Support Act also contains significant reforms in our nation's child support enforcement system. These reforms are designed to ensure that parents who do not live with their children nevertheless meet their responsibilities to them. To improve the adequacy of child support awards, judges and other officials will be required to apply support guidelines developed by their States for setting award amounts. And to help ensure that the child support awarded actually is paid, child support payments will be automatically withheld from the responsible parent's paycheck.

Reflecting the concern we all share over the Federal budget deficit, the Family Support Act contains funding provisions to offset the increased new spending in the bill. The single largest source of the funding comes from a temporary extension of current authority for the Treasury to collect overdue debts owed the Federal Government by reducing Federal tax refunds of individuals not paying those debts on time.

In 1971, when I was Governor of California, we put into law a work-for-welfare requirement similar to the one in the bill before us today. It was called community work experience, and its purpose was to demonstrate to the disadvantaged how ennobling a job could be. And that lesson is as clear today as it was then, and the successes of many fine State programs like that one have made this landmark legislation possible.

As lead Governors on welfare reform for the National Governors' Association, Governors [Michael N.] Castle [of Delaware] and Clinton consistently presented the interests of the States in getting welfare reform enacted. And that interest has been manifested by many States carrying out their own welfare reform programs. Leaders in this effort are Governors [Thomas H.] Kean, Tommy Thompson, [Arch A.] Moore, and [Guy] Hunt [of New Jersey, Wisconsin, West Virginia, and Alaska, respectively] who have paved the way for this legislation through unique welfare reform initiatives in their States. Legislators like Wisconsin's Susan Engeleiter were instrumental in achieving welfare reform and showing Congress how well it works.

Many Members of Congress share the credit for the responsible welfare-to-work and child support enforcement reforms in the Family Support Act. In particular, Senators Moynihan, Armstrong, Dole, and Packwood, and Bentsen, and Representatives Rostenkowski, Hank Brown [R-Colo., Robert H.] Michel [R-Ill., Bill], Frenzel [R-Minn.], and [Thomas J.] Downey [D-N.Y.] played key roles in forging the consensus for this landmark legislation. They and the members of the administration who worked so diligently on this bill will be remembered for accomplishing what many have attempted, but no one has achieved in several decades: a meaningful redirection of our welfare system.

And I think it is time now for me to sign the bill. And I thank all of you, and God bless you all.

SOUTH KOREAN PRESIDENT'S
UNITED NATIONS ADDRESS
October 18, 1988

In an address to the United Nations General Assembly October 18, Roh Tae Woo, president of the Republic of Korea (South Korea), continued his efforts to achieve a reconciliation between his nation and Communist North Korea. The occasion marked the first time a Korean head of state had been invited to speak before the General Assembly. Among those in attendance were North Korean observers and Soviet and Chinese delegates. A North Korean official spoke to the assembly the next day.

The two Koreas participated in the international organization only as observers. North Korea, supported by China and the Soviet Union, blocked South Korea's long quest for full UN membership on the grounds that it would legitimize the Korean peninsula's division.

". . . [W]hat is necessary now is that the leaders of both sides who hold the ultimate responsibilities in their areas meet together without setting any preconditions," President Roh declared. "I hope I can visit Pyongyang [capital of North Korea] as soon as possible." Roh also called for a "consultative conference for peace" among the two Koreas, the United States, the Soviet Union, China, and Japan to end the post-World War II separation of the north and south along the Thirty-eighth Parallel. The division was solidified by the Korean War (1950-1953), in which the United States helped South Korea repel an invasion from the north.

The overture marked one of several occasions since his inauguration February 25, 1988, that Roh had proffered an olive branch to the North Korean government of aging dictator Kim Il Sung. Only July 7 Roh had

*proposed trade, family visits, and student exchanges between the two
nations. Since the peninsula's division, families on opposite sides had not
been able to visit or send mail to one another, and previous talks on such
exchanges had repeatedly broken down. Roh also said his government
would encourage its allies to improve relations with North Korea.*

North Korean Response

*Although it rejected the proposals, North Korea July 21 offered to
discuss a nonaggression pact in August—a month before the summer
Olympic Games opened in Seoul, the South Korean capital. In its letter
to Roh, the North Korean government stated: "Neither to the South nor
the North is confrontation and war beneficial. They cannot be good to the
Olympic Games either." The letter did not call for the withdrawal of the
40,000 U.S. troops stationed in South Korea as a precondition for the
talks, although North Korea continued to protest the American military
presence there.*

*On August 1 Seoul suggested a preliminary meeting to discuss an
agenda, and North Korea joined in planning talks, but they broke off
abruptly August 23. After a lull in these reconciliation efforts, Roh
suggested on October 4 that he meet with President Kim. North Korea's
response was cautious, although the government said in a statement that
the proposal "deserves welcome."*

Anti-U.S. Student Protests

*The diplomatic activity came at a time when the new South Korean
president was facing internal pressure to improve relations with the
North. Roh was elected in December 1987 to a five-year term in Korea's
first open presidential election in sixteen years. Widespread student
protests had forced the former president, Chun Doo Hwan, to agree to
make democratic changes in the government. Roh—head of the ruling
Democratic Justice party—defeated opposition leaders Kim Dae Jung of
the radical Party for Peace and Democracy and Kim Young Sam of the
Reunification Democratic party, but received only 37 percent of the
popular vote in the three-way race.*

*Parliamentary elections that followed in April gave the Democratic
Justice party only 125 of the 299 seats, making Roh the first chief
executive to lose majority control in the National Assembly since South
Korea became a republic in 1948. The Party for Peace and Democracy
captured 70 seats to become the second largest voting bloc.*

*Throughout the year, students continued to demonstrate, often accus-
ing the United States of supporting Chun and working to keep Korea
divided. Riot police quashed the protesters' attempts to hold meetings
with North Korean students and marches in support of reconciliation.
Mindful of the need for Korea to appear stable in the months preceding
the Olympic Games, the public tempered its support for student protest.*

The government was noticeably nervous about the possibility of North Korean terrorist attacks during the games. However, they were held without major incident and provided an international showcase for South Korea's "economic miracle."

In a visit to Seoul July 18, Secretary of State George P. Shultz said the Soviet Union and China had reassured the United States that they would use their influence with North Korea to help make the games safe. North Korea had proposed that it participate in the games, but only as cohost— a condition rejected by the ROK and the International Olympic Committee.

Obstacles to Reconciliation

In his UN address, Roh proposed that both sides agree to "a declaration of nonaggression," and discuss "institutional structures for peaceful relations, mutual contacts and cooperative ventures and, of course, ways of bringing about reunification." Roh's proposal seemed to respond to North Korea's longstanding call for a nonaggression pact and a "confederal" plan for reunification. In an interview the day after his speech, Roh suggested that the United States should consider lifting its trade ban against North Korea and take other "meaningful steps" to improve relations with the Communist north. Shortly before Roh's interview, Kang Sok Ju, North Korean deputy foreign minister, addressed the General Assembly. Roh told his interviewers that North Korea's usual "very strong accusatory tone" had been missing from the address. "I hope this will be a turning point," he said. "We can probe a constructive dialogue with them."

> *Following are excerpts from an address by President Roh Tae Woo, from an English-translated text provided by the South Korean government, delivered before the United Nations General Assembly in New York, October 18, 1988:*

Mr. President, Mr. Secretary-General, distinguished delegates,

Forty-three years ago, as World War II came to an end, the world was taking steps toward the creation of the United Nations with great hope for lasting peace. The new body was to be entrusted with chartering a new international order of peace and stability.

In my country, the end of World War II gave rise to overwhelming jubilation and hope as the Korean people were liberated from the yoke of colonial rule and recovered the land which had been theirs for thousands of years.

The joy of liberation, however, soon turned to despair over the tragic division of our homeland.

As a matter of convenience in the process of disarming the defeated colonial [Japanese] forces, a line of artificial division was drawn through the mid-section of the Korean peninsula along the 38th parallel.

The decision to divide our land was made against the will of the Korean people, dictating the fate of the nation in the decades to come. Overnight, this cruel division turned brother against brother and plunged the Korean peninsula into a violent storm of the Cold War.

On a peaceful Sunday morning in June 1950, war broke out on the Korean peninsula, and soon the whole nation was in flames. Over the next three years, tens of thousands of young people from 20 countries entered the war and eventually over three million lives fell victim to the clash of ideologies. The war also reduced nearly everything on the peninsula to ashes.

Experiencing the battle as a volunteer soldier still wearing my high school uniform, I saw the young and innocent die in the flames of war and came to long for peace and reconciliation. I also came to believe that we must make all possible efforts to end the division and confrontation which were causing such great suffering in our nation.

The conflict ceased in 1952 with the signing of the armistice, but this did not bring about genuine peace. A state of tension and confrontation between the two parts of Korea has persisted ever since.

Even though many seasons have come and gone and the world has changed dramatically over the decades, this hostile confrontation along the Korean Armistice Line has remained frozen in time and continues to be a source of danger which could trigger hostilities involving the whole world.

Beyond these political and strategic implications, the human costs of this standoff have been enormous. Millions of family members—fathers and mothers, husbands and wives, brothers and sisters—have remained separated between the North and the South since the war and have been unable to exchange even letters or phone calls. The emotional strains caused by this situation run deep in both the North and the South of Korea.

Is there no way out of this impasse?

I stand here today to answer this question with a message of hope.

We must henceforth do everything possible to hasten the coming of the springtime for peace and reconciliation on the Korean peninsula.

In this connection, I wish to welcome, on behalf of the Government and people of the Republic of Korea, the timely decision of the General Assembly to adopt the agenda item entitled "Promotion of peace, reconciliation and dialogue in the Korean peninsula.". . .

In the world today, we can see movements toward openness and reconciliation. The Cold War conflicts which dominated the international scene since the end of the Second World War have begun to surrender to the power of human reason and common decency. Mankind's expectations are changing from confrontation to co-existence, from antagonism to reconciliation. . . .

Only three decades ago, we were a poor, agrarian society dependent on other nations' help for survival. We were able to transform ourselves into a newly industrializing nation only through our people's great desire to achieve, together with a passion for education.

We also took advantage of an open and competitive political and economic system which allows individuals to achieve their highest potential. Mankind's inviolate rights and inborn creativity are essential elements for making societal progress.

International trade also has played an important role in our rapid economic growth.

As the twelveth largest trading nation in the world, we are keenly aware of the fact that the growth of world trade has helped promote the rise in income and employment of trading partners. In this, the Republic of Korea has been especially fortunate. So, although the world brought national division and other trials to Korea, it also made it possible for us to grow and make substantial progress. . . .

. . . Serious efforts are also commencing to bring peace and the relaxation of tension to the Korean peninsula, one of the last vestiges of the Cold War. . . .

To achieve this, we need a fresh approach. And that is precisely what I unveiled on July 7th this year.

I have declared that the North and the South of Korea should immediately end all forms of hostile, confrontational relations. For instance, we should immediately cease publicly attacking each other.

I have made clear that we are determined to pursue a relationship of partnership with North Korea. Our cultural and historical unity demands that we devote ourselves to the pursuit of common prosperity and mutual well-being for all Koreans.

In the same declaration, I proposed that we allow not only the reunion of millions of separated family members, but also free exchanges among political, economic and religious leaders as well as ordinary citizens.

Also, I have taken concrete steps to pave the way for free trade between the northern and southern sides of Korea.

We must transform the North-South Korean relationship, so that we can reconnect every roadway, whether a major highway or a little path, linking the two sides which remain disconnected now. Then we could be enabled to go on to develop our common land, by combining our human, technological and financial resources.

If there may be any difficulties for North Koreans in opening their doors just now, I believe that we could work together toward this by building a "city of peace" in the Demilitarized Zone. Within such city, family members who have remained separated for more than three decades could freely reunite. Broad trade and other kinds of exchanges could also be facilitated by establishing in the new "city of peace" such venues as a home for national culture, a center for scholarly exchanges, and a trade center.

Similarly, I stated in the same July 7th declaration that we are determined to end confrontation with North Korea in our external relations.

It is our sincere hope that North Korea participate fully in the international community. Doing so can only benefit the North Korean people, not harm them.

Within the world community, the North and the South must recognize each other and cooperate to promote the common interest of the entire nation.

It is our wish that our allies and friends will contribute to the progress and opening of North Korea by engaging Pyongyang in expanding relations.

It is also our position that those socialist countries with close ties to North Korea continue to maintain positive relations and cooperate with North Korea even as they improve their relations with us.

The pursuit of mutual respect and prosperity through increasing cooperation, however, is not our ultimate goal.

It is a requisite process we must go through in order to build the relationship of trust necessary for the nation's reunification. When such a relationship is firmly established, we can look forward to realizing peaceful reunification. . . .

We must find a common ground to build institutions for peace and create a single national community.

Hence, I have taken particular notice of the fact that President Kim Il Sung has reacted to my proposal for a North-South Korean summit meeting. I hope I can visit Pyongyang as soon as possible.

When the summit meeting does take place, I would like to propose that we agree to a declaration of non-aggression or non-use of force in order to better construct a framework for mutual trust and security. . . .

In this connection, I want to make it absolutely clear that even before a non-aggression declaration is made with the Northern side, the Republic of Korea will never use force first against the North. . . .

Clearly, the problems between the Northern and Southern Korean sides must be dealt with and resolved by the independent efforts of the Korean people themselves.

But due to Korea's geopolitical situation, the problem of durable peace on the Korean peninsula cannot be considered in total isolation from its relations with the surrounding nations.

In order for durable peace to prevail on the Korean peninsula, it is necessary not only for the Northern and the Southern Korean sides to reach rapprochement, but for both of them to build and maintain more rational and normal relations with all the nations that have interest in peace on the Korean peninsula.

The Republic of Korea will continue to maintain and expand close cooperation with her traditional allies and friends including the United States. In particular, we will continue our consultations and common efforts for the maintenance of peace and stability on the peninsula.

In parallel with such efforts, we are also taking positive steps to improve our relations with countries such as the People's Republic of China, the

Union of Soviet Socialist Republics, and many East European nations with which we have had only remote relationships due to our ideological differences. . . .

I find it significant that China, a nation which traditionally was a good neighbor of Korea, is moving to overcome the wall of separation that has lasted for nearly half a century and is expanding its mutual exchanges and cooperation with the Republic of Korea. I have also taken careful notice of the positive signals being made by General Secretary Gorbachev of the Soviet Union. . . .

It is my belief that without peace in Northeast Asia, there cannot be peace in the world, and without cooperation among the area's nations, there cannot commence an era of Pacific prosperity.

Therefore, I take this opportunity to propose a consultative conference for peace among the United States of America, the Union of Soviet Socialist Republics, the People's Republic of China and Japan as well as North and South Korea, in order to lay a solid foundation for durable peace and prosperity in Northeast Asia. . . .

To be sure, it may not be easy to gather these States together at the same table because of the outstanding differences in ideology, social systems and policies among them. . . .

Likewise, the time will certainly come on the Korean peninsula when the brotherhood of all Koreans, North and South, will triumph over our differences, leaving the Korean nation free of tension, conflict and the threat of war.

I believe that the present ordeal will finally come to an end and the blessing of peace and reunification will be bestowed upon the Korean people who, incidentally, have never attempted invasion of a foreign country throughout their five millennia of history.

Upon the day when swords are beaten into plowshares on the Korean peninsula, the opportunity for lasting world peace will be strengthened.

Believing that this day will come, I will continue my efforts, together with my sixty million compatriots, in seeking lasting harmony in our nation.

This is a solemn responsibility of my generation and the dream and passion of our younger generations in Korea. . . .

EPA REPORT OF "GREENHOUSE EFFECT" ON AMERICA'S CLIMATE

October 20, 1988

The hot, dry summer of 1988 aroused public concern over the possibility that a "greenhouse effect" was warming the earth's atmosphere. The greenhouse theory, which had long troubled scientists, asserts that warm infrared rays from the sun are trapped above the planet's surface by a layer of gases, especially carbon dioxide. Many scientists believe that increased levels of carbon dioxide, which is produced by the burning of fossil fuels, have created a steady trend toward higher temperatures.

While some experts attributed the hot weather in 1988 entirely to random climatic fluctuation, extensive research studies at Britain's East Anglia University and the National Aeronautics and Space Administration's Goddard Institute concluded that global temperatures had risen about 0.6 degrees Celsius (about one degree Fahrenheit) over the last century.

The director of the Goddard Institute study, James Hansen, told the Senate Committee on Energy and Natural Resources June 23 that an accelerated warming trend had begun. His calculations were not based on the 1988 weather, although by midsummer the year was already expected to be the world's hottest on record. Hansen said current weather did not sharply change his assessment but it did produce a "sharp change in attention."

The hot summer, and a drought that badly damaged crops in the United States and several other countries, drew public attention to a draft report the Environmental Protection Agency (EPA) released Octo-

ber 20. Entitled "The Potential Effects of Global Climate Change in the United States," the report was prepared in response to a congressional mandate for the agency to study potential health and environmental effects of climate change.

Earlier Studies

The greenhouse theory was first elaborated in papers published in 1896 and 1908 by the Swedish scientist Svante Arrhenius. He calculated that a doubling of the carbon dioxide present in the atmosphere before the Industrial Revolution would increase global temperatures between four and six degrees Celsius (seven to ten degrees Fahrenheit). Although other scientists occasionally noted his work, the prevailing view over the next half century was that the oceans would absorb carbon dioxide as fast as human activity produced it. But in 1957 Roger Revelle and Hans Seuss of the Scripps Institute of Oceanography in La Jolla, California, showed that the upper levels of the ocean could not absorb carbon dioxide as rapidly as had been assumed.

A National Academy of Sciences study in 1979 predicted a possible warming of 2.0 to 3.5 degrees Celsius, and in 1984 an EPA report predicted a global temperature increase of 3.6 degrees Celsius (6.5 degrees Fahrenheit) by 2040. An international conference organized by the United Nations Environmental Programme and the World Meteorological Organization concluded in 1985: "It is now believed that in the first half of the next century a rise of global mean temperature could occur which is greater than any in man's history."

A small minority of scientists continued to dispute some or all aspects of the greenhouse theory. Some said that temperature records had been distorted by readings taken in cities—"urban heat islands." Others argued that the greenhouse gases would produce "feedback effects," such as increased cloud cover, and ameliorate temperature increases. However, researchers claimed that their calculations compensated for such distortions and argued that feedback effects were as likely to increase as to reduce temperatures.

EPA Report

The EPA's draft report was based on fifty-four research projects conducted by government and academic scientists over a two-year period. It concluded that past greenhouse gas emissions had already destined the planet to temperature increases between 1 and 2 degrees Celsius, and that the longstanding upward trend in emissions was expected to continue. Climate change over the next century was expected "at a much faster pace than historically."

Although some scientists had indicated that the impact of global warming may be felt as soon as the next decade, the report said, the full effect of a doubling of carbon dioxide "probably would not be experienced until after 2050." The rate of climate change was "elusive" because of uncertainties about absorption of heat by oceans and about some climate feedback processes. Moreover, the report observed, it was not possible to anticipate how changing technology, science, urban growth, and demographics might "exacerbate or ameliorate" the impact of climate change on society.

The report noted that researchers had not anticipated such results of the 1988 drought as reduced barge shipments due to lower water levels on the Mississippi River or dried up prairie potholes that traditionally served migratory waterfowl. The drought "dramatically reminded us of our vulnerability as a nation," the EPA added, "but it cannot be viewed as a prediction of things to come."

Nevertheless, fear of things to come was unquestionably provoked by the drought. The Worldwatch Institute in Washington, D.C., issued a report in October asking whether the drought-reduced North American harvests in 1980, 1983, and 1988 were "reruns" of the droughts of the 1930s or harbingers of "an agricultural future where summers in mid-continental North America will be far hotter."

Noting that North America was able to maintain grain exports only by selling carryover stocks, Worldwatch warned that "another severe drought in 1989 would reduce exports to a trickle, creating a world food emergency." The concern of the author, Lester R. Brown, the institute president, was additionally expressed in the report's title, "The Changing World Food Prospect: The Nineties and Beyond."

The Department of Agriculture reported that drought conditions reduced U.S. corn production 34 percent below the 1987 level, and soybean production 21 percent. The yield of durum—winter—wheat was cut in half. Many utility companies reported record power demands for cooling purposes in American homes and businesses. Ironically, much of the electricity generated for cooling is derived from the burning of coal and other fossil fuels, which emits carbon dioxide.

The EPA report did not analyze the impact of climate change on other countries, but it noted that "it may be much more difficult for poorer and less mobile societies to respond to climate change." It said the most plausible "adaptive" responses to global warming were increased research, improved long-range planning, development of guidance when impact trends are clear, and "taking no action when it is not obvious that the timing of climate change will affect the resource decision."

Undersecretary of Energy Donna Fitzwater, in congressional testimony, acknowledged that the greenhouse effect is "cause for serious concern," but she added that "scientific uncertainties must be reduced before we commit the nation's economic future to drastic and potentially misplaced policy responses." Schneider conceded that waiting for "more scientific certainty over details" could lead to "having to adapt to a larger, faster-occurring dose of greenhouse gases, acid rain, and ozone depletion."

Following are excerpts from the draft report, "The Potential Effects of Global Climate Change on the United States," issued October 20, 1988, by the Environmental Protection Agency:

This report used regional data from atmospheric models known as general circulation models (GCMs) as a basis for climate change scenarios. The GCMs are large models of the ocean-atmosphere system that provide the best scientific estimates of the impacts of increased greenhouse gas concentrations on climate. . . .

This report uses data from these GCMs as the basis for estimating the potential impacts of climate change. The GCM results are not considered to be predictions, but as scenarios of future climate change. . . .

How quickly climate may change is elusive, because scientists are uncertain both about how rapidly heat will be taken up by the oceans and about some climate feedback processes. Generally scientists assume that current trends in emissions will continue and that climate will change gradually over the next century, although at a much faster pace than historically. Some scientists have indicated that the impact of global warming may be felt as soon as the next decade, but the full effect of the equivalent doubling of CO_2 [carbon dioxide] probably would not be experienced until after 2050. . . .

The results are also inherently limited by our imaginations. Until a severe event occurs such as the drought of 1988, we fail to recognize the close links between our society, the environment, and climate. For example, in this report we did not analyze or anticipate the reductions in barge shipments due to lower river levels, the increases in forest fires due to dry conditions, or the impacts on ducks due to disappearing prairie potholes. . . . The drought dramatically reminded us of our vulnerability as a nation, but it cannot be viewed as a prediction of things to come. . . .

The findings collectively suggest a world that is different from the world that exists today. Global climate change will have significant implications for natural ecosystems; for when, where, and how we farm; for the availability of water to drink and water to run our factories; for how we live in our cities; for the wetlands that spawn our fish; for the beaches we use for recreation; and for all levels of government and industry.

For natural ecosystems (forests, wetlands, barrier islands, national parks) these changes may continue for decades once the process of change is set into motion. As a result, the landscape of North America will change in ways that cannot be fully predicted. The ultimate effects will last for centuries and will be irreversible. Strategies to reverse such impacts on natural ecosystems are not currently available.

Ecological Systems

Changes in Forest Composition Are Likely

Climate change may cause major changes in forest composition and significant reductions in the land area of healthy forests. Higher temperatures may reduce soil moisture levels in many parts of the country. Trees that need wetter soils may die, and their seedlings would have difficulty surviving. A study of forests in northern Mississippi and northern Georgia indicated that seedlings in such areas would not grow because of the dry soil conditions. In central Michigan, forests now dominated by sugar maple and oak may be replaced by grasslands, with some sparse oak trees surviving. In northern Minnesota, the mixed boreal and northern hardwood forest would become all northern hardwood. The process of changes in species composition would most likely continue for centuries.

Declines May Begin in 30 to 80 Years

Forest declines may be visible in as little as a few decades. The studies of forests in the Southeast and Great Lakes indicate that these forests could begin to die back in 30 to 80 years. . . . The health of forests will not be determined by climate change alone. Continued depletion of stratospheric ozone, the presence of tropospheric ozone, and acid deposition will place more stress on forests. In addition, the drier soils expected to accompany climate change could lead to more frequent fires, warmer climates may cause northward migration of forest pests, and pathogens and changes in oxidant formation could reduce the resilience of forests. None of these outcomes was considered by the forest studies in this report. The combined effects of these stressors cannot currently be determined. . . .

Extinction of Species Could Increase

Historic climate changes, such as the ice ages, led to extinction of many species. Thus, it is reasonable to expect the greenhouse effect to lead to a similar result. The differences from prior changes are the expected rate of climate warming and the influence of man, which absent an active program to preserve species, would likely cause a more rapid and greater loss of species. . . .

Impacts on Fisheries Will Vary

Freshwater fish populations may experience growth in some areas and losses in others. Fish in some systems such as the Great Lakes may grow faster and may be able to migrate to new habitats. In addition, higher temperatures may lead to more algal blooms and longer stratification of lakes, which will deplete oxygen levels in shallow areas of the Great Lakes and make them less habitable for fish. Increased amount of plankton, however, could provide more forage for fish. Fish in small lakes and streams may be unable to escape temperatures beyond their tolerances, or their habitat may simply disappear. . . .

Effects on Migratory Birds Will Depend on Impacts on Habitats

Migratory birds are likely to experience mixed effects from climate change, with some arctic-nesting herbivores benefiting and continental nesters and shorebirds suffering. The loss of wintering grounds resulting from sea level rise and changing climate could harm many species as would the loss of inland prairie potholes resulting from potentially increased midcontinental dryness.

Sea Level Rise

A rise in sea level is one of the most certain impacts of climate change. Higher global temperatures will likely lead to thermal expansion of the oceans and melting of glaciers. Published estimates of sea level rise generally range from 0.5 to 2.0 meters by 2100, although some estimates are higher. Rising sea level will drown many coastal wetlands, inundate coastal lowlands, increase coastal flooding, erode beaches, and increase salinity in estuaries. . . .

Given the high property values of developed coastlines, measures to hold back the sea would be justified along most developed shores. Preliminary estimates suggest that the cumulative capital cost of protecting currently developed areas would be $73 to 111 billion (in 1988 dollars) through 2100 for a 1-meter rise. Even with these costs, 7,000 square miles of dryland, an area the size of Massachusetts, could be lost. . . .

INDICTMENT OF FERDINAND AND IMELDA MARCOS

October 21, 1988

Exiled Philippine leader Ferdinand Marcos and his wife, Imelda, were indicted October 21 by a federal grand jury in New York on charges of looting Philippine government funds and illegally concealing their transfer to the United States for investment in choice Manhattan real estate. Marcos abandoned the Philippine presidency in February 1986 under pressure from his countrymen and the U.S. government, and the couple fled to Hawaii at the invitation of President Ronald Reagan. (Philippine Change of Government, Historic Documents of 1986, p. 307)

Eight associates of the Marcoses were also indicted. Among them was Adnan Khashoggi, a prominent Saudi Arabian financier and arms dealer living in Paris. He was accused of helping the Marcoses conceal their art collection and American real estate holdings. Khashoggi previously had figured prominently in the Iran-contra affair. He was identified as a go-between in the ill-fated White House plan to sell Iran weapons to gain the release of American hostages in Lebanon and funnel the sale proceeds to guerrillas (contras) in Nicaragua. He had also been a major contributor to American University in Washington, D.C., where a new sports center was named for him. (Iran-contra Reports, Historic Documents of 1987, p. 891)

The seventy-nine-page, six-count indictment charged the Marcoses, Khashoggi, and four others with racketeering, conspiracy, fraud, and obstruction of justice. The four included two officials of the California Overseas Bank in Los Angeles, of which Marcos was reported to be a co-owner. The bank, itself named as a defendant, was reported to be a conduit for the Marcoses' millions. The three remaining individual defendants faced other charges but not racketeering.

According to the indictment, from 1972—six years after Marcos became president—until the couple left the Philippines, they amassed a personal fortune of $103 million through theft, embezzlement, bribes, and kickbacks. Beginning in 1981, it added, they "engaged in a scheme ... to convert their fraudulently accumulated funds" from Philippine pesos into dollars, transfer them to the United States, and invest in New York real-estate ventures. To maintain their assets, the document continued, the couple used "various deceptive schemes to defraud" U.S. financial institutions and the judiciary system.

If the Marcoses were convicted of racketeering, their assets could be returned to the Philippines, according to Attorney General Richard Thornburgh. President Corazon Aquino, Marcos's successor, had filed a civil suit for the return of his assets and had cooperated in a Justice Department investigation. Because the United States did not have an extradition treaty with the Philippines, the Marcoses could not be forced to return there to stand trial.

According to the grand jury the Marcoses defrauded Citibank and Security Pacific National Bank of more than $165 million in the financing of transactions through which the couple purchased four large Manhattan office buildings.

Contempt Citation, Not-Guilty Plea

On October 19 the U.S. Court of Appeals in New York upheld a contempt ruling that had been issued by U.S. District Court Judge John Walker against the Marcoses on August 11 for failing to respond to grand jury subpoenas requiring their fingerprints, financial records, and other material in the investigation of their activities. The Marcoses had refused to comply on the ground that Ferdinand Marcos was a head of state and therefore had immunity. His argument was rejected.

After the indictments were made, Imelda Marcos flew to New York where she pleaded not guilty to the charges on October 31. The arraignment of Ferdinand Marcos, 71, was postponed for health reasons. A friend, tobacco heiress Doris Duke, put up $5 million in bail for Imelda. On November 3, the Marcoses filed a petition with Supreme Court Justice Thurgood Marshall to halt the contempt citation. However, Marcos and his wife pledged to comply if the petition were rejected.

Reaction and Ramifications

Severina Rivera, general counsel of the Philippine Presidential Commission on Good Government, praised the indictment as sending a "powerful message" to "dictators around the world who hold themselves above the law, loot their country, and abuse public trust for private gain that they can no longer find safe haven in the U.S....." The Marcoses "used their positions of trust to turn the Philippine treasury into their own personal treasure," said James Fox, head of the New York FBI office. He and U.S. Attorney Rudolph W. Guiliani headed the investigation.

Some observers noted that the U.S. drug trafficking charges against President Manuel Noriega of Panama might have even strengthened his resolve not to leave office (Noriega indictment, p. 81), and they expressed concern that the Marcos indictment might dissuade other troubled dictators from accepting U.S. asylum offered as a means of hastening their departure. President Reagan extended asylum to Marcos, who long had been a staunch U.S. ally. However, Reagan did not promise immunity, U.S. officials said. Furthermore, the racketeering charges purportedly resulted from a pattern of activities that continued after the Marcoses came to the United States.

Meeting with reporters on the morning of October 21, Abraham D. Sofaer, the State Department's legal adviser, said, "Obviously, it's of great concern to us to be able to move a country toward a free democracy and away from any kind of dictatorship.... One tool in that process is to be able to offer a safe haven, or certainly a hospitality" to deposed government officials. "On the other hand, no one gets a blank check to violate U.S. law," Sofaer added.

White House spokesman Marlin Fitzwater said Reagan had been advised "that there were no foreign policy considerations to prevent indictment." The president "regrets the need for this" but concluded that the Justice Department had "a very strong case" and should "do what it thought was right," Fitzwater said. He added that the president was "saddened because Marcos was a friend, and a friend of this country...." John J. Tigue, Jr., an attorney for the Marcoses, said, "President and Mrs. Marcos are obviously deeply disappointed at President Reagan's failure to prevent this treatment of a longstanding ally."

> *Following are excerpts from the "Outline of Superseding Indictment" issued by the U.S. attorney's office in Manhattan summarizing the indictments against former Philippine president Ferdinand Marcos, his wife, Imelda, and eight associates, handed down by the U.S. District Court, Southern District of New York, October 21, 1988:*

Ferdinand E. Marcos, former President of the Republic of Philippines, and his wife, Imelda R. Marcos, were indicted today on racketeering and other charges by a federal grand jury sitting in the United States District Court for the Southern District of New York.

Bienvenido Tantoco, Sr., former Philippine ambassador to the Vatican, his wife, Gliceria R. Tantoco, who was the president of Rustans Department Store in the Philippines, Adnan Khashoggi, a businessman and associate of Ferdinand E. Marcos, the California Overseas Bank, an FDIC-insured bank in Los Angeles, Roberto S. Benedicto, Chairman of the Board of the California Overseas Bank, and Rodolfo T. Arambulo, the Bank's former president, were also charged with violations of the Racketeer Influenced and Corrupt Organizations Act ("RICO") and other offenses.

According to the indictment, Ferdinand E. Marcos and his wife, Imelda R. Marcos, engaged in a pattern of racketeering activities that continued through March 1986 when they left the Philippines and came to the United States up to and including the date of the filing of the indictment. As described further in the indictment, the racketeering enterprise included the Marcoses' transfer of $103 million of illegally obtained funds into the United States in order to purchase New York real estate and the defrauding of United States financial institutions of more than $165 million in connection with the purchase and refinancing of those New York properties. . . .

Between 1965 and February 1986 Ferdinand E. Marcos was the President of the Republic of the Philippines. The indictment charges that from approximately 1972 to February 1986 Marcos and his wife accumulated proceeds from the embezzlement, theft, and diversion of Philippine Government funds and the receipt of bribes, kickbacks and gratuities in the form of cash and corporate stock. According to the indictment, the Marcoses concealed these proceeds through various means.

Beginning in September 1981 and continuing to the date of the indictment, the Marcoses engaged in a scheme, as described in the indictment, to convert their fraudulently accumulated funds from Philippine pesos into United States dollars; to transfer these funds from the Republic of the Philippines to the United States; to deposit the recently acquired dollars in United States institutions; to invest these funds in various real estate ventures in New York; and to maintain their assets by using various deceptive schemes to defraud United States financial institutions and the United States judicial system.

There are a number of means described in the indictment by which the Marcoses, with the aid of their co-racketeers, achieved the objects and participated in the affairs of the racketeering enterprise.

From 1981 to 1983, for example, the Marcoses allegedly caused approximately $103 million of their illegally and fraudulently obtained funds to be transferred to confidential accounts, among them accounts maintained in the United States, to purchase certain real property in New York City. The properties purchased, as noted in the indictment, were the Crown Building at 730 Fifth Avenue, the Herald Center at One Herald Square, 40 Wall Street, and 200 Madison Avenue, all in Manhattan. The acts of racketeering set forth in the indictment in connection with the purchase of one or more of these buildings allege involvement not only by the Marcoses, but also by Roberto S. Benedicto, Rodolfo T. Arambulo, Gliceria R. Tantoco and the California Overseas Bank.

The indictment alleges additionally that from 1981 to the present, the Marcoses, Gliceria R. Tantoco and Bienvenido Tantoco, Sr. defrauded two United States banks, Citibank N.A. and the Security Pacific National Bank in Los Angeles, and a mortgage corporation, the Security Pacific Mortgage Corporation, of over $165 million in order to purchase the 200 Madison Avenue property and to purchase and refinance certain other Marcos properties.

Ferdinand E. Marcos, Roberto S. Benedicto, Rodolfo T. Arambulo and the California Overseas Bank are also accused of defrauding the FDIC and fraudulently obtaining FDIC insurance in connection with the California Overseas Bank. It is alleged that the California Overseas Bank is owned and controlled by Ferdinand E. Marcos and Roberto S. Benedicto.

As an additional act of racketeering, the Marcoses are charged with participating in a scheme to purchase and possess the contents of a New York City apartment known as the "Samuels Collection" for $5,950,000. The indictment further accuses the Marcoses of transporting in interstate commerce the funds and certain works of art which they knew to be stolen.

It is alleged, as well, that the Marcoses and their co-racketeers obstructed justice in connection with a civil litigation in New York commenced by the Philippine Government in March 1986 after the Marcoses arrived in Hawaii. The Marcoses, the Tantocos, Adnan Khashoggi and others allegedly agreed to conceal the Marcoses' interest in the four New York properties and to use false documents for that purpose. The false documents, the indictment alleges, which were submitted to a United States District Court, purported to show that Khashoggi had acquired an interest in the Marcos properties prior to March 2, 1986, on which date the Philippine Government obtained a court order forbidding transfer of the properties.

Adnan Khashoggi, in addition to being charged with participating in the scheme to defraud the civil litigants, is accused of obstructing justice. The indictment accuses him of among other things, causing a false document to be submitted to a French judicial officer who was executing the request of the United States District Court for evidence in connection with the criminal investigation of the Marcoses and Khashoggi.

As part of the RICO charges, the Government seeks to forfeit all the property the defendants obtained from their racketeering activity and the indictment notes that this property is subject to restoration to the victims of the racketeering activity.

The indictment specifies each defendant's property that is subject to forfeiture. For the Marcoses that includes the four New York City properties, various foreign bank accounts and other property interests they hold, including their interests in the California Overseas Bank and other companies. For Khashoggi the Government seeks the forfeiture of various bank accounts, interests he may hold in the four New York City properties as well as in a condominium located in the Olympic Towers in Manhattan, and interests in various companies.

Today's charges supersede three prior indictments. The first indictment charged Gliceria R. Tantoco, her brother-in-law, Hector Tantoco, and the Sanmar Export Corporation, of which Gliceria R. Tantoco was president, with conspiracy and mail fraud in connection with a scheme to defraud the City and State of New York of sales tax on the purchase of the Samuels Collection. Sanmar Export Corporation has entered a plea of guilty to these charges. Gliceria R. Tantoco was arrested on these charges in Italy and fled that country pending extradition while released on bail.

The first superseding indictment repeats these charges and names Gliceria R. Tantoco alone for wire fraud and the making of false statements to a bank in connection with bank loans to purchase 200 Madison Avenue and to refinance the Herald Center and the Crown Building. Tantoco has never appeared on these charges, which were sealed until today. She remains a fugitive.

The second superseding indictment names all the defendants charged in the indictment filed today with the exception of Ferdinand E. and Imelda R. Marcos. The defendants named in that indictment were charged with substantially the same offense as those set forth in the indictment returned today.

Ferdinand E. Marcos, Imelda R. Marcos, Gliceria R. Tantoco, Bienvenido Tantoco, Sr., Adnan Khashoggi, Roberto S. Benedicto, Rodolfo T. Arambulo and the California Overseas Bank are each charged in today's indictment with two counts of violating the RICO statute. The individual defendants face up to twenty (20) years in prison on each count in addition to substantial fines and forfeitures. For each RICO count the Bank faces maximum fines of $250,000 in addition to forfeitures.

The Marcoses, Gliceria R. Tantoco, Bienvenido Tantoco, Sr., Adnan Khashoggi, Bienvenido Tantoco, Jr., the son of Gliceria Tantoco and Bienvenido Tantoco, Sr., Karl Bock Peterson, and Jaime Alberto Arias, a Panamanian attorney associated with the Tantocos, are charged with one count of obstruction of justice and one count of mail fraud in connection with the civil litigation in which the Marcoses sought to conceal their interests in the New York buildings after the Marcoses came to the United States. Each defendant faces up to five years in prison on each of these counts.

Adnan Khashoggi faces up to a total of 15 years in prison on the two counts of obstruction of justice for which he is charged, in addition to what he faces on the other counts for which he is charged. . . .

CREATION OF DEPARTMENT OF VETERANS AFFAIRS
October 25, 1988

Bills to elevate the Veterans Administration (VA) to cabinet-level status had been introduced in at least seventeen successive Congresses. Finally, one of the bills survived, winning congressional passage in 1988 to establish the Department of Veterans Affairs (DVA).

President Ronald Reagan signed the bill into law October 25. It designated March 15, 1989, as the change-of-status day. Reagan had endorsed cabinet rank for the VA, although he entered the presidency in 1981 vowing to reduce the size of government and abolish the two newest executive departments, Energy and Education, which had been created during the Carter administration (1977-1981).

Those two departments survived Reagan's tenure, and the creation of the Department of Veterans Affairs added a fourteenth position to the cabinet of his successor, George Bush. The cabinet size increased from four to fourteen in 200 years of government. When George Washington became the first president in 1789, only four persons held cabinet rank, representing the departments of State, Treasury, War (now Defense), and Justice.

The VA, providing services for many of America's 27.4 million veterans and with 240,000 employees, was the largest of all federal independent agencies—agencies whose operations were separate from any of the departments. Its costs, totaling more than $27.6 billion in fiscal year 1988, exceeded those of the Energy, Interior, State, and Commerce departments combined.

Under DVA, existing VA functions were to remain essentially unchanged for administering programs of disability compensation and pensions, education and training, medical care and research, home-loan and life insurance, and for operating 111 national cemeteries. The new department inherited 172 VA hospitals, 231 outpatient clinics, 58 regional offices, 117 nursing homes, 27 domiciliaries, and 189 "outreach" centers for Vietnam-era veterans. Other impressive numbers arose from the guarantee of home loans to eligible veterans. The VA guaranteed 474,400 of these loans in fiscal year 1987, worth $34.7 billion.

The Veterans Administration dated from 1930, but veterans' benefits predate the American Revolution. Following British precedent, the American colonies as early as 1636 enacted laws providing that returning disabled soldiers should be "maintained competently" by the colonies for the rest of their lives. To encourage enlistment, the Continental Congress continued that policy, providing benefits to veterans of the American Revolution and their dependents.

During that time, veterans' affairs passed into and out of various agencies. Congress initially administered a pension law it enacted in 1789. The Secretary of War did so from 1818 until 1849, when the Office of Pensions was moved from the War Department to the newly created Interior Department. In his second Inaugural Address in March 1865, toward the close of the Civil War, President Abraham Lincoln called upon Congress and the American people "to care for him who shall have borne the battle and for his widow, and his orphan"—uttering words later to be carved in stone on the VA's headquarters in Washington, D.C.

Pension Benefits First

Early veterans legislation emphasized pensions; any direct medical and hospital care was provided by states and localities. It was not until 1811 that Congress authorized the first medical facility for veterans, the U.S. Naval Home in Philadelphia, as a "permanent asylum for disabled and decrepit Navy officers, seamen and Marines." In due time, other homes were established to shelter indigent and disabled veterans of America's nineteenth-century wars.

In 1917, during World War I, Congress established disability compensation, insurance for servicemen and veterans, a family allotment program for servicemen, and vocational rehabilitation for the disabled. All except the last of these programs were administered by the Bureau of War Risk Insurance, which had been created in 1914. Another agency, the Public Health Service, provided medical and hospital care. Then in 1930, Congress consolidated three existing agencies into the new Veterans Administration.

The VA served about 4.7 million veterans during its first year; by the end of World War II, in 1945, their numbers had swelled to almost 19 million. To deal with this challenge, VA facilities were substantially en-

larged, and significant new programs, such as the GI bill (signed into law June 22, 1944), were established. New GI bills were enacted for veterans of the Korean War in 1952, and the Vietnam War in 1966.

Debate Over Establishing the DVA

In the aftermath of more wars—and more veterans—pressure mounted for creating a Department of Veterans Affairs. Only a week after Reagan announced his support for a DVA, the House on November 17, 1987, overwhelmingly passed its version of implementing legislation. The Senate followed suit in July 1988. The action came despite a congressionally mandated, nonpartisan report that found "little evidence" such a move would improve government services for veterans. The report, by the National Academy of Public Administration (NAPA), concluded that "there is no compelling reason why the VA ... should be elevated to Cabinet status."

But at a Senate Governmental Affairs Committee hearing March 15, Chairman John Glenn, D-Ohio, said that if cabinet status for the VA was accompanied by management improvements at the agency, "then the case for elevation becomes very, very strong." Another report, also released at the hearing, accused VA officials of "management inattention." This report, from the General Accounting Office (GAO), criticized the decentralized organization of VA services and said high-level managers "have not exercised enough oversight of the field facilities that deliver benefit and medical services to veterans."

Following are excerpts from President Reagan's speech October 25, 1988, at a ceremony at Fort McNair, Washington, D.C., at which he signed into law the bill establishing a cabinet-level Department of Veterans Affairs:

... All those who have served in America's uniform deserve the Nation's thanks. To show our gratitude, I am about to do something I've been looking forward to for a long time: sign the bill that creates a Cabinet-level Department of Veterans Affairs.

It's been 13 years since Army veteran Senator Strom Thurmond [R-S.C.] introduced the bill. We have it this year because Marine veteran Congressman Gerry Solomon [R-N.Y.] worked to make sure the job would be completed before Congress adjourned. And of course, Army veteran Congressman Sonny Montgomery [D-Miss.] was one of the leaders in the fight for the legislation. Others in Congress, especially on the Veterans and Government Operations Committees, helped lead the way. This bill gives those who have borne America's battles, who have defended the borders of freedom, who have protected our nation's security in war and peace—it gives them what they have deserved for so long: a seat at the table in our national affairs.

I've said before that America's debt to those who would fight for her defense doesn't end the day the uniform comes off. For the security of our nation, it must not end. Every time a man or woman enlists in the Army, Navy, Air Force, Marines, or Coast Guard, he or she is ready to lay down his or her life for our nation. We must be ready to show that America appreciates what that means. I like to think that this bill gives Cabinet rank not just to an agency within the Government but to every single veteran. And so, in signing the bill, I'm saying to all our veterans what I say to new Cabinet members: Welcome aboard.

And now I'll quit talking and do a little signing.

STUDY OF CHILD POVERTY
IN AMERICA AND ABROAD
October 26, 1988

A study of children and the elderly in eight Western industrialized nations, released October 26, found that the United States had the highest proportion of children living in low-income families. Although the percentage of elderly Americans below the poverty line had declined between 1976 and 1986, that of children had risen.

The study appeared in a book, The Vulnerable, *produced by the Urban Institute, a nonprofit policy research organization in Washington, D.C., dealing with urban problems. The study, forming a chapter in the book, was written by Timothy Smeeding, professor of public policy and economics at Vanderbilt University's Institute for Public Policy Studies; Barbara Boyle Torrey, chief of the Center for International Research at the U.S. Bureau of the Census; and Martin Rein, professor of social policy at the Massachusetts Institute of Technology. They based their study on information collected by Australia, Britain, Canada, Norway, Sweden, Switzerland, the United States, and West Germany.*

"The two major dependent groups in industrial countries, the young and the elderly, put the greatest demand on public resources and in turn receive most of the public income transfers and services," the authors wrote. "The economic status of these two groups is therefore of particular concern for policymakers." However, the decline in U.S. poverty rates for the elderly and the increase for children "occurred without an explicit policy to favor one group over the other," they noted. Rather, "the reversal was the result of an accumulation of policy decisions interacting with social changes."

Trends in the 1980s

In 1979, the base year for the study, the poverty rate for children in the United States was only slightly higher than for the elderly. By 1986, according to Census Bureau estimates, nearly twenty of every one hundred children were living in poverty and only about twelve of every one hundred elderly persons were. "The international comparisons ... suggest not only that children are at a disadvantage relative to the elderly in the United States, but also that American children have considerably higher poverty rates than the children in all the other countries examined except Australia," the authors concluded.

The authors also pointed out that the United States had the highest percentage of severely poor children (57 percent of all poor children). Compared with the seven other countries studied, the United States not only had a high percentage of children in single-parent families, but also had a high rate of single-parent poverty. It was this combination of circumstances, the authors said, that contributed to the high relative proportion of child poverty in the United States.

Poverty was especially high among young single women with children, as well as among very old single women. For the older women, poverty was prevalent in all eight countries. For the younger group, it was "considerably higher" in the United States than in any of the other countries except Australia. Ninety percent of the single-parent heads of households in the United States were under twenty-five years of age, and nearly two-thirds of them were poor.

Government assistance to the poor populations varied greatly from country to country. Except for Britain, all the countries were judged to be doing an adequate job of helping the elderly overcome or avoid poverty. However, all did less well in providing for poor families with children, and the United States was "conspicuously at the bottom of the list," the authors said.

Third-World Crisis for Children

Globally, an even grimmer picture of child welfare emerged. In the Third World of poor African, Asian, and Latin American countries, child poverty and its attendant ills became more severe in the 1980s, reversing the improvement noted in other decades since the close of World War II, the United Nations Children's Fund (UNICEF) said in its annual report, "The State of the World's Children 1989." It was issued December 20, 1988, initially in New Delhi, India, and subsequently at UN offices in New York.

The report said fourteen million children under age five died throughout the world during 1987, and it attributed half a million of the deaths to "the slowing down of the [economic] development progress [in the poor countries of Afirca, Asia, and Latin America]."

Many of the countries on those three continents, burdened with huge and overdue foreign debts, had cut back their spending for social and health services for the poor. The report called for the lending countries to help the developing countries reduce their debts, and to reallocate their foreign aid so that more assistance could reach the children and other needy persons in the world's poor countries.

Following are excerpts from the conclusions of the chapter, "Patterns of Income and Poverty: The Economic Status of Children and the Elderly in Eight Countries," from the compilation of studies on children and the elderly, entitled The Vulnerable, *released October 26, 1988, by the Urban Institute:*

In the United States over the past decade (1976-86), the official poverty rates for the elderly and for children have diverged considerably, with child poverty rising from 15.8 percent to 19.8 percent and elderly poverty declining from 15.0 percent to 12.4 percent. If noncash transfers in the form of food, housing, or medical care were included in the income definition for determining poverty, the differences between poverty among the elderly and among children would be even wider....

The patterns of income and poverty described here suggest more diversity among eight modern Western industrial nations than generally suspected. The relative economic status of the young and old varies considerably by country. There is, however, more similarity in the economic status of the elderly in the eight countries than of families with children, largely because of the similarity of government programs for the elderly, and the levels of benefits provided through the income tax and transfer systems in general, and the social insurance systems in particular. The economic status of children varies much more than the status of the elderly; so does the variety of transfer approaches and level of benefits provided to poor families.

The poverty of American children contrasts glaringly with the poverty of the young in every other country but Australia (the country with the lowest adjusted median family income among the eight included in the comparison). The poverty rate for American children was 70 percent higher than the rate for children in Canada, our closest neighbor. In fact, American children are not only at a disadvantage relative to American elderly; they are at a disadvantage relative to their peers in all the other countries examined here, except Australia. The reasons for this relative disadvantage seems straightforward:

- The high U.S. rates of poverty and low income for children are due neither to an inordinately high proportion of children in the population share, nor to a measurement quirk ... nor to overall levels of income inequality.

- Neither poor minority populations nor a preponderance of single-parent families adequately explains high U.S. poverty rates for children. Our minorities do have higher poverty rates than the white majority, but so do minorities in other countries. Our poverty rate for majority families with children is still second highest among the countries studied.
- Although the United States has proportionately more single-parent families than several of the other countries have, the American families are economically much more vulnerable. They have both more income inequality and more poverty than similar families elsewhere.
- The income transfer system for families with children in the United States seems to be the main reason for these high poverty rates. It relies on categorical means-tested programs much more than do other countries (with the exception of Australia) to provide benefits to poor children. Despite their presumably more effective targeting, countries that rely on means testing seem politically unable or unwilling to raise benefits high enough to be as effective in moving children out of poverty as universal and social insurance approaches. This situation is particularly glaring in the United States, where the level of benefits in comparison to the poverty line is lower than for all countries except Switzerland.
- The ineffectiveness of the U.S. system is further exacerbated by its categorical nature, which excludes most poor two-parent families with children from public support. Even Australia has a modest universal child allowance program.

The social welfare programs of each country can be seen as a reflection of its social philosophy. Some national programs implicitly favor one group over another. Some programs are considered a right of the beneficiaries (social insurance) or a right of all citizens (universal programs); others are considered a favor (means-tested). Some programs and philosophies may be transferable across borders; others, almost certainly, are not. In particular, the lack of U.S. commitment (through the transfer system) to securing minimum decent standards for poor children stands in sharp contrast to the commitment of other countries studied here. Although the U.S. public safety net does an average-to-above-average job for the otherwise needy elderly, many poor families with children in the United States are largely excluded from the safety net, and those who are not excluded receive inadequate benefits . . . .

November

Amnesty International's Report
   on Human Rights 883

Postelection Statements
   by Bush and Dukakis 891

Palestinian Declaration of Independence 905

Proposals to Overcome
   Savings and Loan Crisis 913

AMNESTY INTERNATIONAL'S REPORT ON HUMAN RIGHTS

November 2, 1988

Amnesty International on November 2 issued its annual report assessing the status of human rights around the world. This London-based, nonprofit organization drew its findings principally from volunteer groups in some sixty countries. The 280-page publication, Amnesty International Report 1988, *listed 135 countries in which it perceived human-rights violations during 1987.*

While not sparing any of the countries entirely, the extent and severity of the violations varied greatly. For example, 600 Swiss citizens were "sentenced to imprisonment or suspended imprisonment for refusing military service." Military service is mandatory in Switzerland, and civilian alternatives are disallowed by the Swiss Constitution. South Africa, in contrast, was a story of gross violations. Amnesty International reported torture and ill-treatment of prisoners, executions, and politically motivated arrests in South Africa's enforcement of its apartheid laws requiring racial separation.

Amnesty International's opposition to capital punishment in all circumstances accounted for the presence of several countries, including the United States, in the report. In February 1987 the organization had issued a special study suggesting that, in practice, the U.S. death penalty was arbitrary, racially biased, and unfair despite elaborate judicial safeguards. Twenty-five Americans were executed in 1987, and at the year's end 1,982 awaited execution, according to the 1988 annual report. Worldwide, it added, 769 prisoners were known to have been put to death in thirty-nine countries, although "the true figures are certainly higher."

The number of victims of all types of abuses varied greatly from country to country. Israeli soldiers "shot and killed" twenty-three Palestinian demonstrators in December 1987 during "violent protests against Israeli occupation" in the West Bank and Gaza. The Ethiopian government held hundreds of political prisoners "without formal charge or trial" in harsh conditions.

Thousands of Iranians "were reported to be detained without trial" in their country. Torture was common in Iran, the report added, and "thousands of people were subjected to lashings and other judicial punishments which constitute torture, or cruel, inhuman or degrading treatment. There were at least 158 executions, although the true number was probably higher as executions of political prisoners continued to occur in secret."

The climate of repression eased in Laos and Afghanistan during 1987. Laos freed hundreds of political prisoners, and in Afghanistan more than "7,000 political prisoners were said by the government to have been released by the end of July [1987], following the announcement of a general amnesty in January." However, there were still reports of people being held without trial, and allegations of torture and executions.

Despite improvements in the Soviet Union, Amnesty International said, "there were as yet no changes in law that would protect Soviet citizens from being imprisoned for peacefully exercising their rights, prevent ill-treatment in places of imprisonment, or abolish the death penalty."

North Korea "disclosed little information about arrests, political trials or imprisonment and the death penalty" for 1987 and Ethiopian authorities did not respond to inquiries concerning the whereabouts of political prisoners who "disappeared" between 1979 and 1986 and "who were believed to have been secretly executed."

The behavior of Korea and Ethiopia was not uncommon, Amnesty International reported. Many countries try to deflect criticism through official "inquiries which never reach a conclusion or end as a whitewash," censorship, and refusing access to reporters. Czechoslovakia, East Germany, and Turkey proscribe sending information abroad that is damaging to national interests. China, Ethiopia, Haiti, and South Africa— among several other countries—hold prisoners in secrecy.

> *Following is the introduction to* Amnesty International Report 1988, *issued November 2, 1988, by Amnesty International Publications:*

This report is a record of Amnesty International's work and concerns throughout the world during 1987. It covers only those matters which fall within Amnesty International's strictly defined mandate: to seek the release of men, women and children detained for their beliefs, colour, sex, ethnic origin, language or religion, provided they have not used or advocated violence; to work for prompt and fair trials for all political prisoners; and to oppose the death penalty and torture without reservation. It is not an exhaustive survey of human rights violations of all kinds.

The content of this report is also restricted by government censorship and secrecy. Recognizing the power of the truth about human rights, governments all too often obstruct the flow of information within and from their countries. Thousands of prisoners are unjustly held, tortured or killed without news of their plight ever reaching the outside world.

This report is limited above all by the impossibility of recording the activities of the hundreds of thousands of members upon whose work to defend human rights Amnesty International is based.

Their actions reflect an idea which, at its birth 27 years ago, was described as "one of the larger lunacies of our time". The idea that ordinary people could help to set free or save from torture or death men and women they had never met, in countries not their own, by writing polite letters to the government involved. It worked.

Those letters, which Amnesty International members write today from a growing number of countries and which have helped to free and save thousands, are based on the Universal Declaration of Human Rights. The Universal Declaration has its 40th anniversary this year.

On 10 December 1948 all the members of the United Nations declared for the first time in history that every human being has inalienable rights. They pledged themselves not only to respect those rights in their own countries, but to protect and promote them in all countries.

Before the Second World War, the international community was only minimally concerned with human rights. International law governed the relations between states and gave virtually no protection to individuals. What governments did to their citizens was essentially their own concern, beyond the reach of international law, and not legitimately subject to the scrutiny of other countries or the international community.

The Universal Declaration of Human Rights and the Charter of the United Nations, from which it flowed, represented a revolutionary development in international law. They established the principle that individuals have the right to be protected by the international community. On the day the Universal Declaration was passed, the President of the United Nations General Assembly predicted that "millions of men, women and children from all over the world, many miles from Paris and New York, will turn for help, guidance and inspiration to this document." And so they have.

Yet the pages of this report show that many of those people have not received the protection that is their right. In at least half the countries of the world, people are locked away for speaking their minds, often after trials that are no more than a sham. In at least a third of the world's nations, men, women and even children are tortured. In scores of countries, governments pursue their goals by kidnapping and murdering their own citizens. More than 120 states have written into their laws the right to execute people convicted of certain crimes, and more than a third carry out such premeditated killings every year.

Amnesty International documents and publicizes this ugly picture of what governments around the world are doing to their citizens 40 years after proclamation of the Universal Declaration for one reason only—to convince more people that something must be done to stop it.

There are many who justify their own inactivity by asserting that 40 years of human rights activity has produced nothing but failure and disillusion.

It is important to respond to the critics not by denying the scale of the challenge that remains but by noting the advances made in the past 40 years.

Today, unlike in 1948, there is a human rights movement that is genuinely worldwide. Amnesty International, for example, now has groups of volunteers working in some 60 countries. More than a thousand other human rights organizations are campaigning for human rights. Some are local human rights groups, others are national, regional or international organizations. In every region of the world, courageous men and women have joined a movement united solely by the conviction that human rights are precious and must be protected.

It is because of this worldwide human rights movement that, more than ever before in world history, governments are exposed to the glare of international publicity—the greatest weapon we have.

It is easy to lose sight of how great an achievement this is. In 1934 more than 30,000 peasants were believed to have been massacred by the army in El Salvador; outside their country this was noticed by only a handful of specialists. Today even one death can set off waves of anger and protest worldwide. The torture and death in 1987 of one student in South Korea— Park Chong-chol—led to publicity, followed by the arrest of police officers and the resignation of government ministers. It doesn't always happen but it can. And it means that no government can be certain that it can hurt or kill its citizens without massive publicity resulting.

The principle of international responsibility is being institutionalized, written into international law and confirmed by practice. The Universal Declaration was followed by the International Covenants on Human Rights and by even more specific instruments like the UN Convention against Torture and Other Cruel, Inhuman or Degrading Treatment or Punishment. And almost unnoticed by the news media, the first mechanisms for enforcement have begun to operate. Since its creation in 1980 by the UN, the Working Group on Enforced or Involuntary Disappearances has acted on more than 15,000 cases of "disappearances" in over 40 countries; in 1987 alone it intervened in more than 1,000 new cases in 14 countries. The Special Rapporteur on summary or arbitrary executions has approached some 60 governments, intervening urgently to try to prevent threatened executions in more than half these cases. The Special Rapporteur on torture has taken action to try to stop torture in more than 30 countries. There have been successes. They are only a beginning but a very important beginning.

Of course there is still a long way to go. Some states have not yet demonstrated their commitment to the international protection of human rights by acceding to the covenants that would bind them in law to protect the rights they claim to respect. Among them are two permanent members of the Security Council, the United States of America and the People's Republic of China. Only 39 states have ratified the Optional Protocol to the Covenant on Civil and Political Rights, which allows individuals to have complaints heard by the Human Rights Committee. Among those which have not ratified the protocol are states whose nationals are currently serving as members of the Human Rights Committee, including the Union of Soviet Socialist Republics and the United Kingdom.

All the states within the United Nations formally subscribe to the Universal Declaration of Human Rights. Yet many of them reveal, by their actions, that they consider the ideas and ideals it enshrines as "subversive". For example, within two weeks of an August 1987 march by 3,000 Colombians proclaiming the right to life, four of the men who led the march had been shot dead by "death squads" apparently connected with the Colombian security forces. The Cuban Government actually confiscated copies of the declaration from a human rights committee when it arrested several of its members in 1986. On Human Rights Day, 10 December 1987, several human rights activists were detained briefly in the German Democratic Republic for trying to hand a declaration to the United Nations Association.

Faced with armed opposition movements, as many governments are, the authorities often choose to forget or ignore their human rights commitments. When armed opposition groups engage in acts of terror, the resulting disruption is frequently used to strengthen the hand of those who see repression as the solution. In many countries the formal authority of an elected government publicly committed to human rights coexists precariously with the power of a military which is prepared to use arbitrary arrest, torture and even murder in the fight against insurgents. Amnesty International condemns the torture and killing of prisoners by anyone, including opposition groups. But whatever the circumstances, it is governments that are responsible for dealing with violent crime, and they must do so without violating the fundamental human rights of their citizens.

In the forefront of the struggle to ensure that governments abide by their obligation are human rights activists. All too many governments respond to attempts to hold them to their commitments with repression, not dialogue.

In every region of the world people are making their contribution to the human rights movement with their freedom and their lives. In China, "democracy movement" activists still languish in jail, some eight years after their arrest. During 1987, in El Salvador, the coordinator of the non-governmental human rights commission was assassinated; in Turkey, the president of the farmers' association was on trial because he said publicly that he wanted an end to torture and the death penalty; in Kenya, the most prominent lawyer prepared to take on political cases was held in jail for most of the year on the grounds that he was a threat to public security; in Tunisia, a leading human rights figure was arrested after giving foreign journalists information on political and human rights issues; in Haiti, a prominent lawyer was shot dead by plainclothes police as he stood with a copy of the new Haitian Constitution in his hand talking to journalists outside a prison. There are other cases that could be reported. That the list is not even longer owes much to governments' fears of publicity damaging to their international "image".

It is because of this fear that governments launch a second form of attack: against the flow of information. Rather than improving their human rights record, governments close the channels of information about the violations. Some states write the prohibition on freedom of information into their laws. For example, laws in Czechoslovakia, the German Democratic Republic and Turkey proscribe sending information abroad which is "damaging" to national interests. Singapore and Malaysia have imposed press laws giving the government absolute discretion to ban or restrict any publication deemed to have engaged in "domestic politics" or to have "alarmed public opinion". These laws have been used to punish people who draw attention to human rights violations. Similarly, in South Korea there is a law making it an offence to give information to foreigners deemed to "insult or slander the state".

The use of incommunicado detention, where prisoners are totally cut off from the outside world, is prevalent in many countries. Without access to lawyers, doctors or relatives, prisoners' chances of alerting the world to abuses against them are greatly diminished. In many countries, among them China, Ethiopia, Haiti, Iran, Iraq, Libya, South Africa, Sri Lanka and Syria, families are often not even told where prisoners are being held, let alone allowed to visit them. The holding of political trials behind closed doors is another way in which states deny the opportunity for public scrutiny of their actions. In 1987 Amnesty International learned of political trials held in secret in many countries, including Bulgaria, China, German Democratic Republic, Guinea, India, Kuwait and Libya. Refusing to grant visas to foreign observers also makes the task of monitoring the human rights record harder.

Censorship of the press and repression of journalists doing their jobs is part of the information war. Amnesty International learned last year of journalists and writers imprisoned because of their writings in the Central African Republic, Jordan, Malawi and South Korea. Journalists were prevented from travelling to areas where they might have observed government agents violating human rights, such as those parts of Bulgaria where ethnic Turks were subjected to an assimilation campaign and the north and east of Sri Lanka where non-combatant Tamil civilians have been deliberately killed in custody by government troops.

Another method of deflecting criticism well-known to officials is to set up inquiries which never reach a conclusion or end as a whitewash. Amnesty International confronts examples of this technique so often that a few examples must serve as illustrations. An official committee set up to investigate certain operations of the Indian provincial police in Meerut, northern India, in May 1987 failed to make public any results. The contents of the committee's report, which was leaked to the press, showed it had failed to investigate detailed allegations of "disappearances" and political killings. In the United Kingdom, the results of an inquiry into three incidents of killings in 1982 of suspected government opponents in Northern Ireland by the security forces had still not been made public by the government. In Israel and the Occupied Territories, an official judicial inquiry into the interrogation methods of the *Shin Bet* (General Security Service), while revealing that the *Shin Bet* had lied to the courts over 16 years about methods used to extract confessions, sanctioned the use of "a moderate measure of physical pressure".

To avoid the threat of public exposure, security forces resort to methods of abuse which are hard to document and designed to obscure who is to blame. Clandestine forces step up their work in Chile; so-called "death squads" composed of police and military operate in plainclothes in El Salvador; government-backed "vigilante" groups surface in the Philippines; and more and more killing takes place in rural militarized zones in Afghanistan.

Evidence of the continuing need to press states to translate declared commitments into practice includes the unending flow of refugees. For the price of raising human awareness while failing to stop massive human rights violations is growing numbers of people seeking protection not in international documents but in fleeing to countries that offer them the chance of survival. Unfortunately, as this report pointed out last year, whatever their rhetoric on human rights, many governments are unwilling to pay the price and are sending people back to places where they face real threats of imprisonment, torture or death.

As with any struggle, what will determine whether the human rights movement goes forward or backwards is, in the end, the balance of forces. Our forces consist not of armies or governments but primarily of the men and women who are prepared to commit themselves to the struggle for human rights. This report demonstrates only too clearly how essential that continuing commitment remains.

POSTELECTION STATEMENTS BY BUSH AND DUKAKIS

November 8 and 9, 1988

With a solid victory assured, George Bush told an election-night gathering of supporters in Houston, Texas: "We can now speak the most majestic words a democracy has to offer: The people have spoken...." Michael S. Dukakis appeared twenty minutes earlier before supporters in Boston, Massachusetts, conceding defeat in the 1988 presidential election. He congratulated Vice President Bush but told his supporters not to cease advocating the issues that his campaign had highlighted. He thanked "everyone who has made this extraordinary experience possible."

Bush and his running mate, Sen. Dan Quayle of Indiana, won the 426 electoral votes of forty states and 54 percent of the nation's popular vote. Bush became the first vice president since Martin Van Buren, in 1837, to be elected directly to the presidency.

Dukakis carried ten states and the District of Columbia for a potential total of 112 electoral votes. He actually received only 111 electoral votes because a so-called "faithless elector," Margaret Leach of West Virginia, cast her electoral college ballot instead for his running mate, Sen. Lloyd Bentsen of Texas.

Dukakis's loss was the fifth defeat for a Democratic presidential candidate in the last six elections. The press interpreted Bush's victory as a personal rather than a Republican party triumph and as lacking a "mandate" for his own program. The Democrats increased their majorities in both houses of Congress, made a net gain of one governorship, and still controlled most of the state legislative chambers.

The vice president promptly extended an olive branch to his defeated foes and to the Democratic-controlled Congress. On election night he spoke of "reaching out" to all Americans, including those who did not support him. Meeting with the press in Houston the following day, November 9, Bush said that he shared with Dukakis and Bentsen "a common interest in building a better America." He congratulated both of them for conducting "a hard-fought campaign."

Dukakis, returning to work as governor of Massachusetts on November 9, acknowledged to questioning reporters that "negative campaigning" by Bush had "hurt us." "I think the distortion of my record contributed a great deal to the defeat, sure," he said. Dukakis seemed to agree with critics who said he waited too long before responding to charges made by Bush. He said, "One of the lessons of this campaign is that you have to respond, you have to respond quickly."

Dukakis announced January 2, 1989, that he would not seek reelection as governor. He said the decision had nothing to do with any plans to try again for the presidency, but he did not rule out such an attempt.

At the Houston press conference, Bush said that "for the most part" he would "bring in a brand new team of people from across the country, and in my view that will reinvigorate the [political] process." He announced that he would appoint his friend and campaign chairman, James A. Baker III, as secretary of state. Baker had served as White House chief of staff under President Ronald Reagan and then as secretary of the Treasury.

Early in the transition period Bush announced his intention to appoint a number of other high-level officials. Returning to Washington, D.C., after a four-day vacation in Florida, Bush said he would ask Nicholas F. Brady to remain as secretary of the Treasury in the new administration. Brady, an investment banker and former senator from New Jersey, had taken that post when Baker left to run Bush's campaign.

Soon afterward, the president-elect named Gov. John H. Sununu of New Hampshire as White House chief of staff, and he invited Attorney General Richard L. Thornburgh, Secretary of Education Lauro F. Cavazos, and CIA Director William H. Webster to continue in those posts. Reagan had appointed Thornburgh in 1987 and Cavazos earlier in 1988.

Although Sununu was viewed as being near the conservative end of the Republican party spectrum, the other officials chosen by Bush early in the transition were seen as political moderates. His early appointments and public statements indicated that his administration would be less ideological than was Ronald Reagan's.

Following is the victory statement by Vice President George Bush on November 8, 1988, and excerpts from press confer-

*ences held November 9, 1988, by Bush in Houston, Texas,
and by Massachusetts Gov. Michael S. Dukakis in Boston:*

BUSH VICTORY STATEMENT

Thank you all very much. What a great welcome. I have just received a telephone call from Governor [Michael] Dukakis, and I want you to know he was most gracious. His call was personal, it was genuinely friendly, and it was in the great tradition of American politics.

We can now speak the most majestic words a democracy has to offer: The people have spoken and with a full heart and with great hopes. I thank all the people throughout America who have given us this great victory.

And I thank Ronald Reagan: I thank him for turning our country around and for being my friend and for going the extra mile on the hustings. He is simply one of the most decent men I have ever met. I want to thank my friend, my running mate Dan Quayle and his family. They have shown great strength under fire, campaigned incessantly. I am proud of him and proud of his family. I want to thank my great friend, Houston's son, James Baker and my campaign chairman Lee Atwater, the national staff, the RNC [Republican National Committee], all of the state chairmen and chairwomen and all of the organizations, and the political clubs. And I especially thank young people who were always up at night, putting up those signs. The people at those telephone banks and the ones who canvassed door to door. And there's a large gathering of volunteers right now at the Washington Hilton. And folks, my heart is with you and many, many thanks for all you've done from our nation's capital.

And I want to talk about my family. The fact is I'd be nothing without them. Our four sons, my daughter Dorothy. And my own Barbara Bush. I guess I shouldn't say she's my own anymore, for soon she'll be the First Lady of all the United States.

And I thank God for the faith He's given me, and as I grow older I'm more aware of the spiritual element in life and I ask for God's help. And I thank the men and women of Texas. The people right here I recognize who started out with me in politics in 1962, and you never lost faith, you never left me and you are a source of my strength. And this is a moving night for all of us, and you can't help but be moved when your country endorses your hopes and your candidacy and the feelings are so personal.

But the decision is larger than that, and now we will move again for an America that is strong and resolute in the world, strong and big-hearted at home. And when I said I want a kinder, gentler nation, I meant it and I mean it.

A campaign is a disagreement, and disagreements divide. But an election is a decision, and decisions clear the way for harmony and peace. And I mean to be a president of all the people, and I want to work for the hopes and interests, not only of my supporters but of the governor's, and of those who didn't vote at all. To those who supported me, I will try to be worthy of your trust, and to those who did not, I will try to earn it, and my hand is out to you, and I want to be your president, too.

I think I know how Governor Dukakis feels. I've lost a few on the way myself, and it hurt. But we both went into the arena and we both fought long and hard. And the governor can take great satisfaction in the fact that his valiant family—Kitty and Kara and Andrea and John—did him proud.

And now I know that we'll come together, as we always have.

Two hundred years of harmony in the oldest, greatest democracy in man's time on Earth.

And I've traveled many miles, reached for many hands, and it's occurred to me that what we were having—the people of America and I—was a conversation, a back and forth, a mutual dialogue, and it cannot go away, not now, not when I need it most.

And so I mean to keep the conversation going. To keep walking toward you, talking with you and reaching for the hand. And one other thing, I'll do my level best to reach out and work constructively with the United States Congress.

And a final word. And a final word about what you mean to me, my friends in this room. Every time Barbara and I come to Texas, it's a homecoming. We were young here. Started out here forty years ago, summer of '48, worked in the oil fields and started a business and went into politics. Forty years. Forty years of work, and caring and friendship. And now I'm going to take that love and friendship—it's all right here in this room—put it in my pocket, take it with me to Washington, where it's sometimes cold, but always gracious, and where God knows there's lots of work to do.

So thank you, God bless you. And one other thing. Once, in days that were a little darker, I made a promise, and now I'll keep it. Thank you, New Hampshire. Thanks for everything.

And God bless America!

Thank you all.

BUSH PRESS CONFERENCE

... To my opponents, again—our opponents—I offer my congratulations for a hard-fought campaign. Both the governor and Senator Bentsen have given a major portion of their own lives to public service, and I have the greatest respect for that commitment, and I know that each one is going to serve the public interest as they see it with the same energy and conviction that they demonstrated so well in this campaign. The very real differences between [us] have been highlighted by the glare of the television lights. But for my part, I've never had any doubt that we share a common interest in building a better America. And that's fundamentally what the American election is all about.

Now, just a few comments on the business of transition. I'm pleased to announce the following initial set of appointments.

I've asked my current chief of staff, Craig Fuller, and my senior campaign adviser, Bob Teeter, to serve as co-directors of the Bush-Quayle transition. Working closely with them will be the counsel to the vice president, Boyden Gray, who will serve as the transition's legal adviser and will be my general counsel in the White House. My former executive assistant and secretary of the Navy, Chase Untermeyer, who will serve as the transition's personnel director, and I expect him to continue that after the transition. And campaign press secretary Sheila Tate will now serve as the press secretary of the transition.

The transition organization will of necessity grow over time, but it is nevertheless my intention to return to the tradition of a somewhat leaner transition organization than we had in 1980, just given the nature of what has to be done. I've asked my friends Bobby Holt of Midland, Texas, and Penne Korth of Washington to co-chair the Inaugural Committee, and they've generously agreed to serve.

And today I can inform you of my first decision regarding my Cabinet. I talked to Secretary of State George Shultz this morning, and he told me that he enthusiastically endorsed my choice for the next secretary of state. George Shultz has given a great deal of extraordinary service to this country, a distinguished career. And he's given us the highest possible standards for public service, and he has helped our president achieve many foreign policy successes. And I salute him.

As his successor, it is my intention to name James A. Baker III. I first persuaded Jim Baker to leave Houston and come to Washington many years ago in the Ford administration when he first came up to the Commerce Department. And since then, he has distinguished himself in every position that he has held. In the Reagan administration, he set a new standard of excellence in his four-year tenure as White House chief of staff and then over three years as secretary of the Treasury in that experience. His 7½ years as a member of the National Security Council, his proven skills as a negotiator and the personal respect in which he is held will allow him again to demonstrate the highest standards of performance as our next secretary of state. . . .

He has big shoes to fill but will get the job done. And I know he feels, as I do, about the distinguished men and women in our Foreign Service. He will lead them and he will work constructively with them to achieve our foreign policy objectives. In these coming months, Jim Baker will not only prepare for his responsibilities, but he'll also serve as an adviser to me on key aspects of the transition.

That said, on the subject of appointments, I note the obvious. President Reagan is still the president of the United States, and I will not be using the transition to try to make or unduly influence decisions that are properly the president's. . . .

As I said in the campaign, I will, for the most part, bring in a brand new team of people from across the country, and in my view that will reinvigorate the process. It will in no way reflect lack of confidence in those who have served President Reagan so well. After this press conference, we head back to Washington, D.C., for a day or two, and then probably on Friday morning, I will head south for perhaps four days and nights, and then back to Washington. . . .

Q: Mr. Vice President, last night, when you celebrated your victory here in Houston, you spoke of reaching out to all Americans, including those who did not support your candidacy. Other than simply calling for unity, what specifically do you intend to do to achieve it?

And, secondly, how do you intend to approach Congress' cooperation you will need, after spending so much of your campaign bashing the Congress?

MR. BUSH: Well, I think the way to heal is to have meetings with various people, maybe those who have not supported us, make very clear through this forum, and others, that I mean what I said, and the American people are wonderful when it comes to understanding when a campaign ends and the work of business begins.

I don't think I was particularly in a "Congress bashing" mode for the most of the campaign, but I will—I have my principles, the American people, in voting for me, voted for certain things.

Congress understands that, and I understand the Congress. I've served in the Congress. And so, I don't think it will be—you know, that they'll do everything my way, and—but I will try very hard because I start with a great respect for the institution in which I served. Yeah, Terry?

Q: Mr. Vice President, what kind of job will you give Dan Quayle in your administration? Will he have the same access to the—all the papers that you saw from President Reagan? And will he—if you could just describe what he would be able to—what he'll do.

MR. BUSH: I haven't formulated in detail, but certainly he will have access to the papers, access to the intelligence, access to the information because it is essential that a vice president be up to speed on every sensitive matter involving the government lest something happen to the president. . . .

Q: Mr. Vice President, in your campaign, you laid out a very ambitious agenda to deal with the Soviet Union—eliminate chemical and biological weapons, conventional weapons, finish the work on strategic arms. Can any of this go forward as long as the Soviets delay their withdrawal from Afghanistan? Do you see any linkage between your plans, looking ahead, and the reality?

MR. BUSH: I would not throw any firm linkage there but, clearly, one of the things I've addressed myself to in this campaign is the need for continued reduction of regional tension. And if the Soviets made a determination not to pull out of Afghanistan, which I doubt they will do, that would throw a complicating factor over the whole relationship. I believe that the Soviets will keep their commitment. . . .

Q: Mr. Vice President, a subject dear to the hearts of conservatives, but less dear to the hearts of Democrats in Congress, in Democrats who still control Congress, is aid, military aid to the Nicaraguan Contras.

You have supported it consistently throughout your campaign, yet you didn't emphasize it consistently throughout your campaign. How high a priority will aid to the Contras be in a Bush administration?

MR. BUSH: It will have a high priority because freedom and democracy in this hemisphere has a high priority, and I know these leaders in this hemisphere. I can't say I know [Nicaraguan leader] Daniel Ortega that well, but I met him a time or two.

And I will press to keep the pressure on the Sandinistas to keep their commitment to the Organization of American States, the commitment being one to democracy and freedom. . . .

Q: Mr. Vice President, now that you've been elected, could you share with us the lessons you learned in the Reagan administration and specifically how you'll run your administration differently?

MR. BUSH: Well, I'll share with you the reason I think our president has been effective. He takes a principled position and stays with it, and he fights for what he believes in.

And true, as somebody suggested, he had the benefit of a Republican Senate when he started, but progress didn't stop when the Republican Senate, when the control changed hands. So, I've learned quite a bit about that. . . .

Q: We've noticed as we followed you in the campaign that you generally stay in rather affluent suburban areas rather than poor inner cities, and not in black neighborhoods at all since the convention. And I wonder, as a symbol, is that a good symbol for a presidency that will try to reach out and touch these people?

MR. BUSH: I think the campaign was properly designed, strategically operated. The message obviously got out to a lot of the American people and I'm very pleased with the amount of the vote. But in a campaign, you obviously have to be sure you get your vote out.

And that doesn't mean you don't want the votes of others because you have to turn out your own people and reach out to as many people as you can. I don't know if you were with us, Saul, at that breakfast in Baltimore put on by Josh Smith, a black businessperson there, on very short notice, a magnificent crowd of people there.

But I had to campaign, set the agenda, set the schedule, and try to win this election. And that is done now, and I had a very nice talk, incidentally, last night, and I want to thank him for it here, from—a phone call from Jesse Jackson, with whom I met as vice president, in the vice president's residency, at least twice without any fanfare, talking about common objectives. . . .

Q: During the last weeks of the campaign, you talked about getting a mandate and about mainstream values in America. Do you believe, with the closeness of the popular vote, that you have a mandate, and could you be specific about what that means you will do?

MR. BUSH: Well, I don't know whether I want to use the word "mandate." I am very pleased with the results, and I don't think it was overly close. I've got to be careful, because I haven't seen the numbers, but I thought the latest I saw was around 54 percent, which I think most people would consider a big win, and with many states.

I think we exceeded—well, I don't know, on the electoral vote, the big, strong support from many, many states. So, I would simply say the American people have spoken, the verdict was clear, and therefore I will take what I think the prime issues of the campaign were, and work constructively with Congress to attain the will of the people. Yeah?

Q: Mr. Vice President, you said throughout the campaign, and as recently as last night, that you want a "kinder, gentler" nation, and that you hear voices of the "quiet people."

Two questions, sir. Beyond the rhetoric and afterglow, what specific programs are you proposing that will make this a "kinder, gentler" nation? And, sir, what are those "quiet people," those "quiet voices," telling you?

MR. BUSH: Well, in the first place, they spoke loud and clear last night, which I was pleased about. Secondly, I think, to go to the first part of your question, I think when I talk about investing in our kids, in the many proposals I've made in that area, that would be an indication of how I will pursue this objective of a "kinder and gentler" nation. I threw in, as you may remember, the whole concept of trying to do the best I possibly can with the environment in that. I used child care as a part of that....

Q: Sir, you campaigned against abortion, for voluntary school prayer, for a line-item veto, for a balanced-budget amendment. Would you make these all top priorities of your administration by pushing either a constitutional amendment or, if Congress rejects that, would you lead an effort for a constitutional convention that would adopt these provisions?

MR. BUSH: I will be selling, setting out the priorities on these and many other issues during the transition, and then I will make clear the major priorities. But on these issues that I've spoken on, I do feel very strongly about them. I have some real reservations about a constitutional convention, however....

Q: Mr. Vice President, you—in the course of the campaign, you've spent quite a bit of time ridiculing liberals, who make up a significant—a significant number of people in the country consider themselves liberals. Do you—and you've created a fair amount of bitterness as a result—what specifically can you say to those people that consider themselves liberals? Are they—

MR. BUSH: I said I want to be president of all the people. And I don't think I've been—was ridiculing. As a matter of fact, I was just trying to get the facts out there. And I think the American people understood that. But I would—I can't do it their way....

I don't plan to suddenly say, "Well, okay, I accept what I call the liberal agenda." That's what this election was about. Come join us. If you've got some good ideas as to how to move this country forward, I need them. . . .

Q: Mr. Vice President, Senator Bentsen complained rather bitterly about the tone of your campaign and spoke of distortions. You, in turn, objected to the Democrats raising the issue of racism. What kind of toll did this race take on your relationship with Bentsen, and will you be able to work with him as chairman of. . . .

MR. BUSH: His call last night, pleading to work together, which is certainly my objective. And—look, this campaign is over. There's no hard feelings about that. The American people are smart. They know a tough-fought campaign on both sides when they see it. . . .

Q: Mr. Vice President, you told the American people to read your lips—no new taxes. But some people on Capitol Hill believe that there will have to be revenue enhancements to reduce the deficit. You've ruled out income tax increases, but will you rule out revenue enhancements to reduce the budget deficits?

MR. BUSH: Well, you'd have to define for me what you mean by "revenue enhancement." I got into a little flap in the campaign because I did support the catastrophic health plan, and there was some charge that that was a tax increase. I don't think it was.

And I'm talking about holding the line on taxes, and I don't plan to deviate, and I think the American people must have understood that when they voted in rather large numbers for my candidacy. . . .

Q: Mr. Vice President, you've—you may well have a chance to appoint one or more Supreme Court justices in your administration. You've promised to appoint men of conservative, moderate views. Would someone who is pro-choice on abortion fit that category in any way?

MR. BUSH: I've said I don't have a litmus test for judges. What I have is a test as to whether, in my view, they will legislate from the bench, in which case I wouldn't want them, or whether they will faithfully interpret the Constitution of the United States, in which case I would. . . .

Q: Mr. Vice President, you said earlier that you were going to provide the intelligence paper to Vice President Quayle. Do you intend to set up with Mr. Quayle the same sort of relationship you had with President Reagan in terms of coming in regularly for lunch and. . . .

MR. BUSH: Yes. I will do that, yes.

Q: Mr. Vice President, in addition to God's help, you're going to need Senator [Robert] Dole's help. And throughout the campaign, he's periodically given you. . . .

MR. BUSH: What order do you place those in?

Q: I'm not sure. But throughout the campaign, he periodically has given you a little whack beside the head, including last night, when he suggested you didn't do enough to elect a Republican Senate. Do you need to have a peace meeting with him? Do you think you can work effectively with him? Or would you like to see a different Republican meeting?

MR. BUSH: I don't think it needs to be a peace meeting. But definitely I will meet with him. He is an effective Republican leader, and I will work with him. And I think that he does a wonderful job out on the campaign trail, and I think that we can work harmoniously together. The question is, we got to get some good support from the Democrats for some of these ideas, but just keep going. Yes?

Q: Mr. Vice President, I'd like to return to the mandate question for a moment. I wonder, to what extent—the mandate question. I wonder, to what extent do you feel that now you can, in effect, create or invent a mandate on the basis that the American people voted for you as an individual rather than for a specific set of programs or policies?

MR. BUSH: I don't know how you sort that out yet, but I do feel that the vote was convincing enough and the margin great enough and the numbers of states carried big enough that it gives a certain confidence to the executive branch of the government that I hope will carry over and influence the Congress with whom I am pledged to work. Thank you all very, very much. Thank you.

DUKAKIS NEWS CONFERENCE

Once again, let me congratulate the vice president on a very decisive victory. At the same time, the Democratic Party is clearly alive and well and very strong. We've added to our majority in the Congress, we've added to our majority in the Senate, and added to our majority of governors.

And what I think this says is that the American people want leadership in Washington that will respond to the concerns of average American families, that will fight battles which are important to fight—for good jobs and decent housing and quality education and drug-free schools, a clean and safe environment, and health care for the American people. All of the things that I tried very hard to emphasize in the campaign. The kind of agenda which I believe most Americans want their government to respond to, want the president and the Congress to respond to.

And I personally will continue to do whatever I can with my fellow governors, with the Congress, with the new administration, here in Massachusetts, to make sure that we respond and respond strongly and well to those concerns and those challenges which face the American people every day, face the people of my state every day, and for which those of us who are elected to public office are elected to do something about. . . .

Q: Governor, some people believe that the state of peace and prosperity and the continuity of Reaganism was so strong that any Democratic nominee would have found it almost impossible to win this year. But, I suppose this morning a lot more people believe that this race was winnable and that, in fact, you blew it. Now, what is your view? Do you think—do you think it was practically winnable, and if so, could you precisely tell us—

MR. DUKAKIS: I think it was neither of the above.

Q: All right. Where do you think you went wrong?

MR. DUKAKIS: Well, there'll be plenty of time for analysis, Sam. At this point, I just (inaudible) activity of being governor of my state again. But, if you look at the results, I think clearly had things gone differently, maybe a different combination of factors, it was winnable.

I think I lost states representing about 133 electoral votes by four percentage points or less. Had we won those states, we'd have had 250 electoral votes and we'd have been very close to a winning majority. But every campaign has its own dynamics, its own ebbs and flows, its high points and its low points, and it's obviously, at least for me, too early to try to go into a detailed analysis.

I gave it my best shot, and we had our good days and our not-so-good days. The last two or three weeks, I hope, gave people a good sense of who Mike Dukakis is and what he believes in, the kind of leadership that he's tried to provide in the course of his political career and wanted to provide as president of the United States. And I'm going to go on now to work with my fellow governors and other elected officials to do everything I can to make good on those ideals and those values. Yeah?

Q: Governor, did you wait too long to answer the negative attacks against you? And a second part to that question, does your defeat mean that future campaigns are going to use negative ads more?

MR. DUKAKIS: Oh, I don't think there's any question that the negativism we had in this campaign is something that had an impact on me, and I hope it doesn't happen, but I fear that this will be a signal now at the national level that this kind of campaigning is effective campaigning. I certainly hope not.

Whether or not I waited too long is something which I'm not sure I'm really the person to judge. . . .

. . . [I]t was important, particularly to somebody who had not been on the national scene, that I give people a sense of what my agenda was, what I wanted to do, what my priorities were. And I tried very hard. . . .

I'm not sure we got through as rapidly as I might have liked, given the nature of the campaign that the Republicans were conducting but, as you recall, I tried to lay out in great detail my plans for our economy, for jobs, for education, for drugs, for housing and health care, for the environment—all of the things that are important to the people of this country and that the next president of the United States must provide leadership on.

And I think, had I failed to do that, then the last two or three weeks, when clearly we were making substantial progress, would have been impossible. Because, had I been saying to the American people at that time, 'I'm on your side,' without having laid out a positive agenda which gave them a sense of what that meant, then the last two or three weeks would not have been as effective as I think they were. So, that's what I tried to do and obviously, the other guy won. . . .

Q: Governor, to follow up on that. You've called this the most negative campaign that you can recall—full of lies. The man who directed that campaign was named by Mr. Bush today to be his secretary—

MR. DUKAKIS: I beg your pardon?

Q: The man who directed the campaign, James Baker, that you called the sleaziest campaign that you can remember was named today by Mr. Bush to be his secretary of state.

MR. DUKAKIS: Uh-hum.

Q: What does that say? What's your reaction to that?

MR. DUKAKIS: I believe in the redemption of souls, Joe. Yes, Bill?

Q: Even Republican souls?

Q: If I could follow up on that. You're very conciliatory today but, during the campaign, you made some very serious charges against the vice president. You said that he was a liar, distorted your record. You said his campaign had elements of racism. Was that campaign rhetoric on your part or did you really mean it? And if you really meant it, what would you say now to your supporters about how they should regard the new president?

MR. DUKAKIS: Well, as a Democrat, obviously, we have a responsibility to work with the administration. After all, Mr. Bush will be our president and will be our president for four years.

On the other hand, there's a responsible opposition. We will have a responsibility to be constructively critical. I hope we can keep it constructively critical. This country faces major challenges over the course of the next four years—debt, deficits, tough economic competition, serious environmental problems that affect not only ourselves but the world, major opportunities and challenges internationally. And they're too important to be lost in a lot of partisan bickering.

So I hope both sides will do everything they can to work together on a progressive agenda for this country. . . .

Q: What do you think is the first problem Mr. Bush is going to have to deal with as President?

MR. DUKAKIS: The federal budget deficit—clearly, it pervades everything we do, will have a crucial impact on our ability to build a strong economic future—to turn that trade deficit around and turn it into a trade surplus, to create economic opportunity on a very strong base in this country.

And that will take a very strong bipartisan effort, because it is so important and is absolutely fundamental. If we can't get that deficit down, and keep borrowing $150, $160 billion a year, and that continues indefinitely, then this country's economic future is going to be seriously jeopardized. . . .

Q: You fared better than either of the last two Democratic nominees, but both candidates lost whole regions of the country, the South and most of the West. What lessons do you draw from this, and what lessons should the party draw from this in the future?

MR. DUKAKIS: Well, obviously I didn't do as good a job as I should have done in reaching out to those regions. We did better in the West, as you know—in the far West—almost took Colorado, that's the first time that's happened in a long time.

And we did better in the Western states, obviously didn't do well in the South. I think my values, the things I care deeply about are things that people in the South care deeply about. And they've demonstrated that on many occasions by electing strong, progressive Democrats as governors and as members of the Senate and the Congress.

But I wasn't successful in getting my message through in the South and in some parts of the West. . . .

Q: Governor, when you ran (inaudible) a number of the issues that you put out in front were in the campaign for some time. On balance now, do you believe that your record is what contributed heavily to your defeat?

MR. DUKAKIS: I think the distortion of my record contributed a great deal to the defeat, sure. I mean, you know, the use of the Willie Horton case, which I have described—I think correctly—as being a very cynical and hypocritical use of that particular case, was one.

The attempt to turn what I've called one of our great achievements— and that is the cleanup of Boston Harbor—into a liability is another. And I could go on, but that goes with the territory.

And I don't think there's any question that the fact that I am a sitting governor of a state that has been successful, and that all my political career I've stood for the kinds of things that I've talked about in the course of the campaign, I think was a plus.

Some 40 million plus people voted for that record and voted for that agenda, and I think that's more than has voted for a Democratic candidate in a long time.

Q: Governor—

MR. DUKAKIS: So, in that sense, we did get through, but—almost doesn't count in politics. Either you win—

Q: Governor—

MR. DUKAKIS: —or you don't. Yes?

Q: Governor, could you just take a minute to describe what you see as George Bush's mandate?

MR. DUKAKIS: I don't see a mandate, not when the House of Representatives has increased its Democratic membership and the Senate has increased its Democratic membership. . . .

The challenge will be for the new president and the administration and the Congress to work together to meet that agenda, and I hope they will do so, and obviously I will do whatever I can to help move that agenda along. . . .

Q: Governor, if another Democratic politician who was trying to run in 1992 came to you for advice—what advice would you give him that, if you had understood it when you started out, it might have been—

MR. DUKAKIS: What do I say to that young man outside of Philadelphia? ... Smile a lot. And respond somewhat more quickly to attacks against you. ... I think it means that you do have to deal with those kinds of attacks, and have to call them for what they are, which, in this case, were distorted and oftentimes absolutely false. Yes?

Q: Governor, some of your staffers have said, if only you had had more time you could have pulled yourself out. Do you believe that? And if so, why didn't you start campaigning the way you did at the end a little earlier?

MR. DUKAKIS: If I had more time, you'd all be in the hospital. And I certainly wasn't going to do that. ...

Q: All right.

MR. DUKAKIS: You know, there has to be a conclusion to every race, and there's a pace to it, and there's a bell lap, and that bell lap is a lap. But, I wouldn't have done that to you guys, I mean, I think too much of you to do that. ...

Q: Governor, in light of the outcome, do you feel any sense of personal bitterness about the negative tone of the campaign, and what you call the lies and distortions?

MR. DUKAKIS: I'm not a bitter person. I look forward. I'm fundamentally an optimist and somebody who believes deeply in this country and in its people. Am I disappointed? Sure I am. It was a distorted campaign. It was a campaign that distorted my record, and I think, did not set high standards for the kind of campaign we wanted for the presidency, and may well set a standard that we live to regret. But I'm not personally bitter. The election was yesterday. We have much to do. I believe in this country. ...

PALESTINIAN DECLARATION OF INDEPENDENCE
November 15, 1988

The Palestine National Council (PNC) met in Algiers November 15 and declared the establishment of an independent Palestinian state. The council, a de facto parliament in exile of the Palestinian movement, issued the declaration as part of a broad political program aimed at recovering land occupied by Israel. An explicit recognition of Israel's right to exist was a crucial part of this program.

Although Palestinian acceptance of Israel was ambiguous at the Algiers conference, it was clarified in a series of statements by Yasir Arafat, chairman of the Palestine Liberation Organization (PLO). Convinced that progress toward peace could be achieved only through Israel's powerful ally, the United States, Arafat sought to satisfy the U.S. government's three conditions for direct talks with the PLO.

These conditions, first enunciated in 1975 in an American-Israeli memorandum of agreement and since 1986 expanded and included in annual foreign aid appropriations laws, prohibited official U.S. contacts with the PLO unless the organization "recognizes Israel's right to exist, accepts United Nations Security Council Resolutions 242 and 338 and renounces use of terrorism."

An address by Arafat to the UN General Assembly, meeting December 13 in a special session in Geneva, failed to satisfy the U.S. government. But a statement Arafat issued the next day prompted President Ronald Reagan to authorize a "diplomatic dialogue" with the PLO. The response stirred deep anxieties in Israel, but elsewhere the prospect of formal

*American-Palestinian talks raised new hope for an end to four decades of
violence and stalemate in that part of the Middle East.*

The Uprising

Stone-throwing Palestinian youths in the Israeli-occupied West Bank
and Gaza had created a situation that made the PLO diplomatic
initiative possible—even necessary. The intifada, or uprising, began in
the occupied territories in December 1987. By the end of 1988, it had cost
the lives of about 300 Palestinians and 12 Israelis. Israeli forces failed to
quell the protests, and their measures succeeded in winning international
sympathy for the Palestinians.

The spectacle of Palestinian youth losing their lives in defiance of
Israeli authority both troubled and inspired the PLO's leaders. They
recognized that they would lose credibility unless they could soon
produce diplomatic results.

The intifada had caused Jordan's King Hussein on July 31 to renounce
his government's claims to the West Bank and to terminate administrative functions it still performed there under Israeli occupation (Hussein's speech, p. 579). Hussein's severance of ties to this territory, which
Jordan ruled from the 1949 Arab-Israeli armistice until its occupation by
Israel in the 1967 war, added to the pressures on the PLO to assert its
leadership.

The PLO felt a need to achieve diplomatic successes lest the uprising
turn toward Islamic fundamentalists, who were uncompromising in their
opposition toward Israel. Radical groups within the PLO slowed Arafat's
search for accommodation with the United States, but they finally
acquiesced in the statement with which he secured U.S.-PLO negotiations. The Soviet Union, eager to improve its relations with the United
States, urged the PLO to meet U.S. demands.

New Palestinian Policy

The Palestinian National Charter, adopted in Cairo in 1968 and
generally regarded as the PLO's basic document, stated: "The partition
of Palestine in 1947 and the establishment of the state of Israel are
entirely illegal, regardless of the passage of time." The charter added
that Palestinians, "expressing themselves by the armed Palestinian
revolution, reject all solutions which are substitutes for the total liberation of Palestine." This position was abandoned at the Algiers conference
when the PNC endorsed UN Resolution 242, adopted by the Security
Council in 1967.

Resolution 242 called for Israel's withdrawal from territories it seized
in the 1967 war in return for Arab acceptance of its "right to live in peace
with secure and recognized boundaries free from threats or acts of force."
Palestinians often based their rejection of Resolution 242 on its call for "a

just settlement of the refugee problem," which they feared classed them as refugees rather than as a people entitled to statehood. Before the Algiers conference, Arafat frequently had hinted at acceptance of 242, but he avoided an unequivocal statement for fear of alienating "rejectionist" guerrilla groups, notably the Popular Front for the Liberation of Palestine, led by George Habash, and the Democratic Front for the Liberation of Palestine, led by Nayef Hawatmeh.

When the PNC accepted Resolution 242, the Palestinians viewed this change as fundamental and were surprised by its cool reception in Washington. Spokesmen for the State Department and President-elect George Bush's transition team called the PLO statement a step forward but still too ambiguous in its recognition of Israel and in its renunciation of terrorism.

Conflict with Arafat

The Reagan administration announced November 26 that it would not grant Arafat a visa to enter the United States to address the UN General Assembly. In a decision closely identified with Secretary of State George P. Shultz, the United States refused the visa on the ground that Arafat "knows of, condones and lends support to" acts of terrorism. The United States had previously attempted to close the PLO's New York mission to the UN by invoking provisions of the Anti-Terrorism Act of 1987, but was barred by a U.S. District Court decision in favor of the PLO. (Order to bar office closing, p. 479)

United Nations Secretary General Javier Pérez de Cuéllar called the visa denial a violation of the freedom-of-access agreement made when the UN headquarters was established in New York. The General Assembly held a special session in Geneva on December 13 to hear Arafat. His exclusion from New York isolated the United States and intensified the world attention being focused on him.

A PLO delegation led by Arafat met with five American Jewish leaders in Stockholm December 6 to explain that the Algiers statement had effectively recognized Israel. Participants issued a joint statement affirming that position. At a news conference Arafat said, "The PNC accepted two states, a Palestinian state and a Jewish state, Israel. Is that clear enough?" He also said that the PNC had "declared its rejection of terrorism in all its forms, including state terrorism." Shultz told reporters that the Stockholm statement "seems to be a little bit further clarification, and I welcome that," but he added, "there's still a considerable distance to go."

United Nations Speech

In his UN speech Arafat dramatically appealed for peace negotiations between Palestinians and Israelis at an international conference that would "respect the right to exist in peace and security for all." He said *that a relaxed international atmosphere had created "a historic, possibly irreplaceable, opportunity" to forge a peace agreement. Arafat condemned terrorism "in all its forms" and proposed that "occupied Palestinian lands" be placed under UN supervision, including a peace-keeping force to "protect the people" and "oversee Israeli withdrawal."*

Prodded by moderate Arab governments as well as by Sweden, Arafat in a press conference in Geneva December 14 made a statement that finally satisfied the United States. That same day Reagan said the conditions for dialogue "have been met," and Shultz authorized the U.S. ambassador to Tunisia, Robert H. Pelletreau, Jr., to meet with the PLO. Shultz said Bush had agreed with the conclusion that Arafat's statement satisfied U.S. conditions for talks. Pelletreau met with PLO representatives in Tunis on December 16, but it was clear that substantive discussion would not begin until President Bush was in office.

U.S.-PLO Talks

The Reagan administration stressed that its decision to meet with the PLO did not imply recognition of a Palestinian state. The administration promised to hold the PLO to its word on terrorism and attempted to reassure Israel of its continuing support. Although a few Israelis welcomed the turn of events, leaders of both the Likud bloc and the Labor party, partners in a new coalition government, expressed dismay over America's willingness to talk with the PLO. But some American Jewish leaders, who had previously hewed closely to Israeli government policies, expressed a cautious acceptance of the talks. The American decision was welcomed by European officials.

Despite hostile reactions in Syria and Iran, and among splinter Palestinian groups outside the PLO, the Arab world felt that a major breakthrough had been achieved. In particular, America's moderate Arab friends were relieved that the United States had strengthened the hand of moderate elements among the Palestinians.

Although the peace process had been given new life, quick results were not expected. In fact, there was fear that deepening anxieties among Israelis, rising hopes among Palestinians, and greater uncertainties among all parties could produce an explosive situation if talks dragged on too long without substantive accomplishment.

> *Following are excerpts in English translation from the Palestine National Council's "Declaration of Independence," asserting statehood for the Palestinian people, adopted at the council's conference in Algiers, November 15, 1988:*

Palestine, the land of the three monotheistic faiths, is where the Palestinian Arab people was born, on which it grew, developed and excelled. The Palestinian people was never separated from or diminished in its integral bonds with Palestine. Thus the Palestinian Arab people ensured for itself an everlasting union between itself, its land and its history. . . .

Despite the historical injustice inflicted on the Palestinian Arab people resulting in their dispersion and depriving them of their right to self-determinination, following upon U.N. General Assembly Resolution 181 (1947), which partitioned Palestine into two states, one Arab, one Jewish, yet it is this Resolution that still provides those conditions of international legitimacy that ensure the right of the Palestinian Arab people to sovereignty.

By stages, the occupation of Palestine and parts of other Arab territories by Israeli forces, the willed dispossession and expulsion from their ancestral homes of the majority of Palestine's civilian inhabitants, was achieved by organized terror; those Palestinians who remained, as a vestige subjugated in its homeland, were persecuted and forced to endure the destruction of their national life.

Thus were principles of international legitimacy violated. Thus were the Charter of the United Nations and its Resolutions disfigured, for they had recognized the Palestinian Arab people's national rights, including the right of Return, the right to independence, the right to sovereignty over territory and homeland.

. . . [F]rom out of the long years of trial in evermounting struggle, the Palestinian political identity emerged further consolidated and confirmed. And the collective Palestinian national will forged for itself a political embodiment, the Palestine Liberation Organization, its sole, legitimate representative recognized by the world community as a whole. . . . And so Palestinian resistance was clarified and raised into the forefront of Arab and world awareness, as the struggle of the Palestinian Arab people achieved unique prominence among the world's liberation movements in the modern era.

The massive national uprising, the *intifada,* now intensifying in cumulative scope and power on occupied Palestinian territories, as well as the unflinching resistance of the refugee camps outside the homeland, have elevated awareness of the Palestinian truth and right into still higher realms of comprehension and actuality. Now at last the curtain has been dropped around a whole epoch of prevarication and negation. The *intifada* has set siege to the mind of official Israel, which has for too long relied exclusively upon myth and terror to deny Palestinian existence altogether. Because of the *intifada* and its revolutionary irreversible impulse, the history of Palestine has therefore arrived at a decisive juncture.

Whereas the Palestinian people reaffirms most definitively its inalienable rights in the land of its patrimony:

Now by virtue of natural, historical and legal rights, and the sacrifices of successive generations who gave of themselves in defense of the freedom and independence of their homeland;

In pursuance of Resolutions adopted by Arab Summit Conferences and relying on the authority bestowed by international legitimacy as embodied in the Resolutions of the United Nations Organizations since 1947;

And in exercise by the Palestinian Arab people of its rights to self-determination, political independence and sovereignty over its territory,

The Palestine National Council, in the name of God, and in the name of the Palestinian Arab people, hereby proclaims the establishment of the State of Palestine on our Palestinian territory with its capital Jersualem (Al-Quds Ash-Sharif).

The State of Palestine is the state of Palestinians wherever they may be. The state is for them to enjoy in it their collective national and cultural identity, theirs to pursue in it a complete equality of rights. In it will be safeguarded their political and religious convictions and their human dignity by means of a parliamentary democratic system of governance, itself based on freedom of expression and the freedom to form parties. The rights of minorities will duly be respected by the majority, as minorities must abide by decisions of the majority. Governance will be based on principles of social justice, equality and non-discrimination in public rights of men or women, on grounds of race, religion, color or sex, under the aegis of a constitution which ensures the rule of law and an independent judiciary. Thus shall these principles allow no departure from Palestine's age-old spiritual and civilizational heritage of tolerance and religious coexistence.

The State of Palestine is an Arab state, an integral and indivisible part of the Arab nation, at one with that nation in heritage and civilization, with it also in its aspiration for liberation, progress, democracy and unity. The State of Palestine affirms its obligation to abide by the Charter of the League of Arab States, whereby the coordination of the Arab states with each other shall be strengthened. It calls upon Arab compatriots to consolidate and enhance the emergence in reality of our state, to mobilize potential, and to intensify efforts whose goal is to end Israeli occupation.

The State of Palestine proclaims its commitment to the principles and purposes of the United Nations, and to the Universal Declaration of Human Rights. It proclaims its commitment as well to the principles and policies of the Non-Aligned Movement.

It further announces itself to be a peace-loving State, in adherence to the principles of peaceful co-existence. . . .

In the context of its struggle for peace in the land of Love and Peace, the State of Palestine calls upon the United Nations to bear special responsibility for the Palestinian Arab people and its homeland. It calls upon all peace- and freedom-loving peoples and states to assist it in the attainment of its objectives, to provide it with security, to alleviate the tragedy of its people, and to help it terminate Israel's occupation of the Palestinian territories.

The State of Palestine herewith declares that it believes in the settlement of regional and international disputes by peaceful means, in accordance with the U.N. Charter and resolutions. Without prejudice to its natural right to defend its territorial integrity and independence, it therefore rejects the threat or use of force, violence and terrorism against its territorial integrity or political independence, as it also rejects their use against the territorial integrity of other states. Therefore, on this day unlike all others, November 15, 1988, as we stand at the threshold of a new dawn, in all honor and modesty we humbly bow to the sacred spirits of our fallen ones, Palestinian and Arab, by the purity of whose sacrifice for the homeland our sky has been illuminated and our Land given life....

Therefore, we call upon our great people to rally to the banner of Palestine, to cherish and defend it, so that it may forever be the symbol of our freedom and dignity in that homeland, which is a homeland for the free, now and always.

PROPOSALS TO OVERCOME SAVINGS AND LOAN CRISIS

November 30, 1988

Federal regulators continued in 1988 to carry out multibillion-dollar bailouts of insolvent lending institutions. This decade-long "crisis" deepened during the year, causing the Federal Home Loan Bank Board to commit $38 billion in assistance to failing savings and loan associations (S&Ls) and, consequently, bankrupt its own insurance fund.

As required by law, the accounts of individual depositors are insured up to $100,000 each from premiums paid by the associations and other nonbank "thrifts" to the Federal Savings and Loan Insurance Corporation (FSLIC), the insurance fund.

The fund's depletion put pressure on Congress and the incoming Bush administration to replenish it with tax dollars. In mid-December, Congress's General Accounting Office (GAO) estimated that $85 billion would be needed by the FSLIC during the next ten years in addition to whatever income would be derived from the insurance premiums that the surviving associations would pay. The Bank Board's estimate was lower, between $45 billion and $50 billion, though still potentially burdensome to a government already confronted with a congressional mandate to bring the federal budget into balance.

Aside from thrifts that the Bank Board forced to close or merge with healthier institutions during the past decade, hundreds of others were insolvent but were allowed to remain open only because the insurance fund had run dry. Outright closure would require the depositors to be paid off. Numerous banks also fell into insolvency and had to be rescued by the Federal Deposit Insurance Corporation (FDIC), the banking industry's counterpart to the FSLIC. But unlike the FSLIC, the banking insurance fund remained solvent despite incurring losses during 1988.

Bank failures, though nationwide, continued to be concentrated in the Southwest, as did many of the S&L failures. Oklahoma and Texas, especially, had been hard hit in recent years by a depressed oil economy, a crippled real-estate market, and in some cases by bank mismanagement and even fraud.

The S&L woes were brought on by unusually high interest rates in the late 1970s and early 1980s. Typically, the institutions were forced to pay higher rates to attract deposits than they were receiving on their long-term investments, usually mortgage loans. To get a better return, many troubled S&Ls made speculative investments that went sour. Government deregulation of the lending institutions gave them more leeway than in the past to make such investments.

The regulatory system encouraged mismanagement by the lending institutions, the Council of Economic Advisers said in its annual report to the president, which was released January 10, 1989. "The irony is that federal government policies led to this debacle," the report said.

In a report the GAO issued November 13, Comptroller General Charles A. Bowsher said "almost a third" of the 3,100 savings and loan institutions were "insolvent or nearly so." He added that "less that $5 billion in tangible capital backs $1.3 trillion of customer deposits; the Federal Savings and Loan Insurance Corporation is insolvent by $14 billion."

Soon afterward, FDIC chairman L. William Seidman suggested that his agency be put in charge of managing the S&L crisis, extending the FDIC's jurisdiction to all lending institutions. Telling a National Press Club audience on November 30 that the FDIC would end the year "with a net worth of approximately $15 billion," he added, "We stand ready to help if this is considered desirable by the administration and the Congress." He outlined a ten-part plan for bringing the situation under control.

The FDIC followed with a report elaborating the proposals, which were being studied by Treasury Department officials in formulating a plan of action for the Bush administration to present to Congress some time early in 1989. At a news conference on January 4, 1989, Seidman said, "We are meeting with Treasury every week. They're aware of the report."

On January 25, President Bush acknowledged that a fee on deposits— to be paid by depositors—was being considered. "I'm not going to say what I'm going to do," Bush told reporters, "but that is one option." According to press reports, the Treasury Department and the White House were discussing the imposition of a twenty-five cent fee on every hundred dollars of deposits. It was estimated that the fee would bring in

$9 billion a year, to be used for liquidating or selling off insolvent thrift institutions. The initial reaction from Congress was decidedly negative, and left doubt whether the plan would be advanced.

> *Following are excerpts from the speech, titled "Deposit Insurance for the Nineties," delivered by FDIC chairman L. William Seidman before the National Press Club in Washington, D.C., November 30, 1988:*

Today we address the problems of deposit insurance because the system as a whole has developed a significant weakness—costs far exceed income. The thrift industry's problems alone now demand funding on a massive scale. That funding requirement appears to exceed the *combined* resources devoted to Europe under the Marshall Plan, and the bailouts of Lockheed, Chrysler, Penn Central, and New York City! . . .

The FDIC will end this year with about a $2 to $3 billion loss—its first such loss. We have spent $7 billion in Texas alone since 1986.

The good news is that the FDIC will end the year with a net worth of approximately $15 billion, and expects to show a half-billion dollar increase in net worth in 1989. We are in a position to handle the problems we can foresee. But obviously we need to control the kinds of losses we've experienced in Texas.

Unfortunately, our sister insurance fund, the FSLIC, is less fortunate and is insolvent. It has been estimated that the cost of restoring it to solvency and a sound financial position will range between $50 and $100 billion. . . .

As a result of this review [of the lending industry by the FDIC], we have developed our commandments.

First, federal deposit insurance is here to stay. Thus our efforts must be aimed at managing the system better.

Second, we must allow the federal insurer to operate as much as possible like a private insurer. This principle is central to improving the system.

Third, the federal insurer's primary mission must be to maintain the integrity of its insurance fund, preventing undue risk taking by insured institutions. This was the essence of the recommendations of President-Elect Bush's Task Group on Regulation of Financial Institutions. We need an independent insurer whose turf and sole focus is preservation of a solvent fund. This structure instills a built-in conservatism into the supervisory process.

The insurer should be independent of the industry it regulates and from chartering authorities—each of which has its own separate mission. Of course, it should be subject to Congressional oversight, but independent of the appropriations process as the Bush Task Group recommended.

Fourth, the insurer should be separately budgeted, and not a part of the regular federal budget. Why? Well, because the federal budget system works backwards for an agency mandated to save for emergencies.

For decades the FDIC has been depositing its unspent premium income in the Treasury. We receive no taxpayer's funds. Are these deposits counted as savings? No, they are counted as income to the government rather than savings put aside for a rainy day.

When it comes time to make a withdrawal to deal with a banking problem, that action is treated as government expenditure. It *should* be treated as a payback of money on deposit.

Thus, the present system is designed so there is no reward for saving. Even worse, there is a penalty for using funds to stop problems early, while they are less costly.

Fifth, the insurer should set insurance premium rates that reflect experience. The deposit insurer, like private insurers, should be able to adjust its premiums to reflect its experience and costs on a continuing basis. While it would be helpful to do this on a bank-by-bank basis, we should start by charging all banks based on the fund's overall experience.

This sort of pay-as-you-go pricing system should help ensure that the deposit insurance fund maintains adequate reserves. It gives bankers a stronger economic incentive to take an interest in promoting firm and forceful supervision to control risk.

Sixth, like a private insurance company, the federal insurer should have the right to decide who shall have federal deposit insurance.

Today, terminating bank insurance can take two years or longer. Meanwhile, the insured institution often continues to deteriorate as losses mount. The insurer must have the clear authority to terminate insurance promptly—that is in six months or less—when the institution threatens the insurance fund. Of course, insured depositors must continue to be protected for a reasonable period once insurance is terminated.

Seventh, all insured institutions should be regulated according to common accounting and supervisory standards. GAAP [Generally Accepted Accounting Principles] ... should govern unless more conservative standards are required.

Eighth, all financial institutions that "buy" federal deposit insurance should be obliged, in addition to paying premiums, to guarantee the insurer against any insurance loss caused by other banks owned by a common parent.

A multibank holding company cannot be allowed to leave federal insurers with the cost of its failed bank subsidiaries, while it walks away with its good banks.

Ninth, we should move toward a banking structure that limits the risk inside the banks to traditional banking activities. Nontraditional activities can be performed outside the bank in its affiliates or subsidiaries. Supervisory "firewalls" can be constructed to insulate the banks from risks associated with those operations. Such a change would contain the insurance risk, and at the same time allow financial firms the necessary freedom to offer a competitive array of products and services.

And tenth, we must improve our ability to supervise financial institutions to control risks.

Concentrations of risk in an institution's portfolios must be limited. FSLIC's and our experiences in the Southwest underscore that point.

Limiting concentration by improving portfolio diversification should involve several elements. Statewide, and hopefully someday, nationwide, branch banking should be encouraged. Diversification, not just by customer, but by loan type and region, should be promoted. And improved secondary markets through securitization should be fostered.

We suggest a new tool to help regulators assess and limit concentration. Establish regional committees comprised of representatives from different supervisory agencies to evaluate the levels of risk present in their respective areas. These Regional Economic Oversight Committees, in regular consultation with industry and academic representatives, should seek to anticipate competitive and economic developments that could lead to trouble down the road.

For example, banks and thrifts all rushed to build office buildings in Austin, Texas, at just about the same time. That resulted today in a city with a decent economy but high levels of unoccupied structures. Regulators and industry representatives working together might have helped prevent that race to folly.

Of course, we should never forget that maintenance of adequate capital is the bedrock of supervision. Once an insured institution's capital falls below an acceptable level, constraints must be placed on asset growth and the ability to engage in new activities.

Above all, supervision must be directed to strong, prompt action to limit risk and loss to the insurance fund.

These are our "Ten Commandments" for a safer and less costly deposit insurance system. A system that is designed to avoid the problems we face today. . . .

No federal insurance system can survive long unless all federal insurers are solvent.

Here are a few of our suggestions. They are given in a spirit of cooperation, and out of a desire to see action now.

First, stop the losses that are taking place among the hopelessly insolvent thrifts. While part of these losses constitute reserving for property value declines that cannot be eliminated, these institutions are reporting losses of over a billion dollars a month.

By our estimate (and as I have said many times, onsite examinations are necessary to support these estimates), the worst twenty percent of the remaining insolvent institutions account for around eighty percent of the growth in losses. We need to close the *worst first,* at an estimated cost of $30 billion. Once these 100 or so worst institutions are liquidated, the other problem institutions can be dealt with over a somewhat longer period. Until that time, these problem institutions must be supervised very closely.

The total bill will be $50 to $100 billion, but the immediate need is for $30 billion to close the worst losers.

Even this initial cost exceeds the resources the thrift industry can shoulder, but it certainly can contribute its part.

Beyond that contribution, the government must find the resources to meet this problem.

Our study contains considerable analysis of potential funding methods. The American Agenda, headed by former Presidents Ford and Carter, outlines a way to spread the cost over a number of years. This proposal should be given serious consideration.

However, it's up to the Treasury Department and Congress to determine which alternative makes the most sense in the overall federal planning. The message today is, the situation requires $30 billion in 1989.

The next question is who gets the money, and who controls how it is spent.

It has been suggested that the FDIC's supervisory and liquidation skills might come in handy in assisting with the problem. We stand ready to help if this is considered desirable by the Administration and the Congress. . . .

Whether there should be some use of FDIC services, or even an administrative merger, is best left to others less prejudiced than we to decide. . . .

December

SEC Report on Corporate Takeovers 921

Gorbachev's Speech to the United Nations . . 927

Interagency Report on Forest-Fire Policy 941

Angola-Namibia Peace Accord 947

Defense Panel's Proposals
    to Close Military Bases 951

SEC REPORT
ON CORPORATE TAKEOVERS
December 4, 1988

Corporate takeovers, a prominent feature of the American economy in the 1980s, reached a pinnacle with the leveraged buyout of RJR Nabisco Inc., the giant food and tobacco company, for $25 billion. The deal, completed December 1, was almost twice as big as the previous largest takeover, Chevron's $13.3 billion acquisition of Gulf Oil in 1984.

These enormous takeovers usually were as controversial as they were spectacular. They tended to be viewed as either a generally beneficial business restructuring or as a drag on industrial development and tax revenues. The concern about the impact of a big takeover increased when it was done primarily with borrowed money, as in the case of RJR Nabisco. Janet L. Norwood, the U.S. commissioner of labor statistics, said the amount of debt produced by buyouts was "absolutely monumental."

Typically, a relatively small amount of equity was used to raise large sums for buyout purposes. Thus, in Wall Street parlance, the small equity becomes a lever in a leveraged buyout—or LBO, as it was sometimes called. By some calculations, the RJR Nabisco deal pushed the total value of buyouts in U.S. industry during 1988 to $90 billion, more than double the previous year's total of $37 billion.

Three days after the RJR Nabisco deal, the Securities and Exchange Commission (SEC) released a sixty-seven-page staff report that cast light on the economic rationale of the takeover boom. The authors of the report, entitled "Do Bad Bidders Become Good Targets?" were Mark L. Mitchell, a senior research scholar at the SEC, and Kenneth Lehn, the

*commission's chief staff economist. The report drew considerable atten-
tion in the nation's business press and was characterized by a New York
Times writer as foreshadowing "the anticipated congressional debate on
the value of takeovers and leveraged buyouts."*

*The takeover frenzy of the 1980s appeared to have its roots in the 1960s
and 1970s when many corporations diversified by acquiring other companies, forming "conglomerates." As time went on, the stock market price of
the conglomerate frequently did not reflect its full value. But the full
value could sometimes be retrieved if the conglomerate were bought and
its assets—whether individual companies, divisions, or products—were
sold to other corporations.*

*In a leveraged buyout, the financing for a takeover often was in the
form of high-interest, highly speculative "junk bonds" whose ultimate
worth depended on a successful outcome of the takeover attempt.*

*The auction of RJR Nabisco began when managers of the conglomerate
decided to "take the firm private" in partnership with investment
bankers Shearson Lehman Hutton. This required buying the outstanding
shares of the company's stock and removing them from public trading.
However, the winning bidders for those shares were not the company
officers but rather a Wall Street firm that specialized in buyouts,
Kohlberg Kravis Roberts & Co. Since it was formed in 1976, the firm had
carried out leveraged buyouts amounting to $40 billion, including the
RJR Nabisco deal.*

*Taking a corporation off the stock market may benefit the owners
because dividend payments on stock are taxed but interest payments on
debt are not. Most economists reasoned, therefore, that the government
loses tax revenues when a company goes private.*

Takeover Study

*In the SEC staff report, Mitchell and Lehn said they studied 412
acquisitions by 288 companies from 1982 to 1986. They determined that
76 of those companies themselves later became targets of takeovers. The
Wall Street Journal commented editorially on December 19 that the
report's conclusions suggested that some corporate raiders were "getting
a taste of their own medicine." It was "no secret that companies that
'grow' by gobbling up other companies sometimes experience digestion
problems," the editorial added. Insofar as takeovers recoup losses taken
by the stockholders because of a company's prior acquisitions, "these
deals promote economic efficiency," Lehn commented to the New York
Times.*

Congressional Response

*At least five committees or subcommittees of the Senate and the House
were planning hearings in 1989 on debt-creating corporate takeovers. But*

it was far from certain that legislation might result. The London-based Economist *magazine commented that it would be a "pity" if the RJR Nabisco LBO "triggers legislation to halt what, for some companies, may be the best opportunity to improve their performance."*

Most legislators and their staff members were also expressing caution. But Rep. Dan Rostenkowski, D-Ill., chairman of the House Ways and Means Committee, said there was a "good possibility" Congress would try to limit tax advantages on borrowing to finance leveraged buyouts.

Sen. John H. Chafee, R-R.I., predicted that Congress would not pass takeover legislation in 1989. "For every cure," Chafee said, "it raises an illness that is worse." An aide to John D. Dingell, D-Mich., chairman of the House Energy and Commerce Committee, was quoted in the press as saying, "We have to be very careful, and the constituency for reform has not yet emerged."

> *Following are excerpts from the report, "Do Bad Bidders Become Good Targets?" by Mark L. Mitchell and Kenneth Lehn, issued December 4, 1988, by the Securities and Exchange Commission:*

Much of the public controversy surrounding corporate takeovers, especially hostile takeovers, concerns the economic rationale for these transactions. Critics contend that takeovers burden corporations with excessive debt, impose heavy costs on employees, local communities, and shareholders in acquiring companies, and often needlessly disassemble highly profitable corporations. Defenders counter with evidence on the significant premiums paid to target shareholders. They assert that these premiums reflect the minimum amount by which the discounted cash flows of target firms are expected to increase, typically by enhancement of the target firms' operating efficiency or a restructuring of their financial claims. . . .

Critics and defenders agree that takeovers result in significant wealth gains for target shareholders. Numerous academic studies document that, on average, the stock price of target firms increases approximately 25-30 percent upon the announcement of tender offers. . . . In short, the evidence shows that corporate takeovers significantly benefit target shareholders.

Critics and defenders of takeovers disagree about the extent to which takeover premiums gauge the resulting efficiency gains. Critics argue that the gains to target shareholders come largely at the expense of other "stakeholders," including bondholders, employees, and local communities. If the losses sustained by these groups more than offset the gains to target shareholders, it is argued, corporate takeovers actually destroy, not create, wealth.

In addition to arguing that hostile takeovers redistribute wealth from other corporate stakeholders to target stockholders, critics also argue that takeover bids are induced, in large part, by a capital market that often undervalues companies. In short, this argument states that inefficient pricing of corporate equity, combined with availability of "junk bond" financing, creates opportunities for corporate raiders to make tender offers for target firms that are efficiently operated, but inefficiently valued. According to this line of reasoning, it is the bidders' heavy reliance on junk bond financing, and not the inefficient organization of the targets, that results in large asset sales following many successful hostile takeovers. Further, it is argued that during the past few years, dozens of major corporations "voluntarily" have sold profitable assets to finance stock repurchases intended to raise their stock prices, and reduce the likelihood of hostile takeovers.

In support of their position, critics cite evidence from studies that examine the pre- and post-takeover accounting profits of target firms. . . . According to critics of hostile takeovers, this evidence suggests that corporate takeovers generally do not enhance the operating efficiency of targets.

Critics of hostile takeovers cite two other pieces of empirical literature in support of their position. First, [Michael E.] Porter (1987) and [David J.] Ravenscraft and [F. M.] Sherer (1987) show that divisions acquired by firms in conglomerate mergers during the 1960s and 1970s frequently were divested following the merger. According to critics, these studies provide further evidence that takeovers generally, and hostile takeovers in particular, do not improve the efficiency with which the target firms' assets are operated. Second, critics often argue that, although takeovers benefit target stockholders, they often diminish the value of acquiring firms. . . .

We argue that the evidence cited above is consistent with a more favorable view of hostile takeovers. Generally, the evidence reviewed above pertains to takeovers during the 1970s and early 1980s, a period during which most takeovers were friendly, and many were conglomerate mergers. This evidence does not directly address the profitability of hostile takeovers during the mid-1980s. A unique feature of hostile takeovers during this period is that many of these transactions were motivated by the acquiring firms' desire to sell a substantial proportion of the target firms' assets. To the extent that these "bust-up" takeovers prune target firms of "poorly" performing assets which the target firms had acquired in earlier takeovers, then these transactions can be viewed, in part, as "undoing" some of the unprofitable takeovers of the 1970s and early 1980s. . . .

The data [studied by the authors] reveal that target firms made acquisitions at a rate that was not significantly different from the corresponding rate for nontarget firms. Per 100 firms, the group of targets made 8.65 acquisitions per annum and the group of nontargets made 8.00 acquisitions per annum. The data also reveal that hostile targets made acquisitions at a faster rate than any other group. Per 100 firms, hostile targets made 10.56 acquisitions per annum and friendly targets made 6.71 acquisitions per annum. Although none of the differences in acquisition rates across these groups is statistically significant, these data indicate that target firms were not making acquisitions at a slower rate than nontargets. . . .

The evidence reported in this paper is relevant for two arguments made by critics of hostile takeovers. First, although critics often lament the advent of hostile "bust-up" takeovers (i.e., takeovers that are followed by large divestitures of the target firms' assets), this evidence is consistent with the view that hostile bust-up takeovers often promote economic efficiency by reallocating the targets' assets to higher valued uses. Second, these results cast new light on evidence concerning the effect of takeovers on the equity value of acquiring firms. Critics of hostile takeovers often argue that although target shareholders fare well in takeovers, these transactions often diminish the equity value of acquiring firms. Our evidence suggests that takeovers can be both a "problem" and a "solution." Although, in the aggregate, we find that the returns to acquiring firms are approximately zero, the aggregate data obscure the fact that the market discriminates between "bad" bidders, who are more likely to become takeover targets, and "good" bidders, who are less likely to become targets. The evidence is consistent with the view that, in part, the proliferation of hostile takeovers in the mid-1980s had its genesis in the failed acquisition strategies of many large corporations. . . .

GORBACHEV'S SPEECH TO THE UNITED NATIONS
December 7, 1988

In a wide-ranging and historic address to the United Nations General Assembly on December 7, Soviet leader Mikhail S. Gorbachev broke with traditional Soviet rhetoric to belittle the role of military force and ideological struggle in world affairs. Underlining that thought, he announced Soviet plans to cut 500,000 of the country's 5.2 million troops by 1991.

Calling in his one-hour speech for "respect for the views and positions of others," Gorbachev seemed to rule out a tenet of communism, that of Soviet foreign intervention in support of the class struggle. "We are not abandoning our convictions, our philosophy, or traditions, nor do we urge anyone to abandon theirs," he said. He supported "a fair rivalry among ideologies" but cautioned that "it should not be extended to relations among states. Otherwise, we would simply be unable to solve any of the world's problems. . . ."

Only a few hours after extolling to the General Assembly the importance of individual liberty as the keystone of world peace, Gorbachev provided the trip's most stunning image: posing with President Ronald Reagan and President-elect George Bush on Governor's Island in New York harbor against the backdrop of the Statue of Liberty. The three leaders had lunched at the Coast Guard-maintained Admiral's House on the island. The two and one-half hour meeting—which Gorbachev had proposed—provided the setting for a mellow farewell between Reagan and Gorbachev. The two leaders' attitudes toward each other had gradually warmed over the years, giving way to expressions of mutual admiration at their 1988 Moscow summit meeting. (Reagan-Gorbachev Summit, p. 353)

"I think we're now at the threshold, present at the birth, of a new phase of our relations," said Gorbachev shortly after the luncheon. Reagan told reporters that the New York meeting achieved "the continuation of what we've accomplished so far...."

Public Relating in Manhattan

Gorbachev carried the feeling of good will into the streets of Manhattan. His motorcade glided past the New York Stock Exchange and up Broadway to Times Square, greeted by a cheering crowd of thousands. Along the way, Gorbachev and his wife, Raisa, made an unexpected stop and alighted from their limousine to greet surprised onlookers—a gesture reminiscent of his visit to Washington, D.C., and Reagan's walk in Red Square. "We saw their faces. We saw their eyes. We saw their friendliness," Gorbachev said.

Gorbachev was the first Soviet party leader to visit New York City since Nikita S. Khrushchev did so in 1960. However, on December 8, the Soviet leader cut short his New York stay by one day and canceled plans to visit Cuba and London, returning home to supervise relief efforts after a devastating earthquake hit Soviet Armenia.

Reactions and Questions

Though he presented his arms-cut decision as a unilateral one, Gorbachev subsequently told reporters that he hoped the United States and its European allies "will also take some steps." Reagan and Bush lauded the Soviet move. "If it is carried out speedily and in full," Reagan told a Washington audience later that day, "history will regard it as important—significant." But he warned against taking the Soviet reductions as a cue for similar U.S. cutbacks. "This still leaves them with superiority in the amount of conventional arms," the president said December 8 at a televised press conference. We're still way below them." West European leaders echoed those thoughts.

From the time Reagan accepted Gorbachev's invitation for a New York meeting, Bush had insisted that he would attend as vice president, but with no intention of engaging in any substantive negotiations. Pressed by reporters after their luncheon meeting, Bush said, "I made it clear ... that I certainly wanted to continue the progress that's been made in the Reagan administration with the Soviets. And I also made it clear that we needed some time, and he [Gorbachev] understood that."

U.S. officials reacted coolly to a plan Gorbachev presented for a cease-fire in Afghanistan, effective January 1, 1989. Some alleged that the Soviets meant to renege on their pledge to withdraw their forces from the country by February 15, under a UN-sponsored agreement signed in

March 1988. Others concluded that Gorbachev was looking to improve the terms of Soviet withdrawal. (Agreements on Afghanistan, p. 257)

In a December 8 editorial entitled, "Gambler, Showman, Statesman," the New York Times *commented: "Amazed Americans can only applaud [Gorbachev's] insistence that the principle of freedom of choice is 'absolute.' Knowledgeable listeners can only smile when he pledges to forgive poor countries their debts to Moscow, knowing that those are very small compared with the billions owed to the West. And people everywhere will hold him to his promise to solve 'human problems, only in a humane way' in his own country.... He risks nothing ... by taking the global stage during the American Presidential transition. He surely understands that neither George Bush nor Ronald Reagan can respond now. Unchallenged, he shrewdly seizes the world's attention."*

Following are excerpts in English translation from the address delivered December 7, 1988, by Soviet leader Mikhail Gorbachev, to the United Nations General Assembly in New York City:

Esteemed Mr. President,
Esteemed Mr. Secretary-General,
Distinguished delegates,

We have come here to show our respect for the United Nations, which increasingly has been manifesting its ability to act as a unique international center in the service of peace and security.

We have come here to show our respect for the dignity of this organization which is capable of accumulating the collective wisdom and will of mankind.

Recent events have been making it increasingly clear that the world needs such an organization, and that the organization itself needs the active involvement of all of its members, their support for its initiatives and actions and their potential and original contributions that enrich its activity.

A little more than a year ago, in an article entitled "Realities and the Guarantees of a Secure World" I set out some ideas on the problems of concern to the United Nations.

The time since then has given fresh food for thought. World developments have indeed come to a crucial point.

The role played by the Soviet Union in world affairs is well-known and, in view of the revolutionary perestroika under way in our country, which contains a tremendous potential for peace and international cooperation, we are now particularly interested in being properly understood.

That is why we have come here to address this most authoritative world body and to share our thoughts with it. We want it to be the first to learn of our new important decisions.

I

What will mankind be like when it enters the twenty-first century? People are already fascinated by this not too distant future. We are looking ahead to it with hopes for the best and yet with a feeling of concern.

The world in which we live today is radically different from what it was at the beginning or even in the middle of this century. And it continues to change as do all its components.

The advent of nuclear weapons was just another tragic reminder of the fundamental nature of that change. A material symbol and expression of absolute military power, nuclear weapons at the same time revealed the absolute limits of that power.

The problem of mankind's survival and self-preservation came to the fore.

We are witnessing the most profound social change.

Whether in the East or the South, the West or the North, hundreds of millions of people, new nations and states, new public movements and ideologies have moved to the forefront of history.

Broad-based and frequently turbulent popular movements have given expression, in a multidimensional and contradictory way, to a longing for independence, democracy and social justice. The idea of democratizing the entire world order has become a powerful sociopolitical force.

At the same time, the scientific and technological revolution has turned many economic, food, energy, environmental, information and population problems, which only recently we treated as national or regional problems, into global ones.

Thanks to the advances in mass media and means of transportation, the world seems to have become more visible and tangible. International communication has become easier than ever before.

Today the preservation of any kind of "closed" societies is hardly possible. This calls for a radical review of approaches to the totality of the problems of international cooperation as a major element of universal security.

The world economy is becoming a single organism, and no state, whatever its social system or economic status, can normally develop outside it.

This places on the agenda the need to devise a fundamentally new machinery for the functioning of the world economy, a new structure of the international division of labor.

At the same time, the growth of the world economy reveals the contradictions and limits inherent in traditional-type industrialization. Its further extension and intensification spell environmental catastrophe.

But there are still many countries without sufficiently developed industries, and some have not yet moved beyond the pre-industrial stage. One of the major problems is whether the process of their economic growth will follow the old technological patterns or whether they can join in the search for environmentally clean production.

And there is another problem: Instead of diminishing, the gap between the developed and most of the developing countries is increasingly growing into a serious global threat.

Hence the need to begin a search for a fundamentally new type of industrial progress—one that would meet the interests of all peoples and states.

In a word, the new realities are changing the entire world situation. The differences and contradictions inherited from the past are diminishing or being displaced. But new ones are emerging.

Some of the past differences and disputes are losing their importance. But conflicts of a different kind are taking their place. . . .

Today, further world progress is only possible through a search for universal human consensus as we move forward to a new world order.

We have come to a point when the disorderly play of elemental forces leads into an impasse. The international community must learn how it can shape and guide developments in such a way as to preserve our civilization, to make it safe for all and more conducive to normal life.

We are speaking of cooperation which could be more accurately termed cocreation and codevelopment.

The formula of development "at the expense of others" is on the way out. In the light of existing realities, no genuine progress is possible at the expense of the rights and freedoms of individuals and nations, or at the expense of nature.

Efforts to solve global problems require a new scope and quality of interaction of states and sociopolitical currents, regardless of ideological or other differences.

Of course, radical changes and revolutionary transformations will continue to occur within individual countries and social structures. This is how it was and how it will be.

But here too, our time marks a change. Internal transformations no longer can advance their national goals if they develop just along "parallel courses" with others, without making use of the achievements of the outside world and of the potential inherent in equitable cooperation.

In these circumstances, any interference in those internal developments, designed to redirect them to someone's liking, would have all the more destructive consequences for establishing a peaceful order. . . .

It is obvious, for instance, that the use or threat of force no longer can or must be an instrument of foreign policy. This applies above all to nuclear arms, but that is not the only thing that matters. All of us, and primarily the stronger of us, must exercise self-restraint and totally rule out any outward-oriented use of force.

That is the first and the most important component of a nonviolent world as an ideal which we proclaimed together with India in the Delhi Declaration and which we invite you to follow.

After all, it is now quite clear that building up military power makes no country omnipotent. What is more, one-sided reliance on military power ultimately weakens other components of national security.

It is also quite clear to us that the principle of freedom of choice is mandatory. Its nonrecognition is fraught with extremely grave consequences for world peace. . . .

This objective fact calls for respect for the views and positions of others, tolerance, a willingness to perceive something different as not necessarily bad or hostile, and an ability to learn to live side-by-side with others while remaining different and not always agreeing with each other.

As the world asserts its diversity, attempts to look down on others and to teach them one's own brand of democracy become totally improper, to say nothing of the fact that democratic values intended for export often very quickly lose their worth.

What we are talking about, therefore, is unity in diversity. If we assert this politically, if we reaffirm our adherence to freedom of choice, then there is no room for the view that some live on each by virtue of divine will while others are here quite by chance. . . .

The new phase also requires de-ideologizing relations among states. We are not abandoning our convictions, our philosophy or traditions, nor do we urge anyone to abandon theirs.

But neither do we have any intention to be hemmed in by our values. That would result in intellectual impoverishment, for it would mean rejecting a powerful source of development—the exchange of everything original that each nation has independently created.

In the course of such exchange, let everyone show the advantages of their social system, way of life or values—and not just by words or propaganda, but by real deeds.

That would be a fair rivalry of ideologies. But it should not be extended to relations among states. Otherwise, we would simply be unable to solve any of the world's problems, such as:

- Developing wide-ranging, mutually beneficial and equitable cooperation among nations;
- Making efficient use of the achievement of scientific and technological revolution;
- Restructuring the world economy and protecting the environment;
- Overcoming backwardness, eliminating hunger, disease, illiteracy and other global scourges.

Nor, of course, shall we then be able to eliminate the nuclear threat and militarism. . . .

In short, the understanding of the need for a period of peace is gaining ground and beginning to prevail. This has made it possible to take the first real steps in creating a healthier international environment and in disarmament. . . .

I am referring to the process of negotiations on nuclear arms, conventional weapons and chemical weapons, and to the search for political approaches to ending regional conflicts.

Of course, I am referring above all to political dialogue—a more intense and open dialogue pointed at the very heart of the problems instead of confrontation, at an exchange of constructive ideas instead of recriminations. Without political dialogue the process of negotiations cannot advance.

We regard prospects for the near and more distant future quite optimistically.

Just look at the changes in our relations with the United States. Little by little, mutual understanding has started to develop and elements of trust have emerged, without which it is very hard to make headway in politics.

In Europe, these elements are even more numerous. The Helsinki process is a great process. I believe that it remains fully valid. Its philosophical, political, practical and other dimensions must all be preserved and enhanced, while taking into account new circumstances.

Current realities make it imperative that the dialogue that ensures normal and constructive evolution of international affairs involve, on a continuous and active basis, all countries and regions of the world, including such major powers as India, China, Japan and Brazil and other countries—big, medium and small. . . .

II

In this specific historical situation, we face the question of a new role for the United Nations. . . .

The recent reinvigoration of its peace-making role has again demonstrated the United Nations' ability to assist its members in coping with the daunting challenges of our time and working to humanize their relations.

Regrettably, shortly after it was established, the organization went through the onslaught of the cold war. For many years, it was the scene of propaganda battles and continuous political confrontation.

Let historians argue who is more and who is less to blame for it. What political leaders today need to do is to draw lessons from that chapter in the history of the United Nations which turned out to be at odds with the very meaning and objectives of our organization.

One of the most bitter and important lessons lies in the long list of missed opportunities. As a result, at a certain point the authority of the United Nations diminished and many of its attempts to act failed.

It is highly significant that the reinvigoration of the role of the United Nations is linked to an improvement in the international climate. . . .

What is needed here is joining the efforts and taking into account the interests of all groups of countries, something that only this organization, the United Nations, can accomplish.

External debt is one of the gravest problems.

Let us not forget that in the age of colonialism the developing world, at the cost of countless losses and sacrifices, financed the prosperity of a large portion of the world community. The time has come to make up for the losses that accompanied its historic and tragic contribution to global material progress.

We are convinced that here, too, internationalizing our approach shows a way out.

Looking at things realistically, one has to admit that the accumulated debt cannot be repaid or recovered on the original terms.

The Soviet Union is prepared to institute a lengthy moratorium of up to 100 years on debt servicing by the least developed countries, and in quite a few cases to write off the debt altogether.

As regards other developing countries, we invite you to consider the following:

- Limiting their official debt, servicing payments depending on the economic performance of each of them or granting them a long period of deferral in the repayment of a major portion of their debt;
- Supporting the appeal of the United Nations Conference on Trade and Development for reducing debts owed to commercial banks;
- Guaranteeing government support for market arrangements to assist in Third World debt settlement, including the formation of a specialized international agency that would repurchase debts at a discount.

The Soviet Union favors a substantive discussion of ways to settle the debt crisis at multilateral forums, including consultations under the auspices of the United Nations among heads of government of debtor and creditor countries.

International economic security is inconceivable unless related not only to disarmament but also to the elimination of the threat to the world's environment. In a number of regions, the state of the environment is simply frightening.

A conference on the environment within the framework of the United Nations is scheduled for 1992. We welcome this decision and are working to have this forum produce results that would be commensurate with the scope of the problem.

But time is running out. Much is being done in various countries. Here again I would just like to underscore most emphatically the prospects opening up in the process of disarmament—for environmental revival.

Let us also think about setting up within the framework of the United Nations a center for emergency environmental assistance. Its function would be to promptly send international groups of experts to areas with a badly deteriorating environment.

The Soviet Union is also ready to cooperate in establishing an international space laboratory or manned orbital station designed exclusively for monitoring the state of the environment.

In the general area of space exploration, the outlines of a future space industry are becoming increasingly clear.

The position of the Soviet Union is well known: Activities in outer space must rule out the appearance of weapons there. Here again, there has to be a legal base. The groundwork for it—the provisions of the 1967 treaty and other agreements—is already in place.

However, there is already a strongly felt need to develop an all-embracing regime for peaceful work in outer space. The verification of compliance with that regime would be entrusted to a world space organization. . . .

The whole world welcomes the efforts of the United Nations organization and its secretary-general Mr. Perez de Cuellar, and his representatives in untying knots of regional problems. . . .

The year 1988 has brought a glimmer of hope in this area of our common concerns as well. This has been felt in almost all regional crises. On some of them, there has been movement. We welcome it, and we did what we could to contribute to it.

I will single out only Afghanistan.

The Geneva accords, whose fundamental and practical significance has been praised throughout the world, provided a possibility for completing the process of settlement even before the end of this year. That did not happen. . . .

I don't want to use this rostrum for recriminations against anyone.

But it is our view that, within the competence of the United Nations, the General Assembly resolution adopted last November could be supplemented by some specific measures.

In the words of that resolution, for the urgent achievement of a comprehensive solution by the Afghans themselves of the question of a broad-based government, the following should be undertaken:

- A complete ceasefire, effective everywhere as of January 1, 1989, and the cessation of all offensive operations or shellings, with the opposing Afghan groups retaining, for the duration of negotiations, all territories under their control;
- Linked to that, stopping as of the same date any supplies of arms to all belligerents;
- For the period of establishing a broad-based government, as provided in the General Assembly resolution, sending to Kabul and other strategic centers of the country a contingent of United Nations peace-keeping forces;
- We also request the Secretary-General to facilitate early implementation of the idea of holding an international conference on the neutrality and demilitarization of Afghanistan.

We shall most actively continue to assist in healing the wounds of the war and are prepared to cooperate in this endeavor both with the United Nations and on a bilateral basis.

We support the proposal to create under the auspices of the United Nations a voluntary international peace corps to assist in the revival of Afghanistan.

In the context of the problem of settling regional conflicts, I have to express my opinion on the serious incident that has recently affected the work of this session. The chairman of an organization which has observer status at the United Nations was not allowed by U.S. authorities to come to New York to address the General Assembly. I am referring to Yasser Arafat.

What is more, this happened at a time when the Palestine Liberation Organization has made a constructive step which facilitates the search for a solution to the Middle East problem with the involvement of the United Nations Security Council.

This happened at a time when a positive trend has become apparent toward a political settlement of other regional conflicts, in many cases with the assistance of the USSR and the United States. We voice our deep regret over the incident and our solidarity with the Palestine Liberation Organization. . . .

. . . I would like to join the voice of my country in the expressions of high appreciation for the significance of the universal declaration of human rights adopted 40 years ago on December 19, 1948.

Today, this document retains its significance. It, too, reflects the universal nature of the goals and objectives of the United Nations.

The most fitting way for a state to observe this anniversary of the declaration is to improve its domestic conditions for respecting and protecting the rights of its own citizens.

Before I inform you on what specifically we have undertaken recently in this respect, I would like to say the following.

Our country is going through a period of truly revolutionary uplifting.

The process of perestroika is gaining momentum. We began with the formulation of the theoretical concept of perestroika. We had to evaluate the nature and the magnitude of problems, to understand the lessons of the past and express that in the form of political conclusions and programs. This was done. . . .

For our society to participate in efforts to implement the plans of perestroika, it had to be democratized in practice. Under the sign of democratization, perestroika has now spread to politics, the economy, intellectual life and ideology.

We have initiated a radical economic reform. We have gained experience. At the start of next year the entire national economy will be redirected to new forms and methods of operation. This also means profoundly reorganizing relations of production and releasing the tremendous potential inherent in socialist property.

Undertaking such bold revolutionary transformations, we realized that there would be mistakes and also opposition, that new approaches would generate new problems. We also foresaw the possibility of slowdowns. . . .

But the guarantee that the overall process of perestroika will steadily move forward and gain strength lies in a profound democratic reform of the entire system of power and administration.

With the recent decisions by the USSR Supreme Soviet on amendments to the Constitution and the adoption of the law on elections we have completed the first stage of the process of political reform.

Without pausing, we have begun the second stage of this process with the main task of improving the relationship between the center and the republics, harmonizing inter-ethnic relations on the principles of Leninist internationalism that we inherited from the great revolution, and at the same time reorganizing the local system of Soviet power....

We have become deeply involved in building a socialist state based on the rule of law. Work on a series of new laws has been completed or is nearing completion.

Many of them will enter into force as early as 1989, and we expect them to meet the highest standards from the standpoint of ensuring the rights of the individual.

Soviet democracy will be placed on a solid normative base. I am referring, in particular, to laws on the freedom of conscience, glasnost, public associations and organizations, and many others.

In places of confinement there are no persons convicted for their political or religious beliefs.

Additional guarantees are to be included in the new draft laws that rule out any form of persecution on those grounds.

Naturally, this does not apply to those who committed actual criminal offenses or state crimes such as espionage, sabotage, terrorism, etc., whatever their political or ideological beliefs.

Draft amendments to the penal code have been prepared and are awaiting their turn. Among the articles being revised are those related to capital punishment.

The problem of exit from and entry to our country, including the question of leaving it for family reunification, is being dealt with in a humane spirit.

As you know, one of the reasons for refusal to leave is a person's knowledge of secrets. Strictly warranted time limitations on the secrecy rule will now be applied. Every person seeking employment at certain agencies or enterprises will be informed of this rule. In case of disputes there is a right of appeal under the law.

This removes from the agenda the problem of the so-called "refuseniks."

We intend to expand the Soviet Union's participation in the United Nations and CSCE human rights monitoring arrangements. We believe that the jurisdiction of the International Court of Justice at the Hague as regards the interpretation and implementation of agreements on human rights should be binding on all states.

We regard as part of the Helsinki process the cessation of jamming of all foreign radio broadcasts beamed at the Soviet Union....

III

Now let me turn to the main issue—disarmament, without which none of the problems of the coming century can be solved....

As you know, on January 15, 1986 the Soviet Union put forward a program of building a nuclear-weapon-free world. Translated into actual negotiating positions, it has already produced material results.

Tomorrow marks the first anniversary of the signing of the INF Treaty [for the reduction of intermediate-range nuclear weapons in Europe]. I am therefore particularly pleased to note that the implementation of the treaty—the elimination of missiles—is proceeding normally, in an atmosphere of trust and businesslike work. . . .

The Soviet leadership has decided to demonstrate once again its readiness to reinforce this healthy process not only by words but also by deeds.

Today, I can report to you that the Soviet Union has taken a decision to reduce its armed forces.

Within the next two years their numerical strength will be reduced by 500,000 men. The numbers of conventional armaments will also be substantially reduced. This will be done unilaterally, without relation to the talks on the mandate of the Vienna meeting.

By agreement with our Warsaw Treaty allies, we have decided to withdraw by 1991 six tank divisions from the German Democratic Republic, Czechoslovakia and Hungary, and to disband them.

Assault landing troops and several other formations and units, including assault crossing units with their weapons and combat equipment, will also be withdrawn from the groups of Soviet forces stationed in those countries.

Soviet forces stationed in those countries will be reduced by 50,000 men and their armaments, by 5,000 tanks.

All Soviet divisions remaining, for the time being, in the territory of our allies are being reorganized. Their structure will be different from what it is now; after a major cutback of their tanks it will become clearly defensive.

At the same time, we shall reduce the numerical strength of the armed forces and the numbers of armaments stationed in the European part of the USSR.

In total, Soviet armed forces in this part of our country and in the territories of our European allies will be reduced by 10,000 tanks, 8,500 artillery systems and 800 combat aircraft.

Over these two years we intend to reduce significantly our armed forces in the Asian part of our country, too. By agreement with the government of the Mongolian People's Republic a major portion of Soviet troops temporarily stationed there will return home.

In taking this fundamental decision the Soviet leadership expresses the will of the people, who have undertaken a profound renewal of their entire socialist society.

We shall maintain our country's defense capability at a level of reasonable and reliable sufficiency so that no one might be tempted to encroach on the security of the USSR and our allies.

By this action, and by all our activities in favor of demilitarizing international relations, we wish to draw the attention of the international community to yet another pressing problem—the problem of transition from the economy of armaments to an economy of disarmament.

Is conversion of military production a realistic idea? I have already had occasion to speak about this. We think that, indeed, it is realistic.

For its part, the Soviet Union is prepared:

- In the framework of our economic reform we are ready to draw up and make public our internal plan of conversion; in the course of 1989 to draw up, as an experiment, conversion plans for two or three defense plants;
- To make public our experience in providing employment for specialists from military industry and in using its equipment, buildings and structures in civilian production.

It is desirable that all states, in the first place major military powers, should submit to the United Nations their national conversion plans.

It would also be useful to set up a group of scientists to undertake a thorough analysis of the problem of conversion as a whole and as applied to individual countries and regions and report to the Secretary-General of the United Nations and, subsequently, to have this matter considered at a session of the General Assembly.

IV

And finally, since I am here on American soil, and also for other obvious reasons, I have to turn to the subject of our relations with this great country. I had a chance to appreciate the full measure of its hospitality during my memorable visit to Washington exactly a year ago....

... [I]n the last few years the entire world could breath a sigh of relief thanks to the changes for the better in the substance and the atmosphere of the relationship between Moscow and Washington.

No one intends to underestimate the seriousness of our differences and the toughness of outstanding problems. We have however, already graduated from the primary school of learning to understand each other and seek solutions in both our own and common interests.

The USSR and the United States have built the largest nuclear and missile arsenals. But it is those two countries that, having become specifically aware of their responsibility, were the first to conclude a treaty on the reduction and physical elimination of a portion of these armaments which posed a threat to both of them and to all others.

Both countries possess the greatest and the most sophisticated military secrets. But it is those two countries that have laid a basis for and are further developing a system of mutual verification both of the elimination of armaments and of the reduction and prohibition of their production.

It is those two countries that are accumulating the experience for future bilateral and multilateral agreements.

We value this. We acknowledge and appreciate the contribution made by President Ronald Reagan and by the members of his administration, particularly Mr. George Shultz.

All this is our joint investment in a venture of historic importance. We must not lose this investment, or leave it idle.

The next U.S. Administration headed by President-elect George Bush will find in us a partner who is ready—without long pauses or backtracking—to continue the dialogue in a spirit of realism, openness and goodwill, with a willingness to achieve concrete results working on the agenda which covers the main issues of Soviet-U.S. relations and world politics.

I have in mind, above all:

- Consistent movement toward a treaty on 50 percent reductions in strategic offensive arms while preserving the ABM Treaty;
- Working out a convention on the elimination of chemical weapons— here, as we see it, prerequisites exist to make 1989 a decisive year;
- And negotiations on the reduction of conventional arms and armed forces in Europe.

We also have in mind economic, environmental and humanistic problems in their broadest sense. . . .

I am concluding my first address to the United Nations with the same feeling that I had when I began it—a feeling of responsibility to my own people and to the world community.

We are meeting at the end of a year which has meant so much for the United Nations and on the eve of a year from which we all expect so much.

I would like to believe that our hopes will be matched by our joint effort to put an end to an era of wars, confrontation and regional conflicts, to aggressions against nature, to the terror of hunger and poverty as well as to political terrorism.

This is our common goal and we can only reach it together.

Thank you.

INTERAGENCY REPORT
ON FOREST-FIRE POLICY
December 14, 1988

The 1988 fire season was severe in the western United States, where many areas experienced their driest summer in more than a century. Fires caused by lightning or the handiwork of man blackened, sometimes destroyed, extensive swaths of forest lands throughout the West. An extraordinary fire situation in and around Yellowstone National Park became a focal point of public concern and for criticism of government agencies in charge of firefighting on public lands. In that area, 249 summer fires burned more than one million acres of forest, most of which was in Yellowstone itself.

This burning of America's oldest and perhaps best-known national park was witnessed by millions of people worldwide in televised news reports. There were anguished responses from the viewers, often directed at what appeared to be inadequate efforts by the government to contain the fires. From people living in some communities near the park who were or felt threatened by the flames, there were cries of outrage—sometimes repeated by state officials and in Congress—over what they termed the "let-burn" policy of the National Park Service and National Forest Service.

Political heat from the fire reached high into the departments of Agriculture and Interior, which oversee the forest and park services, respectively. The secretaries of Agriculture and Interior on September 28 appointed a ten-member Fire Management Policy Review Team representing both services to review the fire-management policies currently in place in national parks and wilderness areas and recommend what, if any, changes, were needed.

The review team issued a report December 14 saying that "the objectives of policies governing prescribed natural fire programs are sound, but the policies themselves need to be refined, strengthened and reaffirmed." These policies, it explained, "permit fires to burn under predetermined conditions." With this recommendation, the review team backed the prevailing belief among environmentalists that in some situations fires may have a beneficial effect.

This thinking came to be accepted by the National Park Service gradually over several decades, extending from the 1950s into the 1970s. It reversed a long-standing policy of exterminating forest fires in all situations and in all conditions—as exemplified by the fire-fighting symbol, Smokey the Bear, who admonished everyone to extinguish their fires and cigarettes with care in the woods.

After a period of sixty days for public comments to be filed, the report was destined to undergo further review in both the Agriculture and Interior departments. Charles Philpot, a coleader of the review team, said at a news conference on December 15 that he did not expect the review to be completed before the next fire season began in the West in May or June 1989.

Spokesmen for environmental groups generally spoke favorably of the report. Paul C. Pritchard, president of the National Parks and Conservation Association, a nongovernmental group, said, "We are pleased they found the fire policy to be sound." George T. Frampton, Jr., president of the Wilderness Society, said the report was "sound and well reasoned."

However, Sen. Steve Symms, R-Idaho, was quoted as saying: "Agencies tend to cover their backsides. I doubt the public will be as gentle with the 'let burn' policy as the review team was." Other criticism of the policy had been voiced by Alan Simpson and Malcolm Wallop, Republican senators from Wyoming, is which much of Yellowstone is situated.

> *Following are excerpts from the Fire Management Policy Review Team's "Report on Fire Management Policy," issued December 14, 1988:*

The Fire Management Policy Review Team finds that:

- The objectives of policies governing prescribed natural fire programs in national parks and wildernesses are sound, but the policies need to be refined, strengthened, and reaffirmed. These policies permit fires to burn under predetermined conditions.
- Many current fire management plans do not meet current policies; the prescriptions in them are inadequate; and decision-making needs to be tightened.
- There are risks inherent in trying to manage fire, but they can be reduced by careful planning and preparation. Use of planned burning

and other efforts to reduce hazard fuels near high value structures and to create fire breaks along boundaries help to reduce risks from both prescribed natural fires and wildfires.

- The ecological effects of prescribed natural fire support resource objectives in parks and wilderness, but in some cases the social and economic effects may be unacceptable. Prescribed natural fires may affect permitted uses of parks and wilderness, such as recreation, and impact outside areas through such phenomena as smoke and stream sedimentation.
- Dissemination of information before and during prescribed natural fires needs to be improved. There needs to be greater public participation in the development of fire management plans.
- Internal management processes, such as training more personnel, developing uniform terminology, and utilizing similar budget structures, would significantly improve fire management.
- Claims were heard that some managers support "naturalness" above all else, allowing fires to burn outside of prescription requirements without appropriate suppression actions.

The Team recommends that:

- Prescribed natural fire policies in the agencies be reaffirmed and strengthened.
- Fire management plans be reviewed to assure that current policy requirements are met and expanded to include interagency planning, stronger prescriptions, and additional decision criteria.
- Line officers certify daily that adequate resources are available to ensure that prescribed fires will remain within prescription, given reasonably foreseeable weather conditions and fire behavior.
- Agencies develop regional and national contingency plans to constrain prescribed fires under extreme conditions.
- Agencies consider opportunities to use planned ignitions to complement prescribed natural fire programs and to reduce hazard fuels.
- Agencies utilize the National Environmental Policy Act requirements in fire management planning to increase opportunities for public involvement and coordination with state and local government.
- Agencies provide more and better training to assure an adequate supply of knowledgeable personnel for fire management programs.
- Agencies review funding methods for prescribed fire programs and fire suppression to improve interagency program effectiveness.
- Additional reseach and analysis relating to weather, fire behavior, fire history, fire information integration, and other topics be carried out so that future fire management programs can be carried out more effectively and with less risk.
- Allegations of misuse of policy be promptly investigated and acted upon as may be appropriate.

Concerns and Views

As stated in the Team's charter, "the objective of the review process is to determine the appropriate fire policies for national parks and wildernesses which addresses the concerns expressed by citizens and public officials about the management of fires on these lands as a result of the Yellowstone fire situation."

To gather information about those concerns, individual members of the team, assisted by representatives of the National Fire Protection Association, the Western Governors Association, and the academic community, met with or called a number of knowledgeable persons, including governors, local government officials, concessioners and outfitters, individuals with businesses in nearby communities, organizations with an interest in parks and wildernesses, academicians, and others. The Team also reviewed letters, summaries of correspondence, and many newspaper and journal articles related to fire management policy.

Policy Options

Fire management policy options range from immediate control of all fires to allowing all wildland fires to burn. The team considered the full range following its discussion with interested parties and agency personnel.

The great majority of comment from knowledgeable people indicated support for the careful use of prescribed burns and prescribed natural fires, in accordance with publicly reviewed management plans. There was also general agreement that such policy must be executed in ways that give the fullest possible assurance that human lives and property or special resources will not be lost or seriously impaired.

Federal Fire Policies

Traditionally, the fire policies of Federal land management agencies were to control all wildland fires as promptly as possible. When initial attack failed in controlling a fire the first day, personnel and equipment were organized to control the fire by 10:00 a.m. the succeeding day. . . .

Following prescribed burning experience in the Everglades in the 1950's, the National Park Service began to change its fire suppression and prescribed burning policies in 1968 to accept a more natural role of fire in park ecosystems. Lightning-caused fires were allowed to burn under specified conditions in Sequoia-Kings Canyon National Parks that year, followed by a similar program in another 7 parks between 1968 and 1972. In the decade that followed, another 26 parks began some parts of the prescribed fire program. . . .

The purpose for this policy change was to restore fire to a more natural ecological role. "Naturalness" is defined as those dynamic processes and components which would likely exist today, and go on functioning, if technological humankind had not altered them. . . .

No ecosystem today is totally unaltered by technological humankind. However, extensive areas in which the achievement and maintenance of naturalness is a basic purpose are increasingly important to humankind. These areas are found primarily in national parks and wildernesses. They serve as invaluable scientific benchmarks; and the uniqueness imparted by their natural qualities is irreplaceable as a source of human inspiration and enjoyment. Those natural qualities differ in each area. They are compromised by the effects of necessary and appropriate provisions for enjoyment of parks, the impacts of other uses under legislative mandates governing non-park wilderness and by potential adverse impacts outside of unit boundaries. Each unit in its management plan describes how it will attain the objective of naturalness.

In those parks and wildernesses where fire has been a historic component of the environment, it is critical to management objectives to continue that influence. An attempt to exclude fire from these lands leads to major unnatural changes in vegetation and wildlife from that which would occur without fire suppression, as well as creating fuel accumulation that can lead to uncontrollable, sometimes very damaging, wildfire. Current fire management policy allows for inclusion of naturally occurring fire on these lands, to the extent possible, as well as the use of prescribed burns to bring these areas back into a more natural condition of fire hazard and occurrence, and to reduce the risk of damage from fire to improvements within these areas and to improvements and resources on adjacent lands.

Lightning fires are permitted to burn in designated zones within 46 areas managed by the National Park Service. Nearly 58 million acres of national parks are classified natural fire zones, including 50 million acres in Alaska alone. A total of 58 national park areas use human-ignited prescribed burns to simulate the role of natural fire in certain ecosystems.

The USDA Forest Service also began allowing lightning-caused fires to play a more natural role in wilderness in 1972, when exceptions to the policy of suppressing all fires were approved by the Chief. By 1976, policy exceptions allowing lightning-caused fires to burn under carefully prescribed conditions had been put into effect in parts of the Selway-Bitterroot, Gila, and Teton wildernesses of Idaho, New Mexico and Wyoming.

In 1978, authority to approve wilderness fire management plans was delegated to Regional Foresters as part of a revised policy that called for "fire management programs" as contrasted with previous "fire control programs." This revision—which is current policy—provided for "well-planned and executed fire protection and fire use programs that are cost effective and responsive to land and resource management goals and objectives."

Forest Service wilderness fire management policy was again revised in 1985, following public review and comment, clarifying wilderness fire management objectives and the use of prescribed fire within wilderness. Forest Service ignited prescribed fires were authorized when necessary to meet the objectives of (1) allowing lightning fires to play their natural role to the extent possible and (2) reducing the risk of wildfire within wilderness to life and property, and to life, property, and resources outside of wilderness to an acceptable level.

The Bureau of Land Management uses prescribed fire extensively to meet resource and fire management objectives. However, the use is almost exclusively through planned ignitions. Prescribed natural fire is generally not used due to the predominance of fuel types having a high rate of spread (i.e. grass and brush) commonly found on Bureau-administered lands. . . .

Results in National Parks

Since the beginning of these programs in 1968 until 1987, more than 1600 lightning-caused fires have been permitted to burn more than 320,000 acres of national park land. Only one serious problem had developed—the Ouzel Fire on the Rocky Mountain National Park which threatened the adjacent community of Allens Park, Colorado. At the same time, more than 1400 prescribed burns were ignited by the park staff in 46 national park areas that covered more than 325,000 acres. The burns were designed mainly to manage vegetation by simulating the natural role of fire in reducing fuel accumulations in order to modify plant succession and to help maintain ecosystem processes. Some of the benchmark fire management programs in national parks are those found in Sequoia-Kings Canyon and Yosemite National Parks in the Sierra Nevada, the Everglades National Park in Florida and Yellowstone and Grand Teton National Parks in the Rockies.

Results in National Forest Wilderness

Since 1972 when the USDA Forest Service began permitting lightning-caused fires to play a more natural role in wilderness, 503 prescribed natural fires have burned nearly 210,000 acres within wilderness areas in the Northern and Intermountain Regions, the Forest Service Regions having the most active prescribed natural fire management programs. Of these fires, 23 became wildfires burning an additional 544,000 acres (14 of these escaped prescribed natural fires occurred in 1988). Four prescribed fires, burning 4,424 acres, have been ignited by the Forest Service in three different wilderness areas since management ignitions were permitted in 1985. . . .

ANGOLA-NAMIBIA PEACE ACCORD
December 22, 1988

Foreign ministers of Angola, Cuba, and South Africa met at the United Nations in New York on December 22 and signed a peace accord calling for the withdrawal of Soviet-backed Cuban forces from Angola and independence for Angola's next-door neighbor, South African-controlled Namibia—the last colony in Africa. The ceremony concluded eight years of on-again, off-again negotiations that had been moderated by the United States.

The three signatory nations had agreed in principle on main points of the accord in July and then to the final details at a meeting of the foreign ministers December 13 in Brazzaville, Congo. The formal signing followed, fittingly, at the United Nations, which was to assume a large role in seeing that the accord's provisions were carried out.

The agreement set a timetable for Cuban troop withdrawal and Namibian independence but left unresolved the thirteen-year conflict between the Marxist Angolan government and Jonas Savimbi's U.S.-supported insurgency. The Angolan civil war, according to UN estimates, had left 60,000 people dead and 750,000 homeless.

Savimbi in 1966 established the National Union for Total Independence of Angola (known by its Portuguese initials as UNITA), to overthrow Portugal's colonial rule. Since then his organization had gained control over much of Angolan territory and the support of at least half of the people. Angola became independent of Portugal in 1975, and called in Cuban troops to prop up the Marxist government.

Economic Necessity for Peace

Assistant Secretary of State Chester Crocker, the architect of the agreement, contended that the Reagan administration's efforts to link Namibian independence to the withdrawal of Cuban troops from Angola provided both sides with an incentive to negotiate a settlement.

The cost of pursuing a military solution to the regional conflict became intolerable for all parties concerned. War-torn Angola ran up huge foreign debts despite assistance from the Soviet Union, which became less inclined to continue with its support. South Africa, plagued by U.S. economic sanctions in response to its apartheid policies, was forced to make budget cuts and reduce its outlays in Namibia. South Africa's control of Namibia had increasingly been challenged by guerrilla forces operating from across the Angolan border.

Namibia, once known as South-West Africa, was a former German colony administered by South Africa under a League of Nations mandate after Germany's defeat in World War I. A United Nations trusteeship replaced the mandate in 1946 but South Africa defied the UN and remained in control. In 1966 the South-West Africa People's Organization (SWAPO) began a guerrilla war of independence.

SWAPO supporters were expected to win a majority of seats in the national legislature in elections scheduled by the peace agreement for November 1, 1989. Nevertheless, Namibia would have no choice but to remain dependent on South African industry and trade. Presumably, from South Africa's standpoint, continued access to Namibian resources and its deep-water port at Walvis Bay was worth the price of granting Namibia its independence.

United Nations Peacekeeping Role

The accord accepted UN Resolution 435, approved by the Security Council in 1978, as the basis for a cease-fire, the phased withdrawal of Cuban troops, and the timetable for Namibian independence. A UN mission was destined to be established by April 1, 1989, to see that the accord was carried out. A peace-keeping force of 9,400 soldiers and civilians was to be assembled by the United Nations to safeguard the integrity of the election in Namibia.

Assuming that Namibian independence moved forward as scheduled, all Cuban troops would leave Angola by mid-1991. The first contingent left early in January 1989; 3,000 more were due to depart by April 1, 1989 and 25,000 by the following November 1.

Following are excerpts from the "Agreement Among the People's Republic of Angola, the Republic of Cuba, and the Republic of South Africa," signed at the United Nations in New York, December 22, 1988:

The government of the People's Republic of Angola, the Republic of Cuba, and the Republic of South Africa. . . .

Affirming the sovereignty, sovereign equality, and independence of all states of southwestern Africa,

Affirming the principle of non-interference in the internal affairs of states,

Affirming the principle of abstention from the threat of use of force against the territorial integrity or political independence of states,

Reaffirming the right of the peoples of the southwestern region of Africa to self-determination, independence, and equality of rights, and of the states of southwestern Africa to peace, development, and social progress,

Urging African and international cooperation for the settlement of the problems of the development of the southwestern region of Africa,

Expressing their appreciation for the mediating role of the Government of the United States of America,

Desiring to contribute to the establishment of peace and security in southwestern Africa,

Agree to the provisions set forth below.

(1) The Parties shall immediately request the Secretary-General of the United Nations to seek authority from the Security Council to commence implementation of UNSCR 435/78 on 1 April 1989.

(2) All military forces of the Republic of South Africa shall depart Namibia in accordance with UNSCR 435/78.

(3) Consistent with the provisions of UNSCR 435/78, the Republic of South Africa and the People's Republic of Angola shall cooperate with the Secretary-General to ensure the independence of Namibia through free and fair elections and shall abstain from any action that could prevent the execution of UNSCR 435/78. The Parties shall respect the territorial integrity and inviolability of borders of Namibia and shall ensure that their territories are not used by any state, organization, or person in connection with acts of war, aggression, or violence against the territorial integrity or inviolability of borders of Namibia or any other action which could prevent the execution of UNSCR 435/78.

(4) The People's Republic of Angola and the Republic of Cuba shall implement the bilateral agreement, signed on the date of signature of this agreement, providing for the redeployment toward the North and the staged and total withdrawal of Cuban troops from the territory of the People's Republic of Angola, and the arrangements made with the Security Council of the United Nations for the on-site verification of that withdrawal.

(5) Consistent with their obligations under the Charter of the United Nations, the Parties shall refrain from the threat or use of force, and shall ensure that their respective territories are not used by any state, organization, or person in connection with any acts of war, aggression, or violence, against the territorial integrity, inviolability

of borders, or independence of any state of southwestern Africa.

(6) The Parties shall respect the principle of non-interference in the internal affairs of the states of southwestern Africa.

(7) The Parties shall comply in good faith with all obligations undertaken in this agreement and shall resolve through negotiation and in a spirit of cooperation any disputes with respect to the interpretation or implementation thereof.

(8) This agreement shall enter into force upon signature. . . .

DEFENSE PANEL'S PROPOSALS TO CLOSE MILITARY BASES

December 29, 1988

Closing unneeded military bases has long been a politically sensitive matter in Congress. The bases often are the economic lifeblood of nearby communities. For a decade, the lawmakers were unwilling to decide which bases should go. Then in 1988 they approved a Defense Department plan to let a blue-ribbon commission of outsiders make the selections. Congress, distancing itself from the selections, could then approve or reject the entire list but not individual bases.

Secretary of Defense Frank C. Carlucci named the twelve-member Defense Secretary's Commission on Base Realignment and Closure on May 3, and the panel presented its report to him on December 29. He approved its recommendations before he left office and Congress had forty-five days, beginning March 1, 1989, to act on them. Former representative Dick Cheney, R-Wyo., succeeded Carlucci on March 17.

Despite protests by some lawmakers from states in which bases were recommended for closing, senior members of the House and Senate armed services committees predicted that Congress would approve the list—or rather take no action and let it become official. Observers noted that lawmakers in the states left untouched by the "hit list" were relieved—and apparently willing to close the selected bases to help protect their own from being shut down. They and other members were under Congress's own mandate to balance the federal budget in the years ahead.

The commission recommended that eighty-six army, navy, and air force installations be shut down, and that five others be closed in part, beginning in 1990. Affected military activities would be moved to fifty-

four other bases. The commission calculated that the measures would save the government $5.6 billion over the next twenty years. Some 58,500 military and civilian jobs at the bases would be eliminated, the report added, but 37,850 new jobs would be created to care for reassigned duties.

"While cost reduction was an important reason for its chartering," the report said, "the Commission decided that the military value of a base should be the preeminent factor in making its decisions." It added that "many bases experienced an erosion of their military value as a result of urban development." Increasingly, urban encroachments had constrained certain training activities, which increasingly require larger and larger tracts of land.

"Modern tactical doctrine, taking advantage of vastly improved equipment capabilities, calls for greatly increased mobility for the operational units of all [armed] services," the report explained. It added that, for instance, an army mechanized battalion needs more than 80,000 acres to practice standard maneuvers, whereas its World War II predecessor required fewer than 4,000 acres.

On the closing list were several installations in or near urban areas that had served generations of soldiers. The Presidio, which long guarded the entrance to San Francisco Bay, was earmarked for closure. In recent years it became headquarters for the Sixth Army and the site of Letterman Army Medical Center. Similarly, all of Fort Sheridan in Chicago except for certain reserve-support facilities would be closed. The closure list included five air force bases, three—George, Mather, and Norton—in California. The Brooklyn (New York) Naval Station would be closed and its operations transfered to nearby Staten Island.

Fort Dix, New Jersey, would cease to be an infantry-training center and would go on "semi-active" status. Fort Meade, Maryland, noted as a weapons-testing site, would lose 9,000 acres and become an administrative center for several military activities in the Washington, D.C., area. In contrast to places like Forts Dix and Meade, many of the installations on the closure list were quite small. One of them, Fort Douglas, was enclosed by the University of Utah campus. Another, called Nike Kansas City 30, consisted of two barracks, a mess hall, and an administrative building.

The commission was composed of businessmen, retired military officers, and former government officals. Its chairmen were Abraham Ribicoff, a former Democratic senator from Connecticut who had served as the state's governor, and Jack Edwards, a former Republican representative from Alabama who was identified with defense issues in Congress.

Following is the Executive Summary from the commission report, "Base Realignments and Closures," presented December 29, 1988 to Secretary of Defense Frank C. Carlucci:

Executive Summary

The Defense Secretary's Commission on Base Realignment and Closure was chartered on May 3, 1988 to recommend military installations within the United States, its commonwealths, territories, and possessions for realignment and closure. The Congress and the President subsequently endorsed this approach through legislation that removed some of the previous impediments to successful base-closure actions.

For over a decade, the Department of Defense has been unable to improve the effectiveness of the military base structure or to realize the significant savings that might have been gained through the realignment and closure of unnecessary or underutilized military bases. This situation is largely the result of 1977 legislation that mandated Congressional approval for any closure affecting 300 or more civilian employees of the Department. In this same legislation, the Department was expressly directed to comply with the procedural requirements of the National Environmental Policy Act for all base-closure decisions.

Despite the absence of closure actions, there is general agreement within the government that the national defense could be improved, and its cost reduced, through a more efficient military base structure. This conclusion was endorsed in 1983 by the President's Private Sector Survey on Cost Control (the Grace Commission), which recommended that a non-partisan, independent commission be established to study the base-closure issue. The Defense Secretary's Commission on Base Realignment and Closure was chartered in the spirit of that recommendation.

This Commission's recommendations for closure and realignment affect 145 installations. Of this number, 86 are to be closed fully, five are to be closed in part, and 54 will experience a change, either an increase or a decrease, as units and activities are relocated. The Commission also makes several additional recommendations that address potential problems in implementing the Commission's closure and realignment recommendations and certain other matters that the Commission has discovered during its review of the military base structure.

From the outset, the Commission sought the most appropriate criteria to govern the nomination of installations for realignment or closure. While cost reduction was an important reason for its chartering, the Commission decided that the military value of a base should be the preeminent factor in making its decisions. With a primary focus on military value and improving the overall military base structure, the Commission elected not to set savings targets. Nevertheless, the Commission estimates the realignment and closure actions recommended in this report should lead to annual savings of $693.6 million and a 20-year savings with a net present value of $5.6 billion.

The Commission's analysis of military installations began with a review of the military force structure and its basing requirements. Representative of the kinds of installation characteristics mandated by force structure are availability of acreage and airspace for realistic combat training and provisions for survivability of strategic forces.

The Commission found that many bases have experienced an erosion of their military value as a result of urban development. The resulting encroachment has forced the modification of missions at many installations. The acquisition of additional land, especially in less populated areas, may be needed to satisfy military requirements.

After a review of the general condition of the military base structure, the Commission began the process of selecting bases for realignment and closure. The data supporting this process were provided by the Services and validated by the Commission and its staff. Installations with similar missions were grouped together to facilitate consistent analysis. The bases were then screened to determine whether the installations were appropriately sized to support current or future requirements and whether their physical attributes were appropriate to accomplish assigned missions.

When it was determined that an installation's mission was impaired, the Commission looked at relocation alternatives. This review focused on the ability of a receiving installation to accommodate and enhance the mission of the units or activities being relocated and whether the costs of the closure and realignment package could be paid back with savings in six years.

As realignment or closure candidates were identified, the Commission took an initial look at environmental impacts. This review was not intended to be a substitute for the environmental analysis required by the Congress during actual implementation of the approved base realignments and closures. As a result of this review, the Commission found that closures generally resulted in positive impacts on the environment rather than negative ones. As individual realignment and closure actions are taken by the Secretary of Defense, full opportunity for public hearings will, of course, be provided.

Besides environmental issues, the public will also be concerned about the economic impact of base closures. The Commission reviewed the history of base closures since 1961 and found that closures were generally less traumatic than people anticipated. In many cases, Defense Department jobs have been replaced by new civilian jobs, and the bases themselves converted to civilian uses. Notwithstanding this record of success, the Commission has recommended to the Secretary of Defense several actions that should be taken to aid local communities in their redevelopment planning.

As a final task, the Commission considered the process for realigning and closing bases in the future, which will be necessary as military strategy and force structure change.

CUMULATIVE INDEX, 1984-1988

A

Abortion. *See also Birth control*
Democratic Party Platform on, 550, 608 (1984)
Presidential Debates on, 861-865 (1984); 722, 723, 736-738, 766-767 (1988)
Reagan Remarks to Right-to-Life Marchers, 53-56 (1985)
Republican Party Platform on, 662, 663, 706 (1984); 642 (1988)
State of the Union, 91-92 (1984); 65 (1988)
Supreme Court Decisions, 559-580 (1986)

Acquired immune deficiency syndrome (AIDS)
AMA Report, 817-832 (1987)
Center for Disease Control Report on AIDS in the Workplace, 733-747 (1985)
Democratic Party Platform on, 564 (1988)
FDA Approval of AZT (azidothymidine), 327-330 (1987)
Institute of Medicine Report, 887-908 (1986)
PHS Report on Aids Education, 319-326 (1987)
Presidential Commission Report, 415-446 (1988)
Presidential Debates on, 730-731 (1988)
Reagan's Budget Message, 9 (1987); 150, 155 (1988)
Republican Party Platform on, 638 (1988)
Supreme Court on Victims of Contagious Disease, 245-252 (1987)
Urban League Report, 55-58 (1987)

Adoption
Republican Party Platform on, 635-636 (1988)

Affirmative action
Black America Report, 58 (1987)
Democratic Party Platform on, 551, 606 (1984)
Kerner Report Updated, 189-190, 193 (1988)

Supreme Court Decisions, 365-385 (1984); 651-678 (1986); 331-349 (1987)

Afghanistan
Negotiated Settlement Agreements, 257-266 (1988)
Reagan-Gorbachev Summit Meeting, 991, 993 (1987); 356, 358, 361 (1988)
State of the Union, 66 (1988)
UN Report on Human Rights, 919-936 (1986)

Africa. *See also specific countries*
Democratic Party Platform on, 641-642 (1984); 568 (1988)
Natural Disasters Report, 973-995 (1984)
Pope John Paul II's Trip, 499-514 (1985)
Republican Party Platform on, 714-715 (1984); 685-686 (1988)

Aged. *See also Medicaid and Medicare*
Democratic Party Platform on, 614-616 (1984)
Economic Advisers' Report, 99-101 (1985)
Republican Party Platform on, 696 (1984); 639-640 (1988)
Supreme Court Decision on Mandatory Retirement, 397-407 (1985)

Agrava, Corazon J., 925-932 (1984)

Agriculture. *See also Food supply*
Bishops' Report on Economic Justice, 1002-1005 (1986)
Democratic Party Platform on, 589-591 (1984); 564-565 (1988)
Economic Report, 142-143 (1984); 124, 126-127 (1987)
Gorbachev at 27th Party Congress, 146, 156-157 (1986)
Natural Disasters Report, 973-995 (1984)
OTA Report on Biotechnology, 287-306 (1986)
Presidential Debates on, 751-752 (1988)
Reagan on Farm Subsidies, 10, 526 (1987); 393 (1988)
Reagan's Budget Message, 10 (1987); 157 (1988)
Republican Party Platform on, 673-679

(1984); 660-664 (1988)
Vice Presidential Debate on, 812-813 (1988)
Sweden's Farm-Animal Rights Law, 347-351 (1988)
Aguilar v. Felton, 433-461 (1985)
Aid to Families with Dependent Children (AFDC)
Kerner Report Updated, 189, 193 (1988)
Revision of Welfare System, 847-852 (1988)
AIDS. *See Acquired immune deficiency syndrome*
Air pollution. *See Pollution*
Airline deregulation. *See also Regulatory reform; Transportation*
Aviation Safety Report, 267-276 (1988)
Economic Advisers' Report, 85-87 (1986); 118, 144-148 (1988)
GAO Report on Air Traffic Safety, 253-266 (1986)
President's Commission on Privatization Report, 233 (1988)
State of the Union Address, 60 (1986)
Ake v. Oklahoma, 207-209 (1985)
Albania
Enver Hoxa death, 325-331 (1985)
Alcoholism. *See also Drug abuse*
Mental Health Report, 833-843 (1984)
Report on Black and Minority Health, 686-687, 698-702 (1985)
Supreme Court on Alcoholism and Veterans' Benefits, 277-285 (1988)
Alfonsin, Raul, 789-791 (1984)
Alzheimer's disease
OTA Report, 391-406 (1987)
Amendments, Constitutional. *See Constitution, U.S.*
American Bar Association
Legal Professionalism Report, 767-778 (1986)
Tort Reform Recommendations, 165-181 (1987)
American Indians. *See Indians, American*
American Iron and Steel Institute v. Natural Resources Defense Council, 427-437 (1984)
American Medical Association
AIDS Report, 817-832 (1987)
Proposed Boxing Ban, 1019-1021 (1984)
American Psychiatric Association, 834 (1984)
Americas Watch Nicaragua Reports, 255-269 (1985)
Amnesty International's Human Rights Report, 883-889 (1988)
Amundsen, Roald, 833 (1988)
Andropov, Yuri V., 145-154 (1984)
Angola
Angola-Namibia Peace Accord, 947-950 (1988)
Antitrust
Supreme Court Decision, 413-426 (1984)

Aquino, Benigno S., 925-932 (1984)
Aquino, Corazon C.
Philippine Cease-fire Agreement, 1037-1046 (1986)
Philippine Change of Government, 307-314 (1986)
Philippine Coup Attempt Thwarted, 843-854 (1987)
Arab states. *See Middle East*
Arafat, Yasir, 905, 907-908 (1988)
Arctic Expedition of 1909
Peary's Polar Notes, 831-833 (1988)
Argentina
Disappeared Persons, 789-793 (1984)
Human Rights Report, 157-158 (1984); 148-149 (1985); 98-100 (1988)
IMF-World Bank Conference, 796-797 (1984)
Arias Sánchez, Oscar
Central American Peace Agreement, 637-648 (1987); 241-243 (1988)
Nobel Peace Prize Speech, 1007-1011 (1987)
Armed forces. *See also Defense Department; Military draft; Veterans*
Interment of Unknown Vietnam Serviceman, 347-352 (1984)
Joint Chiefs of Staff Reorganization, 681, 684-685 (1986)
Pentagon Report on Sexual Harassment, 671-679 (1987)
Republican Party Platform on, 720-723 (1984); 697 (1988)
State of the Union, 86, 87, 92-93 (1984)
Supreme Court on Student Aid/Draft Registration, 493-503 (1984)
Weinberger on Use of Military Force, 1005-1015 (1984)
Arms control. *See also Defense; Intermediate-range Nuclear Forces; Space; Strategic Arms Limitation Treaty; Strategic Arms Reduction Talks; Strategic Defense Initiative*
ABM Treaty Interpretation, 289-317 (1987); 330 (1988)
Bishops on U.S. Economy, 957-972 (1984)
Chernenko Interview, 917-923 (1984)
Democratic Party Platform on, 550-551, 627-630 (1984); 566-567 (1988)
Former Security Officials' Paper on Defense Strategy, 782-784, 789-790 (1986)
Gorbachev, Mikhail S.
27th Party Congress Address, 163-166 (1986)
U.S.-Soviet INF Treaty Statement, 945, 947-950 (1987)
Presidential Debates on, 847, 893, 895-897, 899-900 (1984)
Reagan, Ronald
United Nations Address, 811-829 (1984)
U.S.-Soviet INF Treaty Statement, 945, 947-950 (1987)

Reagan-Gorbachev New Year's Messages, 3-8 (1986)
Reagan-Gorbachev Summit Meetings (Geneva), 749-761 (1985) (Moscow), 353-373 (1988) (Reykjavik), 875-885 (1986) (Washington, D.C.), 995-999 (1987)
Republican Party Platform on, 719-720 (1984); 692-693 (1988)
Scientists/OTA on Star Wars Defense, 257-272 (1984)
State of the Union, 114-115 (1985); 46-47 (1986); 57-58, 67 (1988)
U.S.-Soviet INF Treaty, 945-989 (1987); 57-58, 67 (1988)

Arts and humanities
China/U.S. Accords, 296-298 (1984)
Democratic Party Platform on, 573-574 (1984)
Humanities Education Report, 992-1003 (1984); 681-696 (1987)
Republican Party Platform on, 653 (1988)
State of the Humanities Report, 517-527 (1988)

Asians
Alcoholism and, 701-702 (1985)
California Vote on English as Official Language, 959 (1986)

Assassinations and attempts
Aquino, Benigno S., 925-932 (1984)
CIA Manual, 903-916 (1984)
Gandhi, Indira, 945-949 (1984)

Association for Supervision and Curriculum Development (ASCD), 597-608 (1987)
Association of American Colleges, 127-144 (1985)
Attorneys. *See also American Bar Association*
ABA Commission on Legal Profession, 767-778 (1986)
Supreme Court on Independent Counsel, 465-478 (1988)

Austria
Pope John Paul's Visit, 405-414 (1988)
Waldheim's Inaugural Address, 743-750 (1986)

Aviation Safety Commission Report, 267-276 (1988)

B

Baby M, In Matter of, 373-387 (1987); 71-80 (1988)
Baker, James A., III, 643-652 (1985)
Balanced Budget and Emergency Deficit Control Act. *See Gramm-Rudman-Hollings Act*
Baldus, David C., 464-476 (1987)
Bankruptcy
Supreme Court Decision on Bankruptcy Law, 181-198 (1984)
Banks and banking. *See also Credit; Stocks*

Economic Advisers' Report, 90-91 (1985); 89-91 (1986)
IMF-World Bank Conference, 643-652 (1985)
Savings and Loan Crisis, 913-918 (1988)
Barbie, Klaus, 517-524 (1987)
Barnes, Fred, 848-876 (1984)
Barnes, Michael D., D-Md., 558 (1988)
Batson v. Kentucky, 409-433 (1986)
Belgium
Pope John Paul II's Visit, 365, 374-376 (1985)
Belize
Kissinger Commission Report, 32, 36, 42 (1984)
Bender Foundation, 507-509 (1988)
Bennett, William J., 997-1003 (1984)
Assessing American Education, 297-306 (1988)
Elementary Education Report, 803-817 (1986)
Teaching and Learning Report, 217-238 (1986)
Bentsen, Lloyd, D-Texas
Acceptance Speech, 533, 542-546 (1988)
Presidential Debates on, 750-751 (1988)
Vice Presidential Debate, 799-829 (1988)
Berlin Wall Anniversary, 791-799 (1986)
Bernadin, Joseph, 910 (1986)
Bernardéz, Torres, 341-344 (1984)
Betamax case, 53-80 (1984)
Bethel School District v. Fraser, 731-742 (1986)
Biaggi, Mario, D-N.Y., 498-499 (1988)
Bingaman, Jeff, D-N.M., 850, 853-856 (1986)
Bioethics. *See also Ethics*
Life-sustaining Measures, 275-285 (1984)
New Jersey Court on Surrogates, 71-80 (1988)
OTA Reports on Biotechnology, 351-372 (1987)
Rights of Surrogates, 373-387 (1987)
Vatican Report, 267-287 (1987)
Birth control. *See also Abortion*
Pope John Paul II on, 363 (1985); 25, 35-37 (1986); 170 (1988)
Population Institute Report, 439-462 (1987)
Report on Teenage Pregnancy, 1057-1064 (1986)
Vatican on Bioethics, 267-287 (1987)
World Population Problems, 521-547 (1984)
Blackmun, Harry A.
Abortion, 561, 562-571 (1986)
Alcoholism and Veterans' Benefits, 279, 284-285 (1988)
Exclusionary Rule, 507, 514-515 (1984)
Federal and State Powers, 167-187 (1985)
Labor Union Membership, 415-429 (1985)
Mandatory Budget Cuts, 707, 728-730 (1986)

Nativity Scene, 219, 239 (1984)
Prisoners' Rights, 481 (1984)
Seniority/Affirmative Action, 366, 376-385 (1984)
Sodomy and Privacy, 602-603, 608-614 (1986)
Video Recorders, 54-55, 69-80 (1984)
Blacks. *See also Civil and political rights; Equal opportunity; Minority groups*
Alcoholism, 699-700 (1985)
Democratic Party Platform on, 549, 551, 607-610, 614 (1984)
Diabetes, 702-703 (1985)
Employment
    Economic Advisers' Report, 140 (1988)
    President's Economic Report, 119 (1988)
Kerner Report Updated, 185-194 (1988)
Mental Health Report, 837-838 (1984)
President Botha's Manifesto for the Future, 515-527 (1985)
Report on Black and Minority Health, 685-706 (1985)
South Africa, 99, 102, 369-381 (1986)
Supreme Court Decisions
    Affirmative Action, 365-385 (1984); 651-678 (1986); 331-349 (1987)
    Death Penalty and Race, 463-476 (1987)
Tutu Nobel Prize Speech, 1027-1037 (1984)
Urban League Report, 27-37 (1985); 43-60 (1987)
Block v. Rutherford, 481 (1984)
Boff, Rev. Leonardo, 317, 757 (1986)
Bork, Robert H.
Supreme Court Confirmation Battle, 717-744 (1987)
Bose Corp. v. Consumers Union, 299-312 (1984)
Botha, P. W., 515-527 (1985); 370, 582 (1986)
Bowen, Otis R., 483-484, 1025-1035 (1986); 319-326 (1987)
Bowen v. American Hospital Association, 541-558 (1986)
Bowers v. Hardwick, 601-614 (1986)
Bowman, Isaiah, 832 (1988)
Bowsher v. Synar, 705-730 (1986)
Boyer, Ernest L., 939-958 (1986)
Brady Commission Report, 9-11, 13-33 (1988)
Brazil
Discovery of Mengele, 409-414 (1985)
Presidential Elections, 3-12 (1985)
Brennan, William J., Jr.
Address on Role of Supreme Court, 653-666 (1985)
Adult Theaters, 133-134, 140-144 (1986)
Affirmative Action, 654-676 (1986); 332-333, 335-344 (1987)
Bankruptcy Law, 182-183, 193-199 (1984)
Contagious Diseases, 246-250 (1987)
Creation Science, 566-571 (1987)

Death Penalty and Race, 463, 465, 473-476 (1987)
Disruptive Handicapped Students, 47-56 (1988)
Exclusionary Rule, 506-508, 516-519 (1984)
Labor Union Membership, 415, 424-429 (1985)
Media Libel Law, 252-253 (1984); 364 (1986)
Miranda Rule, 225, 233, 236-250 (1985)
Nativity Scene, 219, 231-239 (1984)
PAC Spending Limits, 279-280, 283-291 (1985)
Public Broadcasting Editorials, 449, 451, 452-461 (1984)
Public School Teachers in Parochial Classes, 433, 436-448, 450-453 (1985)
Secrecy of CIA Sources, 333, 342-344 (1985)
Sex Bias in Education, 202-203, 213-214 (1984)
Sex Discrimination in Commercial Organizations, 467-475 (1984)
Student Newspaper Censorship, 45-46 (1988)
Student Searches, 15, 23-26 (1985)
Students' Free Speech, 739 (1986)
Uncompensated Takings and Land Use, 533-534, 549-553 (1987)
British-Irish Accord on Northern Ireland, 723-732 (1985)
Brokaw, Tom, 806-807, 813-814, 819-820, 826-827 (1988)
Brown, Harold, 781-790 (1986)
Budget, Federal. *See also Gramm-Rudman-Hollings Act; International debt*
Balanced Budget Bill, 803-808 (1985)
CBO/GAO Report on Grace Commission, 169-179 (1984)
Deficit, 53-54 (1986); 124, 126, 128-129 (1988)
Democratic Party Platform on, 559-565 (1984)
Economic Report, 125 (1983); 119-144 (1984); 71-104 (1985); 124-125 (1988)
Economic Summit (London), 355 (1984)
Packard Commission Report on Defense Management, 679-695 (1986)
Presidential Debates on, 849-852, 870-871 (1984); 726-728, 756-758 (1988)
President's Budget Message, 99-117 (1984); 71-78 (1985); 49-58 (1986); 3-15 (1987); 149-163 (1988)
Republican Party Platform on, 669 (1984)
State of the Union, 81, 87-89 (1984); 111-113 (1985); 40, 43-44 (1986); 106, 111 (1987); 58, 61-63 (1988)
Supreme Court on Mandatory Budget Cuts, 705-730 (1986)
Vice Presidential Debate on, 813-814, 825-826 (1988)

Burger, Warren E.
Antitrust Law, 414-422 (1984)
Federal and State Powers, 167-187 (1985)
Legal Professionalism, 767 (1986)
Mandatory Budget Cuts, 706, 708-718 (1986)
Nativity Scene, 217-228 (1984)
Peremptory Challenge, 425-433 (1986)
Prisoners' Rights, 479-485, 488-491 (1984)
Public School Teachers in Parochial Classes, 433-461 (1985)
Resignation, 591-599 (1986)
Secrecy of CIA Sources, 333-342 (1985)
Sex Bias in Education, 202 (1984)
Silent Prayer, 379-395 (1985)
Sodomy and Privacy, 602, 607 (1986)
Student Aid/Draft Registration, 495-500 (1984)
Students' Free Speech, 732, 733-739 (1986)
Use of Deadly Force, 303-315 (1985)
Bush, George
Acceptance Speech, 727-745 (1984); 589-591, 604-613 (1988)
Andropov Death, 145 (1984)
Postelection Statements, 891-904 (1988)
Presidential Debates, 721-783 (1988)
Shultz on Terrorism, 934 (1984)
Transfer of Presidential Power, 491-495 (1985)
Victory Statement, 893-894 (1988)
Business and industry. See also Foreign trade; Minority business; Privatization of government services; Small business
Bhopal Gas Poisoning, 1023-1026 (194); 295-302 (1985)
China-U.S. Accords, 293-294 (1984)
Corporate Management, 971-981 (1986)
Corporate Takeovers, 921-925 (1988)
Democratic Party Platform on, 584-586 (1984)
Donovan Indictment, 803-807 (1984)
President's Commission on Organized Crime, 200-210 (1986)
President's Economic Report, 129, 141-142 (1984); 89-90, 101, 104 (1985); 61, 68, 88-89 (1986)
Supreme Court Decisions
Antitrust Law, 413-416 (1984)
Bankruptcy and Labor, 181-198 (1984)
EPA and Clean Air, 427-437 (1984)
Mandatory Retirement, 397-407 (1985)
Union Membership, 415-429 (1985)
Video Recorders, 53-80 (1984)

C

Cabinet. See Executive branch
Calder and South v. Jones, 247-248, 253-256 (1984)
California
Vote on English as Official Language, 959-962 (1986)

California Federal Savings and Loan v. Guerra, 17-27 (1987)
Cambodia
Human Rights Report, 103-104 (1988)
Cameroon
Disaster Aid Report, 61-77 (1987)
Pope John Paul II's Trip, 500, 504-509 (1985)
Campaign financing. See Government ethics
Canada
Economic Summit, 347-355 (1985); 391-397 (1988)
Pope John Paul II's Visit, 777-787 (1984)
Trade Pact, 571-578 (1988)
Trudeau Farewell, 407-412 (1984)
Cancer
Black and Minority Health Report, 686, 697-698 (1985)
Cigarette Smoking, 1079, 1084-1085 (1986)
Interferon Approval, 481-484 (1986)
Radon Report, 3-8
Capital punishment. See Death penalty
Carlucci, Frank C.
Appointment, 1049 (1986)
Downing of Iranian Airliner, 703-717 (1988)
Military Base Closings, 951-954 (1988)
Carnegie Foundation
Higher Education Report, 583-602 (1985)
Teaching Profession Report, 457-485 (1986)
Undergraduate Colleges Report, 939-958 (1986)
Urban Schools Report, 195-219 (1988)
Carpenter v. United States, 881-889 (1987)
Catholic church. See also Religion
Apostolic Letter on Women, 785-792 (1988)
Bishops on Economic Justice, 983-1011 (1986)
Bishops on U.S. Economy, 957-972 (1984)
Bishops' Report to the Vatican, 571-581 (1985)
Excommunication of Archbishop Lefebvre, 489-494 (1988)
Pope John Paul II's Journeys, 327-338, 399-406, 777-787 (1984); 57-67, 363-376, 499-514 (1985); 23-37, 639-640 (1986); 555-564, 699-716 (1987); 405-414 (1988)
Pope John Paul II's Visit to Rome Synagogue, 339-346 (1986)
Synod of Catholic Bishops, 765-780 (1985)
Theology of Liberation, 759-775 (1984); 317-338, 640-641, 646-649 (1986)
Vatican Disciplining of Father Curran, 757-765 (1986)
Vatican on Bioethics, 267-287 (1987)
Vatican on Pastoral Care of Homosexuals, 909-918 (1986)
Vatican-U.S. Relations, 19-22 (1984)
CBS/Westmoreland Controversy, 159-165 (1985)

Censorship of Student Newspapers, Supreme Court on, 37-46 (1988)

Central America. *See also Latin America; specific countries*
Americas Watch Reports on Nicaragua, 255-269 (1985)
Arias Nobel Peace Prize Speech, 1007-1011 (1987)
Central American Cease-Fire Agreement, 241-245 (1988)
Central American Peace Agreement, 637-648 (1987)
CIA Manual on Guerrilla Warfare, 903-916 (1984)
Democratic Party Platform on, 637-641 (1984); 567-568 (1988)
Kissinger Commission, 31-52 (1984)
Presidential Debates on, 877-880 (1984)
Republican Party Platform on, 662, 707-709 (1984); 675-676 (1988)
State of the Union, 66 (1988)
Vice Presidential Debate on, 807-808 (1988)
Weinberger on Use of Military Force, 1005-1006 (1984)

Central Intelligence Agency. *See also Iran-contra affair*
Americas Watch Reports on Nicaragua, 256-257, 259 (1985)
Guerrilla Warfare Manual, 903-916 (1984)
Iran Arms Deal and Contra Funding, 1013-1024 (1986)
Presidential Debates on, 847 (1984)
Secrecy of Sources, 333-344 (1985)
World Court on Mining Nicaragua Harbors, 339-345 (1984)

***Challenger* Space Shuttle**
Accident Commission Report, 515-539 (1986)
Discovery Tribute, 795-798 (1988)

Chazov, Dr. Yevgeny I., 781-785 (1985)

Cheney, Lynne V., 517-527 (1988)

Chernenko, Konstantin U.
Andropov Death, 145-154 (1984)
Death of, 271-274 (1985)
Doder Interview, 917-923 (1984)

Chevron v. Natural Resources Defense Council, 427-437 (1984)

Children. *See also Education; Family and marital issues; Youth*
Bishops on Economic Justice, 999 (1986)
Child Survival Program, 686 (1988)
Democratic Party Platform on, 569-571 (1984); 560-561 (1988)
Infant Mortality Report, 147-165 (1987)
Republican Party Platform on, 702-703 (1984); 634-636, 638-639, 686 (1988)
Senate on School Prayer, 241-245 (1984)
Supreme Court on Sustaining Handicapped Infants, 541-558 (1986)
Urban Institute Child Poverty Report, 877-880 (1988)

Children's Defense Fund (CDF) Infant Mortality Report, 147-165 (1987)

Chile
Human Rights Report, 149-150 (1985); 102-103 (1986); 193-194 (1987); 100-101 (1988)

China, People's Republic of
Human Rights Report, 165-166 (1984)
Reagan Visit, 287-298 (1984)
Return of Hong Kong, 1045-1050 (1984)
World Population Problems, 540-541 (1984)
Zhao Visit/Technology Accords, 23-30 (1984)

Chirac, Jacques
French Antiterrorist Plan, 829-838 (1986)

Cholesterol, 779-790 (1987)

Chun Doo Hwan, 583-586, 590-594 (1987)

Church and state
Creation Science, 565-576 (1987)
Democratic Party Platform on, 606 (1984)
Pope John Paul II on, 777-787 (1984); 57-67 (1985)
Senate on School Prayer, 241-245 (1984)
Supreme Court Decisions, 379-395, 433-461 (1985); 565-576 (1987)
Vatican on Theology of Liberation, 761 (1984); 317-338, 640-641, 646-649 (1986)

CIA v. Sims and Wolfe, 333-344 (1985)

Cities. *See State and local government*

Civil and political rights. *See also Affirmative action; Equal opportunity; Human rights*
Black America Report, 31-32, 33, 35 (1985) 43-45, 47, 51-52, 58 (1987)
Democratic Party Platform on, 605-613 (1984)
Kerner Report Updated, 185-194 (1988)
Republican Party Platform on, 642-649 (1988)
Supreme Court Decisions
Affirmative Action, 365-385 (1984); 651-678 (1986); 331-349 (1987)
Exclusionary Rule, 505-519 (1984)
Indigents' Rights to Psychiatric Aid, 207-219 (1985)
Prisoners' Rights, 479-491 (1984)
Private Clubs, 399-403 (1988)
Sex Bias in Education, 201-214 (1984)
Sex Discrimination in Commercial Organizations, 465-478 (1984)
Student Searches, 13-26 (1985)
Suspects' Rights, 387-397 (1984); 223-253 (1985)
Use of Deadly Force, 303-315 (1985)
Tutu Nobel Prize Speech, 1027-1037 (1984)

Civil service retirement, 112 (1984)

Claiborne, Harry E.
Impeachment, 849-857 (1986)

Clausen, A. W., 800-802 (1984); 860 (1986)

Cocaine. *See also Drug abuse*

President's Commission on Organized
Crime, 181, 183-187 (1986)
Colombia
Pope John Paul II's Trip, 639-649 (1986)
President's Commission on Organized
Crime, 185-189 (1986)
Commission on Civil Rights
Urban League Report, 45 (1987)
Commission on Minority Participation in
Education and American Life
Kerner Report Updated, 185-187 (1988)
Commission on the Cities
Kerner Report Updated, 185-194 (1988)
Commission on Wartime Relocation and In-
ternment of Civilians, 288-289 (1988)
Common Market. See European Community
(EC)
Commonwealth of Nations Report on South
Africa, 581-590 (1986)
Communications
Democratic Party Platform on, 578-579
(1984)
FCC on Fairness Doctrine, 625-636 (1987)
Supreme Court Decisions
Freedom of the Press, 299-312 (1984)
Media Libel Law, 247-256 (1984); 355-
368 (1986)
Public Broadcasting Editorials, 449-463
(1984)
Video Recorders, 53-80 (1984)
Communists. See individual communist
countries
Compton, Ann, 756-757, 764-765, 772-773,
781 (1988)
Conable, Barber, 861 (1986)
Congress. See also Government ethics;
House of Representatives; Senate
Balanced Budget Bill, 803-808 (1985)
Defense Budget Process, 693-695 (1986)
Reagan's Post-Geneva Summit Address,
751, 756-761 (1985)
Congressional Budget Office (CBO)
Grace Commission, Report on, 169-179
(1984); 231 (1988)
Constitution, U.S.
Ban on Bill of Attainder, 493-503 (1984)
Bicentennial Observance, 765-775 (1987)
1st (First Amendment)
Adult Theaters, 131-144 (1986)
Church and State, 19-22, 217-239, 241-
245 (1984); 379-395, 433-461 (1985);
565-576 (1987)
FCC on Fairness Doctrine, 625-636
(1987)
Freedom of the Press, 299-312 (1984)
Media Libel Law, 247-256 (1984); 355-
368 (1986)
Obscenity, 479-490 (1987)
Press Freedom, 175-182 (1988)
Private Clubs, 399-403 (1988)
Public Broadcasting Editorials, 449-463
(1984)

Religion in School Curriculum, 597-608
(1987)
School Prayer, 241-245 (1984); 379-395
(1985)
Sex Discrimination in Commercial Orga-
nizations, 465-478 (1984)
Student Newspaper Censorship, 37-46
(1988)
Students' Free Speech, 731-742 (1986)
4th (Fourth Amendment)
Exclusionary Rule, 505-519 (1984)
Prisoners' Rights, 479-491 (1984)
Sodomy and Privacy, 601-614 (1986)
Student Searches, 13-26 (1985)
Use of Deadly Force, 303-315 (1985)
5th (Fifth Amendment)
Student Aid/Draft Registration, 493-503
(1984)
Suspects' Rights, 387-397 (1984); 223-
253 (1987)
Uncompensated Takings and Land Use,
531-553 (1987)
6th (Sixth Amendment)
Jury Selection in Capital Cases, 445-456
(1986)
Peremptory Challenge, 409-433 (1986)
8th (Eighth Amendment)
Death Penalty and Race, 463-476 (1987)
Preventive Detention, 491-508 (1987)
10th (Tenth Amendment)
Balanced Budget Amendment, 82, 105,
662 (1984)
Independent Counsel, 465-478 (1988)
Mandatory Budget Cuts, 705-730 (1986)
Republican Party Platform on, 647
(1988)
14th (Fourteenth Amendment)
Death Penalty and Race, 463-476 (1987)
Jury Selection in Capital Cases, 445-456
(1986)
Political Gerrymandering, 615-635
(1986)
Preventive Detention, 491-508 (1987)
Uncompensated Takings and Land Use,
531-553 (1987)
25th (Twenty-fifth Amendment)
Transfer of Presidential Power, 491-495
(1985)
Consumer affairs
Democratic Party Platform on, 583-584
(1984)
Consumers Union, 299-312 (1984)
Contadora Agreement
Administration Reports on Nicaragua,
257, 266-267 (1985)
Central American Peace Agreement, 637-
648 (1987)
Cook, Frederick A., 832-833 (1988)
Coordinating Committee on Multilateral Ex-
port Controls (CoCom)
National Security Export Controls, 29-42
(1987)

Copperweld Corp. v. Independent Tube Corp., 413-426 (1984)
Copyright law and video recorders, 53-80 (1984)
Corporation for Public Broadcasting, 449-463 (1984)
Costa Rica
Central American Peace Agreement, 637-648 (1987)
Kissinger Commission Report, 31-52 (1984)
Vice Presidential Debate on, 807 (1988)
Council of Economic Advisers
Annual Economic Report, 119-144 (1984); 80, 88-104 (1985); 59, 70-92 (1986); 117-119, 125-144 (1987); 126-148 (1988)
Courts, U.S. *See also Supreme Court*
Indigents' Rights to Psychiatric Aid, 207-219 (1985)
Jury Selection in Capital Cases, 445-456 (1986)
Peremptory Challenge, 409-433 (1986)
PLO Office Closing, 479-485 (1988)
Sentencing Commission Report, 407-426 (1987)
Surrogates' Rights, 373-387 (1987); 71-80 (1988)
Covey, Col. Harvey O., 798 (1988)
Credit. *See also Banks and banking*
Economic Advisers' Report, 89-91 (1986)
Federal Credit Programs, 113 (1984); 11-12 (1987)
OTA Report on Biotechnology, 292-294 (1986)
Crime and law enforcement. *See also Courts, U.S.; Supreme Court*
Budget Message, 114 (1983); 111 (1984); 155 (1988)
Cuban Detainee Agreements, 929-937 (1987)
Democratic Party Platform on, 619-621 (1984); 562 (1988)
Donovan, Raymond J., 803-809 (1984)
Meese Criticism of Supreme Court, 480-481, 485-486 (1985)
Philadelphia Police Raid on MOVE Group, 239-251 (1986)
President's Commission on Organized Crime, 179-216 (1986)
President's Commission on Privatization Report, 234 (1988)
Republican Party Platform on, 693-695 (1984); 655-656 (1988)
Sentencing Commission Report, 407-426 (1987)
State of the Union, 92 (1984); 114 (1985)
Supreme Court Decisions
Death Penalty and Race, 463-476 (1987)
Exclusionary Rule, 505-519 (1984)
Miranda Ruling, 387-397 (1984); 223-253 (1985)
Preventive Detention, 491-508 (1987)
Prisoners' Rights, 479-491 (1984)
Student Searches, 13-26 (1985)
Suspects' Rights, 387-397 (1984)
Use of Deadly Force, 303-315 (1985)
U.S.-U.K. Extradition Treaty, 751-756 (1986)
Crowe, Adm. William J., 703-717 (1988)
Cruise missile, ground-launched. *See Intermediate-range Nuclear Forces*
Cuba
Angola-Namibia Peace Accord, 947-950 (1988)
Cuban Detainee Agreements, 929-937 (1987)
Human Rights Report, 158-159 (1984)
International Terrorism, 471-472 (1985)
Kissinger Commission Report, 31, 44-47, 51 (1984)
Cuéllar, Javier Perez de, 610-611 (1987); 531-532 (1988)
Cuomo, Mario M., 648-649 (1984)
Curran, Charles E.
Vatican Disciplining of, 757-765 (1986)

D

Daniloff, Nicholas S., 819-827 (1986)
Darman, Richard G., 971-981 (1986)
Davis v. Bandemer, 615-635 (1986)
Death Penalty
Presidential Debates on, 723, 736-737 (1988)
Supreme Court Decisions, 463-476 (1987)
Debates. *See Presidential election; Vice presidency*
Defense. *See also Arms control; Defense Department; Foreign affairs; Foreign aid; Strategic Arms Limitation Treaty; Strategic Defense Initiative*
ABM Treaty Interpretation, 289-317 (1987); 330 (1988)
Budget, 108 (1984); 51, 55 (1986); 4, 9-10, 14 (1987)
Democratic Party Platform on, 550-551, 566, 621-646 (1984); 566-567 (1988)
Intelligence
CIA Manual on Guerrilla Warfare, 903-916 (1984)
Iran-Contra Reports, 891-928 (1987)
Pentagon Report on Soviet Espionage, 603-614 (1985)
Republican Party Platform on, 698-699 (1988)
Tower Commission Report, 205-242 (1987)
Westmoreland/CBS Controversy, 159-165 (1985)
MX Missile Production, 365-374 (1983); 4 (1987)
National Security Export Controls, 29-42 (1987)
National Security Strategy, 781-790 (1986)

Packard Commission on Defense Management, 679-695 (1986)

Presidential Debates on, 846-847, 880-889, 893-902 (1984); 741-744, 761-764, 767-769, 778-781 (1988)

Republican Party Platform on, 663-664, 718-726 (1984); 688-702 (1988)

Science Board Panel on Strategic Missile Defense, 323-331 (1988)

Scientists/OTA on Star Wars Defense, 257-272 (1984)

Senate Report on Persian Gulf War, 747-755 (1984)

State of the Union, 87, 92-93 (1984); 106-107 (1985); 40, 44 (1986); 57-58, 60, 66-67 (1988)

Supreme Court on Student Aid/Draft Registration, 493-503 (1984)

USS *Stark* Attack, 791-816 (1987)

Vice Presidential Debate on, 827 (1988)

Weinberger on Use of Military Force, 1005-1015 (1984)

Defense Department

Downing of Iranian Airliner, 703-717 (1988)

Joint Chiefs of Staff Reorganization, 679 (1986)

Military Base Closings, 951-954 (1988)

National Security Export Controls, 29-42 (1987)

Packard Commission on Defense Management, 679-695 (1986)

SDI Milestone Panel on Strategic Missile Defense, 323-331 (1988)

Senate Armed Services Report on the Pentagon, 669-683 (1985)

Sexual Harassment Report, 671-679 (1987)

Deficits. *See Budget, Federal*

De Larosière, J., 795-799 (1984)

Delvalle, Eric Arturo, 81 (1988)

Democratic Party

Convention

Bentsen Acceptance Speech, 533, 535, 542-546 (1988)

Dukakis Acceptance Speech, 533-542 (1988)

Jackson Address, 534-535, 546-556 (1988)

Mondale Ferraro Acceptance Speeches, 647-658 (1984)

Election Results, 953-956 (1984)

Platform, 549-646 (1984); 557-569 (1988)

Presidential Debates, 858-861 (1984)

Democratic Reforms

Gorbachev Address to 19th All-Union Soviet Party Conference, 447-464 (1988)

Gorbachev Address to Plenary Session of Soviet Party Congress, 79-104 (1987)

South Korean Leaders Speeches, 583-594 (1987)

Desegregation. *See Civil and political rights; Equal opportunity; Education; Housing*

Developing countries. *See also Foreign aid; United Nations; and specific countries*

Bhopal Gas Poisoning, 1023-1026 (1984)

Bishop's Letter on Economic Justice, 1005-1010 (1986)

Bishops on U.S. Economy, 970-971 (1984)

Child Survival Program, 686 (1988)

Democratic Party Platform on, 644-645 (1984)

Economic Advisers' Report, 78-83 (1986)

Economic Summit Meetings

(Bonn), 353-354 (1985)

(London), 355-364 (1984)

(Toronto), 391, 396-397 (1988)

Environmental Defense Fund on World Bank Project, 859-873 (1986)

IMF-World Bank Conference, 795-802 (1984); 643-652 (1985)

Natural Disasters Report, 973-995 (1984)

Pope's Encyclical on Social Concerns, 165-174 (1988)

Population Institute Report, 439-462 (1987)

Republican Party Platform on, 679-680 (1984)

Third World Debt, 644-645 (1984)

Vatican on Theology of Liberation, 759-775 (1984); 317-338 (1986)

World Population Problems, 521-547 (1984)

Diabetes

Black and Minority Health Report, 686, 697-698 (1985)

Disabled. *See Handicapped*

Disarmament. *See Arms control*

Disasters

Cameroon Aid Report, 61-77 (1987)

Natural Disasters Report, 973-995 (1984)

Discovery **Space Shuttle Tribute to** *Challenger* **Victims,** 795-798 (1988)

Discrimination. *See Affirmative action; Civil and political rights; Equal opportunity; Human rights; Pregnancy Discrimination Act*

Dixon, Alan, D-Ill., 850, 856-857 (1986)

Doder, Dusko, 917-923 (1984)

Donaldson, Sam, 1093-1095 (1986)

Donovan, Raymond J., 803-809 (1984)

Draft, military. *See Military draft*

Drug abuse. *See also Acquired immune deficiency syndrome*

Democratic Party Platform on, 562 (1988)

Economic Summit (Toronto), 394-395 (1988)

Jackson Address to Democratic National Convention, 552-553 (1988)

Mental Health Report, 833-843 (1984)

Nicotine Addiction Report, 309-322 (1988)

Noriega Indictments, 81-92 (1988)

Presidential Commission on the Human Immunodeficiency Virus Epidemic, 416, 435-436 (1988)

Presidential Debates on, 725-726 (1988)
President's Commission on Organized
Crime, 180-200 (1986)
Reagan's Budget Message, 150, 155 (1988)
Reagan's Executive Order on Drug Test-
ing, 839-846 (1986)
Republican Party Platform on, 656-657,
679-680 (1988)
Ueberroth on Drugs in Baseball, 169-175
(1986)
Vice Presidential Debate on, 814-815
(1988)
Due process. *See Constitution, U.S., Four-
teenth Amendment*
Dukakis, Michael S.
Acceptance Speech, 533-542 (1988)
Postelection Statement, 900-904 (1988)
Presidential Debates, 721-783 (1988)
Duvalier, Jean-Claude "Baby Doc," 98-99,
106-107 (1986)

E

Earthscan, 973-975 (1984)
Economic policy. *See also Budget, Federal;
Inflation; Monetary policy*
Annual Economic Report, 119-144 (1984);
79-104 (1985); 59-92 (1986); 117-144
(1987)
Bishops on Economic Justice, 983-1011
(1986)
Bishops on U.S. Economy, 957-972 (1984)
Budget Message, 99-117 (1984); 71-78
(1985); 49-58 (1986); 3-15 (1987); 149-163
(1988)
Common Market Summit, 439-445 (1984)
Democratic Party Platform on, 549, 552-
598 (1984); 559-560 (1988)
Economic Sanctions in Panama, 81 (1988)
Economic Summit Meetings
(Bonn), 347-355 (1985)
(Fontainebleau), 439-445 (1984)
(London), 355-364 (1984)
(Tokyo), 437-444 (1986)
(Toronto), 391-397 (1988)
(Venice), 512 (1987); 525-530 (1987)
Gorbachev's Address to 27th Soviet Party
Congress, 145-146, 152-160 (1986)
IMF-World Bank Conference, 795-802
(1984); 643-652 (1985)
Plunge of the Dollar, 523-530 (1985)
Presidential Debates on, 846-876 (1984)
Republican Party Platform on, 665-680
(1984); 619-621, 632-633 (1988)
Return of Hong Kong to China, 1045-1050
(1984)
State of the Union, 87-88 (1984); 105-117
(1985); 38-45 (1986); 111 (1987)
Stock Market Crash, 833-842 (1987); 9-36
(1988)
Vice Presidential Debate on, 813-814
(1988)

World Population Problems, 521-547
(1984)
Education. *See also Carnegie Foundation*
Assessing American Education, 297-306
(1988)
Black America Report, 30, 36-37 (1985)
Budget Message, 107 (1984); 150, 154
(1988)
Carnegie Report on Urban Schools, 195-
219 (1988)
Democratic Party Platform on, 571-573
(1984); 561-562 (1988)
Department of Education Report on
Teaching and Learning, 217-238 (1986)
Elementary Education, 803-817 (1986)
Higher Education Report, 583-602 (1985)
Humanities Education Report, 992-1003
(1984); 681-696 (1987)
Kerner Report Updated, 190-191, 193
(1988)
Math and Science Education Reports, 377-
390 (1988)
Mental Health Report, 838 (1984)
Pope John Paul II's Canada Trip, 778,
780-783 (1984)
President's Commission on Privatization
Report, 233 (1988)
Religion in Curriculum, 597-608 (1987)
Republican Party Platform on, 689-693
(1984); 649-653 (1988)
State of the Humanities Report, 517-527
(1988)
State of the Union, 91 (1984); 63-64 (1988)
Supreme Court Decisions
Alcoholism and Veterans' Benefits, 277-
285 (1988)
Creation Science, 565-576 (1987)
Disruptive Handicapped Students, 47-
56 (1988)
Public School Teachers in Parochial
Classes, 433-461 (1985)
School Prayer, 91, 241-245, 662 (1984);
379-395 (1985)
Sex Bias, 201-214 (1984)
Student Aid/Draft Registration, 493-503
(1984)
Student Newspaper Censorship, 37-46
(1988)
Student Searches, 13-26 (1985)
Students' Free Speech, 731-742 (1986)
Teaching Profession, 457-485 (1986)
Undergraduate Colleges Report, 939-958
(1986)
U.S. College Curriculum, 127-144 (1985)
Edwards v. Aguillard, 565-576 (1987)
Egypt
Arab Summit Communiqué, 869-874
(1987)
Eighth Amendment. *See Constitution, U.S.*
El Salvador. *See also Central America*
Central American Peace Agreement, 637-
648 (1987)

Human Rights Report, 159-162 (1984); 146, 150-151 (1985); 103-104 (1986); 194-195 (1987)

Kissinger Commission Report, 31-52 (1984)

Vatican on Theology of Liberation, 761 (1984)

Elderly. *See Aged*

Elections. *See also Campaign financing; Voting*
Court on Closed Party Primaries, 1065-1073 (1986)
Democratic Party Platform on, 565 (1988)

Elias, T.O., 341-344 (1984)

Employment and unemployment
Bishops on Economic Justice, 996-998 (1986)
Bishops on U.S. Economy, 958, 967 (1984)
Black America Report, 27-37 (1985)
Budget Message, 107-108 (1984)
Democratic Party Platform on, 574-575 (1984)
Economic Advisers' Report, 143-144 (1987); 118, 126, 139-142 (1988)
Economic Summit (Bonn), 351-352 (1985)
Kerner Report Updated, 187-188, 193 (1988)
President's Economic Report, 119-120, 122-123 (1984); 63 (1986); 118, 119-121 (1988)
Republican Party Platform on, 621-623 (1988)
Sex Segregation in the Workplace, 789-801 (1985)
Smoking in the Workplace, 809-822 (1985)
Supreme Court Decisions
Affirmative Action, 365-385 (1984); 651-678 (1986)
Labor Union Membership, 415-429 (1985)
Mandatory Retirement, 397-407 (1985)
Women in the Labor Force, 143-144 (1987)

Energy policy
Democratic Party Platform on, 592-595 (1984); 565 (1988)
Reagan Budget Message, 109 (1984)
Republican Party Platform on, 662, 672-673 (1984); 665-668 (1988)

English language
California Vote on English as Official Language, 959-962 (1986)

Entitlement programs. *See Welfare and social services*

Environment. *See also "Greenhouse effect"; Pollution*
Bhopal Gas Poisoning, 1023-1026 (1984); 295-302 (1985)
Chernobyl Nuclear Accident, 384, 401-404 (1986)
Democratic Party Platform on, 549, 595-598 (1984); 564 (1988)
Economic Summit Meetings

(Bonn), 354-355 (1985)
(Toronto), 397 (1988)
Environmental Defense Fund on World Bank Project, 859-873 (1986)
EPA Report on "Greenhouse Effect," 861-866 (1988)
Interagency Report on Forest-Fire Policy, 941-946 (1988)
Nuclear War Effects, 541-554 (1985)
OTA Report on Biotechnology, 295-296 (1986)
Ozone Treaty and Scientific Study, 745-764 (1987); 221-228, 397 (1988)
Presidential Debates on, 776-777 (1988)
Republican Party Platform on, 677-678, 685-686 (1984); 668-671 (1988)
State of the Union, 82-83, 90 (1984)
Supreme Court Decisions
EPA and Clean Air, 427-437 (1984)
Uncompensated Takings and Land Use, 531-553 (1987)
Vice Presidential Debate on, 805-806, 817-818 (1988)

Environmental Protection Agency (EPA)
"Greenhouse Effect" on America's Climate, 861-866 (1988)
Supreme Court on Clean Air, 427-437 (1984)

Equal opportunity. *See also Civil and political rights; Equal Rights Amendment*
Democratic Party Platform on, 598-621 (1984); 563 (1988)
Republican Party Platform on, 696-702 (1984); 622-623 (1988)
State of the Union, 92 (1984)
Supreme Court Decisions
Affirmative Action, 365-385 (1984); 651-678 (1986)
Sex Bias in Education, 201-214 (1984)

Equal Rights Amendment (ERA)
Democratic Party Platform on, 607 (1984)
Republican Party Platform on, 662 (1984)

Ethics. *See also Bioethics; Government ethics*
ABA Report on Legal Professionalism, 767-778 (1986)
AMA Proposed Boxing Ban, 1019-1021 (1984)
Bhopal Gas Poisoning, 1023-1026 (1984)
Bishops on Economic Justice, 990-994 (1986)
Bishops on U.S. Economy, 957-972 (1984)
Donovan, Raymond J., 803-809 (1984)
Natural Disasters Report, 973-995 (1984)
Supreme Court on Media Libel Law, 247-256 (1984)
Tutu Nobel Prize Speech, 1027-1037 (1984)

Ethiopia
Human Rights Report, 151-152 (1985); 99-101 (1986); 191-192 (1987)
Natural Disasters Report, 973-995 (1984)

Europe. *See specific countries*
European Community (EC)
   Common Market Summit, 439-445 (1984)
   Economic Summit Meetings
      (Fontainebleau), 439-445 (1984)
      (Tokyo), 437-444 (1986)
      (Venice), 525-530 (1987)
Evans, Daniel J., D.-Wash., 292-293 (1988)
Executive branch. *See also Government re-*
organization
   Supreme Court Decision on Mandatory
      Budget Cuts, 705-730 (1986)
   Transfer of Presidential Power, 491-495
      (1985)
Exports. *See Foreign trade*

F

Fabius, Laurent, 631-634 (1985)
Fabrikant, Jacob I.
   NRC Radon Report, 3-8 (1988)
Fairness doctrine. *See Constitution, U.S.,*
First Amendment
Falwell, Jerry
   Supreme Court on Freedom of the Press,
      175-177 (1988)
Family and marital issues. *See also Chil-*
dren; Youth
   Black America Report, 27-37 (1985)
   Pope John Paul II on, 25, 35-37 (1986)
   Population Institute Report, 439-462
      (1987)
   Republican Party Platform on, 633-636
      (1988)
   State of the Union, 41, 43, 45-46 (1986); 59,
      63-65 (1988)
   Surrogates' Rights, 373-387 (1987); 71-80
      (1988)
   Tutu Nobel Prize Speech, 1027-1037
      (1984)
   Vice Presidential Debate on, 806-807
      (1988)
   World Population Problems, 521-547
      (1984)
Family planning. *See Abortion; Birth control*
Family Support Act of 1988, 847-852 (1988)
Farmers and farming. *See Agriculture*
Federal Aviation Administration (FAA)
   Air Traffic Safety, 253-266 (1986)
   Aviation Safety Commission Report, 267-
      276 (1988)
Federal Communications Commission (FCC)
   Fairness Doctrine, 625-636 (1987)
Federal Communications Commission v.
League of Women Voters of California, 449-
   463 (1984); 626-627 (1987)
Federal Deposit Insurance Corporation
(FDIC)
   Savings and Loan Crisis, 913-918 (1988)
Federal Election Commission v. National Con-
servative Political Action Committee, 277-294
   (1985)

Federal Reserve System
   Economic Advisers' Report, 120-121, 128-
      144 (1984); 72-73 (1986); 117-118, 129-131
      (1988)
   Greenspan Appointment, 511-516 (1987)
   President's Economic Report, 120-121,
      122-128 (1984)
   Volcker Resignation, 511-516 (1987)
Feldstein, Martin, 119-121 (1984)
Fellay, Bernard, 490-492 (1988)
Ferraro, Geraldine
   Acceptance Speech, 647-658 (1984)
   Democratic Party Platform on, 550 (1984)
Fifth Amendment. *See Constitution, U.S.*
Financial policy. *See Economic policy; Infla-*
tion; Monetary policy
Firefighters v. Stotts, 365-385 (1984)
First Amendment. *See Constitution, U.S.*
First English Evangelical Lutheran Church of
Glendale v. County of Los Angeles, 531-546
   (1987)
Fogarty, Rear Adm. William M., 703-717
   (1988)
Food
   Cholesterol Report, 779-790 (1987)
   NIH Heart Disease Report, 1039-1043
      (1984)
Food and Drug Administration (FDA)
   AZT (azidothymidine) approval, 327-330
      (1987)
   TPA (tissue plasminogen activator) ap-
      proval, 875-879 (1987)
Food supply
   Bishops on Economic Justice, 1002-1005,
      1009 (1986)
   Economic Advisers' Report, 83-84 (1986)
   Gorbachev at 27th Party Congress, 146,
      156-157 (1986)
   Hunger in America, 189-205 (1985)
   Natural Disasters Report, 973-995 (1984)
   Nuclear War Effects, 543, 551-554 (1985)
   Presidential Task Force on Food Assis-
      tance, 3-17 (1984)
Ford, Gerald R., 728-729 (1984)
Foreign affairs. *See also Arms control; For-*
eign aid; Foreign trade; Human rights; In-
ternational debt; Iran-contra affair; Sum-
mit conferences; Treaties and agreements
   Americas Watch/Administration Reports
      on Nicaragua, 255-269 (1985)
   Andropov Death, 145-154 (1984)
   Chernenko Interview, 917-923 (1984)
   CIA Guerrilla Warfare Manual, 903-916
      (1984)
   Common Market Summit, 439-445 (1984)
   Democratic Party Platform on, 621-646
      (1984); 566 (1988)
   Gorbachev at 27th Party Congress, 163-
      167 (1986)
   Gromyko-Reagan UN Address, 811-829
      (1984)
   Ireland Forum, 315-326 (1984)

Kissinger Commission Report, 31-52
(1984)
Natural Disasters Report, 973-995 (1984)
Persian Gulf War, Senate Report, 747-755
(1984)
Republican Party Platform on, 663-664,
707-726 (1984); 673-688 (1988)
Return of Hong Kong to China, 1045-1050
(1984)
Shultz on Terrorism, 933-944 (1984)
State of the Union, 83-84 (1984); 115-116
(1985); 40, 47 (1986); 60, 65-66 (1988)
Tutu Nobel Prize Speech, 1027-1037
(1984)
U.S. Reduction of Soviet UN Mission, 267-
272 (1986)
U.S.-U.K. Extradition Treaty, 751-756
(1986)
U.S. Withdrawal from World Court Juris-
diction, 637-641 (1985)
USS *Stark* Attack, 791-816 (1987)
Vatican-U.S. Relations, 19-22 (1984)
World Court on Mining Nicaragua, 339-
345 (1984)
Zhao Visit, 23-30 (1984)
Foreign aid
Child Survival Program, 686 (1988)
Haiti, 939-941 (1987)
Kissinger Commission Report, 31-52
(1984)
Natural Disasters Report, 973-995 (1984)
State of the Union, 115-116 (1985)
Foreign trade. *See also General Agreement
on Tariffs and Trade (GATT); Interna-
tional debt*
Canada-U.S., 58, 65-66, 123; 571-578
(1988)
China-U.S. 23-30 (1984)
China-U.S. Accords, 293-294 (1984)
Democratic Party Platform on, 586-589
(1984); 561 (1988)
Economic Advisers' Report, 140-141
(1984); 95-99 (1985); 117-118, 126 (1987);
118, 142-144 (1988)
Economic Summit Meetings
(Bonn), 354 (1985)
(London), 356, 361 (1984)
IMF-World Bank Conference, 796 (1984)
Japan-U.S. Trade Dispute, 427-437 (1987)
Kissinger Commission Report, 40-42
(1984)
Mexico-U.S., 58, 66 (1988)
Nakasone Speech, 319-323 (1985)
National Security Export Controls, 29-42
(1987)
Poland, Lifting Trade Sanctions Against,
183-188 (1987)
President's Economic Report, 119-120, 124
(1984); 68-69 (1986); 117-118, 122-123
(1987); 123, 125 (1988)
Reagan Trade Bill Vetoes, 339-346 (1988)
Republican Party Platform on, 679-680

(1984); 630-632 (1988)
State of the Union, 115-116 (1985); 44-45
(1986); 58, 65-66 (1988)
Supreme Court on Unitary Taxation of
Multinational Corporations, 645-658
(1983)
Forest Fires. *See Environment*
Fourteenth Amendment. *See Constitution,
U.S.*
Fourth Amendment. *See Constitution, U.S.*
France
Chirac on French Antiterrorist Plan, 829-
838 (1986)
Economic Summit (Bonn), 347-355 (1985)
Greenpeace Affair, 631-634 (1985)
Group of Five Communiqué on the Dollar,
523-530 (1985)
Free speech. *See Constitution, U.S., First
Amendment*
Free trade. *See Foreign trade*
Freedom of Information Act. *See also Press*
Secrecy of CIA Sources, 333-344 (1985)
Fuel. *See Energy Policy*

G

Galarreta, Alfonso de, 490-492 (1988)
Galiber, Joseph L., 803-809 (1984)
Galman, Rolando, 925-932 (1984)
Gandhi, Indira, 945-949 (1984)
Gandhi, Mahatma, 24, 26-28 (1986)
Gandhi, Rajiv, 945-949 (1984); 615-622
(1987)
Garcia, Robert, D-N.Y., 499 (1988)
Gases, Asphyxiating and poisonous. *See also
Natural Gas*
Bhopal Gas Poisoning, 1023-1026 (1984);
295-302 (1985)
Cameroon Disaster Aid Report, 61-77
(1987)
General Accounting Office (GAO)
Grace Commission Report, 169-179 (1984);
231 (1988)
Report on Air Traffic Safety, 253-266
(1986)
**General Agreement on Tariffs and Trade
(GATT),** 142-143, 631 (1988). *See also For-
eign trade*
Genetic engineering. *See also Bioethics*
Interferon Approval, 484-485 (1986)
OTA Report on Biotechnology, 287-288,
296 (1986); 352-353, 356-358 (1987)
Genocide Convention
Senate Ratification of, 115-130 (1986)
Germany, Federal Republic of
Berlin Wall Anniversary, 791-799 (1986)
Common Market Summit, 443 (1984)
Economic Summit (Bonn), 347-355 (1985)
Group of Five Communiqué on the Dollar,
523-530 (1985)
Reagan at Bitburg, 357-362 (1985)

Geyer, Georgie Anne, 876-902 (1984)
Ginsburg, Douglas H., 720 (1987)
Goldwater, Barry, R-Ariz., 729 (1984); 669 (1985); 682 (1986)
Goode, W. Wilson, 239-241 (1986)
Gorbachev, Mikhail S.
  Afghanistan Agreements, 257-258 (1988)
  All-Union Soviet Party Congress, 447-464 (1988)
  Arms Control Proposal, 9-20 (1986)
  Bolshevik Anniversary Speech, 857-868 (1987)
  Chernenko Death, 271-274 (1985)
  Democratic Reforms, 79-104 (1987); 447-464 (1988)
  INF Treaty Statement, 945, 947-950 (1987)
  New Year's Message to U.S., 3-6 (1986)
  Soviet Party Congress, 145-168 (1986); 79-104 (1987)
  Summit Meetings
    (Geneva), 749-761 (1985)
    (Moscow), 353-373 (1988)
    (Reykjavik), 875-885 (1986); 866-867 (1987)
    (Washington, D.C.), 991-1006 (1987)
  United Nations Address, 927-940 (1988)
Government ethics
  Meese Investigation, 495-516 (1988)
  PAC Spending Limits, Supreme Court on, 277-294 (1985)
  Presidential Debates on, 781-782 (1988)
  Republican Party Platform on, 647-649 (1988)
  Vice Presidential Debate on, 808-809, 810, 816-817 (1988)
Government regulations. See Regulatory reform
Government reorganization
  Budget Message, 54-58 (1986); 157-158 (1988)
  Reagan's Reform '88 Program, 152, 159-161
Government spending. See also Budget, Federal
  CBO/GAO Grace Commission Report, 169-179 (1984)
  Economic Advisers' Report, 132-134 (1984)
  Packard Commission Report on Defense Management, 679-695 (1986)
  Presidential Debates on, 849-852 (1984)
  President's Economic Report, 66 (1986); 121-122 (1987); 124-125 (1988)
  Reagan Budget Message, 99-117 (1984)
  Republican Party Platform on, 629-630 (1988)
  State of the Union, 87-88 (1984); 111-113 (1985); 61 (1988)
Grace Commission, 115, 126, 169-179 (1984); 231 (1988)
Gramm-Rudman-Hollings Act. See also Bud-

get, Federal
  Balanced Budget Bill, 803-808 (1985)
  Budget Message, 49-58 (1986); 3-15 (1987); 153, 154 (1988)
  Economic Advisers' Report, 74, 76 (1986)
  President's Economic Report, 66 (1986); 124 (1988)
  State of the Union, 43-44 (1986); 63 (1988)
  Supreme Court Decision, 705-730 (1986)
  Vice Presidential Debate on, 826 (1988)
Grand Rapids School District v. Ball, 433-461 (1985)
Gray, Nellie J., 53-56 (1985)
Great Britain
  British-Irish Accord on Northern Ireland, 723-732 (1985)
  Common Market Summit, 439-445 (1984)
  Economic Summit Meetings
    (Bonn), 347-355 (1985)
    (London), 355-364 (1986)
  Group of Five Communiqué on the Dollar, 523-530 (1985)
  New Ireland Forum, 315-326 (1984)
  Return of Hong Kong to China, 1045-1050 (1984)
  U.S.-U.K. Extradition Treaty, 751-756 (1986)
"Greenhouse effect"
  EPA Report on Global Climate Change, 861-866 (1988)
  Vice Presidential Debate on, 817-818 (1988)
Greenpeace affair, 631-634 (1985)
Greenspan, Alan, 511-516 (1987)
Grenada, 808, 814 (1988)
Groer, Anne, 729-730, 736-737, 744-745, 751 (1988)
Gromyko, Andrei A.
  Chernenko interview, 917-919 (1984)
  UN Address, 811-814, 821-829 (1984)
Grosz, Paul, 409-411 (1988)
Group of Five Communiqué on the Dollar, 523-530 (1985)
Grove City College v. Bell, 201-214 (1984)
Guatemala
  Central American Peace Agreement, 637-648 (1987)
  Human Rights Report, 152 (1985); 104-106 (1986); 195-196 (1987)
  Kissinger Commission Report, 32, 36, 42 (1984)

H

Habib, Philip C., 308 (1986)
Haiti
  AIDS Report, 735 (1985)
  Elections, 939-941 (1987)
  Human Rights Report, 98-99, 106-107 (1986); 191, 196-197 (1987); 101-103 (1988)
Hale, Mother, 117 (1985)

Handicapped
Democratic Party Platform on, 616 (1984)
Pope's Canada Visit, 778-780 (1984)
Republican Party Platform on, 700-701 (1984); 644-645 (1988)
Supreme Court Decisions
Contagious Diseases, 245-252 (1987)
Disruptive Handicapped Students, 47-56 (1988)
Sustaining Handicapped Infants, 541-558 (1986)
Hart, Gary, 549-551 (1984)
Harvard Commission on the Presidential Press Conference, 835-845 (1988)
Harvard University Report on Medicare Reform, 273-285 (1986)
Hauck, Capt. Frederick H., 795, 798 (1988)
Health. *See also Acquired immune deficiency syndrome; Cancer; Heart disease; Medical care; Medicaid and Medicare; Mental health; Radiation*
AMA Proposed Boxing Ban, 1019-1021 (1984)
Alzheimer's Disease Report, 391-406 (1987)
Bhopal Gas Poisoning, 1023-1026 (1984)
Black and Minority Health Report, 685-706 (1985)
Budget Message, 109-110 (1984)
Cholesterol Report, 779-790 (1987)
Doctors on the Terminally Ill, 275-285 (1984)
Food Assistance Report, 3-17 (1984)
Health Costs of Smoking, 615-622 (1985)
Hospital Length of Stay Report, 333-337 (1988)
Interferon Approval, 481-484 (1986)
Involuntary Smoking, 1079-1090 (1986)
Nicotine Addiction Report, 309-322 (1988)
Republican Party Platform on, 683-685 (1984); 636-639, 686 (1988)
Smoking in the Workplace, 809-822 (1985)
Supreme Court on Contagious Diseases, 245-252 (1987)
Health and Human Services Department
AIDS, 733-747 (1985); 887-889 (1986); 319-326 (1987)
AZT Approval, 327-330 (1987)
Catastrophic Illness Expenses, 1025-1035 (1986)
Interferon Approval, 481-485 (1986)
Health Insurance
Presidential Debates on, 729-730 (1988)
Heart disease
Black and Minority Health Report, 686, 697-698 (1985)
Cholesterol Report, 779-790 (1987)
FDA Approval of TPA, 875-879 (1987)
Heart Disease Report, 1039-1043 (1984)
Heckler, Margaret, 685-687 (1985)
Helms, Jesse, R-N.C., 289, 293 (1988)
Hilmers, David C., 797 (1988)

Hinduism
Indira Gandhi Assassination, 945-949 (1984)
Hispanics. *See also Minority groups*
Alcoholism, 700 (1985)
California Vote on English as Official Language, 959 (1986)
Diabetes, 703-704 (1985)
Employment
Economic Advisers' Report, 140 (1988)
President's Economic Report, 119 (1988)
Pope John Paul II's Visit to U.S., 700, 705-707 (1987)
Holocaust
Mengele Discovery, 409-414 (1985)
Pope John Paul in Austria, 405-414 (1988)
Wiesel Nobel Peace Prize, 1075-1078 (1986)
Wiesel Testimony at Klaus Barbie Trial, 517-524 (1987)
Homeless
Presidential Debates on, 734-736 (1988)
Republican Party Platform on, 640-642 (1988)
Vice Presidential Debate on, 806 (1988)
Homosexuals
AIDS, 733-736 (1985); 887 (1986)
Democratic Party Platform on, 549, 612 (1984)
Vatican on Pastoral Care of Homosexuals, 909-918 (1986)
Honduras
Central American Peace Agreement, 637-648 (1987)
Kissinger Commission Report, 32, 36, 42 (1984)
Hong Kong
Return to China Agreement, 1045-1050 (1984)
Honig v. Doe, 47-56 (1988)
Hospitals
Doctors on Terminally Ill, 275-285 (1984)
For-Profit Hospitals, 487-513 (1986)
PHS Report on Length of Hospitalization, 333-337 (1988)
House of Representatives. *See also Congress; Senate*
Iran-Contra Reports, 891-928 (1987)
School Prayer, 241 (1984)
Housing
Democratic Party Platform on, 579-580 (1984); 563 (1988)
Kerner Report Updated, 190, 193 (1988)
Presidential Debates on, 734-736 (1988)
President's Commission on Privatization Report, 231-232 (1988)
Republican Party Platform on, 681-682 (1984); 628-629 (1988)
Hoxha, Enver, 325-331 (1985)
Hudson v. Palmer, 480-481 (1984)
Human immunodeficiency virus (HIV). *See*

Acquired immune deficiency syndrome
Human rights. *See also Civil and political rights*
  Americas Watch, Administration Reports on Nicaragua, 255-269 (1985)
  Amnesty International's Report, 883-889 (1988)
  Argentine "Disappeared" Persons, 789-793 (1984)
  Commonwealth Group on South Africa, 581-590 (1986)
  Democratic Party Platform on, 645-646 (1984); 568 (1988)
  Pope John Paul II, 329, 336-338 (1984)
  Reagan-Gorbachev Summit, 355-356, 359, 371 (1988)
  Republican Party Platform on, 716-717 (1984)
  Senate Ratification of Genocide Convention, 115-130 (1986)
  South African Pass Laws, 369-381 (1986)
  South African Violations, 515-527, 531-540 (1985)
  State Department Reports, 155-168 (1984); 145-157 (1985); 97-113 (1986); 189-204 (1987); 93-115 (1988)
  Tutu Nobel Prize Speech, 1027-1037 (1984)
  UN Report on Afghanistan, 919-936 (1986)
Humanities. *See Arts and humanities*
Hume, Brit, 808-810, 815-816, 821-822 (1988)
Hunger in America Report, 189-205 (1985)
Hunthausen, Raymond G., 757, 985-986 (1986)
Hussein, Jaddam, 747-755 (1984)
Hussein, King of Jordan
  West Bank Speech, 579-585 (1988)
Hussein, Saddam of Iraq
  869-874 (1987); 529-530 (1988)
Hustler **Magazine,** 247-253 (1984); 175-182 (1988)
Hustler Magazine, Inc., et al. v. Falwell, 175-182 (1988)

I

Iceland Summit, 875-885 (1986); 866-867 (1987)
Illegal Aliens. *See Immigration; Refugees*
Immigration. *See also Refugees*
  Cuban Detainee Agreements, 929-937 (1987)
  Democratic Party Platform on, 611 (1984)
  Economic Advisers' Report, 91-93 (1986)
  Immigration Reform and Control Act, 963-969 (1986)
  Reagan-Mondale Presidential Debates on, 889-894 (1984)
  Republican Party Platform on, 703-704 (1984); 647 (1988)
  Supreme Court on Political Asylum, 253-265 (1987)

Immigration and Naturalization Service v. Luz Marina Cardoza-Fonseca, 253-265 (1987)
Impeachments
  Claiborne, Harry E., 849-857 (1986)
  Mecham, Gov. Evan, 249-256 (1988)
India
  Bhopal Gas Poisoning, 1023-1026 (1984); 295-302 (1985)
  Gandhi, Indira, 945-949 (1984)
  Indo-Sri Lankan Accord, 615-622 (1987)
  Pope John Paul II's Trip, 23-37 (1986)
Indians, American
  Alcoholism, 700-701 (1985)
  Democratic Party Platform on, 612 (1984)
  Diabetes, 703 (1985)
  Pope John Paul II's Canada Visit, 778 (1984)
  Reagan-Gorbachev Summit, 365-366 (1988)
  Republican Party Platform on, 702 (1984); 645 (1988)
Indictments
  Donovan, Raymond J., 803-809 (1984)
  Marcos, Ferdinand and Imelda, 867-872 (1988)
  Noriega, Manuel Antonio, 81-92 (1988)
Individual Retirement Accounts (IRAs)
  Economic Report, 124, 135 (1984)
Indochina
  Environmental Defense Fund on World Bank Project, 859-873 (1986)
INF. *See Intermediate-range Nuclear Forces*
Infant mortality
  Black and Minority Health Report, 686-687, 705-706 (1985)
  CDF Report on Infant Mortality, 147-165 (1987)
Inflation. *See also Monetary policy*
  Budget Message, 101-103 (1984); 70-73 (1986); 151 (1988)
  Democratic Party Platform on, 568-569 (1984); 70-73 (1986)
  Economic Advisers' Report, 123-130 (1984); 90-91 (1985)
  President's Economic Report, 119-120, 123-124 (1984); 79-87 (1985); 63-64 (1986)
  Republican Party Platform on, 626 (1988)
  State of the Union, 85-86 (1984); 108 (1987)
Inouye, Daniel K., D-Hawaii, 289, 290-291 (1988)
Insider trading. *See Stock market*
Intelligence. *See Central Intelligence Agency (CIA); Defense*
Intercontinental Ballistic Missile (ICBM)
  Former Security Officials on Defense Strategy, 785-786 (1986)
Interest rates. *See Monetary policy*
Intermediate-range Nuclear Forces (INF)
  Democratic Party Platform on, 566-567 (1988)

Reagan-Gorbachev Summit, 353-355, 358, 367-369 (1988)
State of the Union, 57-58, 67 (1988)
U.S.-Soviet INF Treaty, 945-989 (1987)
International Association of Firefighters v. City of Cleveland, 651-678 (1986)
International Court of Justice
  Genocide Convention Ratification, 116, 121 (1986)
  Mining Nicaraguan Harbors, 339-345 (1984)
  Pope John Paul II's Speech, 365, 369-371 (1985)
  U.S. Withdrawal from Jurisdiction of, 637-641 (1985)
International debt. *See also Foreign trade*
  Economic Advisers' Report, 78-79, 82-83 (1986)
  Reagan's Budget Message, 149 (1988)
  Vice Presidential Debate on, 818-819 (1988)
International Monetary Fund (IMF)
  Economic Advisers' Report, 79-80 (1986)
  IMF-World Bank Conference, 795-802 (1984); 643-652 (1985)
International Physicians for the Prevention of Nuclear War, 781-787 (1985)
Iran
  Arab Summit Communiqué, 869-874 (1987)
  Downing of Iranian Airliner, 703-717 (1988)
  Economic Summit Meetings
    (London), 364 (1984)
    (Venice), 527, 530 (1987)
  Human Rights Report, 155, 162-163 (1984)
  International Terrorism, 470-471 (1985)
  Iran-Iraq Truce, 529-532 (1988)
  Persian Gulf War, 747-755 (1984)
  UN on Iran-Iraq War, 609-613 (1987)
Iran-contra affair
  Iran Arms Deal and Contra Funding, 1013-1024, 1049-1055 (1986)
  Iran-Contra Reports, 891-928 (1987)
  State of the Union, 106, 109-110 (1987)
  Tower Commission Report, 205-242 (1987)
  Vice Presidential Debate on, 807-808 (1988)
Iraq
  Arab Summit Communiqué, 869-874 (1987)
  Attack on USS *Stark*, 791-816 (1987)
  Economic Summit Meetings
    (London), 364 (1984)
    (Venice), 527, 530 (1984)
  Iran-Iraq Truce, 529-532 (1988)
  Persian Gulf War, 747-755 (1984)
  UN on Iran-Iraq War, 609-613 (1987)
Ireland, 315-326 (1984); 723-732 (1985). *See also Northern Ireland*
Israel
  Human Rights Report, 112-113 (1986);
113-115 (1988)
  Hussein's West Bank Speech, 579-585 (1988)
Italy
  Economic Summit (Bonn), 347-355 (1985)

J

Jackson, Jesse L., 549-551 (1984); 27, 32 (1985)
  Democratic National Convention Address, 535, 546-556 (1988)
  Democratic Party Platform, 557-558 (1988)
Japan
  Economic Summit Meetings
    (Bonn), 347-355 (1985)
    (Tokyo), 437-444 (1986)
  Group of Five Communiqué on the Dollar, 523-530 (1985)
  Nakasone Speech on Foreign Trade, 319-323 (1985)
  Nakasone Visit, 427, 429, 433-437 (1987)
  U.S.-Japan Trade Dispute, 427-437 (1987)
Japanese-American Internees Reparations, 287-295 (1988)
Jaruzelski, Wojciech, 555 (1987)
Jaycees, 465-478 (1984)
Jayewardene, Junius, 615-622 (1987)
Jefferson Parish Hospital District v. Hyde, 415 (1984)
Jennings, Peter, 731-733, 738-740, 746-747 (1988)
Jews. *See also Holocaust*
  Pope John Paul II
    Austria Trip, 405-414 (1988)
    Miami Address to Jewish Leaders, 699-700, 702-705 (1987)
    Rome Synagogue, 339-346 (1986)
Jobs. *See Employment and unemployment*
John Paul II
  Apostolic Letter on Women, 785-792 (1988)
  Encyclical on Social Concerns, 165-174 (1988)
  Excommunication of Archbishop Lefebvre, 489-494 (1988)
  Journeys, 327-338, 399-406, 777-787 (1984); 57-67, 363-376, 499-514 (1985); 23-37, 639-649 (1986); 555-564 (1987); 699-716 (1987); 405-414 (1988)
  Vatican on Theology of Liberation, 759, 761, 765 (1984); 317 (1986)
  Visit to Austria, 405-414 (1988)
  Visit to Rome Synagogue, 339-346 (1986)
Johnson v. Transportation Agency, Santa Clara, California, 331-349 (1987)
Jones, Shirley, 247-248, 253-256 (1984)
Jordan
  Hussein's West Bank Speech, 579-585 (1988)
Judiciary. *See Courts, U.S.; Supreme Court*

K

Kalb, Marvin, 876-902 (1984)
Kasten, Bob, R-Wis., 860 (1986)
Kauffman, Bruce W., 240-241, 248-251 (1986)
Keeton v. Hustler Magazine, 247-253 (1984)
Kennedy, Anthony M., 720-721 (1987)
Kerner Commission Report Update, 185-194 (1988)
Khamenei, Ali, 531-532 (1988)
Khomeini, Ayatollah Ruhollah, 747 (1984); 529-531 (1988)
Kirkpatrick, Jeane J., 728 (1984)
Kissinger Commission Report on Central America, 31-52 (1984)
Kohl, Helmut
   Berlin Wall Anniversary, 791-799 (1986)
Kolvenbach, Rev. Peter Haus, 761 (1984)
Kondracke, Morton, 876-902 (1984)
Koop, C. Everett
   Involuntary Smoking Report, 1079-1090 (1986)
   Nicotine Addiction Report, 309-322 (1988)
Korea, South. *See also North Korea*
   Human Rights Report, 109-110 (1986); 199-201 (1987); 104-106 (1988)
   Pope John Paul II Visit, 327-328, 329-332 (1984)
   Roh Tae Woo's UN Address, 853-859 (1988)
   South Korean Leaders on Democratic Reforms, 583-594 (1987)

L

Labor. *See also Employment and unemployment*
   Democratic Party Platform on, 549, 582-583, 608-609 (1984)
   Pope John Paul II's South America Trip, 59-61 (1985)
   President's Commission on Organized Crime, 200-210 (1986)
   Supreme Court Decisions
      Affirmative Action, 651-678 (1986); 331-349 (1987)
      Bankruptcy and Labor, 181-199 (1984)
      Union Membership, 415-429 (1985)
Labor Department
   Donovan, Raymond J., Indictment, 803-809 (1984)
Land Use and Uncompensated Takings
   Supreme Court on, 531-553 (1987)
Latin America. *See also Central America; specific countries*
   Human Rights Report, 155 (1984); 102-108 (1986)
   Pope John Paul II's Journeys, 57-67 (1985)
   Republican Party Platform on, 675-677 (1988)
   State of the Union, 93 (1984); 66 (1988)
   Vatican on Theology of Liberation, 759-

775 (1984)
Law enforcement. *See Crime and law enforcement*
Lebanon
   Presidential Debates on, 884-886 (1984)
Lefebvre, Archbishop Marcel, 400 (1984)
   Excommunication, 489-494 (1988)
Legislative branch. *See Congress*
Lehrer, Jim, 724-754 (1988)
Lehn, Kenneth, 921-925 (1988)
Liability. *See Tort reform*
Libel
   Sharon Libel Verdict, 47-52 (1985)
   Westmoreland/CBS Controversy, 159-165 (1985)
   Supreme Court Decisions
      Freedom of the Press, 299-312 (1984)
      Media Libel Law, 247-256 (1984); 355-368 (1986)
Libya
   Human Rights, 203-204 (1987)
   Reagan on International Terrorism, 470-471 (1985)
   U.S. Air Strike, 347-354 (1986)
Lillestrand, Robert, 832-833 (1988)
Local government. *See State and local government*
Lockhart v. McCree, 445-456 (1986)
Lounge, John M., 797 (1988)
Lown, Dr. Bernard, 781-787 (1985)
Lynch v. Donnelly, 217-239 (1984)

M

Mallerais, Bernard Tissier de, 490-492 (1988)
Malone, James, 571-581 (1985)
Mandela, Nelson, 582, 586-587 (1986)
Marcos, Ferdinand, 925-932 (1984); 98, 110-111, 307, 1037 (1986); 867-872 (1988)
Marcos, Imelda, 867-872 (1988)
Margolis, Jon, 804-805, 810-812, 817-818, 823-825 (1988)
Marijuana. *See Drug abuse*
Marshall, Thurgood
   Closed Party Primaries, 1065, 1066, 1068-1071 (1986)
   Exclusionary Rule, 506 (1984)
   Indigents' Rights to Psychiatric Aid, 208, 210-217 (1985)
   Jury Selection in Capital Cases, 454-456 (1986)
   Labor Union Membership, 415, 424-429 (1985)
   Maternity Leave, 20-26 (1987)
   Miranda Rule, 225, 236-250 (1985)
   PAC Spending Limits, 279, 290-291 (1985)
   Peremptory Challenge, 421-425 (1986)
   Preventive Detention, 491-494, 502-508 (1987)
   Prisoners' Rights, 481, 491 (1984)
   Secrecy of CIA Sources, 333, 342-344 (1985)

Sex Bias in Education, 202 (1984)
Student Aid/Draft Registration, 500-503 (1984)
Student Searches, 15, 23-26 (1985)
Students' Free Speech, 733, 739-740 (1986)
Suspects' Rights, 388, 395-397 (1984)
Marxism
Vatican on Theology of Liberation, 759-775 (1984)
Mashek, John, 726-727, 734-735, 741-742, 749 (1988)
Maternity Leave, 17-27 (1987)
Matsunaga, Spark M., D.-Hawaii, 289-291 (1988)
Mauthausen, Austria
Pope John Paul's Visit, 406-409 (1988)
McCleskey v. Kemp, 463-476 (1987)
McFarlane, Robert, 1015-1016, 1050 (1986)
McKay, James C.
Ethics Investigation of Edwin Meese III, 495-516 (1988)
McKelvey v. Turnage, 277-285 (1988)
McNamara, Robert S., 523-524 (1984)
Mecham, Gov. Evan, 249-256 (1988)
Media. *See Communications; Press*
Medicaid and Medicare
Catastrophic Illness Expenses, 1025-1035 (1986)
Harvard Report on Medicare Reform, 273-285 (1986)
Hospital Length of Stay Report, 333-337 (1988)
President's Commission on Privatization Report, 235 (1988)
Reagan's Budget Message, 152, 157 (1988)
Medical care
AIDS in the Workplace, 733-747 (1985)
AMA Proposed Boxing Ban, 1019-1021 (1984)
Catastrophic Illness Expenses, 1025-1035 (1986)
Court on Sustaining Handicapped Infants, 541-558 (1986)
Democratic Party Platform on, 567-568 (1984); 563-564 (1988)
Doctors on the Terminally Ill, 275-285 (1984)
For-Profit Hospitals, 487-513 (1986)
Heart Disease Report, 1039-1043 (1984)
Hospital Length of Stay Report, 333-337 (1988)
Medicare. *See Medicaid and Medicare*
Meese, Edwin, III, 479-490 (1985); 1014, 1023-1024 (1986); 495-516 (1988)
Mengele, Josef, 409-414 (1985)
Mental Health Report, 833-843 (1984)
Mexican-Americans. *See Hispanics*
Middle East. *See also specific countries*
Arab Summit Communiqué, 869-874 (1987)
Democratic Party Platform on, 636-637 (1984); 567-568 (1988)

Iran Arms Deal, 1013-1024, 1049-1055 (1986)
Persian Gulf War, 747-755 (1984)
Presidential Debates on, 884-886 (1984)
Republican Party Platform on, 711-712 (1984); 683-685 (1988)
Shultz on Terrorism, 933-944 (1984)
UN Resolution on Iran-Iraq War, 609-613 (1987)
Vice Presidential Debate on, 820-821 (1988)
Military. *See also Defense; Defense Department*
Joint Chiefs of Staff, 669-683 (1985)
Military Base Closings, 951-954 (1988)
Organized Crime Commission, 181, 194-195 (1986)
Military aid. *See Foreign aid*
Military draft
Court on Student Aid/Draft Registration, 493-503 (1984)
Minority business
Democratic Party Platform on, 585-586 (1984)
Donovan Indictment, 803-809 (1984)
Minority groups. *See also specific groups*
Affirmative Action, 365-385 (1984); 651-678 (1986)
AMA Proposed Boxing Ban, 1019-1021 (1984)
Bishops' Letter on Economic Justice, 999 (1986)
Black and Minority Health Report, 685-706 (1985)
Employment
Economic Advisers' Report, 140 (1988)
President's Economic Report, 119 (1988)
Kerner Report Updated, 185-194 (1988)
Tutu Nobel Prize Speech, 1027-1037 (1984)
Mitchell, Andrea, 761-762, 769-771, 777-779 (1988)
Mitchell, Mark L., 921-925 (1988)
Mitterrand, François
Economic Summit (Bonn), 348-349 (1985)
Statue of Liberty's Centennial, 697, 702-703 (1986)
Mondale, Walter F.
Acceptance Speech, 647-648 (1984)
Democratic Party Platform, 549-551 (1984)
Election Results, 953-956 (1984)
Presidential Debates, 845-902 (1984)
Monetary policy. *See also Economic policy; Inflation*
Democratic Party Platform on, 568 (1984)
Economic Advisers' Report, 128-129, 134-136 (1984); 91 (1985); 59-60, 76-78 (1986); 117, 128-131 (1988)
Economic Summit Meetings
(Bonn), 354 (1985)

(London), 356-357, 359-361 (1984)
(Venice), 512 (1987); 525-530 (1987)
Greenspan Appointment, 511-516 (1987)
IMF-World Bank Conference, 795-802
(1984); 643-652 (1985)
Plunge of the Dollar, 523-530 (1985)
President's Economic Report, 119-120,
125-126 (1984); 87 (1985)
Republican Party Platform on, 662, 667-
670 (1984)
Stock Market Crash, 833-842 (1987); 9-36
(1988); 132-135 (1988)
Volcker Resignation, 511-516 (1987)
Morocco
Pope John Paul II's Visit, 500, 509-514
(1985)
Morrison v. Olson, 465-478 (1988)
Motion Picture Association of America, 55
(1984)
MOVE Raid in Philadelphia, 239-251 (1986)
Mozambique, 973-995 (1984)
Mulroney, Brian, 407, 408-409 (1984); 571-
574 (1988)
MX Missile
Former Security Officials on Defense
Strategy, 782-783 (1986)

N

Nakasone, Yasuhiro, 319-323 (1985); 427,
429, 433-437 (1987)
Namibia
Angola-Namibia Peace Accord, 947-950
(1988)
UN Resolution on, 356 (1988)
Narcotics. *See Drug abuse*
National Academy of Sciences (NAS)
AIDS Report, 887-908 (1986)
For-Profit Hospitals, 487-513 (1986)
National Security Export Controls Report,
29-42 (1987)
Sex Segregation in the Workplace, 789-801
(1985)
Teenage Pregnancy, 1057-1064 (1986)
**National Advisory Commission on Civil Dis-
orders**
Kerner Report Updated, 185-194 (1988)
**National Aeronautics and Space Administra-
tion (NASA)**
Challenger Accident Commission Report,
515-539 (1986)
Discovery Tribute to *Challenger* Victims,
795-798 (1988)
Ozone Depletion Report, 221-228 (1988)
Ride Commission Report, 649-669 (1987)
**National Assessment of Educational Prog-
ress (NAEP)**
Math and Science Education Reports, 377-
390 (1988)
**National Center for Health Services Re-
search and Health Care Technology Assess-
ment**

Report on Length of Hospitalization, 333-
337 (1988)
*National Collegiate Athletic Assn. v. University
of Oklahoma,* 415 (1984)
National Conference of Catholic Bishops
Pastoral Letter on Economy, 957-972
(1984); 983-1011 (1986)
**National Endowment for the Humanities
(NEH)**
Humanities Education Report, 973-1003
(1984); 681-696 (1987)
State of the Humanities Report, 517-527
(1988)
National Enquirer, 247-248, 253-256 (1984)
National Institute of Mental Health (NIMH)
Mental Health Report, 833-843 (1984)
National Institutes of Health (NIH)
Cholesterol Report, 779-790 (1987)
Heart Disease Report, 1039-1043 (1984)
Reagan's Budget Message, 150, 155 (1988)
National Labor Relations Board v. Bildisco,
181-199 (1984)
National Research Council (NRC)
Radon Report, 3-8 (1988)
National Security Council (NSC). *See also
Defense*
Iran-Contra Reports, 891-928 (1987)
Tower Commission Report, 205-242 (1987)
National Urban League
Black America Report, 27-37 (1985); 43-60
(1987)
Kerner Report Updated, 185-186 (1988)
Natural resources. *See also Energy policy;
Environment; Water policy*
Democratic Party Platform on, 592-598
(1984)
Natural Resources Defense Council, 427-437
(1984)
Navy, U.S.
Pentagon on Sexual Harassment, 671-679
(1987)
Report on USS *Stark* Attack, 791-816
(1987)
Nelson, George D., 798 (1988)
Netherlands
Pope John Paul II's Visit, 363-374 (1985)
Neves, Tancredo, 3-12 (1985)
New Ireland Forum, 315-326 (1984)
New Jersey v. T.L.O., 13-26 (1985)
New York v. Quarles, 387-397 (1984)
*New York State Club Assn., Inc. v. City of New
York et al.,* 399-403 (1988)
Newman, Edwin, 876-902 (1984)
Newman, Frank, 583-602 (1985)
Nguyen, Jean, 116-117 (1985)
Nicaragua. *See also Central America*
Americas Watch, Administration Reports,
255-269 (1985)
Central American Cease-Fire Agreement,
241-245 (1988)
Central American Peace Agreement, 637-
648 (1987)

CIA Manual on Guerrilla Warfare, 903-916 (1984)
Human Rights Report, 164-165 (1984); 146, 153 (1985); 107-108 (1986); 197-198 (1987)
Iran Arms Deal and Contra Funding, 1013-1024, 1049-1055 (1986)
Iran-Contra Reports, 891-928 (1987)
Kissinger Commission Report, 31-52 (1984)
Presidential Debates on, 847, 877-878, 883-884 (1984)
Reagan on International Terrorism, 472 (1985)
State of the Union, 66 (1988)
Tower Commission Report, 205-242 (1987)
U.S. Withdrawal from World Court Jurisdiction, 637-641 (1985)
Vatican on Theology of Liberation, 761 (1984); 318 (1986)
World Court on Mining Harbors, 339-345 (1984)
Nicotine Addiction Report, 309-322 (1988)
Niskanen, William A., 119 (1984); 80 (1985)
Nix v. Williams, 506 (1984)
Nobel Peace Prize
Arias Speech, 1007-1011 (1987)
International Physicians for the Prevention of Nuclear War Speech, 781-787 (1985)
Tutu Speech, 1027-1037 (1984)
Wiesel Speech, 1075-1078 (1986)
Nofziger, Lyn (Franklyn C.), 495, 499 (1988)
Nollan v. California Coastal Commission, 531, 533-534, 547-553 (1987)
Noriega, Manuel Antonio
Grand Jury Indictments, 81-92 (1988)
Vice Presidential Debate on, 814-815 (1988)
North, Oliver, 1015-117, 1050-1052 (1986); 217-218, 225-226, 232-233 (1987). *See also Iran-contra affair*
North Atlantic Treaty Organization (NATO)
Democratic Party Platform on, 633-634 (1984)
Republican Party Platform on, 710-711 (1984), 680-681, 694 (1988)
North Korea. *See also Korea*
Human Rights Report, 198-199 (1987)
Reagan on Terrorism, 471 (1985)
Roh Tae Woo's UN Address, 853-859 (1988)
Northern Ireland
British-Irish Accord on Northern Ireland, 723-732 (1985)
Human Rights Report, 112-113 (1988)
New Ireland Forum, 315-326 (1984)
U.S.-U.K. Extradition Treaty, 751-756 (1986)
Nuclear energy. *See also Energy policy*
Chernobyl Nuclear Accident, 383-407 (1986)

Republican Party Platform on, 667 (1988)
Nuclear weapons. *See also Arms control; Treaties and agreements*
Effects of Nuclear War, 541-554 (1985)
Former Security Officials on Defense Strategy, 781-790 (1986)
Nobel Peace Prize Speech on, 781-787 (1985)
Reagan Trip to China, 288-289, 294-295 (1984)
Nunn, Sam, D-Ga.
ABM Treaty Interpretation, 289-317 (1987)

O

Obscenity. *See Pornography*
Occupational safety
AIDS in the Workplace, 733-747 (1985)
Health Costs of Smoking, 615-622 (1985)
Vice Presidential Debate on, 810-812 (1988)
O'Connor, Sandra Day
Abortion, 562, 579-580 (1986)
Affirmative Action, 676 (1986); 332-333, 340, 346 (1987)
Federal and State Powers, 169, 182-187 (1985)
Media Libel Law, 356-364 (1986)
Miranda Rule, 223-236 (1985)
Nativity Scene, 228-231 (1984)
Political Gerrymandering, 617, 629-63 (1986)
Private Clubs, 403 (1988)
Public School Teachers in Parochial Classes, 433, 448-449, 455-461 (1985)
Sex Bias in Education, 202 (1984)
Sex Discrimination, 468, 475-478 (1984)
Silent Prayer, 380, 387-392 (1985)
Suspects' Rights, 388, 393-395 (1984)
Sustaining Handicapped Infants, 544-558 (1986)
Use of Deadly Force, 304, 312-315 (1985)
Office of Technology Assessment (OTA)
Alzheimer's Disease, 391-406 (1987)
Biotechnology Reports, 287-306 (1986); 351-372 (1987)
Health Costs of Smoking, 615-622 (1985)
Ownership of Human Tissues and Cells, 351-372 (1987)
Star Wars Defense Report, 257 260, 267-272 (1984)
Oil. *See also Energy policy*
Economic Adviser's Report, 118, 127-128 (1987)
Republican Party Platform on, 665-666 (1988)
Okun, Herbert S., 267-272 (1986)
O'Neill, Thomas P., Jr., D-Mass., 39, 42, 753 (1986)
Oregon v. Elstad, 223-253 (1985)
OTA. *See Office of Technology Assessment*

P

Packard Commission on Defense Management
Report, 679-695 (1986)
Republican Party Platform on, 696 (1988)
PACs. *See Political Action Committees*
Pakistan
Afghanistan Agreements, 257-261 (1988)
Palestine Liberation Organization (PLO)
Hussein's West Bank Speech, 579-585 (1988)
Office Closing, 479-485 (1988)
PNC Declaration of Independence, 905-908 (1988)
Palestine National Council (PNC)
Declaration of Independence, 905-911 (1988)
Panama
Kissinger Commission Report, 32, 36, 42 (1984)
Noriega Indictments, 81-92 (1988)
Republican Party Platform on, 677 (1988)
Papua New Guinea
Pope John Paul II's Visit, 328, 332-334 (1984)
Pattern Makers League of North America (AFL-CIO) v. National Labor Relations Board, 415-429 (1985)
Peacemaking efforts. *See also Arms control; Nobel Peace Prize; Treaties and agreements*
Arab Summit Communiqué, 869-874 (1987)
Central American Cease-Fire Agreement, 241-245 (1988)
Central American Peace Agreement, 637-648 (1987)
Indo-Sri Lankan Accord, 615-622 (1987)
Reagan-Gorbachev New Year's Messages, 3-8 (1986)
State of the Union, 114-115 (1985)
UN on Iran-Iraq War, 609-613 (1987)
UN World Conference on Women, 567-570 (1985)
Peary, Robert E., 831-833 (1988)
People's Republic of China (PRC). *See China, People's Republic of*
Peres, Shimon, 498 (1988)
Pershing II Ballistic Missile. *See Intermediate-range Nuclear Forces*
Peru
Pope John Paul II's Visit, 57, 58, 62-67 (1985)
Philadelphia
Investigation of Police Raid on MOVE Group, 239-251 (1986)
Philadelphia Newspapers Inc. v. Hepps, 355-368 (1986)
Philippines
Aquino Assassination Reports, 925-932 (1984)

Aquino Speech on Coup Attempt, 843-854 (1987)
Cease-Fire Agreement, 1037-1046 (1986)
Change of Government, 307-314 (1986)
Human Rights Report, 166-167 (1984); 154-155 (1985); 98, 110-112 (1986); 190-191, 201-202; 106-108 (1988)
Marcos Indictment, 867-872 (1988)
Presidential Debates on, 897-898 (1984)
Physicians Task Force on Hunger in America, 189-205 (1985)
Platforms, Political. *See Democratic Party; Republican Party*
Poindexter, John, 1016, 1049-1050 (1986); 208, 216, 218, 222, 232 (1987). *See also Iran-contra affair*
Poland
Human Rights Report, 153-154 (1985)
Lifting Trade Sanctions, 183-188 (1987)
Pope John Paul II's Visits, 555-564 (1987)
Sentencing of Popieluszko's Slayers, 119-126 (1985)
Polar exploration. *See Arctic Expedition of 1909*
Political Action Committees (PACs)
Spending Limits, 277-294 (1985)
Vice Presidential Debate on, 808-809 (1988)
Political activism
Black America Report, 28, 33 (1985)
Pope John Paul II's Journey to South America, 57, 65-67 (1985)
Pollution. *See also Environment*
Bhopal Gas Poisoning, 1023-1026 (1984)
Radon Report, 3-8 (1988)
Poole, William, 119 (1984); 80 (1985)
Pope v. Illinois, 479-490 (1987)
Pope John Paul II. *See John Paul II*
Popieluszko, Jerzy, 119-126 (1985); 557 (1987)
Population
Population Institute Report, 439-462 (1987)
World Population Problems, 521-547 (1984)
Pornography
Court on Adult Theaters, 131-144 (1986)
Court on Obscenity, 479-490 (1987)
Republican Party Platform on, 636 (1988)
Portugal
Common Market Summit, 443 (1984)
Postal Service, U.S.
Economic Advisers' Report, 88-89 (1986)
President's Commission on Privatization Report, 231, 233-234 (1988)
Poverty. *See also Homeless; Welfare and social services*
Bishops on Economic Justice, 984, 998-1002 (1986)
Bishops on U.S. Economy, 957-972 (1984)
Democratic Party Platform on, 616-618 (1984)

Food Assistance Report, 3-17 (1984)
Hunger in America, 189-205 (1985)
Kerner Report Updated, 185-194 (1988)
Kissinger Commission Report on Central
  America, 31-52 (1984)
Natural Disasters Report, 973-995 (1984)
Pope John Paul II on, 777-778, 785-787
  (1984); 23-37 (1986)
Republican Party Platform on, 657-659
  (1988)
Urban Institute Child Poverty Report,
  877-880 (1988)
Vatican on Theology of Liberation, 759-
  775 (1984); 317-338 (1986)
Vice Presidential Debate on, 806-807
  (1988)
Powell, Lewis F., Jr.
Creation Science, 566, 572-574 (1987)
Death Penalty, 463-473 (1987)
Federal and State Powers, 168-169, 182-
  187 (1985)
Labor Union Membership, 415-424 (1985)
Peremptory Challenge, 410, 412-421 (1986)
Political Asylum, 253-255, 262-265 (1987)
Political Gerrymandering, 617, 632-633
  (1986)
Retirement, 577-581 (1987)
Sex Bias in Education, 202, 210-212 (1984)
Sodomy and Privacy, 602, 607-608 (1986)
Pregnancy and childbirth. *See also Abortion;*
Birth control
CDF Infant Mortality Report, 147-165
  (1987)
Maternity Leave, 17-27 (1987)
Surrogates' Rights, 373-387 (1987); 71-80
  (1988)
Teenage Pregnancy, 1057-1064 (1986)
Vatican on Bioethics, 267-287 (1987)
Pregnancy Discrimination Act
Supreme Court Decisions, 17-27 (1987)
Presidency. *See also individual names*
Harvard Commission on the Presidential
  Press Conference, 835-845 (1988)
Transfer of Presidential Power, 491-495
  (1985)
Vice Presidential Debate on, 809-810, 815-
  816, 819-820 821-825 (1988)
**Presidential Commission on the Human Im-
munodeficiency Virus Epidemic,** 415-446
**Presidential Commission on the Space Shut-
tle Challenger Accident,** 515-539 (1986)
Presidential election, 1984
Debates, 845-902 (1984)
Democratic Party Platform, 549-646
  (1984)
Mondale-Ferraro Acceptance Speeches,
  657-658 (1984)
Reagan-Bush Acceptance Speeches, 727-
  745 (1984)
Republican Party Platform, 661-726
  (1984)
Victory and Concession, 953-956 (1984)

Presidential election, 1988
Bush-Quayle Acceptance Speeches, 589-
  591, 601-613 (1988)
Debates, 721-783 (1988)
Democratic Party Platform, 557-569
  (1988)
Dukakis-Bentsen Acceptance Speeches,
  533-546 (1988)
Postelection Statements, 891-904 (1988)
Republican Party Platform, 615-702
  (1988)
**Presidential Task Force on Market Mecha-
nisms (Brady Commission),** 9-11, 13-33
(1988)
**President's Blue Ribbon Commission on De-
fense Management (Packard Commission),**
679-695 (1988)
President's Commission on Organized Crime,
179-216 (1986)
President's Commission on Privatization,
229-239 (1988)
**President's Private Sector Survey on Cost
Control (Grace Commission),** 115, 126, 169-
179 (1984); 231 (1988)
Press
Daniloff Arrest in Moscow, 819-827 (1986)
Harvard Commission on the Presidential
  Press Conference, 835-845 (1988)
Sharon Libel Verdict, 47-52 (1985)
Supreme Court Decisions
  Freedom of Press, 299-312 (1984); 175-
    182 (1988)
  Media Libel Law, 247-256 (1984)
  Westmoreland/CBS Controversy, 159-
    165 (1985)
Prisons. *See Crime and law enforcement*
Privacy, Right of, 601-614 (1986)
Privatization of government services. *See*
also Business and industry
Economic Advisers' Report, 88-89 (1986)
Presidential Debates on, 740 (1988)
President's Commission on Privatization
  Report, 229-239 (1988)
President's Economic Report, 61, 68
  (1986); 123-124 (1987); 121-122 (1988)
Reagan's Budget Message, 150, 152, 158-
  159 (1988)
Republican Party Platform on, 627 (1988)
Public Health Service (PHS)
Aids Education Report, 319-326 (1987)
Length of Hospitalization Report, 333-337
  (1988)
Puerto Rico
Democratic Party Platform on, 611 (1984);
  565 (1988)
Republican Party Platform on, 646 (1988)

Q

Qaddafi, Muammar
Reagan on U.S. Air Strike Against Libya,
  347-354 (1986)

Reagan on Terrorism, 464-471 (1985)
Quayle, Dan
  Acceptance Speech, 590-591, 601-604
    (1988)
  Presidential Debates on, 749-750 (1988)
  Vice Presidential Debate, 799-829 (1988)

R

Radiation
  Nuclear War Effects, 541-554 (1985)
  Radon Report, 3-8 (1988)
Ratzinger, Cardinal Joseph
  Bioethics, 267-287 (1987)
  Letter to Charles E. Curran, 758-762
    (1986)
  Liberation Theology, 759-775 (1984); 319-
    338 (1986)
  Pastoral Care of Homosexuals, 909-918
    (1986)
Rawlins, Dennis, 831-833 (1988)
Reagan, Ronald
  Constitution Bicentennial Observance,
    765-775 (1987)
  Defense
    Budget Message, 108 (1984); 4, 9-10, 14
      (1987); 152, 156 (1988)
    Defense in Space, 257-272 (1984)
    Department of Veterans Affairs, 873-876
      (1988)
    INF Treaty Statement, 945, 947-950
      (1987)
    MX Missile Basing, 4 (1987)
    State of the Union, 87, 93-94 (1984)
    Terrorism Policy, 463-477 (1985)
  Domestic Affairs
    Administration Policy on Black Ameri-
      ca, 27-37 (1985)
    Education, 201-203 (1984)
    Executive Order on Drug Testing, 839-
      846 (1986)
    Family Support Act, 847-852 (1988)
    Food Assistance Report, 3-17 (1984)
    Immigration Bill, 963-969 (1986)
    Interment of Unknown Vietnam Ser-
      viceman, 347-350 (1984)
    Public Broadcasting Editorials, 449-451
      (1984)
    Remarks to Right-to-Life Marchers, 53-
      56 (1985)
    School Prayer, 241-245 (1984)
    State of the Union, 85-92 (1984)
    Women, 201-203 (1984)
  Economic Affairs
    Balanced Budget Bill, 803-808 (1985)
    Budget Message, 99-117 (1984); 71-78
      (1985); 49-58 (1986); 3-15 (1987); 149-
      163 (1988)
    Economic Report, 119-128 (1984); 79-87
      (1985); 59, 62-69 (1986); 117-124
      (1987); 117-125 (1988)
    Economic Summit Meetings: (London),

355-364 (1984); (Toronto), 392-393
  (1988); (Venice), 525-530 (1987)
Greenspan Appointment, 511-516 (1987)
Inflation, 85, 102-103, 123-124 (1984)
Stock Market Crash, 837-839 (1987); 9-
  36 (1988)
Trade Bill Vetoes, 339-346 (1988)
U.S.-Japan Trade Dispute, 427-437
  (1987)
Volcker Resignation, 511-516 (1987)
  Energy and Environment
    Budget Message, 109 (1984)
    EPA and Clean Air, 427-437 (1984)
  Foreign Affairs
    Administration Reports on Nicaragua,
      255-258, 260-269 (1985)
    Air Strike Against Libya, 347-354 (1986)
    Andropov Death, 145-146, 148-150
      (1984)
    Bitburg Visit, 357-362 (1985)
    Budget Message, 111-112 (1984)
    Canada-U.S. Trade Pact, 571-578 (1988)
    China Trip, 287-298 (1984)
    CIA Manual on Guerrilla Warfare, 903-
      916 (1984)
    Human Rights Policy, 156 (1984)
    Iran Arms Deal and Contra Funding,
      1013-1024, 1049-1055 (1986)
    Kissinger Commission Report, 31-52
      (1984)
    New Year's Message to Soviets, 3-5, 7-8
      (1986)
    Pope John Paul II's Far East Trip, 327
      (1984)
    Presidential Debates on, 846-847, 876-
      902 (1984)
    South Africa Sanctions, 531-540 (1985)
    State of the Union, 92-94 (1984)
    Summits with Gorbachev: (Geneva),
      749-761 (1985); (Moscow), 353-373;
      (Reykjavik), 875-885 (1986); (Washing-
      ton, D.C.), 991-1006 (1987)
    Terrorism Policy, 934-935 (1984); 463-
      477 (1985)
    Trade Bill Vetoes, 339-346 (1988)
    Tutu Nobel Prize Speech, 1028-1029
      (1984)
    United Nations Address, 811-821 (1984);
      707-719 (1985)
    U.S.-Japan Trade Dispute, 427-437
      (1987)
    Vatican-U.S. Relations, 19-22 (1984)
    Weinberger on Use of Military Force,
      1005-1015 (1984)
    World Court on Mining Nicaraguan
      Harbors, 339-345 (1984)
    Zhao Visit, 23-30 (1984)
  Politics
    Acceptance Speech, 127-745 (1984)
    Mondale-Reagan Debate, 845-902
      (1984)
    Republican National Convention Ad-

dress, 589-590, 592-601 (1988)
Republican Party Platform, 661-726 (1984)
Victory Statement, 953-956 (1984)
State of the Union, 81-95 (1984); 105-117 (1985); 39-48 (1986); 105-115 (1987); 47-56 (1988)
Statue of Liberty's Centennial, 697-698, 700-702 (1986)
Supreme Court
Appointments, 591-599 (1986); 720 (1987)
Bork Confirmation Battle, 717-744 (1987)
Transfer of Presidential Power, 491-495 (1985)
Red Cross (Sweden), 973-995 (1984)
Refugees. *See also Immigration*
Cuban Detainee Agreements, 929-937 (1987)
Democratic Party Platform on, 611 (1984)
Pope John Paul II's Thailand Visit, 329, 336-338 (1984)
Republican Party Platform on, 703-704 (1984)
Supreme Court on Political Asylum, 253-265 (1987)
Regional government. *See State and local government*
Regulatory reform. *See also Airline deregulation*
Budget Message, 113-114 (1984); 12 (1987); 158 (1988)
Economic Advisers' Report, 85-89 (1986)
President's Economic Report, 124-125 (1984); 86-87 (1985); 67-68 (1986); 122 (1988)
Republican Party Platform on, 670-671 (1984); 626-627 (1988)
State of the Union, 60-61 (1986)
Supreme Court on Public Broadcasting Editorials, 450 (1984)
Rehnquist, William H.
Adult Theaters, 132, 134-140 (1986)
Affirmative Action, 677-678 (1986)
Appointment to Chief Justice, 591-599 (1986)
Bankruptcy and Labor, 181, 184-193 (1984)
Contagious Diseases, 246, 250-252 (1987)
Federal and State Powers, 169, 182-187 (1985)
Freedom of Press, 310-312 (1984); 175-182 (1988)
Independent Counsel, 465, 469-477 (1988)
Indigents' Rights to Psychiatric Aid, 209, 217-219 (1985)
Jury Selection in Capital Cases, 446-454 (1986)
Media Libel Law, 247-252, 253-256 (1984)
PAC Spending Limits, 278-290 (1985)
Preventive Detention, 491, 494-502 (1987)

Public Broadcasting Editorials, 461-463 (1984)
Public School Teachers in Parochial classes, 433, 449-450, 455, 458-462 (1985)
Suspects' Rights, 388, 389-393 (1984)
Uncompensated Takings and Land Use, 532-540 (1987)
Use of Deadly Force, 304, 312-315 (1985)
Religion. *See also Catholic church*
Apostolic Letter on Women, 785-792 (1988)
Bishops on U.S. Economy, 957-972 (1984); 983-1011 (1986)
Gandhi, Indira, 945-949 (1984)
Meese Criticism of Supreme Court, 479-480, 486-490 (1985)
New Ireland Forum, 315-326 (1984)
Persian Gulf War, 747-748 (1984)
Pope John Paul II, 327-338, 399-406, 777-787 (1984); 363-376, 499-514 (1985); 23-37, 339-346, 639-649 (1986); 555-564; 699-716 (1987)
Presidential Debates on, 846, 855-858 (1984)
Reagan-Gorbachev Summit, 358-359 (1988)
School Curriculum and, 597-608 (1987)
School Prayer, 241-245 (1984); 112-113 (1987)
Supreme Court Decisions
Nativity Scene, 217-239 (1984)
Public School Teachers in Parochial Classes, 433-461 (1985)
School Prayer, 379-395 (1985)
Synod of Catholic Bishops, 765-780 (1985)
Tutu Nobel Prize Speech, 1027-1037 (1984)
U.S. Bishops Report to the Vatican, 571-581 (1985)
Vatican on Theology of Liberation, 759-775 (1984); 317-338 (1986)
Vatican-U.S. Relations, 19-22 (1984)
Republican Party
Convention
Bush Acceptance Speech, 590-591, 604-613 (1988)
Quayle Acceptance Speech, 590-591, 601-604 (1988)
Reagan Address, 589, 592-601 (1988)
Reagan-Bush Acceptance Speeches, 727-745 (1984)
Election Results, 953-956 (1984)
Party Platform, 661-726 (1984); 615-702 (1988)
Rhodesia. *See Zimbabwe*
Ride, Sally K., 649-669 (1987)
Ridings, Dorothy S., 848, 876 (1984)
Rifkin, Jeremy, 228 (1986)
Roberts v. U.S. Jaycees, 465-478 (1984)
Roh Tae Woo
Statement on Democratic Reforms, 583-590 (1987)

UN Address, 853-859 (1988)
Ruckelshaus v. Natural Resources Defense Council, 427-437 (1984)
Rural development. *See Agriculture*

S

Sabato, Ernesto, 789 (1984)
Sahel
  Natural Disasters Report, 973-995 (1984)
Sakharov, Andrei D.
  Release from Exile, 1091-1095 (1986)
Salerno, Anthony (Fat Tony), 491-508 (1987)
SALT. *See Strategic Arms Limitation Treaty*
Saudi Arabia
  Arab Summit Communiqué, 869-874 (1987)
  Persian Gulf War, 752-755 (1984)
Savings and Loans. *See Banks and banking*
Sawyer, Diane, 848-876 (1984)
Scalia, Antonin
  Affirmative Action, 333-334, 346-349 (1987)
  Appointment to Supreme Court, 591-599 (1986)
  Closed Party Primaries, 1065, 1067, 1072-1073 (1986)
  Contagious Diseases, 246, 250-252 (1987)
  Creation Science, 567, 574-576 (1987)
  Disruptive Handicapped Students, 49, 56 (1988)
  Independent Counsel, 468, 477-478 (1988)
  Obscenity, 479-481, 484-485 (1987)
  Private Clubs, 399, 403 (1988)
  Uncompensated Takings and Land Use, 533, 547-549 (1987)
School Board of Nassau County, Florida v. Arline, 245-252 (1987)
Schools. *See Education*
Schwebel, Stephen, 344-345 (1984); 638 (1985)
Science and technology. *See also Space*
  Bhopal Gas Poisoning, 1023-1026 (1984)
  China-U.S. Accords, 23-30, 288-289, 294-295 (1984)
  Economic Summit (Bonn), 355 (1985)
  Gorbachev at 27th Party Congress, 154-155 (1986)
  Math and Science Education Reports, 377-390 (1988)
  National Security Export Controls, 29-42 (1987)
  Nuclear War Effects, 541-554 (1985)
  OTA Report on Biotechnology, 287-306 (1986)
  Pope John Paul II's Canada Visit, 778-785 (1984)
  Reagan's Budget Message, 108 (1984); 155 (1988)
  Report on Soviet Espionage, 603-614 (1985)
  Republican Party Platform on, 653-654 (1988)
  Scientists/OTA on Star Wars Defense, 257-272 (1984)
Search and seizure
  Student Searches, 13-26 (1985)
Securities and Exchange Commission (SEC)
  Corporate Takeovers Report, 921-925 (1988)
Segregation. *See Civil and political rights; Education; Housing*
Selective Service System v. Minnesota Public Interest Research Group, 493-503 (1984)
Senate
  Armed Services Committee Pentagon Report, 669-683 (1985)
  Bork Confirmation Battle, 717-744 (1987)
  Impeachment of Judge Claiborne, 849-857 (1986)
  Iran-Contra Reports, 891-928 (1987)
  Persian Gulf War Report, 747-755 (1984)
  Ratification of Genocide Convention, 115-130 (1986)
  School Prayer Amendment, 241-245 (1984)
  U.S.-U.K. Extradition Treaty, 751-756 (1986)
Sentencing Commission Report, 407-426 (1987)
Separation of powers. *See Constitution, U.S., Tenth Amendment*
Sex Discrimination
  Pentagon on Sexual Harassment, 671-679 (1987)
  Segregation in the Workplace, 789-801 (1985)
  Supreme Court Decisions
    Commercial Organizations, 465-478 (1984)
    Education, 201-214 (1984)
    Maternity Leave, 17-27 (1987)
    Private Clubs, 399-403 (1988)
Shamir, Yitzhak, 47-52 (1985)
Shaw, Bernard, 754-783 (1988)
Shcharansky, Anatoly Borisovich, 93-96 (1986)
Sheet Metal Workers' International Association v. Equal Employment Opportunity Commission, 651-678 (1986)
Sher, Neal, 409-414 (1985)
Shultz, George P.
  Iran Arms Sales, 1015, 1051 (1986)
  Terrorism Speech, 933-944, 1006-1007 (1984)
  U.S. Withdrawal from World Court Jurisdiction, 637-641 (1985)
Sikhism
  Indira Gandhi Assassination, 945-949 (1984)
Simpson, Alan K., R-Wyo., 288, 289, 294-295 (1988)
Singh, Gianizail, 949 (1984)
Sixth Amendment. *See Constitution, U.S.*

Small business. *See also Minority business*
Democratic Party Platform on, 585-586 (1984)
Republican Party Platform on, 671-672 (1984); 623-624 (1988)
Smoking
Health Costs Report, 615-622 (1985)
Involuntary Smoking, 1079-1090 (1986)
Nicotine Addiction Report, 309-322 (1988)
Smoking in the Workplace, 809-822 (1985)
Social Security. *See also Welfare and social services*
Economic Advisers' Report, 100-101 (1985)
Presidential Debates on, 866, 872-873 (1984); 769-771 (1988)
Vice Presidential Debate on, 804-805 (1988)
Social services. *See Welfare and social services*
Sofaer, Abraham D., 49, 639 (1985); 752-753 (1986); 289 (1987)
Solar Energy. *See Energy policy*
Solomon Islands
Pope John Paul II's Visit, 328 (1984)
Sony Corp. of America v. Universal City Studios, 53-80 (1984)
South Africa. *See also Angola; Namibia*
Angola-Namibia Peace Accord, 947-950 (1988)
Apartheid government, 43, 50 (1987)
Commonwealth Group Report, 581-590 (1986)
Democratic Party Platform on, 641-642 (1984); 568 (1988)
Human Rights, 167-168 (1984); 146-147, 155-156 (1985); 99, 101-102 (1986); 190, 192-193 (1987); 94-96 (1988)
Pass Laws, 369-381 (1986)
President Botha's Manifesto for the Future, 515-527 (1985)
Reagan Sanctions, 531-540 (1985)
Tutu Nobel Prize Address, 1027-1037 (1984)
South Korea. *See Korea, South*
Soviet Union
Afghanistan Agreements, 257-266 (1988)
Andropov Death, 145-154 (1984)
Chernenko Death, 271-274 (1985)
Chernenko Interview, 917-923 (1984)
Chernobyl Nuclear Accident, 383-407, (1986)
Daniloff Arrest in Moscow, 819-827 (1986)
Democratic Party Platform on, 634-636, 643 (1984)
Economic Summit Meetings
(London), 357, 362-363 (1984)
(Venice), 526, 528 (1987)
Gorbachev, Mikhail S.
Address to 19th All-Union Conference, 447-464 (1988)
Address to 27th Soviet Party Congress,

145-168 (1986)
Arms Control Proposal, 9-20 (1986)
Bolshevik Anniversary Speech, 857-868 (1987)
Democratic Reforms Speech, 79-104 (1987)
Human Rights Report, 155, 168 (1984); 98, 111-112 (1986); 190, 202-203 (1987); 93-94, 110-112 (1988)
Kissinger Commission Report on Central America, 31, 44-47, 51 (1984)
Presidential Debates on, 880-883 (1984); 744-745 (1988)
Reagan-Gorbachev
INF Treaty Statement, 945, 947-950 (1987)
New Year's Messages, 3-8 (1986)
Summit Meetings, 749-761 (1985); 875-885 (1986); 991-1006 (1987); 353-373 (1988)
Reagan-Gromyko UN Addresses, 811-829 (1984)
Reagan on International Terrorism, 474-475 (1985)
Republican Party Platform on, 709-710 (1984); 677-679 (1988)
Sakharov Release from Exile, 1092-1095 (1986)
Scientists/OTA on Star Wars Defense, 257-272 (1984)
Shcharansky Release, 93-96 (1986)
Soviet Espionage, 603-614 (1985)
State of the Union, 93-94 (1984); 109-111 (1987)
U.S. Reduction of Soviet UN Mission, 267-272 (1986)
U.S. Relations, 707-709, 712-718 (1985)
U.S.-Soviet INF Treaty, 945-989 (1987); 57-58, 67 (1988)
Weinberger on Use of Military Force, 1005-1015 (1984)
Space
Budget Message, 108-109 (1984); 155 (1988)
Challenger Accident Commission Report, 515-539 (1986)
Discovery Tribute to *Challenger* Victims, 795-798 (1988)
Missile Defense
Democratic Party Platform on, 627 (1984)
Iceland Summit, 875-885 (1986)
Presidential Debates on, 847, 893-895 (1984)
Reagan-Gromyko UN Address, 824 (1984)
Scientists/OTA on Star Wars Defense, 257-272 (1984)
Security Officials on Defense Strategy, 782, 784, 786-788 (1986)
Republican Party Platform on, 654-655, 693-694 (1988)

Ride Commission Report to NASA, 649-669 (1987)
State of the Union, 81-82, 89-90 (1984); 113 (1985)
Spain
Common Market Summit, 443 (1984)
Special prosecutors. *See Attorneys*
Sports
AMA Proposed Boxing Ban, 1019-1020 (1984)
Ueberroth on Drugs in Baseball, 169-175 (1986)
Sri Lanka Accord with India, 615-622 (1987)
Star Wars. *See Strategic Defense Initiative*
START. *See Strategic Arms Reduction Talks*
State and local government
Budget Message, 112-113 (1984)
Democratic Party Platform on, 576-577, 582 (1984)
Food Assistance Report, 15-16 (1984)
Philadelphia Police Raid on MOVE Group, 239-251 (1986)
Supreme Court Decisions
Adult Theaters, 131-144 (1986)
Affirmative Action, 365-385 (1984); 651-678 (1986)
Federal Intervention, 167-187 (1985)
Nativity Scene, 217-239 (1984)
Redistricting, 615-635 (1986)
State Department
Human Rights Reports, 155-168 (1984); 145-157 (1985); 97-113 (1986); 189-204 (1987); 93-115 (1988)
Republican Party Platform on, 688 (1988)
U.S. Withdrawal from World Court Jurisdiction, 637-641 (1985)
State of the Union, 81-95 (1984); 105-117 (1985); 39-48 (1986); 105-115 (1987); 57-68 (1988)
Statue of Liberty's Centennial, 697-703 (1986)
Stern, William, 373-387 (1987); 71-80 (1988)
Stevens, John Paul
Address on Role of Supreme Court, 653-654, 666-668 (1985)
Affirmative Action, 332-334, 345-346 (1987)
Antitrust Law, 414, 422-426 (1984)
EPA and Clean Air, 427-437 (1984)
Exclusionary Rule, 507, 515-516 (1984)
Freedom of the Press, 300-309 (1984)
Mandatory Budget Cuts, 707, 718-723 (1986)
Mandatory Retirement, 397-407 (1985)
Media Libel Law, 364-368 (1986)
Miranda Rule, 226, 233, 250-253 (1985)
Obscenity, 479, 485-490 (1987)
Political Asylum, 253-254, 256-261 (1987)
Prisoners' Rights, 480-481, 485-488 (1984)
Public Broadcasting Editorials, 450, 461 (1984)

Sex Bias in Education, 202, 214 (1984)
Silent Prayer, 379-380, 382-387 (1985)
Student Searches, 15, 23-26 (1985)
Students' Free Speech, 740-742 (1986)
Sustaining Handicapped Infants, 543, 545-554 (1986)
Uncompensated Takings and Land Use, 532-533, 541-546 (1987)
Video Recorders, 53-54, 56-69 (1984)
Stevens, Ted, R-Alaska, 291-292 (1988)
Stock market
Economic Advisers' Report on Stock Market Crash, 132-135 (1988)
Stock Market Crash, 833-842 (1987); 9-36 (1988)
Supreme Court on Insider Trading, 881-889 (1987)
Stotts, Carl, 365-385 (1984)
Strategic Arms Limitation Treaty (SALT), 354 (1988)
Security Officials on Defense Strategy, 783, 788-789 (1986)
Strategic Arms Reduction Talks (START)
Reagan-Gorbachev Summit, 353-355, 372-373 (1988)
State of the Union, 58, 67 (1988)
Strategic Defense Initiative (SDI). *See also Space*
Economic Summit (Bonn), 349 (1985)
Iceland Summit, 875-885 (1986); 110 (1987)
Presidential Debates on, 745-746 (1988)
Republican Party Platform on, 690, 692 (1988)
Science Board Panel on Strategic Missile Defense, 323-331 (1988)
Security Officials on Defense Strategy, 782-790 (1986)
State of the Union, 58, 60, 67 (1988)
Substance abuse. *See Alcoholism; Drug abuse; Smoking*
Sudan
Natural Disasters Report, 973-995 (1984)
Summit conferences. *See also Treaties and agreements*
Arab Summit Communiqué, 869-874 (1987)
Common Market Summit, 439-445 (1984)
Economic Summit Meetings
(Bonn), 347-355 (1987)
(London), 355-364 (1984)
(Tokyo), 437-444 (1986)
(Toronto), 391-397 (1988)
(Venice), 525-530 (1987)
Reagan-Gorbachev Summit Meetings
(Geneva), 749-761 (1985)
(Moscow), 353-373 (1988)
(Reykjavik), 875-885 (1986)
(Washington, D.C.), 991-1006 (1987)
Supreme Court. *See also Supreme Court cases*
Abortion, 559-580 (1986)

Adult Theaters, 131-144 (1986)
Affirmative Action, 365-385 (1984); 651-678 (1986); 331-349 (1987)
Alcoholism and Veterans' Benefits, 277-285 (1988)
Antitrust Law, 416-426 (1984)
Appointments, 591-599 (1986); 717-744 (1987); 772-773 (1988)
Bankruptcy and Labor, 181-199 (1984)
Bork Confirmation Battle, 717-744 (1987); 772 (1988)
Closed Party Primaries, 1065-1073 (1986)
Contagious Diseases, 245-252 (1987)
Creation Science, 565-576 (1987)
Death Penalty, 463-476 (1987)
Disruptive Handicapped Students, 47-56 (1988)
EPA and Clean Air, 427-437 (1984)
Exclusionary Rule, 505-519 (1984)
Federal and State Powers, 167-187 (1985)
Freedom of the Press, 299-312 (1984); 175-182 (1988)
Independent Counsel, 465-478 (1988)
Indigents' Rights to Psychiatric Aid, 207-219 (1985)
Insider Trading, 881-889 (1987)
Jury Selection in Capital Cases, 445-456 (1986)
Justices on Role of Supreme Court, 653-668 (1985)
Labor Union Membership, 415-429 (1985)
Mandatory Budget Cuts, 705-730 (1986)
Mandatory Retirement, 397-407 (1985)
Maternity Leave, 17-27 (1987)
Media Libel Law, 247-253 (1984); 355-368 (1986)
Meese Criticism, 479-490 (1985)
Nativity Scene, 217-239 (1984)
Obscenity, 479-490 (1987)
PAC Spending Limits, 277-295 (1985)
Peremptory Challenge, 409-433 (1986)
Political Asylum, 253-265 (1987)
Political Gerrymandering, 615-635 (1986)
Powell's Retirement, 577-581 (1987)
Preventive Detention, 491-508 (1987)
Prisoners' Rights, 479-491 (1984)
Private Clubs, 399-403 (1988)
Public Broadcasting Editorials, 449-463 (1984)
Public School Teachers in Parochial Classes, 433-461 (1985)
School Prayer, 379-395 (1985)
Secrecy of CIA Sources, 333-344 (1985)
Sex Bias in Education, 201-214 (1984)
Sex Discrimination, 465-478 (1984)
Sodomy and Privacy, 601-614 (1986)
Student Aid/Draft Registration, 493-503 (1984)
Student Newspaper Censorship, 37-46 (1988)
Student Searches, 13-26 (1985)
Students' Free Speech, 731-742 (1986)

Suspects' Rights, 387-397 (1984); 223-253 (1985)
Sustaining Handicapped Infants, 541-558 (1986)
Uncompensated Takings and Land Use, 531-553 (1987)
Use of Deadly Force, 303-315 (1985)
Video Recorders, 53-80 (1984)
Supreme Court cases
Aguilar v. Felton, 433-461 (1985)
Ake v. Oklahoma, 207-219 (1985)
American Iron and Steel Institute v. Natural Resources Defense Council, 427-437 (1984)
Batson v. Kentucky, 409-433 (1986)
Bethel School District v. Fraser, 731-742 (1986)
Block v. Rutherford, 481 (1984)
Bose Corp. v. Consumers Union, 299-312 (1984)
Bowen v. American Hospital Association, 541-558 (1986)
Bowers v. Hardwick, 601-614 (1986)
Bowsher v. Synar, 705-730 (1986)
Calder and South v. Jones, 247-248, 253-256 (1984)
Carpenter v. United States, 881-889 (1987)
California Federal Savings and Loan v. Guerra, 17-27 (1987)
Chevron v. Natural Resources Defense Council, 427-437 (1984)
CIA v. Sims and Wolfe, 333-344 (1985)
Copperweld Corp. v. Independence Tube Corp., 413-426 (1984)
Davis v. Bandemer, 615-635 (1986)
Edwards v. Aguillard, 565-576 (1987)
Federal Communications Commission v. League of Women Voters of California, 449-463 (1984)
Federal Election Commission (FEC) v. National Conservative Political Action Committee (NCPAC), 277-294 (1985)
Firefighters v. Stotts, 365-385 (1984)
First English Evangelical Lutheran Church of Glendale v. County of Los Angeles, 531-546 (1987)
Garcia v. San Antonio Metropolitan Transit Authority, 167-187 (1985)
Grand Rapids School District v. Ball, 433-461 (1985)
Grove City College v. Bell, 201-214 (1984)
Hazelwood School District v. Kuhlmeier, 37-46 (1988)
Honig v. Doe, 47-56 (1988)
Hudson v. Palmer, 480-481 (1984)
Immigration and Naturalization Service v. Luz Marina Cardoza-Fonseca, 253-265 (1987)
International Association of Firefighters v. City of Cleveland, 651-678 (1986)
Jefferson Parish Hospital District v. Hyde, 415 (1984)
Johnson v. Transportation Agency, Santa

Clara, California, 331-349 (1987)
Keeton v. Hustler Magazine, 247-253 (1984)
Lockhart v. McCree, 445-456 (1986)
Lynch v. Donnelly, 217-239 (1984)
McCleskey v. Kemp, 463-476 (1987)
McKelvey v. Turnage, 277-285 (1988)
Morrison v. Olson, 465-478 (1988)
National Collegiate Athletic Assn. v. University of Oklahoma, 415 (1984)
National Labor Relations Board v. Bildisco, 181-199 (1984)
New Jersey v. T.L.O., 13-26 (1985)
New York v. Quarles, 387-397 (1984)
New York State Club Association, Inc. v. City of New York et al., 399-403 (1988)
Nix v. Williams, 506 (1984)
Nollan v. California Coastal Commission, 531, 533, 547-553 (1987)
Oregon v. Elstad, 223-253 (1985)
Pattern Makers' League of North America (AFL-CIO) v. National Labor Relations Board, 415-429 (1985)
Philadelphia Newspapers Inc. v. Hepps, 355-368 (1986)
Pope v. Illinois, 479-490 (1987)
Renton v. Playtime Theatres Inc., 131-144 (1986)
Roberts v. U.S. Jaycees, 465-478 (1984)
Ruckelshaus v. Natural Resources Defense Council, 427-437 (1984)
School Board of Nassau Co., Florida v. Arline, 245-252 (1987)
Selective Service System v. Minnesota Public Interest Research Group, 493-503 (1984)
Sheet Metal Workers' International Association v. Equal Employment Commission, 651-678 (1986)
Sony Corp. of America v. Universal City Studios, 53-80 (1984)
Tashjian v. Republican Party of Connecticut, 1065-1073 (1986)
Teamsters Union v. National Labor Relations Board, 181-199 (1984)
Tennessee v. Garner, 303-315 (1985)
Thornburgh v. American College of Obstetricians and Gynecologists, 559-580 (1986)
Traynor v. Turnage, 277-285 (1988)
United States v. Leon, 505-519 (1984)
United States v. Salerno, 491-508 (1987)
Wallace v. Jaffree, 379-395 (1985)
Western Air Lines Inc. v. Criswell et al., 397-407 (1985)
Surgeon General's Report
Involuntary Smoking, 1079-1090 (1986)
Nicotine Addiction Report, 309-322 (1988)
Smoking in the Workplace, 809-822 (1985)
Surrogate mothers. *See Bioethics; Pregnancy and childbirth*
Sweden
Farm-Animal Rights Law, 347-351 (1988)
Red Cross Natural Disasters Report, 973-995 (1984)

Switzerland
Pope John Paul II's Visit, 399-406 (1984)

T

Tashjian v. Republican Party of Connecticut, 1065-1073 (1986)
Taxes
Corporate Management, 971-981 (1986)
Democratic Party Platform on, 566-567 (1984)
Economic Advisers' Report, 133-135 (1987)
Presidential Debates on, 865-868 (1984); 756-758 769-771 (1988)
President's Economic Report, 86 (1985); 66-67 (1986); 121-122 (1987)
Reagan's Budget Message, 102 (1984)
Republican Party Platform on, 667-669 (1984); 624-626 (1988)
State of the Union, 82, 85-86, 88 (1984); 110 (1985); 40, 44 (1986)
Teamsters Union v. National Labor Relations Board, 181-199 (1984)
Technology. *See Science and technology*
Teenage pregnancy. *See Pregnancy and childbirth*
Television
Supreme Court Decisions
Video Recorders, 53-80 (1984)
Westmoreland/CBS Controversy, 159-165 (1985)
Tennessee v. Garner, 303-315 (1985)
Terrorism
Argentine Report on "Disappeared" Persons, 789-793 (1984)
Chirac's Statement on French Antiterrorist Plan, 829-838 (1986)
Economic Summit Meetings
(London), 363-364 (1984)
(Tokyo), 438-439, 443-444 (1986)
(Toronto), 394 (1988)
(Venice), 526-527, 528-529 (1987)
Gorbachev's Address to 27th Soviet Party Congress, 146, 166-167 (1986)
Organized Crime Commission, 181, 187-189 (1986)
Palestine Liberation Organization (PLO) Office Closing, 479-485 (1988)
Presidential Debates on, 885-886 (1984); 746-747 (1988)
Reagan on International Terrorism, 463-477 (1985)
Reagan on U.S. Air Strike Against Libya, 347-354 (1986)
Republican Party Platform on, 725 (1984); 687-688 (1988)
Shultz Speech, 933-944 (1984)
U.S.-U.K. Extradition Treaty, 751-756 (1986)
Weinberger on Use of Military Force, 1005-1015 (1984)

Thailand
Pope John Paul II's Visit, 328-329, 334 (1984)
Thatcher, Margaret
British-Irish Accord, 723-732 (1985)
Third World. *See Developing countries; Foreign aid; Foreign trade; United Nations*
Thornburgh v. American College of Obstetricians and Gynecologists, 559-580 (1986)
Timberlake, Lloyd, 973-995 (1984)
Time Magazine
Sharon Libel Verdict, 47-52 (1985)
Togo
Pope John Paul II's Visit, 500, 501-504 (1985)
Tort reform
American Bar Association Report, 165-181 (1987)
Economic Adviser's Report, 142-143 (1987)
Tower Commission Report, 205-242 (1987)
Trade. *See Foreign trade*
Transportation. *See also Airline deregulation*
Aviation Safety Commission Report, 267-276 (1988)
Budget Message, 110 (1984)
Democratic Party Platform on, 580 (1984)
Economic Advisers' Report, 85-87 (1986)
GAO Report on Air Traffic Safety, 253-266 (1986)
President's Report on Privatization, 230-231, 233, 235, 236 (1988)
Republican Party Platform on, 687-688 (1984); 671-673 (1988)
Traynor v. Turnage, 277-285 (1988)
Treaties and agreements. *See also Arms control; Peacemaking efforts; United Nations*
Afghanistan Agreements, 257-266 (1988)
ABM Treaty Interpretation, 289-317 (1987)
Angola-Namibia Peace Accord, 947-950 (1988)
Ozone Treaty and Scientific Study, 745-764 (1987); 221-228 (1988)
Return of Hong Kong to China, 1045-1050 (1984)
Senate Ratification of Genocide Convention, 115-130 (1986)
U.S.-China, 23-30, 287-298 (1984)
U.S.-Soviet INF Treaty, 945-989 (1987)
U.S.-U.K. Extradition Treaty, 751-756 (1986)
Vatican-U.S. Relations, 19-22 (1984)
Trewhitt, Henry, 876-912 (1984)
Trudeau, Pierre Elliott, 407-412 (1984)
Turkey
Human Rights Report, 156-157 (1985); 108-110 (1988)
Tutu, Desmond, 1027-1037 (1984)
Twenty-fifth Amendment. *See Constitution, U.S.*

U

Ueberroth, Peter V., 169-175 (1986)
Uganda
Human Rights Report, 97-98 (1988)
Underclass. *See Homeless; Poverty*
UNESCO, 967-971 (1984)
Union Carbide Corp., 1023-1026 (1984); 295-302 (1985)
Union of Concerned Scientists, 257-268 (1984)
Union of Soviet Socialist Republics. *See Soviet Union*
United Kingdom. *See Great Britain*
United Nations
Afghanistan Agreements, 257-259, 264-265 (1988)
Angola-Namibia Peace Accord, 947-950 (1988)
Gorbachev Address, 927-940 (1988)
Human Rights in Afghanistan, 919-936 (1986)
International Conference on Population, 521-522, 544-547 (1984)
Iran-Iraq War Resolutions, 609-613 (1987); 529-532 (1988)
Natural Disasters Report, 973-995 (1984)
PLO Office Closing, 479-485 (1988)
Reagan Address to General Assembly, 707-719 (1985)
Reagan-Gromyko Address, 811-829 (1984)
Republican Party Platform on, 715-716 (1984)
Senate Ratification of Genocide Convention, 115-130 (1986)
South Korean President's UN Address, 853-859 (1988)
U.S. Reduction of Soviet Mission, 267-272 (1986)
U.S. Withdrawal from UNESCO, 967-971 (1984)
World Conference on Women, 555-570 (1985)
United States v. Leon, 505-519 (1984)
United States v. Salerno, 491-508 (1987)
Urban affairs. *See also State and local government*
Republican Party Platform on, 659-660 (1988)
Urban Institute, 877-880 (1988)
Urban League. *See National Urban League*
Urbanization and South African Pass Laws, 369-381 (1986)

V

Valenti, Jack, 55 (1984)
Vatican. *See also Catholic church; John Paul II*
Bioethics, 267-287 (1987)
Diplomatic Relations with U.S., 19-22 (1984)

Excommunication of Archbishop Lefeb-
vre, 489-494 (1988)
Pastoral Care of Homosexuals, 909-919
(1986)
Synod of Bishops, 765-780 (1985)
Theology of Liberation, 759-775 (1984);
317-338 (1986)
U.S. Bishops' Report, 571-581 (1985)
Venezuela
Pope John Paul II's Visit, 57, 58, 59-61
(1985)
Ver, Fabian C., 925-932 (1984); 307-308
(1986)
Veterans
Democratic Party Platform on, 616 (1984)
Department of Veterans Affairs (DVA),
873-876 (1988)
Interment of Unknown Vietnam Service-
man, 347-352 (1984)
Republican Party Platform on, 723-724
(1984); 697-698 (1988)
Supreme Court on Alcoholism and Veter-
ans' Benefits, 277-285 (1988)
Vice presidency
Bentsen Nomination Acceptance Speech,
542-546 (1988)
Bush Nomination Acceptance Speech,
727-745 (1984)
Ferraro Nomination Acceptance Speech,
647-658 (1984)
Quayle Nomination Acceptance Speech,
601-604 (1988)
Vice Presidential Debate, 799-829 (1988)
Vietnam war
Interment of Unknown Vietnam Service-
man, 347-352 (1984)
Vincennes, USS
Downing of Iranian Airliner, 703-717
(1988)
Volcker, Paul A., 511-516 (1987)
Voting. *See also Elections; Presidential elec-
tion*
Democratic Party Platform on, 609-610
(1984)
Supreme Court on Redistricting, 615-635
(1986)

W

Waldheim, Kurt
Inaugural Address, 743-750 (1986)
Pope John Paul's Visit to Austria, 405-406
(1988)
Walesa, Lech, 556 (1987)
Wallach, E. Robert, 497-516, (1988)
Wallace v. Jaffree, 379-395 (1985)
Walsh, Lawrence E., 632 (1986)
Walters, Barbara, 848-876 (1984)
Warner, Margaret, 758, 760-768, 774, 776
(1988)
Water policy. *See also Natural resources;
Oceans*

Democratic Party Platform on, 597-598
(1984)
Republican Party Platform on, 678 (1984)
Weakland, Rembert, 957 (1984)
Wedtech Corp., 496-516 (1988)
Weinberger, Caspar W., 1005-1015 (1984)
Welbilt Corp. *See Wedtech Corp.*
Welfare and social services. *See also Medic-
aid and Medicare*
Bishops on Economic Justice, 1000-1002
(1986)
Bishops on U.S. Economy, 957-972 (1984)
CDF Infant Mortality Report, 161-165
(1987)
Democratic Party Platform on, 613-618
(1984)
Economic Advisers' Report, 132-133
(1984)
Family Support Act, 847-852 (1988)
Food Assistance Report, 3-17 (1984)
Mental Health Report, 833-834 (1984)
Presidential Debates on, 738-741, 773-775
(1988)
Republican Party Platform on, 682-685
(1984); 657-659 (1988)
State of the Union, 112 (1987); 64 (1988)
Welfare System Revision, 847-852 (1988)
Western Air Lines Inc. v. Criswell et al., 397-
407 (1985)
Westmoreland, William C., 159-165 (1985)
White, Byron R.
Abortion, 561, 571-579 (1986)
Affirmative Action, 366, 368-376 (1984);
667-676 (1986)
Alcoholism and Veterans' Benefits, 277-
284 (1988)
Exclusionary Rule, 506-514 (1984)
Freedom of Press, 309 (1984); 182 (1988)
Insider Trading, 884-889 (1987)
Mandatory Budget Cuts, 707, 724-728
(1986)
Maternity Leave, 9, 25-27 (1987)
Obscenity, 479-483 (1987)
PAC Spending Limits, 279, 290-294 (1985)
Private Clubs, 399-403 (1988)
Public School Teachers in Parochial Class-
es, 433, 449 (1985)
Redistricting, 617, 618-619 (1986)
Sex Bias in Education, 202, 204-210 (1984)
Student Newspaper Censorship, 37-44
(1988)
Student Searches, 14-23 (1985)
Sustaining Handicapped Infants, 544, 554-
558 (1986)
Use of Deadly Force, 303-311 (1985)
Whitehead, Mary Beth, 373-387 (1987); 71-80
(1988)
Wiesel, Elie
Nobel Peace Prize, 1075-1078 (1986)
Testimony at Klaus Barbie Trial, 517-524
(1987)
Wijkman, Anders, 973-995 (1984)

Wilentz, C. J., 72-80 (1988)
Will, George, 1092-1095 (1986)
Williamson, Richard, 490-492 (1988)
Wilson, William A., 19 (1984)
Winans, R. Foster, 881-889 (1987)
Women. *See also Equal Rights Amendment (ERA)*
   Apostolic Letter on Women, 785-792 (1988)
   Bishops on Economic Justice, 999 (1986)
   Democratic Party Platform on, 549, 607-608 (1984)
   Mental Health Report, 833-834 (1984)
   Pentagon Report on Sexual Harassment, 671-679 (1987)
   Republican Party Platform on, 662, 698-700 (1984); 643 (1988)
   Sex Segregation in the Workplace, 789-801 (1985)
   Supreme Court Decisions
      Sex Bias in Education, 201-214 (1984)
      Sex Discrimination in Commercial Organizations, 465-478 (1984)
   UN World Conference, 555-570 (1985)
   World Population Problems, 521-547 (1984)
Woodruff, Judy, 799-829 (1988)
Working Group on Financial Markets, 9-12, 34-36 (1988)
World Bank
   Environmental Defense Fund on World

Bank Project, 859-873 (1986)
   IMF-World Bank Conference, 643-652 (1985)
   World Population Problems, 521-543 (1984)
World Council of Churches, 399 (1984)
World Court. *See International Court of Justice*
World debt. *See International debt*
World War II
   Mengele Discovery, 409-414 (1985)
   Japanese-American Internees Reparations, 287-295 (1988)
   Pope John Paul's Visit to Austria, 405-411 (1988)
   Wiesel Testimony at Klaus Barbie Trial, 517-524 (1987)

Y

Young, Frank E., 484-485 (1986)
Youth. *See Children; Education*

Z

Zhao Ziyang
   U.S. Visit, 23-30 (1984)
Zimbabwe
   Natural Disasters Report, 973-995 (1984)